D0341869

THE LIBRARY

OF

LITERARY CRITICISM

OF

ENGLISH AND AMERICAN AUTHORS

VOLUME III

1730 - 1784

EDITED BY CHARLES WELLS MOULTON

ASSISTED BY A CORPS OF ABLE CONTRIBUTORS

GLOUCESTER, MASS.

PETER SMITH

1959

REPRINTED 1959
BY
PETER SMITH

To

Edmund Clarence Stedman, A. M., L. H. D., LL. D.

INTRODUCTION.

BOOKS.

Let us consider how great a commodity of doctrine exists in books, how easily, how secretly, how safely they expose the nakedness of human ignorance, without putting it to shame. These are the masters who instruct us without rods and ferules, without hard words and anger, without clothes or money. If you approach them, they are not asleep; if investigating you interrogate them, they conceal nothing: if you mistake them, they never grumble; if you are ignorant, they cannot laugh at you.—BURY, RICHARD DE, 1345?-1473, *Philobiblion.*

He hath never fed of the dainties that are bred in a book; he hath not eat paper, as it were; he hath not drunk ink; his intellect is not replenished; he is only an animal, only sensible in the duller parts. —SHAKESPEARE, WILLIAM, 1588-98, *Love's Labours Lost, Act* iv, *Scene* ii.

Happy, ye leaves! when as those lilly hands,
Which hold my life in their dead-doing might,
Shall handle you, and hold in love's soft bands,
Like captives trembling at the victors sight.
And happy lines! on which, with starry light,
Those lamping eyes will deigne sometimes to look
And reade the sorrowes of my dying spright,
Written with teares in harts close-bleeding book.
And happy rymes! bath'd in the sacred brooke
Of Helicon, whence she derived is;
When ye behold that Angels blessed looke,
My soules long-lacked foode, my heavens blis;
Leaves, lines, and rymes, seeke her to please alone,
Whom if ye please, I care for other none!
—SPENSER, EDMUND, 1595, *Amoretti.*

If I were not a King, I would be a University man; and if it were so that I must be a prisoner, if I might have my wish, I would desire to have no other prison than that library, and to be chained together with so many good authors, *et mortuis magister.*—JAMES I., 1605, *Speech on Visit to the Bodleian Library.*

Libraries are as the shrines where all the relics of the ancient saints, full of true virtue, and that without delusion or imposture, are preserved and reposed.—BACON, FRANCIS LORD, 1605, *The Advancement of Learning.*

I never come into a library (saith Heinsius) but I bolt the door to me, excluding lust, ambition, avarice, and all such vices whose nurse is idleness, the mother of ignorance and melancholy herself; and in the very lap of eternity, among so many divine souls, I take my seat with so lofty a spirit and sweet content that I pity all our great ones and rich men that know not their happiness.—BURTON, ROBERT, 1621, *Anatomy of Melancholy.*

Books are not absolutely dead things, but do contain a progeny of life in them, to be as active as that soul whose progeny they are; nay, they do preserve as in a vial the purest efficacy and extraction of that living intellect that bred them.—MILTON, JOHN, 1644, *Areopagitica.*

Our books. . . . Do not our hearts hug them, and quiet themselves in them even more than in God?—BAXTER, RICHARD, 1650, *The Saint's Everlasting Rest.*

This to a structure led well known to fame,
And called, "The Monument of Vanished Minds,"
Where when they thought they saw in well-sought books
The assembled souls of all that men thought wise,
It bred such awful reverence in their looks,
As if they saw the buried writers rise.
Such heaps of written thought; gold of the dead,
Which Time does still disperse but not devour,
Made them presume all was from deluge freed
Which long-lived authors writ ere Noah's shower.
—DAVENANT, SIR WILLIAM, 1651, *Gondibert.*

Unconfused Babel of all tongues! which e'er
The mighty linguist Fame, or Time, the mighty traveller,
That could speak, or this could hear.
Majestic monument and pyramid!
Where still the shapes of parted souls abide
Embalmed in verse; exalted souls which now
Enjoy those arts they wooed so well below;
Which now all wonders plainly see
That have been, are, or are to be,
In the mysterious library,
The beatific Bodley of the Deity!

—COWLEY, ABRAHAM, 1667? *Ode on the Bodleian Library.*

The spectacles of books.—DRYDEN, JOHN, 1668, *Essay on Dramatic Poetry.*

Bright books! the perspectives to our weak sights,
The clear projections of discerning lights,
Burning and shining thoughts, man's post-hume day,
And track of fled souls, and their milkie way;
The dead alive and busie, the still voice
Of enlarged spirits, kind Heaven's white decoys!
Who lives with you, lives like those knowing flowers,
Which in commerce with light spend all their hours;
Which shut to clouds, and shadows nicely shun,
But with glad haste unveil to kiss the sun.
Beneath you, all is dark and a dead night,
Which whoso lives in, wants both health and sight.
By sucking you, the wise, like bees, do grow
Healing and rich, though this they do most slow,
Because most choicely; for as great a store
Have we of books, as bees of herbs, or more;
And the great task to try, then know, the good,
To discern weeds, and judge of wholesome food,
Is a rare, scant performance. For man dyes
Oft ere 'tis done, while the bee feeds and flyes.
But you were all choice flowers; all set and dressed
By old sage florists, who well knew the best;
And I amidst you all am turned a weed,
Not wanting knowledge, but for want of heed.
Then thank thyself, wild fool, that would'st not be
Content to know,—what was too much for thee!

—VAUGHAN, HENRY, 1678, *Thalia Rediviva.*

Read Homer once, and you can read no more;
For all books else appear so mean, so poor,
Verse will seem prose; but still persist to read,
And Homer will be all the books you need.

—SHEFFIELD, JOHN, 1682, *Essays on Poetry.*

Books like proverbs receive their chief value from the stamp and esteem of ages through which they have passed.—TEMPLE, SIR WILLIAM, 1689–99, *Ancient and Modern Learning.*

We whom the world is pleased to honour with the title of modern authors should never have been able to compass our great design of everlasting remembrance and never-dying fame if our endeavours had not been so highly serviceable to the general good of mankind.—SWIFT, JONATHAN, 1704, *A Tale of a Tub.*

Read we must, be writers ever so indifferent.—SHAFTESBURY, ANTHONY ASHLEY COOPER EARL, 1711, *Characteristics.*

Whence is thy learning? Hath thy toil
O'er books consumed the midnight oil?

—GAY, JOHN, 1727–38, *The Shepherd and the Philosopher, Fables.*

(Query) Whether the collected wisdom of all ages and nations be not found in books?—BERKELEY, GEORGE, 1735–37, *The Querist.*

Nor is there any paternal fondness which seems to savour less of absolute instinct, and which may be so well reconciled to worldly wisdom, as this of authors for their books. These children may most truly be called the riches of their father, and many of them have with true filial piety fed their parent in his old age; so that not only the affection but the interest of the author may be highly injured by those slanderers whose poisonous breath brings his book to an untimely end.—FIELDING, HENRY, 1749, *The History of Tom Jones.*

My neighbours think me often alone, and yet at such times I am in company with more than five hundred mutes, each of whom communicates his ideas to me by dumb signs quite as intelligibly as any person living can do by uttering of words;

and with a motion of my hand I can bring them as near to me as I please; I handle them as I like; they never complain of ill-usage; and when dismissed from my presence, though ever so abruptly, take no offence.—STERNE, LAURENCE, 1775, *Letters*.

Come, Child of Care! to make thy soul serene,
Approach the treasures of this tranquil scene;
Survey the dome, and, as the doors unfold,
The soul's best cure, in all her cares, behold!
Where mental wealth the poor in thought may find,
And mental physic the diseased in mind;
See here the balms that passion's wounds assuage;
See coolers here, that damp the fire of rage;
Here alteratives, by slow degrees control
The chronic habits of the sickly soul;
And round the heart, and o'er the aching head,
Mild opiates here their sober influence shed.
Now bid thy soul man's busy scenes exclude,
And view composed this silent multitude:—
Silent they are—but, though deprived of sound,
Here all the living languages abound;
Here all that live no more; preserved they lie,
In tombs that open to the curious eye.
—CRABBE, GEORGE, 1781, *The Library*.

Knowledge is proud that he has learned so much;
Wisdom is humble that he knows no more.
Books are not seldom talisman and spells.
—COWPER, WILLIAM, 1785, *The Task, bk.* vi.

I adopted the tolerating measure of the elder Pliny—"nullum esse librum tam malum ut non in aliqua parte prodesset."—GIBBON, EDWARD, 1794, *Autobiography*.

A book's a book, although there's nothing in't.
—BYRON, LORD, 1809, *English Bards and Scotch Reviewers*.

What a place to be in is an old library! It seems as though all the souls of all the writers that have bequeathed their labours to the Bodleians were reposing here as in some dormitory or middle state. . . . I seem to inhale learning, walking amid their foliage; and the odour of their old moth-scented coverings is fragrant as the first bloom of the sciential apples which grew amid the happy orchard.—LAMB, CHARLES, 1820, *Oxford in the Long Vacation*.

In my youthful days I never entered a great library . . . but my predominant feeling was one of pain and disturbance of mind,—not much unlike that which drew tears from Xerxes on viewing his immense army, and reflecting that in one hundred years not one soul would remain alive. To me, with respect to the books, the same effect would be brought about by my own death. Here, said I, are one hundred thousand books, the worst of them capable of giving me some pleasure and instruction; and before I can have had time to extract the honey from one-twentieth of this hive in all likelihood I shall be summoned away.—DE QUINCY, THOMAS, 1823–60, *Letters to a Young Man*.

We visit at the shrine, drink in some measure of the inspiration, and cannot easily breathe in other air less pure, accustomed to immortal fruits.—HAZLITT, WILLIAM, 1826, *The Plain Speaker*.

Were I to pray for a taste which should stand me instead under every variety of circumstances, and be a source of happiness and cheerfulness to me during life, and a shield against its ills, however things might go amiss, and the world frown upon me, it would be a taste for reading. Give a man this taste, and the means of gratifying it, and you can hardly fail of making him a happy man; unless, indeed, you put into his hands a most perverse selection of Books. You place him in contact with the best society in every period of history,—with the wisest, the wittiest, the tenderest, the bravest, and the purest characters who have adorned humanity. You make him a denizen of all nations, a contemporary of all ages. —HERSCHEL, SIR JOHN, 1833, *Address at the Opening of the Eton Library*.

It is our duty to live among books.—NEWMAN, JOHN HENRY, 1834, *Tracts for the Times, No.* 2.

Nothing is pleasanter than exploring in a library.—LANDOR, WALTER SAVAGE, 1836, *Pericles and Aspasia*.

In the best books, great men talk to us, give us their most precious thoughts, and pour their souls into ours. God be thanked for books. They are the voices of the distant and the dead, and make us heirs of the spiritual life of past ages. Books are the true levellers. They give to all, who will faithfully use them, the society, the spiritual presence of the best and greatest of our race. No matter how poor I am. No matter though the prosperous of my own time will not enter my obscure dwelling. If the Sacred Writers will enter and take up their abode under my roof, if Milton will cross my threshold to sing to me of Paradise, and Shakespeare to open to me the worlds of imagination and the workings of the human heart, and Franklin to enrich me with his practical wisdom, I shall not pine for want of intellectual companionship, and I may become a cultivated man though excluded from what is called the best society in the place where I live. . . . Nothing can supply the place of books. They are cheering and soothing companions in solitude, illness, affliction. The wealth of both continents would be no equivalent for the good they impart. Let every man, if possible, gather some good books under his roof, and obtain access for himself and family to some social library. Almost any luxury should be sacrificed to this.—CHANNING, WILLIAM ELLERY, 1838, *Self-Culture.*

On all sides, are we not driven to the conclusion that, of the things which men can do or make here below, by far the most momentous, wonderful and worthy are the things we call Books! . . . For indeed, whatever be the outward form of the thing . . . is it not verily, at bottom, the highest act of man's faculty that produces a Book? It is the *Thought* of man; the true thaumaturgic virtue; by which man works all things whatsoever. All that he does, and brings to pass, is the vesture of a Thought.—CARLYLE, THOMAS, 1841, *Heroes and Hero Worship.*

I will bury myself in my books and the devil
may pipe to his own.

—TENNYSON, ALFRED LORD, 1842, *Locksley Hall.*

Lightly as I have spoken of these old books, there yet lingers with me a superstitious reverence for literature of all kinds. A bound volume has a charm in my eyes similar to what scraps of manuscript possess for the good Mussulman. He imagines that those wind-wafted records are perhaps hallowed by some sacred verse; and I, that every new book or antique one may contain the "open sesame,"—the spell to disclose treasures hidden in some unsuspected cave of Truth.—HAWTHORNE, NATHANIEL, 1846, *Mosses from an Old Manse.*

Yet is it just
That here, in memory of all books which lay
Their sure foundations in the heart of man,
. . . .
That I should here assert their rights, attest
Their honours, and should, once for all, pronounce
Their benediction, speak of them as powers
For ever to be hallowed; only less
For what we are and what we may become
Than Nature's self, which is the breath of God,
Of His pure Word by miracle revealed.

—WORDSWORTH, WILLIAM, 1850, *The Prelude.*

It is oppressive to conceive what a world of human thought and human passion is dwelling on the silent and senseless paper, how much of wisdom is ready to make its entrance into the mind that is prepared to give it welcome. . . . Reflecting on what a book can do and ought to do for you—how it may act on your mind, and your mind react on it—and thus, holding communion, you can travel through a wilderness of volumes onward, onward through time, wisely and happily, and with perfect vision of your way, as the woodman sees a path in the forest—a path to his home, while the wanderer, whether standing or staggering, is lost in blind and blank bewilderment.—REED, HENRY, 1855, *Lectures on English Literature from Chaucer to Tennyson.*

The Elzevirs
Have fly-leaves over-written by his hand,
In faded notes, as thick and fine and brown
As cob-webs on a tawny monument
Of the old Greeks,—*Conferenda hæc cum his—*
Corrupte citat—lege potius,—
And so on, in the scholar's regal way
Of giving judgment on the parts of speech,
As if he sate on all twelve thrones up-piled
Arraigning Isreal.
—BROWNING, ELIZABETH BARRETT, 1857, *Aurora Leigh, bk.* v.

We confess a bibliothecaraian avarice that gives all books a value in our eyes; there is for us a recondite wisdom in the phrase, "A book is a book;" from the time when we made the first catalogue of our library, in which "Bible, large, 1 vol.," and "Bible, small, 1 vol.," asserted their alphabetic individuality and were the sole *B*s in our little hive, we have had a weakness even for those checker-board volumes that only fill up; we cannot breathe the thin air of that Pepysian self-denial, that Himalayan selectness, which, content with one bookcase, would have no tomes in it but *porphyrogeniti*, books of the bluest blood, making room for choicer new-comers by a continuous ostracism to the garret of present incumbents. There is to us a sacredness in a volume, however dull; we live over again the author's lonely labors and tremulous hopes; we see him, on his first appearance after parturition, "as well as could be expected," a nervous sympathy yet surviving between the late-severed umbilical cord and the wondrous offspring.—LOWELL, JAMES RUSSELL, 1858-64-90, *Library of Old Authors; Prose Works, Riverside ed., vol.* I, *p.* 292.

In a library we are surrounded by many hundred of dear friends but they are imprisoned by an enchanter in these paper and leathern boxes.—EMERSON, RALPH WALDO, 1870, *Society and Solitude.*

It's mighty hard to write nowadays without getting something or other worth listening to into your essay or your volume. The foolishest book is a kind of leaky boat on a sea of wisdom. Some of the wisdom will get in anyhow.—HOLMES, OLIVER WENDELL, 1872, *The Poet at the Breakfast Table.*

All round the room my silent servants wait—
My friends in every season, bright and dim;
Angels and seraphim
Come down and murmur to me, sweet and low,
And spirits of the skies all come and go
Early and late;
All from the old world's divine and distant date,
From the sublimer few,
Down to the poet who but yester-eve
Sang sweet and made us grieve,
All come, assembling here in order due.
And here I dwell with Poesy, my mate,
With Erato and all her vernal sighs,
Great Clio with her victories elate,
Or pale Urania's deep and starry eyes.
Oh friends, whom chance and change can never harm,
Whom Death the tyrant cannot doom to die,
Within whose folding soft eternal charm
I love to lie
And meditate upon your verse that flows,
And fertilizes wheresoe'er it goes.
—PROCTER, BRYAN WALLER (BARRY CORANWLL), 1874? *An Autobiographical Fragment.*

Every book that we take up without a purpose, is an opportunity lost of taking up a book with a purpose—every bit of stray information which we cram into our heads without any sense of its importance, is for the most part a bit of the most useful information driven out of our heads and choked off from our minds. It is so certain that information, that is, the knowledge, the stored thoughts and observations of mankind, is now grown to proportions so utterly incalculable and prodigious, that even the learned whose lives are given to study, can but pick up some crumbs that fall from the table of truth. They delve and tend but a plot in that vast and teeming kingdom, whilst those whom active life leaves with but a few cramped hours of study can hardly come to know the very vastness of the field before them, or how infinitesimally small is the corner they can traverse at the best.—HARRISON, FREDERIC, 1879-86, *The Choice of Books.*

This union of freedom with authority—of a choice for one's self, and a willingness to believe that the world is right in setting Shakespeare above Swinburne, and Homer above Tupper—is, I believe, the true and the only guide in the selection of books to read. In the long run, nothing but truth, simplicity, purity, and a lofty purpose approves a book to the favor of the ages, and nothing else ought to approve it to the individual reader. Thus the end is reached, and the choice is made, not by taking a book because a "course of reading" commands you to do so, but because you come to see for yourself the wisdom of the selection. The pure and wholesome heart of humanity—that thing which we call conscience—is the guide of the readers as it is of every other class of workers in life.—RICHARDSON, CHARLES FRANCIS, 1881, *The Choice of Books.*

The book is the lens between life and the reader by which he gathers a clear knowledge of the former. There are two elements in this connection. The book receives light, it also gives light. In the consideration of the first the priority of life must be recognized as the priority of the material to the work. Literature which does not show a life below itself, and fundamental, is too shallow to live. Therefore, a man or a people must live before writing. What darkness would fall on the world if this were not so. For literature is a point of departure for new achievements, without which each person would have to start at the bottom and climb the whole hill of knowledge anew. Literature does more than this. It gives life new qualities through style. In Carlyle's "French Revolution," we recognize a revolution which existed in the world, because it existed in his intellect and soul. The same is true of all books. The relations between life and literature are so delicate that if the life is a little too strong for literature, or *vice-versa* they are much disturbed. The former is now the case. The latter was the case when Goethe lived; books were considered sacred. Literature as the food of life appeals to three faculties—curiosity, obedience, and admiration. The perfection of these in Christ makes the Bible the book of books. Literature appeals to the same vitality which gives man knowledge, and so it is the *livest* man who makes the best reader. A good idea is to pursue some topic as deeply as possible.—BROOKS, PHILLIPS, 1886, *Address before New England Sunday-School Assembly.*

From "The Book Hunter" I learnt a reverence for a book, a respect for it as the shrine of wisdom, a regard for it as a thing of beauty in itself. So possessed am I now by this feeling that I find Imogen were fitly punished for ill-treating the book she had been reading while Iachimo was hidden in the chest: she bade her woman, Helen, "fold down the leaf where she had left." To fold down the leaf of a book is to torture a poor dumb friend which cannot protest in self-defense, and for this crime lèse-literature and for other reasons known to the dramatist, Imogen suffered not a little.—MATTHEWS, BRANDER, 1888, *Books That Have Helped Me, p.* 81.

Teach me rightly to admire Milton and Keats, and I will find my own criticism of living poets. Help me to enjoy, however feebly, Homer and Dante, and I will promise not to lose my head over Pollok's "Course of Time," or Mr. Bailey's "Festus." Fire my enthusiasm for Henry Vaughan and George Herbert, and I shall be able to distinguish between the muse of Miss Frances Ridley Havergal and of Miss Christina Rossetti. Train me to become a citizen of the true Republic of Letters, and I shall not be found on my knees before false gods, or trooping with the vulgar to crown with laurel brazen brows.—BIRRELL, AUGUSTINE, 1894, *Essays about Men, Women and Books p.* 227.

CONTENTS.

ENGRAVINGS.

The Library of Literary Criticism of English and American Authors

VOLUME III

Samuel Sewall

1652–1730.

Colonist and judge, son of Henry Sewall and Jane, daughter of Stephen Drummer, was born at Bishopstoke, Hampshire, on 28 March 1652. Emigrating in childhood with his parents to Newbury, Massachusetts, he was educated at a private school and at Harvard, entering in 1667, and graduating B. A. in 1671 and M. A. in 1674. He was then ordained minister, but on his marriage in 1677 was induced to leave that calling, and, under the patronage of his father-in-law, started a printing-press at Boston. He soon became known in public life, and in 1684 was elected a member of the court of assistants for Massachusetts. In 1688 he came to England on business. In 1692 Sewall, as a justice of the peace, was concerned in adjudicating in the Salem witchcraft case, but afterwards bitterly repented of his share in the proceedings, and publicly announced the fact, henceforward spending one day annually in fasting and prayer. He afterwards became one of the regular judges of Massachusetts, and in 1718 chief justice. He retired in 1728, and died at Boston on 1 Jan. 1730. Sewall married, on 28 Feb. 1676, Hannah, daughter of John Hull and Judith Quincy. He left a long line of descendants, the "loyalist" branch of which changed the spelling of the name to "Sewell." Sewall's diary, an interesting and valuable source for the social history of the colony from 1674 to 1729, was first published in the "Collections of the Massachusetts Historical Society," 5th Ser. vol. v. An engraving, from a supposed original portrait (date and artist unknown), forms the frontispiece. Sewall was also author of a phamphlet against slavery, entitled "The Selling of Joseph" (1700).—HARRIS, C. ALEXANDER, 1897, *Dictionary of National Biography, vol.* LI, *p.* 279.

PERSONAL

Stately and slow, with thoughtful air,
His black cap hiding his whitened hair,
Walks the Judge of the great Assize,
Samuel Sewall the good and wise.
His face with lines of firmness wrought,
He wears the look of a man unbought,
Who swears to his hurt and changes not;
Yet, touched and softened nevertheless
With the grace of Christian gentleness,
The face that a child would climb to kiss!
True and tender and brave and just,
That man might honor and woman trust.
—WHITTIER, JOHN GREENLEAF, 1857, *The Prophecy of Samuel Sewall.*

A strong, gentle, and great man was Samuel Sewall, great by almost every measure of greatness,—moral courage, honor, benevolence, learning, eloquence, intellectual force and breadth and brightness.—TYLER, MOSES COIT, 1878, *A History of American Literature,* 1676–1765, *vol.* II, *p.* 99.

Sewall was a representative of the most devout English Puritans, but he was of a submissive, not an aggressive temper. He was honestly attached to the old church and state government of the early settlers. His political and religious principles were thoroughly Puritan, and he had an almost morbid dislike of innovations of all sorts. . . . The character and behavior of Sewall and men like him were the prevailing cause of the overthrow of the charter government.—LODGE, HENRY CABOT, 1878, *The Last of the Puritans, Magazine of American History, vol.* 2, *p.* 645.

Judge Sewall is better known to us in both his outer and inner being, in all his elements, composition, and manifestation of character, in his whole personal, domestic, social, official, and religious life, than is any other individual in our local history of two hundred and fifty years. And this is true not only of himself, but through his pen, curiously active, faithful, candid, kind, impartial, and even just, his own times stand revealed and described to us, as if by thousands of daguerreotypes and repeating telephones.—ELLIS, GEORGE E., 1884, *Address on Samuel Sewall, Oct.* 26.

He was an amiable and honorable man, whose outer and inner life for fifty-six years, laid open upon the pages of his private *Diary*, bears the light as few men's lives could do, but he had a leaning toward creature comforts and respect for shillings and pence prophetic of the Yankee constitution.—BATES, KATHARINE LEE, 1897, *American Literature, p.* 37.

Sewall, though he seems opinionated, narrow, mercenary, and over frugal, as seen by the light of to-day, should be judged by the ethics of historical criticism—that is, regarded in the environment of his age, in the atmosphere and circumstances of Puritan New England. Thus viewed, his was certainly a kindly, wise, thoughtful, prudent, helpful, honourable, and fruitful life. Even those dark days of his life, his brief but sad part in the Salem Witchcraft, are glorified by his noble public penitence therefor in later life.—EARLE, ALICE MORSE, 1897, *"A Puritan Pepys," The Bookman, vol.* 5, *p.* 425.

DIARY

Throughout we find evidences that he was a devout Puritan, a worthy member of the Old South Church in Boston. His prayers and fasts were numerous, and doubtless genuine. His early training in theology gives a flavor, always apparent, to his reflections. It is, however, as difficult to make satisfactory selections from Sewall as it always has been from Pepys or Evelyn. The interest of the work lies not so much in any particular part as in the aggregation of the details of the whole record. In this volume we have the daily life of a Bostonian recorded for fifteen years. We enter imperceptibly into a knowledge of his surroundings, his joys and sorrows, his cares and his successes. We learn when his children are born, when they are ill, and when they die. We know, above all, about the daily occurrences of the town at a time when newspapers were not and the reporter was unimagined.— WHITMORE, W. H., 1878, *Sewall's Diary, The Nation, vol.* 27, *p.* 287.

Judge Sewall's "Diary" is essentially a work of historical reference. It can never be a popular book, or even in considerable demand with general readers. There is too much uninteresting detail in it; nor is the subject in any aspect a large or inviting one. To the student of New England history, however, it is a mine of necessary information.—ADAMS, CHARLES FRANCIS, JR., 1882, *Sewall's Diary, The Nation, vol.* 35, *p.* 77.

In these many pages of Sewall we find traces of austerity, narrowness, bigotry, pettiness, and (in the witchcraft matter) fatal delusion; but we are still more impressed with the writer's sincerity, constant endeavor to do right, and faithful adherence to those principles of duty which are the foundation of society. The little details of his life are no more trivial than would be those of most men, if written down as fully; the records of an old man's courtships, melancholy—amusing as they are,—and it should be said that they ought not to have been printed,—reveal nothing morally discreditable; and even in the witchcraft error, let us not forget that Sewall shared his mistake with hundreds of the most learned and devout men of this time, in both hemispheres; that his part in the executions was no greater than that of others of high standing in England and America; and that, more fully than any of them, he publicly and privately recanted.—RICHARDSON, CHARLES F., 1887, *American Literature,* 1607–1885, *vol.* I, *p.* 108.

It is perhaps the only book of the Colonial period that can be read through with pleasure.—HAWTHORNE, JULIAN AND LEMMON, LEONARD, 1891, *American Literature, p.* 6.

Has been compared with the more famous "Diary" of Samuel Pepys, which it resembles in its confidential character and the completeness of its self-revelation, but to which it is as much inferior in historical interest as "the petty province here" was inferior in political and social importance to "Britain far away." For the most part it is a chronicle or small beer, the diarist jotting down the minutiæ of his domestic life and private affairs, even to the recording of such haps as this: "March 23, I had my hair cut by G. Barret." But it also affords instructive glimpses of public events, such as King Philip's War, the Quaker troubles, the English Revolution of 1688, etc.—BEERS, HENRY A., 1895, *Initial Studies in American Letters, p.* 31.

We have no other book like it; perhaps no other storehouse of old ways and social life so abundant as it. Sewall never took the time or the pains, being too busy, to get himself a well-mannered style and fixed forms as a literary man. Perhaps the exacting, and even narrow, zeal of Puritanism, always unfavorable to art, dissuaded him. Yet there are not lacking passages in his Diary and Letter Book which show his ability to have written the strongest, well-ordered English had he willed it.—CHAMBERLAIN, N. H., 1897, *Samuel Sewall and the World he Lived In, Preface, p.* viii.

Inferior in literary merit to Evelyn and Pepys, Sewall may yet be classed with his two contemporary diarists; resembling the former in the piety which tinges his journal, and the latter in the variety of his scope and the personal, even trivial, nature of much that he records. . . . Like many people who have launched into autobiography, this aged charmer does not know when to close his diary, and his biographer thinks it only right to punish him for his indiscretion by giving to the world some of his later entries along with the rest. Shall we regard his autumnal frivolity as one more proof that human nature will not be denied its rights, and, if forced to conform to a strait-laced Puritanism in its springtime, will kick up its heels in old age?—BICKNELL, PERCY FAVOR, 1897, *A Glimpse of Puritan New England, The Dial, vol.* 23, *pp.* 328, 329.

On the whole, Judge Sewall's diary is not cheerful reading, but the grayness of its atmosphere is mainly due to the unlovely aspect of colonial life, to the rigors of an inclement climate not yet subdued by the forces of a luxurious civilization, and by a too constant consideration of the probabilities of being eternally damned.—REPPLIER, AGNES, 1897, *The Deathless Diary, Varia, p.* 58.

His diary presents a vivid picture of the public and private life of the time, besides disclosing a singularly pure, manly, and gentle character.—NOBLE, CHARLES, 1898, *Studies in American Literature, pp.* 47, 48.

Gives very interesting and sometimes very amusing pictures of the man and the times—the harmless vanity, love of creature comforts, hatred of wigs, and mingled shrewdness and simplicity of the one; the political troubles, quaint customs, sympathetic piety, and abundance of human nature (regenerate and unregenerate) in the other.—BRONSON, WALTER C., 1900, *A Short History of American Literature, p.* 34.

GENERAL

I have called Samuel Sewall "A Puritan Pepys," and the description is by no means so fanciful as might be supposed. From the fact that they were in a measure contemporary, a comparison of the two diarists is obvious, but the first impression is of the strange contrast between them rather than of any similarity. Pepys was twenty years older than Sewall, and his diary ceases nearly six years before that of the latter begins. Pepys lived in London, the great metropolis of a great nation. . . . Between the gay politician of the Restoration and the grave Puritan judge there is a marked and interesting likeness. Possibly certain fixed qualities of mind and character must be common to all good diarists, but, however this may be, if Pepys had been brought up as a Puritan and lived in New England, one cannot help thinking that he would have been much like Sewall.—LODGE, HENRY CABOT, 1884, *Studies in History, pp.* 24, 25.

Justice Sewall was a strong writer on many topics. He was one of the first to protest against African slavery. His little tract, "The Selling of Joseph," a powerful and impassionate plea against this evil, is still readable.—PATTEE, FRED LEWIS, 1896, *A History of American Literature, p.* 45.

Elijah Fenton

1683–1730.

An English poet, dramatist, and biographer; born at Shelton, Staffordshire, May 20, 1683; died in Berkshire, August (not July), 1730. He worked with Pope at the translation of the Odyssey, wrote "Mariamne," a tragedy, and produced a "Hymn to the Sun," with other verse displaying taste and talent.—WARNER, CHARLES DUDLEY, 1897, *ed., Biographical Dictionary of Authors, Library of the World's Best Literature, vol.* XXIX, *p.* 183.

PERSONAL

The lazy Mr. Fenton has obeyed your commands, and wrote for the notes in a huge long letter of at least three lines. I am now in hopes he will not lose the use of writing and speaking. I will tell you a true story: When he was with me at Sturston he often fished; this gave him an opportunity of sitting still, and being silent; but he left it off because the fish bit. He could not bear the fatigue of pulling up the rod and baiting the hook. —BROOME, WILLIAM, 1725–6, *Letter to Alexander Pope, Jan.* 2.

I Intended to write to you on this melancholy subject, the death of Mr. Fenton, before y^rs came; but stay'd to have informed myself & you of ye circumstances of it. All I hear is, that he felt a Gradual Decay, tho so early in Life, & was declining for 5 or 6 months. It was not, as I apprehended, the Gout in his Stomach, but I believe rather a Complication first of Gross Humours, as he was naturally corpulent, not discharging themselves, as he used no sort of Exercise. No man better bore ye approaches of his Dissolution (as I am told) or with less ostentation yielded up to his Being. The great Modesty wch you know was natural to him, and ye great Contempt he had for all Sorts of Vanity & Parade, never appeared more than in his last moments: He had a conscious Satisfaction (no doubt) in acting right, in feeling himself honest, true, & unpretending to more than was his own. So he dyed, as he lived, with that secret, yet sufficient, Contentment. . . . I shall with pleasure take upon me to draw this amiable, quiet, deserving, unpretending Christian and Philosophical character, in His Epitaph. . . . Let us love his Memory, and profit by his example.—POPE, ALEXANDER, 1730, *Letter to the Rev. Mr. Broome, Aug.* 29.

This modest Stone, what few vain Marbles can,
May truly say, Here lies an honest Man:
A Poet, blest beyond the Poet's fate,
Whom Heav'n kept sacred from the Proud and Great:
Foe to loud Praise, and Friend to learned Ease,
Content with Science in the Vale of Peace.
Calmly he look'd on either Life, and here
Saw nothing to regret, or there to fear;
From Nature's temp'rate feast rose satisfy'd,
Thank'd Heav'n that he had liv'd, and that he died.

—POPE, ALEXANDER, 1730, *On Mr. Elijah Fenton; at Easthamstead in Berks.*

Whoever mentioned Fenton, mentioned him with honour. . . . Fenton was tall and bulky, inclined to corpulence, which he did not lessen by much exercise; for he was very sluggish and sedentary, rose late, and when he had risen, sat down to his books or papers. . . Of his morals and his conversation the account is uniform; he was never named but with praise and fondness, as a man in the highest degree amiable and excellent. —JOHNSON, SAMUEL, 1779–81, *Fenton, Lives of the English Poets.*

His character was that of an amiable but indolent man, who drank, in his great chair, two bottles of port wine a day.—CAMPBELL, THOMAS, 1819, *Specimens of the British Poets.*

GENERAL

Sweet Fancy's bloom in Fenton's lay appears,
And the ripe judgment of instructive years.

—SAVAGE, RICHARD, 1729, *The Wanderer.*

As the plan of this play ["Mariamne,"] is regular, simple, and interesting, so are the sentiments no less masterly, and the characters graphically distinguished. It contains likewise many beautiful strokes of poetry.—CIBBER, THEOPHILUS, 1753, *Lives of the Poets, vol.* IV, *p.* 170.

Fenton seems to have had some peculiar system of versification. "Mariamne" is written in lines of ten syllables, with few of those redundant terminations which the drama not only admits but requires, as more nearly approaching to real dialogue. The tenor of his verse is so uniform that it cannot be thought casual; and yet upon what principle he so constructed it, is difficult to discover. . . . Of his petty poems some are very trifling, without any thing to be praised either in the thought or expression. He is unlucky in his competition; he tells the same idle tale with Congreve, and does not tell it so well. He translates from Ovid the same epistle as Pope; but I am afraid not with equal happiness. To examine his performances one by one would be tedious. His translation from Homer into blank verse will find few readers, while another can be had in rhyme. The piece addressed to Lambarde is no disagreeable specimen of epistolary poetry; and his ode to the lord Gower was pronounced by Pope the next ode in the English language to Dryden's "Cecilia." Fenton may be justly styled an excellent versifier and a good poet.—JOHNSON, SAMUEL, 1779–81, *Fenton, Lives of the English Poets.*

A survey of Fenton's works shows a striking reproduction on his part of most of the species of poetry cultivated by Pope. Fenton has a pastoral (*Florelio*) to correspond to Pope's fourth and favourite Pastoral; a paraphrase of the 14th chapter of Isaiah to correspond to Pope's "Messiah"; an epistle from "Sappho to Phœon," Epistles, Prologues, and Translations and Imitations of Horace. Fenton was a thorough master of versification, and excelled Pope in his command of a variety of metres. His "Ode to Lord Gower" (which Pope placed next in merit to Dryden's "St. Cecilia") avoids the faults committed by Pope in his own "Pindaric" essay; and his blank verse translation of the 11th book of the "Odyssey" is dignified without heaviness. Fenton's tragedy of "Mariamne" seems to have owed its success in part to the judicious suggestions of the author of "Oroonoko."—WARD, ADOLPHUS WILLIAM, 1869, *ed., Poetical Works of Alexander Pope, p.* 460, *note.*

No poet, though a man with poetic tastes.—ADAMS, W. H. DAVENPORT, 1886, *Good Queen Anne, vol.* II, *p.* 331.

Fenton is styled by Johnson "an excellent versifier and a good poet." He had, indeed, caught the trick of Pope's versification with such success that it has never been possible to distinguish his share of the version of the "Odyssey" from Pope's by internal evidence. It is questionable whether he deserves the appellation of poet. His most considerable pieces, the "Hymn to the Sun," the ode to Lord Gower, the elegy on Lord Blandford, the "Epistles," are at most agreeable exercises in metre, and his general good taste does not preserve him from some rather ludicrous lapses. Perhaps his most memorable couplet is one in which he completely inverts the conclusions of modern science respecting the origin of the human species:—

> Foes to the tribe from which they trace their clan,
> As monkeys draw their pedigree from man.

His tragedy exhibits considerable ability, but rather that of a playwright than of a poet. Mariamne's fate had already been the subject of one of Calderon's greatest plays, of which Fenton probably never heard. His lighter pieces are not deficient in sprightliness, but the humour is far inferior to that of his model Prior. On the whole he must be classed with those to whom poetry has been rather an amusement than an inspiration or an art. The testimony to his character is very high and uniform. "He was never," says his pupil Orrery, "named but with praise and fondness, as a man in the highest degree amiable and excellent." In face of this evidence, which is amply confirmed by particular anecdotes, the assertion that he spoke ungratefully of Pope may be dinmissed as groundless. He seems to have had no fault except the indolence which shortened his life.—GARNETT, RICHARD, 1889, *Dictionary of National Biography, vol.* XVIII, *p.* 323.

He seems to have been one of those beings who are generally and perhaps rather selfishly beloved, because, while known to possess fine powers, they make little effort to use them in their own behalf. His poems, which occasionally show glimpses of genius, exhibit his character much in the same light as his letters to Broome, suggesting something of Swift's contempt for mankind, mixed with a general kindliness and benevolence, and a strong vein of religious feeling.—COURTHOPE, WILLIAM JOHN, 1889, *The Life of Alexander Pope, Works, ed., Elwin and Courthope, vol.* V, *p.* 196.

Laurence Echard

1670?-1730.

A voluminous historian, at one time very popular, now seldom read. Born at Cassam, near Beccles, in Suffolk, about 1671. His first important work was "The Roman History, from the building of the City to the perfect settlement of the Empire by Augustus Cæsar,"—fourth edition published in 1699. In 1702 was published "A General Ecclesiastical History, from the Nativity of our blessed Saviour, to the establishment of Christianity by human laws, under the emperor Constantine the Great; containing the space of about 313 years; with so much of the Jewish and Roman history as is necessary and convenient to illustrate the work; to which is added a large Chronological Table of all the Roman and ecclesiastical affairs, included in the same period of time." In 1707 Echard became prebendary of Lincoln, and chaplain to the bishop of that diocese, publishing in the same year the first part of his most widely known work, "The History of England, from the first entrance of Julius Cæsar and the Romans." In 1712 Echard was installed archdeacon of Stowe, and in 1718 he published the second and third volumes of his history, bringing the work down to the Revolution. Echard published a number of other original works and translations, now forgotten. He died in 1730.—MOULTON, CHARLES WELLS, 1901.

GENERAL

"The Ecclesiastical History" of Mr. Laurence Echard is the best of its kind in the English tongue.—PRIDEAUX, HUMPHREY, 1716–18, *Connection of the Old and New Testament in the History of the Jews and Neighboring Nations.*

King George hath given 300 libs. to Mr. Laurence Eachard, for his "History of England," which is dedicated to king George. I suppose 'tis a most roguish, whiggish thing, much such as what Kennett writes. I have not read it. Such writers ought to be laid aside. Yet I hear that Dr. Prideaux, dean of Norwich, mightily commends this Eachard's "Church History." But Prideaux is a great whig himself, tho' a good scholar. Indeed Eachard hath a good pen, but he does not look into, much less follow, original authors.—HEARNE, THOMAS, 1718, *Reliquiæ Hearnianæ, ed. Bliss, April* 27, *vol.* II, *p.* 61.

The clearness of your method, and the perspicuity of your language, are two very great excellencies, which I admire. I am singularly pleased with the refreshing divisions of your matter, and the chronological distinction of the several parts of your history. . . . I neither admire many of the authors which you cite, nor your way of citing them: and I have some reason to think I am not singular in either. Many of the authors that are cited by you have so little credit in the world as to be far from giving sufficient warrant to justify your inserting things from them into an history that should give an account to posterity of past transactions. And your way of citing them is liable to very great objections.—CALAMY, EDMUND, 1718, *Letter to Mr. Archdeacon Echard upon occasion of his History of England.*

More distinguished as an historian than a poet.—CIBBER, THEOPHILUS, 1753, *Lives of the Poets, vol.* IV, *p.* 198.

Laurence Echard, A. M., was a person of some estimation amongst his contemporaries, but who is little known to us. —NOBLE, MARK, 1806, *A Biographical History of England, vol.* III, *pp.* 106, 107.

He was familiar with the powerful, was renowned as the chief historian of the time, and might well believe himself destined for immortality. . . . The fame of Echard, so imposing to his contemporaries, has long since passed away. He now neither awakens envy nor merits attention. He was, however, successful in carrying off the emoluments of literature. . . . But no one of Echard's works rises above the level of a third-rate writer, or have found admirers among posterity.—LAWRENCE, EUGENE, 1855, *The Lives of the British Historians, vol.* I.

Echard's "History," though it gave rise to many adverse criticisms, retained its popularity until it was superseded by Tindal's translation of Rapin. It is chiefly remarkable for the insertion of Captain Lindsey's astonishing narrative concerning Cromwell's interview with the devil on the morning of the battle of Worcester.—BARKER, G. F. RUSSELL, 1888, *Dictionary of National Biography, vol.* XVI, *p.* 351.

DANIEL DEFOE

Engraving by Gucht.
From Painting by Taverner.

Daniel Defoe

1661?–1731.

Born [Daniel Foe, name changed to Defoe in 1703,] in Cripplegate, 1660 or 1661. To school at Newington Green, 1674 or 1675. Went into business about 1685 [?]. Sided with Monmouth in Rebellion, 1685. Liveryman of City of London, 26 Jan. 1688. With William's army, 1688. Bankrupt, about 1692 [?]. Accountant to the Commissioners of the Glass Duty, 1695–99. Vigorous partisan of King William. Prosecuted for libelling the Church, 1703. Sentenced to fine, pillory, and imprisonment during Queen's pleasure, July 1703. Stood in pillory, which populace guarded and wreathed with flowers, July 1703. Imprisoned in Newgate. Released from prison, Aug. 1704. Wrote "The Review," Feb. 1704 to June 1713. Sent to Edinburgh as secret agent in favour of Union, autumn 1706. Returned to England, spring 1708. On another mission to Scotland, 1708; again in 1712. Active political controversialist and pamphleteer. Prosecuted for libel and imprisoned, 22 April 1713, but pardoned immediately. Found guilty of libelling Lord Annesley, 12 July 1715, but escaped sentence. Wrote periodical "Mercurius Politicus," 1716–20; edited "Mist's Journal," Aug. 1717 to Oct. 1724. Started "Whitehall Evening Post," 1718, and "Daily Post," 1719; wrote in "Whitehall Evening Post," 1718–20; in "Daily Post," 1719–25; in "Applebee's Journal," 1720–26. Died, in Moorfields, 26 April 1731. Buried in Bunhill Fields. *Works:* A complete list of Defoe's works, numbering upwards of 250, is given in William Lee's "Life of Defoe," 1869. His political, religious, and social Controversial Tracts date from 1694 to 1731. In fiction, some of his best-known works are; "The Life and Strange Surprising Adventures of Robinson Crusoe," 1719; "The Further Adventures of Robinson Crusoe," 1719; "Life of Captain Singleton," 1720; "Moll Flanders," 1722; "Journal of the Plague Year," 1722; "Life of John Sheppard," 1724. *Collected Works:* "A True Collection of the Writings of the Author of The True Born Englishman, Corrected by Himself" (anon.), 1703; "Novels," 1810; "Novels and Miscellaneous Works," 20 vols., 1840–41; "Works," with memoir by Hazlitt, 1840–43. *Life*, by W. Lee, 1869.—SHARP, R. FARQUHARSON, 1897, *A Dictionary of English Authors*, p. 76.

PERSONAL

DANIEL DE-FOE
BORN 1661
DIED 1731
AUTHOR OF
ROBINSON CRUSOE.

This monument is the result of an appeal,
in the "Christian World" newspaper,
to the boys and girls of England, for funds
to place a suitable memorial upon the grave
of
Daniel De-Foe.
It represents the united contributions
of seventeen hundred persons.
Septr. 1870.

—INSCRIPTION ON MONUMENT, ERECTED 1870.

Whereas Daniel De Foe, alias De Fooe, is charged with writing a scandalous and seditious pamphlet, entitled "The Shortest Way with the Dissenters;" he is a middle-sized, spare man, about forty years old, of a brown complexion, and dark brown-coloured hair, but wears a wig; a hooked nose, a sharp chin, gray eyes, and a large mole near his mouth; was born in London, and for many years was a hose-factor, in Freeman's yard, in Cornhill, and now is owner of the brick and pantile works near Tilbury Fort, in Essex. Whoever shall discover the said Daniel De Foe to one of her majesty's principal secretaries of state, or any of her majesty's justices of the peace, so as he may be apprehended, shall have a reward of fifty pounds, which her majesty has ordered immediately to be paid on such discovery.—LONDON GAZETTE, 1702–3, *Proclamation, Jan.* 10.

The person who discovered Daniel Foe—for whom a reward of £50 was promised in the *Gazette*—sends to me for his money, but does not care to appear himself. If, therefore, your lordship will order the sum to be paid to Mr. Armstrong, I will take care that the person shall have it who discovered the said Foe, and upon whose information he was apprehended.—NOTTINGHAM, 1703, *Letter to Godolphin, May; Calendar Treasury Papers, vol.* II, *p.* 153.

One of those authors (the fellow that

was pilloried, I have forgot his name) is indeed so grave, sententious, dogmatical a rogue, that there is no enduring him.—SWIFT, JONATHAN, 1708, *A Letter from a Member of the House of Commons in Ireland to a Member of the House of Commons in England, concerning the Sacramental Test.*

I remember an Author in the World some years ago, who was generally upbraided with Ignorance, and called an "Illiterate Fellow," by some of the *Beau-Monde* of the last Age. . . . I happened to come into this Person's Study once, and I found him busy translating a Description of the Course of the River Boristhenes, out of *Bleau's* Geography, written in *Spanish.* Another Time I found him translating some Latin Paragraphs out of *Leubinitz Theatri Cometici*, being a learned Discourse upon Comets; and that I might see whether it was genuine, I looked on some part of it that he had finished, and found by it that he understood the Latin very well, and had perfectly taken the sense of that difficult Author. In short, I found he understood the *Latin*, the *Spanish*, the *Italian*, and could read the *Greek*, and I knew before that he spoke *French* fluently—*yet this Man was no Scholar.* As to Science, on another Occasion, I heard him dispute (in such a manner as surprised me) upon the motions of the Heavenly Bodies, the Distance, Magnitude, Revolutions, and especially the Influences of the Planets, the Nature and probable Revolutions of Comets, the excellency of the New Philosphy, and the like; *but this Man was no Scholar.* . . . This put me upon wondering, ever so long ago, what this *strange Thing* called a Man of Learning *was*, and what is it that constitutes a *Scholar?* For, *said I*, here's a man speaks five Languages and reads the Sixth, is a master of Astronomy, Geography, History, and abundance of other useful Knowledge (which I do not mention, that you may not guess at the Man, who is too Modest to desire it), and yet, they say *this Man is no Scholar.*—DEFOE, DANIEL, 1720–26, *Applebee's Journal.*

De Foe, a man of talents, but of indifferent character, was the darling of the whig mob, and the contempt of men of genius, because he disgraced himself by every low artfice as a writer. He wrote poetry, and on politics; and was a plagiary.—NOBLE, MARK, 1806, *A Biographical History of England, vol.* II, *p.* 306.

That De Foe was a man of powerful intellect and lively imagination, is obvious from his works; that he was possessed of an ardent temper, a resolute courage, and an unwearied spirit of enterprise, is ascertained by the events of his changeful career: and whatever may be thought of that rashness and improvidence by which his progress in life was so frequently impeded, there seems no reason to withold from him the praise of . . . integrity, sincerity, and consistency.—BALLANTYNE, JOHN, 1810, *ed. De Foe's Novels, Edinburgh ed., Memoir.*

When, or upon what occasion it was, that De Foe made the alteration in his name, by connecting with it the foreign prefix, no where appears. His enemies said, he adopted it because he would not be thought an Englishman; but this notion seems to have no other foundation than the circumstance of his having, in consequence of his zeal for King William, attacked the prejudices of his countrymen, in his well-known satire of "The Trueborn Englishman." Oldmixon intimates, that it was not until after he had stood in the pillory, that he changed his name; and Dr. Browne tells us, that he did it at the suggestion of Harley:

"Have I not chang'd by your advice my name."

But no reliance is to be placed upon the testimony of either of these writers when speaking of De Foe. His motive was, probably, a dislike to his original name, either for its import, or its harshness; or he might have been desirous of restoring it to its Norman origin.—WILSON, WALTER, 1830, *Memoirs of the Life and Times of Daniel De Foe, vol.* I, *p.* 231.

De Foe has left one descendant,—a Crusoe without a Friday,—in an island to him a desert. . . . There are men who may be warmed by the reflected glory of their ancestors; but, however elevated and unclouded, it falls feebly on the deathbed of the forsaken. . . . Daniel De Foe wants no statue, and is far beyond any other want; but, alas, there is one behind who is not so. Let all contribute one penny for one year: poor James De Foe has lived seventy-seven, and his dim eyes cannot look far into another. . . . It was in the power of Johnson to relieve the granddaughter of Milton; Mr. Editor, it is in yours, to prop up the last scion of De Foe. If Milton wrote the grandest poem and the most energetic and eloquent prose of any writer in any country; if he stood erect before Tyranny, and covered with his buckler not England only, but nascent nations; if our great prophet raised in vision the ladder that rose from earth to heaven, with angels upon every step of it; lower indeed, but not less useful, were the energies of De Foe. He stimulated to enterprise those colonies of England which extend over every sea, and which carry with them, from him, the spirit and the language that will predominate throughout the world. Achilles and Homer will be forgotten before Crusoe and De Foe.—LANDOR, WALTER SAVAGE, 1855? *From The Times Newspaper, Life by Forster, p.* 593.

Could the life of this extraordinary man be represented in a dramatic form, we should behold him in the utmost extremes of social position, each explicable by his course as an author. He might be seen the familiar and admired *habitué* of a Puritan coffee-house, ardently discussing the latest news from the seat of war, or the local question of the hour; alternating between his hosier's shop in Cornhill and the Dissenters' chapel at Surrey; in arms for the Duke of Monmouth; one of the handsomely-mounted escort of volunteers who attended William and Mary from Whitehall to the Mansion house; a bankrupt refugee, talking with Selkirk at the Red Lion Tavern in Bristol; the confidential visitor ensconced in the cabinet of William of Orange; the occupant of a cell in Newgate; an honored guest at Edinburgh, promoting the Union; a secret ambassador to the Continent; the delegate of the people, handing to Harley a mammoth petition; the cynosure of a hundred sympathetic and respectful eyes as he stands in the pillory; in comfortable retirement at Newington; and at last a victim of filial ingratitude, his health wasted in noble intellectual toil, dying at the age of seventy. Such are few of the strong contrasts which the mere external drama of De Foe's life presents. . . . While Swift was noting the banquets he attended for the diversion of Stella, Steele dodging bailiffs in his luxurious establishment, Addison, in elegant trim, paying his court to the Countess of Warwick, and Bolingbroke embodying his heartless philosophy in artificial rhetoric, De Foe was wrestling for truth in Cripplegate. . . . His contemporary authors are known to us through elaborate and loving memoirs; their portraits adorn noble galleries; scholars still emulate their works, and glorify them in reviews; while their monumental effigies are clustered in imposing beauty in the venerable Abbey. Our knowledge of De Foe's appearance is chiefly derived from an advertisment describing him as a fugitive.—TUCKERMAN, HENRY T., 1857, *Essays, Biographical and Critical, pp.* 286, 288.

On my visiting that sacred spot of departed patriotism—the last solemn resting-place of the mortal remains of Daniel De Foe, Bunhill Fields Cemetery—I was struck with the condition of the tombstone, which was broken, and the inscriptions, two or three, obliterated by nelgect and the corrosive influence of time and atmosphere. I pointed this gravestone to the sexton:—"That tombstone is broken, and the inscriptions are worn off through the corrosive influence of the atmosphere." "Yes sir, the lightning did it," was the reply. Lightning did it—impossible! The tomb of De Foe requiring lightning from heaven to destroy it! This truly is one way of obliterating the memorial of departed greatness; for De Foe was both great and good—yes, he was a good man. What!—the white reeky haze of the sulphurous exhalations of the vale of Sodom and Gomorrah here? Forbid it, Heaven! Daniel De Foe's last resting-place to be torn up by fire from heaven!—he; one of the first writers on free trade and political economy, and every branch of civil and religious liberty, in all seasons of prosperity or national danger—he; not only statesman but philanthropist—be torn up or disturbed, in his last resting-place, by fire from heaven! Impossible! The tomb is broken of that man, who dared to show to arbitrary powers in church and in state; how to pull their house about their ears—THE SHORTEST WAY.—CHADWICK, WILLIAM, 1859, *The Life and Times of Daniel De Foe, p.* 463.

He was a great, a truly great liar, perhaps the greatest liar that ever lived. His dishonesty went too deep to be called superficial, yet, if we go deeper still in his rich and strangely mixed nature, we come upon stubborn foundations of conscience. . . . Shifty as Defoe was, and admirably as he used his genius for circumstantial invention to cover his designs, there was no other statesman of his generation who remained more true to the principles of the Revolution, and to the cause of civil and religious freedom. No other public man saw more clearly what was for the good of the country, or pursued it more steadily. . . . Defoe cannot be held up as an exemplar of moral conduct, yet if he is judged by the measures that he laboured for and not by the means that he employed, few Englishmen have lived more deserving than he of their country's gratitude. He may have been self-seeking and vain-glorious, but in his political life self-seeking and vainglory were elevated by their alliance with higher and wider aims. Defoe was a wonderful mixture of knave and patriot. Sometimes pure knave seems to be uppermost, sometimes pure patriot; but the mixture is so complex, and the energy of the man so restless, that it almost passes human skill to unravel the two elements. The author of "Robinson Crusoe," is entitled to the benefit of every doubt.—MINTO, WILLIAM, 1879, *Daniel Defoe (English Men of Letters), pp.* 165, 166, 167.

His fate he has earned,
His book we have burned,
That its soul may fly free!
One and all, come and see
Great London's brave show!
Here's to Daniel Defoe!

. . . .

On to the Pillory, ho!
To punish rogue Daniel Defoe!
Pelt him, maidens and men!
For he thinks with a pen,
And his thought is too free!
God bless him! See! See!!
Fill glasses! Fill, ho!
Here's to Daniel Defoe!

—VENABLE, WILLIAM HENRY, 1885, *Defoe in the Pillory; Melodies of the Heart, Songs of Freedom and Other Poems, p.* 132.

The names of Dryden, Addison, Steele, Pope, Johnson conjure up before us the groups of friends which surrounded them, the clubs which they frequented, the disciples who sat admiringly at their feet. But Defoe strides through the press a solitary figure—sternly selfreliant, friendless, uncompanioned—always alone, but always sufficient to himself—less fortunate than the cast-away of his own creation, for he, at least, possessed the affection of a faithful attendant—active with a ceaseless activity, vigorous with a manly strength, but, from first to last, a lonely Man of Letters.—ADAMS, W. H. DAVENPORT, 1886, *Good Queen Anne, vol.* II, *p.* 230.

His connection with Mist forced him to pass himself off as one of the Jacobites, "a generation who, I profess," as he says in his letter in the State Paper Office of 26 April 1718, "my very soul abhores." He had, therefore, to abandon his claims to integrity, and submit to pass for a traitor. No man has a right to make such a sacrifice; and if not precisely a spy, Mist and Mist's friend would hardly draw the distinction.—STEPHEN, LESLIE, 1888, *Dictionary of National Biography, vol.* XIV, *p.* 288.

His fame is world-wide, yet all that is known of him is one or two of his least productions, and his busy life is ignored in the permanent place in literary history which he has secured. His characteristics, as apart from his conduct, are all those of an honest man; but when that most important part of him is taken into the question, it is difficult to pronounce him anything but a knave. His distinguishing literary quality is a minute truthfulness to fact which makes it almost impossible not to take what he says for gospel; but his constant inspiration is fiction—not to say, in some circumstances, falsehood. He spent his life in the highest endeavors that a man can engage in, —in the work of persuading and influencing his country, chiefly for her good, —and he is remembered by a boys' book, which is, indeed, the first of boys' books, yet not much more. Through these contradictions we must push our way before we can reach any clear idea of Defoe, the London tradesman, who, by times, composed almost all the newspapers in London, wrote all the pamphlets, had his finger in every pie, and a share in all that was done, yet brought nothing out of it but a damaged reputation and an unhonored end.—OLIPHANT, M. O. W., 1893, *The Author of "Robinson Crusoe," The Century, vol.* 46, *p.* 740.

It would not be fair to judge Defoe altogether by the moral standard of our own day, but the part he played as a servant and spy of the government would have been an act of baseness in any age, and of this he seems to have been conscious.—DENNIS, JOHN, 1894, *The Age of Pope, p.* 181.

To narrate the career of Daniel Defoe is to tell a tale of wonder and daring, of high endeavour and marvellous success. To dwell upon it is to take courage, and to praise God for the splendid possibilities of life. . . . Defoe is always the hero; his career is as thick with events as a cornfield with corn; his fortunes change as quickly and as completely as the shapes in a kaleidoscope—he is up, he is down, he is courted, he is spurned; it is shine, it is shower, it is *couleur de rose,* it is Stygian night. Thirteen times he was rich and poor. Achilles was not more audacious, Ulysses more subtle, Æneas more pious. . . . *Te Deum laudamus,* that, as before intimated, is the key-note to Defoe's life, and no careful student thereof can help being struck with the frequency with which these three words occur. His whole life was one long cry, "We praise Thee, O Lord." There was nothing of the pessimist in Defoe; and optimism beatified, and that only, could have carried him safely, as it did, through the surges that unceasingly broke upon him. . . . Defoe was temperate in his habits: unlike so many of his contemporaries, he never drank to excess. He did not smoke or take snuff. He considered smoking as "conducive to intemperate drinking;" and in his younger days, thanks to a fine constitution, he rarely troubled the doctor. The theatre, the ball-room, and the card-table were to him the very devil. In manly sports and athletic exercises he had always found an attraction; nor was there wanting in him the Puritan love of horse-play; and his reputation for swordsmanship was always a protection to him. In that "frenzy of the tongue," as he puts it, called swearing he could see "neither pleasure nor profit." He loved a good tale and a merry jest; but "low-prised wit," indulged in at the expense of decency and morals, his soul abhorred. His talk, when he was excited, was pungent with witticisms; but he was in the habit of repeating favourite quotations with too great frequency.—WRIGHT, THOMAS, 1894, *The Life of Daniel Defoe, pp.* 1, 83, 316.

Most of the attacks upon Defoe published of late years have been based upon the work which he did for the Whigs under George I. in the guise of a Tory. But whatever view we may take of that matter, there are points which can be urged in Defoe's favour. There is no reason to think that he wrote in these papers in a manner contrary to his principles; what he undertook, was to prevent others doing so, as far as might be. Neither did he betray the opponents among whom he found himself; on the contrary, he did his utmost to prevent them getting into trouble, or to shield them from punishment. The position was not altogether new to him, for he had been employed on secret services in the previous reign, and he had published ironical pamphlets which had misled members of both parties. It is impossible to believe that Defoe was not himself satisfied that the part he now played was consistent with honour. "No obligation," he says, "could excuse me in calling evil good, or good evil." This was written only a year before the compact with Townshend. The morality or immorality of "secret service" must depend upon the nature of the service required; and there can be no doubt that Defoe held that he could perform these duties without injuring his character. It should be remembered that he was in thorough sympathy with the statesmen by whom he was employed; that there was a real danger to the country in the sedition preached by the Jacobite papers which it was his business to render harmless; and that opposition to the Pretender's cause was a leading principle throughout Defoe's career. His critics seem to forget that even in these easy days there are few public men against whom charges of inconsistency and departure from the literal truth are not brought, rightly or wrongly; and they do not realise the difficulties against which Defoe had to contend.—AITKEN, GEORGE A., 1895, *ed. Defoe's Romances and Narratives, General Introduction, vol.* I, *p.* xxxiv.

It is not of much use to discuss Defoe's moral character, and it is sincerely to be hoped that no more revelations concerning it will turn up, inasmuch as each is more damaging than the last, except to those who have succeeded in taking his true measure once for all. It is that of a man who, with no high, fine, or poetical sentiment to save him, shared to the full the partisan enthusiasm of his time, and its belief that all was fair in politics.—SAINTSBURY, GEORGE, 1898, *A Short History of English Literature, p.* 547.

ESSAY UPON PROJECTS
1698

There was also a book of DeFoe's called an "Essay on Projects," and another of Dr. Mather's, called "Essays to do Good," which perhaps gave me a turn of thinking that had an influence on some of the principal future events of my life.—FRANKLIN, BENJAMIN, 1771–89, *Autobiography, ed. Bigelow.*

It is questionable if there is any other book that has so much benefited mankind in the practical manner as this little essay by the author of "Robinson Crusoe."—PARTON, JAMES, 1864, *Life and Times of Benjamin Franklin, vol.* I, *p.* 45.

It displays Defoe's lively and lucid style in full vigor, and abounds with ingenious thoughts and apt illustrations, though it illustrates also the unsystematic character of his mind.—SAINTSBURY, GEORGE, 1877, *Encyclopædia Britannica, Ninth Edition, vol.* VII.

There is more fervid imagination and daring ingenuity than business talent in Defoe's Essay; if his trading speculations were conducted with equal rashness, it is not difficult to understand their failure. The most notable of them are the schemes of a dictator, rather than of the adviser of a free Government. The essay is chiefly interesting as a monument of Defoe's marvellous force of mind, and the strange mixture of steady sense with incontinent flightiness. There are ebullient sallies in it which we generally find only in the productions of madmen and charlatans, and yet it abounds in suggestions which statesmen might profitably have set themselves with due adaptations to carry into effect. The "Essay on Projects" might alone be adduced in proof of Defoe's title to genius.—MINTO, WILLIAM, 1879, *Daniel Defoe* (*English Men of Letters*), *p.* 18.

TRUE-BORN ENGLISHMEN
1701

A satire which, if written in doggerel verse, and without the wit or pleasantry of Butler's "Hudibras," is a master-piece of good sense and just reflection, and shows a thorough knowledge both of English history and of the English character. It is indeed a complete and unanswerable exposure of the pretence set up to a purer and loftier origin than all the rest of the world, instead of our being a mixed race from all parts of Europe, settling down into one common name and people. Defoe's satire was so just and true, that it drove the cant, to which it was meant to be an antidote, out of fashion; and it was this piece of service that procured the writer the good opinion and notice of King William. It did not, however, equally recommend him to the public. If it silenced the idle and ill-natured clamours of a party, by telling the plain truth, —that truth was not the more welcome for being plain or effectual.—HAZLITT, WILLIAM, 1830, *Wilson's Life and Times of Daniel Defoe, Edinburgh Review, vol.* 50, *p.* 413.

He lost a part of his strength, his facility, and his fancy, when he wrote in verse. Yet, even in verse, he made a lucky, nervous hit, now and then; and the best of his efforts was the "True-born Englishman."—FORSTER, JOHN, 1845, *Daniel De Foe, Edinburgh Review, vol.* 82, *p.* 500.

SHORTEST WAY WITH THE DISSENTERS
1702

On the 29th instant, Daniel Foe, *alias*, De Foe, stood in the pillory before the Royal Exchange in Cornhill, as he did yesterday near the Conduit in Cheapside, and this day at Temple Bar; in pursuance of his sentence given against him at the last sessions at the Old Bailey for writing and publishing a seditious libel, entitled the "Shortest Way with the Dissenters." By which sentence he is also fined 200 marks, to find sureties for his good behaviour for seven years; and to remain in prison till all be performed.—LONDON GAZETTE, 1703, *July* 31.

Perhaps we might be allowed to ask, *why* De Foe, a thorough dissenter of the old Puritan school, should write a mad fire-and-faggot tract against the whole body of dissenters? De Foe's principles were not the ordinary sunshine principles of prosperous mace or sword bearing dissent; but were of the true old persecuted Puritan class—a class doomed to conquest or death in the combat. . . . De Foe's tract has always been held up for a very witty performance; it might be witty, but I cannot see the wit of it, and I never could see the wit of it; but I can conceive a man of De Foe's power of discrimination perceiving the exact position of parties in England; and calculating the effect of a pushing the High Church principles to their extreme length.—CHADWICK, WILLIAM, 1859, *The Life and Times of Daniel De Foe, pp.* 181, 182.

The traditional criticism of this remarkable pamphlet is a most curious example of the way in which thoroughly inappropriate descriptions of books pass from mouth to mouth. Every commentator (with the single exception of Mr. Chadwick) has dilated upon its "exquisite irony." Now, the fact of the matter is, that in "The Shortest Way" there is no irony at all, and, as Defoe's adversaries acutely remarked, irony would never have been pleaded had not the author got into trouble, when of course it suited him *faire flèche de tout bois.* The pamphlet is simply an exposition in the plainest and most forcible terms of the extreme "high-flying" position, and every line of it might have been endorsed, and was endorsed, by consistent high-churchmen. The author's object clearly was by this naked presentation to awaken the dissenters to a sense of their danger, and to startle moderate churchmen by showing them to what end their favourite doctrines necessarily led. For neither of these purposes was irony necessary, and irony, we repeat, there is none. If any lingering doubt from the consensus of authority on the other side remain, let the student read "The Shortest Way" and then turn to Swift's "Modest Proposal" or his "Reasons against Abolishing the Church of England." He will soon see the difference.—SAINTSBURY, GEORGE, 1877, *Encyclopædia Britannica, Ninth Edition, vol.* VII.

A work of high rhetorical art, modeled after the example set by him who imagined the speech of Antony over the dead body of Cæsar. The beginning is calm, gentle, charitable, with a touch of sadness over the fate of those steadfast clergymen who had either to sacrifice their worldly fortunes to their loyalty, or wrong their consciences by accepting the oath to the Revolution Settlement. There is a touch of inevitable yet half-suppressed indignation when the case of the Church in Scotland is casually noticed.—BURTON, JOHN HILL, 1880, *A History of the Reign of Queen Anne, vol.* I, *p.* 94.

The reader will observe a curious resemblance between the style of argument in "Killing No Murder"—incitement to the assassination of a man—which was meant to be taken seriously, and that in "The Shortest Way with the Dissenters" —incitement to the assassination of a party—which was meant to be taken as satire.—MORLEY, HENRY, 1886, *ed., Famous Pamphlets, Introduction, p.* 7.

Defoe's immortal satire, "The Shortest Way with Dissenters," so subtle and restrained as to deceive its victims into the belief that it was written by one of themselves, is a worthy exposure of the narrowness and intolerance which were the curse of High Churchmen; though at the same time it helps one to understand the causes which led to that intolerance, so thoroughly does Defoe present his enemies' case.—DEARMER, PERCY, 1898, *ed., Religious Pamphlets, Introduction, p.* 36.

THE REVIEW
1704-1713

The poor "Review" is quite exhausted, and grown so very contemptible that, though he has provoked all his brothers of the quill, none will enter into a controversy with him. The fellow, who had excellent natural parts, but wanted a small foundation of learning, is a lively instance of those wits who, as an ingenious author says, will endure but one skimming.—GAY, JOHN, 1711, *Present State of Wit.*

One of the leading objects of the "Review," after the discussion of politics, was to correct the vices of the times. Throughout the work, the writer carries on an unsparing warfare against folly and vice, in all their forms and disguises. In forcible terms he inveighs against the fashionable practice of immoderate drinking, the idle propensity to swearing, the little regard that was paid to the marriage vow, and the loose conversation and habits of men in general. In well-pointed satire, he chastises the licentiousness of the stage; and condemns, in strong language, the barbarous practice of duelling. He has also some just remarks upon the rage for gambling speculations, which, in this reign, had risen to a great height. Upon all these subjects, he brings forth his capacious stores of wit and humour to the assistance of grave reasoning, adducing examples occasionally of the flagitious courses he condemns; but with sufficient delicacy to shew that his aim was the reformation, rather than the exposure, of the offender. No man paid a greater regard to those decencies of expression which have so much influence in regulating the intercourses of life; and although few individuals had greater provocation, from the coarse and illiberal writers of the day, yet he rarely suffers his temper to be disturbed, or departs from courtesy of language towards even his bitterest opponents.—WILSON, WALTER, 1830, *Memoirs of the Life and Times of Daniel De Foe, vol.* II, *p.* 201.

Defoe's greatest work, greatest undoubtedly, as to its magnitude, and perhaps, in value and importance; yet the least known of his multifarious writings. . . . When it is remembered, that no other pen was ever employed than that of Defoe, upon a work appearing at such frequent intervals, extending over more than nine years, and embracing, in more than five thousand printed pages, essays on almost every branch of human knowledge, the achievement must be pronounced a great one, even had he written nothing else. If we add that, between the dates of the first and last numbers of the "Review," he wrote and published no less than eighty other distinct works, containing 4727 pages, and perhaps more, not now known, the fertility of his genius must appear as astonishing as the greatness of his capacity for labour. . . . Only those who have read the "Review" can be thoroughly acquainted with Daniel Defoe.—LEE, WILLIAM, 1869, *Daniel Defoe: His Life and Recently Discovered Writings, vol.* I, *pp.* 84, 85.

It is probable that if the five points of bulk, rapidity of production, variety of matter, originality of design, and excellence of style are taken together, hardly any author can show a work of equal magnitude.—SAINTSBURY, GEORGE, 1877, *Encyclopædia Britannica, Ninth Edition, vol.* VII.

While Defoe's "Review," with its invention of the leading article, its splendid versatility, and its fearless criticism of topics of the day, must be granted an important place in the history of journalism; large reservation must be made when it is claimed that its author anticipated Steele. Few writers more than Defoe elude classification. He occupies a tantalizing position at the threshold of two great developments in prose literature, and it is as difficult to deny that the "Review" led the way to the "Tatler" as to maintain that "Pamela" was not influenced by "Crusoe" or "Roxana." . . . It is generally hazardous to appeal against any long-sustained verdict of public literary opinion, but it cannot be admitted that the oblivion into which the "Review" has fallen is a wholly merited one.—LOBBAN, J. H., 1896, *English Essays, Introduction, pp.* xvi, xviii.

APPARITION OF MRS VEAL
1706

An adventurous bookseller had ventured to print a considerable edition of a work by the Reverend Charles Drelincourt, minister of the Calvinist Church in Paris, and translated by M. D'Assigny, under the title of the "Christian's Defence against the Fear of Death, with several directions how to prepare ourselves to die well." But however certain the prospect of death, it is not so agreeable (unfortunately) as to invite the eager contemplation of the public; and Drelincourt's book, being neglected, lay a dead stock on the hands of the publisher. In this emergency he applied to De Foe to assist him (by dint of such means as were then, as well as now, pretty well understood in the literary world) in rescuing the unfortunate book from the literary death to which general neglect seemed about to consign it. De Foe's genius and audacity devised a plan which, for assurance and ingenuity, defied even the powers of Mr. Puff in the *Critic;* for who but himself would have thought of summoning up a ghost from the grave to bear witness in favour of a halting body of divinity? There is a matter-of-fact, businesslike style in the whole account of the transaction, which bespeaks ineffable powers of self-possession. . . . The effect was most wonderful. "Drelincourt upon Death," attested by one who could speak from experience, took an unequalled run. The copies had hung on the book-seller's hands as heavy as a pile of lead bullets. They now traversed the town in every direction, like the same balls discharged from a field-piece. In short, the object of Mrs. Veal's apparition was perfectly attained.—SCOTT, SIR WALTER, c 1821, *Memoir of Daniel De Foe, Miscellaneous Works, vol.* IV, *pp.* 267, 273.

No English writer has ever excelled him in his power of painting fictitious events in the colours of truth. His simple and natural style has much to do with this. "The Relation of Mrs. Veal's Apparition," prefixed to "Drelincourt on Death," affords, perhaps, the best specimen of Defoe's wonderful power of clothing fiction with the garb of truth.—COLLIER, WILLIAM FRANCIS, 1861, *A History of English Literature, p.* 250.

Never, perhaps, has a story been so misunderstood as this apparition of Mrs. Veal. The idle tradition that it was written to promote the sale of Drelincourt's work on "The Fear of Death," has been conclusively disposed of by Mr. Lee, who proves that when "Mrs. Veal" appeared "Drelincourt" was already a popular work in its third edition, and, furthermore, that Mrs. Veal's recommendation, contrary likewise to tradition, did not have any appreciable effect on the sale of "Drelincourt." These traditions, which arose from the fact that the printer of "Drelincourt" was permitted to reprint Defoe's pamphlet in the fourth edition of "Drelincourt," deceived even so acute a critic as Sir Walter Scott. "Drelincourt," which long continued popular, was subsequently printed sometimes with and sometimes without "Mrs. Veal." But there is another erroneous notion concerning "Mrs. Veal" that requires to be dealt with, and that is the assumption that the narrative is a fiction. Whoever will read the story, says Sir Walter Scott, "as told by Defoe himself will agree that, could the thing have happened in reality, so it would have been told." But the extraordinary thing is that nobody should have inquired whether it was not true, that is to say, whether a lady of Defoe's acquaintance, to whom he gives the name of Mrs. Bargrave, did not tell him, and in good faith, this story; and that such was certainly the case, no one who reads carefully Defoe's works on "Magic and Apparitions," can possibly doubt. Defoe, as we shall show, when dealing with those books, believed firmly in apparitions; he had had stories told him which there was no getting over, and this of Mrs. Bargrave's was one of them.—WRIGHT, THOMAS, 1894, *The Life of Daniel Defoe, p.* 131.

The fact that there is no record of Defoe's story being contradicted by contemporary writers might have suggested that it was at least based on fact; for enemies were not slow to blame Defoe for saying that "Robinson Crusoe" and other tales were true. It has become the fashion of late to assume that Defoe was romancing when he said that his narratives were true histories, and the more he has asserted it the more critics have laughed at his skill or abused him for the immorality of his devices, according to the way the matter struck them. This scepticism has been extended to matters relating to Defoe's own life and character, and the late Professor Minto went so far as to say that he was "perhaps the greatest liar that ever lived." The result of this attitude has been a marked change in the common estimate of Defoe, as shown by the chance notices of him in the newspapers. . . . But does not the story told in this paper show that we should be at least as likely to arrive at the truth by believing what Defoe says, in the absence of proof to the contrary?—AITKEN, GEORGE A., 1895, *Defoe's "Apparition of Mrs. Veal," The Nineteenth Century, vol.* 37, *pp.* 99, 100.

FAMILY INSTRUCTOR
1715

My very good friend. Having, at your request, read over the book, called the "Family Instructor," I do, upon several accounts, very much approve of the design of it; and wish I could say any thing to recommend it to the perusal of others. The decay of family religion is very visible, and frequently matter of complaint; and, therefore, I doubt not such an attempt as this will be well received by all serious and thoughtful persons among us. The printer has been faulty to a degree that I am afraid will render the reader very uneasy, and I wish the author had thought fit to communicate his papers to you before they had fallen into such hands; but the substance of the book, however, will command regard; and if I may judge for others by myself, will afford some pleasure and entertainment. —WRIGHT, SAMUEL, 1715, *Defoe's "The Family Instructor," Letter to the Publisher.*

"The Family Instructor" of this author, in which he inculcates weightily his own notions of puritanical demeanour and parental authority, is very curious. It is a strange mixture of narrative and dialogue, fanaticism and nature; but all done with such earnestness, that the sense of its reality never quits us. Nothing, however, can be more harsh and unpleasing than the impression which it leaves. It does injustice both to religion and the world. It represents the innocent pleasures of the latter as deadly sins, and the former as most gloomy, austere, and exclusive. One lady resolves on poisoning her husband, and another determines to go to the play, and the author treats both offences with a severity nearly equal!—TALFOURD, THOMAS NOON, 1842, *On British Novels and Romances, Critical and Miscellaneous Writings, p.* 16.

ROBINSON CRUSOE

1719

The | LIFE | and | Strange Surprizing | ADVENTURES | of | ROBINSON CRUSOE, | Of YORK, Mariner: | Who lived Eight and Twenty Years, all alone in an un-inhabited Island on the | Coast of America, near the Mouth of | the Great River of Oroonoque; | Having been cast on Shore by Shipwreck, where | in all the Men perished but himself. | With | An Account how he was at last as strangely deliver'd by PYRATES. | *Written by Himself.* | LONDON. | Printed for W. Taylor at the *Ship* in *Pater-Noster Row.* MDCCXIX. | —TITLE PAGE OF FIRST EDITION, 1719.

If ever the story of any private man's adventures in the world were worth making public, and were acceptable when published, the Editor on this account thinks this will be so. The wonders of this man's life exceed all that (he thinks) is to be found extant; the life of one man being scarce capable of a greater variety. The story is told with modesty, with seriousness, and with a religious application of events to the uses to which wise men always apply them, viz., to the instruction of others by this example, and to justify and honour the wisdom of Providence in all the variety of our circumstances, let them happen how they will. The Editor believes the thing to be a just history of fact; neither is there any appearance of fiction in it; and, however, thinks, because all such things are despatched, that the improvement of it, as well to the diversion as to the instruction of the reader, will be the same. And as such, he thinks, without farther compliment to the world, he does them a great service in the publication.—DEFOE, DANIEL, 1719, *Robinson Crusoe, Preface.*

The Life and Strange Surprizing Adventures of Mr. D—DeF—, of London, Hosier, who has lived above fifty years by himself, in the Kingdoms of North and South Britain. The various Shapes he has appear'd in, and the Discoveries he has made for the Benefit of his Country. In a Dialogue between *Him, Robinson Crusoe,* and his Man *Friday.* With Remarks Serious and Comical upon the life of Crusoe. *Qui vult decipi, decipiatur.* London. Printed for J. Roberts in Warwick Lane.—GILDON, CHARLES, 1719, *Title Page.*

We may remember that we have been most of us, when Children, wonderfully pleased with the achievements of *Tom Thumb, Jack the Giant-Killer, Don Bellianis of Greece, The Seven Champions of Christendom,* and such like extraordinary Heroes; and many of us, in our more advanced Age, are little less delighted with such Books as, "The Life and Adventures of Robinson Crusoe;" which seems to have had that uncommon Run upon the Town for some Years past, for no other Reason but that it is a *most palpable Lye,* from Beginning to End; and I doubt not that the famous Passage of his *Swimming to Shore* Naked, *with his* Pockets *full of Biscuits,* tho' a most notorious *Blunder* in the Author, has pass'd for a very good Jest, and been received with abundance of Pleasure by many of his Readers.—HOADLEY, BENJAMIN, 1725, *London Journal, Sept.* 4.

Since we must have books, there is one which, to my mind, furnishes the finest of treatises on education according to nature. My Émile shall read this book before any other; it shall for a long time be his entire library, and shall always hold an honorable place. It shall be the text on which all our discussions of natural science shall be only commentaries.

It shall be a test for all we meet during our progress toward a ripened judgment, and so long as our taste is unspoiled, we shall enjoy reading it. What wonderful book is this? Aristotle? Pliny? Buffon? No; it is "Robinson Crusoe."—ROUSSEAU, JEAN JACQUES, 1762–67, *Émile, tr. Worthington, p.* 147.

"Robinson Crusoe" must be allowed, by the most rigid moralists, to be one of those novels which one may read, not only with pleasure, but also with profit. It breathes throughout a spirit of piety and benevolence; it sets in a very striking light . . . the importance of the mechanic arts, which they, who know not what it is to be without them, are apt to undervalue: it fixes in the mind a lively idea of the horrors of solitude, and, consequently, of the sweets of social life, and of the blessings we derive from conversation and mutual aid; and it shows, how, by labouring with one's own hands, one may secure independence, and open for one's self many sources of health and amusement. I agree, therefore, with Rousseau, that this is one of the best books that can be put in the hands of children.—BEATTIE, JAMES, 1783, *Dissertations, Moral and Critical.*

Was there ever yet any thing written by mere man that was wished longer by its readers, excepting "Don Quixote," "Robinson Crusoe," and "The Pilgrim's Progress?"—JOHNSON, SAMUEL, 1784–5, *Piozzi's Anecdotes, No.* 140.

It was the happiness of De Foe, that as many writers have succeeded in relating enterprises by land, he excelled in narrating adventures by sea, with such felicities of language, such attractive varieties, such insinuative instruction, as have seldom been equalled, but never surpassed. —CHALMERS, GEORGE, 1786–1841, *The Life of Daniel De Foe, p.* 78.

"Robinson Crusoe," the favourite of the learned and the unlearned, of the youth and the adult; the book that was to constitute the library of Rousseau's Emilius, owes its secret charm to its being a new representation of human nature, yet drawn from an existing state; this picture of self-education, self-inquiry, self-happiness, is scarcely a fiction, although it includes all the magic of romance; and is not a mere narrative of truth, since it displays all the forcible genius of one of the most original minds our literature can boast. The history of the work is therefore interesting. It was treated in the author's time as a mere idle romance, for the philosophy was not discovered in the story; after his death it was considered to have been pillaged from the papers of Alexander Selkirk, confided to the author, and the honour, as well as the genius, of De Foe were alike questioned. . . . "Robinson Crusoe" was not given to the world till 1719, seven years after the publication of Selkirk's adventures. Selkirk could have no claims on De Foe; for he had only supplied the man of genius with that which lies open to all; and which no one had, or perhaps could have, converted into the wonderful story we possess but De Foe himself. Had De Foe not written "Robinson Crusoe," the name and story of Selkirk had been passed over like others of the same sort; yet Selkirk has the merit of having detailed his own history, in a manner so interesting, as to have attracted the notice of Steele, and to have inspired the genius of De Foe.—DISRAELI, ISAAC, 1791–1824, *Robinson Crusoe, Curiosities of Literature.*

I have for some time past been engaged in an Arabic exercise, which has proved of great utility to me; it is the metamorphosis of the well-known novel of "Robinson Crusoe," into an Arabian tale, adapted to Eastern taste and manners. A young Frank, born at Aleppo, who speaks Arabic like a native, but who neither reads nor writes it, has been my assistant in the undertaking. I take the liberty of sending you here enclosed a copy of this travestied Robinson, or as I call the book in Arabic, Dur el Bakur, the Peal of the Seas.—BURCKHARDT, JOHN LEWIS, 1810, *Travels in Nubia, p.* 28.

Perhaps there exists no work, either of instruction or entertainment, in the English language, which has been more generally read, and more universally admired, than the "Life and Adventures of Robinson Crusoe." It is difficult to say in what the charm consists, by which persons of all classes and denominations are thus fascinated: yet the majority of readers will recollect it as among the first works which awakened and interested their youthful attention; and feel, even in advanced life, and in the maturity of their understanding, that there are still associated with Robinson Crusoe, the sentiments peculiar to that period, when all is new, all glittering in prospect, and when those visions are most bright, which the experience of afterlife tends only to darken and destroy.—BALLANTYNE, JOHN, 1810, *ed. De Foe's Novels, Edinburgh ed., Memoir.*

Never did human being excite more sympathy in his fate than this shipwrecked mariner: we enter into all his doubts and difficulties, and every rusty nail which he acquires fills us with satisfaction. We thus learn to appreciate our own comforts, and we acquire, at the same time, a habit of activity; but, above all, we attain a trust and devout confidence in divine mercy and goodness. The author also, by placing his hero in an uninhabited island in the Western Ocean, had an opportunity of introducing scenes which, with the merit of truth, have all the wildness and horror of the most incredible fiction. *That* foot in the sand—*those* Indians who land on the solitary shore to devour their captives, fill us with alarm and terror, and, after being relieved from the fear of Crusoe perishing by famine, we are agitated by new apprehensions for his safety. The deliverance of Friday, and the whole character of that young Indian, are painted in the most beautiful manner; and, in short, of all the works of fiction that have ever been composed, Robinson Crusoe is perhaps the most interesting and instructive.—DUNLOP, JOHN, 1814–42, *The History of Fiction, vol.* II, *p.* 420.

Compare the contemptuous Swift with the contemned De Foe, and how superior will the latter be found! But by what test?—Even by this; that the writer who makes me sympathize with his presentations with the whole of my being, is more estimable than he who calls forth, and appeals but to, a part of my being—my sense of the ludicrous, for instance. De Foe's excellence it is, to make me forget my specific class, character, and circumstances, and to raise me while I read him, into the universal man.—COLERIDGE, SAMUEL TAYLOR, 1818, *Mythology, Imagination, and Superstition; Miscellanies, Æsthetic and Literary, ed. Ashe, p.* 154.

There scarce exists a work so popular as "Robinson Crusoe." It is read eagerly by young people; and there is hardly an elf so devoid of imagination as not to have supposed for himself a solitary island in which he could act "Robinson Crusoe," were it but in the corner of the nursery. To many it has given the decided turn of their lives, by sending them to sea. For the young mind is much less struck with the hardships of the anchorite's situation than with the animating exertions which he makes to overcome them; and "Robinson Crusoe" produces the same impression upon an adventurous spirit which the "Book of Martyrs" would do on a young devotee, or the "Newgate Calendar" upon an acolyte of Bridewell; both of which students are less terrified by the horrible manner in which the tale terminates, than animated by sympathy with the saints or depredators who are the heroes of their volume. Neither does a re-perusal of "Robinson Crusoe," at a more advanced age, diminish our early impressions. The situation is such as every man may make his own, and, being possible in itself, is, by the exquisite art of the narrator, rendered as probable as it is interesting. It has the merit, too, of that species of accurate painting which can be looked at again and again with new pleasure.—SCOTT, SIR WALTER, c 1821, *Memoir of Daniel De Foe, Miscellaneous Works, vol.* IV, *p.* 279.

What man does not remember with regret the first time that he read "Robinson Crusoe?" Then, indeed, he was unable to appreciate the powers of the writer; or rather, he neither knew nor cared whether the book had a writer at all. He probably thought it not half so fine as some rant of Macpherson about dark-browed Foldath and white-bosomed Strinadona. He now values Fingal and Temora only as showing with how little evidence a story may be believed, and with how little merit a book may be popular. Of the romance of Defoe, he entertains the highest opinion. He perceives the hand of a master in ten thousand touches, which formerly he passed by without notice. But though he understands the merits of the narrative better than formerly, he is far less interested by it. Xury, and Friday, and pretty Poll, the boat with the shoulder-of-mutton sail, and the canoe which could not be brought down to the water's edge, the tent with its hedge and ladders, the preserve of kids, and the den where the old goat died, can never again be to him the realities which they were.—MACAULAY, THOMAS BABINGTON, 1828, *Dryden, Edinburgh Review; Critical and Miscellaneous Essays.*

Few things, in an ordinary life, can come up to the interest which every reader of sensibility must take in the author of "Robinson Crusoe." "Heaven lies about us in our infancy;" and it cannot be denied, that the first perusal of that work makes a part of the illusion:—the roar of the waters is in our ears,—we start at the print of the foot in the sand, and hear the parrot repeat the well-known sounds of "Poor Robinson Crusoe! Who are you? Where do you come from; and where are you going?"—till the tears gush, and in recollection and feeling we become children again! One cannot understand how the author of this world of abstraction should have had any thing to do with the ordinary cares and business of life; or it almost seems that he should have been fed, like Elijah, by the ravens. What boots it then to know that he was a hose-factor, and the owner of a tile-kiln in Essex—that he stood in the pillory, was over head and ears in debt, and engaged in eternal literary and political squabbles?—HAZLITT, WILLIAM, 1830, *Wilson's Life and Times of Daniel Defoe, Edinburgh Review, vol.* 50, *p.* 400.

It has become a household thing in nearly every family in Christendom. Yet never was admiration of any work—universal admiration—more indiscriminately or more inappropriately bestowed. Not one person in ten—nay, not one person in five hundred—has, during the perusal of "Robinson Cruso," the most remote conception that any particle of genius, or even of common talent, has been employed in its creation! Men do not look upon it in the light of a literary performance. Defoe has none of their thoughts—Robinson all. The powers which have wrought the wonder have been thrown into obscurity by the very stupendousness of the wonder they have wrought! We read, and become perfect abstractions in the intensity of our interest; we close the book, and are quite satisfied that we could have written as well ourselves. All this is effected by the potent magic of verisimilitude. Indeed the author of "Crusoe" must have possessed, above all other faculities, what has been termed the faculty of *identification*—that dominion exercised by volition over imagination, which enables the mind to lose its own in a fictitious individuality.—POE, EDGAR ALLAN, 1836, *Marginalia, Works, vol.* VII, *p.* 300.

It sinks into the bosom while the bosom is most capable of pleasurable impressions from the adventurous and the marvellous; and no human work, we honestly believe, has afforded such great delight. Neither the *Iliad* nor the *Odyssey*, in the much longer course of ages, has incited so many to enterprise, or to reliance on their own powers and capacities. It is the romance of solitude and self-sustainment; and could only so perfectly have been written by a man whose own life had for the most part been passed in the independence of unaided thought, accustomed to great reverses, of inexhaustible resource in confronting calamities, leaning ever on his Bible in sober and satisfied belief, and not afraid at any time to find himself Alone, in communion with nature and with God. —FORSTER, JOHN, 1845–58, *Daniel De Foe, Edinburgh Review, Historical and Biographical Essays, vol.* II, *p.* 95.

One of the most truly genial, perfect, and original fictions that the world has ever seen.—SHAW, THOMAS B., 1847, *Outlines of English Literature, p.* 252.

"Robinson Crusoe" is understood to be founded on the real history of Alexander Selkirk, a summary of which, charmingly written, was given to the public by Steele. The greatest genius might have been proud to paint a picture after that sketch. Yet we are not sure that Selkirk's adventure was not an injury, instead of a benefit to De Foe. A benefit it undoubtedly was, to him and to all of us, if it was required in order to put the thought into De Foe's head; but what we mean is, that the world would probably have had the fiction, whether the fact had existed or not. Desert islands and cast-away mariners existed before Selkirk: children have played at hermits and house-building, even before they read "Robinson Crusoe;" and the whole inimitable romance would have required but a glance of De Foe's eye upon a child at play, or at a page in an old book of voyages, or even at his own restless and isolated thoughts. This is a conjecture, however, impossible to prove; and we only throw it out in justice to an original genius. After all, it would make little difference; for Selkirk was not Crusoe, nor did he see the ghost of a human footstep, nor obtain a man Friday. The inhabitant of the island was De Foe himself.—HUNT, LEIGH, 1849, *A Book for a Corner.*

That Robertson, however, had carefully studied the best writers, with a view to acquire genuine Anglicism, cannot be doubted. He was intimately acquainted with Swift's writings; indeed, he regarded him as eminently skilled in the narrative art. He had the same familiarity with Defoe, and had formed the same high estimate of his historical powers. I know, that when a Professor in another University consulted him on the best discipline for acquiring a good narrative style, previous to drawing up John Bell of Antermony's "Travels across Russia to Tartary and the Chinese Wall," the remarkable advice he gave him was to read "Robinson Crusoe" carefully; and when the Professor was astonished, and supposed it was a jest, the historian said he was quite serious: but if "Robinson Crusoe" would not help him, or he was above studying Defoe, then he recommended "Gulliver's Travels."—BROUGHAM, HENRY LORD, 1855, *Robertson, Lives of Men of Letters of the Time of George III.*, p. 273.

"The Life and Adventures of Robinson Crusoe" appeared as far back as the year 1719, and at once rose to the popularity which it has ever since maintained. But it failed to attract the notice of the critics. The men who sat in judgment on the small elegances of the wits of the reign of George I., and marked how sentences were balanced and couplets rounded, could not stoop to notice a composition so humble as a novel, more especially a novel written by a self-taught man. But his singularly vivacious production forced a way for itself, leaving the fine sentences and smart couplets to be forgotten. In a short time it was known all over Europe; several translations appeared simultaneously in France. . . . And such was the rage of imitation which it excited in Germany, that no fewer than forty-one German novels were produced that had Robinson Crusoes for their heroes, and fifteen others that, though equally palpable imitations, had heroes that bore a different name. —MILLER, HUGH, 1856, *Essays*, p. 470.

This novel too, like many of the best ever written, has in it the autobiographical element which makes a man speak from greater depths of feeling than in a purely imaginary story.—STEPHEN, LESLIE, 1875, *Hours in a Library, vol.* I, p. 43.

The vast mass of Defoe's writings received no kindly aid from distinguished contemporaries to float them down the stream; everything was done that bitter dislike and supercilious indifference could do to submerge them. "Robinson Crusoe" was their sole life-buoy.—MINTO, WILLIAM, 1879, *Daniel Defoe (English Men of Letters)*, p. 137.

"Robinson Crusoe," which is a fairy tale to the child, a book of adventure to the young, is a work on social philosophy to the mature. It is a picture of civilization. The essential moral attributes of man, his innate impulses as a social being, his absolute dependence on society, even as a solitary individual, his subjection to the physical world, and his alliance with the animal world, the statical elements of social philosophy, and the germs of man's historical evolution have never been touched with more sagacity, and assuredly have never been idealised with such magical simplicity and truth. It remains, with Don Quixote, the only prose work of the fancy which has equal charms for every age of life, and which has inexhaustible teaching for the student of man and of society.—HARRISON, FREDERIC, 1879–86, *The Choice of Books and Other Literary Pieces*, p. 64.

Grimmelshausen has here introduced an idea which had already played a certain part in Shakspeare's "Tempest," and which Defoe made, fifty years later, the centre of his remarkable work, "Robinson Crusoe." But the idea started by Grimmelshausen remained dormant until it came before the public in a new form from England. Daniel Defoe's "Robinson Crusoe" appeared in 1719; it was at once translated into various languages, and it continued for a long time to call forth numerous imitations in Germany. Foreign nations as well as native districts were made to furnish names for all these Robinsons or Adventurers; there was an Italian, French, Dutch, Norwegian, Saxon, Silesian, Thuringian, Swabian, Brandenburg, and Palatinate Robinson, a Swiss,

Danish, Dresden, and Leipzig Adventurer. The most celebrated achievement of this literature of Robinsonades, which was continued down into the age of Frederick the Great, was a four-volume story, which appeared between 1731 and 1743, and was called "The Island of Felsenburg," after the scene of the narrative. It was written by Johann Gottfried Schnabel, court-agent and newswriter to Count Stolberg. His literary apparatus is on the whole the same as that employed in "Simplicissimus," but he gives still greater scope to ghostly and magical elements, he does not mind repeating himself, and he makes no attempt to introduce any higher thoughts into his fascinating narrative of changeful incidents.—SCHERER, WILHELM, 1883–86, *A History of German Literature, tr. Conybeare, vol.* I, *p.* 392.

While he was not a great artist, he was a wonderful craftsman. That is to say, he studied his fellow-creatures from the point of view of their relations to society; he writes as a reformer with a direct practical end, with the end that was foremost in the minds of his generation, that of promoting civilization. Take his "Robinson Crusoe," for example; full as it is of fine things, as when Robinson sees with terror the print of a human print upon the sand, it is singularly devoid of any expression of the feeling of vast loneliness that would weigh down on the spirit of any such hero in a novel of the present day. The problem that lay before him, and which he accomplished, was how to make himself over from a worthless person into a peaceable, God-fearing citizen. The shadow of the municipal law and of the English Sunday seems to lie over the lonely island. The moral of the book, in short, is this: If a man in solitude, with a few scraps from a wreck and an occasional savage, dog, and cat to help him, can lead so civilized a life, what may we not expect of good people in England with abundance about them? This moral is what now makes the value of the book as a means of education for boys, that they may see, as Rousseau put it, that the stock of an ironmonger is better than that of a jeweller, and glass better than diamonds.—PERRY, THOMAS SERGEANT, 1883, *English Literature in the Eighteenth Century, p.* 310.

No theory as to children's books would be worth much attention which found itself obliged to exclude that memorable work. Although it submits in a certain measure to classification, it is almost *sui generis;* no book of its kind, approaching it in merit, has ever been written. In what, then, does its fascination consist? There is certainly nothing hermetic about it; it is the simplest and most studiously matter-of-fact narrative of events, comprehensible without the slightest effort, and having no meaning that is not apparent on the face of it. And yet children, and grown people also, read it again and again, and cannot find it uninteresting. I think the phenomenon may largely be due to the nature of the subject, which is really of primary and universal interest to mankind. It is the story of the struggle of a man with wild and hostile nature,—in the larger sense an elementary theme,—his shifts, his failures, his perils, his fears, his hopes, his successes. The character of Robinson is so artfully generalized or universalized, and sympathy for him is so powerfully aroused and maintained, that the reader, especially the child reader, inevitably identifies himself with him, and feels his emotions and struggles as his own. The ingredient of suspense is never absent from the story, and the absence of any plot prevents us from perceiving its artificiality. It is, in fact, a type of the history of the human race, not on the higher plane, but on the physical one; the history of man's contest with and final victory over physical nature. The very simplicity and obviousness of the details give them grandeur and comprehensiveness: no part of man's character which his contact with nature can affect or develop is left untried in Robinson. He manifests in little all historical earthly experiences of the race; such is the scheme of the book; and its permanence in literature is due to the sobriety and veracity with which that scheme is carried out. To speak succinctly, it does for the body what the hermetic and cognate literature does for the soul; and for the healthy man, the body is not less important than the soul in its own place and degree. It is not the work of the Creator, but it is contingent upon creation.—HAWTHORNE, JULIAN, 1887, *Confessions and Criticisms, p.* 122.

When a boy I loved those books that

other boys love, and I love them still. I well remember a little scene which took place when I was a child of eight or nine. "Robinson Crusoe" held me in his golden thrall, and I was expected to go to church. I hid beneath a bed with "Robinson Crusoe," and was in due course discovered by an elder sister and a governess, who, on my refusing to come out, resorted to force. Then followed a struggle that was quite Homeric. The two ladies tugged as best they might, but I clung to "Crusoe" and the legs of the bed, and kicked till, perfectly exhausted, they took their departure in no very Christian frame of mind, leaving me panting, indeed, but triumphant.—HAGGARD, H. RIDER, 1887, *Books which Have Influenced Me, p.* 66.

When we read "Robinson Crusoe" we feel that the hero would not naturally have acted in any other way than he actually did. And it is this fact which gives its life to the book. Defoe might have kept his inventive powers in their place and never have gained his reputation for untrustworthiness, and still have given "Robinson Crusoe" to the world as perfect as it is now, no doubt, but we must look at facts as they are and not as we should wish them to be. And the fact is that this immortal story-teller was a man to whom the truth was a stranger. He was seldom straightforward. He was fertile in expedients to pass off falsehood for truth, and it is this gift of invention which, rightfully exercised in "Robinson Crusoe," made, when carried into actual practice in life, so untrustworthy a character as his. . . . In spite of all his faults he was great enough to write for his time, and for all time, "Robinson Crusoe."—ADAMS, OSCAR FAY, 1889, *Dear Old Story-Tellers, pp.* 176, 177.

"Robinson Crusoe" has a place in literature as unassailable as "Gulliver's Travels" or as "Don Quixote." . . . Had he not written "Robinson Crusoe," he would still have held a high place in English literature, because of the other romances that came from his teeming brain, and because of the political tracts, that made so deep and lasting an impression even in that age of famous political tracts. But "Robinson Crusoe" is to his other works like Aaron's serpent, or the "one master-passion in the breast," which the poet has compared with it—it "swallows all the rest."—MCCARTHY, JUSTIN, 1890, *A History of the Four Georges, vol.* II, *pp.* 1, 2.

And if you should ever have any story of your own to tell, and want to tell it well, I advise you to take "Robinson Crusoe" for a model; if you ever want to make a good record of any adventures of your own by sea, or by land, I advise you to take "Robinson Crusoe" for a model; and if you do, you will not waste words in painting sunsets, or in decorating storms and sea-waves; but, without your straining, and by the simple colorless truth of your language, the sunsets will show their glow, and the storms rise and roar, and the waves dash and die along the beach as they do in nature.—MITCHELL, DONALD G., 1890, *English Lands Letters and Kings, From Elizabeth to Anne, p.* 277.

It is one of those immortal stories which appeal equally to the interest and sympathy of any period and any civilised race. —FIELD, MRS. E. M., 1891, *The Child and His Book, p.* 230.

Defoe would hardly recognize "Robinson Crusoe" as "a picture of civilization," having innocently supposed it to be quite the reverse; and he would be as amazed as we are to learn from Mr. Frederic Harrison that his book contains "more psychology, more political economy, and more anthropology than are to be found in many elaborate treatises on these especial subjects," — blighting words which I would not even venture to quote if I thought that any boy would chance to read them, and so have one of the pleasures of his young life destroyed.—REPPLIER, AGNES, 1891, *A Plea for Humor, Points of View, p.* 4.

Defoe's narratives all aim at exhibiting the processes of memory, untouched by the shaping imagination. And unambitious though such an aim may be, it was perhaps a necessary exercise for the modern novel in its infancy. . . . Robinson Crusoe typifies the spirit of the Anglo-Saxon race, and illustrates in epitome the part it has played in India and America. He keeps his house in order, stores the runlets of rum, and converts Friday, telling him that God is omnipotent, that he "could do everything for us, give everything to us, take everything from us." Poor Friday believed in a Great Spirit, and held that "All things say O to him"—an unpractical view that receives no manner of notice from Crusoe, who nevertheless reports their conversations, and honestly admits that he was "run down to the last degree" by some of Friday's theological arguments. But the very deficiencies in the story of Crusoe, and the imagination of Defoe, only gave the writer fuller scope for the exhibition of his particular talent. On a blank canvas small splashes are striking, and Defoe forces the reader to take the deepest interest in the minutest affairs of the castaway. It is a testimony to the practical nature of childhood that the book is so widely regarded as the best boy's book in the world. When the story leaves the magic limits of the island, it must be said the interest flags; and at last, in the "Serious Reflections," subjoined by an afterthought, it positively stagnates. But the main piece of original narrative is a masterpiece, and marks a new era in the writing of prose fiction. —RALEIGH, WALTER, 1894, *The English Novel, pp.* 132, 133.

Jean-Jacques pronounced a splendid eulogy upon the educational qualities of the work, preferring its author to Aristotle, Pliny and Buffon. . . . He saw quite clearly how closely the author of "Robinson Crusoe" had adhered to life, and perceived the lofty teaching he had managed to extract from it. Rousseau raised to its proper position what had been regarded nothing more than a novel, when in reality it was a moral treatise. It was his testimony to its qualities that gave Daniel Defoe's work a place in the philosophical heritage of humanity.—TEXTE, JOSEPH, 1895-99, *Jean-Jacques Rousseau and the Cosmopolitan Spirit in Literature, tr. Matthews, pp.* 127, 128.

Aha, old Crusoe! I see thee now in yonder case smiling out upon me as cheerily as thou didst smile those many years ago when to a little boy thou broughtest the message of Romance! And I do love thee still, and I shall always love thee, not only for thy benefaction in those ancient days, but also for the light and the cheer which thy genius brings to all ages and conditions of humanity.—FIELD, EUGENE, 1895, *The Love Affairs of a Bibliomaniac, p.* 17.

It was an invention, a great, unexpected stroke of British genius, and it was immediately hailed as such by the rest of Europe. It was one of the first English books which was widely imitated on the Continent, and it gave direction and impetus to the new romantico-realistic conception of fiction all over the world. . . . In England, however, the bourgeois romances of Defoe long remained without influence and without prestige, widely read indeed, but almost furtively, as vulgar literature fit for the kitchen and the shop.—GOSSE, EDMUND, 1897, *Short History of Modern English Literature, p.* 227.

"Robinson Crusoe" has proved itself more than a story-book. At the beginning nobody thought it a mere book for children; and there is now something out of the way in that house where it is treated simply as a child's book. Its steady popularity, as great now as ever, is not easily explained by the critics. A boy who likes it need not, probably cannot, tell why he likes it. No, nor can the best critics, by counting the words or telling why the sentences are long or short, explain why the boy ought to like it. What is certain is this, that so many new editions of it are published every year that no librarian pretends to keep the account of them.—HALE, EDWARD EVERETT, 1897, *Robinson Crusoe and Defoe, The Outlook, vol.* 55, *p.* 1031.

The first of my favorite authors of fiction is Daniel Defoe, and he comes to the front as naturally as if he saw a sail upon the horizon and was anxious to discover to what sort of craft it belonged. . . . Defoe's prominence in my mind is based upon his ability to transmute a fictional narrative into a record of facts; things which might have been became, in his hands, things which actually were. But it is to the story itself that his supremacy as a fictional writer is confined; it does not extend to his personages. It is in the relation of a story, not in the delineation of character, that this great author excels. . . . To reduce romance to realism without depriving the former of any of its charms was the example set by Defoe to the writers of English fiction. His characters, his situations, his incidents, his material, and his machinery, have all been surpassed, but his story telling never. . . . I may sum up what I have to say about Defoe in the statement that it is the telling of his story and not the story itself which charms me and holds me to my allegiance. "Robinson Crusoe" is not the best work of English fiction, but it is, in my opinion, the best told story.—STOCKTON, FRANK R., 1897, *My Favorite Novelist and His Best Book, Munsey's Magazine, vol.* 17, *pp.* 351, 352, 353.

"Robinson Crusoe," first edition, 2 vols., 1719. Roxburghe (1812), £1, 4s. Sotheby's (1846), £4, 16s. (with "Serious Reflections," 3 vols., 1719–20). Alfred Crampton, 1896 (3 vols.,) £75. Sir Cecile Domvile, 1897 (part i,) £45, 10s.—WHEATLEY, HENRY B., 1898, *Prices of Books, p.* 246.

Thus ends the authentic history of Alexander Selkirk. He left no children, but representatives of the family from which he sprang are still to be found in his native town. Mr. Davied Gillies, whose mother was a great-grandniece of Selkirk, has commemorated him in a statue which, since its unveiling by the Countess of Aberdeen in 1885, has made the leading feature of Largo for every visitor to the place. If you ask a native where any one lives, the position will almost certainly be indicated from a reference to "the statue." Nor is there any difficulty in identifying the statue, for the sculptor has dressed his Crusoe in the very garb with which necessity first and Defoe afterward adorned him. . . . And Juan Fernandez has its memorial, too. Two thousand feet above the sea-level, on the height which Selkirk called his "Lookout," a handsome tablet commemorates him in the following inscription:

In memory of Alexander Selkirk, mariner, a native of Largo, in the county of Fife, Scotland, who lived on this island in complete solitude for four years and four months. He was landed from the Cinque Ports galley, 96 tons, 18 guns, A. D. 1704, and was taken off in the Duke, privateer, 12th February, 1709. He died Lieutenant of H. M. S. Weymouth, A. D. 1723, aged 47. This tablet is erected near Selkirk's lookout, by Commodore Powell and the officers of H. M. S. Topaze, A. D. 1868.

Thus while Defoe himself remains undistinguished by statue or mark of public favor of any kind, the humble hero whose fame he created is memorialized in two widely separated corners of the globe. —HADDEN, J. CUTHBERT, 1899, *The Making of "Robinson Crusoe," The Century Magazine, vol.* 58, *pp.* 393, 394.

MEMOIRS OF A CAVALIER
1720?

The most life-like account of the Civil Wars in England in the seventeenth century that I know is contained in De Foe's "Memoirs of a Cavalier," which it is impossible to read without believing that it is the work of a writer who had been himself an actor in the scenes which he describes—and which Lord Chatham indeed quoted as a genuine history. And yet it is as much a fiction as Waverley, with its picture of the Rebellion of 1745. —FORSYTH, WILLIAM, 1871, *The Novels and Novelists of the Eighteenth Century, p.* 11.

Almost all the battles and incidents it relates, are so evidently taken from Clarendon and other contemporaries of the Civil Wars (with whose writings I was familiar before I read this work) that I confess I was not so much struck with "The Cavalier" as I expected.—BRAY, ANNA ELIZA, 1883, *Autobiography, ed. Kempe, p.* 190.

Defoe is with me not seldom. The style of these men is refreshing. For narrative, it would be difficult to beat Defoe. "The History of a Cavalier" is a downright masterpiece.—BROWN, THOMAS EDWARD, 1893, *Letters, ed. Irwin, March* 10, *vol.* I, *p.* 173.

It is well known that the Earl of Chatham believed the "Memoirs of a Cavalier" to be genuine history, and said they gave the best account of the Civil War which was extant. Opinions as to the duties of a serious historian have altered much since then; historical romances, if good of their kind, will always be welcome, and will serve other useful ends besides amusements; but nowadays we expect a writer to make it clear whether his work is fact or fiction. Defoe felt perfectly warranted in giving greater point and interest to his narrative by the interposition of an imaginary Cavalier who could describe the events of the time as his own experiences. He thought it much more important that his readers should have before them a striking picture of the chief events of a war than that the story should be of impeccable accuracy, but dull. There is certainly a place in the historical library for such work as Defoe's, and the "Memoirs of a Cavalier" is, from the historical point of view, one of the very best books of its class in existence.—AITKEN, GEORGE A., 1895, *ed. Defoe's Romances and Narratives, Memoirs of a Cavalier, vol.* VII, *Introduction, p.* xviii.

One of the most vivid and apparently genuine military histories ever printed.—SAINTSBURY, GEORGE, 1896, *Social England, ed. Traill, vol.* V, *p.* 86.

MOLL FLANDERS
1722

The various incidents in the eventful life of Moll Flanders, from the time of her seduction to that of her becoming a convict and a quiet settler in Maryland, are those of real life, as exemplified by multitudes of individuals, who have run the career of their vicious propensities. The artless disposition of the narrative, the lively interest excited by unlooked for coincidences, the rich natural painting, the moral reflections, are all so many proofs of the knowledge and invention of the writer; but the facts were furnished him by the annals of Newgate. . . . From the character of the incidents that compose the present narrative, De Foe was fully aware of the objections that would be urged against it by the scrupulous. To conceal a single fact, would have taken so much from the fidelity of the portrait; all that he could do, therefore, was to neutralize the poison, by furnishing the strongest antidotes. Accordingly, whilst he paints the courses of an every-day profligate in their natural colours, he shows us with the same faithfulness their natural tendency; and that, first or last, vice is sure to bring down its own punishment. His villains never prosper; but either come to an untimely end, or are brought to be penitents. In dressing up the present story, he tells us, he had taken care to exclude every thing that might be offensive; but conscious that he had a bad subject to work upon, he endeavours to interest the reader in the reflections arising out of it, that the moral might be more enticing than the fable.—WILSON, WALTER, 1830, *Memoirs of the Life and Times of Daniel De Foe, vol.* III, *pp.* 489, 490.

Of these novels we may, nevertheless, add, for the satisfaction of the inquisitive reader, that "Moll Flanders" is utterly vile and detestable: Mrs. Flanders was evidently born in sin. The best parts are the account of her childhood, which is pretty and affecting; the fluctuation of her feelings between remorse and hardened impenitence in Newgate; and the incident of her leading off the horse from the inn-door, though she had no place to put it in after she had stolen it.—HAZLITT, WILLIAM, 1830, *Wilson's Life and Times of Daniel Defoe, Edinburgh Review, vol.* 50, *p.* 422.

Deals with the sore of society in very much the spirit of M. Zola and his followers. Defoe lays bare the career of an abandoned woman, concealing nothing, extenuating nothing, but also hoping nothing. It could only be when inspired by the hope of amelioration, that such a narrative could be endurable. But Defoe's novel is inspired merely by hope of the good sale which of course it achieved: the morbid way in which he, like M. Zola, lingers over disgusting detail, and the perfunctory manner in which any necessary pieces of morality are introduced, preclude us from attributing any moral purpose to a vivid and clever, but most revolting novel.—ROWLAND, P. F., 1894, *A Comparison, Criticism and Estimate of the English Novelists from* 1700 *to* 1850, *p.* 6.

RELIGIOUS COURTSHIP
1722

As a work of pure and orthodox morality, its progress was slow, but sure. Seven years elapsed before a Second Edition was required; but in 1789, the twenty-first was published, and they have since been innumerable, from the respectable octavo, to the coarse paper publications for cheap distribution. It is still the most popular work ever published on the subject; and would alone secure the lasting fame of its author, independently of any other of his productions. The frame work of the book is skilfully contrived, yet no art whatever is apparent. The reader becomes interested in the welfare of a particular family, and is carried along through the history of its members; sharing their happiness, and, as a friend, touched with their cares and anxieties. It combines the rare advantages of a continuous narrative with those of natural and well sustained dialogue, a form of writing in which Defoe greatly excelled. Like his other works on religion and morality, it is based on the Bible alone, and is equally acceptable to all denominations of orthodox Protestants. It displays, throughout, the characteristics of his best style of writing, and is distinguished as much for its practical utility as for its ability.—LEE, WILLIAM, 1869, *Daniel Defoe: His Life and Recently Discovered Writings, vol.* I, *p.* 357.

For this work both Mr. Wilson and Mr. Lee professed unbounded admiration. To say that I too enjoyed reading it would be untrue. A little of the powder of "admirable unsectarian morality," as Mr. Lee calls it, in a large spoonful of the preserve of fiction could be put up with; but when, as in the case of "Religious Courtship," there is a heaped-up spoonful of this "admirable unsectarian morality," relieved by only the thinnest streak of preserve, one makes wry faces.—WRIGHT, THOMAS, 1894, *The Life of Daniel Defoe, p.* 288.

JOURNAL OF THE PLAGUE YEAR
1722

The "History of the Great Plague in London" is one of that particular class of compositions which hovers between romance and history. Undoubtedly De Foe embodied a number of traditions upon this subject with what he might actually have read, or of which he might otherwise have received direct evidence. The subject is hideous almost to disgust, yet, even had he not been the author of "Robinson Crusoe," De Foe would have deserved immortality for the genius which he has displayed in this work, as well as in the "Memoirs of a Cavalier."—SCOTT, SIR WALTER, c 1821, *Memoir of Daniel De Foe, Miscellaneous Works, vol.* IV, *p.* 255.

Such is the veri-similitude of all the writings of Defoe, that unless we have had some other means of refuting their authenticity than internal evidence, it would be a very difficult task to dispute their claims to credit. Such is the minuteness of detail; such a dwelling is there upon particular circumstances, which one is inclined to think would have struck no one but an actual spectator; such, too, is the plainness and simplicity of style; such the ordinary and probable nature of his materials, as well as the air of conscientiousness thrown over the whole, that it is a much easier thing to say the narrative is tedious, prolix, or dull, than to entertain a doubt of its veracity. All these marks of genuineness distinguish the work before us perhaps more than any other compositions of the same author.—SOUTHERN, H., 1822, *Defoe's History of the Plague, Retrospective Review, vol.* 6, *p.* 2.

Who, in reading his thrilling "History of the Great Plague," would not be reconciled to a few little ones?—HOOD, THOMAS, 1843, *Memorials, vol.* II, *p.* 142.

For the grandeur of the theme and the profoundly affecting familiarity of its treatment, for the thrilling and homely touches which paint at once the moral and the physical terrors of a pestilence, is one of the noblest prose epics of the language.—FORSTER, JOHN, 1845–58, *Daniel De Foe, Edinburgh Review; Historical and Biographical Essays, vol.* II, *p.* 96.

The "Journal of the Plague Year" is in some respects Defoe's masterpiece.—AITKEN, GEORGE A., 1895, *ed. Defoe's Romances and Narratives, A Journal of the Plague Year, vol.* II, *p.* ix.

Of all the prolific Daniel's two hundred and fifty-odd works, none better exhibits his most striking features of style. The minute detail, the irresistible verisimilitude, the awful realism, are all there, and almost persuade us that he saw all that he describes, in spite of our knowledge that he was a boy—though a precocious one—of five, when the pestilence was raging.—SMITH, JOSIAH RENICK, 1895, *New Presentments of Defoe, The Dial, vol.* 19, *p.* 16.

COLONEL JACK
1722

Every wicked reader will here be encouraged to a change, and it will appear that the best and only good end of a wicked and misspent life is repentance. That is this, there is comfort, peace, and oftentimes hope; and, that the penitent shall be returned like the prodigal, and his latter end be better than his beginning.—DE FOE, DANIEL, 1722, *Colonel Jack, Preface.*

The "Life of Colonel Jacque," is a

work excellent in its kind, although less known than some of the author's other performances. If it contains much manner of low-life, it aspires to an elevation of character; whilst the painting is that of nature, and the tendency stirctly virtuous. There is in truth but little that can associate it in character with Moll Flanders; for, if there is a correspondency in some of their actions, the principle that actuated them was widely different, and our hero appears through the greater part of the volume, a personage entitled to some respect.—WILSON, WALTER, 1830, *Memoirs of the Life and Times of Daniel De Foe, vol.* III, *p.* 495.

The Life of Colonel Jack, like its predecessor, is a book that a religious, or even prudent father could not safely place in the hands of his children; yet is there much in the character of the hero that entitles him to respect. . . . Notwithstanding the obvious objections of fastidious delicacy to this book, and paying due respect to the refinement of modern civilization, I venture to doubt whether more good was effected, at the time, even by our author's excellent work on "Religious Courtship," than by "Colonel Jack," remembering the different classes for whom they were respectively written.—LEE, WILLIAM, 1869, *Daniel Defoe: His Life and Recently Discovered Writings, vol.* I, *pp.* 366, 367.

"The History of Colonel Jack" is an unequal book. There is hardly in "Robinson Crusoe" a scene equal, and there is consequently not in English literature a scene superior, to that praised by Lamb, and extracted in Knight's "Half Hours with the Best Authors,"—the scene where the youthful pickpocket first exercises his trade, and then for a time loses his ill-gotten (though for his part he knows not the meaning of the word ill-gotten) gains. But great part of the book, and especially the latter portion, is dull.—SAINTSBURY, GEORGE, 1877, *Encyclopædia Britannica, Ninth Edition, vol.* VII.

COMPLETE ENGLISH TRADESMAN
1725–27

I have now lying before me that curious book by Daniel Defoe, "The Complete English Tradesman." The pompous detail, the studied analysis of every little mean art, every sneaking address, every trick and subterfuge, short of larceny, that is necessary to the tradesman's occupation, with the hundreds of anecdotes, dialogues (in Defoe's liveliest manner) interspersed, all tending to the same amiable purpose, —namely, the sacrificing of every honest emotion of the soul to what he calls the main chance,—if you read it in an *ironical sense*, and as a piece of *covered satire*, make it one of the most amusing books which Defoe ever writ, as much so as any of his best novels. It is difficult to say what his intention was in writing it. It is almost impossible to suppose him in earnest. Yet such is the bent of the book to narrow and to degrade the heart, that if such maxims were as catching and infectious as those of a licentious cast, which happily is not the case, had I been living at that time, I certainly should have recommended to the Grand Jury of Middlesex, who presented "The Fable of the Bees," to have presented this book of Defoe's in preference, as of a far more vile and debasing tendency.—LAMB, CHARLES, 1830? *The Good Clerk, a Character; The Reflector No.* 4.

The plays of Heywood, Massinger, and Ben Jonson, do not give us the citizens of their time more vividly, nor better contrast the staidness and the follies of old and of young, than De Foe has here accomplished for the traders of William and Anne. We are surprised to be told that this book was less popular than others of its class; but perhaps a certain surly vein of satire which was in it, was the reason.—FORSTER, JOHN, 1845–58, *Daniel De Foe, Edinburgh Review, Historical and Biographical Essays, vol.* II, *p.* 92.

He did more by his pen for the benefit of mankind than almost any English author that ever lived; for his "Complete Tradesman" alone is, perhaps, one of the best books ever printed: a work which did much to form the character of the great American, Benjamin Franklin; and was the very work which Franklin might have been supposed to have written—for it is characteristic of Franklin throughout—it is Franklin all over. This work alone ought to have handed down the name of Daniel De Foe with reverence, to the latest posterity of all true Englishmen.—CHADWICK, WILLIAM, 1859, *The Life and Times of Daniel De Foe, p.* 198.

CAPTAIN CARLETON
1728

He put Lord Eliot in mind of Dr. Walter Harte. "I know, (said he,) Harte was your Lordship's tutor, and he was also tutor to the Peterborough family. Pray, my Lord, do you recollect any particulars that he told you of Lord Peterborough? He is a favourite of mine, and is not enough known; his character has been only ventilated in party pamphlets." Lord Eliot said, if Dr. Johnson would be so good as to ask him any questions, he would tell what he could recollect. Accordingly some things were mentioned. "But, (said his Lordship), the best account of Lord Peterborough that I have happened to meet with, is in 'Captain Carleton's Memoirs.' Carleton was descended of an ancestor who had distinguished himself at the siege of Derry. He was an officer; and, what was rare at that time, had some knowledge of engineering." Johnson said, he had never heard of the book. Lord Eliot had it at Port Eliot; but, after a good deal of enquiry, procured a copy in London, and sent it to Johnson, who told Sir Joshua Reynolds that he was going to bed when it came, but was so much pleased with it, that he sat up till he had read it through, and found in it such an air of truth, that he could not doubt of its authenticity; adding, with a smile, (in allusion to Lord Eliot's having recently been raised to the peerage) "I did not think a *young Lord* could have mentioned to me a book in the English history that was not known to me."—JOHNSON, SAMUEL, 1784, *Life by Boswell, June* 27.

It seems to be now pretty generally believed that Carleton's "Memoirs" were among the numberless fabrications of De Foe; but in this case (if the fact indeed be so), as in that of his "Cavalier," he no doubt had before him the rude journal of some officer.—LOCKHART, JOHN GIBSON, 1832–37, *Life of Scott, note.*

I have abstained from stating why I have rejected a multitude of books that have been erroneously attributed to Defoe. My reason for so doing, after conviction that he was not their author, has been that the explanations would have occupied much space, and have added nothing of value to the memoirs of his life. I must, however, briefly notice an important work assigned to him by no less authority than Sir Walter Scott, Walter Wilson, William Hazlitt, Sir G. C. Lewis, and others; and placed conspicuously in all Lists of his writings. I allude to "The Military Memoirs of Captain George Carleton," a volume published on the 27th of July 1728. It was with great misgivings that I first began to entertain doubts as to its paternity; but in order to remove all possible doubt, I read through it, carefully and critically, several times, until, contrary to my inclination, the conviction was forced upon me that Defoe had nothing whatever to do with any part of the work. I found, however, that the same research which overturned its genuineness, furnished much internal and other evidence in favour of its authenticity. Upon this I was led to a further investigation, which admitted no other conclusion than that Captain George Carleton was a real personage, and himself wrote this true and historical account of his own adventures.—LEE, WILLIAM, 1869, *Daniel Defoe: his Life and Recently Discovered Writings, vol.* I, *p.* 438.

That men of the calibre of Lord Stanhope and Lord Macaulay—who were actually trustees of the British Museum, and moreover could probably have obtained ready access to every other collection of MSS. in the kingdom—should have deliberately abstained from making proper investigations into a matter on which they so unhesitatingly and decidedly published their ideas is, I think, one of the curiosities of modern English literature. On the other hand, though the Defoeists had as little solid grounds for denying altogether the personality of Capt. Carleton, yet there is no doubt that they were infinitely nearer the truth; for my researches have made it absolutely certain that in point of history the "Memoirs" of this officer are sheer fiction. . . . The broad outcome of my own scrutiny into the Carleton question lies, I think, in an establishment of the two great facts that the professed author of the "Memoirs" was a living, cashiered officer who actually was personally engaged (though wholly as a volunteer) in some of the operations in which he professes to have taken part; and secondly, that the general accounts of all these actions, together with some vital statements as to his own career, are intentionally untrue.—PARNELL, ARTHUR,

1889, *Defoe and the "Memoirs of Captain Carleton," The Athenæum, March* 2, *pp.* 279, 280.

GENERAL

This paper—"Mercator" . . . was, soon after, discovered to be the production of an ambidextrous mercenary scribbler, employed . . . by the Earl of Oxford, who . . . for this present dirty work allowed him a considerable weekly salary.—BOYER, ABEL, 1735, *History of Queen Anne, p.* 633.

Foe, as well as the Lord Treasurer, had been a rank Presbyterian, and their genius was so near akin that Harley could not but take him into his confidence as soon as he got acquainted with him. He was adored and caressed by that mighty statesman, who gave him, as that mercenary said himself, to the value of one thousand pounds in one year. Foe's business was only to puzzle the cause by mercantile cant and bold sophistry.—OLDMIXON, JOHN, 1739, *History of England, vol.* III, *p.* 519.

The first part of "Robinson Crusoe" is very good.—De Foe wrote a vast many things; and none bad, though none excellent, except this. There is something good in all he has written.—POPE, ALEXANDER, 1742–43, *Spence's Anecdotes, ed. Singer, p.* 196.

Poetry was far from being the talent of De Foe. He wrote with more perspicuity and strength in prose, and he seems to have understood, as well as any man, the civil constitution of the kingdom, which indeed was his chief study. . . . Considered as a poet, Daniel De Foe is not so eminent, as in a political light: he has taken no pains in versification; his ideas are masculine, his expressions coarse, and his numbers generally rough. He seems rather to have studied to speak truth by probing wounds to the bottom, than, by embellishing his versification, to give it a more elegant keenness. This, however, seems to have proceeded more from carelessness in that particular, than want of ability.—CIBBER, THEOPHILUS, 1753, *Lives of the Poets, vol.* IV, *pp.* 315, 324.

De Foe has not yet outlived his century, though he has outlived most of his contemporaries. Yet the time is come, when he must be acknowledged as one of the ablest, as he is one of the most captivating, writers of which this island can boast. Before he can be admitted to this pre-eminence, he must be considered distinctly, as a poet, as a novelist, as a polemic, as a commercial writer, and as a grave historian. As a poet, we must look to the end of his effusions rather than to his execution, ere we can allow him considerable praise. . . . As a novelist, every one will place him in the foremost rank, who considers his originality, his performance, and his purpose. . . . As a polemic, I fear we must regard our author with less kindness, though it must be recollected, that he lived during a contentious period, when two parties distracted the nation, and writers indulged in great asperities. . . . As a commercial writer, De Foe is fairly entitled to stand in the foremost rank among his contemporaries, whatever may be their performances or their fame. . . . As an historian, it will be found, that our author had but few equals in the English language, when he wrote. His "Memoirs of a Cavalier" show how well he could execute the lighter narratives. His "History of the Union" evinces that he was equal to the higher department of historic composition.—CHALMERS, GEORGE, 1786–1841, *The Life of Daniel De Foe, pp.* 94, 95, 96, 97.

The genius of De Foe has never been questioned, but his sphere of information was narrow; and hence his capacity of fictitious invention was limited to one or two characters. A plain sailor, as Robinson Crusoe,—a blunt soldier, as his supposed Cavalier,—a sharper in low life, like some of his other fictitious personages, were the only disguises which the extent of his information permitted him to assume. In this respect he is limited, like the sorcerer in the Indian tale, whose powers of transformation were confined to assuming the likeness of two or three animals only.—SCOTT, SIR WALTER, 1814, *Memoirs of Jonathan Swift.*

After a vain attempt to apply those laws which hold in ordinary cases, we are compelled to regard him as a phenomenon; and to consider his genius as something rare and curious, which it is impossible to assign to any class whatever. Throughout the ample stores of fiction, in which our literature abounds more than that of any other people, there are no works which at all resemble his, either in the design or execution. Without any precursor in the strange and unwonted path he chose, and without a follower, he spun his web of coarse but original materials, which no mortal had ever thought of using before; and when he had done, it seems as though he had snapped the thread, and conveyed it beyond the reach of imitation. —BARKER, C., 1821, *De Foe's Memoirs of a Cavalier, Retrospective Review, vol.* 3, *p.* 355.

The works of De Foe seemed alternately to delight and disgust. His "Robinson Crusoe" is the most enchanting domestic Romance in the world: but his "Fortunes and Misfortunes of Moll Flanders," and his "Life of Col. Jaque," are such low-bred productions, as to induce us to put an instantaneous negative on their admission into our Cabinets.—DIBDIN, THOMAS FROGNALL, 1824, *The Library Companion, p.* 607.

While all ages and descriptions of people hang delighted over the "Adventures of Robinson Crusoe," and shall continue to do so, we trust, while the world lasts, how few comparatively will bear to be told that there exist other fictitious narratives by the same writer. . . . The narrative manner of Defoe has a naturalness about it beyond that of any other novel or romance writer. His fictions have all the air of true stories. It is impossible to believe, while you are reading them, that a real person is not narrating to you everywhere nothing but what really happened to himself. To this the extreme *homeliness* of their style mainly contributes. We use the word in its best and heartiest sense,—that which comes *home* to the reader. . . . The heroes and heroines of Defoe can never again hope to be popular with a much higher class of readers than that of the servant-maid or the sailor. Crusoe keeps its rank only by tough prescription. Singleton, the pirate; Colonel Jack, the thief; Moll Flanders, both thief and harlot; Roxana, harlot and something worse, —would be startling ingredients in the bill of fare of modern literary delicacies. But, then, what pirates, what thieves, and what harlots, are *the thief, the harlot,* and *the pirate* of Defoe! We would not hesitate to say, that in no other book of fiction, where the lives of such characters are described, is guilt and delinquency made less seductive, or the suffering made more closely to follow the commission, or the penitence more earnest or more bleeding, or the intervening flashes of religious visitation upon the rude and uninstructed soul more meltingly and fearfully painted. They, in this, come near to the tenderness of Bunyan; while the livelier pictures and incidents in them, as in Hogarth or in Fielding, tend to diminish that fastidiousness to the concerns and pursuits of common life which an unrestrained passion for the ideal and the sentimental is in danger of producing.—LAMB, CHARLES, 1830, *Defoe's Secondary Novels.*

One of the most original writers of the English nation.—MACKINTOSH, SIR JAMES 1832–34, *History of the Revolution in England in* 1688, *p.* 178.

The "Plan of the English Commerce" is full of information; and, though desultory, is ably written, and contains sundry passages in which the influence of trade and industry in promoting the well-being of the labouring classes and the public wealth is set in the most striking point of view. . . . "Giving Alms no Charity" is written with considerable cleverness. . . . But these arguments are not so conclusive as some have supposed. . . . The truth is, that in matters of this sort De Foe was quite as prejudiced and purblind as the bulk of those around him. He had not read, or if he had read, he had plainly, at all events, profited nothing by, the conclusive reasonings in the Tract on the East India Trade, previously referred to.—MCCULLOCH, JOHN RAMSAY, 1845, *Literature of Political Economy.*

De Foe is our only famous politician and man of letters, who represented, in its inflexible constancy, sturdy dogged resolution, unwearied perseverance, and obstinate contempt of danger and of tyranny, the great Middle-class English character. We believe it to be no mere national pride to say, that, whether in its defects or its surpassing merits, the world has had none other to compare with it. . . . He was too much in the constant heat of the battle, to see all that we see now. He was not a philosopher himself, but he helped philosophy to some wise conclusions. He did not stand at the highest point of toleration, or of moral wisdom; but, with his masculine active arm, he helped to lift his successors over obstructions which had stayed his own advance. He stood, in his opinions and in his actions, alone and apart from his fellow men; but it was to show his fellow men of later times the value of a juster and larger fellowship, and of more generous modes of action.—FORSTER, JOHN, 1845–58, *Daniel De Foe, Edinburgh Review; Historical and Biographical Essays, vol.* II, *p.* 90.

De Foe was in one respect as unvulgar a man as can be conceived; nobody but Swift could have surpassed him in such a work as "Robinson Crusoe;" yet we cannot conceal from ourselves, that something vulgar adheres to our idea of the author of "Moll Flanders," the "Complete English Tradesman," and even of "Robinson" himself. He has no music, no thorough style, no accomplishments, no love; but he can make wonderful shift without them all; was great in the company of man Friday; and he has rendered his shipwrecked solitary immortal.—HUNT, LEIGH, 1849, *A Book for a Corner.*

He is very far from being an immoral writer: but most of his scenes are such as we cannot be benefited by contemplating. Were it not for this serious drawback, several of his stories, depicting ordinary life with extraordinary vigour and originality, and inspired by a never-failing sympathy for the interests and feelings of the mass of the people, might deserve higher honour than the writings of his more refined and dignified contemporaries. Nor is the author's idiomatic English style the smallest of his merits.—SPALDING, WILLIAM, 1852–82, *A History of English Literature, p.* 321.

Daniel De Foe is a most voluminous political writer, and one of the most distinguished of his age and nation. No man ever battled more manfully and consistently for enlightened and liberal sentiments in politics than he did, and few have suffered more grievous and tantalising prosecutions for their steadfast adherence to them.—BLAKEY, ROBERT, 1855, *The History of Political Literature, vol.* II, *p.* 172.

In the main, as all know, he drew upon his knowledge of low English life, framing imaginary histories of thieves, courtesans, buccaneers, and the like, of a kind to suit a coarse, popular taste. He was a great reader, and a tolerable scholar, and he may have taken the hint of his method from the Spanish picaresque Novel, as Swift adopted his from Rabelais. On the whole, however, it was his own robust sense of reality that led him to his style. There is none of the sly humor of the foreign picaresque Novel in his representations of English ragamuffin life; there is nothing of allegory, poetry, or even of didactic purpose; all is hard, prosaic, and matter-of-fact, as in newspaper paragraphs, or the pages of the Newgate Calendar. Much of his material, indeed, may have been furnished by his recollections of occurrences, or by actual reports and registers; but it is evident that no man ever possessed a stronger imagination of that kind which, a situation being once conceived, teems with circumstances in exact keeping with it.—MASSON, DAVID, 1859, *British Novelists and Their Styles, p.* 95.

He had the kind of mind suitable to such a hard service, solid, exact, entirely destitute of refinement, enthusiasm, pleasantness. His imagination was that of a man of business, not of an artist, crammed and, as it were, jammed down with facts. He tells them as they come to him, without arrangement or style, like a conversation, without dreaming of producing an effect or composing a phrase, employing technical terms and vulgar forms, repeating himself at need, using the same thing two or three times, not seeming to suspect that there are methods of amusing, touching, engrossing, or pleasing, with no desire but to pour out on paper the fulness of the information with which he is charged. Even in fiction his information is as precise as in history. He gives dates, year, month and day; notes the wind, north-east, south-west, north-west; he writes a log-book, an invoice, attorneys' and shopkeepers' bills, the number of moidores, interest, specie payments, payments in kind, cost and sale prices, the share of the king, of religious houses, partners, brokers, net totals, statistics, the geography and hydrography of the island, so that the reader is tempted to take an atlas and draw for himself a little map of the place, to enter into all the details of the history as clearly and fully as the author. It seems as though he had performed all Crusoe's labours, so exactly does he describe them, with numbers, quantities, dimensions, like a carpenter, potter, or an old tar. Never was such a sense of the real before or since. —TAINE, H. A., 1871, *History of English Literature, tr. Van Laun, vol.* II, *bk.* iii, *ch.* vi, *p.* 153.

In the fictitious element he was, of course, remarkably strong; his art was undoubtedly good, but it was the art of the inventor, and not the narrator. . . . His energy, his irrepressibility, his misery, all combined to make him one of the strongest writers of his age; but he must yield the palm to Fielding in the art of novel writing.—SMITH, GEORGE BARNETT, 1875, *Henry Fielding, Poets and Novelists, p.* 275.

It may be safely said of Defoe that no author ever wrote with a more entire absence of vanity, with a more ardent wish to instruct and benefit mankind, and with so little expectation of profit or fame. Of his extraordinary creative powers he himself seems not to have been at all conscious. — WYON, FREDERICK WILLIAM, 1876, *The History of Great Britain During the Reign of Queen Anne, vol.* I, *p.* 139.

"Giving Alms no Charity," one of the most admirable of the many excellent tracts of Defoe. No man then living was a shrewder or more practical observer, and he has collected many facts which throw a vivid light on the condition of the labouring poor.—LECKY, WILLIAM EDWARD HARTPOLE, 1877, *A History of England in the Eighteenth Century, vol.* I, *p.* 608.

He was what would have been called in our time, I dare say, a hot-headed radical; and if he had been born a century and a half later, would have made a capital editorial writer for a slashing morning journal, in either New York or Washington.—MITCHELL, DONALD G., 1877, *About Old Story-Tellers, p.* 202.

Defoe was not an accomplished satirist, in the sense of leaving behind the touch of the poisoned sting, that in either of his contemporaries, Swift or Tom Brown, would have revealed the work of his hand. Defoe turns about his victim with a resistless but good-humoured jocularity, showing his strength rather than his venom.—BURTON, JOHN HILL, 1880, *A History of the Reign of Queen Anne, vol.* I, *p.* 94.

He was condemned to imprisonment and set in the pillory on each of the last three days of July 1703. "A Hymn to the Pillory," which he wrote for distribution to the crowd, caught easily the ears and understandings of the people. The flower-girls were about, and Defoe's pillory was strewn with roses. Defoe's pillory is a new starting point for English Literature. With Defoe especially it may be said that we have the beginning of a form of literature written with the desire to reach all readers.—MORLEY, HENRY, 1881, *Of English Literature in the Reign of Victoria, with a Glance at the Past, p.* 68.

There is probably no writer with whose works his life and personality are more intimately connected. It is impossible to consider the one separate from the other. Defoe began to write novels as a tradesman, as a literary hack, and as a reformer. Being dependent on his pen for his bread, he wrote what was likely to bring in the most immediate return. He calculated exactly the value and quality of his wares. He gave to his fictions the same moral object which inspired his own life. His novels followed naturally on his other labors, and partook of their character. It was his custom, on the death of any celebrated person, to write his life immediately, and to send it to the world while public interest was still fresh. But being often unable to obtain complete or authentic information concerning the subject of his biography, he supplemented facts and rumors by plausible inventions. Fiction entered into his biographies, just as biography afterward entered into his novels. But in writing the lives of real individuals Defoe recognized the necessity of impressing his reader with a sense of the truth and exactitude of the narrative. This effect he attained by the use of a literary faculty which he possessed in a degree unequalled by any other writer —that of circumstantial invention. By the multiplication of small, unimportant details, each one of which is carefully dwelt upon, and by the insertion of uninteresting personal incidents and moral reflections, seeming true from their very dulness, he gave to his work a remarkable verisimilitude.—TUCKERMAN, BAYARD, 1882, *A History of English Prose Fiction, p.* 184.

He was a brave, active man, who saw

things as they were and said what he thought; a man battling for liberty, who fought with a wrongdoer, whether friend or foe; the Ishmael of political writing.—DAWSON, GEORGE, 1886, *Biographical Lectures.*

The "Compleat English Gentleman," by Daniel Defoe, which appears now for the first time in print, is preserved, in the author's handwriting, in the manuscript collection of the British Museum, numbered 32,555 of the Additional MSS. John Forster was the first to mention the existence of the work, in his "Biographical Essays," London, 1860, foot-note on page 155. Fuller particulars were made public by William Lee ("Life of Daniel Defoe," London, 1869, pp. 451, 452, and 457), and to these subsequent writers have added nothing further. . . . The work is written in the classic style which has so often been praised in Defoe. His mastery of language in this late work is still as complete and admirable as ever; the sentences flow in an uninterrupted stream, and the author never seems to hesitate except, as indeed often happens, to return to his proper subject after a digression into which his flood of language has carried him. The most obvious peculiarity of his diction is the tendency to write over-long sentences, and to use as many words as possible; but this excessive copiousness of expression rarely or never destroys the lucidity, or even the simplicity, of his language. He never indulges in the clumsy or grotesque classical constructions which characterized many writers of the previous century, nor in the oppressive quotations from Horace, Virgil, and "their chiming train," upon whom so many others still liked to "draw a bill."—BÜLBRING, KARL D., 1890, *ed., The Compleat English Gentleman, Forewords, pp.* ix, xxvi.

'Tis true the poverty of Defoe's heroes sometimes leads them into questionable society, and engages them in more than questionable enterprises. His works are strongly spiced with the *gusto picaresco*, popular long before in Spain, and he relates with evident relish the exploits of his harlots and vagabonds. It may be worth considering whether portions, for instance, of "Colonel Jack" and "Moll Flanders" might not with advantage be published in a convenient duodecimo as a "Pickpocket's Companion, or Complete Guide to the Art of Pilfering." This notwithstanding, the general tendency of Defoe's novels is unexceptionally moral, and his rough homespun is wrought of more lasting, more serviceable material than the gay brocade of most of his contemporaries and predecessors in English fiction.—WARD, WILLIAM C., 1890, *Samuel Richardson, Gentleman's Magazine, N. S., vol.* 44, *p.* 77.

However much we may praise Defoe's writings, however much—which is not always the same thing—we may enjoy them, we cannot choose but regret that he had not more leisure to be brief. His great, his gigantic literary qualities, his gift of narrative, his verisimilitude, his racy vocabulary, his inimitable art of vivid presentation went hand in hand with a lack of all sense of proportion, measure, restraint, form.—WALKLEY, A. B., 1892, *London Daily Chronicle, Feb.* 17.

No man ever wielded his pen with more consummate ease: and no man ever made his style fit so aptly to his theme, and clothe imaginative creations with such an irresistible air of reality, as Defoe. It was impossible that any language could be handled as Defoe handled it, and yet not carry on its face the impress of his genius: but it is nevertheless true that his position is unique, and that we cannot look upon him, as we look upon Dryden or upon Addison, as marking a distinct phase in the development of English prose. —CRAIK, HENRY, 1894, *English Prose, Introduction, vol.* 3, *p.* 5.

His brain was singularly active and fecund. He had his own views upon all the current questions, and he was eager and resolute to say his say about them. And many questions he himself started, and urged upon his age with characteristic pertinacity and vigour. He was an indefatigable journalist, and struck out new lines in journalism, so that he has left a permanent impression upon our periodical press. The leading article may be said to be one of his creations, or a development of one of them. He was a trenchant pamphleteer, and twice received from the government the painful compliment of imprisonment for his brilliant success in that department. In the fierce clamours of his time one may incessantly—one might almost say always—

detect his voice, clear, irrepressible, effective. . . . He had in an eminent degree the gift of ready writing, and this gift he assiduously cultivated, so that to write, and what is more to write with success, was as easy to him as to speak. He never let his gift of ready writing prove his ruin. . . . Defoe kept his gift well in hand. He never permitted himself to be merely self-confident and careless. Nor, after all, incessantly as he wrote, did he ever yield idly to the impulse to say something when in fact he had nothing to say. . . . Within his limits he was an admirable and a most successful artist. He produced precisely the effects he wished to produce and used always his material with singular judgment and skill. We may feel his world of thought somewhat narrow, and, as we enter it, may be keenly aware that there are more things in heaven and earth —so many more!—than are dreamt of in his philosophy; but in that world he is supreme. Thus no one has ever equalled Defoe in the art of literary deception, that is, in the art of making his own inventions pass for realities, in the art of "lying like truth": no one has ever so frequently and completely taken in his readers.—HALES, JOHN W., 1894, *English Prose, ed. Craik, vol.* III, *pp.* 356, 357, 358.

If Locke is, in certain formal respects, the best paragrapher of his day, Defoe is in all respects the worst. He really knows no difference between the sentence and the paragraph; he paragraphs for emphasis only. The sentence of "Robinson Crusoe" is nearly as long as the paragraph of the "Essay on Projects." It would be hard to find another writer of such irregularities in sentence-length. Defoe's coherence in narrative is good, for his pictorial imagination is exceedingly vivid, and his diction and method those of swift, lucid conversation. But in argument all this is changed. Here he neglects every device of transition and pours out his ideas in the most haphazard way. In argument he is vigorous enough, but his vigor is wasted by utter disregard of method.—LEWIS, EDWIN HERBERT, 1894, *The History of the English Paragraph, p.* 108.

Defoe gained a marvellous knowledge of men; in this respect it has been claimed that he surpasses Shakespeare. He had the journalist's faculty for seeing what was of interest to the people, and the skill to stimulate that interest to his own advantage. It cannot be denied that he concocted news most unblushingly, and that he was an adept in preparing the market for his wares.—SIMONDS, WILLIAM EDWARD, 1894, *Introduction to the Study of English Fiction, p.* 40.

In his greatest works Defoe remains, in his own way, unsurpassed; it is when we turn to the tales which are less known that we see how later writers have developed the art of fiction. . . . If Defoe's narratives are generally less thrilling, if there is less humour or sentiment, if there is a want of imagination and a neglect of the aid furnished by picturesque descriptions of scenery or past times, the honour remains to him of having a great share in the education and inspiration of those who carried the art to a higher level than that to which he usually attained. If his range of vision was limited, it was very vivid; and he was so great a master of the simple style of narration, that all his readers, whether illiterate or refined, can understand and find pleasure in his works.—AITKEN, GEORGE A., 1895, *ed. Defoe's Romances and Narratives, General Introduction, vol.* I, *pp.* xlvi, xlvii.

Defoe, for instance, like Le Sage, was a story-teller above all things; he had this precious faculty in the highest degree, and perhaps he had little else.—MATTHEWS, BRANDER, 1896, *Aspects of Fiction, p.* 157.

Despite all his Newgate experiences and his acquaintance with noted felons, Defoe never understood either the weakness or the strength of the criminal type. So all his harlots and thieves and outcasts are decidedly amateurish. A serious transgression of the moral law is to them a very slight matter, to be soon forgotten after a temporary fit of repentance, and a long course of evil living in no wise interferes with a comfortable and respectable old age. His pirates have none of the desperation and brutal heroism of sin. Stevenson's John Silver or Israel Hands is worth a schooner-load of them. —JOHNSON, CHARLES FREDERICK, 1897, *Library of the World's Best Literature, ed. Warner, vol.* VIII, *p.* 4482.

If Steele be the father of fiction, Defoe

is the parent of journalism. Defoe, again, is no paragon. He was a struggling man of restless enterprise, who lived from hand to mouth—a manufacturer, a merchant adventurer, a reformer, and an author. He mastered every practical department except success. William had listened to his schemes of finance. A bankrupt himself, he projected bankruptcy reforms. In the days of the Second George he was still inditing manuals of trade. In Queen Anne's time he conducted the *Review*. It would be difficult to define his politics. He spied for Harley as he had spied for Godolphin. It would be difficult to define his creed. The indignant Dissenter who penned the "Legion" pamphlet was the same who assured Harley, "Nay, even, the Dissenters, like Casha (*sic*) to Cæsar, lift up the first dagger at me. I confess it makes me reflect on the whole body of the Dissenters with something of contempt." The informer against Sacheverell to the Whigs was the same who, in the autumn of 1710, "was concerned to see people spread the grossest absurdities, by which they would make their disgusts at the late changes appear rational." But, with all inconsistencies, he was a patriot and a reformer. By perpetual projects of improvement, by a voluminous trick of emphatic expansion which suited his audience, he appealed to the *bourgeoisie* and the artisan. That religion should be real, that law should be simplified, that commerce should walk honest and erect, he wrestled like a giant and roared like a Stentor.—SICHEL, WALTER, 1901, *Bolingbroke and His Times*, *p.* 120.

Brook Taylor

1685-1731

Mathematician; born at Edmonton, near London, Aug. 18, 1685; entered St. John's College, Cambridge, in 1701; distinguished himself in music, painting, and mathematics; in 1708 worte a treatise on "The Center of Oscillation," which was published in the "Philosophical Transactions" for 1713; in 1712 was chosen a fellow of the Royal Society, of which he became secretary two years later; and in 1715 he had a controversial correspondence with Count Raymond de Montmort upon the philosophical theories of Malebranche. He published "Methodus Incrementorum," etc. (1715), which contains the foundation of the calculus of finite differences and the first announcement of the famous "Taylor's theorem," the latter almost unnoticed by mathematicians until 1772, when Lagrange adopted it as the basis of the differential calculus. Among his other works were "New Principles of Linear Perspective" (1719); and "Contemplatio Philosophica," which was published, with a memoir by his grandson, Sir William Young (1793). Died in London Dec. 29, 1731.—ADAMS, CHARLES KENDALL, *ed.*, 1897, *Johnson's Universal Cyclopædia, vol.* VIII, *p.* 25.

PERSONAL

We have a remarkable evidence of domestic unhappiness annihilating the very faculty of genius itself, in the case of Dr. Brook Taylor, the celebrated author of the "Linear Perspective." This great mathematician in early life distinguished himself as an inventor in science, and the most sanguine hopes of his future discoveries were raised both at home and abroad. Two unexpected events in domestic life extinguished his inventive faculties. After the loss of two wives, whom he regarded with no common affection, he became unfitted for profound studies; he carried his own personal despair into his favourite objects of pursuit, and abandoned them. The inventor of the most original work suffered the last fifteen years of his life to drop away, without hope, and without exertion.—DISRAELI, ISAAC, 1796-1818, *Domestic Infelicity, The Literary Character.*

GENERAL

A single analytical formula in the "Method of Increments" has conferred a celebrity on its author, which the most voluminous works have not often been able to bestow. It is known by the name of Taylor's Theorem, and expresses the value of any function of a variable quantity in terms of the successive orders of increments, whether finite or infinitely small. If any one proposition can be said to comprehend in it a whole science, it is this: for from it almost every truth and every method of the new analysis may be deduced. It is difficult to say, whether the theorem does most credit to the genius of the author, or the power of the language which is capable of concentrating such a vast body of knowledge in a single expression.—PLAYFAIR, JOHN, 1816–19, *Dissertation on the Progress of Mathematical and Physical Science, pt.* ii.

Successively modified, transformed, and extended by Maclaurin, Lagrange, and Laplace, whose names are attached to their respective formulæ.—LESLIE, SIR JOHN, c1830, *Dissertation on the Progress of the Mathematical and Physical Sciences in the Eighteenth Century, Encyclopædia Britannica.*

I have made this extract from a very short tract, called "Contemplatio Philosophica," by Brook Taylor, which I found in an unpublished memoir of his life printed by the late Sir William Young in 1793. It bespeaks the clear and acute understanding of the celebrated philosopher, and appears to me an entire refutation of the scholastic argument of Descartes; one more fit for the Anselms and such dealers in words, from whom it came, than for himself.—HALLAM, HENRY, 1837–39, *Introduction to the Literature of Europe, pt.* iii, *ch.* iii, *par.* 90, *note.*

In 1715 he published his "Methodus Incrementorum Directa et Inversa" (London, 4to), which was in reality the first treatise dealing with the calculus of finite differences. It contained the celebrated formula known as "Taylor's theorem" which was the first general expression for the expansions of functions of a single variable in infinite series, and of which Mercator's expansion of log. $(1 + x)$, Sir Isaac Newton's binomial theorem, and his expansions of sin x, cos x, e^x, &c., were but particular cases. The importance of the discovery was not fully recognised, however, until it was pointed out by La Grange in 1772. In this work Taylor also applied the calculus for the solution of several problems which had baffled previous investigators. He obtained a formula showing that the rapidity of vibration of a string varies directly as the weight stretching it and inversely as its own length and weight. For the first time he determined the differential equation of the path of a ray of light when traversing a heterogeneous medium. He also discussed the form of the catenary and the determination of the centres of oscillation and percussion.—CARLYLE, E. IRVING, 1898, *Dictionary of National Biography, vol.* LV, *p.* 404.

John Gay

1685–1732

Born, at Barnstaple, 1685; baptized 16 Sept. 1685. Educated at Barnstaple Grammar School. For short time apprentice in a London shop; returned to Barnstaple: thence again to London, probably as secretary to Aaron Hill. Sec. to Duchess of Monmouth, 1712–14. Contrib. to "Guardian," 1713. "The Wife of Bath" produced at Drury Lane, 12 May 1713. In Hanover as sec. to Lord Clarendon, 8 June to Sept., 1714. "What-d'ye-Call-it" produced at Drury Lane, 23 Feb. 1715. "Three Hours after Marriage" (written with Pope and Arbuthnot), Drury Lane, 16 Jan. 1717. To Aix with William Pulteney (afterwards Earl of Bath), 1717. At Cockthorpe with Lord Harcourt, 1718. Severe losses in South Sea Bubble. Under patronage of Duchess of Queensberry from 1720. "The Captives" produced at Drury Lane, 15 Jan. 1724; "The Beggar's Opera," Lincoln's Inn Fields, 29 Jan. 1728; sequel, "Polly," forbidden by Lord Chamberlain, 1729; "Acis and Galatea," Haymarket, May 1732; "Achilles" (posthumous), Covent Garden, 10 Feb. 1733. Died, in London, 4 Dec. 1732. Buried in Westminster Abbey. *Works:* "Wine," 1708; "The Present State of Wit" (anon.,) 1711; "The Mohocks" (anon.), 1713; "Rural Sports," 1713; "The Wife of Bath," 1713; "The Fan," 1714; "The Shepherd's Week," 1714; "A Letter to a Lady" (anon.), 1714; "What-d'ye-Call-it," 1715; "A Journey to Exter," 1715; "Court Poems," 1716; "God's Revenge against Punning" (under pseud. of "Sir James Baker"), 1716; "Trivia," 1716; "An Admonition . . . to the famous Mr. Frapp" (under pseud. of "Sir James Baker"), 1717; "Letter to W—L—, Esq.," 1717; "Epistle to Pulteney," 1717; "Three Hours after Marriage" (with Pope and Arbuthnot), 1717; "Two Epistles," [1720?]; "Poems"

(2 vols.), 1720; "A Panegyrical Epistle" (anon.; attrib. to Gay), 1721; "An Epistle to . . . Henrietta, Duchess of Marlborough," 1722; "The Captives," 1724 (2nd edn. same year); "Fables," first series, 1727, second ser., 1738; "The Beggar's Opera," 1728 (2nd and 3rd edns. same year); "Polly," 1729 (another edn. same year); "Acis and Galatea" (anon.), 1732. *Posthumous:* "Achilles," 1733; "The Distress'd Wife,"1743; "The Rehearsal at Goatham," 1754; "Gay's Chair: poems never before printed," 1820. *Collected Works:* "Plays," 1760; "Works" (4 vols.) 1770; ed. by Dr. Johnson (2 vols.), 1779; ed. J. Underhill (2 vols.), 1893. *Life:* by Coxe, 1797; by W. H. K. Wright, in 1889 edn. of "Fables;" by J. Underhill in 1893 edn. of Poems.—SHARP, R. FARQUHARSON, 1897, *A Dictionary of English Authors, p.* 110.

PERSONAL

Mr. Gay.

	£.	s.	d.
12 *May*, 1713			
Wife of Bath	25	0	0
11 *Nov.*, 1714.			
Letter to a Lady	5	7	6
14 *Feb.*, 1714.			
The What d'ye call it?	16	2	6
22 *Dec.*, 1715.			
Trivia	43	0	0
Epistle to the Earl of Burlington	10	15	0
4 *May*, 1717.			
Battle of the Frogs	16	2	6
8 *Jan.*, 1717.			
Three Hours after Marriage . .	43	2	6
The Mohocks, a Farce, 2l. 10s.			
(Sold the Mohocks to him again.)			
Revival of the Wife of Bath . .	75	0	0
	234	10	0

—LINTOT, BERNARD, 1717, *Account-Book.*

Thus Gay, the hare with many friends,
Twice seven long years the court attends:
Who, under tales conveying truth,
To virtue form'd a princely youth:
Who paid his courtship with the crowd,
As far as modest pride allow'd;
Rejects a servile usher's place,
And leaves St. James's in disgrace.
—SWIFT, JONATHAN, 1729, *A Libel on the Reverend Dr. Delany, and His Excellency John Lord Carteret.*

Life is a jest, and all things show it;
I thought so once, but now I know it.
—GAY, JOHN, 1732, *My Own Epitaph.*

Of manners gentle, of affections mild;
In wit, a man; simplicity, a child:
With native humour temp'ring virtuous rage;
Form'd to delight at once and lash the age:
Above temptation, in a low estate,
And uncorrupted, ev'n among the great:
A safe companion, and an easy friend,
Unblam'd thro' life, lamented in thy end.
These are thy honours! not that here thy bust
Is mix'd with heroes, or with kings thy dust;
But that the worthy and the good shall say,
Striking their pensive bosoms—*Here* lies Gay.
—POPE, ALEXANDER, 1732–35, *On Mr. Gay, in Westminster Abbey.*

I often want poor Mr. Gay, and on this occasion extremely. Nothing evaporates sooner than joy untold, or even told, unless to one so entirely in your interest as he was, who bore at least an equal share in every satisfaction and dissatisfaction that attended us. I am not in the spleen, though I write thus; on the contrary it is a sort of pleasure to think over his good qualities: his loss was really great, but it is a satisfaction to have once known so good a man. As you were as much his friend as I, it is needless to ask your pardon for dwelling so long on this subject.—QUEENSBERRY, CATHERINE HYDE DUCHESS, 1734, *Letter to Mr. Howard, Sept.* 28, *Suffolk Papers, vol.* II, *p.* 109.

Gay was quite a natural man, wholly without art or design, and spoke just what he thought, and as he thought it.—He dangled for twenty years about a court, and at last—was offered to be made Usher to the young Princesses.—Secretary Craggs made Gay a present of stock in the South Sea year: and he was once worth twenty thousand pounds, but lost it all again. He got about four hundred pounds by the first "Beggar's Opera," and eleven or twelve hundred by the second.—He was negligent and a bad manager:—latterly the Duke of Queensbury took his money into his keeping, and let him have only what was necessary out of it: and as he lived with them he could not have occasion for much: he died worth upwards of three thousand pounds.—POPE, ALEXANDER, 1737–39, *Spence's Anecdotes, ed. Singer, p.* 161.

The Duchess of Queensberry told me that Gay could play on the flute, and that this enabled him to adopt so happily some airs in the "Beggar's Opera."—WARTON, JOSEPH, 1797, *ed. Pope's Works, vol.* I, *p.* 159.

The most good-natured and simple of

mankind.—MACAULAY, THOMAS BABINGTON, 1843, *Life and Writings of Addison, Critical and Miscellaneous Essays.*

His haunts may be traced, but home of his own he seems never to have had. Gay was an easy, good-natured fellow, but he had no great feeling of independence; and without being able or desirous to say that he was a mean, far less a disgraceful, hanger-on of the great, he was still a hanger-on.—HOWITT, WILLIAM, 1846, *Homes and Haunts of the Most Eminent British Poets, vol.* I, *p.* 158.

In the great society of the wits, John Gay deserved to be a favourite, and to have a good place. In his set all were fond of him. His success offended nobody. He missed a fortune once or twice. He was talked of for court favour, and hoped to win it; but the court favour jilted him. Craggs gave him some South Sea Stock; and at one time Gay had very nearly made his fortune. But Fortune shook her swift wings and jilted him too: and so his friends, instead of being angry with him, and jealous of him, were kind and fond of honest Gay.—THACKERAY, WILLIAM MAKEPEACE, 1853, *The English Humourists of the Eighteenth Century, p.* 146.

His body was brought by the Company of Upholders from the Duke of Queensberry's to Exeter Change, and thence to the Abbey, at eight o'clock in the winter evening [December 23]. Lord Chesterfield and Pope were present amongst the mourners. He had already, two months before his death, desired: "My dear Mr. Pope, whom I love as my own soul: if you survive me, as you certainly will, if a stone shall mark the place of my grave, see these words put upon it:—

> Life is a jest and all things show it:
> I thought it once, but now I know it.

with what else you may think proper." His wish was complied with.—STANLEY, ARTHUR PENRHYN, 1867–96, *Historical Memorials of Westminster Abbey, ch.* iv.

His character is hardly one for which much respect can be entertained. He had a great deal more of the woman about him than the man. He was absurdly helpless; narrowly scanning for its opinion each face he encountered as he pressed forward; gazing ruefully, almost tearfully about him when alone, like some nervous female in the mazes of London. He had no strength of mind; no dignity of sentiment; no power of helping himself. . . . His women friends made a whim of him, as they made a whim of Jocko the monkey, or the black footboy who followed them with their prayer-book to church. His mind was soft, fat, flabby; it was without muscle, or sinew, or sap. He agreed with everybody, always pleasantly smiling as he assented; but assenting perhaps not so much from sycophancy or respect for the society that endured him, as from incapacity to oppose—as from emptiness of original ideas.—RUSSELL, WILLIAM CLARK, 1871, *The Book of Authors, p.* 186.

In character Gay was affectionate and amiable, but indolent, luxurious, and very easily depressed. His health was never good, and his inactive habits and tastes as a gourmand did not improve it. But his personal charm as a companion must have been exceptionable, for he seems to have been a universal favourite, and Pope, Swift, and Arbuthnot (with none of whom he ever quarrelled) were genuinely attached to him.—DOBSON, AUSTIN, 1890, *Dictionary of National Biography, vol.* XXI.

He was one of those fortunate, helpless persons whom everybody helps, and the Duke and Duchess of Queensberry took him into their household, managed his money for him (he had made a good deal by the "Beggar's Opera"), and prevented him from having any need of it. He died at the end of 1732, too lazy even to make a will. The traditional character of him as of a kind of human lapdog, without any vice except extreme self-indulgence, has been little disturbed.—SAINTSBURY, GEORGE, 1898, *A Short History of English Literature, p.* 559.

THE SHEPHERD'S WEEK
1714

These are Mr. Gay's principal performance. They were originally intended, I suppose, as a burlesque on those of Phillips; but perhaps without designing it, he has hit the true spirit of pastoral poetry. In fact he more resembles Theocritus than any other English pastoral writer whatsoever. There runs throughout the whole a strain of rustic pleasantry, which should ever distinguish this species of composition; but how far the antiquated expressions used here may contribute to the humour, I will not determine; for my own part, I could wish the simplicity were preserved, without recurring to such obsolete antiquity for the manner of expressing it.—GOLDSMITH, OLIVER, 1767, *The Beauties of English Poetry.*

But though the proem burlesqued Philips, and the purpose of censure and caricature was evident enough, yet simple speech is better than the false classicism that condemned it; and Gay, being much more of a poet than Ambrose Philips, and in himself, as Pope said, "a natural man, without design, who spoke what he thought," "The Shepherd's Week" made its own mark as pastoral poetry, and, in spite of its Cloddipole and Hobnelia, by its own merit went far to disprove its case.—MORLEY, HENRY, 1879, *A Manual of English Literature, ed. Tyler, p.* 535.

Like Fielding's novel of "Joseph Andrews," the execution of "The Shepherd's Week" was far superior to its avowed object of mere ridicule. In spite of their barbarous "Bumkinets" and "Grubbinols," Gay's eclogues abound with interesting folk-lore and closely-studied rural pictures. We see the country-girl burning hazel-nuts to find her sweet-heart, or presenting the faithless Colin with a knife with a "posy" on it, or playing "Hot Cockles," or listening to "Gillian of Croydon" and "Patient Grissel." There are also sly strokes of kindly satire, as when the shepherds are represented fencing the grave of Blouzelinda against the prospective inroads of the parson's horse and cow, which have the right of grazing in the churchyard; or when that dignitary, in consideration of the liberal sermon-fee,

"Spoke the Hour-glass in her praise—quite out."

These little touches (and there are a hundred more) make us sure that we are reading no mere caricature; but that the country-life of that age of Queen Anne, which her poet loyally declares to be the only "Golden Age," is truly and faithfully brought before us.—DOBSON, AUSTIN, 1880, *English Poets, ed. Ward, vol.* III, *p.* 146.

They may still be glanced at with pleasure.—STEPHEN, LESLIE, 1880, *Pope (English Men of Letters), p.* 114.

The satirical design is evident enough in the affected use of obsolete words, in the absurd bumpkin nomenclature, Buxoma and Blouzelind, Clumsilis and Hobnelia. But Gay's poetic instinct was too much for him. He had a true insight into the picturesque elements of rural life, a wide knowledge of country customs and country superstitions. And so, though only half intending it, he produced no mere parody, but a genuine work of pastoral art, the nearest approach to a realistic pastoral which our literature had yet seen. And here the history of pastoral really closes upon a note curiously significant. The versifiers who followed in the wake of Pope are of no account. But the temper of Gay, so fantastic in his own age, is prophetic enough to us of the tendencies, revolutionary and deep-rooted, which were destined, nearly a century later, to completely transform the English conception of country life as a subject for poetry.—CHAMBERS, EDMUND K., 1895, *English Pastorals, p.* xlvii.

FABLES
1727–38

For a Fable he gives now and then a Tale, or an abstracted Allegory; and from some, by whatever name they may be called, it will be difficult to extract any moral principle. They are, however, told with liveliness; the versification is smooth; and the diction, though now-and-then a little constrained by the measure or the rhyme, is generally happy.—JOHNSON, SAMUEL, 1779–81, *Gay, Lives of the English Poets.*

Gay was sometimes grosser than Prior, not systematically, but inadvertently—from not being so well aware of what he was about; nor was there the same necessity for caution, for his grossness is by no means so seductive or inviting. Gay's "Fables" are certainly a work of great merit, both as to the quantity of invention implied, and as to the elegance and facility of the execution. They, are, however, spun out too long; the descriptions and narrative are too diffuse and desultory; and the moral is sometimes without point. They are more like Tales than fables. The best are, perhaps, the Hare with Many Friends, the Monkeys, and the Fox at the Point of Death.—HAZLITT, WILLIAM, 1818, *Lectures on the English Poets, Lecture* vi.

As a fabulist he has been sometimes hypercritically blamed for presenting us with allegorical impersonations. The mere naked apologue of Æsop is too simple to interest the human mind, when its fancy and understanding are past the state of childhood or barbarism. La Fontaine dresses the stories which he took from Æsop and others with such profusion of wit and *naïveté*, that his manner conceals the insipidity of the matter. "*La sauce vaut mieux que le poisson.*" Gay, though not equal to La Fontaine, is at least free from his occasional prolixity; and in one instance, (the Court of Death,) ventures into allegory with considerable power. Without being an absolute simpleton, like La Fontaine, he possessed a *bonhomie* of character which forms an agreeable trait of resemblance between the fabulists.—CAMPBELL, THOMAS, 1819, *Specimens of the British Poets.*

The most finished productions of our poet, and those to which he will owe his reputation with posterity, are his "Fables,"—the finest in the lanugage. They are written with great spirit and vivacity; the versification is generally smooth and flowing; the descriptions happy and appropriate, and the moral designed to be conveyed is, for the most part, impressive and instructive.—CLEVELAND, CHARLES D., 1848, *A Compendium of English Literature, p.* 414.

Gay's "Fables" carry to many people pleasant memories of the nursery and the schoolroom, where they lightened the weight of graver studies.—BURTON, JOHN HILL, 1880, *A History of the Reign of Queen Anne, vol.* III, *p.* 292.

Thackeray confessed that he had not been able to peruse them since his very early youth; but probably he would have found no difficulty in digesting them if he had made some slight effort. It is true that there is a certain want of variety both in the subject and tone of the fables; but they abound in touches of humour, and are written in an easy style. Many of them are tales and sometimes allegories, rather than fables, properly so called, and in the posthumous collection the fable forms a very small part of each poem. But what can be neater than the description of the election of the Fox as regent to the Lion?—AITKEN, GEORGE A., 1893, *John Gay, Westminster Review, vol.* 140, *p.* 402.

The "Fables" are light and lively, and might safely be recommended to Mr. Chamberlain, who is fond of an easy quotation. To lay them down is never difficult.—BIRRELL, AUGUSTINE, 1894, *Essays about Men, Women and Books, p.* 118.

THE BEGGAR'S OPERA
1728

Dr. Swift had been observing once to Mr. Gay, what an odd pretty sort of thing a Newgate Pastoral might make. Gay was inclined to try at such a thing, for some time, but afterwards thought it would be better to write a comedy on the same plan. This was what gave rise to the "Beggar's Opera." He began on it, and when first he mentioned it to Swift, the Doctor did not much like the project. As he carried it on, he showed what he wrote to both of us; and we now and then gave a correction, or a word or two of advice: but it was wholly of his own writing. When it was done, neither of us thought it would succeed. We showed it to Congreve, who, after reading it over, said, "It would either take greatly, or be damned confoundedly."—We were all at the first night of it, in great uncertainty of the event; till we were very much encouraged by overhearing the Duke of Argyle, who sat in the next box to us, say, "It will do, —it must do!—I see it in the eyes of them."—This was a good while before the first act was over, and so gave us ease soon; for the duke (besides his own good taste) has a more particular knack than any one now living, in discovering the taste of the public. He was quite right in this, as usual; the good nature of the audience appeared stronger and stronger every act, and ended in a clamour of applause.—POPE, ALEXANDER, 1734–36, *Spence's Anecdotes, ed. Singer, p.* 120.

"Cato," it is true, succeeded, but reached not by full forty days the progress and applause of the "Beggar's Opera." Will it however admit of a question which of the two compositions a good writer would rather wish to have been the author of? Yet, on the other side, must we not allow, that to have taken a whole nation, high and low, into a general applause, has shown a power in poetry which, though often attempted in the same kind, none but this one author could ever yet arrive at.—CIBBER, COLLEY, 1739, *An Apology for His Life.*

The effects of the "Beggar's Opera"

on the minds of the people have fulfilled the prognostications of many that it would prove injurious to society. Rapine and violence have been gradually increasing ever since its first representation: the rights of property, and the obligation of the laws that guard it, are disputed upon principle. Every man's house is now become what the law calls it, his castle, or at least it may be said that, like a castle, it requires to be a place of defence; young men, apprentices, clerks in public offices, and others, disdaining the arts of honest industry, and captivated with the charms of idleness and criminal pleasure, now betake themselves to the road, affect politeness in the very act of robbery, and in the end become victims to the justice of their country: and men of discernment, who have been at the pains of tracing this evil to its source, have found that not a few of those, who, during these last fifty years have paid to the law the forfeit of their lives, have in the course of their pursuits been emulous to imitate the manners and general character of Macheath. —HAWKINS, SIR JOHN, 1776, *A General History of the Science and Practice of Music, ch.* cxc, *p.* 875.

Often and often had I read Gay's "Beggar's Opera," and always delighted with its poignant wit and original satire, and if not without noticing its immorality, yet without any offence from it. Some years ago, I for the first time saw it represented in one of the London theatres; and such were the horror and disgust with which it impressed me, so grossly did it outrage all the best feelings of my nature, that even the angelic voice and perfect science of Mrs. Billington lost half their charms, or rather increased my aversion to the piece by an additional sense of incongruity. Then I learned the immense difference between reading and seeing a play.—COLERIDGE, SAMUEL TAYLOR, 1812, *Omniana, ed. Ashe, p.* 386.

It is indeed a masterpiece of wit and genius, not to say of morality. In composing it, he chose a very unpromising ground to work upon, and he has prided himself in adorning it with all the graces, the precision, and brilliancy of style. It is a vulgar error to call this a vulgar play. So far from it that I do not scruple to say that it appears to me one of the most refined productions in the language. The elegance of the composition is in exact proportion to the coarseness of the materials: by "happy alchemy of mind," the author has extracted an essence of refinement from the dregs of human life, and turns its very dross into gold. The scenes, characters, and incidents are, in themselves, of the lowest and most disgusting kind: but, by the sentiments and reflections which are put into the mouths of highwaymen, turnkeys, their mistresses, wives, or daughters, he has converted this motley group into a set of fine gentlemen and ladies, satirists and philosophers. He has also effected this transformation without once violating probability, or "o'erstepping the modesty of nature." In fact, Gay has turned the tables on the critics; and by the assumed license of the mock-heroic style, has enabled himself to *do justice to nature,* that is, to give all the force, truth, and locality of real feeling to the thoughts and expressions, without being called to the bar of false taste and affected delicacy.—HAZLITT, WILLIAM, 1818, *Lectures on the English Poets, Lecture* vi.

This piece has kept possession of the stage for upwards of a century. "Macheath" and "Polly" have been favourite parts with most of our principal vocal performers; and, when well represented, it has rarely failed to draw crowded audiences in every part of the kingdom. Its effects on public morals have been the subject of much discussion and controversy. Soon after its appearance it was praised by Swift, as a piece which placed all kinds of vice in the strongest and most odious light. Others, however, censured it, as giving encouragement not only to vice but to crime, by making a highwayman the hero, and dismissing him at last unpunished. It was even said that its performance had a visible effect in increasing the number of this description of freebooters. The celebrated police magistrate, Sir John Fielding, once told Hugh Kelly, the dramatist, on a successful run of the "Beggar's Opera," that he expected, in consequence of it, a fresh cargo of highwaymen at his office. Upon Kelly's expressing his surprise at this, Sir John assured him, that, ever since the first representation of that piece, there had been, on every successful run, a proportionate number of highwaymen brought to the office, as would appear by the books any morning he chose to look over them. Kelly did so, and found the observation to be strictly correct. . . . Recently, however, the "Beggar's Opera" has been rarely performed. Whether this has arisen from a growing sense of its impropriety, or from the want of fitting representatives of the hero and heroine, we shall not pretend to say. We believe that its licentiousness has contributed, no less than its wit and the beauty of its music, to the favour it has so long enjoyed: but it may be presumed that the time is come, or at least approaching, when its licentiousness will banish it from the stage, notwithstanding its wit and the beauty of its music.—HOGARTH, GEORGE, 1838, *Memoirs of The Musical Drama, vol.* II, *pp.* 50, 55.

We have seen the "Beggar's Opera" degraded from a pungent yet delicate satire upon the Walpoles and Pulteneys to an episode from the Newgate Calendar. Its humor had passed away; its songs had lost their savour; the actors mistook irony for earnest; we seemed to have fallen among thieves and longed to call for the police, and send them packing to Bow-street.—DONNE, WILLIAM BODHAM, 1854–58, *Essays on the Drama, p.* 139.

The "Beggar's Opera" was Gay's ruin. —THOMSON, KATHARINE (GRACE WHARTON), 1862, *The Literature of Society, vol.* II, *p.* 217.

The satire was purely the revenge of a disappointed courtier. Gay had accepted one office from the political Macheath, had long been a suppliant for another, and only talked of Bob Booty because he had not been allowed a larger share of the spoils.—ELWIN, WHITWELL, 1871, *ed., The Works of Alexander Pope, vol.* VII, *p.* 142, *note.*

Of all ballad-operas the first is easily the foremost, excepting only "The Duenna."—MATTHEWS, BRANDER, 1880, *"Pinafore's" Predecessor, Harper's Magazine, vol.* 60, *p.* 501.

The "Beggar's Opera" is, in fact, rather the parody of a comedy interspersed with songs than a true opera, but there are passages in it which, abating some necessary absurdity, are wholly in the comedy vein. The play is unfortunately too gross for a more liberal extract than has been given. In reading the "Beggar's Opera," it is good to remember the wonderful success of the play in its own day. Phrases from it passed as catch-words in society, and its admirable songs were painted on ladies' fans.—CRAWFURD, OSWALD, 1883, *ed., English Comic Dramatists, p.* 204.

It was *Polly*, however, as impersonated by the fascinating Lavinia Fenton (in 1728), that made the success of "The Beggar's Opera." She dressed the part in the most simple manner, and the pathetic naïveté with which she delivered the lines—

> For on the rope that hangs my dear
> Depends poor Polly's life,

had such an effect that applause burst forth from every part of the house. The work had up to this moment gone but poorly. Its triumph was now assured, and the enthusiasm of the public went on increasing until the fall of the curtain. The opera soon made its way to Wales, Scotland, and Ireland. The principal songs were inscribed on fans and screens, and the enemies of foreign art boasted that "The Beggar's Opera" (which is really a semi-burlesque comedy, interspersed with songs set to popular tunes) had driven out the opera of the Italians. —EDWARDS, HENRY SUTHERLAND, 1888, *The Prima Donna: Her History and Surroundings.*

The present age would perhaps rank Gay lowest in that kind of writing in which, in his own time, he achieved a phenomenal success. The "Beggar's Opera" is very coarse homespun compared with the dainty fabrics which have come from the loom of Mr. W. S. Gilbert.—TOVEY, DUNCAN C., 1897, *Reviews and Essays in English Literature, p.* 115.

POLLY

1729

The Duchess of Queensberry is surprised and well pleased that the King has given her so agreeable a command as forbidding her the Court, where she never came for diversion, but to bestow a very great civility on the King and Queen. She hopes that by so unprecedented an order as this, the King will see as few as she wishes at his Court, particularly such as dare to think and speak truth. I dare not do otherwise, nor ought not; nor could I have imagined but that it would have been the highest compliment I could possibly pay the King and Queen, to endeavour to support truth and innocence in their house.

—C. QUEENSBERRY.

P. S. Particularly when the King and Queen told me that they had not read Mr. Gay's play, I have certainly done right then to justify my own behaviour, rather than act like his Grace of Grafton, who has neither made use of truth, honour or judgment in this whole affair, either for himself or his friends.— QUEENSBERRY, CATHERINE HYDE, DUCHESS, 1728–9, *Letter to Mr. Stanhope, Vice-Chamberlain, Feb.* 27.

I suppose you will have some odd account of me, pray let me know what they say of me behind my back? The Duchess of Queensbury, to the great amazement of the admiring world, is forbid the Court, only for being solicitous in getting a subscription for Mr. Gay's sequel of the "Beggar's Opera," which the Court forbid being acted, on account that it reflected on the Government. The Duchess is a great friend of Gay's, and has thought him much injured; upon which, to make him some amends, for he is poor, she promised to get a subscription for his play if he would print it. She indiscreetly has urged the King and Queen in his behalf, and asked subscriptions in the drawing-room, upon which she is *forbid the Court*—a thing never heard of before to one of her rank: one might have imagined *her beauty* would have secured her from such treatment! The Vice-Chamberlain went with the message, and she returned the answer which I have enclosed.—PENDARVES, MRS. M., 1728–29, *Letter to Mrs. Anne Granville, March* 4, *Life and Correspondence of Mrs. Delany, ed. Lady Llanover, vol.* I, *p.* 193.

The inoffensive John Gay is now become one of the obstructions to the peace of Europe, the terror of the ministers, the chief author of the "Craftsman," and all the seditious pamphlets which have been published against the government. He has got several turned out of their places; the greatest ornament of the court (*i. e.* Duchess of Queensberry) banished from it for his sake; another great lady (Mrs. Howard, afterwards Countess of Suffolk) in danger of being chasée likewise; about seven or eight duchesses pushing forward, like the ancient circumcelliones in the church, who shall suffer martyrdom on his account first. He is the darling of the city. . . . I can assure you, this is the very identical Jno. Gay whom you formerly knew and lodged with in Whitehall two years ago.—ARBUTHNOT, JOHN, 1728–29, *Letter to Jonathan Swift, March* 19.

Among the remarkable occurrences of this winter, I cannot help relating that of the Duchess of Queensberry being forbid the Court, and the occasion of it. One Gay, a poet, had written a ballad opera, which was thought to reflect a little upon the Court, and a good deal upon the Minister. It was called "The Beggar's Opera," had a prodigious run, and was so extremely pretty in its kind, that even those who were most glanced at in the satire had prudence enough to disguise their resentment by chiming in with the universal applause with which it was performed. Gay, who had attached himself to Mrs. Howard and been disappointed of preferment at Court, finding this couched satire upon those to whom he imputed his disappointment succeeded so well, wrote a second part to this opera, less pretty but more abusive, and so little disguised that Sir Robert Walpole resolved, rather than suffer himself to be produced for thirty nights together upon the stage in the person of a highwayman, to make use of his friend the Duke of Gafton's authority, as Lord Chamberlain, to put a stop to the representation of it. Accordingly, this *theatrical Craftsman* was prohibited at every playhouse. Gay, irriated at this bar thrown in the way both of his interest and his revenge, zested the work with some supplemental invectives, and resolved to print it by subscription. The Duchess of Queensberry set herself at the head of this undertaking, and solicited every mortal that came in her way, or in whose way she could put herself, to subscribe. To a woman of her quality, proverbially beautiful, and at the top of the polite and fashionable world, people were ashamed to refuse a guinea, though they were afraid to give it. Her solicitations were so universal and so pressing, that she came even into the Queen's apartment, went round the Drawing-room, and made even the King's servants contribute to the printing of a thing which the King had forbid being acted. The King, when he came into the Drawing-room, seeing her Grace very busy in a corner with three or four men, asked her what she had been doing. She answered, "*What* must be agreeable, she was sure, to anybody so humane as his Majesty, for it was an act of charity, and a charity to which she did not despair of bringing his Majesty to contribute." Enough was said for each to understand the other. . . . Most people blamed the Court upon this occasion. What the Duchess of Queensberry did was certainly impertinent; but the manner of resenting it was thought impolitic.—HERVEY, LORD, 1729, *Letter to Swift, Hervey's Memoirs, vol.* I, *chap.* vi.

Which brought in more money to Gay from its not having been allowed to get on the stage than its brilliant predecessor had done after all its unexampled run. The measure of Walpole's wrath was filled by the knowledge that a piece was in preparation in which he was to be held up to public ridicule in the rudest and most uncompromising way. Walpole acted with a certain boldness and cunning. The play was brought to him, was offered for sale to him. This was an audacious attempt at black-mailing; and at first it appeared to be successful. Walpole agreed to the terms, bought the play, paid the money, and then proceeded at once to make the fact that such a piece had been written, and but for his payment might have been played, an excuse for the introduction of a measure to put the whole English stage under restriction, and to brand it with terms of shame. He picked out carefully all the worst passages, and had them copied, and sent round in private to the leading members of all parties in the House of Commons, and appealed to them to support him in passing a measure which he justified in advance by the illustrations of dramatic licentiousness thus brought under their own eyes. By this mode of action he secured beforehand an amount of support which made the passing of his Bill a matter of almost absolute certainty. Under these favorable conditions he introduced his Playhouse Bill.—MCCARTHY, JUSTIN, 1884, *A History of the Four Georges, vol.* II, *chap.* 27.

It may be interesting to note that "Polly" was first seen upon the stage at the Haymarket Theatre on June 19, 1777. A few new songs were upon that occasion introduced, and portions of the dialogue were here and there omitted. But the alterations were not material. Polly Peachum was played by a "gentlewoman (her first appearance)." Perhaps the most remarkable thing about this remarkable *première* was the fact that the Duchess of Queensbury, though extremely old—she died in the following month—attended it. "Polly" was played at the Haymarket again in 1782, and at Drury Lane in 1813.—UNDERHILL, JOHN, 1893, *ed., the Poetical Works of John Gay, vol.* I, *p.* lx.

It is an exceedingly nasty piece, not unworthy of one of the three authors who between them produced that filthiest and most stupid of farces, "Three Hours After Marriage."—BIRRELL, AUGUSTINE, 1894, *Essays about Men, Women and Books, p.* 117.

GENERAL

When fame did o'er the spacious plains
The lays, she once had learn'd, repeat;
All listen'd to the tuneful strains,
And wonder'd who could sing so sweet.
'Twas thus:—The Graces held the lyre,
Th' harmonious frame the Muses strung,
The Loves and Smiles composed the choir,
And Gay transcribed what Phœbus sung.
—GARTH, SAMUEL, 1719? *To Mr. Gay on his Poems.*

I grieve to be outdone by Gay
In my own humorous biting way.
—SWIFT, JONATHAN, 1731, *On the Death of Dr. Swift.*

Gay was a good-natured man, and a little poet.—MONTAGU, LADY MARY WORTLEY, 1740–41, *Spence's Anecdotes, ed. Singer, p.* 176.

As to his genius it would be superfluous to say any thing here, his works are in the hands of every reader of taste, and speak for themselves; we know not whether we can be justified in our opinion, but we beg leave to observe, that all of Gay's performances, his "Pastorals" seem to have the highest finishing; they are perfectly Doric; the characters and dialogue are natural and rurally simple; the language is admirably suited to the persons, who appear delightfully rustic.—CIBBER, THEOPHILUS, 1753, *Lives of the Poets, vol.* IV. *p.* 259.

As a poet, he cannot be rated very high. He was, as I once heard a female critick remark, "of a lower order." He had not in any great degree the *mens divinior* the dignity of genius. Much however must be allowed to the author of a new species of composition, though it be not of the highest kind. We owe to Gay the Ballad Opera; a mode of comedy which at first was supposed to delight only by its novelty, but has now by the experience of half a century been found so well accommodated to the disposition of a popular audience, that it is likely to keep long possession of the stage. Whether this new drama was the product of judgment or of luck, the praise of it must be given to the inventor; and there are many writers read with more reverence, to whom such merit or originality cannot be attributed.—JOHNSON, SAMUEL, 1779–81, *Gay, Lives of the English Poets.*

Oh! what monster mentions Gay? We wish all fame to the memory of him and his panegyrist Sir William Jones. But his "Pastorals" are about as bad as his "Beggar's Opera"—vulgar both—if vulgarity there ever were on earth—in town or country—and we have been miserably awakened from our dream of the Golden Age.—WILSON, JOHN, 1833, *Spenser, Blackwood's Magazine, vol.* 34, *p.* 833.

Mr. Gay's "Fables," which were written to benefit that amiable Prince, the Duke of Cumberland, the warrior of Dettingen and Culloden, I have not, I own, been able to peruse since a period of very early youth; and it must be confessed that they did not effect much benefit upon the illustrious young Prince, whose manners they were intended to molify, and whose natural ferocity our gentle-hearted Satirist perhaps proposed to restrain. But the six pastorals called the "Shepherd's Week," and the burlesque poem of "Trivia," any man fond of lazy literature will find delightful, at the present day, and must read from beginning to end with pleasure. They are to poetry what charming little Dresden china figures are to sculpture: graceful, minikin, fantastic; with a certain beauty always accompanying them. The pretty little personages of the pastoral, with gold clocks to their stockings, and fresh satin ribbons to their crooks and waistcoats and boddices, dance their loves to a minuet-tune played on a bird-organ, approach the charmer, or rush from the false one daintily on their red-heeled tiptoes, and die of despair or rapture, with the most pathetic little grins and ogles; or repose, simpering at each other, under an arbour of pea-green crockery; or piping to pretty flocks that have just been washed with the best Naples in a stream of Bergamot.—THACKERAY, WILLIAM MAKEPEACE, 1853, *The English Humourists of the Eighteenth Century.*

In Gay, as well as with them, unvarnished and sensual drollery has its sway. The people of the north, who are great eaters, always liked country fairs. The vagaries of toss-pots and gossips, the grotesque outburst of the popular and animal mind, put them into good humour. One must be genuinely a worldling or an artist, a Frenchman or an Italian, to be disgusted with them. They are the product of the country, as well as meat and beer: let us try, in order that we may enjoy them, to forget wine, delicate fruits, to give ourselves blunted senses, to become in imagination compatriots of such men. We have become used to the pictures of these drunken clods, which Louis XIV. called "baboons," to these red cooks who scrape their horse-radish, and to the like scenes. Let us get used to Gay; to his poem "Trivia, or the Art of Walking the Streets of London;" to his advice as to dirty gutters, and shoes "with firm, well-hammer'd soles; his description of the amours of the goddess Cloacina and a scavenger, whence sprang the shoeblacks. He is a lover of the real, has a precise imagination, does not see objects on a large scale, but singly, with all their outlines and surroundings, whatever they may be, beautiful or ugly, dirty or clean.—TAINE, H. A., 1871, *History of English Literature, tr. Van Laun, vol.* II, *bk.* iii, *ch.* vii, *p.* 216.

Mr. Dobson fails to emphasize fully many of the characteristics which gave Gay a unique position in his own age, and leaves others entirely unnoticed. Chief among these characteristics were—a form of versification, especially in the couplet, far less rigid and artificial than that employed by any of his contemporaries; a sense of real humour; and, lastly, a feeling for the country and country life not to be found again till the appearance of "The Seasons."—STRACHEY, ST. LOE, 1883, *The Academy, vol.* 23, *p.* 3.

Gay is yet a figure in English letters. As a song-writer he has still a claim on us, and is still able to touch the heart and charm the ear. The lyrics in "Acis and Galatea" are not unworthy their association with Handel's immortal melodies, the songs in "The Beggar's Opera" have a part in the life and fame of the sweet old tunes from which they can never be divided. — HENLEY, WILLIAM ERNEST, 1890, *Views and Reviews, p.* 187.

He had received no regular education, and had, on emerging from obscurity, been too indolent to remedy the defect. A smattering of Latin and a smattering of French and Italian constituted all his stock as a scholar; but, if he owed little to the schools, he owed much to nature—a rich vein of genial humour, wit less abundant, indeed, and less brilliant, than that of his friends Congreve and Pope, but scarcely less pleasing, native grace, and, what were rare with the poets of that age, spontaneity and simplicity. His first experiment had been made in serious poetry, and in serious poetry Gay never rises, even in his happiest moments, above mediocrity.—COLLINS, JOHN CHURTON, 1893, *Jonathan Swift, p.* 96.

Gay's position as a poet is practically determined by his "Fables." It is their popularity and their merit that have secured for him the place in English literature which he now holds. "Trivia" and "The Shepherd's Week" are interesting mainly for the glimpses of town and country life in the eighteenth century which they afford us. Gay's lyrical gifts, which were of a high order, find full expression in "Black Eyed Susan" and similar ballads, and in the songs which form part of his operas and plays. As to his other works, the reader of the following pages will be in a position to criticise them for himself. He will probably marvel at the reputation which Gay enjoyed in his lifetime, and still more in the high position in the hierarchy of English poets that is now accorded to him. And perhaps for the first time he will recognise the force of the statement with which this Memoir begins, and will agree with the writer that time has indeed laid a gentle hand upon the literary fame of John Gay.—UNDERHILL, JOHN, 1893, *ed., The Poetical Works of John Gay, vol.* I, *p.* lxviii.

He had a true vein of happy song, and "Black-eyed Susan" remains with the "Beggar's Opera" to please us still.—BROOKE, STOPFORD A., 1896, *English Literature, p.* 187.

"Black Ey'd Susan, or Sweet William's Farewell" was written by Gay, the author of the "Beggar's Opera," and is included among his published poems. The music was composed by Richard Leveridge, a genial, jovial individual, who published a collection of his songs in 1727. "Black Ey'd Susan" was not issued till 1730. Douglas Jerrold wrote his famous play of the same name in 1824 (revived 1896), it being first produced on Whit Monday of that year at the Surrey Theatre, making all the principals connected with the production, except the author, passing rich. The song is introduced into the piece, and is usually sung by Blue Peter.—FITZ-GERALD, S. J. ADAIR, 1898, *Stories of Famous Songs, p.* 224.

William Lowth

1660–1732

Born at London, Sept. 11, 1661; died at Buriton, Hampshire, May 17, 1732. He was graduated at Oxford, 1683; and became chaplain to Dr. Mew, bishop of Winchester, who made him a prebendary of Winchester, 1696, and rector of Buriton and Petersfield, 1699. His own works were few in number, but weighty in value: "A Vindication of the Divine Authority and Inspiration of the Old and New Testament, in Answer to (Le Clerc's) Five Letters," Oxford, 1692, 3d. ed., 1821, (this brought him into notice); "Directions for the Profitable Reading of the Holy Scriptures," London, 1708, 7th ed., 1799; but his principal work was a "Commentary on the Prophets," London, 1714–23, 4 vols., afterwards collected in one folio volume, and incorporated with Bishop Patrick's Commentary, and frequently reprinted, in that connection, under the caption, "Patrick, Lowth, and Whitby's Commentary." Dr. Lowth was the efficient assistant upon several works which pass under other names, such as Dr. Potter's edition of "Clemens Alexandrinus," Oxford, 1715, 2 vols., enlaregd edition, Venice, 1757, 2 vols.; *Hudson's* "Josephus," Oxford, 1720, 2 vols.; *Reading's* "Historiæ

FRANCIS ATTERBURY

Engraving by Simon, from Painting by Kneller.

HENRY SAINT-JOHN

Engraving by T. A. Dean, from Painting by Kneller.

Ecclesiasticæ," Cambridge, 1720, 3 vols. (reprinted Turin, 1748). A "Life" of Dr. Lowth will be found in the seventh edition of his "Directions, etc."—SCHAFF AND HERZOG, *eds.*, 1883, *Encyclopædia of Religious Knowledge, vol.* II, *p.* 1357.

GENERAL

I mention with pleasure the labours of a respectable prelate, who in this, ["Translation of Isaiah"] as well as in a former work, has very happily united the most critical judgment, with the taste and spirit of poetry.—GIBBON, EDWARD, 1779, *A Vindication of Some Passages in the Fifteenth and Sixteenth Chapters of the History of the Decline and Fall of the Roman Empire.*

Lowth had the amiable accomplishments of a man of parts and a scholar; but in no transcendent degree of eminence in either character.—HURD, RICHARD, 1808? *Commonplace Book, ed. Kilvert, p.* 249.

Lowth is one of the most judicious commentators on the prophets. He never prophesies himself: adheres strictly to the literal meaning of the inspired writer, and is yet generally evangelical in his interpretations. There is not much appearance of criticism; but the original text and other critical aids were doubtless closely studied by the respectable author. It is often quoted by Scott, and, along with Patrick and Whitby (with whom he is associated, though a writer of more spirituality than either), is pronounced by Bishop Watson the best commentary in the English language.—ORME, WILLIAM, 1824, *Bibliotheca Biblica.*

His piety, his diligence, his hospitality, and his beneficence, rendered his life highly exemplary, and greatly enforced his public ministrations.—MILLS, ABRAHAM, 1851, *The Literature and the Literary Men of Great Britain and Ireland, vol.* II, *p.* 238.

Distinguished for his classical and theological attainments, and the liberality with which he communicated his stores to others. . . . His learning is said to have been equally extensive and profound, and he accompanied all his reading with critical and philological remarks.—CHAMBERS, ROBERT, 1876, *Cyclopædia of English Literature, ed. Carruthers.*

The value of his commentary was never very great, and it has been long since entirely superseded. Its tone is pious but cold, and he fails to appreciate the spiritual and poetical character of the prophetical writings, while he is far too eager to discover Messianic interpretations. His knowledge of Hebrew was moreover inadequate. At the same time his exegesis, if shallow, is simple, direct, and brief. The commentary has been highly praised by Bishop Richard Watson and by William Orme. Though less eminent than his son, Robert Lowth, the bishop of London, he was believed to be the profounder scholar. But he was too diffident to undertake any considerable original work, and the wide range and accuracy of his learning was chiefly shown in his contributions to the publications of others. We are told that he carefully read and annotated almost every Greek and Latin author, classical or ecclesiastical, and the stores he had thus collected he dispensed ungrudgingly.—VENABLES, EDMUND, 1893, *Dictionary of National Biography, vol.* XXXIV, *p.* 217.

Francis Atterbury

1662–1732

Francis Atterbury, Bishop of Rochester, was born 6th March 1662, at Milton-Keynes, near Newport-Pagnell, and educated at Westminster, whence in 1680 he passed to Christ Church, Oxford. In 1687 he answered a pseudonymous attack on Protestanism by Obadiah Walker, master of University College; and, taking orders about the same time, won such reputation as a preacher, that he was appointed lecturer of St. Bride's (1691), a royal chaplain, and minister to Bridewell Hospital. Boyle's "Examination of Bentley's Dissertations on the Epistles of Phalaris" (1698), a clever, but shallow performance, was really by Atterbury, who had been the young noblemen's tutor at Christ Church; his defence (1700) of Convocation won him the archdeaconry of Totnes, a canonry of Exeter, and the degree of D. D. In 1704 he was promoted to the deanery of Carlisle; in 1710 was chosen prolocutor of Convocation; in 1712 became Dean of Christ Church; and in 1713 was made Bishop of Rochester and Dean of Westminster. To Atterbury is ascribed, with great likelihood,

Dr. Sacheverel's famous defence (1710) before the Lords; and he was author of the scarcely less famous "Representation of the State of Religion" (1711). He may well have aspired to the primacy; but the death of Queen Anne extinguished his hopes in that direction. His known character and Jacobite leanings made him no favourite with George I. In 1715 he refused to sign the bishop's declaration of fidelity, and in 1722 he was committed to the Tower. A bill of pains and penalties was brought into the House of Commons, and passed in the Lords by 83 to 43. Atterbury, who had defended himself with great ability, was deprived of all his offices, and for ever banished the kingdom. In 1723 he quitted England, and after a short stay at Brussels, settled in Paris, where he died, 15th February, 1732. He was laid in a nameless grave in Westminster Abbey. His works comprise sermons, and letters to Pope, Swift, Bolingbroke and others of his friends.—PATRICK AND GROOME, *eds.*, 1897, *Chambers's Biographical Dictionary, p.* 48.

PERSONAL

I know not what to think of your uneasiness. It shews unlike a Christian, and savours neither of temper nor consideration. I am troubled to remember it is habitual. . . . You make your friends and yourself uneasy: cannot trust Providence. Do your duty and serve God in your station.—ATTERBURY, LEWIS, 1690, *To his Son, Nov.* 1.

Urim was civil, and not void of sense,
Had humour, and a courteous confidence. . . .
But see how ill mistaken parts succeed!
He threw off my dominion, and would read;
Engaged in controversy, wrangled well,
In convocation language could excel,
In volumes proved the Church without defence—
By nothing guarded but by Providence.

—GARTH, SAMUEL, 1699–1714, *The Dispensary, canto i.*

He has so much regard to his congregation, that he commits to his memory what he has to say to them; and has so soft and graceful a behaviour, that it must attract your attention. His person, it is to be confessed, is no small recommendation; but he is to be highly commended for not losing that advantage, and adding to the propriety of speech, which might pass the criticism of Longinus, an action which would have been approved by Demosthenes. He has a peculiar force in his way, and has many of his audience who could not be intelligent hearers of his discourse, were there not explanation as well as grace in his action. This art of his is used with the most exact and honest skill: he never attempts your passions till he has convinced your reason. All the objections which he can form are laid open and dispersed, before he uses the least vehemence in his sermon; but when he thinks he has your head, he very soon wins your heart: and never pretends to show the beauty of holiness, till he hath convinced you of the truth of it.—STEELE, RICHARD, 1709, *The Tatler, No.* 66, *Sept.* 10.

"A little black man of pretty near fifty" "The same." "Ay, A good pleasant man?" "Ay, the same." "Cunning enough?" "Yes." "One that understands his own interest?" "As well as anybody." . . . "A very good face, and abundance of wit. . . . I mean Dr. Atterbury, Dean of Carlisle."—SWIFT, JONATHAN, 1710–11, *Journal to Stella, Jan.* 6.

While yet I can write to you, I must and will correspond with you, till the very moment that it is felony; and when I can no longer write to you, I will write of you. To tell you that my heart is full of your defence is no more than I believe, the worst enemy you have must own of his. You have really without a figure, had all the triumph that ancient eloquence boasts of. Their passions and consciences have done you right, though their votes will not. You have met with the fate, frequent to great and good men, to gain applause where you are denied justice. Let me take the only occasion I have had in the whole series of your misfortunes to congratulate you, and not you alone, but posterity, this noble defence. I already see in what lustre that innocence is to appear to other ages, which this has overborne and oppressed. I know perfectly well what a share of credit it will be to have appeared on your side, or to have been called your friend. I am far prouder of that word you publickly spoke of me than of anything I have yet heard of myself in my whole life.—POPE, ALEXANDER, 1723, *Letter to Bishop Atterbury, May.*

He could hardly account for the

inveterate hatred and malice which some persons bore to the ingenious Bishop of Rochester, unless it was that, infatuated like the wild Americans, they fondly hoped to inherit not only the spoils, but even the abilities of the man they should destroy. —BATHURST, LORD, 1723, *State Trials.*

His behaviour in every station in life has shown him to be a person of the greatest wit, built upon the foundation of good sense and directed by the strictest rules of religion and morality. He was always for maintaining the dignity and privileges of the several offices he bore in the Church, and the just way of behaviour enforced by that steadiness which was natural to him, created him many enemies among the Canons of Christ Church and Prebendaries of Westminster, who naturally must, by their own interest, be obliged to oppose any dean who should maintain the undoubted rights which he ought to enjoy; but it is hoped all those feuds will be at an end in this last-mentioned chapter, by the prudent and just choice his Majesty has made of Dr. Bradford to succeed him. His [Atterbury's] piety towards his children, and his sincerity to his friends, made him justly beloved and respected by both. No other crime can be laid to his charge but that for which he now suffers, which overbalances all his virtues.—WHARTON, DUKE OF? 1723, *True Briton, No.* VIII.

His temper was made up of irascible qualities, and had very little in it of the mild and merciful. His resentment of injuries was quick and lasting, his remembrance of favours done him soon gone. There are few or none of his friends and patrons but what at one time or other he quarrelled with.—STACKHOUSE, THOMAS, 1727, *Memoirs of the Life of Atterbury, p.* 63.

Hail, happy Sire! the pain of life is o'er,
Stranger and wandering pilgrim no more,
At home, at rest, secure in blissful skies,
Where envy drops its snakes, and Fraud its guise.
See seraph guards the starry crown prepare!
See smiling angels fly to greet thee there!

. . . .

When pyramids, unfaithful to their trust,
Crumble to atoms with their founder's dust;
When solid marble mould'ring, wastes away,
And desert lies the monumental clay;
Thou shalt live, to deathless Fame consign'd,
Live like the best and bravest of mankind!

—WESLEY, SAMUEL, 1732, *An Ode on the Death of Bishop Atterbury.*

Atterbury was of a restless aspiring temper, and eager to obtain the highest honours of the church, which he would certainly have acquired, had not queen Anne died. . . . If we may judge from the inflexibility of his character, there is reason to believe that he rejected all offers of promotion, and was never inclined to desert his party.—COXE, WILLIAM, 1798, *Memoirs of Sir Robert Walpole, vol.* I, *p.* 168.

A man distinguished for his learning and his wit, and obnoxious only by his religious bigotry and false ambition.—MACKINTOSH, WALLACE, AND BELL, 1840, *History of England, vol.* X, *p.* 120.

Worthy of high appreciation must be the man who was warmly loved by Pope, revered by Wesley, admired by Steele, and honoured by Swift; who was the centre of the brilliant social circle that included Busby, Dryden, Addison, Prior, Congreve, Gay, Arbuthnot, Garth, Radcliffe, Parnell, Rowe, Dr. William King, Dean Aldrich, Lords Orrery and Stanhope, Drs. John and Robert Freind, Locke, Newton, Bentley, the able critic, and Bingham, the learned divine. Nor was he less an object of regard to the rival interests struggling for pre-eminence at court, represented by Marlborough, Shaftesbury, Sunderland, Godolphin, Halifax, Somers, Landsdowne, Dorset, Harcourt, Bathurst, Bolingbroke, Oxford, Buckingham, Walpole, Carteret, Townshend, and Pulteney —not forgetting the fair candidates for power, the Duchesses of Marlborough, Buckingham, and Queensberry, and Lady Masham. In his own profession he was honoured with the affection of Bishops Trelawney, Gastrell, and Smalridge, and Dr. Sacheverell; though he excited the hostility of Hoadly, Wake, Burnet, and Tenison. Such were his coadjutors and opponents to the period of his arbitrary banishment, when he was obliged to mingle in a new set of associates, who endeavoured to support the claims of the son of James II.—the Dukes of Ormonde and Wharton, Lord Marischal Keith, Lochiel, and the rest of that brilliant staff of adventurers and enthusiasts who sacrificed their fortunes or their lives in his service—including the traitors who took bribes to betray its secrets. Particularly worthy of notice will be found Atterbury's relations with his home circle;

for as he was honoured as a prelate, and esteemed as a statesman, he was loved as a parent. The episode in his career in which his daughter figures, must be classed amongst the most touching ever narrated.—WILLIAMS, FOLKESTONE, 1869, *Memoirs and Correspondence of Francis Atterbury, Preface, vol.* I, *p.* ix.

Francis Atterbury, the most accomplished and eloquent of the Tory clergymen, became Bishop of Rochester, though sorely against the wishes of Anne who, while sympathizing with his doctrine, held in abhorrence the factiousness of his temper.—WYON, FREDERICK WILLIAM, 1876, *The History of Great Britain During the Reign of Queen Anne, vol.* II, *p.* 465.

The most brilliant tribune, orator, and pamphleteer of the High Church party. —LECKY, WILLIAM EDWARD HARTPOLE, 1877, *A History of England in the Eighteenth Century, vol.* I, *p.* 272.

There is no Churchman of the day whose virtues as well as faults stand out in lineaments so clearly marked as those of Atterbury. . . . There is no doubt now as to Atterbury's guilt: but it was then concealed from his friends by a process of Jesuitical prevarication, which leaves on Atterbury's character a worse stain even than that of treason, especially in a case where treason might be so far conscientious, and was at least not uncommon. But Jesuitical as he was in this episode of his life, insincerity was not Atterbury's common failing. He had left amongst the circle a memory which was not without its lasting effect. From him they had imbibed that refusal to subscribe to the tenet of the Whigs which regarded the Revolution as the beginning and end of the Constitution. From his whole character, his love of extremes, his anxiety to play a sensational part in some exciting drama, his resolute refusal to regard prudence or expediency in his bigoted attachment to a cause, even from his fiery vanity, the Bishop was fitted to make a deep and lasting impression upon those amongst whom his life had lain. Warm and loving in all his private relations, with the tenderness of a woman, and the courage, if not the calm judgment, of a man, he held his place in the hearts of his friends, and made it impossible for them to believe that his public acts could be stained by duplicity and treason: and not a little of their indignant protest against the Government of Walpole, not a little of their claim to be the assertors of liberty in an age which bowed before a political autocrat, is to be traced to the work, to the spirit, to the trial, and to the banishment of Atterbury.—CRAIK, HENRY, 1882, *The Life of Jonathan Swift, pp.* 97, 375.

At Marlborough's funeral we see for the last time in high public estate one of the few Englishmen of the day who could properly be named in the same breath with Marlborough. This was Francis Atterbury, the eloquent and daring Bishop of Rochester. . . . His was not a very reverential spirit. There was as little of the temper of pious sanctity in Atterbury as in Swift himself. The allusion to the last scene of pompous vanity might have had another significance, as well as that which Atterbury meant to give to it. Amid the pomp in which Marlborough's career went out the career of Atterbury went out as well, although in a different way, and not closed sublimely by death. . . . Francis Atterbury may rank among the most conspicuous public men of his time. He stands only just beneath Marlborough, and Bolingbroke, and Walpole. . . . Atterbury had, however, among his many gifts a dangerous gift of political intrigue. Like Swift, and Dubois, and Alberoni, he was at least as much statesman as churchman. He had mixed himself up in various intrigues—some of them could hardly be called conspiracies—for the restoration of the Stuarts, and when at last something like a new conspiracy was planned, it was not likely that he would be left out of it. —MCCARTHY, JUSTIN, 1884, *A History of the Four Georges, vol.* I, *pp.* 278, 281, 282.

Atterbury cannot be regarded as a perfect character or as a great divine, but he was a very able man, and in his way a brave, faithful son of the church. If he mingled politics too much with religion it must be remembered in justice to him that the two subjects were so strangely mixed up in that eventful time that it was all but impossible for a public character to disentangle the one from the other. His name will always be a prominent one in the complicated history of the church and nation of England, in the later part of the seventeenth and the early part of the eighteenth century.—OVERTON, JOHN HENRY, 1885, *Dictionary of National Biography, vol.* II, *p.* 237.

BOYLE–BENTLEY CONTROVERSY

"A Short Review of the Controversy bewteen Mr. Boyle and Dr. Bentley," the author of which, I have no hesitation in believing, from the style as well as other evidence, to be Atterbury himself. The professed objects of the piece are, to apologize for Mr. Boyle, and to decry the presumption and ill-manners of his opponent: but from all questions of learning, the only objects in the controversy worth attention, it carefully abstains, and thereby conveys a tacit but perfect confession of Bentley's triumph. Though the style is caustic and polished, yet its general effect is feeble; being little more than a repetition of the criminating charges of Boyle's book, subdued and diluted by an unwilling moderation. Notwithstanding the popularity of Atterbury, this tract produced little or no sensation: in fact, it appears shortly after its birth to have sunk into oblivion.—MONK, JAMES HENRY, 1830, *The Life of Richard Bentley, vol.* I, *p.* 178.

Out came the reply to Bentley, bearing the name of Boyle, but in truth written by Atterbury, with the assistance of Smalridge and others. A most remarkable book it is, and often reminds us of Goldsmith's observation, that the French would be the best cooks in the world if they had any butcher's meat, for that they can make ten dishes out of a nettle top. It really deserves the praise, whatever that praise may be worth, of being the best book ever written by any man on the wrong side of a question of which he was profoundly ignorant. The learning of the confederacy is that of a schoolboy, and not of an extraordinary schoolboy; but it is used with the skill and address of most able, artful, and experienced men; it is beaten out to the very thinnest leaf, and is disposed in such a way as to seem ten times larger than it is. The dexterity with which they avoid grappling with those parts of the subject with which they know themselves to be incompetent to deal is quite wonderful.—MACAULAY, THOMAS BABINGTON, 1836, *Sir William Temple, Edinburgh Review; Critical and Miscellaneous Essays.*

SERMONS

When Willis of Ephraim heard Rochester preach,
Thus Bentley said to him, "I pr'ythee, dear brother,
How likest thou this sermon? 'tis out of my reach."
"His is one way, (said Willis) and ours is another;
I care not for carping; but this I can tell,
We preached very sadly, if he preaches well."
—PRIOR, MATTHEW, 1721? *Doctors Differ, Epigram.*

The day was so bad I could not even go to church here, so the Dean gave us prayers at home, and we read one of Atterbury's sermons; they are at present our Sunday reading, and charming sermons they are: I am not critic deep enough to find fault with them: his *doctrine* to me appears *very good* and his language *elegant and pure.*—DELANY, MRS. (MARY GRANVILLE), 1751, *Autobiography and Correspondence, ed. Llanover, vol.* III, *p.* 37.

Sir John Pringle had expressed a wish that I would ask Dr. Johnson's opinion what were the best English sermons for style. . . . "Atterbury?" *Johnson:* "Yes, Sir, one of the best."—JOHNSON, SAMUEL, 1778, *Life by Boswell, ed. Hill, vol.* III, *p.* 281.

The Sermons of Atterbury attracted great attention from the first, and soon gave rise to controversies which we have merely time to refer to. Hoadley, Burnet, and Wake, were no mean antagonists, but our champion seems never to have been intimidated by numbers or awed by the fear of names.—ALLIBONE, S. AUSTIN, 1854–58, *A Dictionary of English Literature, vol.* I, *p.* 80.

Reading the sermons in cold blood, and deprived of all the charm of delivery, we find them in substance wonderfully like other sermons of the time. The deists are refuted, and virtue is recommended in the ordinary method; though Hoadly discovered traces of the hated sacerdotal taint. The style is not unworthy of the friend and critic of the most brilliant writers of the day; and here and there, as in the sermon on the death of poor Lady Cutts, at the age of eighteen, the pathos has not entirely evaporated. But there are no traces of real power of thought or depth of emotion. They are the performances of a very able man, who is a politician before he is an ecclesiastic, and a Tory more distinctly than a High-Churchman. In other times, Atterbury might have been a Laud or a Wolsey; in the eighteenth century his ambition could end only by sacrificing his talents and energy to the most contemptible of all pretenders. The spirit of the age enervates his religious thought as well as his political principles.—STEPHEN, LESLIE, 1876, *History of English Thought in the Eighteenth Century, vol.* II, *p.* 345.

Unfortunately Atterbury's literary gifts, like his oratory, lack the merit of permanence, and his sermons, more conspicuous for eloquence than for the weightiness of matter, although extremely popular at the time, have long ceased to be read.—DENNIS, JOHN, 1894, *The Age of Pope, p.* 207.

It is a great drop, say, from the sermons of Isaac Barrow to those of Francis Atterbury.—OVERTON, JOHN HENRY, 1897, *The Church in England, vol.* II, *p.* 206.

GENERAL

Though Dr. Atterbury be a man of a very sharp pen, and of very quick parts, yet I do not look upon him to be a man of extraordinary depth. He has not a true genius to the study of antiquities; nor has he taken much pains to make himself a master of our English history. He may be cryed up for a master of style, and 'twill not be denyed; yet this however must be granted withall, that affectation of wit and satyr does not become a grave subject, and Mr. Hooker, bishop Sanderson, and others, are rather to be followed in such sort of writing; whilst the study of witty expressions is to be looked upon as levity, and more proper for juvenile essays. — HEARNE, THOMAS, 1710–11, *Reliquiæ Hearnianæ, ed. Bliss, Jan.* 16, *vol.* I, *p.* 215.

Whose very considerable attainments in classical scholarship were enlivened and decorated by the finest spirit of wit and humor.—CRAIK, GEORGE L., 1861, *A Compendious History of English Literature and of the English Language, vol.* II, *p.* 205.

His diction is not quite so pure as Swift's or Addison's; and it is easy in the sense of fluent and racy, not in the sense of languid.—MINTO, WILLIAM, 1872–80, *Manual of English Prose Literature, p.* 398.

On all quesitons pertaining to the niceties of criticism he was an unerring guide, for his judgment was clear and solid, his perception fine, and his taste pure even to fastidiousness. In no contemporary critic had Pope so much confidence.—COLLINS, JOHN CHURTON, 1893, *Jonathan Swift, p.* 96.

Atterbury's life was one too much engaged in ecclesiastical controversy, in political intrigue, and in schemes of personal ambition, to allow him much time for literature; and what he has left (beyond his correspondence) is small in bulk. But it may always be read with pleasure as the composition of one who studied minutely, and with an eye careful of effect, all the details of style, and the fundamental sincerity of whose nature, with its vivid contrasts of light and shadow, serves to give a certain picturesqueness and variety to his diction. But above all his letters are models of epistolary style.—CRAIK, HENRY, 1894, *English Prose, vol.* III, *p.* 459.

A brilliant and popular preacher, a pleasant letter-writer, a most dangerous controversialist and debater, and a good critic (though he made the usual mistakes of his age about poetry before Waller), Atterbury wrote in a style not very unlike Addison's, though inferior to it.—SAINTSBURY, GEORGE, 1898, *A Short History of English Literature, p,* 542.

Bernard Mandeville

1670?-1733.

Bernard Mandeville: born at Dordrecht (Dort), Holland, about 1670; studied medicine, and took his degree at Leyden, Mar. 30, 1691, after which he settled in London as a physician. Published "Esop Dressed, or a Collection of Fables in Familiar Verse" (1704); a "Treatise of the Hypochondriac and Hysteric Passions" (1711), highly commended by Dr. Johnson; "The Grumbling-hive or Knaves turned Honest" (1705); and in 1714 an enlarged edition, under the title "The Fable of the Bees, or Private Vices Public Benefits" (2d ed., 1723), which was censured by Berkeley and others, and presented as a nuisance by the grand jury of Middlesex. A second part of the "Fable" appeared in 1728, and both parts in 1732. He also published "Free Thoughts on Religion" (1720); "Origin of Honor" (1732); "A Letter to Dion" (1732); and "A Modest Defense of Public Stews" (1740). He was patronized by Lord Macclesfield, and died in London, Jan. 21, 1733.—MARSH, A. R., *rev.*, 1897, *Johnson's Universal Cyclopædia, vol.* V, *p.* 515.

PERSONAL

He lived in obscure lodgings in London, and betook himself to the profession of physic, but was never able to acquire much practice. . . . I once heard a London physician, who had married the daughter of one of that trade, mention him as a good sort of man, and one that he was acquainted with, and at the same time assert a fact, which I suppose he had learned from Mandeville, that the children of women addicted to dram-drinking, were never troubled with the rickets. He is said to have been coarse and overbearing in his manners where he durst be so; yet a great flatterer of some vulgar Dutch merchants, who allowed him a pension. This last information comes from a clerk of a city attorney, through whose hands the money passed.—HAWKINS, SIR JOHN, 1787, *Life of Samuel Johnson, p.* 263, *note.*

FABLE OF THE BEES
1705–28

The fallacy of that book is, that Mandeville defines neither vices nor benefits. . . . I read Mandeville forty, or, I believe, fifty years ago. He did not puzzle me; he opened my views into real life very much.—JOHNSON, SAMUEL, 1778, *Life, ed. Boswell.*

With respect to his capital and offensive paradox, that private vices are public benefits, Mandeville's whole art consists in denominating our passions by the appellation assigned to their vicious excess, and then proving them, under this denomination, useful to society. There is a lively force, and caustic though coarse wit, in his performance, which occasionally reminds one of Paine.—GREEN, THOMAS, 1779–1810, *Diary of a Lover of Literature.*

Mandeville was a man wholly destitute of morality, and without insight into the nature of man or the connexions between bodily and mental soundness and well-being. . . . This book no man would now trouble himself to read.—SCHLOSSER, FREIDRICH CHRISTOPH, 1823, *History of the Eighteenth Century.*

If Shakspeare had written a book on the motives of human actions, it is by no means certain that it would have been a good one. It is extremely improbable that it would have contained half so much able reasoning on the subject as is to be found in the "Fable of the Bees." But could Mandeville have created an Iago? Well as he knew how to resolve characters into their elements, would he have been able to consider those elements in such a manner as to make up a man, a real, living, individual man?—MACAULAY, THOMAS BABINGTON, 1825, *Milton, Edinburgh Review; Critical and Miscellaneous Essays.*

Though licentious, and in many respects objectionable, there are a great number of valuable remarks and of just and profound observations in this work, especially with reference to the improvement of arts and the increase of wealth.—MCCULLOCH, JOHN RAMSAY, 1845, *Literature of Political Economy.*

The book occasioned a great commotion; but it is now generally admitted that, whatever may be the worth, or worthlessness, of the philosophical system propounded in it, the author's object was not an immoral one. Independently altogether of its general principles and conclusions, the work is full both of curious matter and vigorous writing.—CRAIK, GEORGE L., 1861, *A Compendious History of English Literature and of the English Language, vol.* II, *p.* 253.

The work possesses no literary merit. —ANGUS, JOSEPH, 1865, *The Handbook of English Literature, p.* 509.

His humour is the coarsest of the coarse, but he cannot be denied great wit, happy expression, and ingenious illustrations.—MINTO, WILLIAM, 1872–80, *Manual of English Prose Literature, p.* 401.

It represented strongly the increasing tendency to dwell upon the evils of society as a result of over-civilisation, and anticipated the teaching of those philosophers who saw no hope of a return to innocence but by returning to the state of nature. . . . Mandeville argued, not, like Shaftesbury, that all is for good, but that the world is bad, and its whole civilisation fed by evil appetites and evil deeds. The work was, indeed, a first sign of the strength of the reaction that gathered force year after year, until it struck on Europe with the shock of Revolution. But there was nothing in Bernard Mandeville of the fine yearning for a higher life that was to rise above the ruins of all that had been based on human wrong. It was enough for him to maintain steadily that evil was man's good.—MORLEY, HENRY, 1880, *ed., Shorter Works in English Prose, p.* 253.

It would be a relief if we could look upon the work as an ironical satire upon the immorality of the age—a jeering exposure of the prevalent vicious practice by flaunting it in the outrageous extravagance of a theory; but the whole manner of the book, taken along with the appended "Inquiry into the Origin of Moral Virtue," is incompatible with such a supposition. The author has, therefore, been generally and justly interpreted as maintaining desirously a doctrine which is in flagrant antagonism alike with all the history of political society, with the results of economical science, and with the high Hebrew morality on which Christianity founds—the doctrine that the vices of individuals are economically beneficial to society, that it is unrighteousness that exalts a nation, while godliness is a reproach to any people.—MURRAY, J. CLARK, 1887, *The Revived Study of Berkeley, Macmillan's Magazine, vol.* 56, *p.* 171.

Mandeville gave great offence by this book, in which a cynical system of morality was made attractive by ingenious paradoxes. It was long popular, and later critics have pointed out the real acuteness of the writer as well as the vigour of his style, especially remarkable in a foreigner. His doctrine that prosperity was increased by expenditure rather than by saving fell in with many current economical fallacies not yet extinct. Assuming with the ascetics that human desires were essentially evil and therefore produced "private vices," and assuming with the common view that wealth was a "public benefit," he easily showed that all civilisation implied the development of vicious propensities. He argued again with Hobbists that the origin of virtue was to be found in selfish and savage instincts, and vigorously attacked Shaftesbury's contrary theory of a "moral sense." But he tacitly accepted Shaftesbury's inference that virtue so understood was a mere sham. He thus argued, in appearance at least, for the essential vileness of human nature; though his arguments may be regarded as partly ironical, or as a satire against the hypocrisies of an artficial society. In any case his appeal to facts, against the plausibilities of the opposite school, shows that he had many keen though imperfect previsions of later scientific views, both upon ethical and economical questions. Dr. Johnson was much impressed by the "Fable," which, he said, did not puzzle him, but "opened his views into real life very much."—STEPHEN, LESLIE, 1893, *Dictionary of National Biography, vol.* XXXVI, *p.* 21.

The author of the "Fable of the Bees" writes coarsely for coarse readers, and the arguments by which he supports his graceless theory merit the infamy generally awarded to them.—DENNIS, JOHN, 1894, *The Age of Pope, p.* 215.

GENERAL

Mandeville's satires, though general, frequently exhibit strong and lively pictures.—MILLS, ABRAHAM, 1851, *The Literature and the Literary Men of Great Britain and Ireland, vol.* II, *p.* 265.

Mandeville's object being chiefly *negative* and *dialectical* he has left little of positive ethical theory. Virtue he regards as *de facto* an arbitrary institution of society; what it ought to be, he hardly says, but the tendency of his writings is to make the good of the whole to be preferred to private interests. He denies the existence of a moral sense and of disinterestedness. The motive to observe moral rules is pride and vanity fomented by politicians. He does not regard virtue as an independent end, even by association, but considers that pride in its naked form is the ever present incentive to good conduct.—BAIN, ALEXANDER, 1868–72, *Moral Science, p.* 183.

Mandeville is said to have been in the habit of frequenting coffee-houses, and amusing his patrons by ribald conversation. The tone of his writing harmonises with this account of his personal habits. He is a cynical and prurient writer, who seems to shrink from no jest, however scurrilous, and from no paradox, however grotesque, which is calculated to serve the purpose, which he avows in his preface to be his sole purpose, of diverting his readers—readers, it may be added, not very scrupulous in their tastes. . . . Mandeville shares Swift's contempt for the human race; but his contempt, instead of urging him to the borders of madness, merely finds vent in a horse-laugh. He despises himself as well as his neighbours, and is content to be despicable. He is a scoffer, not a misanthrope. You are all Yahoos, he seems to say, and I am a Yahoo; and so—let us eat, drink, and be merry. . . . Tell your fine stories to devotees or school-girls, he seems to say, but don't try to pass them off upon me, who have seen men and cities, and not taken my notions from books.—STEPHEN, LESLIE, 1876, *History of English Thought in the Eighteenth Century, vol.* II, *pp.* 33, 34.

Ay, this same midnight, by this chair of mine,
Come and review thy counsels: art thou still
Staunch to their teaching?—not as fools opine
Its purport might be, but as subtler skill
Could, through turbidity, the loaded line
Of logic casting, sound deep, deeper, till
It touched a quietude and reached a shrine
And recognized harmoniously combine
Evil with good, and hailed truth's triumph—
thine,
Sage dead long since, Bernard de Mandeville!

. . . .

Sage, once more repeat
Instruction! 'Tis a sore to soothe not chafe.
Ah, Fabulist, what luck, could I contrive
To coax from thee another "Grumbling
Hive!"

—BROWNING, ROBERT, 1887, *Parleyings with Certain People of Importance in Their Day, pp.* 23, 26.

The "Fable of the Bees" which, with its more immediate appendices, contains almost everything of Mandeville's that is of importance to any but the curious, is one of those unlucky books which have become known to posterity chiefly by the polemical efforts of others to suppress them. . . . His verse is very uncouth, and his prose is frequently incorrect and never in any way polished; but he makes up for this by many of the merits of Defoe, to whom in character as in period he is very close. Many of his characters—the special knack of the time—possess great felicity and truth of touch; his argument, sophistical as it commonly is, is put with a good deal of surface clearness and cogency; and his illustrations and digressive passages have singular liveliness and force. . . . And though his sudden and not very savoury notoriety tempted him to indulge in long and dull dissertations where the merit of his style is spun too thin to cover the nakedness of his sophistry, he must still at his best remain a striking exemplar of one of the most nervous if not the most elegant periods of English writing, and deserve a place in the division of English prose history which includes Latimer and Bunyan, Defoe and Cobbett.—SAINTSBURY, GEORGE, 1894, *English Prose, ed. Craik, vol.* III, *pp.* 438, 439.

A misanthropical Dutch doctor. . . . Mandeville was a daring thinker, who permitted no traditional prejudice, no habit of decency, to interfere with the progression of his ideas. He was by far the ablest of the English deists, and though all the respectability of his time drew away from him, and voted him, like the grand jury of Middlesex, a public nuisance, he was not without his very distinct influence on the progress of English literature. He was an emancipator of thought, a rude and contemptuous critic of the conventions. In himself base and ugly—for all his writings reveal a gross individuality—the brute courage of Mandeville helped English speculation to slip from its fetters. His style is without elegance, but, what is strange in a foreigner, of a remarkable homeliness and picturesque vigour.—GOSSE, EDMUND, 1897, *Short History of Modern English Literature, p.* 225.

Mandeville is certainly not an innocent writer, but he has been considerably misunderstood both by his contemporaries and by modern critics. His business is the exposure of humbug and hypocrisy, and he does his work consistently and thoroughly, though he dips his pen in a very nasty mixture and carefully poses as a very disreputable person. His taste is as abominable as his style is effective. The essentially satirical character of his work is however concealed by his constant indulgence in paradox, a method which enables him to give a maximum of offence, while keeping in the back-ground a few unexceptionable principles to which he can apppeal in case of need.—SELBY-BIGGE, L. A., 1897, *ed., British Moralists, vol.* I, *Introduction, p.* xv.

Matthew Tindal

1653?-1733

One of the successors of Toland and Shaftesbury in the school of English deists or freethinkers, was born at Beer-Ferrers, in Devonshire, about 1657. He was educated at Lincoln and Exeter Colleges, Oxford: took his A. B. in 1676; shortly after was elected fellow of All-Souls', and was admitted doctor of laws at Oxford in 1685. He retained his fellowship during the reign of James II. by professing the Roman Catholic faith; he afterwards recanted, however, and, adopting revolutionary principles, went to the other extreme, and wrote against the nonjurors. He now became an adovcate, and sat as judge in the court of delegates, with a pension from the crown of £200 per annum. Some time afterwards, considerable attention was drawn to him by his work entitled "The Rights of the Christian Church" (1706-7, 8vo), and the ensuing controversy; but the production which had rendered his name a memorable one was his "Christianity as Old as the Creation" (1730) which provoked replies from Dr. Warburton, Leland, Foster, and Conybeare. . . . Tindal died in London, Aug. 16, 1733, and was interred in Clerkenwell Church. Mr. Tindal also wrote, "An Essay concerning the Power of the Magistrate and the Rights of Mankind in Matters of Religion" (London 1697, 8vo):—"A Defence of the Rights of the Christian Church" (ibid. 1709, 2 pts. 8vo):—"The Nation Vindicated" (ibid. 1711; pt. ii, 1712):—"War with Priestcraft, or the Freethinker's Iliad" (ibid. 1732, 8vo), a burlesque poem.—M'CLINTOCK AND STRONG, *eds.*, 1881, *Cyclopaedia of Biblical, Theological and Ecclesiastical Literature, vol.* X, *pp.* 425, 426.

PERSONAL

This day, at 12 o'clock at noon, St. Marie's great bell rung out for Dr. Matthew Tindall, fellow of All Soul's college, who died this last week out of the college. . . . He was a man of most vile principles, and of no religion, as may appear from many books he wrote and published, in which he had the assistance of the late Mr. Collins, yet without his name to them, amongst which are the "Rights of the Christian Church," and "Christianity as old as the Creation."—HEARNE, THOMAS, 1733, *Reliquiæ Hearnianæ, ed, Bliss, Aug.* 20, *vol.* III, *p.* 102.

CHRISTIANITY AS OLD AS CREATION

1730

If you was here, you would see how I have scribbled over the margins of Tindal's "Christianity as old as the Creation." I think I have him as sure as I had Collins: that is, overturn the pillars of this famous edifice of impiety: which all the writers against him hitherto have left standing; busying themselves only to untile his roof.—WARBURTON, WILLIAM, 1758, *Letters from a Late Eminent Prelate, p.* 267.

This was not only the most important work that deism had yet produced, composed with care, and bearing the marks of thoughtful study of the chief contemporary arguments, Christian as well as Deist, but derives an interest from the circumstance that it was the book to which more than to any other single work, bishop Butler's "Analogy" was designed as a reply.—FARRAR, ADAM STOREY, 1862, *Critical History of Free Thought, Lecture* iv, *p.* 195.

The replies to Tindal, taking them altogether, were unsatisfactory. This may have been owing to a want of definiteness as to the object of his book. It was diffuse in its style, abounding in long quotations, and many subjects were merely alluded to and left for future treatment. . . . Tindal left another volume of his book in manuscript, but it fell into the hands of the Bishop of London, who thought the best way to answer it was to destroy it. Bishop Gibson had made Tindal's work the subject of one of his "Pastoral Letters." He had said the same things against it as Tindal's other opponents, and he said them as well as any of them had done. Gibson was a liberal Churchman as well as an assiduous bishop, and had some of the best qualities of the rational divines of his time, but the world will scarcely forgive him for the sacrilege of destroying the work of one of the most thoughtful men of that age. On the monument erected to his memory in the vestibule of Fulham Church this is not recorded among his noble virtues and the great acts of his life. Could the deed speak, it would say—

"Non ego sum titulis surripienda tuis."
—HUNT, JOHN, 1869, *Matthew Tindal, Contemporary Review, vol.* 10, *p.* 589.

He was about thirty at the time of his first escapade; at the ripe age of nearly fifty, he first attracted notice by a book called "The Rights of the Christian Church," which was a vigorous assault upon his former High Church allies; and he was already past seventy when he produced the first volume of "Christianity as Old as the Creation." The second which should have followed, was quietly burned by Bishop Gibson, into whose hands the MS. fell after the author's death, and who acted on the principle that prevention was better than cure. The first volume, however, had done its work. It has not the force of style or the weight of thought which could secure a permanent place in literature; and has become rather heavy reading at the present day. The arrangement is confused; it is full of repetition. Yet it had the merit of bringing out with great distinctness the most essential position of the deists. Tindal was, in reality, just one stage in advance of Tillotson, Hoadly, Clarke, and other latitudinarian divines from whom he borrowed, and whose authority he freely quotes. He was to Clarke what Toland had been to Locke. The indignation which he produced amongst their followers was the livelier because he seemed to be unmasking their secret thoughts, and formulating the conclusions for which they had already provided the premises. Are you aware, asked some disputant, that the necessary inference from your argument is so and so? Yes, replied his antagonist, but I don't draw it. Tindal insisted upon drawing it, and was reviled, accordingly.—STEPHEN LESLIE, 1876, *History of English Thought in the Eighteenth Century, vol.* I, *p.* 135.

"Christianity as old as the Creation," a work published without his name, and never finished, revealed how deeply and long meditated had been this protest against all positive religion. This book, to my mind, has many and grievous faults. Being in the form of a dialogue between A and B, it commits the Christian cause to one of the greatest weaklings known in controversy. It is radically ambiguous. It has endless repetitions, is full of the fallacy of citation, and is crowded with particular objections to the Old Testament and New that do not belong to its main argument, holding right on, as in the case of the various readings, as if nothing had ever been said on the other side. But with all these drawbacks it compels the breaking up of new ground bearing on the relation of natural religion (so called) to revealed. . . . The ground of Tindal was really the key of the Deistic position; and hence with his defeat the struggle became less close and stubborn.—CAIRNS, JOHN, 1881, *Unbelief in the Eighteenth Century, pp.* 84, 85.

Thomas Woolston

1670–1733

Born at Northampton, England, 1669; died in London, 1732; was educated at Cambridge, and obtained a fellowship there. After attracting an unenviable attention by some other writings, he published, London, 1727–1729, six discourses "On the Miracles of our Saviour," which, on account of their tone of ridicule, gave so much offence that he was prosecuted by the attorney-general, tried, found guilty, and sentenced to one year's imprisonment and to pay a fine of £100. Being unable to pay the fine, he remained in prison and died there shortly after. There is some reason, however, for believing his mind was diseased.—JACKSON, SAMUEL MACAULEY, *ed.*, 1889–91, *Concise Dictionary of Religious Knowledge, p.* 980.

GENERAL

He might at the same rate of arguing have undertaken to prove that there was no such person as Jesus Christ, or his apostles, or that they were only allegorical persons, and that Christianity was never planted or propagated in the world at all.—LELAND, JOHN, 1754–56, *A View of the Deistical Writers, Letter* VIII.

The letters ["Discourses"] were written with a coarseness and irreverence so singular, even in the attacks of that age, that it were well if they could be attributed to insanity. They contain the most undisguised abuse which had been uttered against Christianity since the days of the early heathens. . . . In classifying Woolston with later writers against miracles, he may be compared in some cases, though with striking differences of tone, with those German rationalists, like Paulus, who have rationalized the miracles, but in more cases with those who, like Strauss, have idealized them. His method, however, is an appeal to general probability, rather than to literary criticism.—FARRAR, ADAM STOREY, 1862, *Critical History of Free Thought, Lecture* IV.

No man was ever more thoroughly refuted than Thomas Woolston. It seems a pity that such men as Pearce, Sherlock and Lardner should have been under the necessity of defending Christianity against one who, it is charitable to suppose, was not really sane. It was a pity in many respects that the Deist controversy reached its climax in a madman. Woolston's mind was typical of the minds of a large class which is fairly divided between believers and unbelievers. They can only be Christians while they can lean upon a book, a Church, Primitive antiquity, or some external authority. When this prop fails, they are unbelievers. So long as Woolston could believe in the Fathers, he was a Christian. When he found it impossible to believe Christianity on their authority, he was no more a believer. He had no eye to see the everlasting harmonies. He had no soul to feel that there is a Divine Christ in the miracles, whatever else we may know about them. That spirit which giveth life was more dead to him than the letter which he despised. He wrote against the clergy; perhaps they deserved it. He wrote much against the Gospels, and he could have written much more of the same kind. It is easy to raise a thousand plausible and ingenious objections to anything whatever, and as easy to make a thousand answers as plausible and ingenious, while the thing itself remains where it was.—HUNT, JOHN, 1871, *Religious Thought in England from the Reformation to the End of the Last Century, vol.* II, *p.* 431.

Woolston's discourses, written to prove the miracles of the new testament are as mythical and allegorical as the prophecies of the old, appeared at the same time, and had an enormous sale. Voltaire was much struck by this writer's coarse and hardy way of dealing with the miraculous legends, and the article on miracles in the Philosophical Dictionary shows how carefully he had read Woolston's book.—MORLEY, JOHN, 1872, *Voltaire, p.* 84.

Through six straggling discourses, Woolston attempts to make fun of the miracles. There are, at intervals, queer gleams of distorted sense, and even of literary power, in the midst of his buffoonery. Occasionally he hits a real blot; more frequently he indulges in the most absurd quibbles, and throughout he shows almost as little approximation to a genuine critical capacity as to reverential appreciation of the beauty of many of the narratives. He is a mere buffoon jingling his cap and bells in a sacred shrine; and his strange ribaldry is painful even to those for whom the supernatural glory of the temple has long utterly faded away. Even where some straggling shreds of sense obtrude themselves, the language is obtrusively coarse, and occasionally degenerates into mere slang.—STEPHEN, LESLIE, 1876, *History of English Thought in the Eighteenth Century, vol.* I, *p.* 231.

The discussion in regard to miracles, which immediately followed that as to prophecy, and made, in one sense the most flagrant and noted passages of the Deistical controversy, was unhappily connected with a leader who wanted every quality that could give it a solid and a permanent interest, being either so blunted in his moral perceptions, or, what is more probable, so near to madness in his mental condition, and in any case so destitute of judgment and learning, that the deniers of Christianity in our day would as little consent to be represented by him as his antagonists. This was Thomas Woolston.—CAIRNS, JOHN, 1881, *Unbelief in the Eighteenth Century, p.* 79.

He bore the repute of a sound scholar, a good preacher, a charitable and estimable man. His reading led him to study the works of Origen, from whom he adopted the idea of interpreting the scripture as allegory. . . . The vigour of the discourses is undeniable, and it has been said with some truth that they anticipate the mythical theory of Strauss.—GORDON, ALEXANDER, 1900, *Dictionary of National Biography, vol.* LXII, *p.* 439.

John Dennis

1657–1734

Son of a London saddler, after education at Harrow and at Caius College, Cambridge, travelled in France and Italy, and began his career as a writer in the reign of William III., with "The Passion of Byblis" in 1692, and in the same year "The Impartial Critic; or, some Observations on Mr. Rymer's late Book, entitled a Short View of Tragedy." In 1693 Dennis published "Miscellanies in Verse and Prose." In 1695 he published a poem, "The Court of Death," on the death of Queen Mary; and in 1696, "Letters on Milton and Congreve," and "Letters upon Several Occasions, Written by and between Mr. Wycherley, Mr. Dryden, Mr. Moyle, Mr. Congreve, and Mr. Dennis;" also adverse "Remarks" on Blackmore's "Prince Arthur." In 1697 he published "Miscellaneous Poems;" in 1698 "The Usefulness of the Stage to the Happiness of Mankind, to Government, and to Religion, occasioned by a late Book written by Jeremy Collier, M. A.;" in 1701 a little treatise on the "Advancement and Reformation of Modern Poetry;" and in 1702 an "Essay on the Navy," a tract against Sacheverell's party, "Priestcraft dangerous to Religion and Government," a volume of collected "Works," and, on the death of William III., a poem sacred to his memory, "The Monument." . . . He produced plays also, poor ones: "A Plot and No Plot," in 1697; "Rinaldo and Armida," in 1699; in 1702, "Iphigenia," and "The Comical Gallant; or, the Amours of Sir John Falstaff, with an Essay on Taste in Poetry." . . . In 1711 he attacked Pope in "Reflections Critical and Satirical upon a late Rhapsody called An Essay on Criticism;" and in 1713, on the production of Addison's Cato, Dennis appeared as a hostile critic, with "Remarks upon Cato, a Tragedy." In 1718 Dennis's "Letters" were published in two volumes; and in the same year his "Select Works," consisting of plays, poems, etc., likewise in two volumes.
—MORLEY, HENRY, 1879, *A Manual of English Literature, ed. Tyler, pp.* 511, 512.

PERSONAL

At a meeting of the masters and fellows, Sir Dennis mulcted 3*l.*, his scholarship taken away, and he sent out of the college, for assaulting and wounding Sir Glenham with a sword.—CAMBRIDGE, GESTA BOOK, 1680, *March* 4.

. . . Appius reddens at each word you speak,
And stares, tremendous, with a threatening eye,
Like some fierce tyrant in old tapestry.
—POPE, ALEXANDER, 1711, *Essay on Criticism, pt.* iii, *v.* 585–8.

I observed his room was hung with old tapestry, which had several holes in it, caused, as the old woman informed me, by his having cut out of it the heads of divers tyrants, the fierceness of whose visages had much provoked him. On all sides of his room were pinned a great many sheets of a tragedy called Cato, with notes on the margin with his own hand. The words absurd, monstrous, execrable, were everywhere written in such large characters, that I could read them without my spectacles. By the fire-side lay three farthings worth of small coal in a Spectator, and behind the door huge heaps of papers of the same title, which his nurse informed me she had conveyed thither out of his sight, believing they were books of the black art; for her master never read in them, but he was either quite moped, or in raving fits. There was nothing neat in the whole room, except some books on his shelves, very well bound and gilded, whose names I had never before heard of, nor I believe were anywhere else to be found; such as "Gibraltar, a Comedy;" "Remarks on Prince Arthur;" "The Grounds of Criticism in Poetry;" "An Essay on Public Spirit." The only one I had any knowledge of was a "Paradise Lost," interleaved. The whole floor was covered with manuscripts, as thick as a pastry-cook's shop on a Christmas eve. On his table were some ends of verse and of candles; a gallipot of ink with a yellow pen in it, and a pot of half dead ale covered with a Longinus.
—POPE, ALEXANDER? 1713, *The Narrative of Dr. Robert Norris; Works, ed. Elwin and Courthope, vol.* X, *p.* 453.

His motion is quick and sudden, turning on all sides, with a suspicion of every object, as if he had done or feared some extraordinary mischief. You see wickedness in his meaning, but folly of countenance, that betrays him to be unfit for the execution of it. He starts, stares, and looks round him. This constant shuffle of haste without speed, makes the man thought a little touched; but the vacant look of his two eyes gives you to understand that he could never run out of his wits, which seemed not so much to be lost, as to want employment; they are not so much astray, as they are a wool-gathering. He has the face and surliness of a mastiff, which has often saved him from being treated like a cur, till some more sagacious than ordinary found his nature, and used him accordingly. Unhappy being! terrible without, fearful within! Not a wolf in sheep's clothing, but a sheep in a wolf's.—STEELE, RICHARD, 1720, *The Theatre; Disraeli, Calamities of Authors.*

Say what revenge on Dennis can be had,
Too dull for laughter, for reply too mad.
On one so poor you cannot take the law,
On one so old your sword you scorn to draw.
Uncaged then, let the harmless monster rage,
Secure in dullness, madness, want, and age!
—SAVAGE, RICHARD, ? 1731, *Grub Street Journal, July* 1.

Adieu! unsocial excellence! at last
Thy foes are vanquish'd, and thy fears are pass'd:
Want, the grim recompense of truth like thine,
Shall now no longer dim thy destined shine.
The impatient envy, the disdainful air!
The front malignant, and the captious stare?
The furious petulance, the jealous start,
The mist of frailties that obscured thy heart,
Veil'd in thy grave shall unremember'd lie,
For these were parts of Dennis, born to die!
But, there's a nobler Seity behind,
His reason dies not—and has friends to find!
Though here, revenge and pride withheld his praise,
No wrongs shall reach him through his future days:
The rising ages shall redeem his name;
And nations read him into lasting fame!
—HILL, AARON, 1734, *On the Death of Mr. Dennis.*

It was not literature, then, that made the mind coarse, brutalising the habits and inflaming the style of Dennis. He had thrown himself among the walks of genius, and aspired to fix himself on a throne to which Nature had refused him a legitimate claim. What a lasting source of vexation and rage, even for a long-lived patriarch of criticism! Accustomed to suspend the scourge over the heads of the first authors of the age, he could not sit at a table or enter a coffee-house without exerting the despotism of a literary dictator. How could the mind that had devoted itself to the contemplation of masterpieces, only to reward its industry by detailing to the public their human frailties, experience one hour of amenity, one idea of grace, one generous impulse of sensibility? But the poor critic himself at length fell, really more the victim of his criticism than the genius he had insulted. Having incurred the public neglect, the blind and helpless Cacus in his den sunk fast into contempt, dragged on a life of misery, and in his last days, scarcely vomiting his fire and smoke, became the most pitiable creature, receiving the alms he craved from triumphant genius.—DISRAELI, ISAAC, 1812–13, *Influence of a Bad Temper in Criticism, Calamities of Authors.*

The great opportunities for success and self-praise offered by the stage, it is to be feared, engender more of malice, hatred, and ill-will than is found in other professions. There is an episode, in which Pope figured, which gathers these vices into a small compass in an incredible way. Dennis, the savage critic, grown old and reduced to poverty, was to have a benefit, and bethought him that if he could get his old enemy's (Pope's) patronage for the performance, it would bring money and company. What follows Voltaire might have described. The old critic declared that he knew how to get him to consent. He knew pretty well the vanity of the little gentleman, and would, therefore, solicit him to write a prologue, and that he was sure, notwithstanding their mutual enmity, *the reputation of appearing charitable* would readily induce him to undertake it. He was not deceived. Pope consented, and the play, thus strengthened, produced a good house, while the virtue of forgiveness of enemies was loudly chanted to Pope's honour. Both the world, however, and Dennis were deceived, for the prologue was couched in such terms that every line contained some fine ironical stroke of satire against the poor devil he professed to serve.—FITZGERALD, PERCY, 1882, *A New History of the English Stage, vol.* I, *p.* 323.

The careers of Rymer and Dennis are amongst the saddest and most deplorable stories to be found in the annals of

English literature. If industry ever deserved an acknowledgement, these two men deserved it. If they were not exactly buried in paupers' graves, they at all events spent their last days in great misery—and misery in the earliest part of the last century is not conceivable to the "general reader" of to-day.—ROBERTS, WILLIAM, 1889, *Two Eighteenth Century Critics, The Bookworm, vol.* 2, *p.* 150.

GENERAL

How chang'd from him who made the boxes groan,
And shook the Stage with Thunders all his own!
Stood up to dash each vain PRETENDER'S hope,
Maul the French Tyrant, or pull down the Pope!
If there's a *Briton* then, true bred and born,
Who holds Dragoons and wooden shoes in scorn:
If there's a Critic of distinguished rage;
If there's a Senior, who contemns this age;
Let him to-night his just assistance lend,
And be the *Critic's*, *Briton's*, *Old Man's* Friend.

—POPE, ALEXANDER, 1733, *A Prologue to a Play for Mr. Dennis's Benefit.*

Mr. Dennis, considered as a dramatic writer, makes not so good a figure as in his critical works; he understood the rules of writing, but it is not in the power of every one to carry their own theory into execution. There is one error which he endeavoured to reform, very material for the interest of dramatic poetry. He saw, with concern, that love had got the entire possession of the tragic stage, contrary to the authority of the ancients, and the example of Shakespear. He resolved therefore to deviate a little from the reigning practice, and not to make his heroes such whining slaves in their amours, which not only debases the majesty of tragedy, but confounds most of the principal characters, by making that passion the predominant quality in all. But he did not think it safe at once to shew his principal characters wholly exempt from it, lest so great and sudden a transition should prove disagreeable. He rather chose to steer a middle course, and make love appear violent, but yet to be subdued by reason, and give way to the influence of some other more noble passion; as in Rinaldo, to Glory; in Iphigenia, to Friendship; and in Liberty Asserted, to the Public Good.—CIBBER, THEOPHILUS, 1753, *Lives of the Poets, vol.* IV, *p.* 235.

The universality of applause, however it might quell the censure of common mortals, had no other effect than to harden Dennis in fixed dislike; but his dislike was not merely capricious. He found and shewed many faults; he shewed them indeed with anger, but he found them indeed with acuteness, such as ought to rescue his criticism from oblivion; though, at last, it will have no other life than it derives from the work which it endeavours to oppress.—JOHNSON, SAMUEL, 1779–81, *Addison, Lives of the Poets.*

Pope and Addison had a Dennis; and Dennis, if I mistake not, held up as he had been to scorn and detestation, was a sensible fellow, and passed some censures upon both those writers that, had they been less just, would have hurt them less. —COWPER, WILLIAM, 1786, *Letter to Rev. Walter Bagot, July* 4.

His poetry and politics are now but little regarded; yet, from Dr. Johnson's frequent and long extracts from his critical pieces, it may be fairly presumed, that he did not think meanly of them; and such readers as will not suffer their judgment to be run away with by a regard for names, will think, that even "Cato" itself, was indebted to the enthusiasm of party at the time, for getting rid so easily of Dennis's strictures. He is, perhaps, one of those authors who have not had justice done to them. Dennis was overwhelmed in his own time, and has never been able to recover himself since.—NOBLE, MARK, 1806, *A Biographical History of England, vol.* II, *p.* 257.

Dennis could not be carried beyond the cold line of a precedent, and before he ventured to be pleased, he was compelled to look into Aristotle. His learning was the bigotry of literature. It was ever Aristotle explained by Dennis. But in the explanation of the obscure text of his master, he was led into such frivolous distinctions, and tasteless propositions, that his works deserve inspection, as examples of the manner of a true mechanical critic.—DISRAELI, ISAAC, 1812–13, *Influence of a Bad Temper in Criticism, Calamities of Authors.*

His credit with the public in his day was at least as great as that of Rymer, the formidable champion who had threatened destruction to the "Paradise Lost" in 1677.—GODWIN, WILLIAM, 1815, *Lives of Edward and John Philips, ch.* xi.

We must not forget, that Mr. Dennis laid claims to public esteem, not only as a critic, but as a wit, a politician, and a poet. In the first and the last of these characters, he can receive but little praise, His attempts at gaiety and humour are weighty and awkward, almost without example. His poetry can only be described by negatives; it is not inharmonious, nor irregular, nor often turgid—for the author, too nice to sink into the mean, and too timid to rise into the bombastic, dwells in elaborate "decencies for ever." . . . He was a true-hearted Englishman—with the legitimate prejudices of his country, warmly attached to the principles of the Revolution, detesting the French, abominating the Italian opera, and deprecating as heartily the triumph of the Pretender, as the success of a rival's tragedy. His political treatises, though not very elegantly finished, are made of sturdy and lasting materials. He appears, from some passages in his letters, to have cherished a genuine love of nature, and to have turned, with eager delight, to her deep and quiet solitudes, for refreshment from the feverish excitements, the vexatious defeats, and the barren triumphs, of his critical career.—TALFOURD, THOMAS, NOON, 1820, *John Dennis's Works, Retrospective Review, vol.* 1, *p.* 306.

The fiercest oppugner of puns in ancient or modern times.—LAMB, CHARLES, 1826, *Popular Fallacies.*

He carried heavier metal than Gildon; but he nevertheless belonged to the cuckoo school of "rules of art."—KNIGHT, CHARLES, 1849, *Studies of Shakspere.*

Steele one time gave the title of hangman of the gospel to a furious preacher. He might have called John Dennis the hangman of literature. Indeed he was worse than the hangman, who merely executes a painful but necessary duty. Dennis, on the contrary, indulged in wanton cruelty, and if he had been the functionary referred to, would have treated his victim to a preliminary rehearsal of his office before executing it. —MONTGOMERY, HENRY R., 1862, *Memoirs of the Life and Writings of Sir Richard Steele, vol.* II, *p.* 47.

One of Pope's typical dunces, a dull man outside of his own sphere, as men are apt to be, but who had some sound notions as a critic, and thus became the object of Pope's fear and therefore of his resentment.—LOWELL, JAMES RUSSELL, 1868–90, *Dryden, Prose Works, Riverside ed., vol.* III, *p.* 190.

John Dennis was one of those old campaigners who can boast more scars than laurels; but with whom a long experience in the wars goes to supply the want of regular training or native capacity. As an original author, he occupied a place among the rank and file of his contemporaries. He wrote or altered nine dramatic pieces, among which two comedies are said by an indefatigable and conscientious searcher of such wares to display considerable merit. As a critic, he undoubtedly possessed certain characteristics which would have ensured him the prominence he coveted even in our own times. He was free from that sentiment which with the generality of critics so fatally interferes with a due exercise of the judicial faculty—a respect for success. Indeed he avowed it as his guiding principle in the choice of his victims, to select leading instances of unmerited popularity. —WARD, ADOLPHUS WILLIAM, 1869, *ed. Poetical Works of Alexander Pope, Introductory Memoir, p.* xxiv.

A writer of turgid plays, and of ferocious but not always wholly unjust *critiques.*—WILLIAMS, HOWARD, 1886, *English Letters and Letter-Writers of the Eighteenth Century, p.* 282.

In the literary matters he was a born dissenter. He belonged by nature to the opposition, and the cardinal principle upon which he acted was to find fault with any view that had met with general approval. He could not fail to be at times, right.—LOUNSBURY, THOMAS R., 1891, *Studies in Chaucer, vol.* III, *p.* 141.

Dennis has been resolutely misjudged, in consequence of his foolish attitude towards his younger contemporaries in old age, but in his prime he was a writer of excellent judgment. He was the first English critic to do unstinted justice to Milton and to Molière, and he was a powerful factor in preparing public opinion for the literary verdicts of Addison.—GOSSE, EDMUND, 1897, *Short History of Modern English Literature, p.* 200.

Roger North

1653-1734

Born 1653: died 1734. An English historian, sixth son of Dudley North, fourth Baron North. He was attorney-general to the queen (Mary of Modena). He wrote the abusive "Examen" of White Kennett's "History of England" (1740), the "Lives" of his brothers, "A Discourse on the Study of the Laws" (first printed in 1824), "Memoirs of Music" (first printed in 1846), etc. He is one of the chief authorities on the history of the reigns of Charles II. and James II., and is remembered for his partizanship toward his brothers.—SMITH, BENJAMIN E., *ed.*, 1894-97, *The Century Cyclopaedia of Names, p.* 743.

PERSONAL

Roger North was in no respect a famous man. His estimate of himself, that he was "a plant of a slow growth, and when mature but slight wood and of a flashy growth," is perhaps over-modest, and yet it is evidently not far from the mark. During his early manhood he was, so to speak, in tutelage to his brothers: to John, the future master of Trinity, while at Cambridge; to Francis, the lord chief justice and lord keeper, while at the bar. He never occupied any prominent position, and his fairly successful professional career was the result not so much of his own merit as of his position as "favourite" to the great and successful lawyer, the "bond of the faggot." His mind, though active and from boyhood ingenious, was not very powerful; and though his senses were unsealed and his judgment clear, and though he participated fully in the general zeal for culture which marked the period, his professional duties left him little time to become more than an interested and interesting student of music, mathematics, morals, politics, and a score of other subjects.—AIRY, OSMUND, 1888, *The English Historical Review, vol.* 3, *p.* 174.

Roger North was held in great and increasing respect by his neighbours as an authority on questions of law, and was frequently consulted by the magnates of the county, and sometimes chosen to arbitrate when disputes arose. On one occasion he was called in to settle some difference between Sir Robert Walpole and his mother. The country people called him "Solomon," as in his early days the pamphleteers had styled him "Roger the Fiddler." He retained his vigour and brightness of intellect to the last, and one of his latest letters was written when he was nearly eighty years old, in answer to some one who had applied to him for advice as to the best course of reading for the bar.—JESSOPP, AUGUSTUS, 1895, *Dictionary of National Biography, vol.* XLI, *p.* 178.

He liked painting and yachting as well as the toughest quillets of the old law, and was altogether a character.—SAINTSBURY, GEORGE, 1898, *A Short History of English Literature, p.* 522.

LIVES

Francis, Lord Keeper Guilford, was younger son of the lord North before mentioned. Burnet and Kennet have given no very favourable character of the keeper: his relation, Roger North, has defended him in a very bulky work; which, however, does not contribute much to raise our ideas either of the writer or his subject. If that performance and its companion, the Examen, had nothing else ridiculous in them, it would be sufficient to blast their reputation, that they aim at decrying that excellent magistrate, the lord chief justice Hale; and that Charles the second, and that wretch the duke of Lauderdale, the king's taking money from France, and the seizure of the charter of London, are some of the men, and some of the measures, the author defends! . . . It is very remarkable that two peers of this race have suffered by apologies written for them by two of their own relations; but with this difference naturally attending the performances of a sensible man and a weak one: Dudley, lord North, has shown himself an artful and elegant historian; Roger North, a miserable biographer.—WALPOLE, HORACE, 1758-1806, *A Catalogue of the Royal and Noble Authors of England, Scotland and Ireland, ed. Parke, vol.* III, *p.* 295, *and note.*

Roger North's life of his brother, the lord Keeper, is the most valuable specimen of this class of our literature; it is delightful, and much beyond any other of the writings of his contemporaries.—COLERIDGE, SAMUEL TAYLOR, 1818, *Style, Miscellanies Æsthetic and Literary, ed. Ashe, p.* 180.

This old piece of legal biography, which has been lately republished, is one of the most delightful books in the world. Its charm does not consist in any marvellous incidents of Lord Guilford's life, or any peculiar interest attaching to his character, but in the unequalled naïveté of the writer—in the singular felicity with which he has thrown himself into his subject—and in his vivid delineations of all the great lawyers of his time. He was a younger brother of the Lord Keeper, to whose affection he was largely indebted, and from whom he appears to have been scarcely ever divided. His work, in nice minuteness of detail, and living picture of motive, almost equals the auto-biographies of Benvenuto Cellini, Rousseau, and Cibber. He seems to be almost as intensely conscious of all his brother's actions, and the movements of his mind, as they were of their own. All his ideas of human greatness and excellence appear taken from the man whom he celebrates. There never was a more liberal or gentle penetration of the spirit. He was evidently the most human, the most kindly, and the most single-hearted, of flatterers. There is a beauty in his very cringing, beyond the independence of many. It is the most gentleman-like submission, the most graceful resignation of self, of which we have ever read.—TALFOURD, THOMAS NOON, 1820, *North's Life of Lord Guilford, Retrospective Review, vol.* 2, *p.* 238.

In compiling these affectionate memorials of his brothers, the writer appears to have been chiefly actuated by his regard and veneration for their memory. Having survived them all, he was distressed to find the names of those whom he had so loved and honoured, passing rapidly into oblivion. During their lives, his happiest moments were spent in their society; and after their death, he found his greatest consolation in recording their history. This he has done with a minuteness of detail, which to himself appeared to require an apology, but which, in fact, is one of the most attractive qualities of his style. His writings have the effect of introducing the reader, as it were, into the presence of the party, so lively and natural are the touches of his pen.—ROSCOE, H., 1826, *ed., Lives of the Rt. Hon. Francis North, the Rt. Hon. Dudley North and Dr. John North, Preface, p.* ix.

Roger North's "Life of the Lord-Keeper," which, like Boswell's "Life of Johnson," interests us highly, without giving us a very exalted notion of the author. Notwithstanding its extravagant praise of the hero of the tale, its inaccuracies, and its want of method, it is a most valuable piece of biography, and, with Roger's lives of his brothers, "Dudley and John," and his "Examen," ought to be studied by every one who wishes to understand the history and the manners of the reign of Charles II.—CAMPBELL, JOHN LORD, 1845–56, *Lives of the Lord Chancellors and Keepers of the Great Seal of England, vol.* III, *Life of Lord-Keeper Guilford.*

One of the most entertaining books ["Life of Lord Keeper Guilford"] in our language.—KNIGHT, CHARLES, 1847–8, *Half-Hours with the Best Authors.*

The labour that North bestowed upon the lives of his brothers was extraordinary. The life of the lord keeper was written and rewritten again and again. Defaced though the style is by the use of some unusual words, there is a certain charm about it which few readers can resist, and the "Lives of the Norths" must always remain an English classic and a prime authority for the period with which it deals.—JESSOPP, AUGUSTUS, 1895, *Dictionary of National Biography, vol.* XLI, *p.* 178.

The biographies and autobiography . . . are very good literature, though Dr. Jessopp is hardly warranted in styling them English classics. They are neither planned with classic symmetry nor executed with classic elegance, but are charming from their artless loquacity and the atmosphere of fraternal affection in which they are steeped, as well as most entertaining from their wealth of anecdote and their portraits, partial, but not intentionally unfair, of remarkable men. Two elements in these books are sharply contrasted, the political and the anecdotic. The former affords a melancholy but useful representation of the factious unreason of political parties in that age, especially Roger's, and of the prejudices which kept

Englishmen apart until they learned toleration from Locke and Hoadly.—GARNETT, RICHARD, 1895, *The Age of Dryden*, *p.* 214.

The whole is written in a curious and very piquant style, strangely free from any of the new classicism, but as strangely crossed between the older conceit and the new slang. North is Harrington *plus* L'Estrange.—SAINTSBURY, GEORGE, 1898, *A Short History of English Literature, p.* 522.

John Arbuthnot

1667–1735

Born, at Arbuthnot, Kincardineshire, 1667; baptized 29 April. Educated at [Marischal Coll. ?] Aberdeen. Settled in London, 1691; taught mathematics. At University Coll., Oxford, as Fellow-Commoner, 6 Oct. 1694–96. Took M. D. degree, St. Andrew's University, 11 Sept. 1696. Married, about 1702. F. R. S., 30 Nov. 1704. Physician Extraordinary to Queen Anne, 30 Oct. 1705; Physician in Ordinary, Nov. 1709. Fellow of Roy. Coll. of Physicians, 27 April 1710; Second Censor, 30 Sept. 1723; "Elect," 5 Oct. 1727; Harveian Orator, 18 Oct. 1727. Physician at Chelsea Hospital, 1713. Formed "Scriblerus Club" with Swift, Pope, Gay, and Parnell, 1714. Visits to France, 1714 and 1718. Ill health in later years. Contrib. to "London Magazine," 1732. To Hampstead, 1734. Died, in London, 27 Feb. 1735. Buried in St. James's Church, Piccadilly. *Works:* "Of the Laws of Chance" (anon.), 1692; "Theses Medicæ de Secretione Animali," 1696; "An Examination of Dr. Woodward's Account of the Deluge" (under initials: J. A., M. D.), 1697; "An Essay on the Usefulness of Mathematical Learning," 1701; "Tables of the Grecian, Roman, and Jewish Measures" [1705;] "A Sermon Preach'd . . . at the Mercat-Cross" (anon.), 1706; "Proposals for printing a very curious discourse . . . intitled Ψενδολογια Πολιτεκη" (anon.), 1712; "The History of John Bull" (anon.; in six pamphlets: (i) "Law is a Bottomless Pit;" (ii.) "John Bull in his Senses;" (iii.) "John Bull still in his Senses;" (iv.) "An Appendix" to preceding; (vi.) "Lewis Baboon turned Honest"), 1712; "Three Hours after Marriage" (with Gay and Pope), 1717; "Reasons humbly offer'd by the Company . . . of Upholders" (anon.), 1724; "Tables of Ancient Coins" (anon.), 1727; "Oratio Anniversaria Harvæiana," 1727; "Miscellanies in Prose and Verse" (3 vols.), 1727 (another ed., 4 vols., 1727–32); "An Essay concerning the Nature of Ailments" (2 vols.), 1731–32; "A Brief Account of Mr. John Ginglicutt's Treatise" (anon.), 1731; "An Essay concerning the Effects of Air," 1733; "Γνωθι Σεαυτον," 1734. [A further list of anonymous works *attributed* to Arbuthnot is given in Aitken's "Life and Works" of Arbuthnot, 1892.] *Collected Works:* In 2 vols., 1751 [1750]; enlarged ed., with memoir, 1770. *Life:* By G. A Aitken, 1892.—SHARP, R. FARQUHARSON, 1897, *A Dictionary of English Authors, p.* 7.

PERSONAL

I think him as good a doctor as any man for one that is ill, and a better doctor for one that is well.—POPE, ALEXANDER, 1722, *Letter to the Hon. Robert Digby, Sept.* 1.

O if the world had but a dozen Arbuthnots in it, I would burn my travels! but, however, he is not without fault: there is a passage in Bede highly commending the piety and learning of the Irish in that age, where, after abundance of praises, he overthrows them all, by lamenting that, alas! they kept Easter at a wrong time of the year. So our doctor has every quality and virtue that can make a man amiable or useful, but, alas! he hath a sort of slouch in his walk!—SWIFT, JONATHAN, 1725, *Letter to Mr. Pope, Sept.* 29.

I John Arbuthnott Doctor of Physick thus make my last Will and Testament. I recommend my soul to its mercifull Creator hoping to be saved by the Merits of Jesus Christ, and that I may be found in him not having on my own Righteousness but his which is of ffaith. I leave my body to be decently interred by my ffriends. I leave twenty pounds to each of my two sisters Elizabeth and Anne to Purchase Mourning. I leave my Greek Septuagint and Greek New Testament (the gift of my late Royal Mistress Queen Anne) to my dear son George. And I leave all the rest of my estate Goods and

Chattells to be equally divided amongst my three Children or the Survivors of them immediately after my death in equal parts, reckoning amongst my goods what is owing unto me by my Son George; recommending unto them that mutual love and affection which I thank God I have hitherto observed amongst them. I appoint my Son George my sole Executor of this my last Will and Testament, and earnestly recommend to him the Care and Protection of his dear Sisters, and failing him (which God in his Mercy forbid) the Eldest of my surviving Daughters. I leave to my dearest and most affectionate Brother Robert my Watch.—Jo. Arbuthnott. Signed and Sealed the 5th of November1733 in the presence of Erasmus Lewis, John Bradshaw. —ARBUTHNOT, JOHN, 1733, *Will.*

I regret the loss of Dr. Arbuthnot every hour of the day: he was the best-conditioned creature that ever breathed, and the most cheerful.—LEWIS, ERASMUS, 1737, *Letter to Swift, June* 30; *Swift's Works, ed. Scott, vol* XIX, *p.* 88.

Although he was justly celebrated for wit and learning, there was an excellence in his character more amiable than all his other qualifications. I mean the excellence of his heart. He has shewed himself equal to any of his contemporaries in humour and vivacity; and he was superior to most men in acts of humanity and benevolence; his very sarcasms are the satirical strokes of good nature: they are like flaps of the face given in jest, the effects of which may raise blushes, but no blackness after the blows. . . . He is seldom serious, except in his attacks upon vice, and then his spirit rises with a manly strength and a noble indignation. . . . No man exceeded him in the moral duties of life.—BOYLE, JOHN (LORD ORRERY), 1751, *Remarks on the Life and Writings of Dr. Jonathan Swift, Letter* XX.

His imagination was almost inexhaustible, and whatever subject he treated, or was consulted upon, he immediately overflowed with all that it could possibly produce. It was at anybody's service, for as soon as he was exonerated, he did not care what became of it: insomuch that his sons, when young, have frequently made kites of his scattered papers of hints, which would have furnished good matter for folios. Not being in the least jealous of his fame as an author, he would neither take the time nor the trouble of separating the best from the worst; he worked out the whole mine, which afterward, in the hands of skilful refiners, produced a rich vein of ore. As his imagination was always at work, he was frequently absent and inattentive in company, which made him both say and do a thousand inoffensive absurdities; but which, far from being provoking, as they commonly are, supplied new matter for conversation, and occasioned wit, both in himself and others. His social character was not more amiable than his moral character was pure and exemplary; charity, benevolence, and a love of mankind appeared unaffectedly in all he said or did. . . . He indulged his palate to excess, I might have said to gluttony, which gave a gross plethoric habit of body, that was the cause of his death. He lived and died a devout and sincere Christian.—CHESTERFIELD, LORD, 1763? *Characters, ed. Bradshaw, vol.* III, *pp.* 1411, 1412.

A man estimable for his learning, amiable for his life, and venerable for his piety. Arbuthnot was a man of great comprehension, skilful in his profession, versed in the sciences, acquainted with ancient literature, and able to animate his mass of knowledge by a bright and active imagination; a scholar with great brilliance of wit; a wit who, in the crowd of life, retained and discovered a noble ardour of religious zeal.—JOHNSON, SAMUEL, 1779–81, *Pope, Lives of the English Poets.*

Arbuthnot was forgetful of himself; he was indifferent to the ambitions that prompted jealousy amongst the rest. He watched with the keenest interest the success of his brethren; he guided, suggested, helped; but he remained careless about his own fame. Convinced that amid the crowd of dunces, the best genius of the age was concentred in his own friends, he yet must have seen, as clearly as their detractors, the flaws in the charater of each. In the annals of our literature there are not a few men who have filled something of the part that he did: but none who has filled it with such complete success of self-abnegation. It is a part that earns no wide or high-sounding fame: but it is something in an age of such envenomed detraction, and such vehemence of party hate, to have lived revered and cherished by its men of "light and leading;" to have trained their talents, and to have condoned their faults: to have died without losing their esteem: and yet without one stain, in the midst of very general corruption, on which the keen eyes of political partizans could fasten. —CRAIK, HENRY, 1882, *The Life of Jonathan Swift, p.* 371.

Arbuthnot's acts of kindness were incessant. He seems never to have wearied in doing good to those in distress, and every additional fact about him with which we are favoured serves to deepen the belief that in his character there was no trace of gall.—COURTNEY, W. P., 1892, *The Academy, vol.* 41, *p.* 415.

The manly, learned, lovable, genial, humane, and witty Dr. Arbuthnot, whose sweet face, if such an adjective be permissible in connection with the male sex, would alone have drawn folk to him.—WRIGHT, THOMAS, 1894, *The Life of Daniel Defoe, p.* 184.

THE HISTORY OF JOHN BULL
1712

When I was first called to the office of historiographer to John Bull, he expressed himself to this purpose:—"Sir Humphry Polesworth, I know you are a plain dealer; it is for that reason I have chosen you for this important trust; speak the truth, and spare not." That I might fulfill those, his honorable intentions, I obtained leave to repair to and attend him in his most secret retirements; and I put the journals of all transactions into a strong box, to be opened at a fitting occasion, after the manner of the historiographers of some Eastern monarchs. . . . And now, that posterity may not be ignorant in what age so excellent a history was written (which would otherwise, no doubt, be the subject of its inquiries), I think it proper to inform the learned of future times that it was compiled when Lewis XIV. was King of France, and Philip, his grandson, of Spain; when England and Holland, in conjunction with the Emperor and the allies, entered into a war against these two princes, which lasted ten years, under the management of the Duke of Marlborough, and was put to a conclusion by the treaty of Utrecht under the ministry of the Earl of Oxford, in the year 1713.—ARBUTHNOT, JOHN, 1712, *John Bull, Preface.*

Dr. Arbuthnot was the sole writer of John Bull.—POPE, ALEXANDER, 1734–36, *Spence's Anecdotes, ed. Singer, p.* 109.

It is an ingenious and lively attack upon the war policy of the whigs; and, if it wants the force of Swift's profounder satire, it is an admirably effective and still amusing party squib. It does not seem to be known whether Arbuthnot originated or only adopted the nickname, John Bull.—STEPHEN, LESLIE, 1885, *Dictionary of National Biography, vol.* II, *p.* 63.

The story is told with great humour of the origin of the law-suit; of its success, which caused John Bull to contemplate leaving off his trade to turn lawyer; of the discovery that Hocus had an intrigue with John's wife; of the attorney's bill, which made John angry; and of the methods adopted by the lawyers to dissuade him from making an end of the law-suit by accepting a composition. Arbuthnot appears to have been the first to apply the name of John Bull to the English people, and he drew the character, which has ever since been accepted as a type, of this honest, plain-dealing fellow, choleric, bold, and of a very inconstant temper.—AITKEN, GEORGE A., 1892, *The Life and Works of John Arbuthnot, p.* 45.

"The History of John Bull" is not fitted to attain lasting popularity. It will be read from curiosity and for information; but the keen excitement, the amusement, and the irritation caused by a brilliant satire of living men and passing events can be but vaguely imagined by readers whose interest in the statecraft of the age is historical and not personal.—DENNIS, JOHN, 1894, *The Age of Pope, p.* 177.

MEMOIRS OF MARTIN'S SCRIBLERUS

It has been little read, or when read, has been forgotten, as no man could be wiser, better, or merrier, by remembering it.—JOHNSON, SAMUEL, 1779–81, *Pope, Lives of the English Poets.*

The "Memories of Martinus Scriblerus" were first published in the quarto edition of Pope's works in 1741; they are mainly, if not exclusively, Arbuthnot's, and give the best specimen of his powers. The ridicule of metaphysical pedantry is admirable, though rather beyond popular appreciation. Other passages are directed against the antiquarians and Arbuthnot's old opponent, Woodward, and his supposed discovery of an ancient shield. The account of Scriblerus's education clearly gave some hints to Sterne's "Tristram Shandy."—STEPHEN, LESLIE, 1885, *Dictionary of National Biography, vol.* II, *p.* 63.

The "Memoirs of the extraordinary Life, Works, and Discoveries of Martinus Scriblerus" seems to be almost entirely by Arbuthnot, but he was helped by Pope and others. We have only the first Book, and this was not printed until 1741, six years after Arbuthnot's death, when Pope included it in the volume he issued in that year. He told Spence that the design was carried on much farther than had appeared in print; but it was stopped by the members of the club being dispersed after 1714, or being otherwise engaged. . . . The "Memoirs" are excellent in their kind, and the mock gravity is admirably maintained. Arbuthnot was the most learned of the wits of the time, and the piece is full of out-of-the-way knowledge. Many parts, too, involved an intimate acquaintance with medicine which he alone, of the members of the club, possessed. Most of the humour can be appreciated by any reader, but some of the ridicule poured upon philosophers and others can only be understood thoroughly by persons well read in the authors attacked. I cannot profess to agree with some critics who have placed the "Memoirs" above any other of Arbuthnot's works; they do not seem to me more interesting than the "History of John Bull," and they are marred by coarse touches not usually found in Arbuthnot's writings, though common enough in those of some of his friends. —AITKEN, GEORGE A., 1892, *The Life and Works of John Arbuthnot, pp.* 57, 58.

What Arbuthnot has left us is not only by far the best of his work, but shows how high was the range of his humour, which could unite the grave irony of Swift, in the travesty of an elaborate argument, with the dramatic characterisation of Sterne, who in "Tristram Shandy" has drawn not a little inspiration from the early chapters of Arbuthnot's fragment. The book was not published until 1741, six years after Arbuthnot's death.—CRAIK, HENRY, 1894, *English Prose, vol.* III, *p.* 427.

GENERAL

Seignior Montpelier, who wrote not much but well. He seems to understand the difficulty to maintain an acquired reputation, and is therefore wiser than to hazard the losing of it by a new attempt. —MANLEY, MRS. MARY DE LA RIVIERE, 1709, *New Atalantis.*

The grating scribbler! whose untuned Essays
Mix the Scotch Thistle with the English Bays;
By either Phœbus preordained to ill,
The hand prescribing, or the flattering quill,
Who doubly plagues, and boasts two Arts to kill!

—SMYTH, JAMES MOORE, 1730, *One Epistle to Mr. A. Pope, occasioned by Two Epistles, lately published.*

"Talking of the eminent writers in Queen Anne's reign, he observed, "I think Dr. Arbuthnot the first man among them. He was the most universal genius, being an excellent physician, a man of deep learning, and a man of much humour."—JOHNSON, SAMUEL, 1763, *Life by Boswell.*

The most distinguished collection of letters in the English language, is that of Mr. Pope, Dean Swift, and their friends; partly published in Mr. Pope's works, and partly in those of Dean Swift. This collection is, on the whole, an entertaining and agreeable one; and contains much wit and refinement. It is not, however, altogether free from the fault which I imputed to Pliny's Epistles, of too much study and refinement. In the variety of letters from different persons, contained in that collection, we find many that are written with ease, and beautiful simplicity. Those of Dr. Arbuthnot, in particular, always deserve that praise.—BLAIR, HUGH, 1783, *Lectures on Rhetoric and Belles-Letters, ed. Mills, Lecture* xxxvii, *p.* 416.

Your sentiments of Dr. Arbuthnot agree entirely with mine. He had, I think, more wit and humour, and he certainly had much more virtue and learning, than either Pope or Swift.—BEATTIE, JAMES, 1785, *Letter to Mrs. Montagu, Jan.* 31; *Beattie's Life by Forbes, vol.* II, *p.* 357.

Satire was his chief weapon, and no man knew its value better: it was a true Highland *broad-sword*, calculated to cut and slash on each side; yet so keen was the instrument, that the wound soon healed, unless he meant to destroy, and not to correct.—NOBLE, MARK, 1806, *A Biographical History of England, vol.* III, *p.* 367.

Arbuthnot's style is distinguished from that of his contemporaries, even by a greater degree of terseness and conciseness. He leaves out every superfluous word; is sparing of connecting particles, and introductory phrases; uses always the simplest forms of construction; and is more a master of the idiomatic peculiarities and internal resources of the language than almost any other writer.—HAZLITT, WILLIAM, 1818, *Lectures on the English Poets, Lecture* vi, *p.* 124.

Dr. Arbuthnot possessed, in a high degree, that classical knowledge in which Swift and Pope were deficient. In the publication of these friends, entitled "Miscellanies," which appeared in 1727, Arbuthnot, who wrote most of the lucubrations of Martinus Scriblerus, sometimes endeavoured to ape Bentley's style; and the section called *Virgilius Reformatus* contains a direct burlesque of his emendatory criticism, under the garb of Scriblerus' pretended alterations of the first two books of the Æneid; the short and imperious decrees of this critical *jeu-d'esprit* being particularly designed to ridicule the Notes on Phædrus, which were lately published.—MONK, JAMES HENRY, 1830–33, *The Life of Richard Bentley, vol.* II, *p.* 373.

When his feelings are not specially roused he is genial, lambent, good-humoured; but he was capable of genuine indignation, and sometimes lays on the lash with unsparing severity. His paper on the "Altercation or Scolding of the Ancients" is in very happy humour; his "Art of Political Lying" is more sarcastic.—MINTO, WILLIAM, 1872–80, *Manual of English Prose Literature, p.* 405.

Arbuthnot wrote little, and there is no collected edition of his works; but the little that he did write shows that if he had used his pen more freely he could have won for himself a very high position in literature.—NICOLL, HENRY J., 1882, *Landmarks of English Literature, p.* 184.

His writings to-day have lost something of their original flavor. Only students of the time are likely to recur to them. Their politics are of an outworn fashion. The pedantry they mock at has departed. The allusions required vexatious explanation in endless footnotes. The humor is less direct and palpable than Swift's, the wit less pointed and flashing than Pope's, the sportiveness less dainty and delicate than Gay's. Yet the "History of John Bull" and the "Memoirs of Scriblerus" will long hold their place in the literature of scholars, for their pithy English, their manly sense, their grotesque drollery, their vivid imagination.—RICHARDS, C. A. L., 1892, *An Eighteenth Century Character, The Dial, vol.* 13, *p.* 99.

The truth is that Arbuthnot's literary fame has suffered from causes which must sooner or later preclude any writer from permanent popularity. With two exceptions, the first book of the "Memoirs of Scriblerus" and the inimitable "Epitaph on Chartres," his satires must be unintelligible to a reader not minutely versed in the politics of that time. No satire in itself so intrinsically excellent is so little capable of universal application. His wit, his humour, his sarcasm, exhausting themselves on particular persons and on particular events, now require an elaborate commentary. There is, moreover, nothing either striking or felicitous in his style. The "History of John Bull" and the "Art of Political Lying" will probably not find half a dozen readers in as many years, but we venture to think that out of these readers there will be one or two who will have no difficulty in understanding the position which Arbuthnot once held.—COLLINS, JOHN CHURTON, 1893, *Jonathan Swift, p.* 99.

If we take the lash out of the style of Swift, we have that of John Arbuthnot, who can often hardly be distinguished from his friend and master. Without personal ambition of any kind, no vanity deterred Arbuthnot from frankly adopting, as closely as he could, the manner of the man whom he admired the most. As he was a perfectly sane and normal person, with plenty of wit and accomplishment, and without a touch of misanthropy, Arbuthnot served to popularise and to bring into general circulation the peculiar characteristics of Swift, and to reconcile him with his contemporaries.—GOSSE, EDMUND, 1897, *Short History of Modern English Literature, p.* 225.

Such letters and verses as have come down to us exhibit a talent which, while it modestly blushed as dilettante, competes favourably with the brightest of his age.—SICHEL, WALTER, 1901, *Bolingbroke and His Times, p.* 18.

Samuel Wesley

1662–1735

The father of John Wesley, the founder of Methodism, was the second son of John Wesley, of Whitchurch, and was born at Winterborn Whitchurch, according to Dr. Adam Clarke, in 1666. . . . . He was interested, in 1698 and 1699, in a Society for the Reformation of Manners, which resembled in many respects the societies formed by his son at Oxford, and published a letter in defense of such societies. He expressed the warmest sympathy with the efforts of John and Charles Wesley at Oxford, and wrote, in 1730, that if his son John was the father of a Holy Club, he must be the grandfather of it, and that he would rather any of his sons had such distinction than to be himself styled his Holiness. He was a prolific writer, having relied upon his pen as a source of income from the time he entered college. His first volume of poems, a volume of trifles and conceits, called "Maggots," was published when he was nineteen years of age. Among his other principal works, besides the "Life of Christ," already mentioned, were "Dissertations on the Book of Job," in Latin, "The History of the Old and New Testament," in verse, with illustrations, "Eupolis' Hymn to the Creator," and the poem of "Marlborough, or the Fate of Europe." He was intimately connected with the Athenian Gazette, published by John Dunton, and was its principal contributor. His best known hymns are "Behold the Saviour of Mankind" and "O, Thou who when I did Complain." He died at Epworth, April 22, 1735.—SIMPSON, MATTHEW, *ed.*, 1876, *Cyclopædia of Methodism, pp.* 916, 917.

PERSONAL

No man was ever more suitably mated than the elder Wesley. The wife whom he chose was, like himself, the child of a man eminent among the Non-conformists, and, like himself, in early youth she had chosen her own path: she had examined the controversy between the Dissenters and the Church of England with conscientious diligence, and satisfied herself that the schismatics were in the wrong. The dispute, it must be remembered, related wholly to discipline; but her inquiries had not stopt there, and she had reasoned herself into Socinianism, from which she was reclaimed by her husband. She was an admirable woman, of highly-improved mind, and of a strong and masculine understanding, an obedient wife, an exemplary mother, a fervent Christian. The marriage was blest in all its circumstances: it was contracted in the prime of their youth: it was fruitful; and death did not divide them till they were both full of days. They had no less than nineteen children; but only three sons and three daughters seem to have grown up; and it is probably to the loss of the others that the father refers in one of his letters, where he says, that he had suffered things more grievous than death. —SOUTHEY, ROBERT, 1820, *The Life of Wesley, and the Rise and Progress of Methodism, p.* 8.

Wesley's verse will not lift him high among poets (he was pilloried in the first edition of the "Dunciad," 1728, i. 115), nor has his "Job" given him his expected rank among scholars. He was an able, busy, and honest man, with much impulsive energy, easily misconstrued; his fame is that of being the father of John and Charles Wesley.—GORDON, ALEXANDER, 1899, *Dictionary of National Biography, vol.* LX, *p.* 317.

GENERAL

The author possessed considerable learning, and some poetical talent; but neither his conjectures ["Dissertations on Job"] nor his illustrations throw much light on this ancient poem.—ORME, WILLIAM, 1824, *Bibliotheca Biblica.*

He held the living of Epworth upwards of forty years, and was distinguished for the zeal and fidelity with which he discharged his parish duties. Of his talents and learning, his remaining works afford honourable evidence.—WATSON, RICHARD, 1831, *Life of the Rev. John Wesley, p.* 2.

He was a writer of no inconsiderable merit, though he has not won a place among the immortals, and perhaps did not deserve to do so. There is a sort of perverted ingenuity about most of his literary work. What, for example, could be expected from poems published under the unpromising, not to say repulsive, title of "Maggots," his first juvenile, work? Who *could* answer satisfactorily such profound questions as "What became of the Ark after the Flood?" "How high was Babel's Tower?" "What language was spoken by Balaam's ass?" "Did Peter and Paul use notes when they preached?" which are really not abnormal specimens of the sort of questions which were asked, and laboriously answered, by Mr. Wesley in the *Athenian Gazette*, a kind of seventeenth-century *Notes and Queries*. His poem on Blenheim suggests invidious comparisons with Addison's "Campaign;" and though few will now endorse the estimate which contemporaries formed of the "Campaign," fewer will deny that Addison had a far more elegant and delicate touch than Wesley. His poem on "The Life of Christ" and his "History of the New Testament in Verse" are wonderful *tours de force;* but it required a Milton to do justice to such lofty themes, and Mr. Wesley was no Milton. The extravagant laudations with which the first of these poems was greeted naturally provoked a reaction. The author was put on a pedestal from which a fall was inevitable. His poetry, instead of being admired, began to be laughed at. And yet it was certainly not without merit. His translation of the Great Hallel proved that at any rate one thing the great Laureate Nahum Tate said of him was true; it is far superior to the version Nahum himself has given us; and his last work, the "Dissertations on the Book of Job," shows that the writer, if not a poet, was at any rate a learned divine and an excellent Latin scholar.—OVERTON, JOHN HENRY, 1885, *The Wesley's at Epworth, Longman's Magazine, vol.* 7, *p.* 49.

That this speech ["Sacheverell's"] was the composition of the Rector of Epworth seems to have been universally recognised in Lincolnshire, and, in after years, John Wesley declared positively that his father was its author. Probably he was paid, in some shape or form, for preparing it, although, perhaps, like an old war horse, he scented the battle from afar and did his share of the fighting gratuitously.—CLARKE, ELIZA, 1886, *Susanna Wesley*, *p.* 90.

George Granville

Lord Lansdowne

1667–1735

George Granville, Greenville, or Grenville, Viscount Lansdowne, 1667–1735, a son of Bernard Granville, was educated at Trinity College, Cambridge, where he displayed such extraordinary merit that he was created M. A. at the age of thirteen. He subsequently wrote a number of poems, dramatic pieces, some essays, and minor historical treatises. 1. "The Gallants," C., 1696, 4to. 2. "Heroic Love," T., 1698, 4to. 3. "The Jew of Venice," C., 1701, 4to. 4. "Peleus and Thetis," M., 1701, 4to. 5. "The British Enchantress," D. P., 1706, 4to. 6. "Once a Lover and Always a Lover," C., 1736, 12mo. 7. "Poems on Several Occasions," 1712, 8vo. 8. "A Letter from a Nobleman abroad to his Friends in England," 1722. In Lord Somers's collection. 9. "Genuine Works, in verse and prose," 1732, 2 vols. 4to. 10. "Letter to the Author of Reflections Historical and Political, occasioned by a Treatise in vindication of General Monk and Sir Richard Greenville," 1732, 4to.—ALLIBONE, S. AUSTIN, 1854–58, *A Critical Dictionary of English Literature, vol.* I, *p.* 721.

PERSONAL

Auspicious poet, wert thou not my friend,
How could I envy what I must commend!
But since 'tis Nature's law in love and wit,
That youth should reign and withering age submit,
With less regret those laurels I resign,
Which, dying on my brows, revive on thine.
—DRYDEN, JOHN, 1698, *To Mr. Granville, On his Excellent Tragedy, Called Heroic Love.*

The lustre of his station no doubt procured him more incense, than the force of his genius would otherwise have attracted; but he appears not to have been destitute of fine parts, which were however rather elegantly polished, than great in themselves.—CIBBER, THEOPHILUS, 1753, *Lives of the Poets, vol.* IV, *p.* 249.

A poet and patron of poets, modest on the heads of his own performances, eager for the success of those of others.—WARD,

ADOLPHUS WILLIAM, 1869, *ed., Poetical Works of Alexander Pope, Introductory Memoir, p.* xxi.

GENERAL

'Tis yours, my Lord, to bless our soft retreats,
And call the Muses to their ancient seats;
To paint anew the flow'ry sylvan scenes,
To crown the forests with immortal greens,
Make Windsor-hills in lofty numbers rise,
And lift her turrets nearer to the skies;
To sing those honours you deserve to wear,
And add new lustre to her silver star!
—POPE, ALEXANDER, 1704–13, *Windsor Forest, v.* 283–90.

The "She Gallants," a comedy wrote by Mr. Granville when he was very young; extraordinary witty and well acted; but offending the ears of some ladies who set up for chastity, it made its exit.—DOWNES, JOHN, 1708, *Roscius Anglicanus, p.* 45.

Waller in Granville lives; when Mira sings
With Waller's hand he strikes the sounding strings;
With sprightly turns his noble genius shines,
And manly sense adorns his easie lines.
—GAY, JOHN, 1714, *To Barnard Lintot, Poems.*

Imitated Waller; but as that poet has been much excelled since, a faint copy of a faint master must strike still less.—WALPOLE, HORACE, 1758, *A Catalogue of the Royal and Noble Authors of England, Scotland and Ireland., vol.* IV, *p.* 169.

Granville could not admire without bigotry; he copied the wrong as well as the right from his masters. . . . His little pieces are seldom either sprightly or elegant, either keen or weighty. They are trifles written by idleness, and published by vanity. But his Prologues and Epilogues have a just claim to praise.—JOHNSON, SAMUEL, 1779–81, *Granville, Lives of the English Poets.*

Notwithstanding the many praises lavished on this celebrated nobleman as a poet, by Dryden, by Addison, by Bolingbroke, by our Author, and others, yet candid criticism must oblige us to confess that he was but a feeble imitator of the feeblest parts of Waller.—WARTON, JOSEPH, 1797, *ed. Pope's Works.*

His predominant characteristics were amiability and vanity. His love of distinction incited him to become a dramatist, poet, and politician. He had aspirations without ability, and in none of these capacities did he exhibit any vigour of mind. . . . His plays reflect the worst qualities of the era of Charles II. In tragedy he thought that to be dull and stately was to be classical; in comedy that affected briskness of dialogue was liveliness, and indecent double meanings wit. He made no figure in politics, and owed his post in the Harley administration to his wealth, family, and electioneering influence. His literature, aided by his hereditary advantages, sufficed to procure him a factitious fame while he lived, but his reputation was at an end the moment his works lost the lustre they derived from his social position.—ELWIN, WHITWELL, 1871, *ed., The Works of Alexander Pope, vol.* I, *p.* 325.

Though this tragedy ["Heroic Love"] is not altogether without merit—for the passion of Chryseis is touching, even though the craft used by Ulysses in arousing her jealousy cannot be described as profound—the love-sick King Agamemnon sinks into something very like a parody of passion, and is in no sense what he calls "a gainer" by having exchanged his Homeric for a "heroic" personality.—WARD, ADOLPHUS WILLIAM, 1875–99, *A History of English Dramatic Literature, vol.* III, *p.* 424.

Thomas Hearne

1678–1735

An eminent English antiquary, was born in 1678 in the parish of White Waltham, Berkshire, and had his education at St. Edmund Hall, Oxford, where he graduated B. A. in 1699. Two years later he was appointed to a post in the Bodleian Library of which in 1712 he became second keeper. This office he was obliged to resign in 1716 from his inability to take the oaths to the government, but he continued to live at Oxford occupied entirely with his studies. He died 10th June 1735. Hearne compiled and edited no less than forty-one works, all stamped by painful and laborious learnings, although poor in style and somewhat rambling in method. They are usually marred by the intrusion of irrelevant matter—even his Jacobitism crept into his prefaces; yet they remain solid contributions to bibliography, and their author deserved better than to be gibbeted in the Dunciad as a dull and dusty pedant. His most important books were Reliquiæ Bodleianæ (1703), Leland's Itinerary (9 vols. 1710–12), Leland's Collectanea (6 vols. 1715), A Collection of Curious Discourses upon English Antiquities (1720); and the editions of Camden's Annals (3 vols. 1717), Alured of Beverley (1716), William of Newburgh (1719), Fordun's Scotichronicon (1722), Robert of Gloucester's Chronicle (1724), and that of Peter Langtoft (1725). The Bibliotheca Hearniana was published in 1848; Reliquiæ Hearnianæ, by Philip Bliss, in 1857. The third volume of Remarks and Collections of Thomas Hearne appeared in 1889, edited by C. E. Doble for the Oxford Historical Society. See Impartial Memorials of his life by several hands (1736), and the Lives of Leland, Hearne, and Wood (Oxford, 1772).—PATRICK, DAVID, 1897, *ed. Chambers's Encyclopædia, vol.* V, *p.* 604.

PERSONAL

(?) But who is he, in closet close y-pent,
Of sober face, with learned dust besprent?
Right well mine eyes arede the myster wight,
On parchment scraps y-fed and Wormius hight.
To future ages may thy dulness last,
As thou preserv'st the dulness of the past!

—POPE, ALEXANDER, 1728, *The Dunciad, pt.* iii, *v.* 185–190.

The son of a parish clerk in Berkshire, he was taken while a boy into the service of Mr. Cherry, and employed to clean knives, and help in the kitchen. He neglected his menial duties for books, which brought him into discredit with his fellow-servants, and got him the favour of his master, who sent him to school and college. He was singularly uncouth in his person and manners, his countenance was dull, and he was not a man of powerful intellect. But his industry was unbounded, his passion for poring over classical and mediæval manuscripts intense, and he rendered considerable service to literature by printing the text of many valuable works. Having become Roman catholic and non-juror through independent inquiry, he sacrificed his pecuniary interests to his principles, and had a claim to respect for his integrity even more than for his learning.—ELWIN, WHITWELL, 1872, *ed., The Works of Alexander Pope, vol.* VIII, *p.* 269, *note.*

Prejudiced up to the eyes as this bookworm of bookworms is, even the least of the sympathisers with his ecclesiastical or political opinions cannot refrain from admiring the disinterestedness of his labours. His whole thoughts were centered in the success of his principles, or in the advancement of learning; and he pursued his course with unflagging spirit, although his means at home were but scant and his enemies at the university took advantage of his sympathies with the vanquished cause to hinder his advancement. —COURTNEY, W. P., 1887, *The Academy, vol.* 31, *p.* 4.

Hearne again! May not one wonder what there is in this Hearne that volume after volume of choosings from his handwritten books of jottings is given to the world, in good paper and print? Indeed, the great number of American reader-folk need not take any shame to themselves if they cannot recall the man to mind. . . . We may say that we should like an etching of this steadfast, trusty, possibly a little crabbed, "Jacobite" and (half)? "non-juror." There are many chances to one that he was not handsome, or "distinguished"-looking, or well-dressed; he may have been ungainly, even rawboned and coarse-skinned; but, being a shrewd man, with eyes quick to watch those about him, and the comers and goers, in times when it was "touch-and-go" with any man of any account, we should like a glimpse of him, caught in a twinkling. His wig might be a little awry; a grim smile might float about his tightened lips as he wrote, glibly, how "that old smooth-booted, self-interested, ambitious, paultry Lancaster" (the Vice-Chancellor of the University—and a Whig, of course) had met a rebuff, or mortification; or his brows might have been knitted, and his teeth set, while he put down, in black and white, what "that sneaking, snivelling" wretch, and his likes, were plotting. —LOWELL, R. T. S., 1890, *The Nation, vol.* 50, *pp.* 247, 248.

GENERAL

"Pox on't," says Time to Thomas Hearne,
"Whatever I forget, you learn."

—ANON, 1727, *A Collection of Epigrams.*

The last who has dug deep into the mine was Thomas Hearne, a clerk of

Oxford, poor in fortune, and indeed, poor in understanding. His minute and obscure diligence, his voracious and undistinguishing appetite, and the coarse vulgarity of his taste and style, have exposed him to the ridicule of idle wits. Yet it cannot be denied that Thomas Hearne has gathered many gleanings of the harvest; and if his own prefaces are filled with crude and extraneous matter, his editions will always be recommended by their accuracy and use.—GIBBON, EDWARD, 1794, *An Address, Miscellaneous Works, ed. Sheffield.*

The ridicule and satire which once pursued the person and the publications of the author, are now forgotten; and Hearne stands upon a pedestal which may be said to have truth and honour for its basis. His works, which present us with portions of History, chiefly local, are now coveted by the antiquary, and respected by the scholar. The "old" and the "young," professedly attached to book collecting, can never be thoroughly happy, if their *Hearnëan Series* be not complete. —DIBDIN, THOMAS FROGNALL, 1824, *The Library Companion, p.* 215.

As he grew older his attention was chiefly confined to English history and antiquities, and after publishing the "Itinerary" and "Collectanea" of John Leland he began his well-known series of editions of the English chroniclers; they were all published by subscription, very few copies of each being printed. Their importance to historical students can scarcely be exaggerated, many of them being the only editions that existed till the recent publication of the Rolls Series of historical works, and some being still the only editions in print. Hearne accomplished all this with little help from others, with only the income he derived from his susbcribers, and with the chief authorities of the university looking askance at him. It is satisfactory to know that he lived to see what he had published for 2*l.* 2s. sold for 12*l.* 12s. and that at his death over 1000*l.* was found in his possession. He does not show any grasp of history, and for the most part he contented himself with seeing his manuscripts carefully through the press; but his accuracy is generally to be depended on, though his explanations of words are not always satisfactory. His prefaces do not give the information which would be expected of the contents of the volumes or even of the history and condition of the manuscripts from which he printed. His appendices contain all kinds of extraneous matters, having in most cases no connection with the author they follow. He was certainly wanting in power to distinguish the relative value of what fell in his way; it seemed to him enough that a document was old to induce him to publish it.—LUARD, REV. H. R., 1891, *Dictionary of National Biography, vol.* XXV, *p.* 336.

George Sale

1697?-1736

George Sale, 1680–1736, an English lawyer and a learned Orientalist, was a contributor (of the cosmogony, Oriental papers, &c.) to the "Universal History," to the "General Dictionary, Historical and Critical," and to other works, but is best known by his "Translation from the Original Arabick, with Explanatory Notes, taken from the Most Approved Commentators, with a Preliminary Discourse, of the Koran, commonly called the Alcoran, of Mahomed," Lon., 1734, 4to.—ALLIBONE, S. AUSTIN, 1870, *Dictionary of English Literature, vol.* II, *p.* 1916.

PERSONAL

The learned Sale, who first gave the world a genuine version of the Koran, and who had so zealously laboured in forming that "Universal History" which was the pride of our country, pursued his studies through a life of want—and this great orientalist (I grieve to degrade the memoirs of a man of learning by such mortifications), when he quitted his studies too often wanted a change of linen, and often wandered in the streets in search of some compassionate friend who would supply him with the meal of the day!—DISRAELI, ISAAC, 1812–13, *The Rewards of Oriental Students, Calamities of Authors, note.*

GENERAL

Our honest and learned translator, Sale, . . . who is half a Mussulman. . . . Sale had accurately studied the language and character of his author.—GIBBON,

EDWARD, 1776–88, *History of the Decline and Fall of the Roman Empire.*

Sale's chief work, on which his claim to remembrance principally rests, is his version of the Koran. This first appeared in November 1734, in a quarto volume, and was dedicated to Lord Carteret. While apologising for delay in its publication, he stated that the work "was carried on at leisure times only, amidst the necessary avocations of a troublesome profession." As a translator, he had the field almost entirely to himself. The only full translation of the Koran in any modern language previously published was the despicable French version by André Du Ryer, issued in 1649. A very poor English rendering of Du Ryer's from French was issued by Alexander Ross (1590–1654) in London in the same year. Despite a few errors, Sale's translation is remarkably accurate. Throughout he has made full use of native commentators, as regards both the interpretation of the text and its illustration in the notes. It may perhaps be regretted that he did not preserve the division into verses, as Savary has since done, instead of connecting them into a continuous narrative. Some of the poetical spirit is unavoidably lost by Sale's method. But his version remains the best in any language. His translation was reprinted in octavo in 1764, 1795, 1801, and frequently afterwards. . . . Voltaire wrote in the "Dictionnaire Philosophique" that "the learned Sale had at last enlightened us by a faithful translation of the Alcoran, and a most instructive preface to it." Sale's preliminary discourse and notes display a remarkable acquaintance not only with the works of European writers upon mohammedanism and its history, but also with native Arab literature. The preface and notes are still reckoned among the best sources of information with regard to the faith of Islam and the mohammedan peoples.—LYON, H. THOMSON, 1897, *Dictionary of National Biography, vol.* L, *pp.* 179, 180.

Eustace Budgell

1686–1737

This writer was born August 19, 1686, being the son of Gilbert Budgell, D. D., of St. Thomas, Exeter, by his first wife Mary, only daughter of Bishop Gulston of Bristol. The latter's sister was the wife of Lancelot, and thereby mother of Joseph Addison, thus making the two essayists cousins in the second degree. Eustace Budgell entered Trinity College, Oxford, March 31, 1705. Afterward he entered the Inner Temple, and was called to the bar. His intimacy with Addison rather drew him to literature. Thirty-seven papers in "The Spectator" are, by Drake, ascribed to him. By many he is called an imitator of Addison. He undertook some independent literary ventures. In 1771 the death of his father brought to him a considerable fortune. On the accession of George I., he became under secretary to Addison. In 1717 Addison secured for him the place of accountant general. He lost his fortune in the South Sea speculations. Misfortune followed mishap, along with actions savoring of dishonesty, as in the alleged forging of a will, till he at last, in 1737, May 4, committed suicide by drowning. His life was an active if not a successful one. He did much in the way of pamphlet writing, and had to do with "The Bee" as well as "The Spectator." He was also known as one of the Grub Street writers.—ROE, ALFRED S., 1890, *ed. Sir Roger De Coverley Papers, p.* 9.

PERSONAL

Let Budgel charge low Grubstreet on his quill,
And write whate'er he please except my Will.

—POPE, ALEXANDER, 1735, *Epistle to Dr. Arbuthnot, v.* 378–9.

We talked of a man's drowning himself. *Johnson:* "I should never think it time to make away with myself." I put the case of Eustace Budgell, who was accused of forging a will, and sunk himself in the Thames, before the trial of its authenticity came on. "Suppose sir," said I, "that a man is absolutely sure, that, if he lives a few days longer, he shall be detected in a fraud, the consequence of which will be utter disgrace and expulsion from society." *Johnson:* "Then, Sir, let him go abroad to a distant country; let him go to some place where he is *not* known: Don't let him go to the devil, where he *is* known."—JOHNSON, SAMUEL, 1773, *Life by Boswell.*

From the fate of this misguided man a useful lesson may be drawn; though possessed of considerable abilities, of a competent fortune, of great and powerful connections, and admired and respected in the early period of his life, the pride of self-opinion, and the fury of ungoverned resentment, blasted all his hopes and views, and gradually led him into the commission of errors and extravagances, which at length terminated in gaming, forgery, infidelity, and suicide. —DRAKE, NATHAN, 1804–14, *Essays, Illustrative of the Tatler, Spectator, and Guardian, vol.* III, *p.* 17.

A man of extreme vanity and vindictive feeling.—CHAMBERS, ROBERT, 1876, *Cyclopædia of English Literature, ed. Carruthers.*

GENERAL

As an author where he does not speak of himself, and does not give a loose to his vanity, he is a very agreeable and deserving writer; not argumentative or deep; but very ingenious and entertaining; and his stile is peculiarly elegant, so as to deserve being ranked in that respect with Addison's, and is superior to most of the other English writers.—CIBBER, THEOPHILUS, 1753, *Lives of the Poets, vol.* V, *p.* 14.

He told us that "Addison wrote Budgell's papers in 'The Spectator;' at least mended them so much, that he made them almost his own; and that Draper, Tonson's partner, assured Mrs. Johnson, that the much admired Epilogue to 'The Distressed Mother,' which came out in Budgell's name, was in reality written by Addison." —JOHNSON, SAMUEL, 1776, *Life by Boswell, ed. Hill, vol.* III, *p.* 53.

Budgell was a man of lively talents, a good taste, and a well informed mind. In vigour of intellect he was inferior to Steele, but superior to him in elegant learning.—BISSET, ROBERT, 1793, *A Biographical Sketch of the Authors of the Spectator, p.* 215.

However erroneous or vicious we may esteem the conduct of Budgell, it is with pleasure that we can mention his contributions to the Spectator and Guardian, as displaying both the cheerfulness and gaiety of an innocent mind, and the best and soundest precepts of morality and religion. At the time of their composition, indeed, he was more directly under the influence and direction of his accomplished relation than at any subsequent period of his life, and he then possessed the laudable ambition of doing all that might render him worthy of his affection and support.—DRAKE, NATHAN, 1804–14. *Essays, Illustrative of the Tatler, Spectator and Guardian, vol.* III, *p.* 24.

Budgell was a rough, vigorous, dissipated barrister, who preferred making a figure in the coffee-houses and in literature to the practice of his profession. His humour is comparatively obstreperous, of the Defoe and Macaulay type, which the French seem to consider peculiarly English. It is genial rather from the author's hearty enjoyment of the fun he is making than from any sympathy with the objects of his derision.—MINTO, WILLIAM, 1872–80, *Manual of English Prose Literature, p.* 404.

Thirty-seven numbers of the "Spectator" are ascribed to Budgell; and though Dr. Johnson says that these were either written by Addison, or so much improved by him that they were made in a manner his own, there seems to be no sufficient authority for the assertion. It is true that the style and humour resemble those of Addison; but as the two writers were much together, a successful attempt on Budgell's part to imitate the productions of his friend, was probable enough.—CHAMBERS, ROBERT, 1876, *Cyclopædia of English Literature, ed. Carruthers.*

He shared Addison's lodgings during the last years of Queen Anne, and took a considerable part in the "Spectator." Thirty-seven papers are ascribed to him. They are palpable imitations of Addison's manner. One of them (No. 116) is an account of Sir Roger de Coverley in the hunting-field. Johnson mentions a report that Addison had "mended them so much that they were almost his own." It was also said that Addison was also the real author of an epilogue to Ambrose Philip's "Distressed Mother," the "most successful ever spoken in an English theatre;" and had Budgell's name substituted for his own at the last moment, to strengthen his young cousin's claims to a place.—STEPHEN, LESLIE, 1886, *Dictionary of National Biography, vol.* VII, *p.* 224.

John Strype

1643-1737

John Strype was the son of a German refugee who fled to England on account of his religion, and there followed the business of a silk merchant. The son was born in London, in 1643, and educated at Catherine Hall, Cambridge. At that university, and also at Oxford, he took his master's degree, in 1671. Entering into orders, he became successively curate of Theydon-Boys, in Essex, preacher in Low Leyton, rector of Terring, in Sussex, and lecturer at Hackney. He resigned his clerical charges in 1724, and from that time till his death, which occurred in 1737, he resided at Hackney, with an apothecary, who had married his grand-daughter. Strype was an industrious and even laborious collector of literary antiquities. His works afford ample illustrations of ecclesiastical history and biography, at periods of deep national interest and importance, and they are now ranked among the most valuable of English standard memorials. His writings consist of a "Life of Archbishop Cranmer;" a "Life of Sir Thomas Smith;" a "Life of Bishop Aylmer;" a "Life of Sir John Cheke;" "Annals of the Reformation," in four volumes; a "Life of Archbishop Grindal;" "Life and Letters of Archbishop Parker;" "Life of Archbishop Whitgift;" and "Ecclesiastical Memorials," in three volumes. He also edited Stow's "Survey of London," and part of Dr. Lightfoot's works.—MILLS, ABRAHAM, 1851, *The Literature and the Literary Men of Great Britain and Ireland, vol.* II, *p.* 234.

GENERAL

Of *Strype*, it would be impossible to speak too highly. His labours have supplied us with some of the most necessary, as well as instructive, portions of Church history. . . . A writer, who, all fidelity, and honest and honourable in the letter and spirit of every thing which he wrote, seems, nevertheless, too frequently to have been under the influence of a somnolency which it was impossible to shake off. Strype is a fine, solid, instructive fellow, for a large arm chair, in a gothic study, before a winter's fire; but you must not deposit him on the shelves of your *Tusculum*—to be carried to rustic seats in arbours and bowers; by the side of gurgling streams or rushing cascades. There is neither fancy, nor brilliancy, nor buoyancy, about him; he is a sage to consult, rather than a companion to enliven.—DIBDIN, THOMAS FROGNALL, 1824, *The Library Companion, pp.* 117, *note,* 516.

Honest John Strype.—HALLAM, HENRY, 1837-39, *Introduction to the Literature of Europe, pt.* i, *ch.* v, *par.* 25, *note.*

I have no wish to cavil at what Strype says, and I think no one feels more strongly than I do the value of his work; but really it is one great inconvenience of the careless way in which he wrote, that one cannot bring one passage to correct another, without a high probability of its containing something in itself which needs correction. . . . We are certainly much indebted to Strype for publishing many manuscripts which he found in old collections, but we must receive what he says of them, and from them, with a constant recollection that, in his estimation, one old manuscript appears to have been about as good as another.—MAITLAND, SAMUEL ROFFEY, 1849-99, *Essays on Subjects Connected with the Reformation in England, ed. Hutton, pp.* 31, *note,* 47.

His works have been printed in 27 vols., 8vo. . . . and though valuable as store houses of information, are of the Dryasdust order.—HART, JOHN S., 1872, *A Manual of English Literature, p.* 255.

The most famous antiquary of the period.—MINTO, WILLIAM, 1872-80, *Manual af English Prose Literature, p.* 403.

Strype's lack of literary style, unskilful selection of materials, and unmethodical arrangement render his books tiresome to the last degree. Even in his own day his cumbrous appendixes caused him to be nicknamed the "appendix-monger." His want of critical faculty led him into serious errors, such as the attribution of Edward VI of the foundation of many schools which had existed long before that king's reign. . . . To students of the ecclesiastical and political history of England in the sixteenth century the vast accumulations of facts and documents of which his books consist render them of the utmost value.—GOODWIN, GORDON, 1898, *Dictionary of National Biography, vol.* LV, *p.* 68.

Matthew Green

1696–1737

Matthew Green was born in 1696, and died in 1737; held a position in the Custom House; and was distinguished as a poet and wit. He wrote "The Grotto," and other poems; but his most noted production is "The Spleen," whose cheerful, thoughtful octosyllabics dealt with remedy for the depression of spirits which was said to have its source in the spleen.—MORLEY, HENRY, 1879, *A Manual of English Literature, ed. Tyler*, p. 546.

PERSONAL

We find that he had obtained a place in the Custom house, the duties of which he is said to have discharged with great diligence and fidelity. It is further attested, that he was a man of great probity and sweetness of disposition, and that his conversation abounded with wit, but of the most inoffensive kind. He seems to have been subject to low spirits, as a relief from which he composed his principal poem, "The Spleen."—AIKIN, JOHN, 1820, *Select Works of the British Poets.*

THE SPLEEN

1737

His poem, "The Spleen," was never published during his lifetime. Glover, his warm friend, presented it to the world after his death; and it is much to be regretted, did not prefix any account of its interesting author. It was originally a very short copy of verses, and was gradually and piecemeal increased. Pope speedily noticed its merit, Melmoth praised its strong originality in Fitzosborne's Letters, and Gray duly commended it in his correspondence with Walpole, when it appeared in Dodsley's collection. In that walk of poetry, where Fancy aspires no further than to go hand in hand with common sense, its merit is certainly unrivalled. —CAMPBELL, THOMAS, 1819, *Specimens of the British Poets.*

Such is this singular poem on the "Spleen," which few persons, it is imagined, will once read, without frequent re-perusals, every one of which will be repaid by new discoveries of uncommon and ingenious turns of thought. It possesses that undoubted mark of excellence, the faculty of impressing the memory with many of its strong sentiments and original images: and perhaps not more lines of "Hudibras" itself have been retained by its admirers, than of this poem.—AIKIN, JOHN, 1820, *An Essay on the Poems of Green.*

Something of the quaker may be observable in the stiffness of his versification, and its excessive endeavors to be succinct. His style has also the fault of beng occasionally obscure; and his wit is sometimes more labored than finished. But all that he says is worth attending to. His thoughts are the result of his own feeling and experience; his opinions rational and cheerful, if not very lofty; his warnings against meddling with superhuman mysteries admirable; and he is remarkable for the brevity and originality of his similes. He is of the school of Butler; and it may be affirmed of him as a rare honor, that no man since Butler has put so much wit and reflection into the same compass of lines.—HUNT, LEIGH, 1846, *Wit and Humor*, p. 242.

"The Spleen," a reflective effusion in octosyllabic verse, is somewhat striking from an air of originality in the vein of thought, and from the labored concentration and epigrammatic point of the language; but, although it was much cried up when it first appeared, and the laudation has continued to be duly echoed by succeeding formal criticism, it may be doubted if many readers could now make their way through it without considerable fatigue, or if it be much read in fact at all. With all its ingenious or energetic rhetorical posture-making, it has nearly as little real play of fancy as charm of numbers, and may be most properly characterized as a piece of bastard or perverted Hudibrastic,—an imitation of the manner of Butler to the very dance of his verse, only without the comedy,—the same antics, only solemnized or made to carry a moral and serious meaning.—CRAIK, GEORGE L., 1861, *A Compendious History of English Literature and of the English Language, vol.* II, p. 275.

Green suffered really or poetically from the fashionable eighteenth-century disorder which Pope has so well described in "The Rape of the Lock," and in this "motley piece," as he calls it, he sets forth the various expedients which he employed to evade his enemy. Taken altogether, his precepts constitute a code of philosophy not unlike that advocated in more than one of the Odes of Horace. To observe the religion of the body; to cultivate cheerfulness and calm; to keep a middle course, and possess his soul in quiet; content, as regards the future, to ignore what Heaven withholds,—such are the chief features of his plan. But, in developing his principles he takes occasion to deal many a side-long stroke at imperfect humanity, and not always at those things only which are opposed to his theory of conduct. Female education, faction, law, religious sects, reform, speculation, place-hunting, poetry, ambition,—all these are briefly touched and seldom left unmarked by some quivering shaft of ridicule. Towards the end of the poem comes an ideal picture of rural retirement, which may be compared with the joint version by Pope and Swift of Horace's sixth satire in the second book; and the whole closes with the writer's views upon immorality and a summary of his practice. Regarded as a whole, we can recall few discursive poems which contain so much compact expression and witty illustration. The author was evidently shrewd and observant, and unusually gifted in the detection of grotesque aspects and remote affinities.—DOBSON, AUSTIN, 1880, *English Poets, ed. Ward, vol.* III, *p.* 195.

He is remembered by his poem of "The Spleen;" less known than it deserves to be to modern readers. It contains less than nine hundred lines; is full of happy expressions, and evidently the production of a profound, original, and independent thinker.—SARGENT, EPES, 1880–81, *Harper's Cyclopædia of British and American Poetry, p.* 154.

It was one of the most original works of the day; and I am not sure that anything so good, of the same kind, is to be found in our later literature. There is something of the humour of Butler in its fluent and yet vigorous octosyllabic couplets; but the character of the thought and its mode of expression are Green's own. He was almost Pope's equal in the art of packing a thought into terse and pithy phrases.—ADAMS, W. H. DAVENPORT, 1886, *Good Queen Anne, vol.* II, *p.* 351.

In style and temper he was astonishingly like his French contemporary, J. B. L. Gresset (1709–1777), whose poems, first printed in 1734, it is needless to say Green had never heard of. He is a master of refined philosophic wit and gentle persiflage; his delicate raillery is without the least element of rancour; he addresses a little circle of private friends, and is charming because so easy, natural, and sincere. . . . It calls forth the reader's surprise to note how wide a range of reflection Green's little poem moves across, yet whatever his witty muse touches she adorns. The originality of Matthew Green, the fact that he never wastes a line by repeating a commonplace, together with his fine cheerfulness as of a Jabez, desiring neither poverty nor riches, makes us regret that he left so little behind him, and so narrowly escaped the poppy of oblivion.—GOSSE, EDMUND, 1888, *A History of Eighteenth Century Literature, pp.* 216, 217.

The "Spleen," written in Swift's favourite octosyllabic metre, is one of the best poems of its class.—STEPHEN, LESLIE, 1890, *Dictionary of National Biography, vol.* XXIII, *p.* 51.

GENERAL

All there is of M. Green here, has been printed before; there is a profusion of wit everywhere; reading would have formed his judgment, and harmonised his verse, for even his wood-notes often break out into strains of real poetry and music.—GRAY, THOMAS, 1751, *Letter to Horace Walpole.*

We incline to think that if it be not, as a whole, a *poem*, it sparkles, at least, with some genuine *poetry*. We are far from wishing to exalt Green to the topmost summits of Parnassus, but surely the critic who praised Blackmore, and Pitt, and "Rag Smith" might have spared a word and a smile for the many poetical and brilliant thoughts to be found in the "Spleen." Green's chief power, however, lay not in imagination, nor perhaps even in art, so much as in keen, strong sense, which he has the power, too, of shaping into the most condensed couplets and sharp-edged lines. . . . Pope, when he read the "Spleen," said "there was a great deal of originality in it." There are, here and there, indeed, traces of resemblance to "Hudibras" and to "Alma," but on the whole, Green has a brain, an eye, and a tongue of his own—a brain piercing if not profound—an eye clear if not comprehensive—and an utterance terse and vigorous, if not grand and lyrical.—GILFILLAN, GEORGE, 1858, *ed., The Poetical Works of Armstrong, Dyer and Green, pp*, 236, 237, 238.

A poet of whimsical and dainty vein, who wrote with great sprightliness of humor and lightness of touch.—MINTO, WILLIAM, 1894, *The Literature of the Georgian Era, ed. Knight, p.* 129.

Elizabeth Rowe

1674-1737

Miscellaneous writer, was the daughter of a dissenting minister at Ilchester, where she was born in 1674. She was married to Thomas Rowe, a young littérateur, who lived a few years after; upon which she retired to Frome, where she resided for the remainder of her life. Her principal works are, "Friendship in Death," "Letters, Morals and Entertaining," and "Devout Exercises of the Heart." Died, 1737.—CATES, WILLIAM L. R., 1867, *ed., A Dictionary of General Biography, p.* 975.

PERSONAL

She had the happiest command over her passions, and maintained a constant calmness of temper, and sweetness of disposition, that could not be ruffled by adverse accidents. She was in the utmost degree an enemy to ill-natured satire and detraction; she was as much unacquainted with envy, as if it had been impossible for so base a passion to enter into the human mind. She had few equals in conversation; her wit was lively, and she expressed her thoughts in the most beautiful and flowing eloquence.—CIBBER, THEOPHILUS, 1753, *Lives of the Poets, vol.* IV, *p.* 340.

This highly accomplished woman had a great share of all the personal charms that awaken love, as she had all the virtues to rivet it. Her stature was of the true standard; her hair of the most pleasing colour; and her eyes were inclined to blue, and full of fire: her complexion was fair, and often suffused by a modest blush; her voice was soft, as her manners were gentle: in short, she was all that man can form an idea of excellence and beauty.—NOBLE, MARK, 1806, *A Biographical History of England, vol.* III, *p.* 310.

She made it her duty to soften the anxieties, and heighten all the satisfactions, of his life. Her capacity for superior things did not tempt her to neglect the less honourable cares which the laws of custom and decency impose on the female sex, in the connubial state; and much less was she led by a sense of her own merit, to assume anything to herself inconsistent with that duty and submission which the precepts of Christian piety so expressly enjoin.—HALE, SARAH JOSEPHA, 1852, *Woman's Record, p.* 493.

GENERAL

Let all my pow'rs, with awe profound,
While Philomela sings,
Attend the rapture of the sound,
And my devotion rise on her seraphic wings.
—WATTS, ISAAC, 1706, *To Mrs. Elizabeth Singer.*

I have just finished Mrs Rowe's "Letters from the Dead to the Living"—and moral and entertaining,—I had heard a great deal of them before I saw them, and am sorry to tell you I was much disappointed with them: they are so very enthusiastick, that the religion she preaches rather disgusts and cloys than charms and elevates—and so romantick, that every word betrays improbability, instead of disguising fiction, and displays the Author, instead of human nature.—BURNEY, FRANCES, 1768, *Early Diary, ed. Ellis, vol.* I, *p.* 8.

Her strongest bent was to poetry. So prevalent was her genius this way, that her very prose hath all the charms of verse without the fetters; the same fire and elevation, the same bright images, bold figures, and rich and flowing diction. She could hardly write a single letter but it bore the stamp of the poet.—BURDER, SAMUEL, 1815-34, *Memoirs of Eminently Pious Women, p.* 222.

In the year 1736, Mrs. Rowe published her poem, called "The History of Joseph," to which, at the urgent request of her friend Lady Hertford, she afterwards wrote a sequel, in two books, which was published early in 1737. In this poem there is a larger accumulation of historical knowledge than in all her other compositions put together. Having a natural faculty for narration, she has not only told the story fluently, in easy couplets of heroic verse, but also introduced so many apt illustrations and entertaining episodes as to make the eight first books pleasant reading. The ninth and tenth are of inferior merit, presenting merely a rhymed repetition of Scripture facts, and, consequently, a depreciating recital. . . . Her style, both in prose and verse, was formed on that of Addison, preserving much of the elegance of her model, with still greater ease, copiousness and luxuriance. She wrote with facility, and delighted in the act; but she was not a fastidious critic, and loathed the toil of revision. Her translations from the Italian of Tasso, Guarini, and Rolli and from the French of Racine, are respectable. She is never at a loss for words, and although her mind calls for no exact definitions or fine gradations of meaning, she strikes off the general sense of things successfully. . . . Her hymns want conciseness. —WILLIAMS, JANE, 1861, *The Literary Women of England, pp.* 166, 168, 169.

Mrs. Rowe's most popular literary compositions took an epistolary form, which she employed with much skill. In 1728 she published "Friendship in Death, in twenty Letters from the Dead to the Living" (3rd edit. 1733, 5th edit. 1738, and many other editions until 1816). Here she gave a curiously realistic expression to her faith in the soul's immortality. "Thoughts on Death," translated from the Moral Essays of "Messieurs de Port Royal," was appended. A second epistolary venture, "Letters Moral and Entertaining" (pt. i. 1729, pt. ii. 1731, and pt. iii. 1733), was undertaken with the pious intention of exciting religious sentiment in the careless and dissipated. But the frankess with which Mrs. Rowe's imaginary characters acquaint each other with their profane experiences lends her volumes some secular interest. Dr. Johnson, while commending Mrs. Rowe's "brightness of imagery" and "purity of sentiment" in this work, describes the author as the earliest English writer to employ with success "the ornaments of romance in the decoration of religion." —LEE, SIDNEY, 1897, *Dictionary of National Biography, vol.* XLIX, *p.* 339.

John Asgill

1659–1738

John Asgill, an eccentric writer, born at Hanley Castle, Worcestershire, in 1659, was called to the bar in 1692. Having got into difficulties, he sailed in 1699 for Ireland, where an act for the resumption of forfeited estates promised plenty of lawsuits. His talents gained him a lucrative practice; and in 1703 he obtained a seat in the Irish parliament. Three years before, however, he had published a paradoxical pamphlet, bepraised by Coleridge, to prove that by the rules of English law the redeemed need not die. Much to his own surprise, the Irish parliament voted this a blasphemous libel, and expelled its author from the House. In 1705 he returned to England, and entered the English parliament as member for Bramber, in Sussex. But the fame of his unlucky pamphlet haunted him; for the English House condemned it to be burned by the common hangman, and expelled Asgill in 1707. At last he found peace in the King's Bench and the Fleet, where he died in November 1738.—PATRICK AND GROOME, *eds.*, 1897, *Chambers's Biographical Dictionary, p.* 46.

GENERAL

Nay, there's a wit has found, as I am told,
New ways to heaven, despairing of the old.
He swears he'll spoil the clerk and sexton's trade:
Bells shall no more be rung, nor graves be made,
The hearse and six no longer be in fashion,
Since all the faithful may expect translation.
What think you of the project? I'm for trying.
I'll lay aside these foolish thoughts of dying,
Preserve my youth and vigour for the stage,
And be translated in a good old age.
—ROWE, NICHOLAS, 1700, *The Ambitious Stepmother, Epilogue.*

Asgill was an extraordinary man, and his pamphlet is invaluable. He undertook to prove that man is literally immortal; or rather, that any given living man might probably never die. He complains of the cowardly practice of dying. He was expelled from two Houses of Commons for

blasphemy and atheism, as was pretended; I really suspect because he was a staunch Hanoverian. I expected to find the ravings of an enthusiast, or the sullen snarlings of an infidel; whereas I found the very soul of Swift—an intense half self-deceived humorism. I scarcely remember elsewhere such uncommon skill in logic, such lawyer-like acuteness, and yet such a grasp of common sense. Each of his paragraphs is in itself a whole, and yet a link between the preceding and following; so that the entire series forms one argument, and yet each is a diamond in itself.
—COLERIDGE, SAMUEL TAYLOR, 1831, *Table Talk, July* 30.

If it be true that he nearly attained the age of an hundred (as one statement represents), and with these happy faculties unimpaired, he may have been tempted to imagine that he was giving the best and only convincing proof of his own argument. Death undeceived him, and Time has done him justice at last. For though it stands recorded that he was expelled the House of Commons as being the Author of a Book in which are contained many profane and blaspheous expressions, highly reflecting upon the Christian Religion! nothing can be more certain than that this censure was undeserved, and that his expulsion upon that ground was as indefensible as it would have been becoming, if, in pursuance of the real motives by which the House was actuated, an Act had been passed disqualifying from that time forward any person in a state of insolvency from taking or retaining a seat there. In the year 1760 I find him mentioned as "the celebrated gentleman commonly called Translated Asgill." His name is now seen only in catalogues, and his history known only to the curious.—SOUTHEY, ROBERT, 1834–47, *The Doctor, ed. Warter, ch.* clxxiii, *p.* 456.

On the whole, Asgill does not deserve to be forgotten. His noble crochets, quaint puzzling paradoxes, and vivid faith; his wonderful luck and sang-froid, his absolute sincerity, his inability to bend to a compromise his utter absence of worldly-mindedness, and his remarkable logical dexterity—these shadow him forth as a distinctive figure—that of a man we feel we should like to become better acquainted with. He is a strange compound in creed of what we should now style Swedenborgianism and of views held by those whom we should to-day call advanced Christians. To the latter section of thought would belong his faith in the Christian scheme only on the basis of its universality. With the former system he has much in common. . . . What appears to have greatly offended the orthodox of Asgill's day is a certain jocularity of expression that is evidently natural to him. But the seriousness at the root of his nature is thorough, beyond a doubt; indeed, he gives us the impression of having a faith much like William Blake's—so much a part of his nature, and so deeply rooted within it, that he was somewhat careless as to the form into which he cast it.—COOK, KENINGALE, 1871, *John Asgill, Frazer's Magazine, n. s., vol* 4, *p.* 165.

Asgill's seriousness in the pamphlet on death was doubted at the time. A German traveller in 1710 (Offenbach's "Merkwürdige Reisen," ii. 200) gives a report that it was written in answer to a lady's challenge to show his skill in maintaining paradoxes. The book itself indicates no want of sincerity, though some ludicrous phrases were very unfairly wrested by the committee of the English House of Commons to colour the charge of blasphemy. It interprets the relations between God and man by the technical rules of English law. Death being the penalty imposed by Adam's sin, and Christ having satisfied the law, death could no longer be legally inflicted, and all who claim their rights will be exempt. Asgill professes that, having claimed his discharge, he expects "to make his exit by way of translation." The book is written in pithy detached sentences. Coleridge declares that there is no "genuine Saxon English" finer than Asgill's; thinks his irony often finer than Swift's; and calls him "a consummate artist in the statement of his case." The praise seems excessive, though not groundless; but we may accept Coleridge's conclusion that Asgill was a humorist who did not himself know how far he was serious. Full extracts may be found in Southey's "Doctor." In recent years Asgill found a disciple in a Mr. Tresham Gregg, an Irish clergyman, who republished the pamphlet with some introductory notes.—STEPHEN, LESLIE, 1885, *Dictionary of National Biography, vol.* II, *p.* 160.

George Lillo

1693–1739

Born, in London, 4 Feb. 1693. Assisted his father in jewellery business. Play "Silvia" produced at Drury Lane, 10 Nov. 1730; "The Merchant" (afterwards called: "The London Merchant, or the History of George Barnwell"), Drury Lane, 22 June 1731; "Britannia, or the Royal Lovers," Covent Garden, 11 Feb. 1734; "The Christian Hero," Drury Lane, 13 Jan. 1735; "Fatal Curiosity," Haymarket, 1736; "Marina" (adapted from "Pericles"), Covent Garden, 1 Aug. 1738; "Elmerick," posthumously produced, Drury Lane, 23 Feb. 1740; adaptation of "Arden of Faversham," posthumously produced, Drury Lane, 19 July 1759. Died, in London, 3 Sept. 1739. Buried in St. Leonard's, Shoreditch. *Works:* "Silvia" (anon.), 1731; "The London Merchant," 1731 (2nd edn. same year); "The Christian Hero," 1735; "Fatal Curiosity," 1737; "Marina," 1738. *Posthumous:* "Britannia and Batavia," 1740; "Elmerick," 1740; "Arden of Faversham" (adapted), 1762. *Collected Works:* ed. by T. Davies, with *memoir* (2 vols.), 1775.—SHARP, R. FARQUHARSON, 1897, *A Dictionary of English Authors, p.* 169.

PERSONAL

He had a perfect knowledge of human nature, though his contempt of all base means of application, which are the necessary steps to great acquaintance, restrained his conversation within very narrow bounds. He had the spirit of an old Roman, joined to a primitive Christian He was content with his little state of life, in which his excellent temper of mind gave him an happiness beyond the power of riches; and it was necessary for his friends to have a sharp insight into his want of their services, as well as good inclination, and abilities, to serve him. In short, he was one of the best of men, and those who knew him best, will most regret his loss.—FIELDING, HENRY, 1740, *The Champion.*

As a man he was honourable and just in all the relations of life. Like Richardson, "he kept his shop, and his shop kept him." His disposition was genial, kind, and social; and though prudent and correct himself, he could tolerate error in others, and render assistance to those who too often neglected to assist themselves. —LAWRENCE, FREDERICK, 1855, *The Life of Henry Fielding, p.* 132.

It was at the rehersals for the original production of "Fatal Curiosity" at the Haymarket that Lillo's future editor and biographer, "Tom Davies," who was cast for the part of Young Wilmot, made the acquaintance of the author. He describes Lillo as plain and simple in his address, and at the same time modest, affable, and engaging in conversation. Elsewhere he states him to have been in person lusty, but not tall, and of a pleasing aspect, though deprived of the sight of one eye. —WARD, ADOLPHUS WILLIAM, 1893, *Dictionary of National Biography, vol.* XXXIII, *p.* 254.

GEORGE BARNWELL

1731

A tragedy which has been acted thirty-nine times consecutively at Drury Lane, amidst unflagging applause from a constantly crowded house; which has met with similar success wherever it has been performed; which has been printed and published to the number of many thousand copies, and is read with no less interest and pleasure than it is witnessed upon the stage—a tragedy which has called forth so many marks of approbation and esteem must occasion in those who hear it spoken of one or other of two thoughts: either that it is one of those master-pieces the perfect beauty of which is perceived by all; or that it is so well adapted to the particular taste of the nation which thus delights in it that it may be considered as a certain indication of the present state of that nation's taste.—PRÉVOST, ABBÉ, 1740, *Le Pour et Contre, vol.* III, *p.* 337.

Avaunt, ye small wits, whose quality is not so much delicacy as subtlety and frivolity; ye thankless, hardened hearts, wrecked by excess and overmuch thinking! You are not made for the sweetness of shedding tears!—CLÉMENT DE GENÈVE, 1748, *tr., Le Marchand de Londres.*

As this was almost a new species of tragedy, wrote on a very uncommon subject, he rather chose it should take its fate in the summer, than run among the more hazardous fate of encountering the winter criticks. The old ballad of "George Barnwell" (on which the story was founded) was on this occasion reprinted, and many thousands sold in one day. Many gaily-disposed spirits brought the ballad with them to the play, intending to make their pleasant remarks (as some afterwards owned) and ludicrous comparisons between the antient ditty and the modern drama. But the play was very carefully got up, and universally allowed to be well performed. The piece was thought to be well conducted, and the subject well managed, and the diction proper and natural; never low, and very rarely swelling above the characters that spoke. Mr. Pope, among other persons distinguished by their rank, or particular publick merit, had the curiosity to attend the performance, and commended the actors, and the author; and remarked, if the latter had erred through the whole play, it was only in a few places, where he had unawares led himself into a poetical luxuriancy, affecting to be too elevated for the simplicity of the subject. But the play, in general, spoke so much to the heart, that the gay persons before mentioned confessed, they were drawn in to drop their ballads, and pull out their handkerchiefs. It met with uncommon success; for it was acted above twenty times in the summer season to great audiences; was frequently bespoke by some eminent merchants and citizens, who much approved its moral tendency: and, in the winter following, was acted often to crowded houses: And all the royal family, at several different times, honoured it with their appearance. It gained reputation, and brought money to the poet, the managers, and the performers.—CIBBER, THEOPHILUS, 1753, *Lives of the Poets, vol.* V, *p.* 339.

An admirable piece of work, with a moral which goes more straight to the point than that of any French play I am acquainted with.—ROUSSEAU, JEAN-JACQUES, 1781, *Lettre sur les spectacles, note.*

On the first night of representation, the greatest part of the audience assembled to laugh, and brought with them the old ballad on the subject, as a token of ridicule; but, as the play proceeded, they became attentive, then interested, and, at length, threw down the ancient ditty, and drew forth their handkerchiefs.—INCHBALD, MRS. ELIZABETH, 1806–9, *The British Theatre, vol.* V.

"The Merchant of London" is remarkable from having been praised by Diderot and Lessing, as a model deserving of imitation. This error could only have escaped from Lessing, in the keenness of his hostility to the French conventional tone. For in reality, we must perpetually bear in mind the honest views of Lillo, to prevent us from finding "The Merchant of London" as laughable as it is certainly trival. Whoever possesses so little knowledge of the world and of men ought not to set up for a public lecturer on morals. We might draw a very different conclusion from this piece, from that which the author had in view, namely, that we ought to make young people early acquainted with prostitutes, to prevent them from entertaining a violent passion, and being at last led to steal and murder, for the first wretch who spreads her snares for them, (which they cannot possibly avoid). Besides, I cannot approve of making gallows first visible in the last scene; such a piece ought always to be acted with a place of execution in the background. With respect to the edification to be drawn from a drama of this kind, I should prefer the histories of malefactors, which are usually printed in England at executions; they contain, at least, real facts, instead of awkward fictions.—SCHLEGEL, AUGUSTUS WILLIAM, 1809, *Lectures on Dramatic Art and Literature, tr. Black, Lecture* xiii.

Lillo's domestic tragedies were what she most admired; for "My lady used to declare," said the old servant so often quoted, "that whoever did not cry at George Barnwell must deserve to be hanged."—STUART, LADY LOUISA, 1837, *The Letters and Works of Lady Mary Wortley Montagu, ed. Lord Wharncliffe, Introductory Anecdotes, vol,* I, *p.* 110.

It marks in the history of the stage the same change which Richardson introduced into the novel. Yet the comparison must not be carried too far; they agree in the most devoted respect for morality, but in art poor Lillo is the merest bungler, and by the side of Richardson he makes but a poor show.—PERRY, THOMAS SERGEANT, 1883, *English Literature in the Eighteenth Century, p.* 327.

(At the Theatre Royal, Manchester, "George Barnwell" used within a recent date to be annually performed on Shrove Tuesday). "George Barnwell" retained possession of the English stage for more than a century, and experienced some notable "revivals." Among these need only be mentioned that at Covent Garden on 28 Sept. 1796, when for the sake of her brother Charles Kemble, who appeared as the hero, Mrs. Siddons took the part of Millwood, and induced Miss Pope to act Lucy (Genest, vii. 287–8). Its popularity is further attested by various treatments of the same theme in novel and burlesque, Thackeray's "George de Barnwell" being conspicuous among the latter.—WARD, ADOLPHUS WILLIAM, 1893, *Dictionary of National Biography, vol.* XXXIII, *p.* 253.

Read again to-day, the "master-piece" of this remarkable character seems less sublime. It is a melodrama of a decidedly sombre type, highly moral, and in parts, but in parts only, full of pathos. . . . "Manon" was as yet unwritten, and who shall say that Lillo's play, which Prévost saw performed in London, and spoke of with such enthusiasm, did not count for something in the creation of his romance? However this may be, there is a touch of the rogue about Des Grieux, and Manon is too lovable; the lesson conveyed is less direct and less tragic. The manner in which the humble dissenter George Lillo determined to produce was very different. He aimed at producing a more forcible impression, and wrote, not a dramatic work, but a sermon in the form of a play. Nevertheless, crude as it is from an artistic point of view, this drama contains a presage of something great. . . . "George Barnwell," which in England was regarded as a common and rather vulgar drama of some merit, produced on the continent the impression of a work of genius, and gave the theater a new lease of life. The Germans became as enthusiastic over Lillo as over Shakespeare; Gottsched and Lessing extolled him to the skies, and the latter imitated him in "Sara Sampson." He became one of the classics of the modern drama. Yet, strange as it may seem, even to the Germans he appeared too brutal, and Sébastien Mercier's "Jenneval," a modified but inferior adaption, was played in preference.—TEXTE, JOSEPH, 1895–99, *Jean-Jacques Rousseau and the Cosmopolitan Spirit in Literature, tr. Matthews, pp.* 134, 135, 138.

FATAL CURIOSITY

1736

Long since, beneath this humble roof, this Play,
Wrought by true English Genius saw the day.
Forth from this humble roof it scarce has stray'd;
In prouder Theatres 'twas never play'd.
There you have gap'd, and doz'd o'er many a piece,
Patch'd up from France, or stol'n from Rome or Greece,
Or made of shreds from Shakespeare's Golden Fleece.
There Scholars, simple nature cast aside,
Have trick'd their heroes out in Classick pride;
No Scenes, where genuine Passion runs to waste,
But all hedg'd in by shrubs of Modern Taste.
Each Tragedy laid out like garden grounds,
One circling gravel marks its narrow bounds.
Lillo's plantations were of Forest growth—
Shakespeare's the same — Great Nature's hand in both!
Give me a tale the passions to control,
"Whose slightest word may harrow up the soul!"
A magick potion, of charm'd drugs commixt,
Where Pleasure courts, and Horror comes betwixt!

—COLMAN, GEORGE, 1782, *Prologue to Lillo's Fatal Curiosity, Works, vol.* III, *p.* 233.

Lillo had many requisites for a tragedian; he understood, either from innate taste, or critical study, the advantage to be derived from a consistent fable; and, in the tragedy of the "Fatal Curiosity," he has left the model of a plot, in which, without the help of any exterior circumstances, a train of events operating upon the characters of the dramatic persons, produce a conclusion at once the most dramatic and the most horrible that the imagination can conceive.—SCOTT, SIR WALTER, 1814–23, *Essay on the Drama.*

On the 10th of February, Lillo's most horrible tragedy of the "Fatal Curiosity" was brought out augmented by Mr. Mackenzie in a style sufficiently similar. Henderson and Mrs. Stephen Kemble rendered the audience completely miserable.—BOADEN, JAMES, 1825, *Memoirs of the Life of John Philip Kemble, vol.* I, *p.* 147.

That the play is distinguished by a

homely, genuine pathos, rarely, if ever met with, in the dramatic efforts of the age, will be admitted by every reader. In fact, Lillo was to dramatic, what Crabbe, half a century later, was to narrative poetry. If not a genuis of the highest order, he had strong and healthful sympathies; and at a period when profligacy, fustain, and affectation, held possession of the stage, it is refreshing to turn to his simple humanity and unexceptionable morality.—LAWRENCE, FREDERICK, 1855, *The Life of Henry Fielding, p.* 131.

GENERAL

Nothwithstanding the power of Lillo's works, we entirely miss in them that romantic attraction which invites to repeated perusal of them. They give us life in a close and dreadful semblance of reality, but not arrayed in the magic illusion of poetry. His strength lies in conception of situations, not in beauty of dialogue, or in the eloquence of the passions. Yet the effect of his plain and homely subjects was so strikingly superior to that of the vapid and heroic productions of the day, as to induce some of his contemporary admirers to pronounce that he had reached the acmè of dramatic excellence, and struck into the best and most genuine path of tragedy. . . . It is one question whether Lillo has given to his subjects from private life the degree of beauty of which they are susceptible. He is a master of terrific, but not of tender impressions. We feel a harshness and gloom in his genius even while we are compelled to admire its force and originality.—CAMPBELL, THOMAS, 1819, *Specimens of the British Poets.*

There was more of moral purpose than of genius in his tragedies.—MORLEY, HENRY, 1873, *A First Sketch of English Literature, p.* 838.

Amused the town with some perfectly unreadable plays, principally "George Barnwell" and "The Fatal Curiosity," which are interesting as the first specimens of "*tragedie bourgeoise,*" or modern melodrama. These artless dramas were composed in the interest of morality and virtue, and are the parents of a long line of didactic plays of crime and its punishment. —GOSSE, EDMUND, 1888, *A History of Eighteenth Century Literature, p.* 393.

One of the prominent offenders who followed in Steele's wake was George Lillo whose highly moral tragedies, written for the edification of playgoers, have the kind of tragic interest which is called forth by any commonplace tale of crime and misery. In Lillo's two most important dramas, "George Barnwell," a play founded on the old ballad, and "The Fatal Curiosity," there is a total absence of the elevation in character and language which gives dignity to tragedy. His plays are like tales of guilt arranged and amplified from the Newgate Calendar. The author wrote with a good purpose, and the public appreciated his work, but it is not dramatic art, and has no pretension to the name of literature.—DENNIS, JOHN, 1894, *The Age of Pope, p.* 138.

Daniel Waterland

1683–1740

Born at Wasely, Lincolnshire, England, Feb. 14, 1683; died in London, Dec. 23, 1740. He became a fellow of Magdalen College, Cambridge, 1704, and its master, 1713; Chaplain to George I, 1714; rector of Ellingham, 1713, and of St. Austin and St. Faith, London, 1720; Chancellor of York, 1723; canon of Windsor, 1727; vicar of Twickenham and archdeacon of Middlesex, 1730. He is eminent as a patristic scholar, a champion of orthodoxy, and a fair-minded and unembittered controversialist. Besides much against Dr. Samuel Clarke, Whitby, Middleton, Tindal, and others, he wrote a "Critical History of the Athanasian Creed," Cambridge, 1724, n. e. Oxford, 1870, and a "Review of the Doctrine of Eucharist," 1737, n. e. Oxford, 1868. His works, with a memoir by Bishop Van Mildert, were collected in 11 vols., Oxford, 1823–28, and in 6 vols., 1843 and 1856.—BIRD, FREDERIC MAYER, 1889–91, *Concise Dictionary of Religious Knowledge and Gazetteer, ed. Jackson, p.* 955.

GENERAL

The *Stile* is simple and unadorned, but clear and nervous; and such an *unusual plainness* runs through the whole, that perhaps it is a kind of Stile which never yet appeared; but which wants only to appear, in order to be *admired* and *imitated*.—CLARKE, JOSEPH, 1742, *Sermons on Several Important Subjects of Religion and Morality.*

This great man is the Archimedes of the Christian Church. His Demonstrations, like engines and battering-rams, drive all before them. Neither Dr. Clarke, nor Jackson, nor even Emlyn, could stand before him.—RYLAND, JOHN, 1781, *ed., The Student and Preacher, by Cotton Mather, Supplement.*

Few names, recorded in the annals of the Church of England, stand so high in the estimation of its most sound and intelligent members, as that of Dr. Waterland. During a period remarkable for literary and theological research, and fruitful in controversies upon subjects of primary importance, this distinguished writer acquired, by his labours in the cause of religious truth, an extensive and solid reputation. Nor did the reputation thus acquired die away with those controversies in which he bore so large a share. It has survived the occasions which gave them birth, and still preserves its lustre unimpaired. His writings continue to be referred to by divines of the highest character, and carry with them a weight of authority never attached but to names of acknowledged preëminence in the learned world.—VAN MILDERT, WILLIAM, 1823, *ed., The Works of Daniel Waterland, With Life.*

A learned and able defender of some important points; but little, as far as the author has seen, of evangelical and devout divinity, or the main principle of the gospel,—salvation by grace.—BICKERSTETH, EDWARD, 1844, *The Christian Student.*

Waterland, the most learned of contemporary divines.—STEPHEN, LESLIE, 1876, *The Starting Point of Deism, History of English Thought in the Eighteenth Century, vol.* I, *p.* 86.

Then arose a Christian champion who annihilated those anti-Trinitarians who held a middle ground between the Catholic faith and Humanitarianism pure and simple, as completely as Butler and others annihilated Deism. This was Dr. Waterland, who first appeared in the arena in 1719, and routed Dr. Clarke and his friends from one position after another until he left them no ground to stand upon, except that of admitting the full Divinity of Christ, or regarding Him as a mere man. . . . Dr. Waterland took a comprehensive view of the whole question, and left to posterity not only an effective answer to Dr. Clarke, but a masterly and luminous exposition of a fundamental doctrine of the faith, the equal to which it would be difficult to find in any other author, ancient or modern.—OVERTON, JOHN HENRY, 1897, *The Church in England, vol.* II, *pp.* 226, 227.

Waterland did more than any other divine of his generation to check the advance of latitudinarian ideas within the church of England. His deep and accurate learning and his command of nervous and perspicuous English rendered him unusually formidable as a controversialist. Of mysticism and philosophy he was suspicious, and was therefore reduced to rest the defence of Christianity entirely on external evidence.—RIGG, J. M., 1899, *Dictionary of National Biography, vol.* LIX, *p.* 447.

Thomas Tickell

1686–1740

Born, at Bridekirk, Cumberland, 1686. Matric., Queen's College, Oxford, 16 May 1701; B. A., 1705; M. A., 22 Feb. 1709. Friendship with Addison. Appointed by him Under-Secretary of State, 1717. Married, 1726. Secretary to Lords Justices of Ireland, 1724–40. Died, at Bath, 21 April 1740. *Works:* "A Poem to . . . the Lord Privy Seal on the Prospect of Peace," 1713; Translation of Homer's "Iliad," Bk. I. (pubd. under Tickell's name, but possibly by Addison), 1715; "An Epistle from a Lady in England to a Gentleman at Avignon" (anon.), 1717; "An Ode occasioned by Earl Stanhope's Voyage to France," 1718; "An Ode to the Earl of Sutherland" (anon), 1720; "Kensington Gardens" (anon), 1722; "To Sir G. Kneller" (anon.), 1722; "On Her Majesty's rebuilding the Lodgings of the Black Prince and Henry V. at Queen's College, Oxford," 1733. He *edited:* Addison's Works, 1722, etc. *Collected Works:* ed. by T. Park, 1807.—SHARP, R. FARQUHARSON, 1897, *A Dictionary of English Authors, p.* 281.

PERSONAL

Tickell was not one of those scholars who wear away their lives in a closet. With respect to his personal character, he is said to have been a man of gay conversation, at least a temperate lover of wine and company, and in his domestick relations without censure.—JOHNSON, SAMUEL, 1779–81, *Tickell, Lives of the English Poets.*

Tickell was in his person and manners amiable and pleasing. His habits were rather of a convivial cast; he loved the gay circle and the enlivening glass, but seldom, if ever, passed beyond the limits of temperate indulgence. His conversation was spirited and attractive, and in his family he was regular, affectionate, and kind.—DRAKE, NATHAN, 1804–14, *Essays Illustrative of the Tatler, Spectator and Guardian, vol.* III, *p.* 130.

HOMER'S ILIAD, BOOK I

1715

I must inform the reader that when I begun this first book I had some thoughts of translating the whole "Iliad," but had the pleasure of being diverted from that design by finding that the work was fallen into a much abler hand. I would not, therefore, be thought to have any other view in publishing this small specimen of Homer's "Iliad," than to bespeak, if possible, the favour of the public to a translation of Homer's "Odyssey," wherein I have already made some progress.—TICKELL, THOMAS, 1715, *tr., First Book of the Iliad, To the Reader.*

They tell me, the busy part of the nation are not more divided about Whig and Tory, than these idle fellows of the feather, about Mr. Tickell's and my translation. I (like the Tories) have the town in general, that is, the mob on my side; but it is usual with the smaller party to make up in industry, what they want in number, and that is the case with the little senate of Cato. However, if our principles be well considered, I must appear a brave Whig, and Mr. Tickell a rank Tory. I translated Homer for the public in general, he to gratify the inordinate desires of one man only. We have, it seems, a great Turk in poetry, who can never bear a brother on the throne; and has his mutes too, a set of nodders winkers, and whisperers, whose business 'tis to strangle all other offsprings of wit in their birth. The new translator of Homer, is the humblest slave he has, that is to say, his first minister; let him receive the honours he gives me, but receive them with fear and trembling; let him be proud of the approbation of his absolute Lord, I appeal to the people, as my rightful judges and masters; and if they are not inclined to condemn me, I fear no arbitrary high-flying proceeding, from the small court-faction at Button's. But after all I have said of this great man, there is no rupture between us. We are each of us so civil and obliging, that neither thinks he's obliged: and I for my part treat with him, as we do with the Grand Monarch; who has too many great qualities not to be respected, though we know he watches any occasion to oppress us.—POPE, ALEXANDER, 1715, *Letter to the Hon. James Craggs, July* 15.

It does not indeed want its merit; but I was strangely disappointed in my expectation of a translation nicely true to the original; whereas in those parts where the greatest exactness seems to be demanded, he has been the least careful; I mean the history of ancient ceremonies and rites, &c., in which you have with great judgment been exact.—ARBUTHNOT, JOHN, 1715, *Letter to Pope.*

Be assured I want no new inducement to behave myself like your friend. To be very plain, the University almost in general gives the preference to Pope's Translation; they say his is written with more Spirit, Ornament and Freedom, and has more the air of an original. I inclined some; Hanton &c, to compare the Translation with the Greek; which was done, and it made some small alteration in their opinions, but still Pope was their man. The bottom of the case is this, they were strongly prepossest in Pope's favour, from a wrong notion of your design before the Poem came down; and the sight of yours has not force enough upon them to make them willing to contradict themselves, and own they were in the wrong; but they go far for prejudiced persons, and own yours an excellent translation, nor do I hear any violently affirm it to be worse than Pope's, but those who look on Pope as a miracle, and among those to your comfort Evans is the first, and even these zealots allow that you have outdone

Pope in some particulars. *E. g.* the speech beginning

"Oh sunk in Avarice &c.
And leave a naked" &c.

Upon the whole I affirm the performance has gained you much Reputation, and when they compare you with what they should compare you, with Homer only, you are much admired. It has given I know many of the best judges a desire to see the Odyssies by the same hand, which they talk of with pleasure, and I seriously believe your first piece of that will quite break their partiality for Pope, which your Iliad has weaken'd and secure your success. Nor think my opinion groundlessly swayed by my wishes, for I observe, as Prejudice cools, you grow in favour, and you are a better Poet now than when your Homer first came down. I am persuaded fully that your design cannot but succeed here, and it shall be my hearty desire and endeavour that it may.—YOUNG, EDWARD, 1715, *Letter to Tickell, June* 28.

Addison declared that the rival versions were both good; but that Tickell's was the best that ever was made; and with Addison, the wits, his adherents and followers, were certain to concur. . . . To compare the two translations would be tedious; the palm is now given universally to Pope; but I think the first lines of Tickell's were rather to be preferred; and Pope seems to have since borrowed something from them in the correction of his own.—JOHNSON, SAMUEL, 1779–81, *Tickell, Lives of the English Poets.*

So far as a writer has a right to resent being misjudged by eminent contemporaries, Pope had a right to complain that Addison and his friends should prefer Tickell's version to his own. The translations are substantially executed in the same style, and in that style Pope is incomparably Tickell's superior. Even the passages in which, as Young tells Tickell, Pope's admirers at Oxford were disposed to give Tickell the preference, will not now seem to us to justify any such award. The instances of mean expressions—by far the larger proportion of the faults which Pope finds in Tickell—are in general fairly selected and justly noted. About the places in which Tickell is apparently accused of archaic simplicity, there may be greater room for difference of opinion: but on the whole I believe that Pope's instinct was right, and that in the style which both he and Tickell adopted a vein of "ballad-thinking," however Homeric it may be in itself, was essentially out of place, just as Ambrose Philips' Spenserianisms are not ornaments but blemishes in pastorals, the whole structure of which shows them to be members—unworthy ones, perhaps—of the school of Virgil.—CONINGTON, JOHN, 1860, *Pope's MS., Notes on Tickell's "Homer," Fraser's Magazine, vol.* 62, *p.* 270.

A translation of the first Iliad by Tickell appeared (in June, 1715) simultaneously with Pope's first volume. Pope had no right to complain. No man could be supposed to have a monopoly in the translation of Homer. Tickell had the same right to try his hand as Pope; and Pope fully understood this himself. He described to Spence a conversation in which Addison told him of Tickell's intended work. Pope replied that Tickell was perfectly justified, Addison having looked over Tickell's translation of the first book, said that he would prefer not to see Pope's, as it might suggest double dealing; but consented to read Pope's second book, and praised it warmly. In all this, by Pope's own showing, Addison seems to have been scrupulously fair; and if he and the little senate preferred Tickell's work on its first appearance, they had a full right to their opinion, and Pope triumphed easily enough to pardon them. . . . It was, say Pope's apologists, an awkward circumstance that Tickell should publish at the same time as Pope, and that is about all that they can say. It was, we may reply in Stephenson's phrase, very awkward—for Tickell. In all this, in fact, it seems impossible for any reasonable man to discover anything of which Pope had the slightest ground of complaint.—STEPHEN, LESLIE, 1880, *Pope* (*English Men of Letters*).

ELEGY ON ADDISON

1721

This elegy (by Mr. Tickell) is one of the finest in our language: there is so little new that can be said upon the death of a friend, after the complaints of Ovid, and the Latin Italians, in this way, that one is surprised to see so much novelty in this to strike us, and so much interest to affect.—GOLDSMITH, OLIVER, 1767, *The Beauties of English Poetry.*

Many tributes were paid to the memory of Addison. But one alone is now remembered. Tickell bewailed his friend in an elegy which would do honour to the greatest name in our literature; and which unites the energy and magnificence of Dryden to the tenderness and purity of Cowper.—MACAULAY, THOMAS BABINGTON, 1843, *Life and Writings of Addison, Edinburgh Review; Critical and Miscellaneous Essays.*

The famous elegy is justly ranked among the greatest masterpieces of its kind. In it a sublime and public sorrow for once moved a thoroughly mediocre poet into utterance that was sincere and original. So much dignity, so much pathos, so direct and passionate a distress, are not to be found in any other poem of the period. But when Tickell was not eulogising the majesty and sweetness of Addison, he was but a languid, feeble versifier.—GOSSE, EDMUND, 1880, *English Poets, ed. Ward, vol.* III, *p.* 154.

The poem dedicated to the essayist's memory is perhaps overpraised by Macaulay when he says that it would do honour to the greatest name in our literature, but it proved incontestibly that Tickell, as a poet, was superior to the master whom he so loved and honoured.—DENNIS, JOHN, 1894, *The Age of Pope, p.* 109.

GENERAL

This is not only a state-poem (my ancient aversion), but a state-poem on the peace of Utrecht. If Mr. Pope had wrote a panegyric on it, one could hardly have read him with patience: but this is only a poor short-winded imitator of Addison, who had himself not above three or four notes in poetry, sweet enough indeed, like those of a German flute, but such as soon tire and satiate the ear with their frequent return. Tickell has added to this a great poverty of sense, and a string of translations that hardly become a school-boy. However, I forgive him for the sake of his ballad, which I always thought the prettiest in the world.—GRAY, THOMAS, 1751, *Letter to Horace Walpole, Works, ed. Gosse, vol.* II, *p.* 219.

He has a very happy talent in versification, which much exceeds Addison's, and is inferior to few of the English Poets, Mr. Dryden and Pope excepted.—CIBBER, THEOPHILUS, 1753, *Lives of the Poets, vol.* V, *p.* 19.

Through all Tickell's Works there is a strain of ballad thinking, if I may so express it; and in this professed ballad, ["Colin and Lucy"] he seems to have surpassed himself. It is, perhaps, the best in our language in this way.—GOLDSMITH, OLIVER, 1767, *The Beauties of English Poetry.*

Of his personal character we have little information: he is said to have been a man of gay conversation, at least a temperate lover of wine and company, and in his domestic relations without censure. It may be added, that he was in one respect at least a man of great modesty. He suppressed his share in the Spectator and Guardian, for which no other motive can fairly be assigned, and this he did so successfully, that it is not easy to determine any one paper to be his. Of those which have been attributed to him, upon conjecture, he had no reason to be ashamed; yet it frequently happens that men in advanced and serious life do not look upon their juvenile productions with complacency. If this apology is unsatisfactory, let it be supposed, on the other hand, that he became vain, and thought them beneath him.—CHALMERS, ALEXANDER, 1808-23, *ed., The British Essayists, Preface to the Guardian, p.* 35.

Though it has not much merit as a poem ["Prospect of Peace,"] it presents some noble thoughts on the general subject of peace and the duty of nations to cultivate it among each other, which, if practised, would make the world much better and happier.—CLEVELAND, CHARLES D., 1848, *A Compendium of English Literature, p.* 427.

Nobody writes better grammar than Tickell. His style is always remarkably clear and exact, and the mere appropriateness and judicious collocation of his words, aided by the swell of the verse in his more elaborate or solemn passages, have sometimes an imposing effect.—CRAIK, GEORGE L., 1861, *A Compendious History of English Literature and of the English Language, vol.* II, *p.* 276.

Tickell was what the French call a "Moon" of Addison; yet, poetically speaking, he shone more brightly than his sun, and he had a singular gift at the funeral elegy, those on Addison himself and on Cadogan being of remarkable excellence in their kind.—SAINTSBURY, GEORGE, 1896, *Social England, ed. Traill, vol.* V, *p.* 73.

Tickell was certainly as good a versifier as Addison; but his chief claim to notice, as he himself felt, is that he was Addison's friend.—AITKEN, GEORGE A., 1898, *Dictionary of National Biography, vol.* LVI, *p.* 381.

Edmund Halley

1656–1742

Contemporary with Newton, and second only to him as an astronomer, was Edmund Halley. He was born in London, in the year 1656, and the whole of his long life was devoted to science. He was the author of many discoveries and writings upon watery vapors, tides, and the variation of the magnetic needle. In 1691, he was a candidate for the Savilian professorship of astronomy in the University of Oxford, but failed to get it on account of the belief that some of his views on scientific subjects were inconsistent with Revelation. Twelve years afterwards, having outlived this suspicion, he was elected to the Savilian chair of geometry, and received the title of Doctor of Law. In 1719 he was appointed to the office of astronomer Royal, in which position he continued until his death, in 1742.—JOHNSTON, RICHARD MALCOLM AND BROWNE, WILLIAM HAND, 1872, *English Literature, p.* 189.

PERSONAL

Mr. Edmund Hally, astronomer, born October 29, 1656, London—this nativity I had from Mr. Hally himself. . . . At 9 yeares old, his father's apprentice taught him to write, and arithmetique. He went to Paule's schoole to Dr. Gale: while he was there he was very perfect in the Caelestiall Globes insomuch that I heard Mr. Moxon (the globe-maker) say that if a star were misplaced in the globe, he would presently find it. At . . . he studyed Geometry, and at 16 could make a dyall, and then, he said, thought himselfe a brave fellow. At 16 went to Queen's Colledge in Oxon, well versed in Latin, Greeke, and Hebrew: where at the age of nineteen, he solved this useful probleme in astronomie, never donne before, viz. "from 3 distances given from the sun, and angles between, to find the orbe" (mentioned in the Philosophicall Transactions, Aug. or Sept. 1676, No. 115), for which his name will be ever famous.—AUBREY, JOHN, 1669–96, *Brief Lives, ed. Clark, vol.* I, *p.* 282.

I have no esteem of a man who has lost his reputation, both for skill, candour, and ingenuity, by silly tricks, ingratitude, and foolish prate; and that I value not all, or any of the shame of him and his infidel companions; being very well satisfied, that if Christ and his Apostles were to walk again upon the earth, they should not escape free from the calumnies of their venomous tongues. But I hate his ill manners, not the man. Were he either honest or but civil, there is none in whose company I could rather desire to be.—FLAMSTEED, JOHN, 1692, *Letter to Newton, Feb.* 24.

Being last night with Dr. Halley, he said that he could wish to live seven years longer (if he could be easy) that he might finish a work he had begun, which he believed he could do in that time. Being somewhat lame, he said he wished to have his health perfect to the last without infirmities, and that he would willingly die if such infirmities came on. For why, said he, should a man live to be uneasy both to himself and those about him? What the work above mentioned is neither myself nor the other person with him asked.—HEARNE, THOMAS, 1721, *Reliquiæ Hearnianæ, ed. Bliss, May* 14, *vol.* II, *p.* 129.

In person Halley was "of a middle stature, inclining to tallness, of a thin habit of body, and a fair complexion," and it is added that "he always spoke as well as acted with an uncommon degree of sprightliness and vivacity." His disposition was ardent, generous, and candid; he was disinterested and upright, genial to his friends, an affectionate husband and father, and was wholly free from rancour of jealousy. He passed a life of almost unprecedented literary and scientific activity without becoming involved in a single controversy, and was rendered socially attractive by the unfailing gaity which embellished the more recondite qualities of a mind of extraordinary penetration, compass, and power. One of his admirers was Peter the Great, who in 1697 not only consulted him as to his shipbuilding and other projects, but admitted him familiarly to his table. Portraits of Halley were painted by Murray, Phillips, and Kneller, and engravings from each were published.—CLERKE, MISS A. M., 1890, *Dictionary of National Biography, vol.* XXIV, *p.* 107.

Halley's disposition seems to have been generous and candid, and wholly free from anything like jealousy or rancour. In person he was rather above the middle height, and slight in build; his complexion was fair, and he is said to have always spoken, as well as acted, with uncommon sprightliness. In the *èloge* pronounced upon him at the Paris *Académie dés Sciences*, of which Halley had been made a member in 1719, it was said, "he possessed all the qualifications which were necessary to please princes who were desirous of instruction, with a great extent of knowledge and a constant presence of mind; his answers were ready, and at the same time pertinent, judicious, polite and sincere." Thus we find that Peter the Great was one of his most ardent admirers. He consulted the astronomer on matters connected with shipbuilding, and invited him to his own table. But Halley possessed nobler qualifications than the capacity of pleasing princes. He was able to excite and to retain the love and admiration of his equals. This was due to the warmth of his attachments, the unselfishness of his devotion to his friends, and to a vein of gaiety and good-humour which pervaded all his conversation.—BALL, SIR ROBERT S., 1895, *Great Astronomers, p.* 184.

GENERAL

While we thought that the eulogium of an astronomer, a physicist, a scholar, and a philosopher comprehended our whole subject, we have been insensibly surprised into the history of an excellent mariner, an illustrious traveller, an able engineer, and almost a statesman.—MAIRAN, M., 1742, *Éloge upon Halley.*

The original records of Halley's observations are deposited at Greenwich in four small quarto volumes. Upon the recommendation of Mr. Baily, a manuscript copy of them was taken by the order of the Lords of the Admiralty, and presented to the Astronomical Society, in the year 1832. Mr. Baily has concluded, from a careful inspection of these observations, that they do not possess sufficient value to render it desirable that they should be printed. Maskelyne had already intimated to Delambre, that they were hardly preferable to those of Flamsteed. Halley, indeed, was endowed with a mind of vast compass as well as extraordinary sagacity and power; but he seems to have undervalued those habits of minute attention which are indispensable to the attainment of a high degree of excellence in the practice of astronomical observation.—GRANT, ROBERT, 1852, *History of Physical Astronomy, p.* 479.

Lalande styled Halley "the greatest of English astronomers," and he ranked by common consent next to Newton among the scientific Englishmen of his time. Of eighty-four papers inserted by him in the "Philosophical Transactions" a large proportion expounded in a brilliant and attractive style theories or inventions opening up novel lines of inquiry and showing a genius no less fertile than comprehensive.—CLERKE, MISS A. M., 1890, *Dictionary of National Biography, vol.* XXIV, *p.* 109.

To Halley the World owes a great debt of gratitude—first, for discovering the "Principia;" second, for seeing it through the press; and third, for defraying the cost of its publication out of his own scanty purse. For though he ultimately suffered no pecuniary loss, rather the contrary, yet there was considerable risk in bringing out a book which not a dozen men living could at the time comprehend. It is no small part of the merit of Halley that he recognized the transcendent value of the yet unfinished work, that he brought it to light, and assisted in its becoming understood to the best of his ability. Though Halley afterwards became Astronomer-Royal, lived to the ripe old age of eighty-six, and made many striking observations, yet he would be the first to admit that nothing he ever did was at all comparable in importance with his discovery of the "Principia;" and he always used to regard his part in it with peculiar pride

RICHARD BENTLEY

Engraving by J. Posselwhite, from a Picture by Hudson in Trinity College, Cambridge.

and pleasure.—LODGE, OLIVER, 1893, *Pioneers of Science*, p. 194.

There can be little doubt that the fame as an astronomer which Halley ultimately acquired, great as it certainly was, would have been even greater still had it not been somewhat impaired by the misfortune that he had to shine in the same sky as that which was illumined by the unparalleled genius of Newton. . . . It has often been the good fortune of astronomers to render practical services to humanity by their investigations, and Halley's achievements in this respect deserve to be noted. A few years after he had settled in England, he published an important paper on the variation of the magnetic compass, for so the departure of the needle from the true north is termed. This subject had indeed early engaged his attention, and he continued to feel much interest in it up to the end of his life. With respect to his labours in this direction, Sir John Herschel says: "To Halley we owe the first appreciation of the real complexity of the subject of magnetism. It is wonderful indeed, and a striking proof of the penetration and sagacity of this extraordinary man, that with his means of information he should have been able to draw such conclusions, and to take so large and comprehensive a view of the subject as he appears to have done." In 1692, Halley explained his theory of terrestrial magnetism, and begged captains of ships to take observations of the variations of the compass in all parts of the world, and to communicate them to the Royal Society, "in order that all the facts may be readily available to those who are hereafter to complete this difficult and complicated subject." The extent to which Halley was in advance of his contemporaries, in the study of terrestrial magnetism, may be judged from the fact that the subject was scarcely touched after his time till the year 1811.—BALL, SIR ROBERT S., 1895, *Great Astronomers*, pp. 162, 172.

Richard Bentley

1662–1742

Born, at Oulton, near Wakefield, 27 Jan. 1662. Educated at a day school near Oulton; at Wakefield Grammar School, 1673–76. To St. John's College, Cambridge, as subsizar, 24 May 1676; matriculated, 6 July 1676; Dowman Scholar, 4 Nov. 1678; Constable Scholarship, 1679; B. A., 1680; M. A., July 1683. Master of School at Spalding for short time in 1682. Private tutor to son of Dr. Stillingfleet, 1682–89. Went to reside in Oxford, 1689. Ordained Chaplain to Dr. Stillingfleet, 16 March 1690. First Boyle Lecturer, 1692. Prebend of Worcester, 1692. Keeper of Royal Libraries, 1694. F. R. S., 1694. Chaplain in Ordinary to King, 1695. D. D., Oxford, July 1696. To official residence as Royal Librarian, in St. James's Palace, 1696. Active part in restoring Cambridge University Press. Appointed Master of Trinity College, Cambridge, 1 Feb. 1700. Married Joanna Bernard, 1701. Had four children. Tried before Bishop of Ely for unconstitutional practices as Master of Trinity, 1714, Bishop of Ely died before giving judgment, so trial lapsed. Deprived of degrees by University, having failed to appear in Vice-Chancellor's Court to answer suit of Conyers Middleton respecting fees, 1718. Degrees restored, 26 Mar. 1724. Again tried before Bishop of Ely for proceeding as Master of Trinity, 1733. Deprived of Mastership, 27 April 1734. Execution of sentence prevented by action of Bentley's friends. Paralytic stroke, 1739. Wife died, 1740. He died, 14 July 1742. Buried in Trinity College Chapel. *Works:* "Letter to Mill" (as appendix to the "Chronicle of Malala"), 1691; "The Folly and Unreasonableness of Atheism" (Boyle Lectures), 1693; "Of Revelation and the Messias," 1696; "A Proposal for building a Royal Library," 1697; "Dissertation upon the Letters of Phalaris" (in second edn. of Dr. Wotton's "Reflections upon Ancient and Modern Learning"), 1697; expanded edition, pub. separately, with answer to C. Boyle, 1699; "Emendationes in Menandri et Philemonis Reliquias" (under pseud. of "Phileleutherus Lipsiensis"), 1710; "The Present State of Trinity College," 1710; "Remarks upon a late discourse of Free-Thinking" (anon.), 1713; "A Sermon upon Popery," 1715; "A Sermon preached before Her Majesty," 1717; "Proposals for printing a new edition of the

Greek Testament" (anon.), 1721; "Emendations on the twelve books of Paradise Lost," 1732. *Posthumous:* "Opuscula Philologica," 1781; "R. Bentleii et doctorum virorum Epistolæ," 1807; "Correspondence," ed. by C. Wordsworth (2 vols.), 1842; "Critica Sacra," ed. by A. A. Ellis, 1862. He *edited:* Malala, 1691; Callimachus, 1692; Cicero ("Tusculan Disputations"), 1709; Aristophanes, 1710; Horace, 1711; Terence, 1726; Milton ("Paradise Lost"), 1732. He also at various times annotated: Antigonus, Lucan, Lucretius, Nicander, Ovid, Phædrus, Philostratus, Plautus and Suetonius. *Collected Works:* ed. by Dyce (3 vols.), 1836–38. *Life:* by J. H. Monk (2nd edn.), 1833; by Prof. Jebb ("English Men of Letters" series), 1882.—SHARP, R. FARQUHARSON, 1897, *A Dictionary of English Authors, p.* 23.

PERSONAL

The guardian of the regal library, a person of great valour, but chiefly renowned for his humanity, had been a fierce champion for the moderns; and, in an engagement upon Parnassus, had vowed, with his own hands, to knock down two of the ancient chiefs, who guarded a small pass on the superior rock; but, endeavouring to climb up, was cruelly obstructed by his own unhappy weight, and tendency towards his centre.—SWIFT, JONATHAN, 1698?–1704, *Battle of the Books.*

Bentley will always be an ill-bred pedant; can the leopard change his skin?—PRIOR, MATTHEW, 1713, *Letter to Bolingbroke, July* 13.

Yesterday I heard that, whereas Dr. Bentley talked much of putting out a new edition of Homer, he is now mighty warm about an edition of Ovid; for no other reason but out of spite to Peter Burman, a foreigner, who hath lately published Ovid. Thus does this poor, old, spiteful man turn all his thoughts upon revenge, and spends his time in mere trifles.—HEARNE, THOMAS, 1727, *MS., Aug.* 30.

Bullum is a tall raw-boned man, I believe near six inches and a half high; from his infancy he applied himself, with great industry, to the old Blefuscudian language, in which he made such a progress, that he almost forgot his native Lilliputian: and at this time he can neither write nor speak two sentences, without a mixture of old Blefuscudian. These qualifications, joined to an undaunted forward spirit, and a few good friends, prevailed with the Emperor's grandfather to make him keeper of his library, and a Mulro in the Gomflastru; though most men thought him fitter to be one of the Royal Guards. These places soon helped him to riches, and upon the strength of them he soon began to despise every body, and to be despised by every body. This engaged him in many quarrels, which he managed in a very odd manner; whenever he thought himself affronted, he immediately flung a great book at his adversary, and if he could, felled him to the earth; but if his adversary stood his ground and flung another book at him, which was sometimes done with great violence, then he complained to the Grand Justiciary, that these affronts were designed to the Emperor, and that he was singled out only as being the Emperor's servant. By this trick he got that great officer to favour him, which made his enemies cautious, and him insolent.—ARBUTHNOT, JOHN, 1727, *State of Learning in the Empire of Lilliput.*

Dr. Bentley, when he came to town, was accustomed, in his visits to Lord Carteret, sometimes to spend the evenings with his Lordship. One day old Lady Granville reproached her son with keeping the country clergyman, who was with him the night before, till he was intoxicated. Lord Carteret denied the charge; upon which the lady replied, that the clergyman could not have sung in so ridiculous a manner, unless he had been in liquor. The truth of the case was, that the singing thus mistaken by her Ladyship, was Dr. Bentley's endeavour to instruct and entertain his noble friend, by reciting Terence according to the true *cantilena* of the ancients.—KIPPIS, ANDREW, 1778–93, *ed., Biographia Britannica, vol.* II, *p.* 280.

I had a sister somewhat elder than myself. Had there been any of that sternness in my grandfather, which is so falsely imputed to him, it may well be supposed we should have been awed into silence in his presence, to which we were admitted every day. Nothing can be further from the truth; he was the unwearied patron and promoter of all our childish sports and sallies; at all times ready to detach himself from any topic of conversation to take an interest and bear his part in our amusements. The eager curiosity natural to our age, and the questions it gave birth to, so teazing to many parents, he, on the contrary, attended to and encouraged, as the claims of infant reason never to be evaded or abused; strongly recommending, that to all such inquiries answers should be given according to the strictest truth, and information dealt to us in the clearest terms, as a sacred duty never to be departed from. I have broken in upon him many a time in his hours of study, when he would put his book aside, ring his hand-bell for his servant, and be led to his shelves to take down a picture-book for my amusement. . . . His domestic habits, when I knew him, were still those of unabated study; he slept in the room adjoining to his library, and was never with his family till the hour of dinner; at these times he seemed to have detached himself most completely from his studies; never appearing thoughtful and abstracted, but social, gay, and possessing perfect serenity of mind and equability of temper. He never dictated topics of conversation to the company he was with, but took them up as they came in his way, and was a patient listener to other people's discourse, however trival or uninteresting it might be.—CUMBERLAND, RICHARD, 1806, *Memoirs, vol.* I, *pp.* 9,18.

The habits of Dr. Bentley's domestic life continued in the same simple and uniform course for many years. The greater part of each day he passed in his study, where he breakfasted alone; he joined his family at the other meals, and at ten o'clock for evening prayers; after which they retired for their night's repose. Habited in his dressing-gown, he pursued his studies with the same application as had distinguished the earlier periods of his life. The tempestuous feuds in which he was now embarked appear neither to have deranged his habits, nor affected his health. The only change which they produced in his course of life was by obliging him to make more frequent journeys to London, and pass a longer time at his residence in Cotton House. . . . It appears to me that his passions were not always under the controul, nor his actions under the guidance, of Christian principles; that, in consequence, pride and ambition, the faults to which his nature was most exposed, were suffered to riot without restraint; and that hence proceeded the display of arrogance, selfishness, obstinacy, and oppression, by which it must be confessed that his career was disfigured. That nature however had not denied to him certain amiable qualities of the heart, and that he possessed in a considerable degree many of the social and endearing virtues, is proved beyond a doubt by the warm and steady affection with which he was regarded by his family and his intimate friends.—MONK, JAMES HENRY, 1830–33, *Life of Richard Bentley, vol.* II, *pp.* 117, 416.

In his domestic relations, Bentley was not only blameless, but exemplary; and domestic virtue always brings its own reward. Whatever brawls disturbed him without, "he still had peace at home," nor did he carry his despotic rule and contumelious language to his own fireside; if he called his children names,—they were names of fondness. If he erred, it was in too partial a regard to his kindred or dependents. For forty years he was the affectionate husband of a virtuous wife, who never had reason to complain that his controversies or his lawsuits had soured his temper.—COLERIDGE, HARTLEY, 1833, *Biographia Borealis, p.* 173.

His spirit, daring even to rashness—self-confident, even to negligence—and proud, even to insolent ferocity,—was awed for the first and for the last time—awed, not into meanness or cowardice, but into wariness and sobriety. For once he ran no risks; he left no crevice unguarded; he wantoned in no paradoxes; above all, he returned no railing for the railing of his enemies. In almost everything that he has written we can discover proofs of genius and learning. But it is only here that his genius and learning appear to have been constantly under the guidance of good sense and good temper. —MACAULAY, THOMAS BABINGTON, 1836, *Sir William Temple, Edinburgh Review; Critical and Miscellaneous Essays.*

In the hall of the College, where many celebrated names are commemorated by the portraits on the walls, places of honour are assigned to Bacon, Barrow, Newton, and Bentley. The features of the great scholar speak with singular force from the canvas of Thornhill, who painted him in his forty-eighth year, the very year in which his struggle with the College began. That picture, Bentley's own bequest, is in the Master's Lodge. The pose of the head is haughty, almost defiant; the eyes, which are large, prominent, and full of bold vivacity, have a light in them as if Bentley were looking straight at an impostor whom he had detected, but who still amused him; the nose, strong and slightly tip-tilted, is moulded as if Nature had wished to show what a nose can do for the combined expression of scorn and sagacity; and the general effect of the countenance, at a first glance, is one which suggests power—frank, self-assured, sarcastic, and, I fear we must add, insolent: yet, standing a little longer before the picture, we become aware of an essential kindness in those eyes of which the gaze is so direct and intrepid; we read in the whole face a certain keen veracity; and the sense grows—this was a man who could hit hard, but who would not strike a foul blow, and whose ruling instinct, whether always a sure guide or not, was to pierce through falsities to truth.—JEBB, RICHARD CLAVERHOUSE, 1882, *Bentley (English Men of Letters)*, *p.* 200.

You will think furthermore of this Dr. Bentley as living through all his fierce battles of criticisms and of college mastership to an extreme old age, and into days when Swift and Pope and Steele and Addison were all gone—a gray, rugged, persistent, captious old man, with a great, full eye that looked one through and through, and with a short nose, turned up—as if he always scented a false quantity in the air.—MITCHELL, DONALD G., 1895, *English Lands Letters and Kings, Queen Anne and the Georges*, *p.* 12.

MASTERSHIP OF TRINITY

I find the gentlemen of both Universitys equally amused upon our friend Dr. Bentley's promotion to Trinity College Mastership.—PEPYS, SAMUEL, 1699–1700, *Letter to J. Jackson, Jan.* 22.

We may strip him of his titles, but we never can, we see, of his insolence; he has ceased to be Doctor, and may cease to be Professor, but he can never cease to be Bentley. There he will triumph over the University to the last; all its learning being unable to polish, its manners to soften, or its discipline to tame the superior obstinacy of his genius. . . . There is something so singularly rude and barbarous in his way of treating all mankind, that whoever has occasion to relate it, will, instead of aggravating, find himself obliged to qualify and soften the harshness of his story, lest it should pass for incredible.—MIDDLETON, CONYERS, 1719, *A Full and Impartial Account of the Late Proceedings in the University of Cambridge against Dr. Bentley.*

Between Bentley and his antagonists the differences were vital. Bentley had a good heart; generally speaking, his antagonists had not. Bentley was overbearing, impatient of opposition, domineering, sometimes tyrannical. He had, and deservedly, a very lofty opinion of himself; he either had, or affected, too mean a one of his antagonists. *Sume superbiam quæsitam meritis* was the motto which he avowed. Coming to the government of a very important college, at a time when its discipline had been greatly relaxed and the abuses were many, his reforms (of which some have been retained even to this day) were pushed with too high a hand; he was too negligent of any particular statute that stood in his way; showed too harsh a disregard to the feelings of gentlemen; and too openly disdained the arts of conciliation. Yet this same man was placable in the highest degree; was generous; needed not to be conciliated by sycophantic arts; and, at the first moment when his enemies would make an opening for him to be so, was full of forgiveness. His literary quarrels, which have left the impression that he was irritable or jealous, were (without one exception) upon *his* part mere retorts to the most insufferable provocations; and, though it is true that, when once teased into rousing himself out of his lair, he *did* treat his man with rough play, left him ugly remembrances of his leonine power, and made himself merry with his distressed condition, yet, on the other hand, in his utmost wrath, there was not a particle of malice.—DE QUINCEY, THOMAS, 1830–57, *Richard Bentley, Collected Writings, ed. Masson, vol.* IV, *p.* 122.

The Fellows, as a body, were liable to no such charges as Bentley in his anger brought against them; not a few of them were eminent in the University; and if there were any whose lives would not bear scrutiny, they were at most two or three, usually non-resident, and always without influence. It may safely be said that no large society of that time, in either University, would have sustained an inspection with more satisfactory results. The average College Fellow of that period was a moderately accomplished clergyman, whose desire was to repose in decent comfort on a small freehold. Bentley swooped on a large house of such persons—not ideal students, yet, on the whole, decidedly favourable specimens of their kind; he made their lives a burden to them, and then denounced them as the refuse of humanity when they dared to lift their heads against his insolent assumption of absolute power. They bore it as long as flesh and blood could. For nearly eight years they endured. At last, in December, 1709, things came to a crisis—almost by an accident. . . . It is good to be in sympathy with an illustrious man, but it is better still to be just. The merits of the controversy between Bentley and the Fellows have two aspects, legal and moral. The legal question is simple. Had Bentley, as Master, brought himself within the meaning of the fortieth Elizabethan Statute, and deserved the penalty of deprivation? Certainly he had. It was so found on two distinct occasions, twenty years apart, after a prolonged investigation by lawyers. Morally, the first question is: Was Bentley obliged to break the Statutes in order to keep some higher law? He certainly was not.—JEBB, RICHARD CLAVERHOUSE, 1882, *Bentley (English Men of Letters)*, *pp.* 101 119.

LETTER TO MILL
1691

In order that the truth should be published and proved, we needed the learned daring of Richard Bentley—daring which here, if anywhere, served literature better than the sluggish and credulous superstition of those who wish to be called and deemed critics. Bentley shook off the servile yoke, and put forth that famous "Letter to Mill"—a wonderful monument of genius and learning, such as could have come only from the first critic of his time. —RUHNKEN, DAVID, c1798, *The Hesychius of Alberti, Preface.*

Malelas had been long and anxiously expected by the learned; and his appearance interested them, not from his own merits, which were slender, but from those of the Appendix. The various and accurate learning, and the astonishing sagacity displayed in the "Epistle to Mill," attracted the attention of every person capable of judging upon such subjects. The originality of Bentley's style, the boldness of his opinions, and his secure reliance upon unfailing stores of learning, all marked him out as a scholar to be ranked with Scaliger, Casaubon, and Gataker. Notwithstanding the reluctance with which the pretensions of a new author are usually admitted, and the small number of persons to whom such writings were likely to recommend themselves, we find that the fame of our critic was at once established: in particular, among foreign scholars, the sensation produced by this essay of a young and unknown writer, seems to have been unexampled; and Grævius and Spanheim, the chiefs of the learned world, pronounced him "the rising constellation" of literature, and anticipated the brilliancy of his course. —MONK, JAMES HENRY, 1830–33, *Life of Richard Bentley, vol.* I, *p.* 31.

This short tractate at once placed Bentley at the head of all living English scholars. The ease with which, by a stroke of the pen, he restores passages, which had been left in hopeless corruption by the editors of the "Chronicle," the certainty of the emendation, and the command over the relevant material, are in a style totally different from the careful and laborious learning of Hody, Mill, or Chilmead. To the small circle of classical students it was at once apparent that there had arisen in England a critic, whose attainments were not to be measured by the ordinary academical standard, but whom these few pages had sufficed to place by the side of the great Grecians of a former age.—PATTISON, MARK, 1878, *Encyclopædia Britannica, Ninth ed., vol.* III.

BOYLE LECTURES
1692

One of the most learned and convincing discourses I had ever heard.—EVELYN, JOHN, 1692, *Diary, April* 4.

The reader of these discourses is informed and delighted by the variety of knowledge which they contain, and their close and convincing train of reasoning. The success with which Bentley unmasks the tenets of the atheist, grapples with his arguments, and exposes his fallacies, has never been surpassed, and scarcely equalled, in the wars of controversy. He steadily follows up his antagonist, and never fails to dislodge him from his positions. Various as are the topics which come under discussion, he appears at home in all, and displays a familiarity with metaphysics, natural history, and philosophy, altogether wonderful in a person coming fresh from the field of classical criticism. His ancient learning is introduced in a happy and agreeable manner, when he compares the theories of modern sceptics with those of the heathen philosophers.—MONK, JAMES HENRY, 1830–33, *Life of Richard Bentley, vol.* I, *p.* 39.

As a preacher Bentley could not but occupy a high place in point of depth, and the power of exciting that interest which follows the guidance of a great intellect in the contemplation of the duties of time and the awful realities of eternity. For that style of exhortation which awakens the affections, and secures the convictions of the judgment by the impulses of the heart, the preacher was unequal. He enforced the truths of revelation by the teachings of nature, as expounded by her greatest interpreter, the immortal Newton. A sermon of Bentley's based upon a thesis of Newton's must have been an intellectual gratification not unworthy an angelic auditory. But we fear that in simply "vindicating the ways of God to man," but little would be done to reconcile the heart of man to God. Accurate, precise, and exhaustive he could not fail to be.—ALLIBONE, S. AUSTIN, 1854–58, *A Critical Dictionary of English Literature, vol.* I, *p.* 172.

The Lectures made a deep and wide impression. Soon after they had been published, a Latin version appeared at Berlin. A Dutch version subsequently came out at Utrecht. There was one instance, indeed, of dissent from the general approval. A Yorkshire squire wrote a pamphlet, intimating that his own experience did not lead him to consider the faculties of the human soul as a decisive argument for the existence of a Deity; and, referring to Bentley's observations on this head, he remarked, "I judge he hath taken the wrong sow by the ear."—JEBB, RICHARD CLAVERHOUSE, 1882, *Bentley (English Men of Letters), p.* 32.

DISSERTATIONS ON PHALARIS
1695–99

As the first (Æsop) has been agreed by all ages since, for the greatest master in his kind, and all others of that sort have been but imitations of his original; so I think the "Epistles of Phalaris" to have more race, more spirit, more force of wit and genius, than any others I have ever seen, either ancient or modern. I know several learned men (or that usually pass for such, under the name of critics) have not esteemed them genuine, and Politian with some others have attributed them to Lucian: but I think he must have little skill in painting, that cannot find out this to be an original; such diversity of passions, upon such variety of actions and passages of life and government, such freedom of thought, such boldness of expression, such bounty to his friends, such scorn of his enemies, such honour of learned men, such esteem of good, such knowledge of life, such contempt of death, with such fierceness of nature and cruelty of revenge, could never be represented but by him that possessed them; and I esteem Lucian to have been no more capable of writing, than of acting what Phalaris did. In all one writ, you find the scholar or the sophist; and in all the other, the tyrant and the commander.—TEMPLE, SIR WILLIAM, 1692, *Works, vol.* III, *p.* 463.

The reader of these "Letters" will find less profit in introducing who wrote them than pleasure in enjoying the perusal. As to the authorship, the conflicting opinions of learned men must be consulted—perhaps in vain; as to the worth of the book, the reader can judge best for himself. Lest I disappoint curiosity, however—though the controversy does not deserve keen zeal on either part—I will briefly explain what seems to me probable on both sides of the question. . . . I have collated the "Letters" themselves with two Bodleian manuscripts from the Cantuar and Selden collection; I have also procured a collation, as far as Letter XL., of a manuscript in the Royal Library; the Librarian, with that courtesy which distinguishes him [*pro singulari sua humanitate*], refused me the further use of it. I have not recorded every variation of the MSS. from the printed texts; to do so would have been tedious and useless; but, wherever I have departed from the common reading, my authority will be found in the notes. This little book is indebted to the printer for more than usual elegance; it is hoped that the authour's labour may bring it an equal measure of acceptance.—BOYLE, CHARLES, 1695, *ed., Phalaris, Preface.*

I suspect Mr. Boyle is in the right; for our friend's learning (which I have a great value for) wants a little filing; and I doubt not but a few such strokes as this will do it and him good.—PEPYS, SAMUEL, 1695, *Letters, January.*

Give me leave, sir, to tell you a secret, —that I have spent a whole day upon Dr. Bentley's late volume of scandal, and criticism; for every one may not judge it to his credit to be so employed. He thinks meanly, I find, of my reading, as meanly as I think of his sense, his modesty or his manners. If you have looked into it, sir, you have found that a person, under the pretence of criticism, may take what freedom he pleases with the reputation and credit of any gentleman; and that he need not have any regard for another man's character who has once resolved to expose his own.—KING, WILLIAM, 1698, *Letter to Atterbury, Nichols' Epistolary Correspondence, vol.* IV, *p.* 337.

As a Woman in a little House, that gets a painful livelihood by spinning; if chance her Geese be scattered o'er the Common, she courses round the plain from side to side, compelling, here and there, the stragglers to the flock; they cackle loud, and flutter o'er the campaign: so Boyle pursued, so fled this Pair of Friends. . . . As when a skilful Cook has truss'd a brace of Woodcocks, he, with iron Skewer, pierces the tender sides of both, their legs and wings close pinion'd to their ribs; so was this Pair of Friends transfix'd, till down they fell, join'd in their lives, join'd in their deaths; so closely join'd that Charon would mistake them both for one, and waft them over Styx for half his fare.—SWIFT, JONATHAN, 1698?–1704, *Battle of the Books.*

Before I leave this subject, I will just tell you what Mr. Pope told me, who had been let into the secret, concerning the Oxford performance.—That Boyle wrote only the narrative of what passed between him and the Bookseller, which too was corrected for him; that Friend, the Master of Westminster, and Atterbury wrote the body of the criticisms; and that Dr. King of the Commons wrote the droll argument to prove Dr. Bentley was not the author of the Dissertation on Phalaris, and the Index. And a powerful cabal gave it a surprising run.—Your character of that species of wit, in which Bentley excelled, is just.—WARBURTON, WILLIAM, 1749, *Letters from a Late Eminent Prelate, Aug.* 19, *p.* 11.

I have not enter'd into any of the points of the controversy, as it would be a disagreeable as well as unnecessary task, but shall only observe, that tho' several very specious arguments are brought by doctor Bentley, the strongest of them do only affect particular Epistles; which, as Mr. Boyle observes, "do not hurt the whole body; for in a collection of pieces that have no dependence on each other, as epistles, epigrams, fables, the first number may be increased by the wantonness and vanity of imitators in after-times, and yet the book be authentic in the main, and an original still."—FRANCKLIN, THOMAS, 1749, *ed., Letters of Phalaris, Preface.*

The splendid controversy between Boyle and Bentley was at times a strife of gladiators, and has been regretted as the opprobrium of our literature; but it should be perpetuated to its honour; for it may be considered, on one side at least, as a noble contest of heroism. . . . Wit, ridicule, and invective, by cabal and stratagem, obtained a seeming triumph over a single individual, but who, like the Farnesian Hercules, personified the force and resistance of incomparable strength. "The Bees of Christchurch," as this conspiracy of wits has been called, so musical and so angry, rushed in a dark swarm about him, but only left their fine stings in the flesh they could not wound. He only put out his hand in contempt, never in rage. The Christchurch men, as if doubtful whether wit could prevail against learning, had recourse to the maliciousness of personal satire. They amused an idle public, who could even relish sense and Greek, seasoned as they were with wit and satire, while Boyle was showing how Bentley wanted wit, and Bentley was proving how Boyle wanted learning.—DISRAELI, ISAAC, 1812–13, *Boyle and Bentley, Calamities of Authors.*

On Bentley's memorable performances, the "Dissertations on Phalaris," criticism has been exhausted. In the just arrangement of the matter, in the logical precision of the arguments, and in the readiness and skill with which the most extensive and refined erudition is brought to bear upon the points contested, it is perhaps unrivalled by any single work. Enriched with incidental disquisitions on many different topics of classical learning, it will ever be prized by the student as a storehouse of important information.—DYCE, ALEXANDER, 1836–38, *ed. Bentley's Works.*

The Cambridge giant of criticism replied in an answer which goes by the name of Bentley against Boyle. It was the first great literary war that had been waged in England; and, like that of Troy, it has still the prerogative of being remembered, after the "Epistles of Phalaris" are almost as much buried as the walls of Troy itself. Both combatants were skilful in wielding the sword: the arms of Boyle, in Swift's language, were given him by all the gods; but his antagonist stood forward in no such figurative strength, master of a learning to which nothing parallel had been known in England, and that directed by an understanding prompt, discriminating, not idly sceptical, but still farther removed from trust in authority, sagacious in perceiving corruptions of language, and ingenious, at the least, in removing them; with a style rapid, concise, amusing, and superior to Boyle in that which he had chiefly to boast, a sarcastic wit.—HALLAM, HENRY, 1837–39, *Introduction to the Literature of Europe, pt.* iv, *ch.* i, *par.* 17.

How much do I regret that I have neither learning nor eyesight thoroughly to enjoy Bentley's masterley "Dissertation upon the Epistles of Phalaris!" Many years ago I read the work with infinite pleasure. As far as I know, or rather am able to judge, it is without a rival in that department of literature; a work of which the English nation may be proud as long as acute intellect, and vigorous powers, and profound scholarship shall be esteemed in the world.—WORDSWORTH, WILLIAM, 1837, *Letters, Memoirs by C. Wordsworth, ed. Reed, vol.* II, *p.* 353.

The finest piece of erudite criticism that has ever proceeded from an English pen.—ARNOLD, THOMAS, 1862–87, *A Manual of English Literature, p.* 248.

To any one who has looked into this dead controversy, it is curious to note how the great scholar outrages pure idiomatic English in the criticisms that established his mastership over the Greek.—BURTON, JOHN HILL, 1880, *A History of the Reign of Queen Anne, vol.* III, *p.* 296.

A curious fatality attended on Bentley's adversaries in this controversy. While they dealt thrusts at points where he was invulnerable, they missed all the chinks in his armour except a statement limiting too narrowly the use of two Greek verbs, and his identification of "Alba Graeca" with Buda instead of Belgrade. Small and few, indeed, these chinks were. It would have been a petty, but fair, triumph for his opponents, if they had perceived that, in correcting a passage of Aristophanes, he had left a false quantity. They might have shown that a passage in Diodorus had led him into an error regarding Attic chronology during the reign of the Thirty Tyrants. They might have exulted in the fact that an emendation which he proposed in Isæus rested on a confusion between two different classès of choruses; that he had certainly misconstrued a passage in the life of Pythagoras by Iamblichus; that the "Minos," on which he relies as Plato's work, was spurious; that, in one of the "Letters of Phalaris," he had defended a false reading by false grammar. They could have shown that Bentley was demonstrably wrong in asserting that no writings, bearing the name of Æsop, were extant in the time of Aristophanes; also in stating that the Fable of "The Two Boys" had not come down to the modern world: it was, in fact, very near them—safe in a manuscript at the Bodleian Library. Even the discussion on Zaleucus escaped: its weak points were first brought out by later critics—Warburton, Salter, Gibbon. Had such blemishes been ten times more numerous, they would not have affected the worth of the book; but, such as they were, they were just of the kind which small detractors delight to magnify. In one place Bentley accuses Boyle of having adopted a wrong reading in one of the Letters, and thereby made nonsense of the passage. Now, Boyle's reading, though not the best, happens to be capable of yielding the very sense which Bentley required. Yet even this Boyle and his friends did not discover.—JEBB, RICHARD CLAVERHOUSE, 1882, *Bentley (English Men of Letters), p.* 73.

Bentley replied by publishing, early in 1699, an enlarged Dissertation, which has justly been regarded as marking an epoch not only in the life of the author but also in the history of literature. His victory was really complete, but its effect was not immediately felt in all its fulness. Not one, however, of the Boylean confederacy ever again appeared before the world as a critic, though many years had to elapse before Tyrwhitt could describe the opponents of Bentley as "laid low by the thunderbolt," or Porson pronounce it an "immortal dissertation." Even apart from the merits of the purely controversial portions, it has a permanent value owing to the vast amount of interesting and accurate information which it embodies on points of history and chronology, antiquities; philology, and criticism—such as the age of Pythagoras, the origins of Greek tragedy, the anapæstic metre, and the coinage of Sicily. It is not solely "a masterpiece of controversy" and a "store-house of erudition." It is also an example of critical method, marking the beginning of the *critical* school of classical scholarship, which henceforth prevailed among the leading representatives of learning in England and Holland, until it was succeeded by the *systematic* or *encyclopædic* school of scholarship, which begins in Germany about 1783 with the great name of Friedrich Augustus Wolf.—SANDYS, J. E., 1896, *Social England, ed. Traill, vol.* V, *p.* 64.

HORACE
1711

I am indebted to you, Sir, for the great pleasure and instruction I have received from that excellent performance; though at y[e] same time I cannot but own to you the uneasyness I felt when I found how many things in Horace there were, which, after thirty years' acquaintance with him, I did not understand.—ATTERBURY, FRANCIS, 1712, *Letter to Bentley, April* 19.

Take Bentley's and Jason de Nores' Comments upon Horace, you will admire Bentley more when wrong, than Jason when right.—JOHNSON, SAMUEL, 1776, *Life by Boswell.*

This publication had been long and anxiously expected, and its appearance excited much sensation and surprise. There were found between seven and eight hundred alterations of the common readings of Horace; all of which, contrary to the general practice of classical editors, were introduced into the text. Scholars, having been familiar from their childhood with the works of this poet, were unwilling to believe that they had been all their lives mistaken in those passages which had afforded them unceasing gratification. Many indeed of Bentley's readings are those of old editions and manuscripts; but the greater part are the fruit of his own conjecture, supported by arguments always plausible and ingenious, and not unfrequently convincing. A person, who at first rejects his correction and declares a preference for the old reading, will sometimes be surprised to find his opinion changed on perusing the note, and be compelled to acknowledge the justice of the emendation: and this is a result of his labours which the Doctor anticipated, not without exultation. But while some of his new readings are fairly established, a larger proportion must be confessed to be dubious. Many of his changes are unnecessary, others harsh and improbable. He shows a propensity to confine the limits of poetical licence too closely, and thus to reduce the language of Horace into prose.—MONK, JAMES HENRY, 1830–33, *Life of Richard Bentley, vol.* I, *p.* 313.

On the merits and defects of Bentley's Horace, none but the accomplished scholar can expatiate, and none but professional scholars could feel much interest in the discussion. The intrusion of the conjectural readings into the text has been censured as altogether unwarrantable. Many of them go to crop the most delicate flowers of Horatian fancy, and sheer away the love-locks which the world has doated on. The value of the work consists in the extraordinary display of learning and ingenuity which the defence of these innovations called forth, in the skilful allegation of parallel passages; in the wonderful adroitness with which every line and every letter that supports the proposed change is hunted out from the obscurest corners of Roman literature, and made to bear on the case in point, and in the logical dexterity with which apparent objections are turned into confirmations. Vast as was Bentley's reading, none of it was superfluous, for he turns it all to account; his felicity in fixing his eye at once on what he needed, in always finding the evidence that he wanted, often where no one else would have thought of looking for it, is almost preturnatural. His learning suggested all the phrases that might be admitted in any given passage; but his taste did not always lead him to select the best.—COLERIDGE, HARTLEY, 1833, *Biographia Borealis, p.* 120.

Speaking of Bentley's readings in the mass, one may say that Horace would probably have liked two or three of them—would have allowed a very few more as not much better or worse than his own—and would have rejected the immense majority with a smile or a shudder.—JEBB, RICHARD CLAVERHOUSE, 1882, *Bentley (English Men of Letters), p.* 128.

In this work the editor puts too strict a limit to the author's poetic fancy, and thus too often reduces the poetry of Horace to the level of precise and logical prose. But even the very errors of so great a critic are often instructive, and the commentary abounds in unquestionably valuable hints on grammar and metre, while in the preface we have a serious attempt to deal with the chronology of the poet's works.—SANDYS, J. E., 1896, *Social England, ed. Traill, vol.* v, *p.* 65.

REMARKS ON A LATE DISCOURSE OF FREE-THINKING
1713

Whereas the Reverend Dr. Bentley, Master of Trinity College, besides his other labours published from our press, to the great advancement of learning and honour of this University, has lately, under the borrowed name of "Phileleutherus Lipsiensis," done eminent service to the Christian Religion, and the Clergy of England, by refuting the objections and exposing the ignorance of an impious set of writers, that call themselves Freethinkers—May it please you that the said Dr. Bentley, for his good services already done, have the public thanks of the University; and be desired by Mr. Vice Chancellor, in the name of the whole body, to finish what remains of so useful a work.—UNIVERSITY GRACE BOOK, 1715, *Jan.* 4.

Nothing can be more judicious, or effectual than the manner in which the Doctor takes to pieces the shallow but dangerous performance of the infidel. Not satisfied with replying to particular arguments, he cuts the ground from under his feet, by exposing the fallacious mode of reasoning which pervades them all, and the contemptible sophism which represents all good and great men of every age and country to have been "free-thinkers," and consequently partizans of his own sect. But the happiest of the Remarks are those which display the mistakes and ignorance of Collins in his citations from classical writers. By a kind of fatality, his translations are perpetually inaccurate, and his conception of the originals erroneous: and though most of his blunders are the effects of ignorance, yet not a few seem to arise from a deliberate intention of deceiving his readers. Never was the advantage more conspicuous of a ripe and perfect scholar over a half-learned smatterer: while the latter searches book after book in pursuit of passages favourable to his own theory, the former, familiar with the writings and characters of the authors, and accurately versed in their language, is able to take to pieces the ill-assorted patchwork of irrevelant quotations. These parts of Bentley's work are not only effectual in demolishing his adversary, but are both entertaining and useful to the reader; and to them it is owing that the book has experienced a fate so different from that of other controversial writings: even the ablest and best-written of such pieces generally fall into oblivion along with the dispute which gave them birth; but the "Remarks of Phileleutherus" are still read with the same delight as at their first appearance.—MONK, JAMES HENRY, 1830–33, *Life of Richard Bentley, vol.* I, *p.* 345.

Another, perhaps the only other, book of this polemical tribe which can be said to have been completely successful as an answer, is one most unlike the "Analogy" in all its nobler features. This is Bentley's "Remarks upon a late Discourse of Freethinking, by Phileleutherus Lipsiensis," 1713. Coarse, arrogant, and abusive, with all Bentley's worst faults of style and temper, this masterly critique is decisive. . . . It is rare sport to Bentley, this rat-hunting in an old rick, and he lays about him in high glee, braining an authority at every blow. When he left off abruptly, in the middle of a "Third Part," it was not because he was satiated with slaughter, but to substitute a new excitement, no less congenial to his temper—a quarrel with the University about his fees. A grace, voted 1715, tendering him the public thanks of the University, and "praying him in the name of the University to finish what remains of so useful a work," could not induce him to resume his pen. The "Remarks of Phileleutherus Lipsiensis," unfinished though they are, and trifling as was the book which gave occasion to them, are perhaps the best of all Bentley's performances. They have all the merits of the "Phalaris" dissertation, with the advantage of a far nobler subject. They show how Bentley's exact appreciation of the value of terms could, when he chose to apply it to that purpose, serve him as a key to the philosophical ideas of past times, no less than to those of poetical metaphor. The tone of the pamphlet is most offensive, "not only not insipid, but exceedingly bad-tasted." We can only say the taste is that of his age, while the knowledge is all his own.—PATTISON, MARK, 1860–89, *Religious Thought in England; Essays, ed. Nettleship, vol.* II, *pp.* 95, 97.

EDITION OF PARADISE LOST
1732

Our celebrated author, when he composed this poem, being obnoxious to the Government, poor, friendless, and, what is worst of all, blind with a *gutta serena*, could only dictate his verses to be writ by another. Whence it necessarily follows, that any errors in spelling, pointing, nay even in whole words of a like or near sound in pronunciation, are not to be charged upon the poet, but on the amanuensis.—But more calamities, than are yet mentioned, have happened to our poem: for the friend or acquaintance, whoever he was, to whom Milton committed his copy and the overseeing of the press, did so vilely execute that trust, that Paradise, under his ignorance and audaciousness, may be said to be twice lost. A poor bookseller, then living near Aldersgate, purchased our author's copy for ten pounds, and (if a second edition followed) for five pounds more; as appears by the original bond, yet in being. This bookseller, and that acquaintance, who seems to have been the sole corrector of the press, brought forth their first edition, polluted with such monstrous faults as are beyond example in any other printed book.—But these typographical faults, occasioned by the negligence of this acquaintance, (if all may be imputed to that, and not several wilfully made) were not the worst blemishes brought upon our poem. For this supposed friend (called in these notes the editor), knowing Milton's bad circumstances; who (vii. 26)

"Was fall'n on evil days and evil tongues,
With darkness and with dangers compass'd round
And solitude;"

thought he had a fit opportunity to foist into the book several of his own verses, without the blind poet's discovery. This trick has been too frequently played; but especially in works published after an author's death. And poor Milton in that condition, with threescore years' weight upon his shoulders, might be reckoned more than half dead.—BENTLEY, RICHARD, 1732, *Edition of Milton.*

Did Milton's prose, O Charles, thy death defend?
A furious foe unconscious proves a friend.
On Milton's verse does Bentley comment.—Know
A weak officious friend becomes a foe.
While he but sought his Author's fame to further,
The murderous critic has aveng'd thy murdĕr.
—POPE, ALEXANDER, 1732, *Epigram Occasioned by seeing some sheets of Dr. Bentley's edition of Milton's "Paradise Lost."*

As to Dr. Bentley and Milton, I think the one *above* and ye other *below* all criticism.—POPE, ALEXANDER, 1732, *Letter to Jacob Tonson, June* 7, *Pope's Works, ed. Courthope, vol.* III, *p.* 530.

The generality of my scheme does not admit the frequent notice of verbal inaccuracies; which Bentley, perhaps better skilled in grammar than in poetry, has often found, though he sometimes made them, and which he imputed to the obtrusions of a revisor, whom the author's blindness obliged him to employ; a supposition rash and groundless, if he thought it true; and vile and pernicious, if, as is said, he in private allowed it to be false.—JOHNSON, SAMUEL, 1779–81, *Milton, Lives of the English Poets.*

The classical learning of Bentley was

singular and acute, but the erudition of words is frequently found not to be allied to the sensibility of taste.—DISRAELI, ISAAC, 1791–1824, *"Critical Sagacity," and "Happy Conjecture;" or, Bentley's Milton, Curiosities of Literature.*

The great Bentley, when he undertook the editing of Milton, was far advanced in age, and soon after this work, which formed his last publication, his faculties discovered very evident decline. In many of his former works he has displayed a vigour and sagacity of mind, an extent and accuracy of erudition which are truly wonderful, and which, perhaps, have never been exceeded. But his edition of Milton, though it exhibits many characters of the great critic, must be pronounced to be altogether an egregious failure.—SYMMONS, CHARLES, 1809–10, *The Life of John Milton, p.* 536, *note.*

His edition of Milton had the same merits as his other editions; peculiar defects it had, indeed, from which his editions of Latin classics were generally free; these, however, were due to no decays in himself, but to original differences in the English classic from any which he could have met with in Pagan literature. The romantic, or Christian, poetry was alien to Bentley's taste; he had no more sense or organs of perception for this grander and more imaginative order of poetry than a screaming peacock may be supposed to have for the music of Mozart. Consequently, whatsoever was peculiarly characteristic in it seemed to him a monstrous abortion; and, had it been possible that passages in the same impassioned key should occur in the austere and naked words of the Roman or Grecian muse, he would doubtless have proscribed them as interpolations of monks, copyists, or scholiasts, with the same *desperate hook* which operated so summarily on the text of "Paradise Lost." With these infirmities, and this constitutional defect of poetic sensibility, the single blunder which he committed was in undertaking such a province. The management of it did him honour; for he complied honestly with the constitution of his own mind, and was right in the sense of taking a true view, though undoubtedly from a false station.—DE QUINCEY, THOMAS, 1830–57, *Richard Bentley, Collected Writings, ed. Masson, vol.* IV, *p.* 191.

Bentley's mind was saturated with the authors of antiquity. Their turn of thought, their style of expression, the niceties of their language had been his untiring study from boyhood onwards. To the imaginative poets of England he was a stranger. He was neither accustomed to their ways of thinking, nor their modes of expression, and coming fresh to them when he was close upon seventy he tried them by a standard very unlike their own. An aged, unpliant haughty novice, it was much too late to qualify himself for the commission he had received.—ELWIN, WHITWELL, 1872, *ed., The Works of Alexander Pope, vol.* VIII, *p.* 293, *note,*

Of inspiration, of refined intelligence of delicacy of taste, of any trace of sympathy with the essentials of poetry, his emendations are totally devoid. If, as is sometimes the case, they are felicitous—ingenious, that is to say, without violating poetic propriety—it is by pure accident. In many instances they literally beggar burlesque.—COLLINS, JOHN CHURTON, 1895, *Essays and Studies, p.* 284.

GENERAL

That new and brilliant light of Britain. —GRAEVIUS, JOHN GEORGE, 1697, *ed. Callimachus, Preface.*

A certain Bentley, diligent enough in turning over lexicons.—ALSOP, ANTHONY, 1698, *ed. Æsop.*

To answer the reflexion of a private Gentleman with a general abuse of the Society he belong'd to, is the manners of a dirty Boy, upon a Country-Green.—ATTERBURY, FRANCIS? 1701, *A Short Review.*

While Bentley, long to wrangling schools confin'd,
And but by books acquainted with mankind,
Dares, in the fulness of the pedant's pride,
Rhyme, tho' no genius; tho' no judge, decide;
Yet he, prime pattern of the captious art,
Out tibbalding poor Tibbald, tops his part;
Holds high the scourge o'er each fam'd author's head,
Nor are their graves a refuge for the dead:
To Milton lending sense, to Horace wit,
He makes them write what never poet writ;
The Roman Muse arraigns his mangling pens
And Paradise by him is lost again.
Such was his doom impos'd by Heav'n's decree,
With ears that hear not, eyes shall not see;
The low to swell, to level the sublime,
To blast all beauty, and beprose all rhyme.
—MALLET, DAVID, 1732, *Poem on Verbal Criticism, Addressed to Mr. Pope.*

Mistress! dismiss that rabble from your throne:
Avaunt—is Aristarchus yet unknown?
Thy mighty Scholiast whose unwearied pains
Made Horace dull, and humbled Milton's strains.
Turn what they will to Verse, their toil is vain,
Critics like me shall make it Prose again.
Roman and Greek Grammarians! know your Better,
Author of something yet more great than Letter;
While tow'ring o'er your Alphabet, like Saul,
Stands our Digamma, and o'ertops them all.
—POPE, ALEXANDER, 1742, *Dunciad, bk.* iv., *v.* 209–218.

To have it said and believed that you are the most learned man in England, would be no more than what was said of Dr. Bentley.—CHESTERFIELD, PHILIP DORMER STANHOPE EARL, 1750, *Letters to his Son, Nov.* 1.

Giant as he was in learning, and eagle-eyed in criticism.—COWPER, WILLIAM, 1790, *Letter to Samuel Rose, Feb.* 2.

Its editor, [of Julius Pollux] Hemsterhuis,—(for who at the age of eighteen under values himself?)—was well content with his work. In a short time he received a letter from Bentley, the British Aristarchus, in which the labor bestowed upon the edition by Hemsterhuis was highly commended, and at the same time Bentley's emendations were given of the citations made by Pollux from the comic authors. In restoring these passages Hemsterhuis himself had spared no pains, justly deeming it the most important part of his editorial duty. But, on the perusal of Bentley's emendations, he perceived his own labor to have been in vain, and that Bentley had accomplished the task with almost superhuman sagacity. And what do you suppose were the feelings of Hemsterhuis under these circumstances? He was so disturbed, so dissatisfied with himself, that he resolved to abandon the study of Greek for ever; nor did he, for two months, dare to touch a Greek author.—WOLF, FRIED. AUGUST, 1816, *Litterarische Analecten.*

A name dreaded as well as respected in literature.—SCOTT, SIR WALTER, 1824, *Richard Cumberland.*

In his emendations, as he calls them, both of Milton and of Horace, for one happy conjecture he makes at least twenty wrong, and ten ridiculous. In the Greek poets, and sometimes in Terence, he, beyond the rest of the pack, was often brought into the trail by scenting an unsoundness in the metre. But let me praise him where few think of praising him, or even of suspecting his superiority. He wrote better English than his adversary Middleton, and established for his university that supremacy in classical literature which it still retains.—LANDOR, WALTER SAVAGE, 1828, *Imaginary Conversations, Third Series, Southey and Landor, p.* 466.

In conclusion, I will venture to pronounce Dr. Bentley the greatest *man* amongst all scholars. In the complexion of his character and the style of his powers he resembled the elder Scaliger, having the same hardihood, energy, and elevation of mind. But Bentley had the advantage of earlier polish, and benefited by the advances of his age. He was, also, in spite of insinuations to the contrary, issuing from Mr. Boyle and his associates, favourably distinguished from the Scaligers, father and son, by constitutional good-nature, generosity and placability. I should pronounce him, also, the greatest of *scholars,* were it not that I remember Salmasius. Dr. Parr was in the habit of comparing the Phalaris Dissertation with that of Salmasius "De Lingua Hellenistica." For my own part, I have always compared it with the same writer's "Plinian Exercitations." Both are among the miracles of human talent: but with this difference, that the Salmasian work is crowded with errors; whilst that of Bentley, in its latest revision, is absolutely without spot or blemish.—DE QUINCEY, THOMAS, 1830–57, *Richard Bentley, Collected Writings, ed. Masson, vol.* IV, *p.* 234.

His scheme for an edition of Homer was abandoned, but the germ of all the modern theories on the subject is distinctly developed in his writings. In an article on the Homeric writings, we have ventured to enter our dissent against the prevailing hypothesis of Wolf; but who, at all deeply interested in the writings of the great poet of antiquity, will refuse to acknowledge how infinitely their knowledge has been increased, their delight in the Homeric writings heightened, by the inquiries of that eminent scholar, of Heyne, and of Payne Knight; and what are all these but the acknowledged disciples of Bentley? The whole modern theory of the Homeric versification rests on his discovery of the digamma; and independent of this groundwork of his system, and however imperfect the success of Mr. Knight, who, before the time of Bentley, would have imagined, as he has done, the possibility of restoring the original language in which the Iliad and Odyssey were composed?—BLOOMFIELD, C. J., 1831, *Bishop Monk's Life of Bentley, Quarterly Review, vol.* 46, *p.* 165.

Many things now familiar to young academics (thanks to the labours of Dawes, and Burney, and Parr, and Porson, and Elmsley) were utterly unknown to scholars like Bentley, and to Scaliger before him; and though it might seem an ungracious task, it would not be void either of pleasure or of profit to give select specimens of errors in metre and syntax committed by these illustrious men. —TATE, JAMES, 1834, *Introduction to the Principal Greek Tragic and Comic Metres.*

Whether his name could be safely placed above that of Erasmus, Scaliger, and Hemsterhuys, not to mention any of the renowned scholars of the last generation, may be a question on which the learned of England and other countries might differ. But this we think may be safely said, that if Bentley, in all other things the same, had passed his life in the quiet of a University in Holland or Germany;—if he had redeemed to those studies for which he was born, the time and the talents which he wasted in the petty squabbles of his College mastership, he would unquestionably have made himself, beyond all rivalry, the most celebrated scholar of modern times. . . . Bishop Monk bestows on him the epithet of the Prince of Scholars, and, if we were disposed to deny his title to this proud appellation, we should be at a loss to say who better deserves it. . . . But it cannot be denied by his warmest admirers, that his talent and learning were, even in his literary studies, most wofully misapplied. Of that small portion of leisure for tranquil study, which his contentious spirit left, the greater part was wasted in propping up, with boundless learning and a tact never surpassed, his arbitrary changes in the text of Latin poets. His *forte* was unquestionably Greek; and though he possessed an acuteness of verbal criticism, which has never been equalled, it is greatly to be deplored, that he has not devoted himself to the elucidation of the really great questions, that present themselves in the compass of Grecian literature.—EVERETT, EDWARD, 1836, *Richard Bentley, North American Review, vol.* 43, *pp.* 458, 494.

Bentley, relying upon his own exertions and the resources of his own mind, pursued an original path of criticism, in which the intuitive quickness and subtility of his genius qualified him to excel. In the faculty of memory, so important for such pursuits, he has himself candidly declared that he was not particularly gifted. Consequently he practised throughout life the precaution of noting in the margin of his books the suggestions and conjectures which rushed into his mind during their perusal. To this habit of laying up materials in store, we may partly attribute the surprising rapidity with which some of his most important works were completed.—HALLAM, HENRY, 1837–39, *Introduction to the Literature of Europe, pt.* iv, *ch.* i, *par.* 19.

He stands undoubtedly the very first among all the philological critics of every age and nation, "in shape and gesture proudly eminent." No single individual ever contributed so much to the actual stores of the learned world, or gave so strong an impulse to the study of the ancient classics. With little either of sensibility or imagination, he possessed an understanding which for compass, strength, and subtlety, has rarely been matched.—CUNNINGHAM, G. G., 1840, *ed., Lives of Eminent and Illustrious Englishmen, vol.* IV, *p.* 286.

The greatest scholar that had appeared in Europe since the revival of letters.—MACAULAY, THOMAS BABINGTON, 1843, *Francis Atterbury, Critical and Historical Essays.*

For Bentley he [Porson] preserved through life an unbounded veneration. He calls his work on Phalaris, *immortalis illa de Phalaridis Epistolis Dissertatio*, and omitted no opportunity of praising him. When, in after life, he had made many emendations in Aristophanes, and Bentley's copy of that poet was shown him, containing a number of his corrections in the margin, he is said to have shed tears of joy at finding a large portion of Bentley's conjectures exactly coincide with his own. He once spoke to some scholars at the Gray's Inn Coffee-House, on Bentley's literary character, with such warmth of eulogy that a North Briton, who was present, asked him if Bentley was not a *Scotchman.* "No," replied Porson, "Bentley was a *Greek* scholar." This story is told in more ways than one, but Porson's stress must have been upon the word "*Greek.*"—WATSON, JOHN SELBY, 1861, *The Life of Richard Porson, p.* 28.

Richard Bentley, therefore, becomes in every respect an important name in our sketch, both because he carried the experimental method, which was the method of the age, into a new region, and because he left behind some examples and some warnings as to the right and wrong use of this method. He showed that it must be applied freely and manfully if it is applied at all; he showed, by his failures as well as his successes, that reverence for an author—for any author whatsoever, be it Horace or Milton—is not a restraint upon sound criticism, but is an indispensable condition of it. He showed that the practical habits which belong to an Englishman—his acquaintance with law courts, and with the rules by which lawyers and men of the world try the truth of testimony—may be of the greatest worth in correcting the formal canons of schoolmen, may often give them quite a new character, and prevent them from leading to utterly false conclusions. But he showed also, that this experience may be purchased very dearly; that the man of letters who aspires to be the man of affairs may become involved in petty quarrels and litigations, which weaken the moral strength if they cultivate the acuteness of the mind. A union of his amazing erudition, minute perception, and practical force, with really high aims, would constitute a critic such as the world has not yet seen.—MAURICE, FREDERICK DENISON, 1862, *Moral and Metaphysical Philosophy, vol.* II, *p.* 479.

Bentley is not one among the great classical scholars, but he inaugurates a new era of the art of criticism. He opened a new path. With him criticism attained its majority. When scholars had hitherto offered suggestions and conjectures, Bentley, with unlimited control over the whole material of learning, gave decisions.—MÄHLY, JACOB, 1868, *Richard Bentley, Eine Biographie.*

Incomparably the first critic of the day. —STEPHEN, LESLIE, 1876, *History of English Thought in the Eighteenth Century, vol.* I, *p.* 86.

He had an excellent familiar knowledge of Greek, and was a great interpreter. Yet it must be remembered that he never tried his art upon the more difficult authors. He was better acquainted with the Anthology, Lucian, Suidas, Iamblichus, than with Plato, Thucydides, Sophocles, Æschylus, Pindar, Herodotus, who owe nothing to him. Upon the whole he keeps bad company in literature.— JOWETT, BENJAMIN, 1880–82, *Note Book, Life and Letters, ed. Abbott and Campbell, vol.* II. *p.* 186.

Bentley's reflections upon language, even when in conflict with sound philosophy, are worthy of study, for even the aberrations of true genius are suggestive. When he philosophizes upon the tendency of speech to constant change, in structure as well as in vocabulary, he seems to have a prevision of comparative philology, and we almost wonder that he has nothing to say about "consonantal interchange," "phonetic decay," and the other commonplaces of our modern science.— SHEPHERD, H. E., 1881, *A Study of Bentley's English, American Journal of Philology, vol.* 2, *p.* 27.

Bentley's simple English is racy in a way peculiar to him. It has the tone of a strong mind which goes straight to the truth; it is pointed with the sarcasm of one whose own knowledge is thorough and exact, but who is accustomed to find imposture wrapped up in fine or vague words, and takes an ironical delight in using the very homeliest images and phrases which accurately fit the matter in hand. No one has excelled Bentley in the power of making a pretentious fallacy absurd by the mere force of translation into simple terms; no writer of English has shown greater skill in touching the hidden springs of its native humour.— JEBB, RICHARD CLAVERHOUSE, 1882, *Bentley* (*English Men of Letters*), *p.* 170.

He left no great work; yet what he did in lines of classical criticism could not by any possibility have been better done by others. He supplied interpretations—where the world had blundered and stumbled—which blazed their way to unquestioned acceptance. He mastered all the difficulties of language, and wore the mastership with a proud and insolent self-assertion—a very Goliath of learning, with spear like a weaver's beam, and no son of Jesse to lay him low. . . . When you meet with that name of Bentley you may safely give it great weight in all scholarly matters, and not so much in matters of taste. Trust him in foot-notes to Aristophanes (a good mate for him!) or to Terence; trust him less in foot-notes to Milton, or even Horace (when he leaves prosody to talk of rhythmic *susurrus*).—MITCHELL, DONALD G., 1895, *English Lands Letters and Kings, Queen Anne and the Georges, p.* 11.

Was from the first recognized as a consummate genius by the scholars of Germany, by Græвius and Spanheim, who welcomed him as "novum et lucidum Britanniæ sidus," as "splendidissimum Britanniæ lumen." The many beginnings which he had laid for subsequent critical research among the ancient classical authors were taken up abroad by men like Heyne, Reiz, F. A. Wolf, Gottfried Hermann, and Friedrich Ritschl, in whose hands they have developed into a special school of philology, counting probably over a hundred representatives, many of whom have openly avowed their indebtedness to Bentley.—MERZ, JOHN THEODORE, 1896, *A History of European Thought in the Nineteenth Century, vol.* I, *p.* 169, *note.*

Prince of textual critics.—DOWDEN, JOHN, 1897, *Outlines of the History of the Theological Literature of the Church of England, p.* 207.

John Oldmixon

1673-1742.

Born in Somerset, 1673: died at London, 1742. An English historical writer. He was dull and insipid. He abused Pope in his "Essay on Criticism in Prose" (1728), and was promptly scarified in the "Dunciad" (ii. 283). Among his other works are "The British Empire in America" (1708), "Critical History of England, etc." (1726), "History of England" (1730-39), "Memoirs of the Press, etc." (1742), etc.—SMITH, BENJAMIN E., 1894-97, *ed., The Century Cyclopedia of Names, p.* 756.

PERSONAL

In naked majesty Oldmixon stands,
And Milo-like surveys his arms and hands;
Then, sighing thus, "And am I now three-score?
"Ah why, ye Gods, should two and two make four?"
He said, and climb'd a stranded lighter's height,
Shot to the black abyss, and plung'd downright.
The Senior's judgment all the crowd admire,
Who but to sink the deeper, rose the higher.
—POPE, ALEXANDER, 1728-43, *The Dunciad, bk.* II, *v.* 283, 290.

When we meet with the name of Oldmixon, who thinks of the real man, the tiresome old Whig pamphleteer, with his insipid pastorals and his petulant essays? We think of a figure created entirely by Pope; we think of the aged athlete, "in naked majesty," climbing the side of the stranded lighter, to plunge the deeper into the dreadful sluice of mud. Our interest is quickened, indeed, but not created by the consciousness that there was a real Oldmixon, to whom this figment of Pope's imagination must have given exquisite pain.—GOSSE, EDMUND, 1888, *A History of Eighteenth Century Literature, p.* 124.

GENERAL

Mr. Oldmixon wrote a history of the Stuarts in folio, and a Critical History of England, in two volumes octavo. The former of these pieces was undertaken to blacken the family of the Stuarts. The most impartial writers and candid critics, on both sides, have held this work in contempt, for in every page there breathes a malevolent spirit, a disposition to rail and calumniate: So far from observing that neutrality and dispassionate evenness of temper, which should be carefully attended to by every historian, he suffers himself to be transported with anger: He reviles, wrests particular passages, and frequently draws forced conclusions. A history written in this spirit has no greater claim to a reader's faith.—CIBBER, THEOPHILUS, 1753, *Lives of the Poets, vol.* IV, *p.* 203.

Oldmixon, who was a Whig historian,—if a violent party-writer ought ever to be dignified by so venerable a title,—unmercifully rigid to all other historians, was himself guilty of the crimes with which he so loudly accused others.—DISRAELI, ISAAC, 1812–13, *Authors by Profession, Calamities of Authors, note.*

Oldmixon's assertion, unsupported by evidence, is of no weight whatever.—MACAULAY, THOMAS BABINGTON, 1849, *History of England, ch.* xi, *note.*

His chief work was a history of the reign of the Stuarts in folio, a production which no doubt suggested to Hume the plan and title of his first two volumes. This work, although highly popular in its own time, has had little success with posterity. It wants fidelity, accuracy of research, a pleasing style and a philosophic tone; and it was no doubt a great encouragement to Hume that he had no more formidable rival than the imperfect volumes of Oldmixon. . . . A few lines of bitter satire in the Dunciad have done more to preserve the name of John Oldmixon to posterity than all his own labored productions.—LAWRENCE, EUGENE, 1855, *The Lives of the British Historians, vol.* I, 322.

Oldmixon could do nothing but rant and abuse . . . given to the world the worst history of England that ever was or is ever likely to be written. The student who resorts to his voluminous work for information rises from the perusal with disgust and wonder that a man who lived through a considerable part of the period he professes to pourtray, who was personally acquainted with many of the characters whose actions he undertakes to record, should have contented himself with drawing his materials wholly from party squibs, without contributing one atom of intelligence upon matters which fell under his own observation, or making one comment which is not either extravagantly laudatory or extravagantly abusive.—WYON, FREDERICK WILLIAM, 1876, *The History of Great Britain During the Reign of Queen Anne, vol.* II, *pp.* 262, 327.

John Oldmixon, the pamphleteer, was a waspish person. He was continually attacking somebody, and even ventured to have his fling at Pope, who promptly gibbeted him in "The Dunciad." As he was universally disliked, his verses were usually kept out of the miscellanies of the time; but from his little volume of poems in the manner of Anacreon, published in 1696, I have chosen some dainty trifles.—BULLEN, A. H., 1895, *Musa Proterva, Preface, p.* xii.

His historical work has little value now, and his main object in writing it was to promote the cause of the party. He never hesitated in attacking those on the other side, whether dead or living.—AITKEN, GEORGE A., 1895, *Dictionary of National Biography, vol.* XLII, *p.* 118.

Unfortunately, the great Whig historian and essayist sometimes allowed political bias to influence his brilliant literary productions; and he sacrificed accuracy to his love of rhetorical antithesis. Incomparably superior in attainments and character to Oldmixon (1673–1732), one of the heroes of the "Dunciad," both are remarkable for their overmastering spirit of Whig partisanship, though it is a degradation to Macaulay to imply a comparison in literary style with Oldmixon's dull, careless, and unveracious compilations.—AUBREY, W. H. S., 1896, *The Rise and Growth of the English Nation, vol.* III, *p.* 238.

William Somerville

1675-1742.

Born at the family seat, Edston, Warwickshire, in 1677, (?) (not 1692, as Dr. Johnson states), was admitted to Winchester school in 1690; in the same year became Fellow of New College, Oxford; resigned on succeeding to his patrimonial estate in 1704; divided his time between his justiceship of the peace, his books, hounds, and bottle, and died July 19, 1742. . . . 1. "The Two Springs; a Fable," London, 1725. 2. "Occasional Poems, Translations, Fables Tales," &c., 1727. 3. "The Chace; a Poem, 1735," 4th ed., 1743. . . . 4. "Field Sports; a Poem," 1742, 5. "Hobbinol; or, The Rural Games; a Burlesque Poem in Blank Verse," 1740.—ALLIBONE, S. AUSTIN, 1870, *Critical Dictionary of English Literature, vol.* II, *p.* 2175.

PERSONAL

Our old friend Somerville is dead; I did not imagine I could have been so sorry as I find myself on this occasion. Sublatum fuœrimus, I can now excuse all his foibles; impute them to age and to distressed circumstances. The last of these considerations wrings my very soul to think on; for a man of high spirit, conscious of having (at least in one production) generally pleased the world, to be plagued and threatened by wretches that are low in every sense; to be forced to drink himself into pains of the body in order to get rid of the pains of the mind, is a misery.—SHENSTONE, WILLIAM, 1742, *Letters, p.* 318.

Somerville was a handsome noisy squire, a strapping fellow six feet high, a hard rider, a crack shot. No more characteristic specimen of the sporting country gentleman, pure and simple, could be imagined, or one less likely to develop into a poet. It was, in fact, not until fast living begun to break down his constitution that he took to literature as a consolation. One of his earliest exercises was an epistle addressed to Addison, who had bought a property in Warwickshire, and so had become Somerville's neighbour.—GOSSE, EDMUND, 1880, *English Poets, ed. Ward, vol.* III, *p.* 189.

THE CHASE
1734

To this poem praise cannot be totally denied. He is allowed by sportsmen to write with great intelligence of his subject, which is the first requisite to excellence; and though it is impossible to interest the common readers of verse in the dangers or pleasures of the chase, he has done all that transition and variety could easily effect; and has with great propriety enlarged his plan by the modes of hunting used in other countries.—JOHNSON, SAMUEL, 1779–81, *Somerville, Lives of the English Poets.*

He is strictly and almost solely a *descriptive* poet; and his talent lies in delineating actual scenes with fidelity and spirit, adorning them with the beauties of diction, but leaving them to act upon the imagination by their own force, without aid from the creations of fancy. In classical allusion he is not deficient, but it is of the more common kind; and little occurs in his writings that indicates a mind inspired by that exalted enthusiasm which denotes the genius of superior rank. His versification is generally correct and well varied, and evidently flows from a nice and practised ear. His language is well suited to his subjects, rising and sinking with them, and free from that stiffness and affectation so commonly attendant upon blank verse. It more resembles that of Armstrong, than of Thomson or Akenside.—AIKIN, JOHN, 1820, *A Critical Essay on Somerville's Poem of the Chase.*

Somerville is best known by his poem, entitled the "Chase," which still has considerable popularity. It is written in blank verse, tolerably harmonious, and his descriptions, always accurate, from his own practical knowledge of his subject, are frequently vivid and beautiful.—CLEVELAND, CHARLES D., 1848, *A Compendium of English Literature, p.* 431.

Somerville has the merit of being inspired by a genuine love for the subject. He writes directly from the testimony of his own eyes, and the impulses of his own heart. He has obviously had the mould of his poem suggested by Thomson's "Seasons," but it is the mould only; the thoughts and feelings which are poured into it are his own.—GILFILLAN, GEORGE, 1859, *ed. Somerville Chase, p.* 319.

This epic, which is in four books, discusses in its first part the origin of hunting, the economy of kennels, the physical and moral accomplishments of hounds, and the choosing of a good or bad scenting day. The second book, which possesses more natural language and a finer literary quality than the others, commences with directions for hare-hunting, and closes with a moral reproof of tyranny. In the third book hunting is treated from an antiquarian and an exotic standpoint, while the fourth deals with the breeding of hounds, their diseases and the diseases they cause, such as hydrophobia. It will hardly be guessed from such a sketch of the contents that "The Chase" is a remarkably readable and interesting poem: It is composed in blank verse that is rarely turgid and not very often flat, and the zeal and science of the author give a certain vitality to his descriptions which compels the reader's attention. People that have a practical knowledge of the matters described confess that Somerville thoroughly understood what he was talking about, and that in his easy chair before the fire he "plied his function of the woodland" no less admirably than he had done in the saddle in his athletic youth.—GOSSE, EDMUND, 1880, *English Poets, ed. Ward, vol.* III, *p.* 190.

In "The Chase" Somerville had the advantage of knowing his subject, but knowledge is not poetry, and the interest of the poem is not due to its poetical qualities. He deserves some credit for his skill in handling a variety of metres as well as blank verse, in which his principal poem is written.—DENNIS, JOHN, 1894, *The Age of Pope, p.* 112.

GENERAL

Like Matt. and Swift ye sing with ease,
And can be Waller when you please.
—RAMSAY, ALLAN, 1730? *Answer to Epistle from William Somerville.*

Somerville's fame rests chiefly on "The Chase," a poem of four books in blank verse, to which "Field Sports" may be considered a supplement. It contains a vivid description of his favourite pastime and some lively pictures of animal life. It has always been held in high esteem by sportsmen, and many editions of it have been published, the finest being that of 1796, with illustrations by the brothers Bewick, of whose art it exhibits some of the best examples. The edition of 1800 has designs by Stothard. In 1896 it was reissued with illustrations by Mr. Hugh Thomson. . . . His poems figure in the collections of Johnson, Anderson, Chalmers, Bell, Stanford and Park.—CAMPBELL, G. W., 1898, *Dictionary of National Biography, vol.* LIII, *p.* 257.

John Hervey

Lord Hervey of Ickworth

1696-1743.

John, Lord Hervey (born 1696, died 1743), succeeded to the peerage on the death of his brother in 1723. During the greater part of his career he was a supporter of Sir Robert Walpole. In 1731 he fought a duel with Pulteney, on account of a libel against himself which Pulteney refused to disavow. Both combatants were slightly wounded. In 1740 he was appointed Lord Privy Seal against the wish of the Duke of Newcastle, and we find him subsequently intriguing with Pulteney and Chesterfield against Sir Robert Walpole. In 1743 he distinguished himself by a speech against the Gin Act. Lord Hervey left behind him certain memoirs of his own time, which form a most valuable addition to the history of the period of which they treat. He had the misfortune to offend Pope, who has handed his name down to posterity under the pseudonym of Sporus in the "Prologue to the Satires." Lord Hervey's "Memoirs of the Reign of George II." were first published by Mr. J. W. Croker in 1848.—LOW AND PULLING, 1884, *eds., Dictionary of English History, p.* 564.

PERSONAL

Let *Sporus* tremble--A. What? that thing of silk,
Sporus, that mere white curd of Ass's milk?
Satire or sense, alas! can *Sporus* feel?
Who breaks a butterfly upon a wheel?
P. Yet let me flap this bug with gilded wings,
This painted child of dirt, that stinks and stings;
Whose buzz the witty and the fair annoys,
Yet wit ne'er tastes, and beauty ne'er enjoys:
So well-bred spaniels civilly delight
In mumbling of the game they dare not bite,
Eternal smiles his emptiness betray,
As shallow streams run dimpling all the way.
Whether in florid impotence he speaks,
And, as the prompter breathes, the puppet squeaks;
Or at the ear of *Eve*, familiar Toad,
Half froth, half venom, spits himself abroad,
In puns, or politics, or tales, or lies,
Or spite, or smut, or rhymes, or blasphemies.
His wit all see-saw, between *that* and *this*
Now high, now low, now master up, now miss,
And he himself one vile Antithesis.
Amphibious thing! that acting either part,
The trifling head or the corrupted heart,
Fop at the toilet, flatt'rer at the board,
Now trips a Lady, and now struts a Lord,
Eve's tempter thus the Rabbins have exprest,
A Cherub's face, a reptile all the rest;
Beauty that shocks you, parts that none will trust;
Wit that can creep, and pride that licks the dust.
—POPE, ALEXANDER, 1735, *Epistle to Dr. Arbuthnot.*

Lord Hervey is at this time always with the king, in vast favour. He has certainly parts and wit, but is the most wretched, profligate man that ever was born, besides ridiculous; a painted face and not a tooth in his head: and it is not above six months ago that the king hated him so, that he would not suffer him to be one in his diversions at play. I think 'tis possible that sir Robert Walpole may make some use of him at first, and perhaps the other may have vanity enough to imagine that he may work himself up to be a great man; but that is too mad, I think, to be ever effected, because all the world except sir Robert abhors him, and notwithstanding all the mischiefs sir Robert has done the nation, and myself in particular, which people generally resent in the first place, I had much rather he should continue in power than my lord Hervey.—MARLBOROUGH, SARAH JENNINGS DUCHESS, 1737, *Opinions, ed. Hales, p.* 44.

The last stages of an infirm life are filthy roads, and like all other roads I find the farther one goes from the capital the more tedious the miles grow and the more rough and disagreeable the way. I know of no turnpikes to mend them; medicine pretends to be such, but doctors who have the management of it, like the comissioners for most other turnpikes, seldom execute what they undertake: they only put the toll of the poor cheated passenger in their pockets, and leave every jolt at least as bad as they found it, if not worse. "May all your ways (as Solomon says of wisdom) be ways of pleasantness, and all your paths peace;" and when your dissolution must come may it be like that of your lucky workman. Adieu!—HERVEY, JOHN LORD, 1743, *Letter to Lady Mary Wortley Montagu, June* 18.

You will see in the papers that Lord Hervey is dead—luckily, I think, for himself; for he had outlived his last inch of character.—WALPOLE, HORACE, 1743, *To Sir Horace Mann, Aug.* 14; *Letters, ed. Cunningham, vol.* I, *p.* 264.

Beneath the effeminacy of the Maccaroni, Lord Hervey was one of the few who united to intense *finery* in every minute detail, an acute and cultivated intellect. To perfect a Maccaroni it was in truth advisable, if not essential, to unite some smattering of learning, a pretension to wit, to his super-dandyism; to be the author of some personal squib, or the translator of some classic. Queen Caroline was too cultivated herself to suffer fools about her, and Lord Hervey was a man after her own taste: as a courtier he was essentially a fine gentleman; and, more than that, he could be the most delightful companion, the most sensible adviser, and the most winning friend in the court. His ill health, which he carefully concealed, his fastidiousness, his ultra delicacy of habits, formed an agreeable contrast to the coarse robustness of "Sir Robert," and constituted a relief after the society of the vulgar, strong-minded minister, who was born for the hustings and the House of Commons rather than for the courtly drawing-room.—THOMSON, KATHARINE AND J. C. (GRACE AND PHILIP WHARTON), 1860, *The Wits and Beaux of Society.*

Hervey was a remarkable man. His physical frame was as feeble as that of Voltaire. He suffered from epilepsy and a variety of other ailments. He had to live mainly on a dietary of ass's milk. His face was so meagre and so pallid, or rather livid, that he used to paint and make up like an actress or a fine lady. Pope, who might have been considerate to the weak of frame, was merciless in his ridicule of Hervey. He ridiculed him as Sporus, who could neither feel satire nor sense, and as Lord Fanny. Yet Hervey could appreciate satire and sense; could write satire and sense. He was a man of very rare capacity. He had already distinguished himself as a debater in the House of Commons, and was afterwards to distinguish himself as a debater in the House of Lords. He wrote pretty verses and clever pamphlets, and he has left to the world a collection of "Memoirs of the Reign of George the Second," which will always be read for its vivacity, its pungency, its bitterness, and its keen, penetrating good-sense. Hervey succeeded in obtaining the hand of one of the most beautiful women of the day, the charming Mary Lepell, whose name has been celebrated in more than one poetical panegyric by Pope, and he captivated the heart of one of the royal princesses. The historical reader must strike a sort of balance for himself in getting at an estimate of Hervey's character. No man has been more bitterly denounced by his enemies or more warmly praised by his friends.—MCCARTHY, JUSTIN, 1884, *A History of the Four Georges, vol.* I.

We have said that Lord Hervey was a man of considerable parts, a wit, a ready writer, a keen and amusing observer of character, but when this has been said all has been said. In a lax age his profligacy was notorious. He was a sceptic, and took the greatest delight in wounding the religious susceptibilities of those he came across. In his creed there was nothing great, nothing noble, nothing of good report; all was hollow, artificial, and insincere. As a necessary consequence of his distorted faith, he believed in nothing, except perhaps himself, and in nobody, except perhaps Queen Caroline. —EWALD, ALEXANDER CHARLES, 1885, *Studies Re-Studied, p.* 330.

Hervey was a clever and unprincipled man, of loose morals and sceptical opinions. He was an effective though somewhat pompous speaker, a ready writer, and a keen observer of character. His wit and charm of manner made him a special favourite of women.—BARKER, G. F. RUSSELL, 1891, *Dictionary of National Biography, vol.* XXVI, *p.* 285.

As long as the loathsome traits which are delineated in the character of "Sporus" repel and sicken mankind, so long will the name of John Lord Hervey be infamous. Of the impotence of truth to contend with the fiction of so great an artist as Pope, the result of Mr. Croker's attempt to vindicate Hervey's fame is a striking illustration. In 1848 Mr. Croker published that nobleman's "Memoirs," prefixing an Introduction, in which he proved, as indeed the "Memoirs" themselves proved, that the original of Pope's picture was a man whose genius and temper had been cast rather in the mould of St. Simon and Tacitus than in that of the foppish and loathsome hermaphrodite with whom he had been associated. But the popular estimate of Hervey remains unchanged. He was "Sporus" to our ancestors, who had neither his "Memoirs" nor Mr. Croker's Introduction before them, and he is "Sporus" to us who have both, but who, unfortunately for Hervey, care for neither, and know Pope's verses by heart.—COLLINS, JOHN CHURTON, 1895, *The Porson of Shakspearian Criticism, Essays and Studies, p.* 265.

One has certainly to fortify oneself by the recollection of Horace and his *sic visum Veneri*. Everything that one hears of the brilliant and cynical John Hervey, with his "coffin-face" and his painted cheeks, his valetudinarian, anaemic beauty, and his notorious depravity of life, makes it difficult to understand what particular qualities in him—apart from opportunity and proximity—could possibly have attracted the affection of a young and a very charming woman, who was besides far in advance of her contemporaries in parts and education. Yet it must be remembered that

"—when Hervey the handsome was wedded
To the beautiful Molly Lepell"

(as the ballad has it), he was only four-and twenty.—DOBSON, AUSTIN, 1896, *Eighteenth Century Vignettes, Third Series, p.* 301.

MEMOIRS OF THE REIGN OF GEORGE II

Lord Hervey himself fairly admits that impartiality in such cases as his is not to be expected, and he justifies that confession to its fullest extent; but though we see that his colouring may be capricious and exaggerated—no one can feel the least hesitation as to the substantial and, as to mere facts, the minute accuracy of his narrative. He may, and I have no doubt too often does, impute a wrong motive to an act, or a wrong meaning to a speech; but we can have no doubt that the act or the speech themselves are related as he saw and heard them: and there are many indications that the greater part was written from day to day as the events occurred. I know of no such near and intimate picture of the interior of a court; no other memoirs that I have ever read bring us so immediately, so actually into not merely the presence, but the company of the personages of the royal circle. Lord Hervey is, may I venture to say, almost the *Boswell* of George II. and Queen Caroline—but Boswell without his good nature. He seems to have taken—perhaps under the influence of that "wretched health" of which he so frequently complained—a morbid view of mankind, and to have had little of the milk of human kindness in his temper.—CROKER, JOHN WILSON, 1848, *ed., Memoirs of the Reign of King George the Second, Prefatory and Biographical Notice, vol.* I, *p.* 49.

Lord Hervey, for we put aside his poetical effusions, gave to our own day a present which, one may say, has enriched the treasury of our social literature with some very bad coin. For years his "Diary" was buried; until, at last, the late Mr. Croker, on whose shoulders the mantle of the bitter satirist had fallen, exhumed it and gave it, slightly mangled, to the world. His Lordship's "Diary" is very clever, very revolting, and, we fear, very true. At all events, it is the report of an anatomist who has made deep and daily search into the physiology of princes, princesses, statesmen, and courtiers. He has thoroughly dissected their hearts; and he knows every throb, and its consequence. He has left a picture such as no human skill could have invented nor conceived, and which we must therefore believe to be accurate; but it is told in such cold-blooded terms, it is so dark with the endless delineations of selfishness and turpitude, that we would willingly believe that "Lady Fanny's" mind was diseased, had we not other proofs that the revelations are essentially veracious.—THOMSON, KATHERINE (GRACE WHARTON), 1862, *The Literature of Society, vol.* II, *p.* 232.

Lord Hervey was a person whom the world never appreciates, and does not like. To the English reading public, a courtier and a hater of the clergy is always unacceptable. This antiecclesiastical eighteenth century tone is not forgiven either in Gibbon or in Adam Smith, and to its presence in Lord Hervey's "Memoirs" we must ascribe the fact that they are so little relished. They are, even in the mutilated state in which we have them, one of the best productions in our language of a kind of writing in which the French are so rich, and we so poor. No parallel is intended between Pope's "Satires" and Lord Hervey's "Memoirs" on any other point but the one of flashing a vivid light upon their surroundings during a period little otherwise illuminated. The two books have no other resemblance, and may be obviously contrasted. Lord Hervey paints the Court from St. James's; Pope, at Twickenham, vents the spleen of the opposition. Lord Hervey relates matter of fact in simple prose; Pope deals in distant allusions and veiled sneers. However, such as they are, the two together, Pope and Lord Hervey, mortal foes as they were, are the two most important witnesses of the period in question.—PATTISON, MARK, 1872–89, *Pope and His Editors, Essays, ed. Nettleship, vol.* II, *p.* 352.

Though the portrait of Sporus is described by Johnson as the meanest part of this Epistle, it is difficult to suppose that such would have been his deliberate judgment if he had not been prejudiced in favour of Lord Hervey. The morals of the latter, as displayed by himself in his "Memoirs of the Reign of George II." show that Pope's satire is as just as it is ardent and poetical.—ELWIN, WHITWELL AND COURTHOPE, WILLIAM JOHN, 1881, *eds., The Works of Alexander Pope, vol.* III, *p.* 265, *notes.*

The world owes him some thanks for a really interesting book, the very boldness and bitterness of which enhance to a certain extent its historical value.—McCARTHY, JUSTIN, 1884, *A History of the Four Georges, vol.* I, *chap.* XX.

Of all these *Mémoires pour servir* there are few that can compare, in novelty of information, in humour, in mordant descriptions of character, in hate and cynicism, with the pages of John, Lord Hervey. . . . Throughout the pages of his "Memoirs" detraction is the principal feature. His enemies are of course painted in the blackest colours, their characters picked out in the *aqua fortis* of hate; but even in his descriptions of his friends there is always something spiteful and malicious, which casts into the shade the praise that may have been bestowed. Everybody is a knave or a sycophant; the world revolves upon the axis of humbug, and between the poles of venality and corruption. A politician is one who identifies his own interests with those of the country; a priest is a scheming hypocrite who makes the best of both worlds, and who would sell his soul for a mitre; justice, truth, morality, and all the other attributes of virtue, are only so many masks to conceal motives and to further the cause of self-advancement. We rise from the splenetic pages of Lord Hervey with the feelings of a sane man who has been shut up with the afflicted in mind, and who longs to mix again with his sound and healthy fellows, so as to dispel the morbid associations of the past; or with the feelings of one confined in a hothouse, and who craves for the inspiriting breezes of the moorland.—EWALD, ALEXANDER CHARLES, 1885, *Studies Re-Studied, pp.* 325, 330.

GENERAL

Lord Hervey was not destitute of wit, though some of his lines have been absurdly overpraised. His recriminations on Pope are the best, indeed the only good things he wrote.—RUSSELL, WILLIAM CLARKE, 1871, *The Book of Authors, p.* 180, *note.*

Intellectually he was reckoned one of the most brilliant men of that most intellectually brilliant period. His satires were sharp-edged, clever, and bright, his Parliamentary speeches full of force, and his political pamphlets were "equal to any that ever were written," according to Sir Robert Walpole: moreover, he was a linguist, and had a spice of classic lore. —MOLLOY, J. FITZGERALD, 1882, *Court Life below Stairs, p.* 22.

Hervey's style, though somewhat elaborated, is lively and forcible. Throughout his writings, which in many ways bear a curious resemblance to those of Horace Walpole, a bitter tone of cynicism and a morbid spirit of universal detraction are always apparent.—BARKER, G. F. RUSSELL, 1891, *Dictionary of National Biography, vol.* XXVI, *p.* 286.

He is at his best as a writer when he has to describe some dramatic scene; he can then be terse and vivid, but only to lapse after a few good sentences into his customary mode. His place in a descriptive history of English prose is due to the fact that his writing represents what the English of his time was in the hands of a cultivated man, undistinguished as a master of writing.—STREET, G. S., 1894, *English Prose, ed. Craik, vol.* III, *p.* 614.

Richard Savage

1690?-1743.

Richard Savage, 1690[?]-1743, Born, about 1690 [?]. Play, "Woman's a Riddle," produced at Lincoln's Inn Fields, 4 Dec. 1716; "Love in a Veil," Drury Lane, 17 June 1718; "Sir Thomas Overbury," Drury Lane, 12 June 1723. Condemned to death, for murder in a tavern brawl, Nov. 1727; pardoned, March 1728. Member of Lord Tyrconnel's household, 1728-34. Pension from Queen Caroline, 1732-37. Arrested for debt in Bristol, 10 Jan. 1743. Died in prison there, 1 Aug. 1743. Buried in St. Peter's Churchyard, Bristol. *Works:* "The Convocation," 1717; "Memoirs of Theophilus Keene" (anon.; attrib. to Savage), 1718; "Love in a Veil," 1719; "Sir Thomas Overbury," 1724; "A Poem, sacred to the glorious memory of . . . King George," 1727; "Nature in Perfection," 1728; "The Bastard," 1728; "The Author to be Let" [1728?]; "The Wanderer," 1729; "Verses occasioned by Lady Tyrconnel's Recovery," 1730; "Poem to the Memory of Mrs. Oldfield" (anon.; attrib. to Savage), 1730; "A Collection of Pieces. . . . publish'd on occasion of the Dunciad," 1732; "The Volunteer Laureat" (6 nos.), 1732-37; "On the Departure of the Prince and Princess of Orange," 1734; "The Progress of a Divine," 1735; "Poem on the Birthday of the Prince of Wales," 1735; "Of Public Spirit in regard to Public Works," 1737. *Posthumous:* "London and Bristol Compared," 1744; "Various Poems," 1761. He *edited:* "Miscellaneous Poems and Translations, by several hands," 1726. *Collected Works:* in 2 vols., 1775.—SHARP, R. FARQUHARSON, 1897, *A Dictionary of English Authors, p.* 248.

PERSONAL

Two fathers join'd to rob my claim of one!
My mother too thought fit to have no son!
The senate next, whose aid the helpless own,
Forgot my infant wrongs, and mine alone.
—SAVAGE, RICHARD, 1732, *A Poem on the Queen's Birth-Day.*

It is a long time since I saw him: I have been told some of his friends make complaints of a certain little effect of a *spleen* in his temper, which he is no more able to help, and therefore should no more be accountable for, than the misfortunes to which, in all likelihood, his constitution may have owed it originally.—HILL, AARON, 1736, *Letter to James Thomson, May* 20, *Hill's Works, vol.* I, *p.* 237.

"Why do I breathe? what joy can being give,
When she who gave me life forgets I live!
Feels not these wintry blasts—nor heeds my smart;
But shuts me from the shelter of her heart?
Saw me exposed to want! to shame! to scorn!
To ills!—which make it misery to be born!
Cast me, regardless, on the world's bleak wild,
And bade me be a wretch, while yet a child!

Where can he hope for pity, peace or rest,
Who moves no softness—in a mother's breast?
Custom, law, reason, all! my cause forsake;
And nature sleeps, to keep my woes awake!
Crimes, which the cruel scarce believe can be,
The kind are guilty of, to ruin me!
E'en she who bore me blasts me with her hate,
And, meant my fortune, makes herself my fate!"
—HILL, AARON, c1740, *Verses made for Mr. Savage, and sent to Lady Macclesfield, His Mother.*

I have really taken more pains not to affront him than if my bread had depended on him. He would be to be forgiven, if it was misfortune only, and not pride, that made him captious.—POPE, ALEXANDER, 1741, *Letter to Mallet, Jan.* 25, *Pope's Works, ed. Elwin and Courthope, vol.* X, *p.* 95.

I must be sincere with you, as our correspondence is now likely to be closed. Your language is really too high, and what I am not used to from my superiors; much too extraordinary for me, at least sufficiently so to make me obey your commands, and never more presume to advise or meddle in your affairs, but leave your own conduct entirely to your own judgment. It is with concern I find so much misconstruction joined with so much resentment in your nature. You still injure some whom you had known many years as friends, and for whose intentions I would take upon me to answer; but I have no weight with you, and cannot tell how soon (if you have not already) you may misconstrue all I can say or do; and I see in the case how unforgiving your are, I desire to prevent this in time.—POPE, ALEXANDER, 1743, *Letter to Savage, Pope's Works, ed. Elwin and Courthope, vol.* X, *p.* 102.

Wherever he came his address secured him friends, whom his necessities soon alienated; so that he had, perhaps, a more numerous acquaintance than any man ever before attained, there being scarcely any person eminent on any account to whom he was not known, or whose character he was not in some degree able to delineate. . . . He was of a middle stature, of a thin habit of body, a long visage, coarse features, and melancholy aspect; of a grave and manly deportment, a solemn dignity of mein, but which, upon a nearer acquaintance, softened into an engaging easiness of manners. His walk was slow, and his voice tremulous and mournful. He was easily excited to smiles, but very seldom provoked to laughter. His mind was in an uncommon degree vigorous and active. His judgment was accurate, his apprehension quick, and his memory so tenacious that he was frequently observed to know what he had learned from others in a short time, better than those by whom he was informed, and could frequently recollect incidents, with all their combination of circumstances, which few would have regarded at the present time, but which the quickness of his apprehension impressed upon him. He had the art of escaping from his own reflections, and accommodating himself to every new scene. —JOHNSON, SAMUEL, 1744, *An Account of the Life of Mr. Richard Savage.*

Poor Savage was well remembered to have been as inconsiderate, inconsistent, and inconstant a mortal as ever existed, what he might have said carried but little weight; and, as he would blow both hot and cold, nay, too frequently, to gratify the company present, would sacrifice the absent, though his best friend. . . . I met Savage one summer, in a condition too melancholy for description. He was starving; I supported him, and my father cloathed him, 'till his tragedy was brought on the stage, where it met with success in the representation, tho' acted by the young part of the company, in the summer season; whatever might be the merit of his play, his necessities were too pressing to wait 'till winter for its performance.—CIBBER, THEOPHILUS, 1753, *Lives of the Poets, vol.* V, *p.* 213, *note.*

He was, however, undoubtedly a man of excellent parts; and, had he received the full benefits of a liberal education, and had his natural talents been cultivated to the best advantage, he might have made a respectable figure in life. He was happy in an agreeable temper, and a lively flow of wit, which made his company much coveted; nor was his judgment, both of writing and of men, inferior to his wit; but he was too much a slave to his passions, and his passions were too easily excited. He was warm in his friendships, but implacable in his enmity; and his greatest fault, which is indeed the greatest of all faults, was ingratitude. He seemed to suppose everything due to his merit, and that he was little obliged to any persons for those favours which he thought it their duty to confer on him; it is therefore the less to be wondered at, that he never rightly estimated the kindness of his many friends and benefactors, or preserved a grateful and due sense of their generosity towards him.—BAKER, DAVID ERSKINE, 1764–1812, *Biographia Dramatica, pt.* ii, *vol.* I, *p.* 634.

Ill-fated Savage, at whose birth was giv'n
No parent but the Muse, no friend but Heav'n.
—SHERIDAN, RICHARD BRINSLEY, 1777, *Sir Thomas Overbury, Prologue.*

The history of this man is well known by the life of him written by Johnson; which, if in no other respect valuable, is curious, in that it gives to view a character self-formed, as owing nothing to parental nurture, and scarce any thing to moral tuition, and describes a mind, in which, as in a neglected garden, weeds, without the least obstruction, were suffered to grow into luxuriance: nature had endowed him with fine parts, and those he cultivated as well as he was able; but his mind had received no moral culture, and for want thereof, we find him to have been a stranger to humility, gratitude, and those other virtues that tend to conciliate the affections of men, and insure the continuance of friendship. . . . Savage, as to his exterior, was, to a remarkable degree, accomplished: he was a handsome, well-made man, and very courteous in the modes of salutation. I have been told, that in the taking off his hat and disposing it under his arm, and in his bow, he displayed as much grace as those actions were capable of; and that he understood the exercise of a gentleman's weapon, may be inferred from the use he made of it in that rash encounter which is related in his life, and to which his greatest misfortunes were owing.—HAWKINS, SIR JOHN, 1787, *The Life of Samuel Johnson, p.* 52.

An earl's son, a shoemaker's apprentice, who had seen life in all its forms, who had feasted among blue ribands in Saint James's Square, and had lain with fifty pounds weight of irons on his legs, in the condemned wards of Newgate. This man had, after many vicissitudes of fortune, sunk at last into abject and hopeless poverty. His pen had failed him. His patrons had been taken away by death, or estranged by the riotous profusion with which he squandered their bounty, and the ungrateful insolence with which he rejected their advice. He now lived by begging. He dined on venison and Champagne whenever he had been so fortunate as to borrow a guinea. If his questing had been unsuccessful, he appeased the rage of hunger with some scraps of broken meat, and lay down to rest under the Piazza of Covent Garden in warm weather, and, in cold weather, as near as he could get to the furnace of a glass house. Yet, in his misery, he was still an agreeable companion. He had an inexhaustible store of anecdotes about that gay and brilliant world from which he was now an outcast. He had observed the great men of both parties in hours of careless relaxation, had seen the leaders of opposition without the mask of patriotism, and had heard the prime minister roar with laughter and tell stories not over-decent. During some months Savage lived in the closest familiarity with Johnson; and then the friends parted, not without tears. Johnson remained in London to drudge for Cave. Savage went to the west of England, lived there as he had lived everywhere, and, in 1743, died, penniless and heart-broken, in Bristol gaol.—MACAULAY, THOMAS BABINGTON, 1843, *Samuel Johnson, Critical and Historical Essays.*

Savage is commonly connected with Chatterton, but except in the accident of their poverty, I could never, for my own part, find out any resemblance. As a man, Chatterton was of austere demeanor, and as a poet he was of the highest powers; but Savage as a man was extremely social, and as a poet was not greatly beyond mediocrity. Chatterton died rather than ask relief: Savage did not, indeed, solicit relief, he commanded it.—GILES, HENRY, 1850, *Lectures and Essays, vol.* II, *p.* 305.

Whatever errors there might be in the common tradition of the Countess of Macclesfield's story, it was at least well known that she had a male child whose father was Lord Rivers, and which child had disappeared. Speculation and gossip on the fate of this child were sure to be rife, and were not unlikely to produce a pretender, who, if he could not convince the mother of his claims, might at least find some sympathy and support in the public, who were not so well informed.

A romantic story, a noble birth discovered by accident, an unnatural mother, and a neglected child, could not fail to captivate some persons; and experience shows that the partisans of such claimants are not scrupulous about proof, and that even the claimants themselves, if not checked by exposure, grow at length into a kind of faith in their story, which helps them to sustain their part. I am on the whole, and notwithstanding some circumstances in his favour, to which I would allow due weight, strongly of opinion that this was Savages's case.—THOMAS, W. MOY, 1858, *Richard Savage, Notes and Queries, Second Series, vol.* 6, *p.* 386.

The investigations of Moy Thomas would go to show that the Savage friend of Johnson's early days in London was the most arrant of imposters; and that of all the shame that rests upon him, he can only justly be relieved of that which counts him a child of such a woman as the Countess of Macclesfield. I have dwelt upon the Savage episode, not alone because it provoked one of Johnson's best pieces of prose work, but because it shows how open were his sympathies to such tales of distress, and how quick he was to lift the rod of chastisement upon wrong-doers of whatever degree.—MITCHELL, DONALD G., 1895, *English Lands Letters and Kings, Queen Anne and the Georges, p.* 94.

The by-ways of our literature reek with the memories of sordid tragedies. Ghosts of neglected wits, squalid still, winnow the air in the least disturbed corners. Many a genius has here dwindled, guttered, and gone out, a beggarly unknown garreteer; hustled from earth either to vanish in oblivion or be saturated with post-mortem praise—thin food and fit for a spook to feed on. Gather together these ravelled skeins, these records of souls prodigally wasted, none will fret the heart more than that of Richard Savage, the tale of whose pilgrimage has thrilled many a heart-string. Distressed poets there have been a many, but still the miserable chronicle of this man's privations remains unequalled.—RUSSELL, TOM, 1896, *A Volunteer Laureate, The Gentleman's Magazine, vol.* 280, *p.* 146.

No documents in support of Savage's pretensions have been produced, not even those letters from which he himself claimed to make the discovery. All the details are vague, lacking in names and dates; they cannot be independently authenticated, and long intervals in his early life are left unaccounted for. Research has been unable to confirm the existence of Mrs. Lloyd. In the register of St. Andrew's he is only alloted one godmother, Dorothea Ousley, who married Robert Delgardno at St. James's, Westminster, on 24 Sept. 1698. There is no record of any communication between Savage and Lady Mason, the alleged guardian of his childhood, though she did not die till 1717. Newdigate Ousley, his godfather, who lived till 1714 at Enfield in Middlesex, was unknown to him. Lord Rivers's will is dated fourteen months before his death, and contains no codicil, though Savage asserted that he revoked the legacy to him on his deathbed. His reputed mother (Mrs. Brett) steadily maintained that he was an impostor. When to these considerations is added the fact that Savage, very late in life, contradicted essential details in the published story in a letter to Elizabeth Carter on 10 May 1739, the falsity of his tale seems demonstrated. The chief points in his favour are that Lord Tyrconnel, Mrs. Brett's nephew, after Savage had published his story, received him into his household, and that one at least of Lord Rivers's children, whom he styles his sister, recognised his claim, and corresponded with him in his later years. That Mrs. Brett took no decisive steps to disprove his claims was owing doubtless to her unwillingness to revive the memory of her disgrace, and to the difficulty of obtaining proof of her own child Richard's death.—CARLYLE, E. IRVING, 1897, *Dictionary of National Biography, vol.* L, *p.* 345.

THE BASTARD

1728

A poem remarkable for the vivacious sallies of thought in the beginning, where he makes a pompous enumeration of the imaginary advantages of base birth; and the pathetick sentiments at the end, where he recounts the real calamities which he suffered by the crime of his parents. The vigour and spirit of the verses, the peculiar circumstances of the author, the novelty of the subject, and the notoriety of the story to which the allusions are made, procured this performance a very favourable reception; great numbers were immediately dispersed, and editions were multiplied with unusual rapidity.—JOHNSON, SAMUEL, 1744, *An Account of the Life of Mr. Richard Savage.*

Almost all things written from the heart, as this certainly was, have some merit. The Poet here describes sorrows and misfortunes which were by no means imaginary; and thus there runs a truth of thinking through this poem, without which it would be of little value, as Savage is, in other respects, but an indifferent poet.—GOLDSMITH, OLIVER, 1767, *The Beauties of English Poetry.*

A very forcible piece of writing.—ARNOLD, THOMAS, 1868–75, *Chaucer to Wordsworth, p.* 286.

THE WANDERER
1729

It has been generally objected to "The Wanderer," that the disposition of the parts is irregular; that the design is obscure, and the plan perplexed; that the images, however beautiful, succeed each other without order, and that the whole performance is not so much a regular fabrick, as a heap of shining materials thrown together by accident, which strikes rather with the solemn magnificence of a stupendous ruin, than the elegant grandeur of a finished pile. This criticism is universal, and therefore it is reasonable to believe it at least in a great degree just; but Mr. Savage was always of a contrary opinion, and thought his drift could only be missed by negligence or stupidity, and that the whole plan was regular, and parts distinct. It was never denied to abound with strong representations of nature, and just observations upon life; and it may easily be observed, that most of his pictures have an evident tendency to illustrate his first great position, "that good is the consequence of evil."—JOHNSON, SAMUEL, 1744, *An Account of the Life of Mr. Richard Savage.*

Did you ever read Savage's beautiful poem of "The Wanderer?" If no, do so, and you will see the fault which, I think, attaches to Lord Maxwell—a want of distinct precision and intelligibility about the story, which counteracts, especially with ordinary readers, the effect of beautiful and forcible diction, poetical imagery, and animated description.—SCOTT, SIR WALTER, 1821, *Letter to Allan Cunningham, Apr.* 27.

"The Wanderer" of Savage is a very remarkable production; the more remarkable when we consider the circumstances in which it was composed. Stanzas of it were often written upon cobblers' stalls, and sometimes whole passages were indited in a pauper-lodging. One special quality of the poem is the extreme purity, and moral elevation of sentiment, contrasted with his own practical conduct.—GILES, HENRY, 1850, *Lectures and Essays, vol.* II, *p.* 306.

"The Wanderer" is the poem upon which he evidently bestowed the greatest care. It may be regarded as his own epitaph, written by himself, and embodying the dark phrases of his career, the most vivid of his sensations, and the beauty of his moral sentiments, combined with the want of system, the self-esteem, recklessness, and courage, which alternated in his feelings and conduct.—TUCKERMAN, HENRY T., 1857, *Essays, Biographical and Critical, p.* 196.

Not being compelled to write for bread, he finished it with considerable care, and it forms a very favourable specimen of his powers. It contains much that is feeble, tawdry, and in the meanest taste; but, on the other hand, the versification is fluent, and there are passages of so much vigour and excellence as to justify a belief that, with deeper study, broader culture, and a higher and wider experience of life, its author might have taken a respectable position in the front rank of our minor poets. The commonplace, however, is so mixed up with that which is more forcible and elevated that it is difficult to make quotations.—ADAMS, W. H. DAVENPORT, 1880, *Wrecked Lives, First Series, p.* 252.

GENERAL

Thee, Savage! these (the justly great) admire,
Thee, quick'ning Judgment's phlegm with
Fancy's fire.

—DYER, JOHN, c1743, *To Mr. Savage.*

Though he may not be altogether secure against the objections of the critic, it must however be acknowledged, that his works are the productions of a genius truly poetical; and, what many writers who have been more lavishly applauded cannot boast, that they have an original air, which has no resemblance of any foregoing writer, that the versification and sentiments have a cast peculiar to themselves, which no man can imitate with success, because what was nature in Savage, would in another be affectation. It must be confessed, that his descriptions are striking, his images animated, his fictions justly imagined, and his allegories artfully pursued; that his diction is elevated, though sometimes forced, and his numbers sonorous and majestick, though frequently sluggish and encumbered. Of his style, the general fault is harshness, and its general excellence is dignity; of his sentiments, the prevailing beauty is simplicity, and uniformity the prevailing defect.—JOHNSON, SAMUEL, 1744, *An Account of the Life of Mr. Richard Savage.*

The incidents of his life rather than the creations of his genius have preserved the fame of Savage. His poems are his only writings now recognized, and we find them regularly included in editions of the British anthology. It is, however, but here and there, scattered through a long array of heroics, that we can detect either originality or raciness. Like his life, these effusions are crude and unsustained; they lack finish, completeness, and unity. Deformed by coarseness, and sometimes by obscurity, they often repel taste; and their frequent want of clear and uniform design induces weariness. Their most genuine interest is personal; we naturally associate them with the misfortunes of the author, and the special references are not without a pathetic zest. . . . It is evident that he possessed, in an uncommon degree, what the phrenologists call the organ of wonder, and metaphysical writers a sense of the sublime. In his descriptions of nature and life, we perceive the inspiration of a reflective ideality. His couplets occasionally glow with vital animation, and his choice of epithets is often felicitous. Vigour, fluency, and expressiveness, at times, indicate that there was an original vein in his nature, though too carelessly worked to produce a great and consistent result.—TUCKERMAN, HENRY T., 1857, *Essays, Biographical and Critical, pp.* 195, 196.

Savage's poem called "The Bastard" has some vigorous lines, and some touches of tenderness as well as bursts of more violent passion; but, as a whole, it is crude, spasmodic, and frequently wordy and languid. His other compositions, some of which evince a talent for satire, of which assiduous cultivation might have made something, have all passed into oblivion. The personal history of Savage, which Johnson's ardent and expanded narrative has made universally known, is more interesting than his verse; but even that owes more than half its attraction to his biographer. He had, in fact, all his life, apparently, much more of another kind of madness than he ever had of that of poetry.—CRAIK, GEORGE L., 1861, *A Compendious History of English Literature and of the English Language, vol.* II, *p.* 279.

Created an interest, and had chances in life greater than his personal merits warranted. His poetical pretensions were of no high order, and in most instances his productions were only redeemed by a few vigorous lines.—MONTGOMERY, HENRY R., 1862, *Memoirs of the Life and Writings of Sir Richard Steele, vol.* II, *p.* 166.

His poems are now hopelessly unreadable.—STEPHEN, LESLIE, 1879, *Samuel Johnson* (*English Men of Letters*), *p.* 30.

Savage ostentatiously described himself on his title-pages as "Son of the late Earl Rivers," but it is more than doubtful whether this unwise son knew his own father. It is needful here only to dwell on the fact that at the age of about thirty Savage displayed for two or three years some genuine poetical talent, and published three vigorous works in heroic measure. "The Bastard" (1728), written in real or feigned indignation against his supposed mother, the Countess of Macclesfield, enjoyed a success of scandal; it is short, terse, and effective. In "The Wanderer" (1729) Savage made a very different effort to subdue the public, with a long and serious poem in five books. . . . It is really a kind of prototype of Goldsmith's "Traveller," to which it bears the sort of relation that Dryden is conventionally supposed to bear to Pope. What is mainly noticeable in "The Wanderer" . . . is the influence of Thomson, enlarging the range of poetic observation, and encouraging an exacter portraiture of natural objects. The last book of Savage's poem is remarkably full of brilliant if often crude colour.—GOSSE, EDMUND, 1888, *A History of Eighteenth Century Literature, p.* 217.

Henry Carey

d 1743.

Henry Carey, born in 1685 (1692?) died in London, Oct. 4, 1743. Dramatic composer, said to have been a natural son of George Savile, Marquis of Halifax; pupil of Olaus Westeinson Linnert, of Roseingrave, and of Geminiani. His instruction was limited, and he was obliged to teach for a living. He wrote many musical dramas which were popular in their time, but he is now remembered chiefly by his ballad "Sally in our Alley," and by the attempt to prove him to be the composer of "*God* save the King." Carey may have arranged and perhaps altered this national air, and it is reasonably certain that he first sang it in public, but the melody is probably older than his time. His posthumous son, George Savile Carey (1743-1807), poet and dramatist, tried to substantiate his father's claim to its authorship, but the question still remains undecided. Henry Carey is said to have committed suicide, but this is doubtful. Works—Musical dramas, etc.: "The Contrivances," London, 1715; "Betty," 1732; "Cephalus and Procris," 1733; "The Honest Yorkshireman," 1735; "Nancy," 1739; Six cantatas (1732); "The Musical Century"—one hundred English ballads written and composed by himself (1739-40). He was the author also of plays and poems.—CHAMPLIN, JOHN DENISON, JR., *ed.*, 1888, *Cyclopedia of Music and Musicians, vol.* I, *p.* 270.

PERSONAL

Was a man of facetious temper, resembling Leveridge in many respects. He was a musician by profession, and one of the lower order of poets; his first preceptor in music was Olaus Westeinson Linnert, a German; he received some farther instructions from Roseingrave; and, lastly, was in some sort a disciple of Geminiani. But with all the advantages he might be supposed to have derived from these instructors, the extent of his abilities seems to have been the composition of a ballad air, or at most a little cantata, to which he was just able to set a bass. . . . With all his mirth and good humour, Carey seems to have been at times deeply affected with malevolence of some of his own profession, who, for reasons that no one can guess at, were his enemies: It is true that in some of his poems he manifests a contempt for them, but it is easy to discover that it is dissembled. . . . As a musician Carey seems to have been one of the first of the lowest rank; and as a poet, the last of that class of which D'Urfey was the first, with this difference, that in all the songs and poems written by him on wine, love, and such kind of subjects, he seems to have manifested an inviolable regard for decency and good manners.—HAWKINS, SIR JOHN, 1776, *A General History of the Science and Practice of Music, vol.* II, *pp.* 827, 828.

At the time that this poet could neither walk the streets nor be seated at the convivial board, without listening to his own songs and his own music—for, in truth, the whole nation was echoing his verse, and crowded theatres were applauding his wit and humour—while this very man himself, urged by his strong humanity, founded a "Fund for decayed Musicians"—he was so broken-hearted, and his own common comforts so utterly neglected, that in despair, not waiting for nature to relieve him from the burden of existence, he laid violent hands on himself; and when found dead, had only a half penny in his pocket! Such was the fate of the author of some of the most popular pieces in our language. He left a son, who inherited his misery, and a gleam of his genius.—DISRAELI, ISAAC, 1812–13, *The Despair of Young Poets, Calamities of Authors.*

GOD SAVE THE KING

1740?

On Saturday night last, the audience at the Theatre Royal, Drury Lane, were agreeably surprised by the gentlemen belonging to that house performing the anthem of *God save our noble King.* The universal applause it met with,—being encored with repeated huzzas, sufficiently denoted in how just an abhorence they hold the arbitrary schemes of our insidious enemies, and detest the despotick attempts of Papal power.—DAILY ADVERTISER, 1745, *Monday, Sept.* 30.

The anecdote you mention, respecting your father's being the author and composer of "God Save the King," is certainly true. That most respectable gentleman, my worthy friend and patient, Mr. Smith, has often told me what follows, viz., "That your father came to him with the words and music, desiring him to correct the bass which was not proper; and at your father's request Mr. Smith wrote another bass in harmony." Mr. Smith (John Christopher Smith, Handel's amanuensis), to whom I read your letter this day, repeated the same account, and on this authority I pledged myself for the truth of the statement.—HARINGTON, H., 1795, *Letter to George Savile Carey, June* 13.

Objections may be taken to Carey's claim, because "God save the King" was published anonymously. I do not attach any importance to that fact, because I have before me several others of his songs so printed. The copies were, in all probability, obtained surreptitiously. He complains of this piracy in the preface to the first volume of "The Musical Century," 1737, and states his losses on that account to have averaged nearly 300£ a year. . . . Carey's last musical publication bears date Jan., 1740, and that is the year in which he is stated to have sung "God save the King" at a Tavern in Cornhill. The celebration of Admiral Vernon's victory was certainly an appropriate time for its production. Carey died in October, 1743, and "God save the King" first became extensively popular in October, 1745. It was the rebellion of that year that called forth such repeated expressions of loyalty, and caused so much enthusiasm when the song was sung at all the theatres.—CHAPPELL, WILLIAM, 1855–59, *Popular Music of the Olden Time, vol.* II, *p.* 703.

Its first public performance is said to have been at a dinner in 1740 to celebrate the taking of Portobello by Admiral Vernon (Nov. 20, 1739), when it is said to have been sung by Henry Carey as his own composition, both words and music. The nearest known copy to that date is that in the "Harmonia Anglicana" of 1742 or 43. . . . This is the nearest we can arrive at to the original form of the air and words, and both will be found somewhat different from those with which we are familiar. The fact that Henry Carey was the author of both, is testified to by J. Christopher Smith, Handel's amanuensis, and by Dr. Harington. . . . The Pretender was proclaimed at Edinburgh Sept. 16, and the first appearance of "God save the King" was at Drury Lane, Sept. 28. For a month or so it was much sung at both Covent Garden and Drury Lane; Burney harmonised it for the former, and Arne for the latter. Both words and music were printed, the latter in their present form, in the Gentleman's Magazine, Oct. 1745. How far "God save the King" was complied from older airs will probably never be known. Several exsit with a certain resemblance to the modern tune.—GROVE, GEORGE, 1879, *A Dictionary of Music and Musicians, vol.* I, *p.* 605.

Carey has been credited with the authorship of "God save the Queen." The first known publication of this was in the "Harmonia Anglicana," 1742, where it is anonymous. Carey did not include it in his "Century." It first being popular after his death, during the rebellion of 1745. The actor Victor describes the performance in a contemporary letter to Garrick, and says that it was an old anthem sung in the chapel of James II. when William III. was expected. Arne arranged it for Drury Lane, and Burney for Covent Garden. Burney told Isaac D'Israeli that the authorship was unknown, and gives the same account of its origin as Victor. Fifty years later, Carey's son, George Savile Carey, claimed it for his father in order to justify a request for a pension. His only authority was J. C. Smith, who told Dr. Harington of Bath, on 13 June, 1795, that Henry Carey had brought it to him in order to correct the bass. Smith was the friend of Handel, and had been a collaborator with Carey. A Mr. Townshend is said to have told John Ashley of Bath, who told W. L. Bowles, in 1828, that he had heard Carey sing the anthem at a tavern on occasion of Vernon's capture of Portobello in 1740. Some internal evidence in favor of Carey is suggested in Bowles's "Life of Ken," but the improbability that Carey should have left the authorship unclaimed, that his family should not have claimed it when it became popular, and that Arne (to whom he must have been well known) and Burney should have been unable to discover the authorship at the time, seems to overbalance the small probability of the much later statements, which, moreover, if accepted, do not establish Carey's authorship. —STEPHEN, LESLIE, 1887, *Dictionary of National Biography, vol.* IX, *p.* 71.

Will it ever be definitely known who wrote and composed our national anthem —an anthem that is familiar all the whole wide world over? During the Chicago Exhibition a body of World's Fair representatives of twenty-seven different nationalities, speaking when at home fifteen different languages, crossed the Canadian frontier at Gretna in Manitoba on August 29th, 1893, for the purpose of heartily cheering Queen Victoria and singing "God Save the Queen." Yet, particulars concerning the origin of the melody are so conflicting that we doubt if it will ever be absolutely proved whence it sprang. The vast majority of those who have gone into the subject incline to favour the claim put forward for Henry Carey.—FITZ-GERALD, S. J. ADAIR, 1898, *Stories of Famous Songs, p.* 384.

SALLY IN OUR ALLEY

A vulgar error having long prevailed among many persons, who imagine Sally Salisbury the subject of this ballad, the Author begs leave to undeceive and assure them it has not the least allusion to her, he being a stranger to her very name at the time this Song was composed. For as innocence and virtue were ever the boundaries to his Muse, so in this little poem he had no other view than to set forth the beauty of a chaste and disinterested passion, even in the lowest class of human life. The real occasion was this: a Shoemaker's 'Prentice making holiday with his Sweetheart, treated her with a sight of Bedlam, the puppet-shows, the flying-chairs, and all the elegancies of Moorfields: from whence proceeding to the Farthing-pie-house, he gave her a collation of buns, cheese-cakes, gammon of bacon, stuff'd beef, and bottled ale; through all which scenes the Author dodged them (charmed with the simplicity of their courtship), from whence he drew his little sketch of nature; but being then young and obscure, he was very much ridiculed by some of his acquaintance for this performance; which nevertheless made its way into the polite world, and amply recompensed him by the applause of the divine Addison, who was pleased (more than once) to mention it with approbation.—CAREY, HENRY, 1729, *Sally in Our Alley, Preface.*

Though he had but little skill in music, he had a prolific invention, and very early in his life distinguished himself by the composition of songs, being the author both of the words and the music: one of these, beginning "Of all the girls that are so smart," he set to an air so very pretty, and withal so original, that it was sung by everybody.—HAWKINS, SIR JOHN, 1776, *A General History of the Science and Practice of Music, vol.* II, *p.* 827.

Of all his compositions, the most popular, and that which will transmit his name to posterity, is his ballad of "Sally in our Alley," one of the most striking and original melodies that ever emanated from the brain of a musician.—HUSK, WILLIAM H., 1879, *A Dictionary of Music and Musicians, ed. Grove, vol.* I, *p.* 310.

GENERAL

Carey was a true son of the Muses, and the most successful writer in our language. He is the author of several little national poems. In early life he successfully burlesqued the affected versification of Ambrose Philips, in his baby poems, to which he gave the fortunate appellation of "*Namby Pamby*, a panegyric on the new versification;" a term descriptive in sound of those chiming follies, and now become a technical term in modern criticism. Carey's "Namby Pamby" was at first considered by Swift as the satirical effusion of Pope, and by Pope as the humorous ridicule of Swift. His ballad of "Sally in our Alley" was more than once commended for its nature by Addison, and is sung to this day. Of the national song, "God save the King," it is supposed he was the author both of the words and of the music. He was very successful on the stage, and wrote admirable burlesques of the Italian Opera, in "The Dragon of Wantley," and "The Dragoness;" and the mock tragedy of "Chrononhotonthologos" is not forgotten. Among his Poems lie still concealed several original pieces; those which have a political turn are particularly good, for the politics of Carey were those of a poet and a patriot.—DISRAELI, ISAAC, 1812-13, *The Despair of Young Poets, Calamities of Authors.*

Daniel Neal

1678-1743.

Born at London, Dec. 14, 1678: died at Bath, April 4, 1743. An English historian. He was educated at the Merchant Taylors' School and at the universities of Utrecht and Leyden. In 1706 he settled as an independent clergyman in London. He wrote a "History of New England" (1720), and (his chief work) the "History of the Puritans" (1732-38).—SMITH, BENJAMIN E., *ed.*, 1894–97, *The Century Cyclopedia of Names, p.* 726.

HISTORY OF THE PURITANS
1732-38

Neal opposes a more elaborate history; where these "great and good men," the puritans and the presbyterians, "are placed among the *reformers;*" while their fame is blanched into angelic purity. Neal and his party opined that the protestant had not sufficienlty protested, and that the reformation itself needed to be reformed. They wearied the impatient Elizabeth, and her ardent churchmen; and disputed with the learned James, and his courtly bishops, about such ceremonial trifles, that the historian may blush or smile who has to record them. And when the *puritan* was thrown out of preferment, and seceded into separation, he turned into a *presbyter.* Nonconformity was their darling sin, and their sullen triumph. —DISRAELI, ISAAC, 1791–1824, *"Political Religionism," Curiosities of Literature.*

The most dishonest book in our language, Dodd's "Roman Catholic Church History," *not* excepted. — SOUTHEY, ROBERT, 1823, *Burnet's History of his Own Time, Quarterly Review, vol.* 29, *p.* 166.

Neals' "History of the Puritans" is almost wholly compiled as far as this (Elizabeth's reign) is concerned, from Strype, and from a manuscript written by some Puritan about the time. It was answered by Madox, afterwards bishop of Worcester, in a "Vindication of the Church of England," published anonymously in 1733. Neal replied with tolerable success; but Madox's book is still an useful corrective. Both, however, were, like most controversialists, prejudiced men, loving the interests of their respective factions better than truth, and not very scrupulous about misrepresenting an adversary. But Neal has got rid of the intolerant spirit of the Puritans; while Madox labours to justify every act of Whitgift and Parker.—HALLAM, HENRY, 1827–46, *Constitutional History of England, vol.* I, *ch.* iv, *note.*

A valuable and instructive history, with a strong bias in favour of his subjects, but an upright mind.—BICKERSTETH, EDWARD, 1844, *The Christian Student.*

It contain numerous passages of that homely eloquence, which springs from simple earnestness of feeling, and finds its way directly to the heart. There is occasionally much felicity in the selection of words embodying homely fancies, and which convey the sense by suggesting an image.—WHIPPLE, EDWIN P., 1845, *Neal's History of the Puritans, North American Review, Jan.; Essays and Reviews.*

The whole work was warmly praised by Neal's party, but his occasionally serious misrepresentation or suppression of facts did not pass unchallenged.—MULLINGER, J. BASS, 1894, *Dictionary of National Biography vol.* XL. *p.* 135.

Lewis Theobald

1688-1744.

Lewis Theobald, son of an attorney, at Sittingbourne, in Kent, and bred to the law, published, in 1714, a translation of the "Electra" of Sophocles; and produced in the following year an acted tragedy, the "Persian Princess," written before he was nineteen. His "Perfidious Brother," acted in 1716, was on the model of Otway's "Orphan," In 1715 he published translations of the "Œdipus" of Sophocles, and versions from Aristophanes of "Plutus" and "The Clouds." To these he had added opera, melodrama, and, in 1725, when Pope issued his "Shakespeare," the pantomime of "Harleguin a Sorcerer," before his attack upon Pope's "Shakespeare," in 1726, with a pamphlet, called "Shakespeare Restored; or, Specimens of Blunders Committed and Unamended in Pope's Edition of this Poet." Theobald understood Shakespeare better than Pope did, and lived to show it; but this did not lessen the annoyance of his attack, and, fresh from the smart of it, Pope made Theobald the hero of his "Dunciad." In 1727 Theobald gave work to the critics by producing at Drury Lane, as a play of Shakespeare's, "The Double Falsehood; or, The Distrest Lovers."—MORLEY, HENRY, 1873, *A First Sketch of English Literature*, p. 809.

PERSONAL

A notorious idiot, one hight Whachum, who, from an under spurleather to the law, is become an understrapper to the playhouse.—DENNIS, JOHN, 1717, *Remarks on Pope's Homer*.

SHAKESPEARE RESTORED
1726

In the body of the work he confines himself to animadversions on "Hamlet," but in an appendix of some forty-four closely printed pages in small type he deals similarly with portions of most of the other plays. This work not only exposed the incapacity of Pope as an editor, but gave conclusive proof of Theobald's competence for the task in which Pope had failed. Many of Theobald's most felicitous corrections and emendations of Shakespeare's text are to be found in this, his first contribution to textual criticism.—COLLINS, JOHN CHURTON, 1898, *Dictionary of National Biography, vol.* LVI, *p.* 119.

Pope found a rigorous critic in Lewis Theobald, who, although contemptible as a writer of original verse and prose, proved himself the most inspired of all the textual critics of Shakespeare. Pope savagely avenged himself on his censor by holding him up to ridicule as the hero of the "Dunciad." Theobald first displayed his critical skill in 1726 in a volume which deserves to rank as a classic in English literature. The title runs "Shakespeare Restored, or a specimen of the many errors as well committed as unamended by Mr. Pope in his late edition of this poet, designed not only to correct the said edition but to restore the true reading of Shakespeare in all the editions ever yet publish'd."—LEE, SIDNEY, 1900, *Shakespeare's Life and Work, p.* 175.

EDITION OF SHAKESPEARE
1733

Mr. Theobalds (Mr. Baker tells me) is a very genteel man, and has show'd himself a scholar in his Shakespeare, which I just run over, and might (were it not quite out of my way) have made observations. I noted, however, that he had taken too great liberty. I wish rather he had follow'd the first editions very exactly, be they faulty or not. Shakespeare wanted learning. He was guilty of pseudography, sometimes perhaps designedly. He (Mr. Theobalds) is too bold in bringing his own conjectures into the text, which (it may be) will lay him too open to his adversaries, and make them say Shakespeare wants as much to be restored as ever, and that his edition is not of much greater authority than that of Mr. Pope, who is much inferior to Mr. Theobalds in learning. Mr. Theobalds hath all along, very often justly enough, discovered and reflected upon Mr. Pope's defects, which will, without doubt, nettle Mr. Pope, who, however, may thank himself, he having in his Dunciad (a scurrilous piece against many of the greatest men of the age) treated Mr. Theobalds in a very barbarous manner, for which Mr. Pope is much blamed.—HEARNE, THOMAS, 1734, *Reliquiæ Hearnianæ, ed. Bliss, May* 17, *vol.* III, *p.* 137.

This Tibbald, or Theobald, published an edition of Shakespear, of which he was so proud himself as to say, in one of Mist's Journals, June 8, "That to expose any Errors in it was impracticable." And in another, April 27, "That whatever care might for the future be taken by any other Editor, he would still give above five hundred emendations, that *shall* escape them all."—POPE, ALEXANDER, 1743, *The Dunciad, bk.* i, *v.* 133, *note*.

Mr. Theobald was naturally turned to industry and labour. What he read he could transcribe; but as what he thought, if ever he did think, he could but ill express, so he read on; and by that means got a character of learning without risking to every observer the imputation of wanting a better talent. By a punctilious collation of the old books, he corrected what was manifestly wrong in the later editions by what was manifestly right in the earlier. And this is his real merit, and the whole of it. . . . Nor had he either common judgment to see, or critical sagacity to amend, what was manifestly faulty. Hence he generally exerts his conjectural talent in the wrong place. He tampers with what is sound in the common books, and in the old ones omits all notice of variations the sense of which he did not understand.—WARBURTON, WILLIAM, 1747, *ed. Shakspeare, Preface.*

Pope was succeeded by Theobald, a man of narrow comprehension and small acquisitions, with no native and intrinsic splendour of genius, with little of the artificial light of learning, but zealous for minute accuracy, and not negligent in pursuing it. He collated the ancient copies, and ratified many errors. A man so anxiously scrupulous might have been expected to do more, but what little he did was commonly right.—JOHNSON, SAMUEL, 1760, *ed. Shakspeare's Plays, Preface.*

Among the commentators on Shakspeare, Warburton, always striving to display his own acuteness and scorn of others, deviates more than any one else from the meaning. Theobald was the first who did a little.—HALLAM, HENRY, 1837–39, *Introduction to the Literature of Europe, pt.* iii, *ch.* vi, *par.* 54.

His attempts were limited to the emendation of corrupt passages, and the explanation of obscure ones: the more elevated disquisitions to develop the genius of his author, by principles of criticism applied to his beauties or his defects, he assigned to "a masterly pen." This, at least, was not arrogant. The man who is sensible of his own weakness is safe by not tasking it to the proof. His annotations are amusing from the self-complacency of the writer, who at times seems to have been struck by his now felicitous results; and in truth he was often successful, more than has been honestly avowed by those who have poached on his manor. Theobald exulted over Pope; but he read his triumph in "the Dunciad." The Popeians now sunk the sole merit of the laborious sagacity of "the restorer," as Mr. Pope affectionately called him, to that of "a word-catcher." But "piddling Theobald," branded in the forehead by the immortal "Dunciad," was the first who popularized the neglected writings of Shakespeare. His editions dispersed thirteen thousand copies; while nearly a third of Pope's original subscription edition, of seven hundred and fifty copies, were left unvendible.—DISRAELI, ISAAC, 1841, *Shakespeare, Amenities of Literature.*

In 1733 he produced an edition of Shakspere, in seven volumes octavo, which annihilated Pope's quartos and duodecimos. The title-page of Theobald's Shakspere bore that it was "collated with the oldest copies, and corrected, with Notes." Pope's edition was not again reprinted in London; but of Theobald's there have been many subsequent editions, and Steevens asserts that of his first edition thirteen thousand copies were sold. Looking at the advantage which Pope possessed in the pre-eminence of his literary reputation, the preference which was so decidedly given to Theobald's editions is a proof that the public thought for themselves in the matter of Shakspere.—KNIGHT, CHARLES, 1849, *Studies of Shakspere.*

Theobald, "poor, piddling Tibbald," the first hero of his Dunciad, came after Pope, and is one of the very best editors who have fallen to the lot of Shakespeare. He was the first who did any great service by conjectual emendation, and the judicious use of the quartos.—WHITE, RICHARD GRANT, 1854, *Shakespeare's Scholar, p.* 9.

Strangely enough, it is not the men of highest intellect that have in this way done the most for Shakspeare. Pope was one of his editors; so was Warburton; Johnson another; Malone too, a very able man. Mr. Charles Knight is correct in saying that the best of the old editors of Shakspeare is Theobald.—DALLAS, E. S., 1866, *The Gay Science, vol.* I, *p.* 16.

To be regarded not only as the father of Shakspearian criticism, but as the editor to whom our great poet is most deeply indebted. To speak of any of the eighteenth-century editors in the same breath with him is absurd. In the first place he had what none of them possessed—a fine ear for the rhythm of blank verse, and the nicest sense of the *nuances* of language as well in relation to single words as to words in combination—faculties which, as it is needless to say, are indispensable to an emendator of Shakspeare, or, indeed, of any other poet. In every department of textual criticism he excelled. In its humbler offices, in collation, in transcription, in the correction of clerical errors, he was, as even his enemies have frankly admitted, the most patient and conscientious of drudges. To the elucidation of obscurities in expression or allusion, and for the purposes of illustrative commentary generally, he brought a stock of learning such as has never perhaps been found united in any other commentator on Shakspeare. . . . The proper monument of Theobald is not that cairn of dishonour which the sensitive vanity of Pope, the ignoble and impudent devices of Warburton to build his own reputation on the ruin of another, the careless injustice of Johnson, the mean stratagems of Malone, and the obsequious parrotry of tradition on the part of subsequent writers, have succeeded in accumulating. It is the settled text of Shakspeare. It should be the gratitude of all to whom that text is precious, the gratitude of civilised mankind.—COLLINS, JOHN CHURTON, 1895, *The Porson of Shakspearian Criticism, Essays and Studies, pp.* 275, 315.

GENERAL

Theobald was one of the worms of literature, a painful antiquarian, devoting his feeble powers to the illustration of obscure passages in Shakspeare's writings; useful, indeed, but certainly humble enough to have escaped the martyrdom of a "Dunciad" immorality. The truth is, that private pique had animated Pope in placing Theobald at the head of the dunces. The great poet had himself published an edition of Shakspeare, in which his want of that minute antiquarian knowledge which Theobald undoubtedly possessed was glaringly apparent, a defect which the latter was naturally but too willing to point out. The character given to Theobald in the "Dunciad," though of course exaggerated with all the ingenuity of a rich imagination and an intense jealousy, was in the main appropriate.—SHAW, THOMAS, B., 1847, *Outlines of English Literature, p.* 220.

Lewis Theobald was a type of the class whom Pope was resolved to crush. He was pedantic, poor, and somewhat malignant. He had attempted with equal ill-success original poetry, translation, and play-writing; and had, indeed, no disqualification for the throne of Dulness except his insignificance. Pope, as we have seen, admits this drawback, and candidly avows that the sole reason for Theobald's sudden elevation to the unwelcome dignity was the attack which the latter had made on his edition of "Shakespeare." At first sight, even this personal reason seems inadequate, for Theobald, in his preface to "Shakespeare Restored," speaks of the poet with studied respect. There was, however, a sting in his title,—"Shakespeare Restored, or an Exposure of the Blunders Committed and Unamended in Mr. Pope's late edition,"—which might not unfairly be cited by the poet as a proof of wanton malignity. To this we must add that it was malignity triumphant. Theobald was by nature better qualified than Pope for the task which both had undertaken; and he had exhibited Pope to the world in a position of somewhat ridiculous inferiority.—COURTHOPE, WILLIAM JOHN, 1882, *ed., The Works of Alexander Pope, Introduction to the Dunciad, vol.* IV, *p.* 27.

The fate of Lewis Theobald is without parallel in literary history. It may be said with simple truth that no poet in our own or in any language has ever owed so great a debt to an editor as Shakspeare owes to this man. He found the text of the tragedies and comedies, which is now so intelligible and lucid, in a condition scarcely less deplorable than that in which Aldus found the choruses of Æschylus, and Musurus the parabases of Aristophanes, and he contributed more to its certain and permanent settlement than all the other editors from Rowe to Alexander Dyce. . , . From the publication of the "Dunciad" to the present day he has been the butt of almost every critic and biographer of Shakspeare and Pope. Indeed, the shamelessness of the injustice with which he has been treated by his brother commentators on Shakspeare exceeds belief. Generation after generation it has been the same story. After plundering his notes and appropriating his emendations, some times with, but more generally without, acknowledgment, they all contrive, each in his own fashion, to reproduce Pope's portrait of him. Whenever they mention him, if they do not couple with their remarks some abusive or contemptuous expression, it is with a sort of half-apology for introducing his name. They refer to him, in fact, as a gentleman might refer among his friends to a shoeblack who had just amused him with some witticism while polishing his boots.—COLLINS, JOHN CHURTON, 1895, *Essays and Studies, pp.* 263, 264, 265.

Alexander Pope

1688–1744

1688, (May 21), Birth of Pope. 1700, (Circ), Pope takes up his residence with his father at Binfield. 1704, Commencement of intimacy with Sir Wm. Trumbull, 1705, and Walsh. 1707, First acquaintance with the Blount family. 1709, "Pastorals" published. 1711, "Essay on Criticism," Pope introduced to Gay, 1712, and Addison, "Rape of the Lock" (original edition), "The Messiah." 1713, (April), Addison's "Cato" first acted, "Prologue to Cato." Pope's attack on Dennis reproved by Addison, "Windsor Forest," Pope introduced to Swift, "Ode on St. Cecilia's Day," Pope studies painting under Jervas. (November), Subscription for "Translation of Iliad" opened. 1713–4, Meetings of the Scriblerus Club. 1714, Death of Queen Anne, "Rape of the Lock" (enlarged), "Temple of Fame." 1715, "Iliad" (vol. i). 1715–6, Quarrel with Addison. 1716, (April), Pope settles with his parents at Chiswick, Departure for the East of Lady Mary Wortley Montagu. 1717, "Elegy to the Memory of an Unfortunate Lady," "Epistle of Eloisa to Abelard," "Three Hours after Marriage" produced, First quarrel with Cibber. (October), Death of Pope's father. 1718. Pope settles with his mother at Twickenham, Return from the East of Lady Mary Wortley Montagu. 1720, South-Sea Year, "Iliad" (last volume). 1722, Correspondence with Judith Cowper. 1723, First return of Bolingbroke, Banishment of Atterbury. 1725, Edition of "Shakspere," Pope attacked by Theobald, "Odyssey" (vols. i.-iii.), Second return of Bolingbroke, who settles at Dawley. 1726, "Letters to Cromwell" (Curll), Swift pays a long visit to Twickenham. 1727, (June), Death of George I., "Miscellanies" (vols. i. and ii.); containing, among other pieces by Pope, the "Treatise on the Bathos." 1728, "The Dunciad" (Books i.-iii.). 1730, "Grub Street Journal" (continued by Pope and others till 1737). Quarrels with Aaron Hill and others. 1731, "Epistle on Taste," The remaining "Moral Essay" up to 1735. 1732, "Essay on Man" (Ep. I.), The remaining Epistles up to 1734. (December), Death of Gay. 1733, Quarrel with Lord Hervey. (June), Death of Pope's mother. 1735, "Epistle to Arbuthnot," Death of Arbuthnot, Pope's "Correspondence." (Curll). 1736, Pope's "Correspondence" (Authorised edition). 1737, "Imitations of Horace." 1738, "Epilogue to Satires." 1740. (March), Close of Correspondence with Swift, First meeting with Warburton. 1742. "The New Dunciad" (in four books). 1743, "The Dunciad" (with Cibber as hero). 1744, (May 30), Death of Pope.—WARD, ADOLPHUS WILLIAM, 1869, *ed., The Poetical Works of Alexander Pope, Chronological Table, p.* lii.

PERSONAL

If you have a mind to enquire between Sunninghill and Oakingham, for a young, squab, short gentleman, an eternal writer of amorous pastoral madrigals, and the very bow of the god of Love, you will be soon directed to him. And pray, as soon as you have taken a survey of him, tell me whether he is a proper author to make personal reflections on others. This little author may extol the ancients as much, and as long as he pleases, but he has reason to thank the good gods that he was born a modern, for had he been born of Grecian parents, and his father by consequence had by law the absolute disposal of him, his life had been no longer than that of one of his poems,—the life of half a day.—DENNIS, JOHN, 1711, *Reflections, Critical and Satirical on a Rhapsody, An Essay on Criticism, p.* 29.

Dick Distick we have elected president, not only as he is the shortest of us all, but because he has entertained so just a sense of his stature as to go generally in black, that he may appear yet less; nay, to that perfection is he arrived that he stoops as he walks. The figure of the man is odd enough: He is a lively little creature, with long arms and legs—a spider is no ill emblem of him; he has been taken at a distance for a small windmill.—POPE, ALEXANDER, 1713, *The Little Club, The Guardian, June* 26.

And yet so wonderful, sublime a thing
As the great Iliad, scarce could make me sing,
Except I justly could at once commend
A good companion, and as firm a friend.
—SHEFFIELD, JOHN (EARL OF MULGRAVE), 1717, *On Mr. Pope and His Poems.*

Mr. Pope, the poet, who is now publishing Homer, in English verse, (three

ALEXANDER POPE

Engraving by Geo. T. Doo, R. A.
From a Painting by Richardson.

ALEXANDER POPE

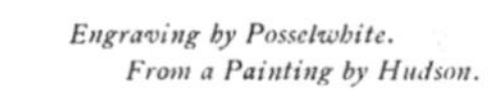

Engraving by Posselwhite.
From a Painting by Hudson.

volumes of the Iliads in 4to. being already come out,) was born in the parish of Binfield, near Ockingham, in Berks. He is a papist, as is also his father, who is a sort of a broken merchant. The said Mr. Pope was patronized and encouraged by the late sir William Trumbull. He lived in Binfield parish till of late, when he removed to Chiswick, in Surrey. He is most certainly a very ingenious man. He is deformed.—HEARNE, THOMAS, 1717, *Reliquiæ Hearnianæ, ed. Bliss, Aug.* 7, *vol.* II, *p.* 50.

Tuneful Alexis on the Thames' fair side,
The Ladies' play-thing, and the Muses' pride;
With merit popular, with wit polite,
Easy, tho' vain, and elegant tho' light:
Desiring, and deserving others' praise,
Poorly accepts a fame he ne'er repays;
Unborn to cherish, sneakingly approves,
And wants the soul to spread the worth he loves.
—HILL, AARON, 1728, *The Progress of Wit.*

. . . Pope, the monarch of the tuneful train!
To whom be Nature's, and Britannia's praise!
All their bright honours rush into his lays!
And all that glorious warmth his lays reveal,
Which only poets, kings, and patriots feel!
Tho' gay as mirth, as curious though sedate,
As elegance polite, as pow'r elate;
Profound as reason, and as justice clear;
Soft as compassion, yet as truth severe;
As bounty copious, as persuasion sweet,
Like Nature various, and like Art complete;
So fine her morals, so sublime her views,
His life is almost equall'd by his Muse.
—SAVAGE, RICHARD, 1729, *The Wanderer, Canto* I.

Mr. Alexander Pope, the poet's father, was a poor ignorant man, a tanner at Binfield in Berks. This Mr. Alex. Pope had a little house there, that he had from his father, but hath now sold it to one Mr. Tanner, an honest man. This Alexander Pope, though he be an English poët, yet he is but an indifferent scholar, mean at Latin, and can hardly read Greek. He is a very ill-natured man and covetous, and excessively proud.—HEARNE, THOMAS, 1729, *Reliquiæ Hearnianæ, ed. Bliss, July* 18, *vol.* III, *p.* 23.

Hail, happy Pope! whose generous mind
Detesting all the statesman kind,
Contemning courts, at courts unseen,
Refused the visits of a queen.
A soul with every virtue fraught,
By sages, priests, or poets taught;
Whose filial piety excels
Whatever Grecian story tells;
A genius for all stations fit,
Whose meanest talent is his wit:
His heart too great, though fortune little,
To lick a rascal statesman's spittle:
Appealing to the nation's taste,
Above the reach of want is placed:
By Homer dead was taught to thrive,
Which Homer never could alive;
And sits aloft on Pindus' head,
Despising slaves that cringe for bread.
—SWIFT, JONATHAN, 1729, *A Libel on the Reverend Dr. Delany, and His Excellency, John Lord Carteret.*

Nor thou the justice of the world disown,
That leaves thee thus an outcast and alone:
For though in law the murder be to kill,
In equity the murder is the will.
Then while with coward hand you stab a name,
And try at least to assassinate our Fame,
Like the first bold assassin be thy lot,
Ne'er be thy guilt forgiven or forgot;
But as thou hat'st be hated by mankind,
And with the emblem of thy crooked mind
Marked on thy back, like Cain, by God's own hand,
Wander like him accursed through the land.
—ANON, 1733, *Verses Addressed to the Imitator of Horace.*

Whose life, severely scann'd, transcends his lays;
For wit supreme is but his second praise.
—MALLET, DAVID, 1733, *Epistle on Verbal Criticism.*

To believe nothing is yours but what you own, would be merely ridiculous. Did you not deny the Dunciad for seven years? Did you not offer a reward of three guineas, by an advertisement in the Post-man, to know the publisher of your version of the First Psalm? and when you were informed, did you ever pay the premium? Did you not publish the Worms yourself? And do you own any of these in the preface of the second volume of your works? In short, sir, your conduct as to your poetical productions is exactly of a piece with what I once met with at the Old Bailey. A most flagrant offender was put upon his trial for a notorious theft, and by his egregious shuffling he put Mr. Recorder Lovel into a violent passion. Sirrah, says he, you have got a trick of denying what you ought to own, and by owning what you might as well deny. "An' please your honour," quoth culprit, "that's the way not to be hanged."—CURLL, EDMUND, 1735, *Epistle, Pope's Literary Correspondence, vol.* II.

Mr. Pope's not being richer may be easily accounted for.—He never had any love for money: and though he was not extravagant in anything, he always delighted, when he had any sum to spare, to make use of it in giving, lending, building, and gardening; for those were the ways in which he disposed of all the overplus of his income.—If he was extravagant in anything it was in his grotto, for that, from first to last, cost him above a thousand pounds.—BLOUNT, MRS., 1737–39, *Spence's Anecdotes, ed. Singer, p.* 160.

To cast a shadow o'er the spotless fame,
Or dye the cheek of innocence with shame;
To swell the breast of modesty with care,
Or force from beauty's eye a secret tear;
And, not by decency or honour sway'd,
Libel the living and asperse the dead.
Prone, *where he ne'er received, to give offence,*
But most averse to merit and to sense;
Base to his foe, but baser to his friend;
Lying to blame, and sneering to commend:
Then let him boast that honourable crime
Of making *those who fear not God, fear HIM*—
When the great honour of that boast is such,
That hornets and mad dogs may boast as much.
Such is th' injustice of his daily theme,
And such the lust that breaks his nightly dream,
That vestal fire of undecaying hate,
Which time's cold tide itself can ne'er abate.
—HERVEY, JOHN LORD, 1742, *The Difference between Verbal and Practical Virtue, exemplified in some Instances both ancient and modern.*

One of his worst mistakes was that unnecessary noise he used to make in boast of his morality. It seemed to me almost a call upon suspicion that a man should rate the duties of plain honesty, as if they had been qualities extraordinary. And, in fact, I saw in some occasions, that he found these duties too severe for practice, and but prized himself upon the character in proportion to the pains it cost him to support it.—HILL, AARON, 1744, *Letter to Richardson, Sept.* 10, *Richardson's Correspondence.*

I can say no more for Mr. Pope (for what you keep in reserve may be worse than all the rest). It is natural to wish the finest writer, one of them, we ever had, should be an honest man. It is for the interest even of that virtue, whose friend he professed himself, and whose beauties he sung, that he should not be found a dirty animal. But, however, this is Mr. Warburton's business, not mine, who may scribble his pen to the stumps and all in vain, if these facts are so. It is not from what he told me about himself that I thought well of him, but from a humanity and goodness of heart, ay, and greatness of mind, that runs through his private correspondence, not less apparent than are a thousand little vanities and weaknesses mixed with those good qualities, for nobody ever took him for a philosopher.—GRAY, THOMAS, 1746, *Letter to Horace Walpole, Feb.* 3.

His voice in common conversation was so naturally musical, that I remember honest Tom Southerne used always to call him "the little nightingale."—BOYLE, JOHN (LORD ORRERY), 1751–53, *Remarks on the Life and Writings of Dr. Jonathan Swift, p.* 207.

"But I have been told of one Pope, is he there?" "It is time enough," replied my guide, "these hundred years; he is not long dead; people have not done hating him yet." "Strange," cried I, "can any be found to hate a man, whose life was wholly spent in entertaining and instructing his fellow-creatures?" "Yes," said my guide, "they hate him for that very reason."—GOLDSMITH, OLIVER, 1762, *A Citizen of the World, In Westminster Abbey, Letter* xiii.

Pope's frame of body did not promise long life; but he certainly hastened his death by feeding much on high-seasoned dishes, and drinking spirits.—KING, WILLIAM, 1763–1818, *Political and Literary Anecdotes of His own Times, p.* 12.

Pope had but one great end in view to render this world supportable to him. That was *Friendship, the peculiar gift of heaven.* This did he nobly deserve and obtain; but for how short a time! Jealousy deprived him of the affection he assiduously sought from Mr. Wycherly, and many others; but Death cruel Death was far more cruel. The dearest ties of his heart all yielded to his stroke. The modest Digby, the gentle virtuous Gay, the worthy Arbuthnot, the exiled Atterbury—but why should I enumerate these excellent men, when their very names dejected me? But in nothing does Pope equally charm me as in his conduct to his mother: it is truly noble.—BURNEY, FRANCES, 1771, *Early Diary, Dec.* 8, *vol.* I, *p.* 140.

Pope, who was all malice, hatred, and uncharitableness; false as a Jesuit; fickle as a fool; mercenary as a waiting woman; and with a prurient fancy, which, had his body permitted it, would have led him into excesses as gross as any that Chartres was accused of.—MONTAGU, EDWARD WORTLEY, 1776? *An Autobiography, vol.* I, *p.* 57.

Pope was, through his whole life, ambitious of splendid acquaintance; and he seems to have wanted neither diligence nor success in attracting the notice of the great; for from his first entrance into the world (and his entrance was very early) he was admitted to familiarity with those whose rank or station made them most conspicuous. . . . He is said to have been beautiful in his infancy; but he was of a constitution originally feeble and weak; and as bodies of a tender frame are easily distorted, his deformity was probably in part the effect of his application. His stature was so low, that, to bring him to the level with common tables, it was necessary to raise his seat. But his face was not displeasing, and his eyes were animated and vivid. . . . When he rose, he was invested in a bodice made of stiff canvas, being scarcely able to hold himself erect till they were laced, and he then put on a flannel waistcoat. One side was contracted. His legs were so slender that he enlarged their bulk with three pair of stockings, which were drawn on and off by the maid; for he was not able to dress or undress himself, and neither went to bed nor rose without help. His weakness made it very difficult for him to be clean. . . . He sometimes condescended to be jocular with servants or inferiors; but by no merriment, either of others or his own, was he ever seen excited to laughter. . . . In the duties of friendship he was zealous and constant; his early maturity of mind commonly united him with men older than himself, and therefore, without attaining any considerable length of life, he saw many companions of his youth sink into the grave; but it does not appear that he lost a single friend by coldness or by injury; those who loved him once, continued their kindness.—JOHNSON, SAMUEL, 1779–81, *Pope, Lives of the English Poets.*

Sir Joshua Reynolds once saw Pope. It was about the year 1740, at an auction of books or pictures. He remembers that there was a lane formed to let him pass freely through the assemblage, and he proceeded along bowing to those who were on each side. He was, according to Sir Joshua's account, about four feet six high; very humpbacked and deformed; he wore a black coat; and according to the fashion of that time, had on a little sword. Sir Joshua adds that he had a large and very fine eye, and a long handsome nose; his mouth had those peculiar marks which always are found in the mouths of crooked persons; and the muscles which run across the cheek were so strongly marked as to appear like small cords. Roubilliac, the statuary, who made a bust of him from life, observed that his countenance was that of a person who had been much afflicted with headache, and he should have known the fact from the contracted appearance of the skin between his eyebrows, though he had not been otherwise apprised of it.—MALONE, EDMUND, 1791, *Maloniana, ed. Prior, p.* 428.

Pope's character and habits were exclusively literary, with all the hopes, fears, and failings, which are attached to that feverish occupation,—a restless pursuit of poetical fame. Without domestic society, or near relations; separated by weak health and personal disadvantages from the gay; by fineness of mind and lettered indolence, from the busy part of mankind, surrounded only by a few friends, who valued these gifts in which he excelled, Pope's whole hopes, wishes, and fears, were centered in his literary reputation. To extend his fame, he laboured indirectly, as well as directly; and to defend it from the slightest attack, was his daily and nightly anxiety. Hence the restless impatience which that distinguished author displayed under the libels of dunces, whom he ought to have despised, and hence too the venomed severity with which he retorted their puny attacks.—SCOTT, SIR WALTER, 1814, *Memoirs of Jonathan Swift.*

No politician studied to obtain his purposes by more oblique directions, or with more intricate stratagems; and Pope was at once the lion and the fox of Machiavel. A book might be written on the Stratagems of Literature, as Frontinus has composed one on War, and among its subtilest heroes we might place this great poet.—DISRAELI, ISAAC, 1814, *Pope, Quarrels of Authors.*

I have hung up Pope, and a gem it is, in my town room; I hope for your approval. Though it accompanies the "Essay on Man," I think that was not the poem he is here meditating. He would have looked up, somehow affectedly, if he were just conceiving "Awake, my St. John." Neither is he in the "Rape of the Lock" mood exactly. I think he has just made out the last lines of the "Epistle to Jervis," between gay and tender,

"And other beauties envy Worsley's eyes."

I'll be d. . . . 'd if that isn't the line. He is brooding over it, with a dreamy phantom of Lady Mary floating before him. He is thinking which is the earliest possible day and hour that she will first see it. What a miniature piece of gentility it is! Why did you give it me? I do not like you well enough to give you anything so good.—LAMB, CHARLES, 1823, *Letter to B. W. Procter, April* 13, *Letters, ed. Ainger, vol.* II. *p.* 74.

As he advanced in life the original complaint ceased to make any further progress, and its effects on his constitution might have been removed by due attention to regimen and exercise; but instead of these,active medicines and stimulating diet were the means he constantly employed of temporarily palliating the exhaustion, and obviating the excitement consequent on excessive mental application. None of his biographers, indeed, allude to his having suffered from indigestion; and it is even possible that he might not have been himself aware of the nature of those anomalous symptoms of dyspepsia, which mimic the form of every other malady; those symptoms of giddiness, langour, dejection, palpitation of the heart, constant headache, dimness of sight, occasional failure of the mental powers, exhaustion of nervous energy, depriving the body of vital heat, and the diminution of muscular strength, without a corresponding loss of flesh, he frequently complains of; and every medical man is aware, that they are the characteristic symptoms of dyspepsia.—MADDEN, R. R., 1833, *The Infirmities of Genius, vol.* I, *p.* 180.

The peculiar fondness of Pope for petty stratagem is well known. He was like one of those gallants whom Swift ridicules as preferring midnight and a window, to prosecute an amour, which could be carried on with equal safety by daylight and the door. Lady Bolingbroke used to tell him that he played the politician about cabbages and turnips; and another of his lady friends accused him of not being able to drink tea without a stratagem.—COOKE, GEORGE WINGROVE, 1835, *Memoirs of Lord Bolingbroke, vol.* II, *p.* 215.

As a Christian, Pope appears in a truly estimable light. He found himself a Roman Catholic by accident of birth; so was his mother; but his father was so upon personal conviction and conversion, —yet not without extensive study of the questions at issue. It would have laid open the road to preferment, and preferment was otherwise abundantly before him, if Pope would have gone over to the Protestant faith. And in his conscience he found no obstacle to that change; he was a philosophical Christian, intolerant of nothing but intolerance, a bigot only against bigots. But he remained true to his baptismal profession, partly on a general principle of honour in adhering to a distressed and dishonoured party, but chiefly out of reverence and affection to his mother. In his relation to women Pope was amiable and gentlemanly, and accordingly was the object of affectionate regard and admiration to many of the most accomplished in that sex. This we mention especially, because we would wish to express our full assent to the manly scorn with which Mr. Roscoe repels the libellous insinuations against Pope and Miss Martha Blount. A more innocent connexion we do not believe ever existed.—DE QUINCEY, THOMAS, c1838–90, *Pope, Works, ed. Masson, vol.* IV, *p.* 277.

His own life was one long series of tricks, as mean and as malicious as that of which he suspected Addison and Tickell. He was all stiletto and mask. To injure, to insult, to save himself from the consequence of injury and insult by lying and equivocating, was the habit of his life. He published a lampoon on the Duke of Chandos; he was taxed with it; and he lied and equivocated. He published a lampoon on Aaron Hill; he was taxed with it; and he lied and equivocated. He published a still fouler lampoon on Lady Mary Wortley Montagu; he was taxed with it; and he lied with more than usual effrontery and vehemence. He puffed himself and abused his enemies under feigned names. He robbed himself of his own letters, and then raised the hue and cry after them. Besides his frauds of malignity, of fear, of interest, and of vanity, there were frauds which he seems to have committed from love of fraud alone. He had a habit of stratagem—a pleasure in outwitting all who came near him. Whatever his object might be, the indirect road to it was that which he preferred. —MACAULAY, THOMAS BABINGTON, 1843, *Life and Writings of Addison, Edinburgh Review; Critical and Miscellaneous Essays.*

By one of those acts which neither science nor curiosity can excuse, the skull of Pope is now in the private collection of a phrenologist. The manner in which it was obtained is said to have been this. On some occasion of alteration in the church, or burial of someone in the same spot, the coffin of Pope was disinterred, and opened to see the state of the remains; that by a bribe to the sexton of the time, possession of the skull was obtained for a night, and *another* skull returned instead of it. I have heard that fifty pounds were paid to mange and carry through this transaction. Be that as it may, the skull of Pope figures in a private museum.—HOWITT, WILLIAM, 1846, *Homes and Haunts of the Most Eminent British Poets, vol.* I, *p.* 197.

Alexander Pope went through doubt, contradiction, confusion, to which yours are simple and light; and conquered. He was a man of light passions with yourselves; infected with the peculiar vices of his day. Narrow, for his age was narrow; shallow, for his age was shallow; a *bon-vivant,* for his age was a gluttonous and drunken one; bitter, furious, and personal, for men around him were such; foul-mouthed often, and indecent, as the rest were. Nay, his very power, when he abuses it for his own ends of selfish spite and injured vanity, makes him, as all great men can be (in words at least, for in life he was far better than the men around him), worse than his age. He can outrival Dennis in ferocity, and Congreve in filth. So much the worse for him in that account which he has long ago rendered up. But in all times and places, as far as we can judge, the man was heart-whole, more and not less righteous than his fellows. With his whole soul he hates what is evil, as far as he can recognise it. With his whole soul he loves what is good, as far as he can recognise that. With his whole soul he believes that there is a righteous and a good God, whose order no human folly or crime can destroy; and he will say so; and does say it, clearly, simply, valiantly, reverently in that "Essay on Man."—KINGSLEY, CHARLES, 1853, *Alexander Smith and Alexander Pope, Fraser's Magazine, vol.* 48, *p.* 457.

The Pope mansion was described by the poet as

"A little house, with trees a row,
And like its master very low."

It has since been raised and transformed into a handsome villa residence. Two of the trees—noble elms—still remain at the gate of the house, and the poet's study has been preserved. On the lawn is a cypress-tree which Pope is said to have planted—a tradition common to all poetical residences. Milton has still an apple-tree at Horton and a mulberry tree at Cambridge; and Shakspeare's mulberry-tree, with the story of its ruthless and Gothic destruction, has a fame almost as universal as his dramas. . . . Part of the forest of Windsor now bears the name of Pope's Wood, and among those tall, spreading beeches with smooth, grey, fluted trunks he first met the Muse and "lisped in numbers." His country retirement and sylvan walks were highly important at this susceptible period of life in the formation of Pope's poetical character. He soon ceased to be a descriptive poet, and, with a weakness observable on other subjects, he depreciated what he did not adopt or prefer. . . . Pope's physical constitution no doubt helped to shape his mental habits, but it was fortunate that he had this early taste of the country. His recollections of Windsor Forest, and of the mornings and sunsets he had enjoyed within its broad circumference of shade, or from the "stately brow" of its historic heights, may be tracked, like the fresh green of spring, along the fiery course of his satire, and through the mazes of his metaphysics. Milton, let us remember, was familiar with the same scenery. Horton is within sight of Windsor, and the great poet must often have listened to the echoes of the royal chase in the forest. —CARRUTHERS, ROBERT, 1853–57, *Life of Pope, pp.* 17, 18.

He had giant energies, and a wretched

field for them; a soul for worship, in an age of unbelief; a heart for love, yet under the ban of a mysterious destiny; and he had to fight his fight under the closest of all restrictions,—the restriction on the very energies of life within him, by disease;—he moved from youth in a cloud of hypochondria. Hercules had the poisoned shirt on him all his life.—HANNAY, JAMES, 1854, *Satire and Satirists, p.* 131.

Thanks to his father, Pope's fortune was enough to place him above dependence. No matter what was the amount of his patrimony, his spirit was independent, and he resolved, from the first, to limit his desires to his means. . . . Pope greedy of money! Why Johnson admits that he gave away an eighth part of his income; and where is the man, making no ostentatious profession of benevolence—subscribing to no charities, as they are called, or few—standing in no responsible position before the world, which indeed he rather scorned than courted, of whom the same can be said? Pope, we suspect, with all his magnificent subscriptions, did not leave behind him so much as he had received from his father. His pleasure was in scattering, not in hoarding, and that on others rather than on himself. He was generous to the Blounts and because one proof has accidentally become known, it has been winged with scandal;—he was generous to his half-sister,—generous to her sons,—generous to Dodsley, then struggling into business,—nobly generous to Savage; for though the weakness and the vice of Savage compelled Pope to break off personal intercourse, he never deserted him. These facts were known to his biographers; and we could add a bead-roll of like noble actions, but that it would be beside our purpose and our limits. Pope, indeed, was generous to all who approached; and though his bodily weakness and sufferings made him a troublesome visitor, especially to servants,—though one of Lord Oxford's said that, "in the dreadful winter of forty, she was called from her bed by him four times in one night," yet this same servant declared, "that in a house where her business was to answer his call, she would not ask for wages." What more could be told of the habitual liberality of a man who never possessed more than a few hundred a year? It startled persons accustomed to the munificence of the noble and the wealthy.—DILKE, CHARLES WENTWORTH, 1854–75, *Pope's Writings, The Papers of a Critic, vol.* I, *pp.* 110, 111.

There is probably no English author whose life can be compared with Pope as a succession of petty secrets and third rate problems. . . . A man whose actions were generally blameless would not have left so many things for his apologists to explain; a man whose character was truthful and simple would not have been the hero of so many enigmatical narratives.—CONINGTON, JOHN, 1858, *Oxford Essays, p.* 2.

Bolingbroke had given to Pope the manuscript of "The Patriot King," and the letter on Patriotism, in order to get five or six copies printed for private circulation. Pope, however, had given orders for fifteen hundred additional copies to be worked off, under the strictest injunctions of secrecy. The secret was kept until Pope's death. Soon afterwards Bolingbroke received a letter from the printer, asking him what was to be done with these fifteen hundred copies? Bolingbroke was astonished to find so much artifice and meanness in his former friend. He requested Lord Marchmont to get all the edition into his hands. . . . The edition was, however, not burnt at the house Lord Marchmont was furnishing in London. He thought it more satisfactory to have the sheets, destroyed under Bolingbroke's own eyes. They were all taken down to Battersea, and burned on the terrace. Bolingbroke himself set fire to the pile. It is impossible to defend Pope. That he greatly admired "The Patriot King," and was afraid so valuable a work would be lost to posterity, unless he took this method of preserving it, as Warburton afterwards alleged, is at best scarcely an excuse. No adequate motive for Pope's conduct has ever been discovered nor imagined. The simplest explanation is the most satisfactory. Stratagem and double-dealing were habitual to him: he could not act straightforwardly, nor understand a straightforward course in others; he frequenlty lied when lying was quite useless to him, and answered no purpose of deception; and when he could not deceive his enemies, he with a weak kind of cunning appears to have taken a pleasure in outwitting his best friends.—MACKNIGHT, THOMAS, 1863, *The Life of Henry St. John, Viscount Bolingbroke, pp.* 666, 667.

It was not, however, the hate of his contemporaries that kept his bust out of the Abbey, but his own deliberate wish to be interred, by the side of his beloved mother, in the central aisle of the parish church of Twickenham: and his epitaph, composed by himself, is inscribed on a white marble tablet above the gallery.—

FOR ONE THAT WOULD NOT BE BURIED IN WESTMINSTER ABBEY

Heroes and kings! your distance keep,
In peace let one poor poet sleep,
Who never flatter'd folks like you:
Let Horace blush, and Virgil too.

The "Little Nightingale," who withdrew from the boisterous company of London to those quiet shades, only to revisit them in his little chariot like "Homer in a nutshell," naturally rests there at last.—STANLEY, ARTHUR PENRHYN, 1867–96, *Historical Memorials of Westminster Abbey, p.* 269.

No author has been more elaborately slandered on principle, or more studiously abused through envy. Smarting dullards went about for years, with an ever-ready microscope, hunting for flaws in his character that might be injuriously exposed; but to-day his defamers are in bad repute. Excellence in a fellow-mortal is to many men worse than death; and great suffering fell upon a host of mediocre writers when Pope uplifted his sceptre and sat supreme above them all.—FIELDS, JAMES, 1871, *Yesterdays with Authors, p.* 6.

Personally we know more about Pope than about any of our poets. He kept no secrets about himself. If he did not let the cat out of the bag, he always contrived to give her tail a wrench so that we might know she was there. In spite of the savageness of his satires, his natural disposition seems to have been an amiable one, and his character as an author was as purely factitious as his style.—LOWELL, JAMES RUSSELL, 1871–90, *Pope, Prose Works, Riverside ed., vol.* IV, *p.* 49.

It is not a pleasant picture one of Pope's biographers has painted of the sickly stunted young poet shut up in his room at Binfield, building himself up with books, reading till the stars twinkle in upon him unheeded, reading while the wonders of the sun-setting and sun-rising pass by unknown. "He is ignorant how the little birds answer each other among the trees, and how the wood-pigeons coo. The mavis and the merle are never singing among the branches, nor is it a 'good greenwood' to the boy-poet." He has nothing to do with the beauty outside; the dews fall not, the balm breathes not, for him. Windsor Forest was the scene, its glades and recesses the surrounding; but in a "curious mental work-shop," as one critic expresses it, the lad lived and laboured, "with his windows shut, we may be sure," and the fever of toil on his worn face: it was a juvenile manufactory, where verse was already turned and returned, and where a correct couplet was reckoned the highest product of earth and heaven. Thus at least modern criticism rates him, and rates his work.—JACOX, FRANCIS, 1872, *Aspects of Authorship, p.* 74.

In Pope, then, we have to do with a remarkably complex character. It will not do simply to brand him as a hypocrite, for the essence of hypocrisy consists in unreality; but behind the falsities of Pope there is an eagerness and intensity which gives them a human interest, and makes us feel, that, in his poetry, we are in contact with the nature of the man himself. To separate that moral nature into various elements, so as to decide how much is deliberately false, how much may be accepted as true, and how much is self-deception, we ought, following his own rule, to examine his

Proper character,
His fable, subject, scope in every page,
Religion, country, genius of his age.

On this principle much of the inconsistency in his conduct will be found to correspond with the union of opposite conditions in his nature: the piercing intelligence and artistic power, lodged in the sickly and deformed frame; the vivid perception of the ridiculous in others, joined to the most sensitive consciousness of his own defects; the passionate desire for fame, aggravated by a fear of being suspected by his countrymen on account of his religion; the conflicting qualities of benevolence and self-love; the predominance of intellectual instinct; the deficiency of moral principle. It might be predicted of a character so highly strung, so variously endowed, so "tremblingly alive" to opinion, and so capable of transformation, that it would exhibit itself in the most diverse aspects, according to the circumstances by which it was tested. And this is just what we find. Perhaps no man of genius was ever more largely influenced by his companions and his surroundings than Pope.—COURTHOPE, WILLIAM JOHN, 1881, *ed., The Works of Alexander Pope, Introduction to The Moral Essays and Satires, vol,* III, *p.* 26.

The deformed and decrepit poet had a grudge against the world. The feelings of this "Homer in a nutshell" were easily hurt, and easily fired. He was keenly alive to his own infirmities. He resented his malformation. He once or twice tries to allude lightly, and by and by, to "the libelled person and the pictured shape;" but the hand winces and the flesh quivers as he writes. There is a smile on the shrunken face, but the pain is intense. There is mockery in the voice, but the excessive bitterness is fitter for tears than for laughter. . . . In the heart of such a man many jealous and angry passions must have lodged. Sometimes he was bowed down by anguish; sometimes he was fiercely excited. And, undoubtedly, there was a *twist* in his mind as in his body. Pope's was, in many aspects, a lofty and generous nature. He was of an intrepid disposition. He could brave power. Let the cowards bully him if they dared! He loved his friends. Yet he was sometimes base. He was familiar with the stealthy and secret arts with which nature arms the weaker animals. Sometimes he practised these arts without excuse, necessity, or provocation.—SKELTON, JOHN, 1883, *The Great Lord Bolingbroke, Essays in History and Biography, pp.* 197, 198.

With the exception of some details recently brought to light with an industry worthy of a better subject, his contemporaries were as well aware of these delinquencies as we are now, only none but his bitter enemies were so earnest in denouncing them.—MINTO, WILLIAM, 1885, *Encyclopdæia Britannica, Ninth ed., vol.* XIX.

Nor can I think that "'twere to consider too curiously, to consider" that the temperament of his ill-conditioned body rather than the temper of his imprisoned mind must be held responsible for the childish trickery and apish furtiveness of such intrigues as have been so sharply cast in his teeth by the successive severity of the three Anglican clergymen who have edited and defamed him as a poet or as man. After the Reverend Mr. Warton came the Reverend Mr. Bowles, and after the Reverend Mr. Bowles comes the Reverend Mr. Elwin. "Hear them! All these against one foreigner!" cries Mr. Browning's Luria; and "See them! All these against one Liberal Catholic!" a lay student may be tempted and permitted to exclaim at sight of so many cassocked commentators opening in full cry upon the trail of this poet. And such a feeling may be indulged without any very sympathetic admiration for the balanced attitude of Pope between a modified sort of conformity and a moderate kind of philosophy.—SWINBURNE, ALGERNON CHARLES, 1886, *Miscellanies, p.* 36.

"An Ape,"—"An Apothecary,"—"The Bard of Twickenham,"—"The Best Poet of England,"—"The Empty Flask,"—"Gunpowder Percy,"—"A Little Druidwight,"—"A Little Liar,"—"The Little Man of Twickenham,"—"The Little Nightingale,"—"A Lurking, Way-Laying Coward,"—"The Most Faultless of Poets,"—"The Nightingale of Twickenham,"—"Paper-Sparing Pope,"—"Poet Pug,"—"The Portentous Cub,"—"Sawney,"—"The Sweet Swan of Thames,"—"The True Deacon of the Craft,"—"The Wasp of Twickenham."—FREY, ALBERT R., 1888, *Sobriquets and Nicknames, p.* 452.

Pope's disease was that of Malvolio and one or two others—he was sick of self-love. He knew himself to be warm-hearted and generous, he forgot he was also vain and disingenuous, and so remembering and thus forgetting, he loved himself unsparingly. A cripple and a Catholic, he was prevented by nature and by law from either active pursuits or the public service. Crazy for praise and fame, and conscious of enormous ability, he determined to make himself felt, as an independent force in verse. Resentful to the last degree, writhing under a dunce's sneer, maddened by a woman's laugh, he grasped his only weapon with a fierce hand and made his hatreds "live along the line." I do not believe any just man can read Dr. Johnson's and Mr. Courthope's Lives of Pope without liking him. Some of the bad poets (e. g. Kirke White) have been better men, but very few of the good ones. —BIRRELL, AUGUSTINE, 1889, *Noticeable Books, The Nineteenth Century, vol.* 26, *p.* 988.

The poor man's life was as weak and crooked as his frail, tormented body, but he had a dauntless spirit, and he fought his way against odds that might well have appalled a stronger nature. I suppose I must own that he was from time to time a snob, and from time to time a liar, but I believe that he loved the truth, and would have liked always to respect himself if he could. He violently revolted, now and again, from abasement to which he forced himself, and he always bit the heel, that trod on him, especially if it was a very high, narrow heel, with a clocked stocking and a hooped skirt above it. I loved him fondly at one time, and afterwards despised him, but now I am not sorry for the love, and I am very sorry for the despite.—HOWELLS, WILLIAM DEAN, 1895, *My Literary Passions, p.* 51.

LADY MARY

To say that he had any right to make love to her is one thing; yet to believe that her manners, and cast of character, as well as the nature of the times, and of the circles in which she moved, had given no license, no encouragement, no pardoning hope to the presumption, is impossible; and to trample in this way upon the whole miserable body of his vanity and humility, upon all which the consciousness of acceptability and glory among his fellow-creatures, had given to sustain himself, and all which in so poor, and fragile, and dwarfed, and degrading a shape, required so much to be so sustained;—assuredly it was inexcusable,—it was inhuman. . . . She had every advantage on her side:—could not even this induce her to put a little more heart and consideration into her repulse? Oh, Lady Mary! A duke's daughter wert thou, and a beauty, and a wit, and a very triumphant and flattered personage, and covered with glory as with lute-string and diamonds; and yet false measure didst thou take of thy superiority, and didst not see how small thou becamest in the comparison when thou didst thus, with laughing cheeks, trample under foot the poor little *immortal!*—HUNT, LEIGH, 1847, *Men, Women and Books, vol.* II, *p.* 196.

The friendship with Pope, conspicuous in the letters written during the embassy, is an unfortunate episode in the life of Lady Mary. All the stories which have gained credence, to the injury of her reputation, are probably due to his subsequent quarrel with her, the hatred and unscrupulousness with which he pursued her, and his fatal power of circulating scandalous insinuations. It is certain that the tenor of her life up to the period of her quarrel with Pope, was wholly unlike that career of profligacy which has been popularly attributed to her since the publication of Pope's Satires and the Letters of Horace Walpole—who, it must be remembered, wrote after Pope's celebrated attacks; and it is no less certain that, on a careful investigation, not one of the charges brought against her will be found to rest on any evidence.—THOMAS, W. MOY, 1861, *ed., Letters and Works of Lady Mary Wortley Montagu, Memoir, vol.* I, *p.* 21.

Why Pope and Lady Mary quarreled is a question on which much discussion has been expended, and on which a judicious German professor might even now compose an interesting and exhaustive monograph. A curt English critic will be more apt to ask why they should *not* have quarreled. We know that Pope quarreled with almost every one: we know that Lady Mary quarreled or half quarreled with most of her acquaintances: why then should they not have quarreled with one another? It is certain that they were very intimate at one time; for Pope wrote to her some of the most pompous letters of compliment in the language. And the more intimate they were to begin with, the more sure they were to be enemies in the end. . . . We only know that there was a sudden coolness or quarrel between them, and that it was the beginning of a long and bitter hatred. In their own times Pope's sensitive disposition probably gave Lady Mary a great advantage,—her tongue perhaps gave him more pain than his pen gave her; but in later times she has fared the worse.—BAGEHOT, WALTER, 1862–89, *Lady Mary Wortley Montagu, Works, ed. Morgan, vol.* I, *pp.* 377, 379.

The stroke, when it came, was delivered on the most sensitive part of the poet's nature. It is quite unnecessary to suppose that he was passionately in love with Lady Mary. The "declarations" which he is constantly making to her in his letters, he made, with as much sincerity, and almost in identical words, to Judith Cowper and Martha Blount; and, in using language of this kind, he was only conforming with the gallantry fashionable in his age. He calls himself in one of his poems the "most thinking rake alive." His love-making was like his description of Stanton-Harcourt, purely ideal, but his vanity and his artistic sensibility were so strong that he was vexed when he was not believed to be in earnest. To have the declaration of his elaborate passion received with laughter, must have been a rude shock to his vanity, and his acute self-consciousness would have no doubt associated Lady Mary's behaviour with his own physical defects. After all his well-considered expressions of devotion, after the exquisite lines in which he had connected her name with his grotto, ridicule was the refinement of torture. It humiliated him in his own esteem, and the recollection of the light mockery, with which she had always met his heroics, added to his sense of insult and injury. These considerations, though they help us to understand the condition of Pope's feelings, afford no excuse whatever for the character of his satire on Lady Mary.—ELWIN, WHITWELL AND COURTHOPE, WILLIAM JOHN, 1881, *ed., The Works of Alexander Pope, vol.* III, *p.* 282.

An incident occurred in connection with this picture that is worth recording, as showing the way artists are sometimes treated by their—so-called—patrons. A collector, of a somewhat vulgar type, had long desired me to paint a picture for him. I showed him the sketch, and, to prove the culture of the gentleman, I may mention the following fact: "What's the subject?" said he. "Lady Mary Wortley Montagu and Pope," said I; "the point taken is when Pope makes love to the lady, who was married at the time, and she laughed at him." "The pope make love to a married woman—horrible!" "No, no, not *the* pope—Pope the poet!" "Well, it don't matter who it was; he shouldn't make love to a married woman, and she done quite right in laughing at him; and if I had been her husband I should —" etc. "Very well," said I, "as you don't like the subject, we will say no more about it. I will paint you something else." "Oh, no," was the reply; "I like to see a woman laugh at a man who makes an ass of himself. I'll take it. What's the figure?"—FRITH, W. P., 1888, *My Autobiography and Reminiscences, vol.* I, *p.* 155.

MARTHA BLOUNT

Patty Blount was red-faced, fat, and by no means pretty. Mr. Walpole remembered her walking to Mr. Bethell's, in Arlington Street, after Pope's death, with her petticoats tucked up like a sempstress. She was the decided mistress of Pope, yet visited by respectable people.—MALONE, EDMUND, 1792, *Maloniana, From Horace Walpole, ed. Prior, p.* 437.

He was never indifferent to female society; and though his good sense prevented him, conscious of so many personal infirmities, from marrying, yet he felt the want of that sort of reciprocal tenderness and confidence in a female, to whom he might freely communicate his thoughts, and on whom, in sickness and infirmity, he could rely. All this Martha Blount became to him; by degrees, she became identified with his existence. She partook of his disappointments, his vexations, and his comforts. Wherever he went, his correspondence with her was never remitted; and when the warmth of gallantry was over, the cherished idea of kindness and regard remained.—BOWLES, WILLIAM LISLE, 1806, *ed. Pope's Works, vol.* I.

Martha Blount was not so kind or so attentive to Pope in his last illness as she ought to have been. His love for *her* seemed blended with his frail existence; and when he was scarcely sensible to any thing else in the world, he was still conscious of the charm of her presence. "When she came into the room," says Spence, "it was enough to give a new turn to his spirits, and a temporary strength to him." She survived him eighteen years, and died unmarried at her house in Berkeley Square, in 1762. She is described, about that time, as a little, fair, prim old woman, very lively, and inclined to gossip. Her undefined connexion with Pope, though it afforded matter for mirth and wonder, never affected her reputation while living; and has rendered her name as immortal as our language and our literature. One cannot help wishing that she had been more interesting, and more worthy of her fame.—JAMESON, ANNA BROWNELL, 1829, *The Loves of the Poets, vol.* II, *p.* 285.

Johnson repeats a story that Martha neglected Pope "with shameful unkindness," in his later years. It is clearly exaggerated or quite unfounded. At any rate, the poor sickly man, in his premature and childless old age, looked up to her with fond affection, and left to her nearly the whole of his fortune. His biographers have indulged in discussions —surely superfluous—as to the morality of the connexion. There is no question of seduction, or of tampering with the affections of an innocent woman. Pope was but too clearly disqualified from acting the part of Lothario. There was not in his case any Vanessa to give a tragic turn to the connexion, which otherwise resembled Swift's connexion with Stella. Miss Blount, from all that appears was quite capable of taking care of herself, and, had she wished for marriage, need only have intimated her commands to her lover. It is probable enough that the relations between them led to very unpleasant scenes in her family; but she did not suffer otherwise in accepting Pope's attentions. The probability seems to be that the friendship had become imperceptibly closer, and that what begun as an idle affectation of gallantry was slowly changed into a devoted attachment, but not until Pope's health was so broken that marriage would then, if not always, have appeared to be a mockery.—STEPHEN, LESLIE, 1880, *Alexander Pope* (*English Men of Letters*).

Miss Blount retained her place in the fashionable world after Pope's death. She lived at last in Berkeley Row, by Hanover Square, and there Swinburne the traveller, her relative, visited her (Roscoe, i, 581 note). He found her a little, neat, fair, prim old woman, easy and gay in her manners. By her will she left the residue of her property to her "dear nephew," Michael Blount, of Mapledurham. She died in 1762, aged 72.—HUMPHREYS, JENNETT, 1886, *Dictionary of National Biography, vol.* V, *p.* 249.

ODE TO SOLITUDE

The first of our author's compositions now extant in print, is an "Ode on Solitude," written before he was twelve years old: Which, consider'd as the production of so early an age, is a perfect masterpiece; nor need he have been ashamed of it, had it been written in the meridian of his genius. While it breathes the most delicate spirit of poetry, it at the same time demonstrates his love of solitude, and the rational pleasures which attend the retreats of a contented country life.—CIBBER, THEOPHILUS, 1753, *Lives of the Poets, vol.* V, *p.* 221.

The close of the seventeenth century forever shut the eyes of John Dryden upon the clouded and fluctuating daylight of our sublunary world. It may have been in the same year, that a solitary boy, then twelve years old, wrote five stanzas which any man might have been glad to have written—and which you have by heart—an "Ode to Solitude,"—conspicuous in the annals of English poetry as the dawn-gleam of a new sun that was presently to arise, and to fill the region that Dryden had left.—WILSON, JOHN, 1845, *Dryden and Pope, Blackwood's Magazine, vol.* 57, *p.* 379.

Pope never wrote more agreeable or well-tuned verses than this interesting effusion of his boyhood. Indeed there is an intimation of sweetness and variety in the versification, which was not borne out afterwards by his boasted smoothness: nor can we help thinking, that had the author of the "Ode on Solitude" arisen in less artificial times, he would have turned out to be a still finer poet than he was. But the reputation which he easily acquired for wit and criticism, the recent fame of Dryden, and perhaps even his little warped and fragile person, tempted him to accept such power over his contemporaries as he could soonest realize. It is observable that Pope never repeated the form of verse in which this poem is written. It might have reminded him of a musical feeling he had lost.—HUNT, LEIGH, 1849, *A Book for a Corner.*

The Odes written by Pope are decidedly of an inferior caste. I need not say how inferior to the immortal "Ode on St. Cecilia's Day," by Dryden, who preceded —or how inferior to Gray or Campbell, who have followed him. The Ode, perhaps, of every species of poetical composition, was the most alien to the genius of Pope.—CARLISLE, GEORGE WILLIAM FREDERICK HOWARD, EARL, 1851–62, *Lectures and Addresses, p.* 15.

PASTORALS
1709

The author seems to have a particular genius for this kind of poetry, and a judgment that much exceeds his years. He has taken very freely from the ancients. But what he has mixed of his own with theirs is no way inferior to what he has taken from them. It is not flattery at all to say that Virgil had written nothing so good at his age. His preface is very judicious and learned.—WALSH, WILLIAM, 1705? *Letter to William Wycherley, April* 20.

He shall bring with him, if you will, a young poet, newly inspired in the neighbourhood of Cooper's Hill, whom he and Walsh have taken under their wing. His name is Pope. He is not above seventeen or eighteen years of age, and promises miracles. If he goes on as he has begun in the Pastoral way, as Virgil first tried his strength, we may hope to see English poetry vie with the Roman, and this swan of Windsor sing as sweetly as the Mantuan. —GRANVILLE, GEORGE (LORD LANSDOWNE), 1706? *Letters, Works of Lord-Lansdowne, vol.* II, *p.* 113.

I have lately seen a pastoral of yours in Mr. Walsh's and Congreve's hands, which is extremely fine, and is generally approved of by the best judges in poetry. I remember I have formerly seen you at my shop, and am sorry I did not improve my acquaintance with you. If you design your poem for the press, no person shall be more careful in printing it, nor no one can give a greater encouragement to it.—TONSON, JACOB, 1706, *Letter to Mr. Pope, April* 20.

Young, yet judicious; in your verse are found
Art strength'ning nature, sense improved by sound.

—WYCHERLEY, WILLIAM, 1709, *To My Friend Mr. Pope, On his Pastorals.*

Neither Mr. Pope's nor Mr. Philips's pastorals, do any great honour to the English poetry. Mr. Pope's were composed in his youth; which may be an apology for other faults, but cannot well excuse the barrenness that appears in them. They are written in remarkably smooth and flowing numbers, and this is their chief merit; for there is scarcely any thought in them which can be called his own; scarcely any description, or any image of nature, which has the marks of being original, or copied from nature herself; but a repetition of the common images that are to be found in Virgil, and in all poets who write of rural themes.—BLAIR, HUGH, 1783, *Lectures on Rhetoric and Belles-Lettres, ed. Mills, Lecture* xxxix.

It is somewhat strange that in the pastorals of a young poet there should not be found a single rural image that is new; but this, I am afraid, is the case in the Pastorals before us. The ideas of Theocritus, Virgil, and Spenser are, indeed, here exhibited in language equally mellifluous and pure; but the descriptions and sentiments are trite and common. To this assertion, formerly made, Dr. Johnson answered, "that no invention was intended." He, therefore, allows the fact and the charge. It is a confession of the very fault imputed to them. There *ought* to have been invention. It has been my fortune from my way of life, to have seen many compositions of youths of sixteen years old, far beyond these Pastorals in point of genius and imagination, though not perhaps of correctness. Their excellence, indeed, might be owing to having had such a predecessor as Pope.—WARTON, JOSEPH, 1797, *ed. Pope's Works.*

Warton's observations are very just, but he does not seem sufficiently to discriminate between the softness of individual lines, which is the chief merit of these Pastorals, and the general harmony of poetic numbers. Let it, however, be always remembered, that Pope gave the first idea of mellifluence, and produced a softer and sweeter cadence than before belonged to the English couplet. Dr. Johnson thinks it will be in vain, after Pope, to endeavour to improve the English versification, and that it is now carried to the *ne plus ultra* of excellence. This is an opinion the validity of which I must be permitted to doubt. Pope certainly gave a more correct and finished tone to the English versification, but he sometimes wanted a variety of pause, and his nice precision of every line prevented, in a few instances, a more musical flow of modulated passages. But we are to consider what he did, not what might be done, and surely there cannot be two opinions respecting his improvement of the couplet though it does not follow that his general rhythm has no imperfection. Johnson seems to have depreciated, or to have been ignorant of, the metrical powers of some writers prior to Pope. His ear seems to have been caught chiefly by Dryden, and as Pope's versification was more equably (couplet with couplet being considered, not passage with passage) connected than Dryden's, he thought therefore that nothing could be added to Pope's versification. I should think it the extreme of arrogance and folly to make my own ear the criterion of music; but I cannot help thinking that Dryden, and of later days, Cowper, are much more harmonious in their general versification than Pope. I ought also to mention a neglected poem, not neglected on account of its versification, but on account of its title and subject—Prior's "Solomon." Whoever candidly compares these writers together, unless his ear be habituated to a certain recurrence of pauses precisely at the end of a line, will not (though he will give the highest praise for compactness, skill, precision, and force, to the undivided couplets of Pope, separately considered)—will not, I think, assent to the position, that in versification "what he found brickwork he left marble." I am not afraid to own, that with the exception of the "Epistle to Abelard," as musical as it is pathetic, the verses of Pope want variety, and on this account in some instances they want both force and harmony. In variety, and variety only, let it be remembered, I think Pope deficient.—BOWLES, WILLIAM LISLE, 1806, *ed. Pope's Works.*

There is no evidence, except the poet's own assertion, to prove that the Pastorals were composed at the age of sixteen. They had been seen by Walsh before April 20, 1705, if any dependence could be placed upon the letter of that date which he wrote to Wycherley, when returning the manuscript, but the letter rests on the authority of Pope alone, and there is reason to question the correctness of the date. . . . Whatever may be the true date of the Pastorals, a portion of them certainly existed before April 20, 1706.—ELWIN, WHITWELL, 1871, *ed., The Works of Alexander Pope, Pastorals, vol.* I, *pp.* 240-41.

The Pastorals have been seriously criticised; but they are, in truth, mere schoolboy exercises; they represent nothing more than so many experiments in versification. The pastoral form has doubtless been used in earlier hands to embody true poetic feeling; but in Pope's time it had become hopelessly threadbare. The fine gentlemen in wigs and laced coats amused themselves by writing about nymphs and "conscious swains," by way of asserting their claims to elegance of taste. Pope, as a boy, took the matter seriously, and always retained a natural fondness for a juvenile performance upon which he had expended great labour, and which was the chief proof of his extreme precocity. He invites attention to his own merits, and claims especially the virtue of propriety. He does not, he tells us, like some other people, make his roses and daffodils bloom in the same season, and cause his nightingales to sing in November; and he takes particular credit for having remembered that there were no wolves in England, and having accordingly excised a passage in which Alexis prophesied that those animals would grow milder as they listened to the strains of his favourite nymph. When a man has got so far as to bring to England all the pagan deities, and rival shepherds contending for bowls and lambs in alternate strophes, these niceties seem a little out of place. . . . We may agree with Johnson that Pope performing upon a pastoral pipe is rather a ludicrous person, but for mere practice even nonsense verses have been found useful.—STEPHEN, LESLIE, 1880, *Alexander Pope, (English Men of Letters), pp.* 23, 24.

I fell in love with Pope, whose life I read with an ardor of sympathy which I am afraid he hardly merited. I was of his side in all his quarrels, as far as I understood them, and if I did not understand them I was of his side anyway. When I found he was a Catholic I was almost ready to abjure the Protestant religion for his sake; but I perceived that this was not necessary when I came to know that most of his friends were Protestants. If the truth must be told, I did not like his best things at first, but long remained chiefly attached to his rubbishing pastorals, which I was perpetually imitating, with whole apparatus of swains and shepherdesses, purling brooks, enameled meads, rolling years, and the like. . . . I could not imitate Pope without imitating his methods, and his method was to the last degree intelligent. He certainly knew what he was doing, and although I did not always know what I was doing, he made me wish to know, and ashamed of not knowing. There are several truer poets who might not have done this; and after all the modern contempt of Pope, he seems to me to have been at least one of the great masters, if not one of the great poets.—HOWELLS, WILLIAM DEAN, 1895, *My Literary Passions, pp.* 49, 50.

Certainly, the controversy as to the respective merits of Pope and Philips has lost its freshness. From the point of view taken in this essay, each had failed alike to appreciate the true conditions and to catch the proper spirit of pastoral. Yet within their own limits, one can hardly deny that the superiority rests with Pope. The contrary judgment were to confuse a rhymester with a man of genius. Pope's manner is intolerably artificial; he bears the graceless yoke of the Miltonic epithet; his matter is a mere pastiche from Virgil and Theocritus, Dryden and Spenser; but for melodious rhythm and dignity of phrase his pastorals reach a point which he never afterwards surpassed. The musical possibilities of the heroic couplet are exhausted in the eclogue entitled "Autumn," and though we may perhaps think the meter inappropriate to the subject, we cannot fail to be sensible of the ease and dignity of the verse.—CHAMBERS, EDMUND K., 1895, *English Pastorals, p.* xlv.

ESSAY ON CRITICISM
1711-12

"The Art of Criticism," which was published some months since, and is a masterpiece in its kind. The observations follow one another like those in Horace's "Art of Poetry," without that methodical regularity which would have been requisite in a prose author. They are some of them uncommon, but such as the reader must assent to, when he sees them explained with that elegance and perspicuity in which they are delivered. As for those which are the most known, and the most received, they are placed in so beautiful a light, and illustrated with such apt allusions, that they have in them all the graces of novelty, and make the reader, who was before acquainted with them, still more convinced of their truth and solidity.—ADDISON, JOSEPH, 1711, *The Spectator, No.* 253, *Dec.* 20.

His precepts are false, or trivial, or both; his thoughts are crude and abortive, his expressions absurd, his numbers harsh and unmusical, his rhymes trivial and common; instead of majesty, we have something that is very mean; instead of gravity, something that is very boyish; and instead of perspicuity and lucid order, we have but too often obscurity and confusion.—DENNIS, JOHN, 1711, *Reflections, Critical and Satirical on a Rhapsody, An Essay on Criticism.*

I dare not say anything of the "Essay on Criticism" in verse; but if any more curious reader has discovered in it something *new* which is not in Dryden's prefaces, dedications, and his "Essay on Dramatic Poetry," not to mention the French critics, I should be very glad to have the benefit of the discovery.—OLDMIXON, JOHN, 1728, *Essay on Criticism in Prose.*

Was the work of his childhood almost; but is such a monument of good sense and poetry as no other, that I know, has raised in his riper years.—BOLINGBROKE, HENRY ST. JOHN LORD, 1735, *On the Study and Use of History.*

I admired Mr. Pope's "Essay on Criticism" at first, very much, because I had not then read any of the ancient critics, and did not know that it was all stolen.—MONTAGU, LADY MARY WORTLEY, 1740-41, *Spence's Anecdotes, ed. Singer, p.* 176.

A work which displays such extent of comprehension, such nicety of distinction, such acquaintance with mankind, and such knowledge both of ancient and modern learning, as are not often attained by the maturest age and longest experience. . . . One of his greatest, though of his earliest, works is the "Essay on Criticism," which, if he had written nothing else, would have placed him among the first critics and the first poets, as it exhibits every mode of excellence that can embellish or dignify didactic composition,—selection of matter, novelty of arrangement, justness of precept, splendour of illustration, and propriety of digression. I know not whether it be pleasing to consider that he has produced this piece at twenty, and never afterwards excelled it: he that delights himself with observing that such powers may be soon attained, cannot but grieve to think that life was ever after at a stand. To mention the particular beauties of the Essay would be unprofitably tedious; but I cannot forbear to observe, that the comparison of a student's progress in the sciences with the journey of a traveller in the Alps, is perhaps the best that English poetry can shew.—JOHNSON, SAMUEL, 1779–81, *Pope, Lives of the English Poets.*

Most of the observations in this Essay are just, and certainly evince good sense, an extent of reading, and powers of comparison, considering the age of the author, extraordinary. Johnson's praise however is exaggerated.—BOWLES, WILLIAM LISLE, 1806, *ed. Pope's Works.*

The quantity of thought and observation in this work, for so young a man as Pope was when he wrote it, is wonderful: unless we adopt the supposition that most men of genius spend the rest of their lives in teaching others what they themselves have learned under twenty. The conciseness and felicity of the expression are equally remarkable. . . . Nothing can be more original and happy than the general remarks and illustrations in the Essay: the critical rules laid down are too much those of a school, and of a confined one.—HAZLITT, WILLIAM, 1818, *Lectures on the English Poets, Lecture* iv.

Which some people have very unreasonably fancied his best performance.—DE QUINCY, THOMAS, c1838–63, *Pope, Works, ed. Masson, vol.* IV, *p.* 260.

The praise that is uppermost in one's mind of the "Essay on Criticism" is its rectitude of legislation. Pope is an orthodox doctor—a champion of the good old cause. . . . It is of the right good *English* temper—thoughtful and ardent—discreet and generous—firm with sensibility—bold and sedate—manly and polished. He establishes himself in well-chosen positions of natural strength, commanding the field; and he occupies them in the style of an experienced leader, with forces judiciously disposed, and showing a resolute front every way of defence and offence.—WILSON, JOHN, 1845, *Dryden and Pope, Blackwood's Magazine, vol.* 57, *p.* 393.

Considered solely as a phenomenon in literary history, the "Essay on Criticism" is doubtless one of the most remarkable instances of precocious genius which the annals of English or of any other literature afford.—WARD, ADOLPHUS WILLIAM, 1869, *ed., Poetical Works of Alexander Pope, p.* 47, *note.*

English literature must become far richer than it is in witty *mots* or rememberable lines before we can afford to throw away the "Essay on Criticism."—PATTISON, MARK, 1872–89, *Pope and His Editors, Essays, ed. Nettleship, vol.* II, *p.* 360.

The "Essay" has many incorrect observations, and, in spite of its own axioms, many bad rhymes, many faulty grammatical constructions. But these cannot weigh against the substantial merit of the performance. They cannot obscure the truth that the poem is, what its title pretends, an "Essay on Criticism," an attempt made, for the first time in English literature, and in the midst of doubts, perplexities, and distractions, of which we, in our position of the idle heirs of that age, can only have a shadowy conception, to erect a standard of judgment founded in justice of thought and accuracy of expression. Nor will it be denied that, as a poem, the critical and philosophical nature of the subject is enlivened by bold, brilliant, and beautiful imagery.—COURTHOPE, WILLIAM JOHN, 1889, *The Life of Alexander Pope, Works, ed. Elwin and Courthope, vol.* V, *p.* 70.

Pope impaired the vitality of English poetry for fifty years by his futile "to advantage dressed," and succeeded in teaching "a school of dolts to smooth, inlay, and clip, and fit," as the excited Keats has it. Horace is very modern, we say; we can read him nowadays with great comfort, with greater comfort than we can get from Pope. Not only is Horace nearer to us in his ideas on language and on style; he understood criticism better than did Pope.—HALE, EDWARD E., JR., 1897, *The Classics of Criticism, The Dial, vol.* 22, *p.* 246.

THE MESSIAH
1712

This is certainly the most animated and sublime of all authors' compositions, and it is manifestly owing to the great original which he copied. Perhaps the dignity, the energy, and the simplicity of the original, are in a few passages weakened and diminished by florid epithets, and useless circumlocutions.—WARTON, JOSEPH, 1797, *ed. Pope's Works.*

All things considered, the "Messiah" is as fine and masterly a piece of composition as the English language, in the same style of verse, can boast. I have ventured to point out a passage or two, for they are rare, where the sublimity has been awakened by epithets; and I have done this, because it is a fault, particularly with young writers, so common. In the most truly sublime images of Scripture, the addition of a single word would often destroy their effect. It is therefore right to keep as nearly as possible to the very words. No one understood better than Milton where to be general, and where particular; where to adopt the very expression of Scripture, and where it was allowed to paraphrase.—BOWLES, WILLIAM LISLE, 1806, *ed. Pope's Works.*

The flamboyant style of his "Messiah" is to me detestable: nothing can be more unlike the simplicity of Christianity. All such, equally with those by whatever hand that would be religious by being miserable, I reject at once, along with all that are merely commonplace religious exercises.—MACDONALD, GEORGE, 1868, *England's Antiphon, p.* 285.

Pope says he was induced to subjoin in his notes the passages he had versified by "the fear that he had prejudiced Isaiah and Virgil by his management." The reputation of Isaiah and Virgil was safe, and no one can doubt that his real reason for inviting the comparison was the belief that he had improved upon them. He imagined that he had enriched the text of the prophet, and did not suspect that the majesty and truth of the original were vitiated by his embroidery.—ELWIN, WHITWELL, 1871, *ed., The Works of Alexander Pope, Messiah, vol.* I, *p.* 308.

Pope's "Messiah" reads to us like a sickly paraphrase, in which all the majesty of the original is dissipated.—PATTISON, MARK, 1880, *The English Poets, ed. Ward, vol.* III, *p.* 60.

His "Messiah" would sound grand to us, if we could for a moment feel that he felt it himself, or forget that it was copied from Virgil's Pollio.—POOR, LAURA ELIZABETH, 1880, *Sanskrit and its Kindred Literatures, p,* 436.

It is an admirable *tour de force,* and should be regarded like his "Pastorals" as an exercise in diction and versification. Though, by the conditions under which he has bound himself, he was forced to lower the grandeur of the Scripture language, the artfulness with which he adapts his imagery to the Virgilian manner, and combines scattered passages of prophecy in a volume of stately and sonorous verse, is deserving of high admiration; and the concluding lines ascend to a height not unworthy of the original they paraphrase. —COURTHOPE, WILLIAM JOHN, 1889, *The Life of Alexander Pope, Works, ed. Elwin and Courthope, vol.* V, *p.* 36.

RAPE OF THE LOCK
1712–14

THE RAPE OF THE LOCK.
An heroi-comical poem.

Nolueram, Belinda, tuos violare capillos,
Sed juvat, hoc precibus me tribuisse tuis.
MART. *Epigr. XII.* 84.

Printed for Bernard Lintott, 1712. 8vo. —TITLE PAGE TO FIRST EDITION, 1712.

How flames the glories of Belinda's hair,
Made by the Muse the envy of the fair!
Less shone the tresses Egypt's princess wore,
Which sweet Callimachus so sung before.
Here courtly trifles set the world at odds,
Belles war with beaux, and whims descend for gods.
The new machines, in names of ridicule,
Mock the grave phrenzy of the chemic fool:
But know, ye fair, a point concealed with art,
The Sylphs and Gnomes are but a woman's heart.
The Graces stand in sight; a Satyr train
Peeps o'er their head, and laughs behind the scene.
—PARNELL, THOMAS, 1717, *To Mr. Pope.*

The stealing of Miss Belle Fermor's hair, was taken too seriously, and caused an estrangement between the two families, though they had lived so long in great friendship before. A common acquaintance and well-wisher to both, desired me to write a poem to make a jest of it, and laugh them together again. It was with this view that I wrote the "Rape of the Lock"; which was well received, and had its effect in the two families.—Nobody but Sir George Brown was angry, and he was a good deal so, and for a long time. He could not bear, that Sir Plume should talk nothing but nonsense.—Copies of the poem got about, and it was like to be printed; on which I published the first draught of it (without the machinery), in a Miscellany of Tonson's. The machinery was added afterwards, to make it look a little more considerable, and the scheme of adding it was much liked and approved of by several of my friends, and particularly by Dr.

Garth: who, as he was one of the best natured men in the world, was very fond of it.—POPE, ALEXANDER, 1737–39, *Spence's Anecdotes, ed. Singer, p.* 147.

I have been assured by a most intimate friend of Mr. Pope's, that the Peer in the "Rape of the Lock" was Lord Petre; the person who desired Mr. Pope to write it, old Mr. Caryl, of Sussex; and that what was said of Sir George Brown in it, was the very picture of the man.—SPENCE, JOSEPH, 1737–39, *Anecdotes, ed. Singer, p.* 148.

The grand characteristic of a poet is his invention, the surest distinction of a great genius. In Mr. Pope, nothing is so truly original as his "Rape of the Lock," nor discovers so much invention. In this kind of mock-heroic, he is without a rival in our language, for Dryden has written nothing of the kind.—CIBBER, THEOPHILUS, 1753, *Lives of the Poets, vol.* V, *p.* 249.

This seems to be Mr. Pope's most finished production, and is, perhaps, the most perfect in our language. It exhibits stronger powers of imagination, more harmony of numbers, and a greater knowledge of the world, than any other of this poet's works: and it is probable, if our country were called upon to shew a specimen of their genius to foreigners, this would be the work here fixed upon.—GOLDSMITH, OLIVER, 1767, *The Beauties of English Poetry.*

The most airy, the most ingenious, and the most delightful of all his compositions. . . . To the praises which have been accumulated on "The Rape of the Lock" by readers of every class, from the critic to the waiting-maid, it is difficult to make any addition. Of that which is universally allowed to use the most attractive of all ludicrous compositions, let it rather be now inquired from what sources the power of pleasing is derived.—JOHNSON, SAMUEL, 1779–81, *Pope, Lives of the English Poets.*

'Tis Pope who sweetly wakes the silver lyre
To melting notes, more musically clear
Than Ariel whisper'd in Belinda's ear.
—HAYLEY, WILLIAM, 1782, *An Essay on Epic Poetry, ep.* iii.

In my eyes, the "Lutrin," the "Dispensary," and the "Rape of the Lock" are standards of grace and elegance, not to be paralleled by antiquity. . . . The "Rape of the Lock," besides the originality of great part of the invention, is a standard of graceful writing.—WALPOLE, HORACE, 1785, *Letter to J. Pinkerton, Letters, ed. Cunningham, vol.* VIII, *pp.* 565, 566.

That exquisite little toilet-bottle of essence, the "Rape of the Lock."—HUNT, LEIGH, 1817, *The Examiner.*

It is the most exquisite specimen of *filigree* work ever invented. It is admirable in proportion as it is made of nothing. . . . It is made of gauze and silver spangles. The most glittering appearance is given to every thing, to paste, pomatum, billets-doux and patches. Airs, languid airs, breathe around; the atmosphere is perfumed with affectation. A toilette is described with the solemnity of an altar raised to the goddess of vanity, and the history of a silver bodkin is given with all the pomp of heraldry. No pains are spared, no profusion of ornament, no splendour of poetic diction, to set off the meanest things. The balance between the concealed irony and the assumed gravity is as nicely trimmed as the balance of power in Europe. The little is made great, and the great little. You hardly know whether to laugh or weep. It is the triumph of insignificance, the apotheosis of foppery and folly. It is the perfection of the mock-heroic.—HAZLITT, WILLIAM, 1818, *Lectures on the English Poets, Lecture* iv.

The most exquisite monument of playful fancy that universal literature offers. —DE QUINCEY, THOMAS, c1838–63, *Pope, Works, ed. Masson, vol.* IV, *p.* 260.

If dramatic pieces be left out of the question, the "Rape of the Lock" is probably one of the longest occasional poems in any literature; and yet French literature itself may be challenged to match the sparkling vivacity of its execution no less than the airy grace of its plot and underplot.—WARD, ADOLPHUS WILLIAM, 1869, *ed., Poetical Works of Alexander Pope, p.* 71, *note.*

Consider "The Rape of the Lock" as a whole; it is a buffoonery in a noble style. —TAINE, H. A., 1871, *History of English Literature, tr. Van Laun, vol.* II, *bk.* iii, *ch.* vii, *p.* 203.

The whole poem more truly deserves the name of a creation than anything

Pope ever wrote. The action is confined to a world of his own, the supernatural agency is wholly of his own contrivance, and nothing is allowed to overstep the limitations of the subject. It ranks by itself as one of the purest works of human fancy; whether that fancy be strictly poetical or not is another matter. If we compare it with the "Midsummer-night's Dream," an uncomfortable doubt is suggested. The perfection of form in the "Rape of the Lock" is to me conclusive evidence that in it the natural genius of Pope found fuller and freer expression than in any other of his poems. The others are aggregates of brilliant passages rather than harmonious wholes.—LOWELL, JAMES RUSSELL, 1871–90, *Pope, Prose Works, Riverside ed., vol.* IV, *p.* 35.

No more brilliant, sparkling, vivacious trifle is to be found in our literature than the "Rape of the Lock," even in this early form. . . . Pope declared, and critics have agreed, that he never showed more skill than in the remodelling of this poem; and it has ever since held a kind of recognized supremacy amongst the productions of the drawing-room muse. . . . The successive scenes are given with so firm and clear a touch—there is such a sense of form, the language is such a dexterous elevation of the ordinary social twaddle into the mock-heroic, that it is impossible not to recognize a consummate artistic power. The dazzling display of true wit and fancy blinds us for the time to the want of that real tenderness and humour which would have softened some hard passages, and given a more enduring charm to the poetry. It has, in short, the merit that belongs to any work of art which expresses in the most finished form the sentiment characteristic of a given social phrase; one deficient in many of the most ennobling influences, but yet one in which the arts of converse represent a very high development of shrewd sense refined into vivid wit.—STEPHEN, LESLIE, 1880, *Alexander Pope* (*English Men of Letters*), *pp,* 39, 40, 42.

Pope's execution is so clever as always to charm us even when his subject is most devoid of interest. The secret of the peculiar fascination of "The Rape of the Lock" lies, I believe, not merely in the art and management, but in the fact that here, for the first time, Pope is writing of that which he knew, of the life he saw and the people he lived with. For Windsor Forest, though he lived in it, he had no eyes; but a drawing-room, a fop, and a belle, these were the objects which struck his young fancy when he emerged from the linen-draper's villa, and he had studied them.—PATTISON, MARK, 1880, *The English Poets, ed. Ward, vol.* III, *p.* 64.

I may as well own frankly that I am unable to admire the poem. It is, of course, clever, but I fail to get such delight from its lines as has rewarded the eminent men who have written about it. It is impossible to avoid the thought that patriotism is in part the cause of this admiration.—PERRY, THOMAS SERGEANT, 1883, *English Literature in the Eighteenth Century, p.* 248.

Blameless in its beauty and perfect in its charm as is that sovereign flower of social satire.—SWINBURNE, ALGERNON CHARLES, 1886, *Miscellanies, p.* 44.

This apparently hazardous experiment was perfectly successful, and the "Rape of the Lock" became what it remains, the typical example of raillery in English verse—the solitary specimen of sustained and airy grace. If it has faults, they are the faults of the time, and not of the poem, the execution of which is a marvel of ease, good humour, and delicate irony. —DOBSON, AUSTIN, 1888, *Alexander Pope, Scribner's Magazine, vol.* 3, *p.* 539.

The "Rape of the Lock" stands as far above "Le Lutrin" as the latter does above "La Secchia Rapita." . . . The style of the "Rape of the Lock" is a happy compound of the best elements of burlesque in Tassoni's and Boileau's manner, with an epic loftiness which is all Pope's own. . . . In his machinery Pope is neither driven like Tassoni to employ obsolete Pagan mythology, nor like Boileau to resort to moral abstractions; by a supreme effort of invention he has made his supernatural agents credible to the modern imagination. Hence he has successfully encountered all those difficulties in the way of mock-heroic poet on which I have dwelt in the foregoing pages. A slight incident of social life has been made the basis of a well-connected epic narrative; the sayings and doings of persons belonging to existing society are invested with heroic dignity; the whole delicate creation breathes a justly diffused moral air, which saves it from the reproach of triviality, without making it obtrusively didactic. Pope has succeeded in embalming a fleeting episode of fashionable manners in a form which can perish only with the English language.—COURTHOPE, WILLIAM JOHN, 1889, *The Life of Alexander Pope, Works, ed. Elwin and Courthope, vol.* V, *pp.* 107, 110, 114.

"The Rape of the Lock" is very witty, but through it all don't you mark the sneer of the contemptuous, unmanly little wit, the crooked dandy? He jibes among his compliments; and I do not wonder that Mistress Arabella Fermor was not conciliated by his long-drawn cleverness and polished lines.—LANG, ANDREW, 1889, *Letters on Literature, p.* 152.

"The celebrated lady herself," the poet wrote, "is offended, and which is stranger, not at herself but me. Is not this enough to make a writer never be tender of another's character or fame?" But Pope, whose praise of women is too often a libel upon them, was not as tender as he ought to have been of the lady's reputation. The offence felt by the heroine of the poem is now unheeded; the dainty art exhibited is a permanent delight, and our language can boast no more perfect specimen of the poetical burlesque than the "Rape of the Lock." The machinery of the sylphs is managed with perfect skill, and nothing can be more admirable than the charge delivered by Ariel to the sylphs to guard Belinda from an apprehended but unknown danger.—DENNIS, JOHN, 1894, *The Age of Pope, p.* 31.

It does not seem to me to furnish very inspiring reading.—MITCHELL, DONALD G., 1895, *English Lands Letters and Kings, Queen Anne and the Georges, p.* 39.

The most brilliant occasional poem in our language.—BROOKE, STOPFORD A., 1896, *English Literature, p.* 184.

We may draw attention to the fact, already averted to, that, poetic excellence and merit altogether apart, "The Rape of the Lock" presents us with the most perfect picture in miniature possible of life at Hampton Court during the reign of Queen Anne. We have already cited at the beginning of this chapter the opening lines of the third canto, beginning with the words, "Close by those meads," etc.: the verses that follow them, with their delicate irony on the fashionable frivolities of the inhabitants of Hampton Court at that time, give us a peep into the interior social life of the palace, than which nothing could be more vivid. . . . Thus it comes about the subject-matter of these pages is associated with the most brilliant and exquisite mock-heroic poem in the English, or perhaps any, language, replete with all the subtlest delicacies of humour, satire, language, and invention, and redolent of the refined and airy graces of the artificial world which it so intimately describes.—LAW, ERNEST, 1897, *Hampton Court, pp.* 358, 359.

Is Pope's masterpiece.—HALLECK, REUBEN POST, 1900, *History of English Literature, p.* 255.

WINDSOR FOREST
1713

WINDSOR FOREST. | To the Right Honorable George, Lord Landsdown. | By Mr. Pope.

Non injussa cano: te nostræ, Vare, myricæ,
Te nemus omne canet; nec Phœbo gratior ulla est,
Quam sibi quæ Vari præscripsit pagina nomen --Virg.

London: Printed for Bernard Lintott, at the Cross-keys, | in Fleet Street. |
—TITLE PAGE OF FIRST EDITION, 1713.

Mr. Pope has published a fine poem called "Windsor Forest." Read it.—SWIFT, JONATHAN, 1713, *Journal to Stella, March* 9.

I should have commended his poem on "Windsor Forest" much more, if he had not served me a slippery trick; for you must know I had long since put him upon this subject, gave several hints, and at last, when he brought it, and read it, and made some little alterations, &c., not one word of putting in my name till I found it in print.—TRUMBULL, SIR WILLIAM, 1713, *Letter to Mr. Bridges, May* 12.

ODE ON ST. CELIA'S DAY
1713

Many people would like my Ode on Music better, if Dryden had not written on that subject. It was at the request of Mr. Steele that I wrote mine; and not with any thought of rivalling that great man, whose memory I do and always have reverenced.—POPE, ALEXANDER, 1734–36, *Spence's Anecdotes, ed. Singer, p.* 119.

Must be reckoned amongst his utter failures.—STEPHEN, LESLIE, 1880, *Alexander Pope (English Men of Letters), p.* 196.

THE TEMPLE OF FAME

1714

The hint of the following piece was taken from Chaucer's "House of Fame." The design is in a manner entirely altered, the descriptions and most of the particular thoughts my own: yet I could not suffer it to be printed without this acknowledgment, or think of a concealment of this nature the less unfair for being common. The reader who would compare this with Chaucer, may begin with his third Book of Fame, there being nothing in the two first books that answers to their title. Whenever any hint is taken from him, the passage itself is set down in the marginal notes.—POPE, ALEXANDER, 1715, *The Temple of Fame, Advertisement.*

It was probably the similarity of taste that induced Pope when young to imitate several of the pieces of Chaucer, and in particular to write his "Temple of Fame," one of the noblest, although one of the earliest of his productions. That the hint of the piece is taken from Chaucer's "House of Fame," is sufficiently obvious, yet the design is greatly altered, and the descriptions, and many of the particular thoughts, are his own; notwithstanding which, such is the coincidence and happy union of the work with its prototype, that it is almost impossible to distinguish those portions which are originally Pope's, from those for which he has been indebted to Chaucer.—ROSCOE, WILLIAM, 1824–47, *ed., The Works of Alexander Pope, vol.* II, *p.* xiv.

Pope, who reproduced parts of the "House of Fame," in a loose paraphrase, in attempting to improve the construction of Chaucer's work, only mutilated it.—WARD, ADOLPHUS WILLIAM, 1880, *Chaucer (English Men of Letters), p.* 96.

One of Pope's least attractive pieces. —DENNIS, JOHN, 1894, *The Age of Pope, p.* 33.

HOMER'S ILIAD

1715–20

I am pleased beyond measure with your design of translating Homer. The trials you have already made and published on some parts of that author have shown that you are equal to so great a task; and you may therefore depend upon the utmost services I can do in promoting this work, or anything that may be for your service. —GRANVILLE, GEORGE (LORD LANSDOWN), 1713, *Letter to Alexander Pope, Oct.* 21.

Then he [Swift] instructed a young nobleman that the best poet in England was Mr. Pope (a Papist), who had begun a translation of Homer into English verse, "for which he must have them all subscribe; for," says he, "the author shall not begin to print till I have a thousand guineas for him."—KENNET, BISHOP, 1713. *Diary, Nov.*

I borrowed your Homer from the bishop, (mine is not yet landed), and read it out in two evenings. If it pleases others as well as me, you have got your end in profit and reputation: yet I am angry at some bad rhymes and triplets; and pray in your next do not let me have so many unjustifiable rhymes to war, and gods. I tell you all the faults I know, only in one or two places you are a little too obscure, but I expected you to be so in one or two-and-twenty. . . . Your notes are perfectly good, and so are your preface and essay.—SWIFT, JONATHAN, 1715, *Letter to Pope, June* 28.

Did I not see when thou first sett'st sail
To seek adventures fair in Homer's land?
Did I not see thy sinking spirits fail,
And wish thy bark had never left the strand?
Even in mid ocean often didst thou quail,
And oft lift up thy holy eye and hand,
Praying the Virgin dear and saintly choir,
Back to the port to bring thy bark entire.
Cheer up, my friend! thy dangers now are o'er;
Methinks,—nay, sure the rising coasts appear;
Hark! how the guns salute from either shore,
As thy trim vessel cuts the Thames so fair:
Shouts answering shouts from Kent and Essex roar,
And bells break loud through every gust of air:
Bonfires do blaze, and bones and cleavers ring,
As at the coming of some mighty king.

—GAY, JOHN, 1720, *To Mr. Pope, Welcome from Greece.*

I have as yet read only to the end of the eighth Iliad; but, as far as I can judge, this is one of the finest translations in the English language; and, what is very extraordinary, it appears to the best advantage when compared with the original. I have read both carefully so far, and written remarks as I went along; and I think I can prove that where Pope has omitted one beauty he has added or improved four. . . . —DODDRIDGE, PHILIP, 1725, *Letter to Rev. Nettleton, Aug.* 5.

All the crime that I have committed is saying that he is no master of Greek; and I am so confident of this, that if he can translate ten lines of Eustathius I'll own myself unjust and unworthy.—BROOME, WILLIAM, 1727, *Letter to Fenton, June* 5.

In order to sink in reputation, let him take it into his head to descend into Homer (let the world wonder, as it will, how the devil he got there), and pretend to do him into English, so his version denote his neglect of the manner how.—THEOBALD, LEWIS, 1728, *Mist's Journal, March* 30.

> Three times I've read your Iliad o'er;
> The first time pleas'd me well;
> New beauties unobserv'd before,
> Next pleas'd me better still,
> Again I tri'd to find a flaw,
> Examin'd ilka line;
> The third time pleas'd me best of a',
> The labour seem'd divine.
> Henceforward I'll not tempt my fate,
> On dazzling rays to stare,
> Lest I should tine dear self-conceit,
> And read and write nae mair.

—RAMSAY, ALLAN, 1728, *To Mr. Pope, Poems, Paisley ed., vol.* I, *p.* 270.

The "Iliad" took me up six years; and during that time, and particularly the first part of it, I was often under great pain and apprehension. Though I conquered the thoughts of it in the day, they would frighten me in the night.—I sometimes, still, even dream of being engaged in that translation; and got about half way through it: and being embarrassed and under dread of never completing it.—POPE, ALEXANDER, 1742–43, *Spence's Anecdotes, ed. Singer, p.* 214.

They can have no conception of his [Homer's] manner, who are acquainted with him in Mr. Pope's translation only. An excellent poetical performance that translation is, and faithful in the main to the original. In some places, it may be thought to have even improved Homer. It has certainly softened some of his rudenesses, and added delicacy and grace to some of his sentiments. But withal, it is no other than Homer modernized. In the midst of the elegance and luxuriancy of Mr. Pope's language, we lose sight of the old bard's simplicity.—BLAIR, HUGH, 1783, *Lectures on Rhetoric and Belles-Lettres, ed. Mills, Lecture* xliii.

Pope's translation is a portrait endowed with every merit, excepting that of likeness to the original. The verses of Pope accustomed my ear to the sound of poetic harmony.—GIBBON, EDWARD, 1794, *Memoirs of My Life and Writings.*

To what a low state knowledge of the most obvious and important phenomena had sunk, is evident from the style in which Dryden has executed a description of Night in one of his Tragedies, and Pope his translation of the celebrated moonlight scene in the "Iliad." A blind man, in the habit of attending accurately to descriptions casually dropped from the lips of those around him, might easily depict these appearances with more truth. Dryden's lines are vague, bombastic, and senseless; those of Pope, though he had Homer to guide him, are throughout false and contradictory. The verses of Dryden, once highly celebrated, are forgotten; those of Pope still retain their hold upon public estimation,—nay, there is not a passage of descriptive poetry, which at this day finds so many and such ardent admirers. Strange to think of an enthusiast, as may have been the case with thousands, reciting those verses under the cope of a moonlight sky, without having his raptures in the least disturbed by a suspicion of their absurdity!—WORDSWORTH, WILLIAM, 1815, *Poetry as a Study.*

In the course of one of my lectures, I had occasion to point out the almost faultless position and choice of words in Pope's original compositions, particularly in his Satires, and Moral Essays, for the purpose of comparing them with his translation of Homer, which I do not stand alone in regarding as the main source of our pseudo-poetic diction.—COLERIDGE, SAMUEL TAYLOR, 1817, *Biographia Literaria.*

The age of Pope was the golden age of poets,—but it was the pinchbeck age of poetry. They flourished in the sunshine of public and private patronage; the art meantime was debased, and it continued to be so as long as Pope continued lord of the ascendant. More injury was not done to the taste of his countrymen by Marino in Italy, nor by Gongora in Spain, than by Pope in England. The mischief was affected not by his satrical and moral pieces, for these entitled him to the highest place among poets of his class; it was by his Homer. There have been other versions as unfaithful; but none were ever so well executed in as bad a style; and no other work in the language so greatly vitiated the diction of English poetry. Common readers (and the majority must always be such) will always be taken by glittering faults, as larks are caught by bits of looking-glass; and in this meretricious translation, the passages that were most unlike the original, which were most untrue to nature, and therefore most false in taste, were precisely those which were most applauded, and on which critic after critic dwelt with one cuckoo note of admiration.—SOUTHEY, ROBERT, 1835, *Life of Cowper, vol.* I, *p.* 313.

Chapman's translation, with all its defects, is often exceedingly Homeric; a praise which Pope himself seldom attained. —HALLAM, HENRY, 1837–39, *Introduction to the Literature of Europe, pt.* ii, *ch.* v, *par.* 73.

Between Pope and Homer there is interposed the mist of Pope's literary artificial manner, entirely alien to the plain naturalness of Homer's manner. . . . In elevated passages he is powerful, as Homer is powerful, though not in the same way; but in plain narrative, where Homer is still powerful and delightful, Pope, by the inherent fault of his style, is ineffective and out of taste.—ARNOLD, MATTHEW, 1861, *On Translating Homer, pp,* 11, 21.

Pope's translations of the Homeric poems are achievements not only unmatched but unapproached. His thorough command over his native tongue gave him an active sense of its capacities and its deficiencies, and therefore he took the two narratives, each with all its parts and their sequence, but he told the two stories in his own way. Passing his early youth in a heroic period, when the bells pealed at short intervals for victory after victory, he had the best of all possible opportunities for drinking in heroic sensations; and with thorough power and efficiency "he sang of battles and the breath of stormy war and violent death." His successors, professing to perform the same work, and to do it more accurately, have in that vain effort made repeated failures. —BURTON, JOHN HILL, 1880, *A History of the Reign of Queen Anne, vol.* III, *p.* 245.

The Pity of it! And the changing Taste
Of changing Time leaves half your Work a Waste!
My Childhood fled your couplet's clarion tone,
And sought for Homer in the Prose of Bohn.
Still through the Dust of that dim Prose Appears
The Flight of Arrows and the Sheen of Spears;
Still we may trace what Hearts heroic feel,
And hear the Bronze that hurtels on the Steel!
But, ah, your Iliad seems a half-pretence,
Where Wits, not Heroes, prove their Skill in Fence,
And great Achilles' Eloquence doth show
As if no Centaur trained him, but Boileau!
—LANG, ANDREW, 1886, *Letters to Dead Authors.*

One hundred and seventy years have since gone by, and many attempts have been made by writers of distinction to supply the admitted deficiencies in Pope's work. Yet his translation of the "Iliad" occupies a position in literature which no other has ever approached. It is the one poem of the kind that has obtained a reputation beyond the limits of the country in the language of which it is written, and the only one that has fascinated the imagination of the unlearned. Many an English reader, to whom the Greek was literally a dead language, has followed through it the action of the Iliad with a livelier interest than that of the "Faery Queen" or of "Paradise Lost." The descriptions of the single combats and the funeral games have delighted many a schoolboy, who has perhaps revolted with an equally intense abhorrence from the syntax of the original.—COURTHOPE, WILLIAM JOHN, 1889, *The Life of Alexander Pope, Works, ed. Elwin and Courthope, vol.* V, *p.* 162.

Many scholars and many poets have scoffed at his translations of Homer, but generations of English schoolboys have learned to love the "Iliad" because of the way in which Pope has told them the story, and as to the telling of a story the judgment of a schoolboy sometimes counts for more than the judgment of a sage. Pope's "Iliad" and "Odyssey" are certainly not for those who can read the great originals in their own tongue, or even for those who have a taste strong and refined enough to enjoy the severe fidelity of a prose translation. But Pope has brought the story of Achilles' wrath, and Helen's pathetic beauty, and Hector's fall, and Priam's agony home to the hearts of millions for whom they would otherwise have no life.—MCCARTHY, JUSTIN, 1890, *A History of the Four Georges, vol.* II, *p.* 262.

We may add that neither its false glitter nor Pope's inability—shared in great measure with every translator—to catch the spirit of the original, can conceal the sustained power of this brilliant work. Its merit is the more wonderful since the poet's knowledge of Greek was extremely meagre, and he is said to have been constantly indebted to earlier translations. Gibbon said that his "Homer" had every merit except that of faithfulness to the original; and Pope, could he have heard it, might well have been satisfied with the verdict of Gray, a great scholar as well as a great poet, that no other version would ever equal his. All that has been hitherto said with regard to Pope and Homer relates to his version of the "Iliad." On that he expended his best powers, and on that it is evident he bestowed infinite pains.—DENNIS, JOHN, 1894, *The Age of Pope, p.* 37.

His translation of Homer resembles Homer as much as London resembles Troy, or Marlborough Achilles, or Queen Anne Hecuba. It is done with great literary art, but for that very reason it does not make us feel the simplicity and directness of his original. It has neither the manner nor the spirit of the Greek, just as Pope's descriptions of nature have neither the manner nor the spirit of nature.—BROOKE, STOPFORD A., 1896, *English Literature, p.* 186,

He could not have turned out a true translation, indeed, when his lack of Greek learning threw him back upon French and Latin versions, upon earlier English translations, or upon assistance of more scholarly but less poetic friends. He worked from a Homer minus Homer's force and freedom, a Homer ornamented with epigrams to suit the taste of the age. His tools were a settled diction and a ready-made style, regular, neat, and terse. The result could never have been Homer, but it is an English poem of sustained vivacity and emphasis, a fine epic as epics went in the days of Anne—"A very pretty poem, Mr. Pope, but not Homer."—PRICE, WARWICK JAMES, 1896, *ed., The Iliad of Homer, Books* i, vi, xxii *and* xxiv, *Introduction, p.* 11.

Although Pope has also a certain rapidity of movement, it is not the smooth, subtly-varied swiftness of Homer, but a jogging and rather monotonous briskness. He impedes the progress of the action, even in his translation, by introducing reflective phrases, fanciful asides, and lingering appreciation of passages elaborated for their own sakes, to their detriment as humble parts of a swift narrative. His eye is not fixed clearly on the moving objects, but on the thoughts and feelings he lets them suggest.—GENTNER, PHILIP, 1899, *Introduction to Pope's Iliad, p.* xi.

ODYSSEY
1725

I think I need not recommend to you further the necessity of keeping this whole matter to yourself, as I am very sure Fenton has done, lest the least air of it prejudice with the town. But if you judge otherwise, I do not prohibit you taking to yourself your due share of fame. Take your choice also in that. . . . The public is both an unfair and a silly judge unless it be trepanned into justice.—POPE, ALEXANDER, 1724, *Letter to Broome, Nov.*

Pope's "Homer's Odyssey," surely a very false, and though ingenious and talented, yet bad translation.—CARLYLE, THOMAS, 1831, *Note Book, Life by Froude, vol.* II, *p.* 78.

He made over 3500£. after paying Broome 500£. (including 100£. for notes) and Fenton 200£.—that is, 50£. a book. The rate of pay was as high as the work was worth, and as much as it would fetch in the open market. The large sum was entirely due to Pope's reputation, though obtained, so far as the true authorship was concealed upon something like false pretences. Still, we could have wished that he had been a little more liberal with his share of the plunder. . . . The shares of the three colleagues in the Odyssey are not to be easily distinguished by internal evidence. On trying the experiment by a cursory reading, I confess (though a critic does not willingly admit his fallibility) that I took some of Broome's work for Pope's, and, though closer study or an acuter perception might discriminate more accurately, I do not think that the distinction would be easy. This may be taken to confirm the common theory that Pope's versification was a mere mechanical trick. Without admitting this, it must be admitted that the external characteristics of his manner were easily caught; and that it was not hard for a clever versifier to produce something closely resembling his inferior work, especially when following the same original. But it may be added that Pope's Odyssey was really inferior to the Iliad, both because his declamatory style is more out of place in its romantic narrative, and because he was weary and languid, and glad to turn his fame to account without more labour than necessary.—STEPHEN, LESLIE, 1880, *Alexander Pope (English Men of Letters), pp.* 79, 80.

ELOISA TO ABELARD
1717

Abelard and Eloisa flourished in the twelfth century; they were two of the most distinguished persons of their age in learning and beauty, but for nothing more famous than for their unfortunate passion. After a long course of calamities, they retired each to a several Convent, and consecrated the remainder of their days to religion. It was many years after this separation, that a letter of Abelard's to a Friend, which contained the history of his misfortune, fell into the hands of Eloisa. This awakening all her Tenderness, occasioned those celebrated letters (out of which the following is partly extracted) which gives so lively a picture of the struggles of grace and nature, virtue and passion.—POPE, ALEXANDER, 1717, *Eloisa to Abelard, Argument.*

O Abelard, ill-fated youth,
Thy tale will justify this truth:
But well I weet, thy cruel wrong
Adorns a nobler poet's song.
Dan Pope, for thy misfortune grieved,
With kind concern and skill has weaved
A silken web; and ne'er shall fade
Its colours; gently has he laid
The mantle o'er thy sad distress:
And Venus shall the texture bless.
He o'er the weeping nun has drawn
Such artful folds of sacred lawn;
That love, with equal grief and pride,
Shall see the crime he strives to hide;
And, softly drawing back the veil,
The god shall to his votaries tell
Each conscious tear, each blushing grace,
That deck'd dear Eloisa's face.
—PRIOR, MATTHEW, 1718, *Alma. Canto II.*

The harmony of numbers in this poem is very fine. It is rather drawn out to too tedious a length, although the passions vary with great judgment. It may be considered as superior to anything in the epistolary way; and the many translations which have been made of it into the modern languages are in some measure a proof of this.—GOLDSMITH, OLIVER, 1767, *The Beauties of English Poetry.*

The epistle of "Eloise to Abelard" is one of the most happy productions of human wit; the subject is so judiciously chosen, that it would be difficult, in turning over the annals of the world, to find another which so many circumstances concur to recommend.—JOHNSON, SAMUEL, 1779–81, *Pope, Lives of the English Poets.*

Mr. Pope's "Eloisa to Abelard" is such a *chef-d'œuvre* that nothing of the kind can be relished after it. Yet it is not the story itself, nor the sympathy it excites in us, as Dr. Johnson would have us think, that constitutes the principal merit in that incomparable poem. It is the happy use he has made of the monastic gloom of the Paraclete, and of what I will call papistical machinery, which gives it its capital charm, so that I am almost inclined to wonder (if I could wonder at any of that writer's criticisms) that he did not take notice of this beauty, as his own superstitious turn certainly must have given him more than a sufficient relish for it.—MASON, WILLIAM, 1788, *Life of William Whitehead, p.* 30.

It is fine as a poem; it is finer as a piece of high-wrought eloquence. No woman could be supposed to write a better love-letter in verse. Besides the richness of the historical materials, the high *gusto* of the original sentiments which Pope had to work upon, there were perhaps circumstances in his own situation which made him enter into the subject with even more than a poet's feeling. The tears shed are drops gushing from the heart; the words are burning sighs breathed from the soul of love. Perhaps the poem to which it bears the greatest similarity in our language is Dryden's "Tancred and Sigismunda," taken from Boccaccio. Pope's "Eloise" will bear this comparison; and after such a test, with Boccaccio for the original author, and Dryden for the translator, it need shrink from no other.—HAZLITT, WILLIAM, 1818, *Lectures on the English Poets, Lecture* iv.

He has rendered this one of the most

impressive poems of which love is the subject; as it is likewise the most finished of all his works of equal length, in point of language and versification.—AIKIN, JOHN, 1820, *Select Works of the British Poets.*

Had Pope never written but this poem, it should suffice to render him immortal, for all the united efforts of art and study, —of perseverance and toil,—could never have produced it, devoid of that exquisite sensibility, without which no poet ever excelled in the pathetic.—M'DERMOT, MARTIN, 1824, *The Beauties of Modern Literature, p.* xxi.

I read it again, and am bored: this is not as it ought to be; but, in spite of myself, I yawn, and I open the original letters of Eloisa to find the cause of my weariness. . . . Declamation and commonplace; she sends Abelard discourses on love and the liberty which it demands, on the cloister and peaceful life which it affords, on writing and the advantages of the post. Antitheses and contrasts, she forwards them to Abelard by the dozen; a contrast between the convent illuminated by his presence and desolate by his absence, between the tranquillity of the pure nun and the anxiety of the culpable nun, between the dream of human happiness and the dream of divine happiness. In fine, it is a *bravura* with contrasts of *forte* and *piano*, variations and change of key. Eloisa makes the most of her theme, and sets herself to crowd into it all the powers and effects of her voice. Admire the *crescendo*, the shakes by which she ends her brilliant *morceaux*. . . . Observe the noise of the big drum, I mean the grand contrivances, for so may be called all that a person says who wishes to rave and cannot. . . . This kind of poetry resembles cookery; neither heart nor genius is necessary to produce it, but a light hand, an attentive eye, and a cultivated taste.—TAINE, H. A,, 1871, *History of English Literature, tr. Van Laun, vol.*, II, *bk.* iii, *ch.* vii, *pp.* 200, 201, 202.

Pope always resembles an orator whose gestures are studied, and who thinks, while he is speaking, of the fall of his robes, and the attitude of his hands. He is throughout academical; and though knowing with admirable nicety how grief should be represented, and what have been the expedients of his best predecessors, he misses the one essential touch of spontaneous impulse. One other blemish is perhaps more fatal to the popularity of the "Eloisa." There is a taint of something unwholesome and effeminate. Pope, it is true, is only following the language of the original in the most offensive passages; but we see too plainly that he has dwelt too fondly upon those passages, and worked them up with especial care. We need not be prudish in our judgment of impassioned poetry; but when the passion has this false ring, the ethical coincides with the æsthetic objection.—STEPHEN, LESLIE, 1880, *Alexander Pope (English Men of Letters), p.* 38.

The "Elegy on the Unfortunate Lady" is good, but I do not find much human feeling in him, except perhaps in "Eloisa to Abelard."—TENNYSON, ALFRED LORD, 1883, *Some Criticism on Poets, Memoirs by his Son, vol.* II, *p.* 287.

His "Eloisa," splendid as is its diction, and vigorous though be the portrayal of the miserable creature to whom the poem relates, most certainly lacks "a gracious somewhat," whilst no less certainly is it marred by a most unfeeling coarseness. A poem about love it may be—a love poem it is not.—BIRRELL, AUGUSTINE, 1887, *Obiter Dicta, Second Series, p.* 106.

In the "Eloisa to Abelard" there is undoubtedly much that no longer rings true to the modern ear; there are passages here and there which it is difficult to think of as having ever rung true to the ear of any man, even to that of the poet himself; there are lines in it, though but a few, which are of a taste that never could be otherwise than false and unsound in any poet of any age; it contains at least one line of which we can agree with Mr. Swinburne in thinking that "no woman could read it without a blush, nor any man without a laugh." Yet he who can read its last hundred lines, with the struggle between love and devotion thrilling and throbbing through them, and not hear in them the true note, the unmistakable cry of human passion, uttered as only poetry can give it utterance, may rest assured that his natural sympathies and sentiments have been dwarfed and sophisticated by theory, and that from dogmatizing overmuch about what poetry ought to be he has blunted some of the sensibilities which should tell him what poetry *is.* —TRAILL, H. D., 1889, *Pope, The National Review, vol.* 14, *p.* 497.

It is unique in English literature for passionate eloquence of language and for melody of numbers. As his imagination dwelt upon the figure of Heloise in her devotion and her despair, as he pictured to himself the conflict in her soul between religious feeling and the memory of earthly passion, he poured his whole soul into his dramatic creation.—COURTHOPE, WILLIAM JOHN, 1889, *The Life of Alexander Pope, Works, ed. Elwin and Courthope, vol.* V, *p.* 135.

A mystery surrounds the "Elegy"—we do not know the circumstances by which it was conceived; but the warmth of "Eloisa" may be largely explained on purely personal grounds, which fact, of course, robs it of much of its significance as an index to Pope's general taste in poetry. No one who reads Pope's correspondence with Lady Mary can avoid the conclusion that the poet embodied in this *Epistle* much of his own sentimental longings; for Pope's attitude toward the brilliant society woman was certainly more than that of conventional gallantry. —PHELPS, WILLIAM LYON, 1893, *The Beginnings of the English Romantic Movement, p.* 24.

EDITION OF SHAKESPEARE
1725

If aught on earth, when once this breath is fled,
With human transport touch the mighty dead,
Shakespear, rejoice! his hand thy page refines;
Now ev'ry scene with native brightness shines;
Just to thy fame he gives thy genuine thought;
So Tully published that Lucretius wrote;
Pruned by his care, thy laurels loftier grow,
And bloom afresh on thy immortal brow.
—BROOME, WILLIAM, 1726, *To Mr. Pope.*

He [Pope] never valued himself upon it enough to mention it in any letter, poem, or other work whatsoever.—AYRE, WILLIAM, 1745, *Memoirs of Pope, vol.* II, *p.* 15.

Mr. Pope discharged his duty so well, as to make his editions the best foundation for all future improvements.—WARBURTON, WILLIAM, 1747, *ed. Shakspeare, Preface.*

Pope, in his edition, undoubtedly did many things wrong, and left many things undone; but let him not be defrauded of his due praise. He was the first that knew, at least the first that told, by what helps the text might be improved. If he inspected the early editions negligently, he taught others to be more accurate. In his preface he expanded with great skill and elegance the character which had been given to Shakespeare by Dryden; and he drew the public attention upon his works, which, though often mentioned, had been little read.—JOHNSON, SAMUEL, 1779–81, *Pope, Lives of the English Poets.*

Pope asserts, that he [Shakspeare] wrote both better and worse than any other man. All the scenes and passages which did not suit the littleness of his taste, he wished to place to the account of interpolating players; and he was in the right road, had his opinion been taken, of mangling Shakspeare in a most disgraceful manner.—SCHLEGEL, AUGUSTUS WILLIAM, 1809, *Dramatic Art and Literature, tr. Black.*

Pope would have given us a mutilated Shakespeare! but Pope, to satisfy us that he was not insensible to the fine passages of Shakespeare, distinguished by inverted commas all those which he approved!—so that Pope thus furnished for the first time what have been called "the *beauties* of Shakespeare"! But, amid such a disfigured text, the *faults* of Shakespeare must have been too apparent! Pope but partially relished, and often ill understood, his Shakespeare; yet, in the liveliest of prefaces, he offers the most vivid delineation of our great bard's *general characteristics.* The *genius of Shakespeare* was at once comprehended by his brother poet; but the *text* he was continually tampering with ended in a fatal testimony, that POPE had no congenial taste for the style, the manner, and the whole native drama, of England.—DISRAELI, ISAAC, 1841, *Shakespeare, Amenities of Literature.*

His Preface is a masterly composition, containing many just views elegantly expressed. The criticism is neither profound nor original; but there is a tone of quiet sense about it which shows that Pope properly appreciated Shakspere's general excellence. He believes, in common with most of his time, that this excellence was attained by intuition, and that the finest results were produced by felicitous accidents.—KNIGHT, CHARLES, 1849, *Studies in Shakspere.*

This was, perhaps, the first decided failure in any of the publications by Pope. He was deficient in some important requisites for the task he had undertaken. The irksome but necessary duty of collation was indifferently performed; he wanted patience, and he could not command all the early copies. He was not sufficiently read in the literature of Shakspeare's contemporaries, and thus missed many points of illustration confirming or elucidating the text. He also somewhat arbitrarily and unwarrantably altered or suppressed lines and passages, which he conceived to have been interpolated or vitiated by the players and transcribers. —CARRUTHERS, ROBERT, 1853–57, *The Life of Alexander Pope, p.* 231.

Rowe was succeeded, as an editor of Shakespeare, by Pope, who published a superb edition, in six volumes, quarto, in 1725. Pope, like most of those authors of eminence in other departments of literature, who have undertaken to regulate the text of Shakespeare, made a very poor editor. He used the quartos somewhat to the advantage, but more to the detriment of his author; foisting into the text that which Shakespeare himself had rejected. He gave us a few good, and several very pretty and plausible conjectural emendations of typographical errors; but he added to these so many which were only exponents of his own conceit and want of kindred appreciation of Shakespeare's genius, that his text, as a whole, is one of the poorest which remain to us. —WHITE, RICHARD GRANT, 1854, *Shakespeare's Scholar, p.* 9.

With a few happy emendations, and with a singularly interesting and well-written Preface, begins and ends all that is of any value in Pope's work as an editor of Shakspeare. For the correction of the text he did as little as Rowe. To its corruption he contributed more than any other eighteenth-century editor, with the exception, perhaps, of Warburton. He professed to have based his text on a careful collation of the quartos and folios. Nothing can be more certain than that his text is based simply on Rowe's, and that he seldom troubled himself to consult either the quartos or the folios. In "correction" his process is simple. If he cannot understand a word, he substitutes a word which he can: if a phrase is obscure to him, he rewrites it.—COLLINS, JOHN CHURTON, 1895, *The Porson of Shakspearan Criticism, Essays and Studies, p.* 295.

Pope had few qualifications for the task, and the venture was a commercial failure. . . . His innovations are numerous, and are derived from "his private sense and conjecture, "but they are often plausible and ingenious. He was the first to indicate the place of each new scene, and he improved on Rowe's subdivision of the scenes.—LEE, SIDNEY, 1900, *Shakespeare's Life and Works, p.* 175.

THE DUNCIAD
1728–43

The | Dunciad | An Heroic Poem | In Three Books. | Dublin | Printed, London Re | printed for A. Dodd. 1728.—TITLE PAGE TO FIRST EDITION, 1728, *May* 28.

There is a general outcry against that part of the poem which is thought an abuse on the Duke of Chandos. Other parts are quarrelled with as obscure and inharmonious; and I am told that there is an advertisement that promises a publication of Mr. Pope's Epistle verified. . . . I am surprised Mr. Pope is not weary of making enemies.—DELANY, PATRICK,1731, *Letter to Sir Thomas Hanmer, Dec.* 23, *Hanmer's Correspondence, p.* 217.

On the 12th of March, 1729, at St. James's, that poem was presented to the King and Queen (who had before been pleased to read it) by the Right Honourable Sir Robert Walpole: and some days after the whole impression was taken and dispersed by several noblemen and persons of the first distinction. It is certainly a true observation, that no people are so impatient of censure as those who are the greatest slanderers: which was wonderfully exemplified on this occasion. On the day the book was first vended, a crowd of authors besieged the shop; entreaties, advices, threats of law, and battery, nay, cries of treason were all employed, to hinder the coming out of the "Dunciad;" on the other side, the booksellers and hawkers made as great efforts to procure it: what could a few poor authors do against so great a majority as the public? There was no stopping a torrent with a finger, so out it came. Some false editions of the book having an owl in their frontispiece, the true one, to distinguish it, fixed in its stead an ass laden with authors. Then another surreptitious one being printed with the same ass, the new edition in octavo returned for distinction to the owl again. Hence arose a great contest of booksellers against booksellers, and advertisements against advertisements; some recommended the "Edition of the Owl," and others the "Edition of the Ass;" by which names they came to be distinguished, to the great honour also of the gentlemen of the "Dunciad."—SAVAGE, RICHARD, 1732, *Account of the Dunciad.*

The Dunciad cost me as much pains as anything I ever wrote.—POPE, ALEXANDER, 1734–36, *Spence's Anecdotes, ed. Singer, p.* 107.

It was a victory over a parcel of poor wretches, whom it was almost cowardice to conquer. A man might as well triumph for having killed so many silly flies that offended him. Could he have let them alone, by this time, poor souls! they had all been buried in oblivion.—CIBBER, COLLEY, 1742, *Letter to Mr. Pope, July* 7, *p.* 12.

The fifth volume contains a correcter and completer edition of the Dunciad than hath been hitherto published, of which, at present, I have only this further to add, that it was at my request he laid the plan of a fourth book. I often told him, it was a pity so fine a poem should remain disgraced by the meanness of its subject, the most insignificant of all dunces,—bad rhymers and malevolent cavillers; that he ought to raise and ennoble it by pointing his satire against the most pernicious of all,—minute philosophers and free-thinkers. I imagined, too, it was for the interest of religion to have it known, that so great a genius had a due abhorrence of these pests of virtue and society. He came readily into my opinion; but, at the same time, told me it would create him many enemies. He was not mistaken, for though the terror of his pen kept them for some time in respect, yet on his death they rose with unrestrained fury in numerous coffee-house tales, and Grub Street libels. The plan of this admirable satire was artfully contrived to show, that the follies and defects of a fashionable education naturally led to, and necessarily ended in, freethinking, with design to point out the only remedy adequate to so destructive an evil.—WARBURTON, WILLIAM, 1751, *ed. Pope's Works.*

He (Dryden) died, nevertheless, in a good old age, possessed of the kingdom of wit, and was succeeded by king Alexander, surnamed Pope. This prince enjoyed the crown many years, and is thought to have stretched the prerogative much farther than his predecessor: he is said to have been extremely jealous of the affections of his subjects, and to have employed various spies, by whom if he was informed of the least suggestion against his title, he never failed of branding the accused person with the word *dunce* on his forehead in broad letters; after which the unhappy culprit was obliged to lay by his pen forever, for no bookseller would venture to print a word that he wrote. He did indeed put a total restraint upon the liberty of the press; for no person durst read anything which was writ without his license and approbation; and this license he granted only to four during his reign, namely, to the celebrated Dr. Swift, to the ingenious Dr. Young, to Dr. Arbuthnot, and to one Mr. Gay, four of his principal courtiers and favourites. But, without diving any deeper into his character, we must allow that king Alexander had great merit as a writer, and his title to the kingdom of wit was better founded, at least, than his enemies have pretended.—FIELDING, HENRY, 1752, *Covent Garden Journal, No.* 23, *March* 21.

"The Dunciad" of Mr. Pope is an everlasting monument of how much the most correct, as well as the most elegant and harmonious, of all the English poets, had been hurt by the criticisms of the lowest and most contemptible authors.—SMITH, ADAM, 1759–61, *Of Duty, The Theory of Moral Sentiments, pt.* iii, *ch.* ii.

I thought you might possibly whip me at the cart's tail in a note in the "Divine Legation," the ordinary place of your literary execution; or pillory me in the "Dunciad," another engine which as legal proprietor, you have very ingeniously and judiciously applied to the same purpose; or perhaps have ordered me a kind of Bridewell correction, by one of your beadles, in a pamphlet.—LOWTH, ROBERT, 1765, *Letter to Warburton.*

"The Dunciad" is blemished by the offensive images of the games; but the poetry appears to me admirable; and, though the fourth book has obscurities, I prefer it to the three others: it has descriptions not surpassed by any poet that ever existed, and which surely a writer merely ingenious will never equal. The lines on Italy, on Venice, on Convents, have all the grace for which I contend as distinct from poetry, though united with the most beautiful.—WALPOLE, HORACE, 1785, *Letter to J. Pinkerton, June* 26.

In richness of ideas, in strength of diction, and in intensity of feeling, this production surpasses all that Pope had previously done, and is perhaps the finest specimen of literary satire which exists in any language in the world. The whole vocabulary of irony is exhausted. The whole universe of contempt is ransacked. We find the combined merits of the most dissimilar satirists—the wild, fearless, inventive, picturesque extravagance of Aristophanes, the bitter irony and cold sarcasm of Lucian, the elegant raillery of Horace, and Juvenal's strange union of moral severity and grim pleasantry.—SHAW, THOMAS B., 1847, *Outlines of English Literature, p.* 218.

The thong with which he lashed them was dreadful; he fired upon that howling crew such shafts of flame, and poison, he slew and wounded so fiercely, that in reading "The Dunciad" and the prose lampoons of Pope, one feels disposed to side against the ruthless little tyrant, at least to pity those wretched little folks upon whom he was so unmerciful. . . . The condition of authorship began to fall from the days of the "Dunciad:" and I believe in my heart that much of that obloquy which has since pursued our calling was occasioned by Pope's libels and wicked wit. Everybody read those. Everybody was familiarised with the idea of the poor devil author. The manner is so captivating, that young authors practise it, and begin their career with satire. It is so easy to write, and so pleasant to read! to fire a shot that makes a giant wince, perhaps; and fancy one's self his conqueror. It is easy to shoot—but not as Pope did—the shafts of his satire rise sublimely.—THACKERAY, WILLIAM MAKEPEACE, 1853, *The English Humourists of the Eighteenth Century.*

It is unquestionable that the poet had received innumerable provocations—the ordinary declarations of envy and hostility against a successful rival; but his true friends, and Atterbury amongst them, considered the work a waste of talent and of feeling. "The rats and mice, and such small deer," of Grub Street, were not worth so much attention. His attacks, too, are indiscriminate. Bentley was despotic and arrogant, but was a profound scholar. It was gross injustice to class him with dunces. Ducket and Aaron Hill were as unjustifiably treated; and the insignificance of the mere scribblers should have been their security. Unfortunately Pope, with much greatness of soul, had some littleness: his vanity would not permit him to be indifferent to criticism that questioned his superiority. It is hard to believe that the same spirit which defended and consoled Atterbury could betray the malevolence that has gibbeted Theobald and Cibber: but the proverb, "Extremes meet," was forcibly illustrated by him. It should be a consolation of his innumerable admirers to know that many a creditable set-off may be found against his personal attacks.—WILLIAMS, FOLKESTONE, 1869, *Memoirs and Correspondence of Francis Atterbury, vol.* II, *p.* 227.

We need much self-command not to throw down this masterpiece as insipid, and even disgusting. Rarely has so much talent been spent to produce greater tedium.—TAINE, H. A., 1871, *History of English Literature, tr. Van Laun, vol.* II, *bk.* iii, *ch.* vii, *p.* 205.

However great his merit in expression, I think it impossible that a true poet could have written such a satire as the "Dunciad," which is even nastier than it is witty. It is filthy even in a filthy age, and Swift himself could not have gone beyond some parts of it. One's mind needs to be sprinkled with some disinfecting fluid after reading it. I do not remember that any other poet ever made poverty a crime. And it is wholly without discrimination. De Foe is set in the pillory forever; and George Wither, the author of that charming poem, "Fair Virtue," classed among the dunces. And was it not in this age that loose Dick Steele paid his wife the finest compliment ever paid to woman, when he said "that to love her was a liberal education?"—LOWELL,

James Russell, 1871–90, *Pope, Prose Works, Riverside ed., vol.* IV, *p.* 49.

Looked at apart from personal questions, the "Dunciad" is the greatest feat of the humorous imagination in English poetry.—Minto, William, 1885, *Encyclopædia Britannica, Ninth ed., vol.* XIX.

Extinct as they may or as they may not be now, it is indisputable that such noisome and unmentionable vermin were daily and nightly "about the path and about the bed" of the great and gallant man who embalmed the types of them for all time in the black-spooted and ill-savoured amber of the "Dunciad." And it was inevitable that the unseemly accident of their "villainous company" or controversy should exasperate as with infectious virulence the habit of mind which physical infirmity or deformity is proverbially liable to engender. Pope was by nature undeniably "malin comme un bossu"—no more and no less: for he surely was not malignant or malevolent; but as surely the untranslatable French epithet hits off the nature of his quality to a hair.—Swinburne, Algernon Charles, 1886, *Miscellanies, p.* 36.

As for Pope, it must be confessed that he led off in the long, cruel, and degrading attacks of poet on poet, of author on author. What can be more venomous, what can be more malignant, than the "Dunciad?"—Besant, Walter, 1898, *The Pen and the Book, p.* 13.

MORAL ESSAYS
1731–35

In the "Moral Poem," I had written an address to our Saviour; imitated from Lucretius's compliment to Epicurus: but omitted it by the advice of Dean Berkley.—One of our priests, who are more narrow-minded than yours, made a less sensible objection to the "Epistle on Happiness:" he was very angry that there was nothing said in it of our eternal happiness hereafter, though my subject was expressly to treat only of the state of man here.—Pope, Alexander, 1734–36, *Spence's Anecdotes, ed. Singer, p.* 107.

These Epistles, in which Poetry has condescended to become the handmaid of Philosophy, to decorate, and set her off to advantage, are written with a spirit and vivacity not exceeded by any production of the kind in any country or language. Their nearest prototypes are the Epistles of Horace and Boileau, and the Satires of Ariosto and Bentivoglio, to none of which they are inferior. In our own language they may be considered as the first attempt to unite sound sense and deep research with the lighter graces of elegant composition, and to promote the cause of virtue and morality by conveying the purest precepts in the most impressive language, and illustrating them by examples which strike the imagination with all the force of reality. As they had in this country no example, so they have as yet had no rival; nor until a genius shall arise that shall unite in himself, in an equal degree, the various endowments by which their author was distinguished, is it likley they ever will.—Roscoe, William, 1824–47, *ed., The Works of Alexander Pope, vol.* IV, *p.* 170.

Warton preferred "Windsor Forest" and "Eloisa" to the "Moral Essays" because they belonged to a higher kind of poetry. Posterity likes the "Moral Essays" better because they are better of their kind. They were the natural fruit of Pope's genius and of his time, while the others were artificial. We can go to Wordsworth for nature, to Byron for passion, and to a score of poets for both, but Pope remains unrivaled in his peculiar field. In other words, we value what is characteristic in the artist; the one thing which he does best, the precise thing which he can do and no one else can.—Beers, Henry A., 1898, *A History of English Romanticism in the Eighteenth Century, p.* 220.

ESSAY ON MAN
1732–34

Let others now translate; thy abler pen
Shall vindicate the ways of God to men;
In Virtue's cause shall gloriously prevail,
When the bench frowns in vain, and pulpits fail.
Made wise by thee, whose happy style conveys
The purest morals in the softest lays.

—Somerville, William, 1732? *To the Author of the Essay on Man.*

The poem of Pope alleviates my troubles and encourages me to be patient?—Rousseau, Jean-Jacques, 1756, *Letter to Voltaire, Aug.* 18.

If I had undertaken to exemplify Pope's felicity of composition before a rigid critic, I should not select the "Essay on Man;" for it contains more lines unsuccessfully laboured, more harshness of diction, more thoughts imperfectly expressed, more levity without elegance, and more heaviness without strength, than will easily be found in all his other works.—JOHNSON, SAMUEL, 1779–81, *Pope, Lives of the English Poets.*

In the year 1763, being at London, I was carried by Dr. John Blair, prebendary of Westminster, to dine at old Lord Bathurst's, where he found the late Mr. Mallet, Sir James Porter, &c. The conversation turning on Mr. Pope, Lord Bathurst told us that the "Essay on Man" was originally composed by Lord Bolingbroke in prose, and that Mr. Pope did no more than put it into verse; that he had read Lord Bolingbroke's manuscript in his own handwriting, and remembered well that he was at a loss whether most to admire the elegance of Lord Bolingbroke's prose or the beauty of Mr. Pope's verse. When Lord Bathurst told this, Mr. Mallet bade me attend, and remember this remarkable piece of information, as by the course of nature I might survive his Lordship and be a witness of his having said so.—BLAIR, HUGH, 1779, *Letter to Boswell, Sept.* 21.

Pope has shown how high poetry can soar on the wings of philosophy.—MARMONTEL, JEAN FRANÇOIS, 1787, *Elêments de Littêrature.*

Dr. Joseph Warton, talking last night at Sir Joshua Reynold's of Pope's "Essay on Man," said that much of his system was borrowed from King's book on the "Origin of Evil." This was first published in Dublin, in Latin, in 1704, and translated into English by Bishop Law, in 1731, not very long before the "Essay on Man" was written. Dr. Warton mentioned that Lord Lyttleton told him that he lived much with Pope at that time, and that Pope was then undoubtedly a Free-thinker; though he afterwards either changed his opinion or thought it prudent to adopt Warburton's explanation and comment, who saw his meaning as he chose to express it, "better than he did himself." Dr. Warton forbore to state this in his "Essay on Pope."—MALONE, EDMOND, 1789, *Jan.* 18, *Life by Prior, p.* 149.

Various and discordant have been the opinions of critics and commentators respecting this celebrated performance. That it possesses a distinguished share of poetic excellence none, however, have yet ventured to deny. M. Voltaire goes so far as to affirm, that to this Essay Pope stands indebted for that pre-eminence which he ascribes to him, when compared with his illustrious predecessor Dryden. But that Pope is actually entitled to this claim of superiority is, at least, very problematical; and if it was allowed, the "Rape of the Lock," the "Epistle of Eloise," the "Eclogue of the Messiah," and some other pieces that might be mentioned, would generally be considered as affording a better foundation for this claim to rest upon than the "Essay on Man," in which poetry holds a subordinate place; and in which it is merely employed, though with the happiest success, to embellish and illustrate the most abstruse lessons of philosophy. . . . It is well known that the general plan of this Essay was originally framed by Lord Bolingbroke, and it is universally believed that Pope was ignorant of the ultimate, and indeed the obvious tendency of his own arguments.—BELSHAM, W., 1799, *Essays Philosophical and Moral, Historical and Literary, vol.* I, *pp.* 346, 347.

The author of the "Essay on Man," from a want of precision in his metaphysical ideas, has unconsciously fallen into various expressions, equally inconsistent with each other and with his own avowed opinions.—STEWART, DUGALD, 1815–21, *First Preliminary Dissertation, Encyclopædia Britannica.*

The "Essay on Man" is not Pope's best work. . . . All that he says, "the very words, and to the self-same tune," would prove just as well that whatever is is *wrong*, as that whatever is is *right.*—HAZLITT, WILLIAM, 1818, *Lectures on the English Poets, Lecture* iv.

Bolingbroke had himself sufficient vigor of imagination and brilliancy of style to have written a prose essay which might engage the attention of persons fond of moral and philosophical speculation; but by judiciously borrowing the Muse of Pope, he has diffused his sentiments on these topics through all classes and ages of English literature; has made them familiar to our early and our mature conceptions; and stamped them in indelible characters on the language of the country. This conversion of a dry and argumentative subject into a splendid and popular one, is a miracle of the poetic art; and an inquiry into the means by which it has been effected will probably go far into the elucidation of that *essential character* of poetical composition which distinguishes it from prose.—AIKIN, JOHN, 1820, *Observations on Pope's Essay on Man.*

The success of this enterprise was astonishing. Be the philosophy what and whose it may, the poem revived to the latest age of poetry the phenomenon of the first, when precept and maxim were modulated into verse, that they might write themselves in every brain, and live upon every tongue. The spirit and sweetness of the verse, the lucid and vivid expressions, the pregnant brevity of the meanings, the marrying of ardent and lofty poetical imaginings to moral sentiments and reflections, of which every bosom is the birth-home, the pious will of the argument, which humbles the proud and rebellious human intellect under the absolute rectitude and benevolence of the Deity—nor, least of all, the pleasure of receiving easily, as in a familiar speech, thoughts that *were* high, and *might be* abstruse, that, at all events, wore a profound and philosophical air—with strokes intervening of a now playful, now piercing, but always adroit wit—and with touches, here and there strewn between, of natural painting, and of apt unsought pathos—these numerous and excellent qualifications met upon the subject of all subjects nearest to all—MAN—speedily made the first great, original, serious writing of Pope a text-book and a manual for its branch of ethico-theosophy, in every house where there were books in England. These powerful excellences of this great poem did more. They inwove its terse, vigorous, clear, significant, wise, loving, noble, beautiful, and musical sentences—east, west, north, south,—with all memories, the mature and the immature—even as in that old brave day of the world or ever books were.—WILSON, JOHN, 1845. *Dryden and Pope, Blackwood's Magazine.*

If the question were asked, What ought to have been the best among Pope's poems? most people would answer, the "Essay on Man." If the question were asked, what is the worst? all people of judgment would say, the "Essay on Man." Whilst yet in its rudiments, this poem claimed the first place by the promise of its subject; when finished, by the utter failure of its execution, it fell into the last.—DE QUINCEY, THOMAS, 1848–58, *The Poetry of Pope, Works, ed. Masson, vol.* XI, *p.* 86.

The "Essay on Man" has been supposed to derive all its worth from the doctrines which Bolingbroke has contributed to it. Might it not be much more fairly described as a stately mausoleum in which these doctrines have been saved from putrefaction? They are not more vague and declamatory in their rhymed than in their prose form, but far more distinct and pointed. The folds of affectation and conceit in which they were wrapped have in great measure been stripped off from them. We now see what there was in them which accorded with the temper of the age, what had a suitableness to the poet's own temper and circumstances, what had a permanent worth.—MAURICE, FREDERICK DENISON, 1862, *Moral and Metaphysical Philosophy, vol.* II, *p.* 452.

Everywhere, in the pulpit, in the coffee-houses, in every pamphlet, argument on the origin of evil, on the goodness of God, and the constitution of the world was rife. Into the prevailing topic of polite conversation Bolingbroke, who returned from exile in 1723, was drawn by the bent of his native genius. Pope followed the example and impulse of his friend's more powerful mind. Thus much there was of special suggestion. But the arguments or topics to the poem are to be traced to books in much vogue at the time; to Shaftesbury's "Characteristics" (1711), King on the "Origin of Evil" (1702), and particularly to Leibnitz, "Essais de Théodicée" (1710).—PATTISON, MARK, 1869, *ed., The Essay on Man, Introduction.*

A great poem should be a natural growth from one root, with all the graceful proportions of nature: Pope in the Essay has packed together, as his editor allows, a number of incongruous doctrines; there is no central thought, no even unity of feelings, to connect them. His art no doubt is great; but it is the art which begins by elaborating the parts, and afterwards endeavours to fit them together by diligently plastering over the interstices; the art of a Milton works from within outwards, fusing all the materials into one solid mass by its own central heat.—MAYOR, J. B., 1870, *Pope's Essay on Man, Contemporary Review, vol.* 14, *p.* 124.

Every word is effective: every passage

must be read slowly; every epithet is an epitome; a more condensed style was never written.—TAINE, H. A., 1871, *History of English Literature, tr. Van Laun, vol.* II, *bk.* iii, *ch.* vii, *p.* 210.

It is a droll illustration of the inconsistencies of human nature, a more profound satire than Pope himself ever wrote, that his fame should chiefly rest upon the "Essay on Man." It has been praised and admired by men of the most opposite beliefs, and men of no belief at all. Bishops and free-thinkers have met here on a common ground of sympathetic approval. And, indeed, there is no particular faith in it. It is a droll medley of inconsistent opinions. It proves only two things beyond a question,—that Pope was not a great thinker; and that wherever he found a thought, no matter what, he could express it so tersely, so clearly, and with such smoothness of versification as to give it an everlasting currency.—LOWELL, JAMES RUSSELL, 1871–90, *Pope, Prose Works, Riverside ed., vol.* IV, *p.* 415.

This philosophy in verse speaks much of God and virtue, but it is decidedly a philosophy of egotism.—SCHERR, J., 1874, *A History of English Literature, p.* 144.

Pope, as the mouthpiece of Spinoza or of Hobbes, might have written an impressive poem, if he had not attained to the level of Lucretius. But the age was not favourable to consistency and thoroughness. The "Essay on Man" remains radically unsatisfactory considered as a whole, though there are many brief passages marked by Pope's special felicity of touch; many in which the moral sentiment is true and tender, and many in which he forgets for a moment the danger of open heterodoxy, and utters with genuine force some of the deeper sentiments which haunt us in this mysterious universe.—STEPHEN, LESLIE, 1876, *History of English Thought in the Eighteenth Century, vol.* II, *p.* 352.

The tedious and stilted effort.—BLACK, WILLIAM, 1879, *Goldsmith (English Men of Letters), p.* 74.

The noblest of his works, the most influential, and the surest guarantee of his immortality.—WELSH, ALFRED H., 1883, *Development of English Literature and Language, vol.* II, *p.* 115.

It is bare justice to say that those who accuse him of merely superficial thinking raise a suspicion that they themselves have been guilty of hasty and careless reading. Nor can they justify their charge by the plea that Pope simply versified the thought of Bolingbroke. What is the explanation of the fact that to-day, though Pope is not read as he ought to be read, the readers of the "Essay on Man" are numbered by thousands, while readers of Bolingbroke,—one of the most brilliant writers of English prose—are numbered by units? No explanation is possible but this,—that Pope, though he may not have originated the intellectual substance of the "Essay" has given to it the finally satisfying expression; and this he could not have done by merely translating it from prose into verse, but only by thinking it, as it were, over again, for no one can rightly utter the thought that he has not made his own.—NOBLE, JAMES ASHCROFT, 1892, *The Sonnet in England and Other Essays, p.* 145.

His attempt to "vindicate the ways of God to man" is confused and contradictory, and no modern reader, perplexed with the mystery of existence, is likely to gain aid from Pope. Nominally a Roman Catholic, and in reality a deist, apart from poetry he does not seem to have had strong convictions on any subject, and was content to be swayed by the opinions current in society. In undertaking to write an ethical work like the "Essay" his ambition was greater than his strength, yet if Pope's philosophy does not "find" us, to use Coleridge's phrase, it did appeal to a large number of minds in his own day, and had not lost its popularity at a later period. The poem has been frequently translated into French, into Italian, and into German; it was pronounced by Voltaire to be the most useful and sublime didactic poem ever written in any language; it was admired by Kant and quoted in his lectures; and it received high praise from the Scotch philosopher, Dugald Stewart. The charm of poetical expression is lost or nearly lost in translations, and while the sense may be retained the aroma of the verse is gone. The popularity of the "Essay" abroad is therefore not easily to be accounted for, unless we accept the theory that the shallow creed on which it is based suited an age less earnest than our own.—DENNIS, JOHN, 1894, *The Age of Pope, p.* 52.

The "Essay on Man" did more to spread English deism in France than all the works of Shaftesbury. At bottom the doctrine is Shaftesbury's, but it is shorn of his aggressiveness, purified from all leaven of scepticism and pantheism, rendered more vague and indefinite, and therefore more poetical.—TEXTE, JOSEPH, 1895–99, *Jean-Jacques Rousseau and the Cosmopolitan Spirit in Literature, tr. Matthews, p.* 117.

IMITATIONS OF HORACE
1737

I have perused the last lampoon of your ingenious friend, and am not surprised you did not find me out under the name of Sappho, because there is nothing I ever heard in our characters and circumstances to make a parallel; but as the town (except you, who know better) generally suppose Pope means me, whenever he mentions that name, I cannot help taking notice of the horrible malice he bears against the lady signified by that name, which appears to be irritated by supposing her writer of the Verses to the Imitator of Horace.—MONTAGU, LADY MARY WORTLEY, 1735, *Letter to Arbuthnot, Jan.* 3.

His imitations of Horace equal their archetypes in elegance, and often surpass them in energy and fire.—BEATTIE, JAMES, 1776–9, *Essays, p.* 19, *note.*

His imitations of Horace are so peculiarly happy, that one is at a loss, whether most to admire the original or the copy; and they are among the few imitations extant, that have all the grace and ease of an original.—BLAIR, HUGH, 1783, *Lectures on Rhetoric and Belles-Lettres, ed. Mills, Lecture* xl.

Few portions of the poetry of Pope have been more popular than these "Imitations of Horace," with their accompanying Prologue and Epilogue. Though the satire be often too severe, and too much tinged with party rancour, or private spleen, the allusions are so apt, and the parallel passages so happy, that every reader must feel gratified in comparing the two poets, and in remarking the exquisite art and address of the *English* satirist, who has never in any instance servilely copied his original, but has merely pursued the train of thought which Horace had suggested; and in so doing has ably filled up the outline which is sometimes but faintly traced on the page of the Roman classic. The Prologue and Epilogue, especially the latter, are still more poignant and keen than the Imitations, to which, perhaps, they were at first, with no great propriety, annexed.—DRAKE, NATHAN, 1804, *Essays Illustrative of the Tatler, Spectator and Guardian, vol.* III, *p.* 103.

They are sometimes nearer to, and sometimes recede from,—in some points fall below, and in others rise above,—the original; and hence the materials are afforded for an interesting comparison between the characteristic aims and endowments of the two satirists.—ARNOLD, THOMAS, 1868–75, *Chaucer to Wordsworth, p.* 303.

In these Pope's verse is as perfect as it is anywhere, and his subject is borrowed, not from his commonplace book, but from his own experiences. He wants the careless ease, the variety, the unemphatic grace of Horace, it is true. But he has many of the qualities of his master, and it is probable that only when men weary of hearing how Horace strolled down the Sacred Way and met an intolerable Bore —only then, or perhaps a little earlier, will they cease to hearken how Alexander Pope bade John Searle bar the door at Twickenham against the inroads of Bedlam and Parnassus. —DOBSON, AUSTIN, 1888, *Alexander Pope, Scribner's Magazine, vol.* 3, *p.* 547.

LETTERS

I have read the collection of letters you mention and was delighted with nothing more than that air of sincerity, those professions of esteem and respect, and that deference paid to his friend's judgment in poetry which I have sometimes seen expressed to others, and I doubt not with the same cordial affection. If they are read in that light, they will be very entertaining and useful in the present age; but in the next, Cicero, Pliny, and Voiture may regain their reputation.—FENTON, ELIJAH, 1726, *Letter to Broome, Sept.*

If I could receive letters from you and Mr. Pope as you had leisure, I would never come in town as long as I live. In that way of conversing I should have all the pleasure that I can possibly propose, without the disappointment when Mr. Pope falls asleep, nor the dread of your taking leave because you are weary.—MARLBOROUGH, SARAH JENNINGS, DUCHESS, 1742, *Letter to Lord Marchmont, March* 15.

There cannot be a stronger proof of his being capable of any action for the sake of gain than publishing his literary correspondence, which lays open such a mixture of dulness and iniquity, that one would imagine it visible even to his most passionate admirers.—MONTAGU, LADY MARY WORTLEY, 1752, *Letter to the Countess of Bute, June* 23.

In all his letters, as well as in those of Swift, there runs a strain of pride, as if the world talked of nothing but themselves.—GOLDSMITH, OLIVER, 1762, *Life of Richard Nash.*

It is a mercy to have no character to maintain. Your predecessor, Mr. Pope, laboured his Letters as much as the "Essay on Man;" and, as they were written to everybody, they do not look as if they had been written to anybody.—WALPOLE, HORACE, 1777, *Letter to Rev. William Mason, March* 13, *Letters, ed. Cunningham, vol.* VI, *p.* 422.

A taint of affectation, more or less strong, runs through the whole of Pope's Letters: those to the ladies, particularly, are stuffed with miserable and frigid attempts to be gay and gallant.—GREEN, THOMAS, 1779–1810, *Diary of a Lover of Literature, p.* 65.

Pope's private correspondence . . . . filled the nation with praises of his candour, tenderness, and benevolence, the purity of his purposes, and the fidelity of his friendship. — JOHNSON, SAMUEL, 1779–81, *Pope, Lives of the English Poets.*

I found this consequence attending, or likely to attend the eulogium you bestowed, —if my friend thought me witty before, he shall think me ten times more witty hereafter; where I joked once, I will joke five times, and for one sensible remark I will send him a dozen. Now this foolish vanity would have spoiled me quite, and would have made me as disgusting a letter-writer as Pope, who seems to have thought that unless a sentence was well-turned, and every period pointed with some conceit, it was not worth the carriage. Accordingly he is to me, except in very few instances, the most disagreeable maker of epistles that I ever met with.—COWPER, WILLIAM, 1780, *To Unwin, June* 8.

Pope very frequently imitated Voiture. . . . The object was to say what meant little, with the utmost novelty in the mode, and with the most ingenious compliment to the person addressed; so that he should admire himself and admire the writer. They are, of course, very tiresome after a short time; yet their ingenuity is not without merit. . . . Voiture seems to have fancied that good sense spoils a man of wit. But he has not so much wit as *esprit;* and his letters serve to exemplify the meaning of that word. Pope, in addressing ladies, was nearly the ape of Voiture. It was unfortunately thought necessary, in such a correspondence, either to affect despairing love, which was to express itself with all possible gayety, or, where love was too presumptuous, as with the Rambouillets, to pour out a torrent of nonsensical flattery, which was to be rendered tolerable by far-fetched turns of thought.—HALLAM, HENRY, 1837–39, *Introduction to the Literature of Europe, pt.* iii, *ch.* vii, *par.* 20.

No one can read them without feeling that they were written for more eyes than those of his correspondents. There is a laboured smartness, a constant exhibition of fine sentiment, which is strained and unnatural. His repeated deprecation of motives of aggrandizement argues "a thinking too precisely" on the very subject; and no man whose chief ambition was to gain a few friends would so habitually proclaim it. These tender and delicate aspirations live in the secret places of the heart. . . . True sentiment is modest.—TUCKERMAN, HENRY THEODORE, 1846, *Thoughts on the Poets, Third ed., p.* 76.

If any of my hearers, as I hope they may, should take a fancy to look at Pope's correspondence, let them pass over that first part of it; over, perhaps, almost all Pope's letters to women; in which there is a tone of not pleasant gallantry, and, amidst a profusion of compliments and politenesses, a something which makes one distrust the little pert, prurient bard. There is very little indeed to say about his loves, and that little not edifying. He wrote flames and raptures, and elaborate verse and prose for Lady Mary Wortley Montagu; but that passion probably came to a climax in an impertinence and was extinguished by a box on the ear, or some such rebuff, and he began on a sudden to hate her with a fervour much more genuine than that of his love had been. It was a feeble, puny grimace of love, and paltering with passion. After Mr. Pope had sent off one of his fine compliments to Lady Mary, he made a second draught from the rough copy, and favoured some other friend with it. He was so charmed with the letter of Gay's, that I have just quoted, that he had copied that and amended it, and sent it to Lady Mary as his own. A gentleman who writes letters *à deux fins*, and after having poured out his heart to the beloved, serves up the same dish *rechauffé* to a friend, is not very much in earnest about his loves, however much he may be in his piques and vanities when his impertinence gets its due. But, save that unlucky part of the Pope Correspondence, I do not know, in the range of our literature, volumes more delightful. You live in them in the finest company in the world. A little stately, perhaps; a little *apprêté* and conscious that they are speaking to whole generations who are listening; but in the tone of their voices—pitched, as no doubt they are, beyond the mere conversation key—in the expression of their thoughts, their various views and natures, there is something generous, and cheering, and ennobling. You are in the society of men who have filled the greatest parts in the world's story—you are with St. John the statesman; Peterborough, the conqueror; Swift, the greatest wit of all times; Gay, the kindliest laughter—it is a privilege to sit in that company.—THACKERAY, WILLIAM MAKEPEACE, 1853, *The English Humourists of the Eighteenth Century.*

I do not hesitate to say that Pope's correspondence, as originally published, has little of either the lighter or the graver merits of familiar letters. I at least remember none more barren of matter, less enlivened by wit, or less explanatory of the history of either the writer or the times.—CROKER, JOHN WILSON, 1857, *Elwin's Pope, vol.* VI, *p.* xxviii.

Every examination into the history of the letters was slight before Mr. Dilke engaged into the laborious task. His familiarity with the books, pamphlets and periodicals of the time could not be exceeded, and his doubts once awakened he accepted nothing upon trust. With an immense amount of research and skill he proceeded to track Pope through his tortuous courses. He laid bare the ramifications of the plot against Curll, which was only known in a few of its prominent particulars. He detected, what none of the editors and biographers had perceived, base manœuvres and deceit which accompanied the publication of the "Letters to and from Dr. Swift." He was originally put upon his investigations by the manuscript collection of Pope's letters to Caryll and these revealed a new set of frauds in the evidence they supplied of letters converted into a fictitious correspondence. His inclination was to favour Pope whenever there was an opening for a liberal interpretation, and it was not from hostility that he exposed the net-work of fraud, and brought out the dark traits of a dishonourable disposition with new and terrible force. He printed his discoveries in the *Athenæum*, and after studying the facts afresh by the light of his essays, I am compelled to adopt his conclusions. The evidence, upon which they rest is often circumstantial and intricate, and cannot be followed to the end without steady attention, and some trial of patience.—ELWIN, WHITWELL, 1871, *ed., The Works of Alexander Pope, vol.* I, *Introduction, p.* xxvii.

Pope, in fact, was evidently ashamed of the attitude which he had so unnaturally adopted to his correspondent. The first man of letters of his day could not bear to reveal the full degree in which he had fawned upon the decayed dramatist, whose inferiority to himself was now plainly recognized. He altered the whole tone of the correspondence by omission, and still worse by addition. He did not publish a letter in which Wycherley gently remonstrates with his young admirer for excessive adulation; he omitted from his own letters the phrase which had provoked the remonstrance; and, with more daring falsification, he manufactured an imaginary letter to Wycherley out of a letter really addressed to his friend Caryll. In this letter Pope had himself addressed to Caryll a remonstrance similar to that which he had received from Wycherley. When published as a letter to Wycherley, it gives the impression that Pope, at the age of seventeen, was already rejecting excessive compliments addressed to him by his experienced friend. By these audacious perversions of the truth, Pope is enabled to heighten his youthful independence, and to represent himself as already exhibiting a graceful superiority to the reception or the offering of incense; while he thus precisely inverts the relation which really existed between himself and his correspondent.—STEPHEN, LESLIE, 1880, *Alexander Pope (English Men of Letters), p.* 17.

GENERAL

I am always highly delighted with the discovery of any rising genius among my countrymen. For this reason I have read over, with great pleasure, the late miscellany published by Mr. Pope, in which there are many excellent compositions of that ingenious gentleman.—ADDISON, JOSEPH, 1712, *The Spectator, No.* 523, *Oct.* 30.

When Pope's harmonious Muse with pleasure roves,
Amidst the plains, the murm'ring streams, and groves,
Attentive Echo pleas'd to hear his songs,
Thro' the glad shade each warbling note prolongs;
His various numbers charm our ravish'd ears,
His steady judgment far out-shoots his years,
And early in the youth the god appears.
—GAY, JOHN, 1714, *To Bernard Lintot, Miscellaneous Poems.*

But in his other works what beauties shine,
While sweetest music dwells on every line!
These he admired, on these he stamped his praise,
And bade them live to brighten future days.
—COOKE, THOMAS, 1725, *Battle of the Poets, f.* 15.

'Tis true, if finest notes alone could show
(Tuned justly high or regularly low)
That we should fame to these mere vocals give,
Pope more than we can offer should receive;
For when some gliding river is in his theme,
His lines run smoother than the smoothest stream.
—STANHOPE, H., 1728, *Progress of Dulness.*

Durgen's sweet Pen, we know, the World admires,
He's bless'd with a kind Muse that never tires;
Skill'd in all antient Tongues, and modern Arts,
A prodigy in Person, and in Parts;
A half-bred Deity, made up of Thought,
A something, but no mortal Man knows what;
A living *Chaos*, whose prolifick Brain,
Does e'ery thing in miniature contain;
Has Wit at Will, and is, without dispute,
A wondrous Creature, neither Man nor Brute;
Who, to delight himself, and vex the Town,
Spent twice three Years in writing one Lampoon;
And, if no Rival does his Scheme defeat,
Will waste six more to make the work compleat;
A task, that when it's finish'd, must command
Laudative Poems from each skilful Hand,
Especially each poor neglected Muse,
His gen'rous Satyr does so kindly use,
Forgetful of the hard unhappy fate
Of Poets more sublime, and Wits more great,
Than those that wrong the Mem'ry of the Dead,
And stifle Conscience for the sake of Bread,
Slander the living, with a spightful Pen,
And prostitute the Fame of worthy Men.
So the proud Cit, possess'd of an Estate,
For nothing good, tho' worshipfully Great,
Triumphs o'er Dealers of a low Degree,
More honest, tho' less prosperous than he.
—WARD, EDWARD, 1729, *Durgen, or, a Plain Satyr upon a Pompous Satyrist.*

In Pope I cannot read a line,
But with a sigh I wish it mine;
When he can in one couplet fix
More sense than I can do in six;
It gives me such a jealous fit,
I cry, "Pox take him and his wit!"
—SWIFT, JONATHAN, 1731, *On the Death of Dr. Swift.*

Pope and Boileau are certainly the two best poets of all the moderns. They both write extremely well; but I should prefer Pope to Boileau, because he excels in what is most material in the character of a poet. Boileau writes more correctly, and better than Pope; but Pope thinks more nobly, and has much more of the true spirit of poetry than Boileau.—RAMSAY, CHEVALIER, 1732–33, *Spence's Anecdotes, ed. Singer, p.* 99.

He is, in my opinion, the most elegant, the most correct poet; and at the same time the most harmonious (a circumstance which redounds very much to the honour of this muse) that *England* ever gave birth to. He has mellowed the harsh sounds of the *English* trumpet to the soft accents of the flute. His compositions may be easily translated, because they are vastly clear and perspicuous; besides, most of his subjects are general, and relative to all nations.—VOLTAIRE, FRANÇOIS MARIE AROUET, 1732? *Letters Concerning the English Nation, p.* 170.

—"Don't you really think so, Sir?"—I think, madam, that he writes verses very well.—"Yes, he writes verses so well, that he is in danger of bringing even good verse into disrepute! from his all tune and no meaning."—MONTAGU, LADY MARY WORTLEY, 1740–41, *Spence's Anecdotes, ed. Singer, p.* 178.

Mr. Pope, as you with equal keenness and propriety express it, is *gone out.* I told a friend of his, who sent me the first news of it, that I was very sorry for his death, because I doubted whether he would live to recover the accident. Indeed it gives me no surprize to find you thinking he was in the wane of his popularity. It arose, originally, but from meditated little personal assiduities, and a certain bladdery swell of management. He did not blush to have the cunning to blow himself up, by help of dull, unconsciousness instruments, whenever he would seem to sail as if his own wind moved him. In fact, if anything was fine, or truly powerful, in Mr. Pope, it was chiefly centered in expression; and that rarely, when not grafted on some other writer's preconceptions. His own sentiments were low and narrow, because always interested; darkly touched, because conceived imperfectly; and sour and acrid, because writ in envy. He had a turn for verse without a soul for poetry. He stuck himself into his subjects, and his muse partook his maladies; which, with a kind of peevish and vindictive consciousness, maligned the healthy and the satisfied.—HILL, AARON, 1744, *Letter to Samuel Richardson.*

This great man is allowed to have been one of the first rank amongst the poets of our nation, and to acknowledge the superiority of none but Shakespear, Milton, and Dryden. With the two former, it is unnatural to compare him, as their province in writing is so very different. Pope has never attempted the drama, nor published an Epic Poem, in which these two distinguished genius's have so wonderfully succeeded. Though Pope's genius was great, it was yet of so different a cast from Shakespear's and Milton's, that no comparison can be justly formed. But if this may be said of the former two, it will by no means hold with respect to the latter, for between him and Dryden, there is a great similarity of writing, and a very striking coincidence of genius.—CIBBER, THEOPHILUS, 1753, *Lives of the Poets, vol.* V, *p.* 247.

I revere the memory of Pope, I respect and honour his abilities; but I do not think him at the head of his profession. In other words, in that species of poetry wherein Pope excelled, he is superior to all mankind: and I only say that this species of poetry is not the most excellent one of the art.—WARTON, JOSEPH, 1756, *Essay on the Genius and Writings of Pope, Preface.*

Pope, the prince of lyric poetry, unrivalled in satire, ethicks, and polished versification.—SMOLLETT, TOBIAS GEORGE, 1757–58, *History of England.*

Had Milton never wrote, Pope would have been less to blame; but when in Milton's genius, Homer, as it were, personally rose to forbid Britons doing him that ignoble wrong, it is less pardonable, by that effeminate decoration, to put Achilles in petticoats a second time. How much nobler had it been, if his numbers had rolled on in full flow, thro' the various modulations of masculine melody, into those grandeurs of solemn sound which are indispensably demanded by the native dignity of heroic song! How much nobler if he had resisted the temptations of that Gothic demon which modern poesy, tasting, became mortal! . . . Harmony, as well as eloquence, is essential to poesy; and a murder of his music is putting half Homer to death. "Blank" is a term of diminution; what we mean by "blank verse" is verse, unfallen, uncursed; verse reclaimed, re-inthroned in the true language of the gods; who never thundered, nor suffered their Homer to thunder, in rhyme.—YOUNG, EDWARD, 1759, *Conjectures on Original Composition, p.* 565.

His great, will not say greatest, merit lay in what we call the mechanic of poetry. —LESSING, GOTTHOLD EPHRAIM, 1759, *Briefe die neueste Litteratur betreffend,* II, *Brief.*

In polish'd numbers and majestic sound,
Where shall thy rival, Pope! be ever found?
But whilst each line with equal beauty flows,
E'en excellence, unvaried, tedious grows.
Nature through all her works, in great degree,
Borrows a blessing from variety.
Music itself her needful aid requires
To rouse the soul, and wake our dying fires.

Still in one key, the nightingale would tease;
Still in one key, not Brent would always please.
—CHURCHILL, CHARLES, 1761, *The Apology, Poems, ed. Tooke, vol.* I, *p.* 76.

Pope's talent lay remarkably in what one may naturally enough term the condensation of thoughts. I think no English poet ever brought so much sense into the same number of lines with equal smoothness, ease, and poetical beauty. Let him who doubts of this peruse the "Essay on Man" with attention.—SHENSTONE, WILLIAM, 1763 ? *Essays on Men and Manners.*

If the opinion of those critics be true, who hold that the highest regions of Parnassus are appropriated to pathos and sublimity, Dryden must after all confess, that he has never ascended so far as his illustrious imitator: there being nothing in the writings of the first so pathetic as the "Epistle of Eloisa," or the "Elegy on the Unfortunate Lady;" nor so uniformly sublime as the "Essay on Man," or the "Pastoral of the Messiah." This last is indeed but a selection and imitation of choice passages; but it bespeaks a power of imitation, and a taste in selection, that Dryden does not seem to have possessed. To all which may I not be permitted to add, what I think I could prove, that the pathos of Homer is frequently improved by Pope, and that of Virgil very frequently debased by Dryden?—BEATTIE, JAMES, 1776-9, *Essays, p.* 18, *note.*

In the last Review, I mean in the last but one, I saw Johnson's critique upon Prior and Pope. I am bound to acquiesce in his opinion of the latter, because it has always been my own. I could never agree with those who preferred him to Dryden; nor with others (I have known such, and persons of taste and discernment too), who could not allow him to be a poet at all. He was certainly a mechanical maker of verses, and in every line he ever wrote, we see indubitable marks of the most indefatigable industry and labour. Writers who find it necessary to make such strenuous and painful exertions, are generally as phlegmatic as they are correct; but Pope was, in this respect, exempted from the common lot of authors of that class. With the unwearied application of a plodding Flemish painter, who draws a shrimp with the most minute exactness, he had all the genius of one of the first masters. Never, I believe, were such talents and such drudgery united. But I admire Dryden most, who has succeeded by mere dint of genius, and in spite of a laziness and carelessness almost peculiar to himself. His faults are numberless, but so are his beauties. His faults are those of a great man, and his beauties are such (at least sometimes), as Pope with all his touching and retouching could never equal.—COWPER, WILLIAM, 1782, *Letter to Rev. William Unwin, Jan.* 5.

Then Pope, as harmony itself exact,
In verse well disciplined, complete, compact,
Gave virtue and morality a grace,
That, quite eclipsing pleasure's painted face,
Levied a tax of wonder and applause,
E'en on the fools that trampled on their laws.
But he (his musical finesse was such,
So nice his ear, so delicate his touch)
Made poetry a mere mechanic art;
And every warbler has his tune by heart.
—COWPER, WILLIAM, 1782, *Table Talk.*

Pope's works are superabundant with superfluous and unmeaning verbage; his translations are even replete with tautology, a fault which is to refinement as midnight is to noon day. What is truly surprizing is, that the fourth book of the "Dunciad," his last publication, is more full of redundancy and incorrectness than his Pastorals, which are his first.—PINKERTON, JOHN (ROBERT HERON), 1785, *Letters of Literature, p.* 64.

All that was wanting to his illustrious predecessor found its consummation in the genius, knowledge, correct sense, and condensation of thought and expression, which distinguish this poet.—MATHIAS, THOMAS JAMES, 1798, *The Pursuits of Literature, Eighth ed., p.* 36.

The fourteenth chapter of Scriblerus, it is true, possesses humour, but the Second Satire from Horace has nothing to palliate its grossness. It were much to be wished also that every future editor would expel not only these offensive pages, but the Imitations likewise of Chaucer and Spenser, neither of which have a particle of merit, and the last impresses an idea of the genius of the poet totally void of all verisimilitude.—DRAKE, NATHAN, 1810, *Essays, Illustrative of the Rambler, Adventurer and Idler, vol.* II, *p.* 143.

Shall I venture to own to you, that in mental power, I give him only the third place among the wits of his time? In talent, that is, in power formed and directed by habit to one sort of exertion, his place may be higher. He had a greater talent for brilliant and sententious verses than perhaps any of his contemporaries had for any other kind of literary excellence. I really think that his great merit is the same with that of a writer of maxims. His observations on life are both sensible and fine, but they are seldom his own; they have not the truth of immediate experience; and in his maxims, like those of his brethern, the truth is always in part sacrificed to the brilliancy; some part of the jewel is cut away in polishing. A talent very inferior to a man's general power of mind, especially when joined to mannerism, strikes me as a sort of knack. Estimated by the two great faculties of the human mind, his place must be where I have assigned it. Swift was as much above him in understanding, as Addison in imagination,—not to mention taste. Both Swift and Addison were more classical writers; that is, their writings approach more near to the models of beauty in their respective kinds.—MACKINTOSH, SIR JAMES, 1811, *Diary, Memoirs ed., Mackintosh, vol.* II, *p.* 101.

The poetic fame of Pope, however, has been the bane of religion; for independent of the seductive lustre which he has given to the dæmonology of Homer, and the unblushing deism of his "Essay on Man," pure heathenism, in spite of a few solitary truths introduced for the sake of the rhyme, ever feeds his lamp and scents his works, which paganise the taste of thousands.—BOGUE, DAVID, AND BENNETT, JAMES, 1812, *History of Dissenters, from the Revolution in* 1688, *to the year* 1808.

But ever since Pope spoiled the ears of the town
With his cuckoo-song verses, half up and half down.

—HUNT, LEIGH, 1814–15, *Feast of the Poets.*

We shall not enter into the question whether Pope had most taste or genius. Perhaps he was destined by nature for bold invention; but in fact he has, in general, imitated with taste. The same thing may be said of Horace, Vida, and Boileau. Pope, like them, was a critic as well as a poet. It is a curious observation that no poet of the first rank has ever spoken of the mechanism of his art, while poets of inferior station have laboriously displayed its rules in verse.—FOSCOLO, UGO, 1818, *Dante, Edinburgh Review, vol.* 29, *p.* 467.

The question, whether Pope was a poet, has hardly yet been settled, and is hardly worth settling; for, if he was not a great poet, he must have been a great prose-writer, that is, he was a great writer of some sort. He was a man of exquisite faculties, and of the most refined taste; and as he chose verse (the most obvious distinction of poetry) as the vehicle to express his ideas, he has generally passed for a poet, and a good one. If, indeed, by a great poet, we mean one who gives the utmost grandeur to our conceptions of nature, or the utmost force to the passions of the heart, Pope was not in this sense a great poet; for the bent, the characteristic power of his mind, lay the clear contrary way.—HAZLITT, WILLIAM, 1818, *Lectures on the English Poets, Lecture* iv.

Pope is a satirist, and a moralist, and a wit, and a critic, and a fine writer, much more than he is a poet. He has all the delicacies and proprieties and felicities of diction—but he has not a great deal of fancy, and scarcely ever touches any of the greater passions. He is much the best, we think, of the classical Continental school; but he is not to be compared with the masters—nor with the pupils—of that Old English one from which there had been so lamentable an apostasy. There are no pictures of nature or of simple emotion in all his writings. He is the poet of town life, and of high life, and of literary life; and seems so much afraid of incurring ridicule by the display of natural feeling or unregulated fancy, that it is difficult not to imagine that he would have thought such ridicule very well directed.—JEFFREY, FRANCIS, 1819–44, *Contributions to the Edinburgh Review, vol.* 2, *p.* 292.

Pope gave our heroic couplet its strictest melody and tersest expression.

D'un mot mis en sa place il enseigne le pouvoir.

If his contemporaries forgot other poets in admiring him, let him not be robbed of his just fame on pretence that a part of it was superfluous. The public ear was long fatigued with repetitions of his manner; but if we place ourselves in the situation of those to whom his brilliancy, succinctness, and animation were wholly new, we cannot wonder at their being captivated to the fondest admiration. . . . But let us look to the spirit that points his antithesis, and to the rapid precision of his thoughts, and we shall forgive him for being too antithetic and sententious. . . . That Pope was neither so insensible to the beauties of nature, nor so indistinct in describing them as to forfeit the character of a genuine poet, is what I mean to urge, without exaggerating his picturesqueness. But before speaking of that quality in his writings, I would beg leave to observe, in the first place, that the faculty by which a poet luminously describes objects of art is essentially the same faculty which enables him to be a faithful describer of simple nature; in the second place, that nature and art are to a greater degree relative terms in poetical description than is generally recollected; and, thirdly, that artificial objects and manners are of so much importance in fiction, as to make the exquisite description of them no less characteristic of genius than the description of simple physical appearances. The poet is "creation's heir."—CAMPBELL, THOMAS, 1819, *An Essay on English Poetry.*

I have loved and honoured the fame and name of that illustrious and unrivalled man, far more than my own paltry renown, and the trashy gingle of the crowd of "schools" and upstarts, who pretend to rival, or even surpass him. . . . The most *perfect* of our poets and the purest of our moralists. . . . He is the moral poet of all civilisation, and as such, let us hope that he will one day be the national poet of mankind. He is the only poet that never shocks; the only poet whose *faultlessness* has been made his reproach.—BYRON, LORD, 1821, *On Bowles's Strictures on the Life and Writings of Pope.*

When he left his own laurel circus at Twickenham, he was lifted into his chariot or his barge; and with weak eyes, and tottering strength, it is physically impossible he could be a *descriptive* bard. Where description has been introduced among his poems, as far as his observation could go, he excelled; more could not be expected. In the descriptions of the cloister, the scenes surrounding the melancholy convent, as far as could be gained by books, suggested by imagination, he was eminently successful; but even here, perhaps, he only proved that he could not go far.—BOWLES, WILLIAM LISLE, 1821, *Two Letters to the Right Honourable Lord Byron.*

Neither time, nor distance, nor grief, nor age can ever diminish my veneration for him, who is the great moral poet of all times, of all climes, of all feelings, and of all stages of existence. The delight of my boyhood, the study of my manhood, perhaps (if allowed to me to attain it) he may be the consolation of my age. His poetry is the Book of Life. Without canting, and yet without neglecting religion, he has assembled all that a good and great man can gather together of moral wisdom clothed in consummate beauty.—BYRON, LORD, 1821, *A Second Letter on Bowles's Strictures on the Life and Writings of Pope.*

It really seems to us absurd, and somewhat conceited to inquire at this time of day, if Pope be really a poet. If the wise men of Europe had not been grossly deceived for the last hundred years, (a pretty fair term of time to settle the pretensions of an author), he is one of the most eminent. It, after all, amounts to a mere verbal dispute; whether our definition of a poet is the same that it was a century ago; as relates to ourselves, we see no reason to doubt it. We study and admire the same great models that were then admired; we acknowledge in Pope the sprightliness of an elegant fancy, graceful dignity of sentiment, a wit unceasing yet never tiring, satire playful yet severe, an accurate taste, a sententiousness of expression neither weakened by affectation, nor clouded by ambiguity, and an uniform polish of language never rivalled. . . . It is not by an indiscriminate commendation of Pope, that we may hope to preserve his poetical character from the unmerited contempt, into which it has fallen of late years; chiefly occasioned by the example of a few captivating but lawless writers. We must meet him on his own ground, which is surely too high to demand the aid of extravagant eulogium; acknowledge his deficiencies, that we may be more readily credited in speaking of his merits; hold him up to imitation as a perspicuous, elegant, and correct writer, abounding in wit and fancy but not sublime; natural but not tender.—PRESCOTT, WILLIAM H., 1821, *Byron's Letter on Pope, North American Review, vol.* 13, *pp.* 468, 470.

Who can be "at fault" with *any* edition, where the text is pure, and the annotations are brief and apposite? There is only *one* feeling, while discoursing of this incomparable poet, which I trust it may be permitted me to avow; that is, that, in the present age of prying research into the documents left of the illustrious dead, no officious zeal, misguided vanity, or base love of lucre, will lead to the publicity of *every thing* yet existing, unrecorded, of the muse of Pope: a name, which should be ever connected with all our better feelings of admiration and gratitude.—DIBDIN, THOMAS FROGNALL, 1824, *The Library Companion, p.* 730.

Pope exhibits more of the accuser than the Judge. Petty interests, and personal malice, instead of a love of justice, and a hatred of vice, appear to be the powers which nerve his arm. The victim is sure to fall beneath his blow, but the deed, however righteous, inspires us with no very affectionate feelings for his executioner.—NEELE, HENRY, 1827–29, *Lectures on English Poetry, p.* 175.

These three writers, Thomson, Collins, and Dyer, had more poetic imagination than any of their contemporaries, unless we reckon Chatterton as of that age. I do not name Pope, for he stands alone, as a man most highly gifted; but unluckily he took the plain when the heights were within his reach.—WORDSWORTH, WILLIAM, 1829, *Letters, Memoirs by C. Wordsworth, ed. Reed, vol.* II, *p.* 217.

Pope formed his style on that of Dryden. He has less enthusiasm, less majesty, less force of thought, than his great model, but he has more delicacy of feeling, more refinement and more correctness. If he never soars to the height which Dryden reached when "the full burst of inspiration came," he never sinks so low as his master ofttimes fell. While soothed by the exquisitely sweet, but somewhat monotonous couplets of Pope, we occasionally long for the bolder and more varied music of Dryden's lines.—DYCE, ALEXANDER, 1831–51, *Memoir of Pope.*

Nothing in the English language can be more perfect than the terseness, elegance, and condensation of Pope's sentiments, diction, and rhyme.—MONTGOMERY, JAMES, 1833, *Lectures on General Literature, Poetry, etc., p.* 302.

Pope was hardly the man to criticise Milton.—COLERIDGE, SAMUEL TAYLOR, 1833, *Table Talk, ed. Ashe, Sept.* 4, *p.* 261.

What fiction has he formed to embody truth? Are not all his illustrations drawn from observance? Even his beautiful "Eloisa" is no original invention; it is the conception of a powerful and passionate fancy,—not invention. The genius is secondary, because it lies solely in the language and versification. But who can put it in the same class with the inventions of Dante, Petrarch, Ariosto, Tasso, Spenser, Shakspeare, and Milton? When Byron wrote "Manfred," and "Cain" and "Heaven and Earth," he was a great inventor: why therefore does he affect to despise himself for not following Pope's model? I am sorry to say, that this seems nothing less than perverse affectation. I have taken the same side on this *Pope-argument* all my life; and,—strangely enough,—made many people angry by it. Pope is an unrivalled favourite with the matter-of-fact people; and they think it an actual affront to them to doubt his preeminence.—BRYDGES, SIR SAMUEL EDGERTON, 1834, *Autobiography, vol.* 1, *p.* 127.

In our own times, not merely has the depreciation of the unities gained ground, but the poets of the age of Anne have been censured as carrying too far the smoothness and correctness of versification. Pope especially, as the foremost of this class, has been nibbled at by men whom, when alive, a single brandish of his pen would have silenced and struck down. He has been denied imagination, variety, true poetic genius, and allowed scarce any thing beyond the talent of harmonious numbers. But his defence has been promptly undertaken by gifted hands, and conducted in a manner worthy of himself and of them. . . . The real truth seems to be, that Pope's was not the highest class of poetry, but that in the second class he deserves to hold the very highest rank. It may also be observed, that this class, though inferior in the scale of merit, is perhaps more generally and permanently pleasing than any other.—STANHOPE, PHILIP HENRY EARL (LORD MAHON), 1836–58, *History of*

England from the Peace of Utrecht to the Peace of Versailles, 1713–1783, *vol.* II, *p.* 218.

It is no use to decide the disputed question as to whether he were a poet or not, in the strict sense of the term; in any case, his was one of the finest heads ever known, full of deep sayings, uttered in the shape of couplets—rhymed couplets.—CARLYLE, THOMAS, 1838, *Lectures on the History of Literature*, *p.* 179.

We will admit to our reader in the confessional, that, however convinced in our innermost opinion of the superiority of Dryden's genius, we have more pleasure in reading Pope than we ever could enjoy or imagine under Pope's master. We incline to believe that Dryden being the greatest poet-power, Pope is the best poet-manual; and that whatever Dryden has done—we do not say conceived, we do not say suggested, but *done*—Pope has done that thing better. For translations, we hold up Pope's Homer against Dryden's Virgil and the world. Both translations are utterly and equally contrary to the antique, both bad with the same sort of excellence; but Pope's faults are Dryden's faults, while Dryden's are not Pope's. We say the like of the poems from Chaucer; we say the like of the philosophic and satirical poems: the art of reasoning in verse is admirably attained by either poet, but practised with more grace and point by the later one. To be sure, there is the "Alexander's Feast" ode, called, until people half believed what they said, the greatest ode in the language! But here is, to make the scales even again, the "Eloisa" with tears on it,—faulty but tender—of a sensibility which glorious John was not born with a heart for. To be sure, it was not necessary that John Dryden should keep a Bolingbroke to think for him: but to be sure again, it is something to be born with a heart, particularly for a poet. We recognise besides in Pope, a delicate fineness of tact, of which the precise contrary is unpleasantly obvious in his great master; Horace Walpole's description of Selwyn, *un bête inspirê* with a restriction of *bête* to the animal sense, fitting glorious John like his crown. Now there is nothing of this coarseness of the senses about Pope; the little pale Queen Anne's valetudinarian had a nature fine enough to stand erect upon the point of a needle like a schoolman's angel; and whatever he wrote coarsely, he did not write from inward impulse, but from external conventionality, from a bad social Swift-sympathy. For the rest, he carries out his master's principles into most excellent and delicate perfection: he is rich in his degree. And there is, indeed, something charming even to an enemy's ear in this exquisite balancing of sounds and phrases, these "shining rows" of oppositions and appositions, this glorifying of commonplaces by antithetic processes, this catching, in the rebound, of emphasis upon rhyme and rhyme; all, in short, of this Indian jugglery and Indian carving upon—cherry-stones!—BROWNING, ELIZABETH BARRETT, 1842–63, *The Book of the Poets.*

Though charity may find much in him that needs to be forgiven, though justice may even sometimes class him with those moral assassins who wear, like Cloten, their daggers in their mouths, yet still great merit cannot be denied to the poet and the man who scourged hypocrisy and baseness, at a time when baseness paved the way to power, and hypocrisy distributed the spoils of fraud.—WHIPPLE, EDWIN P., 1845, *Wit and Humor, Literature and Life*, *p.* 101

It was unlucky for him (if indeed it did not produce a lucky variety for the reading world) that Dryden came immediately before him. Dryden, a robuster nature, was just great enough to mislead Pope and French ascendency completed his fate. Perhaps, after all, nothing better than such a honey and such a sting as this exquisite writer developed, could have been got out of his little delicate pungent nature; and we have every reason to be grateful for what they have done for us. Hundreds of greater pretensions in poetry have not attained to half his fame, nor did they deserve it; for they did not take half his pains.—HUNT, LEIGH, 1846, *Wit and Humour*, *p.* 281.

This prince of poets.—CAMPBELL, JOHN LORD, 1849, *Lives of the Chief Justices of England*, *vol.* II, *ch.* XXX.

The mellifluence of Pope, as Johnson called it, has the defect of monotony. Exquisite in the sweet rising and falling of its clauses, it seldom or never takes the ear prisoner by a musical surprise If Pope be the nightingale of our verse, he displays none of the irregular and unexpected gush of the songster. He has no variations. The tune is delicate, but not natural. It reminds us of a bird, all over brilliant, which pipes its one lay in a golden cage and has forgotten the green wood in the luxury of confinement. But Dryden's versification has the freedom and the freshness of the fields. Pope's modulation is of the ear; Dryden's of the subject.—WILLMOTT, ROBERT ARIS, 1851, *Pleasures, Objects and Advantages of Literature, p.* 79.

I admire Pope in the very highest degree; but I admire him as a pyrotechnic artist for producing brilliant and evanescent effect out of elements that have hardly a moment's life within them. There is a flash and startling explosion, then there is a dazzling coruscation, all purple and gold; the eye aches under the suddenness of a display, that, springing like a burning arrow out of darkness, rushes back into darkness with arrowy speed, and in a moment all is over.—DE QUINCEY, THOMAS, 1851, *Lord Carlisle on Pope, Tait, n. s. vol.* 18, *p.* 311.

No poet ever enjoyed greater popularity, or had more influence on the taste of his age. In versification this was immediate and direct. His style was copied by innumerable imitators, until the public ear was cloyed with the everlasting echo of the heroic couplet. In his own didactic poems Pope was too uniform in his pauses and construction. The reader is apt to be fatigued with the regular recurrence of terse and pointed lines, the balanced verse and striking antithesis, unless attention be closely fixed on the weighty truths, the admirable sentiments, and marvellous felicity of diction which are compressed within these brilliant couplets. But, besides harmonious versification, Pope taught correctness and precision of thought, and brought slovenly execution into irredeemable disgrace. Thomson would not have thrice corrected, and almost rewritten his "Seasons," improving them on each revision, if Pope had not raised the standard of public taste with respect to poetical composition. It has been said by one who is himself a true poet, Professor Aytoun, that Pope founded no school of poetry, or if he did it was soon extinct, driven out by Percy's "Reliques," by Cowper, and Burns. The attempt to rival Pope on his own peculiar ground was hopeless. —CARRUTHERS, ROBERT, 1853–57, *The Life of Alexander Pope, p.* 415.

The taste and sensibilities of Pope, which led him to cultivate the society of persons of fine manners, or wit, or taste, or beauty, caused him to shrink equally from that shabby and boisterous crew which formed the rank and file of literature in his time: and he was as unjust to these men as they to him. The delicate little creature sickened at habits and company which were quite tolerable to robuster men: and in the famous feud between Pope and the Dunces, and without attributing any peculiar wrong to either, one can quite understand how the two parties should so hate each other. As I fancy, it was a sort of necessity that when Pope's triumph passed, Mr. Addison and his men should look rather contemptuously down on it from their balcony; so it was natural for Dennis and Tibbald, and Webster and Cibber, and the worn and hungry pressmen in the crowd below, to howl at him and assail him. And Pope was more savage to Grub-street, than Grub-street was to Pope.—THACKERAY, WILLIAM MAKEPEACE, 1853, *The English Humorists of the Eighteenth Century.*

In Pope's writings, whatsoever he may not find, he will find the very excellencies after which our young poets strive in vain, produced by their seeming opposites, which are now despised and discarded; naturalness produced by studious art; daring sublimity by strict self-restraint; depth by clear simplicity; pathos by easy grace; and a morality infinitely more merciful, as well as more righteous, than the one now in vogue among the poetasters, by honest faith in God. If he be shocked by certain peculiarities of diction, and by the fondness for perpetual antithesis, let him remember, that what seems strange to our day was natural and habitual in his; and that, in the eyes of our grandchildren, Keats's and Shelley's peculiarities will seem as monstrous as Pope's or Johnson's do in ours.—KINGSLEY, CHARLES, 1853, *Alexander Smith and Alexander Pope, Fraser's Magazine, vol.* 48, *p.* 455.

Pope our classical English Satirist. No controversies, as to his being a "poet" or not, will ever drive him from his place by the side of Horace and Juvenal; from his leading position in the group of those great and fine intellects who have in various ages seized the very spirit of human society, and depicted it in their pages, or corrected its corruptions, by the force of their inspiration from the sources of moral truth. For the sake of the finished excellence which proves him to have been a great man and a great artist, we must make what allowances we can for drawbacks which it is impossible to hide and useless to ignore.—HANNAY, JAMES, 1854, *Satire and Satirists, p.* 154.

Pope is once again in the ascendant. For a moment a thin filmy shadow passed over his name and fame; but time has restored "all its original brightness, "and Pope now stands, where he ever will stand, amongst the foremost men in the annals of his country's literature.—DILKE, CHARLES WENTWORTH, 1854–75, *Pope's Writings, The Papers of a Critic, vol.* I, *p.* 94.

He was, some one we think has said, the sort of a person we cannot even conceive existing in a barbarous age. His subject was not life at large, but fashionable life. He described the society in which he was thrown, the people among whom he lived; his mind was a hoard of small maxims, a quintessence of petty observations. When he described character, he described it, not dramatically nor as it is in itself, but observantly and from without; calling up in the mind not so much a vivid conception of the man—of the real, corporeal, substantial being—as an idea of the idea which a metaphysical bystander might refine and excruciate concerning him. Society in Pope is scarcely a society of people, but of pretty little atoms, colored and painted with hoops or in coats,—a miniature of metaphysics, a puppet-show of sylphs. He elucidates the doctrine that the tendency of civilized poetry is towards an analytic sketch of the existing civilization.—BAGEHOT, WALTER, 1855, *William Cowper, Works, ed. Morgan, vol.* I, *p.* 424.

Whatever was his power of imagination, of fancy, his command of language, or flow of verse, his genius had not that spiritual healthfulness which is a characteristic of our greatest English poets. There is, running through all the writings of Pope, a large vein of misanthropy. It was his habit to proclaim contempt of the world, antipathy to his fellow-beings, except a few choice friends, whom he clung to most faithfully.—REED, HENRY, 1855, *Lectures on English Literature, From Chaucer to Tennyson, p.* 234.

Thus poetry is degraded and made ornamental. Pope and his school wrote poetry fit to put round frosted cake.—EMERSON, RALPH WALDO, 1856–84, *English Traits, p.* 242.

Of all English authors he [Porson] seems to have had the greatest liking for Pope. He admired, with all the world, Pope's vigour of thought and accuracy and beauty of language. Mr. Maltby has seen the tears roll down his cheeks while he was repeating Pope's "Epistle to the Earl of Oxford," prefixed to Parnell's Poems. Walking with Maltby and Rogers over Pope's Villa at Twickenham, he exclaimed, "Oh, how I should like to pass the remainder of my days in a house which was the abode of a man so deservedly celebrated!" —WATSON, JOHN SELBY, 1861, *The Life of Richard Porson, p.* 350.

If he be not a universal poet in the most striking sense now, none the less is he really a poet, though belonging to a less vehement, less passionate, less startling class, in an embellished, correct and pure fashion. He is far superior to Boileau in extent of ideas and also in taste for the picturesque.—SAINTE-BEUVE, C. A., 1864–75, *Pope as a Poet, English Portraits, p.* 298.

The time has gone by for Pope to be ranked among the master-geniuses of our literature.—WARD, ADOLPHUS WILLIAM, 1869, *ed. Poetical Works of Alexander Pope, Introductory Memoir, p.* xlvii.

Sententious, acute, brilliant, and felicitous, the servant of an age which he was content to flatter and to please, but never attempted to elevate, who fixed for English poetry that factitious and stilted poetic diction which echoed and re-echoed by imitators till it became ashamed and vexed at its own empty reiterations.—PORTER, NOAH, 1870, *Books and Reading, p.* 262.

The serene and just benevolence which placed Pope, in his theology, two centuries in advance of his time, and enabled him to sum the law of noble life in two lines which, so far as I know, are the most complete, the most concise, and the most lofty expression of moral temper existing in English words:—

Never elated, while one man's oppress'd;
Never dejected, while another's bless'd.

I wish you also to remember these lines of Pope, and to make yourselves entirely masters of his system of ethics; because, putting Shakespeare aside as rather the world's than ours, I hold Pope to be the most perfect representative we have, since Chaucer, of the true English mind; and I think the "Dunciad" is the most absolutely chiselled and monumental work "exacted" in our country. You will find, as you study Pope, that he has expressed for you, in the strictest language and within the briefest limits, every law of art, of criticism, of economy, of policy, and, finally, of a benevolence, humble, rational, and resigned, contented with its allotted share of life, and trusting the problem of its salvation to Him in whose hands lies that of the universe.—RUSKIN, JOHN, 1870, *Lectures on Art, Lecture* iii.

Whatever may be said in his dispraise, he is likely to be quoted as long as the English is a living language.—BRYANT, WILLIAM CULLEN, 1870, *A New Library of Poetry and Song, Introduction.*

He was like those little musicians, infant prodigies, who, brought up at the piano, suddenly acquire a marvellous touch, roll out scales, brilliant shakes, makes the octavos vault with an agility and justice which drive off the stage the most famous artists. . . . In fine, his great cause for writing was literary vanity; he wished to be admired, and nothing more, his life was that of a coquette studying herself in a glass, bedecking herself, smirking, paying compliments to herself, yet declaring that compliments weary her, that painting the face makes her dirty, and that she has a horror of affectation. Pope has no dash, no naturalness or manliness; no more ideas than passions; at least such ideas as a man feels it necessary to write, and in connection with which we lose thought of words. Religious controversy and party quarrels resound about him; he studiously avoids them; amidst all these shocks his chief care is to preserve his writing desk; he is a very lukewarm Catholic, all but a deist, not well aware of what deism means; and on this point he borrows from Bolingbroke ideas whose scope he cannot see, but which he thinks suitable to be put into verse. . . . I wish I could admire Pope's works of imagination, but I cannot. In vain I read the testimony of his contemporaries, and even that of the moderns, and repeat to myself that in his time he was the prince of poets.—TAINE, H. A., 1871, *History of English Literature, tr. Van Laun, vol.* II, *bk.* iii, *ch.* vii, *pp.* 196, 198, 199.

As truly as Shakespeare is the poet of man, as God made him, dealing with great passions and innate motives, so truly is Pope the poet of society, the delineator of manners, the exposer of those motives which may be called *acquired*, whose spring is in institutions and habits of purely worldly origin.—LOWELL, JAMES RUSSELL, 1871–90, *Pope, Prose Works, Riverside ed., vol.* IV, *p.* 31.

He is in a peculiar degree the mirror of the social passions and sentiments, the modes and tone of his day. To comprehend how much this is so, we have only to suppose the ten volumes of Pope's works annihilated. What chasm would be created by the act of destruction! But in what? Not a single discovery, or truth, or thought, or idea, or character, or image, which counts among the treasured possessions of human intelligence, would be thereby lost. But in the history of English literature and life what a gap would be occasioned! There is no other book in the language, the loss of which would obliterate so much personal anecdote, so much scandal, if you will, but also so much true and firm drawing of character and personal relations, such felicitous touches of manners and contemporary tone.—PATTISON, MARK, 1872–89, *Pope and his Editors, Essays, ed. Nettleship, vol.* II, *p.* 351

Dryden was his great model. Perhaps his highest excellence lies in the same direction as that of Dryden lay,—in the power of sketching characters. He, too, was a skillful portrait-painter; but his style is very different from Dryden's. In one instance he has ventured to challenge comparison with his master, in his picture of Villiers of *Zimri*, forlorn and dying. A careful juxtaposition of the two masterpieces will well illustrate the affinities and the differences of their authors.—HALES, JOHN W., 1872, *Longer English Poems, p.* 289.

Pope said that the proper study of mankind was Man. But he approached that study from the side of the intellect alone. It was by the criticism of the understanding, not by the emotion of the heart that he worked on his subject. The result was cold speculation and brilliant satire, and in neither of those tempers is any one fit to write fairly or nobly about the whole of Human Nature; though he is fitted to write about that which Man does, or Man has, up to a certain point. The surface of the "study of mankind" is touched it may be in all its points, but the writer does not penetrate into its depths. It is just the difference between Ben Jonson and Shakespeare: the one not seriously caring for his characters, but only how he may develop them; the other loving, pitying, being personally indignant with his characters: so that in the one we study not men, but the humours of men; in the other we study men, nay mankind. The one creates images of men and dresses them and makes them play their part by strings upon his stage: the other creates living men, and bids them act, and sits by watching them with passion. There is the same kind of difference between Pope's study of man and that study of him to which Wordsworth, Shelley, and Byron have accustomed us.—BROOKE, STOPFORD A,, 1874, *Theology in the English Poets, p.* 20.

His writings resemble those fireworks which, after they have fallen to the ground and been apparently quenched, suddenly break out again into sputtering explosions. The waters of a literary revolution have passed over him without putting him out. Though much of his poetry has ceased to interest us, so many of his brilliant couplets still survive that probably no dead writer, with the solitary exception of Shakespeare, is more frequently quoted at the present day. It is in vain that he is abused, ridiculed, and often declared to be no poet at all.—STEPHEN, LESLIE, 1874, *Hours in a Library, vol.* I, *p.* 90.

Pope's English is not only correct, it is also, as Dryden's is, modern. There is no substantial difference between it and the English of the present day, except that Pope is more exact than most modern authors in the use of words. . . . It is Pope's modernness as well as correctness, that makes him so valuable a model for the student of modern English. I know few better or more valuable lessons in the choice of English words than, after reading a passage of Pope, to shut the book and to have the verses repeated with blanks here and there for the students to fill up. By comparing one's failures with the original, one learns to appreciate the unerring exactitude with which Pope elaborated every couplet till it reached absolute perfection. Pope is one of the few poets whose lines cannot be misquoted with impunity.—ABBOTT, EDWIN A., 1875, *A Concordance to the Works of Alexander Pope, Introduction, pp.* iv, v.

The Poet of the Understanding.—ROSSETTI, WILLIAM MICHAEL, 1878, *Lives of Famous Poets, p.* 132.

Loyal as he was to his friends, he was yet more loyal to his verse. His vanity never led him to literary self-sufficiency; no artist ever showed a truer lowliness before the ideal of his art; no poet ever corrected so much, or so invariably bettered his work by each correction. One of his finest characteristics, indeed, was his high sense of literary dignity. From the first he carried on the work of Dryden by claiming a worth and independence for literature; and he broke with disdain through the traditions of patronage which had degraded men of letters into hangers-on of the great.—GREEN, JOHN RICHARD, 1880, *History of the English People, vol.* IV, *p.* 208.

And not only is Pope's style still popular in the truest sense of the word, but it forms the foundation on which have been built many of the most popular poems in the language. There is scarcely a distinguished poet in the eighteenth century who does not owe something of his style to Pope. However much they may differ from him and from each other, Gray, Collins, Johnson, Goldsmith, and Crabbe all do silent homage to his genius; and if it had not been for the exactness and propriety of metrical expression which Pope erected as a standard, it may well be doubted whether we should have enjoyed the beauty of form which we find in the "Elegy in the Country Churchyard" or the "Ode to Evening;" the striking moral manner that arrests the imagination in the "Vanity of Human Wishes" or the "Deserted Village;" or the dramatic force of the character painting in the "Borough." Added to which, the author of "Childe Harold," the greatest master of idiomatic poetical English that this century has seen, was never wearied in proclaiming his admiration for the genius of Pope, and the extent of his own obligations to him.—COURTHOPE, WILLIAM JOHN, 1881, *ed. The Works of Alexander Pope, Introduction to the Moral Essays and Satires, vol.* III, *p.* xxxvi.

He felt what Cowper calls the "musical finesse" of Pope, and admired single lines and couplets very much; but he found the "regular da da, da da" of his heroic metre monotonous. He quoted

"What dire offense from amorous causes springs."

"Amrus causiz springs," horrible! I would sooner die than write such a line!!—TENNYSON, ALFRED LORD, 1883, *Some Criticisms on Poets, Memoir by his Son, vol.* II, *p.* 286.

When he arrived at the age of discretion, which was at an early period, for he was alert and precocious, he made Dryden his master. He was thought to have bettered the music of Dryden in his more polished numbers, and he certainly carried the art of writing the heroic couplet (as he and his contemporaries understood it) to the highest perfection. The bent of his mind was not poetical, but reflective and didactic. He was witty, sarcastic, merciless,—qualities that are inconsistent with a great genius, or a good heart. It was his misfortune to have a crooked mind in a crooked body, and to learn from woman nothing but the exercise of her foibles.—STODDARD, RICHARD HENRY, 1883, *ed. English Verse, Translations, Introduction, p.* xxx.

It rouses the blood, it kindles the heart, to remember what an indomitable force of heroic spirit, and sleepless always as fire, was inclosed in the pitiful body of the misshapen weakling whose whole life was spent in fighting the good fight of sense against folly, of light against darkness, of human speech against brute silence, of truth and reason and manhood against all the banded bestialities of all dunces and all dastards, all blackguardly blockheads and all blockheaded blackguards, who then as now were misbegotten by malignity on dullness. We are easily tempted and naturally apt to set against the high qualities of such warriors on the side of all men worthy of their help, by way of counterpoise to their glory and subtraction from our own debt of gratitude and esteem, the fierceness of their habitual mood and the foulness of their occasional missiles. We are less apt, possibly, to remember the conditions of their life-long fight.—SWINBURNE, ALGERNON CHARLES, 1886, *Miscellanies, p.* 34.

"But Pope, poor D——l, lied from Hand to Mouth;
Affected, hypocritical, and vain,
A Book in Breeches, and a Fop in Grain;
A Fox that found not the high Clusters sour,
The Fanfaron of Vice beyond his power,
Pope yet possessed"—(the Praise will make you start)—
"Mean, morbid, vain, he yet possessed a Heart!
And still we marvel at the Man, and still
Admire his Finish, and applaud his Skill:
Though, as that fabled Barque, a phantom Form,
Eternal strains, nor rounds the Cape of Storm,
Even so Pope strove, nor ever crossed the Line
That from the Noble separates the Fine!"

—LANG, ANDREW, 1886, *Letters to Dead Authors.*

I do not know, after all, that Pope is greatly esteemed in the present day. He was, like many poets, vain and ill-tempered. Moreover, he had the fault common to so many of his day—he did not know when to leave off. If Pope had not sung to such interminable length he would be more tolerable.—STERRY, J., ASHBY-, 1888, *London Letter, The Book Buyer, vol.* 5, *p.* 338.

Satirist after satirist has chirped like a wren from the head of Pope; where are they now? Where is the great, the terrific, the cloud-compelling Churchill? Meanwhile, in the midst of a generation persistently turned away from all his ideas and all his models, the clear voice of Pope still rings from the arena of Queen Anne.—GOSSE, EDMUND, 1889, *What is a Great Poet? Questions at Issue, p.* 105.

Everyone knows that Byron loved and defended Pope, and looked upon Pope as an impeccable master; and Pope deserved the recognition of Byron. For lucidity, for sharpness and brilliance of phrase, for delicate force and effect, it is hard to surpass the finest work of Pope. But gradually men came to see that Pope's "Essay on Man" was not the last possibility of English poetry.—DAWSON, W. J., 1890, *The Makers of Modern English, Introduction, p.* 2.

Pope's place in English poetry may be taken now as settled. He stands high and stands firmly in the second class: that is, in the class just below Shakespeare and Milton and a very few others. He has been extravagantly censured and extravagantly praised. Byron at one time maintained that he was the greatest English poet, and many vehement arguments have been used to prove that he was not a poet at all. One English critic believed he had settled the question for ever when he described Pope as "a musical rocking-horse." Again and again the world has been told that Pope has disappeared from the sky of literature, but the world looks up, and behold, there is the star shining just as before.—McCARTHY, JUSTIN, 1890, *A History of the Four Georges, vol.* II, *p.* 262.

The mention of Pope reminds me that he is the traditional exemplar of the didactic heresy, so much so that the question is still mooted whether he was a poet at all. As to this, one can give only his own impression, and my adverse view has somewhat changed,—possibly because we grow more sententious with advancing years. Considering the man with his time, I think Pope was a poet; one whose wit and reason exceeded his lyrical feeling, but still a poet of no mean degree. Assuredly he was a force in his century, and one not even then wholly spent. His didacticism was inherent in the stiff, vicious, Gallic drum-beat of his artificial style—so falsely called "classical," so opposed to the true and live method of the antique—rather than in his genius and quality. It is impossible that one with so marked a poetic temperament, and using verse withal as almost his sole mode of expression, should not have been a poet. In the manner of his time, how far above his rivals!—STEDMAN, EDMUND CLARENCE, 1892, *The Nature and Elements of Poetry, p.* 213.

If the poetry of Pope has not the vogue it once had, the fame of the most brilliant of poets is secure. He may not have the homage of the multitude, but he will have in every generation, as long as our language lasts the homage of all who can discern. He stands indeed with Horace, Juvenal, and Dryden at the head of a great department of poetry—the poetry of ethics and satire.—COLLINS, JOHN CHURTON, 1893, *Jonathan Swift, p.* 266.

He was able only to play on one instrument, the heroic couplet. When he attempted any other form of verse the result, if not total failure, was mediocrity. . . . The fine wine of his poetry was rarely free from bitterness in the cup. . . . In poetry Pope takes a first place in the second order of poets. The deficiencies which forbid his entrance into the first rank are obvious. He cannot sing, he has no ear for the subtlest melodies of verse, he is not a creative poet, and has few of the spirit-stirring thoughts which the noblest poets scatter through their pages with apparent unconsciousness. There are no depths in Pope and there are no heights; he has neither eye for the beauties of Nature, nor ear for her harmonies, and a primrose was no more to him than it was to Peter Bell. These are defects indeed, but nothing is more unfair says a great French critic than to judge notable minds solely by their defects, and in spite of them Pope's position is so unassailable that the critic must take a contracted view of the poet's art who questions his right to the title. His merits are of a kind not likely to be affected by time; a lively fancy, a power of satire almost unrivalled, and a skill in using words so consummate that there is no poet, excepting Shakespeare, who has left his mark upon the language so strongly. The loss to us if Pope's verse were to become extinct cannot readily be measured. He has said in the best words what we all know and feel, but cannot express, and has made that classical which in weaker hands would be commonplace. His sensibility to the claims of his art is exquisite, the adaptation of his style to his subject shows the hand of a master, and if these are not the highest gifts of a poet, they are gifts to which none but a poet can lay claim.—DENNIS, JOHN, 1894, *The Age of Pope, pp.* 40, 41, 63.

It appears to me that, in spite of the occasional stains which disfigure his pages —stains attributable rather to the age than to the man—we must regard him as one of the most effective powers for good in English literature. In that great conflict which is waged through the ages between God and the enemies of God, Pope fought strenuously, however ignorantly, on the right side. It is true that his hold upon Christian doctrines was feeble and ill-assured, but it is also true, as one of the most recent and assuredly not one of the least able of his critics has pointed out, that the influence of Catholic teaching may be clearly traced in many of his poems. And it is quite certain that his sympathies were with the defenders of Christianity, which, however imperfect his apprehension of it, he regarded as the complement and perfection of the Theism taught by Nature herself. No one can doubt his earnest sincerity when he proclaims in his magnificent verse that august verities of natural Religion, the Commanding sanctities of Natural Morality. And his exposition is the more penetrative with a certain class of minds—a large class, too—because it is delivered, not by a professed metaphysician, not by an accredited divine, but by a man of the world who, as he himself said of Horace, "without method talks us into sense."—LILLY, WILLIAM SAMUEL, 1894-97, *Essays and Speeches*, p. 21.

Pope, the very high-priest of English Classicism, accepts Classic standards only to ignore them at will.—WYLIE, LAURA JOHNSON, 1894, *Evolution of English Criticism*, p. 66.

With regard to the form of his didactic poetry there is not room for two opinions as to its excellence. The lines have been polished and refined until they are positively brilliant; their lustre may be somewhat metalic, but it is unmistakably real and effective. The expression has been pruned till it is the ideal of succinct epigrammatic utterance; indeed, one could adduce cases where compression has been so eagerly sought that grammar and even sense have been sacrificed.—WILLIAMS, A. M., 1895, *Pope, The Gentleman's Magazine*, vol. 279, p. 370.

I know that this poet works in harness, and has not the free movement of one who gallops under a loose rein; the couplets fetter him; may be they cramp him; but there is a blithe, strong resonance of true metal, in the clinking chains that bind him. No, I do not think that Pope is to be laughed out of court, in our day, or in any day, because he labored at form and polish, or because he loved so much the tingle of a rhyme; I think there was something else that tingled in a good deal that he wrote and will continue to tingle so long as Wit is known by its own name.—MITCHELL, DONALD G., 1895, *English Lands Letters and Kings, Queen Anne and the Georges*, p. 37.

If we are to deny the name of poet *simpliciter* to the master of a versification at once so consummate and to a great extent so novel, to the author of such really magnificent examples of their own kind of verse as the character of Atticus and the conclusion of the "Dunciad," to the man who, for nearly an entire century, gave more poetic pleasure to a greater number of his own countrymen than any other writer—then talk about poetry becomes a mere logomachy.—SAINTSBURY, GEORGE, 1895, *Social England, ed. Traill, vol.* IV, *p.* 575.

To the exuberance of the passions, Voltaire, like Pope, opposes restraint of social obligations. But this restraint is lax and feeble, and Pope still remains one of the inaugurators of the movement which led the age of Rousseau to magnify passion, regarded as the true end of man. Further, he never had anything but pity for that philosophy of the humble-minded which pretends "to chasten men under the pretence of exalting him." For Pope the passionate man alone is complete. He venerates passion as the ruling power in man, not so much because it is moral, as because it is beautiful and renders man more great. That is as much as to say that in certain pages of the "Essay on Man" there is, as it were, a foretaste of Rousseau. Above all, the author makes a complacent parade of that vague and maudlin spirit of benevolence so dear to the whole period. If Pope does not actually cause our tears to flow, he at least excites a certain tender feeling and a certain melting mood, which he regards as creditable to man. Sensitiveness, if it is not virtue, is at least the beginning of virtue.—TEXTE, JOSEPH, 1895-99, *Jean-Jacques Rousseau and the Cosmopolitan Spirit in Literature, tr. Matthews*, p. 117.

Keenly alive to the foibles of his time, and with powers of observation carefully trained by practice, Pope failed as an essayist for lack of sympathetic humour and of ability to conceal his art.—LOBBAN, J. H., 1896, *English Essays, Introduction*, p. xxxv.

I admire not a little of Gray, and a good

deal of Pope. The felicity of Pope's language and the energy seem to be the outcome of a vivid imagination. . . . He will be read till the world, with its insatiable maw, will have got from him all that it wants to get—all that he has to give.—LOCKER-LAMPSON, FREDERICK, 1896, *My Confidences, pp.* 177, 329.

On the whole, it is as a satirist we must think of him, and the second greatest in the language. The gods are in pairs, male and female; and if Dryden was the Mars of English satire, Pope was the Venus—a very eighteenth century Venus, quite as conspicuous for malice as for elegance. If a woman's satire were informed with genius, and cultivated to the utmost perfection of form by lifelong and exclusive literary practice, one imagines it would be much like Pope's. His style seems to me feminine in what it lacks; the absence of any geniality, any softening humour to abate its mortal thrust. It is feminine in what it has, the malice, the cruel dexterity, the delicate needle point which hardly betrays its light and swift entry, yet stings like a bee. Even in his coarseness—as in the "Dunciad"—Pope appears to me female. It is the coarseness of the fine ladies of that material time, the Lady Maries and the rest of them. Dryden is a rough and thick-natured man, cudgelling his adversaries with coarse speech in the heat of brawl and the bluntness of his sensibilities; a country squire, who is apt at times to use the heavy end of his cutting whip; but when Pope is coarse he is coarse with effort, he goes out of his way to be nasty, in the evident endeavour to imitate a man. It is a girl airing the slang of her schoolboy brother. The one thing, perhaps, which differentiates him from a woman, and makes it possible to read his verse with a certain pleasure, without that sense of unrelieved cruelty which repels one in much female satire, is his artist's delight in the exercise of his power.—THOMPSON, FRANCIS, 1897, *Academy Portraits, The Academy, vol.* 52, *p.* 14.

For more than thirty years Pope was so completely the center of political attention in England that he may almost be said to have comprised the poetry of his time. There is no second instance of an English poet preserving for so long a period a supremacy comparable to his. It is possible to defend the position that one or two other versemen of the age did some particular thing better than Pope, though even this requires argument; but it is quite certain that he alone excelled over a wide range of subjects. The fact of Pope's poetical ubiquity, however, is rendered much less miraculous by the consideration that if he triumphed over the entire field, the area of that field was extremely restricted.—GOSSE, EDMUND, 1897, *Short History of Modern English Literature, p.* 207.

Pope's success with the couplet in didactic verse is due to the fact that he never had any consecutive thought to express. Thinking in jets, he naturally wrote in couplets, and his verse falls apart into brilliant epigrams and maxims.—WINCHESTER, C. T., 1899, *Some Principles of Literary Criticism, p.* 265.

His malignities in criticism are introductory to the magisterial method of Johnson and the literary personalities of Southey and Gifford. The canons of his school made "poetry prosaic" and undermined the scientific comparative method of criticism in process of construction during the previous century. But his power shows also in his contribution to literary ethics; the establishment of independent authorship and the consequent destruction of the habit of dedications. After him the influence of patronage waned steadily, till with Johnson it expired. Thereafter, the public and the publisher became arbiters of fate in matters both creative and critical.—GAYLEY, CHARLES MILLS AND SCOTT, FRED NEWTON, 1899, *An Introduction, to the Methods and Materials of Literary Criticism, p.* 409.

In his life we find much to admire and much to condemn; but we cannot deny him the tribute of greatness. . . . As a poet, it is too much to claim that his verses attained the highest imaginative flights, such as we find in Shakespeare and Tennyson. He was not swayed by the fine frenzy, the overmastering convictions, and the tormenting passions that irresistibly force an utterance. He conformed his writings to a conventional form. He sought above all, in imitation of classical models, correctness of style. —PAINTER, F. V. N., 1899, *A History of English Literature, pp.* 240, 257.

Jonathan Swift

1667-1745

Born, in Dublin, 30 Nov. 1667. At school at Kilkenny, 1673-82. Matric., Trin. Coll., Dublin, as Pensioner, 24 April 1682; B. A. 1686. Emigrated to England, and joined his mother at Leicester, 1688. Lived in house of Sir W. Temple, at Moor Park, as his Secretary, and Tutor to Esther Johnson, 1689-92. Entered at Hart Hall, Oxford, 14 June 1692; M. A., 5 July 1692. Ordained Deacon, 18 Oct. 1694; Priest, 13 Jan. 1695. Prebend of Kilroot, Ireland, 1695. Returned to Moor Park, 1696-98. To Dublin, as Chaplain to Earl of Berkeley, 1699; Rector of Agher, and Vicar of Laracor and Rathbeggan, March 1699. Prebend of Dunlavin, 1700. Returned to England with Earl of Berkeley, 1701. B. D. and D. D., Dublin, 1702. Subsequent life spent partly in Ireland, partly in England. Edited "The Examiner," Nov. 1710 to June 1711. Founded the Brothers' Club, 1711; the Scriblerus Club, 1712. Dean of St. Patrick's, 23 Feb. 1713. Friendship with Esther Johnson ("Stella") begun, 1700. Friendship with Esther Vanhomrigh ("Vanessa") begun, 1710; she died, 1723. Contributed to "London," 1734. Mind began to give away, 1737. Died, in Dublin, 19 Oct. 1745. Buried in St. Patrick's Cathedral. *Works:* "A Discourse of the Contests . . . between the Nobles and the Commons, etc." (anon), 1701; "A Tale of a Tub" (anon.), 1704; "Predictions" (under pseud.: "Isaac Bickerstaff"), 1707; "Vindication" of preceding, 1709; "Meditation upon a Broomstick" (anon)., 1710; "A New Journey to Paris" (under pseud. "Sieur Du Baudrier"), 1711; "Miscellanies, 1711; "The Conduct of the Allies" (anon.), 1711; "Some Advice . . . to the Members of the October Club" (anon.), 1712; "Letter to the Lord High Treasurer," 1712; "A Proposal for Correcting . . . the English Tongue," 1721; "Some Reasons to prove that no person is obliged, by his principles as a Whig, to oppose Her Majesty" (anon.), 1712; "The Publick Spirit of the Whigs" (anon.), 1714; "A Preface to the B—p of S—r—m's. Introduction" (under pseud. "Gregory Misosarum"), 1713; "The Conduct of the Purse of Ireland," 1714; "Essays," 1714; "The Art of Punning," 1719; "Proposal for the Universal Use of Irish Manufacturers" (anon.), 1720; "Defence of English Commodities," 1720; "Right of Precedence" (anon.), 1720; "The Wonderful Wonder of Wonders" (anon.) [1720?]; "Letter of Advice to a Young Poet," 1721; "Letter to a Gentleman lately entered into Holy Orders," 1721; "The Journal" (anon.), 1722; "Letter from a Lady of Quality" (anon.), 1724; Two Letters under pseud. "M. B. Drapier," 1724; "Gulliver's Travels" (anon.), 1726; "Cadenus and Vanessa" (anon.), 1726; "The Intelligencer" (with Sheridan), 1729; "The Journal of a Modern Lady" (anon.), 1729; "Proposal for Preventing the Children of the Poor from Being a Burthen, etc." (anon.), 1730; "The Presbyterians' plea . . . examined" (anon.), 1731; "The Advantages proposed by repealing the Sacramental Test, etc.," 1732; "On Poetry" (anon.), 1733; "Scheme for a Hospital for Incurables" (anon.), 1733; "Poems on Several Occasions," 1734; "Proposals for erecting a Protestant Nunnery in the City of Dublin" (anon.), 1736; "The Beast's Confession to the Priest," 1738; "Complete Collection of Genteel and Ingenious Conversation" (under pseud. "Simon, Wagstaff"), 1738; "An Imitation of the Sixth Satire of the Second Book of Horace," 1738; "Verses on the Death of Dr. Swift, written by himself," 1739; "Some Free Thoughts upon the Present State of Affairs" (anon.,) 1741; "Literary Correspondence," 1741; "Three Sermons," 1744; "The Difficulty of Knowing One's Self," 1745. [Also a number of small controversial tracts, anonymous ballads printed on single sheets, etc.] *Posthumous:* "Brotherly Love," 1754; "History of the Four Last Years of the Queen," 1758; "Letters" (3 vols.), 1767; "Letters" (6 vols.), 1761-69; "Sermons" [1790?]. He *edited* Sir W. Temple's Letters, 1700; Sir W. Temple's Works, 1720; Arbuthnot and Pope's "Miscellaneous Works," 1742. *Collected Works:* ed. by Sir Walter Scott (19 vols.), 1814. *Life:* by H. Craik, 1882; by J. Churton Collins, 1895.—SHARP, R. FARQUHARSON, 1897, *A Dictionary of English Authors, p.* 272.

JONATHAN SWIFT

Engraving by W. H. Lizars. From Painting by J. Burgess. Original Picture by Bindon in the Deanery House of St. Patricks, Dublin.

PERSONAL

Hic depositum est corpus
JONATHAN SWIFT, S. T. D.
Hujus Ecclesiæ Cathedralis
Decani
Ubi sæva indignatio
Ulterius
Cor lascerare nequit.
Abi Viator
Et imitare, si potesis,
Strenuum pro virili
Libertatis vindictatorem.
Obiit 19° die mensis Octobris,
A. D. 1745. Anno Ætatis 78.
—SWIFT, JONATHAN, *Epitaph, St. Patrick's Cathedral, Dublin.*

Hee has latine and greek, some french, writes a very good and current hand, is very honest and diligent.—TEMPLE, SIR WILLIAM, 1690, *Letter to Sir Robert Southwell, May* 29.

Now, I know a learned man at this time, an orator in the Latin, a walking Index of books, who has all the libraries in Europe in his head, from the Vatican at Rome to the learned collection of Doctor Salmon at Fleet Ditch; but he is a cynic in behaviour, a fury in temper, unpolite in conversation, abusive in language, and ungovernable in passion. Is this to be learned? Then may I still be illiterate. —DEFOE, DANIEL, 1704–13, *The Review.*

Swift came into the coffee-house, and had a bow from everybody but me. When I came to the antechamber to wait before prayers Dr. Swift was the principal man of talk and business, and acted as Minister of Requests. He was soliciting the Earl of Arran to speak to his brother, the Duke of Ormond, to get a chaplain's place established in the garrison of Hull for Mr. Fiddes, a clergyman in that neighbourhood, who had lately been in jail, and published sermons to pay fees. He was promising Mr. Thorold to undertake with my Lord Treasurer that according to his petition he should obtain a salary of 200*l* per annum, as minister of the English Church at Rotterdam. He stopped F. Gwynne, Esq., going in with the red bag to the Queen, and told him aloud he had something to say to him from my Lord Treasurer. He talked with the son of Dr. Davenant to be sent abroad, and took out his pocket-book and wrote down several things as *memoranda* to do for him. He turned to the fire, and took out his gold watch, and telling him the time of day, complained it was very late. A gentleman said, "it was too fast." "How can I help it," says the Doctor, "if the courtiers give me a watch that won't go right?" Then he instructed a young nobleman that the best poet in England was Mr. Pope (a Papist), who had begun a translation of Homer into English verse for which, he said, he must have them all subscribe. "For," says he, "the author *shall not* begin to print till I *have* a thousand guineas for him." Lord Treasurer, after leaving the Queen, came through the room, beckoning Dr. Swift to follow him; both went off just before prayers.—KENNETT, WHITE, BISHOP OF PETERBOROUGH, 1713, *Diary.*

I could never impute your silence to want of friendship in one whose goodness to me has always been abundantly more than I could deserve. And I do assure you, from the bottom of my heart, there is not a person living I have a greater friendship for than yourself, and shall have to the end of my life.—MASHAM, LADY, 1723, *Letter to Swift.*

Dr. Swift has an odd blunt way, that is mistaken, by strangers, for ill-nature.—'Tis so odd that there's no describing it but by facts.—I'll tell you one that just comes into my head. One evening Gay and I went to see him: you know how intimately we were all acquainted. On our coming in; "Hey-day, gentlemen," says the Doctor, "what's the meaning of this visit? How come you to leave all the great lords, that you are so fond of, to come hither to see a poor Dean?"—Because we would rather see you than any of them.—"Ay, any one that did not know you so well as I do, might believe you. But, since you are come, I must get some supper for you, I suppose?"—No, Doctor, we have supped already.—"Supped already! that's impossible: why, 'tis not eight o'clock yet."—Indeed we have.—"That's very strange: but if you had not supped, I must have got something for you.—Let me see, what should I have had? a couple of lobsters? ay, that would have done very well;—two shillings: tarts; a shilling. But you will drink a glass of wine with me, though you supped so much before your usual time, only to spare my pocket?"—No, we had rather talk with you, than drink with you.—"But if you had supped with me, as in all reason you ought to have done, you must have drank with me.—A bottle of wine; two shillings.—Two and two, is four; and one is five: just two and sixpence a piece. There, Pope, there's half-acrown for you; and there's another for you, sir: for I won't save anything by you I am determined." This was all said and done with his usual seriousness on such occasions; and in spite of everything we could say to the contrary, he actually obliged us to take the money.—POPE, ALEXANDER, 1728-30, *Spence's Anecdotes, ed. Singer, p.* 15.

Violent party-men, who differed in all things besides, agreed in their turn to show particular respect and friendship to this insolent derider of the worship of his country, till at last the reputed writer is not only gone off with impunity, but triumphs in his dignity and preferment.—BLACKMORE, SIR RICHARD, 1716, *Essays, vol.* I, *p.* 217.

The day before we came out of town we dined at Doctor Delany's, and met the usual company. The Dean of St. Patrick's was there *in very good humour;* he calls himself "*my master,*" and corrects me when I speak bad English or do not pronounce my words distinctly. I wish he lived in England, I should not only have a great deal of entertainment from him, but improvement.—PENDARVES, MRS., 1733, *Life and Correspondence of Mrs. Delany, vol.* I, *p.* 407.

When people ask me how I governed Ireland, I say that I pleased Dr. Swift.—CARTERET, LORD, 1736-7, *Letter to Swift, March* 24.

Dean Swift has had a statute of lunacy taken out against him. His madness appears chiefly in most incessant strains of obscenity and swearing,—habits, to which the more sober parts of his life were not absolutely strangers, and of which his writings themselves have some tincture.—YORKE, CHARLES, 1742, *Letter to his Brother, June.*

He assumed more the air of a patron than of a friend. He affected rather to dictate than advise. . . . His hours of walking and reading never varied. His motions were guided by his watch, which was so constantly held in his hand, or placed before him on his table that he seldom deviated many minutes in the daily revolution of his exercises and employments.—BOYLE, JOHN (LORD ORRERY), 1751-53, *Remarks on the Life and Writings of Dr. Jonathan Swift, pp.* 29, 44.

My lord when you consider Swift's singular, peculiar, and most variegated vein of wit, always rightly intended (although not always so rightly directed), delightful in many instances, and salutary even where it is most offensive; when you consider his strict truth; his fortitude in resisting oppression and arbitrary power; his fidelity in friendship; his sincere love and zeal for religion; his uprightness in making right resolutions, and his steadiness in adhering to them; . . . his invincible patriotism, even to a country which he did not love; his very various, well-devised, well-judged, and extensive charities throughout his life, and his whole fortune (to say nothing of his wife's) conveyed to the same Christian purposes. . . . To conclude. No man ever deserved better of his country than Swift did of his. A steady, persevering, inflexible friend; a wise, a watchful, and a faithful counsellor, under many severe trials and bitter persecutions, to the manifest hazards both of his liberty and fortune. He lived a blessing, he died a benefactor, and his name will ever live an honour, to Ireland.—DELANY, PATRICK, 1754, *Observations on Lord Orrery's Remarks on the Life and Writings of Dr. Jonathan Swift, p.* 291.

I know the Dean well, though I never was within-side of his house, because I could not flatter, cringe, or meanly humour the extravagances of any man. . . . I had him often to myself in his rides and walks, and have studied his soul when he little thought what I was about. As I lodged for a year within a few doors of him, I knew his time of going out to a minute, and generally nicked the opportunity. He was fond of company on these occasions, and glad to have any rational man to talk to; for whatever was the meaning of it, he rarely had any of his friends attending him at his exercises. . . . What gave me the easier access to him was my being tolerably well acquainted with our politics and history, and knowing many places, &c., of his beloved England. . . . We talked generally of factions and religion, states, revolutions, leaders and parties: sometimes we had other subjects. Who I was he never knew. Nor did I seem to know he was Dean for a long time, not till one Sunday evening that his verger put me into his seat at St. Patrick's prayers, without my knowing the Doctor sat there. . . . The Dean was proud beyond all other mortals that I have seen, and quite another man when he was known. —AMORY, THOMAS, 1755, *Memoirs of Several Ladies of Great Britain, Preface.*

He could not endure to be treated with any sort of familiarity, or that any man living, his three or four acquaintances with whom he corresponded to the last only excepted, should rank himself in the number of his friends.—SWIFT, DEANE, 1755, *An Essay upon the Life, Writings and Character of Dr. Jonathan Swift, p.* 361.

I remember as I and others were taking with him an evening walk, about a mile from Dublin, he stopped short; we passed on; but perceiving he did not follow us, I went back, and found him fixed as a statue, and earnestly gazing upward at a noble elm, which in its uppermost branches was much withered and decayed. Pointing at it, he said, "I shall be like that tree, and shall die at the top."—YOUNG, EDWARD, 1759, *Letter to Richardson.*

The person of Swift had not many recommendations. He had a kind of muddy complexion, which, though he washed himself with Oriental scrupulosity, did not look clear. He had a countenance sour and severe, which he seldom softened by any appearance of gaiety. He stubbornly resisted any tendency to laughter. . . . His beneficence was not graced with tenderness of civility; he relieved without pity, and assisted without kindness; so that those who were fed by him could hardly love him. . . . Of Swift's general habits of thinking, if his letters can be supposed to afford any evidence, he was not a man to be either loved or envied. He seems to have wasted life in discontent, by the rage of neglected pride, and the languishment of unsatisfied desire. He is querulous and fastidious, arrogant and malignant; he scarcely speaks of himself but with indignant lamentations, or of others but with insolent superiority when he is gay, and with angry contempt when he is gloomy.—JOHNSON, SAMUEL, 1779–81, *Jonathan Swift, Lives of the English Poets.*

Swift was a wild-beast, who worried and baited and worried all mankind almost, because his intolerable arrogance, vanity, pride, and ambition were disappointed.—WALPOLE, HORACE, 1780, *To Sir Horace Mann, Letters, ed. Cunningham, vol.* VII, *p.* 311.

Though the greatness of Swift's talents was known to many in private life, and his company and conversation much sought after and admired, yet was his name hitherto little known in the republic letters. The only pieces which he had then published, were "The Battle of the Books," and "The Contests and Dissentions in Athens and Rome," and both without a name. Nor was he personally known to any of the wits of the age, excepting Mr. Congreve, and one or two more, with whom he had contracted an acquaintance at Sir William Temple's. The knot of wits used at this time to assemble at Button's coffee-house: and I had a singular account of Swift's first appearance there from Ambrose Philips, who was one of Mr. Addison's little senate. He said that they had for several successive days observed a strange clergyman come into the coffeehouse, who seemed utterly unacquainted with any of those who frequented it; and whose custom it was to lay his hat down on a table, and walk backward and forward at a good pace for half an hour or an hour, without speaking to any mortal, or seeming in the least to attend to anything that was going forward there. He then used to take up his hat, pay his money at the bar, and walk away without opening his lips. After having observed this singular behaviour for some time, they concluded him to be out of his senses; and the name that he went by among them, was that of "the mad parson." This made them more than usually attentive to his motions; and one evening, as Mr. Addison and the rest were observing him, they saw him cast his eyes several times on a gentleman in boots, who seemed to be just come out of the country, and at last advanced towards him as intending to address him. They were all eager to hear what this dumb mad parson had to say, and immediately quitted their seats to get near him. Swift went up to the country gentleman, and in a very abrupt manner, without any previous salute, asked him, "Pray, sir, do you remember any good weather in the world?" The country gentleman, after staring a little at the singularity of his manner, and the oddity of the question, answered, "Yes, sir, I thank God I remember a great deal of good weather in my time."—"That is more," said Swift, "than I can say; I never remember any weather that was not too hot, or too cold; too wet or too dry; but however God Almighty contrives it, at the end of the year 'tis all very well." Upon saying this, he took up his hat, and without uttering a syllable more, or taking the least notice of any one, walked out of the coffeehouse; leaving all those who had been spectators of this odd scene staring after him, and still more confirmed in the opinion of his being mad.—SHERIDAN, THOMAS, 1784, *Life of Dean Swift.*

There remains a conjecture which can only be intimated, but which, if correct, will explain much of Swift's peculiar conduct in his intercourse with the female sex. During that period of life when the passions are most violent, Swift boasts of his "cold temper." Since that time, the continual recurrence of a distressing vertigo was gradually undermining his health. It seems, in these circumstances, probable, that the continence which he observed, may have been owing to physical, as well as moral causes. Were such the case, he might seek the society of Vanessa, without the apprehension of exciting passions, to which he was himself insensible; and his separation from Stella, after marriage, might be a matter equally of choice, or of necessity. This much, at least, is certain, that if, according to a saying which Swift highly approved, desire produces love in man, we cannot find any one line in Swift's writings or correspondence, intimating his having felt such a source of passion; nor indeed is there a single anecdote of his life recorded, which indicates his having submitted to what he irreverently terms "that ridiculous passion which has no being but in playbooks or romances." In youth he sought female society merely as a relaxation from unpleasant thoughts. . . . Swift was in person tall, strong and well made, of a dark complexion, but with blue eyes, black and bushy eyebrows, nose somewhat aquiline, and features which remarkably expressed the stern, haughty, and dauntless turn of his mind. He was never known to laugh, and his smiles are happily characterized by the well-known lines of Shakspeare. Indeed, the whole description of Cassius might be applied to Swift:

> He reads much,
> He is a great observer, and he looks
> Quite through the deeds of men.—
> Seldom he smiles, and smiles in such a sort,
> As if he mock'd himself, and scorned his spirit
> That could be moved to smile at anything.

. . . .

His manners in society were, in his better days, free, lively, and engaging, not devoid of peculiarities, but bending them so well to circumstances, that his company was universally courted. When age and infirmity had impaired the elasticity of his spirits and the equality of his temper his conversation was still valued, not only on account of the extended and various acquaintance with life and manners, of which it displayed an inexhaustible fund, but also for the shrewd and satirical humour which seasoned his observations and anecdotes.—SCOTT, SIR WALTER, 1814, *Memoirs of Jonathan Swift.*

His character seems to have been radically overbearing and tyrannical;—for though, like other tyrants, he could stoop low enough where his interests required it, it was his delight to exact an implicit compliance with his humours and fancies, and to impose upon all around him the task of observing and accommodating themselves to his habits, without the slightest regard to their convenience or comfort. . . . Born almost a beggar, and neither very industrious nor very engaging in his early habits, he attained, almost with his first efforts, the very height of distinction, and was awarded by appointments, which placed him in a state of independence and respectability for life. He was honoured with the acquaintance of all that was distinguished for rank, literature, or reputation;—and, if not very generally beloved, was, what he probably valued far more, admired and feared by most of those with whom he was acquainted. When his party was overthrown, neither his person nor his fortune suffered;—but he was indulged, through the whole of his life, in a licence of scurrility and abuse, which has never been permitted to any other writer,—and possessed the exclusive and devoted affection of the only two women to whom he wished to appear interesting. In this *history*, we confess we see but little apology for discontent and lamentation;—and in his *conduct*, there is assuredly still less for misanthropy.—JEFFREY, FRANCIS LORD, 1816, *The Works of Jonathan Swift, Edinburgh Review, vol.* 27, *pp.* 24, 43.

He moves laughter, but never joins in it. He appears in his works such as he appeared in society. All the company are convulsed with merriment, while the dean, the author of all the mirth; preserves an invincible gravity, and even sourness of aspect; and gives utterance to the most eccentric and ludicrous fancies, with the air of a man reading the commination-service.—MACAULAY, THOMAS BABINGTON, 1843, *Life and Writings of Addison, Edinburgh Review; Critical and Miscellaneous Essays.*

The disease under which he laboured so long, and which we have ventured to term "cerebral congestion," might, from the symptoms, be styled by some pathologists "epileptic vertigo," such as that described by Esquirol—an affection to which, it is well known, many men of strong intellect have been subject. For the last few years of his embittered existence, from his seventy-fifth to his seventy-eight year, his disease partook so much of the nature of senile decay, or the *dementia* of old age, that it is difficult, with the materials now at command, to define by any precise medical term his actual state.—WILDE, SIR WILLIAM R., 1845, *On the Closing Years of Swift's Life.*

From Laracor, Swift's remove was to Dublin, where he spent the remainder of his life. Here the deanery has been quite removed, and a modern house occupies its place. The old Cathedral of St. Patrick is a great object connected with his memory here. Though wearing a very ancient look, St. Patrick's was rebuilt after its destruction in 1362, and its present spire was added only in 1750. In size and proportion the cathedral is fine. It is three hundred feet long, and eighty broad. It can not boast much of its architecture, but contains several monuments of distinguished men; among them, those of Swift and Curran. These two are busts. Aloft in the nave hang the banners of the Knights of St. Patrick; and again, in the choir, hang newly-emblazoned banners of the knights; and over the stalls which belong to the knights are fixed gilt helmets, and by each stall hangs the knight's sword. The whole fabric is now undergoing repair, and not before it was needed. Of course, the monuments of highest interest here are those of Swift and Stella. These occupy two contiguous pillars on the south side of the nave. They consist of two plain slabs of marble, in memory of the dean and Mrs. Johnson—Stella. The inscription on the dean's slab is expressive "of that habit of mind which his own disappointments and the oppressions of his country had produced." It was written by himself.—HOWITT, WILLIAM, 1846, *Homes and Haunts of the Most Eminent British Poets, vol.* I, *p.* 230.

Would you have liked to be a friend of the great Dean? . . . If you had been his inferior in parts (and that, with a great respect for all persons present, I fear is only very likely), his equal in mere social station, he would have bullied, scorned, and insulted you; if, undeterred by his great reputation, you had met him like a man, he would have quailed before you, and not had the pluck to reply, and gone home, and years after written a foul epigram about you—watched for you in a sewer, and come out to assail you with a coward's blow and a dirty bludgeon. If you had been a lord with a blue riband, who flattered his vanity, or could help his ambition, he would have been the most delightful company in the world. He would have been so manly, so sarcastic, so bright, odd, and original, that you might think he had no object in view but the indulgence of his humour, and that he was the most reckless, simple creature in the world. How he would have torn your enemies to pieces for you! and made fun of the opposition! His servility was so boisterous that it looked like independence; he would have done your errands, but with the air of patronizing you, and after fighting your battles masked in the street or the press, would have kept on his hat before your wife and daughters in the drawing-room, content to take that sort of pay for his tremendous services as a bravo.—THACKERAY, WILLIAM MAKEPEACE, 1853, *The English Humourists of the Eighteenth Century.*

He was born in Ireland, but would have thought himself insulted if he had been called an Irishman. . . . Was at heart the haughtiest, the most aspiring, the most vindictive, the most despotic of men.—MACAULAY, THOMAS BABINGTON, 1855, *History of England, ch.* xix.

That eccentric and scarcely intelligible man, whose conduct even when kind always differed from that of others in the mode of displaying it.—PRIOR, SIR JAMES, 1860, *Life of Edmond Malone, Editor of Shakespeare, p.* 118.

A man strangely compounded of contrary extremes, uniting many natures within his own. . . . A strenuous and even merciless defender of the Church as by law established, he sometimes brought discredit upon his profession, and upon the institution he so much revered, by the freedom of his behaviour and the recklessness of his wit. A vehement lover of liberty, he was guilty of no compassion for hostile scribblers, whose arrest and punishment he often urged on the Tory leaders; while he constantly inveighed against any relaxation of the disabilities that shut out Dissenters from offices under the Crown. A friend to the principles of the Revolution in the State, he cleaved to the principles of the reaction in the Church; Somers was his friend, while Sacheverell seemed his exemplar. A man of piquant and at times charming manner, of social sensibilities, enjoying company, tolerant of foibles, he was nevertheless a stern censor and an unsparing censurer of the race, which he hated and contemned. A despiser of mankind, incessantly aflame with rage against the cruelties of the dominant and the cowardice of the subject, he was full of good works, such as only the truest and largest benevolence could dictate. A student of economy, parsimonious to a fault in private affairs, in philanthropic and literary relations he was a very Mæcenas for his generous munificence; and many men owed their fortune to one who neither sued nor intrigued for himself. An ardent admirer and tender friend of not a few women, he disappointed the love of two who were deeply and fatally devoted to him, and heartily despised the sex. A marvel of cold purity in his personal life, in his poems and satires he rushed repeatedly into grossness and downright filthiness worthy only of a man who had passed the stage in vice at which sexual pleasures cease to give the desired satisfaction to the appetites. A coward in many trivial matters of daily incident—dreading smallpox and other such mischances of our civilisation—in his public life he was fearless, when freedom of speech brought him face to face with an enraged and tyrannical law. . . . A lover of anonymity, a courtier of obscurity, a despiser of pretence, a hater of show, his genius made him the familiar of Princes, the friend and counsellor of Ministers, the pride of a whole country, the peculiar trust and boast of the poor within its borders. In two things alone was he throughout consistent: in the thorough and even offensive personal independence, into which the unhappy experience of his youth but too harshly trained him; and in the unextinguishable love of liberty, the incorruptible patriotism, that guided his political career from the first to the last. —PURVES, D. LAING, 1868, *The Works of Jonathan Swift, Life, pp.* 38, 39.

When one thinks of the man, the sermons of Dean Swift, although in themselves excellent, seem to be a mockery, and we can fancy them written by the author of a "Tale of a Tub" with a grin of derision on his face.—FORSYTH, WILLIAM, 1871, *The Novels and Novelists of the Eighteenth Century, p.* 22.

He seemed to look upon himself as a superior being, exempt from the necessity of ceremony, entitled to homage, caring neither for sex, rank, nor fame, whose business is to protect and destroy, distributing favours, insults, and pardons. . . . If ever a soul was saturated with the joy of tearing, outraging, and destroying, it was his. Excess of scorn, implacable irony, crushing logic, the cruel smile of the foeman, who sees beforehand the mortal spot in which he will strike his enemy, advances towards him, tortures him deliberately, eagerly, with enjoyment, —such were the feelings which had leavened him, and which broke from him with such harshness that he hindered his own career; and that of so many high places for which he stretched out his hands, there remained for him only a deanery in poor Ireland.—TAINE, H. A., 1871, *History of English Literature, tr. Van Laun, vol.* II, *bk.* iii, *ch.* v, *pp.* 118, 121.

The portrait of him now painted by Jervas confirms the general statement at the time, that his personal appearance was very attractive. Features regular yet striking, forehead high and temples broad and massive, heavy-lidded blue eyes, to which his dark complexion and bushy black eyebrows gave unusual capacity for sternness as well as brilliance, a nose slightly aquiline, mouth resolute with full-closed lips, a handsome dimpled double chin, and over all the face the kind of pride not grown of superciliousness or scorn, but of an easy, confident, calm superiority. Of the dullness which Pope saw sometimes overshadow the countenance of his friend, of the insolence which Young declares was habitual to it, of the harsh, unrelenting severity which it assumes in Bindon's picture at the deanery, there is no trace at present. By one who loved him he was said to have a look of uncommon archness in eyes quite azure as the heavens; and he was himself told by one who did not love him less, that he had a look so awful it struck the gazer dumb; but only the first is in Jervas's picture, the years that are to bring the last being still to come.—FORSTER, JOHN, 1875, *The Life of Jonathan Swift, vol.* I, *p.* 240.

Jonathan Swift remains what he was a century ago, the sphinx of English literature. Prominent, in his own line, as probably no other author ever was before; the observed of all, as the bosom friend of the leading wits and statesmen of the most classic modern age; the most illustrious polemic that the modern world has ever seen, he yet stands to this day, the greatest mystery among distinguished men of letters. Even the secret of Junius, yields, in importance and interest, to that which attaches to the name of the Dean of St. Patrick's. Gifted with the capacity to entrance the intellect of men, and inthrall the passions of women, he seems to have been at home in ridiculing the former, and bringing down the love of the latter to despair. Who, on regarding the portrait of him left by Jervas, which exhibits a noble and placid expanse of brow, serene eyes, and a mouth not noticeable for its bitterness or agitation, could imagine that one of the most restless spirits which ever inhabited a human breast found lodgment there?—SMITH, GEORGE BARNETT, 1876, *Dean Swift, The International Review, vol.* 3, *p.* 306.

We confess to a kindness for Swift. We are not blind to his faults, but to our thinking they are amply redeemed by two valuable traits in his character—namely, the courage he had of his opinions, and the unswerving honesty with which he clung to them. In those characteristics we may perhaps find the clue to the hitherto apparent cruelty with which Swift dwelt with the affections of two such lovable women as Esther Johnson, otherwise Stella, and Esther Vanhomrigh, *alias* Vanessa. . . . Henceforth Swift's life is like that serenade which Don Juan, disguised, sings under a balcony, a melancholy and piteous song, breathing sorrow, distress, misjudged love, but the accompaniment to which is lively, strident, staccato; still the song struggles on, wailing, making itself heard above the false instrument, whose mocking tones want to turn it into derision, and seems to jeer at being obliged to go so slowly and mournfully. Nay, in a measure Swift becomes Don Juan himself, with whom the marble statue, just returned from the graves of Vanessa and Stella, sits down to supper. The Dean remains calm, collected, for some time, but the statue asks his hand; and when with an assumed indifference he has given it, the man is seized with a mortal chill, and falls into convulsions. They get more frequent, and at last send him raving mad, the intervals of frenzy leaving him a mere pitiable idiot. He is like the man who boasted of being inaccessible to superstitious fear, and dreading nothing. One night his friends placed a skeleton in his bed, then went into an adjacent apartment to watch the effect. They heard nothing; but the following morning, when they entered the room, they found him seated playing with the bones. He had lost his reason. Swift had been insensible to all the softer feelings. Memory placed their skeleton in his bed, he played with the bones for more than three years, unconscious of what passed around him. Upon the 19th of October, 1745, God mercifully removed the terrible spectacle, and released the sufferer from his misery, degradation, and shame.—VANDAN, ALBERT D., 1878, *Amours of Great Men, vol.* II, *pp.* 94, 159.

Here was a man endued with an intellect pellucid as well as brilliant; who could not only conceive but see also—with some fine instincts too; whom fortune did not flout; whom circumstances fairly served; but who, from first to last, was miserable himself, who made others miserable, and who deserved misery. . . . He was a man whose mind was never fixed on high things, but was striving always after something which, little as it might be, and successful as he was, should always be out of his reach. It had been his misfortune to become a clergyman, because the way to church preferment seemed to be the readiest. He became, as we all know, a dean—but never a bishop, and was therefore wretched.—TROLLOPE, ANTHONY, 1879, *Thackeray* (*English Men of Letters*), *pp.* 155, 156.

However Jonathan Swift's biographers may explain or apologize for him, I have never yet seen a woman who did not feel for his character both contempt and detestation. A man who could deliberately and for years outrage the feelings and lacerate the hearts of two women whose worse weakness was in the fact that they devotedly loved him, can be looked at in no amiable light by any woman with any chivalry for her sex.—RICHARDSON, ABBY SAGE, 1882, *ed. Old Love Letters*, *p.* 36.

No man had stronger affections than Swift; no man suffered more agony when they were wounded; but in his agony he would commit what to most men would seem the treason of cursing the affections instead of simply lamenting the injury, or holding the affection itself to be its own sufficient reward. The intense personality of the man reveals itself alternately as selfishness and as "altruism." He grappled to his heart those whom he really loved "as with hoops of steel;" so firmly that they became a part of himself; and that he considered himself at liberty to regard his love of friends as he might regard a love of wine, as something to be regretted when it was too strong for his own happiness. The attraction was intense, but implied the absorption of the weaker nature into his own. His friend ships were rather annexations than alliances. . . . Swift showed a complete absence of the ordinary touchiness of authors. His indifference to literary fame as to its pecuniary rewards was conspicuous. He was too proud, as he truly said, to be vain. His sense of dignity restrained him from petty sensibility. When a clergyman regretted some emendations which had been hastily suggested by himself and accepted by Swift, Swift replied that it mattered little, and that he would not give grounds, by adhering to his own opinion, for an imputation of vanity. If Swift was egotistical. there was nothing petty even in his egotism.—STEPHEN, LESLIE, 1882, *Swift* (*English Men of Letters*), *pp.* 31, 58.

The last indignity was reserved for our own century and for philosophers in the Flying Island of the British Association. In 1835, in making alterations under the aisle of St. Patrick's Cathedral, the coffins of Swift and Stella were found side by side. The British Association was holding its meeting in Dublin, and, as the genius of irony would have it, phrenology was then the fashion. Doubtless with the permission of Swift's successor at that day in the deanery of the Cathedral, two dainty toys were provided for the perambulating professors and their fair entertainers. The skulls of Swift and of Esther Johnson went the rounds of the drawing-rooms; they were patted and poised and peeped at; pretty, sentimental speeches and ponderous scientific phrases flew to right and left; here hung "only a woman's hair," and there the condyloid processes projected into the foramen magnum of the occipital bone. The bumps of veneration and amativeness were measured, and it was ascertained that wit was small. Drawings and casts were made. Finally when all the pretty speeches had run dry; and the spectacles were all taken off, and wisdom had departed from the land, the desecrated bones were restored to darkness, to be once more discovered within a few days past, but not again to have their nakedness exposed to the gaping inhabitants of Laputa.—DOWDEN, EDWARD, 1882, *Literature, The Academy, vol.* 22, *p.* 233.

Thou sawest from far the curse thou might'st not stay,
Most mighty spirit, strong to love and hate.
For what great sin, sinned in some former state,
Was thy soul forced to contemplate that day
Which should not at one blow take life away,
But on each vital sense shut gate by gate,
Until thy lord's unfathomable hate,
Supreme, relentless, and which none gainsay,
Left thy great brain confounded in black night,
And wild with pain?

—MARSTON, PHILIP BOURKE, 1883, *Jonathan Swift, Wind-Voices.*

"Cadenus."—"Mr. Dean."—"The English Rabelais."—"This Impious Buffoon."—"Presto."—"The Rabelais of Good

Society."—FREY, ALBERT R., 1888, *Sobriquet and Nicknames, p.* 469.

If Jonathan Swift had entered the room while the Lecture upon him was going forward, he would have eaten William Makepeace Goliath, white waistcoat and all.—QUILLER-COUCH, A. T., 1891, *Adventures in Criticism, p.* 95.

No one who is acquainted with the character of Swift, with his character as it appears in his own writings, as it has been illustrated in innumerable anecdotes, and as it has been delineated by those who were familiar with him, can fail to see that he belonged to the kings of humankind. Like Innocent III, and like Chatham, he was one of those men to whom the world pays instinctive homage. Everything about him indicated superiority. His will was a will of adamant; his intellect was an intellect the power and keenness of which impressed or awed every one who approached him. And to that will and to that intellect was joined a temper singularly stern, daunltess, and haughty. . . . Into a particular account of Swift's last years it would be almost agony to enter. Nothing in the recorded history of humanity, nothing that the imagination of man has conceived, can transcend in horror and pathos the accounts which have come down to us of the closing scenes of his life. His memory was gone, his reason was gone; he recognised no friend; he was below his own Struldbrugs. Day after day he paced his chamber, as a wild beast paces its cage, taking his food as he walked, but refusing to touch it as long as any one remained in the room. During the autumn of 1742 his state was horrible and pitiable beyond expression. At last, after suffering unspeakable tortures from one of the most agonising maladies known to surgery, he sank into the torpor of imbecility. By the mercy of Providence it generally happens that man so degraded is unconscious of his degradation. But this mercy was withheld from Swift. On one occasion he was found gazing at his image in a pier-glass and muttering piteously over and over again, "Poor old man!" On another he exclaimed, frequenlty repeating it, "I am what I am." "He never talked nonsense," says Deane Swift, "nor said a foolish thing." In this deplorable condition he continued for two years, and then maintained unbroken silence till death released him from calamity.—COLLINS, JOHN CHURTON, 1893, *Jonathan Swift, pp.* 70, 235.

It was, no doubt, a case of what you call fatuity, and what doctors call dementia—that is, loss of mental power. There was no delusion, so far as I remember; but there was this peculiarity—the inability to find words for the expression of the poor remains of thought, although phrases did now and then find utterance under unwonted stimulus. It was, in fact, a case of aphasia with dementia, leading to the expectation that, if one could have seen the brain, a clot, or the effects or remains of a clot, would have been found on or about the third frontal convolution. . . . *A.* There is sufficient evidence to render a correct diagnosis of Swift's mental disease possible. *B.* There are records of numerous cases in which the phenomena are parallel. *C.* It is not physically possible that Swift's fatuity at 75 originated from a surfeit of green fruit when he was 23. *D.* The sane part of Swift's life was not likely to have been affected by the latent presence of the insanity.—BUCKNILL, DR., 1893, *Letter in Collin's Life of Swift, Appendix, p.* 270.

A dim light was burning in the back room of a first-floor in Bury Street, St. James's. The apartment it illumined was not a spacious one; and the furniture, adequate rather than luxurious, had that indefinable lack of physiognomy which only lodging-house furniture seems to acquire. There was no fireplace; but in the adjoining parlour, partly visible through the open door, the last embers were dying in a grate from which the larger pieces of coal had been lifted away, and carefully ranged in order on the hobs. Across the heavy high-backed chairs in the bedroom lay various neatly-folded garments, one of which was the black gown with pudding sleeves usually worn in public by the eighteenth-century clergyman, while at the bottom of the bed hung a clerical-looking periwig In the bed itself, and leaning towards a tall wax candle at his side (which, from a faint smell of burnt woollen still lingering about the chamber, must have recently come into contact with the now tucked-back bed-curtain), was a gentleman of forty or thereabouts, writing in a very small hand upon a very large sheet of paper, folded, for greater convenience, into one long horizontal slip. He had dark, fierce-looking eyebrows, a slightly aquiline nose, full-lidded and rather prominent clear eyes, a firmly-cut handsome mouth, and a wide, massive forehead, the extent of which, for the moment, was abnormally exaggerated by the fact that, in the energy of composition, the fur-lined cap he had substituted for his wig had been slightly tilted backwards. As his task proceeded his expression altered from time to time, now growing grave and stern, now inexpressibly soft and tender. Occasionally, the look almost passed into kind of a grimace, resembling nothing so much as the imitative motion of the lips which one makes in speaking to a pet bird. He continued writing until, in the distance, the step of the watch-man, first pausing deliberately, then passing slowly forward for a few paces, was heard in the street below. "Past twelve o'clock!" came a wheezy cry at the window. "*Paaaaast twelvvve o'clock*" followed the writer, dragging out his letters so as to reproduce the speaker's drawl. . . . The personage thus depicted was Jonathan Swift, Doctor of Divinity, vicar of Laracor by Trim, in the diocese of Meath in the kingdom of Ireland, and Prebendary of Dunlavin in St. Patrick's Cathedral.—DOBSON, AUSTIN, 1893, *The Journal to Stella, Longman's Magazine, vol.* 22, *pp.* 30, 31.

Gradually my eyes became accustomed to the subdued light, and right at my feet I saw a large brass plate set in the floor and on it only this:

SWIFT
Died Oct. 19, 1745
Aged 78

On the wall near is a bronze tablet, the inscription of which, in Latin, was dictated by Swift himself: "Here lies the body of Jonathan Swift, Dean of this Cathedral, where fierce indignation can no longer rend his heart. Go! wayfarer, and imitate, if thou canst, one who, as far as in him lay, was an earnest champion of liberty —" Above this is a fine bust of the Dean and to the right is another tablet: "Underneath lie interred the mortal remains of Mrs. Hester Johnson, better known in the world as Stella, under which she is celebrated in the writings of Dr. Jonathan Swift, Dean of this Cathedral. She was a person of extraordinary endowments and accomplishments, in body, mind, and behavior; justly admired and respected by all who knew her on account of her eminent virtues as well as for her great natural and acquired perfections." . . . In 1835 the graves were opened and casts taken of the skulls. The top of Swift's skull had been sawed off at the autopsy, and a bottle in which was a parchment setting forth the facts was inserted in the head that had conceived "Gulliver's Travels." I examined the casts. The woman's head is square and shapely. Swift's head is a refutation of phrenology, being small, sloping, and ordinary. The bones of Swift and Stella were placed in one coffin and now rest under three feet of concrete, beneath the floor of St. Patrick's.—HUBBARD, ELBERT, 1895, *Little Journeys, pp.* 163, 166.

He was a man, I think, who would have infinitely scorned and revolted at many of the apologies that have been made for him. . . . And in that great Court of Justice—which I am old-fashioned enough to believe will one day be held—where juries will not be packed, and where truth will shine, by its own light, withstanding all perversion—and where opportunities and accomplishments will be weighed in even scales against possible hindrances of moral or of physical makeup—there will show, I am inclined to think, in the strange individuality of Swift, a glimmer of some finer and higher traits of character than we are accustomed to assign him.—MITCHELL, DONALD G., 1895, *English Lands Letters and Kings; From Elizabeth to Anne, p.* 339.

He was a profoundly sensitive man, yet he was also matter-of-fact. His honest recognition of things as they were was mitigated by no intervening haze of romance, and no spiritual revelation of distant hopes. . . . His was not a temperament to manufacture ideals; and the times had no ideals to offer. What wonder if fierce wrath filled his great, sad soul; if the worlds of politics, of society, of the great mass of men, seemed to him equally contemptible and pitiful. . . . The social sarcasm of Swift is unequaled in fervor of ironic power, but is also alone among the chief satires of England in the bitterness of its tone. The terrible epitaph which, by his own command, was placed over his tomb speaks of the only peace possible to him.—SCUDDER, VIDA D., 1898, *Social Ideals in English Letters, p.* 97.

Probably no prominent character has been more cruelly misjudged. Popular opinion has been guided by the superficial sketches of Macaulay, Thackeray, and Taine, and has not stopped to consider that a brilliant presentment is not necessar'ly an historical portrait. One has only to study Swift's letters to realize how utterly mistaken is the common view. To estimate him merely by his satires and political writings is to measure a brain and leave out body and soul. In his literary works he is all intellect—cold, even cruel intellect—and the milk of human kindness is turned sour. It is no wonder that the author of "A Tale of a Tub" and "Gulliver's Travels" has acquired the reputation of the bitterest cynic and misanthrope in all literature. It is the merit and virtue of the letters that they reveal the heart of one who in his public writings is mere head.—POOLE, STANLEY LANE —, 1898, *Eighteenth Century Letters, ed. Johnson, Introduction, p.* ix.

The two, like so many others coupled in history, were in truth of opposed temperaments. Prior was vain, Swift proud; Swift uncompromising, Prior accommodating; Prior fanciful, Swift imaginative. Swift was the same electric force whether business or pleasure engaged him. Prior was solemn ("Dutch," De Torcy afterwards termed him) in routine, madcap—indeed reckless—over his cups. Outward appearance heightened the contrast. Swift was of middle height, inclined to be stout, darkly sanguine in complexion, with arch eyes of a piercing blue. He walked "like lightning" to be lean. Prior was tall and thin, lantern-jawed and cavernous. His eyes were dreamy, though his expression was alert. His visage seemed carved out of wood, and he coughed much as he went. He walked to be fat. Swift was a stoic aflame; Prior, an epicurean with dashed ambitions. In Swift's heart of hearts hid Stella, and already lurked Vanessa; in Prior's, Mrs. Anne Durham and the marionettes of vulgar intrigue whom he dignified as "Chloes." Pangs tortured the one, while the other sighed sentiment. Both cried "Vive la bagatelle," but Prior's "bagatelle" was a bubble, Swift's a bullet. In four things, however, the comrades were united—in devotion to the Church interest, in detestation of democratic clamour, in the endowment of a signal style, and in personal admiration for Harley and St. John.—SICHEL, WALTER, 1901, *Bolingbroke and His Times, p.* 284.

STELLA.

This day, being Sunday, January 28, 1727–8, about eight o'clock at night, a servant brought me a note, with an account of the death of the truest, most virtuous, and valuable friend, that I, or perhaps any other person, was ever blessed with. She expired about six in the evening of this day; and as soon as I am left alone, which is about eleven at night, I resolve, for my own satisfaction, to say something of her life and character. . . . She was sickly from her childhood, until about the age of fifteen; but then grew into perfect health, and was looked upon as one of the most beautiful, graceful, and agreeable young women in London, only a little too fat. Her hair was blacker than a raven, and every feature of her face in perfection. . . . Never was any of her sex born with better gifts of the mind, or who more improved them by reading and conversation. Yet her memory was not of the best, and was impaired in the latter years of her life. But I cannot call to mind that I ever once heard her make a wrong judgment of persons, books, or affairs. Her advice was always the best, and with the greatest freedom, mixed with the greatest decency. She had a gracefulness, somewhat more than human, in every motion, word, and action. Never was so happy a conjunction of civility, freedom, easiness, and sincerity. There seemed to be a combination among all that knew her, to treat her with a dignity much beyond her rank; yet people of all sorts were never more easy than in her company. . . . All of us who had the happiness of her friendship agree unanimously, that, in an afternoon or evening's conversation, she never failed, before we parted, of delivering the best thing that was said in the company. Some of us have written down several of her sayings, or what the French call *bons mots*, wherein she excelled beyond belief. She never mistook the understanding of others; nor ever said a severe word, but where a much severer was deserved.—SWIFT,

JONATHAN, 1727–8, *The Character of Mrs. Johnson.*

Stella was the concealed but undoubted wife of Dr. Swift, and if my informations are right, she was married to him in the year 1716 by Dr. Ash, then Bishop of Clogher. . . . Stella was a most amiable woman both in mind and person: She had an elevated understanding, with all the delicacy, and softness of her own sex. Her voice, however sweet in itself, was still rendered more harmonious by what she said. Her wit was poignant without severity: Her manners were humane, polite, easy and unreserved.—Wherever she came, she attracted attention and esteem. As virtue was her guide in morality, sincerity was her guide in religion. She was constant, but not ostentatious in her devotions: She was remarkably prudent in her conversation; She had great skill in music; and was perfectly well versed in all the lesser arts that employ a lady's leisure. Her wit allowed her a fund of perpetual cheerfulness within proper limits. She exactly answered the description of Penelope in Homer.

"A woman, lovliest of the lovely kind,
In body perfect, and compleat in mind."

—BOYLE, JOHN (LORD ORRERY), 1751, *Remarks on the Life and Writings of Dr. Jonathan Swift.*

The general rule, I think, between him and Mrs. Johnson was this: when the Doctor was absent from home she lived at his house; but when he was at home she lodged either somewhere at Trim, or was resident at the house of Dr. Raymond, the vicar of Trim, a gentleman of great hospitality, a friend of Dr. Swift, a man of learning and fine address, with the advantage of a tall, handsome, and graceful person.—SWIFT, DEANE, 1755, *An Essay upon the Life, Writings and Character of Dr. Jonathan Swift, p.* 90.

I was informed by the relict of Bishop Berkeley that her husband had assured her of the truth of Swift's marriage, as the Bishop of Clogher, who had performed the ceremony, had himself communicated the circumstance to him.—BERKELEY, GEORGE MONCK, 1789, *Inquiry into the Life of Dean Swift, Literary Relics.*

Immediately subsequent to the ceremony Swift's state of mind appears to have been dreadful. Delany, (as I have learned from a friend of his relict), being pressed to give his opinion on this strange union, said, that about the time it took place, he observed Swift to be extremely gloomy and agitated; so much so that he went to Archbishop King to mention his apprehensions. On entering the library, Swift rushed out with a countenance of distraction, and passed him without speaking. He found the Archbishop in tears, and upon asking the reason, he said, "You have just met the most unhappy man on earth; but on the subject of his wretchedness you must never ask a question." Swift secluded himself from society for some days. When he reappeared, his intercourse with Stella and Mrs. Dingley was resumed, with the same guarded and cautious attention to prevent the slightest suspicion of a more intimate union with the former; as if such intimacy had not now been legal and virtuous. Stella, therefore, continued the beloved and intimate friend of Swift, the regulator of his household and table on public days, although she only appeared there as an ordinary guest; the companion of his social hours, and his comforter in sickness; but his wife only in name, and even that nominal union a secret from the world.—SCOTT, SIR WALTER, 1814, *Memoirs of Jonathan Swift.*

Notwithstanding Dr. Delany's sentiments of Swift's marriage, and notwithstanding all that Lord Orrery and others have said about it, there is no authority for it but a hearsay story, and that very ill-founded. It is certain that the Dean told one of his friends, whom he advised to marry, that he himself never wished to marry at the time he ought to have entered into that state; for he counted upon it as the happiest condition, especially towards the decline of life, when a faithful, tender friend, is most wanted. While he was talking to this effect, his friend expressed his wishes to have seen him married: the Dean asked why? "Because," replied the other, "I should have the pleasure of seeing your offspring; all the world would have been pleased to have seen the issue of such a genius." The Dean smiled, and denied his being married, in the same manner as before, and said he never saw the woman he wished to be married to. The same gentleman, who was intimate with Mrs. Dingley for ten years before she died, in 1743, took occasion to tell her that such a story was whispered of her friend Mrs. Johnson's marriage with the Dean, but she only laughed at it as an idle tale, founded only on suspicion. . . . Had he been married, he could not have lived in a state of separation from her, he loved her so passionately; for he admired her upon every account that can make a woman amiable or valuable as a companion for life. Is it possible to think that an affectionate husband could first have written, and then have used, those several prayers, by a dying wife with whom he never cohabited, and whose mouth must have been filled with reproaches for denying her all conjugal rights for a number of years, nay, from the very period (1716) that is pretended to be the time of the marriage?—MASON, WILLIAM MONCK, 1820, *History and Antiquities of St. Patrick's Cathedral, near Dublin.*

An eccentric, uncouth, disagreeable young Irishman, who had narrowly escaped plucking at Dublin, attended Sir William as an amanuensis, for twenty pounds a year and his board, dined at the second table, wrote bad verses in praise of his employer, and made love to a very pretty dark-eyed young girl who waited on Lady Giffard. Little did Temple imagine that the coarse exterior of his dependant concealed a genius equally suited to politics and to letters;—a genius destined to shake great kingdoms, to stir the laughter and the rage of millions, and to leave to posterity memorials which can perish only with the English language. Little did he think that the flirtation in his servants' hall, which he perhaps scarcely deigned to make the subject of a jest, was the beginning of a long unprosperous love which was to be as widely famed as the passion of Petrarch or of Abelard. Sir William's secretary was Jonathan Swift, Lady Giffard's waiting-maid was poor Stella.—MACAULAY, THOMAS BABINGTON, 1836, *Life and Writings of Sir William Temple, Edinburgh Review*; *Critical and Miscellaneous Essays.*

Two women whom he loved and injured are known by every reader of books so familiarly that if we had seen them, or if they had been relatives of our own, we scarcely could have known them better. Who has not in his mind an image of Stella? Who does not love her? Fair and tender creature: pure and affectionate heart! Boots it to you now that you have been at rest for a hundred and twenty years, not divided in death from the cold heart which caused yours, whilst it beat, such faithful pangs of love and grief—boots it to you now, that the whole world loves and deplores you? Scarce any man, I believe, ever thought of that grave, that did not cast a flower of pity on it, and write over it a sweet epitaph. Gentle lady!—so lovely, so loving, so unhappy. You have had countless champions, millions of manly hearts mourning for you. From generation to generation we take up the fond tradition of your beauty; we watch and follow your story, your bright morning love and purity, your constancy, your grief, your sweet martyrdom. We knew your legend by heart. You are one of the saints of English story.—THACKERAY, WILLIAM MAKEPEACE, 1853, *The English Humourists of the Eighteenth Century.*

Happy as Swift might have been, his felicity was troubled by an occurrence on which, for a brief space, the fate of poor Stella hung. After her arrival in Ireland she received an offer of marriage. The suitor was a clergyman, a friend of Swift's, named Tisdale, and to his honourable suit there was not a single objection. He was a man of character and talent. Swift's heart beat uneasily at this new difficulty. The proposal was made to him, as the guardian of the blooming Stella. He must, he perceived, either lay it before her, with all its advantages, or offer to her himself. Was there a struggle in that selfish remorseless heart? Let us hope so. To lose Stella must have been terrible. She was then, at eighteen, in the full perfection of a beauty enhanced by intelligence and sweetness. Her hair, raven black, set off the finest features and complexion in the world; and her figure, with a girlish tendency to *embonpoint* was perfect. Poor fated being! She was in Swift's hands, and his empire over her was strengthened, and for ever, by this untoward event. She consented, however, it appears to receive Tisdale as her suitor; but Swift, as her guardian exacted such exorbitant terms for Stella's dower, in case of widowhood, that Tisdale could not comply. His honourable attachment was unsuccessful, and Stella became the enthralled victim of one, who, whilst he often declared he loved "her better than his life a thousand millions of times," took advantage of her unprotected situation to interfere with her best interests. Swift and Tisdale continued, nominally, friends; yet the perfidious Jonathan did not scruple to amuse his friends with epigrams, at the expense of one who had so nearly carried away Stella from her bondage; Swift excusing himself by saying that Tisdale went from house to house to show his wit upon him.—THOMSON, KATHERINE (GRACE WHARTON), 1862, *The Literature of Society, vol.* II, *p.* 171.

It may be interesting enough to mention that in the year 1791 (you will see that I am anything but young, and perhaps admire the memory of a man now in his eighty-eight year), when I was fifteen, and tolerably observant of things said or done before me, I heard a then aged man, the Rev. Dr. Ashe, the rector of Clonard, in the county of Meath, and the descendant (lineally or collaterally) of the Bishop of Clogher (ob. 1717), speak of the Dean's marriage to Stella as having been solemnised by the bishop: this on the family tradition of his lordship's *personal statements.*—SWIFT, EDMUND LENTHALL, 1865, *Letter to John Francis Waller, Jan.* 23.

That Esther Johnson was a beautiful woman, no one who looks upon the portrait will deny. That Swift loved her with all the strength and tenderness of such love as he could feel for woman, no one can doubt. Let the agony of grief and remorse, which thenceforth made his inner life desolate—even when the popular plaudits were ringing around him, and his voice and his pen were controlling measures and baffling governments—win our pity, though they cannot extenuate his faults.—WALLER, JOHN FRANCIS, 1865, *ed. Gulliver's Travels, Life, p.* xxxii.

He married Miss Johnson from duty, but in secret, and on condition that she should only be his wife in name. She was twelve years dying.—TAINE, H. A., 1871, *History of English Literature, tr. Van Laun, vol.* II, *bk.* iii, *ch.* v, *p.* 123.

One final consideration is that the oppressive and disabling nature of Swift's life-long disease has been greatly underrated in the more severe of the criticisms which have been made with regard to his conduct to Esther Johnston. I do not know that labyrinthine vertigo would necessarily incapacitate a man for the performance of marital duties, but it certainly might be a barrier to them more formidable than unprofessional critics are likely to suppose possible. Dr. Beddoes suggested that Swift was impotent from youthful dissipation, of which there is not a tithe of evidence. May not the great and grave disease of which I have adduced such copious evidence have been the real reason why Swift did not live with the woman whom it was certain that he loved with the most tender and persistent devotion?—BUCKNILL, DR. (F. R. S.), 1881, *Dean Swift's Disease, Brain.*

The relation between the two was from the first, so far as the world was concerned, free from all doubt or ambiguity. Stella shared in all Swift's interests, remained his constant companion, and by degrees became the centre of his circle. But they never met alone: they never lived in the same house: and though all his thoughts and cares were shared by her, the bond was never in reality a closer one. And these strict limits of their friendship were so carefully maintained, that slander never ventured to assert otherwise, except in some vulgar outbursts which forgot even appropriateness of attack. Strange and abnormal as were its conditions, fettered and cramped as it was by Swift's pride and waywardness, or by the mysteries of disease, the romance of that mutual devotion still forms one of the threads of the deepest interest running through Swift's dark and somber life.—CRAIK, HENRY, 1882, *The Life of Jonathan Swift, p.* 89.

There has hardly ever been in the world, or out of it, in the illimitable kingdoms of fancy, a more famous pair of lovers than these two. Leila and Majnun, Romeo and Juliet, Petrarch and Laura—repeat what names we may of famous lovers that the fancies of poets have ever adored by the Tigris, or the Avon, or in the shadows of Vaucluse, the names of Swift and Stella are found to appeal no less keenly to heart and brain, to the imagination and to pity. Happy they were not, and could not be. When we read of Swift and Stella the mind naturally turns to that luckless pair of lovers whom Dante saw in the third circle of hell, blown about forever on the racking wind, and finding comfort through the lapse of eternal twilight in the companionship of their common doom: They, too—Swift and Stella—seem driven by the pitiless wind of fate; they have fallen upon evil days; they are greatly gifted, noble, greatly unhappy; they are sustained by their strange, exquisite friendship, by the community of genius, by a tender affection which was out of tune with the time and with their troubled lives. . . . There is nothing in literature more profoundly melancholy than Swift's own eloquent tribute to the memory of his dead wife, written in a room to which he has removed so that he may not see the light burning in the church windows, where her last rites are being prepared.—McCARTHY, JUSTIN, 1890, *History of the Four Georges, vol.* II, *p.* 315.

In Swift's private life Stella and Vanessa occupy a place curiously similar to that held by Oxford and Bolingbroke in his public career. The brilliancy and culture of the first of each pair pleased his imagination. The honesty and plainness of the others won his heart. For a parallel for Swift's affection for Stella there is no better one than that of Hamlet for Ophelia. The Danish prince found in the simplicity and naturalness of the one a relief from the corruption and hollowness of a depraved court. Swift, in the straightforward character, and unassuming devotion of the other, obtained consolation for the folly, perverseness and deceit which his "savage indignation" led him to regard as the dominating qualities of all mankind.—MORIARTY, GERALD P., 1892, *Dean Swift and his Writings, p.* 253.

If there was any person entitled to speak with authority on the subject, that person was assuredly Mrs. Dingley. For twenty-nine years, from the commencement, that is to say, of Swift's intimate connection with Stella till the day of Stella's death, she had been her inseparable companion, her friend and confidante. She had shared the same lodgings with her; it was understood that Swift and Esther were to have no secrets apart from her. When they met, they met in her presence; what they wrote, passed, by Swift's special request, through her hands. Now it is well known that Mrs. Dingley was convinced that no marriage had ever taken place. The whole story was, she said, an idle tale. Two of Stella's executors, Dr. Corbet and Mr. Rochford, distinctly stated that no suspicion of a marriage had ever even crossed their minds, though they had seen the Dean and Esther together a thousand times. Swift's housekeeper, Mrs. Brent, a shrewd and observant woman, who resided at the deanery during the whole period of her master's intimacy with Miss Johnson, was satisfied that there had been no marriage. So said Mrs. Ridgeway, who succeeded her as housekeeper, and who watched over the Dean in his declining years. But no testimony could carry greater weight than that of Dr. John Lyon. He was one of Swift's most intimate friends, and, when the state of the Dean's health was such that it had become necessary to place him under surveillance, Lyon was the person selected to undertake the duty. He lived with him at the deanery; he had full control over his papers; he was consequently brought into contact with all who corresponded with him, and with all who visited him. He had thus at his command every contemporary source of information. Not long after the story was first circulated, he set to work to ascertain, if possible, the truth. The result of his investigations was to convince him that there was absolutely no foundation for it but popular gossip, unsupported by a particle of evidence.—COLLINS, JOHN CHURTON, 1893, *Jonathan Swift, p.* 150.

VANESSA

Hail, blushing goddess, beauteous spring!
Who in thy jocund train dost bring
Loves and graces—smiling hours—
Balmy breezes—fragrant flowers;
Come, with tints of roseate hue,
Nature's faded charms renew!
Yet why should I thy presence hail?
To me no more the breathing gale
Comes fraught with sweets, no more the rose
With such transcendent beauty blows,
As when Cadenus blest the scene,
And shared with me those joys serene.
When, unperceived the lambent fire
Of friendship kindled new desire;
Still listening to his tuneful tongue,
The truths which angels might have sung,
Divine imprest their gentle sway,
And sweetly stole my soul away.
My guide, instructor, lover, friend,
Dear names, in one idea blend;
Oh! still conjoined, your incense rise,
And waft sweet odours to the skies!
—VANHOMRIGH, ESTHER, *Ode to Spring.*

Near twenty years ago I heard from a gentleman now living, with whom Vanessa lived, or lodged, in England, an account of the Dean's behaviour to the unhappy woman, much less to his reputation than the account my Lord [Orrery] gives of that affair. According to this gentleman's account she was not the creature that she became when she was in Ireland, whither she followed him, and, in hopes to make herself an interest with his vanity, threw herself into glare and expense; and, at last, by disappointment, into a habit of drinking, till grief and the effects of that vice destroyed her. You may gather from that really pretty piece of his, Cadenus and Vanessa, how much he flattered her, and that he took great pains to gloss over that affair. I remember once to have seen a little collection of letters and poetical scraps of Swift's, which passed between him and Mrs. Van Homrigh, this same Vanessa, which the bookseller then told me were sent him to be published, from the originals by this lady, in resentment of his perfidy.—RICHARDSON, SAMUEL, 1752, *To Lady Bradshaigh, April* 22, *Correspondence, ed. Barbauld, vol.* VI, *p.* 175.

Though all will confess that the two devoted women, who fell victims to his barbarous selfishness, and whose names are eternally linked with the history of our literature, are far more interesting, from their ill-bestowed, ill-requited, and passionate attachment to *him* than by anything he ever sung or said of *them.* Nay, his longest, his most elaborate, and his most admired poem,—the avowed history of one of his attachments—with its insipid tawdry fable, its conclusion, in which nothing is concluded, and the inferences we are left to draw from it, would have given but an ignominious celebrity to poor Vanessa, if truth and time, and her own sweet nature, had not redeemed her. —JAMESON, ANNA BROWNELL, 1829, *The Loves of the Poets, vol.* II. *p.* 240.

His affection was never free from the egoistic element which prevented him from acting unequivocally, as an impartial spectator would have advised him to act, or as he would have advised another to act in a similar case. And therefore, when the crisis came, the very strength of his affection produced an explosion of selfish wrath, and he escaped from the intolerable position by striking down the woman whom he loved, and whose love for him had become a burden. The wrath was not the less fatal because it was half composed of remorse, and the energy of the explosion proportioned to the strength of the feeling which had held it in check. —STEPHEN, LESLIE, 1882, *Swift* (*English Men of Letters*), *p.* 144.

He lodged close to her mother, and was a frequent guest at her table. Vanessa insensibly became his pupil, and he insensibly became the object of her impassioned affection. Her letters reveal a spirit full of ardour and enthusiasm, and warped by that perverse bent which leads so many women to prefer a tyrant to a companion. Swift, on the other hand, was devoid of passion. Of friendship, even of tender regard, he was fully capable, but not of love. The spiritual realm, whether in divine or earthly things, was a region closed to him, where he never set foot. As a friend he must have greatly preferred Stella to Vanessa; and from this point of view his loyalty to the original object of his choice, we may be sure, never faltered. But Vanessa assailed him on a very weak side. The strongest of all his instincts was the thirst for imperious domination. Vanessa hugged the fetters to which Stella merely submitted. Flattered to excess by her surrender, yet conscious of his binding obligations and his real preference, he could neither discard the one beauty nor desert the other. It is humiliating to human strength and consoling to human weakness to find the Titan behaving like the least resolute of mortals, seeking refuge in temporizing, in evasions, in fortuitous circumstance.—GARNETT, RICHARD, 1887, *Encyclopædia Britannica, Ninth ed., vol.* XXII.

BATTLE OF THE BOOKS
1697?–1704

Swift for the Ancients has argued so well,
'Tis apparent from thence that the Moderns excel.

—BARKER, MRS., 1735, *On the Celebrated Dispute between the Ancients and the Moderns, p.* 285.

A piece exhibiting, perhaps, more than any of his writings, the original vein of humour which distinguishes its author. —COLERIDGE, HARTLEY, 1833, *Biographia Borealis, p.* 79.

Of all that constituted once the so

famous controversy, its prodigious learning and its furious abuse, this triumphant piece of humour alone survives. It was circulated widely before Temple died, and not until four years later appeared in print, as portion of a volume which weakened the side of which the writer had engaged as much as it strengthened that of the enemy. Swift could not help himself. The ancients could show no such humour and satire as the "Tale of a Tub" and the "Battle of the Books."—FORSTER, JOHN, 1875, *The Life of Jonathan Swift, vol.* I, *p.* 104.

So purely popular that it lost nothing by being whetted on the wrong edge.—JEBB, RICHARD CLAVERHOUSE, 1882, *Bentley* (*English Men of Letters*), *p.* 77.

The "Battle of the Books" is the best of the travesties. Nor in the brilliant assault upon great names do we at present see anything more than the buoyant consciousness of power, common in the unsparing judgments of youth, nor edged as yet by any real bitterness. Swift has found out that the world is full of humbugs; and goes forth hewing and hacking with superabundant energy, not yet aware that he too may be conceivably a fallible being, and still less that the humbugs may some day prove too strong for him. —STEPHEN, LESLIE, 1882, *Swift* (*English Men of Letters*), *p.* 36.

Its object is satire, not criticism. Where it touches on the points in dispute, it is in such broad and far-reaching metaphor as that by which he illustrates the "sweetness and light" of the ancients through the fable of the Spider and the Bee, which has supplied a telling phraseology to a phase of latter-day criticism. Like all the satire that Swift ever wrote, it goes directly to the point by its personal reference. For Swift the main issue is one between Temple and Bentley, between the Christchurch wits and Wotton, not between the arguments of the critics. His preference for the ancients was thorough and sincere: but it went deeper than literary criticism.—CRAIK, HENRY, 1882, *The Life of Jonathan Swift, p.* 72.

TALE OF A TUB

1704

I am of your mind as to the Tale of a Tub. I am not alone in the opinion, as you are there; but I am pretty near it, having but very few on my side, but those few are worth a million. However, I have never spoke my sentiments, not caring to contradict a multitude. Bottom admires it, and cannot bear my saying I confess I was diverted with several passages when I read it, but I should not care to read it again. That he thinks not commendation enough.—CONGREVE, WILLIAM, 1704, *Letter to Keally, Oct.* 28.

I beg your Lordship (if the book is come down to Exon), to read "The Tale of a Tub," for, bating the profaneness of it, it is a book to be valued, being an original of its kind, full of wit, humour, good sense, and learning. It comes from Christ Church, and a great part of it is written in defence of Mr. Boyle against Wotton and Bentley. The town is wonderfully pleased with it. . . . The author of "A Tale of a Tub" will not as yet be known; and if it be the man I guess, he hath reason to conceal himself because of the profound strokes in that piece, which would do his reputation and interests in the world more harm than the wit can do him good. I think your lordship hath found out a very proper employment for your pen, which he would execute very happily. Nothing can please more than that book doth here at London. —ATTERBURY, FRANCIS, 1704, *Letters to Bishop Trelawney, June* 15, *July* 1.

He seemed to me to have an unaccountable prejudice against Swift; for I once took the liberty to ask him, if Swift had personally offended him, and he told me, he had not. He said to-day, "Swift is clear, but he is shallow. In coarse humour, he is inferior to Arbuthnot; in delicate humour, he is inferior to Addison. So he is inferior to his contemporaries; without putting him against the whole world. I doubt if the 'Tale of a Tub' was his: it has so much more thinking, more knowledge, more power, more colour, than any of the works which are indisputably his. If it was his, I shall only say, he was *impar sibi.*"—JOHNSON, SAMUEL, 1773, *Life by Boswell, ed. Hill, vol.* V, *p.* 49.

The "Tale of a Tub" is a work, of perhaps greater felicity of wit, and more ludicrous combinations of ideas, than any other book in the world. It is however, written in so strange a style of "banter," to make use of one of the author's words, or rather in so low and anomalous a slang, which perhaps Swift considered as the necessary concomitant of wit; that it is by no means proper to be cited as an example of just composition. —GODWIN, WILLIAM, 1797, *Of English Style, The Enquirer, p.* 444.

The literary merit of the "Tale of a Tub" is great, and, in this respect, exceeding everything which he afterwards produced. The style has more nerve, more imagery, and spirit, than any other portion of his works: the wit and humour are perfectly original, and supported throughout with undiminished vigour; but, it must be confessed, occasionally coarse and licentious; and the digressions exhibit erudition of no common kind, though not always applied in illustration of that side of the question on which justice and impartiality have since arranged themselves.—DRAKE, NATHAN, 1804, *Essays Illustrative of the Tattler, Spectator and Guardian, vol.* III, *p.* 143.

With this for my whole fortune, I was trudging through Richmond in my blue smock-frock, and my red garters tied under my knees, when, staring about me, my eyes fell upon a little book in a bookseller's window, on the outside of which was written "The Tale of a Tub, price threepence." The title was so odd that my curiosity was excited. I had the threepence; but, then, I could not have any supper. In I went and got the little book, which I was so impatient to read, that I got over into a field at the upper corner of Kew Gardens, where there stood a haystack. On the shady side of this I sat down to read. The book was so different from any thing I had ever read before, it was something so new to my mind, that, though I could not understand some parts of it, it delighted me beyond description, and produced what I have always considered a sort of birth of intellect. I read on until it was dark without any thought of supper or bed. . . . My "Tale of a Tub," which I carried about with me wherever I went, and when I—at about twenty years old—lost it in a box that fell overboard in the Bay of Fundy, in North America, the loss gave me greater pain than I have since felt in losing thousands of pounds.—COBBETT, WILLIAM, c1810, *Evening Post.*

"The Tale of a Tub" is, in my apprehension, the masterpiece of Swift; certainly Rabelais has nothing superior, even in invention, nor anything so condensed, so pointed, so full of real meaning, of biting satire, of felicitous analogy.—HALLAM, HENRY, 1837–39, *Introduction to the Literature of Europe, pt.* iv, *ch.* vii., *par.* 61.

An astonishing production, of which the fervid vehement style, sparkling wit, and vivacity of genius, seem to distinguish it above the happiest efforts even of his own restless pen.—ROSCOE, THOMAS, 1841, *ed. The Works of Jonathan Swift, vol.* I, *p.* 42.

It is certainly his most astonishing production. You see a "virgin mind crumbling down with its own riches." It is the wildest, wittiest, wickedest, wealthiest book of its size in British literature.—GILFILLAN, GEORGE, 1855, *A Third Gallery of Portraits, p.* 222.

Although the object of the "Tale of a Tub" was undoubtedly to defend the Church of England, and to ridicule its opponents, it would be difficult to find in the whole compass of literature any production more utterly unrestrained by considerations of reverence or decorum. Nothing in Voltaire is more grossly profane than the passages in Swift about the Roman Catholic doctrine concerning the Sacrament, and the Calvinistic doctrine concerning inspiration. And although the "Tale of a Tub" is an extreme example, the same spirit pervades many of his other performances. His wit was perfectly unbridled. His unrivalled power of ludicrous combination seldom failed to get the better of his prudence; and he found it impossible to resist a jest. It must be added that no writer of the time indulged more habitually in coarse, revolting, and indecent imagery; that he delighted in a strain of ribald abuse peculiarly unbecoming in a clergyman; that he lived in an atmosphere deeply impregnated with scepticism; and that he frequently expressed a strong dislike for his profession.—LECKY, WILLIAM EDWARD HARTPOLE, 1861–71, *The Leaders of Public Opinion in Ireland, p.* 19.

Swift had, indeed, little enough in common with the philosophy of Lucretius. But in both we have the same gloom of cynicism. In both there is the same profound scorn of superstition, and yet the same belief that in superstition we must find the main source of most human action.

In Swift as in Lucretius, the literary instinct has made the general and wide-reaching satire far more strong in its impression than the ostensible object of the book. If we read the "Tale of a Tub" with understanding of its real meaning, we have as little impression, at the end, of the quarrels of Peter and Martin and Jack, as we have, after reading the poem of Lucretius, of the niceties of the Epicurean system. Divided by eighteen centuries, there is yet much in the mental attitude of the two men that brings them close together. Swift's supposed debt to Rabelais is almost proverbial. But, after all, it is more in the following of a recognised vehicle of satire, than in anything else. Swift read Rabelais, as the acknowledged master of a peculiar style of sarcasm. The style has already become antiquated: and yet his adoption of it leaves the essential qualities of the "Tale of a Tub" absolutely unimpaired.—CRAIK, HENRY, 1882, *The Life of Jonathan Swift, p.* 112.

In style, and as an artistic whole, the "Tale of a Tub" is Swift's masterpiece. The satire is more pointed and concise than in "Gulliver," the thought more full and vigorous, the ideas and language more sustained and nervous. But to our modern taste there is much in the story of the three brothers that is painful and repellent. —POOLE, STANLEY LANE-, 1883, *ed. Selections from the Prose Writings of Jonathan Swift, Preface, p.* xxii.

If not the most amusing of Swift's satirical works, the most strikingly original, and the one in which the compass of his powers is most fully displayed. In his kindred productions he relies mainly upon a single element of the humorous—logical sequence and unruffled gravity bridling in an otherwise frantic absurdity, and investing it with an air of sense. In the "Tale of a Tub" he lashes out in all directions. The humor, if less cogent and cumulative, is richer and more varied; the invention too, is more daringly original and more completely out of the reach of ordinary faculties.—GARNETT, RICHARD, 1887, *Encyclopædia Britannica, Ninth ed., vol.* XXII.

The very extraordinary treatise called "A Tale of a Tub" is allowed to rank among the first of its author's productions. It displays his finest qualities of imagination and irony when they were in their freshest and most ebullient condition. . . . The reader is carried along so gaily on this buoyant tide of wit, that he puts the book down with regret to find it ended, when it seemed but just begun. In this, "A Tale of a Tub" forms a surprising contrast to almost all the prose which had preceded it for half a century, the writers of the Restoration, even where they are most correct and graceful, being devoid of this particular sparkle and crispness of phrase. . . . In "A Tale of a Tub" the intellectual interest never halts for a moment. There is infinite variety, and the reader is tantalised by the prodigality of wit, never fatigued for a moment by its expression. In pure style Swift never excelled this his first important essay.—GOSSE, EDMUND, 1888, *A History of Eighteenth Century Literature, pp.* 144, 146.

The reader of such vigorous and effective English, employed with so much directness and point, cannot but sympathize with the feeling which prompted him to say in his old age, when his mind was gradually failing, "Good God, what a genius I had when I wrote that book!" Not only is the book his masterpiece, but it is also his best allegory; indeed one would hazard little in making the assertion that it is the best sustained allegory that ever was written.—GREENE, HERBERT EVELETH, 1889, *The Allegory in Spenser, Bunyan and Swift; Publications of the Modern Language Association of America, vol.* IV, *p.* 168.

I have been wandering through Swift a good deal. The hearty cursing in his "Tale of a Tub" goes straight to my midriff—so satisfying, the best of tonics. For absolute splendour too, commend me to his chapters about the Aeolists!—BROWN, THOMAS EDWARD, 1893, *Letters, ed. Irwin, March* 10, *vol.* I, *p.* 173.

It is a mad, strange, often foul-mouthed book, with thrusts in it that go to the very marrow of all monstrous practices in all ecclesiasticisms; showing a love for what is honest and of good report, perhaps; but showing stronger love for thwacking the skulls of all sinners in high places; and the higher the place the harder is the thwack.—MITCHELL, DONALD G., 1895, *English Lands Letters and Kings, From Elizabeth to Anne, p.* 317.

THE EXAMINER

No modern leader-writer, however common-place, would write such heavy stuff now.—POOLE, STANLEY LANE-, 1883, *ed. Selections from the Prose Writings of Jonathan Swift, Preface, p.* XXV.

At the beginning of November Swift undertook the editorship of the "Examiner," and for upwards of three years he fought the battles of the Ministry as no one had ever yet fought the battles of any Ministry in the world. With a versatility unparalleled in the history of party warfare, he assailed his opponents in almost every form which satire can assume; in Essays which are still read as models of terse and luminous disquisition; in philippics compared with which the masterpieces of Cicero will, in point of vituperative skill, bear no comparison; in pamphlets which were half a century afterwards the delight of Burke and Fox: in ribald songs, in street ballads, in Grubstreet epigrams, in ludicrous parodies. He had applied his rare powers of observation to studying the peculiarities of every class in the great family of mankind, their humours, their prejudices, their passions; and to all these he knew how to appeal with exquisite propriety. He was a master of the rhetoric which casts a spell over senates and tribunals, and of the rhetoric which sends mobs yelling to the tar-barrel or the clubstick. With every weapon in the whole armoury of scorn he was equally familiar. In boisterous scurrility he was more than a match for Oldmixon. In delicate and subtle humour he was more than a match for Addison. In an age when the bad arts of anonymous polemics had been brought to perfection, his lampoons achieved a scandalous pre-eminence. His sarcasm and invective were terrific. His irony made even the Duchess of Marlborough quail; his pasquinades drove Eugene in ignominy from our shores; his broadsides made it perilous for the Opposition to show their faces in the streets. But however remarkable were his abilities as an unscrupulous assailant, his abilities as an unscrupulous advocate were not less consummate. Where his object was persuasion, he was indifferent to everything but effect. He hesitated at nothing. When the testimony of facts was against him, he distorted them beyond recognition. When testimony was wanting, he invented it. When the statements of his opponents admitted of no confutation, he assumed the air of an honest and stout-hearted Englishman who refused to be duped. His diction—plain, masculine, incisive—came home to every one; and the monstrous effrontery of his assumptions was seldom suspected by readers whose reason was enthralled by the circumstantial conclusiveness with which he drew his deductions. In truth, of all writers who have ever entered the arena of party politics, Swift had, in a larger measure than any, the most invaluable of all qualifications—the art of making truth assume the appearance of elaborate sophistry, and the art of making elaborate sophistry assume the appearance of self evident truth.—COLLINS, JOHN CHURTON, 1886, *Bolingbroke, A Historical Study, and Voltaire in England, p.* 59.

The style of Swift's "Examiners" is perfect of its kind and for its purpose. His own rather bald definition of a good style—"proper words in proper places"—expresses the form of these papers precisely, while their matter like the lead of a bullet, is calculated nicely, and only to serve a single object—to go straight and strong and true to its mark. The admiration Swift's political tracts excites is of the kind excited by a steam-engine—admiration of power, precision, and such exquisite adaptation of means to a single end that there is neither waste nor want, friction nor dispersion.—KING, RICHARD ASHE, 1895, *Swift in Ireland, p.* 61.

CONDUCT OF THE ALLIES
1711

The book is, in truth, a miracle of clear and forcible logic.—WYON, FREDERICK WILLIAM, 1876, *The History of Great Britain During the Reign of Queen Anne, vol.* II, *p.* 335.

Swift was now called upon to perform the greatest service ever rendered to an English government by a man of letters. In November, 1711, six weeks after the secret preliminaries had been signed, whilst the States of the confederacy were still doubtful as to the propriety of entering a congress on the base proposed, and whilst the public was still, as he complains, "half bewitched" against a peace,—at the end of November, the meeting of

Parliament being three times postponed to allow the utmost care to be bestowed on the work, and its statements with the conclusions founded on them to sink deeply into the public mind, appeared Swift's political masterpiece, "The Conduct of the Allies." . . . It is impossible to exaggerate the effect produced and the service rendered by the publication of this tract. Written with simple eloquence, presenting throughout its course an unbroken chain of argument in which—granting the author's premise—no flaw could be detected, and enlivened here and there with a touch of his peculiar humour, it had the merit of bringing an abstruse political question down to the level of the plainest understanding. It was disseminated with the utmost industry by the agents of Government. The first edition was all exhausted in a couple of days; the second in five hours; the third and fourth within the week. By the end of the year, a month after its first appearance, it was computed that eleven thousand copies had passed into some reader's hand; and its author relates in his correspondence with pardonable complacency how nothing of the kind had ever made so many converts; how, in the debates that followed, all the Government orators drew their arguments from it; how "every one agreed it was my book" which spirited up the court to its severe resolution against the allies; and how, on the return of peace, the first ambassador accredited to St. James's by the Bourbon King of Spain, on reaching London, "asked to be presented to Dr. Swift," as the man to whom "in all Europe" his royal master and the most Christian King were most indebted.—HARROP, ROBERT, 1884, *Bolingbroke, A Political Study and Criticism, pp.* 113, 116.

The style and tone of this masterly pamphlet are adapted with great skill both to the popular taste and to the reason of thoughtful men.—COLLINS, JOHN CHURTON, 1893, *Jonathan Swift, p.* 88.

Never did publicist render any party such yeoman service as Swift rendered the Tories, and rarely did anyone meet with such scant reward. More than anything else, his "Conduct of the Allies" made the peace of Utrecht acceptable to the nation.—POLLARD, A. F., 1897, *ed. Political Pamphlets, Introduction, p.* xviii.

DRAPIER LETTERS
1724

A proclamation for discovering ye Author of ye Pamphlet intitled A letter to ye whole people of Ireland, by M. B. Drapier, author of the letter to the shopkeepers, &c.

£300 REWARD.

By the Lord Lieutenant and Council of Ireland.

A PROCLAMATION.

Content:

Whereas a wicked and malicious pamphlet, intitled A letter to the whole people of Ireland, by M. B. Drapier, author of the letter to the shopkeepers, &c., printed by John Harding, in Molesworth's Court, in Fishamble Street, Dublin, in which are contained several seditious and scandalous paragraphs highly reflecting upon his Majesty and his ministers, tending to alienate the affections of his good subjects of England and Ireland from each other, and to promote sedition among the people, hath been lately printed and published in this kingdom: We, the Lord Lieutenant and Council do hereby publish and declare that, in order to discover the author of the said seditious pamphlet, we will give the necessary orders for the payment of three hundred pounds sterling, to such person or persons as shall within the specified six months from this date hereof, discover the author of the said pamphlet, so as he be apprehended and convicted thereby. . . .

GOD save the KING.

—*Proclamation Against the Drapier*, 1724, *Oct.* 27.

Let Ireland tell, how wit upheld her cause,
Her trade supported, and supplied her laws;
And leave on Swift this grateful verse engraved,
"The rights a Court Attacked, a poet saved."
Behold the hand that wrought a nation's cure,
Stretched to relieve the idiot and the poor,
Proud vice to brand, or injured worth adorn,
And stretch the ray to ages yet unborn.
—POPE, ALEXANDER, 1737, *Imitations of Horace, bk.* ii, *ep.* i. v. 221–228.

True patriot, her [Ireland's] first, almost her last.—CROKER, JOHN WILSON, 1810, *Ireland Past and Present.*

His object was, not to do good to Ireland, but to vex and annoy the English ministry. To do this however with effect, it was necessary that he should speak to the interests and feelings of some party who possessed a certain degree of power and influence. This unfortunately was not the case in that day with the Catholics; and though this gave them only a stronger title to the services of a truly brave or generous advocate, it was sufficient to silence Swift. They are not so much as named above two or three times in his writings—and then only with scorn and reprobation. In the topics which he does take up, it is no doubt true, that he frequently inveighs against real oppression and acts of indisputable impolicy; yet it is no want of charity to say, that it is quite manifest that this were not his reasons for bringing them forward, and that he had just as little scruple to make an outcry, where no public interest was concerned, as where it was apparent. It was sufficient for him, that the subject was likely to excite popular prejudice and clamour,—or that he had some personal pique or animosity to gratify. The Drapier's letters are sufficient proof of the influence of the former principle.—JEFFREY, FRANCIS LORD, 1816, *The Works of Jonathan Swift, Edinburgh Review, vol.* 27, *p.* 22.

Believing, however erroneously, that Swift had delivered them from a great public danger, their gratitude to him knew no bounds, nor ended even with his powers of mind. "The sun of his popularity," says a great poet, "remained unclouded, even after he was incapable of distinguishing its radiance." The Drapier's Head became a favourite sign; his portrait, we are told, was engraved, woven upon handkerchiefs, and stuck upon medals (not of copper I presume). His health was quaffed at every banquet, his presence everywhere welcomed with blessings by the people. They bore with all the infirmities of genius, all the peevishness of age. In vain did he show contempt and aversion to those who thus revered him: in vain did he deny them even the honour of his birth-place, frequently saying, "I was not dropped in this vile country, but in England." In vain did he sneer at the "savage Old Irish." No insult on his part could weaken their generous attachment. Even at this day, as I am assured, this grateful feeling still survives; and all parties in Ireland, however estranged on other questions, agree in one common veneration for the memory of Swift.—STANHOPE, PHILIP HENRY EARL (LORD MAHON), 1836–58, *History of England from the Peace of Utrecht to the Peace of Versailles,* 1713–1783, *vol.* II., *p.* 67.

Is it fair to call the famous "Drapier's Letters" patriotism? They are masterpieces of dreadful humour and invective: they are reasoned logically enough too, but the proposition is as monstrous and fabulous as the Lilliputian island. It is not that the grievance is so great, but there is his enemy—the assault is wonderful for its activity and terrible rage. It is Samson with a bone in his hand, rushing on his enemies and felling them: one admires not the cause so much as the strength, the anger, the fury of the champion.—THACKERAY, WILLIAM MAKEPEACE, 1853, *The English Humourists of the Eighteenth Century.*

Because Swift takes the Irish, not the English, view of the question,—because he goes to battle armed with the strength of his genius, the fire of his indignation,—he is therefore no patriot! What is it to be a patriot? To sit in the chimney-corner and make fine phrases about loving your country, or to go out and do battle for her? There was nothing in Ireland, in Swift's day, to which the affections could cling. The first thing to be done was to constitute a state worthy of love, the first steps to that end were in resistance to oppressive measures; the first feeling to be encouraged was hatred of the oppressor. It is true that Swift often spoke with contempt of the Irish, and that he regarded his appointment to the Deanery of St. Patrick's as a decree of banishment from civilization and friendship. He showed little sentimental patriotism; but he understood the duties of a patriot, and did his best to discharge them. He may sometimes have displayed the temper of Coriolanus; but, unlike the Roman, he endured unto the end.—HILL, ADAMS SHERMAN, 1868, *The Character of Jonathan Swift, North American Review, vol.* 106, *p.* 86.

The public joy knew no bounds. In a few hours Dublin presented the appearance of a vast jubilee. In a few days there was scarcely a town or a village in Ireland which was not beside itself with exultation. The whole island rang with the praises of the Drapier. It was the Drapier, they cried, who had saved them, it was the Drapier who had taught them to be patriots. Had Swift rescued the country from some overwhelming calamity, had he done all and more than all that the Œdipus of story is fabled to have done for the city of Amphion, popular gratitude could not have gone further. Medals were struck in his honour. A club, the professed object of which was to perpetuate his fame, was formed. His portrait stamped on medallions, or woven on handkerchiefs, was the ornament most cherished by both sexes. When he appeared in the streets all heads were uncovered. If for the first time he visited a town, it was usual for the Corporation to receive him with public honours. Each year, as his birthday came round, it was celebrated with tumultuous festivity. "He became," says Orrery, "the idol of the people of Ireland to a degree of devotion that in the most superstitious country scarcely any idol ever attained." "Spirit of Swift!" exclaimed Grattan on that memorable day when he brought forward his Declaration of Legislative Independence, "Spirit of Swift! your genius has prevailed; Ireland is now a nation." Even now no true Irishman ever pronounces his name without reverence.—COLLINS, JOHN CHURTON, 1893, *Jonathan Swift, p.* 188.

"The Drapier's Letters" are epoch-making in that they first taught Ireland the policy and the power of union, of dogged inert resistance, and of strategically organized and directed agitation. Their effect was, in fact, commensurate with their power, and their power of its kind was supreme. It is the power of a deft, vigorous, intent and unerring-eyed wielder of a hammer, who hits each nail on the head and home without one single feint, or flourish, or one single short, or weak, or wasted stroke. Swift's consummate mastery of the art which conceals art was never shown to such perfection as in these letters, whose naked simplicity is so like naked truth as to be confounded with it. . . . It is, in fact, incontestable that Swift's service to Ireland deserves the distinction he gives it in his epitaph. Look at it how you will, either from the point of view of the need of the service, or of its righteousness, or of its greatness, or of its difficulty, and Swift's work in Ireland is his supreme achievement. When "in the reign of Queen Anne he dictated for a time the policy of the English nation," he had at his back a powerful and compact party, all the influence (then enormous) of the Court, Harley's serviceable cunning and the brilliant intellect of Bolingbroke. But of his work in Ireland he might say with literal truth, "Alone I did it!"—KING, RICHARD ASHE, 1895, *Swift in Ireland, pp.* 108, 202.

The "Drapier's Letters" are as much superior to Junius as Junius is superior to Wilkes.—PAUL, HERBERT, 1900, *The Prince of Journalists, The Nineteenth Century, vol.* 47, *p.* 80.

GULLIVER'S TRAVELS
1726

Here is a book come out, that all our people of taste run mad about; 'tis no less than the united work of a dignified clergyman, an eminent physician, and the first poet of the age; and very wonderful it is, God knows!—great eloquence have they employed to prove themselves beasts, and shew such veneration for horses, that since the Essex quaker, nobody has appeared so passionately devoted to that species; and to say truth, they talk of a stable with so much warmth and affection, I cannot help suspecting some very powerful motive at the bottom of it.—MONTAGU, LADY MARY WORTLEY, 1726, *Letter to the Countess of Mar.*

"Gulliver's Travels," I believe, will have as great a run as John Bunyan. It is in everybody's hands. Lord Scarborough, who is no inventor of stories, told me that he fell in company with a master of a ship, who told him that he was very well acquainted with Gulliver; but that the printer had mistaken; that he lived in Wapping, and not in Rotherhithe. I lent the book to an old gentleman who went immediately to his map to search for Lilliput.—ARBUTHNOT, JOHN, 1726, *Letter to Swift, Nov.* 8.

About ten days ago a book was published here of the Travels of one Gulliver, which has been the conversation of the whole town ever since: the whole impression sold in a week; and nothing is more diverting than to hear the different opinions people give of it, though all agree in liking it extremely. 'Tis generally said that you are the author, but I am told the bookseller declares he knows not from what hand it came. From the highest to the lowest it is universally read, from the cabinet council to the nursery. You may see by this you are not much injured by being supposed the author of this piece. If you are, you have disobliged us, and two or three of your best friends, in not giving us the least hint of it. Perhaps I may all this time be talking to you of a book you have never seen, and which has not yet reached Ireland; if it have not I believe what we have said will be sufficient to recommend it to your reading, and that you will order me to send it to you.—GAY, JOHN, 1726, *Letter to Swift, Nov.* 17.

"Gulliver's Travels" is a book in which the author seems to have called up all his vigilance and skill in the article of style: and, as the plan of his fiction led to that simplicity in which he delighted, no book can be taken as a fairer specimen of the degree of cultivation at which the English language had at that time arrived. Swift was perhaps the man of the most powerful mind of the time in which he lived.—GODWIN, WILLIAM, 1797, *Of English Style, The Enquirer, p.* 446.

This singular work displays a most fertile imagination, a deep insight into the follies, vices, and infirmities of mankind, and a fund of acute observation on ethics, politics, and literature. Its principal aim appears to have been to mortify the pride of human nature, whether arising from personal or mental accomplishments: the satire, however, has been carried too far, and degenerates into a libel on the species. The fourth part, especially, notwithstanding all that has been said in its defence by Sheridan and Berkeley, apparently exhibits such a malignant wish to degrade and brutalize the human race, that with every reader of feeling and benevolence it can occasion nothing but a mingled sensation of abhorrence and disgust. Let us hope, though the tendency be such as we have described, that it was not in the contemplation of Swift; but that he was betrayed into this degrading and exaggerating picture, by that habitual and gloomy discontent which so long preyed upon his spirits, which at length terminated in insanity, and which forever veiled from his eyes the fairest portion of humanity.—DRAKE, NATHAN, 1804, *Essays Illustrative of the Tattler, Spectator and Guardian, vol.* III, *p.* 148.

The genius of Swift converted the sketch of an extravagant fairy tale into a narrative, unequalled for the skill with which it is sustained, and the genuine spirit of satire of which it is made the vehicle.—SCOTT, SIR WALTER, 1814, *Memoirs of Jonathan Swift.*

It would, perhaps, be too much to say that the author had an express design to blacken and culminate human nature, but at least his work displays evident marks of a diseased imagination and a lacerated heart—in short, of that frame of mind which led him in the epitaph he composed for himself, to describe the tomb as the abode, *Ubi saeva indignatio ulterius cor lacerare nequit.* We rise, accordingly, from "Gulliver's Travels," not as from the work of De Foe, exulting in our nature, but giddy, and selfish, and discontented, and, from some parts, I may almost say brutified. The general effect, indeed, of works of satire and humour is perhaps little favourable to the mind, and they are only allowable, and may be read with profit, when employed as the scourges of vice or folly.—DUNLOP, JOHN, 1814–42, *The History of Fiction, vol.* II, *p.* 421.

He has taken a new view of human nature, such as a being of a higher sphere might take of it; he has torn the scales from off his moral vision; he has tried an experiment upon human life, and sifted its pretensions from the alloy of circumstances; he has measured it with a rule, has weighed it in a balance, and found it, for the most part, wanting and worthless, in substance and in show. Nothing solid, nothing valuable is left in his system but virtue and wisdom. What a libel is this upon mankind! What a convincing proof of misanthrophy! What presumption and what *malice prepense,* to show men what they are, and to teach them what they ought to be! What a mortifying stroke, aimed at national glory, is that unlucky incident of Gulliver's wading across the channel and carrying off the whole fleet of Blefuscu! After that, we have only to consider which of the contending parties was in the right. What a shock to personal vanity is given in the account of Gulliver's nurse Glumdalclitch! Still, notwithstanding the disparagement to her personal charms, her good nature remains the same amiable quality as before. I cannot see the harm, the misanthropy, the immoral and degrading tendency of this. The moral lesson is as fine as the intellectual exhibition is amusing.—HAZLITT, WILLIAM, 1818, *Lectures on the English Poets, Lecture* vi.

I think "Gulliver's Travels" the great work of Swift.—COLERIDGE, SAMUEL TAYLOR, 1818, *Wit and Humour; Miscellanies, Æsthetic and Literary, ed. Ashe, p.* 128.

When I was a child scarce any book delighted me more than "Gulliver's Travels;" I have never read it since. I suppose that the charm was in the wonders that it related. Swift's style is plain, and without simile or metaphor, which is a great merit; no author whose power is in the original thought resorts to simile or metaphor.—BRIDGES, SIR SAMUEL EDGERTON, 1834, *Autobiography, vol.* I, *p.* 274.

The part of Dean Swift's satire which relates to the "Stulbrugs" may possibly occur to some readers as bearing upon this topic. That the staunch admirers of that singularly-gifted person should have been flung into ecstasies on the perusal of this extraordinary part of his writings, need not surprise us. Their raptures were full easily excited; but I am quite clear they have given a wrong gloss to it, and heaped upon its merits a very undeserved praise. They think that the picture of the Stulbrugs was intended to wean us from a love of life, and that it has well accomplished its purpose. I am very certain that the dean never had any such thing in view, because his sagacity was far too great not to perceive that he only could make out this position by a most undisguised begging of the question. How could any man of the most ordinary reflection expect to wean his fellow-creatures from love of life by describing a sort of persons who at a given age lost their faculties and became doting, drivelling idiots? Did any man breathing ever pretend that he wished to live, not only for centuries, but even for threescore years and ten, bereaved of his understanding, and treated by the law and by his fellowmen as in hopeless incurable dotage? The passage in question is much more likely to have proceeded from Swift's exaggerated misanthropy, and to have been designed as an antidote to human pride, by showing that our duration is necessarily limited,—if, indeed, it is not rather to be regarded as the work of mere whim and caprice.—BROUGHAM, HENRY LORD, 1835, *A Discourse of Natural Theology, Sect.* v, *note.*

The most admirable satire ever conveyed in a narrative, and the most plausible disguise that fiction ever bore. So well is the style of the old English navigators copied—so much does there seem of their honest simplicity and plain common sense—so consistent is every part of the story—so natural all the events after the first improbability,—that the fable, even in its wildest flights, never loses an air of real truth.—STANHOPE, PHILIP HENRY EARL (LORD MAHON), 1836–58, *History of England from the Peace of Utrecht to the Peace of Versailles,* 1713–1783, *vol.* II, *p.* 228.

Ever and mightiest, breathes from a great
Poet's lute!
Lo! that grim Merriment of Hatred,—born
Of him,—the Master-Mocker of Mankind,
Beside the grin of whose malignant spleen,
Voltaire's gay sarcasm seems a smile serene,—
Do we not place it in our children's hands,
Leading young Hope through Lemuel's fabled
lands?

—BULWER-LYTTON, EDWARD GEORGE LYTTON LORD, 1842, *Eva and Other Poems.*

Undoubtedly the greatest and most durable monument of Swift's style and originality of conception. "Gulliver" being a work of universal satire, will be read as long as the corruptions of human nature render its innumerable ironic and sarcastic strokes applicable and intelligible to human beings; and even were the follies and basenesses of humanity so far purged away that men should no longer need the sharp and bitter medicine of satire, it would still be read with little less admiration and delight for the wonderful richness of invention it displays, and the exquisite art with which the most impossible and extravagant adventures are related—related so naturally as to cheat us into a momentary belief in their reality.—SHAW, THOMAS B., 1847, *Outlines of English Literature, p.* 230.

What a surprising humour there is in these descriptions! How noble the satire is here! How just and honest! How perfect the image! Mr. Macaulay has quoted the charming lines of the poet, where the king of the pigmies is measured by the same standard. We have all read in Milton of the spear that was like "the mast of some tall amiral," but these images are surely likely to come to the comic poet originally. The subject is before him. He is turning it in a thousand ways. He is full of it. . . . As for the humour and conduct of this famous fable, I suppose there is no person who reads but must admire; as for the moral, I think it horrible, shameful, unmanly, blasphemous; and giant and great as this Dean is, I say we should hoot him. Some of this audience may not have read the last part of Gulliver, and to such I would recall the advice of the venerable Mr. Punch to persons about to marry and say "Don't."—THACKERAY, WILLIAM MAKEPEACE, 1853, *The English Humourists of the Eighteenth Century*.

With what power, what genius in ludicrous invention, these stories are written, no one needs to be reminded. Schoolboys, who read for the story only, and know nothing of the satire, read "Gulliver" with delight; and our literary critics, even while watching the allegory and commenting on the philosophy, break down in laughter from the sheer grotesqueness of some of the fancies, or are awed into pain and discomfort by the ghastly significance of others. Of Swift we may surely say, that, let our literature last for ages, he will be remembered in it, and chiefly for his fictions, as one of the greatest and most original of our writers —the likest author we have to Rabelais, and yet with British differences. In what cases one would recommend Swift is a question of large connexions. To all strong men he is and will be congenial, for they can bear to look round and round reality on all sides, even on that which connects us with the Yahoos. Universality is best.—MASSON, DAVID, 1859, *British Novelists and Their Styles*, p. 94.

The reason few persons were angry at Gulliver was that the satire was seldom felicitous enough to wound. Sometimes it is obscure, sometimes revolting and extravagant, and is invariably feeblest when most elaborate. The genius of the book is in the original and diverting incidents, and especially in the skill with which the fabulous is converted into the real. This must always have been the charm of the work, which flags, as Jeffrey remarked, whenever the satire predominates over the story.—ELWIN, WHITWELL, 1871, *ed. The Works of Alexander Pope, vol.* vii, *p.* 86, *note*.

What Swift has really done is to provide for the man who despises his species a number of exceedingly effective symbols for the utterance of his contempt. A child is simply amused with Bigendians and Littleendians; a philosopher thinks that the questions really at the bottom of Church quarrels are in reality of more serious import; but the cynic who has learnt to disbelieve in the nobility or wisdom of the great mass of his species finds a most convenient metaphor for expressing his disbelief. In this way "Gulliver's Travels" contains a whole gallery of caricatures thoroughly congenial to the despisers of humanity.—STEPHEN, LESLIE, 1882, *Swift (English Men of Letters)*, p. 176.

Chivalrous feeling could scarcely breathe in the same atmosphere as Gulliver.—COURTHOPE, WILLIAM JOHN, 1885, *The Liberal Movement in English Literature*, p. 112.

Swift, always among the most original of writers, is nowhere more thoroughly himself than in his enchanting romance of Lemuel Gulliver. Whether we read it, as children do, for the story, or as historians, for the political allusions, or as men of the world, for the satire and philosophy, we have to acknowledge that it is one of the wonderful and unique books of the world's literature.—GOSSE, EDMUND, 1888, *A History of Eighteenth Century Literature*, p. 160.

Swift's great work, after storming the outposts of human policy and human learning, breaks at last in a torrent of contempt and hatred on the last stronghold of humanity itself. The strength of Swift's work as a contribution to the art of fiction lies in the portentous gravity and absolute mathematical consistency wherewith he develops the consequences of his modest assumptions. In the quality of their realism the voyages to Lilliput and Brobdingnag are much superior to the two later and more violent satires; he was better fitted to ridicule the politics of his time than to attack the "men of Gresham," of whose true aims and methods he knew little or nothing; and the imagination stumbles at many of the details of the last book. But the wealth of illustration whereby he maintains the interest of his original conception of pigmies and giants is eternally surprising and delightful.—RALEIGH, WALTER, 1894, *The English Novel*, p. 137.

By a singular dispensation of Providence we usually read the "Travels" while we are children; we are delighted with the marvelous story, we are not at all injured by the poison.—SIMONDS, WILLIAM EDWARD, 1894, *Introduction to the Study of English Fiction*, p. 44.

So ends "Gulliver's Travels." In the verses which he wrote on the subject of his own death, Swift said that perhaps he "had too much satire in his vein," but added that:

> "His satire points at no defect
> But what all mortals may correct."

The imperfections and contradictions in the "Voyage to the Houyhnhnms" are obvious. There is a total want of probability in the general conception, and the Houyhnhnms are made to do many things which it was physically impossible for them to perform. It is difficult to believe that, as some have said, the Houyhnhnm represents Swift's ideal of morality. Houyhnhnm and Yahoo are alike imperfect, and Swift falsely assumes that the natural affections are opposed to reason, instead of showing how the one should be influenced by the other. It is a counsel of despair.—AITKEN, GEORGE A., 1896, *Gulliver's Travels*, p. 396, *note*.

His modern fame mainly rests on "Gulliver's Travels," the object of which, as he said, apart from the three hundred pounds realized, was to vex the world. The sixth chapter of "A Voyage to Brobdingnag" in this immortal book stands unrivalled, unless by More's "Utopia," as an ironical description of English political institutions of the time. —AUBREY, W. H. S., 1896, *The Rise and Growth of the English Nation*, vol. III, p. 112.

The book has maintained its popularity in spite of, rather than on account of its satire, and the first two voyages at least may be read with delight, even by those who know nothing of the persons and events which are held up to ridicule. —DENNIS, G. RAVENSCROFT, 1899, ed. *The Prose Works of Jonathan Swift*.

JOURNAL TO STELLA

It is a wonderful medley, in which grave reflections and important facts are at random intermingled with trivial occurrences and the puerile jargon of the most intimate tenderness.—SCOTT, SIR WALTER, 1814, *Memoirs of Jonathan Swift*.

Never, surely, was there a stranger picture of human character than Swift's daily record of his hopes and fears, his love and his ambition, his small miseries, strange affectations, and tender communings. But it is not an elevating picture as we look upon it; neither the reverend doctor nor the young lady to whom this journal is really addressed rises in our estimation. We are almost inclined to apologize even for the licentiousness of St. John, when we find it plainly recorded for the instruction and amusement of this young lady by her middle-aged companion. The explanation that the manners of Queen Anne's reign were grosser than ours, and that people were much more accustomed to plain speaking, is not at all satisfactory. There are indelicate allusions enough in the Spectator, and in Lady Montague's letters; but nothing like what we find in this journal, written in confidence to a young lady for whom Swift professed the most platonic affection. Coarse jokes and coarse oaths, the plainest allusions and double meanings of the broadest kind, are all mingled together in this strange medley of wit, vanity, affection, and secret history.—MACKNIGHT, THOMAS, 1863, *The Life of Henry St. John, Viscount Bolingbroke*, p. 128.

The delightful, fantastic, secret, childish, infinitely tender babblement, never weary of repeating itself, welling up amidst and around the records of the ruggedest affairs of State, like perennial springs of pure sweet water in a region of savage rocks. He was fighting Titanically a Titanic battle; and night and morning, in bed before he rose, in bed before he slept, he found refreshment and peace in these infantine outpourings of innocent love. The sternest cynics have such soft places in their heart of hearts! incomparably softer than the softness of unctuous sentimentalists; liquid with living fountains where these are boggy with ooze.—THOMSON, JAMES, 1876–81, *Essays and Phantasies*, p. 284.

In reading the "Journal to Stella" we may fancy ourselves waiting in a parliamentary lobby during an excited debate. One of the chief actors hurries out at intervals; pours out a kind of hasty bulletin; tells of some thrilling incident, or indicates some threatening symptom; more frequently he seeks to relieve his anxieties by indulging in a little personal gossip, and only interjects such comments upon politics as can be compressed into a hasty ejaculation, often, as may be supposed, of the imprecatory kind. Yet he unconsciously betrays his hopes and fears; he is fresh from the thick of the fight, and we perceive that his nerves are still quivering, and that his phrases are glowing with the ardour of the struggle. Hopes and fears are long since faded, and the struggle itself is now but a war of phantoms. Yet, with the help of the "Journal" and contemporary documents, we can revive for the moment the decaying images, and cheat ourselves into the momentary persuasion that the fate of the world depends upon Harley's success, as we now hold it to depend upon Mr. Gladstone's.—STEPHEN, LESLIE, 1882, *Swift (English Men of Letters), p.* 81.

His "Journal to Stella" reminds one of Rousseau's "Confessions." The points of similarity between the French infidel and the English Dean are not infrequent.—HUNT, THEODORE W., 1887, *Representative English Prose and Prose Writers, p.* 270.

The "Journal" is almost priceless as a contribution to the literature of the political history of the times, but it possesses a still greater value as a revelation of Swift's personal character. . . . The "Journal to Stella" is the key which opens the impassive mask of the satirist, behind which is disclosed the heart of the man who was sensitive to the delicate charm of a romantic passion, who was capable of disinterested acts of kindness, who was swayed by all those varied emotions which make the whole world kin. —RANDOLPH, HENRY F., 1891, *In London with Dr. Swift, Atlantic Monthly, vol.* 68, *pp.* 486, 487.

Its gossip, its nonsense, its freshness and ease of style, the tenderness concealed, or half-revealed, in its "little language," and the illustrations it supplies incidentally of the manners of the court and town, these are some of the charms that make us turn again and again to its pages with ever-increasing pleasure. We enjoy Swift's egotism and trivialities, as we enjoy the egotism of Pepys or Montaigne, and can imagine the eagerness with which the *Letters* were read by the lovely woman whose destiny it was to receive everything from Swift save the love which has its consummation in marriage. The style of the "Journal" is not that of an author composing, but of a companion talking; and it is all the more interesting since it reveals Swift's character under a pleasanter aspect than any of his formal writings. We see in it what a warm heart he had for the friends whom he had once learnt to love, and with what zeal he exerted himself in assisting brother-authors, while receiving little beyond empty praise from ministers himself.—DENNIS, JOHN, 1894, *The Age of Pope, p.* 166.

Some seven years only divide the close of his almanac and the threshold of "The Journal to Stella," but the gulf between them in attraction is immeasurable. Swift's diary of two worlds—his own and hers whose letters have unfortunately perished—stands out unique, the most entrancing and the most tragic of all extant journals. It haunts one like a refrain. The mere step in style from the quaint affectations of Pepys and the colourless gravity of Evelyn to Swift's nervous diction, his terse impetuosity, his repressed fondness, his emphasised hardness, his little pathetic language, his large indignant irony, is the step from still life to breathing, from lecture to literature, from what must always remain ancient to what will never cease to be modern.—SICHEL, W., 1899, *Men Who Have Kept a Diary, Blackwood's Magazine, vol.* 165, *p.* 74.

POEMS

I heard my father say, that Mr. Elijah Fenton, who was his intimate friend, and had been his master, informed him that Dryden, upon seeing some of Swift's earliest verses, said to him "Young man, you will never be a poet!"—WARTON, JOSEPH, 1756–97, *Essay on the Genius and Writings of Pope.*

Swift, whose muse seems to have been mere misanthropy: he was a cynick rather than a poet; and his natural dryness and sarcastick severity would have been unpleasing had he not qualified them by adopting the extravagant humour of Lucian and Rabelais.—SMOLLETT, TOBIAS GEORGE, 1757–58, *History of England, George I, notes.*

His verse is only, apparently, distinguished by the accident of measure; it has no quality of poetry, and, like his prose, is remarkable for sense and wit.—MACKINTOSH, SIR JAMES, 1811, *Diary, Memoirs ed. Mackintosh, vol.* II, *p.* 182.

As a poet, Swift's post is pre-eminent in the sort of poetry which he cultivated. He never attempted any species of composition, in which either the sublime or the pathetic were required of him. But in every department of poetry where wit is necessary, he displayed, as the subject chanced to require, either the blasting lightning of satire, or the lambent and meteor-like coruscations of frolicsome humour.—SCOTT, SIR WALTER, 1814, *Memoirs of Jonathan Swift.*

His imitations of Horace, and still more his "Verses on his own Death," place him in the first rank of agreeable moralist in verse. There is not only a dry humour, an exquisite tone of irony, in these productions of his pen, but there is a touching, unpretending pathos, mixed up with the most whimsical and eccentric strokes of pleasantry and satire. His "Description of the Morning in London," and of a "City Shower," which were first published in the "Tatler," are among the most delightful of the contents of that very delightful work. Swift shone as one of the most sensible of the poets; he is also distinguished as one of the most nonsensical of them. No man has written so many lack-a-daisical, slip-shod, tedious, trifling, foolish, fantastical verses as he, which are so little an imputation on the wisdom of the writer; and which, in fact, only show his readiness to oblige others, and to forget himself. He has gone so far as to invent a new stanza of fourteen and sixteen syllable lines for Mary the cook-maid to vent her budget of nothings, and for Mrs. Harris to gossip with the deaf old housekeeper. Oh, when shall we have such another Rector of Laracor!—HAZLITT, WILLIAM, 1818, *Lectures on the English Poets, Lecture* vi.

Rhyme and rhythm are only business-like tools, which have served him to press and launch his thought; he has put nothing but prose into them: poetry was too fine to be grasped by those coarse hands. But in prosaic subjects, what truth and force! How this masculine nakedness crushes the artificial poetry of Addison and Pope! There are no epithets; he leaves his thought as he conceived it, valuing it for and by itself, needing neither ornaments, nor preparation nor extension; above the tricks of the profession, scholastic conventionalisms, the vanity of the rhymester, the difficulties of the art; master of his subject and of himself. This simplicity and naturalness astonish us in verse. Here, as elsewhere, his originality is entire, and his genius creative; he surpasses his classical and timid age; he tyrannises over form, breaks it, dare utter anything, spares himself no strong word. Acknowledges the greatness of this invention and audacity; he alone is a superior, who finds everything and copies nothing. . . . He drags poetry not only through the mud, but into the filth; he rolls in it like a raging madman, he enthrones himself in it, and bespatters all passers-by. Compared with his, all foul words are decent and agreeable.—TAINE, H. A., 1871, *History of English Literature, tr, Van Laun, vol.* II, *bk.* iii, *ch.* v, *pp.* 137, 139.

We can hardly assign a place amongst these canary-birds to the satanic muse of Swift. He was a bird of prey in comparison with them, and threw too much of passion and hatred into the most playful of his verses to be ranked with such singers. But what force and command of language, of metre, and of rhyme! what a mastery of all he touched!—SMITH, GEORGE BARNETT, 1875, *English Fugitive Poets, Poets and Novelists, p.* 389.

Swift's poetry is perfect, exactly as the old Dutch artists were perfect painters. He never attempted to rise above this "visable diurnal sphere." He is content to lash the frivolities of the age, and to depict its absurdities. In his too faithful representatons, there is much to condemn and much to admire. Who has not felt the truth and humour of his "City Shower," and his description of "Morning?" Or the liveliness of his "Grand Question Debated," in which the knight, his lady, and the chambermaid, are so admirably drawn?—CHAMBERS, ROBERT, 1876, *Cyclopædia of English Literature, ed. Carruthers.*

Few give themselves the trouble to study his beginnings, and few, therefore, give weight enough to the fact that he made a false start. He, the ground of whose nature was an acrid commonsense, whose eye magnified the canker till it effaced the rose, began as what would now be called a romantic poet. With no mastery of verse, for even the English heroic (a balancing-pole which has enabled so many feebler men to walk the ticklish rope of momentary success) was uneasy to him; he essayed the Cowleian Pindarique, as the adjective was the rightly spelled with a hint of Parisian rather than Theban origin. . . . He who could not be a poet if he would, angrily resolved that he would not if he could. Full-sail verse was beyond his skill, but he could manage the simpler fore-and-aft rig of Butler's octosyllabics. As Cowleyism was a trick of seeing everything as it was not, and calling everything something else than it was, he would see things as they were—or as, in his sullen disgust, they seemed to be,—and call them all by their right names with a resentful emphasis. He achieved the naked sincerity of a Hottentot—nay, he even went beyond it in rejecting the feeble compromise of the breech-clout. Not only would he be naked and not ashamed, but everybody else should be so with a blush of conscious exposure, and human nature should be stripped of the hypocritical fig-leaves that betrayed by attempting to hide its identity with the brutes that perish. His sincerity was not unconscious, but self-willed and aggressive. But it would be unjust to overlook that he began with himself.—LOWELL, JAMES RUSSELL, 1876, *Forster's Life of Swift, The Nation, vol.* 22, *p.* 265.

Generally careless, often harsh, his versification is seldom laboured; his pen may run till it wearies the reader; but we see no reason in fall of energy why Swift's Hudibrastic jingle should cease, any more than why the waves of Spenser's stanza should not roll for ever. The other merits of our author's verse are those of his prose condensation, pith, always the effect, generally the reality, of sincere purpose, and with few exceptions, simplicity and directness. . . . . Swift's tendency to dwell on the meaner, and even the revolting facts of life, pardonable in his prose, is unpardonable in those tributes to Venus Cloacina, in which he intrudes on a lady's boudoir with the eye of a surgeon fresh from a dissecting-room or an hospital. His society verses are like those of a man writing with his feet, for he delights to trample on what others caress. Often he seems, among singing birds, a vulture screeching over carrion.—NICHOL, J., 1880, *English Poets, ed. Ward, vol.* III, *pp.* 36, 38.

Swift's originality appears in the very fact that he requires a new class to be made for him. He justified Dryden's remark in so far as he was never a poet in the sense in which Milton or Wordsworth or Shelley or even Dryden himself were poets. His poetry may be called rhymed prose, and should, perhaps, be put at about the same level in the scale of poetry as "Hudibras." It differs from prose, not simply in being rhymed, but in that the metrical form seems to be the natural and appropriate mode of utterance.—STEPHEN, LESLIE, 1882, *Swift (English Men of Letters), p.* 202.

As a Poet Swift has hardly been appreciated: he has disgusted many readers by his occasional coarseness: but that he was a real poet, and a master of verse, no one can dispute. What a history was his, of Genius crushed by neglect, at last asserting itself: then going out in the dreary, and dismal, light of Insanity. Strange that with his vast intellect, and great ambition, he should not see that, had he kept his writings within the bounds of decency, and had chosen on the whole more serious topics, he must have ranked among the first of British Poets.—FRASER, SIR WILLIAM, 1891, *Hic et Ubique, p.* 22.

How admirable also is his poetry—easy, yet never slip-shod! It lacks one quality only—imagination. There is not a fine phrase, a magical line to be found in it such as may occasionally be found in—let us say—Butler. Yet as a whole, Swift is a far more enjoyable poet than Butler. Swift has unhappily written some abominable verses, which ought never to have been set up in type; but the "Legion Club," the verses on his own death, "Cadenus and Vanessa," the "Rhapsody on Poetry," the tremendous lines on the "Day of Judgment," and many others, all belong to enjoyable poetry, and can never lose their freshness, their charm, their vitality. Amongst the poets of the eighteenth century Swift sits secure, for he can never go out of fashion.—BIRRELL, AUGUSTINE, 1894, *Essays about Men, Women and Books, p.* 7.

CADENUS AND VANESSA
1726

Sr,—I have the Favor of y[r] Lettr of the 7th instant. As to the Poem you mention, I know severall Copyes of it have been given about, and Ld. L[t]. told me he had one. It was written at Windsor near 14 years ago, and dated: It was a Task performed on a Frolick among some Ladyes, and she it was addrest to dyed some time ago in Dublin, and on her Death the Copy shewn by her Executor. I am very indifferent what is done with it, for printing cannot make it more common than it is; and for my own Part, I forget what was in it, but believe it to be onely a cavalier Business, and they who will not give allowances may chuse, and if they intend it maliciously, they will be disappointed, for it was what I expected, long before I left Irel[d]—Therefore what you advise me, about printing it my self is impossible, for I never saw it since I writ it, neither if I had, would I use shifts or Arts, let People think of me as they please. Neither do I believe the gravest Character is answerable for a Private humersome thing which by an accident inevitable, and the Baseness of particular Malice is made publick. I have borne a great deal more, and those who will like me less, upon seeing me capable of having writ such a Trifle so many years ago, may think as they please, neither is it agreeable to me to be troubled with such Accounts, when there is no Remedy and onely gives me the ungratefull Task of reflecting on the Baseness of Mankind, which I knew sufficiently before.—SWIFT, JONATHAN, 1726, *Letter to Mr. Chetwode, Unpublished Letters of Dean Swift, ed. Hill, p.* 189.

This is thought one of Dr. Swift's correctest pieces; its chief merit, indeed, is the elegant ease with which a story, but ill conceived in itself, is told.—GOLDSMITH, OLIVER, 1767, *The Beauties of English Poetry.*

The "Cadenus and Vanessa" is, of itself, complete proof that he had in him none of the elements of poetry. It was written when his faculties were in their perfection, and his heart animated with all the tenderness of which it was ever capable—and yet it is as cold and as flat as the ice of Thulé. Though describing a real passion, and a real perplexity, there is not a spark of fire, nor a throb of emotion in it from one end to the other. All the return he makes to the warm-hearted creature who had put her destiny into his hands, consists in a frigid mythological fiction, in which he sets forth, that Venus and the Graces lavished their gifts on her in her infancy, and moreover got Minerva, by a trick, to inspire her with wit and wisdom. The style is mere prose—or rather a string of familiar and vulgar phrases tacked together in rhyme, like the general tissue of his poetry.—JEFFREY, FRANCIS LORD, 1816, *Works of Jonathan Swift, Edinburgh Review, vol.* 27. *p.* 49.

In the walk of satire and familiar poetry, wit and knowledge of mankind, joined to facility of expression, are the principal requisites of excellence, and in these Swift shines unrivalled. Cadenus and Vanessa may be considered as his chief d'œuvres in that class of poems which is not professedly satirical. It is a poem on manners, and, like one of Marmontel's Contes moraux, traces the progress and circulation of passion, existing between two persons in modern society, contrasted strongly in age, manners, and situation. Yet even here the satirical vein of Swift has predominated. We look in vain for depth of feeling or tenderness of sentiment, although, had such existed in the poet's mind the circumstances must have called it forth. The mythological fable, which conveys the compliments paid to Vanessa, is as cold as that addressed to Ardelia, or to Miss Floyd. It is in short a kind of poetry which neither affects sublimity nor pathos; but which, in the graceful facility of the poet, unites the acute observation of the observer of human nature, to commemorate the singular contest between Cadenus and Vanessa, as an extraordinary chapter in the history of the mind.—MITFORD, JOHN, 1833, *Life of Swift.*

His best piece, "Cadenus and Vanessa," is a poor, threadbare allegory.—TAINE, H. A., 1871, *History of English Literature, tr. Van Laun, vol.* II, *bk.* iii, *ch.* v, *p.* 135.

That exquisitely graceful and original poem which has made the name of Hester Vanhomrigh deathless. She could there read how Venus, provoked by the complaints which were daily reaching her about the degeneracy of the female sex; resolved to retrieve the reputation of that sex, how, with this object, she called into being a matchless maid, who to every feminine virtue united every feminine grace and charm; how, not content with endowing her paragon to all that is proper to woman, the goddess succeeded by a stratagem in inducing Pallas to bestow on her the choicest of the virtues proper to man; how Pallas, angry at being deceived, consoled herself with the reflection that a being so endowed would be likely little to prove obedient to the goddess who had created her; how Vanessa—for such was the peerless creature's name—did not for a while belie the expectations of Pallas, but how at last she was attacked by treacherous Cupid in Wisdom's very stronghold. The flattered girl could then follow in a transparent allegory the whole history of her relation with her friend, sketched so delicately, and at the same time so humorously, that it must have been impossible for her either to take offence or to miss his meaning.—COLLINS, JOHN CHURTON, 1893, *Jonathan Swift*, *p.* 136.

LETTERS

Dean Swift's also are unaffected; and as a proof of their being so, they exhibited his character fully, with all its defects; though it were to be wished, for the honour of his memory, that his epistolary correspondence had not been drained to the dregs, by so many successive publications as have been given to the world.—BLAIR, HUGH, 1783, *Lectures on Rhetoric and Belles-Letters, ed. Mills, Lecture* xxxvii.

Swift's masculine power is manifest in his letters, for affection, unless the affection of rudeness, came not nigh him. There is, too, in his letters, a sad reality, from the connection with that strange control which his stern nature gained over the affections of two women at the same time; his mysterious marriage with one, and the final heart-breaking of them both. —REED, HENRY, 1855, *Lectures on English Literature from Chaucer to Tennyson*, *p.* 405.

Swift's own letters, however, have the true genius ring. In so far as he came under the spirit of the age, and found himself in correspondence with men who would have shuddered at incorrect syntax or bad logic, they are careful compositions. But he was an exceedingly quick writer; and, as most of his letters are addressed to friends of tried fidelity, they afford us a real insight into the man and his being. They describe his manner of life: they show how the solitary chafed against exile without being able to summon up strength to quit it; and they enable us to trace his gradual decline, from attempted resignation, into a bitterness which no philosophy could soothe.—MORIARTY, GERALD P., 1892, *Dean Swift and his Writings*, *p.* 278.

GENERAL

To Jonathan Swift, the most agreeable companion, the truest friend, and the greatest genius of his age, this work is presented by his most humble servant the author.—ADDISON, JOSEPH, 1705, *Inscription to Presentation, Copy of "Travels in Italy."*

O Swift! if fame be life (as well we know
That bards and heroes have esteem'd it so),
Thou canst not wholly die. Thy works will shine
To future times, and life in fame be thine.
—PARNELL, THOMAS, 1713, *To Dr. Swift on his Birthday, Nov.* 30.

This gentleman has the honour (in common with *Rabelais*) of being a priest, and like him laughs at every thing. But in my humble opinion, the title of the *English Rabelais*, which is given the dean, is highly derogatory to his genius. . . . Dean Swift is *Rabelais* in his senses, and frequenting the politest company. The former indeed is not so gay as the latter, but then he possesses all the delicacy, the justness, the choice, the good taste, in all which particulars our giggling rural vicar *Rabelais* is wanting. The poetical numbers of Dean *Swift* are of a singular and almost inimitable taste; true humour, whether in prose or verse, seems to be his peculiar talent; but whoever is desirous of understanding him perfectly, must visit the island in which he was born.—VOLTAIRE, FRANCOIS MARIE AROUET, 1732? *Letters Concerning the English Nation, pp.* 169, 170.

The Spectators, though there are so many bad ones among them, make themselves read still. All Addison's are allowed to be good, and many of Steele's. —Gulliver was received but indifferently, at first, among us; but pleased much after people had entered more into the humour of it.—BOILEAU, ABBÉ, AT TOURS, 1737–39, *Spence's Anecdotes, ed. Singer, p.* 141.

Has stolen all his humour from Cervantes

and Rabelais.—MONTAGU, LADY MARY WORTLEY, 1740–41, *Spence's Anecdotes, ed. Singer, p.* 176.

There is just published Swift's History. . . . Pope and Lord Bolingbroke always told him it would disgrace him, and persuaded him to burn it. Disgrace him indeed it does,—being a weak libel, ill written for style, uninformed, and adopting the most errant mob stories. He makes the Duke of Marlborough a coward, Prince Eugene an assassin, my father remarkable for nothing but impudence, and would make my Lord Somers anything but the most amiable character in the world, if unfortunately he did not praise him while he tries to abuse.—WALPOLE, HORACE, 1758, *To Sir Horace Mann, March* 21; *Letters ed. Cunningham, vol.* III, *p.* 130.

His delight was in simplicity. . . . His style was well suited to his thoughts, which are never subtilised by nice disquisitions, decorated by sparkling conceits, elevated by ambitious sentences, or variegated by far-sought learning. . . . He always understands himself; and his readers always understand him: the peruser of Swift wants little previous knowledge; it will be sufficient that he is acquainted with common words and common things; he is neither required to mount elevations nor to explore profundities; his passage is always on a level along solid ground, without asperities, without obstruction. —JOHNSON, SAMUEL, 1779–81, *Swift, Lives of the English Poets.*

"Now mark, Serena!" (the mild guide began)
"The proudest Phantom of the gloomy clan,
Appointed by this surly Monarch's grace,
High-priest of all this Misanthropic race!
See o'er the crowd a throne of vapour lift
That strange and motly form, the shade of SWIFT!"
"Now shalt thou view" (the guardian Sprite pursues)
"His horrid penance, that each day renews;
Perchance its terrors may o'erwhelm thy sense,
But trust my care to bear thee safely hence!"
—HAYLEY, WILLIAM, 1781, *The Triumphs of Temper, Canto* III, *v.* 587–596.

Nature imparting her satiric gift,
Her serious mirth, to Arbuthnot and Swift,
With droll sobriety they raise a smile
At folly's cost, themselves unmoved the while.
That constellation set, the world in vain
Must hope to look upon their like again.
—COWPER, WILLIAM, 1782, *Table Talk.*

A writer who, with a rich fund of humour, an easy and flowing style, perhaps more correct than that of any of his contemporaries, with habits of observation, and a keen discernment of folly and weakness, was nevertheless ill qualified for this species of composition. His wit was so licentious, that no subject however sacred, and no character however amiable, were safe; his invective has more malignity than virtuous indignation: his characters are drawn in hideous distortion; and perhaps no man ever attempted to ridicule vice or folly with less of the salutary and gentle spirit of correction. . . . SWIFT'S style was, beyond all precedent, pure and precise, yet void of ornament or grace, and partook in some instances of the pride and dogmatism of its author: nor does his Biographer seem to be aware, that his most incorrect composition is his "Proposal for correcting the English tongue."—CHALMERS, ALEXANDER, 1803, *ed. The Tatler, vol.* I, *pp.* 55, 59.

Peace to Swift's faults! his wit hath made them pass,
Unmatch'd by all, save matchless Hudibras!
—BYRON, LORD, 1811, *Hints from Horace.*

Without being distinguished by imagination, subtlety, comprehension, or refinement, he possessed a degree of masterly and correct good sense, almost as rare as genius; if, indeed, we be authorised to withhold the name of genius from so large a measure of any important mental power. Wit was, in him, not so much the effort or the sport of fancy, as the keen edge of that exquisite good sense which laid bare the real ridicule and deformity existing in human life. The distinguishing feature of his moral character was a strong sense of justice, which disposed him to exact with rigour, as well as in general scrupulously to observe, the duties of society. These powerful feelings, exasperated probably by some circumstances of his own life, were gradually formed into an habitual and painful indignation against triumphant wrong, which became the ruling principle of his character and writings. His anger and disgust extended to every physical and moral deformity which human effort could remove; and it cannot be doubted that his severity materially corrected many of them.—MACKINTOSH, SIR JAMES, 1811, *Diary, Memoirs ed. Mackintosh, vol.* II, *p.* 181.

With a quick and sagacious spirit, and a bold and popular manner, he joins an exact knowledge of all the strong and weak parts of every cause he has to manage; and without the least restraint from delicacy, either of taste or of feeling, he seems always to think the most effectual blows the most advisable, and no advantage unlawful that is likely to be successful for the moment. Disregarding all the laws of polished hostility, he uses, at one and the same moment, his sword and his poisoned dagger—his hands, and his teeth, and his envenomed breath,—and does not even scruple, upon occasion, to imitate his own yahoos, by discharging on his unhappy victims a shower of filth, from which neither courage nor dexterity can afford any protection.—Against such an antagonist, it was, of course, at no time very easy to make head; and accordingly his invective seems, for the most part, to have been as much dreaded, and as tremendous as the personal ridicule of Voltaire. Both were inexhaustible, well directed, and unsparing; but even when Voltaire drew blood, he did not mangle the victim, and was only mischievous when Swift was brutal. Any one who will compare the epigrams on M. Franc de Pompignan with those on Tighe or Bettesworth, will easily understand the distinction.—JEFFREY, FRANCIS LORD, 1816, *Works of Jonathan Swift, Edinburgh Review, vol.* 27, *p*, 45.

In Swift's writings there is a false misanthropy, grounded upon an exclusive contemplation of the vices and follies of mankind, and this misanthropic tone is also disfigured or brutalized by his obtrusion of physical dirt and coarseness. . . . Swift's style is, in its line, perfect; the manner is a complete expression of the matter, the terms appropriate, and the artifice concealed. It is simplicity in the true sense of the word.—COLERIDGE, SAMUEL TAYLOR, 1818, *Miscellanies, Æsthetic and Literary, ed. Ashe, pp.* 128, 181.

It is certainly not difficult to perceive throughout all the writings and conduct of Swift, that his avowed dislike to his species was not such a feeling as could lead him to prefer their unhappiness to their welfare, but was a qualified sentiment arising from a quick sense of their vices, follies, and absurdities, which it was his object to correct by a moral caustic; in the same manner as we may presume that in some of his most indelicate poems, his object was not to disgust his readers, but to recommend that due attention to decency and cleanliness, for which he was himself so remarkable.—ROSCOE, WILLIAM, 1824–47, *The Life of Alexander Pope, vol.* I, *p.* 227.

Swift was *anima Rabelaisii habitans in sicco*,—the soul of Rabelais dwelling in a dry place.—COLERIDGE, SAMUEL TAYLOR, 1830, *Table Talk, ed. Ashe, June* 15, *p.* 97.

The apostate politician, the ribald priest, the perjured lover—a heart burning with hatred against the whole human race—a mind richly stored with images from the dunghill and the lazarhouse.—MACAULAY, THOMAS BABINGTON, 1832, *Mahon's War of the Succession, Edinburgh Review; Critical and Miscellaneous Essays.*

Jonathan Swift has been most inappropriately called by Voltaire the English Rabelais. Voltaire relished only the impieties of Rabelais, and his humour, when it is good; but the deep satire on society and man, the lofty philosophy, the grand style, of the *curé* of Mendon, escaped his notice, as he saw only the weak side of Christianity, and had no idea of the intellectual and moral revolution effected in mankind by the gospel. . . . The ages in which the two writers lived produce, moreover, a wide difference between them: Rabelais began his language; Swift finished his.—CHATEAUBRIAND, FRANÇOIS RENÉ VICOMTE DE, 1837, *Sketches of English Literature, vol.* II, *pp.* 245, 246.

By far the greatest man of that time, I think, was Jonathan Swift; Dean Swift, a man entirely deprived of his natural nourishment, but of great robustness; of genuine Saxon mind, not without a feeling of reverence, though, from circumstances, it did not awaken in him, for he got unhappily, at the outset, into the Church, not having any vocation for it. It is curious to see him arranging, as it were, a little religion to himself. . . . He saw himself in a world of confusion and falsehood. No eyes were clearer to see into it than his. He was great from being of acrid temperament: painfully sharp nerves in body as well as soul, for he was constantly ailing, and his mind, at the same time, was soured with indignation at what he saw around him. He took up therefore, what was fittest for him, namely, sarcasm, and he carried it quite to an epic pitch. There is something great and fearful in his irony, for it is not always used for effect, or designedly to depreciate. There seems often to be a sympathy in it with the thing he satirizes; occasionally it was even impossible for him so to laugh at any object without a sympathy with it, a sort of love for it; the same love as Cervantes universally shows for his own objects of merit.—CARLYLE, THOMAS, 1838, *Lectures on the History of Literature, Lecture* x, *p.* 177.

For the qualities of sheer wit and humour, Swift had no superior, ancient or modern. He had not the poetry of Aristophanes, or the animal spirits of Rabelais; he was not so incessantly witty as Butler; nor did he possess the delicacy of Addison, or the good nature of Steele or Fielding, or the pathos and depth of Sterne; but his wit was perfect, as such; a sheer meeting of the extremes of difference and likeness; and his knowledge of character was unbounded. He knew the humour of great and small, from the king down to the cook-maid.—HUNT, LEIGH, 1846, *Wit and Humour.*

Of all men of supereminent genius, Swift appears to have had the least sympathy with what is beautiful, the least enthusiasm for what is sublime. The very force and might of his style consists in its being level, plain, prosaic, logical, and unimaginative. But his taste for images of absolute physical filthiness we believe to be peculiar to him: the *physiologist* might discover its cause.—SHAW, THOMAS B., 1847, *Outlines of English Literature, p.* 232.

At Court the Doctor had no eyes but for the very greatest. Lord Treasurer and Sir John used to call him Jonathan; and they paid him with this cheap coin for the service they took of him. He writ their lampoons, fought their enemies, flogged and bullied in their service, and, it must be owned, with a consummate skill and fierceness. 'Tis said he hath lost his intellect now, and forgotten his wrongs and his rage against mankind. I have always thought of him and of Marlborough as the two greatest men of that age. I have read his books (who doth not know them?) here in our calm woods, and imagine a giant to myself as I think of him,—a lonely fallen Prometheus, groaning as the vulture tears him. Prometheus I saw; but, when first I ever had any words with him, the giant stepped out of a sedan-chair in the Poultry, whither he had come with a tipsy Irish servant parading before him, who announced him,—brawling out his Reverence's name whilst his master below was as yet haggling with his chairmen. I dislike this Mr. Swift. . . . If the greatest satirist the world ever hath seen had writ against Harley, and not for him, what a history had he left behind of the last years of Queen Anne's reign! But Swift, that scorned all mankind, and himself not the least of all, had this merit of a faithful partisan, that he loved those chiefs who treated him well, and stuck by Harley bravely in his fall, as he gallantly had supported him in his better fortune.—THACKERAY, WILLIAM MAKEPEACE, 1852, *The History of Henry Esmond, bk.* iii, *chs.* v, x.

It was a stripped, concentred, irresistible force which dwelt in him—fed, too, by unutterable misery; and hence his power, and hence his pollution. He was strong, naked, coarse, savage, and mud-loving, as one of the huge primeval creatures of chaos. Jeffrey's sense of polish, feeling of elegance and propriety, consciousness of inferiority in most things, and consciousness of superiority in some, all contributed to rouse his ire at Swift; and, unequal as on the whole the match was, the clever Scotchman beat the monster Paddy. One is reminded of Gulliver's contest with some of the gigantic reptiles and wasps of Brobdingnag. Armed with his hanger, that redoubtable traveler made them resile, or sent them wounded away. And thus the memory of Swift bears Jeffrey's steel-mark on it, and shall bear it forever.—GILFILLAN, GEORGE, 1855, *A Third Gallery of Portraits, p.* 194.

How realistic or materialistic in treatment of his subject is Swift. He describes his fictitious persons as if for the police. —EMERSON, RALPH WALDO, 1856, *English Traits, Works, Riverside ed., vol.* v, *p.* 223.

The best and most perfect specimen of ill-humour.—MAURICE, FREDERICK DENISON, 1856, *The Friendship of Books and Other Lectures, p.* 21.

Indubitably one of the most robust minds of his age, Swift, in the first place, went wholly along with his age, nay, tore it along with him faster than it could decorously go, in its renunciation of romance and all "the sublimities." He, a surpliced priest (as Rabelais had also been), a commissioned expositor of things not seen, *was* an expositor of things not seen; but it was of those that are unseen because they have to be dug for down in the concealing earth, and not of those that fill the upward azure, and tremble by their very nature beyond the sphere of vision. The age for him was still too full of the cant of older beliefs, preserved in the guise of "respectabilities;" and, to help to clear it of this, he would fix its gaze on its own roots, and on the physical roots of human nature in general, down in the disgusting and the reputedly bestial. I say this not in the way of judgment, but of fact. It is what we all know of Swift—they who see good in his merciless method, as well as they who abhor it.—MASSON, DAVID, 1859, *British Novelists and Their Styles, p.* 90.

Swift was neither a Cervantes nor a Rabelais; but yet, with something that was peculiar to himself, he combined considerable portions of both. He had more of Cervantes than Rabelais had, and more of Rabelais than was given to Cervantes. There cannot be claimed for him the refinement, the humanity, the pathos, the noble elevation of the Spaniard—all that irradiates and beautifies his satire and drollery as the blue sky does the earth it bends over; neither, with all his ingenuity and fertility, does our English wit and humorist anywhere display either the same inexhaustible abundance of grotesque invention, or the same gayety and luxuriance of fancy, with the historian of the Doings and Sayings of the Giant Gargantua. Yet neither Cervantes nor Rabelais, nor both combined, could have written "The Tale of a Tub," or the "Battle of the Books." The torrent of triumphant merriment is broader and more rushing than anything of the same kind in either. —CRAIK, GEORGE L., 1861, *A Compendious History of English Literature and of the English Language, vol.* II, *p.* 209.

Of the intellectual grandeur of his career it is needless to speak. The chief sustainer of an English Ministry, the most powerful advocate of the Peace of Utrecht, the creator of public opinion in Ireland, he has graven his name indelibly in English history, and his writings, of their own kind, are unique in English literature. It has been the misfortune of Pope to produce a number of imitators, who made his versification so hackneyed that they produced a reaction against his poetry in which it is often most unduly underrated. Addison, though always read with pleasure, has lost much of his old supremacy. A deeper criticism, a more nervous and stimulating school of political writers have made much that he wrote appear feeble and superficial, and even in his own style it would be possible to produce passages in the writings of Goldsmith and Lamb that might be compared without disadvantage with the best papers of the "Spectator." But the position of Swift is unaltered. "Gulliver" and the "Tale of a Tub" remain isolated productions, unrivalled, unimitated, and inimitable.—LECKY, WILLIAM EDWARD HARTPOLE, 1861–71, *The Leaders of Public Opinion in Ireland, p.* 61.

Will nothing but from Greece or Rome
Please me? Is nothing good at home?
Yes; better; but I look in vain
For a Molière or La Fontaine.
Swift, in his humour, was as strong,
But there was gall upon his tongue.
Bitters and acids may excite,
Yet satisfy not appetite.
—LANDOR, WALTER SAVAGE, 1863, *Poems.*

As a man of letters, Swift occupies a high place. The testimony on this subject is ample, sometimes generously offered, sometimes unwillingly extorted. As a satirist and a wit, his power was tremendous. He wielded the thunder-bolt that felled to the earth, and the lightning-flash that scathed, and burned, and shrivelled up its victim. Compared with him Junius is feeble. . . . Swift, too, was an original genius, and no writer was ever less indebted to others, either for the thoughts that he put forward or the style in which he clothed them. And yet few authors were ever less anxious for fame than he: he wrote for an object totally independent of fame, and that object accomplished, he cared little for the means which he had used.—WALLER, JOHN FRANCIS, 1865, *ed. Gulliver's Travels, Life, pp.* xlii, xliii.

It is curious for one who studies the action and reaction of national literatures on each other, to see the humor of Swift and Sterne and Fielding, after filtering through Richter, reappear in Carlyle with a tinge of Germanism that makes it novel, alien, or even displeasing, as the case may be, to the English mind. Unhappily the bit of *mother* from Swift's vinegar-barrel has had strength enough to sour all the rest.—LOWELL, JAMES RUSSELL, 1866–90, *Carlyle, Prose Works, Riverside ed., vol.* II. *p.* 88.

Our greatest English satirist.—HANNAY, JAMES, 1866, *ed., The Poetical Works of Charles Churchill, Memoir, vol.* I, *p.* xxiii.

A hedgehog rolling in filth. . . . Manners of a hangman, the misanthropy of a hypochondriac, and the grin of a tyrant.—SAINT-VICTOR, PAUL DE, 1867, *Hommes et Dieux.*

Swift has the style of a surgeon and a judge, cold, grave, solid, unadorned, without vivacity or passion, manly and practical. He desired neither to please, nor divert, nor to carry people away, nor to touch; he never hesitated, nor was redundant, nor was excited, nor made an effort. He expressed his thoughts in a uniform tone, with exact, precise, often harsh terms, with familiar comparisons, levelling all within reach of his hand, even the loftiest things—especially the loftiest—with a brutal and always haughty coldness. He knows life as a banker knows accounts; and his total once made up, he scorns or knocks down the babblers who dispute it in his presence. . . . He employs the whole force of an excellently armed mind and an excellently tempered character in denying and destroying: all his works are pamphlets.—TAINE, H. A., 1871, *History of English Literature, tr. Van Laun, vol.* II, *bk.* iii, *ch.* v, *pp.* 123, 125.

There is a remarkable determination of purpose in the style of Swift, with perfect transparency; and these are but the reflexes of the natural man, for these were the prominent features of his character. It will be observed that in his writings we rarely meet with a superfluous epithet. . . . Swift is the most English, the most thoroughly national in his diction of all our classic writers. On no occasion does he employ an exotic term, if one indigenous to the language be at hand. He is also sparing of connecting particles and introductory phrases and flourishes, using also the simplest forms of construction; and, moreover, he is master of the idiomatic peculiarities, and lurking, unapparent resources of the language to a degree of perfection that leaves him almost without a competitor. —CLARKE, CHARLES COWDEN, 1871, *On the Comic Writers of England, The Gentleman's Magazine, n. s., vol.* 7, *p.* 437.

Taken as a whole, his writings leave upon our minds a wonderful impression of persistent originality, analogical power, effective eloquence, and wit.—MINTO, WILLIAM, 1872–80, *Manual of English Prose Literature, p.* 358.

That writer had far too high a genius to be commonly understood. Hence many people abuse him instead of loving him; hence the words, beast, man-hater, foul-tongued fellow, applied to him. But Swift understood himself. In his "Tale of a Tub" and "Gulliver" he penned as fine satires as the world ever saw; but in his verses "On a Lady's Bedchamber," and others of the sort, he spoke dirt, and meant to speak dirt, and was too earnest to be satirical.—FRISWELL, JAMES HAIN, 1872, *A Man's Thoughts, p.* 153.

In his works look wherever we may—whether those penned in his happiest, or his most diabolical, moods—he seems to us to be wearing a mask, and to be conscious that he is doing so. We do not refer to a mask which either prevents him from seeing the truth, or from going straight at it, in his writings, but a mask over the inner man, with its affections, its desires, and its ambitions. He appears to us to be constantly saying that everything, by which he is surrounded, is a sham, and that he is compelled, also, to follow the same course of false appearance. This absence of sincerity destroyed his happiness, as it does that of humbler men. . . . Jonathan Swift, though writing upon the gross side of human life, was a writer, nevertheless, who was conscious that he was treading the paths of greatness. Had he always received due encouragement, and had the burden of his life been lightened, there is no knowing of what height he could not have attained in the roll of letters. On the severe and thoroughly caustic side of satire, he has no equal; he is a giant wielding the weapons of ridicule; and had not his existence been so overshadowed by disappointments, it would be hazardous, we repeat, to affirm what triumphs he might not have achieved in English literature. As it is, he enjoys the position of one of its finest and most honored classics.—SMITH, GEORGE BARNETT, 1876, *Dean Swift, The International Review, vol.* 3, *pp.* 311–316.

One of the immortal of the noblest literature of earth, a master of expression, a satirist unequalled before his day and since, feared by his contemporaries and admired by all subsequent writers, he enriched his native tongue with productions distinguished in the last degree by intellectual force and pungency. But to all after-comers he looms up among the crowd of mediocrities, conspicuous no less for sorrows than for brilliant parts, leading the most bitter of lives, dying the most pathetic of deaths that are recorded in the varied tale of English literary history. —GILMAN, NICHOLAS P., 1879, *"Sweetness and Light," Unitarian Review, vol.* 11, *p.* 233.

The small morsel of literature known as "Swift's Directions to Servants," has had, and will continue to have, irresistible attractions to the curious and inquiring. Yet it may safely be said that no one can read it without feeling that, in doing so, he has brought on himself one of the minor misfortunes of life—a something that for some indefinite time will haunt him with such horror as a nightmare-dream may inflict on the first thoughts of morning. It is not that the object of the little book is revolting, or, indeed, anything but commendable. It touches upon morals only obliquely in dealing with the smaller affairs of life; but, so far as it goes, its object is to promote virtue. The preceptor is the absolute antithesis of one wallowing in filth, physical or moral. He is a clean man lifting up his testimony against the abominations that gather around to disgust and torture him. He is jeering and scolding a filthy world with all the vehemence of his rhetoric and sarcasm. But the inexorable logic of the form of irony assumed by him, drags him and his reader through every form of the filthy and the odious that poor fallen human nature is liable to suffer under in domestic life.—BURTON, JOHN HILL, 1880, *A History of the Reign of Queen Anne, vol.* III, *p.* 275.

His indulgence in revolting images is to some extent an indication of a diseased condition of his mind, perhaps of actual mental decay. Delany says that it grew upon him in his later years, and, very gratuitously, attributes it to Pope's influence. The peculiarity is the more remarkable, because Swift was a man of the most scrupulous personal cleanliness. He was always enforcing this virtue with special emphasis. He was rigorously observant of decency in ordinary conversation. Delany once saw him "fall into a furious resentment" with Stella for "a very small failure of delicacy." So far from being habitually coarse, he pushed fastidiousness to the verge of prudery. It is one of the superficial paradoxes of Swift's character that this very shrinking from filth became perverted into an apparently opposite tendency. In truth, his intense repugnance to certain images led him to use them as the only adequate expression of his savage contempt. . . . His intensity of loathing leads him to besmear his antagonists with filth. He becomes disgusting in the effort to express his disgust. As his misanthropy deepened he applied the same method to mankind at large.—STEPHEN, LESLIE, 1882, *Swift (English Men of Letters), p.* 178.

And yet what contradictions! What Titanic pride to strive to see things as a god; to dwarf man's glory or aggrandise his vices with planetary magnifying or diminishing glasses; to distort his features in the concave mirror of the heavens! The Houyhnhnms—Swift's ideas of moral excellence—are calm, rational, benevolent creatures, devoid of passions: and he himself is devoured by scorn and hate. They have not learnt to say the thing that is not: and Swift does not scruple to print monstrous falsehoods for a party purpose. They are modest and cleanly: and Swift flings ordure in the faces of women and of little children. They have tranquil deaths, towards which they move with resignation: and he makes his exit in a rage.—DOWDEN, EDWARD, 1882, *Literature, The Academy, vol.* 22, *p.* 233.

Of his ability it is hard to speak too highly.—PERRY, THOMAS SERGEANT, 1883, *English Literature in the Eighteenth Century, p.* 210.

Swift's satire is as enduring as our language, and will in turn delight and chill and terrify mankind so long as books have power. There is something in this satire that is alone and without exact parallel in literature. It is always in terrible earnest. We smile with Thackeray, for we feel that the humourist is ridiculing himself as much as anybody, and is laughing with us while he pretends to anathematize. With Swift it is no laughing matter. He hates and loathes the meannesses and unrealities of life with the fervour of a prophet of old; he denounces them with the Burden of Moab. Weakness and deception do not amuse but enrage him; he does not pity the feeble race that descends to shams and subterfuge, he despises it heartily. . . . His earnestness is reflected in his style. No English is so pointed and so direct as Swift's. Every sentence is a keen knife that cuts straight to the core; there is no hesitation or swerving; there is never a word wasted. His sentences follow one another logically and equably, in the order dictated by the subject, without any apparent regard for the graces of expression, nor even, sometimes, for the ordinary rules of grammar. —POOLE, STANLEY LANE-, 1883, *ed., Selections from the Prose Writings of Jonathan Swift, Preface, pp.* XV, XVII.

In originality and strength he has no superior, and in irony no equal. He had the genius of insult, as Shakespeare of poetry. Unscrupulous sarcasm and vituperation, crushing logic, knowledge of men and life, vehement expression, made him the most formidable pamphleteer that ever lived. He was deficient in refinement of taste and loftiness of imagination, and lacked the nobility of nature to become a true poet, philosopher, or reformer. The grandeurs of the human spirit escaped him. Palpable and familiar objects, common words, common things, were the sources of his inspiration. Several peculiarities contributed to produce his effect—skillful minuteness of narrative; power to give to fiction the air of truth; the habit of expressing sentiments, the most absurd or atrocious, or sober commonplaces; or relating the most ludicrous and extravagant fancies with an invincible gravity. As a man, he is the most tragic figure in our literature.—WELSH, ALFRED H., 1883, *Development of English Literature and Language, vol.* II, *p.* 104.

Out of his prose, which fills fifteen volumes, only "Gulliver's Travels," the "Tale of a Tub," and the "Journal to Stella," have enough human interest to keep them fresh for many ages. His remaining works have been likened, not quite unjustly, to a row of rusty cannon in an old armoury. Once resistless to beat down and break in pieces, they move us now only by the faint remembrance of the havoc which they have made. Yet we must own that in controversy Swift was at home, and that the pamphlet was a form of expression well suited to his genius. Few men have joined so clear an intellect to a temper so combative. Fewer still who have felt such an agony of angry passion have been able to subdue it to an irony so grave and austere. Since Swift wrote, thousands of able men have used the pen as a weapon of political warfare, and a half-a-dozen of them have become famous. But which of the half-dozen shall we place even second to Swift? Compared with Swift, Junius is a commonplace rhetorician, Cobbett a sturdy clown, Sydney Smith a monotonous humourist. . . . He wrote his political pieces not with the left hand but with the right; and it was the right hand of Achilles.—MONTAGUE, F. C., 1891, *Political Pamphlets by Men of Genius, Murray's Magazine, vol.* 10, *p.* 751.

Swift is the one figure of colossal proportions in the age to which he belonged. Nay, we may go further. Among men whose fame depends mainly on their writings, there is, if we except Aristotle, Shakespeare, and perhaps Bacon, probably no man on record who impresses us with a sense of such enormous intellectual power. He has always the air of a giant sporting among pigmies, crushing or scrutinising, helping or thwarting them, as the mood takes him. Immense strength, immense energy, now frittering themselves away on trifles, now roused for a moment to concentrated action by passion, interest, or benevolence, but never assuming their true proportions, never developing into full activity—this is what we discern in Swift. We feel how miserably incommensurate was the part he played with the part which Nature had fitted him to play, how contracted was the stage, how mighty the capacities of the actor. In his pamphlets, in his two great satires, in his poems, in his correspondence, is the impression of a character which there is no mistaking. And it is not among philosophers, poets, and men of letters that we are to look for its analogy, but among those who have made and unmade nations—among men like Cæsar and men like Napoleon. . . . What figure in that eighteenth century of time is not dwarfed beside this Momus-Prometheus? . . . He was in temper all that Pindar symbolises in Typhon, and all that revolts Plato in the inharmonious and unmusical soul. And so, while his writings bear the impress of powers such as have rarely been conceded to man, they reflect and return with repulsive fidelity the ugliness and discord of the Titanism which inspired them. Without reverence and without reticence, he gloried in the licence which to the Greeks constituted the last offence against good taste and good sense, and out of the indulgence in which they have coined a synonym of shamelessness—the indiscriminate expression of what ought and what ought not to be said.—COLLINS, JOHN CHURTON, 1893, *Jonathan Swift, pp.* 255, 266, 267.

There are few figures in history, and still fewer in literature, which have occupied so great a place in the world's attention, or which retain so strong a hold upon its interests, as that of Jonathan Swift, Dean of St. Patrick's.—OLIPHANT, MARGARET O. W., 1893, *The Author of "Gulliver," The Century, vol.* 24, *p.* 401.

It may well be doubted whether in absolute command over language, any English prose author has ever equalled Swift. His style defies description or classification. It lends itself less than any, to imitation or to parody. It varies according to every mood. Its lucid simplicity is so perfect that its phrases once read, seemed to be only the natural utterances of careless thought, produced effort and without art. Its very neglect of rule, and its frequent defiance of grammatical regularity, help to give to it force and directness. But such a style refuses to transmit the secret of its power, and must needs remain unique and solitary in its kind.—CRAIK, HENRY, 1894, *English Prose, Introduction, vol.* III, *p.* 6.

He was a misanthrope, with deep, though very limited affections, a man frugal to eccentricity, with a benevolence at once active and extensive. His powerful intellect compels our admiration, if not our sympathy. His irony, his genius for satire and humour, his argumentative skill, his language, which is never wanting in strength, and is as clear as the most pellucid of mountain streams—these gifts are of so rare an order, that Swift's place in the literary history of his age must be always one of high eminence. Doubtless, as a master of style, he has been sometimes overpraised. If we regard the writer's end, it must be admitted that his language is admirably fitted for that end. What more then, it may be asked, can be needed? The reply is, that in composition, as in other things, there are different orders of excellence. The kind, although perfect, may be a low kind, and Swift's style wants the "sweetness and light," to quote a phrase of his own, which distinguish our greatest prose writers. It lacks also the elevation which inspires, and the persuasiveness that convinces while it charms. With infinitely more vigour than Addison, Swift, apart from his *Letters*, has none of Addison's attractiveness. No style, perhaps, is better fitted to exhibit scorn and contempt; but its author cannot express, because he does not possess, the sense of beauty.—DENNIS, JOHN, 1894, *The Age of Pope, p.* 174.

No fouler pen than Swift's has soiled our literature. His language is horrible from first to last. He is full of odious images, of base and abominable allusions. It would be a labour of Hercules to cleanse his pages. His love-letters are defaced by his incurable coarseness. This habit of his is so inveterate that it seems a miracle he kept his sermons free from his blackguard phrases. It is a question not of morality, but of decency, whether it is becoming to sit in the same room with the works of this divine. How the good Sir Walter ever managed to see him through the press is amazing. . . . There are, we know, those in whose nature there is too much of the milk of human kindness to enable them to enjoy Swift when he shows his teeth; but however this may be, we confess, if we are to read at all, we must prefer Swift's "Beasts' Confession" to all the sixty-five fables of Gay put together.—BIRRELL, AUGUSTINE, 1894, *Essays about Men, Women and Books, pp.* 2, 118.

Swift's irony, unsurpassable as it is, is cruel to excess, and has little that is Irish about it.—O'DONOGHUE, D. J., 1894, *ed., The Humour of Ireland, Introduction, p.* xvii.

The unity of Swift's paragraphs is usually all that could be desired. Now and then, however, a paragraph will be so long as to obliterate, apparently, any sign of topic. These rare paragraphs are almost inexplicable when compared with his usual sections. Professor Cesare Lombroso would, I fear, find the eccentricity of madness in them, as he did in the inversions of the Dean's conversation. Swift's command of proportion by paragraph punctuation is small. It is noticeable that the proportion of very short sentences (sentences under 15 words) is not large—6.3 per cent. in the "Tale of a Tub," 6.4 per cent. in "Gulliver." The average of the sentence is constant, in works separated even by 28 years: the three books mentioned show a variation of less than a whole word in sentence average, though the paragraph-averages of different books differ enormously. The superb coherence and emphasis of Swift's style are due largely to the straightforward, logical order of the thought, and the skilful placing of important words at the end of a sentence or paragraph. Swift is the first author to show in the paragraph much of what Wendell calls Mass. His sentences often fall at the close like taps of a steam-hammer, and sometimes the taps seem concentrated in one great blow at the end of the paragraph.—LEWIS, EDWIN HERBERT, 1894, *The History of the English Paragraph, p.* 109.

Swift lacked diplomacy. When matters did not seem to progress he grew wrathful, seized his pen and stabbed with it. But as he wrote, the ludicrousness of the whole situation came over him and instead of cursing plain curses, he held his adversary up to ridicule. And this ridicule is so active, the scorn so mixed with wit, the shafts so finely feathered with truth, that it is the admiration of mankind. Vitriol mixed with ink is volatile. Then what? We just run Swift through a coarse sieve to take out the lumps of seventeen century refuse and then we give him to children to make them laugh. Surely no better use can be made of pessimists.—HUBBARD, ELBERT, 1895, *Little Journeys, p.* 147.

It is, indeed, a long and not a very easy inquiry to determine the exact sources of the peculiar charmed sway which he exercises over the best minds; but they may be generally indicated as the combination in him of the wildest and most playful comedy with the sternest tragedy; of a grasp and comprehension of human folly, weakness, baseness, madness, which no man has ever excelled; of an unobtrusive but astonishingly perfect prose style suitable alike for argument, for narrative, for exposition, for invective, for light conversation and talk, and of a most strangely blended character.—SAINTSBURY, GEORGE, 1896, *Social England, ed. Traill, vol.* V, *p.* 79.

Was the keenest of political partisans, for his fierce and earnest personality made everything he did impassioned. But he was far more than a partisan. He was the most original prose writer of his time—the man of genius among many men of talent.—BROOKE, STOPFORD A., 1896, *English Literature, p.* 188.

While it is undeniable that Swift's humour is generally devoid of any touch of sympathy, there is no author of whom it can be more confidently said that he never obtrudes his art. . . . He could easily sustain his style for any time at the same pitch, he could always closely accommodate his manner to his matter, and he could convey his ideas clearly and forcibly without distracting the reader's attention to the excellence of their vehicle of expression. Yet, great as were his powers of shrewd penetration into character, Swift wanted the lighter graces necessary to the essayist. He loved to wage war on man rather than to instruct him, and used wit not to "enliven morality" but to increase the venom of his sting. The Laputans were attended by flappers who awaked them from their day-dreams by gently striking them with a bladder. As contrasted with Swift's method, the methods of Steele and Addison are equally gentle, and yet, as an instrument of social and literary reform the laugh of Steele or the raillery of Addison was far more potent than the loaded bludgeon of Swift.—LOBBAN, J. H., 1896, *English Essays, Introduction, p.* xxxv.

Swift was a bundle of paradoxes—a great churchman who has left not a trace on our ecclesiastical system, an ardent politician who was never more than a fly on the wheel. He is immortal on the one side on which he believes his genius ephemeral; he survives solely, but splendidly, as a man of letters. . . . Swift is the typical instance of the powerlessness of pure intellect to secure any but intellectual triumphs. But even the victories of his brain were tainted; his genius left a taste of brass on his own palate. . . . With no apprenticeship in style, no relation of discipleship to any previous French or English writer, but steeped in the Latin classics, he produced, at the age of thirty, two of the most extraordinary masterpieces of humour and satire which were ever written, the "Tale of a Tub" and the "Battle of the Books."—GOSSE, EDMUND, 1897, *A Short History of Modern English Literature, pp.* 220, 221.

Swift is perhaps the one supreme example of the pamphleteer, and his pamphlets satisfy the characteristic requirements of the form, as the earlier tracts of a time when prose moved less easily could not do.—RHYS, ERNEST, 1897, *Literary Pamphlets, Introduction, vol.* I, *p.* x.

In spite of his failure to realise many of the Christian virtues, Swift's churchmanship amounted to a genuine passion, without being, as his biographer tells us, "either intolerant or tantivy." His *Argument* against *the abolishing of Christianity* brings us face to face with the Deistic movement, which, though it died out before the middle of the century, yet had a curiously lasting effect upon religion in England by virtue of the utilitarian spirit which it helped to engender among the leading Christian apologists, of which spirit Swift's humorous *Argument* might almost seem to be a deliberate parody.—DEARMER, PERCY, 1898, *ed., Religious Pamphlets, Introduction, p.* 37.

Swift, indeed, cannot be imitated. It would be as hopeful to imitate Pindar. His humour is profound; but it is savage, unholy, and unclean. His style is clear, racy, and powerful; but it offers no points for the aspiring essayist. Its perfection is, if not uninteresting, at least uninstructive.—PAUL, HERBERT, 1899, *The Great Tractarian, The Nineteenth Century, vol.* 45, *p.* 456.

Here is a temper cynical, bitter, often almost revolting; yet here again is a most astonishing power in the man to utter himself, and so a style which, with world-wide differences from Addison's, is equally admirable. It is a naked, brawny, almost brutally frank English; but it is Jonathan Swift speaking right on. The ultimate rank of Swift's writings must be measured principally by the permanent value of his truth and the permanent power of his emotion; but his style could hardly be better.—WINCHESTER, C. T., 1899, *Some Principles of Literary Criticism, p.* 197.

William Broome

1689-1745.

William Broome had been educated at Eaton as a foundation scholar, and at Cambridge by the subscription of friends, and was Vicar of Sturston in Suffolk. He had a turn for verse, and, with repute as a Greek scholar, had begun his literary life by taking part in a prose translation of the "Iliad." Introduced to Pope at Sir John Cotton's, in Cambridgeshire, Broome pleased the poet, and was employed in selecting extracts for notes to the "Iliad." Upon the "Odyssey" Broome was a chief helper. He translated eight books,—the second, sixth, eighth, eleventh, twelfth, sixteenth, eighteenth, and twenty-third, and compiled all the notes. . . . Broome published a volume of "Miscellaneous Poems" in 1727, married a rich widow, and became LL. D. at the beginning of the reign of George II. He had several good preferments, and died in 1745.—MORLEY, HENRY, 1879 *A Manual of English Literature, ed. Tyler, p.* 540.

PERSONAL

A clergyman who held several livings and married a rich widow. Unfortunately his independence did not restrain him from writing poetry, for which want of means would have been the only sufficient excuse.—STEPHEN, LESLIE, 1880, *Alexander Pope* (*English Men of Letters*), *p.* 77.

GENERAL

The Parrots are they that repeat another's words, in such a hoarse odd voice, as makes them seem their own.—POPE, ALEXANDER, 1727, *Treatise on the Bathos, ch.* vi.

Of Broome, though it cannot be said that he was a great poet, it would be unjust to deny that he was an excellent versifier; his lines are smooth and sonorous, and his diction is select and elegant.—JOHNSON, SAMUEL, 1779–81, *Broome, Lives of the English Poets.*

Broome was a smooth versifier, without a spark of originality. His style was founded upon Pope's so closely that some of what he thought were his original pieces are mere centos of Pope. He was therefore able, like Fenton, but even to a greater extent, to reproduce the style of Pope with marvellous exactitude in translating the "Odyssey." . . . His early rudeness of manner gave way to a style of almost obsequious suavity, and his letters, though ingenious and graceful, do not give an impression of sincerity. Of his own poems not one has remained in the memory of the most industrious reader, and he owes the survival of his name entirely to his collaboration with Pope.—GOSSE, EDMUND, 1886, *Dictionary of National Biography, vol.* VI, *p.* 442.

He possessed no spark of genius, but was an admirable imitator of other men's style.—COURTHOPE, WILLIAM JOHN, 1889, *The Life of Alexander Pope, Works, eds. Elwin and Courthope, vol.* V, *p.* 197.

Is chiefly known from his association with Pope. . . . His verses are mechanically correct, but are empty of poetry.—DENNIS, JOHN, 1894, *The Age of Pope, p.* 243.

Thomas Southerne

1660-1746.

Thomas Southerne, or Southern, b. at Oxmanton, co. of Dublin, 1660; was admitted a student at Trinity College, Dublin, 1676; entered the Middle Temple, London, 1678, but cultivated dramatic literature in preference to law, and became a popular writer of plays; served a short time in the army, where he attained the rank of captain, and after his retirement continued his literary pursuits,—which were successful both in point of profit (by one play he cleared £700) and as an introduction to the best company (Dryden, Pope, Gray, &c.) of his day. He is said to have died "the oldest and the richest of his dramatic brethren." This would make him neither a Methuselah nor a Crœsus. He died May 26, 1746, in his 86th year. A collection of his plays was published Lon., 1713, 2 vols. 12mo; again, 1721, 2 vols. 12mo; and a better one, under the following title, "Plays written by Thomas Southern, Esq., now first collected, with an Account of the Life and Writings of the Author," 1774, 3 vols. 12mo.—ALLIBONE, S. AUSTIN, 1870, *A Critical Dictionary of English Literature, vol.* II, *p.* 2181.

PERSONAL

An Author of whom I can give no further Account, than that he has two Plays in print.—LANGBAINE, GERARD, 1691, *An Account of the English Dramatick Poets, p.* 489.

We have old Mr. Southern, at a Gentleman's house a little way off, who often comes to see us; he is now seventy-seven years old, and has almost wholly lost his memory; but is as agreeable as an old man can be, at least, I persuade myself so when I look at him, and think of Isabella and Oroonoko.—GRAY, THOMAS, 1737, *Letter to Horace Walpole, Letters, vol.* I, *p.* 8.

Resign'd to live, prepar'd to die,
With not one sin, but poetry,
This day Tom's fair account has run
(Without a blot) to eighty-one.
Kind Boyle, before his poet, lays
A table, with a cloth of bays;
And Ireland, mother of sweet singers,
Presents her harp still to his fingers.
The feast, his tow'ring genius marks
In yonder wild goose and the larks!
The mushrooms shew his wit was sudden
And for his judgment, lo a pudden!
Roast beef, tho' old, proclaims him stout,
And grace, altho' a bard, devout.
May Tom, whom heav'n sent down to raise
The price of prologues and of plays,
Be ev'ry birth-day more a winner,
Digest his thirty-thousandth dinner;
Walk to his grave without reproach,
And scorn a rascal and a coach.

—POPE, ALEXANDER, 1742, *To Mr. Thomas Southern on his Birth-Day.*

Mr. Southern died on the 26th of May, in the year 1746, in the 86th year of his age; the latter part of which he spent in a peaceful serenity, having by his commission as a soldier, and the profits of his dramatic works, acquired a handsome fortune; and being an exact œconomist, he improved what fortune he gained, to the best advantage: He enjoyed the longest life of all our poets, and died the richest of them, a very few excepted.—CIBBER, THEOPHILUS, 1753, *Lives of the Poets, vol.* v, *p.* 330.

I remember him a grave and reserved old gentleman. He lived near Covent Garden, and used to frequent the evening prayers there [at St. Paul's Church], always neat and decently dressed, commonly in black, with his silver sword and silver locks; but latterly he seemed to reside in Westminster.—OLDYS, WILLIAM, c1761, *MS. Notes to Langbaine's Account of the English Dramatick Poets.*

One of those dramatic writers who, without much genius, succeeded in obtaining a considerable name, and justly, by dint of genuine feeling for common nature. He began in Dryden's time, who knew and respected his talents, was known and respected by Pope, and lived to enjoy a similar regard from Gray.—HUNT, LEIGH, 1848, *The Town, p.* 329.

He was a perfect gentleman; he did not lounge away his days or nights in coffee-houses or taverns, but after labor cultivated friendship in home circles, where virtue and modest mirth sat at the hearth. . . . He kept the even tenor of his way, owing no man anything; never allowing his nights to be the marrer of his mornings; and at six-and-eighty carrying a bright eye, a steady hand, a clear head, and a warm heart wherewith to calmly meet and make surrender of all to the Inevitable Angel.—DORAN, JOHN, 1863, *Annals of the English Stage, vol.* I.

GENERAL

In this ["Oroonoko"] piece Mr. Southern has touched the tender passions with so much skill, that it will perhaps be injurious to his memory to say of him, that he is second to Otway. Besides the tender and delicate strokes of passion, there are many shining and manly sentiments in "Oroonoko;" and one of the greatest genius's of the present age, has often observed, that in the most celebrated play of Shakespear, so many striking thoughts, and such a glow of animated poetry cannot be furnished. This play is so often acted, and admired, that any illustration of its beauties here, would be entirely superfluous.—CIBBER, THEOPHILUS, 1753, *Lives of the Poets, vol.* v, *p.* 330.

The repulsive qualities of some of those characters, joined to the little which has been allotted for the heroine to perform, have been obstacles to the attraction of this ["Oroonoko"] drama, and it is seldom acted. Yet, some years past, Mr. Pope, in his very first appearance upon any stage, encountered, and triumphantly overcame, all impediments to the favourable reception of "Oroonoko;" and made the play so impressive, by his talents in the representation of that character, that for many nights it drew to the theatre a crowded audience. . . . If any defect can be attributed to Southern in the tragic fable, either of this play or of "Isabella," it is, that in the one, his first male character wants importance, and in the other, his principal female. Still, in both plays, he makes his tale, a tale of wo, though only a single personage becomes the object of deep concern.—INCHBALD, MRS. ELIZABETH, 1806–9, *The British Theatre.*

Southern's "Fatal Discovery," latterly represented under the name of "Isabella," is almost as familiar to the lovers of our theatre as "Venice Preserved" itself; and for the same reason,—that, whenever an actress of great tragic powers arises, the part of Isabella is as fitted to exhibit them as that of Belvidera. The choice and conduct of the story are, however, Southern's chief merits; for there is little vigor in the language, though it is natural, and free from the usual faults of his age. A similar character may be given to his other tragedy, "Oroonoko;" in which Southern deserves the praise of having, first of any English writer, denounced the traffic in slaves, and the cruelties of their West-Indian bondage. The moral feeling is high in this tragedy, and it has sometimes been acted with a certain success; but the execution is not that of a superior dramatist.—HALLAM, HENRY, 1837–39, *Introduction to the Literature of Europe, pt.* iv, *chap.* vi, *par.* 46.

There is not a little of nature and pathos in Southerne.—SPALDING, WILLIAM, 1852–82, *A History of English Literature, p.* 298.

Neither the thoughts nor the style of his tragedies rise above the common-place.—ARNOLD, THOMAS, 1868–75, *Chaucer to Wordsworth*, p. 314.

The flimsy liveliness of his former comedies failed him in "Money's the Mistress," which is trash too stupid to have forced its way to the stage, except for his previous dramatic reputation.—ELWIN, WHITWELL, 1872, *ed., The Works of Alexander Pope, vol.* VIII, *p.* 111, *note.*

The pathetic plot of this play ["Fatal Marriage"], which is founded on Mrs. Behn's novel of "The Nun, or the Fair Vow-Breaker," may be described as a dramatic treatment of the motive familiar to modern readers from Tennyson's "Enoch Arden" and a larger number of other narrative or dramatic versions than it would be worth while to enumerate. After continuing to command popular favour during the life-time of its author, this tragedy was in 1757 revived by Garrick with great success; nor can we wonder that it should have suited the highly-sentimental tastes of this later age. Yet it would be unjust to Southerne, and it would obscure the continuity in the history of the English seventeenth-century drama, which, however partial and imperfect, should not be overlooked, were we to ignore the remnant of Elisabethan intensity noticeable in the passage, where the thought transiently occurs to Isabella of murdering her first husband on his unexpected return, and in the scene of her lapse into madness.—WARD, ADOLPHUS WILLIAM, 1875–99, *A History of English Dramatic Literature, vol.* III, *p.* 421.

Southerne was a very smart man of business, and he was the first dramatist in England who contrived to make a fortune out of play-writing. He became justly distinguished as a tragic poet. He rebelled against the rant and fustian of the heroic playwrights, and modelled himself upon Otway, whose tenderness is successfully reflected in his scenes, though with some exaggeration. His blank verse runs easily, and owes something to a respectful study of Shakespeare; but we recognise that it is in the process of fossilising into the dead dramatic verse of the succeeding century. Southerne's best plays were produced when the Orange dramatists had completely come to the front, and he answers as a tragic writer to Congreve as a comic one, but with less talent. . . . His comedies are very weak, and strained beyond the custom of the age with cynical indecency.—GOSSE, EDMUND, 1888, *A History of Eighteenth Century Literature, pp.* 62, 63.

Congreve's one tragedy is more often consulted to see what is the context which Johnson praised so highly than for any other reason. Few need go farther. Southerne's two masterpieces, "The Fatal Marriage" and "Oroonoko," are perhaps more unknown still, despite the traditional fame of great actresses in Isabella and Imoinda, the constant references in contemporary and rather later literature to both, and the jokes made on the unlucky second title of "The Fatal Marriage." They have much less elegance of diction than the work of either Rowe or Congreve, but much greater tragic quality; being, in fact, Otway a little further prosed.—SAINTSBURY, GEORGE, 1898, *A Short History of English Literature, p.* 505.

Robert Blair

1699-1746.

Robert Blair; Scottish poet; born in Edinburgh, 1699; a relative of Hugh Blair. He was ordained minister of Athelstaneford in 1731. He wrote a poem of undoubted merit, entitled "The Grave," which was not printed until after his death. Died in Athelstaneford, Feb. 4, 1746.—ADAMS, CHARLES KENDALL, *ed.* 1897, *Johnson's Universal Cyclopædia, vol.* I, *p.* 650.

PERSONAL

I got away time enough next day to reach Haddington before dinner, having passed by Athelstaneford, where the minister, Mr. Robert Blair, author of "The Grave," was said to be dying slowly; or, at any rate, was so austere and void of urbanity as to make him quite disagreeable to young people. His wife, who was in every respect the opposite (a sister of Sheriff Law), was frank and open, and uncommonly handsome; yet, even with her allurements and his acknowledged ability, his house was unfrequented.—CARLYLE, ALEXANDER, 1744–1805–60, *Autobiography*.

THE GRAVE

The door of Death is made of gold,
That mortal eyes cannot behold:
But, when the mortal eyes are closed,
And cold and pale the limbs reposed,
The soul awakes, and, wondering, sees
In her mild hand the golden keys.
The grave is heaven's golden gate,
And rich and poor around it wait:
O Shepherdess of England's fold,
Behold this gate of pearl and gold!
To dedicate to England's Queen
The visions that my soul has seen,
And by her kind permission bring
What I have borne on solemn wing
From the vast regions of the grave.
Before her throne my wings I wave,
Bowing before my sovereign's feet.
The Grave produced these blossoms sweet,
In mild repose from earthly strife;
The blossoms of eternal life.

—BLAKE, WILLIAM, 1808, *Dedication of the Designs to Blair's "Grave" to Queen Charlotte.*

The eighteenth century has produced few specimens of blank verse of so powerful and simple a character as that of "The Grave." It is a popular poem, not merely because it is religious, but because its language and imagery are free, natural and picturesque. The latest editor of the poets has, with singularly bad taste, noted some of this author's most nervous and expressive phrases as vulgarisms, among which he reckons that of friendship "the solder of society." Blair may be a homely and even a gloomy poet in the eye of fastidious criticism; but there is a masculine and pronounced character even in his gloom and homeliness that keeps it most distinctly apart from either dullness or vulgarity. His style pleases us like the powerful expression of a countenance without regular beauty.—CAMPBELL, THOMAS, 1819, *Specimens of the British Poets.*

A brawny contemplative Orson.—BROWNING, ELIZABETH BARRETT, 1842–63, *The Book of the Poets.*

It is a complete and powerful poem, of limited design, but of masterly execution.—MILLS, ABRAHAM, 1851, *The Literature and the Literary Men of Great Britain and Ireland, vol.* II, *p.* 300.

He had found a vein of rich and virgin gold; he had thrown out one mass of ore, and was, as it were, resting on his pickaxe ere recommencing his labour, when he was smitten down by a workman who never rests nor slumbers. Still let us thankfully accept what he had produced; the more as it is so distinctively original, so free from any serious alloy, and so impressively religious in its spirit and tone. This masterpiece of Blair's genius is not a great poem so much as it is a magnificent portion, fragment, or book of a great poem. The most, alike of its merits and its faults, spring from the fact, that it keeps close to its subject—it daguerreotypes its dreadful theme.—GILFILLAN, GEORGE, 1854, *ed., The Poetical Works of Beattie, Blair and Falconer, p.* 124.

This poem met with but little attention at first, but the commendation of Hervey, Pinkerton, and others, brought it into general notice. Of late years it seems to be but little read.—ALLIBONE, S. AUSTIN, 1854–58, *A Critical Dictionary of English Literature, vol.* I, *p.* 202.

It is remarkable for its masculine vigor of thought and expression, and for the imaginative solemnity with which it invests the most familiar truths; and it has always been one of our most popular religious poems.—CRAIK, GEORGE L., 1861, *A Compendious History of English Literature and of the English Language, vol.* II, *p.* 286.

"The Grave" is a complete and powerful poem, of limited design, but masterly execution. The subject precluded much originality of conception, but, at the same time, is recommended by its awful importance and its universal application. The style seems to be formed upon that of the old sacred and puritanical poets, elevated by the author's admiration of Milton and Shakspeare. There is a Scottish Presbyterian character about the whole, relieved by occasional flashes and outbreaks of true genius.—CHAMBERS, ROBERT, 1876, *Cyclopædia of English Literature, ed. Carruthers.*

Blair's singular little poem, which has perhaps been more widely read than any other poetical production of a writer who wrote no other poetry, was, it is said, rejected by several London publishers on the ground that it was "too heavy for the times." As its introducer was Dr. Watts, it is not likely that he suggested it to any but serious members of the trade. "The Grave" thus adds one to the tolerably long list of books respecting the chances of which professional judgment has been hopelessly out. It acquired popularity almost as soon as it was published, and retained it for at least a century; indeed its date is not yet gone by in certain circles. Long after its author's death it obtained an additional and probably a lasting hold on a new kind of taste by the fact of Blake's illustrating it. The artist's designs indeed were, as he expresses it in the beautiful Dedication to Queen Charlotte, rather "visions that his soul has seen" than representations of anything directly contained in Blair's verse. But that verse itself is by no means to be despised. Technically its only fault is the use and abuse of the redundant syllable. The quality of Blair's blank verse is in every respect rather moulded upon dramatic than upon purely poetical models, and he shows little trace of imitation either of Milton, or of his contemporary Thomson. Whether his studies—contrary to the wont of Scotch divines at that time—had really been much directed to the drama, I cannot say; but the perusal of his poem certainly suggests such a conclusion, not merely the licence just mentioned, but the generally declamatory and rhetorical tone helping to produce the impression. The matter of the poem is good. General plan it has none, but in so short a composition a general plan is hardly wanted. It abounds with forcible and original ideas expressed in vigorous and unconventional phraseology, nor is it likely nowadays that this phraseology will strike readers, as it struck the delicate critics of the eighteenth century, as being "vulgar." Vigorous single lines are numerous; and it is at least as much a tribute to the vigour of the poem as to its popularity, that many of its phrases have worked their way into current speech.—SAINTSBURY, GEORGE, 1880, *English Poets, ed. Ward, vol.* III, *p.* 217.

The "Grave" was the first and best of a whole series of mortuary poems. In spite of the epigrams of conflicting partisans, "Night Thoughts" must be considered as contemporaneous with it, and neither preceding nor following it. There can be no doubt, however, that the success of Blair encouraged Young to persevere in his far longer and more laborious undertaking. Blair's verse is less rhetorical, more exquisite, than Young's, and, indeed, his relation to that writer, though too striking to be overlooked, is superficial. He forms a connecting link between Otway and Crabbe, who are his nearest poetical kinsmen. His one poem, the "Grave," contains seven hundred and sixty-seven lines of blank verse. It is very unequal in merit, but supports the examination of modern criticism far better than most productions of the second quarter of the eighteenth century. As philosophical literature it is quite without value; and it adds nothing to theology; it rests solely upon its merit as romantic poetry.—GOSSE, EDMUND, 1886, *Dictionary of National Biography, vol.* V, *p.* 165.

The choice of such a subject as the grave does not necessarily imply anything morbid in the treatment; but it must be admitted that there is a morbid element in Blair's poem. He has no reticence about the worm that surfeits on the damask cheek of beauty, about the awful pangs attending the strong man's dissolution, or about the all-devouring appetite of the "great maneater;" and he has been praised, most injudiciously, for being so out-spoken. Shakespeare has used much the same images; but a comparison of Blair with the parts of "Hamlet" and "Measure for Measure," which he evidently had in his mind in more passages than one, shows at once what a change the stronger imagination has worked, how much more skillful in the execution, how much deeper the moral, how widely-different in consequence the work of the two poets. Yet Blair has learnt not a little, and often has learnt well, from his master; and it is to his honour that he, a Scotch clergyman of a century and a half ago, is found imitating him at all. Often his lines sound simply like distant echoes of Shakespearean lines; but sometimes there is originality combined with a considerable share of Shakespeare's strength. And this is Blair's highest praise. At his best he shows a masculine vigour of language and an austere dignity of imagination more than sufficient to atone for the harshness of his verse, marred, nay, almost ruined, as it is by the abuse of the hypermetrical line. That there is virtue in the poem is proved by its richness in quotable and often-quoted lines—a feature which may be taken as one of the tests of good work.—WALKER, HUGH, 1893, *Three Centuries of Scottish Literature, vol.* II, *p.* 92.

Robert Blair's dull poem of "The Grave."—BROOKE, STOPFORD A., 1896, *English Literature, p.* 213

Pregnant with suggestions that sieze the imagination, and appeal alike to the intellect and the heart. The brevity of the piece is in its favour; there is not a line that flags.—DENNIS, JOHN, 1894, *The Age of Pope, p.* 84.

Francis Hutcheson

1694-1746.

A distinguished philosopher of last century, was the son of a Presbyterian minister in the n. of Ireland, where he was born in 1694. He studied for the church at the university of Glasgow, but shortly after the completion of his theological course, he was induced to open a private academy in the city of Dublin, which proved highly successful. In 1720 he published his "Inquiry into the Original of our Ideas of Beauty and Virtue," etc., which was the means of introducing him to the notice of many influential personages, such as lord Granville, then lord-lieutenant of Ireland, archbishop King, primate Boulter, and others. This work was followed, in 1728, by his "Essay on the Nature and Conduct of the Passions;" and in the year after, he was appointed professor of moral philosophy in the university of Glasgow. Here he died in 1747. His largest and most important works, "A System of Moral Philosophy," was published at Glasgow in 1775 by his son, Francis Hutcheson, M. D., with a preface on the life, writings, and character of the author, by Dr. Leechman, professor of divinity in the same university.—PECK, HENRY THURSTON, *ed.* 1898, *The International Cyclopædia, vol.* VII. *p.* 719.

PERSONAL

He was a good-looking man, of an engaging countenance. He delivered his lectures without notes, walking backwards and forwards in the area of his room. As his elocution was good, and his voice and manner pleasing, he raised the attention of his hearers at all times; and when the subject led him to explain and enforce the moral virtues and duties, he displayed a fervent and persuasive eloquence which was irresistible. Besides the lectures he gave through the week, he, every Sunday at six o'clock, opened his class-room to whoever chose to attend, when he delivered a set of lectures on "Grotius de veritate Religionis Christianæ," which, though learned and ingenious, were adapted to every capacity; for on that evening he expected to be attended, not only by students, but by many of the people of the city; and he was not disappointed, for this free lecture always drew crowds of attendants.—CARLYLE, ALEXANDER, 1744–1805–60, *Autobiography.*

He was all benevolence and affection, none who saw him could doubt of it; his air and countenance bespoke it. It was to such a degree his prevailing temper that it gave a tincture to his writings, which were perhaps as much dictated by his heart as his head; and if there was any need of an apology for the stress that in his scheme seems to be laid upon the friendly and public affections, the prevalence of them in his own temper would at least form an amiable one. . . . If any one should wish to know anything about Dr. Hutcheson's external form, it may be said it was an image of his mind. A stature above middle size, a gesture and manner negligent and easy, but decent and manly, gave a dignity to his appearance. His complexion was fair and sanguine, and his features regular. His countenance and look bespoke sense, spirit, kindness, and joy of heart. His whole person and manner raised a strong prejudice in his favour at first sight.—LEECHMAN, WILLIAM, 1755, *A System of Moral Philosophy, Life.*

In the contingent which the Schools have furnished to the advance-guard of human knowledge, there are many greater figures than Francis Hutcheson's; but few that are more attractive, more complete in symmetry, more noble in sincerity of nature: what he thought, he loved; what he taught, he was. A generous philosophy became in him a generous personality.

With an enthusiasm for truth and goodness, unalloyed by the scholar's fault of jealous property in ideas; with a contempt for nothing but meanness, vice, and wrong; with a transparent unreserve, neither ashamed of an honest admiration, nor afraid to avow a righteous anger; he drew forth what was best in others by simple self-expression; and by the total absence of pretension rendered personal dislike impossible; except with those to whose narrowness of heart and mind his very presence was a rebuke.—MARTINEAU, JAMES, 1885, *Types of Ethical Theory, vol.* II, *p.* 483.

Francis Hutcheson seems to have been noted, even in his earliest years, for the same sweetness of disposition, the same unselfishness, and the same keen intellectual activity that marked him throughout life. . . . His outward aspect did not belie his disposition. Tall and robust of figure, with an open and bright countenance, with a carriage negligent but easy, with unimpaired health, and the subtle charm of absolute simplicity, he made his way to the hearts of his hearers with consummate ease. . . . For the function of public lecturer he was eminently fitted, not by his gift of eloquence alone, but by the electric power of a quick and ready enthusiasm. To the last he refused to write his lectures, and delivered them without notes, "walking," as we are told by Dr. Carlyle, "backwards and forwards in the area of his room." . . . His temper was quick, but so well under control that its vivacity only added to his charm.—CRAIK, SIR HENRY, 1901, *A Century of Scottish History, vol.* II, *pp.* 175, 182, 183.

GENERAL

Dr. Hutcheson had the merit of being the first who distinguished with any degree of precision in what respect all moral distinctions may be said to arise from reason, and in what respect they are founded upon immediate sense and feeling. In his illustrations upon the moral sense he has explained this so fully, and, in my opinion, so unanswerably, that, if any controversy is still kept up about this subject, I can impute it to nothing, but either to inattention to what that gentleman has written, or to a superstitious attachment to certain forms of expression, —a weakness not very uncommon among the learned, especially in subjects so deeply interesting as the present, in which a man of virtue is often loath to abandon, even the propriety of a single phrase which he has been accustomed to.—SMITH, ADAM, 1759–90, *The Theory of Moral Sentiments, pt.* vii, *sec.* iii.

His great and deserved fame, however, rests *now* chiefly on the traditionary history of his academical lectures, which appear to have contributed very powerfully to diffuse, in Scotland, that taste for analytical discussion, and that spirit of liberal inquiry, to which the world is indebted for some of the most valuable productions of the eighteenth century.—STEWART DUGALD, 1811, *Account of the Life and Writings of Adam Smith, note.*

Butler and Hutcheson coincided in the two important positions, that disinterested affections, and a distinct moral faculty, are essential parts of human nature. Hutcheson is a chaste and simple writer, who imbibed the opinions without the literary faults of his master, Shaftesbury. He has a clearness of expression, and fulness of illustration, which are wanting in Butler. But he is inferior to both these writers in the appearance at least of originality, and to Butler especially in that philosophical courage which, when it discovers the fountains of truth and falsehood, leaves others to follow the streams. . . . Hutcheson was the father of the modern school of speculative philosophy in Scotland.—MACKINTOSH, SIR JAMES, 1830, *Second Preliminary Dissertation to Encyclopædia Britannica.*

Butler was a preacher, and Shaftesbury a man of the world, while Hutcheson was a metaphysician by profession. It is not remarkable, therefore, that the doctrine, which the two former merely indicated, should have received from the latter a full dèvelopment under a precise and philosophic form. Shaftesbury and Butler suggested the idea, Hutcheson formed the system, of the moral sense.—JOUFFROY, THÉODORE SIMON, 1840–60, *Introduction to Ethics, tr. Channing.*

His Lectures, which, by their copious illustrations, their amiable tone of feeling, their enlightened views of liberty and human improvement, and their persuasive eloquence, made a deeper impression than the more severe and dry compositions of Butler could ever create, and laid the foundation in Scotland of the modern ethical school.—BROUGHAM, HENRY LORD, 1845–57, *Lives of Philosophers of the Time of George III., p.* 166.

And this leads to what was his most vital experience in college. The more his character and mind matured, the more earnestly did he devote himself to aspirations after moral greatness. He read with delight the Stoics, and was profoundly moved by the stern purity which they inculcated. But the two authors who most served to guide his thoughts at this period were Hutcheson and Ferguson. It was while reading, one day, in the former, some of the various passages in which he asserts man's capacity for disinterested affection, and considers virtue as the sacrifice of private interests and the bearing of private evils for the public good, or as self-devotion to absolute, universal good, that there suddenly burst upon his mind that view of the dignity of human nature, which was ever after to "uphold and cherish" him, and thenceforth to be "the fountain light of all his day, the master light of all his seeing." He was, at the time, walking as he read, beneath a clump of willows yet standing in the meadow a little to the north of Judge Dana's. This was his favorite retreat for study, being then quite undisturbed and private, and offering a most serene and cheerful prospect across green meadows and the glistening river to the Brookline hills. The place and the hour were always sacred in his memory, and he frequently referred to them with grateful awe. It seemed to him, that he then passed through a new spiritual birth, and entered upon the day of eternal peace and joy.—CHANNING, WILLIAM HENRY, 1848, *Memoir of William Ellery Channing, vol.* I, *p.* 63.

Meanwhile Philosophy had distinguished votaries, with Butler at their head. . . . Much inferior in power as well as in clearness, but still useful, in the same field, was Hutcheson, an Irishman who taught in Glasgow, and who has sometimes been called the founder of the Scottish school of mental science.—SPALDING, WILLIAM, 1852–82, *A History of English Literature, p.* 330.

The beginning of the great secular philosophy of Scotland is undoubtedly due to Francis Hutcheson. . . . By his lectures, and by his works, he diffused a taste for bold inquiries into subjects of the deepest importance, but concerning which it had previously been supposed nothing fresh was to be learned; the Scotch having hitherto been taught, that all truths respecting our own nature, which were essential to be known, had been already revealed. Hutcheson, however, did not fear to construct a system of morals according to a plan secular, and no example of which had been exhibited in Scotland before his time. The principles from which he started, were not theological, but metaphysical. They were collected, from what he deemed the natural constitution of the mind, instead of being collected as heretofore, from what had been supernaturally communicated. He, therefore, shifted the field of study. Though he was a firm believer in revelation, he held that the best rules of conduct could be ascertained without its assistance, and could be arrived at by the unaided wit of man; and that, when arrived at, they were, in their aggregate, to be respected as the Law of Nature. This confidence in the power of the human understanding was altogether new in Scotland, and its appearance forms an epoch in the national literature. . . . With a noble and lofty aim did he undertake his task. Venerating the human mind, he was bent on vindicating its dignity against those who disputed its titles. Unhappily, he could not succeed; the prejudices of his time were too strong. Still, he did all that was in his power. He opposed the tide which he was unable to stem; he attacked what it was impossible to destroy.—BUCKLE, HENRY THOMAS, 1862–66, *History of Civilization in England, vol.* III, *pp.* 292, 298.

His style was copious and glowing. He tries to engage the attention of the reader by great abundance of examples and comparisons.—MINTO, WILLIAM, 1872–80, *Manual of English Prose Literature, p.* 430.

The metaphysical doctrines which connect Hutcheson with the so-called Scottish school, and which justify his being considered the precursor of Reid, are the circumstance that he anticipated Reid in his dissent from Locke, and used the term *suggestion* in the same import in which Reid employs it in his Inquiry. . . . Hutcheson also shows his independence of

Locke in his doctrines of axioms.—PORTER, NOAH, 1874, *Philosophy in Great Britain and America, Ueberweg's History of Philosophy, vol.* II, *pp.* 392, 393.

Hutcheson's works got fit audience in his own day, but did not continue to be read much after his death. In his mode and manner of writing he is evidently indebted to the wits of Queen Anne, such as Shaftesbury, Bolingbroke, Pope, and Swift, who were Frenchifying the English tongue, polishing away at once its roughness and its vigor, introducing the French clearness of expression, and, we may add, the French morals. Hutcheson has their clearness, but is without their liveliness and wit. His style is like a well-fenced, level country, in which we are weary walking for any length of time; it is not relished by those who prefer elevations and depressions, and is disliked by those who have a passion for mountains and passes. He ever maintains a high moral tone; but it is doubtful whether he has retained for morality a sufficiently deep foundation. His philosophy is undoubtedly an advance upon that of Locke, and rises unmeasurably above that of those professed followers of Locke in England and France, who in the days of Hutcheson were leaving out Locke's reflection, and deriving all man's ideas from sensation, and all his motives from pleasures and pains. His view of the moral faculty is correct so far as it goes. . . . His view of the moral power falls greatly beneath that of the great English moralists of the previous century, and below that of the school of Clarke in his own day.—MCCOSH, JAMES, 1875, *The Scottish Philosophy, p.* 84.

His writings must have powerfully aided the tendency to detach ethics from thelogy, and to treat questions of morality as an independent branch of investigation, capable of a methodical and scientific handling. Hutcheson's professional and ecclesiastical position was calculated to lend great weight to his example in a matter of this kind. . . . Hutcheson did more than, perhaps, any preceding moralist towards supplying an adequate expression for the moral criterion of actions, affections, and characters. His writings, together with those of Shaftesbury and Hume, undoubtedly pave the way for the general reception, towards the end of the century, of what is now called Utilitarianism. Whether that theory provides a sufficient guide and test of action will always, perhaps, be open to some dispute. But it cannot be questioned, I think, that Hutcheson occupies an important place in its history. Shaftesbury and Hutcheson do not stand in the first rank of philosophers. Neither in the roll of fame nor in that of merit, do they compete with Bacon, Hobbes, Locke, Berkeley, Hume, Descartes, Spinoza, or Kant. But, in the history of literature and philosophy, as in that of war and politics, posterity is often unjust to names of secondary importance, and is apt to pass over considerable services, because the recollection of them is not associated with that of illustrious persons. In the foregoing pages I have endeavoured to repair this injustice in the case of two of our own countrymen, without whose intervention the development of at least one branch of philosophy in English might have been deprived of many of the most characteristic features which we now recognize in it.—FOWLER, THOMAS, 1882, *Shaftesbury and Hutcheson* (*English Philosophers*), *pp.* 238, 239.

The moral sense is his equivalent to Butler's conscience, although his optimism gives a very different character to the resulting doctrine. The chief use of the faculty is to affirm the utilitarian criterion, and he was apparently the first writer to use Bentham's phrase, "The greatest happiness of the greatest number." He may be thus classed as one of the first exponents of a decided utilitarianism as distinguished from "egoistic hedonism." The essence of his teaching is given in his early essays, though more elaborately worked out in the posthumous "system," where he developes a cumbrous psychology of "internal senses." In metaphysics Hutcheson was, in the main, a follower of Locke; but his ethical writings constitute his chief claim to recollection. They did much to promote a psychological study of the moral faculties, though his analysis is superficial, and he is apt to avoid fundamental difficulties. His theology differs little from the optimistic deism of his day.—STEPHEN, LESLIE, 1891, *Dictionary of National Biography, vol.* XXVIII, *p.* 334.

Isaac Watts

1674-1748.

Born, at Southampton, 17 July 1674. Educated at Southampton Grammar School, till 1690. At Dissenters' school in London, 1690-93. Private tutor in family of Sir John Hartopp, at Stoke Newington, 1696-1702. Assistant to Independent Minister at Mark Lane, 1698; Ordained Minister, March 1702. Severe illness, 1703 and 1712. Lived in house of Sir Thomas Abney, at Theobalds, 1712-48. D. D., Edinburgh, and Aberdeen, 1728. Died, at Theobalds, 25 Nov. 1748. Buried in Bunhill Fields. *Works:* "Horæ Lyricæ," 1706; "Essay against Uncharitableness" (anon.), 1707; "A Sermon," 1707; "Hymns and Spiritual Songs," 1707; "Orthodoxy and Charity United," (anon.), 1707; "Guide to Prayer," 1715; "The Psalms of David," 1719; "Divine and Moral Songs," 1720; "The Art of Reading and Writing English," 1721; "Sermons on Various Subjects" (3 vols.), 1721-23; "The Christian Doctrine of the Trinity . . . asserted," 1722; "Death and Heaven," 1722; "The Arian invited to the Orthodox Faith," 1724; "Three Dissertations relating to the Christian Doctrine of the Trinity," 1724; "Logick," 1725; "The Knowledge of the Heavens and Earth made easy," 1726; "Defense against the temptation to Self-Murther," 1726; "The Religious Improvement of Publick Events," 1727; "Essay towards the Encouragement of Charity Schools," 1728; "Prayers composed for the use . . . of Children," 1728; "Treatise on the Love of God," 1729; "Catechisms for Children," 1730; "Humble attempt toward the revival of Practical Religion," 1731; "The Strength and Weakness of Human Reason" (anon.), 1731; "Essay towards a Proof of a Separate State of Souls," 1732; "Short View of the Whole Scripture History," 1732; "Essay on the Freedom of Will," 1732; "Philosophical Essays," 1733; "Reliquiæ Juveniles," 1734; "The Redeemer and the Sanctifier" (anon.), 1736; "The Holiness of Times, Places and People," 1738; "The World to Come," 1738; "A New Essay on Civil Power in Things Sacred" (anon.), 1739; "Essay on the Ruin and Recovery of Mankind," 1740; "Improvement of the Mind," 1741; "A Faithful Enquiry after the . . . Doctrine of the Trinity" (anon.), 1745; "Glory of Christ as God-Man Unveiled" (anon.), 1746; "Useful and Important Questions concerning Jesus" (anon.), 1746; "Evangelical Discourses," 1747; "The Rational Foundation of a Christian Church," 1747. *Posthumous:* "Nine Sermons preached . . . 1718-19," ed. by P. J. Smith, 1812. *Collected Works:* in 6 vols., 1810-11. *Life:* by T. Milner, 1834.—SHARP, R. FARQUHARSON, 1897, *A Dictionary of English Authors, p.* 294.

PERSONAL

We here commit to the ground the venerable remains of one, who being intrusted with many excellent talents by him who is the giver of every good and perfect gift, cheerfully and unweariedly employed them as a faithful steward of the manifold grace of God in his Master's service, approving himself as a minister of Christ in much patience, in afflictions, and distress, by pureness, by knowledge, by long-suffering, by kindness, by love unfeigned, by the word of truth, by the armour of righteousness, by honour and dishonour, by evil report and good report and who, amidst trials from within and from without, was continued by the kind providence of God, and the powerful supports of his grace to a good old age, honoured and beloved by all parties, retaining his usefulness till he had just finished his course, and being at last favoured, according to his own wishes and prayers, with a release from the labours of life into that peaceful state of good men, which commences immediately after death. O how delightful is that voice from heaven which has thus pronounced, "Blessed are the dead who die in the lord, yea, saith the Spirit, that they may rest from their labours, and their works follow them."—CHANDLER, SAMUEL, 1748, *Funeral Sermon.*

By his natural temper he was quick of resentment; but by his established and habitual practice he was gentle, modest, and inoffensive. His tenderness appeared in his attention to children and to the poor. To the poor, while he lived in the family of his friend, he allowed the third part of his annual revenue, though the whole was not a hundred a year; and for

ISAAC WATTS.

Engraving by S. Freeman.

LAURENCE STERNE.

Engraving by W. J. Alais.
Painting by Sir Joshua Reynolds.

the children he condescended to lay aside the scholar, the philosopher, and the wit, to write little poems of devotion, and systems of instruction, adapted to their wants and capacities, from the dawn of reason, through its gradations of advance in the morning of life.—JOHNSON, SAMUEL, 1779–81, *Watts, Lives of the English Poets.*

His stature was beneath the common standard, perhaps not above five feet, or at most five feet two inches, but without any thing like deformity in his frame. His body was spare and lean, his face oval, his nose acquiline, his complexion fair and pale, his forehead low, his cheek bones rather prominent, but his countenance on the whole by no means disagreeable, his eyes were small and grey, and whenever he was attentive or eager, amazingly piercing and expressive, his voice was rather too fine and slender, at least it would have been thought so, if he had been of a larger mould, but it was regular, audible, and pleasant.—GIBBONS, THOMAS, 1780, *Memoir of Dr. Isaac Watts, p.* 322.

In reviewing these discourses it may be justly remarked, that they possess uncommon excellence, and in some respects, notwithstanding the many volumes of sermons since published, have never been exceeded, or even equalled. The beautiful perspicuity and simplicity of their style renders them familiar to the meanest capacities. Their originality of thought, and the happy illustrations that abound in them, discover the genius of the writer; but the fervour of his exhortations, his close addresses to the conscience, and the rich veins of evangelical truth and christian experience in every discourse, shew the christian divine in full proportion. The only thing that can be justly objected to is, that they contain redundancies of expression, and some slight inaccuracies, not exactly conformable to the critical taste of the present age. It is to be remembered, however, that they were written or revised in the chamber of sickness; many of them perhaps with an aching head, and a trembling hand. If they do not, in general, smell of the lamp of study so much as some productions of the present age, they partake more of the holy unction of the gospel.—BURDER, GEORGE, 1810, *ed., The Works of Isaac Watts, Memoir, vol.* I, *p.* XX.

No circumstance, either public or private, tended to provoke in him any angry or acrimonious feelings. Strongly as he was attached to the general principle of nonconformity, there was no bitterness in his dissent; he lived not only in charity with all men, but on terms of good will and friendship with some of the most eminent of the clergy. All parties agreed in rendering justice to the benignity of his disposition, the usefulness of his labours, and the purity of his life.—SOUTHEY, ROBERT, 1834, *Life of Isaac Watts, p.* 19.

We know little of the mother of Dr. Watts, beyond this simple but touching record, and that she was an excellent woman, who, like her son, would seem to have had a taste for poetic numbers; for it is told of her, that when her husband kept a school at Southampton, she used to encourage the boys after their lessons to write verses, and that she used to give those who did so a farthing as a reward. Her own boy would seem to have been a little touched on this point with something of becoming zeal for the poet's honour, for his early composition was this:—

"I write not for a farthing, but to try
How I your farthing writers can defy."

—ELLIS, SARAH STICKNEY, 1859–83, *Mothers of Great Men, Second ed., p* 293.

In the nave of Westminster Abbey, the last resting-place of so many kings, queens, poets, artists, divines, and philosophers, we saw a little tablet of white marble, sacred to the memory of Dr. Watts. On its front is a figure of Watts sitting on a stool, apparently lost in deep thought and meditation. In one hand he holds a pen, and with the other points to a celestial globe, while an angel seems opening to his enraptured senses the "wonders of creation." A bust of the great divine rests upon the monument, and below are the words, "Isaac Watts, D. D., born July 17, 1674, died November 25, 1748."—CLARKE, HELEN F., 1874, *Isaac Watts and his Hymns, Congregational Quarterly, vol.* 16, *p.* 418.

CHRISTIAN DOCTRINE OF THE TRINITY
1722

For my own part I cannot but think that this good man approached as nearly to christian perfection as any mortal ever did in this sublunary state; and therefore

I consider him as a better interpreter of the christian doctrine than the most learned critics, who, proud of their reason and their learning, despised or neglected the very life and soul of christianity, the living, everlasting gospel, the supernatural influence of divine grace; and be it ever remembered, that Dr. Watts was a man who studied the abstrusest sciences, and was as well qualified to become a verbal critic, or a logical disputant on the scriptures, as the most learned among the Doctors of the Sorbonne, or the greatest proficients in polemical divinity. I mention this circumstance for the consideration of those who insinuate that the doctrines of grace cannot be entertained but by ignorant, as well as fanatical persons; by persons uninitiated in the mysteries of philosophy.—KNOX, VICESSIMUS, 1795, *Christian Philosophy.*

Few writers have been more useful, especially in Psalms and Hymns: a fine genius, and deep piety. He fell into some peculiar notions on the Trinity, and was answered by Abraham Taylor, Hurrion, and Edwards. If the wise and good Dr. Watts erred, let all take heed of rash speculations on revealed things.—BICKERSTETH, EDWARD, 1844, *The Christian Student.*

LOGICK
1725

Watts, when he does not bewilder himself and his readers in scholastic subtleties, . . . is very judicious.—GREEN, THOMAS, 1779–1810, *Diary of a Lover of Literature.*

The Logic of Watts, of Duncan, and of others, are worth reading as books, but not as books upon Logic.—HAMILTON, SIR WILLIAM, 1856?–60, *Lectures on Logic, Lecture* ix.

IMPROVEMENT OF THE MIND
1741

An excellent work. It is metaphysics carried into every day life and practice. —BLAKEY, ROBERT, 1848, *History of the Philosophy of Mind, vol.* III, *p.* 244.

The justice of this commendation has generally been acceded to, although more recent inquiries have shown, that some of the views of the mind in the book in question are defective.—UPHAM, THOMAS COGSWELL, 1831–33, *Elements of Mental Philosophy, vol.* II, *p.* 75, *note.*

HYMNS

We come to the greatest name among hymn-writers, for we hesitate not to give that praise to Dr. Isaac Watts, since it has pleased God to confer upon him, though one of the least of the poets of his country, more glory than upon the greatest either of that or of any other, by making his Divine Songs a more abundant and useful blessing than the verses of any uninspired penman that ever lived. In his Psalms and Hymns (for they must be classed together), he has embraced a compass and variety of subjects which include and illustrate every truth of revelation, throw light upon every secret movement of the human heart, whether of sin, nature, or grace, and describe every kind of trial, temptation, conflict, doubt, fear and grief, as well as the faith, hope, charity, the love of joy, peace, labor, and patience of the Christian in all stages of his course on earth; together with the terrors of the Lord, the glories of the Redeemer, and the comforts of the Holy Spirit, to urge, allure, and strengthen him by the way. Then, as in the pages of the evangelist, a word in season for every one who needs it, in whatever circumstance she may require counsel, consolation, reproof, or instruction. We say this, without reserve, of the materials of his hymns, had their execution always been correspondent with the preciousness of these, we should have had a Christian Psalmist, in England, next (and that only in date, not in dignity) to the Sweet Singer of Israel!—MONTGOMERY, JAMES, 1825, *The Christian Psalmist, Introductory Essay.*

Some of his hymns were written to be sung after his sermons, the hymn in each case giving expression to the meaning of the text upon which he had been discoursing. Produced as they were wanted, and for a practical purpose, some of these hymns lack the fire and genius of poetry, and the same must be admitted of some of his other productions.—MILLER, JOSIAH, 1866, *Our Hymns, p.* 82.

The Independents, as represented by Dr. Watts, have a just claim to be considered the real founders of modern English hymnody. No doubt Watts's taste was often faulty, and his style unequal; but more hymns which approached to a very high standard of excellence might be found in his works than in those of any other single writer in the English language.—PALMER, SIR ROUNDELL, 1866, *Lecture on English Church Hymnody.*

We are confirmed in our estimate of the relative value of Watts' hymns by the proportion they bear in nearly all our collections to those of other contributors. Of 1290 hymns in the "Sabbath Hymn Book," 254, as we count, are from Watts, and 56 from Charles Wesley, the next largest contributor. The "Plymouth Collection" has 1374 hymns, of which 218 are from Watts and 81 are from Wesley. In "Songs for the Sanctuary," Dr. Charles S. Robinson's book, there are 1345 hymns, with 198 from Dr. Watts. "Psalms and Hymns," the Connecticut Collection, so called, has 1293 separate pieces, of which 514 are Watts'. The "Psalmist" (Baptist) has 1180, with 301 from Dr. Watts. And so in nearly all the hymn books of the various denominations, with the exception of the Methodist Episcopal and Wesleyan churches; and in their collections, while Wesley leads, Watts is admitted to the second rank. A recent writer in an English magazine, after an examination of 750 different hymn books, ascribes to Dr. Watts the authorship of two-fifths of the hymns which are used in the English-speaking world.—ROBINSON, R. T., 1868, *Dr. Watts' Hymns, Hours at Home, vol.* 7, *p.* 519.

There are lines in those hymns which offend against all good taste. Yet there are wonderful jewels in that oft rubbishy mass of some six hundred religious poems. The man who could write them "ought not to have written as he has written." They "will be sung, I fancy," says the same critic, "so long as men praise God together." And indeed, they are wonderful, wonderful in their firm clear English, their noble sentences, in that true ring which touches every Christian heart.—PRESCOTT, J. E., 1883, *Christian Hymns and Hymn Writers, p.* 97.

I don't know but these bits of moral music may have been hustled out from modern church primers for something more æsthetic; but I am sure that a good many white-haired people—of whom I hope to count some among my readers—are carried back pleasantly by the rhythmic jingle of the good Doctor to those child days when hopes were fresh, and holidays a joy, and summers long; and when flowery paths stretched out before us, over which we have gone toiling since—to quite other music than that of Dr. Isaac Watts. And if his songs are gone out of our fine books, and have fallen below the mention of the dilettanti critics, I am the more glad to rescue his name, as that of an honest, devout, hard-working, cultivated man who has woven an immeasurable deal of moral fibre into the web and woof of many generations of men and women.—MITCHELL, DONALD G., 1895, *English Lands Letters and Kings, Queen Anne and the Georges, p.* 14.

His poetical fame rests on his hymns. At the beginning of the eighteenth century the stern embargo which Calvin had laid on the use in the music of sacred worship of everything except metrical psalms and canticles has been broken by the obscure hymns of Mason, Keach, Barton, and others; and hymns were freely used in the baptist and independent congregations. The poetry of Watts took the religious world of dissent by storm. It gave an utterance, till then unheard in England, to the spiritual emotions, in their contemplation of God's glory in nature and his revelation in Christ, and made hymn-singing a fervid devotional force. The success of Watts's hymns approached that of the new version of the Psalms. Edition followed edition. In the early years of this century the annual output of Watts's hymns, notwithstanding all the wealth of hymn production arising out of methodism, was still fifty thousand copies.—BENNETT, LEIGH, 1899, *Dictionary of National Biography, vol.* LX, *p.* 68.

POEMS

Was nevertheless, if I am in any degree a judge of verse, a man of true poetical ability; careless, indeed, for the most part, and inattentive too often to those niceties which constitute elegance of expression, but frequently sublime in his conceptions, and masterly in his execution.—COWPER, WILLIAM, 1781, *Letter to Rev. John Newton, Sept.* 18, *Works, vol.* II, *p.* 354.

He is emphatically the classic poet of the religious world, wherever the English language is known.—CLEVELAND, CHARLES D., 1848, *A Compendium of English Literature, p.* 480.

I have liked Dr. Watts's "Psalms and

Hymns" ever since the time when, scarcely three years old, I was made to repeat, with his book in my hand, and with such gestures as were prescribed to me, the psalm beginning with the words:—

"Come sound his praise abroad
And hymns of glory sing." . . .

I maintain, for my part, that Dr. Watts has done admirably well what he undertook to do, and the proof, if I wanted any other than the pleasure with which I always read him, I find in the strong hold which his devotional verses have taken on the hearts of men in all conditions of life, and, I think, all varieties of religious belief. . . . The secret of this popularity lies, as it seems to me, in the union of strong feeling with great poetic merit. In what he wrote there are occasional transgressions against good taste, as in his versification of Solomon's Song. There are slovenly lines, and even stanzas, but there is always great fervor and profound earnestness. No poet has ever expressed religious emotions with greater energy. . . . I know very well that poetry of a very moderate degree of merit not unfrequently obtains great popularity on account of its religious character; but I do not recollect an instance in which it has held that popularity long. The devotional verses of Watts have stood the test of time, and it seemed to me due to him that some of the characteristic merits by which they are recommended to the general mind should be pointed out.—BRYANT, W. C., 1864, *The Spirit of the Fair.*

In him the thought is true, the form of its utterance false; the feeling lovely, the word, often to a degree, repulsive. The ugly web is crossed now and then by a fine line, and even damasked with an occasional good poem: I have found two, and only two, in the whole of his seventy-five "Lyrics sacred to Devotion." His objectivity and boldness of thought, and his freedom of utterance, cause us ever and anon to lament that he had not the humility and faith of an artist as well as of a Christian.—MACDONALD, GEORGE, 1868, *England's Antiphon, p.* 281.

Shelley's masterpiece, in the shorter form of lyric (as, if such a judgment be permissible, all things considered, the Editor would hold the "Skylark"), follows Gray's: and in No. 83 we have one of the most stately and musical odes in our or any language. With these, Watts, verses come like the child they describe into a company of kings and conquerors. Indeed, the admirable author of the "Cradle Song" almost apologized for publishing it;—yet within its little sphere, this also is a masterpiece:—Reynolds himself does not paint childhood with a more absolute tenderness.—PALGRAVE, FRANCIS TURNER, 1875, *ed., The Children's Treasury of English Song, p.* 292, *note.*

GENERAL

This, I think, is a just censure on the greatest part of those who have written religious books in English verse; but I except from this number the ingenious Mr. Watts, whose Divine poetry is very laudable, and much superior to all that have gone before him in the lyric kind.—BLACKMORE, SIR RICHARD, 1718, *Preface to a Collection of Poems.*

Happy will be that reader whose mind is disposed, by his verses or his prose, to imitate him in all but his non-conformity, to copy his benevolence to man, and his reverence to God.—JOHNSON, SAMUEL, 1779–81, *Watts, Lives of the English Poets.*

In his literary character, Dr. Watts may be considered as a poet, a philosopher, and a theologian. In the first of these departments, if he did not attain a very high rank, he was, at least, considerably above mediocrity; and his devotional poetry, in particular, possesses a sweetness and simplicity, both in thought and diction, which deservedly acquired for it, especially among the Dissenters, with whom his psalms and hymns are in daily use, an established reputation. His philosophical productions can claim the rare merit of being always practically useful, and have been of the most essential service in the education of youth. His *logic* has received the highest encomium by its admission into the universities; his "Philosophical Essays:" his "Treatise on Education," &c. &c., are conducive to the best purposes of morality and instruction; and on his work entitled "The Improvement of the Mind." . . . In theology the compositions of our author are uncommonly numerous; and every page displays his unaffected piety, the purity of his principles, the mildness of his disposition, and the great goodness of his heart. The style of all his works is perspicuous, correct, and frequently elegant; and, happily for mankind, his labours have been translated and dispersed with a zeal which does honour to human nature; for there are probably few persons who have studied the writings of Dr. Watts without a wish for improvement; without an effort to become a wiser or a better member of society.—DRAKE, NATHAN, 1804, *Essays Illustrative of the Tatler, Spectator and Guardian, vol.* III, *pp.* 338, 339.

Dr. Watts's devotional poetry was for the most part intentionally lowered to the understanding of children. If this was a sacrifice of taste, it was at least made to the best of intentions. The sense and sincerity of his prose writings, the excellent method in which he attempted to connect the study of ancient logic with common sense, and the conciliatory manner in which he allures the youthful mind to habits of study and reflection, are probably remembered with gratitude by nine men out of ten, who have had proper books put into their hands at an early period of their education.—CAMPBELL, THOMAS, 1819, *Specimens of the British Poets.*

Of Watts, the companion of our younger and later years, it is impossible to speak without reverence and respect. His *Hymns* are the charm of our early youth; his *Logic,* the well-known theme of schoolboy study; and his Sermons, Essays, and other theological compositions, are a source of never failing gratification, in the advance, maturity, and decline of life. The man at fourscore may remember, with gratitude, the advantage of having committed the Hymns of this pious man to his infantine memory.— DIBDIN, THOMAS FROGNALL, 1824, *The Library Companion, p.* 65.

There are some reputations that are great merely because they are amiable. There is Dr. Watts; look at the encomiums passed on him by Dr. Johnson: and yet to what, according to his statement, does his merit amount? Why, only to this: that he did that best which none can do well, and employed his talents uniformly for the welfare of mankind. He was a good man, and the voice of the public has given him credit for being a great one. The world may be forced to do homage to great talents, but they only bow willingly to these when they are joined with benevolence and modesty; nor will they put weapons into the hands of the bold and unprincipled sophist to be turned against their own interests and wishes.—NORTHCOTE, JAMES, 1826-7, *Conversations, ed. William Hazlitt, p.* 248.

Watts had inherited a large share of the original temptation,—that inward and spiritual temptation whereby man is incited to pluck the forbidden fruit. He approached too near the veil; and confiding in his own natural and cultivated acuteness, endeavoured sometimes strictly to define what the Scriptures have left indefinite, as if he were possessed of an intellectual prism with which he could decompose the Light of Light. There were times when he was conscious of this. Upon publishing some sermons, many years after they were written, in which he had expatiated on the nature of the Trinity, he confessed in a note that there were "warmer efforts of imagination than riper years could indulge, on a theme so sublime and abstruse."—SOUTHEY, ROBERT, 1834, *Life of Isaac Watts.*

A name never to be uttered without reverence by any lover of pure Christianity or by any well-wisher of mankind.—WILSON, JAMES GRANT, 1876, *The Poets and Poetry of Scotland, vol.* I, *p.* 141.

In his doctrinal writings there are signs of the diffuse sentimentalism which not unfrequently acccompanies a feeble constitution. We may grant to his biographer that there is not an expression in his sermons "that could raise the faintest blush upon the cheek of modesty, or irritate the risibility of the most puerile." The more positive merits discovered by the same admirer will, perhaps, hardly keep the modern reader from somnolency. The sermons, however, show something of the old unction. They appeal strongly to the inward witness of the spirit, with a comparative indifference to the ordinary evidential argument. Unlike most of his contemporaries, he addresses the heart rather than the intellect; and in his hands Christianity is not emasculated Deism, but a declaration to man of the means by which God pleases to work a supernatural change in human nature. The emotional current is still running strongly, though combined with a rather heterogeneous collection of speculative opinions.—STEPHEN, LESLIE, 1876, *History of English Thought in the Eighteenth Century, vol.* II, *p.* 386.

Christopher Pitt

1699-1748.

Deserves a place in the history of English literature from his translation of Virgil. Was born in 1699, educated at Winchester College, and at New College, Oxford. In 1722 was presented to the living of Pimpern, Dorsetshire. In 1724 he resigned his fellowship and retired to Pimpern. He died in 1748. *Works:* "Vida's Art of Poetry, translated into English Verse," 1725. "Poems and Translations," 1727. "The Æneid of Virgil, translated into English Metre," 1740.—MOULTON, CHARLES WELLS, 1901.

PERSONAL

Before strangers he had something of the scholars's timidity or distrust; but when he became familiar, he was in a very high degree cheerful and entertaining. His general benevolence procured general respect, and he had passed a life placid and honourable, neither too great for the kindness of the low, nor too low for the notice of the great.—JOHNSON, SAMUEL, 1779–81, *Pitt, Lives of the English Poets.*

VIRGIL

1740

The impartiality which we have endeavoured to observe through this work, obliges us to declare, that so far as our judgment may be trusted, the latter poet has done most justice to Virgil; that he shines in Pitt with a lustre, which Dryden wanted not power, but leisure to bestow; and a reader, from Pitt's version, will both acquire a more intimate knowledge of Virgil's meaning, and a more exalted idea of his abilities. . . . Mr. Pitt, no doubt, had many advantages above Dryden in this arduous province: As he was later in the attempt, he had consequently the version of Dryden to improve upon. He saw the errors of that great poet, and avoided them; he discovered his beauties, and improved upon them; and as he was not impelled by necessity, he had leisure to revise, correct, and finish his excellent work.—CIBBER, THEOPHILUS, 1753, *Lives of the Poets, vol.* V, *pp.* 301, 307.

Pitt, engaging as a rival with Dryden, naturally observed his failures, and avoided them; and as he wrote after Pope's "Iliad," he had an example of an exact, equable, and splendid versification. With these advantages, seconded by great diligence, he might successfully labour particular passages, and escape many errors. If the two versions are compared, perhaps the result would be, that Dryden leads the reader forward by his general vigour and sprightliness, and Pitt often stops him to contemplate the excellence of a single couplet; that Dryden's faults are forgotten in the hurry of delight, and that Pitt's beauties are neglected in the languor of a cold and listless perusal; that Pitt pleases the critics and Dryden the people; that Pitt is quoted, and Dryden read. He did not long enjoy the reputation which this great work deservedly conferred; for he left the world in 1748.—JOHNSON, SAMUEL, 1779–81, *Pitt, Lives of the English Poets.*

Pitt's translation was included, with high commendation, in Warton's edition of Virgil; but the prevailing opinion of contemporaries, that it rivalled the work of Dryden in beauty while it surpassed it in accuracy, has not been confirmed by subsequent critics.—SECCOMBE, THOMAS, 1896, *Dictionary of National Biography, vol.* XLV, *p.* 342.

James Thomson

1700-1748.

Born at Ednam manse Kelso, 11th Sept. 1700, but brought up at Southdean, Jedburgh. He had studied for the ministry at Edinburgh, when in 1725 he removed to London, and in 1726 published "Winter," the first of his poems on the "Seasons;" it was immediately successful. "Summer" and "Spring" followed in 1727-28, and in 1730 "Autumn" completed the work. In 1729 his "Sophonisba" was produced. One luckless line, "O Sophonisba, Sophonisba O," is still remembered for the parody, "O Jemmy Thomson, Jemmy Thomson O," which killed what little life the piece possessed. His other tragedies were "Agemmnon" (1738), "Edward and Eleonora"

(1739), "Trancred and Sigismunda" (1745), and "Cariolanus" (1748). In 1731 Thomson was chosen to accompany the son of Lord Chancellor Talbot on the Grand Tour. The poem of "Liberty" (1732), inspired by his travels, was dedicated to the Prince of Wales, who in 1737 gave the poet a pension of £100 a year. He also obtained the sinecure post, worth £300 more, of surveyor-general of the Leeward Islands. In 1740 the "Masque of Alfred" was produced before the Prince and Princess of Wales. It contains "Rule Britannia" (claimed also for Mallet.) Thomson's finest work, "The Castle of Indolence," was published in May 1748. He died at Richmond, 27th August following.—PATRICK AND GROOME, *eds.*, 1897, *Chambers's Biographical Dictionary, p.* 914.

PERSONAL

Dear S^r^.

I promised my Friend Mr. Tompson who is now finishing his Subscription in Oxford, all the advantages I could give him; for wch reason I beg leave to introduce him to so valuable an acquaintance as Y^rs^. W^ch^ freedom I hope You will pardon in Dear Sir Y^r^ most obedient and faithful Servt.—YOUNG, EDWARD, 1729, *Letter to Joseph Spence, Apr.* 1; *Spence's Anecdotes, ed. Singer, p.* 298.

Thomson came at last, and disappointed me both by his appearance and conversation. Armstrong bore him down, having got into his sarcastical vein by the wine he had drunk before Thomson joined us. —CARLYLE, ALEXANDER, 1746–1805–60, *Autobiography, p.* 160.

A bard here dwelt, more fat than bard beseems;
Who, void of envy, guile, and lust of gain,
On virtue still, and nature's pleasing themes,
Pour'd forth his unpremeditated strain;
The world forsaking with a calm disdain,
Here laugh'd he careless in his easy seat;
Here quaff'd, encircled with the joyous train,
Oft moralizing sage: his ditty sweet
He loathed much to write, ne car'd to repeat.
—THOMSON, JAMES, 1748, *The Castle of Indolence, s.* lxviii.

The loss of such an agreeable friend as poor Thomson is so much the more shocking that it was unexpected by everybody. He died of a malignant nervous fever, that came upon the back of a tertian; and I had no notice of his being in any danger till I saw it in the most formidable shapes. It is certain nature was oppressed in him with a great load of materials for a disease, not to be easily thrown off by a constitution so much worn as his was; and if he had struggled through that fever, there are many reasons to believe that it must almost unavoidably have been followed by some lingering disease, much worse than a speedy death. This is the most comfortable light in which I can view this shocking loss.—ARMSTRONG, JOHN, 1748, *Letter to John Forbes, Sept.* 3.

Mr. Thomson was at the Leasowes in the summer of 1745, and in the autumn of 1746, and promised when he came again into the country to make a longer visit; but at the time he was expected came an account of his death. It seems he waited too long for the return of his friend, Dr. Armstrong, and did not choose to employ any other physician. He had nothing of the gentleman in his person or address; but he made amends for the deficiency by his refined sense, spirited expressions, and a manner of speaking not unlike his friend Quin. He did not talk a great deal, but after a pause of reflection produced something or other that accounted for his delay. The "Seasons" would make a fine poem in Latin. Its turgid phrases would lose their stiffness, and its vulgar idioms acquire a proper majesty; its propriety and description shine the same.—SHENSTONE, WILLIAM, c1748, *MS. Note in his Copy of the Seasons.*

Meek Nature's Child, again adieu!
The genial meads, assign'd to bless
Thy life, shall mourn thy early doom;
Their hinds and shepherd-girls shall dress,
With simple hands, thy rural tomb.
Long, long, thy stone and pointed clay
Shall melt the musing Briton's eyes:
"O! vales and wild woods, shall he say,
In yonder grave your Druid lies!"
—COLLINS, WILLIAM, 1749, *Ode on the Death of Thomson.*

No party his benevolence confined,
No sect—alike it flow'd to all mankind.
He loved his friends,—forgive this gushing tear,
Alas! I feel I am no actor here,—
He loved his friends with such a warmth of heart,
So clear of interest, so devoid of art,
Such generous friendship, such unshaken zeal,
No words can speak it, but our tears may tell.
O candid truth, O faith without a stain,
O manners gently firm, and nobly plain,

O sympathizing love of others' bliss,
Where will you find another breast like his?
—LYTTELTON, GEORGE LORD, 1749, *Prologue to Thomson's Coriolanus.*

The most benevolent heart that ever warmed the human breast.—SMOLLETT, TOBIAS GEORGE, 1757–58, *History of England, vol.* XIII, *p.* 433.

The Rev. Mr. Riccarton, a man of uncommon penetration and good taste, had very early discovered through the rudeness of young Thomson's puerile essays a fund of genius well deserving culture and encouragement. He undertook therefore, with the father's approbation, the chief direction of his studies, furnished him with the proper books, corrected his performances, and was daily rewarded with the pleasure of seeing his labour so happily employed.—MURDOCH, PATRICK, 1762, *ed., Works of Thomson, p.* 369.

Thomson was of stature above the middle size, and "more fat than bard beseems," of a dull countenance, and a gross, unanimated, uninviting appearance; silent in mingled company, but cheerful among select friends, and by his friends very tenderly and warmly beloved. . . . Among his peculiarities was a very unskilful and inarticulate manner of pronouncing any lofty or solemn composition.—JOHNSON, SAMUEL, 1779–81, *Thomson, Lives of the English Poets.*

So charming Thomson wrote from his lodgings, a milliner's in Bond Street, where he seldom rose early enough to see the sun do more than glisten on the opposite windows of the street.—PIOZZI, HESTER LYNCH, 1789, *Observations and Reflections Made in the Course of a Journey through France, Italy and Germany.*

I was acquainted with the author when I stayed in England. I discovered in him a great genius, and a great simplicity: I liked in him the poet and the true philosopher, I mean the lover of mankind. I think that without a good stock of such a philosophy a poet is just above the fidler, who amuses our ears and cannot go to our soul.—VOLTAIRE, FRANÇOIS MARIE AROUET, 1790, *Letter to Lord Lyttelton, May* 17.

Thomson, the poet, was so extremely indolent, that half his mornings were spent in bed. Dr. Burney having called on him one day at two o'clock, expressed surprise at finding him still there, and asked how he came to lie so long?—"Ecod, mon, because I had no *mot-tive* to rise," was his sole answer. (From Dr. Burney).—MALONE, EDMOND, 1791, *Maloniana, ed. Prior, p.* 415.

He was buried in Richmond Church, under a plain stone without any inscription, and his works formed his only memorial until the erection of the monument in Westminster Abbey, which was opened to public view on the 10th of May, 1762. The cost of it was defrayed by an edition of his works printed, under the superintendence of Murdoch, in two quarto volumes, and published by subscription. It is situated between those of Shakespeare and Rowe; and Thomson appears sitting, leaning his left arm upon a pedestal, and holding a book, with a cap of Liberty, in his right hand. Upon the pedestal is carved a bas-relief of "The Seasons," to which a boy points, offering him a laurel crown. At the feet of the figure is a tragic mask and ancient harp. The whole is supported by a projecting pedestal; and on a panel is inscribed his name, age, and the date of his death, with the lines which are inserted at the commencement of this Memoir, taken from his "Summer." The monument was designed by Adam, and executed by Michael Henry Spang. . . . In person Thomson was rather stout and above the middle size; his countenance was not remarkable for expression, though, in his youth, he was considered handsome, but in conversation his face became animated, and his eye fiery and intellectual. Silent in mixed company, his wit and vivacity seemed reserved for his friends, and in their society he was communicative, playful, and entertaining. Few men possessed in a greater degre the art of creating firm and affectionate friendships. Those with whom he became acquainted at the commencement of his career loved him till its close; and the individuals who had given to his life its sweetest enjoyments watched over his death-bed, and became the guardians of his fame, by superintending the only monuments of which genius ought to be ambitious, a complete edition of his works, and a tablet in Westminster Abbey.—NICOLAS, SIR NICHOLAS HARRIS, 1831–47, *ed., Poetical Works of James Thomson.*

As far as the restless and rapid change of property would permit so near London, the residence of Thomson has been kept from destruction: changed it is, it is true, but that change has been made with a veneration for the Muse in the heart of the new inhabitant. The house of Thomson, in what is called Kew-foot Lane, at Richmond, as shown in the wood-cut in the head of this article, was a simple cottage; behind this lay his garden, and in front he looked down to the Thames, and on the fine landscape beyond. The cottage now appears to be gone, and in the place stands the goodly villa of the earl of Shaftesbury; the cottage, however, is not really gone, it is only swallowed up in the larger house of the present time. After Thomson's death, his cottage was purchased by George Ross, Esq., who, out of veneration for his memory, forbore to pull it down, but enlarged and improved it at the expense of £9000. The walls of the cottage were left, though its roof was taken off, and the walls continued upward to their present height. Thus, what was Thomson's cottage forms now the entrance hall to Lord Shaftesbury's house. . . . The garden of Thomson, which lay behind the house has been preserved in the same manner and to the same extent as his house; the garden and its trees remain, but these now form only part of the present grounds, as the cottage forms only part of the present house.—HOWITT, WILLIAM, 1846, *Homes and Haunts of the Most Eminent British Poets, pp.* 252, 253.

Placid and good-natured in disposition Thomson undoubtedly always was; sluggish and prone to unconventional habits in later years he must have been, or his friends would not have twitted him so excessively on the matter; but a writer who could put to his credit so much admirable and polished poetical work in a somewhat brief career, could not, on the face of it, have been a trifler once upon a day. The storied peach which he so leisurely plucked from his garden-tree at Richmond has enjoyed a celebrity much exceeding its due; in addition, a man who did his writing chiefly at midnight could not with any sort of fairness be expected to be astir at dawn. Thomson has surely borne undeserved reproach, if not libel, on the score of general inertia. . . . A writer who could put so much bright, wholesome, and spiritual thinking into his poetry has inevitably drawn there for himself a character with dominant traits of the best and finest; and, upon the whole, there is no significant reason to conclude that he was materially untrue to the ideal which he thus upheld. Men like Lyttelton and Rundle, moral purists not only in sentiment but in practice, delighted in him. And if a man's letters to his friends are not cunningly devised pieces of deception, then Thomson must be deemed to have been possessed of uncommon goodness of heart.—BAYNE, WILLIAM, 1898, *James Thomson (Famous Scots Series), pp.* 97,107.

THE SEASONS
1726-30

Mr. Thomson's poetical diction in the "Seasons" is very peculiar to him: His manner of writing is entirely his own: He has introduced a number of compound words; converted substantives into verbs, and in short has created a kind of new language for himself. His stile has been blamed for its singularity and stiffness; but with submission to superior judges, we cannot but be of opinion, that though this observation is true, yet is it admirably fitted for description. The object he paints stands full before the eye, we admire it in all its lustre, and who would not rather enjoy a perfect inspection into a natural curiosity through a microscope capable of discovering all the minute beauties, though its exterior form should not be comely, than perceive an object but faintly, through a microscope ill adapted for the purpose, however its outside may be decorated. Thomson has a stiffness in his manner, but then his manner is new; and there never yet arose a distinguished genius, who had not an air peculiarly his own. 'Tis true indeed, the tow'ring sublimity of Mr. Thomson's stile is ill adapted for the tender passions, which will appear more fully when we consider him as a dramatic writer, a sphere in which he is not so excellent as in other species of poetry. —CIBBER, THEOPHILUS, 1753, *Lives of the Poets, vol.* V, *p.* 202.

Of all professed descriptive compositions, the largest and fullest that I am acquainted with, in any language, is Mr. Thomson's "Seasons;" a work which possesses very uncommon merit. The style, in the midst of much splendour and strength, is sometimes harsh, and may be censured as deficient in ease and distinctness. But notwithstanding this defect,

Thomson is a strong and a beautiful describer; for he had a feeling heart, and a warm imagination. He had studied and copied nature with care. Enamoured of her beauties, he not only described them properly, but felt their impression with strong sensibility. The impression which he felt, he transmits to his readers; and no person of taste can peruse any one of his "Seasons," without having the ideas and feelings, which belong to that season, recalled and rendered present to his mind. —BLAIR, HUGH, 1783, *Lectures on Rhetoric and Belles-Lettres, ed. Mills, Lecture* xl.

Of any works which have obtained considerable applause, Thomson's poem of "The Seasons" is the most incorrect. Any reader who understands grammar and classic composition, is disgusted in every page of that poem by faults, which, tho in themselves minute, yet to a refined eye hide and obscure every beauty however great, as a very small intervening object will intercept the view of the sun. This reason makes me very much suspect the fame of the "Seasons" will not be of very long existence; for I know of no work that has inherited long reputation which is deficient in style, as the "Seasons" undoubtedly are to a most remarkable degree. The fact is, that the poem on which the future celebrity of Thomson will be founded is, by a strange fatality, almost totally neglected at this day. That is, his "Castle of Indolence:" a poem which has higher beauties than the "Seasons," without any of the faults which disgrace that work; tho the conclusion even of this is most absurd, and unhappy; and could never have occurred to a writer of taste except in a frightful dream.—PINKERTON, JOHN (ROBERT HERON), 1785, *Letters of Literature, p.* 64.

While virgin Spring, by Eden's flood,
Unfolds her tender mantle green,
Or pranks the sod in frolic mood,
Or tunes the Æolian strains between;
While Summer, with a matron grace,
Retreats to Dryburgh's cooling shade,
Yet, oft delighted, stops to trace
The progress of the spikey blade;
While Autumn, benefactor kind,
By Tweed erects his aged head,
And sees, with self-approving mind,
Each creature on her bounty fed;
While maniac Winter rages o'er
The hills whence classic Yarrow flows,
Rousing the turbid torrent's roar,
Or sweeping, wild! a waste of snows;
So long, sweet Poet of the year!
Shall bloom that wreath thou well hast won,
While Scotia, with exulting tear,
Proclaims that Thomson was her son.
—BURNS, ROBERT, 1791, *Address to the Shade of Thomson.*

Can there be a more charming picture of love in marriage, than that which terminates the first ode of Thomson upon Spring?—STAËL, MADAME DE, 1800, *The Influence of Literature upon Society, ch.* xv.

It is almost stale to remark the beauties of a poem so universally felt; the truth and genial interest with which he carries us through the life of the year; the harmony of succession, which he gives to the casual phenomena of nature; his pleasing transition from native to foreign scenery; and the soul of exalted and unfeigned benevolence which accompanies his prospects of the creation. It is but equal justice to say, that amidst the feeling and fancy of the Seasons, we meet with interruptions of declamation, heavy narrative, and unhappy digression—with a parhelion eloquence that throws a counterfeit glow of expression on common-place ideas—as when he treats us to the solemnly ridiculous bathing of Musidora; or draws from the classics instead of nature; or, after invoking Inspiration from her hermit-seat, makes his dedicatory bow to a patronizing Countess, or Speaker of the House of Commons. As long as he dwells in the pure contemplation of nature, and appeals to the universal poetry of the human breast, his redundant style comes to us as something venial and adventitious—it is the flowing vesture of the druid; and perhaps to the general experience is rather imposing; but when he returns to the familiar narrations or courtesies of life, the same diction ceases to seem the mantle of inspiration, and only strikes us by its unwieldy difference from the common costume of expression.—CAMPBELL, THOMAS, 1819, *Specimens of the British Poets.*

That Thomson's "Seasons" is the original whence our modern descriptive poets have derived that more elegant and correct style of painting natural objects which distinguishes them from their immediate predecessors, will, I think, appear evident to one who examines their several casts and manners. That none of them, however, have yet equalled their master; and that his performance is an exquisite piece, replete with beauties of the most engaging and delightful kind; will be sensibly felt by all of congenial taste:—and perhaps no poem was ever composed which addressed itself to the feelings of a greater number of readers.—AIKIN, JOHN, 1820, *An Essay on the Plan and Character of Thomson's Seasons.*

Are then "The Seasons" and "The Task" Great Poems? Yes.—Why? We shall tell you in two separate articles. But we presume you do not need to be told that that poem must be great, which was the first to paint the rolling mystery of the year, and to shew that all Seasons were but the varied God? The idea was original and sublime; and the fulfilment thereof so complete, that some six thousand years having elapsed between the creation of the world and of that poem, some sixty thousand, we prophesy, will elapse between the appearance of that poem and the publication of another, equally great, on a subject external to the mind, equally magnificent.—WILSON, JOHN, 1831, *An Hour's Talk about Poetry, Blackwood's Magazine, vol.* 30, *p.* 483.

In the whole range of British poetry, Thomson's "Seasons" are, perhaps, the earliest read, and most generally admired. He was the Poet of Nature, and, studying her deeply, his mind acquired that placidity of thought and feeling which an abstraction from public life is sure to produce. . . . His pictures of scenery and of rural life are the productions of a master, and render him the Claude of Poets. "The Seasons" are the first book from which we are taught to worship the goddess to whose service the bard of Ednam devoted himself; and who is there that has reflected on the magnificence of an external landscape, viewed the sun as he emerges from the horizon, or witnessed the setting of that glorious orb when he leaves the world to reflection and repose, and does not feel his descriptions rush upon the mind, and heighten the enjoyment?—NICOLAS, SIR NICHOLAS HARRIS, 1831–47, *ed., Poetical Works of James Thomson.*

No one can read Thomson's "Seasons" with pleasure, and not be the better for it.—BRYDGES, SIR SAMUEL EGERTON, 1834, *Autobiography, vol.* I, *p.* 387.

The finest descriptive poem in the English or perhaps in any language. . . . The work is animated throughout with so gentle yet so genial a glow of philanthropy and religious gratitude, that its parts are, so to say, fused naturally together; the everchanging landscape is harmonised by this calm and elevated, and tender spirit, which throws over the whole a soft and all-pervading glow, like the tint of an Italian heaven.—SHAW, THOMAS B., 1847, *Outlines of English Literature, pp.* 291, 292.

. . . as sweet a bard
(Theocritus and Maro blent in one)
As ever graced the name. . . .
The truthful, soul-subduing lays of him
Whose fame is with his country's being blent,
And cannot die; . . .
Of him who sang the Seasons as they roll,
With all a Hesiod's truth, a Homer's power,
And the pure feeling of Simonides.
—MOIR, DAVID MACBETH, c1851, *Thomson's Birthplace.*

While it is not devoid of sentiment, genial and refined, its more striking characteristic is the large extent and compass of knowledge which it displays. I have looked upon it as pre-eminently valuable, from the fulness and beauty of its teachings in all the prominent departments of Natural History, and have thought, that, by a somewhat ample explanation of those subjects in the notes, a taste may be formed, or matured, in this interesting branch of study, and a foundation laid for prosecuting it with happy success.—BOYD, JAMES ROBERT, 1852, *ed., The Seasons, Preface, p.* 6.

The English poet, from the midst of the luxury and the philosophy of the capital, seeks the country, . . . and though he dedicates his work to a great lady, his feelings are with the people—a people rich and proud of a free fatherland. Like them, he loves its pastures, its forest, and its fields. Thence springs his glowing manner; thence, under a gloomy sky, and in a period of cold philosophy, is his poetry so full of freshness and color.—VILLEMAIN, ABEL FRANÇOIS, 1855, *Cours de Littérature Française.*

It described the scenery and country life of Spring, Summer, Autumn, and Winter. He wrote with his eye upon their scenery, and even when he wrote of it in his room, it was with a "recollected love." The descriptions were too much like catalogues, the very fault of the previous Scotch poets, and his style was always heavy and often cold, but he was the first poet who led the English people into that new world of nature in poetry, which has moved and enchanted us in the work of Wordsworth, Shelley, Keats and Tennyson, but which was entirely impossible for Pope to understand. The impulse he gave was soon followed. Men left the town to visit the country and record their feelings.—BROOKE, STOPFORD, 1876, *English Literature (Primer), p.* 143.

In choosing his subject, therefore, and in the minute loving way in which he dwells upon it, Thomson would seem to have been working in the spirit of his country. But there the Scottish element in him begins and ends. Neither in the kind of landscape he pictures, in the rural customs he selects, nor in the language or versification of his poem, is there much savor of Scottish habits or scenery. His blank verse cannot be said to be a garment that fits well to its subject. It is heavy, cumbrous, oratorical, overloaded with epithets, full of artificial invocations, "personified abstractions," and insipid classicalities. It is a composite style of language formed from the recollection partly of Milton, partly of Virgil's Georgics. Yet in spite of all these obstructions which repel pure taste and natural feeling, no one can read the four books of the "Seasons" through, without seeing that Thomson, for all his false style, wrote with his eye upon Nature, and laid his finger on many a fact and image never before touched in poetry.—SHAIRP, JOHN CAMPBELL, 1877, *On Poetic Interpretation of Nature, p.* 197.

Thomson's descriptions are not always due to the colors thrown upon them by his own hopes and fears for himself; it is only passages here and there that have a direct biographical interest. The gloomy notes of the opening of his poem on Winter are only significant of the mood in which he began the poem; once fairly absorbed in his subject, he seems, as it were, to have been carried on the wings of imagination far above and away from the anxieties of his own life, up into sublime contemplation of the great forces of Nature, and into warm sympathy with the human hardships and enjoyments, horrors and amusements, peculiar to the season.—MINTO, WILLIAM, 1894, *The Literature of the Georgian Era, ed. Knight, p.* 61.

The "Seasons" was at one time, and for many years the most popular volume of poetry in the country. It was to be found in every cottage, and passages from the poem were familiar to every schoolboy. The appreciation of the work was more affectionate than critical, and Thomson's faults were sometimes mistaken for beauties; but the popularity of the "Seasons" was a healthy sign, and the poem, a forerunner of Cowper's "Task," brought into vigorous life, feelings and sympathies that had been long dormant.—DENNIS, JOHN, 1894, *The Age of Pope, p.* 91.

This Scotch poet is wordy; he draws long breaths; he is sometimes tiresome; but you will catch good honest glimpses of the country in his verse without going there —not true to our American seasons in detail, but always true to Nature. The sun never rises in the west in his poems; the jonquils and the daisies are not confounded; the roses never forget to blush as roses should; the oaks are sturdy; the hazels are lithe; the brooks murmur; the torrents roar a song; the winds carry waves across the grainfields; the clouds plant shadows on the mountains.—MITCHELL, DONALD G., 1895, *English Lands Letters and Kings, Queen Anne and the Georges, p.* 75.

"The Seasons" shows that as far as intrinsic worth is concerned the poems are marked with a strange mingling of merits and defects, but that, considered in their historical place in the development of the poetry of nature, their importance and striking originality can hardly be overstated. Though Thomson talked the language of his day, his thought was a new one. He taught clearly, though without emphasis, the power of nature to quiet the passions and elevate the mind of man, and he intimated a deeper thought of divine immanence in the phenomena of nature. But his great service to the men of his day was that he shut up their books, led them out of their parks, and taught them to look on nature with enthusiasm.—REYNOLDS, MYRA, 1896, *The Treatment of Nature in English Poetry, p.* 89.

Between the ages of Pope and Scott, Thomson continued the most popular poet in the English language, and it would be difficult to set a limit to the extent of his influence. His plays, cold and undramatic, were of no great moment; and his political pieces, dreary diatribes and citations, might have remained unwritten. Even his "Castle of Indolence," with its rich archaic setting and its sensuous and languid splendour, must have exercised a charm always only upon the inner few. But his "Seasons" were a new voice on the earth; their imagery, fresh and exuberant, carried men back to the natural wells of delight—the simple enjoyments of sense, the glory of valley and woodland, and the magic and the majesty of the sea. The verse, moreover, in which they were written was the first blank verse of the modern kind.—EYRE-TODD, GEORGE, 1896, *Scottish Poetry of the Eighteenth Century, vol.* I, *p.* 100.

His style is indeed deeply marked by the artificiality of the time; the blank verse moves heavily; warmth and enthusiasm for his great subject are seldom shown. But he has much small, close, and true observation, in which the lines move with a fresh or spontaneous movement—fine but rare genuine touches of Nature.—PALGRAVE, FRANCIS TURNER, 1896, *Landscape in Poetry, p.* 169

Hazlitt called Thomson "the best of our descriptive poets," and the title, in its exact sense, will not with justice be denied him. His claim springs first from the completeness of his devotion to the treatment of external nature; no British poet rivals him in absolute absorption in this subject. No work in the range of British literature approaches "The Seasons" in dealing with Nature in a manner so apt and strenuous. Again, he excels in the expansiveness of his power in transcribing from Nature; his imagination ranges afar, while it depicts with precision; he can treat broad and striking areas with force as well as picturesqueness. A third eminent characteristic is the freshness with which he invests his portrayal. In this he is second to none of the most original of his Scottish precursors.—BAYNE, WILLIAM, 1898, *James Thomson (Famous Scots Series), p.* 114.

We have grown so accustomed to a more intimate treatment and a more spiritual interpretation of nature, that we are perhaps too apt to undervalue Thomson's simple descriptive or pictorial method. Compared with Wordsworth's mysticism, with Shelley's passionate pantheism, with Byron's romantic gloom in presence of the mountains and the sea, with Keats' joyous re-creation of mythology, with Thoreau's Indian-like approach to the innermost arcana—with a dozen other moods familiar to the modern mind—it seems to us unimaginative. Thomson has been likened, as a colorist, to Rubens; and possibly the glow, the breadth, and the vital energy of his best passages, as of Rubens' great canvases, leave our finer perceptions untouched, and we ask for something more esoteric, more intense. Still there are permanent and solid qualities in Thomson's landscape art, which can give delight even now to an unspoiled taste. To a reader of his own generation, "The Seasons" must have come as the revelation of a fresh world of beauty. Such passages as those which describe the first spring showers, the thunderstorm in summer, the trout-fishing, the sheep-washing, and the terrors of the winter night, were not only strange to the public of that day, but were new in English poetry.—BEERS, HENRY A., 1898, *A History of English Romanticism in the Eighteenth Century, p.* 107.

MS. CORRECTIONS OF THE SEASONS

It has long been accepted as a fact among scholars that Pope assisted Thomson in the composition of the "Seasons." Our original authority for the statement is, I suppose, Joseph Warton. Johnson who had heard, through Savage, a great deal about Thomson, does not mention *this*. . . . But if the best authorities at the Museum many years ago were positive that this handwriting is Pope's, their successors at the present time are equally positive that it is not. On this point the opinion of Mr. Warner, whom Mr. W. Y. Fletcher kindly consulted for me, is very decided. Nor does Mr. Courthope, to whom I have shown the volume, recognize the hand as bearing much resemblance to Pope's. Without pretending to an independent judgment upon such matters, I must say that it has all along been perplexing to me how the opinion that this was Pope's handwriting could ever have been confidently entertained. . . . At present I am inclined to believe these notes to be the work of a very intimate and even devoted friend. If space permitted, I think I could show that they were written by a man of finer taste—perhaps of greater poetic gift—

than Thomson himself.—TOVEY, D. C., 1894, *An Interleaved Copy of Thomson's "Seasons," The Athenæum, vol.* 2, *pp.* 131, 132.

"Through the black night that sits immense around." Indeed, throughout "The Seasons" Thomson's indebtedness to his corrector is incalculable; many of the most felicitous touches are due to him. Now, who was his corrector? . . . What has long therefore been represented and circulated as an undisputed fact—namely, that Pope assisted Thomson in the revision of "The Seasons"—rests not, as all Thomson's modern editors, have supposed, on the traditions of the eighteenth century, and on the testimony of authenticated handwriting, but on a mere assumption of Mitford. That the volume in question really belonged to Thomson, and that the corrections are originals, hardly admits of doubt, though Mitford gives neither the pedigree nor the history of this most interesting literary relic. It is of course possible that the corrections are Thomson's own, and that the differences in the handwriting are attributable to the fact that in some cases he was his own scribe, in others he employed an amanuensis; but the intrinsic unlikeness of the corrections made in the strange hand to his characteristic style renders this improbable. In any case there is nothing to warrant the assumption that the corrector was Pope.—COLLINS, JOHN CHURTON, 1897, *A Literary Mare's-Nest, The Saturday Review, vol.* 84, *p.* 118.

(1) There is no one to whom Thomson would have, between 1738 and 1744, so likely applied for criticism and suggestions as his friend and neighbour, the great Mr. Pope. (2) There is no one but Pope who could, at that time, have written verse equal or nearly equal to that of Thomson. (3) If the writing be certainly not that of Pope, as it is not either that of any other known writer who could be supposed to have been the author of such emendations and additions, there remains only to conclude that the real author used an amanuensis. But instead of Mr. Churton Collins's suggestion (which he himself declares to be improbable, and which seems to me utterly untenable) that the notes are Thomson's while employing an amanuensis, I hold by the notion that, whoever the amanuensis, the notes were dictated by Pope.—MOREL, LÉON, 1898, *Thomson and Pope, The Saturday Review, vol.* 86, *p.* 208.

LIBERTY
1732

I do not know a pleasure I should enjoy with more pride than that of filling up the leisure of a well employed year in exerting the critic of your poem; in considering it first, with a view to the vastness of its conception, in the general plan, secondly, to the grandeur, the depth, the unleaning, self-supported richness of the sentiments; and thirdly, to the strength, the elegance, the music, the comprehensive living energy, and close propriety of your expression. I look upon this mighty work as the last stretched blaze of our expiring genius. It is the dying effort of despairing and indignant virtue, and will stand, like one of those immortal pyramids, which carry their magnificence through times that wonder to see nothing round them but uncomfortable desert.—HILL, AARON, 1734, *Letter to Thomson, Feb.* 17.

Liberty called in vain upon her votaries to read her praises, and reward her encomiast: her praises were condemned to harbour spiders, and to gather dust: none of Thomson's performances were so little regarded.—JOHNSON, SAMUEL, 1779–81, *Thomson, Lives of the English Poets.*

His poem on Liberty is not equally good: his Muse was too easy and good-natured for the subject, which required as much indignation against unjust and arbitrary power, as complacency in the constitutional monarchy, under which, just after the expulsion of the Stuarts and the establishment of the House of Hanover, in contempt of the claims of hereditary pretenders to the throne, Thomson lived. Thomson was but an indifferent hater; and the most indispensable part of the love of liberty has unfortunately hitherto been the hatred of tyranny. Spleen is the soul of patriotism, and of public good: but you would not expect a man who has been seen eating peaches off a tree with both hands in his waistcoat pockets, to be "overrun with spleen," or to heat himself needlessly about an abstract proposition.—HAZLITT, WILLIAM, 1818, *Lectures on the English Poets, Lecture* v.

Though the most laboured, and in its author's opinion the best of his productions, "Liberty" was never popular; and perhaps most persons have found it as difficult to read to an end as Dr. Johnson did, who eagerly avails himself of the neglect with which it was treated to indulge in one of those sneers with which his account of Thomson abounds.—NICOLAS, SIR NICHOLAS HARRIS, 1831–47, *ed., Poetical Works of James Thomson.*

The English poet Thomson wrote a very good poem on the Seasons, but a very bad one on Liberty, and that not from want of poetry in the poet, but from want of poetry in the subject.—GOETHE BY ECKERMANN, JOHN PETER, 1832, *Conversations of Goethe, vol.* II, *p.* 427.

The early productions of Thomson are inferior to the beginnings of most poets, and "Liberty" is a composition which has been seldom perused save by editors and proof-readers.—CHILD, FRANCIS J., 1863, *ed., Poetical Works of James Thomson, Advertisement.*

His poem upon "Liberty," which Johnson confesses that he had never read, appears—so far as I have inspected it—to be a series of such sounding commonplaces as Bolingbroke was in the habit of embodying in his political essays. Doubtless, there was some sincerity in such declamation, but clearly there was little passion. It implied contempt for priestcraft, and dislike to the absolute rule of a despot; but not the least desire to upheave and reconstruct society. It is the sentiment of a British Whig, not of Rousseau or Voltaire. The poem on "Liberty" and the plays, in which he indulged the same vein, are as dead as Blackmore.—STEPHEN, LESLIE, 1876, *History of English Thought in the Eighteenth Century, vol.* II, *p.* 360.

Every one who has really endeavoured to read his favourite "Liberty" must endorse Johnson's contemptuous verdict on it. It is not only not good as a whole, but (which is more remarkable) it is scarcely even good in parts. It is with considerable difficulty that one is able to pick out a few lines here and there where the admirable descriptive faculty of the writer has had room to make itself felt.—SAINTSBURY, GEORGE, 1880, *English Poets, ed. Ward, vol.* III, *p.* 169.

The idea at the root of "Liberty" oppressed him from Paris to Rome, and from Rome back to London. And, after all, the sum and substance of his foreign experience produced no worthy result. The poem proved that constitutional freedom was a theme on which his imagination could not range freely, though it could do so intensely, as in "Rule Britannia." A rationalised social philosophy was not the kind of work for which he was fitted, though he himself did not yet, if he ever did, perceive this; but it was decisively demonstrated by the common verdict pronounced upon this one deliberate philosophical poem. . . . The opinion of every succeeding age of readers has reversed the judgment of Thomson on what he considered to be his "noblest work." No other conclusion is possible. In "Liberty" he attempted a task that both in material and scope was not adapted to his powers.—BAYNE, WILLIAM, 1898, *James Thomson (Famous Scots Series), pp.* 82, 84.

THE CASTLE OF INDOLENCE
1748

There is a poem by Thomson, the "Castle of Indolence," with some good stanzas.—GRAY, THOMAS, 1748, *Letter to Thomas Wharton, June* 5, *Works, vol.* II, *p.* 184.

I conclude you will read Mr. Thomson's "Castle of Indolence:" it is after the manner of Spenser; but I think he does not always keep so close to his style as the author of the "School-Mistress," whose name I never knew until you were so good as to inform me of it,—I believe the "Castle of Indolence" will afford you much entertainment; there are many pretty paintings in it; but I think the wizard' song deserves a preference:

"He needs no muse who dictates from the heart."

—HERTFORD, COUNTESS, 1748, *Letter to Lady Luxborough, May* 15.

To the "Castle of Indolence" he brought not only the full nature, but the perfect art, of a poet. The materials of that exquisite poem are derived originally from Tasso; but he was more immediately indebted for them to the "Fairy Queen:" and in meeting with the paternal spirit of Spenser he seems as if he were admitted more intimately to the home of inspiration.—CAMPBELL, THOMAS, 1819, *Specimens of the British Poets.*

A structure of genuine talent, certainly not piled when that "bard, more fat than bard beseems," was, where he delighted to be, on the spot itself, though so witchingly framed for voluptuous ease, that the reader is ready to lie down under its influence,—not, however, to sleep.—MONTGOMERY, JAMES, 1833, *Lectures on General Literature, Poetry, &c., p.* 132.

Not only is the best imitation ever made of the great author of "The Faërie Queen," but one of the most delightful works in the English language.—SHAW, THOMAS B., 1847, *Outlines of English Literature, p.* 294.

"The Castle of Indolence," more thoroughly complete, more delicately finished, and aspiring to a certain plot and story, displays more of the artist, with very little less of the poet, than the "Seasons." It is, certainly, the sweetest piece of poetic seduction in the world. No hymn to Sleep ever was so soft—no "dream within a dream," of rest beyond the dreaming land, was ever so subtle.—GILFILLAN, GEORGE, 1853, *ed. Thomson's Poetical Works, p.* xvii.

No man or boy need hope to be lured into early rising by the study of this poem.—COLLIER, WILLIAM FRANCIS, 1861, *A History of English Literature, p.* 303.

The beauty and purity of imagination, also, diffused over the melodious stanzas of the "Castle of Indolence," make that poem one of the gems of the language.—CRAIK, GEORGE L., 1861, *A Compendious History of English Literature and of the English Language, vol,* II, *p.* 286.

Is an exquisite masterpiece, with not a grain of perishable matter in it. Completely free from all of Thomson's usual faults and less pleasing peculiarities, it is fresh, terse, and natural, perfectly melodious, and has a charming humour rarely displayed by the author in his other pieces, though *indicated* elsewhere, as, for instance, in the hunters' drinking-bout in "Autumn."—CHILD, FRANCIS J., 1863, *ed., Poetical Works of James Thomson, Advertisement.*

One of the most highly-finished and one of the most imaginative of the productions of the eighteenth century.—WALKER, HUGH, 1893, *Three Centuries of Scottish Literature, vol.* II, *p.* 73.

The best poem written between Dryden and Blake. . . . He has penetrated the secret of the verse-paragraph; he has borrowed many of the minor mannerisms; he has adopted (subject to the influence of two generations of reformed English) the classicalised vocabularies. But he has done more than this. He has put the *je ne sais quoi* of personality into his rhythm: so that Thomsonian blank verse is a kind in itself, and stands out among the non-dramatic kinds of the English unrhymed decasyllable as no others do but Milton's own and Tennyson's.—SAINTSBURY, GEORGE, 1896, *Social England, ed. Traill, vol.* V, *pp.* 82, 83.

No work of poetry between the time of Spenser and Thomson is so marked by this absolutely delicate idealising tendency; nothing like it appears again till the time of Keats. We do not hear much about the significance of Thomson's part in setting forth anew the "sweet-slipping movement" and charm of the Spenserian manner as a model for the poets of the nineteenth century literary renaissance; but there can be no doubt about the validity of his right in this matter. In the romantic method, so excellently represented by Thomson, Keats may be taken as the most direct successor who understood the extraordinary richness of the note that was struck in "The Castle of Indolence;" for though there is its mystic glamour in the poetry of Coleridge, Keats, in his work, combines in a more general way, the main aims in the literary design of Thomson.—BAYNE, WILLIAM, 1898, *James Thomson* (*Famous Scots Series*), *p.* 131.

ALFRED
1740

The music of this noble "ode in honour of Great Britain," which, according to Southey, "will be the political hymn of this country as long as she maintains her poetical power," was composed by Dr. Arne for his masque of "Alfred," and first performed at Cliefden House, near Maidenhead, on August 1, 1740. Cliefden was then the residence of Frederick, Prince of Wales, and the occasion was to commemorate the accession of George I., and in honour of the birthday of the young Princess Augusta. The masque gave so much satisfaction that it was repeated on the following night. Dr. Arne afterwards altered it into an opera, and it was so performed at Drury Lane Theatre, on March, 20, 1745, for the benefit of Mrs. Arne. In the advertisements of that performance, and in another of the following month, Dr. Arne entitles "Rule, Britannia," "a *celebrated* ode;" from which it may be inferred that (although the entire masque had not been performed in public), "Rule, Britannia," had then attained popularity. Some detached pieces of the masque had been sung in Dublin, on the occasion of Arne's visit with his wife, but no record of any other public performance has hitherto been discovered. The words of the masque were by Thomson and Mallet, but Thomson seems to have taken the lead in the affair, since, in the newspapers of the day, he alone is mentioned as the author. In the book, the names of Thomson and Mallet are both given. —CHAPPELL, WILLIAM, 1855–59, *Popular Music of the Olden Time, vol.* II, *p.* 686.

The utmost appropriateness accompanies this assignment of the authorship of "Rule Britannia." No more fitting lyrist than he who sang so admirably and so unremittingly of Nature and of man, and the social and industrial glory of his country, could have composed the unchallenged pæan of the nation's greatness.—BAYNE, WILLIAM, 1898, *James Thomson* (*Famous Scots Series*), *p.* 160.

There is no evidence that during their lifetime either Thomson or Mallet claimed the authorship; but this is certain, it was printed at Edinburgh during Mallet's lifetime in the second edition of a well-known song-book entitled "The Charmer," with Thomson's initials appended to it. It is certain that Mallet had friends in Edinburgh, and it is equally certain that he nor any of his friends raised any objection to its assignment to Thomson. In 1743, in 1759 and in 1762 Mallet published collections of poems, but in none of these collections does he lay claim to "Rule Britannia," and though it was printed in song-books in 1749, 1750, and 1761, it is in no case assigned to Mallet. None of his contemporaries, so far as we know, attributed it to him, and it is remarkable that in a brief obituary notice of him which appeared in the "Scots Magazine" in 1765, he is spoken of as the author of the famous ballad "William and Margaret," but not a word is said about this lyric.—COLLINS, JOHN CHURTON, 1897, *The Authorship of "Rule Britannia," The Saturday Review, vol.* 83, *p.* 190.

DRAMAS

The town flocks to a new play of Thomson's, called "Tancred and Sigismunda:" it is very dull; I have read it. I cannot bear modern poetry; these refiners of the purity of the stage and of the incorrectness of English verse are most wofully insipid. I had rather have written the most absurd lines in Lee, than "Leonidas" or "The Seasons;" as I had rather be put into the round-house for a wrong-headed quarrel than sup quietly at eight o'clock with my grandmother.—WALPOLE, HORACE, 1745, *To Sir Horace Mann, March* 29, *Letters, ed. Cunningham, vol.* I, *p.* 347.

Mr. Thomson's tragedies seem to me wisely intricated and elegantly writ; they want perhaps some fire, and it may be that his heroes are neither moving nor busy enough, but taking him all in all, methinks he has the highest claim to the greatest esteem.—VOLTAIRE, FRANÇOIS MARIE AROUET, 1790, *Letter to Lord Lyttelton, May* 17.

Though "Agamemnon" is not a capital play on the whole, and abounds in languid and long declamatory speeches, yet parts of it are striking, particularly Melisander's account of the desert island to which he was banished, copied from the "Philoctetes" of Sophocles; and the prophetic speeches of Cassandra during the moment of Agamemnon's being murdered, well calculated to fill the audience with alarm, astonishment, and suspense at an awful event, obscurely hinted at in very strong imagery. These speeches are closely copied from the "Agamemnon" of Eschylus, as is a striking scene in his "Eleonora" from the "Alcestis" of Euripides. Thomson was well acquainted with the Greek tragedies, on which I heard him talk learnedly when I was once introduced to him by my friend Mr. W. Collins.—WARTON, JOSEPH, 1797, *ed. Pope's Works, vol.* VII, *p.* 10.

The beautiful fancy, the gorgeous diction, and generous affections of Thomson, were chilled and withered as soon as he touched the verge of the Drama; where his name is associated with a mass of verbose puerility, which it is difficult to conceive could ever have proceeded from the author of the "Seasons" and the "Castle of Indolence."—JEFFREY, FRANCIS LORD, 1822–44, *Contributions to the Edinburgh Review, vol.* 2, *p.* 334.

"Tancred and Sigismunda" (founded on a story in "Gil Blas") was the most successful of Thomson's pieces on the stage;

Garrick and Mrs. Cibber appeared in it, and it continued as an acting piece up to 1788, if not later.—ROSSETTI, WILLIAM MICHAEL, 1878, *Lives of Famous Poets*, *p.* 139.

It can only be matter for regret that Thomson wasted so much of his life over compositions in which he was so little qualified to excel. He had not the dramatic faculty. His plays are cold, lifeless, and uninteresting. They are equal in bulk to all his other poetry combined, yet there is hardly a line in the whole for the loss of which the world would be poorer.—WALKER, HUGH, 1893, *Three Centuries of Scottish Literature, vol.* II, *p.* 70.

It ["Sophonisba"] was a poor imitation of Otway, and there was little opportunity in it for the display of the poet's characteristic excellencies; it was nevertheless sold to Millar for 130 guineas, and went through four editions during the year (several translations appeared, a Russian one in 1786). One line of "Sophonisba" at least has defied oblivion. Nat Lee had written "O Sophonisba, Oh!" Thomson expanded the sentiment in the verse

Oh! Sophonisba, Sophonisba, Oh!

the inanity of which was pointed out, not at the theatre, as has generally been assumed, but in an envious little squib, called "A Criticism of the New Sophonisba" (1730). The quick eye of Fielding soon detected the absurdity, which was paraded in his "Tom Thumb the Great," the line "Oh! Huncamunca, Huncamunca, Oh!" appearing as a kind of refrain. It is noticeable that the line "O Sophonisba, I am wholly thine," was not substituted by Thomson until after 1738.—SECCOMBE, THOMAS, 1898, *Dictionary of National Biography, vol.* LVI, *p.* 248.

GENERAL

Poets, like you, their own protectors stand,
Plac'd above aid from pride's inferior hand.
Time, that devours a lord's unlasting name,
Shall land her soundest depth to float your fame. . . .

—HILL, AARON, 1726, *To Mr. James Thomson.*

. . . Thomson, in this praise, thy merit see;
The tongue that praises merit, praises thee.

—SAVAGE, RICHARD, 1729, *The Wanderer, Canto I.*

Tho' Thomson, sweet descriptive bard
Inspiring Autumn sung;
Yet how should we the months regard,
That stopp'd his flowing tongue?
Ah luckless months, of all the rest,
To whose hard share it fell!
For sure his was the gentlest breast
That ever sung so well. . . .
He! he is gone, whose mortal strain
Could wit and mirth refine;
He! he is gone, whose social vein
Surpass'd the power of wine.

—SHENSTONE, WILLIAM, 1748, *Verses to William Lyttleton, Esq.*

. . . The Poet well you know:
Oft has he touch'd your hearts with tender woe:
Oft in this crowded house, with just applause
You heard him teach fair Virtue's purest laws;
For his chaste Muse employ'd her heaven-taught lyre
None but the noblest passions to inspire,
Not one immoral, one corrupted thought,
One line, which, dying, he could wish to blot.

—LYTTELTON, GEORGE LORD, 1749, *Prologue to Thomson's "Coriolanus."*

Thomson was blessed with a strong and copious fancy; he has enriched poetry with a variety of new and original images, which he painted from nature itself, and from his own actual observations; his descriptions have, therefore, a distinctness and truth which are utterly wanting to those of poets who have only copied from each other, and have never looked abroad on the subjects themselves. Thomson was accustomed to wander away into the country for days and for weeks, attentive to each rural sight, each rural sound; while many a poet who has dwelt for years in the Strand has attempted to describe fields and rivers, and has generally succeeeded accordingly.—WARTON, JOSEPH, 1756, *Essay on the Genius and Writings of Pope.*

Mr. Thomson, though, in general, a verbose and affected poet, has told this ["Palemon and Lavinia"] story with simplicity; it is rather given here for being much esteemed by the public than by the editor.—GOLDSMITH, OLIVER, 1767, *The Beauties of English Poetry.*

As a writer, he is entitled to one praise of the highest kind: his mode of thinking, and of expressing his thoughts, is original. His blank verse is no more the blank verse of Milton, or of any other poet, than the rhymes of Prior are the rhymes of Cowley.

His numbers, his pauses, his diction, are of his own growth, without transcription, without imitation. He thinks in a peculiar train, and he thinks always as a man of genius; he looks round on nature and on life with the eye which nature bestows only on the poet; the eye which distinguishes, in every thing presented to its view, whatever there is on which imagination can delight to be detained, and with a mind that at once comprehends the vast and attends to minute.—JOHNSON, SAMUEL, 1779–81, *Thomson, Lives of the English Poets.*

Thomson was admirable in description; but it always seemed to me that there was somewhat of affectation in his style, and that his numbers are sometimes not well harmonized. I could wish too, with Dr. Johnson, that he had confined himself to this country; for when he describes what he never saw, one is forced to read him with some allowance for possible misrepresentation. He was, however, a true poet, and his lasting fame has proved it.—COWPER, WILLIAM, 1788, *Letter to Mrs. King, June* 19.

Lord Buchan is screwing out a little ephemeral fame from instituting a jubilee for Thomson. I fear I shall not make my court to Mr. Berry by owning I would not give him this last week's fine weather for all the four "Seasons" in blank verse. There is more nature in six lines of "L'Allegro" and "Penseroso" than in all the laboured imitations of Milton. What is there in Thomson's of original?—WALPOLE, HORACE, 1791, *To the Miss Berrys, Sept.* 16.

In his poems, those who are able to taste and relish that divine art which raises the man of clay from the soil on which he vegetates to the heaven of sentiment, . . . will delight in seeing the beautiful features of Nature presented to the eyes as spectators and not readers, and after these delightful impressions are over, they will find themselves happier and better than they were before.—BUCHAN, LORD, 1791, *Address at the Coronation of the Bust of Thomson, Sep.* 22.

Thomson, though dear to my heart, was too florid.—HUNT, LEIGH, 1811, *The Feast of the Poets.*

With the wits of Queen Anne this foreign school attained the summit of its reputation; and has ever since, we think, been declining, though by slow and almost imperceptible graduations. Thomson was the first writer of any eminence who seceded from it, and made some steps back to the force and animation of our original poetry. Thomson, however, was educated in Scotland, where the new style, we believe, had not yet become familiar; and lived, for a long time, a retired and unambitious life, with very little intercourse with those who gave the tone in literature at the period of his first appearance. Thomson, accordingly, has always been popular with the much wider circle of readers, than either Pope or Addison; and, in spite of considerable vulgarity and signal cumbrousness of diction, has drawn, even from the fastidious, a much deeper and more constant admiration.—JEFFREY, FRANCIS LORD, 1811, *Ford's Dramatic Works, Edinburgh Review, vol.* 18, *p.* 282.

. . . the strain my Thomson sung,
Delicious dreams inspiring by his note,
What time to Indolence his harp he strung;
. . . .

—SCOTT, SIR WALTER, 1816, *Harold the Dauntless, Introduction.*

He is frequently pedantic and ostentatious in his style, because he had no consciousness of these vices in himself. He mounts upon stilts, not out of vanity, but indolence. He seldom writes a good line but he makes up for it by a bad one. He takes advantage of all the most trite and mechanical common-places of imagery and diction as a kindly relief to his Muse, and as if he thought them quite as good, and likely to be quite as acceptable to the reader, as his own poetry. He did not think the difference worth putting himself to the trouble of accomplishing. He had too little art to conceal his art: or did not even seem to know that there was any occasion for it. His art is as naked and undisguised as his nature; the one is as pure and genuine as the other is gross, gaudy, and meretricious. . . . Thomson is the best of our descriptive poets; for he gives most of the poetry of natural description. Others have been quite equal to him, or have surpassed him, as Cowper for instance, in the picturesque part of his art, in marking the peculiar features and curious details of objects;—no one has yet come up to him in giving the sum total of their effects, their varying influences on the mind.—HAZLITT, WILLIAM, 1818, *Lectures on the English Poets, Lecture* V.

The sweet-souled Poet of the Seasons. . . . —WORDSWORTH, WILLIAM, 1820, *Sonnet, June.*

Thomson is the first of our Descriptive Poets; I had almost said, the first in the world. He is one of the best Poets, and the worst versifiers, that ever existed. To begin with the least pleasing part of our subject, his versification, it is artificial and elaborate; timid and pompous; deserting simplicity, without attaining dignity. It scorns the earth, without being able to soar into the air.—NEELE, HENRY, 1827–29, *Lectures on English Poetry, p.* 180.

Byron and Scott, brilliant as are the pictures which they exhibit, have too exclusively occupied public attention; and there *may* be an admixture of aristocratic fashion in this over ardent display of homage. Thomson, with loftier themes, is the poet of all times, and of every class of readers. I allude more especially to the "Seasons." His "Castle of Indolence," to be fairly appreciated, should be in the hands of those who are accustomed to the refinements of composition—by whom it will ever be esteemed as one of the most impressive and exquisite pieces within the circle of true poesy.—CORNEY, BOLTON, 1841, *Memorandum on the Text of "The Seasons," Gentleman's Magazine, vol.* 111, *p.* 145.

The entire prospect,—one of the finest in England, and eminently characteristic of what is best in English scenery,—enabled me to understand what I had used to deem a peculiarity,—in some measure a defect,—in the landscapes of the poet Thomson. It must have often struck the Scotch reader that in dealing with very extended prospects, he rather enumerates than describes. His pictures are often mere catalogues, in which single words stand for classes of objects, and in which the entire poetry seems to consist in an overmastering sense of vast extant, occupied by amazing multiplicity. . . . Now the prospect from the hill at Hagley furnished me with the true explanation of this enumerative style. Measured along the horizon, it must, on the lowest estimate, be at least fifty miles in longitudinal extent; measured laterally, from the spectator forwards, at least twenty. . . . The real area however must rather exceed than fall short of a thousand square miles: the fields into which it is laid out are small, scarcely averaging a square furlong in superficies. . . . With these there are commixed innumerable cottages, manor-houses, villages, towns. Here the surface is dimpled by unreckoned hollows; there fretted by uncounted mounds; all is amazing, overpowering multiplicity,—a multiplicity which neither the pen nor the pencil can adequately express; and so description, in even the hands of a master, sinks into mere enumeration. The picture becomes a catalogue.—MILLER, HUGH, 1847, *First Impressions of England and its People, pp.* 135, 136.

Thomson writes like a poet who made what he went to find.—HUNT, LEIGH, 1850, *Autobiography, vol.* II, *p.* 205.

A certain careless greatness is the principal element of his genius. He was, as Coleridge truly said, "rather a great than a good poet." Except in passages of the "Castle of Indolence," there is little finish or true polish about his poetry. He did, indeed, labour much at the file, but it was seldom under the presence of a high ideal of Art; and his alterations, like those of John Foster, were often anything but improvement. His great power lay in his deep, glowing, childlike enthusiasm for nature, and in the fulness with which he retained this on to mature manhood; so that, while in understanding he was thirty, in freshness of feeling he was only thirteen. He excelled more in the wide landscape view, than in the cabinet picture or the miniature. He was better at describing the Torrid Zone than a lady bathing—coping with the aggregate terrors of Winter than telling a tale of individual woe. He is more a sublime and sensuous, than he is a refined, spiritualized, or beautiful poet. He resembles rather Byron in all but his elasticity, and the fierce and savage nature that burned in him than such poets as Shelley, who seem half abstracted from earth, and to converse more with its hovering shadows than with its solid substance.—GILFILLAN, GEORGE, 1853, *ed. Thomson's Poetical Works, p.* 16.

Dismissing the ideal shepherds and shepherdesses who formerly trailed their silks, like the ladies in the portraits of the Restoration, over imaginary plains, and rejecting altogether the machinery of the heathen mythology, Thomson addressed himself directly to Nature, and transferred the landscape to his canvas with truthfulness and simplicity.—BELL, ROBERT, 1855, *ed., Poetical Works of James Thomson, vol.* I, *p.* 46.

No poet has ever been more inspired by the love of external nature, or felt with more keenness and delicacy those analogies between the mind and the things it looks upon, which are the fountains of poetic feeling. The faults of Thomson are triteness of thought when he becomes argumentative, and a prevalent pomposity and pedantry of diction; though his later work, "The Castle of Indolence," is surprisingly free from these blemishes.—BOTTA, ANNE C. LYNCH, 1860, *Hand-Book of Universal Literature, p.* 507.

If Young is all art and effort, Thomson is all negligence and nature; so negligent, indeed, that he pours forth his unpremeditated song apparently without the thought ever occurring to him that he could improve it by any study or elaboration, any more than if he were some winged warbler of the woodlands, seeking and caring for no other listener except the universal air which the strain made vocal. As he is the poet of nature, so his poetry has all the intermingled rudeness and luxuriance of its theme. There is no writer who has drunk in more of the inmost soul of his subject. If it be the object of descriptive poetry to present us with pictures and visions the effect of which shall vie with that of the originals from which they are drawn, then Thomson is the greatest of all descriptive poets; for there is no other who surrounds us with so much of the truth of Nature, or makes us feel so intimately the actual presence and companionship of all her hues and fragrances.—CRAIK, GEORGE L., 1861, *A Compendious History of English Literature and of the English Language, vol.* II, *p.* 286.

He is the leading priest in a solemn procession to find God—not in the laws by which he has ordered his creation, but in the beauty which is the outcome of those laws. I do not say there is much of the relation of man to nature in his writing; but thitherward it tends. He is true about the outsides of God; and in Thomson we begin to feel that the revelation of God as *meaning* and therefore *being* the loveliness of nature, is about to be recognized. I do not say—to change my simile—that he is the first visible root in our literature whence we can follow the outburst of the flowers and foliage of our delight in nature: I could show a hundred fibres leading from the depths of our old literature up to the great root. Nor is it surprising that, with his age about him, he too should be found tending to magnify, not God's Word, but his works, above all his name.—MACDONALD, GEORGE, 1868, *England's Antiphon, p.* 292.

Thomson's blank verse, however, is often swollen and bladdery to a painful degree. He seems to have imagined, like many other writers of his time, that blank verse could not support itself without the aid of a stilted phraseology, for that fine poem of his, in the Spenserian stanza, the "Castle of Indolence," shows that when he wrote in rhyme he did not think it necessary to depart from a natural style.—BRYANT, WILLIAM CULLEN, 1870, *A New Library of Poetry and Song, Introduction.*

He was turgid, no good metrist, and his English is like a translation from one of those poets who wrote in Latin after it was dead; but he was a man of sincere genius, and not only English, but European literature is largely in his debt. He was the inventor of cheap amusement for the million, to be had of All-outdoors for the asking. It was his impulse which unconsciously gave direction to Rousseau, and it is to the school of Jean Jacques that we owe St. Pierre, Cowper, Châteaubriand, Wordsworth, Byron, Lamartine, George Sand, Ruskin,—the great painters of ideal landscape.—LOWELL, JAMES RUSSELL, 1871, *A Good Word for Winter, My Study Windows, p.* 29.

He paints all the little things, without being ashamed, for they interest him; takes pleasure in "the smell of the dairy;" you hear him speak of the "insect armies," and "when the envenomed leaf begins to curl," and of the birds which, foreseeing the approaching rain, "streak their wings with oil, to throw the lucid moisture trickling off." He perceives objects so clearly that he makes them visible: we recognise the English landscape, green and moist, half drowned in floating vapours, blotted here and there by violet clouds, which burst in showers at the horizon, which they darken. . . . Thirty years before Rousseau, Thomson had expressed all Rousseau's sentiments, almost in the same style. . . . Like Rousseau, he praised gravity, patriotism, liberty, virtue; rose from the spectacle of nature to the contemplation of God, and showed to man glimpses of immortal life beyond the tomb. Like him, in fine, he marred the sincerity of his emotion and the truth of his poetry by sentimental vapidities, by pastoral billing and cooing, and by such an abundance of epithets, personified abstractions, pompous invocations and oratorical tirades, that we perceive in him beforehand the false and decorative style of Thomas, David, and the Revolution.—TAINE, H. A., 1871, *History of English Literature, tr. Van Laun, vol.* II, *bk.* iii, *ch.* vii, *pp.* 217, 219.

Thomson is one of those minor poets who are read by each successive generation with about equal favor. His fame is as high now as it was during his lifetime, perhaps higher. His descriptions of English scenery, because of their faithfulness to nature, are much read by foreigners, especially by Germans.—HART, JOHN S., 1872, *A Manual of English Literature, p.* 219.

For generations past, as the magic of Nature unrolls its annual recurrences and vicissitudes, some beauty or some majesty has here and there, by this person and by that, been more keenly perceived, more deeply loved, or acknowledged with a more fully realized sense of awe, because of something written by Thomson. He has been one of the concentrators and intensifiers—one of the fixing and fashioning spirits—of that characteristically modern passion, the love of scenery. . . . Our progenitors, to the fourth and fifth step of ascent from our own time, have delighted in Thomson; and, notwithstanding the shifting of literary models, and of the tenor of public taste, our successors, to as remote or a remoter term, may probably do the same.—ROSSETTI, WILLIAM MICHAEL, 1878, *Lives of Famous Poets, p.* 144.

Thomson dared to be true to the face of nature, and to make the delineation of it the all-sufficient object of poetry. And it enhances the merit of the poet that in this, a new form of poetic art, he was thoroughly successful, and influenced the eighteenth century literature of Britain, indeed all British literature since his time. —VEITCH, JOHN, 1878, *The History and Poetry of the Scottish Border, p.* 443.

No competent criticism of any school has ever denied Thomson's claim to a place, high if not of the highest, among poets of the second order. His immense and enduring popularity would settle the question, if it had ever been seriously debated. For the *orbis terrarum* may indeed judge without hesitation on such point, when its judgment is ratified beforehand by many generations. Popularity which outlasts changes of manners and fashions is a testimony to worth which cannot be left out of the account, and Thomson's popularity is eminently of this kind. Neither the somewhat indiscriminate admiration of the romantic style, of which Percy set the fashion, nor the naturalism of Cowper, nor the great revolution championed in various ways by Scott, by the Lakists, and by Byron, nor the still more complete revolution of Shelley and Keats, availed to shake the hold of "The Seasons" on the popular mind.—SAINTSBURY, GEORGE, 1880, *English Poets, ed. Ward, vol.* III, *p.* 168.

For the most part in Thomson, we have mere picturesqueness—a reproduction of Nature for the mere pleasure of reproducing her—a kind of stock-taking of her habitual effects.—MYERS, FREDERIC WILLIAM HENRY, 1880, *Wordsworth (English Men of Letters), p.* 85.

Just at present Thomson's reputation is a pious tradition rather than a visibly potential reality. It seems strange that this should be so, in an age which gives unmistakable and increasing welcome to the apostles of the new naturalism; for it is no exaggeration to say that the discoveries of Jefferies and of Burroughs were well known to Thomson, and that Thomson presented his transcripts of nature with perfect truth, freedom, and beauty, and sublimity of effect. One of the secrets of Thomson's power our new naturalists possess, namely, fulness of knowledge, acquired by careful sympathetic study; but for the felicity of his expression of the phenomena of nature he stands to this day unmatched. His pages are broadcast with these felicities of phrase. Such are his castled clouds, for ever flushing round a flushing sky; the sleepy horror of his waving pines; the still song of his harvests, breathed into the reaper's heart; his sturdy boy grasping the indignant ram by the twisted horns; his lively-shining leopard, the beauty of the waste; his ruddy maid, full as the summer rose blown by prevailing suns; the slender feet of his red-breast, attracted by the table crumbs; his light-footed dews; his isles amid the melancholy main. One does not need to pick and choose; they start from the opened leaves.—HALIBURTON, HUGH, 1893, *James Thomson, Good Words, vol.* 34, *p.* 467.

He was not an idealist; he sought simply to depict what he saw, and what apparently everyone might easily see. On the other hand, if Thomson was a realist, he was assuredly not one of the type to which the garbage of nature is as valuable and as well worthy of description as her noblest scenes. He discriminated. The most commonplace scene was good enough for his verse provided it was perfect of its kind; but decay and dissolution were, to him, matter for reference, not for elaborate portraiture.—WALKER, HUGH, 1893, *Three Centuries of Scottish Literature, vol.* II, *p.* 67.

Thomson must be acknowledged to be one of the greatest of our minor poets—*i. e.*, of those that are ranked next to the great names of Chaucer, Spenser, Shakespeare, Milton, Wordsworth, and Byron. He holds this place in virtue of his vigor of imagination, his broad manly sentiment, the individuality of his verse, and the distinction of his subject. These have given him a remarkable and enduring popularity.—MINTO, WILLIAM, 1894, *The Literature of the Georgian Era, ed. Knight, p.* 68.

It is true that in this work man as a social being still occupies too large a place. Thomson cannot describe winter without giving a sentimental picture of the horrors of cold, nor spring without introducing a hymn to Love. Too frequently also there are suggestions of the "Georgics," and apostrophes to those "who live in luxury and ease," or to "the generous Englishmen" who "venerate the plough." Nevertheless, Thomson has the painter's eye. His winter and his spring are no mere adaptions from Vergil. He has a true and deep understanding of the English landscape. With delicate subtlety he renders the impressions produced by spring or autumn, the charm of the indefinite periods when season gives way to season, the approach of rain, the forebodings of storm, the scudding of heavy clouds across skies grey and overcast. Even in the awkward French version something of the charm of these pictures lingers yet. . . . It is in these grey-toned pictures that Thomson excels. But in others he revels in precision of detail. . . . Occasionally, too, Thomson can command richness of colouring and splendour of imagery. . . . What French author wrote in this style, in 1730?—TEXTE, JOSEPH, 1895–99, *Jean-Jacques Rousseau and the Cosmopolitan Spirit in Literature, tr. Matthews, pp.* 294, 295.

It was Thomson who made the first resistance to the new classical formula, and it is, in fact, Thomson who is the real pioneer of the whole romantic movement, with its return to nature and simplicity. This gift would be more widely recognised than it is if it had not been for the poet's timidity, his easy-going indolence. . . . James Thomson is at the present hour but tamely admired. His extraordinary freshness, his new outlook into the whole world of imaginative life, deserves a very different recognition from what is commonly awarded to him. The "Hymn" which closes the "Seasons" was first published in 1730, when Pope was still rising towards the zenith of his fame. It recalled to English verse a melody, a rapture which had been entirely unknown since Milton's death, more than sixty years before.—GOSSE, EDMUND, 1897, *Short History of Modern English Literature, pp.* 233, 235.

"Jacob Thomson, ein vergessener Dichter des achtzehnten Jahrhunderts"—a forgotten poet of the eighteenth century—such is the title of a recent monograph on the author of "The Seasons" by Dr. G. Schmeding. . . . During the present century there have been no less than twenty editions of his poems, to say nothing of separate editions of "The Seasons;" while his works, or portion of them, have been translated into German, Italian, modern Greek and Russian. Only two years ago M. Léon Morel, in his "J. Thomson, sa vie et ses œuvres," published an elaborate and admirable monograph on this "forgotten poet." And now Mr. Tovey, . . . has given us a new biography of him and a new edition of his works, making, if I am not mistaken, the thirty-second memoir of him and the twenty-first edition of his works which have appeared since the beginning of the century: this is pretty well for a forgotten poet!—COLLINS, JOHN CHURTON, 1897, *A Literary Mare's-Nest, The Saturday Review, vol.* 84, *p.* 117.

As late as 1855 Robert Bell remarked that Thomson's popularity seemed ever on the increase. The date may be taken to mark the turning point in his fame, for since about 1850 he has been unmistakably eclipsed on his own ground, in the favour of the class to whom he was dear, by Tennyson, while in Scotland the commemorative rites which were zealously performed in his honour at Ednam and Edinburgh between 1790 and 1820 (when an obelisk, in the erection of which Scott took a leading part, was erected at the poet's native place) have been supplanted by the cult of Burns. . . . In the possession of the true poetic temperament, he has been surpassed not even by Tennyson.—SECCOMBE, THOMAS, 1898, *Dictionary of National Biography, vol.* LVI, *p.* 252.

When he came to England he found but little entertainment in the landscapes around London, and longed for "the living stream, the airy mountain, and the hanging rock." He portrays with evident delight the changeful aspect of his native watercourses in the various seasons of the year. He knew well the "deep morass" and "shaking wilderness," where many of them "rise high among the hills," and whence they assume their "mossy-tinctured" hue. He traces them as they "roll o'er their rocky channel" until they at last lose themselves in "the ample river" Tweed. He describes them as they appear at sheep-washing time, and dwells on their delights for boys as bathing-places. But it is their wilder moods that dwell most vividly in his memory, when

From the hills
O'er rocks and woods, in broad brown cataracts,
A thousand snow-fed torrents shoot at once.

It is worthy of remark, however, that even though nature is his theme, the poet writes rather as an interested spectator than as an earnest votary. He reveals no passion for the landscapes he depicts. He never appears as if himself a portion of the scene, alive with sympathy in all the varying moods of nature. His verse has no flashes of inspiration, such as contact with storm and spate drew from Burns. It was already however, a great achievement that Thomson broke through the conventionalities of the time, and led his countrymen once more to the green fields, the moors, and the woodlands.—GEIKIE, SIR ARCHIBALD, 1898, *Types of Scenery and their Influence on Literature, p.* 21.

Ambrose Philips

1675?-1749.

Born, in Shropshire [?], 1675 [?]. Early education at Shrewsbury School. To St. John's College, Cambridge, as Sizar, 15 June 1693; B. A., 1696; Fellow of St. John's College, 28 March, 1699 to 24 March 1708; M. A., 1700. Visits to Continent, 1703 and 1710. J. P. for Westminster, 1714. Commissioner for Lottery, 1717. Founded and edited "The Freethinker," 1718-19. To Ireland, as Sec. to Bishop of Armagh, 1724. M. P. for Co. Armagh in Irish Parliament, 1725. Sec. to Lord Chancellor, Dec. 1726. Judge of Prerogative Court, Aug. 1733. Returned to London, 1748. Died there, 18 June 1749. *Works:* "The Life of John Williams," 1700; "Pastorals" (from Tonson's "Miscellany"), 1710; "The Distrest Mother," 1712; "An Epistle to Charles, Lord Halifax," 1714; "Epistle to the Hon. James Craggs," 1717; "Papers from 'The Freethinker'" (3 vols.), 1718-19; "The Briton," 1722; "Humphrey, Duke of Gloucester," 1723; "A Collection of Old Ballads," 1723; "An Ode on the Death of William, Earl Cowper," 1728; "The Tea-Pot" [1725?]; "To the Hon. Miss Carteret," 1725; "To . . . Lord Carteret," 1726; "Codrus," 1728; "Pastorals, Epistles, Odes, etc.," 1748. He *translated:* "The Odes of Sappho," 1713; P. de La Croix's "Persian Tales," 1709.—SHARP, R. FARQUHARSON, 1897, *A Dictionary of English Authors, p.* 226.

PERSONAL

I have had a letter from Mr. Philips, the pastoral poet, to get him a certain employment from lord-treasurer. I have now had almost all the whig-poets my solicitors; and I have been useful to Congreve, Steele, and Harrison; but I will do nothing for Philips; I find he is more a puppy than ever; so don't solicit for him.—SWIFT, JONATHAN, 1711, *Journal to Stella, June* 30.

When simple Macer, now of high renown,
First fought a poet's fortune in the town:
'Twas all th' ambition his high soul could feel,
To wear red stockings, and to dine with Steele.
Some ends of verse his betters might afford,
And give the harmless fellow a good word.
—POPE, ALEXANDER, 1727, *Macer: A Character.*

Ambrose Philips was a neat dresser, and very vain.—In a conversation between him, Congreve, Swift, and others, the discourse ran a good while on Julius Cæsar. After many things had been said to the purpose, Ambrose asked what sort of a person they supposed Julius Cæsar was? He was answered, that from medals, &c., it appeared that he was a small man, and thin-faced.—"Now, for my part," said Ambrose, "I should take him to have been of a lean make, pale complexion, extremely neat in his dress; and five feet seven inches high:" an exact description of Philips himself. Swift, who understood good breeding perfectly well, and would not interrupt anybody while speaking, let him go on, and when he had quite done, said; "And I, Mr. Philips, should take him to have been a plump man, just five feet five inches high; not very neatly dressed, in a black gown with pudding-sleeves."—YOUNG, EDWARD, 1757, *Spence's Anecdotes, ed. Singer, p.* 286.

In 1729 he published by subscription, his poems much enlarged, with the addition of one entitled "Namby Pamby;" the occasion of it was as follows: Ambrose Phillips being in Ireland at the time when lord Carteret was lord lieutenant of Ireland, wrote a poem on his daughter, lady Georgina, now the dowager lady Cowper, then in the cradle; in such a kind of measure, and with such infantine sentiments, as were a fair subject for ridicule: Carey laid hold of this, and wrote a poem, in which all the songs of children at play are wittily introduced, and called it by a name by which children might be supposed to call the author, whose name was Ambrose, Namby Pamby.—HAWKINS, SIR JOHN 1776, *A General History of the Science and Practice of Music, vol.* II, *p.* 828.

Of his personal character all that I have heard is, that he was eminent for bravery and skill in the sword, and that in conversation he was solemn and pompous.—JOHNSON, SAMUEL, 1779–81, *A. Philips, Lives of the English Poets.*

Ambrose Phillips was a stately gentleman who had passed the best portion of his life in lisping dull songs about Chloris and Damon, Strephon and Delia, weak-minded shepherds and bread-and-butter shepherdesses, who made it their silly business to play dismal tunes on oaten reeds to listening flocks of sheep which they called their "fleecy care." To see such a man made a fool of must delight every one. Pope made a fool of him by sending a paper to the "Guardian" brim-ful of good irony, in which while he appeared to praise Phillips as a superior poet to Pope, he left Pope so much the first that Phillips was literally nowhere. The artless and literally Irishman, Steele, was duped by the excellent irony; the astute Addison saw the joke. Phillips was Addison's friend; Addison indeed professed quite an affection for Phillips. He had praised his Pastorals; he had praised his Tragedies. With great demureness, pretending not to see Pope's irony, he had it printed. The ridicule of his friends greatly exasperated Phillips, who hung up a rod at Button's, with which he threatened to beat Pope when he should come to the coffee-house. Pope, who was no coward, laughed contemptuously at Phillips' menaces, called him a rascal, and charged him with robbing the Hanover Club. This double consequence—the discomfiture of Phillips and the quarrel of Pope—was much enjoyed by the virtuous Mr. Addison.—RUSSELL, WILLIAM CLARK, 1871, *ed. The Book of Authors, p.* 155, *note.*

PASTORALS

1710

As to Mr. Phillips's Pastorals, I take the first to be infinitely the best, and the second the worst; and the third is for the greatest part a translation from Virgil's

Daphnis, and I think a good one. . . . In the whole I agree with the "Tatler," that we have no better eclogues in our language. This gentleman, if I am not much mistaken in his talent, is capable of writing very nobly, as I guess by a small copy of his, published in the "Tatler," on the Danish Winter. It is a very lively piece of poetical painting, and I recommend it particularly to your perusal.—POPE, ALEXANDER, 1710, *Letter to Cromwell, Oct.* 28, *Pope's Works, ed. Elwin, vol.* VI, *p.* 106.

In mock heroic poems the use of the heathen mythology is not only excusable, but graceful, because it is the design of such compositions to divert, by adapting the fabulous machines of the ancients to low subjects, and at the same time by ridiculing such kinds of machinery in modern writers. If any are of opinion that there is a necessity of admitting these classical legends into our serious compositions, in order to give them a more poetical turn, I would recommend to their consideration the pastorals of Mr. Philips. One would have thought it impossible for this kind of poetry to have subsisted without fawns and satyrs, wood-nymphs, and water-nymphs, with all the tribe of rural deities. But we see he has given a new life and a more natural beauty to this way of writing, by substituting in the place of these antiquated fables the superstitious mythology which prevails among the shepherds of our own country.—ADDISON, JOSEPH, 1712, *The Spectator, Oct*, 30, *No.* 523.

Theocritus, who left his dominions to Virgil; Virgil, left his to his son Spenser; and Spenser, was succeeded by his eldest-born Philips.—TICKELL, THOMAS, ? 1713, *Guardian No.* 32.

When I remarked it as a principal fault, to introduce fruits and flowers of a foreign growth, the descriptions with the scene lies in our country, I did not design that observation should extend also to animals, or the sensitive life; for Mr. Philips hath with great judgment described wolves in England, in his first Pastoral. Nor would I have a poet slavishly confine himself (as Mr. Pope hath done), to one particular season of the year, one certain time of the day, and one unbroken scene in each eclogue. 'Tis plain, Spenser neglected this pedantry, who, in his pastoral of November, mentions the mournful song of the nightingale.

Sad Philemel her song in tears doth steep.

And Mr. Philips, by a poetical creation, hath raised up finer beds of flowers than the most industrious gardener; his roses, endives, lilies, kingcups, and daffodils, blow all in the same season.—POPE, ALEXANDER, 1713, *The Guardian, No.* 40, *p.* 264.

Notwithstanding the ridicule which Mr. Philips has drawn upon himself, by his opposition to Pope, and the disadvantageous light his Pastorals appear in, when compared with his; yet, there is good reason to believe, that Mr. Philips was no mean Arcadian: By endeavouring to imitate too servilely the manners and sentiments of vulgar rustics, he has sometimes raised a laugh against him; yet there are in some of his Pastorals a natural simplicity, a true Doric dialect, and very graphical descriptions.—CIBBER, THEOPHILUS, 1753, *Lives of the Poets, vol.* V, *p.* 133.

Philips attempted to be more simple and natural than Pope; but he wanted genius to support his attempt, or to write agreeably. He, too, runs on the common and beaten topics; and endeavouring to be simple, he becomes flat and insipid.—BLAIR, HUGH, 1783, *Lectures on Rhetoric and Belles-Letters, ed. Mills, Lecture* XXXIX.

It is not uninstructive to see how tolerable Ambrose is, so long as he sticks manfully to what he really saw. The moment he undertakes to improve on Nature he sinks into the mere court poet, and we surrender him to the jealousy of Pope without a sigh.—LOWELL, JAMES RUSSELL, 1871, *A Good Word for Winter, My Study Windows, p.* 45.

GENERAL

With Philips shall the peaceful valleys ring,
And Britain hear a second Spenser sing.

—TICKELL, THOMAS, 1713, *On the Prospect of Peace.*

All ye poets of the age!
All ye witlings of the stage,
Learn your jingles to reform,
Crop your numbers and conform:
Let your little verses flow
Gently, sweetly, row by row.
Let the verse the subject fit,
Little subject, little wit,
Namby-Pamby is your guide
Albion's joy, Hibernia's pride.

—CAREY, HENRY, 1729, *Namby-Pamby.*

The bard who pilfer'd Pastorals renown,
Who turns a Persian tale for half a Crown,
Just writes to make his barrenness appear,
And strains, from hard-bound brains, eight lines a year.
—POPE, ALEXANDER, 1735, *Epistle to Dr. Arbuthnot, v.* 179–182.

The opening of this poem ["An Epistle to the Earl of Dorset"], is incomparably fine. The latter part is tedious and trifling. —GOLDSMITH, OLIVER, 1767, *The Beauties of English Poetry.*

Of his literary merit nothing great can be said. As a poet he seldom deviates from the path of mediocrity; and, unfortunately for his poetical fame, his quarrel with Pope exposed him to a depreciation in that department beyond what justice would require.—DRAKE, NATHAN, 1804, *Essays Illustrative of the Tatler, Spectator and Guardian, vol.* III, *p.* 269.

A serious and dreary idyllic cockney.—THACKERAY, WILLIAM MAKEPEACE, 1853, *The English Humourists of the Eighteenth Century.*

Although he published three tragedies, is as a dramatist remembered by one of these only, or rather perhaps on account of the celebrity acquired by the "Epilogue" bestowed upon it by the master-spirit of the little literary senate in which Philips had enrolled himself. The characteristically sentimental title of "The Distrest Mother" (acted in 1711) was not intended to conceal the fact that this tragedy was a version of the "Andromaque" of Racine; but the efforts of Steele and Addison to buoy up its theatrical success have succeeded in securing to it a place among the remembered productions of our dramatic literature.—WARD, ADOLPHUS WILLIAM, 1875–99, *A History of English Dramatic Literature, vol.* III, *p.*425.

The "Pastorals" of Philips are certainly poor productions; but he was an elegant versifier, and Goldsmith has eulogised the opening of his "Epistle to the Earl of Dorset" as "incomparably fine." A fragment of Sappho, translated by Philips, is a poetical gem so brilliant, that it is thought Addison must have assisted in its composition.—CHAMBERS, ROBERT, 1876, *Cyclopædia of English Literature, ed. Carruthers.*

Catherine Cockburn

1679-1749.

Mrs. Catherine Cockburn, 1679-1749, was a native of London, a daughter of Captain David Trotter, R. N. In her 17th year her tragedy of "Agnes de Castro" was produced with great success at the Theatre Royal. In 1698 she gave to the world the "Tragedy of Fatal Friendship," and in 1701, "The Unhappy Penitent." In the same year she contributed, with several other ladies, to the Nine Muses; a tribute to the memory of John Dryden. In 1706 her tragedy entitled "The Revolution of Sweden" was acted at the Queen's Theatre. In 1708 she was married to the Rev. Mr. Cockburn, who was subsequently presented to the living of Long-Horsley, Northumberland. In the previous year she returned to the communion of the Church of England, which she had when quite young forsaken for the Church of Rome. In 1726 she pub. a letter to Dr. Holdsworth in vindication of Mr. Locke's Essay respecting the resurrection of the body. In 1747 appeared her "Remarks upon the Principles and Reasonings of Dr. Rutherforth's Essay on the Nature and Obligations of Virtue." In 1751 Dr. Birch pub. an edition of Mrs. Cockburn's Works in 2 vols. 8vo. This collection, however, contains none of her dramatic pieces excepting "The Fatal Friendship."—ALLIBONE, S. AUSTIN, 1854–58, *A Critical Dictionary of English Literature, vol.* I, *p.* 400.

PERSONAL

Mrs. Cockburn was no less celebrated for her beauty, in her younger days, than for her genius and accomplishments. She was indeed small of stature, but had a remarkable liveliness in her eye, and delicacy of complexion, which continued to her death. Her private character rendered her extremely amiable to those who intimately knew her. Her conversation was always innocent, useful and agreeable, without the least affectation of being thought a wit, and attended with a remarkable modesty and diffidence of herself, and a constant endeavour to adapt her discourse to her company. She was happy in an uncommon evenness and cheerfulness of temper. Her disposition was generous and benevolent; and ready upon all occasions to forgive injuries, and bear them, as well as misfortunes, without interrupting her own ease, or that of others, with complaints or reproaches. The pressures of a very contracted fortune were supported by her with calmness and in silence, nor did she ever attempt to improve it among those great personages to whom she was known, by importunities; to which the best minds are most averse, and which her approved merit and established reputation should have rendered unnecessary.—CIBBER, THEOPHILUS, 1753, *Lives of the Poets, vol.* V, *p.* 118.

GENERAL

Posterity, at least, will be so solicitous to know, to whom they will owe the most demonstrative and perspicuous reasonings, upon subjects of eternal importance; and her own sex is entitled to the fullest information about one, who has done such honour to them, and raised our ideas of their intellectual powers, by an example of the greatest extent of understanding and correctness of judgment, united to all the vivacity of imagination. Antiquity, indeed, boasted of its Female Philosophers, whose merits have been drawn forth in an elaborate treatise of Menage.—BIRCH, THOMAS, 1751, *ed. Mrs. Catherine Cockburn's Collected Works.*

But say what matron now walks musing forth
From the bleak mountains of her native north?
While round her brows two sisters of the Nine
Poetic wreaths with philosophic twine!
Hail, Cockburn, hail! even now from reason's bowers
Thy Locke delighted culls the choicest flowers
To deck his great, successful champion's head,
And Clarke expects thee in the laurel shade.
Though long to dark oblivious wants a prey,
Thy aged worth passed unperceived away,
Yet Scotland now shall ever boast thy fame,
While England mourns thy undistinguished name,
And views with wonder, in a female mind,
Philosopher, divine, and poet joined.
—DUNCOMBE, JOHN, 1754, *The Feminead.*

Her poetry has a compression of thought and an ease of style which greatly distinguished it from the verse of most female writers in her time.—ROWTON, FREDERIC, 1848, *The Female Poets of Great Britain, p.* 113.

Although much has been said and written about Locke by the ablest metaphysicians of his age, and of each succeeding generation, it may be questioned whether his own words has ever been more truly construed than by Mrs. Cockburn. What she wrote concerning his opinions during his life was approved by Locke himself; what she wrote of them after his decease was acknowledged to be correct by his most intimate associates, to whom he had frequently and familiarly expounded them.—WILLIAMS, JANE, 1861, *The Literary Women of England, p.* 184.

Mrs. Cockburn was a clever woman, and kept no dull household, though she there wrote a defence of Locke, while her reverend husband was perusing an account of the Mosaic deluge. As a metaphysical and controversial writer, she gathered laurels and abuse in her day, for the latter of which she found compensation in the friendship and admiration of Warburton. She was a valiant woman, too; one, whom asthma and the ills of life could not deter from labor. But death relieved her from all these, in 1749; and she is remembered in the history of literature as a good and well-accomplished woman; the very opposite of Mrs. Behn and all her heroines.—DORAN, JOHN, 1863, *Annals of the English Stage, vol.* I, *p.* 166.

Aaron Hill

1685-1750.

Aaron Hill, 1685-1750, an English poet, dramatist, and miscellaneous writer, a native of London, is better known to the present age from his quarrels with Pope than by his literary compositions. Among other works, he pub.—1. "A History of the Ottoman Empire," 1709. 2. "Elfrid;" a Tragedy, 1709. 3. "Camillus;" a Poem, 1709. 4, 5. "Essays on Beech Oil," 1714-15. 6. "Essays on Coals and Grape-Wines," 1718. 7. "King Henry the Fifth;" a Tragedy, 1723. 8. "The Northern Star;" a Poem, 1725. 9. "Advice to the Poets," 1731. 10. "The Impartial;" a poem. 11. "The Progress of Wit; a Caveat for the use of an Eminent Writer," (a satire upon Pope, who had introduced Hill, rather in a complimentary manner, in the "Dunciad.") 12. "Merope;" a Tragedy, from Voltaire, with alterations, 1749. His Miscellaneous Works—a collection of his best pieces—were published in 1753, 4 vols.; and his Dramatic Works (seventeen in all), with his Life, appeared in 1759, 2 vols.—ALLIBONE, S. AUSTIN, 1854–58, *A Critical Dictionary of English Literature, vol.* I, *p.* 845.

PERSONAL

Merope will be acted on the 9th for the author's bt.—We believe it will be sufficient to draw together a very numerous audience on this occasion to inform our readers that the Gentleman who wrote this Tragedy has been confined to his bed these 8 months past by a lingering and consuming illness; and this only favour which he is to receive from the public, will in all probability be the last.—GENERAL ADVERTISER, 1750, *Feb.* 3.

His person was (in youth) extremely fair, and handsome; his eyes were a dark blue, both bright and penetrating; brown hair and visage oval; which was enlivened with a smile, the most agreeable in conversation; where his address was affably engaging; to which was joined a dignity which rendered him at once respected and admired, by those (of either sex) who were acquainted with him—He was tall, genteelly made, and not thin.—His voice was sweet, his conversation elegant; and capable of entertaining upon various subjects.—His disposition was benevolent, beyond the power of the fortune he was blessed with; the calamities of those he knew (and valued as deserving) affected him more than his own: He had fortitude of mind sufficient to support with calmness great misfortune; and from his birth it may be truly said he was obliged to meet it. . . . His temper, though by nature warm (when injuries were done him) was as nobly forgiving; mindful of that great lesson in religion, of returning good for evil; and he fulfilled it often to the prejudice of his own circumstances. He was a tender husband, friend, and father; one of the best masters to his servants, detesting the too common inhumanity, that treats them almost as if they were not fellow-creatures. His manner of life was temperate in all respects (which might have promis'd greater length of years) late hours excepted; which his indefatigable love of study drew him into; night being not liable to interruptions like the day.—CIBBER, THEOPHILUS, 1753, *Lives of the Poets, vol.* V, *p.* 262.

Mr. Hill in person was tall and genteel; in advanced life, his figure, air, and manner, were gracefully venerable; with a warm and benevolent mind, he had the delicate address and polite manners of the complete gentleman.—DAVIES, THOMAS, 1780, *Memoirs of the Life of David Garrick, vol.* I, *p.* 131.

Few men have so completely mistaken their own abilities as Mr. Hill, who did every thing he ought not to have done: in his youth an historian; in manhood he gave up the superintendence of the public amusements, an office in which he excelled, to be, in a more advanced age, a visionary and unsuccessful projector.—NOBLE, MARK, 1806, *A Biographical History of England, vol.* III, *p.* 300.

One of Pope's Literary Quarrels must be distinguished for its romantic cast. . . . Where, in literary history, can be found the parallel of such an offer of self-immolation? This was a literary quarrel like that of lovers, where to hurt each other would have given pain to both parties. Such skill and desire to strike, with so much tenderness in inflicting a wound; so much compliment, with so much complaint; have perhaps never met together, as in the romantic hostility of this literary chivalry.—DISRAELI, ISAAC, 1814, *Pope, Quarrels of Authors.*

He was reconciled to Pope, and taught the poor poet by experience that his friendship was worse than his enmity. He wrote his letters of criticism; he forced poor Pope to negotiate for him with managers and to bring distinguished friends to the performances of his dreary plays; nay, to read through, or to say that he had read through, one of them in manuscript four times, and made corrections mixed with elaborate eulogy. No doubt Pope came to regard a letter from Hill with terror, though Hill compared him to Horace and Juvenal, and hoped that he would live till the virtues which his spirit would propagate became as general as the esteem of his genius. In short, Hill, who was a florid flatterer, is so complimentary that we are not surprised to find him telling Richardson, after Pope's death, that the poet's popularity was due to a certain "bladdery swell of management." "But," he concludes, "rest his memory in peace! It will very rarely be disturbed by that time he himself is ashes."—STEPHEN, LESLIE, 1880, *Alexander Pope (English Men of Letters)*, *p.* 128.

Hill, though he must be ranked among the literary failures of his age, was a man of some ability and vast energy, who divided his time between theatrical management, dramatic authorship, and commercial and agricultural experiments, which nearly always ended in disaster. Totally destitute of any capacity for self-criticism, he had a thorough confidence in his own powers, and firmly believed that his name would be still remembered when posterity had the sense to realise the utter worthlessness of the works of Mr. Pope.—THOMSON, CLARA LINKLATER, 1900, *Samuel Richardson, A Biographical and Critical Study*, *p.* 77.

GENERAL

In Hill is all that gen'rous souls revere,
To Virtue and the Muse for ever dear.
—SAVAGE, RICHARD, 1729, *The Wanderer, Canto I.*

I need not assure you in many words, that I join my suffrage entirely with Lord B's in general, after a fourth reading of your tragedy of "Cæsar." I think no characters were ever more nobly sustained than those of Cæsar and Brutus in particular. You excel throughout in the greatness of sentiment; and I add, that I never met with more striking sentences, or lively short reprizes. There is almost everywhere such a dignity in the scenes, that instead of pointing out any one scene, I can scarce point out any that wants it, in any degree, except you would a little raise that of the *plebeians* in the last act. That dignity is admirably reconciled with softness, in the scenes between Cæsar and Calputnia: and all those between Cæsar and Brutus are a noble strife between greatness and humanity.—POPE, ALEXANDER, 1738, *Letter to Hill, July* 21; *Pope's Works, ed. Elwin and Courthope, vol.* X, *p.* 61.

When noble thoughts with language pure unite,
To give to kindred excellence its right,
Though unencumber'd with the clogs of rhyme,
Where tinkling sounds for want of meaning chime,
Which, like the rocks in Shannon's midway course,
Divide the sense, and interrupt its force;
Well may we judge so strong and clear a rill
Flows higher from the Muses' sacred *Hill.*
—RICHARDSON, SAMUEL, c1750, *Epigram.*

The play ["Merope"] is certainly the master-piece of Hill, though in many places he retains a swell expression, and an affectation of strength, which destroy all ease and grace; yet he is more natural and simple in his language, upon the whole, in this play, than in any of his dramatic compositions. The second act is finely written. The scenes between Merope and Eumenes is a beautiful exertion of genius, in describing the workings of natural affection in a son and mother unknown to each other.—DAVIES, THOMAS, 1780, *Memoirs of the Life of David Garrick, vol.* I, *p.* 147.

His poetry is in general both pompous and empty enough; and of all he has written, almost the only passage that is now much remembered is a satiric sketch of Pope, in a few lines which have some imitative smartness, but scarcely any higher merit.—CRAIK, GEORGE L., 1861, *A Compendious History of English Literature and of the English Language, vol.* II, *p.* 283.

Although an author of very eccentric genius, whose pen was said to have treated every subject from the Creation to the Day of Judgment (both inclusive), had in him a nobility of soul which shut out anything impure or mean from his literary efforts.—WARD, ADOLPHUS WILLIAM, 1875–99, *A History of English Dramatic Literature, vol.* III, *p.* 430.

Wrote some original dramas, which entitled him, no less than his poems, to the niche he has obtained in the "Dunciad."—CHAMBERS, ROBERT, 1876, *Cyclopædia of English Literature, ed. Carruthers.*

Few men indeed so well known in his own day have sunk into such insignificance in ours. . . . As a poet Hill has the facility in composition exhibited by so many of his contemporaries, and he has occasionally a pretty turn of fancy.—DENNIS, JOHN, 1894, *The Age of Pope, pp.* 104, 106.

A considerable literary dictator in his day, the name of Aaron Hill is now one of the obscurest in the annals of eighteenth century authorship.—BAYNE, WILLIAM, 1898, *James Thomson (Famous Scots Series)*, *p.* 53.

Conyers Middleton

1683-1750

Theologian and classical scholar; born at Richmond, Yorkshire, England, Dec. 27, 1683; graduated at Cambridge 1702, and became a fellow of Trinity College 1706. He was for years engaged in an acrimonious quarrel with Richard Bentley; wrote "A Letter from Rome showing an Exact Conformity between Popery and Paganism" (1729); became principal librarian of Cambridge (1722); was Woodwardian Professor of Mineralogy 1731-34. His best known works are an uncritical and highly eulogistic "Life of Cicero" (1741); "Introductory Discourse" (1747); and the "Free Inquiry" (1748), violent attacks on ecclesiastical miracles. Died at Hildersham, July 28, 1750. —GUDEMAN, ALFRED, 1897, *rev. Johnson's Universal Cyclopædia, vol.* V, *p.* 749.

PERSONAL

You have doubtless heard of the loss I have had in Dr. Middleton, whose house was the only easy place one could find to converse in at Cambridge. For my part I find a friend so uncommon a thing, that I cannot help regretting even an old acquaintance, which is an indifferent likeness of it, and though I don't approve the spirit of his books, methinks 'tis pity the world should lose so rare a thing as a good writer.—GRAY, THOMAS, 1750, *Letter to Thomas Wharton, Aug.* 19, *Works, vol.* II, *p.* 198.

LIFE OF CICERO

1741

The style of Middleton, which is commonly esteemed very pure, is blemished with many vulgar and cant terms; such as, "Pompey had a *month's mind,*" *&c.* He had not been successful in the translations of those many epistles of Tully which he has inserted, which, however curious, yet break the thread of the narration. Mongault and Melmoth have far exceeded him in their excellent translations of these pieces; which are, after all, some of the most precious remains of antiquity. . . . It is a pleasing and useful work, especially to younger readers, as it gives a comprehensive view of a most interesting period in the Roman history, and of the characters principally concerned in those important events.— WARTON, JOSEPH, 1756, *Essay on the Genius and Writings of Pope.*

A man of real taste and politeness. His "Life of Cicero" will live to do him honour when his other works are forgotten.—HURD, RICHARD, 1808? *Commonplace Book, ed. Kilvert, p.* 246.

The style of Middleton is considered to be as pure English as can be read; and whether Hume did, or did not, form his own style upon that of this author, it is certain that the late Mr. Fox (no mean arbiter in literary taste) always spoke warmly of the biography of Cicero, by Middleton; for its style as well as its matter. . . . There was scarcely a family of distinction at the time [of its publication] but what possessed a copy of Middleton's "Cicero."—DIBDIN, THOMAS FROGNALL, 1824, *Library Companion, p.* 520.

Never was there a mind keener or more critical than that of Middleton. Had the doctor brought to the examination of his favourite statesman's conduct but a very small part of the acuteness and severity which he displayed when he was engaged in investigating the high pretensions of Epiphanius and Justin Martyr, he could not have failed to produce a most valuable history of a most interesting portion of time. But this most ingenious and learned man, though

"So wary held and wise
That, as 'twas said, he scarce received
For gospel what the church believed,"

had a superstition of his own. The great Iconoclast was himself an idolater. The great *Avvocata del Diavolo,* while he disputed, with no small ability, the claims of Cyprian and Athanasius to a place in the Calendar, was himself composing a lying legend in honour of St. Tully! He was holding up as a model of every virtue a man whose talents and acquirements, indeed, can never be too highly extolled, and who was by no means destitute of amiable qualities, but whose whole soul was under the dominion of a girlish vanity and a craven fear. Actions for which Cicero himself, the most eloquent and skillful of advocates, could contrive no excuse, actions which in his confidential correspondence he mentioned with remorse and shame, are represented by his biographer as wise, virtuous, heroic.—MACAULAY,

THOMAS BABINGTON, 1834, *Lord Bacon Edinburgh Review; Critical and Miscellaneous Esssays.*

Middleton's "Life of Cicero" may be considered as a most important branch of Roman history. It is an admirable work. The life of that great man spreads over the whole interesting period of the dying convulsions of the Republic. . . . The eventful life of Cicero; his splendid public services; his exalted patriotism; his surprising industry; his immense erudition; his profound sagacity; his incorruptible integrity; his almost Christian philosophy, are thoroughly apparent in his works, and elegantly delineated in Middleton's life of him.—KENT, JAMES, 1853, *Outline of a Course of English Reading.*

Reviewing the whole of the celebrated orator's public career, and the principal transactions of his times—mixing up questions of philosophy, government, and politics with the details of biography, Middleton compiled a highly interesting work, full of varied and important information, and written with great care and taste. An admiration of the rounded style and flowing periods of Cicero seems to have produced in his biographer a desire to attain to similar excellence; and perhaps no author, prior to Johnson's great works, wrote English with the same careful finish and sustained dignity. The graces of Addison were wanting, but certainly no historical writings of the day were at all comparable to Middleton's memoir. — CHAMBERS, ROBERT, 1876, *Cyclopædia of English Literature, ed. Carruthers.*

GENERAL

Dr. Conyers Middleton, of Cambridge, hath just written and put out a twelve penny pamphlett in English, to prove Caxton the first printer in England; and makes the "Ruffinus" or "Hieronymus de Fide," printed in Oxford anno 1468, to be a cheat, as if there were no such book then printed there, or at least if there were such a book printed there, he says, the date should be 1478. He runs down Atkins' book about printing, as he does also the register at Canterbury, making the record to be a forgery, because the register is now wanting. But his whole performance is poor and mean, and tho' he endeavours to rob Oxford of an honour that no one pretended to take from her, yet Middleton *detrahere ausus hærentem capiti, multa cum laude, coronam,* hath plainly shew'd, that he envys us this glory, which no one need wonder at, that considers a much bolder stroke of his lately, which made a great noise, and very deservedly blasted his reputation, which was his book (for he is known to be the author, tho' his name be not to it) to prove that Moses was not an inspired writer. 'Tis certain, that Middleton is an ingenious man, but if he soars at all, and considerable, very uncommon, must be that genius that succeeds.—HEARNE, THOMAS, 1734–5, *Reliquiæ Hearnianæ, ed. Bliss, March* 3, *vol.* III, *p.* 171.

This man was endowed with penetration and accuracy. He saw where his principles led ["Free Inquiry into the Miracles"]; but he did not think proper to draw the consequences.—GIBBON, EDWARD, 1764, *Journal, Feb.* 25.

Dr. Middleton was a man of no common attainments: his learning was elegant and profound, his judgment was acute and polished, his taste was fine and correct: his style was so pure and harmonious, so vigorously flowing without being inflated, that, Addison alone excepted, he seems to me without a rival.—PARR, SAMUEL, 1787, *Bellendus de Statu.*

Conyers Middleton being the original author of the feud which so greatly agitated the University and interested the public, felt himself called upon to vindicate the conduct of the majority, who had so readily embraced his cause. This distinguished writer was not one of those who are early familiar with the press; his present pamphlet happens to be the first published specimen of a style, which for elegance, purity, and ease, yields to none in the whole compass of English literature. In this first essay he showed himself to possess all the talents, and to understand the use of all the weapons of a controversialist. The acrimonious and resentful feeling which prompted every line is in some measure disguised by the pleasing language, the harmony of the periods, and the vein of scholarship which enlivens the whole tract.—MONK, JAMES HENRY, 1830–33, *Life of Richard Bentley, vol.* II, *p.* 67.

This celebrated man was the most malignant of a malignant crew. In his Review of Bentley's Proposals for Editing the

Greek Text of the Greek Testament, he stings like a serpent,—more rancorous party pamphlets never were written. He hated Waterland with the same perfect malignity; and his letters to Warburton, published in a quatro collection of his Miscellaneous Tracts, show that he could combine the part of sycophant, upon occasion, with that of assassin-like lampooner. It is, therefore, no unacceptable retribution in the eyes of those who honour the memory of Dan. Waterland and Bentley, men worth a hecatcomb of Middletons, that the reputation of this venomous writer is now decaying,—upon a belief *at last* thoroughly established that in two at least, and those two the most learned, of his works, he was an extensive plagiarist. —DE QUINCEY, THOMAS, 1857, *Richard Bentley, Collected Writings, ed. Masson, vol.* IV, *p.* 124, *note.*

He was "a man of war from his youth;" and, had his judgment been equal to his learning, he might have obtained a place in the first rank of English letters. . . . If we were disposed to allow his rigid orthodoxy,—and this would be a large demand upon the charity of a theological critic,—it is impossible to deny his passion for controversy. He seems never to have been so much pleased as when, by broaching some startling point of disputation, he succeeds in horrifying the mind of his more orthodox brethren.—ALLIBONE, S. AUSTIN, 1870, *Critical Dictionary of English Literature, vol.* II.

Whatever may be the cause, there is a vein of bitterness in his later controversial writings. Middleton has the tone of a disappointed man. Probably he felt himself to be in a false position. He is more open to the charge of insidious hostility to Christianity than such writers as Tindal and Collins; for, whilst expressing sentiments almost identical with those of the deists, he retained ecclesiastical preferment to the end of his life. Disappointment at the discovery that he had forfeited his chances of higher preferment by overstepping the conventional limits of orthodoxy, and possibly some of the discontent often felt by men doomed to academical retirement whilst ambitious to be regarded as men of the world, may have contributed to sour him. At any rate, we feel a certain suspicion of his loudly expressed claims to disinterested love of truth, and contempt for the trammels of worldly ambition. His best-known book, "The Life of Cicero," is the chief foundation of his claims to a peculiar excellence of style; but his other writings, in spite of the blemishes of sentiment, showed a juster appreciation of the true conditions of the argument than any hitherto noticed, and may be counted as amongst the most powerful agents in the intellectual development of the time. Middleton, who had held his own against Bentley, could not summarily be put down as an ignorant dabbler in matters too deep for him.—STEPHEN, LESLIE, 1876, *History of English Thought in the Eighteenth Century, vol.* I, *p.* 254.

It has been considered that Middleton's covert attacks upon the credibility of miracles and other matters of Protestant creed, marked the beginning of a new tide of critical religious speculation in England. His "Free Inquiry into Miraculous Powers" caused quite a sensation when it appeared in 1747. The arguments of Middleton were ridiculed by Wesley, and scandalised Gray, but they strengthened the hands of Hume, and they helped to mould the conscience of Gibbon.—GOSSE, EDMUND, 1888, *A History of Eighteenth Century Literature, p.* 278.

Following the various lines which the literature of the century presents to us, we find in Middleton a distinct type, which is clearly distinguished from what has gone before, and is carried on consistently in certain features to the end. His learning, within its limits, is clear, practical, and free from pedantry. All his equipment is well assorted and adaptable; there is nothing about it either of cumbrousness or mystery. His style is exact, logical, and full of common sense; if it is bald it therein reflects the limitations of the man.—CRAIK, HENRY, 1895, *ed., English Prose, vol.* IV, *p.* 3.

His place here, however, is that of the most distinguished representative of the absolutely plain style—not colloquial and vernacular like Bentley's, but on the other hand attempting none of the graces which Addison and Berkeley in their different ways achieved—a style more like the plainer Latin or French styles than like anything else in English.—SAINTSBURY, GEORGE, 1898, *A Short History of English Literature, p.* 541.

Henry Saint-John

Viscount Bolingbroke

1678–1751

Born, in London, 1678; baptized 10 Oct. Educated at Eton. Married (i), Frances Winchcombe, 1700. M. P. for Wootton-Bassett, Dec. 1701. Hon. D. D., Oxford, 1702. Sec. for War, 1704. Re-elected M. P. for Wootton-Bassett, 1705. Sec. of State, 1710–14. M. P. for Berkshire, Oct. 1710. Created Viscount Bolingbroke and Baron St. John of Lydiard Tregoze, 7 July 1712. Sec. of State to Pretender, July 1714 to 1716. Abandoned Jacobite Cause, 1716. Wife died, Nov. 1718. Married (ii), Mme. Marie Claire de Villette, May 1720. Restored to favour at English Court, 1723. Resumed political life. Contrib. to "The Craftsman," 1727–34. In later years spent much time in France. Political career ended, 1740. Died, in London, 12 Dec. 1751. Buried at Battersea. *Works:* "Letter to the 'Examiner'" (Anon.), 1710; "Considerations upon the Secret History of the White Staff" (anon.; attrib. to Bolingbroke), 1714; "The Public Spirit of the Whigs" (anon.; with Swift), 1714; "The Representation of the Lord Viscount Bolingbroke" (anon.; attrib. to Bolingbroke), 1715; "Letter . . . to the Dean of St. Patrick's" (anon.), 1715; "The Occasional Writer" (anon.), 1727; "Observations on the Public Affairs of Great Britain," (under pseud.: "W. Raleigh"), 1729: "The Craftsman Extraordinary" (3 pts.; anon.), 1729; "Letter to Caleb Danvers" (under pseud.: "John Trott"), 1730; "A Final Answer to the Remarks on the Craftsman's Vindication" (anon.), 1731; "The Freeholder's Political Catechism" (from "The Craftsman"), 1733; "The Idea of a Patriot King" (anon.), [1735?]; "A Dissertation upon Parties" (from "The Craftsman"), 1735 (2nd edn. same year); "Good Queen Anne Vindicated" (anon.), 1748; "A Collection of Political Tracts" (anon.), 1748; "Letters on the Spirit of Patriotism" (anon.), 1749; "A Familiar Letter to the most impudent man living" (anon.), 1749. *Posthumous:* "Letters on the Study and Use of History" (2 vols.), 1752; "Reflections concerning Innate Moral Principles," 1752; "Letters to Dr. Jonathan Swift," 1752; "Letter to Sir W. Wyndham," 1753; "Reflections on the State of the Nation," 1753; "Introductory Letter to Pope," 1753; "Letters and Correspondence," ed. by G. Parke (4 vols.), 1798. *Collected Works:* ed. by D. Mallet (5 vols.), 1754. *Life:* by T. Macknight, 1863.—SHARP, R. FARQUHARSON, 1897, *A Dictionary of English Authors, p.* 245.

PERSONAL

Thus from the noisy crowd exempt, with ease
And plenty blest, amid the mazy groves,
Sweet solitude! where warbling birds provoke
The silent Muse, delicious rural seat
Of St. John, English Memmius, I presumed
To sing Britannic trophies, inexpert
Of war, with mean attempt; while he, intent
(So Anna's will ordains), to expedite
His military charge, no leisure finds
To string his charming shell; but when return'd,
Consummate Peace shall rear her cheerful head,
Then shall his Churchill, in sublimer verse,
For ever triumph; latest times shall learn
From such a chief to fight, and bard to sing.
—PHILIPS, JOHN, 1705, *Blenheim.*

I think Mr. St. John the greatest young man I ever knew: wit, capacity, beauty, quickness of apprehension, good learning, and an excellent taste; the best orator in the House of Commons, admirable conversation, good nature, and good manners: generous, and a despiser of money. His only fault is talking to his friends in way of complaint of too great a load of business, which looks a little like affectation; and he endeavours too much to mix the fine gentleman and man of pleasure with the man of business. What truth and sincerity he may have I know not. . . . He turns the whole parliament, who can do nothing without him.—SWIFT, JONATHAN, 1711–12, *Journal to Stella.*

O, Bolingbroke! O favourite of the skies,
O born to gifts by which the noblest rise,
Improv'd in arts by which the brightest please,
Intent to business, and polite for ease;
Sublime in eloquence, where loud applause
Hath styl'd thee Patron of a nation's cause.
—PARNELL, THOMAS, 1713, *Essay on the Different Styles of Poetry.*

I am extremely glad to hear that my Lord Treasurer takes care of his health. I hope he will continue to do so; for though I am a poor, discarded mistress, yet my best wishes shall always attend his lordship. I beg my most humble service to him and his lady.—BOLINGBROKE, LADY F., 1713, *Letter to Lord Harley, Aug.* 18.

Oxford was removed on Tuesday: the queen died on Sunday. What a world is this! and how does fortune banter us!—BOLINGBROKE, HENRY SAINT-JOHN LORD, 1714, *Letter to Swift, Aug.* 3.

And so poor Harry is turned out from being Secretary of State, and the seals are given to Mar; and they use poor Harry most unmercifully and call him knave and traitor, and God knows what. I believe all poor Harry's fault was that he could not play his part with a grave enough face; he could not help laughing now and then at such kings and queens.—STAIR, LORD, 1716, *Letter to Horace Walpole, March* 3.

It is necessary that I should make you share my delight at a journey I have made to La Source, the abode of Lord Bolingbroke and Madame de Villette. I have found in this eminent Englishman all the learning of his country, and all the politeness of ours. I have never heard our language spoken with more energy and justice. This man, who has been all his life immersed in pleasure and in business, has, however, found time for learning everything, and retaining everything. He is as well acquainted with the history of the ancient Egyptians as with that of England. He knows Virgil as well as Milton. He loves the poetry of England, France, and Italy; but he loves them differently, because he discerns perfectly the difference of their genius.—VOLTAIRE, FRANÇOIS MARIE AROUET, 1721, *Letter to Thiriot.*

Though you have not signed your name, I know you: you are an infamous fellow, a perjured, ungrateful, unfaithful rascal . . . of so profligate a character, that in your prosperity, nobody envied you, and in your disgrace nobody pities. You were in the interests of France and of the Pope, as hath appeared by your writings, and you went out of the way to save yourself from the gallows. You have no abilities; you are an emancipated slave, a proscribed criminal, and an insolvent debtor. You went out of the way to save yourself from the gallows, and Herostratus and Nero were not greater villains than you. You have been a traitor and should be used like one. And I love my master so well that I will never advise him to use you, lest you should jostle me out of my employment. I know you to be so hot-headed that when you read this you will vent all your malice against me. But do I not value it, for I would rather have you my enemy than my friend. Change your name and be as abusive and scurrilous as you please, I shall find you out. You may change to a flame, a lion, a bull, or a bear, I shall know you, baffle you, conquer you, and contemn you. All your opposition will redound to my honour and glory.—WALPOLE, SIR ROBERT, 1727 *Political Pamphlet.*

Lord Bolingbroke is one of the politest as well as greatest men in the world.—He appeared careless in his talk of religion.—In this he differed from Fenelon: Lord Bolingbroke outshines you, but then holds himself in, and reflects some of his own light, so as to make you appear the less inferior to him.—RAMSAY, CHEVALIER, 1728–30, *Spence's Anecdotes, ed. Singer, p.* 40.

Come then, my friend! my genius! come along;
O master of the poet and the song!
And while the muse now stoops, or now ascends,
To man's low passions, or their glorious ends,
Teach me, like thee in various nature wise,
To fall with dignity, with temper rise;
Formed by thy converse, happily to steer
From grave to gay, from lively to severe;
Correct with spirit, eloquent with ease,
Intent to reason, or polite to please.
Oh! while along the stream of Time thy name
Expanded flies, and gathers all its fame,
Say, shall my little bark attendant sail,
Pursue the triumph, and partake the gale?
When statesmen, heroes, kings, in dust repose,
Whose sons shall blush their fathers were thy foes,
Shall then this verse to future age pretend
Thou wert my guide, philosopher, and friend?

—POPE, ALEXANDER, 1732, *An Essay on Man, Epistle* iv, *v.* 373–390.

I would never be acquainted with Lord Bolingbroke, because I always looked upon him as a vile man.—MONTAGU, LADY MARY WORTLEY, 1740–41, *Spence's Anecdotes, ed. Singer, p.* 176.

As to the Lord Bolingbroke's general character, it was so mixed that he had certainly some qualifications that the greatest men might be proud of, and many which the worst would be ashamed of:

he had fine talents, a natural eloquence, great quickness, a happy memory, and very extensive knowledge; but he was vain, much beyond the general run of mankind, timid, false, injudicious, and ungrateful; elate and insolent in power, dejected and servile in disgrace: few people ever believed him without being deceived, or trusted him without being betrayed: he was one to whom prosperity was no advantage, and adversity no instruction: he had brought affairs to that pass that he was almost as much distressed in his private fortune as desperate in his political views, and was upon such a foot in the world that no king would employ him, no party support him, and few particulars defend him; his enmity was the contempt of those he attacked, and his friendship a weight and reproach to those he adhered to. Those who were most partial to him could not but allow that he was ambitious without fortitude, and enterprising without resolution; that he was fawning without insinuation, and insincere without art; that he had admirers without friendship, and followers without attachment; parts without probity, knowledge without conduct, and experience without judgment. This was certainly his character and situation; but since it is the opinion of the wise, the speculative, and the learned, that most men are born with the same propensities, actuated by the same passions, and conducted by the same original principles, and differing only in the manner of pursuing the same ends, I shall not so far chime in with the bulk of Lord Bolingbroke's contemporaries as to pronounce he had more failings than any man ever had; but it is impossible to see all that is written, and hear all that is said of him, and not allow that if he had not a worse heart than the rest of mankind, at least he must have had much worse luck. —HERVEY, JOHN LORD, 1743? *Memoirs of the Reign of George II, vol.* I, *p.* 71.

In the name of God, whom I humbly adore, to whom I offer up perpetual thanksgiving, and to the order of whose providence I am cheerfully resigned. This is the last Will and Testament of me, Henry St. John, in the Reign of Queen Anne, and by her grace and favour Viscount Bolingbroke, after more than thirty years' proscription, and after the immense losses I have sustained by unexpected events in the course of it, by the injustice and treachery of persons nearest to me, by the negligence of friends, and by the infidelity of servants, as my fortune is so reduced at this time that it is impossible for me to make such disposition and to give such ample legacies as I always intended.—BOLINGBROKE, HENRY SAINT-JOHN VISCOUNT, 1751, *Will.*

HERE LYES
HENRY ST. JOHN,
IN THE DAYS OF QUEEN ANNE
SECRETARY AT WAR, SECRETARY OF STATE,
AND VISCOUNT
BOLINGBROKE.
IN THE DAYS OF KING GEORGE THE FIRST
AND KING GEORGE
THE SECOND
SOMETHING MORE AND BETTER.
HIS ATTACHMENT TO QUEEN ANNE
EXPOSED HIM TO A LONG AND SEVERE
PROSECUTION.
HE BORE IT WITH FIRMNESS OF MIND.
HE PASSED THE LATTER PART OF HIS LIFE
AT HOME,
THE ENEMY OF NO NATIONAL PARTY,
THE FRIEND OF NO FACTION;
DISTINGUISHED UNDER THE CLOUD OF A
PROSCRIPTION
WHICH HAD NOT BEEN ENTIRELY TAKEN OFF,
BY ZEAL TO MAINTAIN THE LIBERTY
AND TO RESTORE THE ANCIENT PROSPERITY
OF GREAT BRITAIN.

—BOLINGBROKE, HENRY SAINT-JOHN VISCOUNT, 1751? *Epitaph, MS., British Museum.*

I believe I have lost an enemy in Lord Bolingbroke. I am sure, Religion, and the State, has. I question whether we shall see any of his MSS. His "Apology for his Public Conduct," which I have seen, affects too many parties, to see the light; and his apology for his private opinions would shock the people too much, as dissolute as they are now grown. His "Letters concerning the use of reading History" (the best of his works, as his "Patriot King," I think, is the worst), I suppose we shall see, because there are printed copies of it in several hands. It is in two volumes, 8vo. It was this work which occasioned his aversion to me. There is a dissertation in it against the canon of Scripture, which I told Mr. Pope was full of absurdities and false reasoning, and would discredit the work: and, at his desire, I drew up a paper of remarks upon it, which Lord Bolingbroke never forgave. He wrote an answer to it in great wrath and much acrimony; but, by the persuasion of a great man, suppressed it. It is possible it may now see the light.—WARBURTON, WILLIAM, 1751, *Letters from a Late Eminent Prelate, Dec.* 29, *p.* 94.

Lord Bolingbroke joined all the politeness, the manners, and the graces of a Courtier, to the solidity of a Statesman, and to the learning of a Pedant.—CHESTERFIELD, PHILIP DORMER STANHOPE EARL, 1752, *Feb.* 20, *Letters to his Son.*

The late lord Bolingbroke, and the lord Carteret, afterwards earl of Granville. But as I know not enough of them to be very particular in their characters, I shall only describe them as they were generally spoken of. They were universally esteemed of the greatest genius for parts and knowledge of any men of the age; the latter thought to be the better scholar, and to have formed his eloquence more upon the ancients, and to have more of their spirit in it, than the former, but the first was far the better writer, and had been a very lively and able speaker in both houses of parliament. He was thought to have more knowledge and skill in the affairs of Europe from his long experience abroad and intimacy there with men of the first rank for business and capacity. But neither of them were thought to know enough for the real temper and constitution of their own country, altho' lord Bolingbroke wrote much on that subject, they were both of them of unbounded spirit and ambition, impatient of restraint, contemning the notion of equality with others in business, and even disdaining to be anything if not the first and highest in power. They were not famed for what is called personal courage, but in the conduct of affairs were deemed bold if not rash, and the lord Bolingbroke was of a temper to overturn kingdoms to make way for himself and his talents to govern the world; whilst the other in projecting the plans of his administration, thought much more of raising a great name to himself all over Europe, and having that continued by historians to all posterity, than of any present domestic popularity or renown whatsoever.—ONSLOW, ARTHUR, c1752, *Remarks on Various Parts of Sir Robert Walpole's Conduct, and Anecdote of the Principal Leaders of the Opposition; Coxe, Memoir of Sir Robert Walpole, vol.* II, *p.* 567.

Sir, he was a scoundrel and a coward: a scoundrel, for charging a blunderbuss against religion and morality; a coward, because he had not resolution to fire it off himself, but left half a crown to a beggarly Scotchman, to draw the trigger after his death!—JOHNSON, SAMUEL, 1754, *Life by Boswell, ed. Hill, vol.* I, *p.* 312.

I own I have small regard for Lord Bolingbroke as an author, and the highest contempt for him as a man. He came into the world greatly favored both by nature and fortune, blest with a noble birth, heir to a large estate, endowed with a strong constitution, and, as I have heard, a beautiful figure, high spirits, a good memory, and a lively apprehension, which was cultivated by a learned education: all these glorious advantages being left to the direction of a judgment stifled by unbounded vanity, he dishonored his birth, lost his estate, ruined his reputation, and destroyed his health, by a wild pursuit of eminence even in vice and trifles.—MONTAGU, LADY MARY WORTLEY, 1755, *Letter to the Countess of Bute, July* 20.

There are some characters that seemed formed by Nature to take delight in struggling with opposition, and whose most agreeable hours are passed in storms of their own creating. The subject of the present sketch was, perhaps, of all others, the most indefatigable in raising himself enemies, to shew his power in subduing them; and was not less employed in improving his superior talents, than in finding objects on which to exercise their activity. His life was spent in a continual conflict of politics, and as if that was too short for the combat, he has left his memory as a subject of lasting contention. . . . Nature seemed not less kind to him in her external embellishments, than in adorning his mind. With the graces of an handsome person, and a face in which dignity was happily blended with sweetness, he had a manner of address that was very engaging. His vivacity was always awake, his apprehension was quick, his wit refined, and his memory amazing:

his subtlety in thinking and reasoning was profound, and all these talents were adorned with an elocution that was irresistible. . . . In whatever light we view his character, we shall find him an object rather properer for our wonder, than our imitation, more to be feared than esteemed, and gaining our admiration without our love. His ambition ever aimed at the summit of power, and nothing seemed capable of satisfying his immoderate desires but the liberty of governing all things without a rival. With as much ambition, as great abilities, and more acquired knowledge than Cæsar, he wanted only his courage to be as successful; but the schemes his head dictated, his heart often refused to execute: and he lost the ability to perform, just when the great occasion called for all his efforts to engage.—GOLDSMITH, OLIVER, 1770, *Life of Lord Bolingbroke.*

The eloquence and ostentation of Bolingbroke could never impose on Arbuthnot: he told his son (whom I once had the honour to converse with at Richmond), that he knew Bolingbroke was an infidel, and a worthless vain man.—BEATTIE, JAMES, 1785, *Letter to Mrs. Montagu, Jan.* 31; *Beattie's Life by Forbes, vol.* II, *p.* 357.

Mr. Burke told me a few days ago that the first Lord Lyttleton informed him, that Lord Bolingbroke never wrote down any of his works but *dictated* them to a secretary. This may account for their endless tautology. In company, according to Lord Lyttleton, he was very eloquent, speaking with great fluency and authority on every subject, and generally in the form of *harangue* rather than colloquial table talk. His company all looked up to him, and very few *dared* to interrupt or contradict him.—MALONE, EDMOND, 1787, *Maloniana, ed. Prior, p.* 375.

Henry lord Bolingbroke was one of the great ornaments of the beginning of the present century. He has been admired as a statesman, an orator, a man of letters and a philosopher. Pope, in the eagerness of his reverence and devotion, foresaw the time when his merits would be universally acknowledged, and assured the world that the "sons" of his personal adversaries, would "blush" for the malignity and injustice of "their fathers." But Pope, though a poet, was no prophet. We every day hear Bolingbroke spoken of by one man or another, with as much contempt as could have been expressed by the most rancorous of his political rivals.—GODWIN, WILLIAM, 1797, *Of Posthumous Fame, The Enquirer p.* 295.

Bolingbroke had beheld the decay of Dryden, and the rise of Pope. It was his fortune to view also the progress of, perhaps, a yet more extraordinary genius. Voltaire was now giving early proofs of those talents which were afterwards to astonish his age in their development, and to disappoint it by their perversion. The English philosopher seems to have been peculiarly successful in winning the confidence and affections of the young. He was regarded by Voltaire with scarcely less esteem and admiration than by Pope. In his society these two illustrious men felt and acknowledged a superior genius; and if he had no claim to excellence in poetry, the art in which they were so preeminent, he surpassed them both in the philosophy which they so admired. . . . Bolingbroke's private, like his public life, offers much subject both for praise and blame. His passions were as fiery as his genius; and in his youth he disdained to control the one, or to regulate the other. Although eminently gifted with those shining qualities which captivate and ensnare, he took little pains to improve the opportunities he possessed; and his intrigues were rather numerous than select. He was not very fastidious in choosing his companions of either sex; but no man was more careful in the selection of a friend. There were few men whom he ever admitted to this distinction, and of these none ever deserted or betrayed him. The ambition which would allow him to brook no equal in the administration of government, prompted him to domineer in private: his friendship was offered only to those whose kindred genius marked them as his equals, and even by these he could never believe that he was loved until he was implicitly obeyed. The estimation in which his friendship was held, appears from the readiness with which the superiority he assumed was conceded: even Pope and Swift owned in him a master.—COOKE, GEORGE WINGROVE, 1835, *Memoirs of Lord Bolingbroke, vol.* II, *pp.* 36, 279.

He looked through the characters of

others with a keen and searching eye. His eloquence, both commanding and rewarding the attention of his hearers, was ready, full, and gushing; according to his own beautiful illustration, it flowed like a stream that is fed by an abundant spring, and did not merely spout forth, like a frothy water, on some gaudy day. His genius was vast and lofty, yet able to contract itself at will—scarcely anything too great for its grasp, and scarcely anything too minute for its care. With such splendid abilities, such active ambition, he might have been the greatest and most useful statesman of his, or, perhaps, of any age. But he utterly wanted virtue. He was no believer in revealed religion, whose tenets he attempted to sap in his writings, and disregarded in his life. He had early rushed into pleasure with an eagerness and excess that might have been forgiven his youth and his ardent passions, had he not afterwards continued them from a miserable personal vanity. He aimed at being the modern Alcibiades—a man of pleasure at the same time as a man of business; sitting up one night to reel at a drunken orgy,—sitting up the next to compose a despatch on which the fate of Europe might hang; at one hour dealing forth his thunderbolts of eloquence to the awe-struck senate,—at another whispering soft words at the ear of yielding beauty! In this unworthy combination he lost all dignity of mind. There ceased to be any consistency between his conduct and his language. No man ever spoke more persuasively of the fatigues of business, yet no man was ever more fretful and uneasy, in retirement. For him, activity was as necessary as air for others. When excluded from public life, there were no intrigues, however low and grovelling, to which he did not stoop in order to return to it. Yet all his writings breathe the noblest principles of independence.—STANHOPE, PHILIP HENRY EARL, 1836–54, *History of England from the Peace of Utrecht to the Peace of Versailles, vol.* I, *p.* 26.

The opinions of posterity as to his character are likely to be as much divided as were those of his contemporaries; and the safe conclusion that can be arrived at is, that he possessed an extraordinary mixture of good and evil, of greatness and meanness, of that which ennobles, as well as that which disgraces morality. . . . His extraordinary talents forced themselves into general notice; his prodigous strength of memory and quick apprehension, his dashing and brilliant style, was the admiration of his friends, and his social disposition rendered their affection equal to their admiration. Formed to excel in whatever he might undertake, he soon became as notorious for his excesses, as he was afterwards eminent for his genius and learning.—TIMPERLEY, C. H., 1842, *ed., Encyclopædia of Literary and Typographical Anecdote, Compiled and Condensed from Nichols's Literary Anecdotes, etc., p.* 681.

He lived in the centre of intrigues which were to shake thrones, and perhaps to form them. He became habituated to the idea that everything could be achieved by dexterity, and that there was no test of conduct except success. To dissemble and to simulate; to conduct confidential negotiations with contending powers and parties at the same time; to be ready to adopt any opinion and to possess none; to fall into the public humour of the moment and to evade the impending catastrophe; to look upon every man as a tool, and never to do anything which had not a definite though circuitous purpose,—these were his political accomplishments; and, while he recognised them as the best means of success, he found in their exercise excitement and delight. To be the centre of a maze of manœuvres was his empyrean. . . . Recklessness with him was a principle of action. He trusted always to his fertile expedients if he failed, and ran the risk in the meanwhile of paramount success—the fortune of those who are entitled to be rash. With all his audacity, which was nearly equal to his craft, he had no moral courage.—DISRAELI, BENJAMIN, (LORD BEACONSFIELD), 1847, *Tancred, ch.* vi.

With two exceptions, . . . Lord Bolingbroke came the nearest of all parliamentary orators who have been particularly recorded to the ideal of a fine rhetorician. It was no disadvantage to him that he was shallow, being so luminous and transparent; and the splendour of his periodic diction, with his fine delivery, compensated his defect in imagery.—DE QUINCEY, THOMAS, 1859, *Rhetoric, Collected Writings, ed. Masson, vol.* X, *p.* 111.

Bolingbroke survived Pope fourteen years. He had resided at Battersea after the death of his father, and here, in 1750, he brought her, who, he said, "had been the comfort of his life," to die. . . . He had lost one who thoroughly admired, comprehended, and loved him. Their tenderness had been signal. The charm of her society, her broken English, her eloquent French, were long remembered by those who knew Lady Bolingbroke. The experience for thirty years of her virtues had shown Lord Bolingbroke the value of woman. A little trait of Lady Bolingbroke, shows her clear perception of the change which came over her once brilliant husband in later days. Walking with her in his own grounds, accompanied by a friend, Bolingbroke began to relate some of the gallantries of his younger days. "He reminds me," said his lady to the friend with them, "of a fine old Roman aqueduct; but, alas! it is in ruins, the water has ceased to flow."—THOMSON, KATHERINE (GRACE WHARTON), 1861, *Celebrated Friendships, vol.* II, *pp.* 210, 211.

In this English Alcibiades, what restless, but what rich vitality!—LYTTON, EDWARD BULWER LORD, 1863–68, *Caxtoniana, Miscellaneous Prose Works, vol.* III, *p.* 88.

Excessive drinking, profane swearing, and loose conversation were not even the worst. It must be confessed that the Secretary outraged the decencies of his situation still more grossly. Though his wife was devotedly attached to him, and though they still lived under the same roof, he was as licentious as in the days of his early youth, when it had been his boast to rival the wild exploits of Rochester. The House of Commons, the War Office, the studies in his country retirement, the development of his genius, the Secretary of State's office, the rivalry with Harley, all the promptings of a high and justifiable ambition had not rendered his life purer than that of the lowest rake about London. On the news of St. John's appointment as Secretary of State spreading through the town, an ancient lady who presided over a mansion of easy virtue, exclaimed with delight, "Five thousand a year, my girls, and all for us!" It is not from his political enemies, from Steele, Addison, or Walpole that we have the most explicit details of St. John's habitual debaucheries. The Secretary's friends have been the most candid. A handsome woman, they all admit, sometimes jestingly and sometimes sadly, was a temptation he never could resist. Rank made no difference whatever in his appreciation. With the same ardour he would make love to a maid of honour about the person of the Queen, or follow in broad daylight a common woman of the town, whose appearance might happen to please him, as he was walking with some friends in the Mall. After this it was an edifying sight to behold the Secretary at his prayers.—MACKNIGHT, THOMAS, 1863, *The Life of Henry St. John, Viscount Bolingbroke, p.* 213.

Three years of eager unwise power, the thirty-five of sickly longing and impotent regret,—such, or something like it, will ever be in this cold modern world the fate of an Alcibiades.—BAGEHOT, WALTER, 1863, *Bolingbroke as a Statesman, Works, ed. Morgan, vol.* III, *p.* 221.

Bolingbroke was capable of intrigue, but not of action. He could cabal with the backstairs, worry his colleagues, negotiate with the men of letters who were of his party, and debauch as far as possible the House of Commons.—ROGERS, JAMES E. THOROLD, 1869, *Historical Gleanings, First series, vol.* I, *p.* 36.

A sceptic and cynic, minister in turn to Queen and Pretender, disloyal alike to both, a trafficker in consciences, marriages, and promises, who had squandered his talent in debauch and intrigues, to end in disgrace, impotence, and scorn.—TAINE, H. A., 1871, *History of English Literature, tr. Van Laun, vol.* II, *bk.* iii, *ch.* iii, *p.* 47.

In conversation he developed that versatility and fire, which distinguish him as a writer; and perhaps he was altogether born rather to be a writer than a statesman.—RANKE, LEOPOLD VON, 1875, *A History of England, vol.* V, *p.* 348.

Adored by Pope—whom he attended on his death-bed, and who considered him the first writer, as well as the greatest man, of his age; hated by Walpole as a political rival; lauded by Swift and Smollett; despised as "a scoundrel and a coward" by Dr. Johnson. His youth had been so wild that his father's congratulation when he was created a viscount was, "Ah,

Harry, I ever said you would be hanged; but now I find you will be *beheaded.*"—HARE, AUGUSTUS J. C., 1878, *Walks in London, vol.* II, *ch.* X.

St. John was the inspired son of genius. He was a being formed on a model that had come into notice in France, where it was copied from the great monarch himself. Its type was the man of pleasure, who can at an instant's notice become the man of affairs. Display, luxury, and riot appeared to ordinary mortals all that such a being was capable of achieving; but let the sudden crisis come, and the call to action, though dragged from the gaming-table or the "midnight modern conversation," as Hogarth has immortalised such scenes, the debauchee became clear in council and prompt in action. —BURTON, JOHN HILL, 1880, *A History of the Reign of Queen Anne, vol.* III, *p.* 75.

We can write with temper of the latter days of the Empire, or of the constitutions of the Medieval Republics; but the reign of Anne still rouses and enlists the passions of partisans. And Bolingbroke has been impartially assailed by every party. It was his misfortune to incur the resentment of the Whigs and the resentment of the Tories. He was attacked by the friends of the Revolution and by the enemies of the Revolution, by the Nonjurors and by the Presbyterian Dissenters, by Williamites and by Jacobites, by Atterbury and by Defoe. The Whigs, he himself declared, had done all they could to expose him for a fool, and to brand him for a knave; and though the Tories had not impeached him for treason to the State, they had impeached him for treason to themselves. "That last burst of the cloud," he exclaimed, "has gone near to overwhelm me." There are some open questions in our Histories as in our Cabinets; and the character of Bolingbroke may still be regarded as an open question —and not improperly. At all events, the writer who maintains that Henry St. John was abler and honester than most of his contemporaries, is not necessarily ventilating a caprice, or airing a paradox.—SKELTON, JOHN, 1883, *The Great Lord Bolingbroke, Essays in History and Biography, p.* 166.

Nor was Bolingbroke's personal character, with all its striking features, one likely to prove attractive to a party of English fox-hunters, whether lay or clerical. . . . His polished manners, his lively wit, his quick perceptions, his facile speech, his ready invention, the ease with which he caught and mimicked the intemperate tone of his rude supporters, his fondness for subterfuge and artifice, his affectation of philosophical indifference to the objects for which he was at the moment most eagerly striving, his vanity, his industry, his simulated idleness, his unfeigned respect for speculative truth, his falseness in all public and personal relations, the vastness and boldness of his political enterprises, the nervous apprehension of physical danger which at the critical moment marred so many of them, the loftiness of his moral conceptions, the looseness and even dirtiness of his private life,—all these things were the marks of a character which in its strange and various traits an Italian of the great age of Florence would have studied with respectful interest, but which repelled the Trullibers and Westerns from its very dissimilarity to their own. In the statesmanship of such a man there is no doubt a natural propensity to indirect and tortuous ways, to sinister intrigues, to organized deceptions, to statements which, when literally true, are calculated and designed to give a false impression, to concealed engagements and sudden surprises. Bolingbroke has himself explained this necessity in a characteristic passage and under a fine simile.—HARROP, ROBERT, 1884, *Bolingbroke, A Political Study and Criticism, p.* 191.

It would, however, be a great mistake to confound Bolingbroke either with fribbles like the second Villiers, whom he resembled in the infirmities of his temper, or with sycophants like Sunderland, whom he resembled in want of principle. His nature had, with all its flaws, been cast in no ignoble mould. The ambition which consumed him was the ambition which consumed Cæsar and Cicero, not the ambition which consumed Harley and Newcastle. For the mere baubles of power he cared nothing. Riches and their trappings he regarded with unaffected contempt. He entered office a man by no means wealthy, and with expensive habits; he quitted it with hands as clean as Pitt's. The vanity which feeds on adulation never touched his haughty spirit. His prey was not carrion. His vast and visionary ambition was bounded only by the highest pinnacles of human glory. He aspired to enroll himself among those great men who have shaped the fortunes and moulded the minds of mighty nations—with the demigods of Plutarch, with the sages of Diogenes. As a statesman he never rested till he stood without a rival on the summit of power. As a philosopher he sought a place beside Aristotle and Bacon, and the infirmities of age overtook him while meditating a work which was to class him with Guicciardini and Clarendon.—COLLINS, JOHN CHURTON, 1886, *Bolingbroke, A Historical Study, and Voltaire in England, p.* 14.

The defect of his nature was, that there was not sufficient ballast for the weight of sail. He would be first always; and not borrow, but found a system. His talents made him lead; there was not enough of judgment, patience, sympathy, or, above all, consistency, to constitute a successful leader. His career, in all its several divisions, had ever the same features. It left a profound impression of force, which may be traced in contemporary literature, but he could never keep his levies long from disbanding. His immediate survivors were unable to explain the sudden decline of the influence of his ideas, when the man, with his contagious strength of will, was gone; posterity cannot understand whence arose his influence at the first.—STEBBING, WILLIAM, 1887, *Some Verdicts of History Reviewed, p.* 152.

The year 1751, which may be said to have opened with the death of poor Frederick, closed with the death of a man greater by far than any prince of the House of Hanover. On December 12 Bolingbroke passed away. . . . There had been a good deal of the spirit of the classic philosopher about him—the school of Epictetus, not the school of Aristotle or Plato. He was a Georgian Epictetus with a dash of Gallicised grace about him. He made the most out of everything as it came, and probably got some comfort out of disappointment as well as out of success. Life had been for him one long dramatic performance, and he played it out consistently to the end.—MCCARTHY, JUSTIN, 1890, *A History of the Four Georges, vol.* II, *ch.* xxxix.

That he was a consummate scoundrel is now universally admitted; but his mental qualifications, though great, still excite differences of opinion. Even those who are comforted by his style and soothed by the rise and fall of his sentences, are fain to admit that had his classic head been severed from his shoulders a rogue would have met with his deserts. He has been long since stripped of all his fine pretences, and morally speaking, runs as naked through the pages of history as erst he did (according to Goldsmith) across Hyde Park.—BIRRELL, AUGUSTINE, 1894, *Essays about Men, Women and Books, p.* 17.

St. Johns's handsome person, and a face in which dignity was happily blended with sweetness, his commanding presence, his fascinating address, his vivacity, his wit, his extraordinary memory, his subtlety in thinking and reasoning, and oratorical powers of the very highest order, contributed to his phenomenal success as a parliamentary orator. Very few fragments of his speeches have come down to us, but from criticisms of those who heard him speak, and from his published writings, they must have been brilliant, sarcastic, and extremely effective, and Lord Chatham said that the loss of his speeches was to be more greatly deplored than the lost books of Livy.—HARDWICKE, HENRY, 1896, *History of Oratory and Orators, p.* 91.

All great men should be judged by the aims and standards of their age. But perhaps no great man ever needed the sympathy of imagination leavening judgment more than Henry St. John, the first Viscount Bolingbroke. He was born to be admired rather than loved, to be dreaded rather than respected. He was unique in a unique period. Statesmanship, eloquence, and adminstrative ability, which in his hot-headed youth compelled the admiration of Swift and the mingled fear and wonder of both Harley and Marlborough, which in his middle age by turns dazzled and embittered Pulteney and Carteret, which awed Walpole and his satellites beneath the mask of their scorn, which nearly succeeded in moulding a loose faction into a magnificent party, which provoked, after his death, the young Burke into indignant imitation, which controlled the reins of Government during the last four years of Queen Anne, and moved the springs of opposition during the first eight years of George the Second, were allied to a literary genius which has left an undying imprint on Pope and Voltaire, a style which kindled Chatham, inspired Gibbon, and preluded Macaulay, a personal fascination and irresistible persuasiveness which enchanted his "dearest foes."—SICHEL, WALTER, 1901, *Bolingbroke and His Times*, p. 1.

THE IDEA OF A PATRIOT KING
1735?

It is a work, sir, which will instruct mankind and do honour to its author; and yet I will take upon me to say that, for the sake of both, you must publish it with caution. The greatest men have their faults, and sometimes the greatest faults; but the faults of superior minds are the least indifferent, both to themselves and to society. Humanity is interested in the name of those who excelled in it; but it is interested before all in the good order of society, and in the peace of the minds of the individuals who compose it. Lord Bolingbroke's mind embraced all objects, and looked far into all, but not without a strong mixture of passions, which will always necessarily beget some prejudices and follow more. And in the subject of *religion* particularly (whatever was the motive that inflamed his passions upon that subject chiefly), his passions were there most strong; and I will venture to say (when called upon as I think to say it), what I have said more than once to himself, with the deference due to his age and extraordinary talents; his passions upon that subject did prevent his otherwise superior reason from seeing that, even in a political light only, he hurt himself, and wounded society by striking at establishments upon which the conduct at least of society depends, and by striving to overturn in men's minds the systems which experience at least has justified, and which at least has rendered respectable, as necessary to public order and private peace, without suggesting to men's minds a better, or indeed any system. You will find this, sir, to be done in a part of the work I mentioned, where he digresses upon the criticism of *Church History*.—HYDE, LORD, 1752, *Letter to David Mallet, March* 7.

This lord had strength and elevation of mind; but he was a sorry philosopher.—GIBBON, EDWARD, 1764, *Journal.*

Possibly the "Patriot King"—his most finished performance—would have thrilled the House of Commons as a speech. Read in cold blood, the weakness of the substance weakens our appreciation of the elegance of the style.—STEPHEN, LESLIE, 1876, *History of English Thought in the Eighteenth Century, vol.* II, *p.* 169.

The most popular and in some ways the most finished of his writings, a party pamphlet devised for a temporary object, an appeal from the statesmanship of the nation to poets and non-jurors and striplings fresh from college, an adroit piece of flattery laid at the feet of the Parliamentary heir, but with a graver meaning and purpose which have secured it a more lasting fame. For this little tract, carefully excluded from general circulation by its author till the eve of his own death, has influenced the speculations of four generations of Englishmen, formed the political creed of George III., created the faction of the King's friends, encouraged the conspirators who broke the power of the Whig nobility, inspired that mixture of the autocratic with the popular which distinguished the rival policy of Chatham and William Pitt, and in our own time fired the imagination of a great minister who aimed at reviving under the phrase *imperium et libertas* its distinctive qualities.—HARROP, ROBERT, 1884, *Bolingbroke, A Political Study and Criticism, p.* 300.

On the composition of the "Patriot King," Bolingbroke took more pains than was usual with him. It is perhaps, in point of execution, his most finished work. But style, though it will do much for a writer, will not do everything. Indeed, Bolingbroke's splendid diction frequently serves to exhibit in strong relief the crudity and shallowness of his matter, as jewels set off deformity.—COLLINS, JOHN CHURTON, 1886, *Bolingbroke, A Historical Study, and Voltaire in England, p.* 208.

His boasted style, though unquestionably lucid, is slipshod and full of platitudes, grandiloquent and yet ineffectual. . . . Criticism now merely smiles at the author's impudent assumption of the airs of a great political philosopher.—GOSSE, EDMUND, 1888, *A History of Eighteenth Century Literature, p.* 174.

A work important equally as a historical document and as a model of style. Chesterfield said that until he read that tract he did not know what the English language was capable of.—PAYNE, E. J., *ed., Select Works of Burke, vol.* I, *p.* xvl.

GENERAL

Lord Bolingbroke is something superior to anything I have seen in human nature. You know I don't deal much in hyperboles: I quite think him what I say.—Lord Bolingbroke is much the best writer of the age. —Nobody knows half the extent of his excellencies, but two or three of his most intimate friends.—Whilst abroad, he wrote "A consolation to a man in exile;" so much in Seneca's style, that, was he living now among us, one should conclude that he had written every word of it. He also wrote several strictures on the Roman affairs (something like what Montesquieu published afterwards) among which there were many excellent observations.—POPE, ALEXANDER, 1734–36, *Spence's Anecdotes, ed. Singer, p.* 127.

I am solicitous to see Lord Bolingbroke's Works. All the writings I have seen of his appeared to me to be copied from the French eloquence. I mean a poor or trite thought dressed in pompous language.—MONTAGU, LADY MARY WORTLEY, 1749, *Letter to the Countess of Bute, Aug.* 22.

> The same sad morn to church and state
> (So for our sins 'twas fixed by fate)
> A double stroke was given;
> Black as the whirlwinds of the north,
> St. John's fell genius issued forth,
> And Pelham fled to heaven.

—GARRICK, DAVID, 1754, *Ode on the Death of Mr. Pelham.*

The works of the late Lord Bolingbroke are just published, and have plunged me into philosophical studies; which hitherto I have not been much used to, or delighted with; convinced of the futility of those researches: but I have read his Philosophical Essay upon the extent of human knowledge, which, by the way, makes two large quartos and a half. He there shows very clearly, and with most splendid eloquence, what the human mind can and cannot do; that our understandings are wisely calculated for our place in this planet, and for the link which we form in the universal chain of things; but that they are by no means capable of that degree of knowledge which our curiosity makes us search after, and which our vanity makes us often believe we arrive at.—CHESTERFIELD, PHILIP DORMER STANHOPE EARL, 1754, *Jan.* 15, *Letters to his Son.*

To this indeed I could say, and it is all that I could say, that my Lord Bolingbroke was a great genius, sent into the world for great and astonishing purposes: that the ends, as well as means of actions in such personages, are above the comprehension of the vulgar. That his life was one scene of the wonderful throughout. That, *as the temporal happiness, the civil liberties and properties of Europe, were the game of his earliest youth, there could be no sport so adequate to the entertainment of his advanced age as the eternal and final happiness of all mankind.*—FIELDING, HENRY, 1754, *Comment on Lord Bolingbroke's Essays.*

Before the Philosophical works of Bolingbroke had appeared, great things were expected from the leisure of a man, who, from the splendid scene of action in which his talents had enabled him to make so conspicuous a figure, had retired to employ those talents in the investigation of truth. Philosophy began to congratulate herself upon such a proselyte from the world of business, and hoped to have extended her power under the auspices of such a leader. In the midst of these pleasing expectations, the works themselves at last appeared in *full body,* and with great pomp. Those who searched in them for new discoveries in the mysteries of nature; those who expected something which might explain or direct the operations of the mind; those who hoped to see morality illustrated and enforced; those who looked for new helps to society and government; those who desired to see the characters and passions of mankind delineated; in short, all who consider such things as philosophy, and require some of them at least in every philosophical work, all these were certainly disappointed; they found the landmarks of science precisely in their former places: and they thought they received but a poor recompense for this disappointment, in seeing every mode of religion attacked in a lively manner, and the foundation of every virtue, and of all government, sapped with great art and much ingenuity. What advantage do we derive from such writings? What delight can a man find in employing a capacity which might be usefully exerted for the noblest purposes, in a sort of sullen labour, in which, if the author could succeed, he is obliged to own, that nothing could be more fatal to mankind than his success?—BURKE, EDMUND, 1756, *A Vindication of Natural Society, Preface.*

No Man of taste can read this noble Author, without being pleased with his manly Style, and strong Imagination. His Imagination appears to me his Characteristic; too much superior to the other Faculties of his mind; and at once the Source of his many Beauties as a Writer, and his many Extravagances as a Reasoner. As a Reasoner, I must place him very low in the learned World. I have hardly ever read an Author, even of the lowest Character, so inconsistent, not only with my Sentiments, which I could easily forgive, but with himself; so full of right Conclusions from wrong Premises, and wrong Conclusions from right Premises; so apt to imagine strongly, and to miscall it strong Reasoning; so sceptical in the midst of Evidence, and so dogmatical and confident in the absence of Evidence; so apt to mistake his own Importance as the Patron of a Cause, for the Importance, and Evidence of the Cause itself, in the View of others. —DAVIES, SAMUEL, 1757, *Letter to Mr. Donald, April* 5, *Princeton Review, vol.* 9, *p.* 351.

With the most agreeable talents in the world, and with great parts, was neither happy nor successful. He wrote against the late king, who had forgiven him; against sir Robert Walpole, who did forgive him; against the Pretender and the clergy, who never will forgive him. He is one of our best writers; though his attacks on all governments and all religions (neither of which views he cared directly to own) have necessarily involved his style in a want of perspicuity. One must know the man before one can often guess his meaning. He has two other faults, which one should not expect in the same writer, much tautology, and great want of connexion.—WALPOLE, HORACE, 1758-1806, *A Catalogue of the Royal and Noble Authors of England, Scotland and Ireland, ed. Park, vol.* V, *p.* 229.

As a moralist therefore, Lord Bolingbroke, by having endeavoured at too much, seems to have done nothing: but as a political writer, few can equal and none can exceed him. And he was a practical politician, his writings are less filled with those speculative illusions, which are the result of solitude and seclusion. He wrote them with a certainty of their being opposed, sifted, examined, and reviled; he therefore took care to build them up of such materials, as could not be easily overthrown: they prevailed at the times in which they were written, they still continue to the admiration of the present age, and will probably last for ever.—GOLDSMITH, OLIVER, 1770, *Life of Lord Bolingbroke.*

Mallet dreamt of getting golden mountains by Bolingbroke's legacy; he was so sanguine in his expectations, that he rejected the offer of three thousand pounds tendered to him by Mr. Millar the bookseller, for the copy-right of that nobleman's works; at the same time, he was so distress'd for cash, that he was forced to borrow money of this very bookseller to pay his stationer and printer. . . . Mallet heartily repented his refusal of Mr. Millar's offer; for the first impression of his edition of Bolingbroke's works was not sold off in twenty years.—DAVIES, THOMAS, 1780, *Memoirs of the Life of David Garrick, vol.* II, *pp.* 47, 48.

Though I may have recourse to this author, sometimes, for examples of style, it is his style only, and not his sentiments, that deserve praise. It is indeed my opinion, that there are few writings in the English language, which, for the matter contained in them, can be read with less profit of fruit, than Lord Bolingbroke's works. His political writings have the merit of a very lively and eloquent style; but they have no other; being, as to the substance, the mere temporary productions of faction and party; no better, indeed, than pamphlets written for the day. His posthumous, or as they are called, his philosophical works, wherein he attacks religion, have still less merit; for they are as loose in the style as they are flimsy in the reasoning. An unhappy instance, this author is, of parts and genius so miserably perverted by faction and passion, that, as his memory will descend to posterity with little honour, so his productions will soon pass, and are, indeed, already passing into neglect and oblivion.—BLAIR, HUGH, 1783, *Lectures on Rhetoric and Belles-Lettres, ed., Mills, Lecture* XV.

His speculative effusions, notwithstanding their splendour of diction and graces of style, are not consulted as containing just axioms or practical precepts; except by those who wish to avail themselves of the laxity of his political tenets, and his affectation of recurring to first principles and abstract doctrines, for the purpose of substituting a capricious and theoretical system, in the place of a well defined and limited government.—COXE, WILLIAM, 1798, *Memoirs of the Life and Administration of Sir Robert Walpole, vol.* I, *p.* 215.

Lord Bolingbroke's, . . . is a style of the highest order. The lofty, rhythmical, full-flowing eloquence of Cicero. Periods of just measure, their members proportioned, their close full and round. His conceptions, too, are bold and strong, his diction copious, polished and commanding as his subject. His writings are certainly the finest samples in the English language, of the eloquence proper for the Senate. His political tracts are safe reading for the most timid religionist, his philosophical, for those who are not afraid to trust their reason with discussions of right and wrong.—JEFFERSON, THOMAS, 1821, *Letter to Francis Eppes, Jan.* 19; *The Writings of Thomas Jefferson, ed. Ford, vol.* X, *p.* 183.

With all the signal faults of his public character, with all the factiousness which dictated most of his writings, and the indefinite declamation or shallow reasoning which they frequently display, they have merits not always sufficiently acknowledged.—HALLAM, HENRY, 1827–41, *The Constitutional History of England, vol.* II, *ch.* XVI.

Lord Bolingbroke, whom Pope idolized (and it pains me that all his idols are not mine) was a boastful empty mouther!—HAZLITT, WILLIAM, 1830? *Men and Manners.*

The best test to use, before we adopt any opinion or assertion of Bolingbroke's, is to consider whether in writing it he was thinking either of Sir Robert Walpole or of Revealed Religion. . . . On most other occasions he may be followed with advantage, as he always may be read with pleasure.—CREASY, SIR EDWARD SHEPHERD, 1831, *Fifteen Decisive Battles of the World, ch.* XI, *note.*

These "Letters on History" bear strong testimony to the tenacity of their author's memory, and to the extent of his reading. His quotations, which are so numerous that upon almost any other subject they would savour of pedantry, were drawn only from his memory and his commonplace book; he had scarcely any of the authors whom he mentions with him at Chantelou. This has indeed betrayed him into some few mistakes. There are several inaccurate quotations, and in more than one instance he has mistaken the name of his author. But these errors were seldom suffered to go unpunished. . . . Bolingbroke's writings are characteristic of himself: the style of the author bears a close resemblance to the character of the man. Brilliant and imaginative, manly and energetic, his power of illustration never renders him frigid or bombastic. His energy never degenerates into coarseness. There is an elegance in his antithesis peculiarly his own; and if it occurs sometimes too frequently, the nervous sentiment it breathes tempts us to overlook the traces of art. His words are selected carefully, and combined with skill; nor is it easy to convict him of a tedious or ill-constructed sentence. But the peculiar charm in Bolingbroke's style is the exact and beautiful propriety of his illustrations. This is characteristic of all his works, but it is more striking in his earlier productions.—COOKE, GEORGE WINGROVE, 1835, *Memoirs of Lord Bolingbroke, vol.* II, *pp.* 175, 263.

As a writer, Lord Bolingbroke is, I think, far too little admired in the present day. Nor is this surprising. His works naturally fail to please us from the false end which they always have in view, and from the sophistical arguments which they are, therefore, compelled to urge.—STANHOPE, PHILIP HENRY EARL, 1836–54, *History of England from the Peace of Utrecht to the Peace of Versailles, vol.* I, *p.* 27.

His poetry is frigid and inharmonious; it never rises above mediocrity, and usually sinks below it. . . . Of the six poetical pieces which are known to be his production, it would be difficult to say which is the most deficient in merit. His own good sense, however,—added to the want of encouragement which his verses met with from his friend Pope, and the actual abuse which was heaped upon them by Swift,—appear to have early convinced him that his genius was ill-suited for poetry.—JESSE, JOHN HENEAGE, 1843, *Memoirs of the Court of England from the Revolution in* 1688 *to the Death of George the Second, vol.* II, *pp.* 92, 93.

Bolingbroke's writings command respect from their mixture of clearness of exposition with power of argument. They form also the transition to the literature of the next age, in turning attention to history. Bolingbroke had great powers of psychological analysis, but he despised the study of it apart from experience. His philosophy was a philosophy of history. In his attacks on revelation we have the traces of the older philosophical school of deists; but in the consciousness that an historical, not a philosophical, solution must be sought to explain the rise of an historical phenomenon such as Christianity, he exemplifies the historic spirit which was rising, and anticipates the theological inquiry found in Gibbon; and, in his examination of the external historic evidence, both the documents by which the Christian religion is attested, and the effects of tradition in weakening historic data, he evinces traces of the influence of the historical criticism which had arisen in France under his friend Pouilly.—FARRAR, ADAM STOREY, 1862, *A Critical History of Free Thought, p.* 144.

Bolingbroke looks down with equally serene scorn upon priests, philosophers, and people. He is not the least anxious to refute divines by a scheme of atheistical philosophy. He refutes them by showing that he can conceive a God as well as they can, and that the God whom he conceives is one whose nature can by no possibility have any affinity with the nature of man; whom it is the most extravagant presumption for man to dream of knowing. Bolingbroke adds nothing to what Hobbes had said and Locke had implied, on the subject, except his own aristocratical air of confidence, and a little abuse of Cudworth, the Platonists and the Schoolmen. He tosses philosophical expositions about as Pope found him tossing the haycocks at his country seat, with infinite grace and condescension. The poet witnessed each performance with equal admiration. No ear could have detected more quickly than his the falsetto in these notes if he had not been bribed, as it was honourable to him that he should be, by an extravagant but real and quite disinterested affection for the musician.—MAURICE, FREDERICK DENISON, 1862, *Moral and Metaphysical Philosophy, vol.* II, *p.* 452.

Had the manuscripts of Bolingbroke's philosophical works been given to the flames, there would have been great expressions of regret from the intellectual world; and yet, although they were looked for with so much impatience, had they never been published at all, his reputation either as a writer or a philosopher would have lost nothing. . . . His published writings on the political controversies of his time still remain; and they will assist us to form a very correct, and even a favourable estimate of what we have lost. For, more than almost those of any other man who ever wrote, St. John's literary works resemble spoken eloquence. They are clearly the compositions of an orator, who, being prevented from addressing an audience by word of mouth, uses the pen as his instrument, and writes what he would have spoken. . . . Their style is, both in its excellencies and defects, thoroughly oratorical; glowing, animated, vehement, and if never bombastic, frequently declamatory, tautological, and diffuse. Graceful and flowing as Bolingbroke in the best of his writings is, he not unfrequently tires the reader with repetitions and amplifications, to which, when set off by his fine person and pleasing intonations, an audience might always listen with interest and delight. . . . Though his memory was so tenacious, that he seldom forgot what he wished to remember, and allusions to the great authors of antiquity are prodigally scatterd throughout his works, he never was a learned man. His information was, in many instances, obviously acquired at second hand; nor did he always make a judicious use of what he indirectly obtained. In his age it was customary to refer much more frequently than in ours to the ancient writers; and quotations and remarks which were then thought extremely clever are now considered only worthy of schoolboys. None of the writers of Queen

Anne's reign abound more in such pedantry than Bolingbroke; and it is more surprising to meet with it in his pages than in those of most of his contemporaries, because he was not so much a professed author as a statesman and a man of business.—MACKNIGHT, THOMAS, 1863, *The Life of Henry St. John, Viscount Bolingbroke, pp.* 66, 69, 131.

His irony is majestic, his lamentations are reserved and masculine. His graces of language are those which become an accomplished statesman. He is not a poet, and he takes from poets no ornament obsolete or far-fetched. . . . His quotations and his images harmonise with the character he assumes. His similes and illustrations are no wanton enrichments of fancy; they support the argument they adorn—like buttresses which, however relieved with tracery, add an air of solidity to the building against which they lean, and, in leaning, prop. Withal, he has been a man of the world's hard business—a leader of party, a chief among the agencies by which opinion is moulded and action is controlled. And therefore, amidst his natural stateliness, there is an absence of pedantry—a popular and genial elegance. His sentences flow loose as if disdainful of verbal care. Yet throughout all their reigns the senatorial decorum. The folds of the toga are not arranged to show off the breadth of the purple hem; the wearer knows too well that, however the folds may fall, the hem cannot fail to be seen.—LYTTON, EDWARD BULWER LORD, 1863–68, *Caxtoniana, Miscellaneous Prose Works, vol.* III, *p.* 87.

Bolingbroke is now little more than a brilliant name, and all the beauties of his matchless style have been unable to preserve his philosophy from oblivion.—LECKY, WILLIAM EDWARD HARTPOLE, 1865, *History of the Rise and Influence of the Spirit of Rationalism in Europe, vol.* I.

In Pope's eyes an indescribable charm attached to the society and personality of this unrepentant Alcibiades. As Bolingbroke discoursed to him on his system of natural theology, clear and shallow as the streamlet in the grotto where they sat, and communicated to him those Essays which he never had the courage to publish, the mind of his friend became imbued with enough of the facile lesson to make him in his own belief the disciple of an exhaustive system, while he was in reality only the acolyte of a sophist and a man of the world.—WARD, ADOLPHUS WILLIAM, 1869, *ed., Poetical Works of Alexander Pope, Introductory Memoir, p.* xxxviii.

He was much too passionate for philosophical speculation. The best metaphysics roused his anger at the first approach, and he stormed against doctrines he had not the patience to comprehend.—ELWIN, WHITWELL, 1871, *ed., The Works of Alexander Pope, vol.* VII, *p.* 328, *note.*

On the whole, it may be said that the reader who, finding how much Bolingbroke was admired by his contemporaries, is led to study his works, will not find much to reward him, except a few happy sentences, such as "Don Quixote believed, but even Sancho doubted."—NICOLL, HENRY J., 1882, *Landmarks of English Literature, p.* 184.

His style may be praised almost without reservation. It is distinguished by the union of those qualities which are in the estimation of critics sufficient to constitute perfection—by elevation, by rapidity, by picturesqueness, by perspicuity, by scrupulous chastity, by the charm of an ever-varying music. It combines, as no other English style has ever combined, the graces of colloquy with the graces of rhetoric. It is essentially eloquent, and it is an eloquence which is, to employ his own happy illustration, like a stream fed by an abundant spring—an eloquence which never flags, which is never inappropriate, which never palls. His fertility of expression is wonderful. Over all the resources of our noble and opulent language his mastery is at once exquisite and unlimited. Of effort and elaboration his style shows no traces. His ideas seem to clothe themselves spontaneously in their rich and varied garb. He had studied, as few Englishman of that day had studied, the masterpieces of French literature, but no taint of Gallicism mars the transcendent purity of his English. His pages are a storehouse of fine and graceful images, of felicitous phrases, of new and striking combinations. As an essayist he is not inferior to his master, Seneca. As a political satirist he is second only to Junius. As a letter-writer he ranks with

Pliny and Cicero, and we cannot but regret that so large a portion of his correspondence is still permitted to remain unpublished. On English prose his influence was immediate and permanent. It would not indeed be too much to say that it owes more to Bolingbroke than to any other single writer.—COLLINS, JOHN CHURTON, 1886, *Bolingbroke, A Historical Study, and Voltaire in England, p.* 15.

Bolingbroke is seen at his best, I think, in his "Letter to Sir William Wyndham" (1752), which may be described as a chapter of autobiographical apologetics. But is he read now-a-days? Is he worth reading (except, of course, to the historical student)? His admirers are obliged to concede that, if he be read, it must be for the *manner* not the *matter*, the *style* not the *thought;* for his historical essays are "thin" in the extreme; his idea of "a Patriot King" is simply that of a patriarchal despot; and his attacks on Christianity would win no approving smile from a modern agnostic. As for his philosophy, you will find it in its most agreeable form in Pope's "Essay on Man." I am not sure that there is very much even in his style. It is unrelieved by felicitous images, and is seldom enriched by happy terms of expression; all that can be said of it is, that it flows easily and clearly, like a pellucid but shallow stream; that in attack it is generally animated, and in defence often dignified. As a man of letters, Bolingbroke owned his whilom reputation to his conspicuousness as a statesman; and as a statesman his influence largely depended, I think, on the attractiveness of his brilliant, restless, wayward, and ambitious personality.—ADAMS, W. H. DAVENPORT, 1886, *Good Queen Anne, vol.* II, *p.* 168.

There is no doubt that, with the exception of the views expressed in "The Patriot King," his ideas died with him. The slight influence exercised by his many writings after his death seems to prove the possession on his part of an immensely strong will. . . . Of the statesmen who are no longer with us there is no name more intimately connected with literature than that of Bolingbroke. There has certainly been no English statesman whose influence, whether for good or for evil, on the whole train of thought and consequently on the productions of two such men as dissimilar as were Pope and Voltaire, has been more marked. A very delightful volume might be written upon Bolingbroke as a man of letters. In an age singularly fertile in prose writers, who were remarkable for the elegance and lucidity of their style, Bolingbroke more than held his own. In an age distinguished for the production of exquisite skill in versification, Bolingbroke was considered competent to revise the proofs of one of the most renowned poems of the greatest master of style in the eighteenth century. In an age when epistolary correspondence, much of which were still regarded as models of letter-writing, was the fashion, Bolingbroke's letters will bear comparison with the correspondence of Lady Mary Montague or with the letters of Pope. The patron of struggling authors, the friend and protector of Dryden, the intimate friend and companion of Pope, Voltaire, and Swift, an author of some of the most interesting political disquisitions ever written, Bolingbroke will be handed down to posterity as a distinguished member of that brotherhood of literary statesmen which includes such men as Burke and Canning, and in our own day has seen added to its ranks Lord Beaconsfield and Mr. John Morley, Lord Iddesleigh and Mr. Gladstone.—HASSALL, ARTHUR, 1889, *Life of Viscount Bolingbroke (Statesmen Series), pp,* 175, 181.

He handled the great and difficult Instrument of written language with such freedom and copiousness, such vivacity and ease, that in spite of much literary foppery and falsetto, he ranks in all that musicians call execution, only below the three or four highest masters of English prose. Yet of all the characters in our history Bolingbroke must be pronounced to be most of a charlatan; of all the writing in our literature, his is the hollowest, the flashiest, the most insincere.—MORLEY, JOHN, 1889, *Walpole, p.* 79.

The first George, though wholly illiterate, yet took it upon himself to despise Bolingbroke, philosopher though he was, and dismissed an elaborate effusion of his as "*les bagatelles.*" Here again the phrase sticks, and not even the beautiful type and lordly margins of Mallet's edition of Lord Bolingbroke's writings, or the stately periods of that nobleman himself, can drive the royal verdict out of my ears. There is nothing real about these writings save their colossal impudence.—BIRRELL, AUGUSTINE, 1894, *Essays about Men, Women and Books, p.* 24.

It may freely be granted that Bolingbroke's style is in some respects vicious; that, as Mr. Gosse says, it is "grandiloquent, and yet ineffectual." These faults affect unfavourably the emphasis of his paragraph; and yet, after every deduction, Bolingbroke is distinctly a modern paragrapher. He knows the value of the short sentence, though he does not use it freely enough. Only 13 per cent. of his sentences fall below the length of 15 words; yet he alternates long propositions and short onos, with telling effect. The unity of his paragraphs is generally unassailable. He looks to the transition between sentences, and, what was then more rare, to the transition between paragraphs. He balances sentences, sometimes to windy lengths, but does not let the coherence seriously suffer. He carefully eschews connectives, indeed rather too carefully. Above all he *depends* more on the paragraph than do his predecessors. He is always making sentences that are unintelligible except in the light of the larger unit. He delights, as Macaulay does, in a preliminary generalization so sweeping and so indefinite as to require a multitude of subsequent propositions to unravel the puzzle. He has deliberately adopted the paragraph unit, and it is evident that from the study of him some of the best English paragraphists, notably Burke and Macaulay, have their cue, slight as that cue is.—LEWIS, EDWIN HERBERT, 1894, *The History of the English Paragraph, p.* 113.

Bolingbroke is one of the few men whose literary reputation has probably been enhanced by the fact that he is rarely read. . . . When from this career we turn to the literary achievement, the glamour is stript off. We cannot deny to him many high literary gifts. His prose style has the easy flow, the rotund and grandiloquent sound, which the habit of the orator gives. His arguments are always specious and often at first presentation persuasive. He sets forth his case with a wonderful harmony of illusion, even when that case is most palpably a perversion of the truth. He maintains without faltering or hesitation an attitude of proud and dignified patriotism, founded upon the fundamental principles of a consistent political creed: and we have only to think of his actual career to estimate the consummate skill of the actor in so doing. His display of reading—much of it necessarily superficial—has all the manner of one careless how he draws upon an inexhaustible store: and yet without a doubt, Bolingbroke relied upon his tact alone in skimming over the thinnest of ice in his copious allusions, and in affecting profound learning. But if his style is easy and flowing it is also tiresome in its tautology. His flowing sentences weary us by their lack of variety, and by the entire absence of the illustration which fancy or imagination might have brought to them. Above all he wants entirely that saving gift of humour which brightens literary controversies and keeps their savour fresh when the subjects have passed into oblivion. Against the approach of such humour Bolingbroke's egotism and affectation set an impenetrable bar. He has not even that literary instinct which enabled such a man as Temple to refresh his reader by digressing into devious ways, and lingering on his road to give his imagination play.—CRAIK, HENRY, 1894, *English Prose, vol.* III, *pp.* 557, 559.

Bolingbroke, perhaps, may be left us, but it is impossible to be very thankful for Bolingbroke. That he was a great orator seems certain, though we have, as in the case of all English parliamentary orators till Burke, next to nothing to prove or disprove the fact. That in his brilliant youth he fascinated and dazzled men of letters from Dryden to Pope, is unquestionable. That he must have had some strange magnetism, as after times have called it, to account for his triumph over the services of Marlborough, the prudery of Anne, the practised wiles of Harley, may be taken for granted. His own day thought him great as a master of philosophy and of style. But a famous sentence, "Who now reads Bolingbroke?" shows how soon this glamour lost its effect; and though several attempts (mostly due to the whimsical fancy of Lord Beaconsfield for him) have of late been made to revive his fame, they have all failed. Nay, most of those who have begun to bless him have ended, if not exactly by cursing, yet with that faint praise the sense of which his adoring friend and bard knew so well. The fact is that whatever Bolingbroke may have been in his youth, before that Tory *débâcle* which his greed of power and party spirit did much to bring about, he was later very much of a sham. His Deism, picked up in France, was utterly shallow; his philosophy, in so far as it was not mere fashionable "philosophism," was shallower still; and his very style was pinchbeck, French polish, veneer — not true metal or solid wood.—SAINTSBURY, GEORGE, 1896, *Social England, ed. Traill, vol.* V, *p.* 84.

It has often been remarked that his writings are substantially orations. Their style has been greatly admired. Chesterfield calls the style "infinitely superior to any one's." Chatham advises his nephew to get Bolingbroke by heart, for the inimitable beauty of his style as well as for the matter. The style, however, does not prevent them from being now exceedingly tiresome, except to persons of refined tastes. The causes are plain. His political theories are the outcome not of real thought, but of the necessities of his political relations. He was in a false position through life. . . . He emits brilliant flashes of perception rather than any steady light, and fails in the attempt to combine philosophical tone with personal ends. His dignified style, his familiarity with foreign politics, and with history especially as regarded by a diplomatist mainly interested in the balance of power, impressed his contemporaries. But his dignity prevents him from rivalling Swift's hard hitting, on the one hand, while his philosophy is too thin on the other to bear a comparison with Burke. —STEPHEN, LESLIE, 1897, *Dictionary of National Biography, vol.* L, *pp.* 142, 143.

Philip Doddridge

1702–1751

Philip Doddridge, D. D., a celebrated dissenting (Independent) divine, and writer of hymns; son of a merchant, and last of twenty children; was born in London June 26, 1702; died at Lisbon Oct. 26, 1751. From infancy he was of infirm constitution. He enjoyed the instructions of pious parents, and early turned his attentions to the ministry. He was first settled at Kibworth in 1723. In 1729 he became assistant at Harborough, and head of an academy by the choice of a general meeting of dissenting ministers. The same year he was called to Northampton: he here continued his activity as teacher, and was very successful. He was forced, by the rapid development of consumptive tendencies, to seek for health in a milder climate. He went to Lisbon, where he died, and lies buried in the English graveyard. . . . Among his works, the most important are "Life of Colonel Gardiner," "The Family Expositor," "A Commentary on the New Testament" (which became a household work in England), and "The Rise and Progress of Religion in the Soul" (1745), which he wrote at the suggestion of Dr. Watts. With the "Pilgrim's Progress," Henry's "Commentary," and Alleine's "Alarm," it has been more extensively used as a stimulus to piety than any other work in the English language. As an author of hymns he was very prolific. Among the more favorite ones are, "Awake, my soul, stretch every nerve," and "Grace, 'tis a charming sound!"—SCHAFF-HERZOG, *eds.*, 1882, *Religious Encyclopaedia, vol.* I, *p.* 652.

PERSONAL

Preached in Dr. Doddridge's pulpit, and the sight of his monument with a very significant inscription, struck my mind with uncommon energy. The congregation is decreased since the doctor's death, as they can find none to supply his place fully. Monday, went in company with Mr. Warburton and Mr. Wilkinson to make private applications among the people, and received about sixteen pounds, of which Mrs. Doddridge procured me three guineas. Dined with her, and found her conversation animated with good sense and piety. She remembered me as a correspondent of the "dear deceased," as she calls the doctor, and treated me with uncommon friendship. I was surprised that she could talk of him with so much composure, notwithstanding her flowing affections. She told me "she never had a more comfortable season, than when returning from Lisbon, on the boisterous ocean, after the doctor's death."—DAVIES, SAMUEL, 1754, *Diary, Aug.* 11.

He had an earnestness and pathos in his manner of speaking, which, as it seemed to be the natural effect of a strong impression of divine truths upon his own heart, tended greatly to affect his hearers, and to render his discourses more acceptable and useful, than if his delivery had been more calm and dispassionate.—ORTON, JOB, 1766, *Memoirs of Rev. Philip Doddridge.*

We mean to say nothing against the doctor's reputation. His fondness was kept within legal bounds, and only overflowed in a double stream of benevolence towards the fair sex,—in a pleasing mixture of piety and gayety,—a double wish to please and to be pleased. But the public were amused to see a name, which had hitherto partaken, however mildly, of the common gloom in which Dissenters stand with the world, suddenly invested with a radiance of gallantry and hilarity, as if Venus had taken an arch pleasure in throwing a light upon him from the clouds, and showing that doctors are men. . . . Dr. Doddridge was an amiable man, of a sprightly blood, and of a hectic temperament, which ultimately threw him into a consumption. His views were too cheerful for his doctrines, which he was accused of accommodating to different companies; that is to say, his charity predominated, and he found out, in his various texts, something to enliven everybody he came nigh. Men of other complexions, who were uneasy with themselves, preached from uneasy texts: he took up the cheerful ones, and made everybody grateful wherever he went, talking to the old of Methusaleh, and comparing the ladies to Eve in Paradise. Accordingly he was adored by all classes and ages. Doors flew open to receive him; men pressed his hands; old ladies fell in love with him, and young ladies, who were not allowed to fall in love, beatified his wife, and wrought ornaments for her person.—HUNT, LEIGH, 1830, *Dr. Doddridge and the Ladies, Wishing-Cap Papers.*

What was the secret of Dr. Doddridge's great success? He had not the rhetoric of Bates, the imagination of Bunyan, nor the massive theology of Owen; and yet his preaching and his publications were as useful as theirs. . . . He was an excellent teacher. At a glance he saw every thing which could simplify his subject, and he had self-denial sufficient to forego those good things which would only encumber it. Hence, like his college lectures, his sermons were continuous and straightforward, and his hearers had the comfort of accompanying him to a goal which they and he constantly kept in view.—HAMILTON, J., 1851, *Philip Doddridge, North British Review, vol.* 14, *p.* 364.

Doddridge was an able and faithful instructor; and by his efficient management, his theological seminary became very flourishing. His course of lectures in the academy embraced a wide range; comprising the ancient classics, French, English literature, geography, moral and natural philosophy, rhetoric, logic, geometry, algebra, trigonometry, conic sections, history, Jewish antiquities, Hebrew, theology, preaching, and the pastoral care. He manifested a great concern for the intellectual, moral, and religious attainments of his students. Besides his daily instructions and counsels to them, he allowed them access to his choice private library, giving them, at the same time, suitable directions respecting the books they should read. It was his earnest desire that his students, on leaving his academy, should not only exhibit a high degree of intellectual culture, but also that fervent piety and active benevolence, which would constrain them to consecrate their lives to the service and glory of God. . . . The remains of Doddridge were interred in the English cemetery at Lisbon, where his grave still remains, and "like Henry Martyn's at Tocat, is to the Christian traveler a little spot of holy ground." A plain monument was first raised over his grave, which in the course of time became decayed. In 1828, the Rev. Thomas Taylor caused a new marble tomb to be erected, with the following inscription: "Philip Doddridge, D. D., died October 26, 1751, aged 50." To this is added: "With high respect for his character and writings, this stone of remembrance was raised upon a former one in decay, in the month of June, 1828, at the desire and expense of Thomas Taylor, of all his numerous pupils the only one living" . . . Dr. Doddridge was of a tall and very slender form, having large features, and a cheerful countenance.

His disposition was amiable; he was extremely kind and full of sympathy; and his manners were easy, agreeable, and courteous. His conversational powers were excellent, his discourse "being at once instructive and entertaining, and not unfrequently rising to the splendid." When engaged in conversation, his countenance was remarkably animated. As a preacher, Doddridge possessed some qualities which rendered his discourses popular, weighty and effective. Graceful and vehement in his gestures, strong and impressive in his language, earnest and pathetic in his address, he was well adapted to instruct the ignorant, to persuade the unbelieving, to arouse the careless, and console the faithful. His vivacity of countenance and manner while in the pulpit, secured the attention of his audience.—HARSHA, D. A., 1864, *Life of Philip Doddridge, pp.* 94, 165, 174.

Doddridge's equipment for the work of his academy was serviceable rather than profound. He had a great and discriminating knowledge of books. Wesley consulted him on a course of reading for young preachers, and received a very detailed reply (18 June 1746). He knew and understood his public; his influence on his pupils was stimulating and liberalising. Doddridge made the use of shorthand, already common, imperative, adapting the system of Jeremie Rich. Each student carried away a full transcript in shorthand of his lectures, as well as of illustrative extracts. The mathematical form of his lectures (in philosophy and divinity), with the neat array of definitions, propositions, and corollaries, was borrowed from Jennings. Jennings, however, lectured in Latin; Doddridge was one of the first to introduce the practice of lecturing in English.—GORDON, ALEXANDER, 1888, *Dictionary of National Biography, vol.* XV, *p.* 161.

THE FAMILY EXPOSITOR

One part of Dr. Doddridge's "Family Expositor," which must have cost him uncommon pains, was his having everywhere interwoven the text with the paraphrase, and carefully distinguished the former from the latter by the Italic character. By his method it is impossible to read the paraphrase without the text; and every one may immediately see, not only the particular clause to which any explication answers, but, also, what are the words of the original, and what merely the sense of the commentator. Nor was our author content with barely inserting the old translation, but gave an entire new version of the whole Testament, the merit and usefulness of which will in many respects be acknowledged. This translation was extracted from the paraphrase, and published in 1765, in two volumes 12mo, with some alterations and improvements by the editor, together with an introduction, and a number of very short notes.—KIPPIS, ANDREW, 1793, *Biographia Britannica.*

Of a book so well known and so generally esteemed as the "Family Expositor," it is scarcely necessary to speak. It is admirably adapted to the object which the author had chiefly in view; and no book can be read in a Christian family with more advantage. . . . The translation frequently corrects the received version; but the paraphrase is often too diffuse, and in the notes he sometimes discovers an anxiety to press a fine thought into the meaning of the sacred writer. His "Harmony," which must have cost him great labour, is often unsatisfactory, has too many transpositions, and is not so judicious in the arrangement as Macknight's.—ORME, WILLIAM, 1824, *Bibliotheca Biblica.*

The "Family Expositor" of Doddridge, should find a place upon the shelf, and upon the table, of every mansion where the moral duties of a christian are enjoined. Doddridge's heart was made up of all the kindlier affections of our nature; and was wholly devoted to the salvation of men's souls. Whatever he did, he appears to have done "to the glory of God." He read, he wrote, he preached —with a zeal, which knew of no abatement, and with an earnestness, which left no doubt of the sincerity of his motives. —DIBDIN, THOMAS FROGNALL, 1824, *The Library Companion, p.* 64.

All works of this kind are at length superseded to a certain extent by others; but if this commentary is at all set aside, it is not from any want of erudition, diligence, or hermeneutical skill and acumen. It still remains a monument to the care, studious toil, and ardent piety of the author; and in regard to the historical books, we are not prepared to say, after all that has been written, that there is even now any single work which we would place before it. This remark we make with some deliberation, after almost weekly resort for many years of parochial exposition, and with a distinct reference, not so much to the popular and devotional, as the strictly learned portions. Measured with respect to the *apparatus biblicus* of the time, Doddridge's Notes remain among the most valuable scholia which we possess on these portions of Scripture; and his suggestions and even conjectures have been confirmed by modern research and comparison as frequently as those of any writer. If sometimes he gives too much place and honour by citations to writers of mediocrity, whose books have not survived, the fault may be forgiven by any one who looks at the catena of hard but perishable German names, adduced by such gatherers after the learned host as Davidson.—ALEXANDER, J. W., 1857, *Writings of Doddridge, Princeton Review, vol.* 29, *p.* 250.

His "Family Expositor," of which the first volume appeared in 1739, is a didactic commment on the New Testament, suited to the taste of a past generation, but too colourless and diffuse to be of permanent value.—GORDON, ALEXANDER, 1888, *Dictionary of National Biography, vol.* XV, *p.* 162.

THE RISE AND PROGRESS OF RELIGION IN THE SOUL
1745

I have no need to give you a large account of his knowledge in the sciences, in which I confess him to be greatly my superior, and as to the doctrines of divinity and the gospel of Christ, I know not any man of greater skill than himself, and hardly one sufficient to be his second. . . . If you have read that excellent performance of his, the "Rise and Progress, &c.," you will be of my mind.—WATTS, ISAAC, c1746, *Letter to Rev. Mr. Longueville.*

I may with truth assure you, that I never was so deeply affected with anything I ever met with as with that book; and I could not be easy till I had given one to every servant in my house.—SOMERSET, DUCHESS OF, 1747, *Letter to Doddridge.*

The religious genius of Doddridge is seen at its best in the powerful addresses which make up his volume "On the Rise and Progress of Religion in the Soul," 1745. This work was planned and prompted by Isaac Watts, who revised a portion of it. Its popularity has been steadily maintained; it has been rendered into a great variety of languages, including Tamil and Syriac.—GORDON, ALEXANDER, 1888, *Dictionary of National Biography, vol.* XV, *p.* 162.

HYMNS

In the number of hymns contributed, Doddridge stands third in the list of contributors to the "New Congregational Hymn Book," having supplied fifty hymns. Like all his other works, they are marked by their self-forgetful devotion to the high cause he served. As hymns, many of them are not above mediocrity, but some are of a high order, and others have some special excellencies. As one thoroughly familiar with the various public occasions in the history of Congregational Churches, Doddridge provided several very useful hymns for such occasions.—MILLER, JOSIAH, 1866, *Our Hymns, p.*117.

Doddridge's hymns have a character of their own. He had not the poetical genius with which his friend Isaac Watts was endowed, and which he so fully appreciated. None of his own metrical compositions have the grandeur of certain psalms and hymns written by him who has been called "the Poet of the Sanctuary." But there is a sweetness and tenderness in Doddridge's versification on devotional subjects, in admirable harmony with his amiable character, which has made him a favourite with all denominations, and has given him a place in the hymnology of English Christendom which he is not likely to lose.—STOUGHTON, JOHN, 1867–81, *History of Religion in England from the Opening of the Long Parliament to the End of the Eighteenth Century, vol.* VI, *p.* 94.

Doddridge deserves our tribute, also, as "the sweet lyrist of God's people." Has he not given voice to the most cherished emotions of the soul? Has he not been with us on our covenant days, and, with exquisite pathos, bid

> The glowing heart rejoice,
> And tell its raptures all abroad.

—SAUNDERS, FREDERICK, 1875, *Evenings with the Sacred Poets, p.* 297.

Beyond all question, the name of Doddridge is to be classed with the names of the most honored of the Poets of the Sanctuary,—Watts, Wesley, Steele, Newton, Cowper, and Kelly—names that will never die.—HATFIELD, EDWIN F., 1884, *The Poets of the Church*, p. 201.

Of the hymns themselves, many, . . . have undergone material alterations before they could be generally adopted. They frequently drop from great heights of pure devotion into prosaic or commonplace expressions. Yet they are so thoroughly excellent in spirit, and oftentimes so admirable in phraseology, that they are indispensable to any collection of sacred verse. They belong with the deepest experiences of the Christian life, and can never be omitted or neglected.—DUFFIELD, SAMUEL WILLOUGHBY, 1886, *English Hymns*, p. 364.

GENERAL

May I remember that I am not to compose an harangue, to acquire to myself the reputation of an eloquent orator, but that I am preparing food for precious and immortal souls, and dispensing the sacred gospel which my Redeemer brought from heaven and sealed with His Blood.—DODDRIDGE, PHILIP, 1742, *The Evil and Danger of Neglecting Men's Souls.*

It gave the author singular pleasure to know that these sermons were the means of convincing two gentlemen, of a liberal education, and distinguished abilities, that Christianity was true and divine; and one of them became a zealous preacher, and an ornament of the religion he had once denied and despised.—MIDDLETON, ERASMUS, 1779–86, *Biographia Evangelica.*

His character and writings will long continue to be revered and honoured by all who prefer scriptural truth to human systems.—MORRELL, REV. T., 1839, *ed. Doddridge's Miscellaneous Works.*

Much may be learned from this learned and devout writer: he has many judicious criticisms on different authors; but there is a tone of excessive candour, bordering upon Latitudinarianism, especially in giving too great weight to objections, when treating upon the Evidences and Doctrines. His criticisms on theological writers in his preaching Lectures, not duly respecting Evangelical Doctrine, fail in discrimination.—BICKERSTETH, EDWARD, 1844, *The Christian Student.*

He is always perspicuous, but often at the cost of energy; and generally harmonious, yet in a sort of inelegant way. We know not how to indicate a fault constantly appearing in his style, and that of other Dissenters of that day, otherwise than by saying it is inordinately genteel. Many turns of expression which temporarily floated on the surface of elegant parlance, are incorporated into his works, and now appear undignified, if not ridiculous. Yet there are occasions upon which his native genius and familiarity with good authors got the better of this mannerism, and produced a diction both beautiful and expressive. And it is beyond a question, that his mode of conveying religious truth was so acceptable in his own time, as to gain the attention of many to sacred subjects, who would otherwise have treated them with disgust.—ALEXANDER, J. W., 1857, *Writings of Doddridge, Princeton Review, vol.* 29, *p.* 256.

He removed to Market Harborough in 1729, and there opened an Academy, and was ordained pastor over the Church in Castle Hill Meeting House, Northampton, in 1730. The four volumes of sermons printed from his MSS. afford a sample of his preaching in that place. In matter evangelical, in arrangement lucid, in imagery tasteful, in diction perspicuous, they must have secured attention and excited interest. Never very great, they were always very good; reminding one of English valleys full of cornfields, gardens, and brooks of water.—STOUGHTON, JOHN, 1867–81, *History of Religion in England, from the Opening of the Long Parliament to the End of the Eighteenth Century, vol.* VI, *p.* 93.

The solid learning, unquestioned piety, and true catholic liberality and benevolence of Dr. Doddridge, secured for him the warm respect and admiration of his contemporaries of all sects.—CHAMBERS, ROBERT, 1876, *Cyclopædia of English Literature, ed. Carruthers.*

His divinity lectures have nothing original, but they possess the merit of skilful selection, and an arrangement which is convenient, if artificial. The same may be said of his courses on the kindred topics of pneumatology (psychology) and ethics.—GORDON, ALEXANDER, 1888, *Dictionary of National Biography, vol.* XV, *p.* 162.

William Whiston

1667-1752

William Whiston, seceder from the Church of England; born at Norton, Leicestershire, Dec. 9, 1667; died in London, Aug. 22, 1752. He graduated at Clare Hall, Cambridge, 1690; became fellow, 1693; chaplain to Bishop Moore, of Norwich, 1694-98; Lowestoft, 1698-1701; then deputy of Sir Isaac Newton, whom he succeeded, 1703, as Lucasian professor of mathematics at Cambridge; expelled, 1710, for Arianism, avowed in an essay on the "Apostolical Constitutions," London, 1708, and persistently maintained by him as the faith of the early church. This essay he reprinted in his "Primitive Christianity Revived," 1711-12, 5 vols. The rest of his life was spent in London, writing, lecturing, and preaching in his own house. He imbibed Baptist and Millenarian tenets, but did not leave the church till 1747, and then as a protest against the Athanasian Creed. He was a model of honesty and disinterestedness, but wayward, erratic, obstinate, intolerant, and violently prejudiced, especially against the memory of Athanasius, whom one of his books (1712) held "Convicted of Forgery." "Paradoxical to the verge of craziness," he spent his life in constant controversy and industrious efforts to propagate his peculiar opinions. His most valuable works are the translation of Josephus, 1737, and a "Life of Dr. Samuel Clarke," 1730. His autobiography appeared in 3 vols., 1749-50.—BIRD, FREDERIC MAYER, 1889-91, *Concise Dictionary of Religious Knowledge and Gazetteer, ed. Jackson, p.* 965.

PERSONAL

Think of a man, who had brilliant preferment within his reach, dragging his poor wife and daughter for half a century through the very mire of despondency and destitution, because he disapproved of Athanasius, or because the "Shepherd of Hermas" was not sufficiently esteemed by the Church of England! Unhappy is that family over which a fool presides. The secret of all Whiston's lunacies may be found in that sentence of his Autobiography, where he betrays the fact of his liability, from youth upwards, to flatulency. What he mistook for conscience was flatulence, which others (it is well known) have mistaken for inspiration. This was his original misfortune: his second was, that he lived before the age of powerful drastic journals. Had he been contemporary with Christopher North, the knout would have brought him to his sense, and extorted the gratitude of Mrs. Whiston and her children.—DE QUINCEY, THOMAS, 1830, *Monk's Life of Bentley, Blackwood's Magazine, vol.* 28, *p.* 451, *note.*

I may add to what precedes that it cannot be settled that, as Granger says, Desaguliers was the first who gave experimental lectures in London. William Whiston gave some, and Francis Hauksbee made the experiments. The prospectus, as we should now call it, is extant, a quarto tract of plates and descriptions, without date. Whiston, in his life, gives 1714 as the first date of publication, and therefore, no doubt, of the lectures. Desaguliers removed to London soon after 1712, and commenced his lectures soon after that. It will be rather a nice point to settle which lectured first; probabilities seem to go in favour of Whiston.—DE MORGAN, AUGUSTUS, 1871-72, *A Budget of Paradoxes, p.* 93.

In Queen Anne's reign his search for a primitive Christianity affected his theology, and brought on him loss of his means of life in the church and university. He taught science; lived, as a poor man, a long and blameless life, until his death, in 1752; and in his writings blended love of nature with the love of God.—MORLEY, HENRY, 1879, *A Manual of English Literature, ed. Tyler, p.* 555.

Whiston was one of the first, if not the first person, to give lectures with experiments in London. He co-operated in some of them with the elder Francis Hauksbee. The first, upon astronomy, were given at Button's coffee-house by the help of Addison and Steele, both of whom he knew well. He amused great men by his frank rebukes. He asked Steele one day how he could speak for the Southsea directors after writing against them. Steele replied, "Mr. Whiston, you can walk on foot and I cannot." When he suggested to Craggs that honesty might be the best policy, Craggs replied that a statesman might be honest for a fortnight, but that it would not do for a month.

Whiston asked him whether he had ever tried for a fortnight. Whiston's absolute honesty was admitted by his contemporaries, whom he disarmed by his simplicity. . . . Whiston belonged to a familiar type as a man of very acute but ill-balanced intellect. His learning was great, however fanciful his theories, and he no doubt helped to call attention to important points in ecclesiastical history. The charm of his simple-minded honesty gives great interest to his autobiography; though a large part of it is occupied with rather tiresome accounts of his writings and careful directions for their treatment by the future republishers, who have not yet appeared. In many respects he strongly resembles the Vicar of Wakefield, who adopted his principles of monogamy. His condemnation of Hoadly upon that and other grounds is in the spirit of Dr. Primrose. It is not improbable that Whiston was more or less in Goldsmith's mind when he wrote his masterpiece.—STEPHEN, LESLIE, 1900, *Dictionary of National Biography, vol.* LXI, *pp.* 11, 13.

GENERAL

The honest, pious, visionary Whiston.—GIBBON, EDWARD, 1776–78, *Decline and Fall of the Roman Empire, ch.* xliii, *note.*

This book ["Short View of Chronology of Old Testament"] partakes largely of the wildness, as well as of the learning, of Whiston, and is now of little importance. . . . The Memoirs of this singular man, published by himself, contain some curious information respecting his times, and afford a view of great honesty and disinterestedness, combined with an extraordinary degree of superstition and love of the marvellous.—ORME, WILLIAM, 1824, *Bibliotheca Biblica, p.* 467.

This admirable translation ["Josephus"] far exceeds all preceding ones, and had never been equalled by any subsequent attempt of this kind.—LOWNDES, WILLIAM THOMAS, 1834, *The Bibliographer's Manual of English Literature, vol.* II, *p.* 1045.

Whiston opposed Burnet's theory, but with one ["New Theory of the Earth"] not less unfounded, nor with less ignorance of all that required to be known.—HALLAM, HENRY, 1837–39, *Introduction to the Literature of Europe, pt.* iv, *ch.* viii, *par.* 32.

Much useful information in this Essay, ["Short View"] but fanciful.—BICKERSTETH, EDWARD, 1844, *The Christian Student.*

Poor Whiston, who believed in every thing but the Trinity.—MACAULAY, THOMAS BABINGTON, 1849, *History of England, ch.* xiv, *note.*

A host of speculators, headed by the eloquent Thomas Burnet and the eccentric William Whiston, both men of genius and learning, but of more fancy than either judgment or knowledge of the subjects which in this instance they undertook to discuss, produced in the last years of the seventeenth and the first of the eighteenth century many theories of the earth, which explained not only its structure, but its origin and its destiny,—in other words, its whole history, past, present, and future,—as well as such a task could be accomplished by the imagination working without materials, and without the aid of any other faculty.—CRAIK, GEORGE L., 1861, *A Compendious History of English Literature and of the English Language, vol.* II, *p.* 184.

Whiston's theological works are now almost forgotten, and he is remembered almost exclusively by his translation of Josephus. This translation has gone through a number of editions, and is still much read, although superseded by the work of Dr. Robert Traill.—HART, JOHN S., 1872, *A Manual of English Literature, p.* 245.

Had he confined himself to mathematical studies, he would have earned a high name in science; but his time and attention were dissipated by his theological pursuits, in which he evinced more zeal than judgment, &c.—CHAMBERS, ROBERT, 1876, *Cyclopædia of English Literature, ed. Carruthers.*

Yet we feel for him something of the pitying kindness which he generally excited in his contemporaries. With a childlike simplicity worthy of the Vicar of Wakefield, he was ready to sacrifice all his prospects rather than disavow or disguise a tittle of his creed. Had that creed been one of greater significance, disciples would have revered him as a worthy martyr, and adversaries regarded him as dangerous in proportion to his virtue. Unluckily it was a creed untenable by any man of sound intellect. It was filled with queer crotchets picked up in various byways of learning, and valued by the collector in proportion to their oddity. Friends and opponents—for he had no enemies—regarded his absurdities with a pitying smile, and were glad to see him pick up a harmless living by giving astronomical lectures and publishing pamphlets on a vast variety of subjects.—STEPHEN, LESLIE, 1876, *History of English Thought in the Eighteenth Century, vol.* I, *p.* 212.

Whiston, notwithstanding the vagaries which characterised his "Theory of the Earth" (an attempt to harmonise the Bible and the Newtonian discoveries), discharged his duties as Lucasian professor with credit, even though appearing as the successor of Newton.—MULLINGER, J. BASS, 1888, *A History of the University of Cambridge, p.* 169.

Joseph Butler

1692-1752

Born, at Wantage, 18 May 1692. Educated at Wantage Latin School, and at Dissenting School at Gloucester and Tewkesbury. To Oriel Coll., Oxford, March 1715; B. A., 11 Oct. 1718; B. C. L., 10 June 1721. Ordained Deacon at Salisbury, Oct. 1718; Priest, Dec. 1718. Preacher at Rolls Chapel, July 1719 to autumn of 1726. Prebendary of Salisbury, 1721. Rector of Houghton-le-Skerne, near Darlington, 1722. Rector of Stanhope in Weardale, 1725. Lived secluded life, mainly occupied in writing "Analogy," published 1736. Chaplain to Lord Talbot, 1733. D. C. L., Oxford, 8 Dec. 1733. Prebendary of Rochester, and Clerk of Closet to Queen Caroline, July 1736. Bishop of Bristol, Aug. 1738. Continued to hold Rochester prebend and Stanhope rectorship till appointed Dean of St. Paul's, 24 May 1740. Clerk of Closet to King, 1746. Bishop of Durham, July 1750. To Bristol and Bath for health. Died, at Bath, 16 June 1752. Buried in Bristol Cathedral. *Works:* "Several Letters to the Rev. Dr. Clarke, from a Gentleman in Gloucestershire" (anon.), 1716; "Letters of Thanks from a Young Clergyman to the Rev. Dr. Hare" (anon.), 1719; "Fifteen Sermons," 1726; "The Analogy of Religion," 1736; "Sermons preached before the Society for Propagating the Gospel," 1739; "Sermon preached before the Lord Mayor," 1740; "Sermon preached before the House of Lords," 1741; "Sermon preached at the annual meeting of the Charity Children," 1745; "Sermon preached before the House of Lords," 1747; "Sermon preached before the Governors of the London Infirmary," 1748; Visitation Charge at Durham, 1751. *Posthumous:* "Some Remains, hitherto unpublished," ed. by E. Steere, 1853. *Collected Works:* ed. by Dr. Kippis, 1804; ed. by Rt. Hon. W. E. Gladstone (2 vols.), 1896. *Life:* by T. Bartlett, 1839; by Samuel Butler, 1896.—SHARP, R. FARQUHARSON, 1897, *A Dictionary of English Authors, p.* 43.

PERSONAL

H. S.
REVERENDUS ADMODUM IN CHRISTO PATER
JOSEPHUS BUTLER, LL. D.
HUJUSCE PRIMO DIŒCESEOS
DEINDE DUNELMENSIS EPISCOPUS.
QUALIS QUANTUSQUE, VIR ERAT
SUA LIBENTISSIMO AGNOVIT ETAS;
ET SI QUID PRÆSULI AUT SCRIPTORI AD FAMAM VALENT
MENS ALTISSIMA, INGENII PERSPICACIS ET SUBACTI VIS
ANIMUSQUE PIUS SIMPLEX CANDIDUS LIBERALIS
MORTUI HAUD FACILE EVANESCET MEMORIA.
OBIIT BATHONIÆ
XVI KAL. JUL. A. D. 1752,
ANNOS NATUS 60.

—FORSTER, NATHANIEL? 1752, *Original Inscription on Tomb, Bristol Cathedral.*

He was my father's friend. I could almost say my remembrance of him goes back some years before I was born, from the lively imagery which the conversations I used to hear in my earliest years have imprinted on my mind. But from the first of my real remembrance, I have ever known in him the kind affectionate friend, the faithful adviser, which he would condescend to when I was quite a child; and the most delightful companion, from a delicacy of thinking, an extreme politeness, a vast knowledge of the world, and a something peculiar to be met with in nobody else. And all this in a man whose sanctity of manners, and sublimity of genius, gave him one of the first ranks among men, long before he was raised to that rank in the world, which must still, if what I painfully fear should

JOSEPH BUTLER.

From the Picture by Vanderbank.

JOHN ARBUTHNOT.

From a Painting in the Possession of the Royal College of Physicians.

happen, aggravate such a loss, as one cannot but infinitely regret the good which such a mind in such a station must have done.—TALBOT, CATHERINE, 1752, *Letter, June* 13.

His life in presence of his God consumed,
Like the bright lamps before the holy shrine.
His aspect pleasing, mind with learning fraught,
His eloquence was like a chain of gold,
That the wild passions of mankind controlled.
—ANON, 1754, *London Magazine, May.*

He was of a most reverend aspect; his face thin and pale; but there was a divine placidness in his countenance which inspired veneration, and expressed the most benevolent mind. His white hair, hung gracefully on his shoulders, and his whole figure was patriarchal.—HUTCHINSON, WILLIAM, 1785–94, *History and Antiquities of the County Palatinate of Durham, vol.* I, *p.* 578.

During the short time that Butler held the see of Durham he conciliated all hearts. In advanced years he retained the same genuine modesty and natural sweetness of disposition which had distinguished him in youth and in retirement. During the performance of the sacred office a divine animation seemed to pervade his whole manner, and lighted up his pale, wan countenance, already marked with the progress of disease, like a torch glimmering in its socket, yet bright and useful to the last.—SURTEES, ROBERT, 1816–40, *History of Durham.*

SACRED
TO THE MEMORY OF JOSEPH BUTLER, D.C.L.,
TWELVE YEARS BISHOP OF THIS DIOCESE
AND AFTERWARDS BISHOP OF DURHAM,
WHOSE MORTAL PART IS DEPOSITED
IN THE CHOIR OF THIS CATHEDRAL.
OTHERS HAD ESTABLISHED
THE HISTORICAL AND PROPHETICAL GROUNDS
OF THE CHRISTIAN RELIGION, AND
THAT SURE TESTIMONY OF ITS TRUTH
WHICH IS FOUND IN ITS PERFECT ADAPTATION
TO THE HEART OF MAN.
IT WAS RESERVED FOR HIM TO DEVELOP
ITS ANALOGY TO THE CONSTITUTION
AND COURSE OF NATURE,
AND LAYING HIS STRONG FOUNDATIONS
IN THE DEPTH OF THAT GREAT ARGUMENT,
THERE TO CONSTRUCT
ANOTHER AND IRREFRAGABLE PROOF:
THUS RENDERING PHILOSOPHY
SUBSERVIENT TO FAITH:
AND FINDING IN OUTWARD AND VISIBLE THINGS
THE TYPE AND EVIDENCE
OF THOSE WITHIN THE VEIL.
BORN A. D., 1692, DIED 1752.
—SOUTHEY, ROBERT, 1834, *Inscription on Monument, Bristol Cathedral.*

One of these [nephews], John, a wealthy and eccentric bachelor, who had more taste for practical mechanics than for metaphysical research, appeared to attach but little value to his uncle's production. Having occasion to borrow an iron vice of his neighbour Mr. Thompson, a shrewd and sensible Scotch solicitor, who spoke in high terms of the "Analogy," and expressed great respect for the author, John Butler proposed that as Mr. Thompson liked the "Analogy," and he himself liked the iron vice, they should make an exchange. To this Mr. Thompson cheerfully assented, and John Butler left him highly pleased, and thinking that he had turned his uncle's present to an excellent account.—BARTLETT, THOMAS, 1839, *Life of Bishop Butler, p.* 95.

Of Butler's personal habits nothing in the way of detail has descended to us. He was never married, and there is no evidence of his ever having spoken to any lady save Queen Caroline. We hear, however, for certain that he was commonly present at her Majesty's philosophical parties, at which all questions, religious and moral, speculative and practical, were discussed with a freedom that would astonish the present generation.—BAGEHOT, WALTER, 1854, *Bishop Butler, Works, ed. Morgan, vol.* II, *p.* 119.

The presence of one of the crowned kings of the realm of Thought haunts one among the hills, along the river bank, all over the pleasant Parish. Joseph Butler is *the* Rector of men's memory, when Stanhope is visited or named. The glory of his fifteen years' occupancy there never can pale from it.—GROSART, ALEXANDER B., 1875, *A Visit to Stanhope, with Memorials of Bishop Butler, Leisure Hour, vol.* 24, *p.* 250.

Underneath the meagre facts of his life, eked out by the few letters left by him or anecdotes told about him, there can be traced the outlines of a great but somewhat severe spirit. He was an earnest and deep thinking Christian, melancholy by temperament, and grieved by what seemed to him the hopelessly irreligious condition of his age. His intellect was profound and comprehensive, thoroughly qualified to grapple with the deepest problems of metaphysics, but by natural preference occupying itself mainly with the practical and moral. Man's conduct in life, not his theory of the universe, was what interested him.—ADAMSON, ROBERT, 1875, *Encyclopædia Britannica, Ninth Edition, vol.* 4.

His liberality to public and private charitable objects was of almost too impulsive a character (reminding us of the tradition of his being unable to refuse a beggar), if a well-known story which was current on the subject be not rather apocryphal. A gentleman is said to have called upon him to ask his aid in some benevolent scheme which he was setting on foot. The bishop approved, and having summoned his steward, asked him how much money he had in the house? "Five hundred pounds, my lord." "Five hundred pounds!" said Butler; "what a shame for a bishop to have so much! Give it away at once—give it to this gentleman, who has a good use for it." In the exercise of the large patronage attached to his new diocese he was strictly conscientious, and took all pains to acquaint himself with the characters and deserts of his clergy. . . . Bishop Butler was a man who lived much to himself, with few intimacies, and apparently by no means a large circle of acquaintance. But there must have been much in his character that was very lovable, for the two or three who had become his friends in early life seem to have been devoted to him. To Edward Talbot's warm interest he owed, instrumentally, his success in life; and Secker watched over him, from the old schooldays to his death at Bath, with more than the tenderness of a brother. His chaplain, Dr. Forster, was much attached to him.—COLLINS, W. LUCAS, 1881, *Butler (Philosophical Classics), pp.* 26, 27.

SERMONS
1729

It must be acknowledged that some of the following Discourses are very abstruse and difficult; or, if you please, obscure; but I must take leave to add, that those alone are judges, whether or no and how far this is a fault, who are judges, whether or no and how far it might have been avoided; those only, who will be at the trouble to understand what is here said, and to see how far the things here insisted upon, and not other things, might have been put in a plainer manner; which yet I am very far from asserting that they could not.—BUTLER, JOSEPH, 1729, *Sermons, Preface; Works, ed. Gladstone, vol.* II, *p.* 4.

His great work on the "Analogy of Religion to the Course of Nature," though only a commentary on the singularly original and pregnant passage of Origen, which is so honestly prefixed to it as a motto, is notwithstanding, the most original and profound work extant in any language, on the Philosophy of Religion. It is entirely beyond our present scope. His ethical discussions are contained in those deep and sometimes dark dissertations which he preached at the Chapel of the Rolls, and afterwards published under the name of "Sermons," while he was yet fresh from the schools, and full of that courage with which youth often delights to exercise its strength in abstract reasoning, and to push its faculties into the recesses of abstruse speculation. . . . In these sermons, he has taught truths more capable of being exactly distinguished from the doctrines of his predecessors, more satisfactorily established by him, more comprehensively applied to particulars, more rationally connected with each other, and therefore more worthy of the name of *discovery*, than any with which we are acquainted; if we ought not, with some hesitation, to except the first steps of the Grecian philosophers towards a theory of morals. . . . There are few circumstances more remarkable than the small number of Butler's followers in Ethics; and it is perhaps still more observable, that his opinions were not so much rejected, as overlooked. It is an instance of the importance of style. No thinker so great was ever so bad a writer. Indeed, the ingenious apologies which have been lately attempted for this defect, amount to no more than that his power of thought was too much for his skill in language. How general must the reception have been of truths so certain and momentous as those contained in Butler's discourses—with how much more clearness must they have appeared to his own great understanding, if he had possessed the strength and distinctness with which Hobbes enforces odious falsehood, or the unspeakable charm of that transparent diction which clothed the unfruitful paradoxes of Berkeley.—MACKINTOSH, SIR JAMES, 1830, *Second Preliminary Disseration to Encyclopædia Britannica.*

In the Sermons which he published, the true foundation of morals is affirmed in the principle of the supremacy of conscience; and though overlaid for a season by the principle of expediency of Paley, which had the disastrous advantage of being recommended to the world by the most popular of writers, truth is once more beginning to show how mighty it is, and Butler's assertion of it to prevail.—BLUNT, J. J., 1839, *Life of Bishop Butler, Quarterly Review, vol.* 64, *p.* 334.

In this travailing to give birth to great thoughts conceived by the spirit, by far the most useful writer to him [Channing] was Butler, whose "Sermons on Human Nature" he regarded as unsurpassed in English for clear, full, and condensed thought, and to which may be traced, perhaps, the germs of some of his most important views.—CHANNING, WILLIAM HENRY, 1848, *Life of William Ellery Channing.*

They are philosophical rather than theological, and ought to be viewed as such. In this respect they have received the unanimous praise of great men; and one of our great seminaries of education, the University of Oxford, sets such a high value upon them, that they are used at this day as the manual of moral philosophy, and are made the subject on which students are examined. Butler is one of the four philosophers with which an exact acquaintance is required there, in all candidates for classical honours; the other three being Plato, Aristotle, and Bacon. —FARRAR, ADAM STOREY, 1862–63, *Bishop Butler, Exeter Hall Lectures, vol.* XVIII, *p.* 343.

His "Sermons on Human Nature" are also of the highest value; they proceed in the same path of reflection, and form a text-book on morals, which, putting aside schemes framed on the fitness of things and the expediency of virtue, builds a sound ethical system on a study of human nature, according to its original constitution, as discoverable through consciousness and observation. Probably, after all that has been written and said on the subject since, these sermons go as far as is possible for human thought under the guidance of enlightened reason. But with the great admiration which Butler's works inspire in most minds, not a few are constrained to confess that his arguments are "wrought out in frost, not in fire." An impassioned style would certainly not befit the kind of reasoning in which Butler was engaged, but more warmth might have been thrown into the colour of the work, imparting to it a glow, which would heighten the impressiveness of the author's logic.—STOUGHTON, JOHN, 1867–81, *History of Religion in England from the Opening of the Long Parliament to the End of the Eighteenth Century, vol.* VI, *p.* 39.

Impressive, then, as the Sermons at the Rolls are, and much as they contain that is precious, I do not think that these sermons, setting forth Butler's theory of the foundation of morals, will satisfy any one who in disquietude, and seeking earnestly for a sure stay, comes to them.—ARNOLD, MATTHEW, 1876, *Bishop Butler and the Zeit-Geist, The Contemporary Review, vol.* 27, *p.* 580.

The "Analogy" is perhaps the most original, if not the most powerful, book ever written in defense of the Christian creed; but it has probably been the parent of much modern Agnosticism, for its method is to parallel every difficulty in revealed religion by a corresponding difficulty in natural religion, and to argue that the two must stand or fall together. Butler's unrivaled sermons on human nature, on the other hand, have been essentially conservative and constructive, and their influence has been at least as strong on character as on belief.—LECKY, WILLIAM EDWARD HARTPOLE, 1890, *Formative Influences, The Forum, vol.* 9, *p.* 381.

Him I believe the march of reform has swept away, hardly to the clearing of men's minds. I do not so much mean the "Analogy" as the wonderful "Sermons." From the "Sermons on Human Nature" one learns, and one does not straightway forget, what manner of man one is.—FREEMAN, EDWARD A., 1892, *A Review of my Opinions, The Forum, vol.* 13, *p.* 152.

The lectures on the "Evidences of Christianity," delivered in January, 1844, the first important book of Dr. Hopkins, bear clear marks of the great influence that Bishop Butler has exercised upon his mind. . . . The lectures from the third to the eighth inclusive are simply the carrying out with fine and yet powerful strokes suggestions that might well arise from the study of the "Analogy." Of this there is an abundance of evidence.—CARTER, FRANKLIN, 1892, *Life of Mark Hopkins, pp.* 136, 137.

His sense of beauty if he possessed it, was absorbed in a supreme allegiance to truth, and his life was that of a Christian philosopher intent upon one object. His sermons, preached, at the Rolls Chapel, which contain the germ of his philosophy, are too closely packed with argument and too recondite in thought to fit them for pulpit discourses.—DENNIS, JOHN, 1894, *The Age of Pope, p.* 236.

ANALOGY
1736

If the reader should meet here with any thing which he had not before attended to, it will not be in the observations upon the constitution and course of nature, these being all obvious; but in the application of them: in which, though there is nothing but what appears to me of some real weight, and therefore of great importance; yet he will observe several things, which will appear to him of very little, if he can think things to be of little importance, which are of any real weight at all, upon such a subject as religion. However, the proper force of the following Treatise lies in the whole general analogy considered together.—BUTLER, JOSEPH, 1736, *The Analogy of Religion, Advertisement; Works, ed. Gladstone, vol.* I, *p.* 1.

The Bishop of Durham (Chandler), another great writer of controversy, is dead too, immensely rich; he is succeeded by Butler of Bristol, a metaphysic author, much patronized by the late Queen: she never could make my father read his book, and which she certainly did not understand herself.—WALPOLE, HORACE, 1750, *Letter to Sir Horace Mann, May* 2; *Letters, ed. Cunningham, vol.* II.

I know no author who has made a more just and a more happy use of this mode of reasoning than Bishop Butler, in his "Analogy of Religion." . . . In that excellent work the author does not ground any of the truths of religion upon analogy, as their proper evidence; he only makes use of analogy to answer objections against them. When objections are made against the truths of religion, which may be made with equal strength against what we know to be true in the course of nature, such objections can have no weight.—REID, THOMAS, 1785, *Essays on the Intellectual Powers of Man, Essay* i, *ch.* v.

To a mind disposed to view with calmness, humility and reverence, *the whole system of Providence*, as far as it is permitted to man to view "the work which God worketh from the beginning to the end," Dr. Butler has unfolded the "Analogy, or *relation* of the Course of Nature to Religion," by which all things are found to proceed in harmony from Him who hath made nothing imperfect. I think this great performance of Butler has peculiar force when it is considered *in the conclusion* of our religious researches, and not as part of the *original* proof; or as Lord Bacon expresses himself, "tanquam portum et sabbathum humanarum contemplationum omnium." . . . Reader, whoever thou art, if thou shouldst approve these *introductory* ideas to this great subject, inexhausted as it is and inexhaustible, prepare thyself, thy understanding, and thy affections. "Te quoque dignum finge Deo!"—MATHIAS, THOMAS JAMES, 1798, *The Pursuits of Literature, Eighth ed., pp.* 204, 205.

Without exception the most unanswerable demonstration of the folly of infidelity that the world ever saw.—WHITE, HENRY KIRKE, 1805, *Letters, Remains, vol.* I, *p.* 154.

In the course of my reading I do not think that any of the books that treat of the evidences of natural and revealed religion were omitted. Of all such works, however, I consider myself to have profited most by Butler's "Analogy," for strengthening my understanding, satisfying my doubts, and suggesting the soundest rules and most becoming temper for the investigation of truth.—SOMERVILLE, THOMAS, 1814–30? *My Own Life and Times,* 1741–1814.

The most argumentative and philosophical defence of Christianity ever submitted to the world.—BROUGHAM, HENRY LORD, 1835, *A Discourse on Natural Theology, pt.* ii, *sec.* iii.

I should think you would gain great benefit, on the whole subject of religion and ethics, from Bishop Butler's "Analogy." It is a very deep work, and, while it requires, will amply repay your study. —NEWMAN, JOHN HENRY, 1840, *Letter to Miss H., Letters, ed. Mozley, vol.* II, *p.* 311.

Having furnished, with a design directly contrary, one of the most terrible of the persuasives to atheism that has ever been produced.—MARTINEAU, JAMES, 1853, *Studies of Christianity.*

In truth, the greatest beauty of any author's style consists in its appropriateness to express his meaning. There is a rough likeness between the style of the "Analogy" and that of a legal document; and it goes deeper than might have been expected. For what makes a deed obscure to the uninitiated? Chiefly the attempt on the part of the framer to exclude all ambiguity. It looks like irony, but it is true, that no written thing, when examined, is clearer than a legal document; and the object, the attained object, of all those obscure phrases is to avoid the possibility of being misunderstood. Therefore it is that, the more one examines into possible meanings of what seemed clearer expressions, the more we shall realise and admire the sound judgment which has preferred what we, at first sight, thought ill-chosen and obscure. Thus it is that careful students of Butler's works generally come, in the end, to have a sort of relish for his peculiar style.—STEERE, EDWARD, 1857, *ed. Butler's Analogy, Preface.*

By the main body of Christian believers he is still considered unanswered and unanswerable, strong as a giant against all the puny attacks of infidelity.—HENNELL, MISS S. S., 1859, *On the Sceptical Tendency of Butler's Analogy.*

It is no paradox to say that the merit of the "Analogy" lies in its want of originality. . . . Its admirable arrangement only is all its own. . . . Its substance are the thoughts of a whole age, not barely compiled, but each reconsidered and digested.—PATTISON, MARK, 1860–69, *Essays, ed. Nettleship, vol.* II, *p.* 75.

The one writer whose reputation stands out pre-eminently above the other apologists is Bishop Butler. His praise is in all the churches. Though the force of a few illustrations in his great work may perhaps have been slightly weakened by the modern progress of physical science, and though objections have been taken on the ground that the solutions are not ultimate, mere *media axiomata;* yet the work, if regarded as adapted to those who start from a monotheistic position, possesses a permanent power of attractiveness which can only be explained by its grandeur as a work of philosophy, as well as its mere potency as an argument. The width and fulness of knowledge displayed in the former respect, together with the singular candour and dignified forbearance of its tone, go far to explain the secret of its mighty influence. When viewed in reference to the deist writings against which it was designed, or the works of contemporary apologists, Butler's carefulness in study is manifest.—FARRAR, ADAM STOREY, 1862, *A Critical History of Free Thought, p.* 157.

The argument is handled with great skill and fairness, and the work has had a more extensive circulation, and exerted a greater influence than any other apologetic treatise of the Modern Church. It supposes however that the objector concedes the truths of ethics and natural religion, and therefore is less effective as a reply to universal skepticism, or to such materialistic systems as those of Hobbes and Bolingbroke, than the work of Conybeare. The purely defensive attitude, moreover, which it assumes, in being content with merely showing that the same difficulty besets the religion of nature that lies against the religion of the Bible, imparts something of a cautious and timid tone to the work, though rendering it an exceedingly difficult one to be replied to.—SHEDD, WILLIAM G. T., 1863, *A History of Christian Doctrine, vol.* I, *p.* 212.

His "Analogy" is so compact and exhaustive, that it has superseded and destroyed the reputation of all the replies to the Deists then current.—MINTO, WILLIAM, 1872–80, *Manual of English Prose Literature, p.* 426.

The objection will naturally be made that to prove so little was surely not worth such profound and elaborate reasoning. But though Butler was ostensibly addressing men who made formal objections to Christianity, he had also in his mind the frivolous freethinkers of his time. Indifference where there was a probability, however small, was unworthy of a reasonable man. And if that indifference was the growth of an immoral life, its danger was serious. It was, therefore, a matter of the greatest importance to convince men that Christianity really had clear demands to be earnestly and impartially examined. Butler also knew the importance in an argument of getting one bit of sure ground, however small.—HUNT, JOHN, 1873, *Bishop Butler, The Contemporary Review, vol.* 22, *p.* 906.

The "Analogy" has been built up like a coral reef by slow accretions of carefully digested matter. The style corresponds to the method. We may say, if we choose to be paradoxical, that the "Analogy" is an almost unique example of a book which has survived, not merely in spite of, but almost by reason of, its faults of style. The paradox, indeed, holds only in so far as the faulty language is indicative of the effort to pack thought more closely than it will easily go. The defect results from a good motive. But it is also characteristic of the lonely thinker who forgets the necessity of expounding with sufficient clearness the arguments which have long been familiar to himself. And, in this sense, it is indicative of a more serious weakness. Butler's mind, like the mind of every recluse, was apt to run in grooves. He endeavoured, as he tells us, to answer by anticipation every difficulty that could be suggested. But, unfortunately, he has always considered them from the same point of view. He has not verified his arguments by varying the centre of thought or contemplating his system from the outside. And thus his reasoning often reminds us of those knots which bind the faster the more they are pulled in a given direction, but fall asunder at the first strain from another quarter.—STEPHEN, LESLIE, 1876, *History of English Thought in the Eighteenth Century, vol.* I, *p.* 279.

I have drawn your attention to the terms of unbounded praise in which the "Analogy" is extolled. It is called *unanswerable.* It is said to be *the most original and profound work extant in any langaage on the philosophy of religion.* It is asserted that, by his "Analogy," Butler *placed metaphysics, which till then had nothing to support them but mere abstraction or shadowy speculation, on the firm basis of observation and experiment.* I have also told you what is to my mind the one sole point of interest for us now, in a work like the "Analogy." To those who search earnestly, amid that break-up of traditional and conventional notions respecting our life, its conduct, and its sanctions, which is undeniably befalling our age, for some clear light and some sure stay, does the "Analogy" afford them? A religious work cannot touch us very deeply as a mere intellectual feat. Whether the "Analogy" was or was not calculated to make the loose Deists of fashionable circles, in the year of grace 1736, feel uncomfortable, we do not, . . . care two straws, unless we hold the argumentative positions of those Deists; and we do not. What has the "Analogy" got to enlighten and help *us?* . . . How unlike, above all, is this motive to the motive always supposed in the book itself of our religion, in the Bible! After reading the "Analogy" one goes instinctively to bathe one's spirit in the Bible again, to be refreshed by its boundless certitude and exhilaration.—ARNOLD MATTHEW, 1876, *Bishop Butler and the Zeit-Geist, The Contemporary Review, vol.* 27, *pp.* 581, 588.

The "Analogy," it would appear, has and can have but little influence on the present state of theology; it was not a book for all time, but was limited to the controversies and questions of the period at which it appeared. Throughout the whole of the "Analogy," it is manifest that the interest which lay closest to Butler's heart was the ethical. His whole cast of thinking was practical.—ADAMSON, ROBERT, 1875, *Encyclopædia Britannica, Ninth edition, vol.* IV.

The book was written with the single purpose of assisting others in what had been the business of his own life, the search after truth. Its reasonings are those with which he had in his own mind overcome doubt. There is no thought about style; no care to give graceful form to sentences intellectually armed with suggestive, defensive, restrictive and otherwise subordinated clauses, so that it has been said that everyone of Butler's sentences is like a well-considered move in chess.—MORLEY, HENRY, 1884, *ed. Butler's Analogy of Religion, Introduction, p.* 8.

Bishop Wilson has well said of the "Analogy" that probably no work in the compass of theology is so full of—to use Bacon's expression—"the seeds of things." For few works have ever been written so suggestive of thought as this. Its author has condensed in it the reading and reflection of more than twenty years, during which time there was scarcely an objection or a difficulty which he had not noted and most carefully considered.—ABBEY, CHARLES J., 1887, *The English Church and Its Bishops,* 1700–1800, *vol.* II, *p.* 56.

The "Analogy" is an isolated work. Even in its own age, when polemical pamphleteering was in fashion, though it was read, it was neither attacked nor defended. It does not refer to any theological movement that preceded it, and it is not the precursor of any subsequent literature. It stands alone, original, inexorably honest and veracious, but unsympathetic, like its silent and unexpansive author.—GOSSE, EDMUND, 1888, *A History of Eighteenth Century Literature, p.* 275.

The involutions of the sentence in the "Analogy" are often impassable, as Emerson would say, and utterly opposed to paragraph structure. Butler is mentioned here merely for the fact that he has a larger percentage of strictly inductive paragraphs than almost any other writer in the language. It may be added that when his sentences are short they usually need the light of the whole section to make their bearing plain.—LEWIS, EDWIN HERBERT, 1894, *The History of the English Paragraph, p.*117.

To do any justice to this great work—the greatest, certainly, which appeared in the eighteenth century—it must be read in the light of the Deism which was then prevalent, for Butler's mind was positively steeped in Deistical literature. If this had been borne in mind, we should never have heard the objection that Butler raised more doubts than he solved; for the doubts were already raised, and Butler did more than any man to solve them.—OVERTON, JOHN HENRY, 1897, *The Church in England, vol.* II, *p.* 224.

GENERAL

He is a most judicious writer, has searched deeply into human nature, and is by some thought obscure; but he thinks with great clearness, and there needs only a deep attention to understand him perfectly.—COCKBURN, CATHERINE, 1738, *Letter to Mrs. Arbuthnot.*

The literary reputation of Bishop Butler in truth is the least of his excellences. . . . He was more than a good writer, he was a good man; and what is an addition even to his eulogy, he was a sincere Christian. His whole study was directed to the knowledge and practice of sound morality and true religion: these he adorned by his life, and had recommended to future ages in his writings; in which, if my judgment be of any avail, he has done essential service to both, as much, perhaps, as any single person since the extraordinary gifts of "the word of wisdom and the word of knowledge" have been withdrawn.—HALIFAX, SAMUEL, 1786, *ed. Butler's Analogy, Preface.*

I am an entire disciple of Butler.—CECIL, RICHARD, 1810, *Remains, p.* 195.

It is true, a man cannot expect constant success in his endeavour, but he is not likely to succeed in any thing that is now even the object of his endeavors. This speaking as if one had something to say, is probably what Bishop Butler means by the expression of a man's writing "with simplicity and in earnest." *His* manner has this advantage, though it is not only inelegant, but often obscure.—WHATELY, RICHARD, 1827–57, *Elements of Rhetoric, pt.* iii, *ch.* iii, *par.* 2.

I have derived greater aid from the views and reasonings of Bishop Butler than I have been able to find besides in the whole range of our extant authorship. —CHALMERS, THOMAS, 1834, *Bridgewater Treatise, Preface.*

Now, of the poetic religion there is nothing in Butler; no one could tell from his writings that the universe was beautiful. If the world were a Durham mine or an exact square, if no part of it were more expressive than a gravel pit or a chalk quarry, the teaching of Butler would be as true as it is now. . . . There was a certain naturalness in Butler's mind which took him straight to the questions on which men differed around him. Generally, it is safer to prove what no one denies, and easier to explain difficulties which no one has ever felt; a quiet reputation is best obtained in the literary *quæstiunculæ* of important subjects. But a simple and straightforward man studies great topics because he feels a want of the knowledge which they contain; and if he has ascertained an apparent solution of any difficulty, he is anxious to impart it to others. He goes straight to the real doubts and fundamental discrepancies,—to those on which it is easy to excite odium and difficult to give satisfaction; he leaves to others the amusing skirmishing and superficial literature accessory to such studies. Thus there is nothing light in Butler; all is grave, serious, and essential,—nothing else would be characteristic of him.—BAGEHOT, WALTER, 1854, *Bishop Butler; Works, ed. Morgan, vol.* II, *pp.* 112, 123.

The genius of Butler was almost equally distinguished by subtilty and comprehensiveness, though the latter quality was perhaps the most characteristic. . . . He could not only recombine, and present in symmetrical harmony, the elements of a complex unity when capable of being subjected to an exact previous analysis,—as in his remarkable sketch of the Moral Constitution of Man,—but he had a wonderfully keen eye for detecting remote analogies and subtle relations where the elements are presented intermingled or in isolation, and insusceptible of being presented as a single object of contemplation previous to the attempt to combine them. . . . All Butler's productions—even his briefest—display much of this "architectonic" quality of mind; in all he not only evinces a keen analytic power in discerning the "differences" (one phase of the philosophical genius, according to Bacon, and hardly the brightest), but a still higher power of detecting the "analogies" and "resemblances of things," and thus of showing their relation and subordination. These peculiarities make his writings difficult; but it makes them profound, and it gives them singular completeness. . . . Butler's composition is almost as destitute of the vivacity of wit as of the graces of imagination. Yet he is by no means without that dry sort of humor, which often accompanies very vigorous logic, and, indeed, is in some sense inseparable from it; for the neat detection of a sophism, or the sudden and unexpected explosiôn of a fallacy, produces much the same effect as wit on those who are capable of enjoying close and cogent reasoning. There is also a kind of simple, grave, satirical pleasantry, with which he sometimes states and refutes an objection, by no means without its piquancy.—ROGERS, HENRY, 1857, *Joseph Butler, Encyclopædia Britannica, Eighth Edition.*

The reason or matter he is producing is palpable and plain enough. But he is so solicitous to find its due place in the then stage of the argument, so scrupulous to give it its exact weight and no more, so careful in arranging its situation relatively to the other members of the proof, that a reader who does not bear in mind that "the effect of the whole" is what the architect is preparing, is apt to become embarrassed, and to think that obscurity which is really logical precision. The generality of men are better qualified for understanding particulars one by one, than for taking a comprehensive view of the whole. The philosophical breadth which we miss in Butler's mode of conceiving is compensated for by this judicial breadth in his mode of arguing, which gives its place to each consideration, but regards rather the cumulative force of the whole. . . . Butler's eminence over his contemporary apologists is seen in nothing more than in that superior sagacity which rejects the use of any plea that it is entitled to consideration singly. In the other evidential books of the time we find a miscellaneous crowd of suggestions of very various value; never fanciful, but often trivial; undeniable, but weak as proof of the point they are brought to prove. Butler seems as if he had sifted these books, and retained all that was solid in them. If he built with brick, and not with marble, it was because he was not thinking of reputation, but of utility, and an immediate purpose. Mackintosh wished Butler had had the elegance and ornament of Berkeley. They would have been sadly out of place.—PATTISON, MARK, 1860–89, *Essays, ed. Nettleship, vol.* II, *pp.* 76, 77.

All his arguments are deduced from the actual experiences of human beings. He will hear of no theories which explain away facts—which start from any other ground than that of facts. He wishes to know what the things mean with which he has to meddle. He wishes to know what he is bound to be and to do, that he may not be in contradiction with himself—that he may not be a practical liar.—MAURICE, FREDERICK DENISON, 1862, *Moral and Metaphysical Philosophy, vol.* II, *p.* 461.

Soon after Bishop Butler's translation to Durham, he assembled his clergy in visitation, and delivered to them that Charge which, from the extraordinary and malicious attacks that were made upon it and the groundless imputations that arose out of it, has obtained more attention than it otherwise would have commanded. Sir James Mackintosh's remark upon Butler has often been quoted, that "no man who thought so well ever wrote so badly;" and this, which is true of the sermons and in a less degree of the "Analogy," is eminently true of the Durham Charge. The style of this document is heavy and inelegant, there is nothing to attract the attention or please the ear. But the matter of the Charge is replete with sound sense and wisdom, exhibiting a perception of the fitness of things far beyond what was common at that day, and likely to provoke the comments of the shallow writers who then boasted themselves as liberal and enlightened.—PERRY, GEORGE G., 1864, *The History of the Church of England, vol.* III, *p.* 370.

There is an old controversy as to whether Butler's style is not unnecessary dark and obscure. He himself defended it on the ground that the questions of which he treated are abstruse and difficult; but the fact that Secker endeavoured to enliven the "Analogy" a little shows that his friends thought his style defective. Sir J. Mackintosh, on the other hand, surely went too far when he said that no thinker so great was ever so bad a writer. There is a simple earnestness and quaint, homely vigour about the "Sermons" which relieve them to a great extent from this reproach. They are certainly not light reading, and some of the phraseology strikes one as artificial and affected; but after the first plunge these defects become less perceptible, while the reader's admiration for the calm, sober wisdom, the chastened temper, and elevated and fervent piety of the writer continually increases.—FYFE, J. HAMILTON, 1874, *Bishop Butler, Good Words, vol.* 15, *p.* 237.

The influence of Butler upon Ethical and Religious philosophy has been powerful wherever the English language is spoken and read, and probably surpasses that of any other single writer. This is not owing to the originality of his doctrines so much as to the compact form in which he has presented the reflections which had been suggested to many minds, and to the cautious and reverent spirit in which he mediates between the claims of independent thought and a revealed communication of Truth. His "Analogy" has been extensively studied and read as a text book in all the seminaries of higher learning, and has largely served to shape and strengthen the religious convictions of the English people. The "Sermons," though less generally read or studied, have exerted a pervading influence upon ethical philosophy. The "Analogy" and "Sermons" have also been efficient in introducing into Christian theology the ethical element, which sometimes it has greatly needed.—PORTER, NOAH, 1874, *Philosophy in Great Britain and America, Ueberweg's History of Philosophy, vol.* II, *p.* 385.

The most patient, original, and candid of philosophical theologians. . . . Butler—and it is the great secret of his power—is always depressed by the heavy burden of human misery and corruption. The horror of sin and death weighs upon his spirits. Our wisest course in life is to "endeavour chiefly to escape misery." Mitigation of sorrow, rather than actual happiness, is all that can be hoped by his sorely tried soul. . . . His special method consists in inferring from nature a Creator distinguished, so to speak, by personal idiosyncrasies. He has to show that the God who made alike the good and the bad instincts, takes part with the good and not with the bad; and, moreover, he has to show this from the inspection of the instincts themselves. Nature is to testify to a special design, not to an impartial and abstract reflection of itself. This is the problem ever present to Butler's mind, and his answer to it is the essence of his writings.—STEPHEN, LESLIE, 1876, *History of English Thought in the Eighteenth Century, vol.* I, *p.* 86, *vol.* II, *pp.* 46, 47.

It is very much to the credit also of Butler's honesty and moderation, that in spite of the tone of something like contempt for the arguments, or want of arguments, of the objectors to whom he addresses himself, he never imputes to them any moral obliquity. . . . If he was wanting in some of the qualifications of the professional advocate,—the suasiveness which carries the jury or the audience with him, as we say—the allowance for their prejudices and weaknesses, the appeals to their better sense, or the professions of respect for their judgment, which go far to make them think that the verdict for which so sensible a speaker asks must be the right one,—he is strong in a point which all authorities, from Aristotle downwards, have laid down as an essential requisite in one who would persuade men—the creating in the minds of those whom he addresses an impression of his own high moral integrity, and earnestness of purpose. In this Butler stands far above the reach of cavil. Objections against both his matter and his manner have been many and various: some have charged him with coldness, and others with enthusiasm.—COLLINS, W. LUCAS, 1881, *Butler* (*Philosophical Classics*), *p.* 174.

Though there is much resemblance between the moral systems of Butler and Shaftesbury, there is hardly room for a charge of plagiarism. Had Butler's system been unfolded in a formal treatise, it would certainly have been strange if Shaftesbury's name had been passed over in silence; but he was hardly bound to mention it either in the text or the scanty notes of a short collection of Sermons, whose primary object was probably religious edification, and the future reputation of which he can scarcely himself have foreseen.—FOWLER, THOMAS, 1882, *Shaftesbury and Hutcheson* (*English Philosophers*), *p.* 151.

Lord Melbourne is truly said to have been "a far greater and abler man than many who have filled a larger space in history." Bishop Butler's case is more noteworthy still. Lord Melbourne, who filled a space in history, was greater than many others who filled a larger space; but Butler was greater than many others who filled a large space in history, although, strange to say, to judge from the records of historians, he filled no space in history at all! White, in his "Eighteen Christian Centuries," does not even so much as mention the name of Sir Isaac Newton, so that it is no wonder that he does not mention the name of so comparatively insignificant an individual as Bishop Butler. Certainly, those whose names are mentioned most frequently in history are by no means always those who have done most for the making of history. And, on the other hand, those whose names appear least prominently in history, or perhaps not at all, are by no means always those who have done least to influence its course. Nevertheless, that Bishop Butler had a weighty influence on the thought of his time, and therefore on subsequent history, there can be no doubt. He arrested the progress of Deism, and by so doing materially affected the future of religion in England.—COPNER, JAMES, 1885, *Sketches of Celibate Worthies, pp.* 211, 212.

He occupies, more nearly perhaps than any other writer, the position of a discoverer in moral theory; nor can its problems ever be accurately discussed without some reference to his thought. But sermons cannot be the depository of a philosophy. He left only the first sketch and the unhewn materials of a systematic structure, and receives his best tribute of honour from those who try to fill in the design, and here and there add a sound stone at a weak place.—MARTINEAU, JAMES, 1885, *Types of Ethical Theory, vol.* II, *p.* 522.

His two books, the "Analogy" and the "Sermons," are not bulky, and exhibit a strange incapacity for clothing thought in fit language. But the thought is always noble, and sometimes it forces the rebellious style into harmony.—SAINTSBURY, GEORGE, 1886, *Specimens of English Prose Style, p.* 177.

Butler was the first philosopher to distinguish between natural and moral benevolence and to maintain that a disposition to make others happy without regard to their character is not merely characterless, but proof of moral perversity. Even God cannot make the wicked happy as he does the righteous. Every form of evolution of the moral from the non-moral encounters Butler.—MAGOUN, GEORGE F., 1887, *A Fountain-Head of English Ethics, Bibliotheca Sacra, vol.* 44, *p.* 118.

The first of these works, the "Analogy," has a world-wide reputation, which every day is constantly increasing. In the second, viz., the "Sermons," the foundation was first laid for a correct theory of morals—to such a degree that Sir James Mackintosh speaks of the doctrines therein laid down as being worthy of the name of *discoveries.* The authorship of these works has placed Bishop Butler upon the highest pinnacle of fame, and his name is justly enrolled among the greatest philosophers the world has ever seen, and he is always to be classed with Shakespeare, Lord Bacon, Sir Isaac Newton, Cuvier, and other distinguished men of extraordinary genius, who are generally recognized as standing intellectually at the head of the human race.—PYNCHON, THOMAS RUGGLES, 1889, *Bishop Butler, a Religious Philosopher for all Time, p.* 13.

In Butler there is a strain of something infinitely higher; a powerful individuality that cannot be stifled, a lucidity that gives to his writings the permanence of classics, and a sincerity and earnestness that illumine his logical acumen with the warm light of genius.—CRAIK, HENRY, 1895, *ed., English Prose, Introduction, vol.* IV, *p.* 4.

His appeals at all times to the reason, and only incidentally to the feelings. There is probably no writer from whose works so little could be pruned always as a mere superfluity of oratory. . . . There is no one who is more successful in infecting his readers with his own ardour and impressing them with a feeling of his entire sincerity.—BONAR, JAME, 1895, *English Prose, ed. Craik, vol.* IV, *p.* 68.

It would be difficult to name a writer who in the prosecution of his work has aimed at, and effected a more absolute self-suppression. His use of the first person singular is rare, and whenever it occurs, we at once perceive that it is a grammatical vehicle, and not the entrance of a caparisoned figure on the stage for presentation to an audience. We attain indeed a solid and rather comprehensive knowledge of the man through his works; but this is owing, if I may so speak, to their moral transparency, which is conspicuous amidst all the difficulties of gaining and keeping a continuous grasp of his meaning. . . . He does not write like a person addicted to any profession or pursuit; his mind is essentially free. He is the votary of truth, and is bound to no other allegiance. . . . The student of Butler will, unless it be his own fault, learn candour in all its breadth, and not to tamper with the truth; will neither grudge admissions nor fret under even cumbrous reserves. But to know what kinds and degrees of evidence to expect or to ask in matters of belief and conduct, and to be in possession of an habitual presence of mind built upon that knowledge, is, in my view, the master gift which the works of Butler are calculated to impart. It can, however, only be imparted to those who approach the study of them as in itself an undertaking; who know that it requires them to pursue it with a whole heart and mind, if they would pursue it profitably; that it demands of them collectedness, concentration, and the cheerful resolve not to be abashed or deterred by difficulty. . . . Undoubtedly, if my counsel were asked, I should advise the intending politician, if of masculine and serious mind, to give to Butler's works, and especially to the "Analogy," a high place among the apparatus of his mental training. . . . Although no one would charge Butler with egotism, yet he is evidently, like Dante, a self-revealing writer. As a man governed by one dominant influence, he wears his heart upon his sleeve. The master passion with him is the love of truth: and it is never leavened, never traversed by any other feeling. . . . Butler assuredly was not made for butterflies to flutter about. He demands the surrender, not to him but to his subject, of the entire man. It has been well said of him that he is as much in earnest, as if he were a gamester. . . . To read them with levity is impossible. The eye may indeed run down the pages, the images of the letters may be formed upon the retina; but the living being that dwells within the brain is unapproached, and either dormant or elsewhere employed. The works of Butler are in this respect like the works of Dante; we must make some kind of preliminary preparation, we must gird up the loins of the mind for the study.—GLADSTONE, WILLIAM EWART,

1896, *Studies Subsidiary to the Works of Bishop Butler, pp.* 2, 3, 5, 6, 86, 88, 138.

Apart from his necessary limitations of knowledge, Butler is for us a master of method only, not a leader of thought. He is incapacitated for the delivery of the message we want to-day by limitations of feeling no less than by limitations of knowledge. He wrote at a period of human thought when "enthusiasm" was a term of reproach, and when it was believed that not only right thinking, but right conduct also, could be arrived at by pure calculation. His whole argument is, and professes to be, a balance of probabilities. There is a balance of probability in favor of Christianity being worth inquiring into; after that, a balance of probability in favor of its truth; further, a balance of probability in favor of its being prudent to obey its behests. This is the whole of his appeal. But, however it may have been in his generation, in ours men are not moved by such cold and prudential calculation.—ARMSTRONG, RICHARD A., 1896, *Mr. Gladstone and Bishop Butler, The New World, vol.* 5, *p.* 704.

He is to be classed, as regards method, with moralists like Shaftesbury and Hutcheson rather than with moralists like Cudworth and Clarke. In his view of human nature he was distinctly influenced by Shaftesbury. He finds in man affections and passions, self-love and disinterested benevolence, and, above the rest and rightly entitled to rule, though not always furnished with power as it is with right, a principle of reflection, or conscience. Taking from the Stoics the position that virtue consists in "following nature," he finds that to follow nature is to obey neither the passions nor "cool self-love," but conscience. In the history of ethics Butler was chiefly influential by his insistence that among the impulses of human nature some are disinterested, aiming either directly at objects or at the good of others, and do not consist of self-love in a more or less disguised form. To some extent Hobbes, against whom all the moralists who argued for primitive benevolent impulses had been contending, is still the opponent in view.—WHITTAKER, THOMAS, 1896, *Social England, ed. Traill, vol.* V, *p.* 44.

George Berkeley

1685–1753

Born, in County Kilkenny, 12 March 1685. To Kilkenny School, 17 July 1696. To Trinity College, Dublin, 21 Mar. 1700; Scholar, 1702; B. A., 1704; M. A., 1707; Fellowship, 9 June 1707; Tutor of College, 1707–24; Sub-lecturer, 1710; Junior Dean, 1710 and 1711; Junior Greek Lecturer, 1712; Divinity Lecturer and Senior Greek Lecturer, 1721; B. D. and D. D., 14 Nov. 1721; Hebrew Lecturer and Senior Proctor, 1722. Visit to England, 1713. Contrib. to "The Guardian," Mar. and Aug. 1713. Chaplain to Lord Peterborough on embassy to King of Sicily, Nov. 1713 to summer of 1714. In London, 1715–16. Abroad 1716–20 (as travelling tutor, Nov. 1716–18). To London, 1720. To Ireland, as chaplain to Lord-Lieutenant, 1721. Legacy left him by Hester Vanhomrigh, 1723. Dean of Derry, May, 1724. In London with project for Missionary College in America, 1724–28. Charter for College obtained, June 1725. Married Anne Forster, 1 Aug. 1728. To America, 4 Sept. 1728. Remained there till 1731. Scheme failed, owing to impossibility of obtaining promised grant from English Govt. In London, 1732–34. Consecrated Bishop of Cloyne, 19 May 1734. At Cloyne, 1734–52. Retired and went to England, Aug. 1752. Lived in Oxford, 1752–53; died there, 14 Jan. 1753; buried at Ch. Ch. *Works:* "Arithmetica absque Algebra aut Euclide demonstrata," 1707; "Mathematica" (anon.), 1707; "Essay towards a new theory of Vision," 1709 (2nd edn. same year); "Treatise concerning the Principles of Human Knowledge," 1710; "Passive Obedience," 1712 (2nd edn. same year); "Three Dialogues between Hylas and Philonous," 1713; "De Motu," 1721; "Essay towards preventing the Ruin of Great Britain" (anon.), 1721; "Proposal for the better Supplying of Churches in our Foreign Plantations" (anon.), 1725; "Sermon before Soc. for Propagation of Gospel," 1732; "Alciphron" (anon.), 1732 (2nd. edn. same year); "Theory of Vision . . . vindicated and explained" (anon.), 1733; "The Analyst" (anon.), 1734; "A Defence of Free-thinking in Mathematics" (anon.), 1735; "Reasons for not replying to Mr. Walton's Full Answer, etc." (anon.), 1735; "The Querist," 1735–37; "A Discourse addressed to Magistrates" (anon.), 1736; "A Chain of Philosophical Reflections . . . concerning the virtues of Tar-Water, etc," 1744 (2nd and 3rd edns. same year; 4th, 1746; 5th, 1748; all of these under the title of "Siris"); "Letter to Thomas Prior" [on the virtues of tar-water] (anon.), 1744; "Letter to the Roman Catholics of the Diocese of Cloyne," 1745; Second Letter to Thomas Prior, 1746 (the first and second letters together, as appx. to Prior's "Authentick Narrative," 1746); "Two Letters, the one to T. Prior . . . the other to Dr. Hales" [on the virtues of tar-water], 1747; "A word to the Wise" (anon.), 1749; "Maxims concerning Patriotism," 1750; "Further Thoughts on Tar-Water," in "Bentley's Miscellany," 1752; "A Miscellany containing several tracts on various subjects," 1752. *Posthumous:* Letter (written 1741) to Sir J. James on the Roman Catholic Controversy, 1850. *Collected Works:* in 2 vols., ed. by J. Stock, 1784; in 2 vols., ed. by G. N. Wright, 1843; complete edn., with *life* by Prof. Fraser, 1871.—SHARP, R. FARQUHARSON, 1897, *A Dictionary of English Authors, p.* 23.

PERSONAL

I went to court to-day, on purpose to present Mr. Berkeley, one of your Fellows of Dublin College, to Lord Berkeley of Stratton. That Mr. Berkeley is a very ingenious man, and great philosopher; and I have mentioned him to all the ministers, and have given them some of his writings, and I will favour him as much as I can. This I think I am bound to, in honour and conscience, to use all my little credit toward helping forward men of worth in the world.—SWIFT, JONATHAN, 1713, *Journal to Stella, April* 12.

Yesterday arrived here Dean Berkeley, of Londonderry, in a pretty large ship. He is a gentleman of middle stature, of an agreeable, pleasant, and erect aspect. He was ushered into the town with a great number of gentlemen, to whom he behaved himself after a very complaisant manner. 'Tis said he proposes to tarry here with his family about three months.—NEW ENGLAND WEEKLY COURIER, 1729, *January* 24, *Newport Letter.*

Whereas the Revnd Dean Berkeley has lately produced a valuable collection of books, and sent them to Harvard College, voted y^{t} ye thanks of ye Corporation be returned by ye President to ye Dean for the above donation, procured and sent by him, and y^{t} he be desired to make proper acknowledgements, on behalf of ye Corporation, to those gentlemen who have contributed to so literal a benefaction.—PRESIDENT AND FELLOWS OF HARVARD COLLEGE, 1733, *Sept.* 3.

Manners with Candour are to *Benson* giv'n,
To *Berkeley*, ev'ry Virtue under Heav'n.
—POPE, ALEXANDER, 1738, *Epilogue to the Satires, Dialogue* ii, *v.* 72–73.

The newspapers say the Bishop of Cloyne, is dead; there is (if so) *a great man gone.* His country people are much disobliged at his settling his son at Oxford, and think that an university that trained him up was worthy of his son.—DELANY, MARY GRANVILLE, 1753, *Letter to Mrs. Dewes, Jan.* 23; *Correspondence, ed. Llanover, vol.* III, *p.* 197.

In this respect I would with pleasure do justice to the memory of a very great though singular sort of man, Dr. Berkeley, known as a philosopher, and intended founder of a University in the Bermudas, or Summer Islands. An inclination to carry me out on that expedition, as one of the young professors on his new foundation, having brought us often together, I scarce remember to have conversed with him on that art, liberal or mechanic, of which he knew not more than the ordinary practitioners. With the widest views, he descended into a minute detail, and begrudged neither pains nor expense for the means of information. He travelled through a great part of Sicily on foot; clambered over the mountains and crept into the caverns to investigate its natural history, and discover the causes of its volcanoes; and I have known him sit for hours in forgeries and founderies to inspect their successive operations. I enter not into his peculiarities, either religious or personal; but admire the extensive genius of the man, and think it a loss to the Western World that his noble and exalted plan of an American University was not carried into execution. Many such spirits in our country would quickly make learning wear another face.—BLACKWELL, THOMAS, 1753–55, *Memoirs of the Court of Augustus, vol.* II, *p.* 277.

[Newport] Three miles from the town, is an indifferent wooden house, built by Dean Berkeley, when he was in these parts: the situation is low, but commands a fine view of the ocean, and of some wild rugged rocks that are on the left hand of it. They relate here several stories of the Dean's wild and chimerical notions, which, as they are characteristic of that extraordinary man, deserve to be taken notice of: one, in particular, I must beg the reader's indulgence to allow me to repeat to him. The Dean had formed the plan of building a town upon the rocks which I have just now taken notice of, and of cutting a road through a sandy beach which lies a little below it, in order that ships might come up and be sheltered in bad weather. He was so full of this project, as one day to say to one Smibert, a designer, whom he had brought over with him from Europe, on the latter's asking some ludicrous question concerning the future importance of the place:—"Truly you have very little foresight, for, in fifty years time, every foot of land in this place will be as valuable as the land in Cheapside." The Dean's house, notwithstanding his prediction, is at present nothing better than a farm-house, and his library is converted into the dairy.—BURNABY, ANDREW, 1759–60, *Travels through the Middle Settlements in North America.*

He was idolised in England before he set off for America. He used to go to St. James's two days a-week to dispute with Dr. Samuel Clarke before Queen Caroline, then Princess of Wales, and had a magnificent gold medal presented to him by George the Second; but he complained of the drudgery of taking part in these useless disputes.—BERKELEY, GEORGE MONCK, 1789, *Literary Relics, Preface.*

Berkeley, afterwards the celebrated Bishop of Cloyne, owed to Swift those introductions which placed him in the way of promotion.—SCOTT, SIR WALTER, 1814, *Memoirs of Jonathan Swift.*

Malebranche, it will give you pleasure to hear, *was* murdered. The man who murdered him is well known: it was Bishop Berkeley. The story is familiar, though hitherto not put in a proper light. Berkeley, when a young man, went to Paris, and called on Père Malebranche. He found him in his cell cooking. Cooks have ever been a *genus irritabile;* authors still more so: Malebranche was both: a dispute arose; the old father, warm already, became warmer; culinary and metaphysical irritations united to derange his liver: he took to his bed, and died. Such is the common version of the story: "So the whole ear of Denmark is abused." The fact is that the matter was hushed up, out of consideration for Berkeley, who (as Pope justly observes) had "every virtue under heaven:" else it was well known that Berkeley, feeling himself nettled by the waspishness of the old Frenchman, squared at him; a *turn-up* was the consequence: Malebranche was floored in the first round; the conceit was wholly taken out of him; and he would perhaps have given in; but Berkeley's blood was now up, and he insisted on the old Frenchman's retracting his doctrine of Occasional Causes. The vanity of the man was too great for this; and he fell a sacrifice to the impetuosity of Irish youth, combined with his own absurd obstinacy.—DE QUINCEY, THOMAS, 1827–54, *On Murder Considered as One of the Fine Arts; Works ed. Masson, vol.* XIII, *p.* 32.

Ancient learning, exact science, polished society, modern literature, and the fine arts, contributed to adorn and enrich the mind of this accomplished man. All his contemporaries agreed with the satirist in ascribing

"To Berkeley every virtue under heaven."

Adverse factions and hostile wits concurred only in loving, admiring, and contributing to advance him. The severe sense of Swift endured his visions; the modest Addison endeavoured to reconcile Clarke to his ambitious speculations. His character converted the satire of Pope into fervid praise, even the discerning, fastidious, and turbulent Atterbury said, after an interview with him, "So much understanding, so much knowledge, so much innocence, and such humility, I did not think had been the portion of any but angels, till I saw this gentleman." . . . Of the exquisite grace and beauty of his diction, no man accustomed to English composition can need to be informed. His works are, beyond dispute, the finest models of philosophical style since Cicero. Perhaps they surpass those of the orator, in the wonderful art by which the fullest light is thrown on the most minute and evanescent parts of the most subtile of human conceptions. Perhaps, also, he surpassed Cicero in the charm of simplicity. —MACKINTOSH, SIR JAMES, 1830, *Second Preliminary Dissertation to Encyclopædia Britannica.*

There are few men of whom England has better reason to be proud than of George Berkeley, Bishop of Cloyne. To extraordinary merits as a writer and thinker, he united the most exquisite purity and generosity of character; and it is still a moot-point whether he was greater in head or heart.—LEWES, GEORGE HENRY, 1845–46, *Biographical History of Philosophy, p.* 547.

It may be said of Berkeley, without exaggeration, that, in point of virtue and benevolence, no one of the sons of men has exceeded him. Whether we consider his public or his private life, we pause in admiration of efforts uncommonly exalted, disinterested, and pure.—CLEVELAND, CHARLES D., 1848, *A Compendium of English Literature, p.* 512.

Whenever a letter of Bishop Berkeley's appears, it shows him always the pure, the gentle, and the virtuous, the gentleman and the divine, the most beautiful character of that generation, the moral footprints of whose life are to this day visible on American soil.—REED, HENRY, 1855, *Lectures on English Literature from Chaucer to Tennyson, p.* 405.

No prominent man of that day enjoyed so many permanent and eligible friendships. Satire, then so much in vogue, was melted into kindness, and criticism softened to eulogy, when his name occurred in verse, letter, or conversation. Swift could not sympathize with his dreams, yet he earnestly advocated his cause. Addison laid aside his constitutional reserve to promote Berkeley's wishes. Pope made an exception in his favor, and suffered encomium to remain on his musical page unbalanced by censure. "I take you," says one of his letters, inviting the dean to Twickenham, "to be almost the only friend I have that is above the little vanities of the town." Atterbury declared, after an interview with him: "So much understanding, so much innocence, and such humility, I did not think had been the portion of any but angels, until I saw this gentleman." It is related by Lord Bathurst, that, on one occasion, when several members of the Scriblerius Club met at his house to dine, it was agreed to rally Berkeley, who was also invited, upon his American scheme. The latter heard the merry banter with the utmost good-nature, and then asked permission to reply; and, as his noble host afterwards declared, "displayed his plan with such an astonishing and animating fiery eloquence and enthusiasm, that they were struck dumb, and, after some pause, rose all up together, with earnestness, exclaiming, 'Let us set out immediately!'" When he determined to make Oxford his abode, he tendered the resignation of the bishopric of Cloyne; but the king refused to accept it, declaring that he "should live where he pleased and die a bishop." "He is," writes Warburton, "a great man, and the only visionary I ever knew that was."—TUCKERMAN, HENRY T., 1857, *Essays Biographical and Critical, p.* 251.

Bishop Berkeley was not only a philosopher, he was a man. His being was not starved upon the meagre fare of speculation, but nourished by all the generous currents of existence. A life full of active service to his kind, full of the warm impulses of a spontaneous, frank, open-hearted Irish nature—a sensibility so keen as to lead him even to Quixotisms and oddities of kindness—give such a warm background to his philosophy as no other great thinker within our recollection can equal. A man who is ready, at an age when men are supposed to consider their own comfort, to sacrifice himself in one of the least comfortable of missions—a man moved in later years to pause in his philosophy in order to promulgate tar-water—grand specific for all the physical ills of humanity—one who feared neither poverty nor neglect nor derision for what seemed to him at the moment the best he could do for his fellow creatures,—is such a man as is rarely met with in the sphere of philosophy. No mental system has called forth such contemptuous criticism, rude laughter, and foolish condemnation—none has been denounced as so visionary and unreal; yet Berkeley is the one philosopher of modern times who brings the race within the warmest circle of human sympathies, and casts a certain interest and glow of light from his own nature upon metaphysics themselves.—OLIPHANT, MARGARET, 1869, *Historical Sketches of the Reign of George II., Blackwood's Magazine, vol.* 105, *p.* 4.

The man who stands out as one of the noblest and purest figures of his time: that Berkeley from whom the jealousy of Pope did not withhold a single one of all "the virtues under heaven;" nor the cynicism of Swift, the dignity of "one of the first men of the kingdom for learning and virtue;" the man whom the pious Atterbury could compare to nothing less than an angel; and whose personal influence and eloquence filled the Scriblerus Club and the House of Commons with enthusiasm for the evangelization of the North American Indians; and even led Sir Robert Walpole to assent to the appropriation of public money to a scheme which was neither business nor bribery.—HUXLEY, THOMAS HENRY, 1871, *Bishop Berkeley on the Metaphysics of Sensation, Macmillan's Magazine, vol.* 24, *p.* 147.

Yale College is fortunate in the possession of a portrait of Berkeley, painted in this country by Smibert, an English artist, who accompanied Berkeley to this country. The Berkeley Divinity School honors him in its name. The seat of the University of California, at the extreme limit of that westward course of empire to which Berkeley's eyes were turned, is, owing to the happy suggestion of the present President of the Johns Hopkins University, most appropriately named Berkeley, and the portrait of the philosopher adorns its walls. There will be academic shrines to his memory in this country as long as our land shall endure.—MORRIS, GEORGE S., 1880, *British Thought and Thinkers, p.* 231.

The greatest of the sons of Ireland who came to us in those days was George Berkeley, and he, like Penn, reposed hopes for humanity on America. Versed in ancient learning, exact science, and modern literature, disciplined by travel and reflection, adverse factions agreed in ascribing to him "every virtue under heaven." Cherished by those who were the pride of English letters and society, favored with unsolicited dignities and revenues, he required for his happiness, not fortune or preferment, but a real progress in knowledge. The material tendencies of the age in which he lived were hateful to his purity of sentiment; and having a mind kindred with Plato and the Alexandrine philosophers, with Barclay and Malebranche, he held that the external world was wholly subordinate to intelligence; that true existence can be predicted of spirits alone.—BANCROFT, GEORGE, 1883, *History of the United States, pt.* iii, *ch.* xv.

Though it be true, therefore, that—philosophy apart—Berkeley effected little; though he did not write enough to rank in the first class among men of letters, nor perform enough to be counted a successful man of action; though he was neither a great social power, nor a great missionary, nor a great ecclesiastic, it is also true that scarce any man of his generation touched contemporary life at so many points. In reading his not very voluminous works we find ourselves not only in the thick of every great controversy—theological, mathematical, and philosophical—which raged in England during the first half of the eighteenth century, but we get glimpses of life in the most diverse conditions: in the seclusion of Trinity College, Dublin, in the best literary and fashionable society in London, among the prosperous colonists of Rhode Island, among the very far from prosperous peasants and squireens of Cork. And all this in the company of a man endowed with the subtlest of intellects, lit up with a humour the most delicate and urbane.—BALFOUR, ARTHUR JAMES, 1897, *Berkeley's Works, ed. Sampson, Biographical Introduction, p.* ix.

UNIVERSITY OF BERMUDA

It is now about ten months since I have determined to spend the residue of my days in Bermuda, where I trust in Providence I may be the mean instrument of doing great good to mankind. . . . The reformation of manners among the English in our Western plantations, and the propagation of the Gospel among the American savages, are two points of high moment. The natural way of doing this is by founding a college or seminary in some convenient part of the West Indies, where the English youth of our plantations may be educated in such sort as to supply their churches with pastors of good morals and good learning—a thing (God knows) much wanted. In the same seminary a number of young American savages may also be educated till they have taken the degree of Master of Arts. And being by that time well instructed in the Christian religion, practical mathematics, and other liberal arts and sciences, and early imbued with public-spirited principles and inclinations, they may become the fittest instruments for spreading religion, morals, and civil life among their countrymen, who can entertain no suspicion or jealousy of men of their own blood and language, as they might do of English missionaries, who can never be well qualified for that work.—BERKELEY, GEORGE, 1723, *Letter to Sir John Percival, March.*

He is an absolute philosopher with regard to money, titles, and power, and for three years past has been struck with a notion of founding an university at Bermudas, by a charter from the Crown. He has seduced several of the hopefullest young clergymen and others here, many of them well provided for, and all of them in the fairest way of preferment; but in England his conquests are greater, and I doubt will spread very far this winter. He showed me a little tract which he designs to publish, and there your Excellency will see his whole scheme of a life academico-philosophical of a college founded for Indian scholars and missionaries, where he most exorbitantly proposeth a whole hundred pound a-year for himself, forty pounds for a fellow, and ten for a student. His heart will break if his deanery be not taken from him and left to your Excellency's disposal. I discourage him by the coldness of courts and ministers, who will interpret all this as impossible and a vision, but nothing will do. And therefore I do humbly entreat your Excellency either to use such persuasions as will keep one of the first men in this kingdom for learning and virtue quiet at home, or assist him by your credit to compass his romantic design, which, however, is very noble and generous, and directly proper for a great person of your excellent education to encourage.—SWIFT, JONATHAN, 1724, *Letter to Lord Carteret, Sept.* 3.

But in the meantime no news or bad news came from England. The money from which the endowment of the Bermuda College was to have come was otherwise appropriated; and Sir Robert Walpole, on being finally appealed to, made answer, that of course the money would be paid *as soon as suited the public convenience*, but, as a friend, he counselled Dean Berkeley to return home and not to wait that far-off contingency. Thus the whole chivalric scheme broke down. Berkeley had wasted four years in the blank existence of the little New England town, had "expended much of his private property," and spent infinite exertions and hopes in vain. A long period before his actual setting-out had been swallowed up in negotiations to obtain this futile charter and unpaid grant. He gave up, on the whole, some seven years of the flower and prime of his life to the scheme thus cruelly and treacherously rendered abortive. It is so that England treats the generous movements and attempted self-devotion of her sons. Had it been a factory or a plantation, there might have been some hope for Berkeley; but a college with only ideal advantages, mere possibilities of influence and evangelisation,—what was that to Walpole, or to the slumbrous prosaic nation over which he ruled?—OLIPHANT, MARGARET, 1869, *Historical Sketches of the Reign of George II., Blackwood's Magazine, vol.* 105, *p.* 21.

With a character like that of Berkeley, and a scheme so calculated to strike the imagination and the finer sentiments of men, it is natural that there should be little but reprobation for the unimaginative and unsympathetic minister by whom Berkeley's project was crushed. But a word of justice remains to be spoken, even here, on the side of the prosaic practical sense by which the business of the world is carried on. The truth is, that Berkeley's project never commended itself to the practical tact of men. From the first announcement of it in Swift's letters to Lord Carteret down to the callous mockery of Walpole's advice, the project is treated very generally as a visionary's dream, which is not to be laughed down simply out of respect for the visionary's character, and for the purity of the motives out of which his dream arose. Even Blackwell of Aberdeen, and the other scholars who at first proposed to act under Berkeley in his new university, all drew back at the last, and left their principal to go out as a lonely pioneer. Berkeley's scheme in fact, ignored one essential condition of success: it was altogether unnecessary, for the work he planned had long been carried on by men better fitted to cope with all its requirements than the best selection of scholars from the universities of the Old World. The Puritan settlers of New England had, soon after their arrival, recognised the importance of the work which Berkeley's biographers sometimes give him the credit of having been the first to conceive. Harvard College was started nearly a century before Berkeley left England, and even Yale dates back to his boyhood. It seems strange that, before entering on his romantic task, he either did not find out, or did not appreciate, the nature of the work which these institutions were already performing in the field that was to be cultivated by his own labours.—MURRAY, J. CLARK, 1887, *The Revived Study of Berkeley, Macmillan's Magazine, vol.* 56, *p.* 169.

The scheme seems now so impracticable that we may well wonder how any single person, let alone the representatives of a whole nation, could be found to support it. In order that religion and learning might flourish in America, the seeds of them were to be cast in some rocky islets severed from America by nearly six hundred miles of stormy ocean. In order that the inhabitants of the mainland of the West Indian colonies might equally benefit by the new university, it was to be placed in such a position that neither could conveniently reach it.—BALFOUR, ARTHUR JAMES, 1893, *Essays and Addresses, p.* 69.

Berkeley's American visit was, in its plan, its execution, and its fruit, much more than it seemed to the public eye, either at that time or since; and while it was a thing that could have been projected only by an idealist and a moral enthusiast —such as Berkeley was—it must be pronounced, even on cool survey, a mission of chivalric benevolence certainly, but also of profound and even creative sagacity. In its boldness and its generosity it was dictated by an apostolic disinterestedness and courage to which, of course, that age was unaccustomed, and which places it in the light of an almost comic incongruity with the spirit of the time in which it occurred. In the history of our colonial period it forms a romantic chapter. But, in order to understand it, we need first to understand Berkeley himself, as well as his attitude toward the period he lived in. —TYLER, MOSES COIT, 1895, *Three Men of Letters, p.* 11.

A NEW THEORY OF VISION
1709

Two clergymen have perused your book —Clarke and Whiston. Not having myself any acquaintance with these gentlemen, I can only report at second hand they think you a fair arguer and a clear writer, but they say your first principles you lay down are false. They look upon you as an extraordinary genius, but say they wish you had employed your thoughts less upon metaphysics, ranking you with Father Malebranche, Norris, and another whose name I have forgot—all of whom they think extraordinary men, but of a particular turn, and their labours of little use to mankind on account of their abstruseness. This may arise from these gentlemen not caring to think after a new manner, which would oblige them to begin their studies anew, or else it may be the strength of prejudice.—PERCIVAL, SIR JOHN, 1710, *Letter to Berkeley, Oct.*

He published this metaphysic notion, that *matter* was not a *real thing;* nay, that the common opinion of its *reality* was groundless, if not ridiculous. He was pleased to send Dr. Clarke and myself, each of us, a book. After we had both perused it, I went to Dr. Clarke, and discoursed with him about it to this effect: that I, being not a metaphysician, was not able to answer Mr. Berkeley's subtile *premises,* though I did not at all believe his absurd *conclusion.* I therefore desired that he, who was deep in such subtilities, but did not appear to believe Mr. Berkeley's conclusions, would answer him: which task he declined.—WHISTON, WILLIAM, 1730, *Life of Samuel Clarke.*

The first attempt that ever was made to distinguish the immediate and natural objects of sight, from the conclusions we have been accustomed from infancy to draw from them; a distinction from which the nature of vision hath received great light, and by which many phænomena in optics, before looked upon as unaccountable, have been clearly and distinctly resolved.—REID, THOMAS, 1764, *An Inquiry into the Mind.*

The doctrine concerning the original and derivative functions of the sense of sight, which, from the name of its author, is known as Berkeley's "Theory of Vision," has remained, almost from its first promulgation, one of the least disputed doctrines in the most disputed and most disputable of all sciences, the Science of Man. This is the more remarkable, as no doctrine in mental philosophy is more at variance with first appearances, more contradictory to the natural prejudices of mankind. Yet this apparent paradox was no sooner published, than it took its place, almost without contestation, among established opinions; the warfare which has since distracted the world of metaphysics, has swept past this insulated position without disturbing it; and while so many of the other conclusions of the analytical school of mental philosophy, the school of Hobbes and Locke, have been repudiated with violence by the antagonist school, that of Common Sense or innate principles, this one doctrine has been recognised and upheld by the leading thinkers of both schools alike. Adam Smith, Reid, Stewart, and Whewell (not to go beyond our own island) have made the doctrine as much their own, and have taken as much pains to enforce and illustrate it, as Hartley, Brown, or James Mill.—MILL, JOHN STUART, 1842–50, *Bailey on Berkeley's Theory of Vision, Dissertations and Discussions, vol.* II, *p.* 84.

Berkeley's "Essay towards a New Theory of Vision" is the chronological and also a logical introduction to his metaphysical philosophy. It is virtually an inquiry into the nature and origin of our conception of Extension in Space, that distinctive characteristic of the material world. The "Essay" was the first fruits of Berkeley's philosophical studies at Dublin. It was also the first elaborate attempt to demonstrate that our apparently immediate visual perceptions of space, and of bodies existing in it apart from our organism, are actually suggestions induced by the constant association of visible ideas, and of certain organic sensations which accompany vision, with objects presented in our tactual experience. Various circumstances contribute to make this "Essay" more perplexing to the reader than any of Berkeley's other works.—FRASER, A. C., 1871, *ed., The Works of George Berkeley, vol.* I, *pp.* 1, 4.

THE PRINCIPLES OF HUMAN KNOWLEDGE
1710

It was only by degrees that this scheme of Berkeley's philosophy attracted the attention due to so original and ingenious a mode of conceiving the Universe. A fragment of metaphysics, by a young and almost unknown author, published at a distance from the centre of English intellectual life, was apt to be overlooked. In connection with the "Essay on Vision," however, it drew enough of regard to carry its author with *éclat* on his first visit to London, three years after the publication of the "Principles." He then published the immortal "Dialogues between Hylas and Philonous," in which the absurdity of Absolute Matter is illustrated, and the doctrine defended against objections, in a manner meant to recommend to popular acceptance what, on the first statement, seemed an unpopular paradox.—FRASER, ALEXANDER CAMPBELL, 1871, *ed. The Works of George Berkeley, vol.* I, *p.* 130.

Which rank among the most exquisite examples of English style, as well as among the subtlest of metaphysical writings; and the final conclusion of which is summed up in a passage remarkable alike for literary beauty and for calm audacity of statement.—HUXLEY, THOMAS HENRY, 1871, *Bishop Berkeley on the Metaphysics of Sensation, Macmillan's Magazine, vol.* 24, *p.* 149.

The treatise, "Of the Principles of Human Knowledge," is probably the most entertaining metaphysical work in the English language, and many men who turn away disgusted from ordinary presentations of philosophical doctrines, have read it with amusement if not with satisfaction. —ALEXANDER, ARCHIBALD, 1885, *The Idealism of Bishop Berkeley, The Presbyterian Review, vol.* 6, *p.* 307.

HYLAS AND PHILONOUS
1713

The characteristic of his intellect was extraordinary subtlety rather than solid judgment. He had, perhaps, too warm an imagination to arrive at sound and sober conclusions. . . . His style has always been esteemed admirable; simple, felicitous, and sweetly melodious. The dialogues are sustained with great skill. —MINTO, WILLIAM, 1872–80, *Manual of English Prose Literature, p.* 402.

In this work Berkeley first displayed his wonderful skill as a manipulator of the English language, which had never been employed for the discussion of philosophical ideas with anything like so much grace and refinement.—GOSSE, EDMUND, 1888, *A History of Eighteenth Century Literature*, p. 198.

A book marked by that consummate beauty of style for which he is distinguished.—DENNIS, JOHN, 1894, *The Age of Pope*, p. 222.

ALCIPHRON, OR THE MINUTE PHILOSOPHER

1732

The style and manner of this work are built on the model of Plato, and may be justly deemed one of the most happy imitations of the Grecian philosopher, of which our language can boast. There was in Berkeley, indeed, much of the sublimity, the imagination, and enthusiasm, which characterize the genius of Plato.—DRAKE, NATHAN, 1804, *Essays Illustrative of the Tatler, Spectator and Guardian*, vol. III, p. 69.

Now,—I want you, and *pray you* to read Berkeley's "Minute Philosopher;" I want you to learn that the religious belief which Wordsworth and I hold, and which —I am sure you know in my case, and will not doubt in his—no earthly considerations would make us profess if we did not hold it, is as reasonable as it is desirable; is in its historical grounds as demonstrable as any thing can be which rests upon human evidence; and is, in its life and spirit, the only divine philosophy, the perfection of wisdom; in which, and in which alone, the understanding and the heart can rest. —SOUTHEY, ROBERT, 1829, *Letter, Oct., Life and Correspondence by C. C. Southey*, ch. xxxii.

Berkeley's "Minute Philosopher" is the least admirable performance of that admirable writer. The most characteristic part is the attempt to erect a proof of theology upon his own peculiar metaphysical theory. The remainder consists for the most part of familiar commonplaces, expressed in a style of exquisite grace and lucidity, but not implying any great originality.—STEPHEN, LESLIE, 1876, *History of English Thought in the Eighteenth Century*, vol. II, p. 43.

In this noble composition the author combats, through his own method, the different types of infidelity current at the time. Berkeley's conception of the nature of religion was more spiritual than that which was prevalent in his day.—FISHER, GEORGE PARK, 1896, *History of Christian Doctrine*, p. 386.

The elegance and easiness of the style, and the freshness and beauty of the descriptions of natural scenery by which the tedium of the controversy is relieved, render this not only a readable, but a fascinating book; but Berkeley falls into the usual error of men who write on controversial subjects in the dialogistic form. He makes his adversaries state their case much more weakly than they would really have done; the giants he raises, only to knock down, are weak-kneed giants. Certainly the same may be said of Tindal, the chief of the Deists; but faults on one side do not justify similar faults on the other.—OVERTON, JOHN HENRY, 1897, *The Church in England*, vol. II, p. 225.

"Alciphron" was, and is likely to be, the most generally enjoyed of Berkeley's volumes. It is simply and variously entertaining with merits that far out-balance its defects. It has to be remembered that "Alciphron" is not directed against the specific doctrines of Deists or Atheists, so much as against the general influence of such writers on people unwilling to think for themselves, yet willing because of their more doubtful lives to deny the existence of God. Deep and close argument throughout would have helped his special object but little; and those who condemn the work as shallow seem to forget this. The "Analogy" of Butler and the "Alciphron" of Berkeley are as different in special aim as any two works on one subject can possibly be; and to expect the same result from each is strangely perverse and unreasonable. Were its philosophical value even less, it would still be eagerly read, for in an age of delicate and symmetrical prose, it stands distinguished by its delicacy and its symmetry.—SAMPSON, GEORGE, 1898, ed., *Works of George Berkeley*, vol. II, p. 148.

GAUDENTIO DI LUCCA

1737

"Gaudentio di Lucca" is generally, and I believe, on good grounds, supposed to be the work of the celebrated Berkeley,

Bishop of Cloyne, one of the most profound philosophers and virtuous visionaries of his age. . . . The style of this work is extremely pure, and some of the incidents, especially that of the Grand Vizier's daughter, who was afterwards sultana, exceedingly well managed. The portrait of the English Freethinker, towards the end of the work, is skillfully drawn and the absurdity of the arguments of Hobbes very humorously displayed.—DUNLOP, JOHN, 1814–42, *The History of Fiction, vol.* II, *pp.* 421, 422.

This well-known fiction, which has long been erroneously ascribed to Bishop Berkeley, was in fact the work of Simon Berington, a Catholic priest. The statement in the *Gent. Mag.* which assigns to him the authorship of this work, is confirmed by the traditions of his family in Herefordshire, as I have ascertained from authentic information. — LEWIS, SIR GEORGE CORNEWALL, 1852, *On the Methods of Observation and Reasoning in Politics, vol.* II, *p.* 273, *note.*

Berkeley's Bermuda enterprise, his former connection with Italy, his fondness for Plato, some vague resemblance in the ingenuity of the fancy, and the amiable spirit of "Gaudentio di Lucca," may have given rise to the supposition that he was the author. There is not sufficient ground in the qualities of the work, in the absence of any definite testimony, to justify this conjecture.—FRASER, ALEXANDER CAMPBELL, 1871, *Life and Letters of George Berkeley, vol.* IV, *p.* 252.

SIRIS

1744–47

Though we are so backward in some sorts of intelligence, we are perfectly acquainted with the virtues of tar-water; some have been cured as they think, and some made sick by it; and I do think it is a defect in the good bishop's recommendation of it, that he makes it a Catholicon; but I daresay he is confident he believes it such.—HERRING, THOMAS, 1744, *Letter to Duncombe.*

It is impossible to write a letter now without tincturing the ink with tar-water. This is the common topic of discourse, both among the rich and poor, high and low; and the Bishop of Cloyne has made it as fashionable as going to Vauxhall or Ranelagh. . . . However, the faculty in general, and the whole posse of apothecaries are very angry both with the author and the book, which makes many people suspect it is a good thing.—DUNCOMBE, WILLIAM, 1744, *Letter to Archbishop Herring, June.*

We are now mad about tar-water, on the publication of a book that I will send you, written by Dr. Berkeley, Bishop of Cloyne. The book contains every subject from tar-water to the Trinity; however, all the women read and understand it no more than they would if it were intelligible. A man came into an apothecary's shop the other day, "Do you sell tar-water?" "Tar-water!" replied the apothecary, "why I sell nothing else!" —WALPOLE, HORACE, 1744, *Letter to Sir Horace Mann, May 2d; Letters, ed. Cunningham, vol.* I, *p.* 303.

Was an enthusiast in many affairs of life, not confined to religion and the education of youth. He invaded another of the learned professions, Medicine. . . . He published a book called "Siris, . . . or Tar-Water." . . . He ought to have checked this officious genius (unless in his own profession-way he had acquired this nostrum by inspiration) from intruding into the affairs of a distinct profession. —DOUGLASS, WILLIAM, 1748–53, *Summary, Historical and Political of the British Setlements in North America.*

From a pedestal so low and abject, so culinary, as Tar Water, the method of preparing it, and its medicinal effects, the dissertation ascends, like Jacob's ladder, by just gradations, into the Heaven of Heavens and the thrones of the Trinity. —DE QUINCEY, THOMAS, 1834–54, *Samuel Taylor Coleridge, Collected Works, ed. Masson, vol.* II, *p.* 153.

Whenever his feelings were enlisted in behalf of a theory or an enterprise, he derived an argument or a charm from the most distant associations. One of the last of his favorite ideas was a faith in the curative qualities of tar-water, which had proved useful in a malady under which he suffered. His treatise on the subject deserves no mean rank among the curiosities of literature. The research, ingenuity, and scholarship, elicited by his ardent plea for this specific, evince a patient and elaborate contemplation seldom manifest in the discussion of the most comprehensive questions. He analyzes the different balsams, from the balm of Gilead to amber; he quotes Leo Africanus to describe the process of making tar on Mount Atlas, and compares it with that used in New England; he cites Herodotus and Pliny, Theophrastus and Plato, Boerhaave and Evelyn; he surveys the whole domain of vegetable physiology, points out the relation of volatile salts to the economy of the blood, and discusses natural history, the science of medicine, chemistry, and the laws of life, space, light, and the soul itself,—all with ostensible reference to the virtues of tar-water. He enumerates every conceivable disease as a legitimate subject of its efficacy; and, while thus prolix and irrelevant, fuses the whole with good sense, fine rhetoric, and graceful zeal.—TUCKERMAN, HENRY T., 1857, *Essays Biographical and Critical, p.* 248.

On the whole, the scanty speculative literature of these islands in the last century contains no other work nearly so remarkable; although curiously it has been much overlooked even by those curious in the history and bibliography of British philosophy. Every time we open its pages we find fresh seeds of thought. There is the unexpectedness of genius in its whole movement. It breathes the spirit of Plato and the Neoplatonists, in the least Platonic generation of English history since the revival of letters, and it draws this Platonic spirit from a thing of sense so commonplace as Tar. It connects tar with the highest thoughts in metaphysics and theology, by links which involve some of the most subtle botanical, chemical, physiological, optical, and mechanical speculations of its time.—FRASER, ALEXANDER CAMPBELL, 1871, *ed., The Works of George Berkeley, vol.* II, *p.* 343.

"Siris' is one of the most extraordinary books ever written; certainly the most amazing work in the literature of British philosophy. . . . "Siris" is among the greatest of Berkeley's works; yet it is not to be numbered with the more closely reasoned works of his earlier years. It is rather the unstudied murmurings of a cultured and persuasive philosopher who in the evening of his life has fallen a-musing. One would as soon turn to Sir Thomas Browne for exact science as to "Siris;" but who seeks in "Siris" delicate food for meditation will not seek in vain. The actual value of its speculation may not be great; yet the whole range of Berkeley's works contains nothing more completely characteristic of its author; more subtle and suggestive in matter and more harmonious and splendid in style.—SAMPSON, GEORGE, 1898, *ed., Works of George Berkeley, vol.* III, *p.* 198.

GENERAL

And coxcombs vanquish Berkeley with a grin.
—BROWN, JOHN, 1746? *Essay on Satire, pt.* ii, *l.* 224.

Doctor Berkeley, Bishop of Cloyne, a very worthy, ingenious, and learned man, has written a book to prove that there is no such thing as Matter, and that nothing exists but in idea: that you and I only fancy ourselves eating, drinking, and sleeping; you at Leipsig, and I at London: that we think we have flesh and blood, legs, arms, &c., but that we are only spirit. His arguments are, strictly speaking, unanswerable; but yet I am so far from being convinced by them, that I am determined to go on to eat and drink, and walk and ride, in order to keep that *matter*, which I so mistakenly imagine my body at present to consist of, in as good plight as possible.—CHESTERFIELD, PHILIP DORMER STANHOPE EARL, 1748, *Letters to his Son, Sept.* 27, *No.* 132.

And indeed most of the writings of that very ingenious author form the best lessons of skepticism which are to be found among the ancient or modern philosophers, Bayle not excepted.—HUME, DAVID, 1758, *Academical or Sceptical Philosophy, note.*

After we came out of the church, we stood talking for some time together of Bishop Berkeley's ingenious sophistry to prove the non-existence of matter, and that every thing in the universe is simply ideal. I observed, that though we are satisfied his doctrine is not true, it is impossible to refute it. I never shall forget the alacrity with which Johnson answered, striking his foot with mighty force against a large stone, till he rebounded from it, "I refute it *thus*." This was a stout exemplification of the *first truths of Père Bouffier*, or the *original principles* of Reid and of Beattie; without admitting which we can no more argue in metaphysicks, than we can argue in mathematicks without axioms. To me it is not conceivable how Berkeley can be answered by pure reasoning; but I know that the nice and difficult task was to have been undertaken by one of the most luminous minds of the present age (Edmund Burke), had not politicks "turned him from calm philosophy aside." What an admirable display of subtilty, united with brilliance, might his contending with Berkeley have afforded us!—JOHNSON, SAMUEL, 1763, *Life by Boswell, ed. Hill, vol.* I, *p.* 545.

It has often given me great pain to see Bishop Berkeley, a most pious and learned man, overturn the main foundations of all religion and all knowledge, by the most extravagant scepticism concerning the real existence of matter, in some of his writings; and then fancy, that in others he could, by any force of argument, establish the evidences of Christianity, which are a perpetual appeal to the truth of our senses, and grounded on a supposition, that they cannot deceive us in those things which are the proper and natural objects of them, within their due limits. Can one wonder, that the sceptics should lay hold of the former in answer to the latter? And can any more useful service be done to Christianity, than to shew the fallacy of such whimsies as would make the body of Christ, which his disciples saw and felt, no body at all? and the proof of his resurrection, from the testimony of their senses, a mere delusive idea?—LYTTELTON, GEORGE LORD, 1770, *Letter to Beattie, Oct.* 6; *Forbes, Life of Beattie, vol.* I, *p.* 228.

The substance, or at least the foundation, of Berkeley's argument against the existence of matter, may be found in Locke's essay, and in the "Principia" of Descartes. And if this be conclusive, it proves that to be false which every man must necessarily believe every moment of his life to be true, and that to be true which no man since the foundation of the world was ever capable of believing for a single moment.—BEATTIE, JAMES, 1773, *Essay on the Nature and Immutability of Truth, pt.* ii, *ch.* ii.

Of the intellectual powers of the Bishop, it may be observed, that, though strong and acute in no common degree, they were frequently mingled with too much enthusiasm and imagination for the purposes of strict philosophical ratiocination. His knowledge, however, was of great compass, and extended to all the useful arts and occupations of life; of which, it has been said, that there was scarcely one, liberal or mechanic, of which he knew not more than the ordinary practitioners.—DRAKE, NATHAN, 1804, *Essays Illustrative of the Tatler, Spectator and Guardian, vol.* III, *p.* 75.

A man uniformly so amiable as to be ranked among the first of human beings; a writer sometimes so absurd that it has been doubted whether it was possible he could be serious in the principles he laid down. His actions manifested the warmest zeal for the interests of Christianity, while some of his writings seemed intended to assist the cause of infidelity. Yet the respect which all who knew Dr. Berkeley have felt for his excellent character, has rescued him in some measure from this imputation, and he will deservedly be handed down to posterity as an able champion of religion, although with a love of paradox, and somewhat of the pride of philosophy, which his better sense could restrain.—CHALMERS, ALEXANDER, 1808–23, *ed., The British Essayists, Preface to the Guardian, p.* 17.

Possessing a mind which, however inferior to that of Locke in depth of reflection and in soundness of judgment, was fully its equal in logical acuteness and invention, and in learning, fancy, and taste far its superior. Berkeley was singularly fitted to promote that reunion of Philosophy and of the Fine Arts which is so essential to the prosperity of both. . . . With these intellectual and moral endowments, admired and blazoned as they were by the most distinguished wits of his age, it is not surprising that Berkeley should have given a popularity and fashion to metaphysical pursuits which they had never before acquired in England.—STEWART, DUGALD, 1815–21, *First Preliminary Dissertation to Encyclopædia Britannica.*

When Bishop Berkeley said there was no matter,
And prov'd it—'twas no matter what he said:
They say his system 'tis in vain to batter,
Too subtle for the airiest human head.
And yet who can believe it? I would shatter
Gladly all matters down to stone or lead,
Or adamant, to find the world a spirit,
And wear my head, denying that I wear it.
—BYRON, LORD, 1823, *Don Juan, canto* xi, *s.* i.

Berkeley can only be confuted, or answered, by one sentence. So it is with Spinoza. His premiss granted, the deduction is a chain of adamant.—COLERIDGE, SAMUEL TAYLOR, 1827, *Table Talk, ed. Ashe, July* 23, *p*. 56.

Berkeley, the strongest, the honestest thinker among our English metaphysicians—Berkeley, who loved truth with his whole heart and soul, and who, in pursuing it, was as humble as he was courageous—Berkeley, who, though he reasoned from narrow premises, and therefore never discovered the whole breadth and universality of the principles which he sought after, yet was able, such was the spirituality of his intellect, even out of that narrow system, which conducted every one else who reasoned from it to materialism, to bring the other and far more important side of truth—Berkeley, whose understanding, indeed, missed the "circumference," but who found the "centre" in his heart.—MAURICE, FREDERICK DENISON, 1828, *Life by Maurice, vol*, I, *p*. 82.

Among all philosophers, ancient or modern, we are acquainted with none who presents fewer vulnerable points than Bishop Berkeley. His language, it is true, has sometimes the appearance of paradox; but there is nothing paradoxical in his thoughts, and time has proved the adamantine solidity of his principles. With less sophistry than the simplest, and with more subtlety than the acutest of his contemporaries, the very perfection of his powers prevented him from being appreciated by the age in which he lived. The philosophy of that period was just sufficiently tinctured with common sense to pass current with the vulgar, while the common sense of the period was just sufficiently coloured by philosophy to find acceptance among the learned. But Berkeley, ingenious beyond the ingenuities of philosophy, and unsophisticated beyond the artlessness of common sense, saw that there was no sincerity in the terms of this partial and unstable compromise; that the popular opinions, which gave currency and credence to the theories of the day, were not the unadulterated convictions of the natural understanding; and that the theories of the day, which professed to give enlightenment to the popular opinions, were not the genuine offspring of the speculative reason. In endeavouring to construct a system in which this spurious coalition should be exposed, and in which our natural convictions and our speculative conclusions should be more firmly and enduringly reconciled, he necessarily offended both parties, even when he appeared to be giving way to the opposite prejudices of each. He overstepped the predilections both of the learned and the unlearned. His extreme subtlety was a stumbling-block in the path of the philosophers; and his extreme simplicity was more than the advocates of common sense were inclined to bargain for. . . . The peculiar endowment by which Berkeley was distinguished, far beyond his predecessors and contemporaries, and far beyond almost every philosopher who has succeeded him, was the eye he had *for facts*, and the singular pertinacity with which he refused to be dislodged from his hold upon them.—FERRIER, JAMES FREDERICK, 1842-6, *Berkeley and Idealism, Lectures, vol*. II, *pp*. 291, 293.

Although the several treatises of the author in defence of Christianity,—in support of the diffusion of knowledge,—on discovering new means for the alleviation of human suffering,—and on promoting the study of metaphysics and mathematics, have obtained the applause of the learned, yet their association with his new and difficult theory in pneumatology militated so far against their reception with the public in general, that one perfect edition only of his works has hitherto ever appeared. This was a circumstance much to be regretted, since no other writer, of the literary age in which he flourished, has left more able, original, or useful advice, in religion, philosophy, and politics.—WRIGHT, G. N., 1843, *ed., The Works of George Berkeley, Preface, vol*. I, *p*. iii.

If, then, Berkeley is more rigorous in his analysis of facts, and more ingenious and plausible in his hypothesis, than his antagonists suppose, shall we pronounce his Idealism satisfactory and true? Hume said of it, that it admitted of no answer, but produced no conviction. And we have met with no final refutation of it. Yet, inasmuch as it is the irresistible belief of mankind that objects are not dependent either upon our perception of them, or upon the perception of any other mind, for their existence—that objects exist *per se*, and would continue to exist if all minds were annihiliated—Berkeley's theory never can produce conviction. Reid, therefore, was right in standing by this universal and irresistible belief. He was egregiously wrong, however, in supposing that he answered Berkeley by an appeal to this irresistible belief. It does not follow that a belief which is irresistible must be true. This maxim, so loudly proclaimed by the Scotch school, is refuted by several well-known facts in philosophy. Thus—to take the most striking example—the belief that the sun revolved round the earth, was for many centuries irresistible, and false. Why may not Berkeley have been a metaphysical Copernicus, who, by rigorous demonstration, proved the belief of mankind in the existence of matter to be irresistible and false? Reid has no answer to give. He can merely say, "I side with the vulgar;" but he might have given the same answer to Copernicus. Many illustrious men (Bacon among them) ridiculed the Copernican theory; but all the dogmatism, ridicule, and common sense in the world could not affect that theory. Why, we repeat, may not Berkeley have been a metaphysical Copernicus? To prove that he was not, you must prove his reasoning defective; to prove this, you must show wherein his error lies, and not wherein his theory is at variance with your belief. . . . One great result of Berkeley's labors was the lesson he taught of the vanity of ontological speculations. He paved the way to that skepticism which, gulf-like, yawns as the terminal road of all consistent Metaphysics.—LEWES, GEORGE HENRY, 1845–46, *Biographical History of Philosophy, pp.* 563, 568.

The only metaphysical writer of the time, besides Locke and Hume, who has maintained a very high name in philosophical history. He forms a solitary—it might seem a singular—exception to what has been said of the prosaic and unmetaphysical character of this moralizing age. The two peculiar metaphysical notions which are connected with Berkeley's name, and which, though he did not originate, he propounded with a novelty and distinctness equal to originality, have always ranked as being on the extreme verge of rational speculation, if not actually within the region of unfruitful paradox and metaphysical romance. These two memorable speculations, as propounded by Berkeley in the "Alciphron," come before us not as a Utopian dream, or an ingenious play of reason, but interwoven in a polemic against the prevailing unbelief. They are made to bend to a most practical purpose, and are Berkeley's contributions to the Deistical controversy. The character of the man, too, was more in harmony with the plain utilitarian spirit of his time than with his own refining intellect. He was not a closet-thinker, like his master Malebranche, but a man of the world and of society, inquisitive and well informed in many branches of practical science. Practical schemes, social and philanthropic, occupied his mind more than abstract thinking. In pushing the received metaphysical creed to its paradoxical consequences, as much as in prescribing "tar-water," he was thinking only of an immediate "benefit to mankind." He seems to have thought nothing of his argument until he had brought it to bear on the practical questions of the day.—PATTISON, MARK, 1860–89, *Religious Thought in England, Essays, ed. Nettleship, vol.* II, *p.* 110.

The most subtle metaphysician who has ever written in English.—BUCKLE, HENRY THOMAS, 1861, *History of Civilization in England, vol.* II, *p.* 217.

As to Berkeley, it is of the less consequence, because I was early lent a good three-volume edition of his works by a noble friend, who was formerly a pupil of mine, and who, after about twenty-five years, reclaimed the loan not very long ago; so that I had leisure to become sufficiently impregnated with Berkeley's teaching, for one who has never aspired to be *himself* a *teacher* of Philosophy. In fact, when I was rather young, namely, in 1832, I allowed Coleridge (at Highgate) to see that I was at that time a regular Berkeleyan; and *he* was pleased to say—for our several interviews, of that year and the following, of which some were long, were not *all* monologues on his part—he allowed me to make a remark now and then, and actually modified his discourse to meet it: "Oh, sir, you will grow out of that!" In *some* respects that prophecy has been since fulfilled; but out of *love* and *reverence* for the great and good Bishop, I trust that I shall *never* grow.—HAMILTON, SIR WILLIAM ROWAN,

1864, *Letter, Life, ed. Graves, vol.* III, *p.* 177.

The greatest modern master of the Socratic dialogue.—LECKY, WILLIAM EDWARD HARTPOLE, 1865, *History of the Rise and Influence of the Spirit of Rationalism in Europe, vol.* II, *ch.* iv.

His claim to the name of metaphysician transcends those of most of his countrymen. He, first of his nation, dealt face to face with ideas as distinguished from scholastic fancies and common notions, and thus gave them their place in the order of mind; and this to exhaustive issues, as his English predecessors in thought had failed to do. His idealism is the purest which the British Isles have produced.—ALCOTT, A. BRONSON, 1869, *Concord Days, p.* 236.

The whole of Berkeley's doctrine on the nature of the Material Substance and of the External Universe is contained in the single proposition, that "Matter is a Phenomenon," i. e. that its *Esse* is *Percipi.* This discovery respecting the essential constitution of the Material Substance, first made by Berkeley and never afterwards abandoned by deep-thinking men, is now, under some one expression or another part and parcel of every metaphysical system and of the convictions of every metaphysician, whether he happens to be aware that it is Berkeley's doctrine or not. Indeed many, we may even say most, of those who hold the doctrine in foreign countries, are not aware that it is so. The hardest work of the Berkeleian advocate is often to make people aware that what they hold is Berkeley's doctrine. The tenet itself never presented any real difficulty to the metaphysician except as the disturber of something preconceived, and it is entirely a mistake which leads one or two writers to fancy that the doctrine, after it was once promulgated, was ever a neglected one. Such is never the fate of what is true. The ablest metaphysicians held the doctrine even before it was recognized as a discovery of science. Does it not seem frivolous to say that they abandoned it after they discovered it to be a scientific fact? —SIMON, T. COLLYNS, 1869, *Berkeley's Doctrine on the Nature of Matter, Journal of Speculative Philosophy, vol.* III, *p.* 336.

Berkeley has suffered more than perhaps any other great modern philosopher from misunderstanding. He lived through the most prosaic and least metaphysical age since the revival of letters: he was himself the greatest metaphysician in his own age. When reflection returned to the springs of thought and feeling, his philosophical language had in some measure lost the meaning which he intended, and no adequate attempt has since been made to recover his point of view, or to recognise the intellectual influence which, partly originating in him, has since been silently modifying all the deeper thought of the time in physics and in metaphysical philosophy. Is an unknowing and unknown something called Matter, or is Intelligence the supreme reality; and are men the transient results of material organization, or are they immortal beings? This is Berkeley's implied question. His answer to it, although, in his own works, it has not been thought out by him into its primary principles, or sufficiently guarded in some parts, nevertheless marks the beginning of the second great period in modern thought, that in which we are living. The answer was virtually reversed in Hume, whose exclusive phenomenalism, reproduced in the Positivism of the nineteenth century, led to the Scotch conservative psychology, and to the great German speculation which Kant inaugurated. It is as a spiritual philosopher, having warm and true sympathy in all human life, that Bishop Berkeley must be looked at, and not at all as a professional ecclesiastic. His writings and his life centre in speculative philosophy. But they radiate from it in various practical and fruitful directions; for his inclination was to what is concrete, at first in a more polemical, but afterwards in a meditative spirit. In their form, his works are numerous and occasional, not individually bulky or systematic. —FRASER, ALEXANDER CAMPBELL, 1871, *ed., The Works of George Berkeley, Preface, vol.* I, *p.* vii.

He believed in truth, and sought it in independent thought, not in tradition. He had no narrow or dogmatic creed, and no ecclesiastical spirit, but sought good and truth everywhere, and recognized them wherever he found them. The key to his philosophy is to be found in an instinctive revolt against the abstractions of scholastic tradition.—SUMNER, WILLIAM G., 1871, *The Life and Works of Bishop Berkeley, The Nation, vol.* 13, *p.* 59.

It may surprise those who have imbibed the popular prejudice against Berkeley as a paradoxical visionary, to hear him described as an advocate of common sense. But in truth, as his editor has observed, Berkeley has suffered more perhaps than any other great modern philosopher from misunderstanding.—MANSEL, HENRY LONGUEVILLE, 1871, *On the Idealism of Berkeley*; *Letters, Lectures and Reviews*, *p.* 382.

Of what is called "the philosophy of Berkeley," it is enough to say here, that, in a phase and a mode of statement suited to his own time and to the shape in which materialism found acceptance, it was an adequate antagonistic presentment of the claims of a high and pure spiritualism. The absurd popular apprehension of his philosophy found expression in the facile assertion that Berkeley denied the existence of the material world, and referred our idea of it to a simple illusion of the senses. So far was he from such an absurdity as this, that he maintained that he was proving the actual existence of the material world by a new and positive method, when he affirmed that we must primarily and equally allow for the fidelity and reality of those intellectual and spiritual faculties of our own, by which we take cognizance of it and apprehend it.—ELLIS, GEORGE E., 1871, *Life of Bishop Berkeley, Old and New, vol.* 4, *p.* 597.

If the facilities afforded by Professor Fraser's labours induce those who are interested in philosophy or in the history of philosophy to study Berkeley's speculations as they issued from his own mind, we think it will be recognised that of all who, from the earliest times, have applied the powers of their minds to metaphysical inquiries, he is the one of greatest philosophic genius: though among these are included Plato, Hobbes, Locke, Hartley, and Hume; Descrates, Spinoza, Leibnitz, and Kant. For, greatly as all these have helped the progress of philosophy, and important as are the contributions of several of them to its positive truths, of no one of them can it be said as of Berkeley, that we owe to him three first-rate philosophical discoveries, each sufficient to have constituted a revolution in psychology, and which by their combination have determined the whole course of subsequent philosophical speculation; discoveries, too, which were not, like the achievements of many other distinguished thinkers, merely refutations of error, and removal of obstacles to sound thinking, but were this and much more also, being all of them entitled to a permanent place among positive truths. These discoveries are—1. The doctrine of the acquired perceptions of sight. . . . 2. The non-existence of abstract ideas. . . . 3. The true nature and meaning of the externality which we attribute to the objects of our senses.—MILL, JOHN STUART, 1871, *Berkeley's Life and Writings, The Fortnightly Review, vol.* 16, *pp.* 505, 506.

To me it appears that idealism has retrograded, not advanced, since Berkeley; and that if we want to study the system at its best, we must go back to the fountain-head of it. For his system there is a great deal to be said; for systems derived from it very much less.—NOEL, RODEN, 1872, *The Philosophy of Perception, The Contemporary Review, vol.* 20, *p.* 72.

The last touch that finishes does not always turn out of hand *for*, but often out of hand *from*, use; and it is just possible that this perfect edition of the *works* of Berkeley appears precisely at the moment that the *work* of Berkeley ceases to function anywhere—orbis terrarum anywhere. The course of Berkeleianism has been this. It functioned historically according to power, in its own day, upon a few; but was soon almost entirely neglected. The revival of poetry in England gradually restored in every larger heart the feeling of religion, and, where this feeling could not at the same time reconcile itself with all the elements of positive religion, Berkeleianism was felt to supply an intellectual want. Such want, though with considerable modification of form, it may be said, to some extent, still to supply. But, side by side with it, as equal companion of the nurture, this want must now be content to accept its own opposite; for the entire matter with which Messrs. Mill and Bain seek to indoctrinate their readers at present is to to be found in the earliest writings of Berkeley, and especially in his very first, the "New Theory of Vision." —STIRLING, JAMES HUTCHISON, 1873, *Professor Fraser's Berkeley, Journal of Speculative Philosophy, vol.* 7, *p.* 3.

One of the most subtle and original

English metaphysicians. . . . Berkeley's new conception marks a distinct stage of progress in human thought. His true place in the history of speculation may be seen from the simple observation that the difficulties or obscurities in his scheme are really the points on which later philosophy has turned. He once for all lifted the problem of metaphysics to a higher level, and, in conjunction with his great successor, Hume, determined the form into which later metaphysical questions have been thrown.—ADAMSON, ROBERT, 1875, *Encyclopædia Britannica, Ninth edition, vol.* III.

Acutest of English metaphysicians and most graceful of philosophic writers.—STEPHEN, LESLIE, 1876, *History of English Thought in the Eighteenth Century, vol.* I, *p.* 86.

Berkeley had no hesitation in preferring a sensationalist theory of knowing to a materialistic theory of being: indeed, the former recommended itself to him mainly as a weapon against the latter. . . . Berkeley, no doubt, thought that if he could rid the world of material substance, he would thus establish the absolute reality of spirit. He did not observe that the weapon he had so hastily taken up was double-edged, and that in rejecting Locke's materialistic ontology, he was rejecting all ontology whatever and reducing reality to a series of feelings, which by this reduction were emptied of all intelligible meaning.—CAIRD, EDWARD, 1877, *A Critical Account of the Philosophy of Kant, p.* 61.

The above sentences from Edwards, avowing Idealism, were written nine or ten years before Berkeley came to America. Moreover, Edwards was not the man to conceal his intellectual obligations; and the name of Berkeley nowhere occurs, as far as I can discover, in all the ten volumes of Edwards's printed writings. It seems more probable that the peculiar opinions which Edwards held in common with Berkeley, were reached by him through an independent process of reasoning and somewhat in the same way that they were reached by Berkeley, who, as Professor Fraser says, "proceeded in his intellectual work on the basis of postulates which he partly borrowed from Locke, and partly assumed in antagonism to him."—TYLER, MOSES COIT, 1878, *A History of American Literature,* 1676–1765, *vol.* II, *p.* 183, *note.*

Berkeleian Idealism is of all speculative theories concerning the external world the one which, perhaps, most quickly and easily commends itself to the philosophic enquirer. The greater number of persons who dabble in such subjects have been idealists at one period of their lives if they have not remained so; and many more, who would not call themselves idealists, are nevertheless of opinion that though the existence of matter is a thing to be believed in, it is not a thing which it is possible to prove. The causes of this popularity are, no doubt, in part, the extreme simplicity of the reasoning on which the theory rests, in part its extreme plausibility, in part, perhaps, the nature of the result which is commonly thought to be speculatively interesting without being practically inconvenient. For it has to be observed, that the true idealist is not necessarily of opinion that his system properly understood, in any way contradicts common sense. It destroys, no doubt, a belief in substance; but then substance is a metaphysical phantom conjured up by a vain philosophy: the Matter of ordinary life it supposes itself to leave untouched.—BALFOUR, ARTHUR JAMES, 1879, *A Defence of Philosophic Doubt, p.* 178.

The truest, acutest philosopher that Great Britain has ever known.—MORRIS, GEORGE S., 1880, *British Thought and Thinkers, p.* 233.

Whether Berkeley's doctrine be true or false, it is certain that he has an important place in the development of English thought, and that his opinions have reappeared in different forms, embodied in the systems of men who are ordinarily thought to be entirely opposed to the philosophy which he defended. Some who have begun with materialism have ended by reproducing the doctrines contained in the "Principles of Human Knowledge," and the University of Edinburgh, which at one time learned philosophy from Berkeley's most able opponent, is now favored with the teaching of Berkeley's most sympathetic expounder.—ALEXANDER, ARCHIBALD, 1885, *The Idealism of Bishop Berkeley, The Presbyterian Review, vol.* 6, *p.* 301.

The absolute spiritualism of Berkeley is a unitary, homogeneous system, unquestionably superior to the hybrid philosophies of Descartes and Wolff. Nay, it is, in my opinion, the only metaphysic that may be successfully opposed to materialism, for it alone takes into consideration the partial truth of its objections. It overcomes the dualism of substances, and thus satisfies the most fundamental demand of the philosophical spirit,—the demand for unity. In this respect it has all the advantages of radical materialism without being hampered by its difficulties. It greatly resembles the system of Leibniz, but excels it in clearness, consistency, boldness, and decision. Leibniz's opinions on matter, space, and time are undecided, conciliatory, and even obscure. Berkeley shows no sign of hesitation. An earnest and profoundly honest thinker, he tells us, in a straightforward manner, that the existence of matter is an illusion; that time is nothing, abstracted from the succession of ideas in our minds; that space cannot exist without the mind; that minds alone exist; and that these perceive ideas either by themselves or through the action of the all-powerful Spirit on which they depend. . . . He is both a thorough-going theologian and a philosopher; his interests are both scientific and religious, and he attacks materialism not only as a theoretical error but as the source of the most serious heresies.—WEBER, ALFRED, 1892–96, *History of Philosophy, tr. Thilly, pp.* 397, 398.

One of the sanest and noblest of English philosophers. . . . Pope's age produced a few great masters of style, and among them Berkeley holds an undisputed place. He succeeded, too, in the most difficult department of intellectual labour, since to express abstruse thought in language as beautiful as it is clear is the rarest of gifts.—DENNIS, JOHN, 1894, *The Age of Pope, pp.* 226, 229.

In his enthusiasm and in his eloquence he kept alive the torch that had been handed on to him from the theologians of another day; in his lucid clearness he added a new element, in which he was akin to the more scientific thought of his own age; and in the richness of his imagination, in the perfection of his philosophic style, he attains to that uniqueness which is the chief attribute of genius.—CRAIK, HENRY, 1895, *ed., English Prose, Introduction, vol.* IV, *p.* 5.

In all philosophical writing there is a certain antinomy. By so much as it is popular, figurative, literary, imaginative, it seems to lack philosophical precision; by so much as it is technical, austere, unliterary, and what has been called "jargonish," it loses humanity and general appeal. If the golden mean was ever hit between these extremes it seems to have been hit in the style of Berkeley. Take the most popular expositions of it as in "Alciphron" and "Siris," the less popular as in the "Theory of Visions," or "Hylas and Philonous," compare them together, note their excellencies, and if any can be detected allow for their defects, and such a philosophical medium as nowhere else exists will, I believe, be found. A crystalline clearness, a golden eloquence, a supreme urbanity, a mixture of fancy and logic which is nowhere else discernible except in Plato, an allowance for sentiment and unction which exists side by side with a readiness to play the game of sheer rough-and-tumble argument at any moment and with any adversary; a preciseness of phrase which is never dull or dry; a felicity of ornament and illustration which never condescends to the merely popular or trivial, and is never used to cloak controversial feebleness; an incapacity of petulance, and an omnipresence of good breeding—these are the characteristics of the style of Berkeley.—SAINTSBURY, GEORGE, 1895, *English Prose, ed. Craik, vol.* IV, *p.* 27.

William Hamilton

1704–1754

William Hamilton (1704–54), born probably at his father's estate of Bangour near Uphall, Linlithgowshire, contributed to Ramsay's "Tea-table Miscellany" (1724). He joined in the Jacobite rising of the '45, and on its collapse escaped to Rouen, but was permitted to return in 1749 and to succeed to the family estate. He died at Lyons. The first collection of his poems was edited by Adam Smith in 1748 (fuller ed. 1760). One poem—"The Braes of Yarrow"—will never die.—PATRICK AND GROOME, *eds.*, 1897, *Chambers's Biographical Dictionary, p.* 457.

PERSONAL

Hamilton's mind is pictured in his verses. They are the easy and careless effusions of an elegant and a chastened taste; and the sentiments they convey are the genuine feelings of a tender and susceptible heart, which perpetually owned the dominion of some favourite mistress, but whose passion generally evaporated in song, and made no serious or permanent impression.—TYTLER, ALEXANDER FRASER (LORD WOODHOUSELEE), 1807, *Memoirs of the Life and Writings of the Hon. Henry Home of Kames, bk.* i, *ch.* iii.

The praise of elegance is all that can be given to his verses. In case any reader should be immoderately touched with sympathy for his love sufferings, it is proper to inform him, that Hamilton was thought by the fair ones of his day to be a very inconstant swain. A Scotch lady, whom he teased with his addresses, applied to Home, the author of Douglas, for advice how to get rid of them. Home advised her to affect to favour his assiduities. She did so, and they were immediately withdrawn.—CAMPBELL, THOMAS, 1819, *Specimens of the British Poets.*

THE BRAES OF YARROW

Amid the generally vague verbiage of his descriptions, one effort of his genius stands out in vividness of human colouring, in depth and simplicity of feeling, and even to some extent in powerful and characteristic touches of scenery. This is a poem which owes its inspiration to the Yarrow. In fact it was suggested by the older poem of "The Dowie Dens." It breathes the soul of the place, and it is so permeated by the spirit of its history and traditions that, when all the other writings of the author shall have fallen into oblivion, there will still be a nook in memory and a place in men's hearts for "The Braes of Yarrow."—VEITCH, JOHN, 1878, *The History and Poetry of the Scottish Border, p.* 452.

The secret of the enduring popularity of this ballad is its somewhat feminine sentiment and the sweetness of fancy it displays. That which delighted Wordsworth was the note of sincerity in reference to nature, a note rare enough then in England, but common to all the Scotch poets of the time. The poem is marred by that want of force which proved to be Hamilton's defect in all he ever wrote.—WALKER, HUGH, 1893, *Three Centuries of Scottish Literature, vol.* II, *p.* 51.

It stands out, one of the few genuine inheritors of the spirit of ancient folksong. —EYRE-TODD, GEORGE, 1896, *Scottish Poetry of the Eighteenth Century, vol.* I, *p.* 125.

GENERAL

The chief beauty of these "Elegies" certainly consists in their being written by a man who intimately felt the subject; for they are more the language of the heart than of the head. They have warmth, but little poetry, and Mr. Hamilton seems to have been one of those poets, who are made so by love, not by nature.—CIBBER, THEOPHILUS, 1753, *Lives of the Poets, vol.* V, *p.* 308.

Johnson, upon repeated occasions, while I was at Ashbourne, talked slightingly of Hamilton. He said there was no power of thinking in his verses; nothing that strikes one; nothing better than what you generally find in magazines; and that the highest praise they deserved was, that they were very well for a gentleman to hand about among his friends.—BOSWELL, JAMES, 1777, *Life of Johnson, ed. Hill, vol.* III, *p.* 170.

As a first adventurer in English literature, rejecting altogether the scholastic school of poetry, Mr. Hamilton must be allowed to have obtained no ordinary success. In his language he shows nearly all the purity of a native; his diction is various and powerful, and his versification but rarely tainted with provincial errors. He delights indeed in a class of words, which though not rejected by the best English writers, have a certain insipidity which only a refined English ear, perhaps, can perceive; such as *beauteous, dubious, duteous,* and even *melancholious!* The same peculiarity may be remarked of most of the early Scottish writers in the English language.—CHAMBERS, ROBERT, 1832–35–55, *A Biographical Dictionary of Eminent Scotsmen, ed. Thomson, vol.* III, *p.* 10.

His first and best strains were dedicated to the lyric muse; and the most attractive feature of his poetry is its pure English style, accompanied with a somewhat ornate poetical diction. He possessed more fancy than feeling, and in this respect his amatory songs resemble those of the poets of Charles the Second's court.

—MILLS, ABRAHAM, 1851, *The Literature and the Literary Men of Great Britain and Ireland, vol.* II, *p.* 319.

Besides conventional lyrics of comparatively small account, Hamilton wrote various notable poems. In "Contemplation, or the Triumph of Love," warmly praised in the "Lounger," by Professor Richardson and Henry Mackenzie, there is much ingenuity of reflection and illustration, in rhymed octosyllabics evincing structural skill and dexterity. The translations from Greek and Latin poets—notably those from Horace—display both scholarship and metrical grace. "The Parting of Hector and Andromache," from the first Iliad, has the distinction of being the earliest Homeric translation into English blank verse. The "Episode of the Thistle," ingeniously explaining the remote origin of the Scottish national emblem—"the armed warrior with his host of spears"—is not without a measure of epic force and dignity. The winter piece in the third of four odes, besides its intrinsic merits, probably inspired the opening passage of the first introduction in "Marmion." But the prominent and thoroughly individual feature of the poem is what Wordsworth, in that heading to "Yarrow Unvisited," calls "the exquisite ballad of Hamilton." Scott, in his introductory remarks to the "Dowie Dens of Yarrow" (*Border Ministrelsy*, iii. 145), says: "It will be, with many readers, the greatest recommendation of these verses, that they are supposed to have suggested to Mr. Hamilton of Bangour the modern ballad beginning,

Busk ye, busk ye my bonny, bonny bride."

If for this poem alone, Hamilton will not be forgotten.—BAYNE, THOMAS, 1890, *Dictionary of National Biography, edited by Leslie Stephen and Sidney Lee, vol.* XXIV, *p.* 222.

Hamilton seems to have had a great deal of force and passion which he deliberately repressed—perhaps thinking the age would not stand it—perhaps himself ashamed of it.—PHELPS, WILLIAM LYON, 1893, *The Beginnings of the English Romantic Movement, p.* 35.

Thomas Carte

1686–1754

Thomas Carte: historian; born at Clifton, near Rugby, England, in April, 1686; educated at University College, Oxford. He became a priest and Jacobite. During the rebellion of 1715 a large reward was offered for his arrest, but he escaped to France. His chief work is a "History of England" (4 vols., 1747–55), which is prized for its facts, but is not well written. Many volumes of his manuscripts are preserved in the Bodleian Library at Oxford. Died April 7, 1754.—ADAMS, CHARLES KENDALL, *ed.*, 1897, *Johnson's Universal Cyclopaedia, vol.* II, *p.* 100.

PERSONAL

About thirty-two years of age, of a middle stature, a raw-boned man, goes a little stooping, a sallow complexion, with a full grey or blue eye, his eyelids fair, inclining to red, and commonly wears a light-coloured peruke.—PROCLAMATION IN GAZETTE, 1722, *Aug.* 15.

Carte possessed a strong constitution, capable of incessant labor. He often wrote from early morning until night, taking only a cup of tea in the interval. Then he would eat heartily and enjoy his late dinner. He was gay and jovial, careless in his dress and appearance. In his writings there is little to be praised except their laborious accuracy, and the chief value of his collections and history consists in their having prepared the way for the more gifted Hume.—LAWRENCE EUGENE, 1855, *The Lives of the British Historians, vol.* I, *p.* 326.

GENERAL

Your history ["Duke of Ormonde"] is in great esteem here. All sides seem to like it. The dean of St. Patrick's (Swift) honours you with his approbation. Any name after his could not add to your satisfaction. But I may say, the worthy and the wise are with you to a man, and you have me into the bargain.—BOYLE, JOHN (LORD ORRERY), 1736? *Letter to Carte.*

Carte's "Life of the Duke of Ormonde" is considered as a book of authority; but it is ill written. The matter is diffused in too many words; there is no animation, no compression, no vigour. Two good volumes in duodecimo might be made out of the two (three) in folio.—JOHNSON, SAMUEL, 1773, *Life by Boswell, Oct.* 8.

Although the author died before the publication of the last volume, in 1755—intending to bring his work down to the Restoration—yet he lived long enough to witness its success, and the victory which he had obtained over its numerous opponents, and the shame attached to those who had withdrawn their original patronage. This work will live long and always be consulted.—DIBDIN, THOMAS FROGNALL, 1824, *The Library Companion.*

Of borrowers from Carte, Hume is one of the largest, and would have acted with more justice by frank acknowledgments of his obligations. It is amusing to observe the cavalier manner in which he incidentally alludes to Carte in his *notes* as "a late author of great industry and learning, but full of prejudices and of no penetration." The two authors occupy the same relative position as those of the laborious miner and the skilful polisher of the precious metal, which but for the assiduity of the former might still be undistinguished beneath the clod. But those who wish to gather all the gold must still revert to Carte.—ALLIBONE, S. AUSTIN, 1854–58, *A Critical Dictionary of English Literature, vol.* I, *p.* 347.

It was not prepossessing in point of style; but it was so great an advance on previous histories, in the extent of the original material used and quoted, that it would have commanded success but for an unlucky note, inserted at p. 291, on a passage concerning the unction of our kings at their coronation. In this note (which his friends vainly pleaded was not by his hand), he asserted his belief in the cure of king's evil in the case of a man named Christopher Lovel of Bristol, by the touch of the Pretender, or, as he called him, "the eldest lineal descendant of a race of kings who had, indeed, for a long succession of ages cured that disease by the royal touch." The cure was said to have been effected at Avignon in November 1716. This raised a storm among the anti-Jacobite party. Carte was attacked in several pamphlets, and a writer in the "Gentleman's Magazine" (1748, p. 13) professed to have investigated the case and found it, of course, entirely false. The man had been temporarily cured by the change of air and regimen, but had suffered a relapse on his return and died when on a second voyage. The practical result to Carte was the withdrawal of the grant from the common council of London by a unanimous vote on 7 April 1748 (Gent. Mag. 1748, p. 185), and an immediate neglect of his work. In spite of such discouragement he persisted in his enterprise, and the next two volumes appeared in 1752, and a fourth in 1755, after his death.—SHUCKBURGH, E. S., 1887, *Dictionary of National Biography, vol.* IX, *p.* 193.

Henry Fielding

1707–1754

Born, at Sharphan Park, Somersetshire, 22 April 1707. Family moved to East Stour, Dorsetshire, 1710. Educated at Eton [1719?–1725?]. At Leyden, studying Law [1725–27?]. Returned to London. First play, "Love in several Masques," produced at Drury Lane, Feb. 1728. Probably returned to Leyden for a short time in 1728. Prolific writer of plays, 1727–37. Married Charlotte Craddock, 1735 [?]. Manager of Haymarket Theatre, 1736–37. Entered Middle Temple, 1 Nov. 1737; called to Bar, 20 June 1740. Edited "The Champion," with J. Ralph; contrib. articles, 27 Nov. 1739 to 12 June 1740. Revised his play, "The Wedding Day," for Garrick; produced 17 Feb. 1743. Wife died, 1743 [?]. Ed. "The True Patriot," 5 Nov. 1745 to 10 June 1746. Edited "The Jacobite's Journal," Dec. 1747 to Nov. 1748. Married Mary Daniel, 27 Nov. 1747. Lived at Twickenham. Moved to house in Bow Street, when appointed J. P. for Westminster, Dec. 1748. Chairman of Quarter Sessions, Hick's Hall, May 1749. Ed. "Covent Garden Journal," Jan. to Nov. 1752. Severe illness, winter of 1749, and spring of 1754. Moved to Ealing, May 1754. To Lisbon for health, July 1754. Died there, 8 Oct. 1754; buried in English cemetery there. *Works:* "Love in several Masques," 1728; "Rape upon Rape" (anon.), 1730 (another edition called: "The Coffee-house Politicians," 1730); "The Temple Beau," 1730; "The Author's Farce" (under pseud. "H. Scriblerus Secundus"), 1730; "Tom Thumb" (by "Scriblerus Secundus"), 1730 (with additional act, 1731); "The Welsh Opera" (by "Scriblerus Secundus"), 1731 (2nd edn. same year, called: "The Grub Street Opera"); "The Letter-Writers" (by "H. Scriblerus Secundus"), 1731; "The Lottery" (anon.), 1732; "The Modern Husband," 1732; "The Covent Garden Tragedy" (anon.), 1732; "The Debauchees" (or "The Old Debauchees;" anon.), 1732; "The Mock Doctor" (anon.; from Molière), 1732; "The Miser," 1733; "The Intriguing Chambermaid," 1734 (from Regnard); "Don Quixote in England," 1734; "An Old Man taught Wisdom," 1735; "The Universal Gallant," 1735; "Pasquin," 1736; "The Historical Register for the Year 1736" (anon.), 1737; "Eurydice," 1737; "Tumble-down Dick," 1737; "The Vernon-aid" (anon.), 1741; "The Crisis," (anon.), 1741; "Miss Lucy in Town" (anon.), 1742; "Letter to a Noble Lord" (respecting preceding; anon.), 1742; "The History of the Adventures of Joseph Andrews" (2 vols.; anon.), 1742 (2nd edn. same year); "A Full Vindication of the Duchess Dowager of Marlborough" (anon.), 1742; "Plutus" (from Aristophanes, with W. Young), 1742; "The Wedding Day," 1743; "Miscellanies" (including "Jonathan Wild," 3 vols.), 1743 (2nd edn. same year); "Proper Answer to a Scurrilous Libel," 1747; "The History of Tom Jones" (6 vols.), 1749; "A Charge delivered to the Grand Jury," 1749; "A True State of the Case of Bosavern Penlez," 1749; "An Enquiry into the Causes of the late Increase of Robbers, etc.," 1751; "Amelia," 1751; "Examples of the Interposition of Providence," 1752; "Proposals for making an effectual Provision for the Poor," 1753; "A clear State of the Case of Elizabeth Canning," 1753. *Posthumous:* "Journal of a Voyage to Lisbon," 1755; "The Fathers," 1778. He *translated:* Ovid's "Art of Love," under title of "The Lover's Assistant," 1859; and *edited:* the 2nd edn. of Sarah Fielding's "Adventures of David Simple," 1744, and "Familiar Letters," 1747. *Collected Works:* ed. by Murphy, in 4 vols., 1762; ed. by Chalmers, in 10 vols., 1806; ed. by Roscoe, 1840; ed. by Herbert, 1872; ed. by Leslie Stephen, 10 vols. 1882; ed. by G. Saintsbury, 12 vols. 1893. *Life:* by F. Lawrence, 1855; by Austin Dobson, 1883.—SHARP, R. FARQUHARSON, 1897, *A Dictionary of English Authors*, p. 99.

PERSONAL

HENRICI FIELDING
A SOMERSETENSIBUS APUD GLASTONIAM
ORIUNDI,
FIRI SUMMO INGENIO,
EN QUÆ RESTRANT!
STYLO QUO NON ALIUS UNQUAM,
INTIMA QUI POTUIT CORDIS RESERARE,
MORES HOMINUM
EXCOLENDOS SUSCEPIT.
VIRTUTI DECOREM, VITIO FŒDITATEM
ASSERUIT, SUUM CUIQUE TRIBUENS;
NON QUIN IPSE SUBINDE IRRETIRETUR
EVITANDIS—
ARDENS IN AMICITIA, IN MISERIA
SUBLEVANDA EFFUSUS,
HILARIS, URBANUS, ET CONJUX, ET PATER
ADAMATUS,
ALIIS, NON SIBI VIXIT.
VIXIT: SED MORTEM VICTRICEM VINCIT.
DUM NATURA
DURAT, DUM SÆCULA CURRUNT,
NATURÆ PROLEM SCRIPTIS PRÆ SE FERENS,
SUAM ET SUÆ GENTIS EXTENDET FAMAM.
—INSCRIPTION ON TOMB, *English Cemetery, Lisbon.*

F——g, who *yesterday* appear'd so rough,
Clad in *coarse Frize*, and plaister'd down with
Snuff,
See how his *Instant* gaudy Trappings shine;
What *Play-house* Bard was ever seen so fine!
But this, not from his *Humour* flows, you'll
say,
But mere *Necessity*;—for last Night lay
In *Pawn*, the *Velvet* which he wears to-Day.
—ANON, 1735, *Seasonable Reproof.*

These so tolerated companies gave encouragement to *a broken wit* to collect a fourth company, who for some time acted plays in the Haymarket. . . . This enterprising person, I say (whom I do not choose to name, unless it could be to his advantage, or that it were of importance), had sense enough to know that the best plays with bad actors would turn but to a very poor account, and therefore found it necessary to give the public some pieces of an extraordinary kind, the poetry of which he conceived ought to be so strong that the greatest dunce of an actor could not spoil it: he knew, too, that as he was in haste to get money, it would take up less time to be intrepidly abusive than decently entertaining; that to draw the mob after him he must rake the channel and pelt their superiors. . . . Such then was the mettlesome modesty he set out with; upon this principle he produced several frank and free farces, that seemed to knock all distinctions of mankind on the head—religion, laws, government, priests, judges, and ministers, were all laid flat, at the feet of this *Herculean* satirist! this Drawcansir in wit, who spared neither friend nor foe! who, to make his poetical fame immortal, like another Erostratus, set fire to his stage by writing up to an act of parliament to demolish it. I shall not give the particular strokes of his ingenuity a chance to be remembered by reciting them; it may be enough to say, in general terms, they were so openly flagrant that the wisdom of the legislature thought it high time to take a proper notice of them.—CIBBER, COLLEY, 1740, *Apology.*

I wish you had been with me last week when I spent two evenings with Fielding and his sister, who wrote "David Simple:" and you may guess I was very well entertained. The lady, indeed, retired pretty soon, but Russell and I sat up with the poet till one or two in the morning, and were inexpressibly diverted. I find he values, as he justly may, his "Joseph Andrews" above all his writings. He was extremely civil to me, I fancy on my father's account. — WARTON, JOSEPH, 1746, *Letter to Thomas Warton, Oct.*

He [Rigby] and Peter Bathurst t'other night carried a servant of the latter's, who had attempted to shoot him, before Fielding; who, to all his other vocations, has, by the grace of Mr. Lyttelton, added that of Middlesex justice. He sent them word he was at supper, that they must come next morning. They did not understand that freedom, and ran up, where they found him banqueting with a blind man, a whore, and three Irishmen, on some cold mutton and a bone of ham, both in one dish, and the dirtiest cloth. He never stirred nor asked them to sit. Rigby, who had seen him so often come to beg a guinea of Sir C. Williams, and Bathurst, at whose father's he had lived for victuals, understood that dignity as little, and pulled themselves chairs; on which he civilised.—WALPOLE, HORACE, 1749, *Letter to George Montagu, May* 18; *Letters, ed. Cunningham, vol.* II, *p.* 162.

I dined with him (Ralph Allen) yesterday, where I met Mr. Fielding,—a poor emaciated, worn-out rake, whose gout and infirmities have got the better even of his buffoonery.—HURD, RICHARD, 1751, *Letter to Balguy, March* 19.

I advise Mr. Spondy to give him the refusal of this same pastoral; who knows but he may have the good fortune of being listed in the number of his beef-eaters, in which case he may, in process of time, be provided for in the Customs or the Church; *when he is inclined to marry his own cook-wench his gracious patron may condescend to give the bride away; and may finally settle him, in his old age, as a trading Westminster Justice.*—SMOLLETT, TOBIAS GEORGE, 1751, *Adventures of Peregrin Pickle.*

I am sorry for H. Fielding's death, and not only as I shall read no more of his writings, but I believe he lost more than others, as no man enjoyed life more than he did, though few had less reason to do so, the highest of his preferment being raking in the lowest sinks of vice and misery. I should think it a nobler and less nauseous employment to be one of the staff-officers that conduct the nocturnal weddings. His happy constitution (even when he had, with great pains, half demolished it) made him forget everything when he was before a venison pasty, or over a flask of champaigne; and I am persuaded he has known more happy moments than any prince upon earth. His natural spirits gave him rapture with his cook-maid, and cheerfulness when he was starving in a garret. There was a great similitude between his character and that of Sir Richard Steele. He had the advantage both in learning and, in my opinion, genius: they both agreed in wanting money in spite of all their friends, and would have wanted it, if their hereditary lands had been as extensive as their imagination; yet each of them so formed for happiness, it is pity he was not immortal.—MONTAGU, LADY MARY WORTLEY, 1755, *Letter to the Countess of Bute, Sept.* 22.

Mr. Fielding had not been long a writer for the stage, when he married Miss Craddock, a beauty from Salisbury. About that time, his mother dying, a moderate estate, at Stower, in Dorsetshire, devolved to him. To that place he retired with his wife, on whom he doated, with a resolution to bid adieu to all the follies and intemperances to which he had addicted himself in the career of a town-life. But unfortunately a kind of family-pride here gained an ascendant over him; and he began immediately to vie in splendour with the neighbouring country 'squires. With an estate not much above two hundred pounds a-year, and his wife's fortune, which did not exceed fifteen hundred pounds, he encumbered himself with a large retinue of servants, all clad in costly yellow liveries. For their master's honour, these people could not descend so low as to be careful in their apparel, but, in a month or two, were unfit to be seen; the 'squire's dignity required that they should be new-equipped; and his chief pleasure consisting in society and convivial mirth, hospitality threw open its doors, and in less than three years, entertainments, hounds, and horses, entirely devoured a little patrimony, which, had it been managed with economy, might have secured to him a state of independence for the rest of his life. . . . His passions, as the poet expresses it, were trembling alive all o'er: whatever he desired, he desired ardently; he was alike impatient of disappointment, or ill-usage, and the same quickness of sensibility rendered him elate in prosperity, and overflowing with gratitude at every instance of friendship or generosity: steady in his private attachments, his affection was warm, sincere, and vehement; in his resentments, he was manly, but temperate, seldom breaking out in his writings into gratifications of ill humour, or personal satire. It is to the honour of those whom he loved, that he had too much penetration to be deceived in their characters; and it is to the advantage of his enemies, that he was above passionate attacks upon them. Open, unbounded, and social in his temper, he knew no love of money; but, inclining to excess even in his very virtues, he pushed his contempt of avarice into the opposite extreme of imprudence and prodigality. When young in life he had a moderate estate, he soon suffered hospitality to devour it; and when in the latter end of his days he had an income of four or five hundred a-year, he knew no use of money, but to keep his table open to those who had been his friends when young, and had impaired their own fortunes. Though disposed to gallantry by his strong animal spirits, and the vivacity of his passions, he was remarkable for tenderness and constancy to his wife, and the strongest affection for his children.—MURPHY, ARTHUR, 1762, *An Essay on the Life and Genius of Henry Fielding, Esq., Works, ed. Chalmers, vol.* I, *pp.* 44, 82.

If I could not discover the place of Camoens' interment, I at last found out the grave and tombstone of the author of "Tom Jones." Fielding, who terminated his life, as is well-known, at Lisbon, in 1754, of a complication of disorders, at little more than forty-seven years of age, lies buried in the cemetery appropriated to the English factory. I visited his grave, which was already nearly concealed by weeds and nettles. Though he did not suffer the extremity of distress under which Camoens and Cervantes terminated their lives, yet his extravagance—a quality so commonly characteristic of men distinguished by talents—embittered the evening of his days.—WRAXALL, SIR NATHANIEL WILLIAM, 1815, *Historical Memoirs of My own Time, from* 1772 *to* 1784.

Nor was she (Lady Mary Wortley Montagu) a stranger to that beloved first wife, whose picture he drew in his "Amelia," where, as she said, even the glowing language he knew how to employ did not do more than justice to the amiable qualities of the original, or to her beauty, although this had suffered a little from the accident related in the novel—a frightful overturn, which destroyed the gristle of her nose. He loved her passionately, and she returned his affection. . . . His biographers seem to have been shy of disclosing that after the death of this charming woman, he married her maid. And yet the act was not so discreditable to his character as it may sound. The maid had few personal charms, but was an excellent creature, devotedly attached to her mistress, and almost broken-hearted for her loss. In the first agonies of his own grief, which approached to frenzy, he found no relief but from weeping along with her; nor solace when a degree calmer, but in talking to her of the angel they mutually regretted. This made her his habitual confidential associate, and in process of time he began to think he could not give his children a tenderer mother, or secure for himself a more faithful housekeeper and nurse. At least, this was what he told his friends; and it is certain that her conduct as his wife confirmed it, and fully justified his good opinion.—STUART, LADY LOUISA, 1837, *Letters and Works of Lady Mary Wortley Montagu, ed. Wharncliffe, Introductory Anecdotes.*

Let travellers devote one entire morning to inspecting the Arcos and the Mai das agoas, after which they may repair to the English church and cemetery, Pere-la-chaise in miniature, where, if they be of England, they may well be excused if they kiss the cold tomb, as I did, of the author of "Amelia," the most singular genius which their island ever produced, whose works it has long been the fashion to abuse in public and to read in secret.—BORROW, GEORGE, 1843, *The Bible in Spain.*

I cannot offer or hope to make a hero of Harry Fielding. Why hide his faults? Why conceal his weaknesses in a cloud of periphrasis? Why not show him, like him as he is, not robed in a marble toga, and draped and polished in a heroic attitude, but with inked ruffles, and claret stains on his tarnished lace coat, and on his manly face the marks of good fellowship, of illness, of kindness, of care, and wine. Stained as you see him, and worn by care and dissipation, that man retains some of the most precious and splendid human qualities and endowments. He has an admirable natural love of truth, the keenest instinctive antipathy to hypocrisy, the happiest satirical gift of laughing it to scorn. His wit is wonderfully wise and detective; it flashes upon a rogue and lightens up a rascal like a policeman's lantern. He is one of the manliest and kindliest of human beings: in the midst of all his imperfections, he respects female innocence and infantine tenderness, as you would suppose such a great-hearted, courageous soul would respect and care for them. He could not be so brave, generous, truth-telling as he is, were he not infinitely merciful, pitiful, and tender. He will give any man his purse—he cannot help kindness and profusion. He may have low tastes, but not a mean mind; he admires with all his heart good and virtuous men, stoops to no flattery, bears no rancour, disdains all disloyal arts, does his public duty uprightly, is fondly loved by his family, and dies at his work.—THACKERAY, WILLIAM MAKEPEACE, 1853, *The English Humourists of the Eighteenth Century.*

The day of reckoning came. In a very short time Fielding found that all was spent and gone—all swallowed up in the abyss of ruin! It seemed like a dream, a wild, incoherent vision. The roar of mirth, the deafening cheer, the splendid liveries, prancing horses, staring rustics, full-mouthed dogs, faded before him like some "insubstantial pageant." He had been generous, hospitable, profuse; and what was his reward? Those who had sat at meat with him now ridiculed his extravagance. Even the gaping boors of the neighbourhood cracked their heavy jokes at his expense. The prudent gentlemen and ladies who had not scrupled to sit at his jovial board, and partake of his cheer, now shook their heads, and gravely condemned his prodigality. Those of his more ambitious neighbours whom he had recently outshone in splendour, rejoiced in his downfall, without attempting to conceal their satisfaction. In the midst of all these untoward circumstances, he had to escape from his creditors as best he might, and to seek for happiness and a livelihood in some other sphere. How bitterly Fielding cursed his folly, and how penitently he bewailed his imprudence, can be well imagined. His sorrow—now, alas! unavailing—was not unmixed with feelings of resentment. The jealousy with which he had been regarded in the height of his ostentatious career, and the treatment he experienced in his reverses, long rankled in his breast. He could not easily forget the sneers and slights of those whom in his heart he so much despised; and from this time forth, therefore, the Squirearchy of England had to expect little mercy at his hands.—LAWRENCE, FREDERICK, 1855, *The Life of Henry Fielding, p.* 75.

Henry Fielding was at Lyme Regis, Dorsetshire, for the purpose of carrying off an heiress, Miss Andrew, the daughter of Solomon Andrew, Esq., the last of a series of merchants of that name at Lyme. The young lady was living with Mr. Andrew Tucker, one of the Corporation, who sent her away to Modbury in South Devon, where she married an ancestor of the present Rev. Mr. Rhodes, of Bath, who possesses the Andrew property. The circumstances about the attempt of Henry Fielding to carry off the young lady, handed down in the ancient Tucker family, were doubted by the late Dr. Rhodes, of Shapwick, &c. Since his death, I have found an entry in the old archives of Lyme about the fears of Andrew Tucker, Esq., as to his safety, owing to the behaviour of Henry Fielding and his attendant or man. According to the tradition of the Tucker family, Sophia Western was intended to portray Miss Andrew.—ROBERTS, GEORGE, 1855, *Letter to the Athenæum, Nov.*

In person Fielding was tall and large, being upwards of six feet high, and he seems to have attached much value to physical power, for he forms all his heroes after his own likeness. In consequence probably of his formation, he appears to have had a high relish for animal enjoyments. . . . That previous to his marriage he ran headlong into every species of dissipation, is, I fear, not to be doubted; but, as I have endeavoured to show, we have no proof that his life was otherwise than regular after his marriage. Had he, for example, been unfaithful to his adored wife, such was his innate candour that we can hardly doubt but he would have seized some occasion of confessing and deploring it. Even in his most licentious days, he never lost his respect for religion and virtue.—KEIGHTLEY, THOMAS, 1858, *On the Life and Writings of Henry Fielding, Fraser's Magazine, vol.* 57, *pp.* 209, 210.

Fielding protests on behalf of nature; and certainly to see his actions and his persons, we might think him made expressly for that: a robust, strongly built man, above six feet high, sanguine, with an excess of good humor and animal spirits, loyal, generous, affectionate, and brave, but imprudent, extravagant, a drinker, a roysterer, ruined as it were by heirloom, having seen the ups and down of life, bespattered, but always jolly. . . . Force, activity, invention, tenderness, all overflowed in him. He had a mother's fondness for his children, adored his wife, became almost mad when he lost her, found no other consolation than to weep with his maid-servant, and ended by marrying that good and honest girl, that he might give a mother to his children; the last trait in the portrait of his valiant plebeian heart, quick in telling all, possessing no dislikes, but all the best parts of man, except delicacy. We read his books as we drink a pure, wholesome, and rough wine, which cheers and fortifies us, and which wants nothing but bouquet.—TAINE, H. A., 1871, *History of English Literature, tr. Van Laun, vol.* II, *bk.* iii, *ch.* vi, *p.* 170.

And what was his reward, after wasting disappointments? The then not very reputable post of Middlesex magistrate at Bow Street. But, to his credit be it told, the corrupt practices which disgraced that important though subordinate seat of criminal justice were swept away by his judicious and indefatigable management, and from being a nest rather for the nursing care of some delinquents than for their utter extermination, it became in his hands the dread of incorrigible evil doers; while the weary and heavy-laden met with compassionate consideration. Of these facts there is no one but must feel assured who has read what may be called his dying words, which are so impressively told in his "Voyage to Lisbon"—his last resting place.—BROWNE, JAMES P., 1872, *ed., Miscellanies and Poems by Henry Fielding, Preface, p.* xviii.

Fielding was no hero. Ginger was hot in the mouth with him, and he was always apt to prefer the call of pleasure to the call of duty.—NICOLL, HENRY J., 1882, *Landmarks of English Literature, p.* 221.

I do not deny that Fielding's temperament was far from being over nice. I am willing to admit, if you will, that the woof of his nature was coarse and animal. I should not stop short of saying that it was sensual. Yet he liked and admired the highest and best things of his time—the art of Hogarth, the acting of Garrick, the verse of Pope. He is said indeed to have loved low company, but his nature was so companionable and his hunger for knowledge so keen, that I fancy he would like any society that was not dull, and any conversation, however illiterate, from which he could learn anything to his purpose.—LOWELL, JAMES RUSSELL, 1883–90, *Fielding, Address on Unveiling the Bust of Fielding, Taunton, Sept.* 4; *Prose Works, Riverside ed., vol.* VI, *p.* 59.

The real monument which Fielding's

memory most needs is one that does not ask for the chisel of any sculptor or the voice of any orator. It is, moreover, a memorial which it would neither be difficult to raise nor pecuniarily unprofitable. That memorial is a complete edition of his writings. Though one hundred and thirty years have gone by since his death, this act of justice to his reputation has never yet been performed. Apparently, it has never once been contemplated. A portion of his work—and, in a certain way, of work especially characteristic—is practically inaccessible to the immense majority of English-speaking men. We are the losers by this neglect more than he. The mystery that envelops much of Fielding's career can never be cleared away, the estimate of his character and conduct can never be satisfactorily fixed, until everything he wrote has been put into the hands of independent investigators pursuing separate lines of study.—LOUNSBURY, THOMAS R., 1884, *Open Letters, The Century, vol*, 27, *p*. 635.

He was too frank, may be; and dared
Too boldly. Those whose faults he bared,
Writhed in the ruthless grasp that brought
Into the light their secret thought.
Therefore the Tartuffe-throng who say
"*Couvrez ce sein,*" and look that way,—
Therefore the Priests of Sentiment,
Rose on him with their garments rent.
Therefore the gadfly swarm whose sting
Plies ever round some generous thing,
Buzzed of old bills and tavern-scores,
Old "might-have-beens" and "heretofores;"—
Then, from that garbled record-list,
Made him his own Apologist.
And was he? Nay,—let who has known
Nor Youth nor Error, cast the stone!
If to have sense of Joy and Pain
Too keen,—to rise, to fall again,
To live too much,—be sin, why then,
This was no Phœnix among men.
But those who turn that later page,
The journal of his middle-age,
Watch him serene in either fate,—
Philanthropist and Magistrate;
Watch him as Husband, Father, Friend,
Faithful, and patient to the end;
Grieving, as e'en the brave may grieve,
But for the loved ones he must leave:
These will admit—if any can—
That 'neath the green Estrella trees,
No Artist merely, but a Man,
Wrought on our noblest island-plan,
Sleeps with the alien Portuguese.

—DOBSON, AUSTIN, 1880, *Henry Fielding, At the Sign of the Lyre.*

We dimly make out that the chief incident of Fielding's dramatic career was his share in a quarrel between Cibber, then manager, and certain actors to whom, as Fielding thought, Cibber had behaved unfairly. Cibber, the smart, dapper little Frenchified coxcomb, was just the type of all the qualities which Fielding most heartily despised; and they fell foul of each other with great heartiness. On the other hand, he was equally enthusiastic on behalf of his friends. Chief among them were Hogarth, whose paintings are the best comment on Fielding's novel, and Garrick, whom, though of very different temperament, he admired and praised with the most cordial generosity. "Harry Fielding," as his familiars call him, was no doubt a wild youth, but to all appearance a most trustworthy and warm-hearted friend.—STEPHEN, LESLIE, 1897, *Henry Fielding, Library of the World's Best Literature, ed. Warner, vol.* X, *p*. 5696.

DRAMAS

'Twas from a sense of this concluding jumble, this unnatural huddling of events, that a witty friend of mine, who was himself a dramatic writer, used pleasantly, though perhaps rather freely, to *damn the man who invented fifth acts*. . . . So said the celebrated Henry Fielding, who was a respectable person both by education and birth. . . . His "Joseph Andrews" and "Tom Jones" may be called masterpieces in the *comic epopée*, which none since have equalled, though multitudes have imitated; and which he was peculiarly qualified to write in the manner he did, both from his *life*, his *learning*, and his *genius*. Had his life been less irregular (for irregular it was, and spent in a promiscuous intercourse with persons of *all* ranks), his pictures of human-kind had neither been so various nor so natural. Had he possessed less of literature, he could not have infused such a spirit of classical elegance. Had his genius been less fertile in wit and humour, he could not have maintained that uninterrupted pleasantry which never suffers his reader to feel fatigue.—HARRIS, JAMES, 1750, *Philological Inquiries, pt*. ii.

Though it must be acknowledged, that in the whole collection there are few plays likely to make any considerable figure on the stage hereafter, yet they are worthy of being preserved, being the works of a genius, who, in his wildest and most inaccurate productions, yet occasionally displays the talent of a master. Though in the plan of his pieces he is not always regular, yet is he often happy in his diction and style; and, in every groupe that he has exhibited, there are to be seen particular delineations that will amply recompense the attention bestowed upon them. — MURPHY, ARTHUR, 1762, *An Essay on the Life and Genius of Henry Fielding, Esq., Works, ed. Chalmers, vol.* I, *p.* 14.

Can any reason be assigned, why the inimitable Fielding, who was so perfect in Epic fable, should have succeeded so indifferently in Dramatic? Was it owing to the peculiarity of his genius, or of his circumstances? to any thing in the nature of Dramatic writing in general, or of that particular taste in Dramatic Comedy which Congreve and Vanburgh had introduced, and which he was obliged to comply with? —BEATTIE, WILLIAM, 1776–9, *Essays on Poetry and Music, p.* 102, *note.*

Fielding was a comic writer, as well as a novelist; but his comedies are very inferior to his novels: they are particularly deficient both in plot and character. The only excellence which they have is that of the style, which is the only thing in which his novels are deficient. The only dramatic pieces of Fielding that retain possession of the stage are, "The Mock Doctor" (a tolerable translation from Moliere's *Medecin malgrelui*), and his "Tom Thumb," a very admirable piece of burlesque.—HAZLITT, WILLIAM, 1818, *On the Comic Writers of the Last Century, Lecture* viii.

While it must be acknowledged that Fielding's genius was not decidedly dramatic, it was something that he escaped disapprobation, though he was at times received with indifference. — ROSCOE, THOMAS, 1840, *Life and Works of Henry Fielding.*

Notwithstanding the ill fate which attended "Pasquin," I venture to pronounce it a work of the highest talent, if genius be not the more appropriate word. The humour is excellent; nor do I think that the satire in it at all oversteps the fair bounds of comic writing. . . . Fielding's other burlesque, "Tom Thumb," had better fortune, and still keeps possession of the stage. It is, however, the barbaric version of Kane O'Hara which is represented; and they who wish to appreciate this genuine specimen of good-humoured ridicule, must look to Fielding's pages, and not to the theatre. Indeed, in any form, "Tom Thumb" is a play rather to be read than to be seen. Tom Thumb and Glumdalca ought to be left to our imagination, and not to the Property-man. If the popularity of this work of Fielding's pen is to be ascertained by a common test, the number of quotations from it, that are universally current, it will be rated very high indeed.—CREASY, SIR EDWARD, 1850–76, *Memoirs of Eminent Etonians, p.* 318.

Of all Fielding's dramatic pieces "Pasquin" seems deserving of the highest praise, and it touches pretty freely upon the political corruptions of the times. Considered in the light of a satire alone it may be pronounced very successful, showing its author as usual at his best in the unsparing use of the lash.—SMITH, GEORGE BARNETT, 1875, *Poets and Novelists, p.* 301.

None of Fielding's plays, with the exception, perhaps, of his adaptation of the "Miser," can be said to have "kept the stage;" few even of the students of literature have read them, and those who have read them have dismissed them too hastily. The closest students these plays have ever had were the dramatists of the following generation, whose works, notably those of Sheridan, contain many traces of their assiduity. The tradition about his writing scenes after his return from tavern carousals on the papers in which his tobacco had been wrapt, and his cool reception of Garrick's desire that he should alter some passage in the "Wedding-Day," have helped the impression that they were loose, ill-considered, ill-constructed productions, scribbled off hastily to meet passing demands. There is only a fraction of truth in this notion. That the plays are not the work of a dull plodder or a mechanician of elaborate ingenuity goes without saying; but, though perhaps rapidly considered and rapidly constructed, they are neither ill-considered nor ill-constructed, and bear testimony to the large and keen intelligence, as well as the overflowing humor and fertile wit of their author.—MINTO, WILLIAM, 1879, *Fielding, Encyclopædia Britannica, vol.* IX.

The dramatic pieces that he wrote during his early period were, it is true, shamefully gross, though there are humorous hints in them that have been profitably worked up by later writers; but what strikes me most in them is that there is so little real knowledge of life, the result of personal experience, and that the social scenery and conception of character are mainly borrowed from his immediate predecessors, the dramatists of the Restoration. In grossness his plays could not outdo those of Dryden, whose bust has stood so long without protest in Westminster Abbey. As to any harm they can do there is little to be apprehended, for they are mostly as hard to read as a Shapira manuscript.—LOWELL, JAMES RUSSELL, 1883–90, *Fielding, Address on Unveiling the Bust of Fielding, Taunton, Sept.* 4; *Prose Works, Riverside ed., vol.* VI, *p.* 58.

As a dramatist he has no eminence; and though his plays do not deserve the sweeping condemnation with which Macaulay once spoke of them in the House of Commons, they are not likely to attract any critics but those for whom the inferior efforts of a great genius possess a morbid fascination. Some of them serve, in a measure, to illustrate his career; others contain hints and situations which he afterwards worked into his novels; but the only ones that possess real stage qualities are those which he borrowed from Regnard and Molière. "Don Quixote in England," "Pasquin," the "Historical Register," can claim no present consideration commensurate with that which they received as contemporary satires, and their interest is mainly antiquarian; while "Tom Thumb" and the "Covent-Garden Tragedy," the former of which would make the reputation of a smaller man, can scarcely hope to be remembered beside "Amelia" or "Jonathan Wild."—DOBSON, AUSTIN, 1883, *Fielding* (*English Men of Letters*), *p.* 176.

JOSEPH ANDREWS
1742

I have myself, upon your recommendation, been reading "Joseph Andrews." The incidents are ill laid and without invention; but the characters have a great deal of nature, which always pleases even in her lowest shapes. Parson Adams is perfectly well; so is Mrs. Slipslop, and the story of Wilson; and throughout he shows himself well read in Stage-Coaches, Country Squires, Inns, and Inns of Court. His reflections upon high people and low people, and misses and masters, are very good.—GRAY, THOMAS, 1742, *Letter to Richard West.*

The worthy parson's learning, his simplicity, his evangelical purity of heart and benevolence of disposition, are so admirably mingled with pedantry, absence of mind, and with the habit of athletic and gymnastic exercise, then acquired at the universities by students of all descriptions, that he may be safely termed one of the richest productions of the Muse of Fiction. — SCOTT, SIR WALTER, 1820, *Henry Fielding.*

Joseph Andrews is a hero of the shoulder-knot: it would be hard to canvass his pretentions too severely, especially considering what a patron he has in Parson Adams. That one character would cut up into a hundred fine gentlemen and novel heroes!—HAZLITT, WILLIAM, 1830? *Men and Manners.*

While, however, it is highly probable that he had Cervantes in his eye, it is certain that the satiric and burlesque portion of "Joseph Andrews" was suggested to him by the perusal of Richardson's "Pamela," on the overwrought refinement and strained sentiment of which it affords a humorous commentary in the adventures of her professed brother, the hero. Besides its intrinsic wit and excellence, it has thus a twofold attraction in the comic and burlesque spirit it maintains throughout, in the same way as the adventures of the Spanish knight and his squire, however ludicrous in themselves, are relished with a double zest for the contrast they offer to the dignified bearing and marvellous deeds of the old Paladins. How exquisitely Fielding has caught the humour, assumed gravity, and delicate satire of his prototype, they who have compared the two master-pieces will readily admit; and that he loses nothing in point of originality.—ROSCOE, THOMAS, 1840, *Life and Works of Henry Fielding.*

Resemblances have been found, and may be admitted to exist, between the Rev. Charles Primrose and the Rev. Abraham Adams. They were from kindred genius; and from the manly habit which Fielding and Goldsmith shared of discerning what was good and beautiful in the homeliest aspects of humanity. In the parson's saddle-bag of sermons would hardly have been found this prison-sermon of the vicar; and there was in Mr. Adams not only a capacity for beef and pudding, but for beating and being beaten, which would ill have consisted with the simple dignity of Doctor Primrose. But unquestionable learning, unsuspecting simplicity, amusing traits of credulity and pedantry, and a most Christian purity and benevolence of heart, are common to both these masterpieces of English fiction; and are in each with such exquisite touch discriminated, as to leave no possible doubt of the originality of either.—FORSTER, JOHN, 1848–54, *The Life and Times of Oliver Goldsmith, vol.* I, *ch.* xiii.

Joseph Andrews, though he wears Lady Booby's cast-off livery, is, I think, to the full as polite as Tom Jones in his fustian-suit, or Captain Booth in regimentals. He has, like those heroes, large calves, broad shoulders, a high courage, and a handsome face. The accounts of Joseph's bravery and good qualities; his voice, too musical to halloo to the dogs; his bravery in riding races for the gentlemen of the county, and his constancy in refusing bribes and temptation, have something affecting in their *naïveté* and freshness, and prepossess one in favour of that handsome young hero. The rustic bloom of Fanny, and the delightful simplicity of Parson Adams are described with a friendliness which wins the reader of their story: we part with them with more regret than from Booth and Jones.—THACKERAY, WILLIAM MAKEPEACE, 1853, *The English Humourists of the Eighteenth Century.*

The character of Mr. Abraham Adams is the most delightful in the whole range of English fiction. It is the embodiment of Christianity in all its noblest bearings—the grandest delineation of a pattern priest which the world has yet seen.—LAWRENCE, FREDERICK, 1855, *The Life of Henry Fielding, p.* 155.

It is a piece of admirable art, but composed of the basest materials, like a palace built of dung. "Amelia" is not so corrupt, but it is often coarse, and, as a whole, very poor and tedious. "Joseph Andrews" is by far the most delightful of his writings. With less art than "Tom Jones," it has much more genius. Parson Adams is confessedly one of the most original and pleasing characters in fiction. Goldsmith's "Vicar of Wakefield," Joseph Cargill in "St. Ronan's Well," are both copied from him, but have not a tithe of his deep simplicity and delicious *bonhommie.* We predict that, in a century hence, "Joseph Andrews" will alone survive to preserve Fielding's name.—GILFILLAN, GEORGE, 1855, *A Third Gallery of Portraits, p.* 231.

What is London in the mouths of Hume, and Richardson, and Boswell? A place of elegant manners, refined ideas, general enlightenment, knowledge, enterprise, wealth, liberality. What are London and England in the pictures of Hogarth and the pages of Fielding? "No better than they should be," certainly: full of poverty, low vice, coarse indulgence, and sheer brutality, relieved now and then by exhibitions of good sense, courage, and love of learning. Parson Adams, the simple-minded clergyman in "Joseph Andrews," who goes up to London to sell his sermons to some publisher, and meets on the way to and from the country with as many adventures as Don Quixote himself, is a literary creation of unsurpassed merit; nor are the personages that surround him, though less interesting, drawn with less ability.—ARNOLD, THOMAS, 1868–75, *Chaucer to Wordsworth, p.* 372.

The type which shows best the force and the limits of Fielding's genius is Parson Adams. He belongs to a distinguished family, whose members have been portrayed by the greatest historians. He is a collateral descendant of Don Quixote, for whose creation Fielding felt a reverence exceeded only by his reverence for Shakespeare. The resemblance is, of course, distant, and consists chiefly in this, that the parson, like the knight, lives in an ideal world, and is constantly shocked by harsh collision with facts. He believes in his sermons instead of his sword, and his imagination is tenanted by virtuous squires and model parsons instead of Arcadian shepherds, or knight-errants and fair ladies. His imagination is not exalted beyond the limits of sanity, but only colours the prosaic realities in accordance with the impulses or a tranquil benevolence. . . . If the ideal hero is always to live in fancy-land and talk in blank verse, Adams has clearly no right to the title; nor, indeed, has Don Quixote. But the masculine portraiture of the coarse realities is not only indicative of intellectual vigour, but artistically appropriate. The contrast between the world and its simple-minded inhabitant is the more forcible in proportion to the firmness and solidity of Fielding's touch.—STEPHEN, LESLIE, 1874–79. *Hours in a Library, Second Series, pp.* 195, 197.

It was not without reason that Fielding added prominently to his title-page the name of Mr. Abraham Adams. If he is not the real hero of the book, he is undoubtedly the character whose fortunes the reader follows with the closest interest. . . . Not all the discipline of hog's blood and cudgels and cold water to which he is subjected can deprive him of his native dignity; and as he stands before us in the short great-coat under which his ragged cassock is continually making its appearance, with his old wig and battered hat, a clergyman whose social position is scarcely above that of a footman, and who supports a wife and six children upon a cure of twenty-three pounds a year, which his outspoken honesty is continually jeopardising, he is a far finer figure than Pamela in her coach-and-six, or Bellarmine in his cinnamon velvet.—DOBSON, AUSTIN, 1883, *Fielding (English Men of Letters), pp.* 73, 74.

JOURNEY FROM THIS WORLD TO THE NEXT
1743

"The Journey from this World to the Next," is to me an unpleasing fiction. The main requisite for such a fiction is precisely that in which Fielding was most deficient—a poetic imagination. It will therefore rarely, I think, be read for pleasure, but it may be for information, for it is a fund of acute satire and profound observation on human nature.— —KEIGHTLEY, THOMAS, 1858, *On the Life and Writings of Henry Fielding, Fraser's Magazine, vol.* 57, *p.* 212.

The Lucianic history called "A Journey from this World to the Next;" this begins with a very sprightly satire, culminating in the author's entrance into Elysium; unhappily, when in a charming vein, he meets Julian the Apostate, who soliloquises, not always very amusingly, for one hundred and forty pages. Julian relinquishes his position to Anne Boleyn, and the fragment presently closes. There are some exceedingly fine passages in the shapeless work.—GOSSE, EDMUND, 1888, *A History of Eighteenth Century Literature, p.* 253.

JONATHAN WILD
1743

"Jonathan Wild" is assuredly the best of all the fictions in which a villain is throughout the prominent character. But how impossible it is by any force of genius to create a sustained attractive interest for such a groundwork, and how the mind wearies of, and shrinks from, the more than painful interest, the μισητὸν, of utter depravity, — Fielding himself felt and endeavoured to mitigate and remedy by the (on all other principles) far too large a proportion, and too quick recurrence, of the interposed chapters of moral reflection, like the chorus in the Greek tragedy,—admirable specimens as these chapters are of profound irony and philosophic satire.—COLERIDGE, SAMUEL TAYLOR, 1832, *Notes on Books and Authors; Miscellanies, Æsthetic and Literary, ed. Ashe, p.* 339.

"The Life of Jonathan Wild" has proved a perfect *crux* to the critics, a proof perhaps that it may have a recondite sense. It is not the real life of that villain, which may be found in the "Newgate Calendar," or in Watson's "Life of Fielding;" it seems rather to be an attempt at forming the *ideal* of perfect and consummate villainy, absorbed in self and unchecked by feeling or remorse.—KEIGHTLEY, THOMAS, 1858, *On the Life and Writings of Henry Fielding, Fraser's Magazine, vol.* 57, *p.*213.

It was written for a special purpose; it fulfilled that purpose admirably; but beyond that fact, and that it contains much of its author's sarcastic genius, the fragment is not in any other aspect very noticeable.—SMITH, GEORGE BARNETT, 1875, *Poets and Novelists, p.* 296.

This has never been a favourite among Fielding's readers, because of its caustic cynicism and the unbroken gloom of its tone, but it is equal to the best he has left us in force and originality. It is the history of an unmitigated ruffian, from his baptism by Titus Oates to his death at Newgate on "the Tree of Glory." The story is intended to mock those relations in which biographers lose themselves in pompous eulogies of their subjects, for their "greatness," without consideration of any "goodness," by showing that it is possible to write the history of a gallows-bird in exactly the same style of inflated gusto. The inexorable irony which is sustained all through, even when the most detestable acts of the hero are described, forms rather a strain at last upon the reader's nerves, and no one would turn to "Jonathan Wild" for mere amusement. But it shows a marvellous knowledge of the seamy side of life, the author proving himself in it to be as familiar with thieves and their prisons as in "Joseph Andrews" he had been with stage-coaches and wayside taverns; while nothing could be more picturesque than some of the scenes with Blueskin and his gang, or than the Petronian passages on board ship.—GOSSE, EDMUND, 1888, *A History of Eighteenth Century Literature, p.* 253.

In "Jonathan Wild" above all Fielding indulges to the full his taste for clearness and unity of intellectual structure. . . . Fielding conducts his narrative under the dominant influence of one prevailing purpose, in the service of which he employs all his irony, never suffering the reader for one moment to forget the main thesis, which is stated at the beginning of the story, restated at the close and illustrated with matchless skill throughout. This thesis is in effect that the elements of "greatness," in the common acceptation of the term, when divorced from that plain goodness of heart which is little likely to foster ambition, are the same in the thief and in men eminent in more reputable professions, as those can testify "who have lived long in cities, courts, gaols, or such places." In sketching the history of Wild, and showing how his career of selfish villainy might have been marred at innumerable points by the slightest liability to humane feeling, Fielding's polished irony achieves a triumph, and presents a picture of almost "perfect diabolism." The humour of the author is at its grimmest in this work, not so much in depicting Wild, the horror of whose character is almost forgotten in its artistic unity, as in sundry subordinate details.—RALEIGH, WALTER, 1894, *The English Novel, pp.* 167, 168.

His brave, generous nature could never give up a belief in virtue or in the substantial happiness of a good heart. He could see, as he proved by Jonathan Wild, into the very soul of a thorough villain, the depth beyond depth of treachery and sensuality that can be embodied in human form. His moral is, as he puts it, that a man may "go to heaven with half the pains which it costs him to purchase hell." The villain, even as things go, naturally overreaches himself. Knowledge of the world takes the gloss off much; but it properly leads to a recognition of the supreme advantage of unworldly simplicity.—STEPHEN, LESLIE, 1897, *Henry Fielding, Library of the World's Best Literature, ed. Warner, vol.* X, *p.* 5701.

TOM JONES
1749

I have been very well entertained lately with the two first volumes of "The Foundling," written by Mr. Fielding, but not to be published till January (1749). If the same spirit runs through the whole work, I think it will be much preferable to "Joseph Andrews."—HERTFORD, LADY (DUCHESS OF SOMERSET), 1748, *Letter to Lady Luxborough.*

Meanwhile, it is an honest pleasure, which we take in adding, that (exclusive of one wild, detach'd, and independent Story of a *Man of the Hill*, that neither brings on Anything, nor rose from Anything that went before it). All the changeful windings of the Author's Fancy carry on a course of regular Design; and end in an extremely moving Close, where Lives that seem'd to wander and run different ways, meet, All, in an instructive Center. The whole Piece consists of an inventive Race of Disappointments and Recoveries. It excites Curiosity, and holds it watchful. It has just and pointed Satire; but it is a partial Satire, and confin'd, too narrowly: It sacrifices to Authority and Interest. Its *Events* reward Sincerity, and punish and expose Hypocrisy; shew Pity and Benevolence in amiable Lights, and Avarice and Brutality in very despicable ones. In every Part It has Humanity for its Intention: In too many, it *seems* wantoner than It was meant to be: It has bold shocking Pictures; and (I fear) not unresembling ones, in high Life, and in low. And (to conclude this too adventurous Guess-work, from a Pair of forward Baggages) woud, every where (we think), *deserve* to please, —if stript of what the Author thought himself most sure to *please by*. And thus, Sir, we have told you our sincere opinion of "Tom Jones." . . . Your most profest Admirers and most humble servants. — HILL, ASTRÆA AND MINERVA, 1749, *Letter to Samuel Richardson, July* 27.

I must confess, that I have been prejudiced by the Opinion of Several judicious Friends against the truly coarse-titled "Tom Jones;" and so have been discouraged from reading it.—I was told, that it was a rambling Collection of Waking Dreams, in which Probability was not observed: And that it had a very bad Tendency. And I had Reason to think that the Author intended for his Second View (His *first*, to fill his Pocket, by accommodating it to the reigning Taste) in writing it, to whiten a vicious Character, and to make Morality bend to his Practices. What Reason had he to make his Tom illegitimate, in an Age where Keeping is become a Fashion? Why did he make him a common—What shall I call it? And a Kept Fellow, the Lowest of all Fellows, yet in Love with a Young Creature who was traping [trapesing?] after him, a Fugitive from her Father's House?—Why did he draw his Heroine so fond, so foolish, and so insipid?—Indeed he has one excuse—He knows not how to draw a delicate Woman—He has not been accustomed to such Company,—And is too prescribing, too impetuous, too immoral, I will venture to say, to take any other Byass that a perverse and crooked Nature has given him; or Evil Habits, at least, have confirm'd in him. Do Men expect Grapes of Thorns, or Figs of Thistles? But, perhaps, I think the worse of the Piece because I know the Writer, and dislike his Principles both Public and Private, tho' I wish well to the *Man*, and Love Four worthy Sisters of his, with whom I am well acquainted. And indeed should admire him, did he make the Use of his Talents which I wish him to make. For the Vein of Humour, and Ridicule, which he is Master of, might, if properly turned, do great Service to ye Cause of Virtue. But no more of this Gentleman's Work, after I have said, That the favourable Things, you say of the Piece, will tempt me, if I can find Leisure, to give it a Perusal.—RICHARDSON, SAMUEL, 1749, *Letter to Astræa and Minerva Hill, Aug.* 4.

Unfortunate *Tom Jones!* how sadly has he mortify'd Two sawcy Correspondents of your making! They are with me now: and bid me tell you, You have spoil'd 'em Both, for Criticks.—Shall I add, a Secret which they did not bid me tell you?—They, Both, fairly *cry'd*, that You shou'd think it possible they cou'd approve of Any thing, in Any work, that had an *Evil Tendency*, in any Part or Purpose of it. They maintain their Point so far, however, as to be convinc'd they say, that *you* will disapprove this over-rigid Judgment of those Friends, who cou'd not find a Thread of Moral Meaning in "Tom Jones," quite independent of the Levities they justly censure.—And, as soon as you have Time to read him, for yourself, tis there, pert Sluts, they will be bold enough to rest the Matter.—Mean while, they love and honour you and your opinions.—HILL, AARON, 1749, *Letter to Samuel Richardson, Aug.* 11.

There is lately sprung up amongst us a species of narrative poem, representing likewise the characters of common life. It has the same relation to comedy that the epic has to tragedy, and differs from the epic in the same respect that comedy differs from tragedy; that is, in the actions and characters, both which are much nobler in the epic than in it. It is therefore, I think, a legitimate kind of poem; and, accordingly, we are told, Homer wrote one of that kind, called "Margites," of which some lines are preserved. The reason why I mention it is, that we have, in English, a *poem* of that kind (for so I will call it), which has more of character in it than any work, antient or modern, that I know. The work I mean is, "The History of Tom Jones," by Henry Fielding, which, as it has more personages brought into the story than any thing of the poetic kind I have ever seen; so all those personages have characters peculiar to them, insomuch, that there is not even an host or an hostess upon the road, hardly a servant, who is not distinguished in that way; in short I never saw any thing that was so much animated, and, as I may say, *all alive* with characters and manners, as "The History of Tom Jones." — MONBODDO, LORD (JAMES BURNET), 1779–99, *Of the Origin and Progress of Language, vol.* III, *p.* 134.

I never saw Johnson really angry with me but once. I alluded to some witty passages in "Tom Jones;" he replied, "I am shocked to hear you quote from so vicious a book. I am sorry to hear you have read it: a confession which no modest lady should ever make. I scarcely know a more corrupt work!" He went so far as to refuse to Fielding the great talents which are ascribed to him, and broke out into a noble panegyric on his competitor, Richardson; who, he said, was as superior to him in talents as in virtue; and whom he pronounced to be the greatest genius that had shed its lustre on this path of literature.—MORE, HANNAH, 1780, *Memoirs, vol.* I, *p.* 168.

In "Tom Jones," his greatest work, the artful conduct of the fable, and the subserviency of all the incidents to the winding up of the whole, deserve much praise. —BLAIR, HUGH, 1783, *Lectures on Rhetoric and Belles-Lettres, ed. Mills, Lecture* xxxvii.

A book seemingly intended to sap the foundation of that morality which it is the duty of parents and all public instructors to inculcate in the minds of young people, by teaching that virtue upon principle is imposture, that generous qualities alone constitute true worth, and that a young man may love and be loved, and at the same time associate with the loosest women. His morality, in respect that it resolves virtue into good affections, in contradiction to moral obligation and a sense of duty, is that of lord Shaftesbury vulgarised, and is a system of excellent use in palliating the vices most injurious to society. He was the inventor of that cant-phrase, goodness of heart, which is every day used as a substitute for probity, and means little more than the virtue of a horse or a dog; in short, he has done more towards corrupting the rising generation than any writer we know of.—HAWKINS, SIR JOHN, 1787, *Life of Samuel Johnson, p.* 214.

I have already given my opinion of Fielding; but I cannot refrain from repeating here my wonder at Johnson's excessive and unaccountable depreciation of one of the best writers that England has produced. "Tom Jones" has stood the test of publick opinion with such success, as to have established its great merit, both for the story, the sentiments, and the manners, and also the varieties of diction, so as to leave no doubt of its having an animated truth of execution throughout. —BOSWELL, JAMES, 1791, *Life of Johnson, ed. Hill, vol.* II, *p.* 201.

The nobility of the Spencers has been illustrated and enriched by the trophies of Marlborough; but I exhort them to consider the Faëry Queen as the most precious jewel of their coronet. Our immortal Fielding was of the younger branch of the Earls of Denbigh, who drew their origin from the Counts of Habsburgh, the lineal descendants of Ethrico, in the seventh century, Duke of Alsace. Far different have been the fortunes of the English and German divisions of the Family of Habsburgh, the former, the knights and sheriffs of Leicestershire, have slowly risen to the dignity of a peerage; the latter, the Emperors of Germany and Kings of Spain, have threatened the liberty of the old and invaded the treasures of the new world. The successors of Charles V. may disdain their brethren of England; but the romance of "Tom Jones," that exquisite picture of human manners, will outlive the palace of the Escurial, and the imperial eagle of the house of Austria.—GIBBON, EDWARD, 1793, *Memoirs of My Life and Writings, p.* 4.

"Tom Jones," cannot be considered simply a novel: the abundance of philosophical ideas, the hypocrisy of society, and the contrast of natural qualities, are brought into action with an infinity of art; and love, as I have observed before, is only a vehicle to introduce all these.— —STAËL, MADAME DE, 1800, *The Influence of Literature upon Society, ch.* XV.

Fielding had all the ease which Richardson wanted, a genuine flow of humour, and a rich variety of comic character; nor was he wanting in strokes of an amiable sensibility, but he could not describe a consistently virtuous character, and in deep pathos he was far excelled by his rival. When we see Fielding parodying "Pamela," and Richardson asserting, as he does in his letters, that the run of "Tom Jones" is over, and that it would soon be completely forgotten: we cannot but smile on seeing the two authors placed on the same shelf, and going quietly down to posterity together.—BARBAULD, ANNA LÆTITIA, 1804, *ed., The Correspondence of Samuel Richardson, vol.* I, *p.* lxxix.

Tom Jones's warmth and generosity do not appear to me of that kind which qualify a man for adorning domestic life.—BRUNTON, MARY, 1811, *Self-Control.*

As a story, "Tom Jones" seems to have only one defect, which might have been so easily remedied, that it is to be regretted that it should have been neglected by the author. Jones, after all, proves illegitimate, when there would have been no difficulty for the author to have supposed that his mother had been privately married to the young clergyman. This would not only have removed the stain from the birth of the hero, but, in the idea of the reader, would have given him better security for the property of his uncle Allworthy. In fact, in a miserable continuation which has been written of the history of Tom Jones, the wrong headed author (of whom Blifil was the favourite), has made his hero bring an action against Tom after the death of Mr. Allworthy, and oust him from his uncle's property. —DUNLOP, JOHN, 1814–42, *The History of Fiction, vol.* II, *p.* 407.

Shall I say which was the first book that most strongly excited my curiosity, and interested my sensibility? It was "Tom Jones." My female Mentor tantalized me without mercy. She would let me have but one volume at a time; and not only would not afford me any clue to the concluding catastrophe, but rather put me upon a wrong scent. Sometimes too when my impatience of expectation was at the very highest point possible, the succeeding volume was mislaid, was lent, was not impossibly lost. However, after a long and most severe trial, after hating Blifil with no common hatred, forming a most friendly intimacy with Patridge, loving Sophia with rapturous extravagance, I complacently accompanied dear wicked Tom to the nuptial altar. I endeavoured of course to procure the other productions of this popular author, but I well remember that I did not peruse any of them, no not within a hundred degrees of the satisfaction, which the Foundling communicated.—BELOE, WILLIAM, 1817, *The Sexagenarian, vol.* I, *p.* 13.

The felicitous contrivance, and happy extrication of the story, where every incident tells upon and advances the catastrophe, while, at the same time, it illustrates the characters of those interested in its approach, cannot too often be mentioned with the highest approbation. The attention of the reader is never diverted or puzzled by unnecessary digressions, or recalled to the main story by abrupt and startling recurrences; he glides down the narrative like a boat on the surface of some broad navigable stream, which only winds enough to gratify the voyager with the varied beauty of its banks. . . . The vices and follies of Tom Jones, are those which the world soon teaches to all who enter on the career of life, and to which society is unhappily but too indulgent; nor do we believe, that, in any one instance, the perusal of Fielding's Novel has added one libertine to the large list, who would not have been such, had it never crossed the press.—SCOTT, SIR WALTER, 1820, *Henry Fielding.*

Many people find fault with Fielding's "Tom Jones" as gross and immoral. For my part, I have doubts of his being so very handsome from the author's always talking about his beauty, and I suspect he was a clown, from being constantly assured he was so very genteel. Otherwise, I think Jones acquits himself very well both in his actions and speeches, as a lover and as a *trencherman*, whenever he is called upon.—HAZLITT, WILLIAM, 1830? *Men and Manners, p.* 217.

Manners change from generation to generation, and with manners morals appear to change,—actually change with some, but appear to change with all but the abandoned. A young man of the present day who should act as Tom Jones is supposed to act at Upton, with Lady Bellaston, &c., would not be a Tom Jones; and a Tom Jones of the present day, without perhaps being in the ground a better man, would have perished rather than submit to be kept by a harridan of fortune. Therefore, this novel is, and indeed, pretends to be, no exemplar of conduct. But, notwithstanding all this, I do loathe the cant which can recommend "Pamela" and "Clarissa Harlowe" as strictly moral, though they poison the imagination of the young with continued doses of *tinct. lyttæ*, while Tom Jones is prohibited as loose. I do not speak of young women; but a young man whose heart or feelings can be injured, or even his passions excited, by aught in this novel, is already thoroughly corrupt. There is a cheerful, sunshiny, breezy spirit, that prevails everywhere, strongly contrasted with the close, hot, day-dreamy continuity of Richardson.—COLERIDGE, SAMUEL TAYLOR, 1832, *Notes on Books and Authors, Miscellanies Æsthetic and Literary, ed. Ashe, p.* 337.

In point of general excellence "Amelia" has commonly been considered, no less by critics, perhaps, than by the public, as decidedly inferior to "Tom Jones." In variety and invention it assuredly is so. Its chief merit depends less on its artful and elaborate construction than on the interesting series it presents of domestic paintings, drawn, as we have remarked, from his own family history. It has more pathos, more moral lessons, with far less vigour and humour, than either of its predecessors. But we agree with Chalmers, that those who have seen much of the errors and distresses of domestic life will probably feel that the author's colouring in this work is more just, as well as more chaste, than in any of his other novels. The appeals to the heart are far more forcible.—ROSCOE, THOMAS, 1840, *Life and Works of Henry Fielding.*

His "Tom Jones" is quite unrivalled in plot, and is to be rivalled only in his own works for felicitous delineation of character.—TALFOURD, THOMAS NOON, 1842, *On British Novels and Romances, Critical and Miscellaneous Writings, p.* 13.

In "Tom Jones," Fielding has comprehended a larger variety of incidents and characters under a stricter unity of story than in "Joseph Andrews;" but he has given to the whole a tone of worldliness which does not mar the delightful simplicity of the latter. As an expression of the power and breadth of his mind, however, it is altogether his greatest work, and, in the union of distinct pictorial representation with profound knowledge of practical life, is unequalled by any novel in the language.—WHIPPLE, EDWIN P., 1849, *The Life and Works of Henry Fielding, North American Review, vol.* 68, *p.* 70.

While at Tulnavert school, I formed one of those schoolboy friendships, which are so common among lads such as we were, for a young class-fellow called William Short. He asked me to go home and spend a few nights with him, an invitation which I gladly accepted. His father lived in a wild mountainous district and possessed a large tract of rough mountain

ground. When I went there I felt astonished at the undoubted evidences of his wealth. While on this visit I saw for the first time an odd volume of "Tom Jones;" but I have not the slightest intention of describing the wonder and the feeling with which I read it. No pen could do justice to that. It was the second volume; of course the story was incomplete, and, as a natural consequence, I felt something amounting to agony at the disappointment —not knowing what the *dénouement* was. —CARLETON, WILLIAM, 1869, *Autobiography, Life by O'Donoghue, vol.* I, *p.* 74.

The only great English epic of that century is the prose Odyssey of which Mr. Tom Jones is the hero.—DOWDEN, EDWARD, 1880, *Southey (English Men of Letters), p.* 51.

The book breathes health. The convention of the time did not forbid a direct picturing of its evil; but the coarse scenes in Fielding's novels are given always for what they are, with no false gloss upon them. Whenever Tom Jones sins against the purity of his love for Sohpia his wrong doing is made in some way to part him from her, and when he pleads toward the close of the story, the difference between men and women, and the different codes of morality by which they are judged in society, Fielding makes Sophia answer, "I will never marry a man who is not as incapable as I am myself of making such a distinction." The charm of genius enters into the whole texture of thought in Fielding's novels. A page of his is to a page of Richardson's as silk to sackcloth. —MORLEY, HENRY, 1881, *Of English Literature in the Reign of Victoria, with a Glance at the Past, p.* 88.

Novelists who have undertaken to write the life of a hero or heroine have generally considered their work completed at the interesting period of marriage, and have contented themselves with the advance in taste and manners which are common to all boys and girls as they become men and women. Fielding, no doubt, did more than this in "Tom Jones," which is one of the greatest novels in the English language, for there he has shown how a noble and sanguine nature may fail away under temptation and be again strengthened and made to stand upright.—TROLLOPE, ANTHONY, 1882–83, *An Autobiography, ch.* xvii.

Like "Don Quixote," "Tom Jones" is the precursor of a new order of things—the earliest and freshest expression of a new departure in art. But while "Tom Jones" is, to the full, as amusing as "Don Quixote," it has the advantage of a greatly superior plan, and an interest more skilfully sustained. The incidents which, in Cervantes, simply succeed each other like the scenes in a panorama, are, in "Tom Jones," but parts of an organised and carefully-arranged progression towards a foreseen conclusion. As the hero and heroine cross and recross each other's track, there is scarcely an episode which does not aid in the moving forward of the story. Little details rise lightly and naturally to the surface of the narrative, not more noticeable at first than the most everyday occurrences, and a few pages farther on become of the greatest importance. . . . What a brave wit it is, what a wisdom after all, that is contained in this wonderful novel! Where shall we find its like for richness of reflection—for inexhaustible good-humour—for large and liberal humanity? Like Fontenelle, Fielding might fairly claim that he had never cast the smallest ridicule upon the most infinitesimal of virtues; it is against hypocrisy, affectation, insincerity of all kinds, that he wages war. And what a keen and searching observation—what a perpetual faculty of surprise—what an endless variety of method!—DOBSON, AUSTIN, 1883, *Fielding, pp.* 118, 126.

At every corner there is a conspicuous finger post intended to point out the roads along which approbation and disapprobation are expected to travel. In reading "Tom Jones" we know at once that we are intended to like Tom and to hate Blifil, and the emotional attitude we are requested to take at the beginning we are compelled to retain until the end. There are light and shade, but they are not intermingled as in real life and in the most typical nineteenth century fiction, for all the sunlight falls on one place and all the shadow on another. Tom Jones is by no means a perfect character, but he is clearly an embodiment of Fielding's ideal, and one may say—if the bull be pardonable—we are meant to feel that if he were more perfect he would be less so.—NOBLE, JAMES ASHCROFT, 1886, *Morality in English Fiction, p.* 15.

In "Tom Jones," a novel of which the respectable profess that they could stand the dulness if it were not so blackguardly, and the more honest admit that they could forgive the blackguardism if it were not so dull—in "Tom Jones," with its voluminous bulk and troops of characters, there is no shadow of a gentleman, for Allworthy is only ink and paper.—STEVENSON, ROBERT LOUIS, 1888, *Some Gentlemen in Fiction, Scribner's Magazine, vol.* 3, *p.* 766.

The Epic of Youth, by a master of comedy. In the prime of his manhood, speaking from a full and ripe experience, but with the zest of youthfulness still easily within the reach of memory and sympathy, Fielding gives in this book his sonorous verdict on human life and human conduct. Whether regarded for its art or for its thought, whether treated as detached scenes of the human comedy, as an example of plot-architecture, or as an attempt at the solution of certain wide problems of life, no truer, saner book has ever been written.—RALEIGH, WALTER, 1894, *The English Novel, p.* 170.

"Tom Jones" is a marvel of invention, character, and wit, of which readers never weary; with its amusing scenes and adventures, its sparkling sketches of high and low life, its genial satire, and its scorn of meanness and hypocrisy. He has stronger claims to be a writer of history than the authors of many elaborate fictions known under that name.—AUBREY, W. H. S., 1895, *The Rise and Growth of the English Nation, vol.* III, *p.* 121.

The scenes are still constructed as in comedy. As we read on, it is as if we were assisting at the representation of a score of comedies, parallel and successive; some pathetic, some burlesque, others possessing the gay wit of Vanbrugh and Congreve—all of which, after a skilfully manipulated revolution of circumstances, are united in a brilliant conclusion. Instead of being burdened, as were the earlier epic romancers, with a number of narratives to be gathered up in the last chapters, Fielding in the main becomes his own story-teller throughout. Character is unfolded, and a momentum is given to his plot by direct, not reported, conversations. All devices to account for his subject-matter, such as bundles of letters, fragmentary or rat-eaten manuscripts, found by chance, or given to the writer in keeping, are brushed aside as cheap and silly. Fielding throws off the mask of anonymity, steps out boldly, and asks us to accept his omniscience and omnipresence.—CROSS, WILBUR L., 1899, *The Development of the English Novel, p.*45.

AMELIA
1751

Methinks I long to engage you on the side of this poor unfortunate book, which I am told the fine folks are unanimous in pronouncing to be very sad stuff.—CARTER, ELIZABETH, 1751, *Letters.*

You guess that I have not read "Amelia." Indeed I have read but the first volume. I had intended to go through with it; but I found the characters and situations so wretchedly low and dirty, that I imagined I could not be interested for any one of them; and to read and not care what became of the hero and heroine, is a task I thought I would leave to those who had more leisure than I am blessed with. . . . Booth, in his last piece, again himself; Amelia, even to her noselessness, is again his first wife. His brawls, his jarrs, his gaols, his spunging-houses, are all drawn from what he has seen and known. As I said (witness also his hamper plot) he has little or no invention: and admirably do you observe, that by several strokes in his "Amelia" he designed to be good, but knew not how, and lost his genius, low humour, in the attempt.—RICHARDSON, SAMUEL, 1752, *Letter to Mrs. Donnellan, Correspondence, ed. Barbauld, vol.* IV, *p.* 60.

"Amelia," which succeeded "Tom Jones" in about *four* years, has indeed the marks of genius, but of a genius beginning to fall into its decay. The author's invention in this performance does not appear to have lost its fertility; his judgment, too, seems as strong as ever; but the warmth of imagination is abated; and, in his landscapes, or his scenes of life, Mr. Fielding is no longer the colourist he was before. . . . And yet "Amelia" holds the same proportion to "Tom Jones" that "The Odyssey" of Homer bears, in the estimation of Longinus, to the "Iliad." A fine vein of morality runs through the whole; many of the situations are affecting and tender; the sentiments are delicate; and, upon the whole, it is "The Odyssey," the moral and pathetic work, of Henry Fielding.—MURPHY, ARTHUR, 1762, *An Essay on the Life and Genius of Henry Fielding, Esq.*

Of all his novels, it leaves the finest impression of quiet, domestic delight, of the sweet home feeling, and the humanities connected with it. We have not the glad spring or the glowing summer of his genius, but its autumnal mellowness and mitigated sunshine, with something of the thoughtfulness befitting the season. Amelia herself, the wife and mother, arrayed in all matronly graces, with her rosy children about her, is a picture of womanly gentleness and beauty, and unostentatious heroism, such as never leaves the imagination in which it has once found a place.—WHIPPLE, EDWIN P., 1849, *The Life and Works of Henry Fielding, North American Review, vol.* 68, *p.* 76.

However this may be, I think that of all the novels of that period, "Amelia" is the one which gives the most generally truthful idea of the manners and habits of middle-class society then. There is little, if any, exaggeration or caricature, and I have no doubt that Fielding intended faithfully to depict society, such as he knew it, with its merits and its faults; its licentious manners, and domestic virtues; its brawls, its oaths, its prisons, and its masquerades.—FORSYTH, WILLIAM, 1871, *The Novels and Novelists of the Eighteenth Century, p.* 273.

Amelia, whose portrait Fielding drew from that of his second wife, has, indeed, been always a favourite character with readers; but the same cannot be said about her husband, Booth, who, we may suppose, was intended to represent Fielding himself. If so, the likeness which he drew is certainly not a flattering one. Thackeray preferred Captain Booth to Tom Jones, because he thought much more humbly of himself than Jones did, and went down on his knees and owned his weaknesses; but most will be inclined to agree with Scott, who declares that we have not the same sympathy for the ungrateful and dissolute conduct of Booth which we yield to the youthful follies of Jones. However, after all necessary deductions have been made, "Amelia" must be pronounced a wonderful work, full of that rich flow of humour and deep knowledge of human nature which charm us in "Tom Jones" and "Joseph

Andrews."—NICOLL, HENRY J., 1882, *Landmarks of English Literature, p.* 219.

In "Amelia," things get better; all things get better; it is one of the curiosities of literature that Fielding, who wrote one book that was engaging, truthful, kind, and clean, and another book that was dirty, dull, and false, should be spoken of, the world over, as the author of the second and not the first, as the author of "Tom Jones," not of "Amelia."—STEVENSON, ROBERT LOUIS, 1888, *Some Gentlemen in Fiction, Scribner's Magazine, vol.* 3, *p.* 766.

On the whole one likes Booth. If he sins he is heavily punished, and his conscience never becomes hardened. He is irresponsible, but he is not a fool. Fielding was a true artist when he put this born soldier into circumstances that needed the attainments of a man of business, and showed thereby that the qualities which were winning for us our colonial empire would not ensure financial success to their possessor. There is no subject on which our author waxes more indignant than the ingratitude shown by the Government to officers of distinguished merit who were so unfortunate as to lack interest in high places. But Booth's military training is apparent throughout the book. As far as his own sufferings are concerned he has plenty of pluck; it is the misery of those dear to him that disturbs his fortitude. When Amelia tries to deter him from foreign service for her sake, his tender heart is torn for his wife, while his honour as a soldier bids him go. And honour wins the day in spite of Amelia's entreaties. This man, after all, has some spirit, and is not simply a foolish prodigal, alternately uxorious and licentious.—THOMSON, CLARA, 1899, *A Note on Fielding's "Amelia," The Westminster Review, vol.* 152, *p.* 585.

GENERAL

Sick of her fools, great *Nature* broke the jest,
And *Truth* held out each character to test,
When *Genius* spoke: Let Fielding take the pen!
Life dropt her mask, and all mankind were men.
—CAWTHORN, THOMAS, 1749, *Gentleman's Magazine.*

Through all Mr. Fielding's inimitable comic romances we perceive no such thing as personal malice, no private character dragged into light; but every stroke is copied from the volume which nature has unfolded to him; every scene of life is by him represented in its natural colours, and every species of folly or humour is ridiculed with the most exquisite touches. A genius like this is perhaps more useful to mankind than any class of writers; he serves to dispel all gloom from our minds, to work off our ill-humours by the gay sensations excited by a well-directed pleasantry, and in a vain of mirth he leads his readers into a knowledge of human nature.—SMART, CHRISTOPHER, 1752, *The Hilliad, Preface.*

We have [says Mr. Bookseller] another writer of these imaginary histories, one who has not long since descended to these regions. His name is Fielding; and his works, as I have heard the best judges say, have a true spirit of comedy, and an exact representation of nature, with fine moral touches. He has not indeed given lessons of pure and consummate virtue, but he has exposed vice and meanness with all the powers of ridicule.—MONTAGU, ELIZABETH, 1760–65, *Dialogues of the Dead, by Lord Lyttelton, No.* 28.

Fielding being mentioned, Johnson exclaimed, "he was a blockhead;" and upon my expressing my astonishment at so strange an assertion, he said, "What I mean by his being a blockhead is that he was a barren rascal." BOSWELL.—"Will you not allow, Sir, that he draws very natural pictures of human life?" JOHNSON.—"Why, Sir, it is of very low life. Richardson used to say, that had he not known who Fielding was, he should have believed he was an hostler. Sir, there is more knowledge of the heart in one letter of Richardson's, than in all 'Tom Jones.' I, indeed, never read 'Joseph Andrews'."—JOHNSON, SAMUEL, 1772, *Life by Boswell, April* 6, *ed. Hill, vol.* II, *p.* 199.

Of the Comic Epopee we have two exquisite models in English, I mean the "Amelia" and "Tom Jones" of Fielding. The introductory part of the latter follows indeed the historical arrangement, in a way somewhat resembling the practice of Euripides in his prologues, or at least as excusable: But, with this exception, we may venture to say, that both fables would bear to be examined by Aristotle himself, and, if compared with those of Homer, would not suffer in the comparison.

This author, to an amazing variety of probable occurrences, and of characters well drawn, well supported, and finely contrasted, has given the most perfect unity, by making them all co-operate to one and the same final purpose. It yields a very pleasing surprise to observe, in the unravelling of his plots, particularly that of "Tom Jones," how many incidents, to which, because of their apparent minuteness, we have scarce attended as they occurred in the narrative, are found to have been essential to the plot. And what heightens our idea of the poet's art is, that all this is effected by natural means, and human abilities, without any machinery. —BEATTIE, JAMES, 1776–9, *Essays on Poetry and Music, p.* 102, *note.*

The cultivated genius of Fielding entitles him to a high rank among the classics. His works exhibit a series of pictures drawn with all the descriptive fidelity of a Hogarth. They are highly entertaining, and will always be read with pleasure.—KNOX, VICESIMUS, 1777, *Essays, Moral and Literary.*

Mr. Fielding's novels are highly distinguished for their humour; a humour which, if not of the most refined and delicate kind, is original, and peculiar to himself. The characters which he draws are lively and natural, and marked with the strokes of a bold pencil. The general scope of his stories is favourable to humanity and goodness of heart.—BLAIR, HUGH, 1783, *Lectures on Rhetoric and Belles-Lettres, ed. Mills, Lecture* xxxvii.

It always appeared to me that he estimated the compositions of Richardson too highly, and that he had an unreasonable prejudice against Fielding. In comparing those two writers, he used this expression: "that there was as great a difference between them as between a man who knew how a watch was made, and a man who could tell the hour by looking on the dial-plate." This was a short and figurative state of his distinction between drawing characters of nature and characters only of manners. But I cannot help being of opinion, that the neat watches of Fielding are as well constructed as the large clocks of Richardson, and that his dial-plates are brighter. Fielding characters, though they do not expand themselves so widely in dissertation, are as just pictures of human nature, and I will venture to say, have more striking features, and nicer touches of the pencil; and though Johnson used to quote with approbation a saying of Richardson's, "that the virtues of Fielding's heroes were the vices of a truly good man," I will venture to add, that the moral tendency of Fielding's writings, though it does not encourage a strained and rarely possible virtue, is ever favourable to honour and honesty, and cherishes the benevolent and generous affections. He who is as good as Fielding would make him, is an amiable member of society, and may be led on by more regulated instructors, to a higher state of ethical perfection.—BOSWELL, JAMES, 1791–93, *Life of Johnson, ed. Hill, vol.* II, *p.* 55.

Fielding will forever remain the delight of his country, and will always retain his place in the library of Europe, notwithstanding the unfortunate grossness which is the mark of an uncultivated taste, and which, if not yet entirely excluded from conversation, has been for some time banished from our writings, where, during the best age of national genius, it prevailed more than in those of any other polished nation.—MACKINTOSH, SIR JAMES, 1815, *Godwin's Lives of Milton's Nephews, Edinburgh Review, vol.* 25, *p.* 485.

Fielding's novels are, in general, thoroughly his own; and they are thoroughly English. What they are most remarkable for, is neither sentiment, nor imagination, nor wit, nor even humour, though there is an immense deal of this last quality; but profound knowledge of human nature, at least of English nature, and masterly pictures of the characters of men as he saw them existing. This quality distinguishes all his works, and is shown almost equally in all of them. As a painter of real life, he was equal to Hogarth; as a mere observer of human nature, he was little inferior to Shakspeare, though without any of the genius and poetical qualities of his mind. His humour is less rich and laughable than Smollett's; his wit as often misses as hits; he has none of the fine pathos of Richardson or Sterne; but he has brought together a greater variety of characters in common life, marked with more distinct peculiarities, and without an atom of caricature, than any other novel writer whatever.—HAZLITT, WILLIAM, 1818, *On the English*

Novelists, Lectures on the English Comic Writers, Lecture vi.

Of all the works of imagination, to which English genius has given origin, the writings of Henry Fielding are, perhaps, most decidedly and exclusively her own. They are not only altogether beyond the reach of translation, in the proper sense and spirit of the word, but we even question, whether they can be fully understood, or relished to the highest extent, by such natives of Scotland and Ireland, as are not habitually and intimately acquainted with the characters and manners of Old England. Parson Adams, Towwouse, Partridge, above all, Squire Western, are personages as peculiar to England, as they are unknown to other countries. Nay, the actors, whose character is of a more general cast, as Allworthy, Mrs. Miller, Tom Jones himself, and almost all the subordinate agents in the narrative, have the same cast of nationality, which adds not a little to the verisimilitude of the tale. The persons of the story live in England, travel in England, quarrel and fight in England; and scarce an incident occurs, without its being marked by something, which could not well have happened in any other country. . . . Fielding, the first of British novelists, for such he may surely be termed. . . . The celebrated Henry Fielding, father of the English Novel.—SCOTT, SIR WALTER, 1820, *Henry Fielding*.

The prose Homer of human nature.—BYRON, LORD, 1821, *A Journal in Italy, Jan.* 4.

Fielding conceived life as it was, with great strength and distinctness, and brought out into clear light those contrasts which are indeed now well enough known, but which were then remarked by none, because England was regarded as a paradise—a Utopia. He showed with such power the difference between appearance and truth—between a flattering clergy and true religion, that the lovers of sentimentality and the multitude, who are always willing to have their eyes bound that they may dream pleasantly, were in some measure driven from himself to his countryman Richardson, the discoverer of a conventional morality. We cannot therefore wonder that Fielding, who died in 1754, found a public in Germany much later than Richardson, whose moralizing and sentimental heroes and heroines had already become the fashion by means of Rousseau, at the same time with the idyllic dreams of Gessner. We must possess good practical sense and a knowledge of pure old English life, and of the abuses of its hierarchy and clergy, to understand Fielding, to estimate a "Joseph Andrews" and a "Tom Jones," and to find pleasure in them; whereas we have only need of indefinite general notions and sensibility, to admire Richardson's "Pamela," and his "Sir Charles Grandison."—SCHLOSSER, FREDERICK CHRISTOPH, 1823–43, *History of the Eighteenth Century, tr. Davison, vol.* II, *pp.* 60.

Have you read Fielding's novels? they are genuine things; though if you were not a decent fellow, I should pause before recommending them, their morality is so loose.—CARLYLE, THOMAS, 1823, *Early Letters, ed. Norton, p.* 293.

I find, in the last conversation I saw, you make me an admirer of Fielding, and so I am; but I find great fault with him too, I grant he is one of these writers that I remember; he stamps his characters, whether good or bad, on the reader's mind. This is more than I can say of every one. For instance, when Godwin plagues me about my not having sufficient admiration of Wordsworth's poetry, the answer I give is, that it is not my fault, for I have utterly forgotten it; it seemed to me like the ravelings of poetry. But to say nothing of Fielding's immorality, and his fancying himself a fine gentleman in the midst of all his coarseness, he has oftener described *habits* than *character*. For example, Western is no character; it is merely the language, manners, and pursuits of the country squire of that day; and the proof of this is, that there is no Squire Western now. Manners and customs wear out, but characters last for ever.—NORTHCOTE, JAMES, 1826–7, *Conversations, ed. William Hazlitt*.

Try what you can remember about Fielding for me. The "Voyage to Lisbon" is the most remarkable example I ever met with of native cheerfulness triumphant over bodily suffering and surrounding circumstances of misery and discomfort.—SOUTHEY, ROBERT, 1830, *Letter to Caroline Bowles, Feb.* 15; *Correspondence, ed. Dowden, p.* 184.

What a master of composition Fielding

was! Upon my word, I think the Œdipus Tyrannus, the Alchemist, and Tom Jones, the three most perfect plots ever planned. And how charming, how wholesome, Fielding always is! To take him up after Richardson, is like emerging from a sick room heated by stoves, into an open lawn, on a breezy day in May.—COLERIDGE, SAMUEL TAYLOR, 1834, *Table Talk, ed. Ashe, July* 5, *p.* 294.

After dinner indulged myself with several chapters of "Tom Jones." I can only believe, when I read Fielding, that persons speak in utter ignorance of his wit, humour, profound thought, satire, and truth of character when they set Scott above him, or even compare the two writers.—MACREADY, WILLIAM CHARLES, 1837, *Diary, Feb.* 26, *Reminiscences, ed. Pollock, p.* 410

There is not in Fielding much of that which can properly be called ideal—if we except the character of Parson Adams; but his works represent life as more delightful than it seems to common experience, by disclosing those of its dear immunities, which we little think of, even when we enjoy them. How delicious are all his refreshments at all his inns! How vivid are the transient joys of his heroes, in their chequered course—how full and over-flowing are their final raptures.—TALFOURD, THOMAS NOON, 1842, *On British Novels and Romances, Critical and Miscellaneous Writings, p.* 13.

Fielding within the range of his mind, approaches near absolute perfection; and if he had possessed as keen a sense of the supernatural as the natural, he might have taken the highest rank among great constructive and creative minds; but he had no elevation of soul, and little power of depicting it in imagination. As it is, however, the life-like reality of the characters and scenes he has painted, indicates that his genius was bounded by nothing but his sentiments.—WHIPPLE, EDWIN P., 1844, *Novels and Novelists, Literature and Life, p.* 46.

Is the forthcoming critique on Mr. Thackeray's writings in the "Edinburgh Review" written by Mr. Lewes? I hope it is. Mr. Lewes, with his penetrating sagacity and fine acumen, ought to be able to do the author of "Vanity Fair" justice. Only he must not bring him down to the level of Fielding—he is far, far above Fielding. It appears to me that Fielding's style is arid, and his views of life and human nature coarse, compared with Thackeray's.—BRONTË, CHARLOTTE, 1847, *Letter to W. S. Williams, Dec.* 23; *Charlotte Brontë and her Circle, ed. Shorter, p.* 407.

What a wonderful art! What an admirable gift of nature, was it by which the author of these tales was endowed, and which enabled him to fix our interests, to waken our sympathy, to seize upon our credulity, so that we believe in his people —speculate gravely upon their faults or their excellencies, prefer this one or that, deplore Jones's fondness for drink and play, Booth's fondness for play and drink, and the unfortunate position of the wives of both gentlemen—love and admire those ladies with all our hearts, and talk about them as faithfully as if we had breakfasted with them this morning in their actual drawing-rooms, or should meet them this afternoon in the Park! What a genius! what a vigour, what a bright-eyed intelligence and observation! what a wholesome hatred for meanness and knavery! what a vast sympathy! what a cheerfulness! what a manly relish of life! what a love of human kind! what a poet is here!—watching, meditating, brooding, creating! What multitudes of truths has that man left behind him! What generations he has taught to laugh wisely and fairly! What scholars he has formed and accustomed to the exercise of thoughtful humour and the manly play of wit! What a courage he had! What a dauntless and constant cheerfulness of intellect, that burned bright and steady through all the storms of his life, and never deserted its last wreck! It is wonderful to think of the pains and misery which the man suffered; the pressure of want, illness, remorse which he endured; and that the writer was neither malignant nor melancholy, his view of truth never warped, and his generous human kindness never surrendered.—THACKERAY, WILLIAM MAKEPEACE, 1853, *The English Humourists of the Eighteenth Century*

With all his faults, Fielding was one of the greatest novelists that England ever produced. If he were often licentious in sentiment and coarse in expression, these were in no small degree the faults of his times and the true reflex of the society which he portrayed; but his merits were all his own. He painted with the heart of a genius and the hand of an artist. Every character is conceived with truth and delineated with vigour. From the lady of fashion to the chambermaid; from the dissipated man of the town to the humble parson—all are portraits; and though some of them are likenesses of a class that has passed away or been greatly changed, others present to us features that will be fresh in every age, and last for all time.—WALLER, JOHN FRANCIS, 1870, *Pictures from English Literature, p.* 47.

He imitates the emphatic style; ruffles the petticoats and bobs the wigs; upsets with his rude jests all the seriousness of conventionality. If you are refined, or simply well dressed, don't go along with him. He will take you to prisons, inns, dunghills, the mud of the roadside; he will make you flounder among rollicking, scandalous, vulgar adventures, and crude pictures. He has plenty of words at command, and his sense of smell is not delicate. . . . Ladies will do well not to enter here. This powerful genius, frank and joyous, loves boisterous fairs like Rubens; the red faces, beaming with good humour, sensuality, and energy, move about his pages, flutter hither and thither, and jostle each other, and their overflowing instincts break forth in violent actions. Out of such he creates his chief characters. He has none more life-like than these, more broadly sketched in bold and dashing outline, with a more wholesome colour. . . . Cervantes, whom you imitate, and Shakspeare, whom you recall, had this refinement, and they have painted it; in this abundant harvest, with which you fill your arms, you have forgotten the flowers. We tire at last of your fisticuffs and tavern bills. You flounder too readily in cowhouses, among the ecclesiastical pigs of Parson Trulliber. We would fain see you have more regard for the modesty of your heroines; wayside accidents raise their tuckers too often; and Fanny, Sophia, Mrs. Heartfree, may continue pure, yet we cannot help remembering the assaults which have lifted their petticoats. You are so rude yourself, that you are insensible to what is atrocious. You persuade Tom Jones falsely, yet for an instant, that Mrs. Waters, whom he has made his mistress, is his mother, and you leave the reader long buried in the shame of this supposition. And then you are obliged to become unnatural in order to depict love; you can give but constrained letters; the transports of your Tom Jones are only the author's phrases. For want of ideas he declaims odes. You are only aware of the impetuosity of the senses, the upwelling of the blood, the effusion of tenderness, but not of the nervous exaltation and poetic rapture. Man, such as you conceive him, is a good buffalo; and perhaps he is the hero required by a people which is itself called John Bull.—TAINE, H. A., 1871, *History of English Literature, tr. Van Laun, vol.* II, *bk.* iii, *ch.* vi, *pp.* 171, 172, 176.

There never was a subtler or a more sagacious observer than Fielding, or who better deserved what is generously said of him by Smollett, that he painted the characters and ridiculed the follies of life with equal strength, humour, and propriety. But might it not be said of him, as of Dickens, that his range of character was limited; and that his method of proceeding from a central idea in all his leading people, exposed him equally to the charge of now and then putting human nature itself in place of the individual who should only be a small section of it? —FORSTER, JOHN, 1872–74, *Life of Charles Dickens, ch.* xiv.

Fielding, in his public capacity of magistrate, as well as in the public career he pursued, had an infinite variety of characters come under his notice; and his order of mind and natural tendency being that of studying the evolutions of human action, the whole animus of his genius was directed to that order of delineation. Hence is to be noticed in his novels how very meagre are his descriptions of scenery, particularly of rural scenery. Compare them with Walter Scott's, whose order of mind was absolutely panoramic. Scott was a true poet. Fielding had very little *external* imagination, and even less fancy; he never went out of the scenes in which he had been accustomed to move. He busied himself solely with human nature; and rarely has any one turned his studies to more ample account than he. Its principles, and general, intimate, and remote feelings, acting under particular circumstances and impressions, move him to an intense degree. They were ever present with him.—CLARKE, CHARLES COWDEN, 1872, *On the Comic Writers of England, The Gentleman's Magazine, n. s., vol.* 8, *p.* 558.

Although Fielding was dramatic, in so far as conversation and incident led the story on from point to point with a certain degree of system, combined with spontaneity, he did not carry the dramatic movement far enough. When all was over, his tale would remain but a rambling, aimless concatenation, terminating in nothing but an end of the adventures. His great powers lay in the observation of manners and natures; but he was content to offer the results of this observation in a crude, digressive form, somewhat lacking—if it may be said—in principle. He was fond of whipping in and out among his characters, in person, and did so with a sufficiently cheery and pleasant defiance of all criticism; but the practice injured his art, nevertheless. In a word, he seems to have written as much for his own amusement as for that of his reader; and although he seduously endeavoured to identify these two interests, he did not hestitate, when he felt like discharging a little dissertation of love, or classical learning, or what not, to do this at any cost, either of artistic propriety or the reader's patience. And, worst of all, he frequently dissected his *dramatis personæ* in full view of the audience, giving an epitome of their characters off-hand, or chattering garrulously about them, when the mood took him. These short-comings withheld from him the possibility of grouping his keen observations firmly about some centre of steady and assimilative thought. With Fielding, nothing crystallized, but all was put together in a somewhat hastily gathered bundle; and the parts have a semi-detached relation.—LATHROP, GEORGE PARSONS, 1874, *Growth of the Novel, The Atlantic Monthly, vol.* 33, *p.* 686.

His surpassing merits have compelled even his most pronounced foes to assign him a lofty place in the art which he adorned. Attempts to depreciate his genius, because the moral backbone was lacking in some of his characters, have been repeatedly made, but with no permanent effect upon his renown. For ourselves, we affirm at the outset that we consider him the Shakspeare of novelists. . . . He is at the head of his race. Other novelists may show a particular aptitude, he is the one being who has no aptitudes, for his art is universal. The temple he has reared has no dwarfed or stunted columns; it is perfect and symmetrical, and of towering and magnificent dimensions. Years have not defaced its beauty or shaken its foundations. Another tribute to those already paid to this great king of fiction—more ephemeral, perhaps, than some, but as sincere as any—is now laid at his feet. Henry Fielding might have been a better man, but it is impossible not to love him, and to recognise shining through him that glorious light of genius which grows not dim with Time, but whose luminous presence is ever with us to cheer, to reprove, to delight, and to elevate.—SMITH, GEORGE BARNETT, 1875, *Poets and Novelists, pp.* 253, 305.

He despises the Pharisee, and has a considerable compassion for the sinner; but then there are sins of different degrees of turpitude. The doctrine of male chastity, expounded in "Pamela," struck him as simply ridiculous; but though a man was not bound to be a monk, he was not to be a seducer or a systematic voluptuary. He would be the last man to attack marriage, and his ideal woman, though made of very solid flesh and blood, is pure in conduct, if tolerably free in speech. His view reflects the code by which men of sense generally govern their conduct, as distinguished from that by which they affect to be governed in language. His respect for facts is, in this sense, as marked as Jonhson's. He refuses to be imposed upon by phrases.— STEPHEN, LESLIE, 1876, *History of English Thought in the Eighteenth Century, vol.* II, *p.* 377.

Our great eighteenth century novelists have won a place in the abiding literature of the world—a place beside the poets more specially so called. Their knowledge of human nature, their humour, their dramatic skill, their pathos, make them peers of those who have used the forms of verse, and it is in the form and not in substance that they may rank below the masters of the creative art in verse. First among them all is the generous soul of Fielding, to whom so much is forgiven for the nobleness of his great heart. On him and on the others there rests the curse of their age, and no incantation can reverse the sentence pronounced upon those who deliberately stoop to the unclean. It is a grave defect in the splendid tale of "Tom Jones"—of all prose romances the most rich in life and the most artistic in construction—that a Bowdlerised version of it would be hardly intelligible as a tale. Grossness, alas! has entered into the marrow of its bones. Happily, vice has not; and amidst much that is repulsive, we feel the good man's reverence for goodness, and the humane spirit's honour of every humane quality, whilst the pure figure of the womanly Sophia (most womanly of all women in fiction) walks in maiden meditation across the darkest scenes, as the figure of the glorified Gretchen passes across the revel in the Walpurgis-Nacht.—HARRISON, FREDERIC, 1879–86, *The Choice of Books and Other Literary Pieces, p.* 63.

I do not believe that Henry Fielding was ever in love.—STEVENSON, ROBERT LOUIS, 1881, *Virginibus Puerisque and Other Papers.*

After the lapse of more than a century and a half, still disputes with Scott and one or two others the proud position of the greatest of English writers of fiction.—NICOLL, HENRY J., 1882, *Landmarks of English Literature, p.* 214.

Fielding is often censured by moralists for the coarseness of his novels. But had he not been coarse he would not have been true. He described life as it was in the eighteenth century, as he had seen it in the ups and downs of a checkered career. His characters were taken from the higher ranks and the lower. He placed the house, the amusements, the habits of a country-gentleman before the reader with the faithfulness of a man who had hunted, feasted, and got drunk with country-gentlemen. He described the miserable prisons of his time as he only could who had mingled with their degraded inmates, and had exerted his power as a police magistrate to break up the gang of ruffians who infested the streets. Thus Fielding's novels have a high historical, as well as a literary value. Mr. Lecky has testified to their importance in a reconstruction of the past by placing "Amelia" among his authorities. Squire Allworthy, Squire Western, Tom Jones, Parson Adams, are characters to be studied by whoever would understand social life in the eighteenth century. The lovely Sophia, the modest Fanny, and above all Amelia, whom Thackeray considered "the most charming character in English fiction," are portraits in the gallery of history.—TUCKERMAN, BAYARD, 1882, *A History of English Prose Fiction, p.* 204.

Certainly Fielding's genius was incapable of that ecstasy of conception through which the poetic imagination seems fused into a molten unity with its material, and produces figures that are typical without loss of characteristic individuality, as if they were drawn, not from what we call real life, but from the very source of life itself, and were cast in that universal mould about which the subtlest thinkers that have ever lived so long busied themselves. Fielding's characters are very real persons; but they are not types in the same sense as Lear and Hamlet. They seem to be men whom we have seen rather than men whom we might see if we were lucky enough, men who have been rather than who might have been. . . . He at least does not paint the landscape as a mere background for the naked nymph. He never made the blunder of supposing that the Devil always smelt of sulphur. He thought himself to be writing history, and called his novels Histories, as if to warn us that he should tell the whole truth without equivocation. He makes all the sins of his heroes react disastrously on their fortunes. He assuredly believed himself to be writing with an earnest moral purpose in his two greater and more deliberately composed works, and indeed clearly asserts as much. I also fully believe it, for the assertion is justified by all that we know of the prevailing qualities of his character, whatever may have been its failings and lapses, if failings and lapses they were. . . . Fielding, then, was not merely, in my judgment at least, an original writer, but an originator. He has the merit, whatever it may be, of inventing the realistic novel, as it is called.—LOWELL, JAMES RUSSELL, 1883–90, *Fielding, Address on Unveiling the Bust of Fielding, Taunton, Sept.* 4; *Prose Works, Riverside ed., vol.* VI, *pp.* 55, 61, 64.

Probably his only legacy to mankind, certainly his chief one, is the picture he has set before us of English society in his generation. We see pretty much what we should have seen as lookers-on. In vindicating the novel against the loftier pretensions of professed historians, he asserted that "in their productions nothing is true but the names and the dates, whereas in mine everything is true but the names and dates." Without going so far, still, as the novel embodies substantially the remarks of the ablest observers upon their contemporaries, we may admit his claim to be a writer of history, who, more faithfully than many historians proper, has given us the very form and presence of the times. In his own age, when coarseness was less offensive, he did, as a humorist, the good that mere pleasure can do. His humor, however, is in this age situated where those who are refined or well-dressed will not care to enter. In this direction, as in others, his influence has ceased to be felt. This is the criterion of a truly great man,—that his life has been deepened and chastened by sorrow, enabling him to discern the inner heart of things, so that there rises out of him a kind of universal Psalm; his thought is in our thoughts, and the fruit of his genius scatters its seed across continents and centuries.—WELSH, ALFRED H., 1883, *Development of English Literature and Language, vol.* II, *p.* 156.

Our English Novel's pioneer!
His was the eye that first saw clear
How, not in natures half-effaced
By cant of Fashion and of Taste,—
Not in the circles of the Great,
Faint-blooded and exanimate,—
Lay the true field of Jest and Whim,
Which we to-day reap after him.
No:—he stepped lower down and took
The piebald People for his Book!

—DOBSON, AUSTIN, 1885, *Henry Fielding, At the Sign of the Lyre.*

Fielding's moral strength lay in the keen insight which enabled him to detect, and the healthy common sense which prompted him to spurn a false, artificial, and altogether inadequate ideal; his weakness lay in a certain want of elevation, which expressed itself in an implied denial of any ideal whatsoever. His theory of life seems to have been that men and women are weak creatures; that any very lofty code of morals is nothing but a collection of counsels of perfection altogether unrealizable in life; and that the highest possibilities of virtue are attained by the man who enjoys himself honestly with the least harm to any one, and is always ready to be charitable to the frailties of others because he knows he has so many of his own. His creed is, in fact, that of the average man of the world in all ages; it is not elevated but it is at least sincere; and if we cannot pay to those who hold it the compliment implied by a large moral demand we can at least say of them that they practice what they preach, and we can acquit them of the too common crime of poisoning the moral atmosphere of the world with the stench of whited sepulchre.—NOBLE, JAMES ASHCROFT, 1886, *Morality in English Fiction, p.* 19.

Ripe fruit from fields of life new-tilled,—
Bright guineas from the mint new-milled,—
The trophies of his genius blaze
Through three half centuries of haze—
We hear the very larks that trilled
When Fielding wrote.

—LÜDERS, CHARLES HENRY, 1888, *When Fielding Wrote, American, March* 31.

There is somewhat inexpressibly heartening, to me, in the style of Fielding. One seems to be carried along, like a swimmer in a strong, clear stream, trusting one's self to every whirl and eddy, with a feeling of safety, of comfort, or delightful ease in the motion of the elastic water. He is a scholar, nay more, as Adams had his innocent vanity, Fielding has his innocent pedantry. He likes to quote Greek (fancy quoting Greek in a novel of to-day!) and to make the rogues of printers set it up correctly. He likes to air his ideas on Homer, to bring in a piece of Aristotle—not hackneyed—to show you that if he is writing about "characters and situations so wretchedly low and dirty," he is yet a student and a critic. —LANG, ANDREW, 1889, *Letters on Literature, p.* 38.

Fielding's portrait-painting is rough at the best. But his error is over-statement and not the fatal error of suppression, and at any rate he gives a true social picture of his time.—LEWIN, WALTER, 1889, *The Abuse of Fiction, The Forum, vol.* 7, *p.* 667.

He is before all things else a writer to be studied. He wrote for the world at large and to the end that he might be read eternally. His matter, his manner, the terms of his philosophy, the quality of his ideals, the nature of his achievement, proclaim him universal. Like Scott, like Cervantes, like Shakespeare, he claims not merely our acquaintance but an intimate and abiding familiarity. He has no special public, and to be only on nodding terms with him is to be practically dead to his attraction and unworthy his society. He worked not for the boys and girls of an age but for the men and women of all time; and both as artist and as thinker he commands unending attention and lifelong friendship. He is a great inventor, an unrivalled craftsman, a perfect master of his material. His achievement is the result of a life-time of varied experience, of searching and sustained observation, of unwearying intellectual endeavour. The sound and lusty types he created have an intellectual flavour peculiar to themselves. His novels teem with ripe wisdom and generous conclusions and beneficient examples.—HENLEY, WILLIAM ERNEST, 1890, *Views and Reviews, p.* 231.

He looked on naked Nature unashamed,
And saw the Sphinx, now bestial, now divine,
In change and rechange; he nor praised nor blamed,
But drew her as he saw with fearless line.
Did he good service? God must judge, not we;
Manly he was, and generous and sincere;
English in all, of genius blithely free:
Who loves a Man may see his image here.
—LOWELL, JAMES RUSSELL, 1890, *Inscription for a Memorial, Bust of Fielding.*

There is this to be said for him as a moralist, that he threw no sentimental halo over vice, that he honored true worth in manhood and in womanhood, that his Parson Adams, his Squire Allworthy, and his Amelia are among the most lovable characters in fiction, and that no satirist ever exposed meanness, hypocrisy, and kindred vices with healthier scorn and ridicule.—MINTO, WILLIAM, 1894, *The Literature of the Georgian Era, ed. Knight, p.* 109.

Theoretically, Fielding denies the existence of the typical hero as commonly conceived, and is, of course, warmly applauded by the great Mr. Thackeray for his opportune discovery; but, as matter of fact, Fielding does make a hero out of Tom Jones, and, from beginning to end, very obviously exalts into heroic attributes the very vices which he politely deprecates and for which he artfully apologizes. The truth is, that while Fielding thus displays the manners of the times, he chooses from preference and sympathy to depict the bad manners of his time rather than the best. Perhaps we need not quarrel with the author's taste: he certainly comprehended life and character, and was in his art, when that was at its highest, far in advance of his rival Richardson. The author of "Joseph Andrews" and "Tom Jones" may not be entitled to claim the highest place among the British novelists, but he certainly deserves to rank among the most vigorous and faithful, as he is, doubtless, one of the most popular of English realists. —SIMONDS, WILLIAM EDWARD, 1894, *An Introduction to the Study of English Fiction, p.* 49.

As a master of style, Fielding has a claim on our admiration, apart from all the other attributes of his genius. It seems strange in regard to Fielding to set aside all the wealth of human sympathy, all the range of humour, all the vividness of character-drawing, and to restrict ourselves solely to the one aspect that interests us here, his place as a writer of prose. His style reflects much that is distinctive of his genius, its massive carelessness, its strong simplicity, its clearness of outline, and its consummate ease. But above all things he repeats two leading characteristics of his age, its irony and its scholarship. Fielding was from first to last a man of letters, as the character was conceived in his time—without pedantry, without strain, without the constraint of subtlety, but always imbued with the instinct of the scholar, never forgetting that, in the full rush of his exuberant fancy and his audacious humour, he must give to his style that indescribable quality that makes it permanent, that forces us to place it in the first rank of literary effort, that, even when irregular, pleads for no allowance on the score of neglect of art. He challenges comparison on merely literary grounds with the best models of literary art, and he is no loser by the comparison.—CRAIK, HENRY, 1895, *ed., English Prose, Introduction, vol.* IV, *p.* 10.

There are only two other writers whom I at least should rank with Fielding in the very topmost class of English novelists. And both Scott and Thackeray were notoriously careless in the mint and anise and cumin of style. . . . He might, if his education and early practice had been different, have written with more formal correctness and yet none the worse; he could hardly, if the paradox may be pardoned, have written otherwise than he did and yet have written much the better. Of no one is the much-quoted and much-misquoted maxim of Buffon more justified than of him. His style is exactly suited to his character and his production—which latter, be it remembered, considering the pleasures of his youth and the business of his age, was very considerable. No fault of his style can ever, either in the general reader or in the really qualified critic, have hindered the enjoyment of the best part of his work; and like the work itself the style in which it is clothed is eminently English. It is English no less in its petty shortcomings of correctness, precision, and grace, than in its mighty merits of power and range. Of the letter Fielding may be here and there a little neglectful; in the spirit he always holds fast to the one indispensable excellence, the adjustment of truth and life to art.—SAINTSBURY, GEORGE, 1895, *English Prose, ed. Craik, vol.* IV, *pp.* 114, 115.

If Richardson was "womanish," Fielding was masculine with a vengeance; gross, too, in a way, which always will, and always should, keep his books outside the pale of decent family reading. Filth is filth, and always deserves to be scored by its name—whatever blazon of genius may compass it about. I have no argument here with the artists who, for art's sake, want to strip away all the protective kirtles which the Greek Dianas wore: but when it comes to the bare bestialities of such tavern-bagnois as poor Fielding knew too well, there seems room for reasonable objection, and for a strewing of some of the fig-leaves of decency.—MITCHELL, DONALD G., 1895, *English Lands Letters and Kings, Queen Anne and the Georges, p.* 67.

His desultory criticism is as sound as it is original, and whatever differences of opinion there may be as to the value of his fiction, there can be none as to the faithfulness with which he adheres in his novels to the theories which his essays propound.—LOBBAN, J. H., 1896, *English Essays, Introduction, p.* xl.

Fielding, in each of his works, but in "Tom Jones" pre-eminently, is above all things candid and good-humoured. He is a lover of morals, but he likes them to be sincere; he has no palliation for their rancid varieties. He has his eye always on conduct; he is keen to observe not what a man pretends or protests, but what he does, and this he records to us, sometimes with scant respect for our susceptibilities. But it has been a magnificent advantage for English fiction to have near the head of it a writer so vigorous, so virile, so devoid of every species of affectation and hypocrisy. In all the best of our later novelists there has been visible a strain of sincere manliness which comes down to them in direct descent from Fielding, and which it would be a thousand pities for English fiction to relinquish.—GOSSE, EDMUND, 1897, *Short History of Modern English Literature, p.* 244.

John Conybeare

1692–1755.

John Conybeare, D. D., 1692-1755, admitted a battler of Exeter College, 1708; Fellow, 1710; Rector of St. Clemet's, Oxford, 1724; Rector of Exeter College, 1730; Dean of Christ Church, 1732; Bishop of Bristol, 1750. "Sermon on Miracles," 1722. Highly esteemed. "Sermon," 1724. "Subscription to Articles of Religion," a Sermon, 1726. Very celebrated. "Defence of Revealed Religion," in answer to Tindal's "Christianity as Old as the Creation," 1732. An admirable confutation. Three editions in a year. Other sermons. After the bishop's death a collection of his sermons was published for the benefit of his family, in 2 vols. 8vo, 1757, on a subscription list of 4600 copies.—ALLIBONE, S. AUSTIN, 1854–58, *A Critical Dictionary of English Literature, vol.* I, *p.* 420.

PERSONAL

On Friday last (Jan. 26) about noon came very privately into Oxford, in a coach and four, Dr. John Conybeare, rector of Exeter coll., being not met by so much as one soul, and yesterday, at 10 o'clock in the morning, he was installed dean of Christ Church, but very little or no rejoycing was shewed on the occasion. He owes this piece of preferment to Mr. [he is not a university Dr.] Edmund Gibson, bp. of London, who hath some private by-ends in view, to whom he dedicated his "Reply to Christianity as old as the Creation," which book (I am told, for I have not read it) is spun out to a great length, whereas all that is material might have been brought into about a sheet of paper.—HEARNE, THOMAS, 1732-33, *Reliquiæ Hearnianæ, ed. Bliss, vol.* III, *p.* 92.

As a bishop he was unfortunately disabled, through almost all his episcopate, by severe illness. Otherwise he would have been a valuable accession to his bench. "I rejoice," said Berkeley, "in his promotion. His writings and character raise him high in my esteem." He lived on terms of intimate friendship with James Foster and some other leading Nonconformists.—ABBEY, CHARLES J., 1887, *The English Church and its Bishops,* 1700-1800, *vol.* II, *p.* 68.

GENERAL

Conybeare is a temperate and able writer, but there is little in his book ["Defence of Religion"] to distinguish it from expositions of the same argument by other contemporary divines of the average type.—STEPHEN, LESLIE, 1887, *Dictionary of National Biography, vol.* XII, *p.* 61.

Conybeare avoids all the scurrility and personality which mar too many of the works written on both sides, and discusses, in calm and dignified, but at the same time luminous and impressive, language, the important question which Tindal had raised.—OVERTON, JOHN HENRY 1897, *The Church in England, vol.* II, *p.* 222.

Thomas Wilson

1663-1755.

Born at Burton in Cheshire, studied at Trinity College, Dublin, and, chaplain to the Earl of Derby, became Bishop of Sodor and Man in 1697. For fifty-eight years he governed his diocese with constant care. His "Principles of Christianity" (1707), commonly called the Manx Catechism—the first book printed in Manx—and his "Instruction for the Indians," written for Oglethorp's Georgia plantation scheme, were combined to form "The Knowledge of Christianity made easy to the Meanest Capacities" (1755). His name best survives in his "Short Instructions for the Lord's Supper" (1736) and "Sacra Privata" (1800). Other books are "Parochialia, or Instructions for the Clergy" (1788), and "Maxims of Piety" (1789). He instituted a Manx translation of the Bible (1772-75.) The best edition of his works is that by Keble (1847-52), with a Life (reprinted 1863).—PATRICK AND GROOME, *eds.*, 1897, *Chambers's Biographical Dictionary, p.* 977.

PERSONAL

The people of the island were so thoroughly persuaded of his receiving a larger portion of God's blessing, that they seldom began harvest till he did; and if he passed along the field, they would leave their work to ask his blessing, assured that that day would be prosperous. Nor was this opinion confined to the obscure corner of the world where he lived. In Warrington, even in London, there are those who can remember crowds of persons flocking round him, with the cry of "Bless me too, my Lord."—CRUTTWELL, CLMENT, 1785, *Life of Wilson.*

His charity was unbounded. It influenced his sentiments, it formed his character, it regulated his life . . . he was utterly free from bigotry . . . he possessed a truly Catholic spirit. With the few Dissenters who resided in his diocese he maintained a friendly intercourse. Such of them as were pious in their lives he treated with marks of particular kindness. In this respect he resembled Archbishop Usher, who lived in habits of intimacy with the learned Nonconformist, Mr. Baxter. "Si in necessariis sit unitas, in non necessariis libertas; in utrisque caritas, optimocerte loco essent res nostrae." Bishop Wilson was so great a friend of toleration that the Roman Catholics that resided on the island were not unfrequently at his sermons and prayers, and the Dissenters in the diocese, who were without a minister of their own persuasion, attended even the

Communion service, having obtained permission from the Bishop to stand or sit, as their consciences directed.—STOWELL, HUGH, 1819, *The Life of Bishop Wilson.*

As far as man can judge of man, few persons ever went out of this world more thoroughly prepared for the change than Bishop Wilson, not only in heart and conscience, but in comparatively trifling arrangements. He had even provided his coffin long before hand.—KEBLE, JOHN, 1863, *Life of Thomas Wilson.*

No name in the long history of the English episcopate is more honourable than that of Thomas Wilson. For no less than fifty-nine years, from 1696 to 1755, he administered the see of Sodor and Man in a way which excited, as it well might the amazement and admiration of all churchmen to whom his fame was known. Nor was his repute confined to England. Cardinal Fleury, shortly before his death in 1743, sent a special messenger to him. He had heard, he said, about him, and he felt the more interest in the account because they were the oldest, and he believed also the two poorest bishops in Europe. He hoped that it might be possible he would accept an invitation from him, and pay him a visit in France. Fleury likewise procured an order that no French privateer—for the war of the Austrian succession was then at his height —should ravage the Isle of Man. Queen Anne and George I. both offered him bishoprics, and Queen Caroline was specially anxious to keep him in England. "Nay," said the bishop, "I will not leave my wife in my old age, because she is poor." In his own diocese he was honoured with a reverence which sometimes almost bordered upon superstition. —ABBEY, CHARLES J., 1887, *The English Church and its Bishops,* 1700–1800, *vol.* I, *p.* 138.

GENERAL

Bishop Wilson's "Maxims" deserve to be circulated as a religious book, not only by comparison with the cartloads of rubbish circulated at present under this designation, but for their own sake, and even by comparison with the other works of the same author. Over the far better known "Sacra Privata" they have this advantage, that they were prepared by him for his own private use, while the "Sacra Privata" were prepared by him for the use of the public. The "Maxims" were never meant to be printed, and have on that account,—like a work of, doubtless, far deeper emotion and power, the "Meditations" of Marcus Aurelius, something peculiarly sincere and first-hand about them. Some of the best things from the "Maxims" have passed into the "Sacra Privata;" still, in the "Maxims," we have them as they first arose; and whereas, too, in the "Sacra Privata" the writer speaks very often as one of the clergy, and as addressing the clergy, in the "Maxims" he almost always speaks soley as a man. I am not saying a word against the "Sacra Privata," for which I have the highest respect; only the "Maxims" seem to me a better and a more edifying book still.—ARNOLD, MATTHEW, 1869, *Culture and Anarchy, Preface, p.* iv.

Wilson, the "Apostolic," was a man of the old sacerdotal type, full of simplicity, tenderness, devotion, and with a sincere belief, inoffensive because alloyed by no tincture of pride or ambition, in the sacred privileges of the Church. Amongst his scattered reflections there are many of much beauty in expression as in sentiment. They imply a theology of that type of which à-Kempis is the permanent representative; less ascetic, inasmuch as Wilson had the good fortune to be a married man instead of a monk; and, of course, less vivid, as he was one born out of due time. His superstitions—for he is superstitious —no more provoke anger than the simple fancies of a child; and we honour him as we should honour all men whose life and thoughts were in perfect harmony, and guided by noble motives. To read him is to love him; he helps us recognise the fact that many of the thoughts which supported his noble nature in its journey through life may be applicable in a different costume to the sorrows and trials which also change their form rather than their character; but we see with equal clearness that he has little or nothing to say upon the speculative difficulties of the time. He may be passed over with the remark that his example proves conclusively that a genuine Christian theologian in the most characteristic sense of the term might still be found under the reign of George II. in the Isle of Man.—STEPHEN, LESLIE, 1876, *History of English Thought in the Eighteenth Century, vol.* II, *p.* 384.

Gilbert West

1703-1756.

Gilbert West (1700?-1756) translated the Odes of Pindar (1749), prefixing to the work,—which is still our standard version of Pindar—a good dissertation on the Olympic games. New editions of West's Pindar were published in 1753 and 1766. He wrote several pieces of original poetry, included in Dodsley's collection. One of these, "On the Abuse of Travelling," a canto in imitation of Spenser (1739) is noticed by Gray in enthusiastic terms. West was also author of a prose work, "Observations on the Resurrection," for which the university of Oxford conferred on him the degree of LL. D.; and Lyttelton addressed to him his treatise on St. Paul. Pope left West a sum of £200, but payable after the death of Martha Blount, and he did not live to receive it. By all his contemporaries, this accomplished and excellent man was warmly esteemed; and through the influence of Pitt, he enjoyed a competence in his latter days, having been appointed (1752) one of the clerks of the privy council, and under-treasurer of Chelsea Hospital.—CHAMBERS, ROBERT, 1876, *Cyclopædia of English Literature, ed. Carruthers.*

PERSONAL

Perhaps it may not be without effect to tell, that he read the prayers of the public liturgy every morning to his family, and that on Sunday evening he called his servants into the parlour, and read to them first a sermon, and then prayers. Crashaw is now not the only maker of verses to whom may be given the two venerable names of *Poet* and *Saint*.—JOHNSON, SAMUEL, 1779-81, *West, Lives of the English Poets.*

GENERAL

Now I talk of verses, Mr. Walpole and I have frequently wondered you should never mention a certain imitation of Spenser, published last year [May, 1739], by a namesake of yours, with which we are all enraptured and enmarvailed.—GRAY, THOMAS, 1740, *Letter to Richard West, July* 16, *Works, ed. Gosse, vol.* II, *p.* 90.

Lord Cobham's West has published his translation of Pindar; the poetry is very stiff, but prefixed to it there is a very entertaining account of the Olympic games, and that preceded by an affected inscription to Pitt and Lyttelton.—WALPOLE, HORACE, 1749, *Letter to George Montagu, May* 18; *Letters, ed. Cunningham, vol.* II, *p.* 163,

He hath not made use [in his "Observations on the Resurrection"] of strained and arbitrary suppositions, but such as seem clearly to arise from the accounts of the evangelists, carefully considered and compared.—LELAND, JOHN, 1754-56, *A View of the Deistical Writers, Lecture* xi.

See a learned and judicious discourse on the Olympic games which Mr. West has prefixed to his translation of Pindar. . . . Affords much curious and authentic information.—GIBBON, EDWARD, 1776-78, *Decline and Fall of the Roman Empire, ch.* xxx, xl, *notes.*

Of his translations I have only compared the first Olympic ode with the original, and found my expectation surpassed, both by its elegance and its exactness. He does not confine himself to his author's train of stanzas; for he saw that the difference of the languages required a different mode of versification. The first strophe is eminently happy; in the second he has a little strayed from Pindar's meaning. . . . A work of this kind, must in a minute examination, discover many imperfections; but West's version, so far as I have considered it, appears to be the product of great labour and great abilities. His "Institution of the Garter" (1742) is written with sufficient knowledge of the manners that prevailed in the age to which it is referred, and with great elegance of diction; but, for want of a process of events, neither knowledge nor elegance preserve the reader from weariness. His "Imitations of Spenser" are very successfully performed, both with respect to the metre, the language and the fiction; and being engaged at once by the excellence of the sentiments, and the artifice of the copy, the mind has two amusements together.—JOHNSON, SAMUEL, 1779-81, *West, Lives of the English Poets.*

I shall endeavor to account for the decline of poetry after the age of Shakspeare and Spenser, in spite of the great exceptions during the Commonwealth, and to trace the effect produced by the restorers of a better taste, of whom Thomson and Gilbert West are to be esteemed as the chief.—SOUTHEY, ROBERT, 1805, *Letter to Grosvenor C. Bedford, April* 13, *Correspondence, ed. C. C. Southey, ch.* xi.

The poems of West, indeed, had the merit of chaste and manly diction; but they were cold, and, if I may so express it, only dead-colored.—COLERIDGE, SAMUEL TAYLOR, 1817, *Biographia Literaria, ch.* i.

His work is noticed here on account of the luminous and satisfactory manner in which he has harmonized the several accounts of the evangelical history of the resurrection. — HORNE, THOMAS HARTWELL, 1818–39, *A Manual of Biblical Bibliography.*

This is one of the acutest and best-reasoned works which have appeared in English on the Resurrection of Christ. —ORME, WILLIAM, 1824, *Bibliotheca Biblica.*

West's two imitations of Spenser are excellent, not merely as Johnson seems to say, for their ingenuity, but for their fulness of thought and vigor of expression. —COLERIDGE, HENRY NELSON, 1843? *ed. Coleridge's Biographia Literaria, ch.* I, *note.*

Besides other verse, he published a translation of a portion of the odes of Pindar, which had long considerable reputation, but is not very Pindaric, though a smooth and sonorous performance. The one of his works that has best kept its ground is his prose tract entitled "Observations on the Resurrection," a very able and ingenious disquisition.—CRAIK, GEORGE L., 1861, *A Compendious History of English Literature and of the English Language, vol.* II, *p.* 283.

He has left some name in theology by his "Observations on the Resurrection," and in poetry by his translation of Pindar, and his "Imitations of Spenser." His writings in both kinds are the productions of a cultivated rather than of a vigorous mind, and the criticism of Coleridge on his poems exactly describes the general character of his works.—ELWIN, WHITWELL, 1872, *ed., The Works of Alexander Pope, vol.* VIII, *p.* 347, *note.*

Colley Cibber

1671-1757.

Born, in London, 6 Nov. 1671. Educated at Grantham Free School, 1682-87. Not long after enlisting in forces of Earl of Devonshire he abandoned army, and in 1690 went to London and joined company of Theatre Royal. First appeared as an actor, 1691; at Theatre Royal, 1691-95. Married Miss Shore, 1692. Followed Betterton to new theatre in Little Lincoln's Inn Fields, 1695. Wrote prologue for opening of theatre. His first play "Love's Last Shift" produced there, Jan. 1696. At Haymarket, 1706-08. At Drury Lane, 1708-32. Share in patent of Drury Lane, March 1708. Concerned with management of Haymarket, 1709-10; of Drury Lane, 1710-33. Appointed Poet Laureate, 3 Dec. 1730. Retired from stage, 1733. Reappeared on one or two occasions afterwards; last appearance, 15 Feb. 1745. Died, 12 Dec. 1757. Buried in vault of Danish Church (now British and Foreign Sailors' Church), Whitechapel. *Works:* "Love's Last Shift," 1694; "A Poem on the Death of Queen Mary," 1695; "Woman's Wit," 1697 (another edn., under title of "The Schoolboy," anon., 1707); "Xerxes," 1699; acting version of Shakespeare's "King Richard III.," 1700; "Love makes a Man," 1701; "She Would and she Would not," 1703; "The Careless Husband," 1705; "Perolla and Izadora," 1706; "The Comical Lovers" (anon.), 1707; "The Double Gallant," 1707; "The Lady's Last Stake," [1708]; "The Rival Fools," [1709]; "Cinna's Conspiracy" (anon.; attributed to Cibber), 1713; "Myrtillo," 1715; "Hob; or the Country Wake," 1715; "Venus and Adonis," 1716; "The Non-Juror," 1718; "Ximena," 1718; "Plays" (2 vols.), 1721; "The Refusal," 1721; "Cæsar in Egypt," 1725; "The Provoked Husband" (with Vanbrugh), 1728; "The Rival Queens," 1729; "Love in a Riddle," 1719 [1729]; "Damon and Phillida" (anon., founded on preceding), 1729; "A Journey to London" (adapted from Vanbrugh), 1730; "An Ode for His Majesty's Birth-Day," 1731; "An Ode to His Majesty for the New Year," 1731; "Chuck," 1736; "Apology," 1740; "A Letter. . . . to Mr. Pope," 1742; "The Egotist; or, Colley upon Cibber," 1743; "Another

Occasional Letter to Mr. Pope," 1744; "Papal Tyranny in the Reign of King John" (founded on Shakespeare's "King John"), 1745; "The Temple of Dulness" (anon.; attributed to Cibber), 1745; "The Character and the Conduct of Cicero," 1747; "The Lady's Lecture," 1748. *Dramatic Works:* in 4 vols., 1760.—SHARP, R. FARQUHARSON, 1897, *A Dictionary of English Authors*. p. 55.

PERSONAL

Round him much Embryo, much Abortion lay,
Much future Ode, and abdicated Play;
Nonsense precipitate, like running Lead,
That slipp'd through Cracks and Zigzags of the Head;
All that on Folly Frenzy could beget,
Fruits of dull Heat, and Sooterkins of wit,
Next, o'er his Books his eyes begin to roll,
In pleasing memory of all he stole,
How here he slipp'd, how there he plunder'd snug,
And suck'd all o'er, like an industrious Bug.
. . . .
High on a gorgeous seat, that far outshone
Henley's gilt tub, or Fleckno's Irish throne,
Or that where on her Curls the public pours,
All-bounteous, fragrant grains and golden showers,
Great Cibber sate: The proud Parnassian sneer,
The conscious simper, and the jealous leer,
Mix on his look: All eyes direct their rays
On him, and crowds turn coxcombs as they gaze.
—POPE, ALEXANDER, 1743, *The Dunciad, bks:* i, ii.

Colley Cibber, Sir, was by no means a blockhead; but by arrogating to himself too much, he was in danger of losing that degree of estimation to which he was entitled. His friends gave out that he *intended* his birth-day Odes should be bad: but that was not the case, Sir; for he kept them many months by him, and a few years before he died he shewed me one of them, with great solicitude to render it as perfect as might be, and I made some corrections, to which he was not very willing to submit.—JOHNSON, SAMUEL, 1763, *Life by Boswell, ed. Hill, vol.* I, *p.* 464.

Though his voice as an actor was occasionally harsh and unmusical, more particularly in tragedy, he was a fine reciter of comedies in private. Foote and Murphy, both excellent judges, have given testimony of this; particularly the latter, who heard him read the scenes of *Lord* and *Lady Townly* in "The Provoked Husband" to Mrs. Woffington. It is true, his voice partook of the *old school*, and therefore differed in some respect from that familiarity in modern dialogue which Garrick introduced; but it was, upon the whole, a fine picture of the manners of the age in which the play was written, and had a very impressive effect.—FOOTE, SAMUEL, 1777? *Memoirs, ed. Cooke, vol.* II, *p.* 201.

Colley, we are told, had the honour to be a member of the great club at White's; and so, I suppose, might any other man, not quite unknown, who wore good cloaths, and paid his money when he lost it. But on what terms did Cibber live with this society? Why, he feasted most sumptuously, as I have heard his friend Victor say with an air of triumphant exultation, with Mr. Arthur and his wife, and gave eighteen pence for his dinner. After he had dined, when the clubroom door was opened, and the laureate was introduced, he was saluted with the loud and joyous acclamation of "O King Coll! Come in, King Coll! Welcome, welcome, King Colley!" And this kind of gratulation, Mr. Victor thought, was very gracious and very honourable.—DAVIES, THOMAS, 1780, *Memoirs of the Life of David Garrick, vol.* II, *p.* 353.

For my part, I can almost believe that Cibber was a *modest man*! as he was most certainly a man of genius. Cibber had lived a dissipated life, and his philosophical indifference, with his careless gaiety, was the breastplate which even the wit of Pope failed to pierce. During twenty years' persecution for his unlucky Odes, he never lost his temper; he would read to his friends the best things pointed against them, with all the spirit the authors could wish; and would himself write epigrams for the pleasure of hearing them repeated while sitting in coffee-houses; and whenever they were applauded as "Palpable hits!"—"Keen!"—"Things with a spirit in them!"—he enjoyed these attacks on himself by himself. If this be vanity, it is at least "Cibberian." It was, indeed, the singularity of his personal character which so long injured his genius, and laid him open to the perpetual attacks of his contemporaries, who were mean enough to ridicule undisguised foibles, but dared not be just to the redeeming virtues of his genius.—DISRAELI, ISAAC, 1814, *Pope and Cibber, Quarrels of Authors.*

He flourished in wig and embroidery, player, poet, and manager, during the Augustan age of Queen Anne, somewhat earlier and somewhat later. A most egregious fop, according to all accounts, he was, but a very pleasant one notwithstanding, as your fop of parts is apt to be. Pope gained but little in the warfare he waged with him, for this plain reason, that the great poet accuses his adversary of dulness, which was not by any means one of his sins, instead of selecting one of the numerous faults, such as pertness, petulance, and presumption, of which he was really guilty.—MITFORD, MARY RUSSELL, 1851, *Recollections of a Literary Life*, p. 264.

Of Colley Cibber it is sufficient here to state that he was not merely a popular actor, but one of the most remarkable men of his age. His professional cleverness was so great that it can be described as only falling short of genius; and as a dramatist, his admirable judgment made up for his deficiencies in the art of composition, so that few writers of comedy have achieved greater temporary triumphs. With all his talents, however, it was his fate to earn the hearty contempt of most of his contemporaries whose good opinion was worth having, and in the fulness of his fame his self-sufficiency and arrogance exposed him to all the shafts of satire. . . . If the character of Cibber were as contemptible as "The Dunciad" and Fielding's writings represent it, much printer's ink was thrown away in blackening it.—LAWRENCE, FREDERICK, 1855, *The Life of Henry Fielding*, pp. 15, 123.

Worn-out, tawdry, with a shabby fine laced coat, and dirty tattered ruffles, taking snuff vehemently, and applauding as if he were in the stage-box one moment, weeping as if he were on the stage the next,—behold Colley Cibber; now in the very yellowest and searest of the leaf, to which old age is likened; still writing, still acting his own plays, and still frequenting the table of Samuel Richardson, to eat at another man's expense, and to pay back the coin of flattery. But he is Poet Laureate; and that office imposes on the worthy, but somewhat tuft-hunting Samuel Richardson.—THOMSON, KATHERINE (GRACE WHARTON), 1862, *The Literature of Society*, vol. II, p. 240.

Among them all, Colley kept his own to the last. A short time before the last hour arrived, Horace Walpole hailed him on his birthday with a good-morrow, and "I am glad, sir, to see you looking so well." "Egad, sir," replied the old gentleman, all diamonded and powdered and dandified, "at eighty-four it is well for a man that he can look at all." . . . And now he crosses Piccadilly and passes through Albemarle Street, slowly but cheerfully, with an eye and a salutation for any pretty woman of his acquaintance, and with a word for any "good fellow" whose purse he has lightened, or who has lightened his, at dice or whist. And so he turns into the adjacent square; and as his servant closes the door, after admitting him, neither of them wots that the master has passed over the threshold for the last time, a living man. In December, 1757, I read in contemporary publications that "there died at his house in Berkeley Square, Colley Cibber, Esq., Poet Laureate."—DORAN, JOHN, 1863, *Annals of the English Stage*, vol. II, ch. ii.

No life illustrates more curiously the history of the stage than that of Colley Cibber, and no figure stands out more conspicuously in that sort of turbulence and war which the actor of his era had to wage. His strange career shows us that the actor was as marked a figure off the stage as upon it.—FITZGERALD, PERCY, 1882, *A New History of the English Stage*, vol. I, p. 320.

DRAMAS

Cibber has written a great many comedies; and though in several of them there be much sprightliness, and a certain pert vivacity peculiar to him, yet they are so forced and unnatural in the incidents, as to have generally sunk into obscurity, except two which have always continued in high favour with the public, "The Careless Husband," and "The Provoked Husband." The former is remarkable for the polite and easy turn of the dialogue; and, with the exception of one indelicate scene, is tolerably moral, too, in the conduct and in the tendency. The latter, "The Provoked Husband," (which was the joint production of Vanbrugh and Cibber), is, perhaps, on the whole, the best comedy in the English language. It is liable, indeed, to one critical objection, of having a double plot; as the incident of the

Wronghead family, and those of Lord Townley's, are separate and independent of each other. But this irregularity is compensated by the natural characters, the fine painting, and the happy strokes of humour with which it abounds. We are, indeed, surprised to find so unexceptionable a comedy proceeding from two such loose authors; for, in its general strain, it is calculated to expose licentiousness and folly; and would do honour to any stage.—BLAIR, HUGH, 1783, *Lectures on Rhetoric and Belles-Lettres, ed. Mills, Lecture* xlvii, *p.* 541.

His "Double Gallant," which has been lately revived, though it cannot rank in the first, may take its place in the second or third class of comedies. It abounds in character, bustle, and stage-effect. It belongs to what may be called the composite style; and very happily mixes up the comedy of intrigue, such as we see it in Mrs. Centlivre's Spanish plots, with a tolerable share of the wit and spirit of Congreve and Vanbrugh. As there is a good deal of wit, there is a spice of wickedness in this play, which was a privilege of the good old style of comedy, not altogether abandoned in Cibber's time. . . . The characters in the "Double Gallant" are well kept up. At-All and Lady Dainty are the two most prominent characters in this comedy, and those into which Cibber has put most of his own nature and genius. They are the essence of active impertinence and fashionable frivolity. Cibber, in short, though his name has been handed down to us as a byword of impudent pretension and impenetrable dulness by the classical pen of his accomplished rival, who, unfortunately, did not admit of any merit beyond the narrow circle of wit and friendship in which he himself moved, was a gentleman and a scholar of the old school; a man of wit and pleasantry in conversation, a diverting mimic, an excellent actor, an admirable dramatic critic, and one of the best comic writers of his age.—HAZLITT, WILLIAM, 1818, *On the Comic Writers of the Last Century, Lecture* viii.

Steele's "Conscious Lovers" is the first comedy which can be called moral; Cibber, in those parts of the "Provoked Husband" that he wrote, carried this farther; and the stage afterwards grew more and more refined, till it became languid and sentimental.—HALLAM, HENRY, 1837–39, *Introduction to the Literature of Europe, pt.* iv, *ch.* vii, *par.* 2, *note.*

In selecting the play of "King Richard the Third," I have, upon mature consideration, decided on adopting the well-known version of Colley Cibber, instead of going back to the original text of Shakespeare. That text has been practically declared by the greatest ornaments of the drama, less fitted in its integrity for representation on the stage than almost any other generally acted play of the great poet; whilst, on the other hand, the tragedy, as modified by Cibber, being rather a condensation than an alteration of Shakespeare (the interpolations themselves being chiefly selections from his other plays), has been pronounced one of the most admirable and skilful instances of dramatic adaptations ever known. David Garrick made his first appearance in London, in 1741, in Colley Cibber's version of "King Richard the Third;" and Henderson adopted the same play; the classical John Kemble followed deliberately in the wake of his great predecessors; and to these succeeded George Frederick Cooke, and my late father, Edmund Kean. With such distinguished precedents for my guide, I might well hesitate in reverting, on the present occasion, to the original text, even if their judgment had not been sanctioned by the voice of experience, and were it not also a fact that the tragedy of "King Richard the Third," as adapted by Cibber, is most intimately associated with the traditionary admiration of the public for those renowned and departed actors. There may be a question as to the propriety of tampering at all with the writings of our bard: but there can be none that as an *acting* play, Colley Cibber's version of "King Richard the Third," evinces great dramatic judgment, and a consummate acquaintance with scenic effect.—KEAN, CHARLES, 1854, *Life and Theatrical Times, ed. Cole, vol.* II, *p.* 101.

"The Careless Husband" doubtless contains things which may seem out of harmony with this intention, and the principal situation would justly be resented by a modern audience. But the purpose of this play is genuinely moral—viz. to exhibit the triumph of pure long-suffering affection, when its object is a man not spoilt at heart. There is true pathos in the character of Lady Easy, and one may forgive her husband as one forgives Fielding's heroes, or Steele in actual life. It cannot be justly said that such a picture is an apology for vice, though doubtless it fails to treat vice from the loftiest of standpoints. The execution is upon the whole admirable; and the quarrels of Lady Betty Modish and Lord Morelove, with Lord Foppington and Lady Graveairs intervening, are in the best style of later English comedy. Lady Betty in particular is a most delightful coquette—with a heart; and the Lord Foppington of this play, who is not a mere *replica* of Vanbrugh's development of Cibber's Sir Novelty, is one of the best easy-going fools ever invented.—WARD, ADOLPHUS WILLIAM, 1875-99, *A History of English Dramatic Literature, vol.* III, *p.* 486.

Those, however, who, after listening to the incomparable language of Shakespeare, and witnessing the superiority of this magnificent play, can ever again tolerate the rubbish which has usurped its place for a century and a half, can have little pretensions to taste.—BAKER, H. BARTON, 1877, *Colley Cibber Versus Shakespeare, The Gentleman's Magazine, vol.* 240, *p.* 351.

Cibber's alteration of "Richard III." has brought down on him almost as much contumely as did the "Dunciad;" and yet his interpolations are excellent mock turtle—so excellent that Charles Reade says that the most admired passages in what literary humbugs who pretend they know Shakespeare by the closet, not the stage, accept as Shakespeare's "Richard," are Cibber's. How many of us have quoted the lines, "Now, by St. Paul, the work goes bravely on!" and "Off with his head—so much for Buckingham!" in blissful unconsciousness that Shakespeare never wrote them! Here is a quotation that has pardonably misled thousands, for it has a sonorous ring of which Cibber's treble seems incapable:

Perish that thought! No, never be it said
That Fate itself could awe the soul of Richard!
Hence, babbling dreams! you threated here in vain;
Conscience avaunt! Richard's himself again!
Hark! the shrill trumpet sounds to horse! away!
My soul's in arms and eager for the fray!

—HUNTINGTON, H. A., 1878, *A Predecessor of Tennyson, Lippincott's Magazine, vol.* 21, *p.* 571.

Cibber's best service to the stage was his "Apology for his Life," the most entertaining and graphic record of the actors and actresses of a remarkable period that perhaps exists in any language. Cibber was a good actor, something of a fine gentleman, so far as fine clothes and foppish manners go to the "make up" of that character. He was also one of the "wits" of his time, and having the laws of stagecraft at his finger ends, and understanding the requirements of audiences, he was enabled to compound a successful comedy, "She wou'd and she wou'd not," where the brisk give-and-take of the dialogue is borrowed from the dramatists of Charles II.'s age, and the bustling plot taken from a Spanish original. His comedies are the smart plays of a clever man whom circumstances, not natural genius, made a playwright. They do not quite possess the ring of true comedy.—CRAWFURD, OSWALD, 1883, *ed., English Comic Dramatists, p.* 110.

Cibber's plays are lighter than thistledown, and mark the rupture between dramatic writing and literature. But they are praiseworthy for their comparative innocence, and for the absence of such cynicism as Collier denounced.—GOSSE, EDMUND, 1888, *A History of Eighteenth Century Literature, p.* 70.

It was only as Poet Laureate, for he could not write poetry, that Cibber displayed his inferiority. . . . Of poetry there is no trace in the five volumes of his dramatic works; there are few touches of nature, and little genuine wit, but these defects are to some extent supplied by sparkling dialogue and lively badinage. Cibber is often sentimental, and when he is sentimental he is odious. His attempts to express strong emotion and honourable feeling excite laughter instead of sympathy, and on this account it is difficult to accept without some deduction Mr. Ward's favourable judgment of "The Careless Husband," which, if it be one of the cleverest of Cibber's dramas, is also one of the most conspicuous for this defect. Here, as elsewhere, Cibber should have left sentiment alone.—DENNIS, JOHN, 1894, *The Age of Pope, pp.* 196, 197.

Most are fairly lively, but hardly any is really literature.—SAINTSBURY, GEORGE,

1898, *A Short History of English Literature, p.* 496.

APOLOGY
1740

And Cibber himself is the honestest man I know, who has writ a book of his confessions, not so much to his credit as St. Augustine's, but full as true and as open. Never had impudence and vanity so faithful a professor. I honour him next to my Lord.—POPE, ALEXANDER, 1742-3, *Letter to Lord Orrery; Pope's Works, eds. Elwin and Courthope, vol.* VIII, *p.* 509.

He was not, indeed, a very wise or lofty character—nor did he affect great virtue or wisdom—but openly derided gravity, bade defiance to the serious pursuits of life, and honestly preferred his own lightness of heart and of head, to knowledge the most extensive or thought the most profound. He was vain even of his vanity. At the very commencement of his work, he avows his determination not to repress it, because it is part of himself, and therefore will only increase the resemblance of the picture. Rousseau did not more clearly lay open to the world the depths and inmost recesses of his soul, than Cibber his little foibles and minikin weaknesses. The philosopher dwelt not more intensely on the lone enthusiasm of his spirit, on the alleviations of his throbbing soul, on the long draughts of rapture which he eagerly drank in from the loveliness of the universe, than the player of his early aspirings for scenic applause, and all the petty triumphs and mortifications of his passion for the favour of the town.—TALFOURD, THOMAS NOON, 1820-42, *Cibber's Apology for His Life, Critical and Miscellaneous Writings, p.* 72.

His well-known account of his own life; or his "Apology for his Life," as he modestly or affectedly calls it, is an amusing piece of something higher than gossip; the sketches he gives of the various celebrated actors of his time are many of them executed, not perhaps with the deepest insight, but yet with much graphic skill in so far as regards those mere superficial characteristics that meet the ordinary eye.—CRAIK, GEORGE L., 1861, *A Compendious History of English Literature and of the English Language, vol.* II, *p.* 275.

Remains to-day one of the best books ever written about the stage.—MATTHEWS, BRANDER, 1880, *"Pinafore's" Predecessor, Harper's Magazine, vol.* 60, *p.* 502.

That entrancing "Apology" with its delightful pictures of his theatrical contemporaries, is as fresh as ever. It will be read when greater poets than he have sunk into oblivion, and thus perpetuate the name of one of the most remarkable characters of a by-gone epoch.—ROBINS, EDWARD, JR., 1895, *Echoes of the Playhouse, p.* 129.

GENERAL

The most undaunted Mr. Colley Cibber; of whom let it be known, when the people of this age shall be ancestors, and to all the succession of our successors, that to this present day they continue to outdo even their own out-doings: and when the inevitable hand of sweeping Time shall have brushed off all the works of to-dav, may this testimony of a contemporary critic to their fame, be extended as far as to-morrow.—POPE, ALEXANDER, 1727, *Martinus Scriblerus, or, the Art of Sinking in Poetry, Works, eds. Elwin and Courthope, vol.* X, *p.* 405.

Augustus still survives in Maro's strain,
And Spenser's verse prolongs Eliza's reign;
Great George's act let tuneful Cibber sing;
For Nature form'd the Poet for the King.

—JOHNSON, SAMUEL, 1741, *Life by Boswell, ed. Hill, vol.* I, *p.* 173.

He seems to me full as pert and as dull as usual ["Cicero"]. There are whole pages of common-place stuff, that for stupidity might have been wrote by Dr. Waterland, or any other grave divine, did not the flirting saucy phrase give them at a distance an air of youth and gaiety.—GRAY, THOMAS, 1747, *Letter to Horace Walpole, Works, ed. Gosse, vol.* II, *p.* 169.

Cibber's merits as an author are of no mean degree; for independently of the comedy which still keeps possession of the stage, notwithstanding the great advance in refinement since the period of its production, the masterly portraitures which he has given of his theatrical contemporaries must ever establish him as a critic of first-rate pretensions. Valuable and numerous as are the delineations of society and manners of the period in which Cibber flourished, none are more spirited than those which we owe to his pen, both in the *dramatis personæ* of his comedies, and the admirable sketches of living characters with whom he associated; and possessing so many and such high claims to consideration, it seems peculiarly hard that he should appear to be indebted to the stigma attached to his name for any part of his well-earned celebrity.—DUNHAM, S. ASTLEY, 1838, *ed., Literary and Scientific Men of Great Britain and Ireland, vol.* III, *p.* 276.

Pope has made himself ridiculous, as he generally did in his petty malice, by making Theobald the hero of the Dunciad, because he had convicted Pope of gross ignorance of Shakspeare. He now made himself ridiculous a second time, by exalting to that dull eminence, Colley Cibber, one of the wittiest and most sprightly authors of the day. Cibber's letter of remonstrance to Pope was unanswerable. —ALLIBONE, S. AUSTIN, 1854–58, *A Critical Dictionary of English Literature, vol.* I, *p.* 383.

Who makes himself a conspicuous ass. —FORSYTH, WILLIAM, 1871, *The Novels and Novelists of the Eighteenth Century, p.* 246.

Although Cibber was not a good poet, he was persevering and consistent, and his integrity has never been questioned. As an actor and author he excelled in comedy; to say that he did not succeed in tragedy is no detraction from his other merits. Wanting all the higher attributes of a poet, his Laureate Odes were never collected, simply because they were not worthy of preservation.—HAMILTON, WALTER, 1879, *The Poets Laureate of England, p.* 172.

All things considered, both in this controversy [with Fielding] and the later one with Pope, Cibber did not come off worst. His few hits were personal and unscrupulous, and they were probably far more deadly in their effects than any of the ironical attacks which his adversaries, on their part, directed against his poetical ineptitude or halting "parts of speech." Despite his superlative coxcombry and egotism, he was, moreover, a man of no mean abilities. His "Careless Husband" is a far better acting play than any of Fielding's, and his "Apology," which even Johnson allowed to be "well-done," is valuable in many respects, especially for its account of the contemporary stage. In describing an actor or actress he had few equals—witness his skilful portraits of Nokes, and his admirably graphic vignette of Mrs. Verbruggen as that "finish'd Impertinent," Melantha, in Dryden's "Marriage à-la-Mode."—DOBSON, AUSTIN, 1883, *Fielding (English Men of Letters), p.* 66.

Cibber's "Odes" are among the most contemptible things in literature.—KNIGHT, JOSEPH, 1887, *Dictionary of National Biography, vol.* X, *p.* 358.

One of the most delightful autobiographies ever written, and a comedy which is in its way a masterpiece, have been powerless to counteract, nay even to modify, the impression left on the world by the portrait for which Pope made Colley Cibber sit.—COLLINS, JOHN CHURTON, 1895, *Essays and Studies, p.* 264.

Edward Moore

1712-1757.

Born at Abingdon, England, March 22, 1712: died at South Lambeth, London, March 1, 1757. An English dramatist and fabulist, third son of Thomas Moore, a dissenting clergyman. He failed in business as a linen-draper in London, and began as a writer with his "Fables for the Female Sex" in 1744. "The Foundling," a comedy, was produced at Drury Lane on Feb. 13, 1748; "Gil Blas," a comedy, in 1751; and "The Gamester," in which Garrick appeared (and which he partly wrote), at Drury Lane on Feb. 7, 1753. In 1753 he was made editor of "The World," a popular paper, which had Lord Lyttelton, Lord Bath, Lord Chesterfield, Soame Jenyns, Horace Walpole, and Edward Lovibond as contributors. His only son, Edward, was educated and pensioned by Lord Chesterfield.—SMITH, BENJAMIN E., *ed.* 1894–97, *The Century Cyclopedia of Names, p.* 704.

PERSONAL

Let us not then aggravate those natural inconveniences by neglect; we have had sufficient instances of this kind already. Sale and Moore will suffice for one age at least. But they are dead, and their sorrows are over.—GOLDSMITH, OLIVER, 1759, *Present State of Polite Learning.*

GENERAL

Mr. Moore was a poet that never had justice done him while living; there are few of the moderns have a more correct taste, or a more pleasing manner of expressing their thoughts. It was upon these Fables he chiefly founded his reputation, yet they are by no means his best production.—GOLDSMITH, OLIVER, 1767, *The Beauties of English Poetry.*

His style is easy and unaffected, and always appropriate to his subjects, which have great variety. If he had not more knowledge of the world than some of his predecessors, he could at least employ it very agreeably. He had professed that the paper had contained *novelty* of ridicule, and it must be allowed that he seldom betrays the servile copyist, when treating of those subjects which had been handled by others. . . . Moore excelled principally in assuming the serious manner for the purposes of ridicule, or of raising idle curiosity . . . However trite his subject, he enlivens it by original turns of thought. Some of the papers are mere exercises of humour, which have no direct moral in view, and for this he in one place offers an apology, or at least acknowledges that he aimed at no higher purpose than entertainment. In the last paper, the conclusion of the work is made to depend on a fictitious accident which is supposed to have happened to the author, and occasioned his death. When the papers were collected in volumes, Mr. Moore superintended the publication, and actually died while this last paper was in the press.—CHALMERS, ALEXANDER, 1808–23, *The British Essayists, vol.* 22, *The World, vol.* I, *Historical and Biographical Preface, pp.* 22, 23.

Of the papers of Moore, which form more than a fourth of the whole work, ["World,"] the characteristic is a grave and well-sustained irony, that not unfrequently displays a considerable share of original humour. The style which he has adopted, if not very correct or elegant, is, however, easy and perspicuous, and not ill suited to the general nature of his subjects.—DRAKE, NATHAN, 1810, *Essays Illustrative of the Rambler, Adventurer, and Idler, vol.* II, *p.* 263.

The "Fables" of Moore rank next to those of Gay, but are inferior to them both in choice of subject and in poetical merit.—CHAMBERS, ROBERT, 1876, *Cyclopædia of English Literature, ed. Carruthers.*

His "Fables for the Female Sex" have an excellent moral turn, but are somewhat deficient in the sprightliness which is especially demanded in that species of composition. . . . His domestic tragedy, "The Gamester," . . . though it set tradition at nought by being written in prose, was on the whole a success. The prologue and some of the most admired passages, including the greater part of the scene between Lewson and Stukely in the fourth act, were written by Garrick, who played the principal part. The piece ran with applause for eleven nights, and has since kept the stage.—RIGG, J. M., 1894, *Dictionary of National Biography, vol.* XXXVIII, *p.* 347.

The most noticeable except the "Rambler" and the "Adventurer" (a sort of imitation "Rambler," edited by Hawkesworth, the great ape of Johnson, and contributed to by Johnson himself) was the "World," which appeared between 1753 and 1756. This is noteworthy, because an attempt was made to make it a distinct "journal of society." The editor, Edward Moore, was a man of letters of some ability, who played the main part of "Adam Fitz Adam"—the *eidolon* who, according to the etiquette of the scheme, was supposed to produce the paper—very fairly. Its interest for us consists in the fact that among the contributors were some of the very chief of those men of fashion, Chesterfield, Horace Walpole, Soame Jenyns, Hanbury Williams, who at the time affected literature.—SAINTSBURY, GEORGE, 1898, *A Short History of English Literature, p.* 620.

David Hartley

1705–1757

David Hartley, 1705–1757. Born, at Luddenden, Halifax, June (?) 1705; baptized, 21 June. At Bradford Grammar School. To Jesus College, Cambridge, as "ordinary sizar," 21 April 1722; B. A., 14 Jan. 1726; Fellow, 13 Nov. 1727 to 8 June 1730; M. A., 17 Jan. 1729. Married, June 1730. Married second time, Nov. 1735;

settled in London. Removed to Bath, May 1742. Died there, 28 Aug. 1757. *Works:* "Some Reasons why the Practice of Inoculation ought to be introduced into the town of Bury," 1733; "Ten Cases of Persons who have taken Mrs. Stephens's Medicines," 1738; "A View of the present Evidence for and against Mrs. Stephens's Medicines," 1739; "De Lithotriptico a Joanna Stephens nuper invento," 1741; "Observations on Man," 1749; "Ad . . . R. Mead, Epistola," 1751. *Posthumous:* "Prayers, and Religious Meditations," 1809. *Life* : by his son, in 1791 edn. of "Observations on Man."—SHARP, R. FARQUHARSON, 1897. *A Dictionary of English Authors, p.* 126.

PERSONAL

His person was of the middle size and well proportioned. His complexion fair, his features regular and handsome. His countenance open, ingenuous, and animated. He was peculiarly neat in his person and attire. He was an early riser, and punctual in the employments of the day; methodical in the order and disposition of his library, papers, and writings, as the companions of his thought.—HARTLEY, DAVID, 1791, *ed., Observations on Man, Life.*

I now devoted myself to poetry and to the study of ethics and psychology; and so profound was my admiration at this time of Hartley's "Essay on Man," that I gave his name to my first born.—COLERIDGE, SAMUEL TAYLOR, 1817, *Biographia Literaria, ch.* x.

Hartley died on the 25th of August, 1757, aged fifty-two, and left a name so distinguished for piety and goodness, that it in a great measure shielded his doctrines from the reprobation they have often incurred when promulgated by others.—LEWES, GEORGE HENRY, 1845–46, *Biographical History of Philosophy, p.* 604.

Hartley's was a quiet, useful, unromantic life,—unromantic in all respects, except in that steady devotion to truth and fact which tinges the most uneventful life with a hue of romance,—too often of pathos. Eminently typical of the century in which he lived,—comfortable, and ready to comfort others,—disposed to ponder and wait, not very prone to action, unambitious,—he was always in a mood to make allowances for the frailty of others, and to take things as they came, while he was utterly destitute of the "passion for reforming the world," which possessed James Mill. On the other hand, if his life was not lit by other aims as that of his great successor, he had all the compensating advantages incidental to a lack of enthusiasm. While he was not to the same extent as Mill the cause of good to unseen masses of men, he made far more friends and intimates out of those whom he did know. The bitterness and violence, which in Mill's case were engendered by consuming earnestness, were unknown to him. No zeal could eat him up. His philosophical system was not converted by him into a dogma or discipline; by thus having no practical reference, while it won him no partisans, it made him no enemies. Though accurate and precise in his reasoning, and methodical in his daily habits, Hartley was far removed alike from pedantry and fussiness. He was polished and gay in society, and eloquent in conversation, without becoming importunate or a bore; and he was entirely without the vices of pride, selfishness, sensuality, or disingenuousness.—BOWER, GEORGE SPENCER, 1881, *Hartley and James Mill* (*English Philosophers*), *p.* 6.

GENERAL

Hartley has investigated the principal of Association more deeply, explained it more accurately, and applied it more usefully, than even his great and venerable predecessor, Mr. Locke.—PARR, SAMUEL, 1774, *Sermon on Education.*

This tract is printed from the second volume of Dr. Hartley's "Observations on Man;" it is written with singular closeness of thought, and to be well understood must be read with great attention. —WATSON, RICHARD, 1785, *Collection of Theological Tracts Selected from Various Authors.*

He thus united all the talents of his own mind for natural and moral science, conformably to that universal system of final morality, which he inculcates, by which each effort of sensation or science in the various gradations of life must be esteemed defective, until it shall have attained to its corresponding moral consummation. It arose from the union above mentioned, of talents in the moral science with natural philosophy, and particularly from the professional knowledge of the human frame, that Dr. Hartley was enabled to bring into one view the various arguments for his extensive system, from the first rudiments of sensation through the maze of complex affections and passions in the path of life, to the final, moral end of man.—HARTLEY, DAVID, 1791, *ed., Observations on Man, Life.*

It was a reference to "Dr. Hartley's Observations on Man," in the course of our Lectures, that first brought me acquainted with that performance, which immediately engaged my closest attention, and produced the greatest, and in my opinion the most favourable effect on my general turn of thinking through life. It established me in the belief of the doctrine of Necessity, which I first learned from Collins; it greatly improved that disposition to piety which I brought to the academy, and freed it from the rigour with which it had been tinctured. Indeed, I do not know whether the consideration of Dr. Hartley's theory contributes more to enlighten the mind, or improve the heart; it affected both in so supereminent a degree. — PRIESTLEY, JOSEPH, 1795, *Autobiography, ed. Rutt, p.* 24.

The intentions of both [Bonnet and Hartley] are allowed, by those who best knew them, to have been eminently pure and worthy; but it cannot be said of either, that his metaphysical writings have contributed much to the instruction or to the improvement of the public. On the contrary, they have been instrumental in spreading a set of speculative tenets very nearly allied to that sentimental and fantastical modification of Spinozism which for many years past has prevailed so much and produced such mischievous effects in some parts of Germany.—STEWART, DUGALD, 1815–21, *First Preliminary Dissertation, Encyclopædia Britannica.*

It is fashionable to smile at Hartley's vibrations and vibratiuncles; and his work has been re-edited by Priestly, with the omission of the material hypothesis. But Hartley was too great a man, too coherent a thinker, for this to have been done, either consistently or to any wise purpose. For all other parts of his system, as far as they are peculiar to that system, once removed from their mechanical basis, not only lose their main support, but the very motive which led to their adoption.—COLERIDGE, SAMUEL TAYLOR, 1817, *Biographia Literaria, ch.* vi.

It is the first attempt to join the study of intellectual man to that of physical man.—COUSIN, VICTOR, 1828–29, *Course of the History of Modern Philosophy, tr. Wight.*

The capital fault of Hartley is that of a rash generalization, which may prove imperfect, and which is at least premature. All attempts to explain instinct by this principle have hitherto been unavailing: many of the most important processes of reasoning have not hitherto been accounted for by it.—MACKINTOSH, SIR JAMES, 1830, *Second Preliminary Dissertation, Encyclopædia Britannica.*

The writer who has built most upon Hobbes, and may be reckoned, in a certain sense, his commentator, if he who fully explains and develops a system may deserve that name, was Hartley. . . . Hartley also resembles Hobbes in the extreme to which he has pushed the nominalist theory, in the proneness to materialize all intellectual processes, and either to force all things mysterious to our faculties into something imaginable, or to reject them as unmeaning, in the want, much connected with this, of a steady perception of the difference between the Ego and its objects, in an excessive love of simplifying and generalizing, and in a readiness to adopt explanations neither conformable to reason nor experience, when they fall in with some single principle, the key that was to unlock every ward of the human soul.—HALLAM, HENRY, 1837–39, *Introduction to the Literature of Europe, pt.* iii, *ch.* iii, *par.* 153.

While acknowledging the defect of Hartley's system, let us not forget its excellence. If the doctrine of Association was not first applied by him, it was by him first made a physiologico-psychological basis. He not only applied it to the explanation of mental phenomena; he applied it, and with great ingenuity, to those physiological phenomena which still interest and perplex philosophers, namely the voluntary and involuntary actions. His twenty-first proposition, and the elucidations which follow, deserve to be read, even in the present day.—LEWES, GEORGE

HENRY, 1845–46, *Biographical History of Philosophy, p.* 608.

That there is great value to be attached to much which Hartley has drawn from the law of association, and that he has afforded an explanation of many phenomena, before very imperfectly understood, cannot be denied. The very ardour, however, with which he threw himself into his system, and the very closeness with which he analysed the facts in the case, necessarily imparted a one-sidedness to his philosophy, and led to the neglect of some other facts equally important.—MORELL, J. D., 1846–47, *An Historical and Critical View of Speculative Philosophy of Europe in the Nineteenth Century.*

A majority, probably, of those who have followed his track of thought have considered his Theopathy and his Christianity were rather extraneous grafts upon the rest of his teaching. It has puzzled them to discover what these had to do with the spinal marrow or the white medullary substance of the brain. But there have been others, and perhaps more than we know of, who have taken, along with the associations and the vibrations, Hartley's whole conception of a moral sense which recognizes beauty and revolts at deformity, and his belief of a divine revelation which touches chords that respond to it in the nature of man. Some have for a time been enabled through him to attain perceptions of the harmony of the world which have afterwards blended with principles that seem most to clash with his. And perhaps his illustrations of the facts of association will be welcomed most cordially by those who most demand a ground for association which he has not discovered to them. Perhaps the moralist and metaphysician are destined to receive the greatest aid from the anatomist and physiologist in tracing the vibratiuncles in the human body to those vibrations which they find first within, and which are produced, as their hearts tell them, by an invisible Musician.—MAURICE, FREDERICK DENISON, 1862, *Moral and Metaphysical Philosophy, vol.* II, *p.* 478.

Hartley clearly distinguished the *synchronous* and *successive* cases or forms of association. He also noticed that the strength of associations is twofold, depending on the vividness of the feelings or ideas associated, and the frequency with which any association is repeated. He shows that as ideas become complex, so they become decomplex by association. Indeed, it would be difficult to find any distinction or principle of the more recent forms of the associational psychology which was not anticipated by Hartley. The more recent discoveries in physiology and in the comparative sciences of nature are more largely used by the later writers, as Bain and H. Spencer, but always in the interest of the principles common to themselves and Hartley.—PORTER, NOAH, 1874, *Philosophy in Great Britain and America, Ueberweg's History of Philosophy, vol.* II, *p.* 388.

The difference between Hartley and the older metaphysicians may be described by saying that, with them the type of all reasoning is to be found in pure mathematics, whilst with him it is to be found applied mathematics. He seeks to do for human nature what Newton did for the solar system. Association is for man what gravitation is for the planets; and as Newton imagined that God's will must be the efficient cause of gravitation, so Hartley imagined the same will to be the cause of those movements in the human organism which are the immediate cause of all mental phenomena. He is about the last writer who affects the mathematical form common to the metaphysicians of the previous generation, but in his mind the analogy is not with the pure mathematics which, dealing with ideas of space and time, seem to have an *a priori* validity, but with those laws of motion which he would have asserted (as indeed he would have asserted of all axiomatic truths) to be derived from experience.—STEPHEN, LESLIE, 1876, *History of English Thought in the Eighteenth Century, vol.* II, *p.* 66.

The styles of the two philosophers were as dissimilar as possible. Hartley was gifted with the "copia fandi," while Mill's style and mode of reasoning were severely simple. The two, indeed, were alike in their formal and scholastic methods, and in their love of packing their doctrines into a syllogism or pocket formula. But Hartley was not prevented by these precise and orderly habits from giving free vent to those sentiments, which Mill and his school would have scorned as sentimentalities, nor from many a gay excursus into a variety of intellectual domains, from which the austerer bent of the latter restrained him. Hartley's rambling and gossiping style, his queer mathematical mysticism (which Mr. Leslie Stephen notices), his medical fancies and digressions, his theories of biblical interpretation, his minute observations of the customs of young children, and the inferior animals, his interest in philosophical languages and dictionaries, his liking for theology and discussion of the theopathetic faculties,—all these were foreign to the mental habits and constitution of James Mill. The preciseness of method apparently reflected in Hartley's Propositions, Corollaries, and Scholia did not extend beneath the surface, whereas that observable in Mill's works was radical, and answered to a certain analytical twist in his mind. Indeed the mathematical forms of the former, when applied to the abstrusest and most ethereal subjects, serve rather, by quaintness of contrast, to intensify our recognition of his love of mysticism than to suggest his predilection for formalism.—BOWER, GEORGE SPENCER, 1881, *Hartley and James Mill (English Philosophers), p.* 215.

His [Coleridge's] greatest favourite among the modern metaphysicians was Hartley, "he of mortal tribe wisest," as he calls him in the "Religious Musings." —BRANDL, ALOIS, 1886–87, *Samuel Taylor Coleridge and the English Romantic School, tr. Eastlake, p.* 53.

Hartley is in the highest sense of the phrase a man of one book, which he began to write before he was twenty-five, published when he was forty-four, and continued to revise until his death. This is his "Observations on Man, His Fame, Duty, and Expectations" (1749). He defined his own contribution to moral philosophy in these words: "I take it to be proved from the doctrine of association, that there is, and must be, such a thing as pure disinterested benevolence; also a just account of the origin and nature of it." A side doctrine of his which was much discussed is the theory of vibrations, and of man as a cluster of "vibratiuncles." —GOSSE, EDMUND, 1888, *A History of Eighteenth Century Literature, p.* 295.

Jonathan Edwards

1703–1757

Edwards was born October 5th, 1703, in East Windsor, Connecticut. He was the son of Rev. Timothy and Esther Stoddard Edwards; was graduated at Yale College in 1720; studied theology at New Haven; from August 1722 to March 1723 preached in New York; from 1724 to 1726 was a tutor at Yale; on the 15th of February, 1727, was ordained at Northampton, Massachusetts; in 1750 was dismissed from the church there, and in 1751 removed to Stockbridge, Massachusetts. He was called to Princeton in 1757, and died there March 22d, 1758.—SMYTH, EGBERT C., 1897, *Jonathan Edwards, Library of the World's Best Literature, ed. Warner, vol.* IX, *p,* 5178.

Sermon on Man's Dependence, 1731; Sermon on Spiritual Light, 1734; first Revival at Northampton, 1735; "Narrative of Surprising Conversions," 1736; publishes sermons on Justification, etc., 1738; The Great Awakening, 1740; Sermon at Enfield, 1741; publishes "Distinguishing Marks," etc., 1741; "Thoughts on the Revival," 1742; "Religious Affections," 1746; troubles at Northampton, 1749; publication of "Qualifications for Full Communion," 1749; "Reply to Williams," 1752; "The Freedom of the Will," 1754; treatises written on "Virtue and End of Creation," 1755; publication of treatise on "Original Sin," 1758.—MOULTON, CHARLES WELLS, 1901.

PERSONAL

On the Sabbath felt wonderful satisfaction in being at the house of Mr. Edwards. He is a son himself and hath also a daughter of Abraham for his wife. A sweeter couple I have not seen. Their children were dressed, not in silks and satins, but plain, as becomes the children of those who in all things ought to be examples of Christian simplicity. She is a woman adorned with a meek and quiet spirit, and talked so feelingly and so solidly of the things of God, and seemed to be such an helpmeet to her husband, that she caused me to renew those prayers which for some months I have put up to God, that He would send me a daughter of Abraham to be my wife. I find upon

DAVID HARTLEY

Engraving by J. Heath.
Painting by Shackelwell.

JONATHAN EDWARDS

Engraving by A. B. Walter.

many accounts it is my duty to marry. Lord, I desire to have no choice of my own. Thou knowest my circumstances.—WHITEFIELD, GEORGE, 1740, *Diary, The Great Awakening.*

I have a constitution in many respects peculiarly unhappy, attended with flaccid solids, vapid, sizy, and scarce fluids, and a low tide of spirits; often occasioning a kind of childish weakness and contemptibleness of speech, presence, and demeanor, with a disagreeable dulness and stiffness, much unfitting me for conversation, but more especially for the government of a college. This makes me shrink at the thoughts of taking upon me, in the decline of life, such a new and great business, attended with such a multiplicity of cares, and requiring such a degree of activity, alertness, and spirit of government; especially as succeeding one so remarkably well qualified in these respects, giving occasion to every one to remark the wide difference. I am also deficient in some parts of learning, particularly in algebra, and the higher parts of mathematics, and in the Greek classics; my Greek learning having been chiefly in the New Testament. . . . My method of study, from my first beginning the work of the ministry, has been very much by writing; applying myself, in this way, to improve every important hint; pursuing the clue to my utmost, when any thing in reading, meditation, or conversation, has been suggested to my mind, that seemed to promise light in any weighty point; thus penning what appeared to me my best thoughts, on innumerable subjects, for my own benefit. The longer I prosecuted my studies in this method, the more habitual it became, and the more pleasant and profitable I found it. The farther I travelled in this way, the more and wider the field opened, which has occasioned my laying out many things in my mind, to do in this manner, if God should spare my life, which my heart hath been much upon; particularly many things against most of the prevailing errors of the present day, which I cannot with any patience see maintained (to the utter subverting of the Gospel of Christ) with so high a hand, and so long continued a triumph, with so little control, when it appears so evident to me that there is truly no foundation for any of this glorying and insult.—EDWARDS, JONATHAN, 1757, *Letter to the Trustees of the College of New Jersey, Oct.* 19.

On Wednesday, the 22d of last month, died of inoculation at Nassau Hall, an eminent servant of God, the reverend and pious Mr. Jonathan Edwards, president of the College of New Jersey; a gentleman of distinguished abilities and of a heavenly temper of mind; a most rational generous, catholic and exemplary Christian, admired by all who knew him for his uncommon candour and disinterested benevolence; a pattern of temperance, meekness, candour and charity; always steady, solemn and serene; a very judicious and instructive preacher, and most excellent divine. And as he lived cheerfully resigned to the will of Heaven, so he died, or rather, as the Scriptures emphatically express it with regard to good men, he fell asleep in Jesus, without the least appearance of pain.—BOSTON GAZETTE, 1758, *April* 10.

The loss sustained by his death, not only by the College of New Jersey, but by the church in general, is irreparable. I do not think our age has produced a divine of equal genius or judgment.—ERSKINE, JOHN, 1758, *Letter to Rev. Mr. McCulloch, Erskine's Life, ed. Wellwood, p.* 224.

M. S.
Reverendi admodum Viri,
Jonathan Edwards, A. M.,
Collegii Novæ Cæsareæ Præsidis.
Natus apud Windsor, Connecticutensium,
V. Octobris,
A. D. MDCCIII. S. V.
Patre reverendo Timotheo Edwards oriundus;
Collegio Yalensi educatis;
Apud Northampton sacris initiatus, XV.
Februarii,
MDCCCXXVI—VII.
Illinc dimissus XXII.
Junii, M. D. C. C. L.
Et Munus Barbaros instituendi accepit.
Præses Aulæ Nassovicæ creatus XVI.
Februarii,
MDCCLVIII.
Defunctus in hoc Vico XXII, Martii
sequentis, S. N.
Ætatis LV. heu nimis brevis!
Hic jacet mortalis pars.
Qualis Persona, quæris, Viator?
Vir corpore procero, sed gracili,
Studiis intentissimis, abstinentiâ, et sedulitate Attenuato.
Ingenii acumine, Judicio acri, et Prudentiâ
Secundus nemini Mortalium.
Artium liberalium et Scientiarum peritiâ

insignis,
Criticorum sacrorum optimus, Theologus eximius,
Ut vix alter æqualis; Disputator candidus;
Fidei Christianæ Propugnator validus et invictus;
Concionator gravis, serius, discriminans,
Et. Deo ferente, successu
Felicissimus.
Pietate præclarus, Moribus suis severus,
Ast aliis æquus et benignus.
Vixit dilectus, veneratus—
Sed, ah! lugendus
Moriebatur.
Quantos gemitus discedens ciebat!
Heu Sapientia tanta! heu Doctrin a et Religio!
Amissum plorat Collegium, plorat et Ecclesia;
At, eo recepto, gaudet
Coelum.
Abi, Viator, et pia sequere vestigia.

—INSCRIPTION ON MONUMENT, 1758, *Princeton Cemetery.*

He studied the Bible more than all other books, and more than most other divines do. He took his religious principles from the Bible, and not from any human system of body or of divinity. Though his principles were Calvinistic, yet he called no man father. He thought and judged for himself, and was truly very much of an original.—HOPKINS, SAMUEL, 1759, *Life of Edwards, p.* 47.

In his youth he appeared healthy, and with a good degree of vivacity, but was never robust. In middle life, he appeared very much emaciated, by severe study, and intense mental application. In his person he was tall of stature—about six feet one inch—and of a slender form. He had a high broad, bold forehead, and an eye unusually piercing and luminous; and on his whole countenance, the features of his mind—perspicacity, sincerity, and benevolence—were so strongly impressed, that no one could behold it, without at once discovering the clearest indications of great intellectual and moral elevation. —DWIGHT, SERENO EDWARDS, 1829, *Life of Jonathan Edwards.*

The person of Mr. Edwards, . . . was tall and slender. He was a little more than six feet in stature. His countenance was strongly marked with intelligence and benignity; and his manners were peculiarly expressive of modesty, gentleness, and Christian dignity. His voice, in public speaking, was rather feeble, and he had little or no gesture. Yet such were the gravity of his manner, the weight and solemnity of his thoughts, and the evident earnestness of his delivery, that few preachers were listened to with more fixed attention, or left a more deep and permanent impression. Mr. Edwards was the father of *eleven* children; *three sons* and *eight daughters.* One of these, his second daughter, died eleven years before him, in the 17th year of her age. All the rest survived him, and some of them a number of years. One only of his sons became a minister of the Gospel. This was his *second* son, *Jonathan*, who greatly resembled his venerable father in metaphysical acuteness, in ardent piety, and in the purest exemplariness of Christian deportment.—MILLER, SAMUEL, 1837, *Life of Jonathan Edwards, Sparks's Library of American Biography, vol.* VIII, *p.* 168.

He reminded you of Milton's line, "The ground burns frore, and cold performs the effect of Fire." A signal instance of this is recorded. A large congregation, including many ministers, were assembled to hear a popular preacher, who did not fulfil his appointment. Edwards was selected to fill this place, principally because, being in the habit of reading his discourses, he happened to have a sermon ready in his pocket. He ascended the pulpit accordingly, amid almost audible marks of disappointment from the audience, whom, however, respect for the abilities and character of the preacher prevented from leaving the church. He chose for his text, "Their foot shall slide in due time," and began to read in his usual quiet way. At first he had barely their attention; by and by he succeeded in riveting every one of them to his lips; a few sentences more, and they began to rise by twos and threes; a little farther, and tears were flowing; at the close of another, particularly deep groans were heard, and one or two went off in fits; and ere he reached the climax of his terrible appeals, the whole audience had risen up in one tumult of grief and consternation. And, amid all this, there stood the calm, imperturbable man, reading on as softly and gently as if he were in his own study. And, in reading the sermon, we do not wonder at the impression it produced upon an audience constituted as that audience must have been. It is a succession of swift thunder-claps, each

drowning and deafening the one which preceded it. We read it once to a distinguished *savant*, who, while disapproving of its spirit, was compelled, literally, to shiver under the "fury of its power."
—GILFILLAN, GEORGE, 1845, *Sketches of Modern Literature and Eminent Literary Men.*

He was commanding as a pulpit teacher, not for grace of person; he was slender and shy; not for elocution; his voice was thin and weak; not for any trick of style; no man more disdained and trampled on it:—but from his immense preparation, long forethought, sedulous writing of every word, touching earnestness and holy life. ·He was not a man of company; he seldom visited his hearers. Yet there was no man whose mental power was greater. Common consent set him at the head of his profession. Even in a time of rapture and fiery excitement he lost no influence.—ALEXANDER, JAMES. W., 1846? *Centennial Discourse at the College of New Jersey.*

As a preacher Edwards has been rarely if ever excelled since the days of the apostles. His manner was not oratorical, and his voice was feeble; but this was of little account, with so much directness and richness of thought, and such overwhelming power of argument, pressed home upon the conscience of the heart. In vain did any one attempt to escape from falling a prey under his mighty appeal. It was in the *application* of his subject that he specially excelled. The part of the sermon before this was only preparatory. Here was the stretching out of the arms of the discourse, to borrow a figure, upon the hearts and lives of his audience.—FISH, HENRY C., 1856, *History and Repository of Pulpit Eloquence, vol.* II, *p.* 395.

Of the religion called "evangelical," he was perhaps, the most perfect exemplification that ever existed. The child was father of the man. We see him, as a boy of ten, building a booth in a swamp near his father's house, to which he and two of his companions used to go regularly to pray. In his eleventh year, we read of his demonstrating, with a kind of solemn jocularity, the absurdity of an opinion which had been advanced by a boy of his own age, that the soul was material, and remained in the grave with the body till the resurrection. At twelve, we find him beginning a letter to one of his sisters thus: "Through the wonderful goodness and mercy of God, there has been in this place a very remarkable outpouring of the Spirit of God." He proceeds to inform his sister that he "has *reason to think* it is in some measure diminished, but he hopes not much, and that above thirty persons came commonly a Mondays to converse with father about their souls." At the same time, he exhibited in things not religious, an intelligence truly remarkable. He wrote, in his twelfth year, an elaborate description of "the wondrous way of the working of the forest spider," which shows that he possessed a rare talent for the observation of nature. One of the greatest of natural philosophers was lost to the world when Jonathan Edwards became a theologian. . . . Nobler than any of his works was the life of this good man.—PARTON, JAMES, 1858, *The Life and Times of Aaron Burr, pp.* 27, 28.

Was the man who could utter such blasphemous sentiments—for so they undoubtedly appear to us—a being of ordinary flesh and blood? One would rather have supposed his solids to be of bronze, and his fluids of vitriol, than have attributed to them the character which he describes. That he should have been a gentle, meditative creature, around whose knees had clung eleven "young vipers" of his own begetting, is certainly an astonishing reflection. And yet, to do Edwards justice, we must remember two things. In the first place, the responsibility for such ghastly beliefs cannot be repudiated by anyone who believes in the torments of hell.—STEPHEN, LESLIE, 1874–79, *Hours in a Library, vol.* I, *p.* 326.

Edwards was pre-eminently a student. Tall in person, and having even a womanly look, he was of delicate constitution. He was, however, so temperate and methodical in his living that he was usually in good health, and able to give more time to study than most men. Twelve or thirteen hours of every day were commonly allotted to this. So devoted was he to his work as a student that he was most unwilling to allow anything to disturb it. Though he was careful to eat regularly and at certain fixed hours, yet he would postpone his meals for a time if he was so engaged in study that the interruption of eating would interfere with the success of his thinking. He was so miserly also in his craving for time that he would leave the table before the rest of the family and retire to his room, they waiting for him to return again when they had finished their meal, and dismiss them from the table with the customary grace.—EGGLESTON, N. H., 1874, *A New England Village, Harper's Magazine, vol.* 43, *p.* 823.

Such, in intellectual attainments and in spiritual quality, was Jonathan Edwards, when, at the age of twenty-four, he entered upon his work as minister of a parish on the frontiers of civilization. The remainder of his life was what he expected it to be,—an experience of labor and of sorrow; but always borne by him with meek and cheerful submission. He had ill health, domestic griefs, public misrepresentation, alienation of friends, persecution, even poverty. In 1751, he was so poor that his daughters had to earn money for household expenses by making fans, laces, and embroidery; and he himself, for lack of paper, had to do his writing, mostly on the margins of pamphlets, on the covers of letters, and on the remnants that his daughters could spare him from the silk-paper used by them in the manufacture of fans. Nevertheless, through it all, he bated not a jot of heart or hope, but still bore up and steered right onward. His chief business was in his study; and there he usually worked thirteen hours a day. Even out of the study, his mind was not at rest; when, for exercise, he rode on horseback, or walked in the woods, he kept on at his tasks of thought; in order that he might not forget anything that he had wrought out in these excursions, he was accustomed to pin a bit of paper upon his coat, for every idea that was to be jotted down on his return; and it was noticed that, sometimes, he would come home with his coat covered over with these fluttering memorials of his intellectual activity.—TYLER, MOSES COIT, 1878, *A History of American Literature*, 1676–1765, *vol.* II, *p.* 187.

His countenance is not such as we should expect a polemical theologian to wear, but is more like that of St. John, according thus with the deep mystical vein of which we have spoken. He is the *doctor angelicus* among our theologians, and, had he lived in the thirteenth century instead of the eighteenth, he would have been decorated by admiring pupils with such a title. If it be true that, in the last century, Berkeley, Hume, and Kant, are the three great names in philosophy, there might have been added to the brief catalogue, had he chosen to devote himself exclusively to metaphysics, the name of Jonathan Edwards.—FISHER, GEORGE PARK, 1879, *The Philosophy of Jonathan Edwards, North American Review, vol.* 128, *p.* 303.

Remarkable as were the intellectual developments of Edwards in his early life there was nothing sickly or premature about them. The greatness of his youth was only proportionate to the greatness of his manhood. His paper on the "Habits of Spiders," written before he was thirteen years old, was a very remarkable production for a boy, but no more remarkable than those which were issuing from his pen at the age of fifty. He came of a sturdy and long-lived race, and except for that fatal experiment of inoculation for the small-pox, in March, 1758, he would naturally have continued till a ripe old age. His father died at 89, his mother at 99. His grandfather Stoddard died at 85, and his grandmother Stoddard at 92. Of his sisters, Esther lived to be 72; Mary, 75; Martha, 77; Eunice, 83; Ann, 91. It was during the years just preceding his death that his great works, those that secured him his world-wide fame, had been produced, and it is certainly natural to believe, if life and health had been continued, that other works, in the same general ranges of thought but with still higher ranges of power, would have been forthcoming.—TARBOX, I. N., 1884, *Jonathan Edwards as a Man, New Englander, vol.* 43, *p.* 630.

If we study Jonathan Edwards with proper sympathy, we must pronounce his life a great life. Though his character was colored by Puritan austerity, and his religious experience involved what many believe to have been morbid emotions, there is no questioning the fact of his masterful intellect and his stainless integrity. . . . Among the many able preachers of America, he stands as one of the greatest. He dwelt habitually on the weightiest doctrines of the Christian faith; and in his treatment of them there is a Miltonic grasp of thought and vigor of language. He was not eloquent in manner or expression; his voice was weak, and he kept his eyes closely fixed on his manuscript.—PAINTER, F. V. N., 1897, *Introduction to American Literature, pp.* 51, 54.

While Edwards' official connection with Princeton was short and came to an almost tragic close, it is yet true that in an important sense Princeton became the residuary legatee of his name and fame. His spirit has continued to be one of the moulding forces of the college's life. The things in which he believed have been, in the main, the things in which Princeton has believed, and the type of religious life and experience which he prized most highly is the type that has always dominated the religious life and history of Princeton. The library of Edwards graces the University's shelves; his portrait and statue dignify and beautify her walls, and among the presidents of the past he holds a place as one of the trinity of greatest names, Edwards, Witherspoon, McCosh.—ORMOND, ALEXANDER T., 1901, *Jonathan Edwards, A Retrospect, ed. Gardiner, p.* 81.

A unique opportunity was afforded for an attempt at appreciation from this broader point of view by the unveiling of a Memorial to Edwards in the First Church in Northampton on Friday, 22d of June, 1900, just a hundred and fifty years after his dismissal. This is not the only memorial of Edwards in Northampton. In spite of its ancient quarrel, the town has never been wanting in regard for its greatest inhabitant. The noble elm which tradition says he planted is still reverently preserved on the site of his dwelling and protected, as far as possible, from the ravages of time. Near the grave of his friend David Brainerd in the old burying-ground a citizen of the town years ago erected a stone inscribed to the memory of "The American Theologian," and of his Scotch admirer, Dr. Chalmers. Not far off, by one of the gateways, a granite monument contains the names of Jonathan Edwards, his wife, and all their children side by side with one of a similar character recording the names of his son-in-law, Timothy Dwight, his wife, and their children. Worthiest of all tributes to his memory, erected not merely to perpetuate his name, but to continue the supreme work of his life, the promotion in varied forms of Christian service of the glory of God in the salvation of men, is the Edwards Church, founded in 1833, a daughter of the First Church, and one of the most flourishing of the religious societies of the town. The Memorial now placed in the First Church is a bronze tablet, set in a massive frame of green-stained oak, and containing a two-thirds length relief figure of Edwards, life size or larger, represented as if preaching. On the panel beneath the figure is the simple inscription:—

In Memory of
Jonathan Edwards
Minister of Northampton
From February 15 1727 to June 22 1750
The Law of Truth was in his Mouth and
Unrighteousness was not Found in His Lips
He walked with me in peace and
uprightness
And Did Turn Many away from Iniquity
Mal. 2:6.

The tablet was erected under authorization of the parish, but the cost was defrayed by public subscription. The Memorial, therefore, represents neither the contrition nor the pride of the local church, but rather a widely spread, and to a certain extent newly awakened regard for the genius and character of its subject and a sympathetic interest in what appealed to many as a simple act of historic justice.—GARDINER, H. NORMAN, 1901, *ed. Jonathan Edwards, A Retrospect, Introduction, p.* vii.

RELIGIOUS AFFECTIONS
1746

The title of the "Treatise on the Religious Affections" might naturally lead us to expect a large expression of those tenderer feelings with which Edwards was, no doubt, naturally endowed. But in point of fact, if a sermon of Edwards is like a nail driven through a human heart, this treatise is just what clinches it. It is a sad thought how many souls it must have driven to despair. For after having equipped the underground laboratory of "revenging justice" with a complete apparatus of torture, such as to think of suggests nothing but insanity, he fills the unhappy believer's mind with so many doubts and scruples that many a pious Christian after reading it must have set himself down as a castaway. No warmth of feeling, no joy in believing, no love of religious exercises, no disposition to praise and glorify God, no assurance of faith, can be depended on as a "gracious affection;" for "as the Devil can counterfeit all the saving operations that are preparatory to grace,"—in short, render every humble Christian so doubtful of his own state that "the peace which passeth all understanding" becomes a phrase without meaning.—HOLMES, OLIVER WENDELL, 1880, *Jonathan Edwards, International Review, vol.* 9, *p.* 19.

The sermon on the "Distinguishing Marks of a Work of the True Spirit of God" was followed by the treatise entitled "Some Thoughts Concerning the Present Revival of Religion, and the way in which it ought to be acknowledged and promoted" (1742); and four years later, by the elaborate work on "Religious Affections." The latter sums up all that Edwards had learned, through his participation in the movement whose beginnings and early stages are described in the "Narrative," and by his long-continued and most earnest endeavor to determine the true hopes of the spiritual life which had enlisted and well-nigh absorbed all the powers of his mind and soul. It is a religious classic of the highest order, yet, like the "De Imitatione Christi," suited only to those who can read it with independent insight. They who can thus use it will find it inexhaustible in its strenuous discipline and spiritual richness, light, and sweetness. Its chief defect lies in its failure to discover and unfold the true relation between the natural and the spiritual, and to recognize the stages of Christian growth, the genuineness and value of what is still "imperfect Christianity."—SMYTH, EGBERT C., 1897, *Jonathan Edwards, Library of the World's Best Literature, ed. Warner, vol.* IX, *p.* 5176.

THE FREEDOM OF THE WILL
1754

He was not indebted to any other writer for the most important part of his materials, which he appears to have drawn almost entirely from his own reflections and resources. Though in many points he coincides with the opinions of authors, whose productions do not appear to have reached him, it is impossible to deny, that the structure and ingenuity of his arguments are his own, or to withhold from him the praise of an original writer.—WELLWOOD, SIR HENRY MONCREIFF, 1818, *An Account of the Life and Writings of John Erskine, p.* 217.

A masterpiece of metaphysical reasoning.—COLLIER, WILLIAM FRANCIS, 1861, *A History of English Literature, p.* 537.

The foundation of the literature of independent America was laid in a book which was published while it was still a subject of the British crown. Even at the end of a century, during which that literature has been sustained by much vigorous native genius, and has been cultivated by influences from France and Germany, as well as from the old country, the treatise of Jonathan Edwards on "The Freedom of the Will," still remains its most original and in some respects its most important product. . . . The treatise on "The Freedom of the Will," as a great philosophical and theological treatise, has had only an influence in England over a very limited circle. It has been presented to us in feeble dilutions, specially prepared for our market. But *this* part of his philosophy—*this* doctrine of motives—has had a most serious influence—a most debasing influence—on our religious morality in all directions. It has incorporated itself as easily into the Arminian as into the Calvinistical teaching. It has entered into alliance with the practical Mammonism which is undermining our national life. It has combined with the morbid tendencies of those who pore over their own mental conditions—hindering action, fostering superstition. All these consequences would have shocked Edwards; for many of them his copyists are mainly answerable. In his own country he retains, and must always retain, a great power. We should imagine that all American theology and philosophy, whatever changes it may undergo, and with whatever foreign elements it may be associated, must be cast in his mould. New Englanders who try to substitute Berkeley, or Butler, or Malebranche, or Condillac, or Kant, or Hegel, for Edwards, and to form their minds upon any of them, must be forcing themselves into an unnatural position, and must suffer from the effort. On the contrary, if they accept the starting point of their native teacher, and seriously consider what is necessary to make that teacher consistent with himself—what is necessary that the divine foundation upon which he wished to build may not be too weak and narrow for any human or social life to rest upon it—we should expect great and fruitful results from their inquiries to the land which they must care for most, and therefore to mankind.—MAURICE, FREDERICK DENISON, 1862, *Moral and Metaphysical Philosophy, vol.* II, *pp.* 469, 472.

The book upon the "Freedom of the Will," which is his main title to philosophical fame, bears marks of the conditions under which it was composed, and which certainly did not tend to confer upon an abstruse treatise any additional charm. Edwards' style is heavy and languid; he seldom indulges in an illustration, and those which he gives are far from lively; it is only at rare intervals that his logical ingenuity in stating some intricate argument clothes his thought in language of corresponding neatness. He has, in fact, the faults natural to an isolated thinker. He gives his readers credit for being familiar with the details of the labyrinth in which he had wandered till every intricacy was plainly mapped out in his own mind, and frequently dwells at tiresome length upon some refinement which probably never occurred to anyone but himself. A writer who, like Hume, is at once an acute thinker and a great literary artist, is content to aim a decisive blow at the vital points of the theory which he is opposing, and leaves to his readers the task of following out more remote consequences; Edwards, after winning the decisive victory, insists upon attacking his adversary in every position in which he might conceivably endeavour to entrench himself.—STEPHEN, LESLIE, 1874–79, *Hours in a Library, vol.* I, *p.* 315.

Has been subjected to the severest criticism by the ablest theologians and philosophers from time to time, yet in its main positions it still remains apparently as impregnable as ever.—PATTON, J. H., 1876, *Primer of English Literature by Brooke, Appendix, p.* 169.

The reader of this celebrated treatise may well admire the sleuthhound-like sagacity and tenacity with which the keen-scented reasoner follows the devious tracks of his adversaries; yet he can hardly help feeling that a vast number of words have been expended in proving over and over again a proposition which, as put by the great logician, is self-evident. In fact, Edwards has more than once stated his own argument with a contemptuous brevity, as if he felt that he had been paying out in farthings what he could easily hand us in the form of a shilling. . . . In spite of any general assertions of Edwards to the contrary, we find our wills tied up hand and foot in the logical propositions which he knots inextricably about them; and yet when we lay down the book, we feel as if there was something left free after all. We cannot help saying *E pur si muove.*—HOLMES, OLIVER WENDELL, 1880, *Jonathan Edwards, International Review, vol.* 9, *pp.* 10, 11.

Witness President Edwards's definition of "necessity." The "Essay on the Will" hinges on a pure invention in the meaning attached to that word. Edwards's idea of necessity, as he defines it, is not the English idea, is not the popular idea: it never was. It was not his own idea outside of the "Essay on the Will." In his sermons he falls back, as other men of sense do, upon the popular idea. Even in the "Essay on the Will" he forgets his definition, and in some sections speaks of "necessity" and "freedom" as the common sense of men understands them. No preacher can accept Edwards's definition of "necessity," and preach it as the philosophical basis of his theology, without lapsing into fatalism. But no preacher can preach "necessity," as Edwards himself preaches it in his sermons, without preaching the freedom of the human will to the full dictates of human consciousness. The most conclusive answer to the weak point in Edwards's essay is the strong point in Edwards's sermons.—PHELPS, AUSTIN, 1883, *English Style in Public Discourse, p.* 31.

That masterpiece of earthly reasoning. —GARNETT, RICHARD, 1888, *Life of Ralph Waldo Emerson, p.* 77.

My father's library—that of a Presbyterian minister—was a bristling phalanx of puritanic writers. The eight volumes of Edwards's works stood in the first rank, and were backed by other productions less able, but not lighter of digestion. My mother—my father died early —with a patient, humble, and devout mind, was able to derive daily and hourly nourishment from Scott's "Commentaries," Doddridge's "Rise and Progress of Religion in the Soul," and Baxter's "Saints' Rest;" but to me, even in the moments of religious fervor, these books were always chips. They were the ever-returning, undeniable proof of the depravity of the natural heart, that so obstinately rejected them. Nor was it because I was unwilling to put hard work upon them, if only it brought any return. To me, the best thing in this library was Edwards's "Treatise on the Will," though I have cast that out, shred by shred, till not a trace of it remains in my spiritual constitution.—BASCOM, JOHN, 1888, *Books That Have Helped Me*, p. 33.

Like Butler's "Analogy," it belongs among the few great books in English theology. It may claim the great and peculiar honor of having first opened up to the world a new subject of interest,—the neglected and almost unknown sphere of the human will in its vast extent and mystery. It attempted to fill an empty niche in the corridors of human thought. From an historical point of view, no one can question its significance. Whether its importance is now more than historical, it is fairly open to doubt. The book is a difficult one to read, and this difficulty has been generally supposed to lie in the nature of the subject rather than in the author's method of exposition. But the close scrutiny to which it has been subjected has revealed a confusion in Edwards' mind as one source of the difficulty which the student encounters.—ALLEN, ALEXANDER V. G., 1889, *Jonathan Edwards (American Religious Leaders)*, p. 287.

Is not a web of pure logic, but of schoolman's logic, reinforced and illustrated by Biblical quotation, without too much regard to the original meaning and purposes of the passages cited. As literature, it is idiomatic and simple to baldness. The English is a mingling of philosophical phrases with the every-day talk of common people. "Do not" is "don't;" "have not" is "han't;" "them" is generally "em;" "cannot" is "can't," etc. There is not a word of ornament, nor a sentence that looks rhetorical; no quotable passages, only a steady and urgent progress from certain propositions to certain conclusions. In spite of occasional quibbles, the mental "grip" is astonishing; so that the reader is drawn on, however much against his will, to admit the plausibility of doctrines which his moral sense rejects. The definitions leave something to be desired; but, all deductions made, this is undoubtedly the ablest of Calvinistic works.—UNDERWOOD, FRANCIS H., 1893, *The Builders of American Literature, First Series*, p. 42.

It is now but little read, for we no longer see the subject from Edwards's point of view. But it remains a monument of intellectual effort. To this day it is probably the most direct and subtle treatise on a philosophical theme written by any American. It justifies the assertion of more than one European critic that no work of the eighteenth century surpasses it in the vigor of its logic or in the sharpness of its argument.—MATTHEWS, BRANDER, 1896, *An Introduction to the Study of American Literature*, p. 20.

ORIGINAL SIN
1758

One of the most revolting books that have ever proceeded from the pen of man. —LECKY, WILLIAM EDWARD HARTPOLE, 1865, *History of the Rise and Influence of the Spirit of Rationalism in Europe, vol.* I, *ch.* iv, *note*.

If there is any literary interest in the treatise on "Original Sin," it lies in the revelation of Edwards' character. He was penetrated with the mystic's conviction of some far-reaching, deep-seated alienation which separates man from God. Out of his ideal of the divine perfection springs his consciousness of sin. But his conception of sin is after all lacking in what may be called an ethical motive. He defines sin as a negation,—the absence of reality. But in this negation he seems to include the infinite gulf which divides the creature from the Creator. All imperfection, finiteness as contrasted with the infinite, the interest in earthly things or all which is not God,—these, as well as the lack of entire disinterested devotion, or the darker vices which disfigure human life, enter into Edwards' conception of sin.—ALLEN, ALEXANDER V. G., 1889, *Jonathan Edwards (American Religious Leaders)*, p.311.

GENERAL

There are some things in your New England doctrine and worship, which I do not agree with; but I do not therefore condemn them, or desire to shake your belief or practice of them. We may dislike things that are nevertheless right in themselves. I would only have you make me the same allowance, and have a better opinion both of morality and your brother. Read the pages of Mr. Edwards's late book, entitled "Some Thoughts concerning the present Revival of Religion in New England," from 367 to 375, and when you judge of others, if you can perceive the fruit to be good, don't terrify yourself that the tree may be evil; but be assured it is not so, for you know who has said, "Men do not gather grapes of thorns and figs of thistles." I have no time to add, but that I shall always be your affectionate brother.—FRANKLIN, BENJAMIN, 1743, *Letter to His Sister, July* 28; *Writings, ed. Sparks, vol,* VII, *p.* 8.

When posterity occasionally comes across them [his writings] in the rubbish of libraries, the rare characters who may read and be pleased with them will be looked upon as singular and whimsical, as in these days an admirer of Suarez, Aquinas or Dionysius Areopagita.—STILES, EZRA, 1787, *Diary, Aug.* 10, *ed. Dexter, vol.* III, *p.* 275.

But, my chief bane, my apostolic foe,
In life, in labours, source of every woe,
From scenes obscure did heav'n his Edwards call,
That moral Newton, and that second Paul.
He, in clear view, saw sacred systems roll,
Of reasoning worlds, around their central soul;
Saw love attractive every system bind,
The parent linking to each filial mind;
The end of heav'n's high works resistless shew'd,
Creating glory, and created good;
And, in one little life, the gospel more
Disclos'd, than all earth's myriads kenn'd before,
Beneath his standard, lo! what numbers rise,
To care for truth and combat for the skies!
Arm'd at all points, they try the battling field,
With reason's sword, and faith's ethereal shield.

—DWIGHT, TIMOTHY, 1797, *The Triumph of Infidelity.*

That most acute reasoner, Jonathan Edwards.—HALL, ROBERT, 1799, *Modern Infidelity Considered, Miscellaneous Works, ed. Gregory, p.* 284, *note.*

A profound searcher into the genuine sources of truth, well versed in the Holy Scriptures, a close and minute reasoner, a strenuous defender of holiness and the rights of God; plain and perspicuous in his method, unadorned but prolix in his language. On the whole, a most excellent writer, both practical and controversial.—WILLIAMS, EDWARD, 1800, *The Christian Preacher.*

In the New World the state of society and of manners has not hitherto been so favourable to abstract science as to pursuits which come home directly to the business of human life. There is, however, *one* metaphysician of whom America has to boast, who, in logical acuteness and subtility, does not yield to any disputant bred in the universities of Europe. I need not say, that I allude to Jonathan Edwards. But, at the time when he wrote, the state of America was more favourable than it now is, or can for a long period be expected to be, to such inquiries as those which engaged his attention; inquiries (by the way) to which his thoughts were evidently turned, lest by the impulse of speculative curiosity, than by his anxiety to defend the theological system in which he had been educated, and to which he was most conscientiously and zealously attached. The effect of this anxiety in sharpening his faculties, and in keeping his polemical vigilance constantly *on the alert,* may be traced in every step of his argument.—STEWART, DUGALD, 1815–21, *First Preliminary Dissertation on the Progress of Philosophy, Encyclopædia Britannica.*

Jonathan Edwards, as a philosopher, as well as a divine, had few equals, and no superior, among his contemporaries. His works will live as long as powerful reasoning, genuine religion, and the science of the human mind, continue to be objects of respect. . . . "The Treatise on Religious Affections" discovers his profound acquaintance with the nature of genuine religion, and with all the deceitful workings of the human heart. "The Inquiry into the Freedom of the Human Will" displays the talent of the author as a metaphysician, and his accurate knowledge of the Arminian and Calvinistic controversy. His "Defence of the Christian Doctrine of Original Sin," designed partly as an answer to a work on that subject by Dr. John Taylor of Norwich, discovers the same high qualities which belong to his former works, with a greater portion of excellent critical interpretation of the Scripture. His style, it is to be regretted, repels many from the examination of his writings; but a little perseverance and attention will render it familiar to a diligent student, and the effect of his close and convincing reasoning will prove eminently beneficial to the understanding. —ORME, WILLIAM, 1824, *Bibliotheca Biblica.*

This remarkable man, the metaphysician of America, was formed among the Calvinists of New England, when their stern doctrine retained its vigorous authority. His power of subtile argument, perhaps unmatched, certainly unsurpassed among men, was joined, as in some of the ancient Mystics, with a character which raised his piety to fervour.—MACKINTOSH, JAMES, 1830, *Second Preliminary Dissertation, Encyclopædia Britannica.*

No sooner does he sit down to investigate a subject, than his passions seem as completely hushed as though their breath had never ruffled the soul; its surface looks as tranquil, as motionless, and we may add, as cold as a sea of ice, and the turbulence of passion seems as little likely to disturb the fixed calm of the one as the winds of heaven to raise tempests in the other. — ROGERS, HENRY, 1834, *Essay on the Life and Genius of Jonathan Edwards, p.* 19.

To theological students his works are almost indispensable. In all the branches of theology, didactic, polemical, casuistic, experimental, and practical, he had few equals, and perhaps no superior. The number and variety of his works show the intenseness of his industry and the uncommon strength of his intellectual powers, "The Inquiry into the Will" is a masterly work, which, as a specimen of exact analysis, of profound or perfect abstraction, of conclusive logic, and of calm discussion, will long support its high reputation, and will continue to be used as a classic material in the business of intellectual education.—LOWNDES, WILLIAM THOMAS, 1839, *British Librarian.*

Universal history does but seek to relate "the sum of all God's works of providence." In 1739, the first conception of its office, in the mind of Jonathan Edwards, . . . was nobler than the theory of Vico: more grand and general than the method of Bossuet, it embraced in its outline the whole "work of redemption"—the history of the influence of all moral truth in the gradual regeneration of humanity.—BANCROFT, GEORGE, 1840–76–83, *History of the United States, pt.* iii, *ch.* xvi.

Seeds from Edwards have taken root in strange fields. A single stalk from his philosophy has shed beauty and perfume over wastes of modern speculation. Many, of whose opinions all is dross that is not borrowed from him, have exhibited the poverty of their natural powers in assaults upon his system; and others, incapable of penetrating beyond the shell of his logic, and understanding the beauty of his life and doctrine, have done him much greater injury by professing to be of his school.—GRISWOLD, RUFUS WILMOT, 1845, *The Prose Writers of America.*

Edwards's writings, as a whole, display an exceedingly strong and comprehensive memory, great force and perspicuity of thought, and powers of ratiocination equalled by few of that or any other age. These powers, which he possessed in so eminent a degree, were still further strengthened by the most unceasing exertion. His intellectual labors knew no relaxation, and so fixedly that his mind becomes associated with one branch of enquiry, that his whole existence may be said to have been absorbed in it. His mind, shut out as it were by his processes of abstraction from the contemplation of the external world, seemed to concentrate its whole energies in the analysis of those materials which lie deep buried within. The subjection of his being to one particular train of thought, placed his passions and feelings so perfectly under control as to give him the appearance of an individual without those ordinary emotions which characterize the human family; hence we find him under the most exciting circumstances as calm and collected as if he were perfectly indifferent as to the result of his investigations.—WYNNE, JAMES, 1850, *Lives of Eminent Literary and Scientific Men of America, p.* 167.

The pages of Edwards especially I have read with so solemn and deep an interest as listening to a great and holy man. —CAMPBELL, J. MCLEOD, 1856, *Nature of the Atonement, p.* 54.

We owe much to Edwards in the way of

harmonizing the theology of the Bible with the reason and the moral intuition of man. Some find that theology hard to be understood, and therefore treat it as a mystery, not to be investigated. Some, failing to reconcile it with their reason or their intuitions, reject it, and the Bible with it. Some seek to explain away the more obvious theology of the Bible, derogating from the authority of the book, and using it only as it may serve their own rational eclecticism. Edwards did neither. While he saw the doctrines and their difficulties he mastered both, and held fast by his moral intuitions on the one hand, and the doctrines of the Bible on the other, till he bound them together by a compact and glowing chain of logic. —THOMPSON, JOSEPH P., 1861, *Jonathan Edwards, Bibliotheca Sacra, vol.* 18, *p.* 837.

I may have the usual bias of a discoverer and editor. But I shall be surprised if this treatise ["Treatise on Grace,"] do not at once take rank with its kindred one, on "The Religious Affections." There is in it, I think, the massive argumentation of his great work on "The Will;" but there is, in addition, a fineness of spiritual insight, a holy fervour not untinged with the pathetic "frenzy" of the English Mystics, as of Peter Sterry and Archbishop Leighton, and—especially towards the close—a rapturous exultation in the "excellency and loveliness" of God, a *glow* in iteration of the wonder and beauty and blessedness of Divine Love, and a splendor of assertion of the CLAIMS, so to speak, of God the Holy Spirit, which it would be difficult to over-estimate.—GROSART, ALEXANDER B., 1865, *Selections from the Unpublished Writings of Jonathan Edwards of America, Introduction.*

He was a thorough Calvinist, but such a Calvinist that he hesitated not to differ from Calvin wherever *he* seemed to differ from the Scriptures. The Saybrook Platform was drawn (chiefly through the agency of the Trustees of the Saybrook Collegiate School, which he afterwards entered) when he was five years of age. The "Westminster Catechism" in Latin and "Ames's Theological Theses" were recited, as a college exercise, when he was a student. He respected these venerable symbols, but his own thinking went immeasurably beyond them. His massive and majestic intellect was too great to be bound by human authority; it reverenced the Infinite Intellect too much to be governed, in its methods or results, by the opinions of men. . . . He was the most progressive thinker of his age. When Franklin opposed the new method of inoculation, Edwards offered himself as a subject for it, and actually died from the secondary fever resulting. He might have been called a new-measure man in religion,—afraid of nothing that worked good and was agreeable to the Scriptures. He convinced a generation that feared more than they knew about revivals of their utility and benefit.—MAGOUN, G. F., 1869, *President Edwards as a Reformer, The Congregational Quarterly, vol.* 11, *p.* 269.

His controversial acuteness and subtlety in drawing distinctions entitle his works to their high rank. He had little turn for style. Dry and precise, without either felicity or ornament, his writings are calculated to repel all but hard students of their particular subjects.—MINTO, WILLIAM, 1872–80, *Manual of English Prose Literature, p.* 430.

In the middle of the eighteenth century, he is still in bondage to the dogmas of the Pilgrim Fathers; he is as indifferent to the audacious revolt of the deists and Hume as if the old theological dynasty were still in full vigour; and the fact, whatever else it may prove, proves something for the enduring vitality of the ideas which had found an imperfect expression in Calvinism. Clearing away the crust of ancient superstition, we may still find in Edwards' writings a system of morality as ennobling, and a theory of the universe as elevated, as can be discovered in any theology. That the crust was thick and hard, and often revolting in its composition, is, indeed, undeniable; but the genuine metal is there, no less unmistakably than the refuse.—STEPHEN, LESLIE, 1874–79, *Hours in a Library, vol.* I, *p.* 344.

I am glad to hear of your reading. The effect produced on you by Jonathan Edwards is very similar to that produced on me when I took the same mental bath. His was a mind whose grasp and intensity you cannot help feeling. He was a poet in the intensity of his conceptions, and some of his sermons are more terrible than Dante's "Inferno."

—STOWE, HARRIET BEECHER, 1874, *Letter to her Son, May; Life by C. E. Stowe, p.* 406.

Edwards was distinguished for the early development of his metaphysical tastes and ability, and for the freedom, even to audacity, with which he attempted to adjust the Calvinists theology to the principles and conclusions of a reasoned philosophy. As a consequence he not only established a new and independent school of Calvinistic theology, which has been known as the New England or the Edwardian Theology, but contributed very largely to the development of speculative tastes, and of confidence in speculative inquiries among the scholars of America. The influence of this school has not been inconsiderable upon theology and philosophy in Great Britain, where the name of Edwards has been familiarly known from the first appearance of his Treatise on the Will. . . . The impulse and direction to the speculations of Edwards were furnished by Locke. He mastered Locke's Essay when he was thirteen years old, studying it with a keener delight than "a miser feels when gathering up handfuls of silver and gold." But he was not exclusively a student of Locke, as might be inferred from his secluded situation and limited opportunities. He was a zealous reader of most of the writers accessible in the English language, and was familiar with the course of speculation in the mother country, reading the writers of all schools with equal ardor, and never abandoning the confident belief that whatever is true in theology could be shown to be both true and reasonable in philosophy. Edwards was at once a scholastic and a mystic; a scholastic in the subtlety of his analysis and the sustained vigor of his reasonings, and a mystic in the sensitive delicacy of his emotive tenderness and the idealistic elevation of his imaginative creations, which at times almost transfigures his Christian faith into the beatific vision.—PORTER, NOAH, 1874, *Philosophy in Great Britain and America, Ueberweg's History of Philosophy, vol.* II, *p.* 443.

I *was* especially interested in Jonathan Edwards, with whom (except in his physical notions of hell) I have great sympathy—a case of *reversion* I suppose, to some Puritan ancestor. If he had only conceived of damnation as a spiritual state, the very horror of which consists (to our deeper apprehension) in its being delightful to who is in it, I could go along with him altogether. What you say of his isolation is particularly good, and applies to American literature more or less even yet. —LOWELL, JAMES RUSSELL, 1876, *Letter to Leslie Stephen, Letters, ed. Norton, vol.* II, *p.* 165.

By his power of subtle argument, his religious fervour, and his peculiar doctrines respecting free-will, Edwards has obtained a high and lasting reputation. He has perhaps never been surpassed as a dialectician.—CHAMBERS, ROBERT, 1876, *Cyclopædia of English Literature, ed. Carruthers.*

As a theologian, as a metaphysician, as the author of "The Inquiry into the Freedom of the Will," as the mighty defender of Calvinism, as the inspirer and the logical drill-master of innumerable minds in his own country, and in Great Britain, he, of course, fills a large place in ecclesiastical and philosophical history. But even from the literary point of view, and in spite of his own low estimate of his literary merits, he deserves high rank. He had the fundamental virtues of a writer, —abundant thought, and the utmost precision, clearness, and simplicity in the utterance of it; his pages, likewise, hold many examples of bold, original, and poetic imagery; and though the nature of his subjects, and the temper of his sect, repressed the exercise of wit, he was possessed of wit in an extraordinary degree, and of the keenest edge. In early life, he was sadly afflicted by the burden of checking the movements of this terrible faculty; but later, it often served him in controversy, not as a substitute for argument, but as its servant; enabling him, especially in the climaxes of a discussion, to make palpable the absurdity of propositions that he had already shown to be untenable.—TYLER, MOSES COIT, 1878, *A History of American Literature,* 1676–1765, *vol.* II, *p.* 191

Franklin snatched from heaven its electric fire; Edwards pierced the skies to an eternal realm. Both were among the most famous of their age—New-World prodigies that had made themselves powerful on both sides of the Atlantic. The fame of Edwards had spread from his quiet New England town to Glasgow and

Edinburgh long before his treatise on the Will startled Boswell's inquisitive intellect. Franklin expended in practical labors the hours that Edwards gave to holy musings and speculative lore. Yet it is doubtful which of these clear intellects was of the greater weight in human affairs; whether Edwards, composing his rare work in silent study, was not more of the philosopher than Franklin, founding his schools and planning his library; whether Franklin has not preached with more success even than the gifted pastor of Northampton the lesson of humanity and benevolence to endless generations. Upon a close comparison they will not appear altogether unlike.—LAWRENCE, EUGENE, 1880, *A Primer of American Literature, p.* 33.

Puritanism to such men was a girdle, not a fetter; it held them together and made them march forward in line, instead of straggling along without aim or purpose. But in time the girdle became a chain; the people began to fret under it and threw it off; and this was the very period at which Edwards and Franklin appeared. The one contended stoutly for the old faith, in all its strictness and with all its alarming penalties for sin; the other, with genial and prudent good nature, sought to introduce a milder sway, more friendly to the general development of mankind. Both were powerful forces, and had other forces more powerful behind them; but the time had come for puritanism to withdraw from the scene, and the controversial writings of Edwards furnished the salvo of theological artillery under cover of which the army of the Puritans fell back in good order, leaving the field to Democracy and the philanthropists.—SANBORN, F. B., 1883, *The Puritanic Philosophy and Jonathan Edwards, The Journal of Speculative Philosophy, vol.* 17, *p.* 421.

But after all criticisms have been made upon Edwards as philosopher and theologian, it remains that he strongly expressed an idea of the might and majesty of God, and of his august government of the universe. Again, some of his conclusions anticipated, and are in close argument with, the dicta of modern science. Evolution, heredity, natural laws, as expounded by Darwin, Spencer, or Galton, teach not less truly than did Edwards the potency, almost the inflexibility, of inheritance and environment. Dr. Holmes, the most strenuous anti-Calvinist in recent American literature, in his "Mechanism in Thoughts and Morals," sometimes seems to join hands with the eighteenth-century philosopher, sprung, like himself, from sturdy Connecticut ministerial stock. —RICHARDSON, CHARLES F., 1887, *American Literature,* 1607–1885, *vol.* I, *p.* 146.

Having made these qualifications, it only remains to add that Edwards may be justly called the father of modern Congregationalism. If he seemed to have been defeated by his expulsion from Northampton, his expulsion made the issue clear and he triumphed in his fall. Most of the Puritan churches accepted his principles, banished the Half-way Covenant, and took on the form which they still retain. As one by one they went over to his side, they found it hard to understand how there ever could have existed a different practice. It became the custom to refer to the times of the Theocracy as "those unhappy days when things secular and religious were strangely mixed up in New England." And yet the Congregational churches have never been able to escape altogether from the effects of that "unhappy" connection, if so it must be regarded. It has given them a certain distinction, the consciousness of which they prize. They have continued to retain a sense of relationship to the state, and to feel themselves responsible for its welfare. Nor have the cases been rare in which its clergy have given themselves to political and legislative duties, as if a natural and congenial work.—ALLEN, ALEXANDER V. G., 1889, *Jonathan Edwards (American Religious Leaders), p.* 270.

In the passionate effort of Edwards to revive the pristine force of orthodox Calvinism, the theology of the fathers reached the highest point. It was sincere, it was terribly earnest, it was almost impregnably logical; but it was so highly developed that even though we knew nothing of its circumstances we might shrewdly guess it to be, like so many great works of art, essentially a thing of the past. In point of fact, we know its circumstances.—WENDELL, BARRETT, 1893, *Stelligeri and Other Essays Concerning America, p.* 121.

New England at this time possessed, in

Jonathan Edwards, the most subtle metaphysical reasoner that America has ever produced.—FRASER, ALEXANDER CAMPBELL, 1894, *Berkeley (Philosophical Classics), p.* 138.

His writings belong to theology rather than literature, but there is an intensity and a spiritual elevation about them, apart from the profundity and acuteness of the thought, which lift them here and there into the finer ether of purely emotional or imaginative art. . . . In Edwards's English all is simple, precise, direct, and business-like.—BEERS, HENRY A., 1895, *Initial Studies in American Letters, pp.* 34, 36.

Jonathan Edwards is a thinker difficult to appreciate and very easy to misunderstand. His faults lie on the surface, while his merits are to be discovered only by sympathetic study. He is not only the greatest of all the thinkers that America has produced, but also the highest speculative genius of the eighteenth century. . . . Take him all in all, in the beauty of his character, in the elevation of his thought, his claim to stand amid the great thinkers of the world is indisputable. In England here we have just been making welcome the new edition of Bishop Butler's works—edited by the statesman who in his retirement shows his undiminished vigour and reveals his lifelong interest in theology—and I have been comparing Butler's answer to Tindal with Edwards's, with the result that I am forced to confess that while the rigour and vigour of inexorable logic and the strength which comes from a concentration due to the careful exclusion of all irrelevant matter are with Butler, the elevation, the insight, the oversight, the feeling of the magnitude of the problem, and the forecast of the lines along which the ultimate answer must move are all with Edwards.—FAIRBAIRN, A. M., 1896, *Jonathan Edwards, The Prophets of the Christian Faith, pp.* 147, 165.

The style of his writing is obscure and heavy in the extreme. He aimed only at the exact expression of his thought and seems to have made no effort to attain clearness. His lifelong habit of writing down his thoughts as they occurred to him, and his other habit of pursuing any line of thought to its end, no doubt aided him in thinking, but his isolation and his lack of experience in the oral discussion of philosophical questions prevented his realization of the necessity of clear statement. In some of his sermons he rises almost to eloquence, and there his sentences are well constructed and full of energy, but this is true of none of his philosophical works.—JONES, ADAM LEROY, 1898, *Early American Philosophers, p.* 49.

Edwards is an example of the power of the unrhetorical rhetoric. His most marked rhetorical means were negative; he instinctively avoided what was likely to stand between him and his hearer, and so his personality had full sway. But Edwards' literary significance at present lies chiefly in the fact that he was a New Englander who made the world aware of the New England mind. That he should have been a theologian was natural; so was Cotton Mather, chiefly, who had performed a somewhat similar service half a century before. Each had presented what had long been the dominant factor in New England life.—HALE, EDWARD EVERETT, JR., 1898, *American Prose, ed. Carpenter, p.* 15.

One of the great philosophical intellects of the world. . . . If he could have given himself to literature, science, or pure philosophy, mankind would be the richer. Yet as it is, he is one of the very few American writers whose fame is world wide. — BRONSON, WALTER C., 1900, *A Short History of American Literature, pp.* 33, 34.

This sifting process must be applied to Edwards. As a whole, Edwards is incredible, impossible. He is nearly as much in the wrong as he is in the right. He carries his vast treasure in the earthen vessel of radical inconsistency and fundamental error. No single treatise of Edwards can to-day commend itself in its entireness to the free and informed mind. In his treatment of the Will, the Religious Affections, the Nature of Virtue, the History of Redemption, God's Final End in Creation, the scheme and process of salvation, the Christian church cannot follow him as a whole, and those who insist upon all or none do their best to make it none. Only wise criticism, large and generous interpretation, the careful winnowing of the chaff from the wheat, the clear discrimination of the precious and imperishable in Edwards from the worthless and deplorable, can restore him to his legitimate pre-eminence among American theologians.—GORDON, G. A., 1901, *Jonathan Edwards, A Retrospect, ed. Gardiner.*

More and more, as I have returned from time to time to the study of Edwards' writings, have I been impressed with his intellectual powers and with the sanctity of his character. It is a pity that in this country so many of "the merely literary"—as Newman would style them—appear to know nothing of his writings save passages in the Enfield sermon. They would find, if they looked for them, in Jeremy Taylor, "the Shakespeare of preachers," delineations of future torment which rival the pictures of terror in that sermon. It is beyond question that Edwards was a theological genius of the first order. He was, besides, an eminently holy man. He mixed, in his soul and in his writings, with the rigor of Calvin the sweetness of St. Francis. He is the Saint of New England.—FISHER, GEORGE P., 1901, *Jonathan Edwards, A Retrospect, ed. Gardiner, p.* 78.

Theophilus Cibber

1703–1758

Theophilus Cibber, son of Colley Cibber (born 1703, died 1758), actor and dramatist, wrote "The Lover" (1730); "Pattie and Peggie" (an adaptation into English of Allan Ramsay's "Gentle Shepherd"), (1730); "The Mock Officer" (1733); and other pieces. "The Lives of the Poets of Great Britain and Ireland from the time of Dean Swift" (1753), were attributed to his pen, but Dr. Johnson was of opinion that the work was written by Robert Shiels, a Scotchman.—ADAMS, W. DAVENPORT, 1877, *Dictionary of English Literature, p.* 152.

PERSONAL

Theo. Cibber was in his person far from pleasing, the features of his face were rather disgusting—his voice had the same shrill treble, but without that musical harmony, which his father was master of —yet still an apparent good understanding and quickness of parts, a perfect knowledge of what he ought to represent, together with a vivacity in his manner, and a kind of effrontery, which was well adapted to the characters he represented, pretty amply compensated these deficiencies—(*Biog. Dram.*)—he had merit in a variety of characters, but he was so apt to mix false spirit and grimace with his acting that he often disgusted the judicious spectator—Ancient Pistol was his best character; in that part he assumed a ridiculous importance of deportment, with turgid action, long immeasurable strides, extravagant grimaces; and the sonorous cant of the old Tragedizers, so that it was impossible not to laugh at so extravagant a figure—(*Davies and Dram. Censor*)—he must have been totally inadequate to many of the parts which he played in Tragedy.—GENEST, P., 1832, *Some Account of the English Stage,* 1660–1830, *vol.* IV, *p.* 532.

It is recorded that Colley, taking the air one day, encountered his hopeful offspring, who was superbly attired. Cibber, knowing that Theophilus was penniless, surveyed him with contempt. "I pity you, sir!" He said. "Better pity my tailor!" was the reply. Theophilus was at least consistent. He conducted all his affairs on "pity my tailor" principles. This theory of life envolved him in perpetual embarrassments, but he lost nothing of his native audacity. He had talents, and amongst them was a capacity for abusive rhetoric, which was carefully cultivated. But the enterprise which established his fame was his attempt to obtain five thousand pounds for damages to his injured honour as a husband. The jury, having reason to believe that he had been a party to the intrigue, awarded him ten pounds. This sum did not enable him to satisfy his creditors, and he spent some little time in prison.—AUSTIN, L. F., 1878, *Theophilus Cibber v. Garrick, The Theatre, N. S., vol.* I, *p.* 122.

LIVES OF THE POETS

He told us, that the book entitled "The Lives of the Poets," by Mr. Cibber, was entirely compiled by Mr. Shiels, a Scotchman, one of his amanuenses. "The bookseller (said he), gave Theophilus Cibber, who was then in prison, ten guineas, to allow *Mr. Cibber* to be put upon the title page, as the authour; by this, a double imposition was intended; in the first place, that it was the work of a Cibber at all; and, in the second place, that it was the work of old Cibber.—JOHNSON, SAMUEL, 1776, *Life by Boswell, ed. Hill, vol.* III, *p.* 34.

This account is very inaccurate. The following statement of facts we know to be true, in every material circumstance:—Shiels was the principal collector and digester of the materials for the work: but as he was very raw in authourship, an indifferent writer in prose, and his language full of Scotticisms, Cibber, who was a clever, lively fellow, and then soliciting employment among the booksellers, was engaged to correct the style and diction of the whole work, then intended to make only four volumes, with power to alter, expunge, or add, as he liked. He was also to supply *notes*, occasionally, especially concerning those dramatic poets with whom he had been chiefly conversant. He also engaged to write several of the Lives: which, (as we are told), he, accordingly, performed. He was farther useful in striking out the Jacobitical and Tory sentiments, which Shiels had industriously interspersed wherever he could bring them in:—and, as the success of the work appeared, after all, very doubtful, he was content with twenty-one pounds for his labour beside a few sets of the books, to disperse among his friends.—ANON, 1792, *Monthly Review, May.*

Cibber's lives are not ill-written, and deserve a better fame than they seem to have attained.—BRYDGES, SIR SAMUEL EGERTON, 1800, *ed. Phillips's Theatrum Poetarum Anglicanorum, Preface, p.* lvi.

In 1753 appeared "An Account of the Lives of the Poets of Great Britain and Ireland," 5 vols. 12mo, with the name of "Mr. Cibber" on the title-page of the first volume, and with Theophilus Cibber's name attached to the later volumes. Dr. Johnson told Boswell that Cibber, who was then in the king's bench, accepted ten guineas from the booksellers for allowing them to prefix his name to the lives, and that he had no hand in the authorship of the book, which was mainly written by Robert Shiels (Johnson's amanuensis); but the truth is that Cibber revised and improved the whole work and wrote some of the lives himself, receiving from the booksellers an honorarium of twenty guineas.—BULLEN, A. H., 1887, *Dictionary of National Biography, vol.* X, *p.* 362.

James Hervey

1714–1758

James Hervey, author of "Meditations among the Tombs," was born at Hardingstone, near Northampton, on 26th February 1714. The facts of his life are few. He was educated at Northampton and Lincoln College, Oxford, and was first curate and afterwards incumbent of Weston-Favel and Collingtree, both near Northampton. He died on Christmas-day 1758. Hervey adopted a Calvinistic creed, and in the 18th century his works, though not distinguished by any extraordinary qualities, enjoyed great favour with the people. The best of them are "Meditations and Contemplations" (1746), including his most famous production, "Meditations among the Tombs," and also "Reflections on a Flower Garden" and "A Descant on Creation;" "Contemplations on the Night and Starry Heavens" (1747); and "Theron and Aspasio, or a Series of Dialogues and Letters on the Most Important Subjects" (3 vols. 1755). This last gave rise to the Sandemanian controversy as to the nature of saving faith. A complete edition of his works, with a memoir, appeared in 1797. See also his Life and Letters (2 vols. 1760).—PATRICK, DAVID, *ed.*, 1897, *Chambers's Encyclopædia, vol.* V, *p.* 696.

PERSONAL

A more gentle, pious, unworldly spirit than that of James Hervey it is difficult to conceive. He was never known to be in a passion; he made a solemn vow to dedicate all the profits of his literary work to pious and charitable uses, and scrupulously performed it. He was naturally disinclined to controversy, though from a sense of duty he threw himself into the hottest and most unsatisfactory of all controversies. The simplicity of his character is a strange contrast to the artificiality of his best-known writings; but in his correspondence and his sermons he uses a simpler and therefore more pleasing style. His popularity as a writer never led him to take a false view of his own powers; when it was at its height he frankly confessed that he was not a man of strong mind, and that he had not power for arduous researches.—OVERTON, J. H., 1891, *Dictionary of National Biography, vol.* XXVI, *p.* 283.

GENERAL

Have you met with two little volumes which contain four contemplations written by a Mr. James Hervey, a young Cornish or Devonshire clergyman? The subjects are upon walking upon the tombs, upon a flower-garden, upon night, and upon the starry heavens. There is something poetical and truly pious in them.—HERTFORD, LADY (DUCHESS OF SOMERSET), 1748, *Letter to Lady Luxborough.*

He wished to have more books, and, upon inquiring if there were any in the house, was told that a waiter had some, which were brought to him; but I recollect none of them, except Hervey's "Meditations." He thought slightingly of this admirable book. He treated it with ridicule, and would not allow even the scene of the dying Husband and Father to be pathetick. I am not an impartial judge; for Hervey's "Meditations" engaged my affections in my early years. He read a passage concerning the moon, ludicrously, and shewed how easily he could, in the same style, make reflections on that planet, the very reverse of Hervey's representing her as treacherous to mankind. He did this with much humour; but I have not preserved the particulars.—JOHNSON, SAMUEL, 1773, *Life by Boswell, Oct.* 24, *ed. Hill, vol.* V, *p.* 400.

Among serious readers, the estimate of their most excellent author, on points far more important than those that relate to the art of authorship, has been, and will ever remain, invariable. There can be very few individuals, whose opinion would be worth hearing, that will not speak with delight of his exalted piety, of his zeal for such views of the Christian religion as animated our venerable and heroic reformers, and the worthiest of their successors, and of the exemplary purity of his life. In addition to this, his writings manifest an understanding of a respectable order; and have been exceeded, we believe, by very few books in extent of beneficial influence. His "Meditations," especially, have contributed more, it is probable, than any other book, to the valuable object of prompting and guiding serious minds, of not the superior rank in point of taste, to draw materials of devotional thought from the scenery of nature. An immense number of persons, have been taught by him, to contemplate vicissitude and phænomena of the seasons, the flowers of the earth, and the stars of heaven, with such pious and salutary associations, as would not otherwise have been suggested to their minds: and the value of these associations is incalculable, on the double ground of enlargement of thought, and devotional tendency. Hervey ranks, therefore, among the high benefactors of his age.—But in turning to the more strictly literary estimate of his writings, there is no averting the heavy charges which critics, without one dissenting voice, bring against his style. No one qualified in the smallest degree to judge of good writing, ever attempts to controvert the justice with which they pronounce that style artificial, timid, and gaudy, loaded with an inanimate mass of epithets, and in short, very fine, without being at all rich.—FOSTER, JOHN, 1811, *Hervey's Letters, The Eclectic Review, vol.* 14, *p.* 1021.

The bloated style and peculiar rhythm of Hervey, which is poetic only on account of its utter unfitness for prose, and might as appropriately be called prosaic, from its utter unfitness for poetry.—COLERIDGE, SAMUEL TAYLOR, 1817, *Biographia Literaria, ch.* xxiii.

The author of "The Doctor" says that some styles are *flowery*, but that the Meditationist's is a *weedy* style; alluding, I suppose, to its luxuriant commonplace, and vulgar showiness, as of corn-poppies and wild mustard. But Hervey seems to have been a simple earnest clergyman, with his heart in his parish.—COLERIDGE, SARA, 1847, *ed. Coleridge's Biographia Literaria, ch.* xxiii.

Hervey's "Meditations" (1746–7), for example, was one of the most popular books of the century; and it bears to Shaftesbury the same kind of relation which Young bears to Pope. Hervey was an attached disciple of Wesley; and a man of some cultivation and great fluency of speech. He tried to eclipse the worldly writers in their own style of rhetoric. The worship of nature might be combined with the worship of Jehovah. He admires the "stupendous orbs," and the immortal harmonies, but he takes care to remember that we must die, and meditates, in most edifying terms, amongst the tombs. Such works can hardly be judged by the common literary canons. Writings which are meant to sanctify imaginative indulgences by wresting the ordinary language to purposes of religious edification are often, for obvious reasons, popular beyond their merits. Sacred poetry and religious novels belong to a world of their own. To the profane reader, however, the fusion of deistical sentiment and evangelical truth does not seem to have thoroughly effected. There is the old falsetto note which affects us disagreeably in Shaftesbury's writings. Hervey, after all, lives in the eighteenth century, and though as his "Theron and Aspasia" proves, he could write with sufficient savour upon the true Evangelical dogmas, the imaginative symbolism of his creed is softened by the contemporary currents which blend with it.—STEPHEN, LESLIE, 1876, *History of English Thought in the Eighteenth Century, vol.* II, *p.* 438.

John Dyer

1700?–1758

Poet, born near Llandilo, and educated at Westminster, abandoned law for art, and in 1727 published "Grongar Hill," remarkable for simplicity, warmth of feeling, and exquisite descriptions of scenery. He next travelled in Italy, returned in bad health to publish the "Ruins of Rome" (1740), took orders, and in 1741 became vicar of Catthorpe, Leicestershire, which he exchanged later for the Lincolnshire livings of Belchford, Coningsby, and Kirkby-on-Bain. "The Fleece" (1757), a didactic poem, is praised by Wordsworth in a sonnet.—PATRICK AND GROOME, *eds.*, 1897, *Chambers's Biographical Dictionary, p.* 324.

PERSONAL

Dodsley, the bookseller, was one day mentioning it ["The Fleece"] to a critical visitor, with more expectation of success than the other could easily admit. In the coversation the author's age was asked; and being represented as advanced in life, "He will," said the critic, "be buried in woolen."—JOHNSON, SAMUEL, 1779–81, *Dyer, Lives of the English Poet.*

Mr. Dyer was a man of uncommon understanding and attainments, but so modest and reserved, that he frequently sat silent in company for an hour, and seldom spoke unless appealed to; in which case he generally showed himself most intimately acquainted with whatever happened to be the subject.—MALONE, EDMOND, 1791, *Maloniana, ed. Prior, p.* 419.

He is represented as a man of excellent private character, and of sweet and gentle-dispositions. He was beloved by, and he loved, a man who had latterly few friends, Richard Savage, and exchanged with him complimentary poems. He was the friend of Aaron Hill, of Hughes, of Akenside, and of various other contemporary authors.—GILFILLAN, GEORGE, 1858, *ed., The Poetical Works of Armstrong, Dyer and Green, p.* 107.

GRONGAR HILL

1727

"Grongar Hill" is the happiest of his productions: it is not indeed very accurately written; but the scenes which it displays are so pleasing, the images which they raise so welcome to the mind, and the reflections of the writer so consonant to the general sense or experience of mankind, that when it is once read, it will be read again.—JOHNSON, SAMUEL, 1779–81, *Dyer, Lives of the English Poets.*

Of English poets, perhaps none have excelled the ingenuous Mr. Dyer in this oblique instruction, into which he frequently steals imperceptibly in his little descriptive poem entitled "Grongar Hill," where he disposes every object so as it may give occasion for some observation on human life. Denham himself is not superior to Mr. Dyer in this particular.—WARTON, JOSEPH, 1782, *Essay on Pope, vol.* I, *p.* 35.

In the "Grongar Hill" of Dyer we have, likewise, a lyric effusion equally spirited and pleasing, and celebrated for the fidelity of its delineation; the commencement, however, is obscure and even ungrammatical, and his landscape not sufficiently distinct, wanting what the artist would term proper keeping. It is nevertheless a very valuable poem and has secured to its author an envied immortality.—DRAKE, NATHAN, 1798–1820, *Literary Hours, vol.* II, *p.* 35.

The poet cannot trust himself frankly to describe Nature for her own sake, like Wordsworth or Shelley. — PALGRAVE, FRANCIS TURNER, 1896, *Landscape in Poetry, p.* 171.

THE FLEECE
1757

The woolcomber and the poet appear to me such discordant natures, that an attempt to bring them together is to *couple the serpent with the fowl.* . . . Let me, however, honestly report whatever may counterbalance this weight of censure. I have been told that Akenside, who, upon a poetical question, has a right to be heard, said, "That he would regulate his opinion of the reigning taste by the fate of Dyer's 'Fleece,' for, if that were ill received, he should not think it any longer reasonable to expect fame from excellence."—JOHNSON, SAMUEL, 1779–81, *Dyer, Lives of the English Poets.*

This beautiful, but too much neglected poem, had ere this attracted the admiration it so justly merits, had not the stearn critique of Dr. Johnson intervened to blast its rising fame. A juster relish of the excellences of poetry, and a more candid style of criticism, may be considered as a characteristic of several of the first literary men of the present day; and, but for the hard censure of the author of the Rambler, the pages of Dyer would now, perhaps, have been familiar to every lover and judge of nervous and highly finished description. As it is, however, they are seldom consulted, from an idea, that little worthy of applause would gratify the inquirer.—DRAKE, NATHAN, 1798–1820, *Literary Hours, vol.* I, *No.* xii, *p.* 160.

The witticism on his "Fleece," related by Dr. Johnson, that its author, if he was an old man, would be buried in wollen, has, perhaps, been oftener repeated than any passage in the poem itself.—CAMPBELL, THOMAS, 1819, *Specimens of the British Poets.*

There is a sluggishness in the general motion of the verse which has injured the popularity of the poem. Milton's blank verse is sometimes heavy, but whenever he gets great, his lines become wheels instinct with spirit, and they bicker and burn, to gain the expected goal. Thomson, too, in his higher moods, shakes off his habitual sleepiness, and you have the race of an elephant, if not the swiftness of an antelope. But Dyer, even when bright, is always slow, and, in this point, too, resembles Wordsworth, whose "Excursion" often glows, but never rushes, like a chariot wheel. On the whole, to recur to the figure of Gideon's Fleece, Dyer's poem is by turns very dry and very dewy; now very dark, and anon sparkling with genuine poetry. . . . On the whole, we think "the Fleece" rather an unfortunate subject for a poem, although the fact that Dyer has made so much of it, and won praise from even fastidious critics, is no slight evidence that he possessed a strong and vivid genius.—GILFILLAN, GEORGE, 1858, *ed., The Poetical Works of Armstrong, Dyer and Green, pp.* 113, 114.

GENERAL

Has more of poetry in his imagination than almost any of our number; but rough and injudicious.—GRAY, THOMAS, 1751, *Letter to Horace Walpole; Works, ed. Gosse, vol.* II, *p.* 220.

Though hasty Fame hath many a chaplet culled
For worthless brows, while in the pensive shade
Of cold neglect she leaves thy head ungraced,
Yet pure and powerful minds, hearts meek and still,
A grateful few, shall love thy modest Lay,
Long as the shepherd's bleating flock shall stray
O'er naked Snowdon's wide aërial waste;
Long as the thrush shall pipe on Grongar Hill!
—WORDSWORTH, WILLIAM, 1810–15, *To the Poet, John Dyer.*

Dyer's is a natural and true note, though not one of much power or compass. What he has written is his own; not borrowed from or suggested by "others' books," but what he has himself seen, thought, and felt. He sees, too, with an artistic eye, while at the same time his pictures are full of the moral inspiration which alone makes description poetry. —CRAIK, GEORGE L., 1861, *A Compendious History of English Literature and of the English Language, vol.* II, *p.* 276.

Is, or was, known as the author of "Grongar Hill" (1727), and "The Fleece" (1757). The latter is in blank verse, and totally worthless; the former, however, is a pretty poem of description and reflection, breathing that intoxicating sense of natural beauty which never fails to awaken in us some sympathy, and an answering feeling of reality.—ARNOLD, THOMAS, 1868–75, *Chaucer to Wordsworth*, *p.* 286.

Is not a painter who would constrain words to be the medium of his art; he is a poet. He has a heart that listens, an eye that loves; his landscape is full of living change, of tender incident, of the melody of breeze and bird and stream. . . . The farmer still collecting his scattered sheaves under the full-orbed harvest moon, the strong-armed rustic plunging in the flood an unshorn ewe, the carter on the dusty road beside his nodding wain, the maiden at her humming wheel, delight Dyer's imagination no more than do the Sheffield smiths near the glaring mass "clattering their heavy hammers down by turns," the builder, trowel in hand, at whose spell Manchester rises and spreads like Carthage before the eyes of Æneas, the keen-eyed factor inspecting his bales, the bending porter on the wharf where masts crowd thick. The poet's ancestors, as he is pleased to record in verse, were weavers, who, flying from the rage of superstition, brought the loom to

"that soft tract
Of Cambria, deep-embayed, Dimetian land,
By green hills fenced, by ocean's murmur
lull'd."

From them he obtained a goodly heritage—his love of freedom and his love of industry. He honoured traffic, the "friend to wedded love;" he honoured England for her independence and her mighty toil; America, for her vast possibilities of well-being. He pleaded against the horrors of the slave trade. He courted the favour of no lord. And, in an age of city poets, he found his inspiration on the hillside and by the stream.—DOWDEN, EDWARD, 1880, *English Poets, ed. Ward, vol.* III, *p.* 208.

Dyer's love of scenery at a period when the taste was out of fashion may give him some claim to remembrance. . . . Dyer's longer poems are now unreadable, though there is still some charm in "Grongar Hill" and some shorter pieces. He is probably best known by the sonnet addressed to him by Wordsworth.—STEPHEN, LESLIE, 1888, *Dictionary of National Biography, vol.* XVI, *p.* 287.

It seems odd that the extreme awkwardness of the opening lines of "Grongar Hill," and a certain grammatical laxity running through the work of Dyer, should have been treated with so much lenity by critic after critic. . . . Dyer's Welsh landscapes, with their yellow sun, purple groves, and pale blue distance, remind us of the simple drawings of the earliest English masters of water colour, and his precise mode of treating outdoor subjects, without pedantry, but with a cold succession of details, connects him with the lesser Augustans through Somerville. As the gentleman predicted, Dyer is buried in the "woolen" of his too-laborious "Fleece."—GOSSE, EDMUND, 1888, *A History of Eighteenth Century Literature.*

In an ease of composition which runs into laxity he reminds us occasionally of George Wither. His chief merit is, that while independent of Thomson, he was inspired by the same love, and wrote with the same aim. Dyer is not content with bare description, but likes to moralize on the landscape he surveys.—DENNIS, JOHN, 1894, *The Age of Pope*, *p.* 113.

Thomas Prince

1681–1758

A Congregational minister, pastor of the Old South Church in Boston, 1718–58, and one of the most fair-minded, accurate historical writers that America has had. His library now forms a separate collection in the Boston Public Library. "Earthquakes of New England" (1755); "Chronological History of New England."—ADAMS, OSCAR FAY, 1897, *A Dictionary of American Authors*, *p.* 304.

PERSONAL

The 22d of October [1758], will be remembered as a remarkable day in the history of the Town, and not only of Boston, but of New England; for on that day died the Rev. Mr. Thomas Prince, a benefactor of his country; leaving a name which will be venerated to the remotest ages, if literature shall then be valued; a name which may with pride be emulated by the inquirers after historical knowledge, and the admirers of precision and accuracy in the paths of history.—DRAKE, SAMUEL G., 1855, *History and Antiquities of Boston, p.* 646.

He was pronounced by Dr. Chauncy the most learned scholar, with the exception of Cotton Mather, in New England, and maintained a high reputation as a preacher, and as a devout and amiable man. Six of his manuscript sermons were published after his death, by Dr. John Erskine, of Edinburgh.—DUYCKINCK, EVERT A. AND GEORGE L., 1855–65–75, *Cyclopædia of American Literature, ed. Simons, vol.* I, *p.* 87.

That 22d of October was the Sabbath; the day on which his collection of Psalms and Hymns was used, for the first time, by his people. The lips of their beloved pastor were forever sealed; but they still had his life and spirit embalmed in those sacred poems, to be with them, guiding them and comforting them. In the twinkling of an eye, had he been changed; mortality had blossomed into immortality; his own sweetest thoughts awoke in music on the tongues of his weeping congregation, as he sank into that blessed sleep which Christ giveth to His beloved. The mystery of the two lives was made perfect by his departure, for he still praised God in the voices of the living, though gone to be a member of the choir of angels.—MANNING, J. M., 1859, *Thomas Prince, The Congregational Quarterly, vol.* I, *p.* 16.

He was a man of most tolerant and brotherly spirit; his days were filled by gentle and gracious and laborious deeds; he was a great scholar; he magnified his office and edified the brethren by publishing a large number of judicious and nutritious sermons; he also revised and improved the New England Psalm Book, "by an endeavor after a yet nearer approach to the inspired original, as well as to the rules of poetry;" he took a special interest in physical science, and formed quite definite opinions about earthquakes, comets, "the electrical substance," and so forth. For all these things, he was deeply honored in his own time, and would have been deeply forgotten in ours, had he not added to them very unique performances as an historian. No American writer before Thomas Prince, qualified himself for the service of history by so much conscious and specific preparation; and though others did more work in that service, none did better work than he. The foundation of his character as a historian was laid in reverence, not only for truth, but for precision, and in willingness to win it at any cost of labor and of time. He likewise felt the peculiar authority of originals in historical testimony, and the potential value, for historical illustration, of all written or printed materials whatsoever; and while he was yet a college-boy, driven by the sacred avarice of an antiquarian and a bibliographer, he began to gather that great library of early American documents, which kept growing upon his hands in magnitude and in wealth as long as his life lasted, and which, notwithstanding the ravages of the time, of British troops, of book-borrowers, and of book-thieves, still remains for him a barrier against oblivion, and for every student of early American thought and action, a copious treasurer-house of help.—TYLER, MOSES COIT, 1878, *A History of American Literature*, 1676–1765, *vol.* II, *p.* 144.

GENERAL

Some may think me rather too critical, others that I relate some circumstances too minute. As to the first, I think a Writer of Facts cannot be too critical: It is Exactness I aim at, and would not have the least mistake, if possible, pass to the World. . . . As to the Second, those Things which are too minute with Some, are not so with Others. . . . And there's none who attentively reads a History either ancient or modern, but in a great many Cases, wishes the Writer had mentioned some minute Circumstances, that were then commonly known, and thought too needless or small to be noted.—PRINCE, THOMAS, 1736, *A Chronological History of New England.*

The most important event of 1735, in this connection, was the issue of the first volume of the "Chronological History of New England." . . . The list of manuscript authorities to which he refers is indeed extensive and most valuable, and though several of them have since been printed, their publication does not detract from the worth of his labors in arranging them, or alter our appreciation of his honesty and exactness in transcribing them.

If we add to the work to be performed the necessity of examining the numerous letters and papers collected by him, and the chronological letters and registers sent to him by the various New England clergymen, we shall no longer wonder at the small number of theological tracts produced by him, but we shall feel surprised at the possibility of his paying any attention to all his clerical duties. In fact, without the strong impulse of a pious trust imposed upon him, he could hardly have written his history in the time he occupied upon it. . . . The work was too learned or too precise to suit the taste of the public, and the second volume, after a languishing life through three Parts, perished for want of patronage in 1755. Though the author had been so poorly appreciated, he had made very extensive preparations to continue his labors, and the cover of the last Part bore an Advertisement soliciting information from the public to enable him to render his book complete.—WHITMORE, W. H., 1860, *Life and Labors of Thomas Prince, North American Review, vol.* 91, *pp.* 368, 369, 371.

He was a devotee to historical accuracy, a knight-errant of precise and unadorned fact, an historical sceptic before the philosophy of historical scepticism was born.—TYLER, MOSES COIT, 1878, *A History of American Literature*, 1676–1765, *vol.* II, *p.* 146.

The author was a slow worker and a busy man; there was waiting for such work as his a real but not an enthusiastic nor a lasting welcome; and he apparently allowed his zeal to flag towards the close of his life. In what he did he displayed the internal qualities needed in an historian: painstaking care for accuracy, and a philosophic temper; and though his book is somewhat forbidding in form and lacking in beauty of style, it marked an improvement upon the slipshod work of Morton. Prince was the direct forerunner of the eminent list of Boston historians; his name is fitly commemorated by one of the historical societies of that city. —RICHARDSON, CHARLES F., 1887, *American Literature*, 1607–1885, *vol.* I, *p.* 114.

In his love of accuracy and original sources Prince belongs to the contemporary "erudite" school of historians, who all over Europe were amassing, with a painstaking and critical spirit that was new, vast stores of material for the rewriting of history.—BRONSON, WALTER C., 1900, *A Short History of American Literature, p.* 36, *note.*

Allan Ramsay

1686–1758

Born, at Leadhills, near Crawford, Lanarkshire, 15 Oct. 1686. Educated at village school at Crawford. Apprenticed to a wig-maker in Edinburgh, 1701. At conclusion of apprenticeship, set up in business. Married Christian Ross, 1712. Mem. of Jacobite "Essay Club," 1712–15. Prolific writer of occasional poetry. Started business as a bookseller, 1716 [?]. Drama, "The Gentle Shepherd," performed in Edinburgh, 1729. Built a theatre in Edinburgh, 1736; closed it 1737. Retired from business, 1755. Died, in Edinburgh, 7 Jan. 1758. Buried in Old Greyfriars Churchyard. *Works:* "The Battel" (anon.), 1716; "Tartana" [1717?]; "Scots Songs," 1718; "The Scriblers Lash'd," 1718; "Christ's Kirk on the Green," 1718; "Elegies on Maggie Johnson, John Cowper and Lucky Wood," 1718; "Content," 1720; "The Prospect of Plenty," 1720; "Robert, Richy and Sandy," 1721; "Poems" (2 vols.), 1721–28; "Fables and Tales," 1722; "A Tale of Three Bonnets" (anon.), 1722; "The Fair Assembly," 1723; "Health," 1724; "The Tea-Table Miscellany" (3 vols.), 1724-27; "The Ever Green" (2 vols.), 1724; "The Gentle Shepherd," 1725; "A Scots Ode to the British Antiquarians" [1726]; "New Miscellany of Scots Songs," 1727; "A Collection of Thirty Fables," 1730; "The Morning Interview," 1731; "An Address of Thanks from the Society of Rakes" (anon.), 1734; "Collection of Scots Proverbs," 1737; "Hardyknute," by Lady Wardlaw, completed by Ramsay, 1745; "The Vision" (anon.), 1748. *Collected Works:* in 3 vols., 1851. *Life:* by O. Smeaton, 1896.—SHARP, R. FARQUHARSON, 1897, *A Dictionary of English Authors, p.* 235.

JOHN GAY

From Painting by William Aikman.

ALLAN RAMSAY

Engraving by William Howison.
From Painting by William Aikman.

PERSONAL

The personal history of Allan Ramsay is marked by few circumstances of striking interest; yet, independently of his poetry, he cannot be reckoned an insignificant individual who gave Scotland her first circulating library, and who established her first regular theatre.—CAMPBELL, THOMAS, 1819, *Specimens of the British Poets.*

Allan Ramsay knew his friends Gay and Somerville as well in their writings, as he did when he came to be personally acquainted with them; but Allan, who had bustled up from a barber's shop into a bookseller's was "a cunning shaver;" and nobody would have guessed the author of the "Gentle Shepherd" to be penurious. —HUNT, LEIGH, 1850, *Autobiography.*

Allan Ramsay was not a man to be patronised; he had too good an opinion of himself; he was too contented with his lot in the world; and it can hardly be questioned that when he went to this or the other nobleman's house he considered the favour reciprocal and the obligation mutual. This frank jovial little man did not abate one whit of his dignity in any one's presence; and his good nature, his liberality of opinion, his ready palliation for other people's shortcomings, were something unusual at that time for one in his station, and served to render him a general favourite. — BLACK, WILLIAM, 1864, *A Poetical Barber, Once a Week, vol.* 11, *p.* 614.

He was one of the poets to whom, in a pecuniary point of view, poetry had been really a blessing, and who could combine poetic pursuits with those of an ordinary business. He possessed that turn of mind which Hume says it is more happy to possess than to be born to an estate of ten thousand a year—a disposition always to see the favourable side of things.— WILSON, JAMES GRANT, 1876, *The Poets and Poetry of Scotland, vol.* I, *p.* 104.

To the Castlehill Allan Ramsay retired in his later years, and there in the lodging built for himself on this novel Parnassus, he sported anew with the Muses to whom he had paid his devoirs in earlier years, sometimes in less prudent fashion. There in 1743 the "Poet's Nest" was built, which still stands surrounded by private garden and civic pleasure grounds, looking across the bed of the old Nor Loch on as magnificent a landscape and civic foreground as poet could desire. According to the tale told to me by Mr. Alexander Smellie,—the son of Burns's old cronie, author of "The Philosophy of Natural History,"—the poet applied to the Crown for a grant of as much land on the Castlehill as would suffice him to build a cage for his *burd, i. e.* his wife. On the site apportioned to him he erected the octagonal structure, still forming the centre of Ramsay Lodge, which, before it received its later additions, looked not unlike a large parrot's cage.—WILSON, DANIEL, 1878, *Reminiscences of Old Edinburgh, vol.* II, *p.* 130.

At fifteen, he stood alone in the world, an orphan in a strange city, friendless and penniless, entirely dependent for the means of earning a livelihood on the prospect of being wig-weaver. He gradually raised himself to a position of honour and wealth, became the associate and friend of some of the most eminent men in his neighbourhood, and the correspondent of several of the leading literary men of his time, gave his son a costly training in art both at home and abroad, and left his children well-provided in an easy independency. His enterprise is another feature of his conduct. He abandoned the trade to which he had been bred, and by which he was securing an independency, for one of which he had little but an onlooker's knowledge, and found without assistance his advantage in the exchange. Then he was the first to introduce that system of lending out books which is now known as the Circulating Library. He was further the first person to erect a house in Edinburgh for dramatic representations, and though the undertaking failed, and almost ruined him, it failed only through the bigotry and timidity of the city rulers. If the house had been licensed there is no doubt that it would have been both a profitable venture and a liberalising agency.—ROBERTSON, J. LOGIE, 1886, *ed., Poems by Allan Ramsay* (*Canterbury Poets*), *Biographical Introduction, p.* xlvii.

Allan Ramsay is believed to lie under a birch-tree almost in front of the tablet to his memory, on the south side of the Greyfriars' Church, although there is no stone to mark his grave.—HUTTON, LAURENCE,

1891, *Literary Landmarks of Edinburgh, p.* 30.

Perhaps as good an idea as any, of the personal appearance of the poet, is to be got from his statue by Sir John Steel which stands close by the monument to Scott in Princes Street Gardens; but references to his short, active figure, his round humourous face, dark twinkling eyes, and mouth ever ready with a merry epigram, live in all the Edinburgh reminiscences of his time. Of all the great personages, indeed, who at that day came and went on the plainstones of Edinburgh, none is remembered more pleasantly and affectionately than the genial bookseller-poet.—EYRE-TODD, GEORGE, 1896, *Scottish Poetry of the Eighteenth Century, vol.* I, *p.* 40.

Existing portraits, including the one most valued for its fidelity to the original, that by his son, Allan Ramsay, the artist (Portrait-painter in Ordinary to King George III.), show him to have possessed features that were delicate and sharply chiselled, keen dark eyes, a mobile, sensitive mouth, a complexion dark almost to swarthiness, and a high rounded forehead. To these items may be added those others coming as side-lights, thrown on a man's character and individuality by the passing references of contemporaries. From such sources we learn that his face was one whereon were writ large, contentment with himself and with the world, as well as a certain pawky shrewdness and unaffected *bonhomie.* This expression was largely induced by the twinkling of his beadlike eyes, and the lines of his mouth, which curved upwards at the corners; almost imperceptibly, it is true, yet sufficiently to flash into his countenance that subtle element of humourous *canniness* which has been accepted by many as the prime attribute of his character. . . . His figure was thickset, but had not as yet acquired the squatness of later days. If in the years to come he grew to resemble George Eliot's portrait of Mr. Casson, when the inevitable penalty of sedentariness and good living has to be paid in increasing corpulence, he never lost his tripping gait which in early manhood earned for him the *sobriquet* of "Denty Allan." In deportment and dress he was "easy, trig and neat," leaning a little to vanity's side in his manners, yet nathless as honourable, sound-hearted, clean-souled a gentleman as any that lounged around Edinburgh Cross of a sunny Saturday afternoon. Such was the youth that presented himself to bonny Kirsty Ross at her father's tea-table. . . . His lovableness and generosity notwithstanding, Ramsay's vanity and self-complacency meets us at every turn. To omit mentioning it would be to present an unfaithful portrait of the honest poet. On the other hand, justice compels one to state that, if vain, he was neither jealous nor ungenerous. He was always ready to recognise the merits of others, and his egoism was not selfishness. Though he might not care to deny himself to his own despite for the good of others, he was perfectly ready to assist his neighbour when his own and his family's needs had been satisfied.—SMEATON, OLIPHANT, 1896, *Allan Ramsay* (*Famous Scots Series*), *pp.* 12, 62.

FABLES AND TALES
1722

"The Monk and the Miller's Wife" would of itself be his passport to immortality as a comic poet. In this capacity he might enter the lists with Chaucer and Boccacio with no great risk of discomfiture. Though far their inferior in acquired address, his native strength was perhaps not widely disproportionate. . . . A story of more festive humour could not have been devised. The characters are sustained with consummate propriety; the manners are true to nature; and poetic justice is not strictly observed in the winding up of the piece.—TYTLER, ALEXANDER FRASER (LORD WOODHOUSELEE), 1800, *Remarks on the Genius and Writings of Allan Ramsay, pp.* lxxii, lxxiii.

THE TEA-TABLE MISCELLANY
1724–27

The object of "The Tea Table Miscellany" was to please the public, not to instruct the inquirer into the history of Scottish songs; and all who have ever handled it with a historical object in view have had in consequence to lament the vagueness and meagerness of the information supplied. Nothing is told but the bare fact that a song is old, old with additions, or new—sometimes not so much as that. In what way recovered, or how old, or on what ground it was believed to be old, are questions to which there is no answer in Ramsay. He cannot however be blamed for not accomplishing what he never attempted, or for being blind to that which none of his contemporaries perceived. "The Tea Table Miscellany," faulty as it is from the point of view of literary history, was and long remained without rival as a collection of Scottish songs; and it has preserved much that otherwise would probably have been lost. The success of Ramsay too, encouraging others, like Oswald and Thomson, to labour in the same field, led indirectly to the recovery and preservation of other pieces.—WALKER, HUGH, 1893, *Three Centuries of Scottish Literature, vol.* II, *p.* 6.

THE EVERGREEN
1724

But the first editor who seems to have made a determined effort to preserve our ancient popular poetry was the well-known Allan Ramsay, in his Evergreen, containing chiefly extracts from the ancient Scottish Makers, whose poems have been preserved in the Bannatyne Manuscript, but exhibiting amongst them some popular ballads.—SCOTT, SIR WALTER, 1802–3, *ed., Minstrelsy of the Scottish Border, Introductory Remarks on Popular Poetry.*

But for the publication of the "Evergreen," the world might never have learnt to doubt the veracity of Allan Ramsay. On the other hand, had the "Evergreen" not come down to us, the "Vision"—its principal attraction—would have been wanting, and the poet would have lost one of the noblest of his laurels. It is better, perhaps, as it is. At any rate it is certain, that what Ramsay has lost in character, he has gained in poetic fame. The world deals mercifully with literary frauds, the more so, perhaps, as the world is likely to be a gainer by them. On the other hand, who does not feel for those gentlemen who spent years of their lives in fruitless researches, all because a Ramsay would not own that he was the author of the "Vision," or a Chatterton that he wrote the "Rowley Manuscripts"? Perhaps the less we say on the matter the better for our author, who certainly deserves enough at our hands to be spared any unnecessary reproaches. There are spots on the sun; our author was not without his. His gravest fault was that he was a dishonest editor. We must not forget, however, that he wrote one of the finest pastorals in any language and that the authorship of the "Gentle Shepherd" is a passport to immortality as good as any that has been signed of late years.—MACKAY, CHARLES, 1870, *ed., The Poetical Works of Allan Ramsay, Life, p.* iv.

THE GENTLE SHEPHERD
1725

I spoke of Allan Ramsay's "Gentle Shepherd," in the Scottish dialect, as the best pastoral that had ever been written; not only abounding with beautiful rural imagery, and just and pleasing sentiments, but being a real picture of manners; and I offered to teach Dr. Johnson to understand it. "No, sir," said he; "I won't learn it. You shall retain your superiority by my not knowing it."—JOHNSON, SAMUEL, 1773, *Life by Boswell.*

The greater part of Ramsay's "Gentle Shepherd" is written in a broad Scotch dialect. The sentiments of that piece are natural, the circumstances interesting; the characters well drawn, well distinguished, and well contrasted; and the fable has more probability than any other pastoral drama I am acquainted with. To an Englishman, who had never conversed with the common people of Scotland, the language would appear only antiquated, obscure, or unintelligible; but to a Scotchman who thoroughly understands it, and is aware of its vulgarity, it appears *ludicrous;* from the contrast between *meanness* of phrase, and *dignity* or *seriousness* of sentiment. This gives a farcical air even to the most affecting parts of the poem; and occasions an impropriety of a peculiar kind, which is very observable in the representation. And accordingly, this play, with all its merit, and with a strong national partiality in its favour, has never given general satisfaction upon the stage. — BEATTIE, JAMES, 1776–9, *On Laughter and Ludicrous Composition, Essays on Poetry and Music, p.* 382.

It is a great disadvantage to this beautiful poem, that it is written in the old rustic dialect of Scotland, which, in a short time, will probably be entirely obsolete, and not intelligible; and it is a farther disadvantage, that it is so entirely informed on the rural manners of Scotland, that none but a native of that country can thoroughly understand or relish it. But, though subject to those local disadvantages, which confine its reputation within narrow limits, it is full of so much natural description, and tender sentiment, as would do honour to any poet. The characters are well drawn, the incidents affecting, the scenery and manners lively and just. It affords a strong proof, both of the power which nature and simplicity possess, to reach the heart in every sort of writing; and of the variety of pleasing characters and subjects, with which pastoral poetry, when properly managed, is capable of being enlivened.—BLAIR, HUGH, 1783, *Lectures on Rhetoric and Belles-Lettres, ed. Mills, Lecture* xxxix.

Exhibited rusticity without vulgarity, and elegant sentiment without affectation. —ROSCOE, WILLIAM, 1795, *Life of Lorenzo de 'Medici.*

One of the finest pastoral comedies in any language; and which could have been only produced by art, co-operating with genius, in a propitious moment for shepherdish poetry. — CHALMERS, GEORGE, 1800, *ed., The Poems of Allan Ramsay, Life, vol.* I, *p.* xxvii.

To every Englishman, and, I trust, to every Scotsman not of fastitidous refinement, the dialect of the "Gentle Shepherd" will appear to be most perfectly consonant to the characters of the speakers and the times in which the action is laid. To this latter circumstance the critics I have just mentioned seem not to have been sufficiently attentive. The language of this pastoral is not precisely the Scotish language of the present day: the poet himself spoke the language of the beginning of the century, and his persons were of the age preceding that period. To us their dialect is an antiquated tongue, and, as such, it carries with it a Doric simplicity. But when we consider both the characters and the times, it has an indispensable propriety; and to have given the speakers in the "Gentle Shepherd" a more refined and polished dialect, or more modern tone of conversation, would have been a gross violation of truth and nature. —TYTLER, ALEXANDER FRASER (LORD WOODHOUSELEE), 1800, *Remarks on the Genius and Writings of Allan Ramsay, p.* c.

The Gentle Shepherd stands quite apart from the general pastoral poetry of modern Europe. It has no satyrs, no featureless simpletons, nor drowsy and still landscapes of nature, but distinct characters and amusing incidents. The principal shepherd never speaks out of consistency with the habits of a peasant; but he moves in that sphere with such a manly spirit, with so much cheerful sensibility to its humble joys, with maxims of life so rational and independent, and with an ascendancy over his fellow swains so well maintained by his force of character, that if we could suppose the pacific scenes of the drama to be suddenly changed into situations of trouble and danger, we should, in exact consistency with our former idea of him, expect him to become the leader of the peasants, and the Tell of his native hamlet. Nor is the character of his mistress less beautifully conceived. She is represented, like himself, as elevated, by a fortunate discovery, from obscure to opulent life, yet as equally capable of being the ornament of either. A Richardson or a D'Arblay, had they continued her history, might have heightened the portrait, but they would not have altered its outline. Like the poetry of Tasso and Ariosto, that of the "Gentle Shepherd" is engraved on the memory of its native country. Its verses have passed into proverbs; and it continues to be the delight and solace of the peasantry whom it describes.—CAMPBELL, THOMAS, 1819, *Specimens of the British Poets.*

Shepherd. I hae some thocht o' writing a play—a Pastoral Drama.

North. What, James! after Allan Ramsay—after the "Gentle Shepherd?"

Shepherd. What for no? That's a stupid apophthegm, though you said it. I wad hae mair variety o' characters, and inceedents, and passions o' the human mind in my drama—mair fun, and frolic, and daffin—in short, mair o' what you, and the like o' you, ca' coorseness;—no sae muckle see-sawing between ony twa individual hizzies, as in Allan; and, aboon a' things, a mair natural and wise-like catastrophe. My peasant or shepherd lads should be sae in richt earnest, and no turn out Sirs and Lords upon you at the hinder end o' the drama. No but that I wad aiblins introduce the upper ranks intil the wark; but they should stand abeigh frae the lave of the characters,—by way o' contrast, or by way o' "similitude in dissimilitude," as that haverer Wordsworth is sae fond o' talking and writing about. Aboon a' things, I wus to draw the pictur o' a perfect and polished Scotch gentleman o' the auld schule.—WILSON, JOHN, 1825, *Noctes Ambrosianæ, ed. Mackenzie, vol.* II, *p.* 60.

One of the most remarkable and truly national Scottish poets is Allan Ramsay, whose "Gentle Shepherd" is perhaps the only modern pastoral which can be compared to the exquisite creations of Theocritus. It is the first successful solution of that difficult problem, to represent rustic manners as they really are, and at the same time so as to make them attractive and graceful. The difficulty of the task will best be appreciated by reflecting on the innumerable failures, from Virgil down to Shenstone, which crowd the annals of literature. But the rustic pictures of Allan Ramsay breathe the freshness of real country life—they have an atmosphere of nature, the breezy freshness of the fields; he has revived the magic of Theocritus, and given us a glimpse into the interior life of the real shepherds, with their artless vigour and unsophisticated feelings.—SHAW, THOMAS B., 1847, *Outlines of English Literature, p.* 313.

Allan Ramsay is the prince of the homely pastoral drama. . . . Allan Ramsay is not only entitled to the designation we have given him, but in some respects is the best pastoral writer in the world. . . . Allan Ramsay's poem is not only a probable and pleasing story, containing charming pictures, much knowledge of life, and a good deal of quiet humour, but in some respects it may be called classical, if by classical is meant ease, precision, and unsuperfluousness of style. Ramsay's diction is singularly straightforward, seldom needing the assistance of inversions; and he rarely says anything for the purpose of "filling up;"—two freedoms from defect the reverse of vulgar and commonplace; nay, the reverse of a great deal of what pretends to be fine writing, and is received as such. We confess we never tire of dipping into it, "on and off," any more than into Fletcher, or Milton, or into Theocritus himself, who, for the union of something higher with true pastoral, is unrivalled in short pieces. The "Gentle Shepherd" is not a forest, nor a mountainside, nor Arcady; but it is a field full of daisies, with a brook in it, and a cottage "at the sunny end;" and this we take to be no mean thing, either in the real or the ideal world. Our Jar of Honey may well lie for a few moments among its heather, albeit filled from Hybla. There are bees, "look you," in Habbie's How. Theocritus and Allan shake hands over a shepherd's pipe.—HUNT, LEIGH, 1848, *A Jar of Honey from Mount Hybla, ch.* viii.

Allan Ramsay's pastoral play of "The Gentle Shepherd" deserves Hogg's censure, for it has the fault of being in rhyme, which is not the language of common, to say nothing of pastoral, life. The *dénouement*, accurately described in the text, is forced and unnatural. He scarcely merits the title of "the Scottish Theocritus."—MACKENZIE, R. SHELTON, 1854, *ed., Noctes Ambrosianæ, vol.* II, *p.* 61, *note.*

The finest existing specimen of its class.—COLLIER, WILLIAM FRANCIS, 1861, *A History of English Literature, p.* 290.

Any one at all acquainted with the literature of the age in which Ramsay lived, is, on reading for the first time "The Gentle Shepherd," at once struck with its peculiar freshness and naturalness: summer breezes seem to be rushing through its pages, scented with odours of bean-blossom and clover. His pictures of country scenery are most life-like and pleasing; his characters talk frankly and openly, without set forms of speech, and without that coarseness which so frequently disfigures the writings of contemporary authors. An excellent piece of dramatic composition, "The Gentle Shepherd" is also a thoroughly genial and satisfactory book for the fire-side, or for a summer afternoon's ramble; the Scotticisms with which it abounds give it an air of quaintness, and rarely obscure the text even for southern readers; while there is throughout a healthy, cheerful tone, refreshing as the blowing of July winds.—BLACK, WILLIAM, 1864, *A Poetical Barber, Once a Week, vol.* 11, *p.* 615.

The feelings of our age may be now and then offended by a freedom of speech that borders on coarseness, but that the texture of the poem is stirring and human hearted is proved by the hold it still retains on the Scottish peasantry. If here and there a false note mars the truth of the human manners, as when Scotch Lowland shepherds talk of playing on reeds and flutes, the scenery of "The Gentle Shepherd" is true to Nature as it is among the Pentland Hills.—SHAIRP, JOHN CAMPBELL, 1877, *On Poetic Interpretation of Nature, p.* 195.

With genuine freshness and humour, but without a trace of burlesque, transferred to the scenery of the Pentland Hills the lovely tale of Florizel and Perdita. The dramatic form of this poem is only an accident, but it doubtless suggested an experiment of a different kind to the most playful of London wits.—WARD, ADOLPHUS WILLIAM, 1877, *Drama, Encyclopædia Britannica, vol.* VII.

Though it now reads like a conventional drama, seemed like a breath of fresh air to those who first read it. All the wits of the time admired it, and justly.—PERRY, THOMAS SERGEANT, 1883, *English Literature in the Eighteenth Century, p.* 389.

In his creations the people recognised themselves, and the scenes amid which they moved—their every-day life, their loves, their aspirations were all mirrored in its pages. Their emulation was roused, and Patie and Peggy have lived as an ideal hero and heroine in the minds of many a Scottish lad and lass. It must be remembered that "The Gentle Shepherd" does not pretend to convey any exalted philosophy of life or morals. It is purely and simply a love story, and its "summons" to lads and lasses to "pu' the gowan in its prime" is no more "pagan" than similar advice given in higher quarters. There are, of course, some suggestions of coarseness in it; it would not be the graphic portraiture of peasant life of the eighteenth century that it is, if there were not; but for the time at which it was written it is singularly free from such blemishes, and its teaching is on the side of contentment and virtue.—TULLOCH, W. W., 1886, *Allan Ramsay and "The Gentle Shepherd," Good Words, vol.* 27, *p.* 678.

Even Burns had not the universal acceptance, the absolute command of his audience, which belonged to honest Allan. There were politicians and there were ecclesiastics, and good people neither one nor the other, who shook their troubled heads over the ploughman who would not confine himself to the daisy of the field or the Saturday night's observances of the Cottar, but was capable of Holy Willie and the Holy Fair. But Ramsay had no gainsayer, and "The Gentle Shepherd" was the first of books in most Lowland homes. Its construction, its language and sentiments, are all as commonplace as could be imagined, but it is a wholesome, natural, pure, and unvarnished tale, and the mind that brought it forth (well aware of what pleased his public) and the public who relished and bought it, give us a better view of the honest tastes and morals of the period than anything else which has come to us from that time. There has always been a good deal of drinking, and other vices still less consistent with purity of heart, in Scotland. Now and then we are frightened by statistics that give us a very ill name; but it is difficult to believe that if the national heart had been corrupt "The Gentle Shepherd" could have afforded it such universal and wholesome delight.—OLIPHANT, MRS. MARGARET O. W., 1890, *Royal Edinburgh, p.* 459.

"The Gentle Shepherd" is the work of a poet, and gives a higher impression of Ramsay's power than his songs alone would warrant.—DENNIS, JOHN, 1894, *The Age of Pope, p.* 121.

Kindled by the theories and the practice of the English wits and poets, Allan Ramsay wrote real pastoral poetry, exhibiting the customs, the dress, the games, the domestic sorrows, the loves, and the lives of real shepherds. And the "Gentle Shepherd" awoke the genius of Burns. —MINTO, WILLIAM, 1894, *The Literature of the Georgian Era, ed. Knight, p.* 31.

Deserves praise rather for the intention than for the performance of his "Gentle Shepherd." A very few lines of genuine Scotch landscape are here placed among conventional and uninteresting dialogue; like his songs, his Pastoral does not rise above the trite half-classical phrases from which Burns could not always detach himself.—PALGRAVE, FRANCIS TURNER, 1896, *Landscape in Poetry, p.* 169.

To the fact that Ramsay has painted Scotland and Scottish rustics as they are, and has not gone to the hermaphrodite and sexless inhabitants of a mythical Golden Age for the characters of his great drama, the heart of every Scot can bear testimony. Neither Burns, supreme though his genius was over his predecessors, nor Scott, revelling as he did in patriotic sentiments as his dearest possession, can rival Ramsay in the absolute truth wherewith he has painted Scottish rustic life. He is at one and the same time the Teniers and the Claude of Scottish pastoral—the Teniers, in catching with subtle sympathetic insight the precise "moments" and incidents in the life of his characters most suitable for representation; the Claude, for the almost photographic truth of his reproductions of Scottish scenery.—SMEATON, OLIPHANT, 1896, *Allan Ramsay.*

It is better adapted for the study than for the stage, in large measure because ideal actors for it are simply impossible. The action is slow and languid, and the interest aroused is mainly sentimental. At first it was without songs, and the lyrics afterwards interspersed are not brilliant. The poem is remarkable for its quick and subtle appreciation of rural scenery, customs, and characters; and, if the plot is slightly artificial, the development is skilful and satisfactory. In its honest, straightforward appreciation of beauty in nature and character, and its fascinating presentation of homely customs, it will bear comparison with its author's Italian models, or with similar efforts of Gay.—BAYNE, THOMAS, 1896, *Dictionary of National Biography, vol.* XLVII, *p.* 231.

GENERAL

Hail, Caledonian bard! whose rural strains
Delight the listening hills, and cheer the
    plains!
Already polished by some hand divine,
Thy purer ore what furnace can refine?
. . . .
To follow Nature is by rules to write,
She led the way and taught the Stagirite.
. . . .
By the same guide instructed how to soar,
Allan is now what Homer was before.
—SOMERVILLE, WILLIAM, 1718? *To Allan Ramsay.*

O fam'd and celebrated Allan!
Renowned Ramsay! canty callan!
There's nowther Highlandman nor Lawlan,
    In poetrie,
But may as soon ding doun Tantallan
    As match wi' thee,
For ten times ten, and that's a hunder,
I ha'e been made to gaze and wonder,
When frae Parnassus thou didst thunder
    Wi' wit and skill;
Wherefore I'll soberly knock under,
    And quat my quill.

Of poetry the hail quintessence
Thou hast suck'd up, left nae excrescence
To petty poets, or sic messens,
    Tho' round thy stool
They may pick crumbs, and lear some lessons
    At Ramsay's school.
—HAMILTON, WILLIAM, 1719, *Epistle to Allan Ramsay.*

Ramsay was a man of strong natural parts, and a fine poetical genius, of which his celebrated pastoral, "The Gentle Shepherd," will ever retain a substantial monument; and though some of his songs may be deformed by far-fetched allusions and pitiful conceits, "The Lass of Peattie's Mill," "The Yellow-Hair'd Laddie," "Fairwell to Lochabar," and some others, must be allowed equal to any, and even superior, in point of pastoral simplicity, to most lyric productions, either in the Scotish or any other language. As an editor, he is, perhaps, reprehensible, not only on account of the liberties he appears to have taken with many of the earlier pieces he published, in printing them with additions, which one is unable to distinguish, but also for preferring songs written by himself, or the "ingenious young gentlemen" who assisted him, to ancient and original words, which would, in many cases, all circumstances considered, have been probably superior, or, at least, much more curious, and which are now irretrievable. In short, Ramsay would seem to have had too high an opinion of his own poetry, to be a diligent or faithful publisher of any other person's.
—RITSON, JOSEPH, 1794, *Scotish Songs.*

Thou paints auld Nature to the nines,
In thy sweet Caledonian lines;
Nae gowden stream thro' myrtles twines,
    Where Philomel,
While nightly breezes sweep the vines,
    Her griefs will tell;
In gowany glens thy burnie strays,
Where bonnie lasses bleach their claes;
Or trots by hazelly shaws and braes,
    Wi' hawthorns gray,
Where blackbirds join the shepherd's lays,
    At close o' day.
Thy rural loves are nature's sel';
Nae bombast spates o' nonsense swell;
Nae snap conceits, but that sweet spell
    O' witchin' love,
That charm that can the strongest quell,
    The sternest move.
—BURNS, ROBERT? 1796? *Poem on Pastoral Poetry.*

Green be the pillow of honest Allan, at

whose lamp Burns lighted his brilliant torch.—SCOTT, SIR WALTER, 1802-3, *ed., Minstrelsy of the Scottish Border, Introductory Remarks on Popular Poetry.*

Ramsay, to be sure, is ideal enough; but there are good ideas and bad ideas. To be snatched from the commonplaces of life that one might "ride on the curl'd clouds," or penetrate the solitudes of a poet's imagination, is good; but it is not so to leave the busy facts of society merely to get on the platitude of a barren tableland. Out of a proper reverence to my master's opinion, I have looked again and again at the "Gentle Shepherd," and I am so unfortunate as to think it the flattest rubbish I ever read. "Prove and Love" in plenty. Take any one page of Browne's "Pastorals," or Jonson's "Shepherd," or Fletcher's "Shepherdess"—see the fancy, the imagination, the exquisite truth of landscape painting; and then browze on the insipid leaves of the Scotch bookseller if you can.—OLLIER, CHARLES, 1844, *Correspondence of Leigh Hunt, vol.* II, *p.* 66.

The simple tenderness of Crawford, the fidelity of Ramsay, and the careless humor of Fergusson.—PRESCOTT, WILLIAM HICKLING, 1826, *Scottish Song, Biographical and Critical Miscellanies.*

It is hardly possible to ignore the fact that Allan Ramsay is by no means so highly esteemed at present as he was in the eighteenth century. The greater brilliancy of Burns has thrown his glory into the shade. He is no longer, as he was a hundred and fifty years ago, the national poet of Scotland. Many good and true Scotsmen know little about him but his name; and scholars south of the Tweed think it quite sufficient to have dipped into his *chef-d'œuvre* with the assistance of a dictionary. But Allan Ramsay has become, if not a popular, at any rate a classic author, and no student of literature can be said to have fairly finished his education who has not read the "Gentle Shepherd."—MACKEY, CHARLES, 1870, *ed., The Poetical Works of Allan Ramsay, Life, p.* i.

After Milton died (1674), rural life and Nature, for more than half a century, disappeared from English poetry. . . . It was in the Scottish poet, Allan Ramsay that the sense of natural beauty first reappeared. Since his day Nature, which, even when felt and described in earlier English poetry, had held a place altogether subordinate to man, has more and more claimed to be regarded in poetry as almost coequal with man.—SHAIRP, JOHN CAMPBELL, 1877, *On Poetic Interpretation of Nature, pp.* 192, 194.

It is as a painter of manners with keen, sly, humorous observation, and not as a lyrist, that Ramsay deserves to be remembered. We can well understand Hogarth's admiration for him. His elegies on *Maggie Johnstone* and *Lucky Wood*, and his anticipation of the "Road to Ruin" in the "Three Bonnets" were after Hogarth's own heart. But the life that he painted in the Scotch capital as he saw it with his twinkling eye, broad sense of fun, and "pawky" humour, was too coarse to have much interest for any but his own time. In a happy hour for his memory, he conceived the idea of describing the life which he had known in his youth in the country. —MINTO, WILLIAM, 1880, *The English Poets, ed. Ward, vol.* III, *p.* 161.

Ramsay created his own audience, and it is wonderful how rapidly it grew and how widely it extended. There is scarcely any better proof of the accuracy and piquancy of his descriptions, and the thoroughly representative and national character of his sentiments and language, than is afforded by this undeniable fact. It is true there was a small reading public to welcome such a collection as Watson's, and to form such a nucleus as a new and original genius might successfully utilise. But it is just as true that he had no such audience as was waiting in Edinburgh for Fergusson, and in lowland Scotland for Burns. These later singers were indebted to him for several advantages, not the least of which was an audience already familiarised with that freedom of subject and sentiment in which both of them, though in unequal degrees, excelled.—ROBERTSON, J. LOGIE, 1886, *ed., Poems by Allan Ramsay (Canterbury Poets), Biographical Introduction, p.* xxxiii.

He gave up the outside of the head for the inside, by becoming a bookseller and a publisher. . . . Most of Ramsay's original songs were poor, but he preserved the habit of writing in the Doric dialect, and as an editor and collector of national poetry he did thoroughly efficient and valuable work.—GOSSE, EDMUND, 1888,

A History of Eighteenth Century Literature, p. 139.

He is really one of the most remarkable figures in the early history of Romanticism. In both his creative and critical work, he threw his influence decidedly against the age. He brought before the public some thoroughly Romantic poetry, and stands as one of the pioneers among ballad collectors. — PHELPS, WILLIAM LYON, 1893, *The Beginnings of the English Romantic Movement, p.* 126.

For any trace of the inevitable in his verse the reader will look in vain. The higher imagination was a gift denied to him; yet with comparatively commonplace powers he exercised an influence which many men far more richly endowed have vainly striven to attain. It is to this, fully as much as to the intrinsic worth of his verse, considerable as its merit often is, that he owes his interest. . . . He had predecessors, indeed he was so little of an original genius that he would probably never have written had there not been a popular demand for the kind of verse he supplied. The language of political economy is well applied to it, for there never was a clearer case in literature of the operation of economic laws. But except Ramsay, there was no one who displayed any sustained capacity to furnish what was wanted.—WALKER, HUGH, 1893, *Three Centuries of Scottish Literature, vol.* II, *pp.* 9, 24.

No Scottish poet, probably, has been subjected at once to praise so much beyond his merits and to distract so grossly unjust to his deserts, as Allan Ramsay. While by some it has been averred that he was merely a time-serving manufacturer of verse, who wrote what would sell, by others he had been extolled as not only the first but as one of the greatest of the singers of a new era. Burns himself spoke of Ramsay's "Gentle Shepherd" as the "most glorious poem ever written." Neither the eulogy nor the disparagement perhaps has been exactly just; but if indeed, as has been said of him, he appears to some to have been less a poet born than one made by circumstances, it must also at least be said that by what he did for the muse of his country he merits a place in Scottish poetic history little behind that of the greatest makers, Barbour, Henryson, Dunbar, Lyndsay, and Burns.—EYRE-TODD, GEORGE, 1896, *Scottish Poetry of the Eighteenth Century, vol.* I, *p.* 38.

The characteristic touch of humour blended with romance, that formed its most distinctive feature, was preserved with a certain freshness and verve, by the individuality of Ramsay, and his sympathy with the realities of life and with nature made him keep in touch with what was the most valuable inheritance of Scottish song. His geniality won for him the favour of the leading spirits of the nation. His revival of the older forms harmonised not with the taste only, but with the deeper feelings of his day; and whatever the limitations of his genius, the author of the "Gentle Shepherd" claims the profound gratitude of his nation as one who transmitted a tradition, and who passed on the torch through the hands of Robert Fergusson to the more powerful arm and more commanding genius of Burns.—CRAIK, SIR HENRY, 1901, *A Century of Scottish History, vol.* II, *p.* 32.

Sir Charles Hanbury Williams

1708-1759.

Sir Charles Hanbury Williams, third son of John Hanbury (the son added Williams to his name in compliance with the will of his godfather, Charles Williams, Esq., of Caerleon), was born in 1709, and educated at Eton; married to Lady Frances Coningsby, 1732; M. P. for Monmouth, 1733, and became a hearty supporter of Sir Robert Walpole, aiding him by his lampoons and pasquinades on his enemies as well as by his votes; Paymaster of the Marines, 1739; in 1746 made Knight of the Bath, and soon afterwards appointed Envoy to the Court of Dresden; minister at Berlin from 1749 to 1751, when he returned to Dresden; subsequently minister of St. Petersburg, where his eventual want of success and habits of dissipation reduced him to a wreck both in mind and body; died, it was supposed by his own hand, Nov. 2, 1759. He was the author of No. 3 of *The World.* 1. "The Odes of Sir Charles Hanbury Williams, Knight of the Bath," (edited by J. Ritson), 1755, 1780, 1784. 2. "Poems by

C. H. Williams, 1763. 3. "The Works of the Right Honourable Sir Charles Hanbury Williams, K. B., from the Originals in the Possession of his Grandson, the Earl of Essex, with Notes by Horace Walpole, Earl of Orford, London, Ed. Jeffery," 1822, 3 vols. The falsehoods of the title-page and preface, and subsequent apology of the publisher, are noticed in London Quarterly Review, xxvii.—ALLIBONE, S. AUSTIN, 1871, *A Critical Dictionary of English Literature, vol.* III, *p.* 2735.

PERSONAL

I enquired after my old acquaintance Sir Charles Williams, who I hear is much broken, both in his spirits and constitution. How happy might that man have been, if there had been added to his natural and acquired endowments a dash of morality: If he had known how to distinguish between false and true felicity; and, instead of seeking to increase an estate already too large, and hunting after pleasures that have made him rotten and ridiculous, he had bounded his desires of wealth, and followed the dictates of his conscience. His servile ambition has gained him two yards of red ribbon, and an exile into a miserable country, where there is no society and so little taste that I believe he suffers under a dearth of flatterers. This is said for the use of your growing sons, whom I hope no golden temptations will induce to marry women they can not love, or comply with measures they do not approve.—MONTAGU, LADY MARY WORTLEY, 1758, *Letter to the Countess of Bute, July* 17.

He goes about again: but the world, especially a world of enemies, never care to give up their title to a man's madness, and will consequently not believe that he is yet in his senses.—WALPOLE, HORACE, 1758, *Letter to Sir Horace Mann, Apr.* 14; *Letters, ed. Cunningham, vol.* III, *p.* 132.

GENERAL

He spoke contemptuously of our lively and elegant, though too licentious, Lyrick bard, Hanbury Williams, and said, "he had no fame, but from boys who drank with him."—JOHNSON, SAMUEL, 1773, *Life by Boswell, Sept.* 24, *ed. Hill, vol.* V, *p.* 305.

His verses were highly prized by his contemporaries, and the letters of his friend Mr. Fox (the first Lord Holland), abound with extravagant commendations of his poetical talents; but in perusing those which have been given to the public, and those which are still in manuscript, the greater part are political effusions, or *licentious lampoons*, abounding with local wit and temporary satire, eagerly read at their appearance, but little interesting to posterity.—COXE, WILLIAM, 1801, *History of Monmouth, vol.* II, *p.* 279.

It's with great pleasure I beg your acceptance of Sir Charles Hanbury Williams' works. . . . How pious, how canting and insincere people are become! I know it will give you great pleasure in hearing his Majesty has ordered one; three of the Cabinet Ministers have purchased copies; the Earl of Lonsdale six copies; also many great ladies, which shows their great sense. There are much more indecent poems in Pope and Prior.—JEFFERY, EDWARD, 1822, *Letter to Mr. Upcot.*

We . . . are ready to make some allowances for Sir Charles Hanbury Williams, and although his pieces are, as we have said, the grossest ever *published*, they probably are not much grosser than many others which were *circulated* in his day; and his reputation now stands so disgracefully distinguished rather through the indiscretion and effrontery of his publishers than through any superior wickedness of his own. We should have thought a new edition of his works not only pardonable, but laudable and useful, if it had been made the opportunity of separating his better from his worse productions, and consigning the latter to obscurity and oblivion. It may not be even now too late. Some of Sir Charles' verses must live; they are not merely witty and gay, but they are the best examples of a particular class of poetry, and are not without their importance in the history of social manners and political parties. We wish that they were collected into a volume, which one could open without being shocked by the juxtaposition of the horrors to which we have alluded. . . . Sir Charles, without any effort on his part, has achieved a lasting fame. He will be always mentioned, and, if a decent edition be published, often read; but of the present work we are obliged to say, notwithstanding the respectable names which the editor has entrapped into his title-page and dedication, that it is a disgrace to good manners, good morals, and literature, and that no man of sense and no woman of delicacy can allow it to be seen on their table.—CROKER, JOHN WILSON? 1822, *Sir Charles Hanbury, Williams's Works, The Quarterly Review, vol.* 28, *pp.* 49, 59.

The lampoons of Sir Charles Williams are now read only by the curious, and, though not without occasional flashes of wit, have always seemed to us, we must own, very poor performances.—MACAULAY, THOMAS BABINGTON, 1833, *Walpole's Letters to Sir Horace Mann, Edinburgh Review, vol.* 58, *p.* 233.

His principal importance as an ally to the minister consisted in his power of writing, almost extempore, light pasquinades and tart lampoons on their political opponents, as each passing event prompted either the spirit of malice or the spirit of fun. The greater part of these have lost their interest; for squibs can only sparkle for a time. But some of Sir Charles's lighter compositions are still popular, and several, which are unconnected with politics, are pleasing for their grace and smartness. His ballad, written in 1740, on Lady Ilchester asking Lord Ilchester how many kisses he would have, is a very successful song.—CREASY, SIR EDWARD, 1850–75, *Memoirs of Eminent Etonians, p.* 312.

Of the conversational humour of Sir Charles Hanbury Williams, very few traces have survived; but of his facetious talent in literary composition we have abundant evidence. We meet, in Walpole's correspondence, numerous traces of his popularity as a writer of quizzical verses—most of them were political satires directed against the enemies of his patron Sir Robert Walpole, and some of these are disfigured with allusions, and even with words, that are extremely objectionable; he also sometimes indulged in satirical squibs on ladies, and on persons whose insignificance should have shielded them from such attacks.—WARBURTON, ELIOT, 1852, *Memoirs of Horace Walpole, vol.* II, *p.* 116.

Time has robbed his satires of their point, by burying in oblivion the circumstances that gave rise to them. A single specimen of his writings is all that was deemed worthy of place in this volume.—PARTON, JAMES, 1856–84, *The Humorous Poetry of the English Language, p.* 687.

His political squibs are some of the most lively and vigorous in our language.—CUNNINGHAM, PETER, 1856, *ed. Letters of Horace Walpole, vol.* I, *p.* 160, *note.*

Witty Excellency Hanbury did not succeed at Berlin on the "Romish-King Question," or otherwise; and indeed went off rather in a hurry. But for the next six or seven years he puddles about, at a great rate, in those Northern Courts; giving away a great deal of money, hatching many futile expensive intrigues at Petersburg, Warsaw (not much at Berlin, after the first trial there); and will not be altogether avoidable to us in this coming, as one could have wished. Besides, he is Horace Walpole's friend and select London wit: he contributed a good deal to the English notions about Friedrich; and has left considerable bits of acrid testimony on Friedrich, "clear words of an Eyewitness," men call them, —which are still read by everybody; the said Walpole, and others, having since printed them, in very dark conditions. Brevity is much due to Hanbury and his testimonies, since silence in the circumstances is not allowable. —CARLYLE, THOMAS, *History of Friedrich II. of Prussia, bk.* XVI, *ch.* V.

Among all these butterflies of song, Sir Charles Hanbury Williams takes the place of a wasp, if not of a veritable hornet. He was the Pasquin of his age, and a master of violent stinging invective in hard verse. In his own age no one dared to collect the savage lyrics of Williams, which were first presented to the world in 1822.—GOSSE, EDMUND, 1888, *A History of Eighteenth Century Literature, p,* 229.

Burke alluded to him as "the polished courtier, the votary of wit and pleasure." Walpole regarded him as a model for the gilded youth of his day. . . . His occasional verse forms a not unworthy link between Prior and Gay, and Cowper and Canning. Yet the writings of Hanbury Williams were not thought to come up to the sparkle of his conversation, of which some idea may perhaps be gathered from the earlier letters of his friend Horace Walpole.—SECCOMBE, THOMAS, 1900, *Dictionary of National Biography, vol.* LXI, *p.* 382.

William Collins

1721-1759.

Born, at Chichester, 25 Dec. 1721. Probably educated first at Chichester. Scholar of Winchester College, 19 Jan. 1733. Contributed verses to "Gentleman's Magazine" (Jan. and Oct. 1739), while still at school. Matriculated at Queen's College, Oxford, 22 March 1740; Demyship at Magdalen College, 29 July 1741; B. A., 18 Nov. 1743. Visit to uncle in Flanders. Thought of entertaining Army or Church, but eventually devoted himself to literature in London. Failing health; visit to France; lived with sister at Chichester on his return. For a time in a madhouse at Chelsea. Visit to Oxford, 1754. Died at Chichester, 12 June 1759. Buried, at St. Andrew's Church, Chichester. *Works:* "Persian Eclogues" (anon.), 1742 (another edn., anon., entitled "Oriental Eclogues," 1757); "Odes," 1747 [1746]; "Verses humbly addressed to Sir Thomas Hammer" (anon.), 1743. *Posthumous:* "An Ode on the Popular Superstitions of the Highlands," 1788. *Collected Works:* ed. by Langhorne, with *Life*, 1765, etc.; ed. by Mrs. Barbauld, 1797; ed. by A. Dyce, 1827; ed. by Moy Thomas, with *Life*, 1858.—SHARP, R. FARQUHARSON, 1897, *A Dictionary of English Authors, p.* 62.

PERSONAL

Ye who the merits of the dead revere,
Who hold misfortune sacred, genius dear,
Regard this tomb, where Collins, hapless name,
Solicits kindness with a double claim.
Though nature gave him, and though science taught
The fire of fancy, and the reach of thought,
Severely doomed to penury's extreme,
He pass'd in maddening pain life's feverish dream,
While rays of genius only served to show
The thickening horror, and exalt his woe.
Ye walls that echoed to his frantic moan,
Guard the due records of this grateful stone;
Strangers to him, enamoured of his lays,
This fond memorial to his talents raise.
For this the ashes of a bard require,
Who touched the tenderest notes of pity's lyre;
Who joined pure faith to strong poetic powers;
Who, in reviving reason's lucid hours,
Sought on one book his troubled mind to rest,
And rightly deemed the book of God the best.
—HAYLEY, WILLIAM AND SARGENT, JOHN, *Inscription on Collins's Monument.*

How little can we venture to exult in any intellectual powers or literary attainments, when we consider the condition of poor Collins. I knew him a few years ago, full of hopes and full of projects, versed in many languages, high in fancy, and strong in retention. This busy and forcible mind is now under the government of those who lately would not have been able to comprehend the least and most narrow of its designs. What do you hear of him? are there hopes of his recovery? or is he to pass the remainder of his life in misery and degradation? perhaps with complete consciousness of his calamity.——JOHNSON, SAMUEL, 1754, *Letter to Joseph Warton, March* 8.

The neglected author of the Persian eclogues, which, however inaccurate, excel any in our language, is still alive. Happy, if *insensible* of our neglect, not *raging* at our ingratitude.— GOLDSMITH, OLIVER, 1759, *An Enquiry into the Present State of Polite Learning.*

In stature somewhat above the middle size; of a "brown" complexion, keen expressive eyes, and a fixed sedate aspect, which from intense thinking had contracted an habitual frown.—LANGHORNE, JOHN, 1765–81, *The Poetical Works of William Collins, Memoir.*

William Collins, the poet, I was intimately acquainted with, from the time he came to reside at Oxford. . . . As he brought with him, for so the whole turn of his conversation discovered, too high an opinion of his school acquisitions, and a sovereign contempt for all academic studies and discipline, he never looked with any complacency on his situation in the university, but was always complaining of the dulness of a college life. . . . When poverty overtook him, poor man, he had too much sensibility of temper to bear with his misfortunes, and so fell into a most deplorable state of mind. How he got down to Oxford, I do not know; but I myself saw him under Merton wall, in a very affected situation, struggling, and conveyed by force, in the arms of two or three men, towards the parish of St. Clement, in which was a house that took in such unhappy objects; and I always understood that, not long after, he died in confinement; but when, or where, or where he was buried, I never knew. Thus was lost to the world this unfortunate person, in the prime of life, without availing himself of fine abilities, which, properly improved, must have raised him to the top of any profession, and have rendered him a blessing to his friends, and an ornament to his country. Without books, or steadiness or resolution to consult them if he had been possessed of any, he was always planning schemes for elaborate publications, which were carried no farther than the drawing up of proposals for subscriptions, some of which were published; and in particular, as far as I remember, one for a "History of the Darker Ages." He was passionately fond of music; good natured and affable; warm in his friendships, and visionary in his pursuits; and, as long as I knew him, very temperate in his eating and drinking. He was of moderate stature, of a light and clear complexion, with grey eyes, so very weak at times as hardly to bear a candle in the room; and often raising within him apprehensions of blindness.—WHITE, GILBERT? 1781, *Gentleman's Magazine.*

He was an acceptable companion everywhere; and, among the gentlemen who loved him for a genius, I may reckon the Doctors Armstrong, Barrowby, and Hill, Messrs. Quin, Garrick, and Foote, who frequently took his opinion on their pieces before they were seen by the public. He was particularly noticed by the geniuses who frequented the Bedford and Slaughter's Coffee Houses. From his knowledge of Garrick he had the liberty of the scenes and green-room, where he made diverting observations on the vanity and false consequence of that class of people; and his manner of relating them to his particular friends was extremely entertaining.—RAGSDALE, JOHN, 1783, *Letter to William Hymers, July.*

In illustration of what Dr. Johnson has related, that during his last malady he was a great reader of the Bible, I am favoured with the following anecdote from the Reverend Mr. Shenton, Vicar of St. Andrews, at Chichester, by whom Collins was buried: "Walking in my vicaral garden one Sunday evening, during Collins's last illness, I heard a female (the servant, I suppose) reading the Bible in his chamber. Mr. Collins had been accustomed to rave much, and make great moanings; but while she was reading, or rather attempting to read, he was not only silent but attentive likewise, correcting her mistakes, which indeed were very frequent, through the whole of the twenty-seventh chapter of Genesis." I have just been informed, from undoubted authority, that Collins has finished a "Preliminary Dissertation" to be prefixed to his "History of the Restoration of Learning," and that it was written with great judgment, precision, and knowledge of the subject. —WARTON, THOMAS, 1783, *Letter to William Hymers, July.*

I have lately finished eight volumes of Johnson's "Prefaces, or Lives of the Poets." In all the number I observe but one man—(a poet of no great fame,—of whom I did not know that he existed till I found him there), whose mind seems to have had the slightest tincture of religion; and he was hardly in his senses. His name was Collins. He sunk into a state of melancholy, and died young. Not long before his death, he was found at his lodgings in Islington by his biographer, with the New Testament in his hand. He said to Johnson, "I have but one book; but it is the best." Of him, therefore, there are some hopes.—COWPER, WILLIAM, 1784, *Letter to Mr. Newton, March* 19.

Glide gently, thus for ever glide,
O Thames! that other bards may see
As lovely visions by thy side
As now, fair river! come to me.
O glide, fair stream! for ever so,
Thy quiet soul on all bestowing,
Till all our minds for ever flow
As thy deep waters now are flowing.
Vain thought!—Yet be as now thou art,
That in thy waters may be seen
The image of a poet's heart,
How bright, how solemn, how serene!
Such as did once the Poet bless,
Who murmuring here a later ditty,
Could find no refuge from distress
But in the milder grief of pity.
Now let us, as we float along,
For *him* suspend the dashing oar;
And pray that never child of song
May know that Poet's sorrows more.
How calm! how still! the only sound,
The dripping of the ear suspended!
—The evening darkness gathers round
By virtue's holiest Powers attended.

—WORDSWORTH, WILLIAM, 1789, *Remembrance of Collins.*

What was the result of his literary life? He returned to his native city of Chichester in a state almost of nakedness, destitute, diseased, and wild in despair, to hide himself in the arms of a sister. . . . At Chichester, tradition has preserved some striking and affecting occurrences of his last days; he would haunt the aisles and cloisters of the cathedral, roving days and nights together, loving their

Dim religious light.

And, when the choristers chanted their anthem, the listening and bewildered poet, carried out of himself by the solemn strains, and his own too susceptible imagination, moaned and shrieked, and awoke a sadness and a terror most affecting amid religious emotions; their friend, their kinsman, and their poet, was before them, an awful image of human misery and ruined genius!—DISRAELI, ISAAC, 1812–13, *Literary Disappointments, Calamities of Authors.*

He wrote an "Ode on the Passions," in which, after dwelling on Hope, Fear, Anger, Despair, Pity, and describing them with many picturesque circumstances, he dismisses Love with a couple of lines, as dancing to the sound of the sprightly viol, and forming with joy the light fantastic round. Such was Collins' idea of love!—JAMESON, ANNA BROWNELL, 1829, *The Loves of the Poets, vol.* 2, *p.* 311.

Collins's person was of the middle size and well formed; of a light complexion, with gray, weak eyes. His mind was deeply imbued with classical literature, and he understood the Italian, French, and Spanish languages. He was well read, and was particularly conversant with early English writers, and to an ardent love of literature he united, as is manifest from many of his pieces, a passionate devotion to Music, that

"——Sphere-descended maid,
Friend of Pleasure, Wisdom's aid."

—NICOLAS, SIR HARRIS NICHOLAS, 1831? *ed. Collins's Poetical Works, Memoir.*

Much speculation has taken place as to the causes of Collins's irresolution; but human motives are not easily determined. The evidences are too many to doubt, that he was at this time indolent and undecided; but fond of pleasure and eager for excitement. His truest friend has spoken of habits of dissipation and long association with "fortuitous companions." But his studies were extensive, and his scholarship commanded the respect of learned men. As with his friends the Wartons, his taste led him to the study of the older English writers. He was acquainted with the riches of the Elizabethan poets at a time when few English students strayed beyond Cowley; and he read in the Italian, French, and Spanish languages those poems and romances which, to the more sober taste of Johnson, "passed the bounds of nature." At this time he composed his Odes, upon which his fame rests.—THOMAS, W. MOY, 1858–92, *ed., The Poetical Works of William Collins, p.* xix.

PERSIAN ECLOGUES
1742

The following eclogues, written by Mr. Collins, are very pretty; the images, it must be owned, are not very local; for the pastoral subject could not well admit of it. The description of Asiatic magnificence and manners is a subject as yet unattempted amongst us, and, I believe, capable of furnishing a great variety of poetical imagery.—GOLDSMITH, OLIVER, 1767, *The Beauties of English Poetry.*

Mr. Collins wrote his Eclogues when he was about seventeen years old, at Winchester school, and, as I well remember, had been just reading that volume of Salmon's Modern History which described Persia; which determined him to lay the scene of these pieces, as being productive of new images and sentiments. In his maturer years he was accustomed to speak very contemptuously of them, calling them his Irish Eclogues, and saying they had not in them one spark of Orientalism; and desiring me to erase a motto he had prefixed to them in a copy he gave me:

—quos primus equis oriens afflavit anhelis.—
Virg.

He was greatly mortified that they found more readers and admirers than his Odes. —WARTON, JOSEPH, 1797, *ed. Pope's Works, vol.* I, *p.* 61.

His "Hassan, or the Camel-Driver," is, I verily believe, one of the most tenderly sublime, most sweetly descriptive poems in the cabinet of the Muses.—DRAKE, NATHAN, 1798–1820, *Literary Hours, vol.* I, *No.* xvi, *p.* 260.

Collins published his "Oriental Eclogues" while at college, and his lyrical poetry at the age of twenty-six. Those works will abide comparison with whatever Milton wrote under the age of thirty. If they have rather less exuberant wealth of genius, they exhibit more exquisite touches of pathos. Like Milton, he leads us into the haunted ground of imagination; like him, he has the rich economy of expression haloed with thought, which by a single few words often hints entire pictures to the imagination. . . . The pastoral eclogue, which is insipid in all other English hands, assumes in his a touching interest, and a picturesque air of novelty. It seems that he himself ultimately undervalued those eclogues, as deficient in characteristic manners; but surely no just reader of them cares any more about this circumstance than about the authenticity of the tale of Troy.—CAMPBELL, THOMAS, 1819, *Specimens of the British Poets.*

Although he has so exquisitely described the Passions, the greatest want of his poetry *is* passion. He has the highest enthusiasm, but little human interest. His figures are warm with the breath of genius, but there is little of the life's-blood of heart about them. Hence his "Oriental Eclogues," although full of fine description, are felt to be rather tame and stiff.—GILFILLAN, GEORGE, 1854, *ed., The Poetical Works of Goldsmith, Collins and T. Warton, p.* 83.

The "Persian Eclogues" have much of the rich and peculiar diction of Collins. He is said, on more than one authority, to have expressed his dissatisfaction with them, by calling them his "Irish Eclogues;" but in this he no doubt simply referred to some remarkable blunders in his first edition.—THOMAS, W. MOY, 1858–92, *ed., The Poetical Works of William Collins, p.* lvi.

For tenderness, simplicity, and grace, must be pronounced as amongst the most beautiful pastoral poetry which we possess.—WALLER, J. F., 1881, *Boswell and Johnson, Their Companions and Contemporaries,* 123.

ODE TO LIBERTY
1747

After an overture worthy of Milton's or of Handel's "Agonistes," a prelude that peals as from beneath the triumphal hand of the thunder-bearer, steadily subsides through many noble but ever less and less noble verses, towards a final couplet showing not so much the flatness of failure as the prostration of collapse.—SWINBURNE, ALGERNON CHARLES, 1880, *The English Poets, ed. Ward, vol.* III, *p.* 282.

ODE TO EVENING

In his address to Evening, he has presented us with the first fortunate specimen of the blank ode. Nothing but his own ode on the Popular Superstitions of the Highlands of Scotland can exceed the fine enthusiasm of this piece; the very spirit of Poussin and Claude breathe throughout the whole, mingled indeed with a wilder and more visionary train of idea, yet subdued and chastened by the softest tones of melancholy.—DRAKE, NATHAN, 1798–1820, *Literary Hours, vol.* II, *No.* XXV, *p.* 36.

If Collins live by the reputation of one, more than of another, performance, it strikes me that his "Ode to Evening" will be that on which the voice of posterity will be more uniform in praise. It is a pearl of the most perfect tint and shape. —DIBDIN, THOMAS FROGNALL, 1824, *The Library Companion, p.* 733, *note.*

His "Ode to Evening" is, perhaps, the most original of his odes. The fine tone of tranquil musing that pervades it is felt by every poetic reader. A subdued and peaceful spirit breathes through it, as in the solitude and stillness of a twilight country. The absence of rhyme leaving the even glow of the verse unbroken, and the change at the end of each stanza into shorter lines, as if the voice of the reader dropped into a lower key, contribute to the effect. To those who feel its spirit the living world is far away, and even the objects in the surrounding landscape, by which the picture is completed, are seen only in their reflection in the poet's mind. The bat and the beetle which are abroad in the dusky air; the brown hamlets and dim-discovered spires; the springs that have a solemn murmur, and the dying gales, are but images of that rapt and peaceful mood. It must, however, be acknowledged that some obscurity in the invocation arises from the long inversion of the sense, by which that which in logical order is the first sentence in the poem is carried over to the last two lines of the fourth stanza.—THOMAS, W. MOY, 1858–92, *ed., The Poetical Works of William Collins, p.* liv.

The most perfect and original poem of Collins, as well as the most finely appreciative of Nature, is his Ode to Evening. No doubt evening is personified in his address as "maid composed," and "calm votaress," but the personification is so delicately handled, and in so subdued a tone, that it does not jar on the feelings, as such personifications too often do. . . . There is about the whole ode a subdued twilight tone, a remoteness from men and human things, and a pensive evening musing, all the more expressive, because it does not shape itself into definite thoughts, but reposes in appropriate images.—SHAIRP, JOHN CAMPBELL, 1877, *On Poetic Interpretation of Nature, pp.* 207, 208.

Displays a sustained power of painting landscape effects which Collins does not repeat elsewhere.—GOSSE, EDMUND, 1888, *A History of Eighteenth Century Literature, p.* 233.

Collins is best known by his Ode on "The Passions," but incomparably his finest and most distinctive work is the "Ode to Evening." The superior popularity of "The Passions" is easily explained. It might be recited at a penny reading, and every line of its strenuous rhetoric would tell; every touch would be at once appreciated. But the beauties of the "Ode to Evening" are of a much stronger kind, and the structure of it is infinitely more complicated. . . . It is a poem to be taken into the mind slowly; you cannot take possession of it without effort. Give a quiet evening to it; return to it again and again; master the meaning of it deliberately part by part, and let the whole sink into your mind softly and gradually, and you will not regret the labor. You will find yourselves in possession of a perpetual delight, of a music that will make the fall of evening forever charming to you.—MINTO, WILLIAM, 1894, *The Literature of the Georgian Era, ed. Knight, pp.* 93, 94.

THE PASSIONS

"The Ode to the Passions" is, by universal consent, the noblest of Collins's productions, because it exhibits a much more extended invention, not of one passion only, but of all the passions combined, acting, according to the powers of each, to one end. The execution, also, is the happiest, each particular passion is drawn with inimitable force and compression. Let us take on Fear and Despair, each dashed out in four lines, of which every word is like inspiration. Beautiful as Spenser is, and sometimes sublime, yet he redoubles his touch too much, and often introduces some coarse feature or expression, which destroys the spell. Spenser, indeed, has other merits of splendid and inexhaustible invention, which render it impossible to put Collins on a par with him: but we must not estimate merit by mere quantity: if a poet produces but one short piece, which is perfect, he must be placed according to its quality. And surely there is not a single figure in Collins's "Ode to the Passions" which is not perfect, both in conception and language. He has had many imitators, but no one has ever approached him in his own department.—BRYDGES, SIR SAMUEL EGERTON, 1831? *An Essay on the Genius and Poems of Collins.*

All that Collins has written is full of imagination, pathos, and melody. The defect of his poetry in general is that there is too little of earth in it: in the purity and depth of its beauty it resembles the bright blue sky. Yet Collins had genius enough for anything; and in his ode entitled "The Passions," he has shown with how strong a voice and pulse of humanity he could, when he chose, animate his verse, and what extensive and enduring popularity he could command.—CRAIK, GEORGE L., 1861, *A Compendious History of English Literature and of the English Language, vol.* II, *p.* 284.

Its grace and vigour, its vivid and pliant dexterity of touch, are worthy of all their long inheritance of praise; and altogether it holds out admirably well to the happy and harmonious end.—SWINBURNE, ALGERNON CHARLES, 1880, *The English Poets, ed. Ward, vol.* III, *p.* 282.

GENERAL

In simplicity of description and expression, in delicacy and softness of numbers, and in natural and unaffected tenderness, they are not to be equalled by anything of the pastoral kind in the English language. —LANGHORNE, WILLIAM, 1765–81, *The Poetical Works of William Collins, Memoir.*

Attempt no number of the plaintive Gay,
Let me like midnight cats, or Collins sing.

—CHATTERTON, THOMAS, 1770? *February, An Elegy.*

His diction was often harsh, unskilfully laboured, and injudiciously selected. He affected the obsolete, when it was not worthy of revival; and he puts his words out of the common order, seeming to think, with some later candidates for fame, that not to write prose is certainly to write poetry. His lines commonly are of slow motion, clogged and impeded with clusters of consonants. As men are often esteemed who cannot be loved, so the poetry of Collins may sometimes extort praise when it gives little pleasure.—JOHNSON, SAMUEL, 1779–81, *Collins, Lives of the English Poets.*

One of our most exquisite poets, and of whom, perhaps, without exaggeration it may be asserted, that he partook of the credulity and enthusiasm of Tasso, the magic wildness of Shakspeare, the sublimity of Milton, and the pathos of Ossian. —DRAKE, NATHAN, 1798–1820, *Literary Hours, vol.* I, *No.* iii, *p.* 49.

There was Collins, 'tis true, had a good deal to say,
But the dog had no industry.
—HUNT, LEIGH, 1811, *The Feast of the Poets.*

Like Collins, ill-starr'd name!
Whose lay's requital was that tardy Fame,
Who bound no laurel round his living head,
Should hang it o'er his monument when dead.
—SCOTT, SIR WALTER, 1813, *The Bridal of Triermain.*

He had that true *vivida vis*, that genuine inspiration, which alone can give birth to the highest efforts of poetry. He leaves stings in the minds of his readers, certain traces of thought and feeling, which never wear out, because nature had left them in his own mind. He is the only one of the minor poets of whom, if he had lived, it cannot be said that he might not have done the greatest things. The germ is there. He is sometimes affected, unmeaning and obscure; but he also catches rich glimpses of the bowers of Paradise, and has lofty aspirations after the highest seats of the Muses. With a great deal of tinsel and splendid patchwork, he has not been able to hide the solid sterling ore of genius. In his best works there is an attic simplicity, a pathos, and fervour of imagination, which make us the more lament that the efforts of his mind were at first depressed by neglect and pecuniary embarrassment, and at length buried in the gloom of an unconquerable and fatal malady. . . . I should conceive that Collins had a much greater poetical genius than Gray: he had more of that fine madness which is inseparable from it, of its turbid effervescence, of all that pushes it to the verge of agony or rapture.—HAZLITT, WILLIAM, 1818, *Lectures on the English Poets, Lecture* vi.

The most accomplished Scholar, and the most original Poet of his age.—NEELE, HENRY, 1827–29, *Lectures on English Poetry, p.* 213.

It is not, however, inconsistent with a high respect for Collins, to ascribe every possible praise to that unrivaled production, the "Ode to the Passions," to feel deeply the beauty, the pathos, and the sublime conceptions of the Odes to Evening, to Pity, to Simplicity, and a few others, and yet to be sensible of the occasional obscurity and imperfections of his imagery in other pieces, to find it difficult to discover the meaning of some passages, to think the opening of four of his odes which commence with the common-place invocation of "O thou," and the alliteration by which so many lines are disfigured, blemishes too serious to be forgotten, unless the judgment be drowned in the full tide of generous and enthusiastic admiration of the great and extraordinary beauties by which these faults are more than redeemed. That these defects are to be ascribed to haste it would be uncandid to deny; but haste is no apology for such faults in productions which fill a hundred pages, and which their author had ample opportunities to remove.—NICOLAS, SIR HARRIS NICHOLAS, 1831? *ed. Collins's Poetical Works, Memoir.*

When Collins is spoken of as one of the *minor* poets, it is a sad misapplication of the term. Unless he be minor because the number and size of his poems is small, no one is less a minor poet. In him every word is poetry, and poetry either sublime or pathetic. He does not rise to the sublimity of Milton or Dante, or reach the graceful tenderness of Petrarch; but he has a visionary invention of his own, to which there is no rival. As long as the language lasts, every richly gifted and richly cultivated mind will read him with intense and wondering rapture; and will not cease to entertain the conviction, from his example, if from no other, that true poetry of the higher orders is real inspiration.—BRYDGES, SIR SAMUEL EGERTON, 1831? *An Essay on the Genius and Poems of Collins.*

That he should never before have heard of Collins, shows how little Collins has been heard of in his life-time; and that Cowper, in his knowledge of contemporary literature, was now awakening, as it were, from a sleep of twenty years. In the course of those years Collins's Odes, which were utterly neglected on their first appearance, had obtained their due estimation. . . . It should also be remembered, that in the course of one generation these poems, without any adventitious aid to bring them into notice, were acknowledged to be the best of their kind in the language. Silently and imperceptibly they had risen by their own buoyancy, and their power was felt by every reader who had any true poetic feeling.—SOUTHEY, ROBERT, 1835, *Life of Cowper*, p. 321.

If we admire the genius and skill which have compressed into the few pages of Gray's collected poems so many noble images, so many exquisite movements of harmony, and so much splendour and propriety of diction, we shall find that an intense susceptibility for beauty has concentrated into the yet smaller compass of Collins's productions a quantity and depth of loveliness of a kind even more permanently attractive to the reader. If Gray was the more accomplished artist, Collins was the more *born poet*. In Collins the first thing we remark is the inimitable felicity of his expression. Gray's lovely and majestic pictures are careful, genial, artistic paintings of nature; those of Collins are the images of nature in the *camera obscura*. Gray is the light of day; Collins is the Italian moonlight—as bright almost, but tenderer, more pensive, more spiritual,—

"Dusk, yet clear;
Mellow'd and mingling, yet distinctly seen."

—SHAW, THOMAS B., 1847, *Outlines of English Literature*, p. 298.

The Odes of Collins are fuller of the fine and spontaneous enthusiasm of genius, than any other poems ever written by one who wrote so little. We close this tiny volume with the same disappointed surprise, which overcomes us when a harmonious piece of music suddenly ceases unfinished. His range of tones is very wide: it extends from the warmest rapture of self-entranced imagination, to a tenderness which makes some of his verses sound like gentle weeping. The delicacy of gradation with which he passes from thought to thought, has an indescribable charm, though not always unattended by obscurity; and there is a marvellous power of suggestion in his clouds of allegoric imagery, so beautiful in outline, and coloured by a fancy so purely and ideally refined. His most popular poem, "The Passions," can hardly be allowed to be his best: of some of his most deeply marked characteristics it conveys no adequate idea. Readers who do not shrink from having their attention put to the stretch, and who can relish the finest and most recondite analogies, will delight in his Ode entitled "The Manners," and in that, still nobler and more imaginative, "On the Poetical Character." Every one, surely, can understand and feel the beauty of such pieces as the Odes "To Pity," "To Simplicity," "To Mercy." Nor does it require much reflection to fit us for appreciating the spirited lyric "To Liberty;" or for being entranced by the finely-woven harmonies and the sweetly romantic pictures, which, in the "Ode to Evening," remind us of the youthful poems of Milton.—SPALDING, WILLIAM, 1852–82, *A History of English Literature*, p. 341.

With some occasional exaggeration and over-luxuriance, this author's language is for the most part exquisitely musical and refined. — ARNOLD, THOMAS, 1868–75, *Chaucer to Wordsworth*, p. 357.

There belong to Collins a new intensity of emotion, a vividness of personification, a broader sweep of imagination, which decidedly distinguish his composition from that of his cotemporaries, and impart to the reader a sense of larger, freer, gladder motion. As a vigorous bird proportions his curves of flight to his power of muscle, so Collins adopts a more varied and continuous rhythm. His successive impulses gather up and weave together more lines, and we are borne on the strong wing of a single image through a series of varying melodies, that will not fall apart into brief, measured stanzas.—BASCOM, JOHN, 1874, *Philosophy of English Literature*, p. 216

What a notion it gives us of the power of poetry that this poor mad-house patient is able at the distance of more than a hundred years to so possess our minds with his own emotion, that we never cease to see amid the skirts of these dim woodlands* his retreating figure!—NADAL, E. S., 1876, *Two Poems of Collins, Scribner's Monthly, vol.* 12, *p.* 220.

Without making odious comparisons, it may be fair to say that Collins's odes are more liked than Gray's. They have less the air of artificiality, and they have less the form of a mosaic, which is naturally suggested to us by Gray's borrowing from his predecessors. Where there are traces of labored elegance in Gray, we have often in Collins the apparently swift choice of the right epithet, for he certainly conceals his art. . . . Collins, however, mastered his instrument, and his odes survive to show that, even in a dreary period of literary history, the man may arise who proves that the poetical tradition, though obscured, is not wholly lost.—PERRY, THOMAS S., 1880, *Gray, Collins and Beattie, Atlantic Monthly, vol.* 46, *p.* 815.

Living both in the age and after an age of critical poetry, Collins, always alien alike from the better and from the worse influences of his day, has shown at least as plentiful a lack of any slightest critical instinct or training as ever did any poet on record, in his epistle to Hanmer on that worthy knight's "inqualifiable" edition of Shakespeare. But his couplets, though incomparably inferior to Gray's, are generally spirited and competent as well as fluent and smooth. The direct sincerity and purity of their positive and straightforward inspiration will always keep his poems fresh and sweet to the senses of all men. He was a solitary song-bird among many more or less excellent pipers and pianists. He could put more spirit of colour into a single stroke, more breath of music into a single note, than could all the rest of his generation into all the labours of their lives. And the sweet name and the lucid memory of his genius could only pass away with all relics and all records of lyric poetry in England. — SWINBURNE, ALGERNON CHARLES, 1880, *The English Poets, ed. Ward, vol.* III, *p.* 282.

There are very few poets from whose wheat so little chaff has been winnowed as from that of Collins. His entire existing work does not extend to much more than fifteen hundred lines, at least two-thirds of which must live with the best poetry of the century. Collins has the touch of a sculptor; his verse is clearly-cut and direct; it is marble-pure, but also marble-cold. Each phrase is a wonder of felicitous workmanship, without emphasis, without sense of strain. His best strophes possess an extraordinary quiet melody, a soft harmonious smoothness as of some divine and aerial creature singing in artless, perfect, numbers for its own delight. . . . The intellectual quality of Collins is not so strongly marked as his pure and polished art; but he had sympathy with fine things unpopular in his own lifetime. He was a republican and a Hellenist and a collector of black-letter poetry, in an age that equally despised what was Greek and what was Gothic. It may perhaps be allowed to be an almost infallible criterion of a man's taste for the highest forms of poetic art to inquire whether he has or has not a genuine love for the verses of William Collins.—GOSSE, EDMUND, 1888, *A History of Eighteenth Century Literature, pp.* 233, 235.

There is the chink of true and rare poetic metal in his verse, and it is fused by an imagination capable of intense heat and wonderful flame.—MITCHELL, DONALD G., 1895, *English Lands Letters and Kings, Queen Anne and the Georges, p.* 161.

Men like Thomas Gray and William Collins attempted to "revive the just designs of Greece," not only in fitness of language, but in perfection of form. They are commonly placed together, but the genius of each was essentially different. What they had in common belonged to the age in which they lived, and one of these elements was a certain artificial phrasing from which they found it difficult to escape. Both sought beauty more than their fellows, but Collins found it more than Gray. He had the greater grace and the sweeter simplicity, and his "Ode to Simplicity" tells us the direction in which poetry was going. His best work, like "The Ode to Evening," is near to Keats, and recalls that poet's imaginative way. His inferior work is often rude and his style sometimes obscure, but when he

*Richmond Churchyard.

is touched by joy in "ecstatic trial," or when he sits with Melancholy in love of peace and gentle musing, he is indeed inspired by truth and loveliness.—BROOKE, STOPFORD A., 1896, *English Literature*, p. 214.

Johnson, a good and true friend of Collins, and though an untrustworthy critic of purely romantic poetry, likely to be conciliated rather than revolted by the classical form of the odes, broke the truth bluntly when he said that Collins's inversion of phrase savoured of the mistake that "if you do not write prose you will write poetry." In no true poet known to me, not in Rossetti, not in Donne, is the drawback of artificial poetic diction so obnoxious as in Collins. And the reason is clear. He *was* a true poet, a poet of the truest, who, unluckily for him, was singing in the spirit of one age with the tongue of another. He is trying to say Shibboleth, but he cannot; and though he says Sibboleth with exquisite grace, it is Sibboleth still.—SAINTSBURY, GEORGE, 1896, *Social England, ed. Traill, vol.* V, *p.* 263.

The landscape of Collins was apparently much influenced by Greek poetry. His work reminds us of the great, rugged, sublime, choral songs, of the audacious metaphors of Æschylus.—PALGRAVE, FRANCIS TURNER, 1896, *Landscape in Poetry, p.* 173.

Collins is among the choicest of English lyrical poets. There is a flute-like music in his best odes—such as the one "To Evening," and the one written in 1746—"How sleep the brave," which are sweeter, more natural, and more spontaneous than Gray's.—BEERS, HENRY A., 1898, *A History of English Romanticism in the Eighteenth Century, p.* 168.

Benjamin Hoadly

1676–1761

Born at Westerham, Kent, in 1697 became a fellow of Catherine Hall, Cambridge, in 1701 lecturer of St. Mildred in the Poultry, and in 1703 rector of St. Peter-le-Poer. Hoadly figures amongst the principal controversial writers of the 18th century, defending the cause of civil and religious liberty against both crown and clergy, and carrying on a controversy with Dr. Atterbury on the obedience due to the civil power by ecclesiastics. In 1710 he was presented to the rectory of Streatham, and in 1715 was made Bishop of Bangor. In 1717 he preached before the king a sermon on "My kingdom is not of this world," in which he sought to show that Christ had not delegated His powers to any ecclesiastical authorities. This originated the Bangorian Controversy, which branched off into such a multiplicity of side-issues that the main question became lost. The dispute had, however, one important consequence—the indefinite prorogation of Convocation. In 1721 Hoadly was translated to Hereford, in 1723 to Salisbury, and in 1734 to Winchester. His son published his "Collected Works" in 1773, with Life.—PATRICK AND GROOME, *eds.*, 1897, *Chambers's Biographical Dictionary, p.* 492.

PERSONAL

Calling at Bull's on Ludgate Hill, he forced me to his house at Hampstead to dinner among a great deal of ill company; among the rest Mr. Hoadly, the Whig clergyman, so famous for acting the contrary part to Sacheverell.—SWIFT, JONATHAN, 1710, *Journal to Stella, Sept.* 13.

> O nurse of Freedom, Albion, say,
> Thou tamer of despotic sway,
> What man, among thy sons around,
> Thus heir to glory hast thou found?
> What page, in all thy annals bright,
> Hast thou with purer joy survey'd
> Than that where truth, by Hoadly's aid,
> Shines through imposture's solemn shade,
> Through kingly and through sacerdotal night?
> . . . .
> We attend thy reverend length of days
> With benediction and with praise,
> And hail thee in our public ways
> Like some great spirit famed in ages old.

—AKENSIDE, MARK, 1754, *To the Right Rev. Benjamin Lord Bishop of Winchester.*

Benjamin Hoadly was probably the best hated clergyman of the century amongst his own order. His titles to the antipathy of his brethren were many and indisputable. A clergyman who opposes sacerdotal privileges is naturally the object of a sentiment such as would be provoked by a trades-unionist who should defend the masters, or a country squire who should protect poachers.—STEPHEN, LESLIE, 1876, *History of English Thought in the Eighteenth Century, vol.* II, *p.* 152.

As a preacher, where the subject was not one of a purely argumentative character, Hoadly was not successful. He said of his lectureship in the City, which he held between 1694 and 1704, that he preached it down to 30£ a year and then resigned. To stir the soul and warm the feelings was quite beyond his reach; and though, in his calm, dispassionate manner, he could reason with force upon the blessing of a life of Christian principle, this of itself can never sway the heart of a great congregation. Moreover, his style, though frequently rising into impressive dignity, was often diffuse and involved. . . . In private life he possessed a genial and happy temperament. Easy in manner and not wanting in humour, he was fond of society, but never so content as in the midst of his own family. Milner speaks of the "incongruous association of emblems" on his tomb at Winchester—the pastoral crosier and the democratic pike and cap—the Scriptures and Magna Charta. The pike, if it is indeed there, is incongruous enough; and the pastoral staff is suggestive of Hoadly's grossest defect. But the rest may well represent those elements in the bishop's character which make up for much that was wanting in it—his love of liberty, his love of justice, his reverence—exclusive to a fault—for the authority of Holy Writ. —ABBEY, CHARLES J., 1887, *The English Church and Its Bishops*, 1700–1800, *vol.* II, *pp.* 3, 19.

GENERAL

Mr. Hoadly, the Bishop of Bangor, has, in the Sermon for which he is so ill-treated, done like an Apostle, and asserted the true dominion established by our Blessed Saviour.—STEELE, RICHARD, 1717, *Letter to Lady Steele, June* 21.

Verily *Benjamin*, thou hast done well in that thou hast openly declared the iniquity of those who have armed themselves with unlawful power, and have exercised tyranny over their brethren, saying, ye must join with us, otherwise ye shall go to prison; or otherwise you shall have no honour, or part or lot among us: Whereas King Jesus never left any such commandment. But it remaineth as a difficulty, or doubt unto us who are Friends, how thou canst lay a confederacy with these men! Verily, *Benjamin*, if thou come not out from among them, thou wilt give occasion to wicked men to say of thee, that thou hast said that in thy teaching office which thou wilt not put in practice in thy person. Wherefore, friend *Benjamin*, as I know that the truth hath been spoken by thee, I warn thee for thy good, that thou come out speedily from among them; lay down thy painted vestments and profane trinkets, the ensigns of that usurpation upon thy Lord and Master's kingdom, which thou hast so faithfully borne thy testimony against.—Blessed art thou, O *Benjamin*, in that thou hast borne thy testimony against these things. Wherefore I know, that leaving behind thee all these wicked and erroneous opinions, and bearing witness to the truth, thou will at length join thyself unto us, and I rejoice over thee in this, that thou art enlightened to know the truth. Friend *Timothy* greeteth thee in like manner; as also *James* the aged, a lover of those who forsake the errors of the wicked. In a word, all Friends greet thee, and speak well of thee. Fare thee well.—DEFOE, DANIEL, 1717, *A Declaration of Truth to Benjamin Hoadly.*

I see no reason for such a prodigious outcry upon the "Plain Account." I really think it a very good book, as orthodox as Archbishop Tillotson. His prayers are very long, but in my opinion some of the best compositions of the sort that ever I read; and if I could bring my mind to that steady frame of thinking with regard to the Deity that is presented by him, I believe I should be so far as happy as my nature is, perhaps, capable of being. —HERRING, THOMAS, 1735, *Letter to Duncombe, Nov.* 17.

The object of Whig Idolatry and Tory abhorrence; and at every weapon of attack and defence, the Nonjuror, on the ground which is common to both, approves himself at least equal to the Prelate.*—GIBBON, EDWARD, 1793, *Autobiography, Memoirs of my Life and Writings.*

The style of Hoadly's controversial treatises is strong and logical, but without any of the graces of composition; and hence they have fallen into comparative oblivion. There can be no doubt, however, that the independent and liberal position that he maintained, aided by his station in the church, tended materially to stem the torrent of slavish submission

*Berkeley.

which, at that time, prevailed in the Church of England.—MILLS, ABRAHAM, 1851, *The Literature and the Literary Men of Great Britain and Ireland, vol.* II, *p.* 275.

His style is in general vigorous and caustic; he seems careless of elegance, and his dry sarcasms have lost their interest. — MINTO, WILLIAM, 1872–80, *Manual of English Prose Literature, p.* 398.

Was a prelate of great controversial ability, who threw the weight of his talents and learning into the scale of Whig politics, at that time fiercely attacked by the Tory and Jacobite parties. . . . There can be no doubt that the independent and liberal mind of Hoadly, aided by his station in the church, tended materially to stem the torrent of slavish submission which then prevailed in the church of England.—CHAMBERS, ROBERT, 1876, *Cyclopædia of English Literature, ed. Carruthers.*

His style is the style of a bore; he is slovenly, awkward, intensely pertinacious, often indistinct, and, apparently at least, evasive; and occasionally (I am thinking especially of his arguments with his old enemy Atterbury) not free from a tinge of personal rancour. He preached his first lectureship down to 30*l.* a year, as he candidly reports, and then thought it time to resign. A perusal of his writings renders the statement easily credible. The three huge folios which contain his ponderous wranglings are a dreary wilderness of now profitless discussion. We owe, however, a vast debt of gratitude to the bores who have defended good causes, and in his pachydermatous fashion Hoadly did some service, by helping to trample down certain relics of the old spirit of bigotry.—STEPHEN, LESLIE, 1876, *History of English Thought in the Eighteenth Century, vol.* II, *p.* 153.

This very able man, who possessed all the moral and intellectual qualities of a consummate controversialist, had for some years been rapidly acquiring the position which Burnet had before held in the Low Church ranks. His latitudinarianism, however, was of a more extreme and emphatic character, and he greatly surpassed Burnet in the incisive brilliancy of his controversial writing, though he was far inferior to him in learning and versatility, in depth and beauty of character, and in the discharge of his episcopal duties,—LECKY, WILLIAM EDWARD HARTPOLE, 1877, *A History of England in the Eighteenth Century, vol.* I, *p.* 270.

As a writer, he is both furious and tiresome, and almost the only purely literary interest we have in him centres around his friendship for Steele.—GOSSE, EDMUND, 1888, *A History of Eighteenth Century Literature, p.* 196.

Hoadly, so dexterous as a controversialist, does not shine as a teacher of positive theology. There is a coldness and heaviness about his utterances, and his style is sometimes so involved that we can appreciate Pope's satirical description of "Hoadly with his periods of a mile." . . . His dogmatic theological writings have no great merit. His political essays are clear and forcible, but they are disfigured by frequent adulation of the king and royal family. The letters to Lady Sundon show that he was well able to flatter influential personages in the state.—PERRY, G. G., 1891, *Dictionary of National Biography, vol.* XXVII, *p.* 20.

His sermons are well-constructed and lucid. There is in them no tedious splitting of texts nor minute casuistry. He expounds the general principles of religion forcibly and earnestly, without dwelling on doctrinal minutiæ. They are clear, vigorous, and brief. Without being rhetorical or brilliant they are pleasant reading; calm, well-sustained and logical. He attacks the Church of Rome with severity, but without asperity, recognising her as the acme of the ecclesiasticism against which he was constantly at war. In controversy he is temperate, controlled, and dignified. He never stoops to petty personalities, but holds to the point at issue without flinching. Bishop Hoadly is not a star of the first magnitude. His writings are not among the classics of English literature. He does not rank with Hooker, Jeremy Taylor, and Baxter. Nevertheless he deserves an honourable place among English men of letters. Possibly had he been a high churchman like Warburton he would have enjoyed his literary deserts and more. As it is, he suffers like others of his school of theological thought, and finds himself passed over for inferior writers who better adapted themselves to the dominant views.—FITZROY, A. I., 1894, *English Prose, ed. Craik, vol.* III, *p.* 548.

William Law

1686-1761

William Law, born a grocer's son at Kingscliffe, Northamptonshire, in 1686, entered Emmanuel College, Cambridge, in 1705, and became a fellow in 1711. He was unable to subscribe the oath of allegiance to George I., and forfeited his fellowship. About 1727 he became tutor to the father of Edward Gibbon, and for ten years was "the much-honoured friend and spiritual director of the whole family." The elder Gibbon died in 1737, and three years later Law retired to Kingscliffe, and was joined by his disciples, Miss Hester Gibbon, sister of his pupil, and Mrs. Hutcheson. The two ladies had a united income of about £3000 a-year, and most of this they spent in works of charity. About 1733 Law had begun to study Jacob Boehme, and most of his later works are expositions of his mysticism. He died April 9, 1761. Law won his first triumphs against Bishop Hoadly in the famous Bangorian controversy with his "Three Letters" (1717). His "Remarks on Mandeville's Fable of the Bees" (1723) is a masterpiece of caustic wit and vigorous English. Only less admirable is the "Case of Reason" (1732), in answer to Tindal the Deist. But his most famous work remains in the "Serious Call to a Devout and Holy Life" (1729), which profoundly influenced Dr. Johnson and the Wesleys. There are two collected editions of his works —that of 1762 and that by Moreton (1893 *et seq.*). See Walton's "Notes and Materials for a Complete Biography" (1848), Overton's "William Law, Nonjuror and Mystic" (1881), and the Rev. Dr. A. Whyte's "Characters of William Law" (1892).—PATRICK AND GROOME, *eds.*, 1897, *Chambers's Biographical Dictionary, p.* 576.

PERSONAL

One Mr. Lawes, A. M., of Cambridge, was lately degraded by the means of Dr. Adams, head of King's College, who complained to the present lord-treasurer (who was zealous for his degradation) upon account of some queries in his speech called tripos speech, such as, Whether the sun shine when it is in an eclipse? Whether a controverted son be not better than a controverted successor? Whether a dubious successor be not in danger of being set aside? With other things of the same nature.—HEARNE, THOMAS, 1713, *Diary, July* 13.

Mr. Law was in stature rather over than under the middle size; not corpulent, but stout made, with broad shoulders; his visage was round, his eyes grey; his features well proportioned, and not large; his complexion ruddy, and his countenance open and agreeable. He was naturally more inclined to be merry than sad. In his habit he was very regular and temperate. —TIGHE, RICHARD, 1813, *Life and Writings of the late Rev. William Law, p.* 30.

A thorough man, full of human infirmities, but a grand specimen of humanity, and a noble monument of the power of divine grace in the soul.—OVERTON, JOHN HENRY, 1881, *William Law, Nonjuror and Mystic, p.* 4.

Law rose at five for devotion and study; the household assembled for prayers at nine; dinner was at twelve in summer and at one in winter, and was followed by devotion. At tea-time Law joined the family, eating only a few raisins, and talking cheerfully, without sitting down. After tea the servants read a chapter of the Bible, which Law explained. He then took a brisk walk in the fields, and after another meal, again followed by prayers, he retired to his room, took one pipe and a glass of water, and went to bed at nine. They attended the church services on Wednesdays, Fridays, and Sundays; saw a few friends, and occasionally took an airing, Mrs. Hutcheson in her "coach," Law and Miss Gibbon riding on horseback. Law, in order to begin the day by an act of charity, distributed the milk of four cows to his poor neighbours. He tasted the soup which was daily prepared for the poor, and his only displays of irritability were on occasions of its being not well enough made. He loved music, and maintained that every one could be taught to sing well enough for devotional purposes. He was fond of dumb animals, and liked to free birds from their cages. He was a lover of children, and has devoted much space in his writings to advice upon their education. He had a small room for a study, which Canon Overton describes as part of "a most commodious bedroom," and altogether a "most convenient little smuggery." He had a large library, chiefly of theological books, and was an untiring student in several languages. The hearthstone of his room was worn away in two places by the rubbing of his chilly feet. . . . Law never allowed his portrait to be taken. He is described by Tighe, who visited Kings Cliffe for information, as rather over the middle height, stoutly made, but not fat, with a round face, grey eyes, ruddy complexion, and a pleasant expression. His manners were unaffected, though with a certain gravity of appearance, induced by a "clerical hat with loops let down, a black coat, and grey wig."—STEPHEN, LESLIE, 1892, *Dictionary of National Biography, vol.* XXXII, *p.* 238.

UNLAWFULNESS OF STAGE ENTERTAINMENT

The wild enthusiasm of Law's pamphlet would afford matter of scorn and laughter to infidels and freethinkers, and render our most sacred religion still more contemptible among them!—DENNIS, JOHN, 1726, *The Stage Defended from Scripture.*

Decidedly the weakest of all his writings, and most of his admirers will regret that he ever published it. Regarded merely as a composition, it is very inferior to his usual standard. Unlike himself, he gives way to passion and seems quite to lose all self-control; unlike himself, he indulges in the most violent abuse; and unlike himself he lays himself open to the most crushing retorts. He makes no distinction whatever between the use and abuse of such entertainments.—OVERTON, JOHN HENRY, 1881, *William Law, Nonjuror and Mystic, p.* 37.

REMARKS ON THE FABLE OF THE BEES

1723

The first section of Law's remarks is one of the most remarkable philosophical essays he had ever seen in English. Now this section has all the highest beauty of his (Law's) polemical compositions, and a weight of pithy right reason, such as fills one's heart with joy. I have never seen, in our language, the elementary grounds of a rational ideal philosophy, as opposed to empiricism, stated with nearly the same clearness, simplicity, and force.—STERLING, JOHN, 1854, *Letter to F. D. Maurice, "Remarks on the Fable of the Bees," Introduction.*

"Remarks on the Fable of the Bees"—the most caustic of all his writings. It is hardly more than a pamphlet, but it is a perfect gem in its way, exhibiting in miniature all the characteristic excellencies of the writer—a thorough perception of the true point at issue, and a close adherence to it, a train of reasoning in which it would be hard to find a single flaw, a brilliant wit, and a pure and nervous style.—OVERTON, JOHN HENRY, 1881, *William Law, Nonjuror and Mystic, p.* 32.

CHRISTIAN PERFECTION

Law's "Christian Perfection" fell into my hands by providence; and after reading it over and over, I recommended it so heartily to a friend of mine near London, that he procured eighteen copies for each of our parochial libraries; I have recommended it to my clergy after the most affecting manner, as the likeliest way to bring them to a most serious temper.—WILSON, BISHOP THOMAS, 1729, *Letter to Lady Elizabeth Hastings, Sept.* 13.

In this work Law begins that crusade against all kinds of human learning which henceforth almost amounted to a life-long craze with him. The most illiterate of Methodist preachers did not express a more sublime contempt of mental culture than this refined and cultured scholar. Every employment which is not of a directly religious tendency is contemptible in his eyes. . . . The "Christian Perfection" is a somewhat melancholy book: the brighter side of Christianity is certainly not brought out into full relief; Law's own character was, particularly at this period, of the stern, austere type, and his book reflects his character.—OVERTON, JOHN HENRY, 1881, *William Law, Nonjuror and Mystic, pp.* 46, 47.

You know what a book it was with the men of eighty years ago. But I had no idea of its merits. Written about the beginning of the eighteenth century by a *Jocobite Nonconformist*, its doctrine is what I suppose would now be called high-flown. But the style is excellent, the logic tenacious, the wit never-failing. Of logic there is almost a Βαναυρία even to mood and figure. It is refreshing to feel oneself for a moment in the grip of such an athlete. But I will not affect to be indifferent to the subject-matter. I think it does me good.—BROWN, THOMAS EDWARD,

1894, *Letter to S. T. Irwin, June* 15, *Letters, vol.* II, *p.* 44.

SERIOUS CALL TO A HOLY LIFE
1729

"When at Oxford, I took up 'Law's Serious Call to a Holy Life,' expecting to find it a dull book (as such books generally are), and perhaps to laugh at it. But I found Law quite an overmatch for me; and this was the first occasion of my thinking in earnest of religion, after I became capable of rational inquiry." From this time forward religion was the predominant object of his thoughts; though, with the just sentiments of a conscientious Christian, he lamented that his practice of its duties fell far short of what it ought to be.—JOHNSON, SAMUEL, 1729, *Life by Boswell, ed. Hill, vol.* I, *p.* 78.

Before I went to the University I met with Mr. Law's "Serious Call," but had not money to purchase it. Soon after my coming up to the University, seeing a small edition of it in a friend's hand, I soon purchased it. God worked powerfully upon my soul, as He has since upon many others, by that and his other excellent treatise upon "Christian Perfection."—WHITEFIELD, GEORGE, 1770? *Life and Times by Robert Philip.*

Mr. Law's "Serious Call," a book I had hitherto treated with contempt, was carelessly taken up by me. But I had no sooner opened it than I was struck with the originality of the work, and the spirit and force of argument with which it is written. . . . By the perusal of it, I was convinced, that I was guilty of great remissness and negligence; that the duties of secret devotion called for far more of my time and attention, than had been hitherto allotted to them; and that, if I hoped to save my own soul, and the souls of those that heard me, I must in this respect greatly alter my conduct, and increase my diligence in seeking and serving the Lord.—SCOTT, THOMAS, 1779, *The Force of Truth, pt.* ii.

I must beg leave to differ from those who would utterly discard Mr. Law's writings, and to assert that we have not perhaps in the language of a more masterly performance in its way, or a book better calculated to promote a concern about religion, than Mr. Law's "Serious Call to a Devout and Holy Life."—STILLINGFLEET, JAMES, 1785, *Life of Thomas Adam.*

A treatise which will hardly be excelled, if it be equalled, in the English tongue, either for beauty of expression or for justness and depth of thought.—WESLEY, JOHN, 1789, *Sermon* cxviii, *On a Single Eye.*

Mr. Law's master-work, the "Serious Call," is still read as a popular and powerful book of devotion. His precepts are rigid, but they are founded on the gospel: his satire is sharp, but it is drawn from the knowledge of human life; and many of his portraits are not unworthy of the pen of La Bruyere. If he finds a spark of piety in his reader's mind, he will soon kindle it to a flame; and a philosopher must allow that he exposes, with equal severity and truth, the strange contradiction between the faith and practice of the Christian world. Under the names of Flavia and Miranda he has admirably described my two aunts—the heathen and the christian sister.—GIBBON, EDWARD, 1794, *Memoirs of My Life and Writings.*

May be read with pleasure even by the purely literary critic. Perhaps, indeed, there is a touch of profanity in reading in cold blood a book which throughout palpitates with the deepest emotion of its author, and which has thrilled so many sympathetic spirits. The power can only be adequately felt by readers who can study it on their knees; and those to whom a difference of faith renders that attitude impossible, doubt whether they are not in a position somewhat resembling that of Mephistopheles in the cathedral. When a man is forced by an overmastering impulse to lay bare his inmost soul, the recipient of the confession should be in harmony with the writer. The creed which is accepted by Law with such unhesitating faith, and enables him to express such vivid emotions, is not exactly my own; and, if I do not infer that respectful silence is the only criticism possible, I admit that any criticism of mine is likely enough to be inappreciative. One who had yielded to the fascination would alone be qualified fully to explain its secret. And yet no one, however far apart from Law's mode of conceiving of the universe, would willingly acknowledge that he is insensible to the thoughts interpreted into his unfamiliar dialect.—STEPHEN, LESLIE, 1876, *History of English Thought in the Eighteenth Century, vol.* II, *p.* 394.

We shall understand Law's power over his generation, if we remember that the "Serious Call" was the first manifesto of Evangelicism. In all its strength and in all its weakness that appeal contained in embryo what we may not inaptly describe as the Religion of Death—the religion that, regarding our sojourn in this world as an anomalous episode in the career of eternity, makes it an object to strip it as bare as possible of everything but the anticipation of departure.—WEDGWOOD, JULIA, 1878, *William Law, the English Mystic, The Contemporary Review, vol.* 31, *p.* 93.

As a composition, it is difficult to speak too highly of it. The epithets which Wesley applied to its writer, "strong" and "elegant," express exactly two out of its many excellences. As one reads it, one feels under the guidance of a singularly strong man. There is no weak, mawkish sentimentality, no feeble declamation, no illogical argument. It is like a strong man driving a weighty hammer with well-directed blows. Every stroke tells, and you cannot evade its force. And both in style and matter it is a singularly elegant composition. There are no offences against good taste, no slipshod sentences, no attempts at fine writing in it. Its illustrations (though, perhaps a little too frequent) are always apposite, and often very beautiful. . . . If Law had written nothing whatever except the "Serious Call," he would have written quite enough to deserve a prominent and honoured place in English literature; and, what is better still, he would have written quite enough to earn the gratitude of all who value true piety.—OVERTON, JOHN HENRY, 1881, *William Law, Nonjuror and Mystic, pp.* 118, 119.

The "Serious Call" had an immediate and strong influence on many thoughtful men, and Law's book stimulated in no common measure the religious life of the country.—DENNIS, JOHN, 1894, *The Age of Pope, p.* 233.

GENERAL

Mr. William Law, after writing so excellently upon the vanity of the world and the follies of human life (on which subjects he has no superior), has left us nothing to depend upon but imagination, and reduced the whole evidence of Christianity to fancied impulses and inspiration, so as to render the sacraments useless and the means of grace contemptible.—JONES, WILLIAM, 1756, *Catholic Doctrine of the Trinity Proved, p.* 13.

In our family he had left the reputation of a worthy and pious man, who believed all that he professed, and practised all that he enjoined. The character of a nonjuror, which he maintained to the last, is a sufficient evidence of his principles in church and state; and the sacrifice of interest to conscience will be always respectable. His theological writings, which our domestic connexion has tempted me to peruse, preserve an imperfect sort of life, and I can pronounce with more confidence and knowledge on the merits of the author. His last compositions are darkly tinctured by the incomprehensible visions of Jacob Behmen; and his discourse on the absolute unlawfulness of stage-entertainments is sometimes quoted for a ridiculous intemperance of sentiment and language . . . The sallies of religious frenzy must not extinguish the praise which is due to Mr. William Law as a wit and a scholar. His argument on topics of less absurdity is specious and acute, his manner is lively, his style forcible and clear; and, had not his vigorous mind been clouded by enthusiasm, he might be ranked with the most agreeable and ingenious writers of the times.—GIBBON, EDWARD, 1794? *Memoirs of My Life and Writings.*

About this time Wesley became personally acquainted with William Law, a man whose writings completed what Jeremy Taylor, and the treatise "De Imitatione Christi," had begun. When first he visited him, he was prepared to object to his views of Christian duty as too elevated to be attainable; but Law silenced and satisfied him by replying, "We shall do well to aim at the highest degrees of perfection, if we may thereby at least attain to mediocrity." Law is a powerful writer: it is said that few books have ever made so many religious enthusiasts as his "Christian Perfection" and his "Serious Call:" indeed, the youth who should read them without being perilously affected, must have either a light mind or an unusually strong one. But Law himself, who has shaken so many intellects, sacrificed his own at last to the reveries and rhapsodies of Jacob Behmen. Perhaps the art of engraving was never applied to a more extraordinary purpose, nor in a more extraordinary manner, than when the nonsense of the German shoemaker was elucidated in a series of prints after Law's designs, representing the anatomy of the spiritual man. His own happiness, however, was certainly not diminished by the change: the system of the ascetic is dark and cheerless; but mysticism lives in a sunshine of its own, and dreams of the light of heaven; while the visions of the ascetic are such as the fear of the devil produces, rather than the love of God.—SOUTHEY, ROBERT, 1820, *The Life of John Wesley, p.* 37.

He was a moral philosopher as well as a theologian, and the man who would combat his statements or escape from his practical conclusions has more to do than shut his eyes to the evidence of revelation. —YOUNG, DAVID, 1838, *ed., Serious Call to a Holy Life.*

By drawing attention to Jacob Behmen, Law has in too many instances only been preparing a tomb for his own works.—KELTY, MARY ANN, 1838, *ed., Spiritual Fragments Selected from the Works of William Law, Memoir, p.* xvii.

I am surprised that Johnson should have pronounced William Law no reasoner. Law did indeed fall into great errors; but they were errors against which logic affords no security. In mere dialectical skill he had very few superiors. That he was more than once victorious over Hoadly no candid Whig will deny.—MACAULAY, THOMAS BABINGTON, 1855, *History of England, ch.* xiv, *note.*

A word or two should find place here concerning the fate of Behmen's doctrine. . . . His best representative in England is William Law. That nonjuring clergyman was elevated and liberalised by his intercourse with the mind of the German mystic, and well did he repay the debt. Law may be said to have introduced Behmen to the English public, both by his services as a translator, and by original writings in advocacy of his leading principles. As might be expected, the education and more practical Englishman frequently expresses the thoughts of the Teuton with much more force and clearness than their originator could command. Several other Englishmen, then and subsequently, speculated the same track. But they met with small encouragement, and their names are all but forgotten. Here and there some of their books are to be found among literary curiosities, whose rarity is their only value. If any would make acquaintance with Behmen's theology, unvexed by the difficulties of his language or the complexity in which he involves his system, let them read Law.—VAUGHAN, ROBERT ALFRED, 1856–60, *Hours with the Mystics, vol.* II, *p.* 288, *note.*

That excellent man, though somewhat cloudy writer.—ARNOLD, THOMAS, 1862–87, *A Manual of English Literature, p.* 260.

William Law has far higher merits than those of the mystic. As a controversialist, among the most logical, keen, exact, and conclusive that the Church of England has produced; as a moralist, plain, impressive, exalted; as a champion of practical religion in the midst of a material, scoffing, and corrupted age—he challenges the admiration of all good men.—PERRY, GEORGE G., 1867, *William Law and His Influence on His Age, The Contemporary Review, vol.* 6, *p.* 133.

Letters to Hoadly may fairly be put on a level with the "Lettres Provinciales" of Blaise Pascal,—both displaying equal power, wit, and learning.—EWING, ALEXANDER, 1869? *ed. Present-Day Papers on Prominent Questions in Theology.*

The immense influence upon the cultivated English student of the rugged, uncouth writings of Jacob Behmen, the Gorlitz shoemaker, "the Teutonic Theosopher," is at first appearance a curious phenomenon. But in Germany the case is abundantly paralleled. Arndt and Andreas, Spener and Francke, Zinzendorf, Novalis, Kahlman, and Schlegel were all more or less indebted to him. Nor can it be wondered at. For amid all his unintelligible verbiage, amid extraordinary fancies, which sometimes seem like the uncontrolled ramblings of insanity, are scattered passages of great beauty and remarkable spiritual insight. And truly there is a golden thread running through it all. For William Law his writings had a surpassing fascination. He mastered the language in order to read them in the original Dutch, translated and published them in folio, and filled his mind with the thoughts which had inspired them.

Although the turbid stream was not altogether infiltrated by its passage through Law's clear and logical intellect, yet he sifted out much of the dregs, while he remained in firm possession of the treasure. To many of his contemporaries it seemed as though he had ruined himself as a divine. They turned with aversion from the too often frequent remains of Behmen's strange jargon. But as soon as it has escaped from this the stream is clear and pure. In the opinion, not indeed of all, but of many competent judges, Law gains far more than he loses by his studies, both of the mystical theology in general, and in particular of Behmen.—ABBEY, CHARLES J., 1887, *The English Church and Its Bishops*, 1700–1800, *vol.* I, *p.* 294.

Among all the divines, the one who wrote most vigorously is perhaps that very ingenious and powerful Tertullian of the dissenters, William Law.—GOSSE, EDMUND, 1888, *A History of Eighteenth Century Literature, p.* 396.

The logical power shown in Law's controversial writings surpasses that of any contemporary author, unless Bentley be an exception. His assaults upon Hoadly, Mandeville, and Tindal could only have failed to place him in the front rank because they diverged too far from the popular theories. He was the most thoroughgoing opponent of the dominant rationalism of which Locke was the great exponent, and which, in his view, could lead only to infidelity. He takes the ground (see especially his answer to Tindal) of the impotence of human reason, and some points anticipates Butler's "Apology."—STEPHEN, LESLIE, 1892, *Dictionary of National Biography, vol.* XXXII, *p.* 239.

Sombre and yet eloquent; instinct with feelings; at once severe and grim in his earnestness, and copious in the range of his imagination.—CRAIK, HENRY, 1895, *ed., English Prose, Introduction, vol.* IV, *p.*5.

Masters of English Prose are not so plentiful that we can afford to allow one who stands in the very first rank to slip into oblivion. And it would be difficult to find many who combine as Law does so much vigour and raciness of thought and diction, so pure and luminous a style, such brilliant, if somewhat grim, humour, such pungent sarcasm, such powers of reasoning. There is, indeed, a stern severity about the writer which is very characteristic of the man; but it is equally characteristic that amid this sternness he sometimes breaks out into passages of sweet tenderness, which are all the more touching from their contrast with the ruggedness of their surroundings. . . . He never loses sight of his subject, and, granting his premises, it is impossible to put a pin's point between his deductions from them. He is, moreover, a singularly equal writer, unlike the good Homer, he never nods, never descends below himself. One might take passages almost at random, and yet convey as favourable an impression of him, as by carefully selecting specimens which shew him at his best. —OVERTON, JOHN HENRY, 1895, *English Prose, ed. Craik, vol.* IV, *pp.* 42, 43.

Law represents, moreover, the best type of pamphleteer that religious controversy has produced. A Latitudinarian himself in a higher sense of that ill-used word, he had the deepest sympathy with those who were outside his communion, saying once that he would like the truth no less because Ignatius Loyola, or John Bunyan, or George Fox were very zealous for it. Who else could have written such words at that time? Or who else could have said in an age, when controversy was still deformed by virulent personalities, that "by the grace of God he would never have any personal contention with anyone?" To those words he kept faithful in the face of great provocation, and therefore he deserves a place of peculiar honour in the strangely assorted crowd of pamphleteers.—DEARMER, PERCY, 1898, *ed., Religious Pamphlets, Introduction, p.*39.

In the goodly succession of the masters of the eighteenth-century style, William Law has an indisputable place, and one could almost wish at times that his theme had not been religion, so that his power as a writer might have been recognised. If he had bantered and satirised and handled the *lacrimæ rerum*, as he was very well able to do, in papers like the *Spectator*, the *Tatler* and the *Rambler*, his place in literature would not have been doubtful. But because he was occupied with religion, counted man as an immortal soul, and used his powers to promote the eternal welfare of men, he is left among the preachers and that dull kind of creature, instead of being ranked among the wits and men of letters. If we mark the eighteenth-century style as in its golden age with Steele and Addison, Pope and Swift, and if we admit it overripe in Gibbon and Dr. Johnson, there is a silver, or a mellow, period which reaches to the middle of the century. Fielding is the most famous reputation of this silver age; Berkeley is the most gifted writer; but William Law is its consummate representative. In him the seriousness and humor of the essayists still blend; in him the weight and stateliness of Burke and Gibbon are already perceptible; and Johnson's gravity, though not his ponderousness, is the ballast of the style.—HORTON, ROBERT F., 1899, *Among My Books, Literature, vol.* 5, *p.* 221.

Samuel Richardson

1689-1761

Samuel Richardson, 1689-1761. Born, in Derbyshire, 1689. Apprenticed to a stationer, 1706. Afterwards employed as compositor at a printing works. Set up as a printer on his own account, 1719. Married (i.) Martha Wilde. She died, 25 Jan. 1731. Married (ii.) Elizabeth Leake. Began novel writing, 1739. Master of Stationers' Company, 1754. Died, in London, 4 July 1761. Buried in St. Bride's Church. *Works:* "Pamela" (anon.), 1741-42; "Clarissa"' (anon.), 1748; "The History of Sir Charles Grandison" (anon.), 1754 (2nd edn. same year). *Posthumous:* "Correspondence," ed. by A. L. Barbauld (6 vols.), 1804. He *edited:* "A Tour thro' . . . at Great Britain,"1742; Sir T. Roe's "Negotiations in his Embassy to the Ottoman Porte," 1746; "The Life . . . of Balbe Berton" [1760?]. *Collected Works:* ed. by E. Mangin (19 vols.), 1811; ed. by Leslie Stephen (12 vols.), 1883.——SHARP, R. FARQUHARSON, 1897, *A Dictionary of English Authors, p.* 239.

PERSONAL

As I had never formed any great idea of a printer by those I have seen in Ireland, I was very negligent of my dress, any more than making myself clean; but was extremely surprised when I was directed to a house of very grand outward appearance, and had it been a palace, the beneficent master deserved it. I met a very civil reception from him, and he not only made me breakfast, but also dine with him and his agreeable wife and children. After dinner he called me into his study and showed me an order he had received to pay me twelve guineas, which he immediately took out of his escritoire and put into my hand; but when I went to tell them over, I found that I had fourteen, and, supposing the gentleman had made a mistake, I was for returning two of them, but he with a sweetness and modesty almost peculiar to himself, said he hoped I would not take it ill, that he had presumed to add a trifle to the bounty of my friend. I really was confounded till recollecting that I had read "Pamela," and been told it was written by one Mr. Richardson, I asked him whether he was not the author of it. He said he was the editor: I told him my surprise was now over, as I found he had only given to the incomparable "Pamela" the virtues of his own worthy heart.—PILKINGTON, LETITIA, 1748, *Memoirs, vol.* II.

Short; rather plump than emaciated, notwithstanding his complaints; about five foot five inches; fair wig; lightish cloth coat, all black besides; one hand generally in his bosom, the other a cane in it, which he leans upon under the skirts of his coat usually, that it may imperceptibly serve him as a support, when attacked by sudden tremors or startings, and dizziness, which too frequently attack him, but, thank God, not so often as formerly; looking directly foreright, as passers-by would imagine, but observing all that stirs on either hand of him without moving his short neck; hardly ever turning back; of a light-brown complexion; teeth not yet failing him; smoothish faced, and ruddy-cheeked; . . . a grey eye, too often overclouded by mistinesses from the head; by chance lively; very lively it will be, if he have hope of seeing a lady whom he loves and honours; his eye always on the ladies.—RICHARDSON, SAMUEL, 1749, *Letter to Mrs. Belfour.*

Poor Mr. Richardson was seized on Sunday evening with a most severe paralytic stroke. How many good hearts will be afflicted by this in many more countries than England! To how many will he be an inexpressible loss! But to consider him at present as lost to himself and perhaps with some sense of that loss is most grievous. It sits pleasantly upon my mind that the last morning we spent together was particularly friendly and quiet and comforting. It was the twenty-eighth of May—he looked then so well! One has long apprehended some stroke of this kind; the disease made its gradual approaches by that heaviness which clouded the cheerfulness of his conversation, that used to be so lively and so instructive; by the increased tremblings which unfitted that hand so peculiarly formed to guide the pen; and by perhaps the querulousness of temper most certainly not natural to so sweet and so enlarged a mind, which you and I have lately lamented as making his family at times not so comfortable as his principles, his study and his delight to diffuse happiness wherever he could, would otherwise have done. Well, his noble spirit will soon now I suppose be freed from its corporeal encumbrance; it were a sin to wish against it, and yet how few such will be left behind.—TALBOT, MISS, 1761, *Letter to Mrs. Carter, Correspondence, vol.* II, *p.* 209.

If ever warm benevolence was dear,
If ever wisdom gained esteem sincere,
Or genuine fancy deep attention won
Approach with awe the dust—of Richardson.
What though his muse, through distant regions known,
Might scorn the tribute of this humble stone;
Yet pleasing to his gentle shade, must prove
The meanest pledge of Friendship, and of Love;
For oft will these, from venal throngs exiled,
And oft will Innocence, of aspect mild,
And white-robed Charity, with streaming eyes,
Frequent the cloister where their patron lies.
This, reader, learn; and learn from one whose woe
Bids her wild verse in artless accents flow:
For, could she frame her numbers to commend
The husband, father, citizen, and friend;
How would her muse display, in equal strain,
The critic's judgment, and the writer's vein!
Ah, no, expect not from the chiselled stone
The praises, graven on our hearts alone.
There shall his fame a lasting shrine acquire;
And ever shall his moving page inspire
Pure truth, fixt honour, virtue's pleasing lore;
While taste and science crown this favoured shore.

—CARTER, ELIZABETH, 1761, *Epitaph on Richardson.*

At Mr. Nairne's, he drew the character of Richardson, the authour of "Clarissa," with a strong yet delicate pencil. I lament much that I have not preserved it; I only remember that he expressed a high opinion of his talents and virtues; but observed, that "his perpetual study was to ward off petty inconveniences, and procure petty pleasures; that his love of continual superiority was such, that he took care to be always surrounded by women, who listened to him implicitly, and did not venture to controvert his opinions; and that his desire of distinction was so great, that he used to give large vails to the Speaker Onslow's servants, that they might treat him with respect."—JOHNSON, SAMUEL, 1773, *Life by Boswell, Nov.* 11–20, *ed. Hill, vol.* V, *p.* 451.

A literary lady has favoured me with a characteristick anecdote of Richardson. One day at his country-house at Northend, where a large company was assembled at dinner, a gentleman who was just returned from Paris, willing to please Mr. Richardson, mentioned to him a very flattering circumstance,—that he had seen his "Clarissa" lying on the King's brother's table. Richardson observing that part of the company were engaged in talking to each other, affected then not to attend to it. But by and by, when there was a general silence, and he thought that the flattery might be fully heard, he addressed himself to the gentleman, "I think, Sir, you were saying something about,—" pausing in a high flutter of expectation. The gentleman provoked at his inordinate vanity, resolved not to indulge it, and with an exquisite sly air of indifference answered, "A mere trifle, Sir, not worth repeating!" The mortification of Richardson was visible, and he did not speak ten words more the whole day. Dr. Johnson was present, and appeared to enjoy it much.—BOSWELL, JAMES, 1780, *Life of Samuel Johnson, ed. Hill, vol.* IV, *p.* 34, *note.*

Richardson's conversation was of the preceptive kind, but it wanted the diversity of Johnson's, and had no intermixture of wit or humour. Richardson could never relate a pleasant story, and hardly relish one told by another: he was ever thinking of his own writings, and listening to the praises which, with an emulous profusion, his friends were incessantly bestowing on them, he would scarce enter into free conversation with any one that he thought had not red "Clarissa," or "Sir Charles Grandison," and at best, he could not be said to be a companionable man. Those who were unacquainted with Richardson, and had red his books, were led to believe, that they exhibited a picture of his own mind, and that his temper and domestic behaviour could not but correspond with that refined morality which they inculcate, but in this they were deceived. He was austere in the government of his family, and issued his orders to some of his servants in writing only. His nearest female relations, in the presence of strangers, were mutes, and seemed to me, in a visit I once made him, to have been disciplined in the school of Ben Jonson's Morose, whose injunction to his servant was, "Answer me not but with your leg." In short, they appeared to have been taught to converse with him by signs; and it was too plain to me, that on his part, the most frequent of them were frowns and gesticulations, importing that they should leave his presence. I have heard it said, that he was what is called a nervous man; and how far nervosity, with so good an understanding as he is allowed to have possessed, will excuse a conduct so opposite to that philanthrophy which he laboured to inculcate, I cannot say: his benevolence might have taken another direction, and in other instances be very strong; for I was once a witness to his putting into the hand of Mr. Whiston the bookseller, ten guineas for the relief of one whom a sudden accident had made a widow.—HAWKINS, SIR JOHN, 1787, *Life of Samuel Johnson*, *p.* 384.

He was delighted by his own works. No author enjoyed so much the bliss of excessive fondness. I heard from the late Charlotte Lenox the anecdote which so severely reprimanded his innocent vanity, which Boswell has recorded. This lady was a regular visitor at Richardson's house, and she could scarcely recollect one visit which was not taxed by our author reading one of his voluminous letters, or two or three, if his auditor was quiet and friendly.—DISRAELI, ISAAC, 1791–1824, *Richardson, Curiosities of Literature.*

Richardson, the author of "Clarissa," had been a common printer, and possessed no literature whatever. He was very silent in company, and so vain that he never enjoyed any subject but that of himself or his works. He once asked Douglas, Bishop of Salisbury, how he liked "Clarissa." The bishop said he could never get beyond the Bailiff scene. The author, thinking this a condemnation of his book, looked grave; but all was right when the bishop added, it affected him so much that he was drowned in tears, and could not trust himself with the book any longer. Richardson had a kind of club of women about him—Mrs. Carter, Mrs. Talbot, &c.—who looked up to him as to a superior being; to whom he dictated and gave laws; and with whom he lived almost entirely. To acquire a facility of epistolary writing he would on every trivial occasion write notes to his daughters even when they were in the same house with him.—(Bishop Douglas and Dr. Johnson).—MALONE, EDMOND, 1792, *Maloniana, ed. Prior, p.* 439.

Richardson was, in person, below the middle stature, and inclined to corpulency; of a round, rather than oval, face, with a fair ruddy complexion. His features, says one, who speaks from recollection, bore the stamp of good nature, and were characteristic of his placid and amiable disposition. He was slow in speech, and, to strangers at least, spoke with reserve and deliberation; but, in his manners, was affable, courteous, and engaging, and when surrounded with the social circle he loved to draw around him, his eye sparkled with pleasure, and often expressed that particular spirit of archness which we see in some of his characters, and which gave, at times, a vivacity to his conversation, not expected from his general taciturnity and quiet manners.—BARBAULD, ANNA LÆTITIA, 1804, *ed. The Correspondence of Samuel Richardson, Life vol.* I, *p.* clxxvi.

His moral character was in the highest degree exemplary and amiable. He was temperate, industrious, and upright; punctual and honourable in all his dealings; and with a kindness of heart, and a liberality and generosity of disposition, that must have made him a very general favourite, even if he had never acquired any literary distinction.—He had a considerable share of vanity, and was observed to talk more willingly on the subject of his own works than on any other. The lowness of his original situation, and the lateness of his introduction into polite society, had given to his manners a great shyness and reserve; and a consciousness of his awkwardness and his merit together, rendered him somewhat jealous in his intercourse with persons in more conspicuous situations, and made him require more courting and attention than every one was disposed to pay. He had high notions of parental authority, and does not seem always quite satisfied with the share of veneration which his wife could be prevailed on to shew for him. He was particularly partial to the society of females; and lived, indeed, as Mrs. Barbauld has expressed it, in a flower-garden of ladies. —JEFFREY, FRANCIS LORD, 1804, *Richardson, Edinburgh Review, vol.* 5, *p.* 31.

He was unceasingly industrious; led astray by no idle views of speculation, and seduced by no temptations to premature expenditure. Industry brought independence, and, finally, wealth in its train; and that well-won fortune was husbanded with prudence, and expended with liberality. A kind and generous master, he was eager to encourage his servants to persevere in the same course of patient labour by which he had himself attained fortune; and it is said to have been his common practice to hide half-a-crown among the types, that it might reward the diligence of the workman who should first be in the office in the morning. His hospitality was of the most liberal, as well as the most judicious kind. . . . The predominant failing of Richardson seems certainly to have been vanity; vanity naturally excited by his great and unparalleled popularity at home and abroad, and by the continual and concentred admiration of the circle in which he lived. Such a weakness finds root in the mind of every one who has obtained general applause, but Richardson, the gentleness of whose mind was almost feminine, was peculiarly susceptible of this feminine weakness, and he fostered and indulged its growth, which a man of firmer character would have crushed and restrained.—SCOTT, SIR WALTER, 1821, *Samuel Richardson.*

His own manners were strict and formal with regard to his family, probably because he had formed his notions of life from old books, and also because he did not well know how to begin to do otherwise (for he was naturally bashful), and so the habit continued through life. His daughters addressed him in their letters by the title of "Honoured Sir," and are always designating themselves as "ever dutiful." Sedentary living, eternal writing, and perhaps that indulgence in the table, which, however moderate, affects a sedentary man twenty times as much as an active one, conspired to hurt his temper (for we may see by his picture that he grew fat, and his philosophy was in no respect as profound as he thought it); but he was a most kind-hearted generous man; kept his pocket full of plums for children, like another Mr. Burchell; gave a great deal of money away in charity, very handsomely too; and was so fond of inviting friends to stay with him, that when they were ill, he and his family must needs have them to be nursed.—HUNT, LEIGH, 1848, *The Town, p.* 90.

The great author was accustomed to be adored. A gentler wind never puffed mortal vanity. Enraptured spinsters flung tea-leaves around him, and incensed him with the coffee-pot. Matrons kissed the slippers they had worked for him. There was a halo of virtue around his nightcap. All Europe had thrilled, panted, admired, trembled, wept o'er the pages of the immortal little kind honest man with the round paunch. Harry came back quite glowing and proud at having a bow from him. "Ah," says he, "my lord, I am glad to have seen him!"—THACKERAY, WILLIAM MAKEPEACE, 1858, *The Virginians, ch.* xxvi.

Good Samuel Richardson—for you really were a good man, in a higher sense to your mind than your own "Sir Charles Grandison"—forgive me if I cannot forbear a smile now and then at your little vanities, so inseparable from the adulation of your "ladies" of every degree, from the precise Mrs. Chapone to the erring Mrs. Pilkington; for men of various morals, from Dr. Young to Colley Cibber. You are, perhaps, amongst the most famous of those who have been writers as well as publishers; but you command my admiration from the fact that you never neglected the duties of your station to surrender yourself to the temptation that beset the man who depends upon authorship alone for holding a firm standing in social life.—KNIGHT, CHARLES, 1865, *Shadows of the Old-Booksellers, p.* 146.

He was a printer and bookseller, a joiner's son, who at the age of fifty, and in his leisure moments, wrote in his shop parlour: a laborious man, who, by work and good conduct, had raised himself to a competency and sound information; delicate, moreover gentle, nervous, often ill, with a taste for the society of women, accustomed to correspond for and with them, of reserved and retired habits, whose only fault was a timid vanity. He was severe in principles, and had acquired perspicacity by his rigour.—TAINE, H. A, 1871, *History of English Literature, tr. Van Laun, vol.* II, *bk.* iii, *ch.* vi, *p.* 159.

Richardson died of apoplexy, July 4, 1761, in this house in Parson's Green, and was buried, at his own request, by the side of his first wife, in the Church of St. Bride, in Fleet Street. A large stone in the pavement of the middle aisle, near the centre of the church, and by the side of the pews numbered 12 and 13 in 1885, records the fact that he lies beneath it. The parish, during the century or more that has elapsed since his death, has not had interest enough in the Father of the English Novel to erect a tablet to his memory; and the stone above him, placed there by the loving hands of his family, is concealed from the public by the coarse matting that generally covers it.—HUTTON, LAURENCE, 1885, *Literary Landmarks of London, p.* 255.

It may safely be said of Richardson that, after attaining to independence, he did more good every week of his life—for he was a wise and most charitable man—than Fielding was ever able to do throughout the whole of his.—BIRRELL, AUGUSTINE, 1892, *Res Judicatæ, p.* 7.

PAMELA
1741–42

Bless'd be thy powerful pen, whoe'er thou art,
Thou skill'd great moulder of the master'd heart!
Where hast thou lain conceal'd? or why thought fit,
At this dire period, to unveil thy wit?
. . . .
Sweet Pamela! for ever blooming maid!
Thou dear enlivening (yet immortal) shade
Why are thy virtues scatter'd to the wind?
Why are thy beauties flash'd upon the blind!
What though thy fluttering sex might learn from thee,
That merit forms a rank above degree?
That pride, too conscious, falls from every claim,
While humble sweetness climbs beyond its aim.
—HILL, AARON, 1740? *To the Unknown Author of the Beautiful New Piece, called "Pamela."*

Two booksellers, my particular friends [Mr. Rivington and Mr. Osborne] entreated me to write for them a little volume of Letters in a common style, on such subjects as might be of use to those country readers who were unable to indite for themselves. "Will it be any harm," said I, "in a piece you want to be written so low, if we should instruct them how they should think and act in common cases as well as indite?" They were the more urgent for me to begin the little volume for this hint. I set about it; and, in the progress of it, writing two or three letters to instruct handsome girls who were obliged to go out to service, as we phrase it, how to avoid the snares that might be laid against their virtue, the above story recurred to my thought; and hence sprung "Pamela."—RICHARDSON, SAMUEL, c1760, *Correspondence, ed. Barbauld, vol.* I, *Introduction, p.* liii.

A work, usually found in the servant's drawer, but which, when so found, has not unfrequently detained the eye of the mistress, wondering all the while by what secret charm she was induced to turn over a book, apparently too low for her perusal, and that charm was—Richardson.—BARBAULD, ANNA LÆTITIA, 1804, *Life of Samuel Richardson.*

Taking the general idea of the character of a modest and beautiful country girl, and of the ordinary situation in which she is placed, he makes out all the rest, even to the smallest circumstance, by the mere force of a reasoning imagination. It would seem as if a step lost would be as fatal here as in a mathematical demonstration. The development of the character is the most simple, and comes the nearest to nature that it can do, without being the same thing. The interest of the story increases with the dawn of understanding and reflection in the heroine; her sentiments gradually expand themselves, like opening flowers.—HAZLITT, WILLIAM, 1818, *On the English Novelists,*

Lectures on the English Comic Writers, Lecture vi.

Thought what fame was on reading in a case of murder that "Mr. Wych, grocer at Tunbbridge, sold some bacon, flour, cheese, and, it is believed some plums, to some gipsy woman accused. He had on his counter (I quote faithfully) a book, the 'Life of Pamela,' which he was tearing for waste-paper, &c. In the cheese was found, &c., and a leaf of 'Pamela' wrapt around the bacon!" What would Richardson, the vainest and luckiest of *living* authors (*i. e.*, while alive)—he who, with Aaron Hill, used to prophesy and chuckle over the presumed fall of Fielding (the prose Homer of human nature), and of Pope (the most beautiful of poets)—what would he have said, could he have traced his pages from their place on the French prince's toilets (see Boswell's "Johnson") to the grocer's counter and the gipsy murderess's bacon!!!—BYRON, LORD, 1821, *A Journal in Italy, Jan.* 4.

It will be Richardson's eternal praise, did he merit no more, that he tore from his personages those painted vizors, which concealed, under a clumsy and affected disguise, everything like the natural lineaments of the human countenance, and placed them before us barefaced, in all the actual changes of feature and complexion, and all the light and shade of human passion. It requires a reader to be in some degree acquainted with the huge folios of inanity, over which our ancestors yawned themselves to sleep, ere he can estimate the delight they must have experienced from this unexpected return to truth and nature.—SCOTT, SIR WALTER, 1821, *Samuel Richardson.*

I do not remember a more whimsical surprise than having been once detected—by a familiar damsel—reclined at my ease upon the grass, on Primrose Hill (her Cythera), reading—"Pamela." There was nothing in the book to make a man seriously ashamed at the exposure; but as she seated herself down by me, and seemed determined to read in company, I could have wished it had been—any other book. We read on very sociably for a few pages; and, not finding the author much to her taste, she got up, and—went away. Gentle casuist, I leave it to thee to conjecture whether the blush (for there was one between us) was the property of the nymph or the swain in this dilemma. From me you shall never get the secret.—LAMB, CHARLES, 1834? *Detached Thoughts on Books and Reading.*

It would be idle to say that a work which was so extensively read, does not possess merits of a very high order. But, on the other hand, it is clear, that however great its attractions, they were much over-estimated and over-praised. The moral teaching which received the approbation of Pope and Sherlock should not be lightly spoken of; yet, with all due deference to such great authorities, it may be questioned whether many readers have risen from the perusal of Richardson's novel with more elevated notions of female honour than they before entertained. His morality was that of the age—rather the virtue of prudence than principle.—LAWRENCE, FREDERICK, 1855, *The Life of Henry Fielding, p.* 152.

This first novel is a flower—one of those flowers which only bloom in a virgin imagination, at the dawn of original invention, whose charm and freshness surpass all that the maturity of art and genius can afterwards cultivate or arrange.—TAINE, H. A., 1871, *History of English Literature, tr. Van Laun, vol.* II, *bk.* iii, *ch.* vi, *p.* 160.

I have already given the substance of the first two volumes in which the rich squire, Mr. B. (as he is called throughout the novel), finally marries and takes home the girl who had been the servant of his wife and against whom, ever since that lady's death, he had been plotting with an elaborate baseness which has never before been, and I sincerely hope will never hereafter be described. By this action Mr. B. has in the opinion of Richardson, of his wife, the servant-girl and the whole contemporary world, saturated himself with such a flame of saintliness as to have burnt out every particle of any little misdemeanor he may have been guilty of in his previous existence; and I need only read you an occasional line from the first four letters of the third volume in order to show the marvelous sentimentality, the untruth towards nature, and the purely commercial view of virtue and of religion which make up this intolerable book.—LANIER, SIDNEY, 1881, *The English Novel, p.* 178.

The name, "Pamela, or Virtue Rewarded," sounds like a tract, and

"Pamela" is, indeed, a very long tract. —TUCKERMAN, BAYARD, 1882, *A History of English Prose Fiction, p.* 195.

Few writers—it is a truism to say so—have excelled him in minute analysis of motive, and knowledge of the human heart. About the final morality of his heroine's long-drawn defence of her chastity it may, however, be permitted to doubt; and, in contrasting the book with Fielding's work, it should not be forgotten that, irreproachable though it seemed to the author's admirers, good Dr. Watts complained (and with reason) of the indelicacy of some of the scenes.—DOBSON, AUSTIN, 1883, *Fielding (English Men of Letters), p.* 71.

While the story of "Pamela" suffers as a story from the slowness of movement which, in a less degree (though the slowness is even greater), injures that of Clarissa, the former heroine, unlike the latter, is herself as severe a sufferer *as* a heroine from the delay. Her figure, to begin with, is one which will not stand much de-romanticizing. Mrs. Pamela's virtue, though no doubt quite sincere and genuine, is (as of course it should be) of a very soubrettish type, exceedingly, not to say pharisaically, self-conscious, not refined or elevated by the slightest admixture of delicacy, and obviously associated with a very shrewd eye to the main chance. All this, of course, is true enough to Nature; but truth to Nature becomes useless unless it falls into the impartial hands of Art.—TRAILL, HENRY DUFF, 1883–97, *Samuel Richardson, The New Fiction, p.* 116.

Sir John Herschel tells an amusing anecdote illustrating the pleasure derived from a book, not assuredly of the first order. In a certain village the blacksmith had got hold of Richardson's novel, "Pamela, or Virtue Rewarded," and used to sit on his anvil in the long summer evenings and read it aloud to a large and attentive audience. It is by no means a short book, but they fairly listened to it all. "At length, when the happy turn of fortune arrived, which brings the hero and heroine together, and sets them living long and happily according to the most approved rules, the congregation were so delighted as to raise a great shout, and procuring the church keys, actually set the parish bells ringing."—LUBBOCK, SIR JOHN, 1887, *A Song of Books, The Pleasures of Life, First Series, p.* 53.

His "Pamela" survives, not as the virtuous serving-maid he tried to portray, but as a perfectly true picture of an atrocious prude, who well knew how to play her cards to advantage.—LEWIN, WALTER, 1889, *The Abuse of Fiction, The Forum, vol.* 7, *p.* 668.

Along with its uncouthness, moreover, Richardson's novel is not without some excellent features of its own. It is prolix to tediousness, but there is at the same time considerable ingenuity in invention. There is an almost painful elaboration of expression, and the phraseology is stilted, but there is consistency in the portraits, and the attempt at character painting is not without a degree of success. Pamela exerts a steady influence for good, until all about her are converted by the power of her example. The wicked Mr. B. succumbs, and even the notorious Mrs. Jewkes is won to penitence and the path of virtue. It is the fashion to laugh, as Fielding did, at this tedious, moralizing, sentimental story; and yet there is a good deal in it that is both homely and wholesome. Richardson plainly did not possess the art that may be claimed by Fielding or Smollett or Sterne; but he was sincere, and honestly pure in his aim, which is more than can be said of any one of the other three.—SIMONDS, WILLIAM EDWARD, 1894, *Study of English Fiction, p.* 46.

Pamela, indeed, may be virtuous, but she is anything but pure-minded; and in this lies her security? Unsuspecting innocence may easily become the prey of vice, but the reader feels that if Pamela falls, it will be with her eyes open. And the worst of it is that in spite of her oft-repeated protestations against her master's wickedness, she is supposed all the time to have a secret leaning to him, and dreads nothing more than to incur his anger. . . . Putting aside these grave faults of taste and morality, there can be no doubt that the heroine is a masterpiece of characterisation. To this is due the pathetic and moving effect produced by her sufferings; she is so life-like that one feels the same kind of interest in them as in those of a real person. . . . A book the defects of which can hardly be over-stated; whose warped morality, glaring want of taste, and improbability of incident, would seem sufficient to obscure all the merit that cannot be denied to it. It is only when we remember that both plan and subject matter were entirely original, and that the sentiments and treatment correspond to the ordinary tone of lower middle-class feeling at the time, that we can comprehend or sympathise with the immense enthusiasm it excited. It inaugurated a new school of fiction, and if its permanent popularity in England was somewhat impaired by the speedy publication of Fielding's parody, its effect on the literary development of France and Germany, where many imitations were produced, was of the greatest importance. —THOMSON, CLARA LINKLATER, 1900, *Samuel Richardson, A Biographical and Critical Study, pp.* 157, 166, 170.

CLARISSA HARLOWE
1748

When I tell you I have lately received this Pleasure (*i. e.*, of reading a new master-piece), you will not want me to inform you that I owe it to the author of "Clarissa." Such Simplicity, such Manners, such deep Penetration into Nature; such Power to raise and alarm the Passions, few Writers, either ancient or modern, have been possessed of. My Affections are so strongly engaged, and my Fears are so raised, by what I have already read, that I cannot express my Eagerness to see the rest. Sure this Mr. *Richardson* is Master of all that Art which *Horace* compares to Witchcraft

—Pectus inaniter angit,
Irritat, mulcet, falsis terroribus implet
Ut Magus.—

—FIELDING, HENRY? 1748, *Jacobite's Journal, No.* 5.

I begin by a confession which ought to do some credit to my honesty because it might do little honour to my discernment. Of all the imaginative works I have read, and my self-conceit does not lead me to except my own, none have given me greater pleasure than the one now submitted to the public.—PRÉVOST, ABBÉ, 1751, *ed. Clarissa Harlowe, Preface.*

I was such an old fool as to weep over "Clarissa Harlowe," like any milkmaid of sixteen over the ballad of the "Lady's Fall." To say truth, the first volume softened me by a near resemblance of my maiden days; but on the whole 'tis most miserable stuff. Miss How, who is called a young lady of sense and honour, is not only extremely silly, but a more vicious character than Sally Martin, whose crimes are owing at first to seduction, and afterwards to necessity; while this virtuous damsel, without any reason, insults her mother at home and ridicules her abroad; abuses the man she marries; and is impertinent and impudent with great applause. Even that model of affection, Clarissa, is so faulty in her behaviour as to deserve little compassion. Any girl that runs away with a young fellow, without intending to marry him, should be carried to Bridewell or to Bedlam the next day. Yet the circumstances are so laid, as to inspire tenderness, notwithstanding the low style and absurd incidents; and I look upon this and "Pamela" to be two books that will do more general mischief than the works of Lord Rochester.—MONTAGU, LADY MARY WORTLEY, 1752, *Letter to the Countess of Bute, March* 1.

I do not think that the age can show a more faithful, more delicate, more spirited touch. We do not read, we *see* what he describes.—MARMONTEL, JEAN FRANÇOIS, 1758, *Mercure de France, August.*

I yet remember with delight the first time it came into my hands. I was in the country. How deliciously was I affected! At every moment I saw my happiness abridged by a page. I then experienced the same sensations those feel who have long lived with one they love, and are on the point of separation. At the close of the work I seemed to remain deserted.—DIDEROT, DENIS, 1761, *Éloge on Richardson, tr. Disraeli.*

This novel may display more talent than Sir Charles Grandison (though, when I recollect the character of Clementina, I should be disposed to contest even this point), but it has certainly interested and delighted me less. Till the grand catastrophe we are exasperated to maddening impatience by the incessant and varied persecutions of the helpless heroine.—GREEN, THOMAS, 1779–1810, *Diary of a Lover of Literature.*

The character of Lothario seems to have been expanded by Richardson into that of Lovelace; but he has excelled his original in the moral effect of the fiction. Lothario, with gaiety which cannot be hated, and bravery which cannot be despised, retains too much of the spectator's kindness. It was in the power of Richardson alone, to teach us at once esteem and detestation; to make virtuous resentment overpower all the benevolence which wit, and elegance, and courage, naturally excite; and to lose at last the hero in the villain.—JOHNSON, SAMUEL, 1779–81, *Rowe, Lives of the English Poets*.

The plot, as we have seen, is simple, and no under-plots interfere with the main design. No digression, no episodes. It is wonderful that without these helps of common writers he could support a work of such length. With Clarissa it begins—with Clarissa it ends. We do not come upon unexpected adventures and wonderful recognitions, by quick turns and surprises; we see her fate from afar, as it were through a long avenue, the gradual approach to which, without ever losing sight of the object, has more of simplicity and grandeur than the most cunning labyrinth that can be contrived by art. . . . As the work advances, the character rises; the distress is deepened; our hearts are torn with pity and indignation; bursts of grief succeed one another, till at length the mind is composed and harmonized with emotions of milder sorrow; we are calmed into resignation, elevated with pious hope, and dismissed glowing with the conscious triumphs of virtue.—BARBAULD, ANNA LÆTITIA, 1804, *Life of Richardson, pp.* lxxxiii, lxxxiv.

Richardson has strengthened Vice, from the mouth of Lovelace, with entangling sophistries and abstruse pleas against her adversary Virtue, which Sedley, Villiers, and Rochester wanted depth of libertinism enough to have invented.—LAMB, CHARLES, 1808, *Specimens of Dramatic Poets*.

The effect of the death of Clarissa—or of Mary Stuart—on the heart, by no means depends on the fact that the one really died, but on the vivacity of the exhibition by the two great painters, Hume and Richardson. . . . I have been reading "Clarissa Harlowe," and my frame is so easily disturbed, that a few of the most common sentences in the first hundred pages of the first volume have brought tears from me. . . . I have just finished poor "Clarissa," and my body is too weak for writing a criticism—even if my mind had power for it. She left her father's house on the 10th of April, and died on the 7th of September. —MACKINTOSH, SIR JAMES, 1811–12, *Journal, Life by Mackintosh, vol.* II, *chs.* ii, iii.

Except by "Clarissa Harlowe," I was never so moved by a work of genius as by "Othello." I read seventeen hours a day at "Clarissa," and held the book so long up, leaning on my elbows in an armchair, that I stopped the circulation and could not move. When Lovelace writes, "Dear Belton, it is all over, and Clarissa lives," I got up in a fury and wept like an infant, and cursed and d——d Lovelace till exhausted. This is the triumph of genius over the imagination and heart of its readers.—HAYDON, BENJAMIN ROBERT, 1813, *Autobiography, March* 3.

But though the character of Lovelace may not perhaps be objectionable in its moral tendency, there is no representation, in the whole range of fiction, which is such an outrage on verisimilitude. Such a character as Lovelace not only never existed, but seems incompatible with human nature. Great crimes may be hastily perpetrated where there is no strong motive for their commission, but a long course of premeditated villainy has always some assignable object which cannot be innocently attained.—DUNLOP, JOHN, 1814–42, *The History of Fiction, vol.* II, *p.* 404.

Clarissa is, however, his masterpiece, if we except Lovelace. If she is fine in herself, she is still finer in his account of her. . . . I should suppose that never sympathy more deep or sincere was excited than by the heroine of Richardson's romance, except by the calamities of real life. The links in this wonderful chain of interest are not more finely wrought, than their whole weight is overwhelming and irresistible. Who can forget the exquisite gradations of her long dying-scene, or the closing of the coffin-lid, when Miss Howe comes to take her last leave of her friend; or the heart-breaking reflection that Clarissa makes on what was to have been her wedding-day? —HAZLITT, WILLIAM, 1818, *On the English Novelists, Lectures on the English Comic Writers, Lecture* vi.

The work on which his fame as a classic of England will rest forever. . . . The publication of "Clarissa" raised the fame of the author to the height. No work had appeared before, perhaps none has appeared since, containing so many direct appeals to the passions, stated too in a manner so irresistible. And high as his reputation stood in his own country, it was even more exalted in those of France and Germany, whose imaginations are more easily excited, and their passions more easily moved by tales of fictitious distress, than are the cold-blooded English.—SCOTT, SIR WALTER, 1821, *Samuel Richardson.*

Blest be the shade of Richardson, who bequeathed to us the divine Clarissa, shining through sufferings, glorious in her fall, and almost visible in her ascent to the regions of immortality. Matchless creation of the only mind that ever conceived and drew truly a Christian heroine, with all her sex's softness, loveliness, and grace, and all the self-devotion, undeviating rectitude, and lively faith of the primitive martyrs! What are his numerous blemishes but dust in the balance when compared to his endless beauties? But then his faults are obvious to every common mind, and no common mind takes in his merits.—GRANT, MRS. ANNE, 1826, *Letter to Mrs. Hook, Feb.* 13; *Memoir and Correspondence, ed. Grant, vol.* III, *p.* 70.

It is wonderful how the cause is seen in the effect. So we find it in Richardson. "Clarissa" is a story in the midst of temptation; but he comes clear and triumphantly out of the ordeal, because his own imagination is not contaminated by it. If there had been the least hint of an immoral tendency, the slightest indication of a wish to inflame the passions, it would have been all over with him. The intention will always peep out—you do not communicate a disease if you are not infected with it yourself.—NORTHCOTE, JAMES, 1826–7, *Conversations, ed. William Hazlitt.*

"Clarissa," is a treatise on strategy. Twenty-four volumes to describe the siege and capture of a heart: It is worthy of Vauban.—VIGNY, ALFRED DE, 1833, *Journal d'un poète.*

He had, in fact, the power of making any set of notions, however, fantastical, appear as "truths of holy writ," to his readers. This he did by the authority with which he disposed of all things and by the infinite minuteness of his details. His gradations are so gentle, that we do not at any one point, hesitate to follow him, and should descend with him to any depth before we perceive that our path had been unequal. By the means of this strange magic, we become anxious for the marriage of Pamela with her base master; because the author has so imperceptibly wrought on us the belief of an awful distance between the rights of an esquire and his servant, that our imaginations regard it in the place of all moral distinctions. After all, the general impression made on us by his works, is virtuous. Clementina is to the soul a new and majestic image, inspired by virtue and by love, which raises and refines its conceptions. She has all the depth and intensity of the Italian character, with all the purity of an angel. She is at the same time one of the grandest of tragic heroines, and the divinest of religious enthusiasts. Clarissa alone is above her. . . . Clarissa Harlowe is one of the books which leave us different beings from those which they find us. "Sadder and wiser" do we arise from its perusal. —TALFOURD, THOMAS NOON, 1842, *On British Novels and Romances, pp.* 12, 13.

I read the last volume of Clarissa, which I have not opened since my voyage from India in the Lord Hungerford. I nearly cried my eyes out.—MACAULAY, THOMAS BABINGTON, 1850, *Life and Letters, Diary, April* 15, *ed. Trevelyan.*

I spoke to him [Lord Macaulay] once about "Clarissa." "Not read 'Clarissa!' " he cried out. "If you have once thoroughly entered on 'Clarissa,' and are infected by it, you can't leave it. When I was in India, I passed one hot season at the hills, and there were the governor-general, and the secretary of government, and the commander-in-chief, and their wives. I had 'Clarissa:' with me; and, as soon as they began to read, the whole station was in a passion of excitement about Miss Harlowe and her misfortunes and her scoundrelly Lovelace! The governor's wife seized the book, and the secretary waited for it, and the chief justice could not read it for tears!" He acted the whole scene: he paced up and down the Athenæum library: I daresay he could have spoken pages of the book,—of that book, and of what countless piles of others!—THACKERAY, WILLIAM MAKEPEACE, 1860, *Nil Nisi Bonum, Cornhill Magazine, Vol.* 1, *p.* 133.

Nothing can exceed the finished manner in which every personage of this splendid fiction is placed before the reader. The bashaw-father; the weak, amiable, depressed mother; the brutish brother; the sister who could never forgive the slight to her own attractions; the uncles; the hideous suitor whom her family wished Clarissa to marry; even the maid-servant —nay more, even the dead grandfather, —are your very intimate acquaintance. They remind one of those quaint old cabinet pictures, family portraits, which we see hung about near one grand painting—a Correggio, perhaps, or a Raphael—delineating the purest and most perfect form of female loveliness. The portraits are out of keeping with this gem of the collection; they are too inferior even to act as foils: And so it is that we wonder how such a being as Clarissa could have been reared amid persons so thoroughly common-minded as the generality of her kinsfolk; so above that world which was all in all to them, and to rise in which was the great aim of their existence.—THOMSON, KATHERINE (GRACE WHARTON), 1862, *The Literature of Society, vol.* II, *p.* 243.

It is like a deluge of very weak and lukewarm green tea, breakfast cup after breakfast cup. After the first of the four volumes, into which the Tauchnitz edition is divided, we gave way. I was much interested with Richardson's method, and admired the particularity with which he puts his characters upon the canvas, and makes them live more in the smallest circumstances of daily life. By force of accumulated details they acquire fulness and reality. But when they come to act, when all the minutiæ of their internal hesitations and emotions are insisted on with wearisome prolixity, one begins to feel that what one wants in Art is something other than the infinite particulars of life. Then Richardson, to my mind, is essentially a bourgeois, his imagination mediocre, his sentiment mawkish.—SYMONDS, JOHN ADDINGTON, 1868, *Life by Brown, vol.* II, *p.* 19.

Here is an old stationer, fat, well to do, loving money and good living, vain as a peacock, worried to death by small critics who continually gave him dyspepsia and agonies of indigestion, and only soothed by the highly spiced flattery and the spiteful reprisals on his enemies of a circle of foolish female friends; here is, to all appearance, one of the most unfit men in the world, who, after making money till he is fifty, is led by the paltry ambition of making more, to write a work which turns out to be utterly different from his first intention, and to prove the author a great moralist, who has the most intimate acquaintance with the human heart, its passions, foibles, strength, and virtues; who can describe almost as minutely as Defoe; who can teach while he amuses, and instruct the heart in virtue while he drives away the admiration for vice; who is powerful, tragic, pathetic, and eminently original; and whose art is so great that his readers follow their enchanter through eight long volumes, heaving a sigh of regret when they lay them down; while the student of morality pronounces them to have been a benefit to the human race.—FRISWELL, JAMES HAIN, 1869, *Essays on English Writers, p.* 271.

He was a respectable tradesman, . . . a good printer, . . . a comfortable soul, . . . never owing a guinea nor transgressing a rule of morality, . . . and yet so much a poet, that he has added at least one character (Clarissa Harlowe) to the inheritance of the world, of which Shakespeare need not have been ashamed—the most celestial thing, the highest imaginative effort of his generation.—OLIPHANT, MARGARET O. W., 1869, *Historical Sketches of the Reign of George Second, ch.* x.

You cannot read through twenty pages of "Clarissa" without feeling that you are mainly in the company, not of the preacher Richardson, but of real live men and women, whose movements, and sentiments, and motives are of importance to watch, and one of whom, the heroine, is a creature to inspire that deep interest always felt in any creature perfectly beautiful: her we can follow into the profoundest misfortunes, and still "in the midmost heart of grief" can "clasp a secret joy." To show, too, that Richardson felt what other artists feel, that a work of art must be mainly beautiful, the figure of Clarissa is made to occupy a place in his picture far more prominent than any one else; and a vast deal of the material which goes to make up the minor figures grouped about this central perfection, and distributed over the distance and middle distance, a great proportion of the narrative upon which our ideas of the rest are formed, comes to us polarised through the medium of Clarissa's noble and lucid mind; so that, while we are frequently disgusted with the matter, we never lose sight of the perfection of Clarissa, whether as actor or narrator.—FORMAN, HENRY BUXTON, 1869, *Samuel Richardson as Artist and Moralist, Fortnightly Review, vol.* 12, *p.* 434.

There is no need that you should shout to make us afraid; that you should write out the lesson by itself, and in capitals, in order to distinguish it. We love art, and you have a scant amount of it; we want to be pleased, and you don't care to please us. You copy all the letters, detail the conversations, tell everything, prune nothing; your novels fill many volumes; spare us, use the scissors; be a literary man, not a registrar of archives. Do not pour out your library of documents on the high-road. Art is different from nature; the latter draws out, the first condenses. Twenty letters of twenty pages do not display a character; but one sharp word does. You are rendered heavy by your conscience, which drags you along step by step and low on the ground; you are afraid of your genius; you rein it in; you dare not use loud cries and frank words for violent moments. You flounder into emphatic and well-written phrases; you will not show nature as it is, as Shakspeare shows it, when, stung by passion as by a hot iron, it cries out, rears, and plunges over your barriers. You cannot love it, and your punishment is that you cannot see it.—TAINE, H. A., 1871, *History of English Literature, tr. Van Laun, vol.* II, *bk.* iii, *ch.* vi, *p.* 169.

To me, I confess, "Clarissa Harlowe" is an unpleasant, not to say odious book. . . . If any book deserved the charge of "sickly sentimentality," it is this, and that it should have once been so widely popular, and thought admirably adapted to instruct young women in lessons of virtue and religion, shows a strange and perverted state of the public taste, not to say public morals.—FORSYTH, WILLIAM, 1871, *The Novels and Novelists of the Eighteenth Century, pp.* 215, 216.

Unfortunately, Macaulay's stay on the Neilgherries [in 1834] coincided with the monsoon. "The rain streamed down in floods. It was very seldom that I could see a hundred yards in front of me. During a month together I did not get two hours walking." He began to be bored, for the first and last time in his life: while his companions, who had not his resources, were ready to hang themselves for very dulness. . . . There were no books in the place except those that Macaulay had brought with him; among which, most luckily, was "Clarissa Harlowe." Aided by the rain outside, he soon talked his favourite romance into general favor. . . . An old Scotch doctor, a Jacobin and a freethinker, who could only be got to attend church by the positive orders of the governor-general, cried over the last volume until he was too ill to appear at dinner. The chief secretary—afterward, as Sir William Macnaghten, the hero and the victim of the darkest episode in our Indian history—declared that reading this copy of "Clarissa" under the inspiration of its owner's enthusiasm was nothing less than an epoch in his life. After the lapse of thirty years, when Ootacamund had long enjoyed the advantage of book-club and a circulating library, the tradition of Macaulay and his novel still lingered on with a tenacity most unusual in the ever-shifting society of an Indian station. — TREVELYAN, GEORGE OTTO, 1876, *The Life and Letters of Lord Macaulay, ch.* vi, 1834–38, *pp.* 333, 334.

Nowhere in either English fiction or poetry is there drawn a figure more beautiful, intense, and splendid than that of Clarissa. . . . Is probably, with all its many defects, the grandest prose tragedy ever penned.—NICOLL, HENRY, 1882, *Landmarks of English Literature, pp.* 211, 212.

By the universal acknowledgment of novel-readers, Clarissa is one of the most sympathetic, as she is one of the most lifelike, of all the women in literature, and Richardson has conducted her story with so much art and tact, that her very faults canonise her, and her weakness crowns the triumph of her chastity.—GOSSE, EDMUND, 1888, *A History of Eighteenth Century Literature, p.* 248.

"Pamela" and "Clarissa" are both terribly realistic; they contain passages of horror, and are in parts profoundly pathetic, whilst "Clarissa" is desperately courageous. Fielding, with all his swagger and bounce, gold lace and strong language, has no more of the boldness than he has of the sublimity of the historian of Clarissa Harlowe. . . . "Clarissa Harlowe" has a place not merely amongst English novels, but amongst English women.—BIRRELL, AUGUSTINE, 1892, *Res Judicatæ, pp.* 3, 20.

Let each to be judged after his kind: to break the glass of Richardson's hot house and let in the common air would only be to kill the tropical plants that he has grown under those fostering limitations; his characters live in a sick-room, but they would die in the open air. Any one who has once learnt to breathe in those confines must feel the beauty and charm of the sentimental growths that there luxuriate; a detached scene from "Clarissa" may jar on the critical sense, but read through, the book carries the reader clear of daily life, creates its own canons, and compels intent admiration.—RALEIGH, WALTER, 1894, *The English Novel, p.* 160.

It has been truly said that "Clarissa Harlowe" is to "La Nouvelle Héloïse" what Rousseau's novel is to "Werther;" the three works are inseparably connected, because the bond between them is one of heredity. But while "Werther" and "Héloïse" are still read "Clarissa" is scarcely read at all, and this, beyond doubt, is the reason that, while no one thinks of disputing Goethe's indebtedness to Rousseau, it is to-day less easy to perceive the extent to which Rousseau is indebted to Richardson.—TEXTE, JOSEPH, 1895–99, *Jean-Jacques Rousseau and the Cosmopolitan Spirit in Literature, tr. Matthews, p.* 208.

If the story of Clarissa still lives, it is not by virtue of any of the subordinate characters, but by reason of the one matchless central figure, who stands unrivalled among the other inventions of her creator. And, as long as the English language is spoken or its literature read, the "divine Clarissa" will hold her own among the noblest of its ideal women, with Imogen, and Portia, and Cordelia. Torn from the proud pedestal of maidenhood, dragged in an unclean company through foul and miry ways, a sacrifice to vanity rather than to lust, she loses none of her charm or potency. For through her there speaks the authentic voice of the best women of all ages, who refuse to disassociate love and respect from the most sacred of human relationships, or to subject themselves to the humiliation of a union unsanctioned by these motives.—THOMSON, CLARA LINKLATER, 1900, *Samuel Richardson, A Biographical and Critical Study, p.* 207.

SIR CHARLES GRANDISON
1754

Will you permit me to take this opportunity, in sending a letter to Dr. Young, to address myself to you? It is very long ago that I wished to do it. Having finished your "Clarissa" (oh, the heavenly book!) I could have prayed you to write the history of a manly Clarissa, but I had not courage enough at that time. I should have it no more to-day, as this is only my first English letter—but I have it! It may be because I am now Klopstock's wife (I believe you know my husband by Mr. Honorst), and then I was only the single young girl. You have since written the manly Clarissa without my prayer. Oh, you have done it to the great joy and thanks of all your happy readers! Now you can write no more, you must write the history of an angel.—KLOPSTOCK, MADAME FRIEDRICH GOTTLIEB, 1757, *Letter to Richardson, Nov.* 29.

Richardson has sent me his "History of Sir Charles Grandison," in four volumes octavo, which amuses me. It is too long, and there is too much mere talk in it. Whenever he goes *ultra crepidam*, into high life, he grossly mistakes the modes; but, to do him justice, he never mistakes nature, and he has surely great knowledge and skill both in painting and in interesting the heart.—CHESTERFIELD, PHILIP DORMER STANHOPE LORD, 1753, *Letter to David Mallett, Nov.* 5.

I have now read over Richardson—he sinks horribly in his third volume (he does so in his story of Clarissa). When he talks of Italy, it is plain he is no better acquainted with it than he is with the kingdom of Mancomugi. He might have made his Sir Charles's amour with Clementina begin in a convent, where the pensioners sometimes take great liberties; but that such familiarity should be permitted in her father's house, is as repugnant to custom, as it would be in London for a young lady of quality to dance on the ropes at Bartholomew fair: Neither does his hero behave to her in a manner suitable to his nice notions. It was impossible a discerning man should not see her passion early enough to check it, if he had really designed it. His conduct puts me in mind of some ladies I have known, who could never find out a man to be in love with them, let him do or say what he would, till he made a direct attempt, and then they were so surprised, I warrant you!—MONTAGU, LADY MARY WORTLEY, 1755, *Letter to the Countess of Bute, Oct.* 20.

Do you never read now? I am a little piqued that you say nothing of Sir Charles Grandison; if you have not read it yet, read it for my sake. Perhaps Clarissa does not encourage you; but in my opinion it is much superior to Clarissa.—GIBBON, EDWARD, 1756, *Letter to Mrs. Porten, Miscellaneous Works, p.* 227.

A masterpiece of the most healthy philosophy. . . . Antiquity, can show nothing more exquisite.—MARMONTEL, JEAN FRANÇOIS, 1758, *Mercure de France, August.*

You admire Richardson, monsieur le marquis; how much greater would be your admiration, if, like me, you were in a position to compare the pictures of this great artist with nature; to see how natural his situations are, however seemingly romantic, and how true his portraits, for all their apparent exaggeration!—ROUSSEAU, JEAN-JACQUES, 1767, *Letter to Marquis de Mirabeau.*

I don't like those long and intolerable novels "Pamela" and "Clarissa." They have been successful because they excite the reader's curiosity even amidst a medley of trifles; but if the author had been imprudent enough to inform us at the very beginning that "Clarissa" and "Pamela" were in love with their persecutors, everything would have been spoiled, and the reader would have thrown the book aside.—VOLTAIRE, FRANÇOIS MARIE AROUET, 1767, *Letter, May* 16.

Who will not one of them submit
To be Sir Charles' devoted slave;
And, blindlings still, will not admit
All the Dictator's teachings brave.
But sneer and jeer, and run away,
And hear no more he has to say.

—GOETHE, JOHANN WOLFGANG, 1768, *Epistle to Frederika Oeser; Grimm's Life of Goethe, tr. Adams, p.* 152.

M. de Voltaire, in his numerous writings, which I have read and re-read, has avoided, so far as I know, all mention of Richardson, whether favourable or otherwise, though he has treated of every other writer, however obscure. . . . It is impossible that the author of "Nanine" should fail to appreciate "Pamela;" he has certainly read "Clarissa" and "Grandison," poems to which antiquity can produce no worthy rival. He must know that these masterpieces of feeling, truth, and moral teaching have found readers of both sexes, in every country and of every age. I suppose that, since M. de Voltaire's manner of writing is diametrically opposed to Richardson's, the silence he has preserved in regard to this author of genius is founded on principle.—MERCIER, SÉBASTIEN, 1773, *Essai sur l'art dramatique, p.* 326.

Clarissa! with Heaven itself radiant in your saintly beauty; free, in all your pain, alike from hatred and from bitterness, suffering without a groan, and perishing without a murmur; beloved Clementina! pure, and heavenly soul, who, amidst the harsh treatment of an unjust household, never lost your innocence with the loss of your reason;—your eyes, bright souls, hold me with their charm; your sweet likeness hastens to fill my fairest dreams!—CHÉNIER, MARIÈ-ANDRÉ, 1794? *Elégie,* xiv.

Throughout the entire composition, the author exhibits great powers of mind; but especially in describing the agitations caused by the passion of love in the bosom of the amiable and enthusiastic Clementina; whose madness is so finely drawn, that Doctor Warton thought it superior to that of Orestes in Euripides; and heightened by more exquisite touches of nature even than that of Shakspeare's Lear. Amongst other beauties in this work may be counted, the truth and delicacy with which the author has sketched the numberless portraits it contains, the innocent love of Emily Jervois, the imposing effect with which Sir Charles is introduced, and the great art shewn in keeping him constantly in view.—MANGIN, EDWARD, 1810, *ed., The Works of Samuel Richardson, Sketch, vol.* I, *p.* xxii.

Sir Charles Grandison, whom I look upon as the prince of coxcombs; and so much the more impertinent as he is a moral one. His character appears to me "ugly all over with affectation." There is not a single thing that Sir Charles Grandison does or says all through the book from liking to any person or object but himself, and with a view to answer to a certain standard of perfection for which he pragmatically sets up. He is always thinking of himself, and trying to show that he is the wisest, happiest, and most virtuous person in the whole world. He is (or would be thought) a code of Christian ethics: a compilation and abstract of all gentlemanly accomplishments. There is nothing I conceive, that excites so little sympathy as this inordinate egotism; or so much disgust as this everlasting self-complacency. Yet his self-admiration, brought forward on every occasion as the incentive to every action and reflected from all around him, is the burden and pivot of the story.—HAZLITT, WILLIAM, 1830? *Men and Manners.*

But as my friend, Sir Charles Grandison, has no other sin to answer for than that of being very long, very tedious, very old-fashioned, and a prig, I cannot help confessing that, in spite of these faults, and perhaps because of them, I think there are worse books printed, now-a-days and hailed with delight among critics feminine, than the seven volumes that gave such infinite delight to the beauties of the court of George the Second.—MITFORD, MARY RUSSELL, 1851, *Recollections of a Literary Life, p.* 412.

Of fiction, read Sir Charles Grandison. —RUSKIN, JOHN, 1857, *The Elements of Drawing, Appendix.*

Other works, of a very different character, fell into my hands about this time. Sir Charles Grandison, despite its stately formality, did me good. I think its tone of old-fashioned, homely chivalry has a healthy influence on young people.—OWEN, ROBERT DALE, 1873, *A Chapter of Autobiography, Atlantic Monthly, vol.* 31, *p.* 450.

In this novel is one of the most powerful of all our author's delineations—the madness of Clementina. Shakspeare himself has scarcely drawn a more affecting or harrowing picture of high-souled suffering and blighting calamity. The same accumulation of details as in "Clarissa," all tending to heighten the effect and produce the catastrophe, hurry on the reader with breathless anxiety, till he has learned the last sad event, and is plunged in unavailing grief. This is no exaggerated account of the sensations produced by Richardson's pathetic scenes. He is one of the most powerful and tragic of novelists; and that he is so, in spite of much tediousness of description, much repetition and prolixity of narrative, is the best testimony to his art and genius.—CHAMBERS, ROBERT, 1876, *Cyclopædia of English Literature, ed. Carruthers.*

"Sir Charles Grandison," published, in 1753, was Richardson's most celebrated romance. The hero is a huge compendium of noble qualities, in whose possible existence every one firmly believed. My uncle Jacob used to tell me of having, as a child, seen his mother absorbed in reading "Sir Charles Grandison." And such reading was no trifling matter; it required much time and thought. These romances came like great events into our life, which at that time had little to do with political agitations. The translations spread in every direction among us. The marvellously broad and plain treatment of universally-useful and well-understood moral problems made a thorough knowledge of these romances almost a duty as well as an enjoyment. There seemed to be no more agreeable way of appropriating to oneself a life experience of the noblest kind than this convenient and most innocent one. Romances of this kind proved the best form in which to comprise all that might be conducive to genuine moral training. They came in as a supplement when the sermon from the pulpit had not fulfilled its task; and for this reason a great number of the romance writers belonged to the clerical profession.—GRIMM, HERMAN, 1877–80, *The Life and Times of Goethe, tr. Adams, p.* 152.

It would be allowing too much, however, to the third of Richardson's romances, "Sir Charles Grandison," to say that it reaches the same level of ideal portraiture as "Clarissa Harlowe." In delineating, at the request of his friends, as he tells us, "the man of true honour," in the person of this irreproachable baronet, Richardson had no such dramatic contrast to inspire him as in his second and greatest romance. Sir Hargrave Pollexfen is but a commonplace and vulgar foil to the virtues of the hero, and there is no thread of pathos or of tragedy running through the story, or indeed appearing in it, except episodically, to give play to the author's strongest powers. Sir Charles Grandison shows himself a man of true honours, in eight volumes; and that is about all that can be said of the romance. Unlike, "Clarissa," its narrative can not be said to hang fire through the diffuseness of the narrator's method; for in strictness of language it contains no narrative at all.—TRAILL, HENRY DUFF, 1883–97, *Samuel Richardson, The New Fiction, p.* 134.

With Sir Charles Grandison I am unacquainted—there are many impediments in this brief life of man; I have more than once, indeed, reconnoitred the first volume with a flying party, but always decided not to break ground before the place till my seige guns came up; and it's an odd thing—I have been all these years in the field, and that powerful artillery is still miles in the rear. . . . As to Sir Charles at least, I have the report of spies; and by the papers in the office of my Intelligence Department, it would seem he was a most accomplished baronet. I am the more ready to credit these reports, because the spies are persons thoroughly accustomed to the business; and because my own investigations of a kindred quarter of the globe ("Clarissa Harlowe") has led me to set a high value on the Richardsonians.—STEVENSON, ROBERT LOUIS, 1888, *Some Gentlemen in Fiction, Scribner's Magazine, vol.* 3, *p.* 766.

In "Sir Charles Grandison" the story is arrested while the characters are displayed, contrasting their thoughts, plans, and sentiments. And there is an incessant doubling back on what has gone before; first a letter is written describing what "Has passed," this letter is communicated by its recipient to a third character, who comments on it, while the story waits. This constant repercussion of a theme or event between one or more pairs of correspondents produces a structure of story very like "The House that Jack Built." Each writer is narrating not events alone, but his or her reflections on previous narrations of the same events. And so, on the next-to-nothing that happened there is superimposed the young lady that wrote to her friend describing it, the friend that approved her for the decorum of the manner in which she described it, the admirable baronet that chanced to find the letter approving the decorum of the young lady, the punctilio of honour that prevented the admirable baronet from reading the letter he found, and so on. It is very lifelike, but life can become at times a slow affair, and one of the privileges of the novel-writer is to quicken it. This privilege Richardson foregoes.—RALEIGH, WALTER, 1894, *The English Novel, p.* 151.

GENERAL

This author never deluges the pavement with blood; he does not transport you into distant lands; he does not expose you to the cannibalism of savages; he never loses himself in magic realms. The world where we live is the scene of his action; the basis of his drama is reality; his persons possess all possible actuality; his characters are taken from the midst of society; his incidents from the manners of all polite nations; the passions that he paints are such as I have myself felt; the same objects inspire them, and they have the energy which I know them to possess. The misfortunes and afflictions of his heroes are of the same kind as continually threaten me; he illustrates the ordinary progress of things around me. Without this art my mind, yielding with difficulty to imaginary descriptions, the illusion would be but momentary, and the impression weak and transitory. . . . I still remember the first time that I chanced upon the works of Richardson. I was in the country. How deliciously did their perusal affect me. With every passing minute I saw my happiness diminish by a page. Very soon I experienced the same sensation as men feel who have lived together in intimate friendship and are on the point of separation. At the end I felt as if I were left all alone. . . . He bequeathed to me a lasting and pleasing melancholy; sometimes my friends perceive it and ask me, What is the matter with you? You are not the same as usual; what has happened to you? They question me about my health, my fortune, my relations, my friends. O my friends, "Pamela," "Clarissa," and "Grandison," are three great dramas! Torn from reading them by important business, I felt an overwhelming distaste for it; I neglected my work and returned to Richardson. Beware of opening these enchanting books when you have any important duties to perform. . . . O Richardson, Richardson, first of men in my eyes, you shall be my reading at all times! Pursued by pressing need; if my friend should fall into poverty; if the limitations of my fortunes should prevent me from giving fit attention to the education of my children, I will sell my books; but you shall remain on the same shelf as Moses, Euripides and Sophocles, and I will read you by turns.—DIDEROT, DENIS, 1761, *Eloge de Richardson, Works, vol.* V, *pp.* 212, 227.

Those deplorably tedious lamentations, "Clarissa" and "Sir Charles Grandison," which are pictures of high life as conceived by a bookseller, and romances as they would be spiritualized by a Methodist teacher. . . . Many English books, I conclude, are to be bought at Paris. I am sure Richardson's Works are, for they have stupified the whole French nation: I will not answer for our best authors.—WALPOLE, HORACE, 1764–65, *Letters, ed. Cunningham, vol.* IV, *pp.* 305, 396.

Erskine. "Surely, Sir, Richardson is very tedious." *Johnson.* "Why, Sir, if you were to read Richardson for the story, your impatience would be so much fretted that you would hang yourself. But you must read him for the sentiment, and consider the story as only giving occasion to the sentiment."—JOHNSON, SAMUEL, 1772, *Life by Boswell, April* 6, *ed. Hill, vol.* II, *p.* 200.

The most moral of all our novel writers is Richardson, the author of Clarissa, a writer of excellent intentions, and of very considerable capacity and genius; did he not possess the unfortunate talent of spinning out pieces of amusement into an immeasurable length.—BLAIR, HUGH, 1783, *Lectures on Rhetoric and Belles-Lettres, ed. Mills, Lecture* xxxvii.

He was a man of no learning nor reading, but had a vivid imagination, which he let loose in reflections on human life and manners, till it became so distended with sentiments, that for his own ease, he was necessitated to vent them on paper. In the original plan of his "Clarissa," it was his design, as his bookseller once told me, to continue it to the extent of twenty-four volumes, but he was, with great difficulty, prevailed on to comprise it in six. The character of Richardson as a writer is to this day undecided, otherwise than by the avidity with which his publications are by some readers perused, and the sale of numerous editions. He has been celebrated as a writer similar in genius to Shakespeare, as being acquainted with the inmost recesses of the human heart, and having an absolute command of the passions, so as to be able to affect his readers as himself is affected, and to interest them in the successes and disappointments, the joys and sorrows of his characters. Others there are who think that neither his "Pamela," his "Clarissa," nor his "Sir Charles Grandison" are to be numbered among the books of rational and instructive amusement, that they are not to be compared to the novels of Cervantes, or the more simple and chaste narrations of Le Sage, that they are not just representations of human manners, that in them the turpitude of vice is not strongly enough marked, and that the allurements to it are represented in the gayest colours; that the texture of all his writings is flimsy and thin, and his style mean and feeble; that they have a general tendency to inflame the passions of young people, and to teach them that which they need not to be taught; and that though they pretend to a moral, it often turns out a bad one. The cant terms of him and his admirers are sentiment and sentimentality.—HAWKINS, SIR JOHN, 1787, *Life of Samuel Johnson, p.* 216.

The Shakspeare of novelists.—DISRAELI, ISAAC, 1791–1824, *Richardson, Curiosities of Literature.*

He has drawn in Lovelace and Grandison models of a debauched and of an elevated character. Neither of them is eminently calculated to produce imitation; but it would not perhaps be adventurous to affirm that more readers have wished to resemble Lovelace, than have wished to resemble Grandison.—GODWIN, WILLIAM, 1797, *Of Choice in Reading, The Enquirer, p.* 134.

Richardson's good people in short are too wise and too formal, ever to appear in the light of desirable companions, or to excite in a youthful mind any wish to resemble them. The gaiety of all his characters is extremely girlish and silly, and is much more like the prattle of spoiled children, than the wit and pleasantry of persons acquainted with the world. The diction throughout, is heavy, vulgar, and embarrassed; though the interest of the tragical scenes is too powerful to allow us to attend to any inferior consideration.—JEFFREY, FRANCIS LORD, 1804, *Richardson's Life and Correspondence, Edinburgh Review, vol.* 5, *p.* 44.

Richadson has perhaps lost, though unjustly, a part of his popularity at home; but he still contributes to support the fame of his country abroad. The small blemishes of his diction are lost in translation. The changes of English manners, and the occasional homeliness of some of his representations, are unfelt by foreigners.—MACKINTOSH, SIR JAMES, 1815, *Godwin's Lives of Milton's Nephews, Edinburgh Review, vol.* 25, *p.* 485.

Voltaire, Rousseau, and Diderot made a frequent and arbitrary use of romance, as being a form eminently adapted to the conveyance of certain peculiar ideas of their own. But if this form be regarded as a distinct poetic species, as regular narrative in prose, sketching the transient features of society, it will be found that, in this respect, too, French writers have frequently copied from English models, but have seldom, if ever, equalled them. In point of originality and power of representation Richardson perhaps occupies the highest place in this peculiar style of composition. If he, likewise, has become antiquated, if his striving after the ideal was not attended with special success owing to exactness of details occasionally tedious, we have a proof of the incompatibility of direct poetic connexion with the hard realities of life, though disguised in prosaic garb. If his genius availed not to solve the problem, it was because its solution was little short of impracticable.—SCHLEGEL, FREDERICK, 1815–59, *Lectures on the History of Literature, p.* 311.

The loaded sensibility, the minute detail, the morbid consciousness of every thought and feeling in the whole flux and reflux of the mind, in short, the self-involution and dream-like continuity of Richardson. —COLERIDGE, SAMUEL TAYLOR, 1817, *Biographia Literaria; ch.* xxiii.

Richardson's nature is always the nature of sentiment and reflection, not of impulse or situation. He furnishes his characters, on every occasion, with the presence of mind of the author. He makes them act, not as they would from the impulse of the moment, but as they might upon reflection and upon a careful review of every motive and circumstance in their situation. They regularly sit down to write letters; and if the business of life consisted in letter-writing, and was carried on by the post (like a Spanish game at chess), human nature would be what Richardson represents it. All actual objects and feelings are blunted and deadened by being represented through a medium which may be true to reason, but is false in nature. He confounds his own point of view with that of the immediate actors in the scene; and hence presents you with a conventional and factitious nature, instead of that which is real. . . . Richardson's wit was unlike that of any other writer—his humour was so too. Both were the effect of intense activity of mind—laboured, and yet completely effectual.—HAZLITT, WILLIAM, 1818, *On the English Novelists, Lectures on the English Comic Writers, Lecture* vi.

The power of Richardson's painting in his deeper scenes of tragedy, never has been, and probably never will be, excelled. Those of distressed innocence, as in the history of Clarissa and Clementina, rend the very heart; and few, jealous of manly equanimity, should read them for the first time in presence of society. In others, where the same heroines, and particularly Clarissa, display a noble elevation of soul, rising above earthly considerations and earthly oppression, the reader is perhaps as much elevated towards a pure sympathy with virtue and religion, as uninspired composition can raise him. His scenes of unmixed horror, as the deaths of Belton and of the infamous Sinclair, are as dreadful as the former are elevating; and they are directed to the same noble purpose, increasing our fear and hatred of vice, as the former are qualified to augment our love and veneration of virtue.—SCOTT, SIR WALTER, 1821, *Samuel Richardson.*

If Richardson's style is not good—and of this we foreigners are no judges,—he will not live, for it is only by style that a writer lives. . . . But if Richardson has been forsaken only for vulgar expressions, unendurable by elegant society, he may revive; the revolution which is taking place, by lowering the aristocracy and raising the middling classes, will render less perceptible, or remove altogether, the traces of lowly habits and of an inferior language. — CHATEAUBRIAND, FRANÇOIS RENÉ VISCOUNT DE, 1837, *Sketches of English Literature, vol.* II, *p.* 296, 297.

This work of Richardson's, and his "Pamela" were written purposely to guide the morals of the young, and of the latter it was said, Pamela is like snow; she covers all things with her whiteness. Snow, when much trodden under a warm sun, is soon converted into slop—which coalesces ere long into mud and mire; in this respect the moral lessons of Pamela and Clarissa do indeed resemble snow; they seem fitted to stir up the mud of the soul—"the earthly mire" of its nature—than permanently to cleanse and whiten it.—COLERIDGE, SARA, 1847, *ed. Coleridge's Biographia Literaria, ch.* xxiii, *note.*

Accustomed as we are to a more fiery, rapid, highly-coloured, and *wide-awake* mode of narration, we have in some measure lost our relish for the manner of this accomplished artist, who produces his effect by an uninterrupted accumulation of touches individually imperceptible, by an agglomerative, not a generative process. If our great modern works of creative fiction may be compared to the rapid and colossal agency of volcanic fire, the productions of Richardson may resemble the slow and gradual formation of an alluvial continent, the secular accumulation of minute particles deposited by the gentle yet irresistible current of a river. If the volcanic tract—the offspring of fire—be sublimely broken into thunder-shattered mountain-peak and smiling valley, yet the level delta is not less fertile or less adorned by its own mild and luxuriant beauty.—SHAW, THOMAS B., 1847, *Outlines of English Literature, p.* 258.

Richardson too often paints the impossible in character, but he is unrivalled in the elaborateness of representation.—SANFORD, SIR DANIEL KEYTE, 1848, *On the Rise and Progress of Literature.*

The greatest and perhaps the most unconscious of Shakespeare's imitators.—VILLEMAIN, ABEL FRANÇOIS, c1858? *Eighteenth Century, Lesson* xxvii.

We do not read Richardson's novels much now; and it cannot be helped that we do not. There are the novels of a hundred years between us and him; time is short; and novels of eight or ten volumes, written in the tedious form of letters, and recording conversations and meditations in which the story creeps on inch by inch, without so much as an unexpected pistol-shot or a trick of Harlequin and Pantaloon to relieve the attention, have little chance against the brisker and broader fictions to which we have been accustomed. We have to remember, however, not only that, a hundred years ago, Richardson's novels were read everywhere, both in Britain and on the continent, with a protracted sense of fascination, a leisurely intensity of interest, such as no British author of prose stories had ever commanded before, but also that almost every thoughtful critic who has read Richardson since has spoken of him as, all in all, one of the masters of our literature. Johnson would not allow Fielding to be put in comparison with Richardson; and, whenever Lord Macaulay names Richardson, it is as a kind of prose Shakespeare. When we read Richardson for ourselves, we can see the reasons which have led to. so high an opinion. His style of prose fiction is perhaps more original than that of any other novelist we have had. . . . He writes on and on in a plain, full, somewhat wordy style, not always grammatically perfect; but every page is a series of minute touches, and each touch is from a thorough conception of the case which he is representing. In minute inquisition into the human heart, and especially the female heart, and in the exhibition of conduct as affected from day to day by growing complications of feeling and circumstance, Richardson is a master.—MASSON, DAVID, 1859, *British Novelists and Their Styles, pp.* 107, 115.

The conceptions of character in Lovelace, Clarissa, Clementina, are founded in the preference of generals to particulars; that is, they are enduring types of great subdivisions in the human family, wholly irrespective of mutations in scene and manners. The knowledge of the world manifested in the creation and completion of such characters is subtler and deeper than Smollett or even Fielding exhibits in his lusty heroes and buxom heroines. Despite the weary tediousness of Richardson's style, the beauties which relieve it are of a kind that bear translation or paraphrase into foreign languages with a facility, which is perhaps the surest test of the inherent substance and cosmopolitan spirit of imaginative writings. The wit and hardihood of Lovelace, the simplicity and *naïveté* of Clarissa, the lofty passion of Clementina, find an utterance in every language, and similitudes in every civilized race.—LYTTON, EDWARD BULWER LORD, 1863-68, *Caxtoniana, Miscellaneous Prose Works, vol.* III, *p.* 453.

Her [Jane Austen's] knowledge of Richardson's works was such as no one is likely again to acquire. . . . Every circumstance narrated in "Sir Charles Grandison," all that was ever said or done in the cedar parlour, was familiar to her; and the wedding days of Lady L. and Lady G. were as well remembered as if they had been living friends.—LEIGH, JAMES EDWARD AUSTEN, 1869, *A Memoir of Jane Austen, p.* 84.

I am working at Richardson now, and will send you the paper by the end of the week. I suppose I ought to be ashamed to confess that, tedious as he often is, I feel less difficulty in getting through him than in reading Fielding, and that as a matter of taste I actually prefer Lovelace to Tom Jones! I suppose that is one of the differences between men and women which even Ladies' Colleges will not set to rights.—OLIPHANT, MARGARET O. W., 1869, *Letters, p.* 221.

He combines whilst he observes; his meditation develops the ideas of the moralist. No one in this age has equalled him in these detailed and comprehensive conceptions, which, grouping to a single end the passions of thirty characters, twine and colour the innumerable threads of the whole canvas, to bring out a figure, an action, or a lesson.—TAINE, H. A., 1871, *History of English Literature, tr. Van Laun, vol.* II, *bk.* iii, *ch.* vi, *p.* 160.

That Richardson (with all his twaddle) is better than Fielding, I am quite certain. There is nothing at all comparable to Lovelace in all Fielding, whose characters are common and vulgar types; of Squires, Ostlers, Lady's maids, etc., very easily drawn. — FITZGERALD, EDWARD, 1871, *Letters, vol.* I, *p.* 335.

It is not unpleasant to think that the ladies of that time, by the way in which they petted, coaxed, and humoured him, conferred an innocent pleasure upon the truest of all the delineators of their sex, except perhaps Balzac, who, if he knows it better, is more unfortunate in his knowledge.—CURWEN, HENRY, 1873, *A History of Booksellers, p.* 56.

He started from a didactic point of view, and represented men as they ought to be within the social circumstances of the England of his time. His fluency is extraordinary, but his composition is monotonous.—SCHERR, J., 1874, *A History of English Literature, tr. M. V., p.* 152.

Here is a man, we might say, whose special characteristic it was to be a milksop—who provoked Fielding to a coarse hearty burst of ridicule—who was steeped in the incense of useless adulation from a throng of middle-aged lady worshippers—who wrote his novels expressly to recommend little unimpeachable moral maxims, as that evil courses lead to unhappy deaths, that ladies ought to observe the laws of propriety, and generally that it is an excellent thing to be thoroughly respectable; who lived an obscure life in a petty coterie in fourth-rate London society, and was in no respect at a point of view more exalted than that of his companions. What greater contrast can be imagined in its way than that between Richardson, with his second-rate eighteenth century priggishness and his two-penny-tract morality, and the modern school of French novelists, who are certainly not prigs, and whose morality is by no means that of tracts? We might have expected *à priori* that they would have summarily put him down, as, a hopeless Philistine. Yet Richardson is idolised by some of their best writers, Balzac, for example, and George Sand, speak of him with reverence; and a writer who is, perhaps, as odd a contrast to Richardson as could well be imagined—Alfred de Musset—calls Clarissa *le premier roman du monde.* What is the secret which enables the steady old printer, with his singular limitation to his own career of time and space, to impose upon the Byronic Parisian of the next century? Amongst his contemporaries Diderot, the atheistic author of one of the filthiest novels extant expresses an almost fanatical admiration for his purity and power, and declares characteristically that he will place Richardson's works on the same shelf with those of Moses, Homer, Euripides, and other favourite writers; he even goes so far as to excuse Clarissa's belief in Christianity on the ground of her youthful innocence.—STEPHEN, LESLIE, 1874–92, *Hours in a Library, vol.* I, *p.* 48.

But the fact that Richardson commenced to write at fifty years of age, precludes the idea of his having possessed lofty creative genius: talent may slumber, as in his case, but genius never.—SMITH, GEORGE BARNETT, 1875, *Henry Fielding, Poets and Novelists, p.* 276.

While he was in Zurich, Wieland had been a rapturous admirer of Richardson's novels; he joined with Gillert and many others in admiring the faultless heroes set before the world by this novelist, Pamela and Clarissa and Grandison, and he even took the materials for a drama from one of these stories.—SCHERER, WILHELM, 1883–86, *A History of German Literature, tr. Conybeare, vol.* II, *p.* 44.

Richardson has a certain standard, the standard of the respectability of the day, and he tries to raise his readers to it both by showing them what a fine thing his ideal looks when it is endowed with life, and by pointing out that the path of virtue is the path of safety, which cannot be forsaken without peril of imminent disaster. Unfortunately Richardson spoils by his eargerness the moral as well as the artistic effect of his books. He is so bent on showing us that virtue is intrinsically admirable and a good investment into the bargain that he becomes absolutely incredible, and we laugh instead of being convinced. His most morally impressive book is that which is also artistically the greatest—the book which telling of the heroic virtue of Clarissa shows us how it found its reward not in the cheap splendours amidst which we bid farewell to his earliest heroine, but in the solemn quiet of the grave, where the wicked Lovelace can no more trouble her, and she, the weary one, may lie at rest.—NOBLE, JAMES ASHCROFT, 1886, *Morality in English Fiction, p.* 16.

The fashion of this world passeth away. Only a hundred and forty years ago, a group of ladies, chiefly young girls just grown up, might have been found seated in a summer-house of a large garden of North End, Hammersmith, working or drawing, and listening eagerly to a stout old gentleman who was reading to them from a manuscript. The ladies were Miss Mulso (afterwards Mrs. Chapone), Miss Highmore, Miss Fielding, and several others; the old gentleman was Richardson, the book was "Clarissa." No one will dispute the severe propriety of any of these ladies, yet the far laxer standard which regulates the conduct of their great-granddaughters forbids "Clarissa" even to be taken by them from the library bookshelf, much less to be positively read aloud, unexpurgated, in full family conclave. . . . Yet the books that formed the interest and delight of our grandmothers cannot be wholly improper food for such of their descendants as have reached years of discretion. Therefore I, whose teens have long been a matter of history, may sit down to record the impressions made on me by Richardson's novels. —LANG, MRS. ANDREW, 1889, *Morals and Manners in Richardson, The National Review, vol.* 14, *p.* 321.

Richardson has to be not skimmed but studied; not sucked like an orange, nor swallowed like a lollipop, but attacked *secundum artem* like a dinner of many courses and wines. Once inside the vast and solid labyrinth of his intrigue, you must hold fast to the clue which you have caught upon entering, or the adventure proves impossible, and you emerge from his precincts defeated and disgraced. And by us children of Mudie, to whom a novel must be either a solemn brandy-and-soda or as it were a garrulous and vapid afternoon tea, adventures of that moment are not often attempted.—HENLEY, WILLIAM ERNEST, 1890, *Views and Reviews, p.* 216.

Richardson's great forte consists in the art of making his characters *live;* in this particular he has rarely been rivalled, never, I think, excelled, by other authors. He employs not the mental dissecting-knife of modern writers. He affects not to analyze with a pretence of profoundity the implexicable workings of the mind. His method, on the contrary, is that of nature herself. The characters of his creations are revealed to us, like those of our friends, in what they say and do; and with so much of nature, so much of consistency, in the representation, that they grow into our intimacy as our friends themselves; they excite our love, our esteem, our compassion, or it may be our scorn, our detestation, as if they were veritably sentient and sensible beings. In a word, the persons of Richardson's novels are no mere problems in psychology, but, relatively to the reader's affections, real creatures of flesh and blood, a consummation far more difficult of attainment.—WARD, WILLIAM C., 1890, *Samuel Richardson, Gentleman's Magazine, N. S., vol.* 44, *p.* 78.

The position, therefore, of Richardson in our literature is that of a great Nonconformist. He was not manufactured according to any established process. If I may employ a metaphor borrowed from his own most honourable craft, he was set up in a new kind of type.—BIRRELL, AUGUSTINE, 1892, *Res Judicatæ, p.* 7.

No men were ever more absolutely antipathetic—more fundamentally and radically antagonistic than Richardson with his shrinking, prudish, careful, self-searching nature, and Fielding with his large, reckless, generous, exuberant temperament. Their literary methods were no less opposed. The one, with the schooling of a tradesman, was mainly a *spectator ab intra;* the other, with the education of a gentleman, mainly a *spectator ab extra.* One had an unrivalled knowledge of Woman; the other an unrivalled experience of Man. To Richardson's subjective gifts were added an extraordinary persistence of mental application, and a merciless power of cumulative details; to Fielding's objective faculty, the keen perceptions of a humorist, and a matchless vein of irony. Both were reputed to have written *"le premier roman du monde."* Each has been called by his admirers the Father of the English Novel. It would be more exact to divide the paternity:—to speak of Richardson as the Father of the Novel of Sentiment, and Fielding as the Father of the Novel of Manners.—DOBSON, AUSTIN, 1893, *Richardson at Home, Scribner's Magazine, vol.* 14, *p.* 383.

It is true that the novel was developed, and not created; but it is not more true of Richardson's novel than of any other new species of composition, such as Marlowe's tragedy, or Scott's romantic tale, or Byron's personal epic. All alike are developed, not created, in the sense of having many affinities with the kind of literature immediately anterior to them. Thus in the novel of manners there are two elements—there is a description of ordinary character, and there is a plot-interest —*i. e.*, there is a story. Both of these elements are found in the generation before Richardson, but not in combination. It was he that combined them in his novel of manners, and therefore is he entitled to the praise of having invented a new species of composition.—MINTO, WILLIAM, 1894, *The Literature of the Georgian Era, ed. Knight, p.* 104.

There was no machinery, no plot, no classicism, no style—but sentiment in abundance and vast prolixity, and ever-recurring villainies, and "pillows bedew'd with tears." The particularity and fulness of his descriptions were something wonderful; every button on a coat, every ring on the fingers, every tint of a ribbon, every ruffle on a cap, every ruffle of emotion, every dimple in a cheek is pictured, and then—the "pillows bedew'd with tears."—MITCHELL, DONALD G., 1895, *English Lands Letters and Kings, Queen Anne and the Georges, p.* 64.

Richardson could not aspire to any literary graces; his resources were too few and his methods too simple for such an ambition. But in his delicate and discriminating character drawing he inevitably developed a new literary appliance. He was bound to eschew theory, to avoid any cataloguing of characteristics, to lay aside the old modes of the seventeenth-century Theophrastuses, and to subordinate his drawing of character to his story. He must perforce be simple, and proceed step by step, discarding all pedantry, and allowing the character to reveal itself with the inevitableness of reality.—CRAIK, HENRY, 1895, *ed., English Prose, Introduction, vol.* IV, *p.* 9.

His style, at its worst, is diffuse, clumsy, and involved; and, at its best, is no more than blunt, direct, and unaffected. When his characters are discussing the "social problems" of their day the diction is no better than the average contemporary pamphleteer's. His vocabulary is commonplace, shows no trace of selection, and is disfigured by that abuse of the current poetical phraseology into which even a Thomson was sometimes betrayed, and by force of which tears are transformed into "pearly fugitives." We are not, indeed, to look to Richardson for that nameless quality of style which is the property of a scholar and a gentleman, such as Fielding was; for Richardson belongs to neither category. On the other hand, it would be grossly unfair to be blind to the great knack of extremely racy and idiomatic colloquial English which he displays in his dialogue; or to grudge him the merits of straightforwardness and spirit; or to refuse to admit that at times he shows complete command over the instrument of modern powers and compass. The effects, indeed, which he more than once achieves seem out of all proportion to the poverty of his means. —MILLAR, J. H., 1895, *English Prose, ed. Craik, vol.* IV, *p.* 58.

To-day the works of Richardson are entirely forgotten. Of these once famous novels the public no longer knows anything beyond the titles. Even the critics scarcely pay any attention to the man who was considered the greatest of all English writers in point of pathos, and if "Tom Jones," the "Vicar of Wakefield" and "Robinson Crusoe" are still read, "Clarissa Harlowe" is read no more than "Clélie" or "Le Grand Cyrus." This neglect may be explained, but it cannot be justified. Richardson's work must always be of the highest importance in the history of fiction, by reason of the magnitude of the revolution he effected. His very faults even, obvious as they are, stamp him with originality. —TEXTE, JOSEPH, 1895–99, *Jean-Jacques Rousseau and the Cosmopolitan Spirit in Literature, tr. Matthews, p.* 165.

I do not for one moment believe that it was the blithe and brutal coarseness of Fielding's novels that exiled them from the female heart, that inconsistent heart which never fluttered over the more repellent indecency of "Pamela." Insidious influences were at work within the dovecotes. The eighteenth-century woman, while less given to self-analysis and self-assertion than her successor to-day, was just as conscious of her own nature, its resistless force, its inalienable laws, its permanent limitations; and in Richardson she recognized the artist who had divined her subtleties, and had given them form and color. His correspondence with women is unlike anything else the period has to show. To him they had an independence of thought and action which took the rest of mankind a hundred years longer to concede; and it is not surprising to see the fervent homage this stout little tradesman of sixty received from his female flatterers, when we remember that he and he alone in all his century had looked into the rebellious secrets of their hearts with understanding and with reverence.—REPPLIER, AGNES, 1897, *Varia, p.* 202.

What was Richardson's addition to literature may be described in a condensed form as a combination of art in the progress of a narrative, force in the evolution of pathos, and morality founded upon a profound study of conduct. Of the group, he was the one who wrote least correctly; Richardson, as a pure man of letters, is the inferior, not merely of Fielding and Sterne, but of Smollett. He knows no form but the tedious and imperfect artifice of a series of letters. He is often without distinction, always without elegance and wit; he is pedantic, careless, profuse; he seems to write for hours and hours, his wig thrown over the back of a chair, his stockings down at heel. But the accidents of his life and temperament had inducted him into an extraordinary knowledge of the female heart; while his imagination permitted him to clothe the commonplace reflections of very ordinary people in fascinating robes of simple fancy. He was slow of speech and lengthy, but he had a magic gift which obliged every one to listen to him. The minuteness of Richardson's observations of common life added extremely to the pleasure which his novels gave to readers weary of the vagueness, the empty fustian of the heroic romances. His pages appealed to the instinct in the human mind which delights to be told over again, and told in scrupulous detail, that which it knows already. His readers, encouraged by his almost oily partiality for the moral conventions, gave themselves up to him without suspicion, and enjoyed each little triviality, each coarse touch of life, each prosaic circumstance, with perfect gusto, sure that, however vulgar they might be, they would lead up to the triumph of virtue. What these readers were really assisting at was the triumph of anti-romantic realism.—GOSSE, EDMUND, 1897, *Short History of Modern English Literature, p.* 242.

Richardson's expressed, and beyond the slightest doubt his sincere, purpose in all was, not to produce works of art, but to enforce lessons of morality. Yet posterity, while pronouncing his morals somewhat musty and even at times a little rancid, has recognised him as a great, though by no means an impeccable artist. —SAINTSBURY, GEORGE, 1898, *A Short History of English Literature*, p. 600.

We are not likely to overestimate the historical position of Richardson; we are more likely to underestimate it. Moreover, in the logical sequence of minor incident, "Clarissa Harlowe" has been excelled only by the maturest work of George Eliot. And yet the weaknesses and shortcomings of Richardson are apparent, and were apparent in his own time. His ethical system was based upon no wide observation or sound philosophy; it was the code of a Protestant casuist. He was a sentimentalist, creating pathetic scenes for their own sake and degrading tears and hysterics into a manner. His language was not free from the affectations of the romancers; even his friends dared tell him with caution and circumlocution that he was fond of the nursery phrase. He was unacquainted, as he said himself, with the high life he pretended to describe.—CROSS, WILBUR L., 1899, *The Development of the English Novel*, p. 42.

To the smaller details of his art, it need hardly be said, Richardson paid no attention whatever. He has no style at all; he wrote just as he talked, and as he composed those innumerable epistles on which we have drawn so largely. His sentences are often quite invertebrate, and innocent of anything that could do duty for a predicate, the finite verb being replaced by a participle or adjective. He never troubles about the symmetry of his paragraphs, and he never wastes time in compressing into ten words what is easier to say in twenty. There is no nice choice of epithet, nor fastidious rejection of the trite or homely; if he had been more careful he could never have been so prolix. And there is not in his books what has often redeemed the style of writers no less homely in their way, that appeal to, and constant illustration by means of natural beauty, which elevate the novels of a writer so much inferior to him as Mrs. Radcliffe.—THOMSON, CLARA LINKLATER, 1900, *Samuel Richardson, A Biographical and Critical Study*, p. 263.

Thomas Sherlock

1678–1761

Thomas Sherlock, D. D.: bishop and author; son of Dean William Sherlock; b. in London, England, in 1678; educated at Eton; graduated at Cambridge 1697; was master of the Temple forty-nine years (1704–53); was made a prebendary of London 1713, vice-chancellor of Cambridge 1714, dean of Chichester Nov., 1715, prebendary of Norwich, 1719, Bishop of Bangor Feb. 4, 1728, of Salisbury 1734, and of London 1748, having declined in 1747 the Archbishopric of Canterbury. He took an active part in the Bangorian controversy in opposition to Dr. Hoadly (1716), wrote several controversial works on Christian evidences, of which the most celebrated were "The Use and Intent of Prophecy" (1725) and "Tryal of the Witnesses of the Resurrection of Jesus" (1729), and published four volumes of his "Discourses at the Temple Church" (1754–58), which gained him a high reputation as a pulpit orator. D. in London, July 18, 1761. His *Works* were edited by T. S. Hughes, D. D. (London, 5 vols., 1830).—JACKSON, SAMUEL MACAULEY, *rev.*, 1897, *Johnson's Universal Cyclopædia, vol.* VII, *p.* 473.

PERSONAL

Though his voice was not melodious, but accompanied rather with a thickness of speech, yet were his words uttered with so much propriety, and with such strength and vehemence, that he never failed to take possession of his whole audience and secure their attention. This powerful delivery of words so weighty and important as his always were, made a strong impression on the minds of his hearers, and was not soon forgot.—NICOLLS, REV., 1762, *Funeral Sermon, Gentleman's Magazine*, p. 23.

In the Bangorian controversy Sherlock took a leading part against Hoadly, and was often considered his most formidable antagonist. He was not only a principal contributor to its voluminous literature, but was prominent in the committee of

Convocation which drew up the charge against the bishop. The part he had taken gave offence at court, and he was removed from the list of king's chaplains. Nichols says that in later life he disapproved of what he had written, and would not have it reprinted. Bishop Newton, however, says he had been assured by those who lived with Sherlock most, and knew him best, that this assertion was wholly groundless. Sherlock was often matched against Hoadly in less serious encounters. They often met in that curious palæstra of theological controversy, Queen Caroline's drawing-room.—ABBEY, CHARLES J., 1887, *The English Church and Its Bishops*, 1700–1800, *vol.* II, *p.* 50.

An ambitious and popular man, Sherlock was an industrious and efficient bishop. He cultivated kindly relations with the dissenters and was in favour of comprehension. . . . He pleaded after the '45 for justice to the Scots episcopalian clergy. His works were "not less esteemed among catholics than among protestants," and several were translated into French.—HUTTON, W. H., 1897, *Dictionary of National Biography, vol.* LII, *p.* 94.

GENERAL

Sherlock's style is very elegant, though he has not made it his principal study.—JOHNSON, SAMUEL, 1778, *Life by Boswell, ed. Hill, vol.* III, *p.* 281.

The genius of our language gives us an advantage in the use of this figure. . . . I shall give a remarkably fine example, from a sermon of Bishop Sherlock's, where we shall see natural religion beautifully personified, and be able to judge from it, of the spirit and grace which this figure, when well conducted, bestows on a discourse. I must take notice, at the same time, that it is an instance of this figure, carried as far as prose, even in its highest elevation, will admit, and therefore suited only to compositions where the great efforts of eloquence are allowed. . . . This is more than elegant; it is truly sublime. The whole passage is animated; and the figure rises at the conclusion, when natural religion, who, before, was only a spectator, is introduced as speaking by the centurion's voice. It has the better effect too, that it occurs at the conclusion of a discourse, where we naturally look for most warmth and dignity. Did Bishop Sherlock's sermons, or, indeed, any English sermons whatever, afford us many passages equal to this, we should oftener have recourse to them for instances of the beauty of composition.—BLAIR, HUGH, 1783, *Lectures on Rhetoric and Belles-Lettres, ed. Mills, Lecture* xvi.

The Sermons of Sherlock, though censured by Mr. Church, are master-pieces of argument and eloquence. His "Discourses on Prophecy" and the "Trial of the Witnesses" are perhaps the best defences of Christianity in our language. —WARTON, JOSEPH, 1797, *ed. Pope's Works.*

The elegance of Sherlock is rather to be found in his ideas; and it is chiefly from a confusion of mind in his readers, that it has been transferred from its proper seat, and ascribed to his composition. His manner is for the most part close to his subject, and he disdains everything impertinent and merely ornamental; but he is usually hard, scholastic and even somewhat repellent in his language. His famous parallel between Christ and Mahomet, which is perhaps the only truly eloquent passage in his works, is indeed happily expressed.—GODWIN, WILLIAM, 1797, *Of English Style, The Enquirer*, *p.* 460

Without departing for a moment from the sobriety of an accomplished prose writer, he often produces the effect of the sublimest poetry.—WAYLAND, D. S., 1824, *Sherlock's Discourses, Preface.*

Having already laid up vast stores of knowledge, having his judgment ripe, and an ambition equal to his abilities, he soon surpassed the most eminent preachers of the day in true pulpit oratory. For his variety of matter and judicious arrangement of it, for the strength and solidity of his reasoning, for his force of language, for his flow of natural and manly eloquence, we may safely appeal to those admirable Discourses which have long ministered delight and consolation to the Christian: they hold no secondary rank among the writings of our Divines.—HUGHES, T. S., 1830, *ed., The Works of Bishop Sherlock, vol.* I, *p.* xix.

Thomas Sherlock was superior to his father, both in general intellectual ability and in special literary faculty; and he had the advantages of an almost finished style put ready into his hands. But he paid for this by being the contemporary of more distinguished writers in his own fields, and by the fact that the pulpit, though still powerful, was less powerful than it had been, and that the gradual "taming" process, of which Tillotson had set the example, had brought its exercises close to the uninteresting. As a mere writer he could not vie with Addison or Swift; as a writer in controversial divinity he could not vie with Law on one side or Berkeley on another. Nevertheless, he exhibited the earlier form of eighteenth-century prose in a very good measure, and showed its capacities in the various uses to which he applied it.—SAINTSBURY, GEORGE, 1894, *English Prose, ed. Craik, vol.* III, *p.* 300.

William Oldys

1696–1761

William Oldys, (1696–1761), bibliographer, natural son of Dr. Oldys, Chancellor of Lincoln. For about ten years Oldys was librarian to the Earl of Oxford, whose valuable collection of books and MSS. he arranged and catalogued, and by the Duke of Norfolk he was appointed Norroy King-of-arms. His chief works are a "Life of Sir Walter Raleigh," prefixed to Raleigh's "History of the World" (1736); "The British Librarian" (1737); "The Harleian Miscellany" (1753), besides many miscellaneous literary and bibliographical articles.—PATRICK AND GROOME, *eds.* 1897, *Chambers's Biographical Dictionary, p.* 704.

PERSONAL

Alas!—Oldys was an outcast of fortune, and the utter simplicity of his heart was guileless as a child's—ever open to the designing. The noble spirit of a Duke of Norfolk once rescued the long-lost historian of Rawleigh from the confinement of the Fleet, where he had existed, probably forgotten by the world, for six years. It was by an act of grace that the duke safely placed Oldys in the Heralds' College as Norroy King of Arms. But Oldys, like all shy and retired men, had contracted peculiar habits and close attachments for a few; both these he could indulge at no distance. He liked his old associates in the purlieus of the Fleet, who he facetiously dignified as "his Rulers," and there, as I have heard, with the grotesque whim of a herald, established "The Dragon Club."—DISRAELI, ISAAC, 1791–1824, *Oldys and His Manuscripts, Curiosities of Literature.*

Nothing, I firmly believe, would ever have biassed him to insert any fact in his writings he did not believe, or to supress any he did. Of this delicacy he gave an instance at a time when he was in great distress. After his publication of the life of Sir Walter Raleigh, some booksellers, thinking his name would sell a piece they were publishing, offered him a considerable sum to father it, which he rejected with the greatest indignation.—GROSE, FRANCIS, 1793, *The Olio.*

Was equally noted for his love of "old books" and regard for "old wine," or rather strong ale. "Old friends" he too often disgusted by his deep potations: *e. g.* at the funeral of the Princess Caroline. He made large literary collections, and aided any who asked his assistance in their books, but published little himself.—ALLIBONE, S. AUSTIN, 1870, *A Critical Dictionary of English Literature, vol.* II, *p.* 1453.

Oldys was connected with the College of Arms for nearly five years. His library was a large room up one flight of stairs in Norroy's apartments, in the west wing of the college. His notes were written on slips of paper, which he afterwards classified and deposited in parchment bags suspended on the walls of his room. In this way he covered several quires of paper with laborious collections for a complete life of "Shakespeare" and from these notes Isaac Reed made extracts which are included among the "Additional Anecdotes" appended to Rowe's life of the poet. At this period Oldys frequently passed his evenings at the house of John Taylor the oculist of Hatton Garden, where he always preferred the fireside in the kitchen, so that he might not be obliged to mingle with the other visitors. His last literary production was "The Life of Charles Cotton," prefixed to Sir John Hawkins's edition of Walton's "Complete Angler," 1760. He died at his apartments in the College of Arms on 15 April

1761, and was buried on the 19th in the north aisle of the church of St. Benet, Paul's Wharf. His friend John Taylor on 20 June 1761, administered as principal creditor, defrayed the funeral expenses, and obtained possession of his official regalia, books, and valuable manuscripts. —COOPER, THOMPSON, 1895, *Dictionary of National Biography, vol.* XLII, *p.* 122.

GENERAL

If its author ["British Librarian"], who is of all men living the most capable, would pursue and perfect this plan, he would do equal justice to the living and to the dead.—CAMPBELL, JOHN, 1754, *Rational Amusement.*

Oldys lived in the back ages of England; he had crept among the dark passages of Time, till, like an old gentleman-usher, he seemed to be reporting the secret history of the courts which he had lived in. He had been charmed among their masques and revels, had eyed with astonishment their cumbrous magnificence, when knights and ladies carried on their mantles and their cloth of gold ten thousand pounds' worth of ropes of pearls, and buttons of diamonds; or, descending to the gay court of the second Charles, he tattled merry tales, as in that of the first he had painfully watched, like a patriot or a loyalist, a distempered era. He had lived so constantly with these people of another age, and had so deeply interested himself in their affairs, and so loved the wit and the learning which are often bright under the rust of antiquity, that his own uncourtly style is embrowned with the tint of a century old. But it was this taste and curiosity which alone could have produced the extraordinary volume of Sir Walter Rawleigh's life; a work richly inlaid with the most curious facts and the juxtaposition of the most remote knowledge; to judge by its fulness of narrative, it would seem rather to have been the work of a contemporary. . . . At the close of every century, in this growing world of books, may an Oldys be the reader for the nation! Should he be endowed with a philosophical spirit, and combine the genius of his own times with that of the preceding, he will hold in his hand the claim of human thoughts, and, like another Bayle, become the historian of the human mind!—DISRAELI, ISAAC, 1791–1824, *Oldys and His Manuscripts, Curiosities of Literature.*

Well versed in English antiquities, a correct writer, and a good historian. —BRYDGES, SIR SAMUEL EGERTON, 1800, *ed. Phillip's Theatrum Poetarum Anglicanorum, p.* lxvii.

My additions to the notes of Oldys in the "Harleian Miscellany" will not be very numerous, for no editor could ever have been more competent to the undertaking than he was; but a successive editor must *seem* at least to have done something more than his predecessor.—PARK, THOMAS, 1807, *Letter to Sir Samuel Egerton Brydges.*

Oldys's interleaved Langbaine is re-echoed in almost every recent work connected with the belles-lettres of our country. Oldys himself was unrivalled in this method of illustration; if, besides his Langbaine, his copy of "Fuller's Worthies" . . . be alone considered! This Oldys was the oddest mortal that ever scribbled for bread. Grose, in his *Olio,* gives an amusing account of his having "a number of small parchment bags inscribed with the names of the persons whose lives he intended to write; into which he put every circumstance and anecdote he could collect, and from thence drew up his history."—DIBDIN, THOMAS FROGNALL, 1809, *The Bibliomania, p.* 64, *note.*

This distinguished writer and indefatigable antiquary, whose extended life was entirely devoted to literary pursuits, and whose copious and characteristic accounts of men and books, have endeared his memory to every lover of English literature. If Oldys possessed not the erudition of Johnson or of Mattaire, he had at least equal patience of investigation, soundness of judgment, and accuracy of criticism, with the most eminent of his contemporaries. One remarkable trait in his character was the entire absence of literary and posthumous fame, whilst he never begrudged his labour or considered his toil unproductive, so long as his researches substantiated Truth, or promoted the study of the History of Literature, which in other words is the history of the mind of man. Hence the very sweepings of his library have since been industriously collected, and enrich the works of Malone, Ritson, Read, Douce, Brydges, and others, and will always serve, as it were, for landmarks to those following in his wake. In his own peculiar departments of literature—history and biography—he has literally exhausted all the ordinary sources of information; and when he lacked the opportunity to labour himself, or to fill up the circle of his knowledge, he has nevertheless pointed out to his successors new or unexplored mines, whence additional *facts* may be gleaned, and the object of his life—the development of Truth—be secured.—THOMS, W. J., 1862, *Memoir of William Oldys, Notes and Queries, Third Series, vol.* I, *p.* 85.

George Bubb Dodington

Lord Melcombe

1691–1762

George Bubb Dodington (later Baron Melcombe). Born in Dorset, England, 1691: died at Hammersmith, July 28, 1762. An English politician. He was the son of George Bubb, but adopted the name of Dodington on inheriting an estate in 1720 from an uncle of that name. In 1715 he entered Parliament, where he acquired the reputation of an assiduous place-hunter. He was created Baron Melcombe of Melcombe Regis, Dorsetshire, in 1761. He patronized men of letters, and was complimented by Edward Young, Fielding, and Richard Bentley. He left a diary covering the period from 1749 to 1761, which was published in 1784.—SMITH, BENJAMIN E., *ed.* 1894–97, *The Century Cyclopædia of Names, p.* 330.

PERSONAL

Though Folly, robed in purple, shines,
Though Vice exhausts Peruvian mines,
Yet shall they tremble, and turn pale,
When Satire wields her mighty flail;
Or should they, of rebuke afraid,
With Melcombe seek hell's deepest shade,
Satire, still mindful of her aim,
Shall bring the cowards back to shame.
—CHURCHILL, CHARLES, 1762, *The Ghost, bk.* iii, *v.* 923–30.

When he passed from Pall-Mall to La Trappe it was always in a coach, which I could not but suspect had been his ambassadorial equipage at Madrid, drawn by six fat unwieldy black horses, short-docked, and of colossal dignity. Neither was he less characteristic in apparel than in equipage; he had a wardrobe loaded with rich and flaring suits, each in itself a load to the wearer, and of these I have no doubt but many were cœval with his embassy above mentioned, and every birth-day had added to the stock. In doing this he so contrived as never to put his old dresses out of countenance, by any variations in the fashion of the new; in the meantime, his bulk and corpulency gave full display to a vast expanse and profusion of brocade and embroidery, and this, when set off with an enormous tye-periwig and deep-laced ruffles, gave the picture of an ancient courtier in his gala habit, or Quin in his stage dress. Nevertheless, it must be confessed this style, though out of date, was not out of character, but harmonized so well with the person of the wearer, that I remember when he made his first speech in the House of Peers as Lord Melcombe, all the flashes of his wit, all the studied phrases and well-turned periods of his rhetoric lost their effect, simply because the orator had laid aside his magisterial tye, and put on a modern bag-wig, which was as much out of costume upon the broad expanse of his shoulders, as a cue would have been upon the robes of the Lord Chief Justice.—CUMBERLAND, RICHARD, 1806, *Memoirs Written by Himself, vol.* I, *p.* 185.

Cumberland, in his own memoirs, has introduced a humorous sketch of lord Melcombe, which appears to be drawn from the life. His passion for magnificence and display was quite puerile, and his eccentricities were scarcely rational: yet we are told that he had an ornamented fancy, and a brilliant wit, was an elegant Latin classic, well versed in history ancient and modern, and that his favourite, prose writer was Tacitus. But upon the whole, his character appears to have been concisely summed up by sir E. Brydges, that he was a heartless man, with a very powerful capacity.—PARK, THOMAS, 1806, *ed. Walpole's Royal and Noble Authors, vol.* IV, *p.* 282.

He is a character typical in many respects of his age; utterly unconscientious and cheerfully blind to his unconscientiousness; and a liberal rather than discriminating patron of literary men.—WARD, ADOLPHUS WILLIAM, 1869, *ed. Poetical Works of Alexander Pope, p.* 279, *note.*

LADY MARY WORTLEY MONTAGU

Engraving by W. Greatbatch,
from Original Miniature.

EDWARD YOUNG

Drawing by J. Thurston, Engraving
by W. C. Edwards. Original
Picture by Highmore.

Doddington's vanity was extreme. He prided himself upon his person, manners, and ancestry, though he was ugly, awkward, and the son of an obscure father. . . . This concentration of self-esteem was expressed in a superb bearing, which, when it took the form of distant civility, would have been very irritating to Pope.—ELWIN, WHITWELL, 1871, *ed., The Works of Alexander Pope, vol.* VII, *p.* 319, *note.*

DIARY

Although it may reflect a considerable degree of honour on his Lordship's abilities, yet, in my opinion, it shews his political conduct (however palliated by the ingenuity of his own pen), to have been wholly directed by the base motives of avarice, vanity, and selfishness. . . . I am aware that, in treating the character of my Author thus freely, I shall appear as an extraordinary Editor, the practice of whom has generally been, to prefer flattery to truth, and partiality to justice. But it may be worth considering whether my method or the common one is the less injurious to the character of an author; and whether the reader may not be more inclined to overlook or pardon those errors, which he is previously instructed to expect, than he would be, if every page contradicted the favourable impressions, which the Editor had been industriously labouring to fix on his mind. —WYNDHAM, HENRY PENRUDDOCKE, 1784, *ed. The Diary of George Bubb Dodington, pp.* viii, x.

It had been well for lord Melcombe's memory, if his fame had been suffered to rest on the tradition of his wit, and the evidence of his poetry. The posthumous publication of his own Diary has not enlarged the stock of his reputation, nor reflected more credit on his judgment than on his steadiness. Very sparingly strewed with his brightest talent, wit; the book strangely displays a complacency in his own versatility, and seems to look back with triumph on the scorn and derision with which his political levity was treated by all to whom he attached or attempted to attach himself. He records conversations in which he alone did not perceive, what every reader must discover, that he was always a dupe. And so blind was his self-love, that he appears to be satisfied with himself, though he relates little but what tended to his disgrace: as if he thought the world would forgive his inconsistencies as easily as he forgave himself. Had he adopted the French title *Confessions*, it would have seemed to imply some kind of penitence. But vain-glory engrossed Lord Melcombe. He was determined to raise an altar to himself; and for want of burnt-offerings, lighted the pyre, like the great author (Rousseau), with his own character. However, with all its faults and curtailments, the book is valuable.—WALPOLE, HORACE, 1796, *A Catalogue of the Royal and Noble Authors of England, Scotland and Ireland, vol.* IV, *p.* 276.

The Diary of Dodington, Lord Melcombe, must by no means be neglected, for by its means we are allowed a slight glance into the intrigues and cabals of the times. It is generally amusing, and sometimes important.—SMYTH, WILLIAM, 1840, *Lectures on Modern History.*

Lady Mary Wortley Montagu

1689–1762

Montagu (*Lady* Mary Wortley), 1689–1762. Born [Mary Pierrepont; Lady Mary in 1690, when her father became Earl of Kingston], in London, 1689; baptized, 26 May. Early taste for literature. Married to Edward Wortley Montagu, 12 Aug. 1712. In favour at Court. Friendship with Pope begun. In Vienna with her husband (appointed Ambassador to the Porte), Sept. 1716 to Jan. 1717; in Constantinople, May 1717 to June 1718. Returned to England, Oct. 1718. Estrangement from Pope, 1722. Lived abroad, apart from husband, July 1739–1762. Died, in England, 21 Aug. 1762. *Works:* "Court Poems" (anon.; surreptitiously published), 1716 (misdated 1706 on title-page); authorised edn., as "Six Town Eclogues" (under initials: Rt. Hon. L. M. W. M.), 1747. *Posthumous:* "Letters of Lady M——y W———y M——e" (3 vols.), 1763; "Poetical Works of the Right Hon. Lady M———y W———y M——e," 1781.—SHARP, R. FARQUHARSON, 1897, *A Dictionary of English Authors, p.* 201.

PERSONAL

SACRED TO THE MEMORY OF
THE RIGHT HONORABLE
LADY MARY WORTLEY MONTAGU,
WHO HAPPILY INTRODUCED FROM TURKEY
INTO THIS COUNTRY
THE SALUTARY ART
OF INOCULATING THE SMALLPOX.
CONVINCED OF ITS EFFICACY
SHE FIRST TRIED IT WITH SUCCESS
ON HER OWN CHILDREN
AND THEN RECOMMENDED THE PRACTICE
OF IT
TO HER FELLOW-CITIZENS.
THUS BY HER EXAMPLE AND ADVICE
WE HAVE SOFTENED THE VIRULENCE
AND ESCAPED THE DANGER OF THIS MALIGNANT DISEASE.
TO PERPETUATE THE MEMORY OF SUCH
BENEVOLENCE
AND TO EXPRESS HER GRATITUDE
FOR THE BENEFIT SHE HERSELF RECEIVED
FROM THIS ALLEVIATING ART,
THIS MONUMENT IS ERECTED BY
HENRIETTA INGE—
RELICT OF THEODORE WILLIAM INGE, ESQ.,
AND DAUGHTER OF SIR JOHN WROTTELSEY,
BART.,
IN THE YEAR OF OUR LORD 1789.

—INSCRIPTION ON CENOTAPH, *Litchfield Cathedral.*

The boy was engrafted last Tuesday, and is at this time singing and playing, very impatient for his supper, I pray God my next may give as good an account of him. I cannot engraft the girl, her nurse has not had the small-pox.—MONTAGU, LADY MARY WORTLEY, 1718, *Letter to Mr. Montagu, March* 23.

The playful smiles around the dimpled mouth,
That happy air of majesty and truth;
So would I draw (but oh! 'tis vain to try,
My narrow genius does the power deny).
The equal lustre of the heavenly mind,
Where every grace with every virtue's joined;
Learning not vain, and wisdom not severe,
With greatness easy, and with wit sincere,
With just description shew the soul divine,
And the whole princess in my work should shine.

—POPE, ALEXANDER, 1720, *On the Picture of Lady Mary Wortley Montagu, by Kneller.*

What lady's that to whom he gently bends?
Who knows not her? Ah, those are Wortley's eyes.
How art thou honoured, numbered with her friends;
For she distinguishes the good and wise.

—GAY, JOHN, 1727, *Mr. Pope's Welcome from Greece.*

Thus in the dame each nobler grace we find,
Fair Wortley's angel accent, eyes, and mind.

—SAVAGE, RICHARD, 1729, *The Wanderer, C. V.*

A woman of as fine a genius, and endu'd with as great a strength of mind as any of her sex in the *British* kingdoms.—VOLTAIRE, FRANÇOIS MARIE AROUET, 1732? *Letters Concerning English Nation.*

Her dress, her avarice, and her impudence must amaze any one that never heard her name. She wears a foul mob that does not cover her greasy black locks, that hang loose, never combed or curled, an old mazarine blue wrapper, that gapes open and discovers a canvas petticoat. Her face swelled violently on one side with the remains of a ——, partly covered with a plaister, and partly with white paint, which for cheapness she has bought so coarse.—WALPOLE, HORACE, 1740, *Letter to Conway, Sept.* 25; *Letters, ed. Cunningham, vol.* I, *p.* 57.

There is more fire and wit in all the writings of that author than one meets with in almost any other; and whether she is in the humour of an infidel or a devotee, she expresses herself with so much strength that one can hardly persuade oneself she is not in earnest on either side of the question. Nothing can be more natural than her complaint of the loss of her beauty [*vide* the "Saturday" in her "Town Eclogues"]; but as that was only one of her various powers to charm, I should have imagined she would only have felt a very small part of the regret that many other people have suffered on a like misfortune; who have nothing but the loveliness of their persons to claim admiration; and consequently, by the loss of that, have found all their hopes of distinction vanish much earlier in life than Lady Mary's;—for if I do not mistake, she was near thirty before she had to deplore the loss of beauty greater than I ever saw in any face beside her own.—HERTFORD, LADY (DUCHESS OF SOMERSET), 1741, *Letters: Little Memoirs of the Eighteenth Century, by Paston, p.* 33.

Now I must tell you a story of Lady Mary. As she was on her travels, she had occasion to go somewhere by sea, and (to save charges) got a passage on board a man of war: the ship was (I think) Commodore Barnet's. When he had landed her, she told him, she knew she was not to offer to pay for her passage, but in consideration of his many civilities intreated him to wear a ring for her sake, and pressed him to accept it, and he did. It was an emerald of remarkable size and beauty. Some time after, as he wore it, some friend was admiring it, and asked him how he came by it. When he heard from whom it came, he laughed and desired him to shew it to a jeweller, whom he knew. The man was sent for. He unset it; it was a paste not worth forty shillings.—GRAY, THOMAS, 1761, *Letter to Thomas Wharton, Jan.* 31.

Lady Mary Wortley is arrived. I have seen her. I think her avarice, her dirt, and her vivacity are all increased. Her dress, like her language, is a *galimatias* of several countries; the groundwork rags, and the embroidery nastiness. She needs no cap, no handkerchief, no gown, no petticoat, no shoes. An old black laced hood represents the first; the fur of a horseman's coat, which replaces the third, serves for the second; a dimity petticoat is deputy, and officiates for the fourth; and slippers act the part of the last.—WALPOLE, HORACE, 1762, *Letter to George Montagu, Feb.* 2; *Letters, ed. Cunningham, vol.* III, *p.* 480.

She does not look older than when she went abroad, has more than the vivacity of fifteen, and a memory which, perhaps, is unique. Several people visited her out of curiosity, which she did not like. I visited her because her husband and mine were cousin-germans. Though she had not any foolish partiality for her husband or his relations, I was very graciously received, and you may imagine entertained, by one who neither thinks, speaks, acts, or dresses, like anybody else. Her *domestick* is made up of all nations, and when you get into her drawing-room, you imagine you are in the first story of the Tower of Babel. An Hungarian servant takes your name at the door; he gives it to an Italian, who delivers it to a Frenchman; the Frenchman to a Swiss, and the Swiss to a Polander; so that, by the time you get to her ladyship's presence, you have changed your name five times, without the expense of an act of parliament. —MONTAGU, ELIZABETH, 1762, *A Lady of the Last Century, p.* 129.

To Congreve she was all brightness, life and spirit; her silvery laugh sounded like divinest melody; but when I stood before her, scarcely daring to look into those eyes for that sacred love after which I pined, she was cold, severe, and silent. When Pope was near, when Wharton was by her side, gazing at her with his large and earnest eyes, how beautiful she appeared; all her genius shone out of her spirit face; her features glowed with animation; her tongue spake in softest accents, and she seemed a something more than earthly. But when the visitor departed, a magic change came over her—she froze, as it were, into marble; she grew cold, still, selfish, unfeeling, capricious, and exacting. One reads in old romances of a beautiful damsel discovered in a forest by some brave, errant knight; she weeps, she prays, she smiles, she fascinates. The gallant adventurer vows to devote his life to her service; she leads him to her bower, or to some faërie castle. Something in her appearance suddenly awakens suspicion, and the noble knight clutches his good sword Excalibar within his mailed hand, and mayhap as an additional precaution lifts up a prayer to God and the Virgin. Scarcely has he done it, when a transformation is seen—a mighty transformation indeed; and the virgin disappears, and he sees only a venomous serpent looking at him with deadly eyes, as Lucifer looked on Eve, and hissing forth cold poison. Such was the difference between my mother before her visitors, and my mother with her son.—MONTAGU, EDWARD WORTLEY, 1776? *An Autobiography, vol.* I, *p.* 97.

Mr. Horace Walpole remembers Lady M. W. Montague perfectly well, having passed a year with her at Florence. He told me this morning that she was not handsome, had a wild, staring eye, was much marked with the smallpox, which she endeavoured to conceal, by filling up the depressions with white paint. She was a great mischief-maker, and had not the smallest regard for truth. Her first gallant after her marriage was Lord Stair, our ambassador at Paris. Worsdale, the painter, told Mr. Walpole that the first cause of quarrel between her and Pope was her borrowing a pair of sheets from the poet, which, after keeping them a fortnight, were returned to him unwashed. —MALONE, EDMOND, 1789, *Maloniana, ed. Prior, March* 8, *p.* 149.

Lady Mary had Lord Byron's fate. . . . Lord Byron was a moody, fiery, brooding child,—full of passion, obstinacy, and irregularity, in his teens;—Lady Mary was a single-thinking, classical, daring, inspired girl long under one-and-twenty. Lord Byron at a plunge formed his own spreading circles on the glittering still-life lake of fashionable society: Lady Mary with her beauty and her genius effected the same result by the same impetuosity. Lady Mary made, as it would appear, a cold unsatisfactory marriage, but, it must be admitted, with one possessed of a patience untainted by genius:—Lord Byron iced himself into the connubial state, but shuddered at its coldness. The press, and the poets, and the prosers united with serene ferocity against both. Both, alas! were

"Souls made of fire and children of the sun,
With whom revenge was virtue!"

Their revenge was mutual-minded. Misunderstood, calumniated, they quitted the land which was not worthy of them. Genius-born, they both passed to the east; and to them we owe the most sensible,—the most passionate,—the most voluptuous,—and the most inspired pictures of "the land of the citron and myrtle," that have ever waked the wish and melted the heart of us southron readers.—REYNOLDS, HAMILTON, 1837, *A Critical Gossip with Lady Mary Wortley Montagu, Bentley's Miscellany, vol.* I, *p.* 140.

The most entertaining, fascinating, witty and brilliant of her sex; learned, accomplished, graceful and beautiful, the irresistible Lady Mary Pierrepont gave from her earliest years promise of what she afterwards became. At eight years old she was a toast, and the fame of her beauty and talents spread from that time, every fresh year adding to her attractions, and luring new admirers, until the crowd of those who followed in her train filled every country through which she passed. She was the very impersonation of all the beauties and enslavers which poets and romancers feign: she might have sat for the portrait of the most finished fine lady, the most enchanting coquette; and she probably, in effect, supplied many a writer with such a heroine as was the fashion of her day. Yet, with the admirers innumerable, and all appliances and means to boot that should have enabled her to make a happy marriage, the charming Lady Mary was unhappy in the choice she made. She possessed so many useful virtues, had so much philanthropy and feeling, that it is impossible but that she would have made a good wife, even in spite of the danger she had run of being spoilt by indulgence and adulation, if she had met with a man of suitable mind, who would have appreciated her good qualities; but Mr. Wortley was a cold, severe, unimaginative person, who, marrying her, a youthful beauty and coquette, should have known how, judiciously, to correct her errors, and brought forth the excellencies which existed in her mind; instead of treating her with the sullen neglect to which, from an early period of her marriage, he condemned her. . . . It is to be regretted that she made a match so unsuitable to her; for had she fortunately married a man of a different character from the cold, harsh, severe person, for whom she gave up all her early brilliant prospects, no doubt she would have been as valuable in domestic life, as she was admirable in literary attainments, and fascinating in the qualities which delight the world.—COSTELLO, LOUISA STUART, 1844, *Memoirs of Eminent Englishwomen, vol.* IV, *pp.* 231, 400.

And so farewell, poor, flourishing, disappointed, reconciled, wise, foolish, enchanting Lady Mary! Fair English vision in Turkland; Turkish vision in ours; the female wit of the days of Pope; benefactress of the species; irritating satirist of the circles. Thou didst err for want of a little more heart,—perhaps for want of finding enough in others, or for loss of thy mother in infancy,—but thy loss was our gain, for it gained us thy books, and thy inoculation. Thy poems are little, being but a little wit in rhyme, *vers de société;* but thy prose is much,—admirable, better than acute, idiomatical, off-hand, conversational without inelegance, fresh as the laugh on the young cheek, and full of brain. The conventional show of things could not deceive thee: pity was it that thou didst not see a little farther into the sweets of things unconventional,—of faith in the heart, as well as in the blood and good sense! Lovable, indeed, thou wert not, whatever thou mightst have been rendered; but admirable thou wert, and ever wilt thou be thought so, as long as pen writeth straight-forward, and sense or Sultana hath a charm.—HUNT, LEIGH, 1847, *Men, Women and Books, vol.* II, *p.* 218.

Had Lady Mary Wortley lived in the days of heathen Greece or Rome, such service as she performed in the introduction of inoculation, would have enrolled her name among the deities who have benefited mankind. But in Christian England, her native land, on which she bestowed such a vital blessing, and through it, to all the people of the West, what has been her recompense? We read of princely endowments bestowed by the British government upon great generals; of titles conferred and pensions granted, through several generations, to those who have served their country; of monuments erected by the British people to statesmen and warriors, and even to weak and worthless princes; but where is the national monument to Lady Mary Wortley Montagu? Is it in Westminster Abbey? Or has it been only by the private bounty of a woman that her good deed has a record? On the pages of history, and in the annals of medicine, the name of Lady Montagu must find its place; but should not England be proud to honor her noble daughter, whose memory, from royal palace to pauper's hut, ought to be held in grateful affection?—HALE, SARAH J., 1856, *ed., The Letters of Lady Mary Wortley Montagu, Memoir, p.* xvii.

We doubt whether at any moment of his life, Mr. Wortley was a loving and affectionate husband. So far as we can fathom his character, he appears to have been a man of shrewd good sense, upright and honourable, but of a mean and penurious nature, which after his father's death, and when the possible million of which he died possessed loomed in the distance, became an all-absorbing passion. In the eyes of the "wits," Lady Mary was remarkably mean; in the eyes of her husband she was extravagant. — DILKE, CHARLES WENTWORTH, 1861–75, *Lady Mary Wortley Montagu, The Papers of a Critic, vol.* I, *p.* 354.

The members of the very exclusive Kit-Kat Club assembled in council at the commencement of the London Season, 1698, to nominate the lady who should be their standing toast for the current year—have her honoured name inscribed upon their drinking-glasses, and her portrait painted in Kit-Kat fashion,—were considerably puzzled for a choice; when the Earl of Dorchester, afterwards Duke of Kingston, suggested the eldest of his three daughters, the Lady Mary Pierrepont. This proposition being demurred to, inasmuch as the said Lady Mary Pierrepont was personally unknown to the members of the club, the Earl volunteered to go at once and bring her there for approval. He soon returned, bringing with him a beautiful child of about eight years of age, the Lady Mary in question, who was received with acclamation, declared the toast of the year, and remained throughout the banquet, receiving the compliments and caresses of the members with a delightful ease far more womanly than childlike,—so early responsive to opportunity was her gay coquetry of nature. The emotions of gratified vanity excited upon this occasion left an indelible impression on her mind. "Pleasure were too poor a word," she exclaims, "to express my sensations: never again throughout my life have I spent so happy a day." There is an unconscious self-revelation in these few words rarely observable in her ladyship's clever and elaborate correspondence with all its artistic confidences, and here and there apparent *abandon.*—RUSSELL, WILLIAM, 1864, *Extraordinary Women, p.* 143.

Whatever esteem we may feel for the talents and merits, whatever toleration we may be inclined to extend over the eccentricities and audacities, of such women as Lady Mary Wortley Montague, it is the rankest and most nauseous cant of hypocritical chivalry to pretend that they have a right to expect the same tender and reverent forbearance which all but the vilest of men and subscribers feel for "any woman, womanly."—SWINBURNE, ALGERNON CHARLES, 1886, *Miscellanies, p.* 42.

The fact seems to have been that Lady Mary, like many of the men of the eighteenth century, had developed the intellectual and practical side of her nature at the expense of the emotions. There is no proof that she was ever in love with anyone but her husband; and her affection for him began in intellectual companionship, and consisted to a considerable extent in respect, with a touch of fear. Her love-letters are full of business details, plain speaking, and close reasoning. Her lover gives her up rather than violate his principles as to marriage settlements, and she heartily approves him. All this is very sensible, but it is hardly the note of passion, even allowing for the undemonstrative character of the age. Family affection was not strongly developed in Lady Mary: her father's death leaves little impression on her. He had neglected her; why should she mourn for him? Her religion, again, was the Whig Christianity of the day, the moderately rationalistic, tolerant half-deism of the Georgian Bishops; she never speaks but with contempt of past mystics or present Methodists. Patriotism had little hold on her—she was cosmopolitan; and though English defeats galled her a little, English victories left her cold. All her failings—coarseness of phrase, coldness of feeling, want of consideration in the use of her wit, even the slovenliness of dress into which she fell—are the faults of a nature too merely intellectual. One may say that she was all her days a traveller, regarding the world of life as she did the lands through which she journeyed. The joys of existence were but the chance of a fine day, or a good inn on the road; its griefs but the breaking of a wheel, the discomfort of a hovel—all alike to be borne with quietly, because they would be gone and almost forgotten to-morrow. Friends, relations even, were but travelling-companions—here to-day, gone to-morrow.—ROPES, ARTHUR R., 1892, *ed., Lady Mary Wortley Montagu, Select Passages from Her Letters, Introduction, p.* 30.

There is in Litchfield Cathedral a cenotaph representing Beauty weeping the loss of her Preserver; it was placed there by some grateful person to perpetuate the memory of the Lady Mary's benevolence in introducing inoculation; and I think it is the only eulogy to be found on any memorial tablet of this strange, witty, beautiful, indiscreet, studious, unhappy, disappointed woman.—MITCHELL, DONALD G., 1895, *English Lands Letters and Kings.*

The lady who bears in English literature the courtesy title of "Lady Mary," without any necessary addition, was, oddly enough, connected with Evelyn by blood and with Pepys by marriage.—SAINTSBURY, GEORGE, 1898, *A Short History of English Literature, p.* 642.

POEMS

The letters of Gold, and the curious illumining of the Sonnets, were not a greater token of respect than what I have paid to *your Eclogues;* they lie inclosed in a monument of red Turkey, written in my fairest hand; the gilded leaves are opened with no less veneration than the pages of the Sibyls; like them, locked up and concealed from all profane eyes, *none but my own* have beheld these sacred remains of yourself; and I should think it as great a wickedness to divulge them, as to scatter abroad the ashes of my ancestors.—POPE, ALEXANDER, 1717, *Letter to Lady Mary Wortley Montagu.*

The town is an owl, if it don't like Lady Mary, and I am surprised at it; we here are owls enough to think her eclogues very bad; but that I did not wonder at.—GRAY, THOMAS, 1751, *Letter to Horace Walpole; Works, ed. Gosse, vol.* II, *p.* 222.

Of her poetical talents it may be observed, that they were usually commanded by particular occasions, and that when she had composed stanzas, as any incident suggested them, little care was taken afterwards; and she disdained the scrupulous labour, by which Pope acquired a great degree of his peculiar praise. But it should be remembered, that the ore is equally sterling, although it may not receive the highest degree of polish of which it is capable. She attempted no poem of much regularity or extent. In the "Town Eclogues," which is the longest, a few illegitimate rhymes and feeble expletives will not escape the keen eye of a critic. The epistle of Arthur Gray has true Ovidian tenderness, the ballads are elegant, and the satires abound in poignant sarcasms, and just reflections on the folly and vices of those whom she sought to stigmatize. There is little doubt, but that if Lady Mary had applied herself wholly to poetry, a near approximation to the rank of her contemporary bards would have been adjudged to her, by impartial posterity.—DALLAWAY, J., 1803, *ed., The Works of Lady Mary Wortley Montagu, Memoirs, vol.* I, *p.* 97.

She was an extraordinary woman; she could translate *Epictetus*, and yet write a song worthy of Aristippus.—BYRON, LORD, 1821, *A Second Letter on Bowles's Strictures on Pope, note.*

She had beauty for the fashionable,

satire for the witty, knowledge for the learned, and intelligence for the politician. She was not too refined to shrink from what we now consider the coarseness of that time. Many of her verses themselves are scarcely adapted for our decorous pages.—BAGEHOT, WALTER, 1862, *Lady Mary Wortley Montagu, Works, ed. Morgan, vol.* I, *p.* 374.

How coarsely, and even lewdly, she herself could write is proved in the "Epistle from Arthur Grey, the Footman;" a composition which a penny street ballad-monger would now blush to own; and added to its offences against decency is the cruelty of holding up the poor lady, whose notoriety was already sufficiently dreadful, to further ribaldry. Nor does this poem stand alone; the "Town Eclogues" and others of her fugitive pieces are almost equally gross.—BAKER, H. BARTON, 1877, *A Representative Lady of the Last Century, The Gentleman's Magazine, vol.* 241, *p.* 86.

If some of Lady Mary Wortley Montagu's "Town Eclogues" were attributed to Pope and Gay, and by them not disclaimed, the circumstance may be taken as proof that her verse was thought very good, in its day. It was by no means equal to her prose, nevertheless it sparkled with a considerable amount of satirical wit, as indeed anything from her pen could hardly fail to do. . . . Save for certain of the graces which adorn our modern *vers de société*, her poems have not much about them to please the modern taste.—ROBERTSON, ERIC S., 1883, *English Poetesses, pp.* 37, 47.

In many respects, though hard and mannish in temper, Lady Mary was eminent for width of view and for a mind open to the whole intellectual horizon. Her "Town Eclogues," printed in 1716 in heroic verse, are so rich and sparkling that they almost place Lady Mary among the poets, but they are of astounding freedom of thought and language.—GOSSE, EDMUND, 1888, *A History of Eighteenth Century Literature, p.* 205.

LETTERS

The publication of these letters will be an immortal monument to the memory of Lady Mary Wortley Montagu, and will shew, as long as the English language endures, the sprightliness of her wit, the solidity of her judgment, the elegance of her taste, and the excellence of her real character. These letters are so bewitchingly entertaining that we defy the most phlegmatic man on earth to read one without going through with them, or, after finishing the third volume, not to wish there was twenty more of them.—SMOLLETT, TOBIAS GEORGE, 1763, *Critical Review.*

They have entertained me very much. What fire, what ease, what knowledge of Europe and of Asia! Her account of the manners of the Turkish women is indeed different from any thing we have yet seen. —GIBBON, EDWARD, 1764, *Private Letters.*

The letters of Lady Mary Wortley Montague are not unworthy of being named after those of Madame de Sevigné. They have much of the French ease and vivacity; and retain more the character of agreeable epistolary style, than perhaps any letters which have appeared in the English language.—BLAIR, HUGH, 1783, *Lectures on Rhetoric and Belles-Lettres, ed. Mills, Lecture* xxxvii.

Lady Mary Wortley Montague is a remarkable instance of an author nearly lost to the nation: she is only known to posterity by a chance publication; for such were her famous Turkish letters, the manuscript of which her family once purchased with an intention to suppress, but they were frustrated by a transcript. The more recent letters were reluctantly extracted out of the family trunks, and surrendered in exchange for certain family documents, which had fallen into the hands of a bookseller. Had it depended on her relatives, the name of Lady Mary had only reached us in the satires of Pope. The greater part of her epistolary correspondence was destroyed by her mother (?); and what that good and Gothic lady spared, was suppressed by the hereditary austerity of rank, of which her family was too susceptible. The entire correspondence of this admirable writer and studious woman (for once, in perusing some unpublished letters of Lady Mary's, I discovered that "she had been in the habit of reading seven hours a day for many years") would undoubtedly have exhibited a fine statue, instead of the torso we now possess; and we might have lived with her ladyship, as we do with Madame de Sévigné.—DISRAELI, ISAAC, 1791–1824,

Of Suppressors and Dilapidators of Manuscripts, Curiosities of Literature.

The great charm of her letters is certainly the extreme ease and facility with which every thing is expressed, the brevity and rapidity of her representations, and the elegant simplicity of her diction. While they unite almost all the qualities of a good style, there is nothing of the professed author in them: nothing that seems to have been composed, or to have engaged the admiration of the writer. She appears to be quite unconscious either of merit or of exertion in what she is doing; and never stops to bring out a thought, or to turn an expression, with the cunning of a practised rhetorician.—JEFFREY, FRANCIS LORD, 1803–1844, *Lady Mary Wortley Montagu, Contributions to the Edinburgh Review, vol.* IV, *p.* 427.

Are lively and ingenious, but not natural. —MACKINTOSH, SIR JAMES, 1808, *Memoirs, ed. Mackintosh, Journal, June* 10, *p.* 404.

Her letters have been compared with those of Madame de Sevigné, but they do not at all resemble them. The latter have a calm, quiet interest, a sweetness, an ingenuous tenderness, a natural simplicity, which powerfully recommend them to us in those moments when we ourselves are calm or melancholy. Lady Montague's have infinitely more nerve and vigour, excite a far deeper interest, but of an equivocal and painful cast, and while, in a certain sense, they amuse and gratify, inspire aversion for their writer. On the other hand, Madame de Sevigné is a person whom one would like to have known. She is garrulous, she frequently repeats herself; but it is maternal love which causes the error. In one word, we admire the talents of Lady Montague, but we love the character of Madame de Sevigné.—ST. JOHN, JAMES AUGUSTUS, 1830, *The Lives of Celebrated Travellers, vol.* II, *p.* 100.

Lady Mary wrote admirable letters; *letters*—not dissertations, nor sentimental *effusions*, nor strings of witticisms, but real letters; such as any person of plain sense would be glad to receive. Her style, though correct and perspicuous, was unstudied, natural, flowing, spirited; she never used an unnecessary word, nor a phrase savouring of affectation; but still she meant to write well, and was conscious of having succeeded.—STUART, LADY LOUISA, 1837, *The Letters and Works of Lady Mary Wortley Montagu, ed. Lord Wharncliffe, Introductory Anecdotes, vol.* I, *p.* 109.

We cannot but suspect, also, that every reperusal of Lady Mary's "Letters" will tend to a doubt whether her merit has not been somewhat exaggerated. When they first appeared, a traveller and an author of Lady Mary's rank and sex was a double wonder—which was much increased by Lady Mary's personal circumstances, and by the vivacity, spirit, and boldness of her pen. But now that the extraneous sources of admiration have run dry, we confess that the intrinsic value of the letters seems less striking; and that if we were to deduct from Lady Mary's pleasantry and wit, those passages which a respectable woman ought not, perhaps, to have written, we should very considerably reduce her claims to literary eminence. The additional letters now produced will add little to Lady Mary's fame, and take little from her reputation. They exhibit her neither wittier nor looser than she was already known to be—on the contrary, the pleasantry and the coarseness being diluted as it were, by a large addition of very commonplace matter, the *peculiarities* of Lady Mary appear on the whole, we think, less pungent than in the earlier editions. — CROKER, JOHN WILSON, 1837, *Lady Mary Wortley Montagu's Letters, Quarterly Review, vol.* 58, *p.* 148.

The best and truest type of English character is exhibited in the letters of Lady Mary Wortley Montagu; in which are found united practical good sense, candour, honesty, and truth, combined with a noble self-sacrifice for the object of her love. The best love-letters by far are those written by women.—MARTEL, CHARLES, 1859, *ed., Love-Letters of Eminent Persons, Second ed., p.* vi.

One great charm of Lady Mary Wortley Montagu's letters, is their being perfectly natural: but then, it is a shrewd, thinking, sensible woman who is natural, not an ordinary being. On whatever subject she touches, we see that she has the grandeur of mind to rise above art.—THOMSON, KATHARINE (GRACE WHARTON), 1862, *The Literature of Society, vol.* II, *p.* 233.

Lady Mary made good use of her position in the front of the herd of tourists;

she told us what she saw in Turkey,—all the best of what she saw, and all the most remarkable things,—and told it very well. —BAGEHOT, WALTER, 1862, *Lady Mary Wortley Montagu, Works, ed. Morgan, vol.* I, *p.* 380.

"Keep my letters," she writes to one of her correspondents, "they will be as good as Madame de Sévigné's forty years hence;" and her prediction has been amply fulfilled. It has been alleged that the essential difference between these two celebrated letter-writers is this, that "the Frenchwoman speaks out of the abundance of her *heart*, and the Englishwoman out of the clearness of her *head.*" —SETON, GEORGE, 1870, *Gossip about Letters and Letter-Writers, p.* 48.

It is impossible to admire too much the grace, ease, and liveliness that breathe through these charming letters. The idiomatic purity and simplicity of the language attests, in conjunction with these qualities, the fundamental simplicity of the lady's character. A thread of sound English sense, too, seems to be carried through the whole literary product, and seems to be the principal prop whereby it is supported.—KEEGAN, P. Q., 1877, *Mrs. Lucy Hutchinson and Ladg Mary Wortley Montagu, Victoria.*

Her rank as the best letter-writer of her sex in English is undisputed.—SAINTSBURY, GEORGE, 1886, *Specimens of English Prose Style, p.* 174.

If one looks in Lady Mary's letters for scandal and coarseness, for occasional flippancy and an affectation of cynicism, these blemishes are easily discovered: they were faults of her time, training, and circumstances. The breadth of view, freedom from prejudice, and intelligent observation also to be found there, the touches of serious thought and tenderness which slip out, as it were, almost against the writer's will, may fairly be credited to herself. The extracts from the letters given here have been chosen rather to illustrate her disposition than her intellect. Her character is still somewhat severely judged, but no one calls her wit in question now.—MAYER, GERTRUDE TOWNSHEND, 1894, *Women of Letters, vol.* I, *p.* 161.

Yet the last, and crowning element in her own genius, and therefore in her own style, was her truthfulness to herself, to her foibles and to her convictions. She was one of those born to talk, with tongue or with pen; and never did her self-knowledge boil over so uncontrollably as when accident led her to study, and of course to comment on, the system of "La Trappe." She had seen too much, and knew too much, to be *naïve*; but though she could philosophise very reasonably and very effectively on the training and disciplining of the mind, she was not afraid of betraying the contradictions in her own nature. This frankness of feeling, to which her gay but not dishevelled spontaneity of utterance corresponded, makes her always good company; it is only in her earliest letters that there linger traces of the affectation rarely absent altogether from the writings of the young. The humour of her Turkish and later letters has a true ring. And, although few women (whether literary or other) have suffered more than she suffered, in part, may be, through the vivacity of her own temper and the freedom of her own pen,—she had a brave heart; and her high spirit, like all qualities which are of rarer growth, faithfully reflects itself in the current of her style. —WARD, ADOLPHUS WILLIAM, 1894, *English Prose, ed. Craik, vol.* III, *p.* 601.

She lacks, perhaps, some of the finer graces of style; but her letters have that one supreme charm, beyond all other letters ever published, or ever written perhaps—they are herself. Take up her volumes and you see not only—or chiefly —the chameleon world she portrayed, but the woman who portrays it. There she is, with her stout, shrewd, wise old face, looking at you through the pages. Are you a humbug of any kind? Be sure Mary has found you out, as she found out the little weak points of St. John Lord Bolingbroke, Samuel Richardson, the great dean of St Patrick's, and the false prudes of society. She will quarrel with you—for sixpence. She will tell you a jolly, imprudent, scandalous story before she has known you five minutes; and laugh that loud, candid laugh of hers at quite a doubtful joke. Mention the immortal name of a little crooked poet, and the old eyes will flash fire, hate, and rage; and the name of his Britannic Majesty's Ambassador to the Porte, and there will come a something on the old face that will warn you that Mary knows how to hold that imprudent tongue of hers sometimes, and on one subject at least to keep the world at bay. She has been dead—is it a hundred years?—with a fine cenotaph to her memory in Litchfield Cathedral; and as she stands beside you, you can hear her old heart still beating life, fight and courage. You can see the human sadness underneath the twinkle in the eyes, and remember how she is all her life battling the demon Melancholy, and vanquishing him, and laughing at him prostrate, and fighting and vanquishing him again, when he gets up, newly armed (as he always does), the next day or the day after that. The firm mouth will soften into a rare tenderness at the mention of her Ladyship of Bute. Who is it says that Mary is close-fisted about money, careless about person and reputation, malignant, shameless, vile? What does it matter who says it? When you read the letters you look up at her, not doubting, and lean across a century to take her hand.—TALLENTYRE, S. G., 1899, *Lady Mary Wortley Montagu, Longman's Magazine.*

GENERAL

It requires but small familiarity with the originals of the private correspondence of those days, to perceive that Lady Mary's standards of delicacy and propriety were simply those of her time. Even in the present day considerable differences on these points are observable among nations equally civilised; and wonderment at the unconsciousness betrayed by the one of the feeling of the other, is frequently to be found on both sides. In the gradual change of manners the English people of Lady Mary's time have become to us, in some degree, as aliens and objects of curious observation, whose points of divergence from our standards it is in like manner hard to forgive. It is not of course pretended that good morals are dependent upon time or place; but we may learn at least from these analogies that it is unwise to expect that any men or women should in these matters be far above the spirit of the society in which it is their lot to live.—THOMAS, W. MOY, 1861, *ed., The Letters and Works of Lady Mary Wortley Montagu, Preface, vol.* I, *p.* vii.

Lady Mary Wortley Montague, who was in her time "the pink of fashion," and who is compared to Madame de Sévnigé, has such a serious mind, such a decided style, such a precise judgment, and such a harsh sarcasm, that you would take her for a man.—TAINE, H. A., 1871, *History of English Literature, tr. Van Laun, vol.* II, *bk.* iii, *ch.* vii, *p.* 203.

There is little to be said about Lady Mary Wortley's writings. Her life and soul and curious personality live in her letters. In her verses there is only the artificial reflex of an age and style of the highest artificiality, with sparkles of wit, no doubt, and full of the wonderful clearness of a keen-eyed, quick, observing woman of the world. But she too, like most other persons with whom one comes in contact in the long vistas of history, is in herself more interesting, more curious, a thousand times closer to us, than any of her works.—OLIPHANT, MARGARET O.W., 1868, *Historical Sketches of the Reign of George II., Blackwood's Magazine, vol.* 104, *p.* 25.

Her intellect, with all the brightness of steel, had also its hardness; wit, taste, and breeding she possessed in abundance, but she had little heart, and wanting natural sensibility, she had also a certain coarseness of moral perception.—COURTHOPE, WILLIAM JOHN, 1889, *The Life of Alexander Pope, Pope's Works, eds. Elwin and Courthope, vol.* V, *p.* 140.

John Byrom

1692–1763

John Byrom (1692–1763) was a Manchester man, who became a fellow of Trinity College, Cambridge, and fell in love with the daughter of the great Bentley. A melodious *Pastoral*, celebrating that lady under the name of Phebe, was printed in the 605th "Spectator," and is the best known of Byrom's writings. He became a physician, and then a professional stenographer, liking to describe himself as "Inventor of the Universal English Short-hand," and a votary of the "Tachygraphic Goddess." Late in life he became deeply impressed by the views of the religious mystic, Law, and in 1751 he versified the views of that apostle in an essay in heroic rhyme, entitled

"Enthusiasm." The poems of Byrom were first published after his death, in two volumes, printed at Manchester in 1773; his "Journals" first saw the light in 1854-57. His verse is of a highly miscellaneous character; the bulk of it is religious, and even polemical; the remainder is made up of apologues, epigrams, epistles, pastoral songs, dialogues and Lancashire dialect, tales and descriptions.—GOSSE, EDMUND, 1888, *A History of Eighteenth Century Literature, p.* 214.

PERSONAL

Byrom's is a figure rather curious than notable, rather amiable than striking. He had many turns and accomplishments, and many holds upon life. He loved learning, for instance, and had scholarship enough to write with point upon scholarly subjects. Again, it is certain that he was a man who could love; for he gave over medicine and the chance of medical honours merely to follow up and win the lady he was wooing to wife. Then, as became Weston's successful rival, the teacher who had improved upon Weston's own system, and had Hoadley and Chesterfield for his pupils, he was keenly interested in stenography, and not only lectured on it to his classes (his lectures, by the way, are said to have been full of matter and of wit), but read papers about it before the Royal Society. Also, he was curiously versed in theology and philosophical divinity; he held advanced opinions on the dogmas of predestination and imputed righteousness; he is known for a disciple of William Law, a student of Malebranche and Madame Bourignon, a follower of Jacob Boehmen, for whose sake he learned German, and some of whose discourse he was at the pains of running into English verse. And above all was he addicted to letters and the practice of what he was pleased to think poetry. Add to this, that he was a good and cheerful talker, whose piety was not always punproof ("Hic jacet Doctor Byfield, volatilis olim, tandem fixus"), but who was capable on occasion of right and genuine epigram, and the picture is complete. As revealed in it, Byrom is the very type and incarnation of the ingenious amateur.—HENLEY, WILLIAM ERNEST, 1880, *English Poets, ed. Ward, vol.* III, *p.* 230.

A Jacobite, a mystic, a shorthand pundit, a physician, and a very interesting person.—SAINTSBURY, GEORGE, 1896, *Social England, ed. Traill, vol.* V, *p.* 80.

He died a few years later (1763). He was not buried as the law directed, in woolen. His executors had to pay £5 as a fine. As Byrom does not appear to have left any verses to justify the failure, we may perhaps assume that the omission was not due to any final whim of his own. He would hardly have missed such a chance for a poem. Few kindlier men have been buried either in woolen or linen.—STEPHEN, LESLIE, 1898, *Studies of a Biographer, vol.* I, *p.* 104.

GENERAL

Read Dr. Byrom's poems. He has all the wit and humour of Dr. Swift, together with much more learning, a deep and strong understanding, and above all a serious vein of piety. A few things in the second volume are taken from Jacob Behmen, to whom I object. But setting these things aside, we have some of the finest sentiments that ever appeared in the English tongue; some of the noblest truths expressed with the utmost energy of language, and the strongest colours of poetry. —WESLEY, JOHN, 1773, *Journal.*

He is certainly a man of genius, plunged deep into the rankest fanaticism. His poetical epistles show him both.—WARBURTON, WILLIAM, 1751-52, *Letter to Bishop Hurd.*

Their oddity indeed well entitles them to the room which they fill. This writer has been compared of late to the Spanish Friar, Luys de Escobar, for the manner of which he treated of all subjects in easy verse, pouring forth extempore lines upon any thing which came in his way; his opinion of one sermon, his abstract of another, the Passive Participle's Petition to the Printer of the Gentleman's Magazine; remarks on any book or pamphlet of the day; critical remarks on several passages in Horace, in which various readings are proposed in rhyme, versification of collects, and of passages from his favourite divines Law and Jacob Behmen! His head seems to have been a rhyming machine which fell to work upon whatever came into it. One poem entitled "Careless Content" is so perfectly in the manner of Elizabeth's age, that we can hardly believe it to be an imitation, but are almost disposed to think that Byrom had transcribed it from some old author, and that the transcript being found among his papers, was printed among his works.—SOUTHEY, ROBERT, 1814, *Chalmers's English Poets, Quarterly Review, vol.* 11, *p.* 491.

And now we come upon a strange little well in the desert. Few flowers indeed shine upon its brink, and it flows with a somewhat unmusical ripple: it is a well of the water of life notwithstanding, for its song tells of the love and truth which are the grand power of God. . . . Here we have yet again a mystical thread running radiant athwart both warp and woof of our poetic web; the mystical thinker will ever be found the reviver of religious poetry; and although some of the seed had come from afar both in time and space, Byrom's verse is of indigenous growth. Much of the thought of the present day will be found in his verses. —MACDONALD, GEORGE, 1868, *England's Antiphon, p.* 287.

Possessed of great wit and rich humor, he is the author of some of our best epigrams; and his poems run through all styles and subjects, "from grave to gay, from lively to severe." He wrote verse carelessly and with great fluency, published next to nothing, and was utterly indifferent to reputation; had he chosen, he might have won high poetic rank. As it is, one or two hymns and several lighter pieces from his pen are still well known: and the fortunate possessor of his somewhat scarce "Poems" will find in them much to amuse, to edify, and to instruct. . . . One-half his poems are distinctively religious: the thought in these belongs rather to our time than to that in which he lived. Often free, it is always reverent, and generally sound; his pages, besides the wholesome flavor of a genial personality, are informed by an ardent and yet a reasoning faith. Among the English authors who have fallen short of absolute greatness, there is perhaps none who better deserves, or is likely longer to retain, honorable mention and kindly remembrance.—HART, JOHN S., 1872, *A Manual of English Literature, p.* 311.

John Byrom had considerable merits, both as a man and an author; but there is a certain absurdity about him in both capacities which rather mars them. . . . At the early age of twenty-three, Byrom wrote a pastoral entitled "Colin and Phœbe," or, as he generally terms it, from its first line: "My time, O ye Muses, &c.," which had the honour of being inserted in the eighth volume of the "Spectator," with the complimentary remark of the editor, "It is so original, that I do not much doubt it will divert my readers." It *is* a diverting little piece, prettily conceived and smoothly written, equal, in fact, to the best pastorals of Shenstone or Philips, and nearly equal to those of Gay. . . . But, after all, Byrom's lucid intervals are rare (that is to say in this department; some of his hymns are good); the residuum of true poetry in his metrical essays is nearly drowned amid the grotesque and prosaic doggerel by which it is surrounded. And the admiration in which his verses were held by men of undoubted ability can only be accounted for by the fact that Byrom wrote in an age singularly barren in poetic genius.—OVERTON, JOHN HENRY, 1881, *William Law, Nonjuror and Mystic, pp.* 61, 363.

One Byrom, born in 1691, has left several hymns, which are more remarkable for their metaphysics than their melody. —SAUNDERS, FREDERICK, 1885, *Evenings with the Sacred Poets, p.* 294.

After early poverty, he lived a retired blameless literary life on his property by Manchester. One of the many men of strong feeling in whom faith burned like "a hidden flame" through the eighteenth century.—PALGRAVE, FRANCIS TURNER, 1889, *ed. The Treasury of Sacred Song, p.* 349, *Note.*

Byrom wrote rhyme with ease and on subjects with which poetry has nothing to do.—DENNIS, JOHN, 1894, *The Age of Pope, p.* 243.

His practice of throwing every possible subject into verse, very often of the swinging trisyllabic kind, of which he was a great lover and a very clever practitioner, has not improved the poetical merit of his work; but he had much more diffuse poetry in him than all but one or two of his contemporaries, and his voluminous work, which has had the good fortune to secure two admirable editors, is singularly interesting to read, and furnishes sidelights on the time only inferior to those of the greatest memoir-writers.—SAINTSBURY, GEORGE, 1898, *A Short History of English Literature, p.* 577.

William Shenstone

1714–1763

William Shenstone (1714-63), born at the Leasowes, Hales Owen, Worcestershire, studied at Pembroke College, Oxford, in 1737 published anonymously "Poems upon various Occasions," in 1741 "The Judgment of Hercules," and next year "The Schoolmistress." In 1745 he succeeded his father in the Leasowes. His success in beautifying his little domain attracted visitors from all quarters, and brought him more fame than his poetry, but involved him in pecuniary embarrassments. "The Schoolmistress" has secured for him a permanent if humble place among English poets. His other works are mostly insignificant; but his "Pastoral Ballad" has touches of exquisite tenderness. See Life by Dr. Johnson prefixed to Shenstone's "Essays on Men and Manners" (new ed. 1868), and that by G. Gilfillan to an edition of his "Poems" (1854).—PATRICK AND GROOME, *eds.*, 1897, *Chambers's Biographical Dictionary, p.* 851.

PERSONAL

His appearance surprised me, for he was a large, heavy, fat man, dressed in white clothes and silver lace, with his gray hairs tied behind and much powdered, which, added to his shyness and reserve, was not at first prepossessing. His reserve and melancholy (for I could not call it pride) abated as we rode along, and by the time we left him at the Admiral's, he became good company,—Garbett, who knew him well, having whispered him, that though we had no great name, he would find us not common men.—CARLYLE, ALEXANDER, 1758, *Autobiography, ch.* ix.

He was no economist; the generosity of his temper prevented him from paying a proper regard to the use of money: he exceeded, therefore, the bounds of his paternal fortune, which, before he died, was considerably encumbered. But when one recollects the perfect paradise he had raised around him, the hospitality with which he lived, his great indulgence to his servants, his charities to the indigent, and all done with an estate not more than three hundred pounds a year, one should rather be led to wonder that he left anything behind him than to blame his want of economy. He left, however, more than sufficient to pay his debts; and by his will appropriated his whole estate for that purpose.—DODSLEY, RICHARD, 1764–69, *ed. Shenstone's Works, Preface.*

I have read an octave volume of Shenstone's "Letters;" poor man! He was always wishing for money, for fame, and other distinctions; and his whole philosophy consisted in living against his will in retirement, and in a place which his taste had adorned, but which he only enjoyed when people of note came to see and commend it. His correspondence is about nothing else but this place and his own writings, with two or three neighbouring clergymen, who wrote verses too. —GRAY, THOMAS, 1769, *Letter to Mr. Nicholls, June* 24.

The pleasure of Shenstone was all in his eye; he valued what he valued merely for its looks; nothing raised his indignation more than to ask if there were any fishes in his water. . . . He is represented by his friend Dodsley as a man of great tenderness and generosity, kind to all who were within his influence, but if once offended not easily appeased; inattentive to economy, and careless of his expenses: in his person he was larger than the middle size, with something clumsy in his form; very negligent of his clothes, and remarkable for wearing his grey hair in a particular manner; for he held that the fashion was no rule of dress, and that every man was to suit his appearance to his natural form. His mind was not very comprehensive, nor his curiosity active; he had no value for those parts of knowledge which he had not himself cultivated.—JOHNSON, SAMUEL, 1779–81, *Shenstone, Lives of the English Poets.*

Dr. Warton, in his "Essay on Pope," has mentioned that three of our celebrated poets died singular deaths. He might have added Shenstone to the number. He had a housekeeper who lived with him in the double capacity of maid and mistress; and being offended with her on some occasion, he went out of the house and set all night in his post-chaise in much agitation, in consequence of which he caught a cold that eventually caused his death.—MALONE, EDMOND, 1783, *Maloniana, ed. Prior, p.* 340.

Mr. Shenstone was too much respected in the neighbourhood to be treated with rudeness: and though his works (frugally as they were managed), added to his manners of living, must necessarily have made him exceed his income, and, of course, he might sometimes be distressed for money, yet he had too much spirit to expose himself to insults from trifling sums, and guarded against any great distress by anticipating a few hundreds; which his estate could very well bear, as appeared by what remained to his executors after the payment of his debts and his legacies to his friends, and annuities of thirty pounds a year to one servant, and six pounds to another: for his will was dictated with equal justice and generosity. —GRAVES, RICHARD, 1788, *Recollections of Some Particulars of the Life of William Shenstone.*

He was not formed to captivate; his person was clumsy, his manners disagreeable, and his temper feeble and vacillating. The Delia who is introduced into his elegies, and the Phillis of his pastoral ballad, was Charlotte Graves, sister to the Graves who wrote the "Spiritual Quixotte." There was nothing warm or earnest in his admiration, and all his gallantry is as vapid as his character. He never gave the lady who was supposed, and supposed herself, to be the object of his serious pursuit, an opportunity of accepting or rejecting him; and his conduct has been blamed as ambiguous and unmanly. His querulous declamations against women in general, had neither cause nor excuse; and his complaints of infidelity and coldness are equally without foundation. He died unmarried.—JAMESON, ANNA BROWNELL, 1829, *The Loves of the Poets, vol.* ii, *p.* 311.

The Leasowes now belongs to the Attwood family, and a Miss Attwood resides there occasionally; but the whole place bears the impress of desertion and neglect. The house has a dull look; the same heavy spirit broods over the lawns and glades; and it is only when you survey it from a distance, as when approaching Halesowen from Hagley, that the whole presents an aspect of unusual beauty. It is said to be the favorite resort of the members of the Society of Friends. —HOWITT, WILLIAM, 1846, *Homes and Haunts of the Most Eminent British Poets, vol.* I.

THE SCHOOLMISTRESS

1742

The "Schoolmistress" is excellent in its kind and masterly.—GRAY, THOMAS, 1751, *Letter to Horace Walpole, Works, ed. Gosse, vol.* ii, *p,* 219.

This poem is one of those happinesses in which a poet excels himself, as there is nothing in all Shenstone which any way approaches it in merit; and, though I dislike the imitations of our English poets in general, yet, on this minute subject, the antiquity of the style produces a very ludicrous solemnity.—GOLDSMITH, OLIVER, 1767, *The Beauties of English Poetry.*

The inimitable "School-Mistress" of Shenstone is one of the felicities of genius; but the purpose of this poem has been entirely misconceived. . . . The "School-Mistress" of Shenstone has been admired for its simplicity and tenderness, not for its exquisitely ludicrous turn! This discovery I owe to the good fortune of possessing the original edition of "The School-Mistress," which the author printed under his own directions, and to his own fancy. To this piece of LUDICROUS POETRY, as he calls it, "lest it should be mistaken," he added a LUDICROUS INDEX, "purely to show fools that I am in jest." But "the fool," his subsequent editor, who, I regret to say, was Robert Dodsley, thought proper to surpress this amusing "ludicrous index," and the consequence is, as the poet foresaw, that his aim has been "mistaken." —DISRAELI, ISAAC, 1791–1824, *Shenstone's School-Mistress, Curiosities of Literature.*

Shenstone's "Schoolmistress" has not indeed the point and condensation of Goldsmith's "Schoolmaster," but its spirit is the same; and there is besides about it a certain soft, warm, slumberous charm, as if reflected from the good dame's kitchen fire. The very stanza seems murmuring in its sleep.—GILFILLAN, GEORGE, 1854, *ed., The Poetical Works of William Shenstone, p.* xxiii.

Owes much of its attraction to its archaisms.—MARSH, GEORGE P., 1860, *Lectures on the English Language, p.* 540.

PASTORAL BALLAD

1743

Mr. Shenstone's pastoral ballad, in four parts, may justly be reckoned, I think, one of the most elegant poems of this kind which we have in English.—BLAIR, HUGH, 1783, *Lectures on Rhetoric and Belles-Lettres, ed. Mills, Lecture* xxxix.

The "Pastorals" of Shenstone were singularly popular in their day, and are still admired by the young. Whatever charm they possess is owing to their smooth and easy language, their simple equable fluency, and also to the true but slender vein of natural sentiment, which makes us forget their intolerable mawkishness and the absurd affectation of the persons and manners of their shepherds and shepherdesses.—SHAW, THOMAS B., 1847, *Outlines of English Literature, p.* 299.

This picture of the old dame is very real, but better than "The Schoolmistress" I like a pastoral by Shenstone, which, although written in a jingling, rather common-place measure has a taste of the old ballad in it and recalls the fresh days of poetry. This pastoral is in four parts—Absence, Hope, Solicitude, Disappointment, and is addressed to Phylis, by the Shepherd Corydon. — RICHARDSON, ABBY SAGE, 1881, *Familiar Talks on English Literature, p.* 301.

GENERAL

Nor can the Muse, while she these scenes surveys,
Forget her Shenstone, in the youthful toil
Associate; whose bright dawn of genius oft
Smooth'd my incondite verse: whose friendly voice
Call'd me from giddy sports to follow him
Intent on better themes—call'd me to taste
The charms of British song, the pictured page
Admire, or mark his imitative skill.
—JAGO, RICHARD, 1767, *Edge Hill, bk.* iii.

That water-gruel bard Shenstone, who never wrote anything good but his "Schoolmistress."—WALPOLE, HORACE, 1778, *To Rev. William Mason, Letters, ed. Cunningham, vol.* VII, *p.* 54.

His diction is often harsh, improper and affected; his words ill-coined or ill-chosen; and his phrase unskilfully inverted.—JOHNSON, SAMUEL, 1779–81, *Shenstone, Lives of the English Poets.*

Why have the "Elegies" of Shenstone, which forty years ago formed for many of us the favourite poems of our youth, ceased to delight us in mature life? It is perhaps that these Elegies, planned with peculiar felicity, have little in their execution. They form a series of poetical truths, devoid of poetical expression; truths,—for notwithstanding the pastoral romance in which the poet has enveloped himself, the subjects are real, and the feelings could not, therefore, be fictitious. . . . These Elegies, with some other poems, may be read with a new interest, when we discover them to form the true Memoirs of Shenstone. Records of querulous but delightful feelings! whose subjects spontaneously offered themselves from passing incidents; they still perpetuate emotions, which will interest the young poet, and the young lover of taste.—DISRAELI, ISAAC, 1791–1824, *Shenstone Vindicated, Curiosities of Literature.*

His Letters show him to have lived in a continual fever of petty vanity, and to have been a finished literary coquet. He seems always to say, "You will find nothing in the world so amiable as Nature and me: come, and admire us."—HAZLITT, WILLIAM, 1818, *Lectures on the English Poets, Lecture* vi.

His genius is not forcible, but it settles in mediocrity without meanness. His pieces of levity correspond not disagreeably with their title. His "Ode to Memory" is worthy of protection from the power which it invokes. Some of the stanzas of his "Ode to Rural Elegance" seem to recall to us the country-loving spirit of Cowley, subdued in wit, but harmonized in expression. From the commencement of the stanza in that ode, "O sweet disposer of the rural hour," he sustains an agreeable and peculiarly refined strain of poetical feeling. The ballad of "Jemmy Dawson," and the elegy on "Jessy," are written with genuine feeling. With all the beauties of the Leasowes in our minds, it may be still regretted, that instead of devoting his whole soul to clumping beeches, and projecting mottoes for summer-houses, he had not gone more into living nature for subjects, and described her interesting realities with the same fond and *naïve* touches which give so much delightfulness to his portrait of the "School-mistress."—CAMPBELL, THOMAS, 1819, *Specimens of the British Poets.*

Shenstone's pathetic and affecting ballad of "Jemmy Dawson" has drawn tears from every person of sensibility, or possessing the feelings of humanity; and it will continue to be admired as long as the English language shall exist.—COLLET, STEPHEN, 1823, *Relics of Literature, p.* 159.

Surely it is an accomplishment to utter a pretty thought so simply that the world is forced to remember it; and that gift was Shenstone's, and he the most poetical of country gentlemen. May every shrub on the lawn of Leasowes be evergreen to his brow!—BROWNING, ELIZABETH BARRETT, 1842-63, *The Book of the Poets.*

Shenstone was naturally an egotist, and, like Rousseau, scarce ever contemplated a landscape without some tacit reference to the space occupied in it by himself.—MILLER, HUGH, 1847, *First Impressions of England and Its People, p.* 129.

Shenstone was deficient in animal spirits, and condescended to be vexed when people did not come to see his retirement; but few men had an acuter discernment of the weak points of others and the general mistakes of mankind, as anybody may see by his "Essays;" and yet in those "Essays" he tells us, that he never passed a town or village, without regretting that he could not make the acquaintance of some of the good people that lived there. —HUNT, LEIGH, 1848, *A Jar of Honey from Mount Hybla, p.* 173.

Nothing can appear more flat than many of Shenstone's pathetic verses. They are written usually in that sing-song, die-away measure, of which "Pity the sorrows of a poor old man" is the everlasting type. Here and there a happy epithet or well-chosen image relieves the insipidity of the strain; but in general a thorough Laura-Matildaish tone, so admirably satirised in "Rejected Addresses," palls upon the ear with a dulcet but senseless monotone. . . . Some of his essays are pleasing, but devoted to quiet moralising or some insignificant theme.—TUCKERMAN, HENRY T., 1849, *Characteristics of Literature, p.* 40.

There is much sweetness and grace in the verses of Shenstone; they formed part of the intellectual food which nourishes the strong soul of Burns.—ARNOLD, THOMAS, 1878, *English Literature, Encyclopædia Britannica, Ninth Edition.*

Shenstone is our principal master of what may perhaps be called the artificial-natural style in poetry; and the somewhat lasting hold which some at least of his poems have taken on the popular ear is the best testimony that can be produced to his merit. . . . It is difficult to believe that Shenstone ever gave much study to his work, or that he possessed any critical faculty. His elegies, though not always devoid of music, are but dreary stuff, and his more ambitious poems still drearier. His attempts at the style of Prior and Gay are for the most part valueless. Yet when all this is discarded, "My banks they are furnished with bees," and a few other such things, obstinately recur to the memory and assert that their author after all was a poet. . . . As concerns the formal part of poetry, his management of the anapaestic trimeter is unquestionably his chief merit. In the Spenserian stanza he is commendable, and dates fortunately prevent the charge that if "The Castle of Indolence" had not been written neither would "The Schoolmistress." His anapaests are much more original. The metre is so incurably associated with sing-song and doggerel, that poems written in it are exposed to a heavy disadvantage, yet in the first two pastoral ballads at any rate this disadvantage is not much felt. Shenstone taught the metre to a greater poet than himself, Cowper, and these two between them have written almost everything that is worth reading in it, if we put avowed parody and burlesque out of the question.—SAINTSBURY, GEORGE, 1880, *The English Poets, ed. Ward, vol.* III, *pp.* 271, 272.

Most of his verse is artificial and unreal, and has rightly been forgotten, but what remains is of permanent interest. He is best known by the "Schoolmistress," a burlesque imitation of Spenser, which was highly praised by Johnson and by Goldsmith; but many will value equally, in its way, the neatly turned "Pastoral Ballad, in four parts," written in 1743, which is supposed to refer to the author's disappointment in love, or the gently satirical "Progress of Taste," showing "how great a misfortune it is for a man of small estate to have much taste." Burns warmly eulogised Shenstone's elegies, which are also to some extent autobiographical, though it is difficult to say how far they are sincere.—AITKEN, GEORGE A., 1897, *Dictionary of National Biography, vol.* LII, *p.* 50.

JOHN ARMSTRONG

Drawing by J. Thurston. Engraving by F. Engleheart, from Miniature bv Shelley.

CHARLES CHURCHILL

JAMES THOMSON

Charles Churchill

1731-1764

Charles Churchill, 1731-1764. Born, in Westminster, Feb. 1731. Educated at Westminster School, 1739-49 (?). Made a "Fleet marriage" with Miss Scot, 1748. Entered at Trinity College, Cambridge, 1749, but did not take up residence. Ordained Curate to South Cadbury, Somersetshire, 1753. Ordained Priest, 1756; took curacy under his father at Rainham. Succeeded father at his death to curacy and lectureship of St. John's Westminster. Added to small income by tuition. Separation from his wife, Feb. 1761. Contrib. to "The Library," 1761. Resigned lectureship in consequence of protests of parishioners, Jan. 1763. Assisted Wilkes in editing "The North Briton," 1762-63. Copious publication of satires and poems. At Oxford during Commemoration, 1763. Died, at Boulogne, 4 Nov. 1764. Buried in St. Martin's Churchyard, Dover. *Works:* "The Rosciad" (anon.), 1761; "The Apology, addressed to the Critical Reviewers," 1761; "Night" (anon.), 1761; "The Ghost," bks. i., ii. (anon.), 1762; bk. iii., 1762; bk. iv., 1763; "The Prophecy of Famine," 1763; "The Conference," 1763; "An Epistle to W. Hogarth," 1763; "The Author," 1763; "Poems," 1763; "Gotham," 1764; "The Duellist," 1764 (2nd edn. same year); "The Candidate," 1764; "The Times" (anon.), 1764; "Independence" (anon.), 1764; "The Farewell" (anon.), 1764. *Posthumous:* "Sermons" (possibly by his father), 1765. *Collected Works:* in 4 vols., 1765; in 4 vols., 1774; in 2 vols., with *life*, 1804.—SHARP, R. FARQUHARSON, 1897, *A Dictionary of English Authors, p.* 54.

PERSONAL

No more he'll sit in foremost row before the astonish'd pit; in brawn Oldmixon's rival as in wit; and grin dislike, and kiss the spike; and giggle, and wriggle; and fiddle, and diddle; and fiddle-faddle, and diddle-daddle.—MURPHY, ARTHUR, 1761, *Ode to the Naiads of Fleet Ditch.*

Whenever I am happy in the acquaintance of a man of genius and letters, I never let any mean ill-grounded suspicions creep into my mind to disturb that happiness: whatever he says, I am inclined and bound to believe, and, therefore, I must desire you not to vex yourself with unnecessary delicacy upon my account. I see and read so much of Mr. Churchill's spirit, without having the pleasure of his acquaintance, that I am persuaded that his genius disdains any direction, and that resolutions once taken by him will withstand the warmest importunities of his friends. At the first reading of his "Apology," I was so charmed and raised with the power of his writing, that I really forgot that I was delighted when I ought to have been alarmed; this puts me in mind of the Highland officer, who was so warmed and elevated by the heat of the battle that he had forgot, till he was reminded by the smarting, that he had received no less than eleven wounds in different parts of his body.—GARRICK, DAVID, 1761, *Letter to Robert Lloyd.*

A bear, whom, from the moment he was born,
His dam despised, and left unlick'd in scorn;
A Babel, which, the power of Art outdone,
She could not finish when she had begun;
An utter Chaos, out of which no might,
But that of God, could strike one spark of light.

Broad were his shoulders, and from blade to blade
A H——might at full length have laid;
Vast were his bones, his muscles twisted strong;
His face was short, but broader than 'twas long;
His features, though by Nature they were large,
Contentment had contrived to overcharge,
And bury meaning, save that we might spy
Sense lowering on the penthouse of his eye;
His arms were two twin oaks; his legs so stout
That they might bear a Mansion-house about;
Nor were they, look but at his body there,
Design'd by Fate a much less weight to bear.

O'er a brown cassock, which had once been black,
Which hung in tatters on his brawny back,
A sight most strange, and awkward to behold,
He threw a covering of blue and gold.
Just at that time of life, when man, by rule,
The fop laid down, takes up the graver fool,
He started up a fop, and, fond of show,
Look'd like another Hercules turn'd beau.

—CHURCHILL, CHARLES, 1764. *Independence, v.* 149-174.

Churchill the poet is dead,—to the great joy of the Ministry and the Scotch, and to the grief of very few indeed, I believe; for such a friend is not only a dangerous but a ticklish possession.. . . . Churchill had great powers; but, besides the facility of outrageous satire, almost all his compositions were wild and extravagant, executed on no plan, and void of the least correction.—WALPOLE, HORACE, 1764, *To Sir Horace Mann, Nov.* 15; *Letters, ed. Cunningham, vol.* IV, *p.* 291.

Your Lordship knows that . . . owed the greatest share of his renown to the most incompetent of all judges, the mob; actuated by the most unworthy of all principles, a spirit of insolence; and inflamed by the vilest of all human passions, hatred to their fellow citizens. Those who joined the cry in his favour seemed to me to be swayed rather by fashion than by real sentiment. He therefore might have lived and died unmolested by me; confident as I am, that posterity, when the present unhappy dissensions are forgotten, will do ample justice to his real character. But when I saw the extravagant honours that were paid to his memory, and heard that a monument in Westminster Abbey was intended for one, whom even his admirers acknowledge to have been an incendiary and a debauchee, I could not help wishing that my countrymen would reflect a little on what they were doing, before they consecrated, by what posterity would think the public voice, a character which no friend to *virtue* or to *true taste* can approve.—BEATTIE, JAMES, 1765, *On the Report of a Monument to be Erected in Westminster Abbey to the Memory of a Late Author.*

Had he not been himself so severe a censor, his private irregularities would have been softened down to the eccentricities of genius, and his midnight parties would have been dignified with the amiable attributes of social enjoyment, "the feast of reason and the flow of soul;" instead of which, they were blazoned abroad as the orgies of brutal intemperance, and the scenes of vulgar and depraved gratification.—TOOKE, WILLIAM, 1804-44, *ed., The Poetical Works of Charles Churchill.*

I stood beside the grave of him who blazed
The comet of a season, and I saw
The humblest of all sepulchres, and gazed
With not the less of sorrow and of awe
On that neglected turf and quiet stone,
With name no clearer than the names unknown,
Which lay unread around it.
—BYRON, LORD, 1816, *Churchill's Grave.*

The unexpected death of a man in the flower of his age, who during four years had been one of the most conspicuous persons in England, and certainly the most popular poet, occasioned a strong feeling among the part of the public to whose political prepossessions and passions he had addressed himself. Some of his admirers were inconsiderate enough to talk of erecting a monument to him in Westminster Abbey; but if permission had been asked it must necessarily have been refused; it would indeed have been not less indecent to grant, than to solicit such an honour for a clergyman who had thrown off his gown, and renounced, as there appeared too much reason to apprehend, his hope in Christ. His associates undoubtedly wished to have it believed that he had shown as little regard to religion in the last hours, as in the latter years of his life; and though they obtained Christian burial for him, by bringing the body from Boulogne to Dover, where it was interred in the old cemetery which once belonged to the collegiate church of St. Martin, they inscribed upon his tombstone, instead of any consolatory or monitory text, this epicurean line from one of his own poems,

Life to the last enjoyed, here Churchill lies.

Wilkes erected a monument to his friend's memory, in the grounds of his cottage at Sandham, in the Isle of Wight. It was a broken pillar, fluted, and of the Doric order, nine feet high, five feet in diameter, placed in a grove, with weeping willows, cypresses, and yews behind, laurels beside it, and bays, myrtles, and other shrubs in the foreground. A tablet, on the pillar, bore this inscription:

CAROLO CHURCHILL,
AMICO JUCUNDO,
POETÆ ACRI,
CIVI OPTIME DE PARTRIA MERITO
P.
JOHANNES WILKES.
M DCC LXV.

The same words he inscribed upon a sepulchral alabaster urn, sent him from Rome by the Abbe Winckelman, who was then the superintendent of the antiquities in that city.—SOUTHEY, ROBERT, 1835, *Life of Cowper, vol.* I, *p.* 325.

Pope had a tall Irishman to attend him when he published the "Dunciad," but Churchill was tall enough to attend himself. One of Pope's victims, by way of delicate reminder, hung up a birch rod at

Button's; but Churchill's victims might see their satirist any day walking Covent-Garden unconcernedly, provided with a bludgeon by himself. . . . The restraint he had so long submitted to, once thrown aside, and the compromise ended, he thought he could not too plainly exhibit his new existence to the world. He had declared war against hypocrisy in all stations, and in his own would set it no example. The pulpit had starved him on forty pounds a-year; the public had given him a thousand pounds in two months; and he proclaimed himself, with little regard to the decencies in doing it, better satisfied with the last service than the first. This was carrying a hatred of hypocrisy beyond the verge of prudence; indulging it indeed, with the satire it found vent in, to the very borders of licentiousness. He stripped off his clerical dress by way of parting with his last disguise, and appeared in a blue coat with metal buttons, a gold-laced waistcoat, a gold-laced hat, and ruffles.—FORSTER, JOHN, 1845–55, *Charles Churchill, pp.* 43, 44.

Possessed of powers and natural endowments which might have made him, under favourable circumstances, a poet, a hero, a man, and a saint, he became, partly through his own fault, and partly through the force of destiny, a satirist, an unfortunate politician, a profligate, died early; and we must approach his corpse, as men do those of Burns and Byron, with sorrow, wonder, admiration, and blame, blended into one strange, complex, and yet not unnatural emotion. Like them, his life was short and unhappy—his career triumphant, yet checquered—his powers uncultivated—his passions unchecked—his poetry only a partial discovery of his genius—his end sudden and melancholy—and his reputation, and future place in the history of letters, hitherto somewhat uncertain. And yet, like them, his very faults and errors, both as a man and a poet, have acted, with many, as nails, fastening to a "sure place" his reputation and the effect of his genius. . . . For the errors of Churchill, as a man, there does not seem to exist any plea of palliation, except what may be found in the poverty of his early circumstances, and in the strength of his later passions. The worst is, that he never seems to have been seduced into sin through the bewildering and bewitching mist of imagination. It was naked sensuality that he appeared to worship, and he always sinned with his eyes open. Yet his moral sense, though blunted, was never obliterated; and many traits of generosity and good feeling mingled with his excesses.—GILFILLAN, GEORGE, 1855, *ed., The Poetical Works of Charles Churchill, pp.* iii, xv.

The details of his life and conversation perished with his contemporaries; and at this moment we know him less familiarly than almost any man of equal celebrity in his whole century. . . . We need only say that his person had the rough vigour of his mind. There were incidents in his life which cannot be defended, and which he did not attempt to defend. His passions were strong, and his morals too often loose. But if there was much to blame in Churchill, there was also a great deal to admire and respect. He was an honest man, a brave man, and a generous man; and many far inferior characters, with less excuse from circumstances, have gone through life in the enjoyment of perfectly respectable reputations.—HANNAY, JAMES, 1866, *ed., The Poetical Works of Charles Churchill, Memoir, pp.* xxix, xxxi.

After Hogarth had made a caricature of Wilkes with his squint, Churchill wrote a savage "Epistle to William Hogarth," who, in return, impaled him with almost the only fame he now has: he represented Churchill as a bear in torn clerical bands, and paws in ruffles, holding a pot of porter in one hand, and a club, inscribed with "Lyes" and "North Briton," in the other, and a pug-dog using his poems as a bone. Beneath was written: "The Bruiser C. Churchill (once the Rev.), in the character of a Russian Hercules, regaling himself after having killed the monster Caricature, that so sorely galled his virtuous friend, the heaven-born Wilkes."—CONWAY, M. D., 1870, *South-coast Saunterings in England, Harper's Magazine, vol.* 40, *p.* 375.

Churchill had been a clergyman "through need, not choice" (Dedication to Sermons). Conscientious biographers alone have read the published sermons attributed to him, and they pronounce them to be unreadable. Churchill himself says that "sleep at his bidding, crept from pew to pew." His first biographers say that he discharged his duties well, which probably means that he had as yet caused no scandal. His marriage was now coming to the usual end of such alliances. His wife was as "imprudent" as himself, if nothing worse; and in February 1761 a formal separation took place. Churchill's references to her imply that he was heartily tired of her.—STEPHEN, LESLIE, 1887, *Dictionary of National Biography, vol.* x, *p.* 309.

GENERAL

He talked very contemptuously of Churchill's poetry, observing, that "it had a temporary currency, only from its audacity of abuse, and being filled with living names, and that it would sink into oblivion." I ventured to hint that he was not quite a fair judge, as Churchill had attacked him violently. *Johnson.* "Nay, Sir, I am a very fair judge. He did not attack me violently until he found I did not like his poetry; and his attack on me shall not prevent me from continuing to say what I think of him, from an apprehension that it may be ascribed to resentment. No, Sir, I called the fellow a blockhead at first, and I will call him a blockhead still. However, I will acknowledge that I have a better opinion of him now, than I once had; for he has shewn more fertility than I expected. To be sure, he is a tree that cannot produce good fruit: he only bears crabs. But, Sir, a tree that produces a great many crabs is better than a tree which produces only a few."—JOHNSON, SAMUEL, 1763, *Life by Boswell, ed. Hill, vol.* I, *p.* 485.

The loss of Churchill I shall always reckon the most cruel of all afflictions I have suffered. I will soon convince mankind that I knew how to value such superior genius and merit. I have more than half finished the projected edition of Churchill, and my thoughts now turn towards printing it, which I find cannot be done here.—WILKES, JOHN, 1765, *Letter to Miss Wilkes, May* 21, *from Naples.*

He was a great admirer of Dryden, in preference to Pope; and indeed the quick turns of thought, strength of expression, with the variety of versification in his own works, are no mean proofs that he studied and copied Dryden's manner. He held Pope so cheap, that one of his most intimate friends assured me, that he had some thoughts of attacking his poetry; and another gentleman informed me, that in a convivial hour he wished the bard of Twickenham was alive, that he might have an opportunity to make him bring forth all his art of poetry, for he would certainly have a struggle with him for preeminence. Of Churchill we may say without hesitation, that he was a man of genius, and of a temper firm and undaunted; often led away by pleasure, but at times strenuously active. His thoughts issued from him with ease, rapidity, and vigour.—DAVIES, THOMAS, 1780, *Life of David Garrick, vol.* I. *p.* 317.

Surly and slovenly, and bold and coarse,
Too proud for art, and trusting in mere force,
Spendthrift alike of money and of wit,
Always at speed, and never drawing bit,
He struck the lyre in such a careless mood,
And so disdain'd the rules he understood,
The laurel seem'd to wait on his command;
He snatch'd it rudely from the Muses' hand.
—COWPER, WILLIAM, 1782, *Table Talk.*

I have read him twice, and some of his pieces three times over, and the last time with more pleasure than the first. . . . He is indeed a careless writer for the most part; but where shall we find in any of those authors who finish their works with the exactness of a Flemish pencil, those bold and daring strokes of fancy, those numbers so hazardously ventured upon and so happily finished, the matter so compressed and yet so clear, and the colouring so sparingly laid on, and yet with such a beautiful effect? In short, it is not his least praise, that he is never guilty of those faults as a writer which he lays to the charge of others. A proof that he did not judge by a borrowed standard, or from rules laid down by critics, but that he was qualified to do it by his own native powers, and his great superiority of genius. For he that wrote so much, and so fast would, through inadvertence hurry unavoidably, have departed from rules which he might have founded in books, but his own truly poetical talent was a guide which could not suffer him to err.—COWPER, WILLIAM, 1786, *Letter to Mr. Unwin.*

Blotting and correcting was so much Churchill's abhorrence, that I have heard from his publisher he once energetically expressed himself, that *it was like cutting away one's own flesh.* This strong figure sufficiently shows his repugnance to an author's duty. Churchill now lies neglected, for posterity will only respect those who

"——File off the mortal part
Of glowing thought with Attic art."
Young.

I have heard that this careless bard, after a successful work, usually precipitated the publication of another, relying on its crudeness being passed over by the public curiosity excited by its better brother. He called this getting double pay, for thus he secured the sale of a hurried work. But Churchill was a spendthrift of fame, and enjoyed all his revenue while he lived; posterity owes him little, and pays him nothing!—DISRAELI, ISAAC, 1791–1824, *Literary Composition, Curiosities of Literature.*

A certain simplicity of style—and easy unaffected English—which disclaims the correction of minute blemishes, immingles much of the idiomatic dialect of conversation—which avoids the set of phrases and dancing master steps of practised versifiers—these constitute Churchill's highest merit, and confer on his writings the atticism which preserves them.—TAYLOR, WILLIAM, 1804, *Critical Review, May.*

The powers of Churchill have been unable to protect him from the oblivion into which his poems are daily sinking, owing to the ephemeral interest of political subjects, and his indolent negligence of severe study and regularity.—SCOTT, SIR WALTER, 1805, *The Life of John Dryden.*

Churchill's Satires on the Scotch, and Characters of the Players, are as good as the subjects deserved: they are strong, coarse, and full of an air of hardened assurance.—HAZLITT, WILLIAM, 1818, *Lectures on the English Poets, Lecture* vi.

Churchill may be ranked as a satirist immediately after Pope and Dryden, with perhaps a greater share of humour than either. He has the bitterness of Pope, with less wit to atone for it; but no mean share of the free manner and energetic plainness of Dryden.—CAMPBELL, THOMAS, 1819, *Specimens of the British Poets.*

That many of the objects of Churchill's satire were morally and politically obnoxious to it, few will have the hardihood to deny. That some of them were too severely treated, we may admit; but where is the proof that Churchill did not, however erroneously, imagine that he was justified in the language which he used? Who is there that believes the stupidity and worthlessness of every individual who suffered under the lash of Dryden and Pope; yet who ever thought that Dryden and Pope ought to be accused of wilful falsehood? With respect to Churchill, there is this powerful fact on his side, that bribes and preferments were vainly offered to purchase his silence; and he who resists such inducements is not likely to be a man who has "little veneration for truth!" He may be a mistaken fanatic, but he must be an honest one.—DAVENPORT, R. A., 1822, *The British Poets, Chiswick, ed., vol.* LXI, *Life, p.* 25.

Of him it was said by one greater far, that he "blazed the meteor of a season." For four years—during life—his popularity—in London and the suburbs—was prodigious; for forty—and that is a long time after death—he was a choice classic in the libraries of aging or aged men of wit upon town; and now, that nearly a century has elapsed since he "from his horrid hair shook pestilence and war" o'er slaves and Scotsmen, tools and tyrants, peers, poetasters, priests, pimps, and players, his name is still something more than a mere dissyllable, and seems the shadow of the sound that Mother dullness was wont to whisper in her children's ears when fretting wakefully on her neglected breasts. . . . There is an air of power in his way of attacking any and every subject. He goes to work without embarrassment, with spirit and ease, and is presently in his matter, or in some matter, rarely inane. It is a part, and a high part of genius, to design; but he was destitute of invention. The self-dubbed champion of liberty and letters, he labours ostentatiously and energetically in that vocation; and in the midst of tumultuous applause, ringing round a career of almost uninterrupted success, he seldom or never seems aware that the duties he had engaged himself to perform —to his country and his kind—were far beyond his endowments—above his conception. His knowledge either of books or men was narrow and superficial. In no sense had he ever been a student. His best thoughts are all essentially commonplace; but, in uttering them, there is almost always a determined plainness of words, a free step in verse, a certain boldness and skill in evading the trammel of the rhyme, deserving high praise; while often, as if spurning the style which yet does not desert him, he wears it clinging about him with a sort of disregarded grace.—WILSON, JOHN, 1845, *Supplement to Mac-Flecnoe and the Dunciad, Blackwood's Magazine, vol.* 58, *pp.* 372, 373.

It is not by the indifferent qualities in his works that Charles Churchill should be, as he has too frequently been, condemned. Judge him at his best; judge him by the men he followed in this kind of composition; and his claim to the respectful and enduring attention of the students of English poetry and literature, becomes manifest indeed. Of the gross indecencies of Sir Charles Hanbury Williams, he has none. He never, in any one instance, that he might fawn upon power or trample upon weakness, wrote licentious lampoons. There was not a form of mean pretence, or servile assumption, which he did not denounce. Low, pimping politics, he abhorred: and that their vile abettors, to whose exposure his works are so incessantly devoted, have not carried him into utter oblivion with themselves, sufficiently argues for the sound morality and permanent truth expressed in his manly verse. He indulged too much in personal invective, as we have said; and invective is too apt to pick up, for instant use against its adversaries, the first heavy stone that lies by the wayside, without regard to its form or fitness. —FORSTER, JOHN, 1845-55, *Charles Churchill, p.* 54.

Churchill's opinions are worth attending to, though he expresses them with vehemence, and by wholesale.—HUNT, LEIGH, 1848, *The Town, p.* 294.

Churchill, by want and rage impell'd to write,
Whose muse was anger, and whose genius spite,
With satire meant to stab, and not to heal,
The morbid, bloated, feverish commonweal;
Too proud to yield to humble virtue's rule,
Smote half the world with reckless ridicule.
Wit, honour, sense, to him did Heaven impart,
But not the last, best gift, a pious heart.
He blazed awhile in fortune, fame, and pride,
But unrespected lived, untimely died.

—COLERIDGE, HARTLEY, 1849, *Sketches of English Poets, Poems, vol.* II, *p.* 303.

Perhaps the writer who, if not by what he did himself, yet by the effects of his example, gave the greatest impulse to our poetry at this time, was Churchill. . . . If we put aside Thomson, Churchill, after all deductions, may be pronounced, looking to the quantity as well as the quality of his productions, to be the most considerable figure that appears in our poetry in the half-century from Pope to Cowper. But that is, perhaps, rather to say little for the said half-century than much for Churchill.—CRAIK, GEORGE L., 1861, *A Compendious History of English Literature and of the English Language, vol.* II, *p.* 305.

Was of the blood of the Juvenals and Drydens, though a poor relation as it were; and with all his carelessness, roughness, and even common-place, has those brilliant flashes of insight, and spontaneous felicities of expression, by which every true critic at once distinguishes the man of natural power from the man of mere cultivation. He rarely gives perfect satisfaction to the student, and never long-continued satisfaction; but the kind of pleasure he gives in his best moments is akin to that given by the greatest writers of his kind. There are some who, with less dross, turn out worse metal. Churchill is frequently dull, but never mediocre; and if he is wearisome in one paragraph, is as likely as not to make up for it by being wonderful in the next. All satirists, it has been said, take with more or less directness either after Horace or Juvenal. Churchill is a Juvenalian; a suckling of the Roman wolf; fierce but jolly; savage yet not unkindly. Of course, too, he has points in common with all the great satirists, for they have the distant likenesses of a clan as well as the nearer likenesses of a family. He has the Aristophanic heartiness, though not the Aristophanic poetry; the good-fellowship of Horace, with far less subtlety and familiar grace; a good deal of Dryden's vigour and eye for the points of a satirical portrait, but inferior penetration of glance, and far less comprehensive sweep, whether of reasoning power, poetic humour, or fancy.—HANNAY, JAMES, 1866, *ed., The Poetical Works of Charles Churchill, Memoir, p.* XXX.

He had a surprising extemporary vigour of mind; his praise carries great weight of blow; he undoubtedly surpassed all contemporaries, as Cowper says of him, in a certain rude and earth-born vigor; but his verse is dust and ashes now, solemnly inurned, of course, in the Chalmers columbarium, and without danger of violation. His brawn and muscle are fading traditions, while the fragile, shivering genius of Cowper is still a good life on the books of the Critical Insurance Office. "It is not, then, loftiness of mind that puts one by the side of Virgil?" cries poor old Cavalcanti at his wit's end. Certainly not altogether that. There must be also the great Mantuan's art, his power, not only of being strong in parts, but of making these parts coherent in an harmonious whole, and tributary to it.—LOWELL, JAMES RUSSELL, 1866–90, *Carlyle; Prose Works, Riverside ed., vol.* II, *p.* 80.

Churchill was a man of much generous impulse; and the reader can still enjoy the vigour of many passages in his poems, although their absolute subject-matter, combined with their length, is a bar to general perusal now-a-days.—ROSSETTI, WILLIAM MICHAEL, 1872, *ed., Humourous Poems, p.* 226.

Churchill was inspired by both the motives which, according to the two great Latin satirists, are the parents of satire; but his indignation did not burn with the pure flame of Juvenal, and his impecuniosity, unlike the honorable poverty of Horace, was the child of his vices. Writing to live, he did not write so that his works should live after him. Dashing off a poem a month, in order to catch a perennial stream of half-crowns from his eager and insatiable readers, he vehemently declared that to blot, prune, or correct was like the cutting-away of his own flesh.

"Little of books, and little known of men,
When the mad fit comes on, I seize the pen;
Rough as they run, the ready thoughts set down;
Rough as they run, discharge them on the town."

With his quiver of darts so unpolished that they could not escape the rust, tipped with venom that long ago had lost its sting, Churchill, "the scourge of bad men, and hardly better than the very worst," easily and rapidly stormed in his lifetime the citadel of Fame, but he was not of those whose names are engraved upon its bulwarks.—TREVELYAN, GEORGE OTTO, 1880, *The Early History of Charles James Fox, p.* 149.

The celebrity of the smart verse making of Churchill marks a low point in English taste. It nearly secured him a poet's monument in Westminster Abbey; and it actually secured a poet's rank for a petulant rhymer without a spark of the poet's imagination, of cold heart, natural bad taste, and very little knowledge of that narrow world which he so impudently lampooned. Nothing in Churchill reveals a gleam of genial feeling, or justifies the suspicion that he could take any pleasure in what refines or elevates. If we may believe his own account of himself, nature had given him little enough, beyond an ugly face, a sour temperament and a bitter tongue. Yet he was not dissatisfied. He was very willing to be taken for what he was: and if he could not win liking and respect, he was content to be feared. In all this there must have been something of affectation. Yet it is only too clear that the coarse texture of his mind was impermeable to the kindlier and worthier influences of his time. . . . Cowper, we know, had a real admiration for him. His earliest work the "Rosciad," is his best, because in it he most adhered to good models. His later works will serve the student as a rich mine of all sorts of errors in taste and judgment. In proportion as he abandoned himself to his own guidance, his work degenerated, and the poverty of his thought appeared; and in three years he had literally written himself out. But in all that he wrote there is a certain fierce manliness which wins attention, and even sympathy for his untutored brain and unsoftened heart, and this effect is heightened by the story of his life and death. —PAYNE, E. J., 1880, *The English Poets, ed. Ward, vol.* III, *pp.* 389, 391.

The satirist who towered for a moment so high above his contemporaries, and who leaves upon us the same impression of greatness as a knock-kneed giant at a country fair may leave. The Rev. Charles Churchill (1731–1764) has faded to the merest shadow of himself, and the writer who of all others aimed at being virile, robust, and weighty, has come to be regarded as the ideal of a pasteboard hero. . . . Feared and admired for his force, with his tempest of uncouth and vituperative verse, his rattling facility, and his reckless swaggering courage to support him,

Churchill exercised a genuine power so long as he lasted, and to some of his contemporaries he appeared another Dryden. But he was really scarcely an Oldham. His work is crude and unfinished to excess, he has no ear and no heart, and he fails to please us the moment that our surprise at his violence is over. His latest works are positively execrable, whether in morals or in style, and he alternates in them between the universal attribution of hypocrisy to others, and the cynical confession of vice in himself. He is a very Caligula among men of letters; when he stings his Muse to the murder of a reputation, he seems to cry "Ita feri, ut se mori sentiat." The happiness of others is a calamity to him; and his work would excite in us the extremity of aversion, if it were not that its very violence betrays the exasperation and wretchedness of its unfortunate author. Even more than Goldsmith, Churchill exemplifies the resolute return to the forms of poetic art in vogue before the age of Thomson and Gray. —GOSSE, EDMUND, 1888, *A History of Eighteenth Century Literature, pp.* 322, 324.

The trifling subject and the venomous personalities of "The Rosciad" cannot hide its vigour, the occasional acuteness of its criticisms, and above all the return, in the management of the couplet, from the exquisite but rather shrilling treble of Pope to the manly range of Dryden.—SAINTSBURY, GEORGE, 1898, *A Short History of English Literature, p.* 584.

Robert Dodsley

1703–1764

Robert Dodsley, 1703–1764, is noted both as an author and a publisher. He began life as apprentice to a tradesman, and afterwards he was a footman. His first publication, made when he was twenty-nine years old, was a collection of poems, called "The Muse in Livery, or The Footman's Miscellany." His next essay was a drama, "The Toy Shop." The manuscript being sent to Pope for examination, he pronounced a warm verdict of approval, which led to its being played at Covent Garden Theatre. Dodsley then opened a bookstore, and was successful in the business. He combined it, however, with authorship and with the patronage of authors. He wrote several other plays. "The King and the Miller of Mansfield;" "The Blind Beggar of Bethnal Green;" "Cleone, a Tragedy," besides numerous poems. He published a "Collection of Old Plays," 12 vols., and wrote "The Economy of Human Life," etc. But the greatest service he did to literature was his establishment of the Annual Register, begun in 1758 at the suggestion of Edmund Burke (who had the charge of it for some time) and continued to the present time.—HART, JOHN S., 1872, *A Manual of English Literature, p.* 228.

PERSONAL

"Cleone" was well acted by all the characters, but Bellamy left nothing to be desired. I went the first night, and supported it, as well as I might; for Doddy, you know, is my patron, and I would not desert him. The play was very well received. Doddy, after the danger was over, went out every night to the stage-side, and cried at the distress of poor Cleone.—JOHNSON, SAMUEL, 1759, *Letter to Bennet Langton.*

He was a generous friend, an encourager of men of genius; and acquired the esteem and respect of all who were acquainted with him. It was his happiness to pass the greater part of his life with those whose names will be revered by posterity, by most of whom he was loved as much for the virtues of his heart as he was admired on account of his excellent writings.—REED, ISAAC, 1780, *ed., Select Collection of Old Plays.*

Robert Dodsley died in 1764, when on a visit to Mr. Spence, who was a prebendary of the Cathedral of Durham. He was buried in the Abbey Churchyard there; and his epitaph was written by this warm and constant friend:—

"If you have any respect
for uncommon industry and merit,
regard this place,
in which are deposited the remains of
Mr. Robert Dodsley;
who, as an Author, raised himself
much above what could have been expected
from one in his rank of life,
and without a learned education;
and who, as a man, was scarce
exceeded by any in integrity of heart,
and purity of manners and conversation.

He left this life for a better,
Sept. 25, 1764,
In the 61st year of his age."
—KNIGHT, CHARLES, 1865, *Shadows of the Old Booksellers, p.* 213.

Personally Dodsley is an attractive figure. Johnson had ever a kindly feeling for his "patron," and thought he deserved a biography. His early condition lent a factitious importance to some immature verse, and his unwearied endeavours for literary fame gained him a certain contemporary fame. Some of his songs have merit—"One kind kiss before we part" being still sung—and the epigram on the words "one Prior" in Burnet's "History" is well known. As a bookseller he showed remarkable enterprise and business aptitude, and his dealings were conducted with liberality and integrity. He deserves the praise of Nichols as "that admirable patron and encourager of learning."—TEDDER, H. R., 1888, *Dictionary of National Biography, vol.* XV, *p.* 173.

GENERAL

The first edition of the present volumes was one of the many excellent plans produced by the late Mr. Robert Dodsley; a man to whom literature is under so many obligations that it would be unpardonable to neglect this opportunity of informing those who may have received any pleasure from the work, that they owe it to a person whose merit and abilities raised him from an obscure situation in life to affluence and independence.—REED, ISAAC, 1780, *ed., Select Collection of Old Plays.*

His plan of republishing "Old English Plays" is said to have been suggested to him by the literary amateur Coxeter, but the execution of it leaves us still indebted to Dodsley's enterprise.—CAMPBELL, THOMAS, 1819, *Specimens of the British Poets.*

"Dodsley's Collection" turned out to be a chance "medley:" unskilled in the language and the literature and the choice of his dramatists, he, as he tells us, "by the assistance of a little common sense, set a great number of these passages right;" that is, the dramatist of the dull "Cleone" brought down the ancient genius to his own; and, if he became intelligible, at least he was spurious. If, after all, some parts were left unintelligible, the reader must consider how many such remain in Shakespeare.—DISRAELI, ISAAC, 1841, *Shakespeare, Amenities of Literature.*

Good DODSLEY honest, bustling, hearty soul,
A foot-man, verse-man, prose-man, bibliopole;
A menial first beneath a lady's roof,
Then Mercury to guttling Dartineuf,
His humble education soon complete,
He learnt good things to write, good things to eat.
Then boldly ventured on the buskin'd stage,
And show'd how toys may help to make us sage:
Nay, dared to bite the great with satire's tooth,
And made a Miller tell his King the truth.
In tragic strain he told Cleone's woes,
The touching sorrows and the madd'ning throes
Of a fond mother and a faithful wife.
He wrote "The Economy of Human Life."
For flights didactic then his lyre he strung,
Made rhymes on Preaching, and blank verse on Dung;
Anon with soaring weary, much at his ease,
Wrote Epigrams, and Compliments, and Kisses.
All styles he tried, the tragic, the comic, lyric,
The grave didactic and the keen satiric;
Now preach'd and taught as sober as a dominie,
Now went pindaric-mad about Melpomene;
Now tried the pastoral pipe and oaten stop,
Yet all the while neglected not his shop.
Fair be his fame, among a knavish clan
His noblest title was an honest man.
A bookseller, he robb'd no bard of pelf,
No bard he libell'd, though a bard himself.
—COLERIDGE, HARTLEY, 1849, *Sketches of English Poets, Poems, vol.* II, *p.* 307.

Dodsley attempted literary fame in many branches, but among all his productions nothing is so well known as his "Select Collection of Old Plays," 1744, dedicated to Sir Clement Cotterel Dormer, who probably contributed some of its contents. The great ladies who first patronised Dodsley had not forgotten him, and the subscription list displays a host of aristocratic names. The art of collation was then unknown, and when he first undertook the work the duties of an editor of other than classical literature were not so well understood as in more recent times. . . . His most important commercial achievement was the foundation of the "Annual Register" in 1758, which is still published.—TEDDER, H. R., 1888, *Dictionary of National Biography, vol.* XV, *pp.* 171, 172.

Edward Young

1683-1765

Born at Upham, Hants, June 1683. At Winchester School, 1694-99. Matric. New Coll., Oxford, 3 Oct. 1702. Soon afterwards removed to Corpus Christi Coll. Law Fellowship, All Soul's Coll., 1706; B. C. L., 23 April, 1714; D. C. L., 10 June 1719. Tutor to Lord Burleigh, for a short time before 1719. Play "Busiris" produced at Drury Lane, March 1719; "The Brothers," Drury Lane, 1753. Ordained, 1727; Chaplain to George II., April 1728; Rector to Welwyn, Herts, 1730-65. Married Lady Elizabeth Leigh, 27 May 1731. Clerk of Closet to Princess Dowager, 1751. Died, at Welwyn, 5 April 1765. Buried there. *Works:* "Epistle to . . . Lord Lansdown," 1713; "A Poem on the Lord's Day,"1713 (2nd edn. same year); "The Force of Religion," 1714; "On the Late Queen's Death," 1714; "Oratio habita in Coll. Omnium Animarum," 1716; "Paraphrase on part of the Book of Job," 1719; "Busiris," 1719; "Letter to Mr. Tickell," 1719; "The Revenge," 1721; "The Universal Passion" (6 pts.: anon.), 1725-28; "The Instalement," 1726; "Cynthio" (anon.), 1727; "Ocean," 1728; "A Vindication of Providence," 1728 (2nd edn. same year); "An Apology for Princes," 1729; "Imperium Pelagi" (anon.), 1730; "Two Epistles to Mr. Pope" (anon.), 1730; "The Sea-Piece," 1730; "The Foreign Address," 1734; "Poetical Works" (2 vols.), 1741; "The Complaint; or, Night Thoughts on Life, Death, and Immortality" (anon.; 9 pts.), 1742-46; "The Consolation" (anon.), 1745; "Reflections on the Public Situation of the Kingdom," 1745; "The Brothers" (anon.), 1753; "The Centaur not Fabulous" (anon.), 1755; "An Argument drawn from the circumstance of Christ's Death," 1758; "Conjectures on Original Composition" (anon.), 1759 (2nd edn. same year); "Resignation" (anon.), 1762; "Works" (4 vols.), 1764. *Posthumous:* "The Merchant," 1771. *Collected Works:* "Complete Works," ed. by Dr. Doran (2 vols.), 1854.—SHARP, R. FARQUHARSON, 1897, *A Dictionary of English Authors, p.* 307.

PERSONAL

Must torture his invention
To flatter knaves or lose his pension.
—SWIFT, JONATHAN, 1745? *Rhapsody on Poetry.*

I have a great joy in Dr. Young, whom I disturbed in a reverie. At first he started, then bowed, then fell back into a surprise; then began a speech, relapsed into his astonishment two or three times, forgot what he had been saying; began a new subject, and so went on. I told him your Grace desired he would write longer letters; to which he cried, "Ha!" most emphatically, and I leave you to interpret what it meant. He has made a friendship with one person here, whom I believe you would not imagine to have been made for his bosom friend. You would, perhaps, suppose it was a bishop or dean, a prebend, a pious preacher, a clergyman of exemplary life; or if a layman, of most virtuous conversation, one that has paraphrased St. Matthew, or wrote comments on St. Paul. . . . You would not guess that this associate of the Doctor's was—old Cibber! Certainly, in their religious, moral, and civil character there is no relation; but in their dramatic capacity there is some. . . . The waters have raised his spirits to a fine pitch, as your Grace will imagine when I tell you how sublime an answer he made to a very vulgar question. I asked him how long he stayed at the Wells: he said, As long as my rival stayed;—as long as the sun did.—MONTAGU, ELIZABETH, 1745, *Letter to the Duchess of Portland.*

The impertinence of my frequent visits to him was amply rewarded; forasmuch as, I can truly say, he never received me but with agreeable open complacency; and I never left him but with profitable pleasure and improvement. He was one or other, the most modest, the most patient of contradiction, and the most informing and entertaining I ever conversed with—at least, of any man who had so just pretensions to pertinacity and reserve.—HILDESLEY, BISHOP, 1760, *Letter to Richardson, Nov.* 11; *Richardson's Correspondence, vol.* V, *p.* 142.

When he had determined to go into orders he addressed himself, like an honest man, for the best directions in the study of theology. But to whom did he apply? It may, perhaps, be thought, to Sherlock or Atterbury; to Burnet or

Hare. No! to Mr. Pope; who, in a youthful frolic, recommended Thomas Aquinas to him. With this treasure he retired, in order to be free from interruption, to an obscure place in the suburbs. His director hearing no more of him in six months, and apprehending he might have carried the jest too far, sought after him, and found him out just in time to prevent an irretrievable derangement.—RUFFHEAD, OWEN, 1769, *Life of Pope, p.* 291, *note.*

There are who relate, that, when first Young found himself independent, and his own master at All Souls, he was not the ornament to religion and morality which he afterwards became. . . . They who think ill of Young's morality, in the early part of his life, may perhaps be wrong; but Tindal could not err in his opinion of Young's warmth and ability in the cause of religion. Tindal used to spend much of his time at All Souls. "The other boys," said the atheist, "I can always answer, because I always know whence they have their arguments, which I have read a hundred times; but that fellow Young is continually pestering me with something of his own." After all, Tindal and the censurers of Young may be reconcilable. Young might, for two or three years, have tried that kind of life in which his natural principles would not suffer him to wallow long. If this were so, he has left behind him not only his evidence in favour of virtue, but the potent testimony of experience against vice.—CROFT, JR., HERBERT, 1780, *Young, Lives of the English Poets by Samuel Johnson.*

That there was an air of benevolence in his manner, but that he could obtain from him less information than he had hoped to receive from one who had lived too much in intercourse with the brightest men of what had been called the Augustan age of England; and that he shewed a degree of eager curiosity concerning the common occurrences that were then passing, which appeared somewhat remarkable in a man of such intellectual stores, of such an advanced age, and who had retired from life with declared disappointment in his expectations. — LANGTON, BENNET, 1781, *Boswell's Life of Johnson, ed. Hill, vol.* IV, *p.* 69.

We stopped at Welwin, where I wished much to see, in company with Johnson, the residence of the authour of "Night Thoughts," which was then possessed by his son, Mr. Young. . . . We went into the garden, where we found a gravel walk, on each side of which was a row of trees, planted by Dr. Young, which formed a handsome gothic arch. Dr. Johnson called it a fine grove. I beheld it with reverence. We sat some time in the summer-house, on the outside wall of which was inscribed "*Ambulantes in horto audiebant vocem Dei;*" and in reference to a brook by which it is situated, "*Vivendi rectè qui prorogat horam,*" &c. I said to Mr. Young that I had been told his father was cheerful. "Sir," said he, "he was too well bred a man not to be cheerful in company; but he was gloomy when alone. He never was cheerful after my mother's death, and he had met with many disappointments." Dr. Johnson observed to me afterwards "That this was no favourable account of Dr. Young; for it is not becoming in a man to have so little acquiescence in the ways of Providence as to be gloomy because he has not obtained as much preferment as he expected, nor to contine gloomy for the loss of his wife. Grief has its time."—BOSWELL, JAMES, 1781, *Life of Johnson, ed. Croker, ch.* lxxiii.

Young, whose satires give the very anatomy of human foibles, was wholly governed by his housekeeper. She thought and acted for him, which probably greatly assisted the "Night Thoughts," but his curate exposed the domestic economy of a man of genius by a satirical novel. If I am truly informed, in that gallery of satirical poets in his "Love of Fame," Young has omitted one of the most striking—his own! While the poet's eye was glancing from "earth to heaven," he totally overlooked the lady whom he married, and who soon became the object of his contempt; and not only his wife, but his only son, who when he returned home for the vacation from Winchester school, was only admitted into the presence of his poetical father on the first and the last day; and whose unhappy life is attributed to this unnatural neglect:—a lamentable domestic catastrophe, which, I fear, has too frequently occurred amidst the ardour and occupations of literary glory.—DISRAELI, ISAAC, 1796–1818, *Domestic Life, The Literary Character.*

The outline of Young's character is too distinctly traceable in the well-attested facts of his life, and yet more in the self-betrayal that runs through all his works, for us to fear that our general estimate of him may be false. For, while no poet seems less easy and spontaneous than Young, no poet discloses himself more completely. Men's minds have no hiding-place out of themselves—their affections do but betray another phase of their nature. And if, in the present view of Young, we seem to be more intent on laying bare unfavourable facts than on shrouding them in "charitable speeches," it is not because we may have any irreverential pleasure in turning men's characters the seamy side without, but because we see no great advantage in considering a man as he was *not*. Young's biographers and critics have usually set out from the position that he was a great religious teacher, and that his poetry is morally sublime; and they have toned down his failings into harmony with their conception of the divine and the poet. For our own part, we set out from precisely the opposite conviction—namely, that the religious and moral spirit of Young's poetry is low and false; and we think it of some importance to show that the "Night Thoughts" are the reflex of a mind in which the higher human sympathies were inactive. This judgment is entirely opposed to our youthful predilections and enthusiasm. The sweet garden-breath of early enjoyment lingers about many a page of the "Night Thoughts," and even of the "Last Day," giving an extrinsic charm to passages of stilted rhetoric and false sentiment, but the sober and repeated reading of maturer years has convinced us that it would hardly be possible to find a more typical instance than Young's poetry, of the mistake which substitutes interested obedience for sympathetic emotion, and baptizes egoism as religion.—ELIOT, GEORGE, 1857, *Worldliness and Other-Worldliness: The Poet Young; Essays.*

One of the greatest sycophants of a very adulatory age; a self-seeking, greedy, worldly man.—NICOLL, HENRY J., 1882, *Landmarks of English Literature, p.* 196.

It was a curious chance which brought together the future author of the "Night Thoughts" and the future author of "La Pucelle;" it was a still more curious circumstance that they should have formed a friendship which remained unbroken, when the one had become the most rigid of Christian divines, and the other the most daring of anti-Christian propagandists. Many years afterwards Young dedicated to him in very flattering terms one of the most pleasing of his minor poems —the "Sea Piece."—COLLINS, JOHN CHURTON, 1886, *Bolingbroke, A Historical Study, and Voltaire in England, p.* 244.

He closed his long career, rich indeed through his marriage with the Earl of Lichfield's daughter, Lady Elizabeth Lee, but petulant, proud, and solitary. The insatiable ambition of Young has been the theme of many moralists, and the tendency of his personal character was indubitably parasitic; but it would be easy to show, on the other hand, that he really was, to an eminent degree, what Hobbes calls an "episcopable" person, and that his talents, his address, his loyalty, and his moral force were qualities which not only might, but for the honour of the English Church should, have been publicly acknowledged by preferment.—GOSSE, EDMUND, 1888, *A History of Eighteenth Century Literature, p.* 210.

NIGHT THOUGHTS
1742–46

The title of my poem (Night Thoughts) not affected; for I never compose but at night, except sometimes when I am on horseback. — YOUNG, EDWARD, 1758, *Spence's Anecdotes, ed. Singer, p.* 288.

I will venture to say that in point of depth this poet is what Homer and Pindar are in point of grandeur. I should find it difficult to explain the effect produced upon me by my first perusal of this work. I might experience much the same impression in the heart of the desert on a dark and stormy night, when the surrounding blackness is pierced at intervals by flashes of lightning.—BISSY, COMTE DE, 1762, *Journal étranger, Feb.*

A great poet, who is certain to share the immortality of Swift, Shaftesbury, Pope, Addison, and Richardson.—LETOURNEUR, PIERRE, 1769, *Les Nuits d'Young.*

Sir, you have conferred a high honour on my old acquaintance Young; the taste of the translator appears to be better than the author's. You have done all that could be done in the way of bringing order into this collection of confused and bombastic platitudes. . . . I think that every foreigner will prefer your prose to the poetry of one who is half poet and half priest, like this Englishman. —VOLTAIRE, FRANÇOIS MARIE AROUET, 1769, *Letter to Letourneur, June* 7.

It is all too full of tolling bells, tombs, mournful chants and cries, and phantoms; the simple and artless expression of true sorrow would be a hundred times more effective.—GRIMM, FREDERICK MELCHIOR, 1770, *Correspondance litterarie, May.*

Looked into Young's "Night Thoughts:" debased throughout with many poor and puerile conceits; such as making "the night weep dew over extinct nature;" the revolving spheres, "a horologe machinery divine;" "each circumstance armed with an aspic, and all a hydra woe;" "each tear mourn its own distinct distress, and each distress heightened by the whole." Frigidity and tumour, obscurity and glare, are the two apparently opposite but striking faults of this popular and imposing poem: yet parts are in good taste: he glows with a natural and genial warmth in describing the charms of social intercourse and the blessings of friendship, towards the close of the 2d Night; and the passage in the 4th, beginning, "O my coævals, remanants of yourselves," is animated and sublime. Johnson perhaps caught his "panting Time toiled after him in vain," from Young's "and leave Praise panting in the distant vale."—GREEN, THOMAS, 1779–1810, *Diary of a Lover of Literature, p.* 67.

No writer, ancient or modern, had a stronger imagination than Dr. Young, or one more fertile in figures of every kind. His metaphors are often new, and often natural and beautiful. But his imagination was strong and rich, rather than delicate and correct. Hence, in his "Night Thoughts," there prevails an obscurity, and a hardness in his style. The metaphors are frequently too bold, and frequently too far pursued; the reader is dazzled, rather than enlightened; and kept constantly on the stretch to keep pace with the author.—BLAIR, HUGH, 1783, *Lectures on Rhetoric and Belles-Lettres, ed. Mills, Lecture* XV.

To all the other excellencies of "Night Thoughts" let me add the gre.. and peculiar one, that they contain not only the noblest sentiments of virtue, and contemplations on immortality, but the *Christian Sacrifice*, the *Divine Propitiation,* with all its interesting circumstances, and consolations to "a wounded spirit," solemnly and poetically displayed in such imagery and language, as cannot fail to exalt, animate, and soothe the truly pious. No book whatever can be recommended to young persons, with better hopes of seasoning their minds with *vital religion,* than Young's "Night Thoughts."—BOSWELL, JAMES, 1791–93, *Life of Johnson, ed. Hill, vol.* IV, *p.* 71.

With powers inferior to Milton, turgid, obscure, and epigrammatic, yet with occasional sallies of imagination, and bursts cf sublimity that course along the gloom with the rapidity and brilliancy of lightning, Young has in his "Night Thoughts" become a favourite not only with the multitude here, but with many of the nations upon the Continent; for, with the bulk of mankind, there is little discrimination between the creative energy of Milton, and the tumid declamation of Young, or between the varied pauses of highly-finished blank-verse and a succession of monotonous lines. Young has, however, the merit of originality: for few authors who have written so much have left fainter traces of imitation, or in the happy hour of inspiration more genuine and peculiar excellence.—DRAKE, NATHAN, 1798–1820, *Literary Hours, vol.* I, *No.* xviii, *p.* 287.

There is nothing of entertaining succession of parts in the "Night Thoughts." The poem excites no anticipation as it proceeds. One book bespeaks no impatience for another, nor is found to have laid the smallest foundation for new pleasure when the succeeding Night sets in. The poet's fancy discharges itself on the mind in short *ictuses* of surprise, which rather lose than increase their force by reiteration; but he is remarkably defective in progressive interest and collective effect. The power of the poem, instead of "*being in the whole,*" lies in short, vivid and broken gleams of genius; so that if we disregard particular lines, we shall but too often miss the only gems of ransom which the poet can bring as the price of his relief from surrounding tedium. . . . After all, the variety and extent of reflection in the "Night Thoughts" is to a certain degree more imposing than real. They have more metaphorical than substantial variety of thought. Questions which we had thought exhausted and laid at rest in one book, are called up again in the next in a Proteus metamorphosis of shape, and a chamelion diversity of colour. Happily the awful truths which they illustrate are few and simple. Around those truths the poet directs his course with innumerable sinuosities of fancy, like a man appearing to make a long voyage, while he is in reality only crossing and recrossing the same expanse of water.—CAMPBELL, THOMAS, 1819, *Specimens of the British Poets.*

I asked how it would be accounted for that Dr. Young's "Night Thoughts" were less estimated than formerly. Mr. Hall replied, "Dr. Young is destined to immortality. I cannot account for the taste of the age in preferring a light and trifling literature, which, being all glare, affords no food for the mind. Another age will properly appreciate the genius of Young." —GREENE, JOHN, 1832, *Reminiscences of Rev. Robert Hall.*

Young's great poem is a notable instance of the want of reserve and poetical economy. In the poetry of Cowper, Burns, Crabbe, we have abundance of sadness, and it is all the more truly and deeply sad, because it seems to come unsought, nay, rather shunned. The poet's soul appears to crave the sunshine: he "does not love the shower nor seek the cold," but only yields to mournful reflections because they force themselves upon him in a world of woe. But when Young so resolutely makes love to Gloom and sets his cap at Melancholy, we suspect that both are in masquerade, and that blooming forms are beneath the sable stole; when he surrounds his head with cypress, we image a snug velvet cap under the dusky wreath; when he "sits by a lamp at mid-day, and has skulls, bones, and instruments of death for the ornaments of his study," we feel disposed to think that he makes sin, death, and sorrow a poetical amusement, and takes up these topics because they offer facilities for impressive writing more than to relieve their pressure on a burdened heart. —COLERIDGE, SARA, 1847, *ed. Coleridge's Biographia Literaria, ch.* xxiii, *note.*

We commend his masterpiece to readers, partly, indeed, for its power,—a power that has hitherto rather been felt than acknowledged, rather admired in silence than analysed; but principally because, like "The Temple" of Herbert, it is holy ground. The author, amid his elaborate ingenuities, and wilful though minor perversities, never ceases to love and to honour truth; in pursuit of renown, he is never afraid to glory in the Cross of our Lord Jesus Christ; and if his flights of fancy be at times too wild, and if his thoughts be often set to the tune of the tempest, it is a tempest on whose wings, to use his own simple but immortal words, "The Lord is abroad."—GILFILLAN, GEORGE, 1853, *ed. Young's Night Thoughts, Life, p.* xxvii.

Although some have called its sublimity "fustian," and its melancholy artificial, its combinations grotesque, its phraseology involved, and its reasoning sometimes confused, it stands, on the whole, as a monument of the inexhaustible wit (in the proper sense of the word) and genius of the author. Its moral is expressly directed against that of Pope in his "Essay on Man," wherein the world was taught to be content with the present, without troubling itself about the hereafter. A great portion of Pope's poem consists merely of a versified translation of Pascal's "Thoughts and Maxims;" but the sentiments of Young are, with one or two exceptions, entirely original.—DORAN, JOHN, 1854, *ed., The Complete Works of Rev. Edward Young, Life.*

Young, with his knowledge of the world and meditative piety, had enthusiasm and vivacity, and was able, like the lion instanced by Longinus, to lash himself into constant fits of sublimity, in which he frequently causes us to forget the effort, though we are not seldom reminded of it. The cardinal defect of his character and of his poetry would appear to be a lack of reverence,—of that modest, quiet, teachable spirit, which, when associated with genius, is capable of receiving and giving forth the noblest utterances of inspiration. . . . Too much of the "Night Thoughts" is rant, scolding, and fury. It is on many pages a truculent, tumultuous poem, filled with a sort of vinous, bacchanalian piety. The sacred Muse of Young goes forth shouting and frantic with some leaves of the thyrsus yet about her from the revels of the Duke of Wharton.—DUYCKINCK, E. A., 1854, *Edward Young, North American Review, vol.* 79, *pp.* 273, 274.

In my youthful days Young's "Night-Thoughts" was a very favourite book, especially with ladies: I knew more than one lady who had a copy of it in which particular passages were marked for her by some popular preacher.—ROGERS, SAMUEL, 1855, *Table Talk, p.* 34.

But never sit I quiet long
Where broider'd cassock floats round Young;
Whose pungent essences perfume
And quirk and quibble trim the tomb;
Who thinks the holy bread too plain,
And in the chalice pours champagne.
—LANDOR, WALTER SAVAGE, 1858, *Apology for Gebir.*

In his last years he [Herder] longed for nothing more earnestly than for some great high thought on which he might live. Klopstock's "Odes," Young's "Night Thoughts," and Müller's "Relics" were, next to the Bible, especially the prophets, the last food of his soul.—HAGENBACH, KARL RUDOLF, 1865, *German Rationalism; its Rise, Progress and Doctrine, tr. Gage and Stuckenberg, ch.* xiv, *p.* 177.

The poem is a mighty and magnificent sermon, preached as from a graveyard, on the vanity and brevity of life and the worthlessness and folly of an ill-spent career; in the divine love to sinners; and the great propitiation offered for them; and on the bright hopes of a new and happy existence which Christianity has opened up. It startles by its scenes of death, its dark picture of the sting of death, and its glimpses into another world, where the Judge is omniscient and just. It reprobates in stern and withering language the unsatisfactoriness of infidelity, and expatiates in glowing and transcendant terms on the doctrine of immortality. The imagery of night is drawn with intense solemnity,—its darkness and its vast canopy studded with the host of heaven, all telling of the great God, and proclaiming his majesty, that man may be awed and brought in faith to the acceptance of that salvation by which he rises above the fear of dissolution, experiences at length a blessed resurrection, and is happy forever in the contemplation and enjoyment of his Saviour. The thought and style are unequal. Splendid declamation fills many a page, though it is usually mixed or followed up with close, bold, grappling appeal. The pointed antithesis may be set off against the diluting amplifications. What is original is far more than a compensating for what reminds one of Pope or Milton. The argument, always powerful, is sometimes rather ingenious than solid; and several descriptions border on hyperbole or extravagance. The lines are occasionally rugged, but the work has been always and deservedly popular, as well from its theme as for his treatment of it; and Young's muse, with her skulls and stars, her cross and her crown, has no rival, and has had no successor.—EADIE, JOHN, 1866, *Imperial Dictionary of Universal Biography, vol.* VI, *p.* 1407.

There is a fine, fluent, sermonising vein about Young; but a flavour of cant hangs about his most ambitious efforts. To use a phrase of the day, he is a sad "Philistine;" and, through the admiration long felt or professed for him, his influence must have much tended to propagate false taste.—ARNOLD, THOMAS, 1868–75, *Chaucer to Wordsworth, p.* 356.

Perhaps the best compliment ever paid to the "Night Thoughts" is the fact that Edmund Burke committed many portions of it to memory.—JENKINS, O. L., 1876, *The Student's Handbook of British and American Literature, p.* 222.

Young was one of the cleverest men who ever wrote English verse, but the cleverness extinguishes the imagination. The "Night Thoughts," owing in great measure to its subject, has enjoyed a vast popularity, in spite of its offences against all literary canons of taste. . . . The substance is everywhere commonplace; and Young shows his inferiority to Pope by inventing phrases for copybooks, where Pope coins proverbs for cultivated thinkers. The love of gloom, of the imagery of the grave, and the awful mysteries of life, which animated our older writers, is not absent, but it is turned to account by this clever man of the world with such ingenuity, that we become aware of the shallowness of his feeling. How hollow are the enjoyments of this world, and how deep the surrounding mystery! is the ostensible sentiment. What a clever fellow I am, and what a shame it is that I was not made a bishop! is the sentiment plainly indicated in every line. Can I not say as many smart things about death and eternity as anybody that ever wrote? Am I not a good orthodox reasoner, instead of a semi-deist like that sinner Pope? We see, as we read, the very type of the preacher of a period when the old mythology, no longer credible or really imposing to the imagination, is still regarded as capable of, at least, an ostensible demonstration, and may afford a sufficient excuse for any quality of intellectual ingenuity.—STEPHEN, LESLIE, 1876, *History of English Thought in the Eighteenth Century, vol.* II, *pp.* 362, 363.

His poem is a wilderness of reflection, through which his fertile fancy scatters flowers of every hue and odor. Its strength is in the vast number of noble and sublime passages, maxims of the highest practical value, everlasting truths.—WELSH, ALFRED H., 1883, *Development of English Literature and Language, vol.* II, *p.* 133.

Notwithstanding the morbid spirit which pervades and overshadows much of his poetry, depriving it somewhat of its potency, it yet abounds with grand imagery and impressive eloquence. Had the poet but infused a little star-light into his "Night Thoughts" they would have possessed a tenfold charm. — SAUNDERS, FREDERICK, 1887, *The Story of Some Famous Books, p.* 85.

It had great currency in England, and was admired, and translated, and read largely upon the Continent. For many a year, a copy of Young's mournful, magniloquent poem, bound in morocco and gilt-edged, was reckoned one of the most acceptable and worthy gifts to a person in affliction. But of a surety it has not the same hold upon people in this century that it had in the last. There are eloquent passages in it—passages almost rising to sublimity. His love of superlatives and of wordy exaggerations served him in good stead when he came to talk of the shortness of time, and the length of eternity, and the depth of the grave, and the shadows of death. Amidst these topics he moved on the great sable pinions of his muse with a sweep of wing, and a steadiness of poise, that drew a great many sorrowing and pious souls after him. —MITCHELL, DONALD G., 1895, *English Lands Letters and Kings, Queen Anne and the Georges, p.* 18.

An eloquent interpreter of the melancholy of his age. . . . The theme of the author of "Night Thoughts" is the old opposition between the social and the natural man. Every other element in the book—its expression of fellowship with nature, its appeal to the human conscience, its sincere conviction of man's miserable condition, has since been expressed by many others whose voices are more persuasive than his. Yet it may be that, if we carry our minds back to 1742 and 1744—the years in which Young's collection of poems appeared—and especially if we reflect on the condition of French lyrical poetry just at that time, we shall feel, even to-day, the partly vanished charm of such lines as these:

O majestic Night!
Nature's great ancestor! Day's elder-born!
And fated to survive the transient sun!

. . . .

Can we not recognise, in these lines, something of the true poet that at times was revealed in Edward Young? Are our wearied perceptions entirely proof against the spell which so fascinated our fathers? —TEXTE, JOSEPH, 1895–99, *Jean-Jacques Rousseau and the Cosmopolitan Spirit in Literature, tr. Matthews, pp.* 304, 310, 311.

He is not a seer, or a prophet, or an enthusiast; but a clever phrasemonger and a disappointed place-hunter, who, in his extreme verbal solicitude about the next world, contrived to keep a sharp eye upon present interests.—AUBREY, W. H. S., 1896, *The Rise and Growth of the English Nation, vol.* III, *p.* 115.

It is difficult to give even a guess whether this remarkable poem will ever recover much or anything of the great reputation which it long held, and which, for two generations at least, it has almost entirely lost. It has against it, the application of phrase and even of thought, merely of an age, to the greatest and most lasting subjects, and a tone only to be described as the theatrical-religious. Its almost unbroken gloom frets or tires according to the mood and temperament of the reader. On the other hand, the want of sincerity is always more apparent than real, and the moral strength and knowledge of human nature, which were the great merits of the eighteenth century, appear most unmistakably. Above all, the poem deserves the praise due to very fine and, in part at least, very original versification. If Young here deserts the couplet, it is, as we have seen, by no means because he cannot manage it; it is because he is at least partly dissatisfied with it, and sees that it will not serve his turn. And his blank verse is a fine and an individual kind. Its fault, due, no doubt, to his practice in drama, is that it is a little too declamatory, a little too suggestive of soliloquies in an inky cloak with footlights in front. But this of itself distinguishes it from the blank verse of Thomson, which came somewhat earlier. It is not a direct imitation either of Milton or of Shakespeare, and deserves to be ranked by itself.—SAINTSBURY, GEORGE, 1898, *A Short History of English Literature*, *p.* 561.

SATIRES

Young's Satires were in higher reputation when published than they stand in at present. He seems fonder of dazzling than pleasing; of raising our admiration for his wit, than our dislike of the follies he ridicules.—GOLDSMITH, OLIVER, 1776, *Works, ed. Cunningham, vol.* III, *p.* 439.

The chief fault in the satires of Young appear to have arisen from a too great partiality to antithesis and epigrammatic point: occasionally used, they give weight and terseness to sentiment; but, when profusely lavished, offend both the judgment and the ear. The poet likewise, instead of faithfully copying from human life, has too often had recourse to the sources of a fertile imagination; hence his pictures, though vividly and richly coloured, are defective in that truth of representation which can alone impart to them a due degree of moral influence.—DRAKE, NATHAN. 1804, *Essays Illustrative of the Tatler, Spectator and Guardian, vol.* III, *p.* 252.

Young is not a satirist of a high order. His satire has neither the terrible vigour, the lacerating energy of genuine indignation, nor the humour which owns loving fellowship with the poor human nature it laughs at; nor yet the personal bitterness which, as in Pope's characters of Sporus and Atticus, ensures those living touches by virtue of which the individual and particular in Art becomes the universal and immortal. Young could never describe a real complex human being; but what he *could* do with eminent success, was to describe with neat and finished point obvious *types* of manners rather than of character,—to write cold and clever epigrams on personified vices and absurdities. There is no more emotion in his satire than if he were turning witty vices on a waxen image of Cupid, or a lady's glove.—ELIOT, GEORGE, 1857, *Worldliness and Other-Worldliness: The Poet Young; Essays.*

DRAMAS

Dr. Young's "Revenge," is a play which discovers genius and fire; but wants tenderness, and turns too much upon the shocking and direful passions.—BLAIR, HUGH, 1783, *Lectures on Rhetoric and Belles-Lettres, ed. Mills, Lecture* xlvi.

Young, Thomson, and others who followed the same wordy and declamatory system of composition, contributed rather to sink than exalt the character of the stage. The two first were both men of excellent genius, as their other writings have sufficiently testified; but, as dramatists they wrought upon a false model, and their productions are of little value. —SCOTT, SIR WALTER, 1814–23, *Essay on The Drama.*

His tragedy of the "Revenge" is monkish and scholastic. Zanga is a vulgar caricature of Iago.—HAZLITT, WILLIAM, 1818, *Lectures on the English Poets, Lecture* vi.

Young's Tragedies of the "*Revenge,*" "*Busiris,*" and the "*Brothers,*" are evidently the productions of no ordinary mind. For high and eloquent declamation, they are equal to any thing which the French School has produced, either in its native soil, or in our imitative Country. Though the first is the only one of these three Tragedies which keeps possession of the Stage, yet "*Busiris*" appears to me to possess the most merit. The principal character is drawn with as much force and decision as *Zanga*, but has more of real human nature in its composition. *Zanga* is a fine Poetical study; the grandeur of the conception, and the power of the execution, are equal; but it has not much of truth or Nature in its composition. Compare it with the *Iago* of Shakspeare, of which it is evidently a copy, and it is like comparing a lay figure with a Statue. One is a fitting vehicle to convey to us the drapery of the Poet's fancy, and the folds and forms in which he chooses to array it; but the other has the truth and power of Nature stamped upon every limb.—NEELE, HENRY, 1827–29, *Lectures on English Poetry, p.* 144.

The literary genius of E. Young (1681–1765), on the other hand, possessed vigour and variety enough to distinguish his tragedies from the ordinary level of Augustan plays; in one of them he seems to challenge comparison in the treatment of his theme with a very different rival; but by his main characteristics as a dramatist he belongs to the school of his contemporaries.—WARD, ADOLPHUS WILLIAM, 1878, *Drama, Encyclopædia Britannica, vol.* VII.

On 18 April 1721 the "Revenge," which ran for only six nights, was acted at the same theatre. The play, a variation upon the theme of "Othello," afterwards had a long popularity on the stage. The character of Zanga, Young's Iago, gave opportunity for effective rant; although Young's mixture of bombast and epigrammatic antithesis is apt to strike the modern reader as it struck Fielding.—STEPHEN, LESLIE, 1900, *Dictionary of National Biography, vol.* LXIII, *p.* 369.

GENERAL

I know nothing else but a new edition of Dr. Young's Works. If your lordship thinks like me, who hold that even in his most frantic rhapsodies there are innumerable fine things, you will like to have this edition.—WALPOLE, HORACE, 1757, *To the Earl of Strafford, July* 5; *Letters, ed. Cunningham, vol.* III, *p.* 89.

I don't know whether you have seen Dr. Young's "Conjectures on Original Composition." He is the finest writer of nonsense of any of this age. . . . But the wisest and kindest part of his work is advising writers to be original, and not imitators; that is, to be geniuses rather than blockheads.—WARBURTON, WILLIAM, 1759, *To. Dr. Hurd, May* 17; *Letters from Late Eminent Prelate.*

Where, to crown the hoary bard of night,
The Muses and the Virtues all unite?

—BEATTIE, JAMES, 1765, *On the Report of a Monument to be Erected to the Memory of a Late Author.*

Of Young's poems it is difficult to give any general character; for he has no uniformity of manner: one of his pieces has no great resemblance to another. He began to write early, and continued long; and at different times had different modes of poetical excellence in view. His numbers are smooth sometimes, and sometimes rugged; his style is sometimes concatenated, and sometimes abrupt; sometimes diffusive, and sometimes concise. His plans seem to have started in his mind at the present moment, and his thoughts appeared the effect of chance, sometimes adverse, and sometimes lucky with very little operation of judgment. . . . His versification is his own; neither his blank nor his rhyming lines have any resemblance to those of former writers; he picks up no hemstitch, he copies no favourite expressions; he seems to have laid up no stores of thought or diction, but to owe all of the fortuitous suggestions of the present moment. Yet I have reason to believe, that, when once he had formed a new design, he then laboured it with very patient industry; and that he composed with great labour, and frequent revisions.—JOHNSON, SAMUEL, 1779–81, *Young, Lives of the English Poets.*

Young judges of human life as if he did not belong to it; his thoughts seem to have risen above himself, to search for an imperceptible spot in the immensity of the creation, where he might observe, himself unseen,

——What is the world?—a grave:
Where is the dust which has not been alive?

—STAËL, MADAME DE, 1800, *The Influence of Literature upon Society, ch.* XV.

Though incapable either of tenderness or passion, he had a richness and activity of fancy that belonged rather to the days of James and Elizabeth, than to those of George and Anne:—But then, instead of indulging it, as the older writers would have done, in easy and playful inventions, in splendid descriptions, or glowing illustrations, he was led, by the restraints and established taste of his age, to work it up into strained and fantastical epigrams, or into cold and revolting hyperboles. Instead of letting it flow gracefully on, in an easy and sparkling current, he perpetually forces it out in jets, or makes it stagnate in formal canals;—and thinking it necessary to write like Pope, when the bent of his genius led him rather to copy what was best in Cowley and most fantastic in Shakespeare, he has produced something which excites wonder instead of admiration, and is felt by every one to be at once ingenious, incongruous, and unnatural.—JEFFREY, FRANCIS LORD, 1811–44, *Ford's Dramatic Works, Contributions to the Edinburgh Review, vol.* II, *p.* 293.

The strained thoughts, the figurative metaphysics and solemn epigrams of Young.—COLERIDGE, SAMUEL TAYLOR, 1817, *Biographia Literaria, ch.* xxiii.

Young is a gloomy epigrammatist. He has abused great powers both of thought and language. His moral reflections are sometimes excellent; but he spoils their beauty by overloading them with a religious horror, and at the same time giving them all the smart turns and quaint expressions of an enigma or repartee in verse.—HAZLITT, WILLIAM, 1818, *Lectures on the English Poets, Lecture* vi.

Young is too often fantastical and frivolous; he pins butterflies to the pulpit-cushion; he suspends against the grating of the charnel-house coloured lamps and comic transparencies,—Cupid, and the cat and the fiddle; he opens a storehouse filled with minute particles of heterogeneous wisdom and unpalatable goblets of ill-concocted learning, contributions from the classics, from the schoolmen, from homilies, and from farces. What you expected to be an elegy turns out an epigram; and when you think he is bursting into tears he laughs in your face. Do you go with him into his closet, prepared for an admonition or a rebuke, he shakes his head, and you sneeze at the powder and perfumery of the rebuke. Wonder not if I prefer to his pungent essences the incense which Cowper burns before the altar.—LANDOR, WALTER SAVAGE, 1828, *Imaginary Conversations: Southey; Conversations, Third Series, Landor's Works, vol.* IV, *p.* 73.

Young has founded a bad school, and was not himself a good master. . . . Young, whom the phantom of the world pursues, even among the tombs, betrays, in his declamations on death, merely a disappointed ambition: he takes his peevishness for melancholy. There is nothing natural in his tenderness, nothing ideal in his grief: it is always a heavy hand moving slowly over the lyre.—CHATEAUBRIAND, FRANÇOIS RENÉ, VICOMTE DE, 1831, *Sketches of English Literature, vol.* II, *p.* 251.

A grander writer by spasms than by volitions.—BROWNING, ELIZABETH BARRETT, 1842–63, *The Book of the Poets.*

In him the intellect had an undue predominance over the imagination and the sensibility; and hardly does he raise up before us some grand image of death, of power, or of immortality, than he turns aside to seek after remote and fantastic allusions, which instantly destroy the potent charm. Few writers are so unequal as Young, or rather, few writers of such powerful and acknowledged genius were ever so deficient in comparative or critical taste. To him every idea seemed good, provided only it was strong, original, and ingenious; and as his subject was precisely the one least suited to this species of intellectual sword-play, the conceits, unexpected analogies, and epigrammatic turns of which he was so fond, are as offensive and incongruous as would be the placing of the frippery fountains and clipped yews and trim parterres of Versailles among the glaciers and precipices of Alpine scenery. . . . It would be unjust were we to refuse our tribute of acknowledgment and admiration to the vast richness and fertility of imagination displayed by this powerful writer: it is the fertility of a tropical climate; or, rather, it is the abundant vegetation of a volcanic region; flowers and weeds, the hemlock and the vine, the gaudy and noxious poppy and the innocent and life-supporting wheat —all is brought forth with a boundless and indiscriminate profusion.—SHAW, THOMAS B., 1847, *Outlines of English Literature, p.* 224.

He had nothing of Donne's subtle fancy, and as little of the gayety and playfulness that occasionally break out among the quibbles and contortions of Cowley. On the other hand, he has much more passion and pathos than Cowley, and, with less elegance, perhaps makes a nearer approach in some of his greatest passages to the true sublime. But his style is radically an affected and false one; and of what force it seems to possess, the greater part is the result not of any real principle of life within it, but of mere strutting and straining.—CRAIK, GEORGE L., 1861, *A Compendious History of English Literature and of the English Language, vol.* II, *p.* 285.

Doubtless there are brilliant flashes of imagination in his poems; seriousness and elevation are not wanting; we can even see that he aims at them; but we discover much more quickly that he makes the most of his grief, and strikes attitudes.—TAINE, H. A., 1871, *History of English Literature, tr. Van Laun, vol.* II, *bk.* iii, *ch.* vii, *p.* 221.

There is scarcely a stanza of the so-called "Odes" which does not read like an admirable and intentional burlesque. The author seems by his rhymes to have had no ear at all, and his gross and fulsome flattery is unspeakably nauseous. —SAINTSBURY, GEORGE, 1880, *The English Poets, ed. Ward, vol.* III, *p.* 222.

His influence was not so pure as that of Thomson. The author of "Night Thoughts" was an artist of a force approaching that of genius, but his error was to build that upon rhetoric which he should have based on imagination. The history of Young is one of the most curious in the chronicles of literature. Born far back in the seventeenth century, before Pope or Gay, he wrote in the manner of the Anne wits, without special distinction, through all the years of his youth and middle life. At the age of sixty he collected his poetical works, and appeared to be a finished mediocrity. It was not until then, and after that time, that, taking advantage of a strange wind of funereal enthusiasm that swept over him, he composed the masterpiece by which the next generation knew him, his amazingly popular and often highly successful "Night Thoughts."—GOSSE, EDMUND, 1897, *Short History of Modern English Literature, p.* 237.

David Mallet

1705?–1765

David Mallet, was born in 1698 near Crieff, the son of a farmer. Janitor at Edinburgh High School in 1717–18, he then studied at the university; in 1720 became a tutor, from 1723 to 1731 in the family of the Duke of Montrose, living mostly in London and changed his name "from Scotch Malloch to English Mallet." In 1723 the adaptation of two old ballads into "William and Margaret" gained him a reputation as a poet, which he enhanced by "The Excursion" (1728). To please Pope, Mallet reviled Pope's critics in "Verbal Criticism" (1733). In 1740 he published a mediocre Life of Bacon; in 1742 another poem, "The Hermit, or Amyntor and Theodora," and the same year became under-secretary to Frederick, Prince of Wales. To gratify Bolingbroke he heaped abuse upon his dead friend Pope in a preface to Bolingbroke's "Patriot King," and he edited Bolingbroke's works: at the bidding of the ministry he directed the popular rage for the loss of Minorca upon Admiral Byng, and the "price of blood," says Dr. Johnson, "was a pension which he retained till his death." He received a legacy of £1000 from the Duchess to write a Life of Marlborough, but never penned a line. He also tried his hand at play-writing. "Mustapha" pleased for a while in 1739; "Eurydice" (1731) and "Elvira" (1763), tragedies, were failures. "Alfred, a Masque" (1740), was written in conjunction with Thomson, and one of its songs, "Rule Britannia," was claimed for both. Mallet died 21st April 1765.—PATRICK AND GROOME, *eds.*, 1897, *Chambers's Biographical Dictionary, p.* 623.

PERSONAL

As a fellow who, while Mr. Pope lived, was as diligent in licking his feet, as he is now in licking your lordship's; and who, for the sake of giving himself an air of importance, in being joined with you, and for the vanity of saying "the Author and I,"—"the Editor and me,"—has sacrificed all his pretensions to friendship, honour, and humanity. — WARBURTON, WILLIAM, ? 1749, *A Letter to the Lord Viscount B——ke, Occasioned by his Treatment of a Deceased Friend.*

Mallet's boasts should not, I imagine, have much effect with those who know him; for, from the knowledge I have of him, I feel an unaccountable propensity to believe the contrary of what he tells me.—WEDDERBURN, ALEXANDER (LORD LOUGHBOROUGH), 1764, *Letter to David Hume, Oct.* 28.

His stature was diminutive, but he was regularly formed; his appearance, till he grew corpulent, was agreeable, and he suffered it to want no recommendation that dress could give it. His conversation was elegant and easy. The rest of his character may, without injury to his memory, sink into silence.—JOHNSON, SAMUEL, 1779-81, *Mallet, Lives of the English Poets.*

Mr Mallet and his lady appeared to all the world to be the happiest couple in it, and I desire to have no doubt that they really were what they wished the world should think them. However, Mrs. Mallet, to her excessive love, joined the most consummate prudence. Every shilling of her fortune, which amounted to seven or eight thousand pounds, she settled upon herself; but then she took all imaginable care that Mr. Mallet should appear like a gentleman of distinction, and, from her great kindness, always chose herself to purchase everything that he wore; hat, stockings, coat, waist-coat, &c., were all of her own choice, and at her own cost; and so was the warmth of her fondness, that she took care all the world should know the pains she bestowed on her husband's dress.—DAVIES, THOMAS, 1780, *Memoirs of the Life of David Garrick, vol.* II, *p.* 47.

When Bolingbroke died and bequeathed the publication of his works to Mallet, Johnson observed:—"His Lordship has loaded a blunderbuss against Religion, and has left a Scoundrel to pull the trigger." Being reminded of this a few years ago, the Doctor exclaimed, "Did I really say so?" "Yes, Sir." He replied, "I am heartily glad of it."—STEEVENS, GEORGE, 1785, *Johnsoniana, European Magazine, Jan.*

A minute life of Mallet might exhibit a curious example of mediocrity of talent, with but suspicious virtues, brought forward by the accident of great connexions, placing a bustling intriguer much higher in the scale of society than "our philosophy ever dreamt of."—DISRAELI, ISAAC, 1814, *Bolingbroke, Mallet and Pope, Quarrels of Authors, note.*

Into Bolingbroke's relations with the cur Mallet we have no intention of entering. To the influence of that unprincipled adventurer and most detestable man is, we believe, in a large measure, to be attributed almost everything which loaded his latter years with reproach—the assault on Pope, the unseemly controversy with Warburton, the determination to prepare for posthumous publication what he had not the courage to publish during life.—COLLINS, JOHN CHURTON, 1886, *Bolingbroke, A Historical Study, and Voltaire in England, p.* 213.

He was a venal writer, a treacherous friend, a dishonest man.—WALKER, HUGH, 1893, *Three Centuries of Scottish Literature, vol.* II, *p.* 85.

He did a large amount of dirty work, and appears to have made a good income by it.—DENNIS, JOHN, 1894, *The Age of Pope, p.* 118.

WILLIAM AND MARGARET
1724

I am never more delighted than when I meet with an opportunity to unveil obscure merit, and produce it into notice. . . . My having taken up, in a late perambulation, as I stood upon the top of Primrose Hill, a torn leaf of one of those Halfpenny Miscellanies which are published for the use and pleasure of our nymphs of low degree and known by the name of *Garlands*. . . . I fell unexpectedly upon a work, for so I have no scruple to call it, which deserves to live forever! and which (notwithstanding its disguise of coarse brown paper, almost unintelligible corruptions of the sense from the blunders of the press, with here and there an obsolete low phrase which I have altered for the clearer explanation of the author's meaning) is so powerfully filled throughout with that blood-curdling chilling influence of Nature working on our passions (which Criticks call the sublime) that I have never met it stronger in Homer himself; nor even in that prodigious English genius, who has made the Greek our countryman. The simple title of this piece was "William and Margaret." *A Ballad.* I am sorry that I am not able to acquaint my Reader with his name to whom we owe this melancholy piece of finished Poetry; under the humble title of a Ballad.—HILL, AARON, 1724, *The Plain Dealer, July* 24.

After what you have said of "William and Margaret," I flatter myself that you will not be displeased with an account of the incident which gave birth to that ballad. Your conjecture that it was founded on the real history of an unhappy woman is true. . . . It was some time after this that I chanced to look into a comedy of Fletcher's called "The Knight of the Burning Pestle." The place I fell upon was where old Merrythought repeats these verses:—

When it was grown to dark midnight,
And all were fast asleep,
In came Margaret's grimly ghost,
And stood at William's feet.

which I fancy was the beginning of some ballad commonly known at the time this author wrote. These lines, naked of ornament, and simple as they are, struck my fancy; I closed the book, and bethought myself that the unhappy adventure I have mentioned above, which then came fresh into my mind, might naturally raise a tale upon the appearance of this ghost. It was then midnight. All around me was still and quiet. These concurring circumstances worked my soul to a powerful melancholy. I could not sleep. And at that time I finished my little poem, such as you see it here.—MALLOCH, DAVID, 1724, *Letter to the Plain Dealer, July* 24.

Poor Mallet! I pity his misfortune and feel for him probably more than he does for himself at present. His "William and Margaret," his only good piece of poetry, is torn from him, and by the evidence of old Manuscripts turns out to be the work of the celebrated Andrew Marvel composed in the year 1670.—GIBBON, EDWARD, 1776, *Private Letters, vol.* I, *p.* 283.

The ballad supposed to be lost has been lately recovered, in a copy of the date 1711, with the title "William and Margaret, an Old Ballad," and turns out to be substantially the piece which Mallet published as his own in 1724, Mallet's changes being comparatively slight. "William and Margaret" is simply "Fair Margaret and Sweet William" rewritten in what used to be called an elegant style. —CHILD, FRANCIS JAMES, 1885, *ed., The English and Scottish Popular Ballads, pt.* iii, *p.* 199.

David Mallet's literary reputation is chiefly due to a piece of poetry which he never wrote. "William and Margaret" was one of the most popular ballads of the eighteenth century. It appeared in nearly all the numerous miscellanies, both poetic and musical; it was read, sung, and recited on all sides. It was even parodied. With the exception of a few skeptical and unimportant personages, its authorship was universally attributed to Mallet, and men like James Thomson, Dr. Johnson, and Bishop Percy gave him the weight of their authority. The ballad floated all the rest of Mallet's literary performances, and he died a famous man. . . . As has been said, it was "William and Margaret" that established Mallet's literary reputation; and it is only within a few years that his claim to its authorship has been successfully assailed. We shall see unfolded one of the prettiest cases of literary forgery on record, as well as one of the meanest, for it took a great deal of deliberate lying on Mallet's part to make good his claim. . . . The proof of the forgery did not come till the year 1878, when a black-letter copy of the old ballad of "William and Margaret" was brought to light. This copy bears a Queen Anne stamp, and *on this stamp* rests the evidence against Mallet. In 1711 an act of Parliament was passed requiring stamps upon newspapers. This Act was not meant to apply to ballads, and, as Mr. Chappell says, "they were speedily excepted from its operation." This ballad is exactly the same as the one published in Mallet's works, with the exception of a few verbal alterations. It could not have been written by Mallet, for he would have been more than a marvel of precocity to produce such a thing at the age of eleven or twelve years. This Queen Anne stamp completely disposes of Mallet's claim; and thus it is altogether probable that "William and Margaret," as it stands, is one of the old English ballads, and not an eighteenth century production at all. . . . "William and Margaret" has an importance, independent of its authorship, as contributing to the early hidden growth of the English Romantic movement. Its great popularity in "the age of prose and reason" shows that there was a love for poetry of this kind, however much fashion condemned it in the abstract. For its introduction to the public, we must be grateful to Aaron Hill —a pompous, short-sighted person—and Allan Ramsay—a sturdy, unscrupulous, half-vulgar fellow. They builded better than they knew.—PHELPS, WILLIAM LYON, 1893, *The Beginnings of the English Romantic Movement, Appendix II., pp.* 177, 180, 182.

Mr. Child says that Mallet passed off as

his own, with very slight changes, a ballad called "William and Margaret," a copy of which, dated 1711, has been discovered. But the resemblances between the two poems scarcely seem to justify Mr. Child's criticism, though Gibbon's statement confirms it. The writer of the article on Mallet, in the "Dictionary of National Biography," throws no doubts upon Mallet being the author of "William and Margaret," nor does the writer on Marvell, in the same series, lay any claim for Marvell to its authorship. Thomas, better known as "Hesiod," Cooke, who published his "Life and Writings of Andrew Marvell" in 1726, and who not only disliked Mallet, but characterised his "William and Margaret" as "trash," nowhere suggests that Mallet was not the author.—PROTHERO, ROWLAND E., 1896, *Private Letters of Edward Gibbon, vol.* I, *p.* 283, *note.*

GENERAL

The nauseous affectation of expressing everything pompously and poetically, is nowhere more visible than in a poem lately published, entitled "Amyntor and Theodora."—WARTON, JOSEPH, 1756, *Essay on the Genius and Writings of Pope, vol.* I, *p.* 147.

Next Mallet came; Mallet who knows each art
The ear to tickle and to soothe the heart;
Who with a goose-quill, like a magic rod,
Transforms a Scotish peer into a god.
Oh! matchless Mallet, by one stroke to clear,
One lucky stroke, four hundred pounds a year.
Long round a court poor Gay dependent hung
(And yet more trimly has the poet sung),
Twice six revolving years vain hoping pass'd,
And unrewarded went away at last.
—SHAW, CUTHBERT, 1766, *The Race.*

As a writer, he cannot be placed in any high class. There is no species of composition in which he was eminent. His Dramas had their day, a short day, and are forgotten; his blank verse seems to my ear the echo of Thomson. . . . His works are such as a writer, bustling in the world, showing himself in public, and emerging occasionally from time to time into notice, might keep alive by his personal influence; but which, conveying little information, and giving no great pleasure, must soon give way, as the succession of things produce new topics of conversation and other modes of amusement.—JOHNSON, SAMUEL, 1779–81, *Mallet, Lives of the English Poets.*

Mallet's literary reputation did not live long, and one contemporary at least was not too severe in calling him a "whiffler in poetry" (Cooke). Johnson told Goldsmith that he "had talents enough to keep his literary reputation alive as long as he himself lived," and he has worked out the same idea in his criticism in the "Lives." His lack of originality justified the sorry joke of the aggrieved Theobald, "that there is no more conceit in him than in a mallet" (edit. of *Shakespeare*, 1733, Pref. lii); and Hume's dictum, that "he was destitute of the pathetic," would not be difficult to prove. At times his lines show the cadence of Pope's verse (e. g. "Verbal Criticism"), and his tragedies echo the fuller rhythm of his friend's "Seasons;" but his *motif* is always poor. His early ballad of "William and Margaret," and the claim set up on his behalf to the authorship of the national ode of "Rule Britannia," alone give him any title to posthumous recognition.—SMITH, G. GREGORY, 1893, *Dictionary of National Biography, vol.* XXXV, *p.* 427.

Was little better than a mere parrot.—WALKER, HUGH, 1893, *Three Centuries of Scottish Literature, vol.* II, *p.* 49.

It is a far cry from Mallet's "System of Runic Mythology" to William Morris' "Sigurd the Volsung" (1877), but to Mallet belongs the credit of first exciting that interest in Scandinavian antiquity which has enriched the prose and poetry not only of England but of Europe in general. Gray refers to him in his notes on 'The Descent of Odin," and his work, continued to be popular authority on its subject for at least half a century. Scott cites it in his annotations on "The Lay of the Last Minstrel" (1805).—BEERS, HENRY A., 1898, *A History of English Romanticism in the Eighteenth Century, p.* 191.

"Edwin and Emma," though not so good, was long as famous as "William and Margaret," and all but a few of Mallet's more numerous pieces in the lighter style show the grace and wit which belongs to the now too-much-neglected lighter verse of the eighteenth century.—SAINTSBURY, GEORGE, 1898, *A Short History of English Literature, p.* 578.

James Grainger

1721?-1766

Born probably at Duns, Berwickshire, in 1721(?): died at St. Christopher, West Indies, Dec. 16, 1766. A Scottish physician and poet. After 1753 he settled in London, where he became intimate with Johnson and other famous men. In 1759 he went to the West Indies. He published a number of works, including essays, etc., on medicine. Among his poems are an "Ode on Solitude" (in Dodsley's collection, 1755), and "The Sugar Cane" (1764). He translated part of Ovid's "Epistles" (1758), and the "Elegies of Tibullus" and the poems of Sulpicia (1759). He assisted, with others, Charlotte Lenox in her translation of Brumoy's "Théâtre des Grecs" (1759).—SMITH, BENJAMIN E., *ed.* 1894–97, *The Century Cyclopedia of Names, p.* 453.

PERSONAL

A man of modesty and reserve and in spite of a broad provincial dialect, extremely pleasing in his conversation. He was tall, and of a lathy make; plain-featured, and deeply marked with small-pox; his eyes were quiet and keen; his temper generous and good-natured; and he was an able man in the knowledge of his profession.—ANON, 1773, *Westminster Review.*

In person he was tall and of "a lathy make," plain-featured, and deeply marked with the small-pox. Despite a broad provincial accent his conversation was very pleasing. By his wife he left two daughters, Louise Agnes, and Eleanor. The latter was married in 1798 to Thomas Rousell of Wandsworth. A foul attack on Mrs. Grainger, imputing her husband's premature death to grief at the discovery of her immorality, was published during her lifetime in the "Westminster Magazine" for December 1773. Percy sent an indignant denial to the "Whitehall Evening Post," and threatened legal proceedings, upon which the libel was withdrawn and apologised for in January 1774. Grainger bequeathed his manuscripts to Percy.—GOODWIN, GORDON, 1890, *Dictionary of National Biography, vol.* XXII, *p.* 369.

GENERAL

Johnson said, that Dr. Grainger was an agreeable man; a man who would do any good that was in his power. His translation of "Tibullus," he thought, was very well done; but "The Sugar-Cane," a poem, did not please him; for, he exclaimed, "What could he make of a sugar-cane? One might as well write the 'Parsley-bed, a Poem;' or 'The Cabbage-garden, a Poem.'"—JOHNSON, SAMUEL, 1776, *Life by Boswell, ed. Hill, vol.* II, *p.* 520.

Mr. Chalmers censures Grainger for having chosen the sugar cane as the subject of a didactic poem: "connected," he says, "as an English merchant may be with the produce of the West Indies, it will not be easy to persuade the reader of English poetry to study the cultivation of the sugar plant, merely that he may add some new imagery to the more ample stores which he can contemplate without study or trouble." The critic's objection is not to the kind of poem, but to the particular subject; now it would be impossible to select any subject for that kind which is capable of being so richly and variously adorned. If Grainger has invoked the muse to sing of rats, and metamorphosed, in Arcadian phrase, negro slaves into swains, the fault is in the writer, not in the topic. The arguments which he has prefixed are indeed ludicrously flat and formal.—SOUTHEY, ROBERT, 1814, *Chalmers's English Poets, Quarterly Review, vol.* XI, *p.* 489.

The novelty of West Indian scenery inspired him with the unpromising subject of the Sugar-cane, in which he very poetically dignifies the poor negroes with the name of "*Swains.*"—CAMPBELL, THOMAS, 1819, *Specimens of the British Poets,.*

Grainger possess'd a true poetic vein,
But why waste numbers on a Sugar-cane?
Say, Doctor, why, since those who only need
Thy blank instructions, sure will never read?
—COLERIDGE, HARTLEY, 1849, *Sketches of English Poets, Poems, vol.* II, *p.* 304.

The two exact contemporaries of Akenside claim mention here only on the strength of one fine lily apiece—James Grainger a didactic West Indian sugar-planting physician, having published in 1755 an "Ode to Solitude," before he began to sing of canes and swains in tedious couplets.—GOSSE, EDMUND, 1888, *A History of Eighteenth Century Literature, p.* 312.

Thomas Birch

1705–1766

Thomas Birch was born in the parish of St. John, Clerkenwell, on the twenty-third of November, 1705. His father was a quaker, coffee-mill maker, but the son's fondness for learning early became so great, that, rather than follow the calling of his father, he left his home, became assistant in Hernel Hampstead school, and there received his education. He had hitherto adhered to the tenets of the quakers, but he now abandoned them, and was soon after ordained, by the bishop of Salisbury. He rose very rapidly in the church, and being honoured with the degree of a doctor of divinity, by the Marischal College of Aberdeen, he became a very considerable personage. He died by a fall from his horse, between London and Hampstead, on the ninth of January, 1766. Dr. Birch wrote the "Historical Memoirs and Lives" of Queen Elizabeth, Raleigh, Boyle, Tillotson, and Henry, Prince of Wales, besides a "History of the Royal Society," of which he was one of the secretaries. He was a diligent explorer of records and public papers: he threw light on history, but was destitute of taste, and the skill of historical arrangement.—MILLS, ABRAHAM, 1851, *The Literature and the Literary Men of Great Britain and Ireland, vol.* II, *p.* 529.

PERSONAL

The mental endowments of Dr. Birch were singular; he had a great eagerness after knowledge, and a memory very retentive of facts; but his learning, properly so called, bore no proportion to his reading; for he was in truth neither a mathematician, a natural philosopher, a classical scholar, nor a divine; but, in a small degree, all, and though lively in conversation, he was but a dull writer. Johnson was used to speak of him in this manner: "Tom is a lively rogue; he remembers a great deal, and can tell many pleasant stories; but a pen is to Tom a torpedo, the touch of it benumbs his hand and his brain: Tom can talk; but he is no writer." . . . In the midst of all his labours and pursuits, Dr. Birch preserved an even temper of mind, and a great cherfulness of spirits. Ever desirous to learn, and willing to communicate, he was uniformly affable, courteous, and disposed to conversation. His life was spent without reproach, but terminated by an unhappy accident, a fall from his horse on the Hampstead road, on the 9th day of January, 1766.—HAWKINS, SIR JOHN, 1787, *Life of Samuel Johnson, p.* 209.

GENERAL

Dr. Birch being mentioned, he said, he had more anecdotes than any man. I said, Percy had a great many; that he flowed with them like one of the brooks here. *Johnson.*—"If Percy is like one of the brooks here, Birch was like the river Thames. Birch excelled Percy in that, as much as Percy excels Goldsmith."—BOSWELL, JAMES, 1773, *The Journal of a Tour to the Hebrides, ed. Hill, Sept.* 24, *p.* 290.

Was a worthy, good-natured soul, full of industry and activity, and running about like a young setting-dog in quest of anything, new or old, and with no parts, taste, or judgment.—WALPOLE, HORACE, 1780, *To Rev. William Cole, Feb.* 5; *Letters, ed. Cunningham, vol.* VII, *p.* 326.

Dr. Birch was a writer with no genius for composition, but one to whom British history stands more indebted than to any superior author; his incredible love of labour, in transcribing with his own hand a large library of manuscripts from originals dispersed in public and in private repositories, has enriched the British Museum by thousands of the most authentic documents of genuine secret history.—DISRAELI, ISAAC, 1791–1824, *True Sources of Secret History, Curiosities of Literature.*

An industrious and faithful Dryasdust.—MINTO, WILLIAM, 1872–80, *Manual of English Prose Literature, p.* 434.

He collected a great amount of materials, literary and historical, and deserves honourable mention in any retrospect of British literature.—CHAMBERS, ROBERT, 1876, *Cyclopædia of English Literature, ed. Carruthers.*

Walpole's censure, though exaggerated, rests on a bias of truth, but the fact remains that, in spite of their wearisome minuteness of detail and their dulness of style, the works of Dr. Birch are indispensable to the literary or historical student.—COURTNEY, W. P., 1886, *Dictionary of National Biography, vol.* V, *p.* 69.

John Leland

1691–1766

John Leland, D. D., 1691–1766, a Presbyterian minister, settled in Dublin, is distinguished as a writer of apologetics. Some of his works in defence of Christianity are considered as among the best that have ever been written. The following are the chief: "A Defence of Christianity," in answer to Tindal; "The Divine Authority of the Old and New Testament Asserted," in answer to Morgan; "Remarks on Christianity not Founded on Argument," in answer to Dodwell; "Remarks on Bolingbroke's Letters on the Study and Use of History;" "A View of the Deistical Writers," "The Advantage and Necessity of the Christian Revelation," etc. Leland's "View of the Deistical Writers" is especially celebrated.—HART, JOHN S., 1872, *A Manual of English Literature, p.* 258.

GENERAL

Every one who wishes to make himself master of the Deistical controversy will carefully study Leland's "Divine Authority of the Old and New Testament" and his "View of the Deistical Writers;" yet Leland's greatest and most useful work is his "Necessity and Advantages of the Christian Revelation." He who desires to know the full value of the Bible should above all things study this book. It contains the latest and maturest thoughts of the very able author.—WILLIAMS, EDWARD, 1800, *The Christian Preacher.*

Leland's "Advantages and Necessity of the Christian Revelation" is a work full of information as to the state of religion among the Heathen. His other works in defence of religion are useful. . . . An able champion of the Christian faith.—BICKERSTETH, EDWARD, 1844, *The Christian Student.*

His "View of the Deistical Writers" (1754), a brief work written in a spirit of praiseworthy moderation, is still a textbook for students of divinity. His great work, "On the Advantage and Necessity of a Christian Revelation" (1764), is long since forgotten. — MINTO, WILLIAM, 1872–80, *Manual of English Prose Literature p.* 427.

Is ["View of the Deistical Writers"] a solid and valuable treatise, and is still regarded as one of the best confutations of infidelity.—CHAMBERS, ROBERT, 1876, *Cyclopædia of English Literature, ed. Carruthers.*

The question raised by such books as Leland's is how such writing can ever have been popular.—STEPHEN, LESLIE, 1876, *History of English Thought in the Eighteenth Century, vol.* I, *p.* 158.

William Thompson

1712?–1766?

Graduated at Queen's College, Oxford (of which he became Fellow), 1738; succeeded to the livings of South Westen and Hampton Poyle, Oxfordshire; became Dean of Raphoe, Ireland, and died there about 1766. In 1734 and 1736 he wrote "Stella, sive Amores, Tres Libri, and Six Pastorals," none of which he included in his collective edition of his "Poems." He afterwards published: 1. "Sickness; a Poem," London, 1745. 2. "Gondibert and Birtha; a Tragedy," 1751. 3. "Gratitude; a Poem," Oxford, 1756. See No. 4. 4. "Poems on several Occasions; to which is added Gondibert and Birtha, a Tragedy," 1758, 2 vols. Of more than ordinary merit. His "Hymn to May," and his "Nativity," (in which he is thought to approach Spenser), and his poem on "Sickness," were once highly valued. . . . He superintended an edition of Bishop Joseph Hall's "Virgidemarium," Oxford, 1753, and left MS. "Notes and Observations on William Browne's Works," which appeared in the edition of 1772, London, 3 vols., edited, when published, by T. Davies, the publisher.—ALLIBONE, S. AUSTIN, 1870, *A Critical Dictionary of English Literature, vol.* III, *p.* 2395.

PERSONAL

Concerning William Thompson, we may add to the short notices collected by Mr. Chalmers, that he was educated at Appleby school, under Yates, a man who obtained the appellation of the Northern Busby. Yates would always insist upon his spelling his name without the *p*, saying, you could *thomp, thomp*, upon one's ear with your *Thompson*. The poet, however, persisted in retaining a letter which serves at least the purpose of distinguishing his written name from that of the author of the Seasons.—SOUTHEY, ROBERT, 1814, *Chalmer's English Poets, Quarterly Review, vol.* XI, *p.* 490.

GENERAL

Among those who have written in the style of Spenser, I do not hesitate to name Thompson as being one of the most successful. His three poems, the "Epithalamium," the "Nativity," and the "Hymn to May," especially the last two, have many of the qualities which distinguish the captivating poet whose manner he adopted. In his "Hymn to May" he displays such an exuberance of rich imagery, such a felicity of fanciful description, and he pours forth his feelings in so joyous a spirit, and in strains so flowing, that the charms and praises of the delightful season which inspires him, were never sung with more elegance, or more animation. Of the minor poems it is necessary to say little more than that, with a few exceptions, they do not discredit the talent of the writer. The panegyric on Pope is rather overcharged; and it is curious that the poet should have chosen to celebrate Pope in blank verse, and Glover in rhyme. —DAVENPORT, R. A., 1822, *The Poems of William Thompson, Chiswick, ed., Life, p.* 14.

William Thompson is a poet almost completely forgotten to-day, but he was one of the best of the Spenserians. Little is known of his life; the dates of his birth and death are uncertain; but he was born in the early part of the century, and died before 1767. He was a careful and enthusiastic student of the old English poets. From early youth he admired Spenser and imitated him in three poems. Although Thompson was really filled with the Romantic spirit, it is worthy of note that he was also extravagantly fond of Pope—another instance of the unconsciousness of English Romanticism. Besides Thompson's Spenserian imitations, he wrote a number of graceful songs, and his "Ode Brumalis" shows him to have been an intense lover of Shakespere. He might also have been classed among the blank-verse school, for he wrote a long poem in that measure, with the not particularly attractive title of "Sickness." He wrote in the stanza of the "Fairy Queen" not for his idle amusement, or to exercise his poetic ingenuity, but because his mind was richly stored with the treasures of old English poetry.—PHELPS, WILLIAM LYON, 1893, *The Beginnings of the English Romantic Movement, pp.* 57, 61.

Thompson was a close imitator of Spenser, and marred his work by the needless use of archaic words and phrases. His "Hymn to May," his "Nativity," and his poem on "Sickness" were once highly esteemed.—CARLYE, E. IRVING, 1898, *Dictionary of National Biography, vol.* LVI, *p.* 227.

Laurence Sterne

1713–1768

Born, at Clonmel, 24 Nov. 1713. At school at Halifax, 1723–31. Matriculated Jesus College, Cambridge, 1732; Sizarship, July 1733; Scholar, July 1734; B. A., Jan. 1736; M. A., 1740. Ordained Deacon, March 1736; Priest, Aug. 1738. Vicar of Sutton-on-the-Forest, Yorks., 1738. Prebendary of York Cathedral, Jan. 1741. Married Elizabeth Lumley, 30 March 1741. Vicar of Stillington, 1741. Curate of Coxwold, Yorks., 1760. Lived mainly in France, 1762–67. Died, in London, 18 March 1768. Buried in Burial Ground of St. George's, Hanover Square. *Works:* "The Case of Elijah and the Widow of Zarephath considered," 1747; "The Abuses of Conscience," 1750; "The Life and Opinions of Tristram Shandy" (9 vols.), 1759–67; "The Sermons of Mr. Yorick" (7 vols.), 1760–69; "A Sentimental Journey through France and Italy, by Mr. Yorick" (2 vols.), 1768. *Posthumous:* "The History of a Good Warm Watch-coat," 1769; "Letters . . . to his Most Intimate Friends," ed. by his daughter (3 vols.), 1775; "Letters from Yorick to Eliza," 1775; "Letters to his Friends on various occasions," 1775; "Original Letters, never before published," 1788; "Seven Letters written by Sterne and his Friends, hitherto unpublished" (priv. ptd.), 1844. *Collected Works:* ed. by G. Saintsbury (6 vols.), 1894. *Life:* by P. H. Fitzgerald, 1864.—SHARP, R. FARQUHARSON, 1897, *A Dictionary of English Authors, p.* 269.

PERSONAL

"Tristram Shandy" is still a greater object of admiration, the man as well as the book. One is invited to dinner, where he dines, a fortnight beforehand. His portrait is done by Reynolds, and now engraving. "Tristram Shandy," Dodsley gives £700 for a second edition, and two new volumes not yet written; and to-morrow will come out two volumes of "Sermons" by him. Your friend, Mr. Hall has printed two Lyric Epistles, one to my Cousin Shandy on his coming to town, the other to the grown gentlewomen, the Misses of York: they seem to me to be absolute madness.—GRAY, THOMAS, 1760, *Letter to Thomas Wharton, April* 22; *Works, ed. Gosse, vol.* III, *p.* 36.

It having been observed that there was little hospitality in London;—*Johnson:* "Nay, Sir, any man who has a name, or who has the power of pleasing, will be generally invited in London. The man, Sterne, I have been told, has had engagements for three months." *Goldsmith:* "And a very dull fellow." *Johnson:* "Why, no, Sir."—JOHNSON, SAMUEL, 1760, *Life by Boswell, ed. Hill, vol.* II, *p.* 254.

The fellow himself is an irrecoverable scoundrel.—WARBURTON, WILLIAM, 1761, *To Dr. Hurd, Dec.* 27; *Letters from a Late Eminent Prelate.*

Lord Ossory told us that the famous Dr. Sterne dyed that morning; he seem'd to lament him very much. Lord Eglinton said (but not in a ludicrous manner), that he had taken his "Sentimental Journey." —COKE, LADY MARY, 1768, *Letters and Journals, vol.* II, *p.* 216.

Shall pride a heap of sculptured marble raise,
Some worthless, unmourned, titled fool to praise,
And shall we not by one poor gravestone learn
Where genius, wit, and humor sleep with Sterne?
— GARRICK, DAVID, 1779? *Epitaph on Laurence Sterne.*

The celebrated writer Sterne, after being long the idol of this town, died in a mean lodging without a single friend who felt interest in his fate except Becket, his bookseller, who was the only person that attended his interment. He was buried in a graveyard near Tyburn, belonging to the parish of Marylebone, and the corpse being marked by some of the *resurrection men* (as they are called), was taken up soon afterwards and carried to an anatomy professor of Cambridge. A gentleman who was present at the dissection told me, he recognized Sterne's face the moment he saw the body.—MALONE, EDMOND, 1783, *Maloniana, ed. Prior, p.* 373.

In the month of January, 1768, we set off for London. We stopped for some time at Almack's house, in Pall-mall. My master afterwards took Sir James Gray's house in Clifford-street, who was going ambassador to Spain. He now began housekeeping, hired a French cook, house-maid, kitchen-maid, and kept a great deal of the best company. About this time, Mr. Sterne, the celebrated author, was taken ill at the silk-bag shop in Old Bond-street. He was sometimes called Tristram Shandy, and sometimes Yorick, a very great favourite of the gentleman's. One day my master had company to dinner, who were speaking about him: the Duke of Roxburgh, the Earl of March, the Earl of Ossory, the Duke of Grafton, Mr. Garrick, Mr. Hume, and Mr. James. "John," said my master, "go and inquire how Mr. Sterne is to-day." I went, returned, and said, "I went to Mr. Sterne's lodging—the mistress opened the door—I enquired how he did. She told me to go up to the nurse; I went into the room, and he was just a-dying. I waited ten minutes; but in five, he said, "Now it is come!" He put up his hand, as if to stop a blow, and died in a minute. The gentlemen were all very sorry, and lamented him very much.—MACDONALD, JAMES, 1790, *The Life of a Footman.*

We are well acquainted with Sterne's features and personal appearance, to which he himself frequently alludes. He was tall and thin, with a hectic and consumptive appearance. His features, though capable of expressing with peculiar effect the sentimental emotions by which he was often affected, had also a shrewd, humorous, and sarcastic character, proper to the wit and the satirist, and not unlike that which predominates in the portraits of Voltaire. His conversation was animated, and witty; but Johnson complained that it was marked by licence, better suiting the company of the Lord of Crazy Castle, than of the great moralist. It has been said, and probably with truth, that his temper was variable and unequal, the natural consequence of an irritable bodily frame, and continued bad health. But we will not readily believe that the parent of Uncle Toby could be a harsh, or habitually bad-humoured man. Sterne's letters to his friends, and especially to his daughter, breathe all the fondness of affection; and his resources, such as they were, seem to have been always at the command of those whom he loved.—SCOTT, SIR WALTER, 1821, *Laurence Sterne.*

So infamous was his private character, that when he entered the pulpit to preach in York Minister, of which he was a prebend, many of the congregation rose from their seats and left the cathedral. His conduct and temper so much provoked his wife, a loving and patient woman, that she was compelled to live away from him. With health so broken that his continued existence appeared almost miraculous, he entered into an intrigue with a married woman, and, at the age of 54, openly speculating on the prospect of marrying her, when his own wife as well as the lady's husband should die! The only redeeming feeling in his life, was his devoted love for his daughter, for whom, however, he made not the slightest provision. He died, in lodgings in London, and his attendants robbed him of his gold shirt-buttons as he lay helpless in bed. His letters, which fully expressed his profligacy, were published, seven years after his death, by his daughter—so reduced to poverty by his extravagance that she was compelled to barter his reputation for bread. It is almost inexplicable how such a man as Sterne could have lived so loosely and produced such a pure-minded original as My Uncle Toby, and such a faithful serving man as Corporal Trim, maternal grandfather to Sam Weller, in all probability.—MACKENZIE, R. SHELTON, 1854, *ed., Noctes Ambrosianæ, vol.* IV, *p.* 214, *note.*

His patient courtship shows that he was truly in love with his wife. Their marriage, in the face of inauspicious circumstances, proves that they were both in earnest; and his frank acknowledgment, a year after, that he was tired of his conjugal partner, argues no uncommon experience, but a rare and unjustifiable candor.—TUCKERMAN, HENRY T., 1857, *Essays, Biographical and Critical, p.* 318.

And Irishman by birth, and a Yorkshire clergyman by profession, but with a somewhat unclerical, if not a cracked reputation.—MASSON, DAVID, 1859, *British Novelists and Their Styles, p.* 106.

The body of the unfortunate Mr. Sterne was but a poor prize for purposes of dissection. He speaks of his spider legs himself, and the portrait and description of him give one the idea of a lean and emaciated presence.—COLLINS, CHARLES, ALLSTON, 1860, *Poet's Corner, Macmillan's Magazine, vol.* 2, *p.* 133.

What a close to Yorick's strange career, which began in wanderings, and brought him back thus finally to his old University! There is even a grim lurid Shandeism over the scene, a charnel-house humour in that recognition of the strange lean Yorick features—more lean in death—upon the dissecting table. But the evidence on which the story is founded seems too convincing not to be accepted. There had been many indistinct shapes of the statement—some improbable—but all pointing indistinctly in that direction. — FITZGERALD, PERCY, 1864, *The Life of Laurence Sterne, vol.* II, *p.* 406.

Hair-brained, light-hearted, and sanguine,—pleased with himself, his whims, follies, and foibles,—he treated misfortune as a passing guest, and even extracted amusement from it while it stayed. He tells us that it was by mirth that he fenced against his physical infirmities, persuaded that every time a man laughed he added something to his fragment of life; and so at Paris he laughed till he cried, and believed that his lungs had been improved by the process as much as by the change of air.—MATHEWS, WILLIAM, 1881, *Literary Style, p.* 74.

As to the nature of Sterne's love-affairs I have come, though not without hesitation, to the conclusion that they were most, if not all of them, what is called, somewhat absurdly, Platonic. In saying this, however, I am by no means prepared to assert that they would all of them have passed muster before a prosaic and unsentimental British jury as mere indiscretions, and nothing worse. . . . But, as I am not of those who hold that the conventionally "innocent" is the equivalent of the morally harmless in this matter,

I cannot regard the question as worth any very minute investigation. I am not sure that the habitual male flirt, who neglects his wife to sit continually languishing at the feet of some other woman, gives much less pain and scandal to others, or does much less mischief to himself and the objects of his adoration, than the thorough-going profligate; and I even feel tempted to risk the apparent paradox that, from the artistic point of view, Sterne lost rather than gained by the generally Platonic character of his amours. For, as it was, the restraint of one instinct of his nature implied the over-indulgence of another which stood in at least as much need of chastenment. If his love-affairs stopped short of the gratification of the senses, they involved a perpetual fondling and caressing of those effeminate sensibilities of his into that condition of hyper-æsthesia which, though Sterne regarded it as the strength, was in reality the weakness, of his art.—TRAILL, H. D., 1882, *Sterne (English Men of Letters)*, *pp.* 28, 29.

This burial-ground of St. George's Hanover Square, situated in Oxford Street, between Albion and Stanhope Streets, is not so wretched and deserted as Mr. Traill describes it. It is green and well cared for. Entirely shut out from the streets by high walls and houses, its very existence unknown to the thousands who pass by it daily, it is as quiet, secluded, and peaceful as a country churchyard, and in refreshing contrast with some of the modern garish cemeteries of the metropolis. Sterne's memorial, a high but plain flat stone, stands next to the centre of the west wall of the grounds, under a spreading flourishing old tree, whose lower branches and leaves almost touch it. The inscription is worth preserving, and is here given entire:—

"Alas, Poor Yorick.
Near to this Place
Lies the body of
The Reverend Laurence Sterne
Dyed September 13 1768
Aged 53 Years.
Ah! Molliter, ossa quiescant.

If a sound head, warm heart and breast humane,
Unsully'd worth, and soul without a stain,
If mental powers could ever justly claim
The well won tribute of immortal fame,
Sterne was the Man who with gigantic stride
Mow'd down luxuriant follies far and wide,
Yet what though keenest knowledge of mankind
Unseal'd to him the Springs that move the mind.
What did it boot him, Ridicul'd, abus'd
By foes insulted and by prudes accus'd.
In his, mild reader view thy future fate,
Like him despise what t'were a sin to hate.

This monumental stone was erected to the memory of the deceased by two *Brother Masons*, for although he did not live to be a member of their *Society*, yet all his uncomparable Performances evidently prove him to have acted by *Rule* and *Square;* they rejoice in this opportunity of perpetuating his high and unapproachable character to after ages.—W. & S."—HUTTON, LAURENCE, 1885, *Literary Landmarks of London*, *p.* 293.

Of all the classical English writers, there is no other, perhaps, who fares so hardly in the present age as Sterne. It would scarcely be an exaggeration to say that his faults, both as man and author, are the very faults for which this age has the least charity, and that his virtues, both as man and author, are those which at present are least esteemed. Sterne is undeniably loose, sometimes even indecent, in his writings, and, viewed in the light of a parish priest, he falls infinitely below what is now required of a person in that position. The Rev. Laurence Sterne probably never in his life presided at a mothers' meeting, or held a week-day service, or fasted for the sake of religion. Moreover, Sterne's reputation has received some savage thrusts from writers who were competent to do it great injury. . . . Above all, Sterne failed to take either himself or the world seriously; and that, from our present point of view, is almost an unpardonable fault. If Sterne had formulated his paganism in a system, writing two or three dull, serious volumes about it; if, instead of flirting with every pretty woman who came in his way, he had simply broken two or three hearts for his own edification, after the manner of Goethe,—if such had been his course, we would find it easier to appreciate him.—MERWIN, HENRY CHILDS, 1894, *The Philosophy of Sterne, Atlantic Monthly*, *vol.* 74, *pp.* 521, 522.

At Coxwold, fourteen miles from York and in the deeper depths of the shire, that we find many remaining objects that were associated with his work and with that portion of his life which chiefly concerns the literary world. . . . Within the hamlet we find a low-eaved road-side inn, and by it the shaded green where rural festivals were held, and where, to celebrate the coronation of George III., Sterne had an ox roasted whole and served with great quantities of ale to his parishioners. Just beyond, Sterne's church stands intact upon a gentle eminence, overlooking a lovely pastoral landscape bounded by verdant hills. The church dates from the fifteenth century and is a pleasing structure of perpendicular Gothic style, with a shapely octagonal tower embellished with fretted pinnacles and a parapet of graceful design. One window has been filled with stained glass, but Sterne's pulpit remains, and the interior of the edifice is scarcely changed since he preached here his quaint sermons. The walls are plain; the low ceiling is divided by beams whose intersections are marked by grotesque bosses; the whole effect is depressing, and to the sensitive "Yorick"—haunted as he was by habitual dread that his ministrations might provoke a fatal pulmonary hemorrhage—it must have been dismal indeed. Among the effigied tombs of the Fauconbergs which line the chancel we find that of Sterne's friend who gave him this living. Beyond the church and near the highway stands the quaint and picturesque old edifice where dwelt Sterne during the eight famous years of his life. In his letters he calls it Castle Shandy, and in all the countryside it is now known as Shandy Hall, shandy meaning in the local dialect crack-brained. It is a long, rambling, low-eaved fabric, with many heavy gables and chimmeys, and steep roofs of tiles. —WOLFE, THEODORE F., 1895, *A Literary Pilgrimage, pp.* 113, 114.

Sterne's reasoning faculty was incapable of controlling his constitutional sensitiveness to pain and pleasure. His deficiency in self-control induced a condition of moral apathy, and was the cause alike of the indecency and of the sentimentality which abounded in "Tristram Shandy" and the "Sentimental Journey." Both the indecency and the sentimentality, faithfully and without artifice reflected Sterne's emotional nature. The indelicate innuendoes which he foists on sedate words and situations, and the tears that he represented himself as shedding over dead asses and caged starlings, had an equally spontaneous origin in what was in him the normal state of his nerves. In itself—with the slightest possible reference to the exciting object—his sensibility evoked a pleasurable nervous excitement, and the fulness of the gratification that it generated in his own being discouraged him from seeking to translate its suggestions into act. The divorce of sensibility from practical benevolence will always justify charges of insincerity. All that can be pleaded in extenuation in Sterne's case is that he made no secret that his conduct was the sport of his emotional impulses, and, obeying no other promptings, was guided by no active moral sentiment. Gravity, he warned his readers, was foreign to his nature. Morality, which ordinarly checks the free play of feeling and passion by the exercise of virtuous reason, lay, he admitted, outside his sphere. Such infirmities signally unfitted him for the vocation of a teacher of religion, but his confessions remove hypocrisy from the list of his offences. His declared temperament renders it matter for surprise not that he so often disfigured his career as a husband and author by a wanton defiance of the accepted moral canons, but that he achieved so indisputable a nobility of sentiment as in his creation of Uncle Toby, and so unselfish a devotion as in his relations with his daughter. He was no "scamp" in any accepted use of the term, as Thackeray designates him. He was a volatile, self-centered, morally apathetic man of genius, who was not destitute of generous instincts.—LEE, SIDNEY, 1898, *Dictionary of National Biography, vol.* LIV, *p.* 216.

TRISTRAM SHANDY
1759–67

This day is published, printed on superfine writing paper, and a new letter, in two volumes, price 5s., neatly bound, *The Life and Opinions of Tristram Shandy, Gentleman. York.* Printed for and sold by John Hinxham (successor to the late Mr. Hilyard), Bookseller in Stonegate; J. Dodsley, in Pall-mall; and Mr. Cooper, in Paternoster-row, London; and by all the booksellers in Great Britain and Ireland.—PUBLICK ADVERTISER, 1760, *Jan.* 1.

Never poor wight of a Dedicator had less

hopes from his Dedication than I have from this of mine; for it is written in a bye-corner of the kingdom, and in a retir'd thatch'd house, where I live in a constant endeavour to fence against the infirmities of ill health, and other evils of life, by Mirth; being firmly persuaded, that every time a man smiles,—but much more so when he laughs,—it adds something to this Fragment of Life. I humbly beg, Sir, that you will honour this Book by taking it—(not under your Protection, —it must protect itself, but)—into the country with you; where, if I am ever told it has made you smile, or can conceive it has beguiled you of one moment's pain, —I shall think myself as happy as a Minister of State;—perhaps, much happier than any one (one only excepted) that I have read or heard of.

I am, great sir,
(and, what is more to your honour)
I am, good sir,
Your Well-wisher, and
most humble Fellow-subject.
THE AUTHOR.

—STERNE, LAURENCE, 1760, *The Life and Opinions of Tristram Shandy, Gent., Dedication.*

At present nothing is talked of, nothing admired, but what I cannot help calling a very insipid and tedious performance: it is a kind of novel, called "The Life and Opinions of Tristram Shandy;" the great humour of which consists in the whole narration always going backward. . . . It makes one smile two or three times at the beginning, but in recompense makes one yawn for two hours. The characters are tolerably kept up, but the humour is for ever attempted and missed.—WALPOLE, HORACE, 1760, *To Sir David Dalrymple, April* 4; *Letters, ed. Cunningham, vol.* III, *p.* 298.

There is much good fun in it, and humour sometimes hit and sometimes missed.—GRAY, THOMAS, 1760, *Letter to Thomas Wharton, July; Works, ed. Gosse, vol.* III, *p.* 53.

However, I pride myself in having warmly recommended "Tristram Shandy" to all the best company in town, except that of Arthur's. I was charged in a very grave assembly, as Doctor Newton can tell him, for a particular patronizer of the work, and how I acquitted myself of the imputation, the said Doctor can tell him. . . . If Mr. Sterne will take me with all my infirmities I shall be glad of the honour of being well known to him; and he has the additional recommendation of being your friend.—WARBURTON, WILLIAM, 1760, *Letter to David Garrick, March* 7.

"Bless me,"cries the man of industry, "now you speak of an epic poem, you shall see an excellent farce. Here it is; dip into it where you will, it will be found replete with true modern humour. Strokes, Sir: it is filled with strokes of wit and satire in every line." *Do you call all these dashes of the pen strokes,* repiled I, *for I must confess I can see no other?* "And pray, Sir," returned he, "what do you call them? Do you see anything good now-a-days that is not filled with strokes—and dashes?—Sir, a well-placed dash makes half the wit of our writers of modern humour. I bought the last season a piece that had no other merit upon earth than nine hundred and ninety-five breaks, seventy-two ha ha's, three good things and a garter. And yet it played off, and bounced, and cracked, and made more sport than a fire-work." . . . There are several very dull fellows, who, by a few mechanical helps, sometimes learn to become extremely brilliant and pleasing; with a little dexterity in the management of the eyebrows, fingers, and nose. By imitating a cat, a sow and pigs; by a loud laugh, and a slap on the shoulder, the most ignorant are furnished out for conversation. But the writer finds it impossible to throw his winks, his shrugs, or his attitudes, upon paper; he may borrow some assistance, indeed, by printing his face at the title page; but without wit to pass for a man of ingenuity, no other mechanical help but downright obscenity will suffice. By speaking to some peculiar sensations, we are always sure of exciting laughter, for the jest does not lie in the writer, but in the subject.—GOLDSMITH, OLIVER, 1762, *A Citizen of the World.*

Nothing odd will do long. "Tristram Shandy" did not last.—JOHNSON, SAMUEL, 1776, *Life by Boswell, ed. Hill, vol.* II, *p.* 521.

From beginning to end a piece of buffoonery after the style of Scarron.—VOLTAIRE, FRANÇOIS MARIE AROUET, 1777, *Journal de politique et de littérature, Apr.* 25.

Voltaire has compared the merits of Rabelais and Sterne as satirists of the abuse of learning, and I think has done neither of them justice. This great distinction is obvious: that Rabelais derided absurdities then existing in full force, and intermingled much sterling sense with the grossest parts of his book; Sterne, on the contrary, laughs at many exploded opinions and forsaken fooleries, and contrives to degrade some of his most solemn passages by a vicious levity. Rabelais flew a higher pitch, too, than Sterne. Great part of the voyage to the Pays de Lanternois, which so severely stigmatizes the vices of the Romish clergy of that age, was performed in more hazard of fire than water.—FERRIAR, JOHN, 1798–1812, *Illustrations of Sterne, with other Essays.*

If we consider Sterne's reputation as chiefly founded on "Tristram Shandy," he must be regarded as liable to two severe charges:—those, namely, of indecency, and of affectation. Upon the first accusation Sterne was himself peculiarly sore, and used to justify the licentiousness of his humour by representing it as a mere breach of decorum, which had no perilous consequence to morals. The following anecdote we have from a sure source:—Soon after Tristram had appeared, Sterne asked a Yorkshire lady of fortune and condition whether she had read his book. "I have not, Mr. Sterne," was the answer; "and, to be plain with you, I am informed it is not proper for female perusal."—"My dear good lady," replied the author, "do not be gulled by such stories; the book is like your young heir there (pointing to a child of three years old, who was rolling on the carpet in his white tunics), he shows at times a good deal that is usually concealed, but it is all in perfect innocence!" This witty excuse may be so far admitted; for it cannot be said that the licentious humour of "Tristram Shandy" is of the kind which applies itself to the passions, or is calculated to corrupt society. But it is a sin against taste, if allowed to be harmless as to morals. A handful of mud is neither a firebrand nor a stone; but to fling it about in sport, argues coarseness of mind, and want of common manners.—SCOTT, SIR WALTER, 1821, *Laurence Sterne.*

To my mind, Uncle Toby is the most perfect specimen of a Christian gentleman that ever existed. . . . Sir Charles Grandison is not to be compared to him. Mr. Shandy, an admirably-drawn character also, is cleverer than Uncle Toby; but "My Uncle" is the wisest man.—LESLIE, CHARLES ROBERT, 1840, *Autobiographical Recollections, p.* 318.

If I were requested to name the book of all others which combined wit and humour under their highest appearance of levity with the profoundest wisdom, it would be "Tristram Shandy."—HUNT, LEIGH, 1846, *Wit and Hnmour.*

One of the most fascinating, witty, and dangerous works that has ever been penned in the English language. It is fascinating from its nature and truth. Its wit is like no other man's wit. It is dangerous because, interwoven with an apparent simplicity of narrative is an insidious indelicacy, which it almost requires a commentary to point out; an indelicacy which never sullied one page of Goldsmith, and from which our great Scott would have shrunk in disgust. Take away this taint, if it be possible to do so, and "Tristram Shandy" is full of exquisite home scenes, and of touching incidents, and noble sentiments.—THOMSON, KATHERINE (GRACE WHARTON), 1862, *The Literature of Society, vol.* II, *p.* 290.

Even Jean Paul, the greatest of German humorous authors, and never surpassed in comic conception or in the pathetic quality of humor, is not to be named with his master, Sterne, as a creative humorist. What are Siebenkäs, Fixlein, Schmelzle, and Fibel, (a single lay-figure to be draped at will with whimsical sentiment and reflection, and put in various attitudes), compared with the living reality of Walter Shandy and his brother Toby, characters which we do not see merely as puppets in the author's mind, but poetically projected from it in an independent being of their own?—LOWELL, JAMES RUSSELL, 1866–90, *Lessing; Prose Works, Riverside ed., vol.* II, *p.* 170.

Figure to yourself a man who goes on a journey, wearing on his eyes a pair of marvellously magnifying spectacles. A hair on his hand, a speck on a tablecloth, a fold of a moving garment, will interest him: at this rate he will not go very far; he will go six steps in a day, and will not quit his room. So Sterne writes four volumes to record the birth of his hero. He perceives the infinitely little, and describes the imperceptible. A man parts his hair on one side: this, according to Sterne, depends on his whole character, which is a piece with that of his father, his mother, his uncle, and his whole ancestry; it depends on the structure of his brain, which depends on the circumstance of his conception and his birth, and these on the fancies of his parents, the humour of the moment, the talk of the preceding hour, the contrarieties of the last curate, a cut thumb, twenty knots made on a bag; I know not how many things besides. . . His book is like a great storehouse of articles of *virtu*, where the curiosities of all ages, kinds, and countries lie jumbled in a heap; texts of excommunication, medical consultations, passages of unknown or imaginary authors, scraps of scholastic erudition, strings of absurd histories, dissertations, addresses to the reader. His pen leads him; he has neither sequence nor plan; nay, when he lights upon anything orderly, he purposely contorts it; with a kick he sends the pile of folios next to him over the history he has commenced, and dances on the top of them.—TAINE, H. A., 1871, *History of English Literature, tr. Van Laun, vol.* II, *bk.* iii, *ch.* vi, *pp.* 179, 180.

It is to be hoped that Sterne made a judicious choice of the passages his daughter was to copy, and which his wife was to hear read. His admonition, when he sends to his Lydia, when far away from him, the Spectator and Metastassio, would tend to show that he would not expose her to the influence of the indelicate parts: and the virtuous and sedate character of his wife would not be likely to relish the innuendos and *double entendres* of his too prurient imagination; for she was not one of those fashionable ladies, who, he says, would read Tristram in the closet, though not in the drawing-room. Indeed his allusion to uncle Toby's character, only, would imply that he had kept out of their view those offensive passages, which outraged decency, even at a time when manners were not so remarkable for moral refinement as happily they are at the present day.—BROWNE, JAMES P., 1873, *ed., The Works of Laurence Sterne, Preface, vol.* I, *p.* viii.

In going over the list, a short list in any case, of the immortal characters in fiction, there is hardly any one in our literature who would be entitled to take precedence of him. To find a distinctly superior type, we must go back to Cervantes, whom Sterne idolised and professed to take for his model. But to speak of a character as in some sort comparable to Don Quixote, though without any thoughts of placing him on the same level, is to admire that he is a triumph of art. Indeed, if we take the other creator of types, of whom it is only permitted to speak with bated breath, we must agree that it would be difficult to find a figure even in the Shakespearean gallery more admirable in its way. Of course, the creation of a Hamlet, an Iago, or a Falstaff implies an intellectual intensity and reach of imaginative sympathy altogether different from anything which his warmest admirers would attribute to Sterne. I only say that there is no single character in Shakespeare whom we see more vividly and love more heartily than Mr. Shandy's uncle.—STEPHEN, LESLIE, 1880, *Hours in a Library, The Cornhill Magazine, vol.* 42, *p.* 88.

As to its morality, I know good people who love the book; but to me, when you sum it all up, its teaching is that a man may spend his life in low, brutish, inane pursuits and may have a good many little private sins on his conscience,—but will nevertheless be perfectly sure of heaven if he can have retained the ability to weep a maudlin tear over a tale of distress; or, in short, that a somwehat irritable state of the lachrymal glands will be cheerfully accepted by the Deity as a substitute for saving grace or a life of self-sacrifice.—LANIER, SIDNEY, 1881, *The English Novel, p.* 187.

A singular and brilliant medley of wit, sentiment, indecency, and study of character. . . . His borrowed plumage and his imitation of Rabelais' style apart, Sterne had originality, a gift at all times rare, and always, perhaps, becoming rarer. As a humorist, he is to be classed with Fielding and Smollett, but as a novelist, his position in the history of fiction is separate and unique. . . . The combination of sentiment, pathos, and humour which Sterne sometimes reached with remarkable success, is particularly apparent in every incident which concerns the celebrated Captain Toby Shandy, for the creation of which character this author may most easily be forgiven his indecencies and his literary thefts.—TUCKERMAN, BAYARD, 1882, *A History of English Prose Fiction, pp.* 231, 233.

Sterne carried the humorous novel to its furthest extreme. . . . The humorous novel, in its narrowest sense, stood chiefly under the influence of Sterne's "Tristram Shandy." Sterne's want of form, his endless digressions, his witty, learned fascinating reflections crammed full of allusions and quotations, his mixture of the pathetic and the comic,—all this attracted writers like Hippel and Jean Paul, and incited them to imitation.—SCHERER, WILHELM, 1883–86, *A History of German Literature, tr. Conybeare, vol.* II, *pp.* 288, 289.

Genuine sentiment was as strange to Sterne the writer as to Sterne the man; and he conjures up no tragic figure that is not stuffed with sawdust and tricked out in the rags of the greenroom. Fortunately, there is scant opportunity for idle tears in "Tristram Shandy."—WHIBLEY, CHARLES, 1894, *Introduction to the Life and Adventures of Tristram Shandy.*

I should have said, with hesitation, that it was one of the most popular books in the language. Go where you will amongst men—old and young, undergraduates at the Universities, readers in our great cities, old fellows in the country, judges, doctors, barristers—if they have any tincture of literature about them, they all know their "Shandy" at least as well as their "Pickwick." What more can be expected? "True Shandeism," its author declares, "think what you will against it, opens the heart and lungs." I will be bound to say Sterne made more people laugh in 1891 than in any previous year; and, what is more, he will go on doing it—" 'that is, if it please God,' said my Uncle Toby." — BIRRELL, AUGUSTINE, 1894, *Essays about Men, Women and Books, p.* 38.

Whose Toby Shandy is one of the finest compliments ever paid to human nature. —LOCKER-LAMPSON, FREDERICK, 1896, *My Confidences, p.* 336.

The story of "Tristram Shandy" wanders like a man in a labyrinth, and the humor is as labyrinthine as the story. It is carefully invented, and whimsically subtle; and the sentiment is sometimes true, but mostly affected. But a certain unity is given to the book by the admirable consistency of the characters.—BROOKE, STOPFORD A., 1896, *English Literature, p.* 202.

"Tristram Shandy," like Charles the Second, has been an unconscionably long time in dying. It would be an exaggeration to say that Mr. Disraeli was the last man who read "Rasselas," or that no man living has read "Irene." But references to these classical compositions would in the best educated company fall exceedingly flat, whereas Uncle Toby's sayings are as well known as Falstaff's, and the "sub-acid humour" of Mr. Shandy plays, like the wit of Horace, round the cockles of the heart. It is now a pure curiosity of literature that men have lived who imputed dulness to "Tristram Shandy." . . . Those who do not feel the charm of the book cannot be taught it, and those who feel it resent being told what it is. It is impalpable and indefinable, like one of those combinations of colour at sunset for which there are no words in the language and no ideas in the mind. There have been few greater masters of conversation than Sterne, and in what may be called the art of interruption no one has ever approached him. He is one of the makers of colloquial English, and thousands who never heard of Shandy Hall repeat the phrases of the Shandy brothers. Of all English humourists except Shakespeare, Sterne is still the greatest force, and that the influence of Parson Yorick is not extinct may be seen in almost every page of the "Dolly Dialogues."—PAUL, HERBERT, 1896, *Sterne, The Nineteenth Century, vol.* 40, *pp.* 995, 1009.

It is indeed a strange book, certainly not everybody's book. To start with, it is often tedious, sometimes silly, not seldom downright nasty. It does not begin at the end, because it has no end to begin at; but it does begin very nearly as far on as it ever gets, and goes back great distances in between. If anything at all happens—and it is possible to disentangle two or three events—it happens quite out of its right order; if the vehicle moves at all, it is with the cart before the horse; it is purposely so mixed up that a page of uninterrupted narrative is hardly to be found in it. It is a mass of tricks and affectations, some amusing, and some very wearisome. To say that it has no plot is nothing; it takes the utmost pains to persuade you that it has not a plan. It is sometimes obviously and laboriously imitative. Its pathos, sometimes superb, is sometimes horribly maudlin. We must not ask for good taste, and can by no means rely on decency; there is even a preserve spirit of impropriety which seizes occasions and topics apparently quite innocent. This is not a complete catalogue of its sins; these are only a few points which occur to an old friend, a few characteristics which it is well to mention, lest those who do not know the book should suffer too severe a shock on making its acquaintance. For the difficulty with it is in the beginning; to read it the first time is almost hard; every reading after that goes more easily. Nevertheless, although there are, I believe, fanatic admirers who read all of it every time, I am not of those. I think I have earned the right to skip, and I exercise it freely, without qualms of conscience. What's the use of being on intimate terms with a book if you cannot have that liberty?—HAWKINS, ANTHONY HOPE, 1897, *My Favorite Novelist and His Best Book, Munsey's Magazine, vol.* 18, *p.* 352.

THE SERMONS OF MR. YORICK
1760–69

Have you read his sermons (with his own comic figure at the head of them)? they are in the style, I think, most proper for the pulpit, and shew a very strong imagination and a sensible heart, but you see him often tottering on the verge of laughter, and ready to throw his periwig in the face of his audience.—GRAY, THOMAS, 1760, *Letter to Thomas Wharton, July; Works, ed. Gosse, vol.* III, *p.* 53.

An excellent writer. His sermons will bear a comparison with any in the English language. — SCOT, DAVID, 1825, *Discourses.*

With many serious blemishes, and leavened with much affectation, they are still earnest, dramatic, practical, and simple sermons, with prodigious life and dramatic power and which, when set off by voice and manner, must have been entertaining and instructive. Besides them, the tame conventionalities of Blair read feebly indeed. And there is in them a triumphant answer to those charges of plagiarism which have been so often swung from hoarse and jangling critical bells.—FITZGERALD, PERCY, 1864, *The Life of Laurence Sterne, vol.* I, *p.* 210.

Sterne was a pagan. He went into the Church; but Mr. Thackeray—no bad judge —said most justly that his sermons "have not a single Christian sentiment." They are well expressed, vigorous moral essays; but they are no more. . . . There is not much of heaven and hell in Sterne's sermons; and what there is, seems a rhetorical emphasis which is not essential to the argument, and which might perhaps as well be left out.—BAGEHOT, WALTER, 1864, *Sterne and Thackeray, Works, ed. Morgan, vol.* II, *p.* 159.

The critics who find wit, eccentricity, flashes of Shandyism, and what not else of the same sort in these discourses, must be able—or so it seems to me—to discover these phenomena anywhere. To the best of my own judgment the Sermons are—with but few and partial exceptions—of the most commonplace character; platitudinous with the platitudes of a thousand pulpits, and insipid with the *crambe repetita* of a hundred thousand homilies.—TRAILL, H. D., 1882, *Sterne (English Men of Letters), p.* 55.

Sterne's sermons are as a rule professional efforts on common-sense lines, and mainly interest the literary critic by the perspicuity, orderliness, and restrained eloquence of which they prove his literary style to be capable.—LEE, SIDNEY, 1898, *Dictionary of National Biography, vol.* LIV, *p.* 219.

SENTIMENTAL JOURNEY
1768

Sterne has published two little volumes, called "Sentimental Travels." They are very pleasing, though too much dilated, and infinitely preferable to his tiresome "Tristram Shandy," of which I never could get through three volumes. In these there is great good-nature and strokes of delicacy.—WALPOLE, HORACE, 1768, *To George Montagu, March* 12; *Letters, ed. Cunningham, vol.* V, *p.* 91

I am now going to *charm* myself for the third time with poor Sterne's "Sentimental Journey."—BURNEY, FRANCES, 1769, *Early Diary, ed. Ellis, vol.* I, *p.* 45.

Sentimental? what is that? It is not *English;* he might as well say, *Continental.* —WESLEY, JOHN, 1772, *Journal, Feb.* 11.

And with this pretty dance and chorus, the volume artfully concludes. Even here one cannot give the whole description. There is not a page in Sterne's writing but has something that were better away, a latent corruption—a hint, as of an impure presence. Some of that dreary *double entendre* may be attributed to freer times and manners than ours, but not all. The foul Satyr's eyes leer out of the leaves constantly: the last words the famous author wrote were bad and wicked—the last lines the poor stricken wretch penned were for pity and pardon.—THACKERAY, WILLIAM MAKEPEACE, 1853, *The English Humourists of the Eighteenth Century, Lecture* VI.

The very idea of the book combines the humorous and the pathetic, in that conscious, playful way which individualizes Sterne among English authors.—TUCKERMAN, HENRY T., 1857, *Essays, Biographical and Critical, p.* 330.

There is no better painting of first and easy impressions than that book; after all which has been written on the *ancient régime*, an Englishman at least will feel a fresh instruction on reading these simple observations. They are instructive *because* of their simplicity. . . . In two points the "Sentimental Journey," viewed with the critic's eye and as a mere work of art, is a great improvement upon "Tristram Shandy." The style is simpler and better; it is far more connected: it does not jump about, or leave a topic *because* it is interesting; it does not worry the reader with fantastic transitions, with childish contrivances and rhetorical intricacies.—BAGEHOT, WALTER, 1864, *Sterne and Thackeray, Works, ed. Morgan, vol.* II, *pp.* 178, 180.

He loves to suck melancholy out of any passing event "as a weasel sucks eggs;" but he also delights to thrust constantly before our eyes the cap and bells; not that he intends the smile to compete with the tear, but that he prides himself on his personal freedom from the torturing sensibilities over which he claims to have absolute command. Immediately after one of his famous sentimental outbursts, he tells us how good the inn is at Moulines. This is an outrage of a kind he delighted to perpetrate. It seems to say: "Behold! what a master I am! How I can harrow up your feelings! and now I'm off to eat a mutton-chop." It is the grimace of a bad actor before the tragic business is over, before he quits the stage, and while his face is still turned towards his audience.—CAINE, HALL, 1882, *Sterne, The Academy, vol.* 22, *p.* 322.

Frenchmen, who are either less awed than we by lecturers in white waistcoats, or understand the methods of criticism somewhat better, cherish the "Sentimental Journey" (in spite of its indifferent French) and believe in the genius that created it. But the Briton reads it with shyness, and the British critic speaks of Sterne with bated breath, since Thackeray told it in Gath that Sterne was a bad man, and the daughters of Philistia triumphed. —QUILLER-COUCH, A. T., 1891, *Adventures in Criticism, p.* 98.

GENERAL

Could I, whilst Humour held the quill,
Could I digress with half that skill;
Could I with half that skill return,
Which we so much admire in Sterne,
Where each digression, seeming vain,
And only fit to entertain,
Is found, on better recollection,
To have a just and nice connexion.
—CHURCHILL, CHARLES, 1762, *The Ghost, bk.* iii, *v.* 967–74.

Of Sterne and Rousseau it is difficult to speak without being misunderstood; yet it is impossible to deny the praise of wit and originality to Yorick, or of captivating eloquence to the philosopher of vanity. Their imitators are below notice. —MATHIAS, THOMAS JAMES, 1798, *The Pursuits of Literature, Eighth ed., p.* 59.

A most impure and whimsical writer, whose very humanity is unnatural.—HALL, ROBERT, 1802, *Reflections on War.*

I have very few heresies in English literature. I do not remember any serious one, but my moderate opinion of Sterne. —MACKINTOSH, SIR JAMES, 1811, *Journal, May* 31, *Life by Mackintosh, vol.* II, *p.* 102.

Sterne, for whose sake I plod through miry ways
Of antic wit, and quibbling mazes drear,
Let not thy shade malignant censure fear,
If aught of inward mirth my search betrays.
Long slept that mirth in dust of ancient days,
Erewhile to Guise or wanton Valois dear.
—FERRIAR, JOHN, 1812, *Illustrations of Sterne, with other Essays.*

His style is . . . at times the most rapid, the most happy, the most idiomatic, of any that is to be found. It is the pure essence of English conversational style. His works consist only of *morceaux*,—of brilliant passages. I wonder that Goldsmith, who ought to have known better, should call him "a dull fellow." His wit is poignant, though artificial; and his characters (though the groundwork of some of them had been laid before) have yet invaluable original differences; and the spirit of the execution, the master-strokes constantly thrown into them, are not to be surpassed. It is sufficient to name them:—Yorick, Dr. Slop, Mr. Shandy, My Uncle Toby, Trim, Susanna, and the Widow Wadman. In these he has contrived to oppose, with equal felicity and originality, two characters, one of pure intellect and the other of pure good nature, in My Father and My Uncle Toby. There appears to have been in Sterne a vein of dry, sarcastic humour, and of extreme tenderness of feeling; the latter sometimes carried to affectation, as in the tale of Maria, and the apostrophe to the recording angel, but at other times pure and without blemish. The story of Le Fevre is perhaps the finest in the English language. My Father's restlessness, both of body and mind, is inimitable. It is the model from which all those despicable performances against modern philosophy ought to have been copied, if their authors had known anything of the subject they were writing about. My Uncle Toby is one of the finest compliments ever paid to human nature. He is the most unoffending of God's creatures; or, as the French express it, *un tel petit bon homme!* Of his bowling green, his sieges, and his amours, who would say or think any thing amiss! —HAZLITT, WILLIAM, 1818, *Lectures on the English Comic Writers, Lecture* vi.

The style employed by Sterne is fancifully ornamented, but at the same time vigorous and masculine, and full of that animation and force which can only be derived by an intimate acquaintance with the early English prose-writers. In the power of approaching and touching the finer feelings of the heart, he has never been excelled, if indeed he has ever been equalled; and may be at once recorded as one of the most affected, and one of the most simple of writers,—as one of the greatest plagiarists, and one of the most original geniuses, whom England has produced.—SCOTT, SIR WALTER, 1821, *Laurence Sterne.*

I think highly of Sterne—that is, of the first part of "Tristram Shandy:" for as to the latter part about the widow Wadman, it is stupid and disgusting; and the "Sentimental Journey" is poor, sickly stuff. There is a great deal of affectation in Sterne, to be sure; but still the characters of Trim and the two Shandies are most individual and delightful. Sterne's morals are bad, but I don't think they can do much harm to any one whom they would not find bad enough before. Besides, the oddity and erudite grimaces under which much of his dirt is hidden take away the effect for the most part; although, to be sure, the book is scarcely readable by women.—COLERIDGE, SAMUEL TAYLOR, 1833, *Table Talk, ed. Ashe, Aug.* 18, *p.* 251.

He terribly failed in the discharge of his duties, still, we must admire in him that sportive kind of geniality and affection, still a son of our common mother, not cased up in buckram formulas as the other writers were, clinging to forms, and not touching realities. And, much as has been said against him, we cannot help feeling his immense love for things around him; so that we may say of him, as of Magdalen, "much is forgiven him, because he loved much." A good simple being after all. — CARLYLE, THOMAS, 1838, *Lectures on the History of Literature, ed. Greene, p.* 179.

We think that, on the whole, Mackenzie is the first master of this delicious style. Sterne, doubtless, has deeper touches of humanity in some of his works. But there is no sustained feeling,—no continuity of emotion,—no extended range of thought, over which the mind can brood, in his ingenious and fantastical writings. His spirit is far too mercurial and airy to suffer him tenderly to linger over those images of sweet humanity which he discloses. His cleverness breaks the charm which his feeling spreads, as by magic, around us. His exquisite sensibility is ever counteracted by his perception of the ludicrous and his ambition after the strange. No harmonious feeling breathes from any of his pieces. He sweeps "that curious instrument, the human heart," with hurried fingers, calling forth in rapid succession its deepest and its liveliest tones, and making only marvellous discord. His pathos is, indeed, most genuine while it lasts; but the soul is not suffered to cherish the feeling which it awakens.—TALFOURD, THOMAS NOON, 1842, *Critical and Miscellaneous Writings.*

Sterne was a very selfish man; according to Warburton, an irreclaimable rascal; yet a writer unexcelled for pathos and charity.—WHIPPLE, EDWIN P., 1846–71, *Authors, Literature and Life, p.* 34.

Sterne, though he could not equal Fielding in fluent wit, is a paragon of lucky quaintness, and in pathos is approached by Mackenzie alone.—SANDFORD, SIR DANIEL KEYTE, 1848, *On the Rise and Progress of Literature.*

He fatigues me with his perpetual disquiet, and his uneasy appeals to my risible or sentimental faculties. He is always looking in my face, watching his effect, uncertain whether I think him an impostor or not; posture-making, coaxing, and imploring me. "See what sensibility I have—own now that I am very clever—do cry, now; you can't resist this!" The humour of Swift and Rabelais, whom he pretended to succeed, poured from them as naturally as song does from a bird; they lose no manly dignity with it, but laugh their hearty great laugh out of their broad chests as nature bade them. But this man—who can make you laugh, who can make you cry too—never lets his reader alone, or will permit his audience repose: when you are quiet, he fancies he must rouse you, and turns over head and heels, or sidles up and whispers a nasty story. The man is a great jester, not a great humourist. He goes to work systematically and of cold blood, paints his face, puts on his ruff and motley clothes, and lays down his carpet and tumbles on it.—THACKERAY, WILLIAM MAKEPEACE, 1853, *The English Humourists of the Eighteenth Century, Lecture* vi.

No novelist has surpassed Sterne in the vividness of his descriptions, none have eclipsed him in the art of selecting and grouping the details of his finished scenes. And yet, next to Shakspeare, he is the author who leaves the most to the imagination of the reader. . . . With all this abstinence from explanatory comment at one time, he indulges in it to excess at another. He constantly takes upon himself to act the part of a showman, and disagreeably reminds us that the characters are his puppets. It is the same with his style. It is frequently deformed by insufferable affectation; and then, again, is remarkable for its purity, its ease, its simplicity, and its elegance. The composition of the inimitable story of LeFever is only second to its pathos. The marble leaves, the blank chapters, the false numbering of the pages to indicate that a portion is torn away, are, with a hundred puerilities, only so many proofs that it is possible for great genius to be combined with equal folly. His propensity to provoke curiosity for the mere pleasure of balking it, by running off into digressions, is a sorry jest unworthy a man of wit, and which, however much it might amuse the writer, excites no hilarity in the reader.—ELWIN, WHITWELL, 1854, *Sterne, Quarterly Review, vol.* 94, *p.* 346.

As an author, he has been the father of an immense family of fiction writers. Goethe has had him in his eye, both in the "Sorrows of Werter" and in "Wilhelm Meister." Rousseau derived a great deal from him. Jean Paul Richter, although possessing far more sincerity and depth of spirit, has copied his affected manner. The Minerva Press was long his feeble echo. Southey's "Doctor" was very much in his style; and the French novelists are still employed in imitating his putrid sentimentalism, although incapable of his humor and pathos.—GILFILLAN, GEORGE, 1855, *A Third Gallery of Portraits, p.* 231.

The humour of Sterne is not only very different from that of Fielding and Smollett, but is something unique in our literature. He also was a professed admirer of Cervantes; to as large an extent as Swift he adopted the whimsical and perpetually digressive manner of Rabelais; and there is proof that he was well acquainted with the works of preceding humorists less familiarly known in England. But he was himself a humorist by nature—a British or Irish Yorick, with differences from any of those who might have borne that name before him after their imaginary Danish prototype; and, perpetually as he reminds us of Rabelais, his Shandean vein of wit and fancy is not for a moment to be regarded as a mere variety of Pantagruelism. There is scarcely anything more intellectually exquisite than the humour of Sterne. To very fastidious readers much of the humour of Fielding or of Smollett might come at last to seem but buffoonery; but Shakespeare himself, as one fancies, would have read Sterne with admiration and pleasure.—MASSON, DAVID, 1859, *British Novelists and Their Styles*, *p.* 145.

There is not much humor, indeed, any where out of Shakspeare and Cervantes which resembles or can be compared with that of Sterne. It would be difficult to name any writer but one of these two who could have drawn Uncle Toby or Trim. Another common mistake about Sterne is, that the mass of what he has written consist of little better than nonsense or rubbish,—that his beauties are but grains of gold glittering here and there in a heap of sand, or, at most, rare spots of green scattered over an arid waste. Of no writer could this be said with less correctness. Whatever he has done is wrought with the utmost care, and to the highest polish and perfection. With all his apparent caprices of manner, his language is throughout the purest idiomatic English; nor is there, usually, a touch in any of his pictures that could be spared without injury to the effect. And, in his great work, how completely brought out, how exquisitely finished, is every figure, from Uncle Toby and Brother Shandy, and Trim, and Yorick, down to Dr. Slop, and Widow Wadman, and Mrs. Bridget, and Obadiah himself! Who would resign any one of them, or any part of any one of them?—CRAIK, GEORGE L., 1861, *A Compendious History of English Literature and of the English Language, vol.* II, *p.* 299.

I know not if any of his contemporaries, mighty prose-writers though they were, had, on the whole, so subtle and fine a perception of the various capacities of our language as the author of "Tristram Shandy." With what finger—how light and how strong —he flies over the keys of the instrument! What delicate elegance he can extract from words the most colloquial and vulgate; and again, with some word unfamiliar and strange, how abruptly he strikes on the universal chords of laughter. He can play with the massive weights of our language as a juggler plays with his airy balls. In an age when other grand writers were squaring their periods by rule and compass, he flings forth his jocund sentences loose and at random; now up towards the stars, now down into puddles; yet how they shine where they soar, and how lightly rebound when they fall! But I should have small respect for the critic who advised the youthful author to emulate the style of Sterne. Only writers the most practised could safely venture on occasional, restrained, imitation of his frolicsome zoneless graces.—LYTTON, EDWARD BULWER LORD, 1863-68, *Caxtoniana, Miscellaneous Prose Works, vol.* III, *p.* 85.

He is a great author; certainly not because of great thoughts, for there is scarcely a sentence in his writings which can be called a thought; nor from sublime conceptions which enlarge the limits of our imagination, for he never leaves the sensuous,—but because of his wonderful sympathy with and wonderful power of representing simple human nature.—BAGEHOT, WALTER, 1864, *Sterne and Thackeray, Works, ed. Morgan, vol.* II, *p.* 162.

The merits of Sterne may be discussed as much as anyone likes, but he has a substantive existence: he is there, with his own character, and with a certain rank and prestige as a founder. Everything about him is odd—his life, his personality, his work. . . . To sum up, Sterne is a tale-teller of the first order and excellent in sentimental scenes. But he has the faults of his style: he abuses the trick of interesting the heart in trifles: he enlarges little things too much: he scarcely ever declaims, but he sometimes whimpers.—SCHERER, EDMOND, 1870–91, *Laurence Sterne, or The Humorist; Essays on English Literature, tr. Saintsbury, pp.* 150, 164.

We know of no English author, the perusal of whose works brings more mingled feelings than Laurence Sterne's. Delight and disgust, admiration and sorrow, the blush of outraged modesty and the throb of excited sensibility, are alternately called forth; and the final sentiment that remains on the mind is the wish that we could expunge from our literature more than one-half of what he has written. A very necromancer of language, he uses the spirit-words which he evokes obedient to his will, now as the ministers of prurient fancies and ribald equivoques, now to convulse us with laughter at some pleasant, harmless humour, or stir the deepest feelings of our nature at the tale of sorrow—uttering words of wisdom with a carelessness that looks almost like levity, and dealing with the virtues, the vices, the foibles of human nature as freely as the anatomist does with the human body.—WALLER, JOHN FRANCIS, 1870, *Pictures from English Literature*, p. 53.

There is more originality of manner, and more mannerism in his originality; more sudden and unaffected strokes of nature, and more palpable affectation; more genuinely idiomatical power, and conversational ease in his style, and more constrained and far-fetched attempts to be unconstrained and easy, than in any eminent classical writer of our language that I am acquainted with.—CLARKE, CHARLES COWDEN, 1872, *On the Comic Writers of England, The Gentleman's Magazine, n. s. vol.* 8, *p.* 575.

A perfect literary artist.—SAINTSBURY, GEORGE, 1886, *Specimens of English Prose Style, p.* 199.

Sterne is in many respects the most eccentric of our prosaists. M. Scherer would have it that he is wilfully sensational and meretricious — a literary mountebank. I should like to find some method in his madness, even to a point where he seems maddest: *i. e.*, his habit of making a chapter of a few words. Chapter xiii, vol. ii, of "Tristram," contains one paragraph, three sentences (in dialogue)—a total of 29 words. Chapter xxvii, vol. iii, has two paragraphs, four sentences, 83 words. Chapter v, vol. v, has one paragraph, one sentence, 16 words. Chapter xxxix, vol. v, one paragraph, two sentences, 30 words. There are a dozen other chapters similar in length to these. All this is freakish enough, but is not so very odd in view of Sterne's long study of French models, from which he had learned the trick of the tiny paragraph. He chose to emphasize a thought by paragraphing it, as Anglo-Saxon scribes had done, long before—and it was but one bold step further, in the process of emphasis by mechanical means, to make a chapter of the paragraph as he had made a paragraph of the sentence. It is hardly to the point for a critic to complain that these chapters are logically incomplete. Sterne was analyzing, not logically, but rhetorically; fastening attention on these small stadia simply for the imaginative suggestions involved in their pregnant brevity. I must, for one, confess to thinking the thing sometimes shrewdly done. Sterne is a lawless wight, but his recusancy has given us some things both quaint and good. There is little else of importance to note of Sterne's paragraphs. In managing dialogue he follows Fielding. — LEWIS, EDWIN HERBERT, 1894, *The History of the English Paragraph, p.* 119.

Laurence Sterne was a born humorist, but his humor was the humor of whimsicality, and at times his oddity grows wearisome. He is too artful to be sympathetic, and his artifice is too obvious. Besides, he is over-fond of innuendo; slyly playing back and forth, he now pretends an innocence more impertinent than diverting, and now suggests that his reader is deeper in the mire than he is; always exhibiting a genius in the art with which he stimulates the latent wickedness whose presence in weak human nature this worldly Ecclesiastes understands all too well.—SIMONDS, WILLIAM EDWARD, 1894, *An Introduction to the Study of English Fiction, p.* 51.

There is a singular blend of two qualities in Sterne's writing, as in his character. Humour and pathos are never in their nature far apart; in Sterne they are almost inextricably combined. His laughter and his tears are both so facile, and their springs lie so near together, that the one almost infallibly provokes the other; he will laugh at sorrow and find matter of sentiment in a comical mishap. It is his keenest pleasure to juggle with these effects; a solemn occasion is to him an irresistible provocative to burlesque, and his pathetic sensibility responds to a touch so light that to a less highly strung nature his tears will seem affected. Yet herein lies the delicacy of his writing, and of those exquisite effects, the despair of many a more robust artist, which are as hard to describe as an odour is to remember. His reader must be incessantly on the alert for surprises; it is only prudent, at a funeral where Parson Sterne officiates, for the guest to attend with a harlequin's suit beneath his decent garb of black, prepared for either event.—RALEIGH, WALTER, 1894, *The English Novel, p.* 195.

Though at the present day we do not take Sterne very seriously, his contemporaries not only appreciated him as a humorist, but delighted especially in the depth and originality of his genius, in his "gloomy and mournful appearance," and in what his translator called "an aroma of sentiment, and a suppleness of thought, impossible to define." By his countrymen he was praised for his joyous spirit, while in France he was looked upon as a kind of prophet of the new religion just brought into fashion by Rousseau, the religion of the *self*. . . . Sterne's reputation increased when it crossed the water. The Germans hailed him as a philosopher. Lessing was taken with him, and when Sterne died, wrote to Nicolai that he would gladly have sacrificed several years of his own life if by so doing he could have prolonged the existence of the sentimental traveller. Goethe writes: "Whoever reads him, immediately feels that there is something free and beautiful in his own soul." The philosophy of Sterne is the most brilliant invention of eighteenth century anglomania.—TEXTE, JOSEPH, 1895–99, *Jean-Jacques Rousseau and the Cosmopolitan Spirit in Literature, tr. Matthews, pp.* 281, 282.

He was a Cambridge man and well taught;—of abundant reading, which he made to serve his turn in various ways, and conspicuously by his stealings; he stole from Rabelais; he stole from Shakespeare; he stole from Fuller; he stole from Burton's "Anatomy of Melancholy;" not a stealing of ideas only, but of words and sentences and half-pages together, without a sign of obligation; and yet he did so wrap about these thefts with the strings and lappets of his own abounding humour and drollery, as to give to the whole—thieving and Shandyism combined—a stamp of individuality. Ten to one that these old authors who had suffered the pilfering, would have lost cognizance of their expressions, in the new surroundings of the Yorkshire parson; and joined in the common grin of applause with which the world welcomed and forgave them.—MITCHELL, DONALD G., 1895, *English Lands Letters and Kings, Queen Anne and the Georges, p.* 216

He is colloquial and slipshod, a chartered libertine in language; losing all sense of dignity in his affectation and whimsical conceits; eccentric not from impulse but from wayward artificiality, ruffled into petty and vanishing emotion by every breath of pathos, however false and tawdry; noisy in his childish depreciation of conventionality and order; but yet, withal, imbued with the same cynicism, aiming at the same indifference of demeanour, impressed by the same sense of the "ridiculous tragedy" of human life —above all, with the same vein of humour, but of a richness and fertility which has scarcely ever been approached, and which Chesterfield could never, even remotely, rival. With all his carelessness of diction, with all his affected contempt of scorn, Sterne wrote for a literary age; even in his wildest extravagances he knows how to attune his language to the mood of the moment, and to make it a fitting dress for the most wayward, the most fitful, the most perplexing, and yet the most invincible wit which fancy ever contrived. —CRAIK, HENRY, 1895, *ed., English Prose, Introduction, vol.* IV, *p.* 6.

To talk of "the style" of Sterne is almost to play one of those tricks with language of which he himself was so fond. For there is hardly any definition of the word which can make it possible to describe him as having any style at all. It is not only that he manifestly recognised no external canons whereto to conform the expression of his thoughts, but he had apparently no inclination to invent and observe, except indeed in the most negative of senses, any style of his own. The "stlye of Sterne," in short, is as though one should say: "The form of Proteus." . . . Chaotic as it is in the syntactical sense, it is a perfectly clear vehicle for the conveyance of thought. We are rarely at a loss for the meaning of one of Sterne's sentences, as we are, for very different reasons, for the meaning of one of Macaulay's. And his language is so full of life and colour, his tone so animated and vivacious, that we forget we are reading and not listening, and we are as well disposed to be exacting in respect to form as though we were listeners in actual fact. Sterne's manner, in short, may be that of a bad and careless writer, but it is the manner of a first-rate talker; and this of course enhances rather than detracts from the unwearying charm of his wit and humour.—TRAILL, H. D., 1895,

English Prose, ed. Craik, vol. IV, *pp.* 207, 208.

Many critics and writers of eminence—Mr. Carlyle, M. Taine, Mr. Elwin, Mr. Traill—have tried to analyse Sterne's style and methods, contrasting him with Rabelais, Cervantes, Fielding and Dickens. The truth is, our author was so capricious and even fragmentary and disorderly in his system that comparison is impossible. The writers just named were really "monumental" in their handling of their characters, and completed their labour before issuing it to the world. Sterne sent forth his work in fragments, and often wrote what was sheer nonsense to fill his volumes. He allowed his pen to lead him, instead of he himself directing his pen. The whole is so incomplete and disjointed that cosmopolitan readers have not the time or patience to piece the various scraps together. . . . He has given to the world a group of living *characters*, which have become known and familiar even to those who have not read a line of "Tristram." These are My Uncle Toby, Mr. and Mrs. Shandy, Yorick—his own portrait—and Dr. Slop. There are choice passages, too, grotesque situations and expressions which have become part of the language. Mr. Shandy, I venture to think, is the best of these creations, more piquant and attractive even than My Uncle Toby, because more original and more difficult to touch. It is in this way that Sterne has made his mark, and may be said to be better known than read. A great deal has been written on the false and overstrained sentiment of his pathetic passages such as in the "Story of Le Fever," "Maria of Moulines," "The Dead Ass," and other incidents. No doubt these were somewhat artificially wrought, but it must be remembered they followed the tone of the time. His exquisite humour is beyond dispute, the Shandean sayings, allusions, topics, etc., have a permanent hold; and, as they recur to the recollection, produce a complacent smile, even though the subject be what is called "broad."—FITZGERALD, PERCY, 1896, *The Life of Laurence Sterne, Preface, vol.* I, *p.* xi.

Sterne was not a moralist in the mode of Richardson or of Fielding; it is to be feared that he was a complete ethical heretic; but he brought to his country as gifts the strained laughter that breaks into tears, and the melancholy wit that saves itself by an outburst of buffoonery. He introduced into the coarse and heavy life of the eighteenth century elements of daintiness, of persiflage, of moral versatility; he prided himself on the reader's powerlessness to conjecture what was coming next. A French critic compared Sterne, most felicitously, to one of the little bronze satyrs of antiquity in whose hollow bodies exquisite odours were stored. He was carried away by the tumult of his nerves, and it became a paradoxical habit with him to show himself exactly the opposite of what he was expected to be. You had to unscrew him for the aroma to escape. His unseemly, passionate, pathetic life burned itself away at the age of fifty-four, only the last eight of which had been concerned with literature. Sterne's influence on succeeding fiction has been durable but interrupted. Ever and anon his peculiar caprices, his selected elements, attract the imitation of some more or less analogous spirit. The extreme beauty of his writing has affected almost all who desire to use English prose as though it were an instrument not less delicate than English verse. Nor does the fact that a surprising number of his "best passages" were stolen by Sterne from older writers militate against his fame, because he always makes some little adaptation, some concession to harmony, which stamps him a master, although unquestionably a deliberate plagiarist.—GOSSE, EDMUND, 1897, *Short History of Modern English Literature, p.* 244.

It was a sad day for English fiction when a writer of genius came to look upon the novel as the repository for the crotchets of a lifetime. This is the more to be lamented when we reflect that Sterne, unlike Smollett, could tell a story in a straightforward manner when he chose to do so. Had the time he wasted in dazzling his friends with literary fireworks been devoted to a logical presentation of the wealth of his experiences, fancies, and feelings, he might have written one of the most perfect pieces of composition in the English language. As it is, the novel in his hands, considered from the standpoint of structure, reverted to what it was when left by the wits of the Renaissance.—CROSS, WILBUR L., 1899, *The Development of the English Novel, p.* 71.

Sarah Fielding

1710–1768

Sarah Fielding (1710–1768), novelist, the third daughter of Edmund Fielding by his first wife, and sister of Henry Fielding was born at East Stour, Dorsetshire, 8 Nov. 1710. She published her first novel, "The Adventures of David Simple in search of a Faithful Friend," in 1744. Her brother contributed a preface in the second edition in the same year, and he wrote another three years later to a collection of "Familiar Letters between the principal characters in David Simple and some others." This originally appeared in 1747, and contains five letters by Henry Fielding (pp. 294–351). A third volume was added to "David Simple" in 1752. She joined with Miss Collier (daughter of Arthur Collier) in "The Cry, a Dramatic Fable," Dublin, 1754. She wrote also "The Governess," 1749; "History of the Countess of Dellwyn," 1759; "Lives of Cleopatra and Octavia," 1757; "History of Ophelia," 1785; and Xenophon's "Memoirs of Socrates; with the Defence of Socrates before his Judges," 1762, translated from the Greek, in which some notes and possibly a revision were contributed by James Harris of Salisbury.—STEPHEN, LESLIE, 1889, *Dictionary of National Biography, vol.* XVIII, *p.* 426.

PERSONAL

Her unaffected manners, candid mind,
Her heart benevolent, and soul resign'd;
Were more her praise than all she knew or thought,
Though Athen's wisdom to her sex she taught.

—HOADLY, JOHN, 1768? *Inscription on Monument.*

GENERAL

I amuse myself as well as I can with reading. I have just gone through your two volumes of "Letters;" have reperused them with great pleasure, and found many beauties in them. What a knowledge of the human heart! Well might a critical judge of writing say, as he did to me, that your late brother's knowledge of it was not (fine writer as he was) comparable to yours. His was but as the knowledge of the outside of a clockwork-machine, while yours was that of all the finer springs and movements of the inside.—RICHARDSON, SAMUEL, 1756, *Letter to Sarah Fielding, Dec.* 7.

Before taking our leave of the novels and novelists of the ancient *régime*, let us not omit to mention Sarah Fielding, the sister of the author of "Tom Jones," who, in her day, was a writer of no small celebrity, but whose books have now long been forgotten by all save the curious student of English literature. Her chief work was a novel written in imitation of "Gil Blas," the title of which will sufficiently describe its character: "The Adventures of David Simple, containing an Account of his Travels through the Cities of London and Westminster, in the Search of a Real Friend, by A Lady." In was the forerunner—doubtless the suggester—of several better works bearing similar titles and following the same general plan.—BALDWIN, JAMES, 1883, *English Literature and Literary Criticism, Prose, p.* 205.

The pale moon who attended these three main luminaries. Her "David Simple," published in 1742, in two volumes, is not a great, but it is certainly an unduly neglected, book. Not only does its rank in time, as the third English novel, give it interest, but it displays a certain prim grace of construction, and a considerable refinement in the analysis of character. It takes a place midway between the work of Richardson and that of her brother, less morbid than the former, less gusty than the latter, and of course much feebler than either. The sedate wavering of David Simple between the rival passions of Camilla and Cynthia might, it may be suggested, have served Richardson as a hint for the conduct of Sir Charles Grandison. Sarah Fielding, it is to be regretted, made no further serious effort in fiction; perhaps her brother's genius dazzled her. But she had a genuine talent of her own. —GOSSE, EDMUND, 1888, *A History of Eighteenth Century Literature, p.* 264.

Oblivion has odd caprices, and in literature, as in the world at large, we are sometimes at a loss when we try to discern the definite unfitness which has interfered with survival. Sarah Fielding, praised—and justly praised—in her lifetime by Richardson on the one hand, and by her brother, Henry Fielding, on the other, is probably not known at this moment to a dozen readers. She has become one of those writers whose good things any man may steal without fear of detection. Yet the good things are plentiful, and any leisurely reader may find it very much worth his while to bestow a few hours upon "David Simple" or "Ophelia," or even the "Familiar Letters." Leisurely, however, he must be; and he will do well to bear in mind the observation made by Dr. Johnson upon a greater than Sarah Fielding. "Why, sir," said the Doctor, "If you were to read Richardson for the story your impatience would be so much fretted that you would hang yourself." Miss Fielding is not, indeed, as long-winded as her admired friend Richardson (it is only the immortals who can be that, and survive), but she has the comfortable prolixity of her day, and is by no means in a hurry to get on to the next incident. It is for the sprightly narrative, the happy phrase, the ironical turn of mind, that these volumes are worth reading.—BLACK, CLEMENTINA, 1888, *Sarah Fielding, The Gentleman's Magazine, vol.* 265, *p.* 485.

Miss Fielding's slight knowledge of the world disabled her from giving fresh life to the picaresque romance.—RALEIGH, WALTER, 1894, *The English Novel, p.* 181.

Richardson sang of chastity; Fielding sang of patience; "David Simple" is an exaltation of friendship. The episode of Dumont and Stainville is as noble and tender as the mediæval Story of Palamon and Arcite. Its place in English fiction is as a little companion piece to "Pamela" and "Amelia."—CROSS, WILBUR L., 1899, *The Development of the English Novel, p.* 77.

It ["David Simple"] is an exceedingly dull book, boasting of little or no construction, and intended to exemplify the misfortunes and ill-usage which are sure to befall those who judge others by their own high moral standards. . . . The book had a considerable run, but at the present day it can be regarded only as a literary curiosity. — THOMSON, CLARA LINKLATER, 1900, *Samuel Richardson, A Biographical and Critical Study, p.* 111.

Joseph Spence

1699–1768

Joseph Spence, anecdotist, born at Kingsclere, Hants, 25th April 1699, from Winchester passed to New College, Oxford, and became a fellow in 1722, professor of poetry (1727), rector of Birchanger and Great Harwood, professor of Modern History (1737), and a prebendary of Durham (1754). He secured Pope's friendship by his "Essay on Pope's Odyssey" (1727), and began to record Pope's conversation and anecdotes of other friends and notabilities. In 1736 he edited Sackville's "Gorboduc," and in 1747 published his "Polymetis." He was drowned at Byfleet, Surrey, August 20, 1768. The best edition of the "Anecdotes" is by Singer (1820; 2d ed. 1858), with memoir.—PATRICK AND GROOME, *eds.*, 1897, *Chambers's Biographical Dictionary, p.* 870.

PERSONAL

Mr. Spence is the completest scholar either in solid or polite learning, for his years, that I ever knew. Besides, he is the sweetest tempered gentleman breathing.—PITT, CHRISTOPHER, 1728, *Letter.*

Here lie the Remains of
Joseph Spence, M. A.
Regius Professor of Modern History in the University of Oxford,
Prebendary of Durham,
And Rector of Great Horwood, Bucks.
In Whom Learning, Genius, and Shining Talents
Tempered with Judgment,
And Softened by the most Exquisite Sweetness of Manners,
Were greatly Excelled by his Humanity;
Ever ready to Assist the Distressed
By Constant and Extensive Charity to the Poor,
And by Unbounded Benevolence to All:
He Died Aug. 20, 1768,
In the 70th Year of His Age.

—LOWTH, ROBERT, 1768? *Inscription on Tablet, Byfleet Church.*

At Captain M'Lean's, I mentioned Pope's friend, Spence. JOHNSON. "He was a weak conceited man. BOSWELL. "A good scholar, Sir?" JOHNSON. "Why, no, Sir." BOSWELL. "He was a pretty scholar." JOHNSON. "You have about reached him." —BOSWELL, JAMES, 1773, *The Journal of a Tour to the Hebrides, ed. Hill, Oct.* 15.

As I knew Mr. Joseph Spence, I do not think I should have been so much delighted as Dr. Kippis with reading his letters. He was a good-natured, harmless little soul, but more like a silver penny than a genius. It was a neat, fiddle-faddle bit of sterling, that had read good books, and kept good company, but was too trifling for use, and only fit to please a child.—WALPOLE, HORACE, 1780, *Letter to Rev. William Cole, May* 19; *Letters, ed. Cunningham, vol.* VII, *p.* 366.

There was a moral loveliness in the character and the life of Spence, which could not fail to engage the affections of such an elegant scholar as Lowth, and those of many other men of genius. Cultivating literature and the arts with the ardour and the playfulness of a lover, it was fortunate that the vicissitudes of life rendered him a traveller.—DISRAELI, ISAAC? 1820, *Spence's Anecdotes of Books and Men, Quarterly Review, vol.* 23, *p.* 404.

Spence's benevolence was most liberal and unconfined; distress of every sort, and in every rank of life, never preferred its claim to his attention in vain: and he is described by one who knew him well, to have had a heart and a hand ever open to the poor and the needy. . . . Spence was in person below the middle size, his figure spare, his countenance benignant, and rather handsome, but bearing marks of a delicate constitution. As in his childhood he had been kept alive by constant care and the assistance of skilful medical aid, he did not expect that his life would have been protracted beyond fifty years. But he possessed those greatest of all blessings, a cheerful temperament, a constant flow of animal spirits, and a most placable disposition. These, with the happy circumstances in which he was placed, and the active nature of his gardening amusements, prolonged its date to his 70th year: when he was unfortunately drowned in a canal in his garden at Byfleet. Being, when the accident occurred, quite alone, it could only be conjectured in what manner it happened; but it was generally supposed to have been occasioned by a fit, while he was standing near the brink of the water. He was found flat upon his face at the edge, where the water was too shallow to cover his head, or any part of his body.—SINGER, SAMUEL WELLER, 1820–58, *ed. Spence's Anecdotes, Observations and Characters of Books and Men, pp.* xxvii, xxxi.

Phesoj Enceps, in the Rev. James Ridley's novel "Tales of the Genii," is Joseph Spence. The sobriquet is an imperfect anagram.—FREY, ALBERT R., 1888, *Sobriquets and Nicknames, p.* 271.

His generosity towards all kinds of persons is warmly eulogised, and he continued to be a friend to struggling authors, especially to Dodsley before his prosperous bookselling days. One of his earliest friends, Christopher Pitt, and one of the latest, Shenstone, unite in their testimony to his gentleness and urbanity. Gardening continued to be his favourite recreation; he also made several tours in England. His health failed during the later years of his life, and when, on 20 Aug. 1768, he was found dead in a canal in his garden, there were rumours of suicide, but the cause of death was more probably a fit. He was buried in Byfleet church, where there is a monument with an inscription by Bishop Lowth.—GARNETT, RICHARD, 1898, *Dictionary of National Biography, vol.* LIII, *p.* 337.

GENERAL

I am indebted to this learned and amiable man, on whose friendship I set the greatest value, for most of the anecdotes relating to Pope, mentioned in this work, which he gave me when I was making him a visit at Byfleet, in 1754.—WARTON, JOSEPH, 1756, *Essay on the Genius and Writings of Pope.*

A man whose learning was not very great, and whose mind was not very powerful.—JOHNSON, SAMUEL, 1779–81, *Pope, Lives of the English Poets.*

The Anecdotes of Pope, compared with Boswell's Memoirs of Johnson, want life and spirit, and connexion. They furnish curious particulars, but minute and disjointed:—They want picturesque grouping and dramatic effect. We have the opinions and sayings of eminent men: but they do not grow out of the occasion: we do not know at whose house such a thing happened, nor the effect it had on those who were present. The conversations seldom extend beyond an observation and a reply. We have good things served up in sandwiches; but we do not sit down, as in Boswell, to "an ordinary of fine discourse."—There is no eating and drinking going on. . . .

There is a gap between each conclusion, and at the end of every paragraph we have a new labour to begin. They are not scenes, but soliloquies, with which we are presented: And in reading through the book, we do not seem travelling along a road, but crossing a series of stepping stones: consequently, we do not get on fast with it. It is made up of shreds and patches, and not cut out of the entire piece; something like the little caps into which the tailor in Don Quixote cut his cloth, and held them up at his fingers' ends. In a word, the living scene does not pass before us;—we have notes and slips of paper handed out by one of the company, but we are not ourselves admitted to their presence, nor made witnesses of the fray.—HAZLITT, WILLIAM, 1820, *Spence's Anecdotes, Edinburgh Review, vol.* 33, *p.* 305.

Spence had much of Boswell's curiosity and hero-worship, but there is neither insight into character in his pages, nor any trace of the dramatic skill which makes Boswell's narrative so delightful. At the same time there is every indication that he strove to give the sayings of the poet, as far as possible, in his own words.—DENNIS, JOHN, 1894, *The Age of Pope, p.* 205.

Although inadequate from the first, ["Polymetis"] and long ago superseded, it remains an agreeable book, owing to the urbanity of its old-fashioned scholarship, the justice of some incidental observations, and its affluent stores of quotations; and, as an intellectual if heterogeneous banquet, may be compared with the "Deipnosophists" of Athenæus.—GARNETT, RICHARD, 1898, *Dictionary of National Biography, vol.* LIII, *p.* 337.

Thomas Secker

1693-1768.

Thomas Secker, born at Sibthorpe, in Nottinghamshire, in 1693, was educated for a Dissenting minister, but afterwards changed his views, and entered the Church, taking holy orders in Dec. 1722, and was soon afterwards made rector of Houghton-le-Spring. Having been rapidly promoted, he was consecrated Bishop of Bristol in 1735, was translated to Oxford in 1737, was made Dean of St. Paul's in 1750, and Archbishop of Canterbury in 1758. Many volumes of his sermons and charges were published during his lifetime, and several collected editions of his works have appeared. He died August 3, 1768. A review of his life and character, by Bishop Porteus, appeared in 1797.—TOWNSEND, GEORGE H., 1870, *The Every-Day Book of Modern Literature, vol.* 1, *p.* 429.

PERSONAL

Speak, look, and move with dignity and ease,
Like mitred Secker, you'll be sure to please.
—PITT, CHRISTOPHER, 1748? *Art of Preaching.*

When Secker preaches the church is crowded.—HERVEY, JAMES, 1753–55, *Theron and Aspasio.*

As a clergyman Secker had greatly won the attachment of his people. Whiston spoke of him "as an indefatigable pastor," and Horace Walpole allows that he was "incredibly popular" in his parish. As a bishop he commanded for the most part respect and esteem rather than any warm feeling. That he was generally thought very highly of is indeed very evident. Richard Newton, mentioning his recent death, speaks of him as "that great and excellent prelate." "Few bishops equal to him," said Johnson of Connecticut. But with many he was not at all popular. He was criticised as being rather haughty and imperious, and of showing too much of an air of prelatical dignity. That he was especially distant towards his old Nonconformist friends seems to be disproved by the undoubted cordiality of his relations towards Doddridge, Leland, Lardner, and Chandler. He was somewhat stiff, formal, and precise, and often seemed reserved and cold. Porteus acknowledges this, but says that it generally rose from the bodily pain, depression, and fatigue to which he was subject, and that faults were often laid to his charge which did not really belong to his character.—ABBEY, CHARLES J., 1887, *The English Church and Its Bishops*, 1700–1800, *vol.* II, *p.* 43.

GENERAL

E'en in a bishop I can spy desert;
Secker is decent, Rundel has a heart.
—POPE, ALEXANDER, 1738, *Epilogue to the Satires, Dialogue,* ii, *v.* 70–71.

You will find nowhere, perhaps, a nobler

specimen of practical preaching than is to be met with in the sermons of Archbishop Secker. —OWEN, HENRY, 1766, *Short Directions to Young Students in Divinity and Candidates for Holy Orders.*

When occasion calls for it, he is pathetic, animated, nervous; rises to that true sublime which consists not in pomp of diction, but in grandeur of sentiment, expressed with simplicity and strength.—PORTEUS, BEILBY, 1770-97, *Life of Archbishop Secker.*

What his discourses wanted of gospel was made up by a tone of fanaticism that he still retained.—WALPOLE, HORACE, 1797, *Memoirs of the Last Ten Years of the Reign of King George II.*

A name never to be uttered but with reverence, as the great exemplar of metropolitan strictness, erudition, and dignity. —MATHIAS, THOMAS JAMES, 1798, *The Pursuits of Literature, Eighth ed. p.*, 304.

As a celebrated prelate, Secker follows Tillotson. . . . Like Tillotson, also, he departed too much from primitive peculiarities of the gospel, though far preferable to most of his Episcopal contemporaries.—WILLIAMS, EDWARD, 1800, *The Christian Preacher.*

A candid, wise, and practical writer; his Charges useful; superior to most in his day.—BICKERSTETH, EDWARD, 1844, *The Christian Student.*

As a writer Secker is distinguished by his plain good sense. The range of his knowledge was wide and deep. He was a good hebraist, and he wrote excellent Latin. The works which he has left to the Lambeth library are valuable quite as much from his manuscript annotations as for their own worth. Judging by his printed sermons, one would hardly rank him among the great pulpit orators of the English church. But he purposely, his biographer tells us, composed them with studied simplicity, and the reader missed the tall commanding presence, and the good voice and delivery of the preacher. —OVERTON, JOHN HENRY, 1897, *Dictionary of National Biography, vol.* LI, *p.* 172.

Nathaniel Lardner

1684-1768.

Nathaniel Lardner, D. D.: Clergyman; born at the Hall House, Hawkhurst, Kent, England, June 6, 1684; studied at Utrecht and Leyden 1699-1703; was a private tutor; became assistant to his father; was from 1729 to 1751 assistant minister in the Presbyterian meeting-house in Poor Jewry Lane, Crutched Friars, London. He became partially deaf in 1723, and after 1753 could hear nothing. Died at the Hall House, Hawkhurst, Sunday, July 24, 1768. He is chiefly remembered as author of "The Credibility of the Gospel History" (14 vols., 1727-55), first delivered as a series of lectures at the Old Jewry, and still a standard work. As a supplement he issued a similar work on the apostles (3 vols., 1756-57). Other less known but important works are "Letter on the Logos" (1759, distinctly Socinian), a work which converted Priestley; "Jewish and Heathen Testimonies to the Truth of the Christian Religion" (1764-67, 4 vols.); a "History of Heretics of the First Two Centuries" (1780), etc. See his "Works" with biography by A. Kippis (11 vols., London, 1788; reprinted 5 vols., 1815; 10 vols., 1829; 10 vols., 1838).—ADAMS, CHARLES KENDALL, *ed.* 1897, *Johnson's Universal Cyclopaedia, vol.* V, *p.* 109.

PERSONAL

When he thought it his duty, and for the honour of revelation, to call in question common opinions, he did it with unaffected candour and modesty, and, at the same time, with that integrity and simplicity, which, if it did not bring over his adversary, never offended him. He was respectful without ceremony, friendly without officiousness, and obliging without mean compliances. He preserved a dignity of character without reserve, and united the acuteness of the critic with the manners of a gentleman and the spirit of a Christian. The Goodness of his temper excited a prejudice in favour of his principles; and as his writings were free from acrimony, his life was clear of reproach. On the whole, when I consider his ardour for truth, yet tenderness for error, his learning mixed with so much diffidence and humility, his zeal tempered with so much prudence, and his faith accompanied with so much benevolence; when I observe the simplicity of his deportment, his uniform and unaffected piety, his attachment to his Divine master, and good-will of mankind, I cannot help saying, "This was the disciple whom Jesus loved."—RADCLIFF, EBENEZER, 1788, *The Life of Dr. Nathaniel Lardner.*

His want of popularity as a preacher was partly due to indistinct enunciation; he slurred his words and dropped his voice, defects to which his deafness rendered him insensible. From about 1753 "the only method of conversing with him was by writing," and he amused himself when alone with looking over the sheets covered with miscellaneous jotlings of his visitors.—GORDON, ALEXANDER, 1892, *Dictionary of National Biography, vol.* XXXII, *p.* 148.

THE CREDIBILITY OF THE GOSPEL HISTORY
1727–57

On this occasion it is proper to mention Dr. Lardner's excellent work of the "Credibility of the Gospel-History;" in the second part of which—consisting of several volumes—he hath made a full and accurate collection of the passages which are to be found in the writers of the first ages of the Christian Church relating to the four Gospels, and other sacred books of the New Testament. This he hath executed with so much fidelity and diligence, and with such exactness of judgment, that the English reader who hath not opportunity to consult the originals will be able to judge for himself, upon considering the passages of the original authors, which are very faithfully translated. This affordeth so clear and continued a proof of their having been generally received in the earliest ages of the Christian Church, that one would hope it should put an end to this part of the controversy.—LELAND, JOHN, 1754–56, *A View of the Principal Deistical Writers, vol.* I, *Letter* iv.

It is, indeed, an invaluable performance, and has rendered the most essential service to the cause of Christianity. Whoever peruses this work, will find it replete with admirable instruction, sound learning, and just and candid criticism.—KIPPIS, ANDREW, 1788, *Life of Dr. Nathaniel Lardner.*

The services which Dr. Lardner rendered to the cause of Christianity are well known and very considerable. His extensive and accurate investigations into the credibility of the gospel history have left scarcely any thing more to be done or desired. Subsequent writers on the evidences of Christianity have generally availed themselves of Lardner's collection of testimonies, deeming it useless to verify his quotations or add to their number. His sentiments on the doctrinal part of Christianity did not injure his reasoning as an historian, but they probably influenced his selection of quotations from the early Christian writers. "The History of the Writers of the New Testament" Bishop Watson republished in the second volume of his Tracts. The first part of the "Credibility" was translated into Latin by the celebrated Wolfius. It was also translated into Dutch and German. Walch eulogizes it as *insigne opus.*—ORME, WILLIAM, 1824, *Bibliotheca Biblica.*

A very candid and learned but Arian writer. He impartially goes through the principal fathers, showing their testimonies to the Scriptures.—BICKERSTETH, EDWARD, 1844, *The Christian Student.*

This vast quarry of learning supplied Paley with the material for his more neat and substantial "Evidences."—MINTO, WILLIAM, 1872–80, *Manual of English Prose Literature, p.* 428.

When Christianity was driven by it to appeal to the bar of learning, it chanced that the one eminent scholar who did most to refute the assertions of the Deists, and to satisfy the English mind on the ground of history, was the eminent Unitarian scholar, Lardner, whose great work in defence of historical Christianity is a standard to this day. I do not say how far his argument satisfies the scientific thinkers and historical students of our time, who have shifted their ground a good deal from that of a hundred years ago. I only say that, when modern Unitarianism came to take shape, and began to be known under its own name, it was as a defence of Christianity on the grounds of reason against the attacks of reason.—ALLEN, JOSEPH HENRY, 1882, *Our Liberal Movement in Theology, p.* 11.

GENERAL

Have you read over Dr. Lardner on the Logos? It is, I think, scarcely possible to read it, and not be convinced.

—COLERIDGE, SAMUEL TAYLOR, 1796, *Letter to Mr. Poole.*

The manner of this writer gives me pleasure: he has been called the "laborious Lardner," and laborious he must have been; but he never seems to me to labour. He is always easy and unembarrassed.—HEY, JOHN, 1796, *Lectures in Divinity Delivered in the University of Cambridge.*

In the applause of Dr. Lardner all parties of Christians are united, regarding him as the champion of their common and holy faith. Archbishop Secker, Bishops Porteus, Watson, and Tomline, and Doctors Jortin, Hey, and Paley, of the Anglican church, Doctors Doddridge, Kippis, and Priestley, amongst the Dissenters, and all foreign Protestant biblical critics, have rendered public homage to his learning, his fairness, and his great merits as a Christian apologist. The candid of the literati of the Romish communion have extolled his labours; and even Morgan and Gibbon, professed unbelievers, have awarded to him the meed of faithfulness and impartiality. With his name is associated the praise of deep erudition, accurate research, sound and impartial judgment, and unblemished candour. The publication of his works constituted a new æra in the annals of Christianity; for, by collecting a mass of scattered evidences in favour of the authenticity of the evangelical history, he established a bulwark on the side of truth which infidelity has never presumed to attack.—HORNE, THOMAS HARTWELL, 1818–39, *A Manual of Biblical Bibliography.*

Lardner's works contain a mine of theological learning; in which the Student may toil till he is weary—and from which he cannot fail to bring away much that is curious and edifying.—DIBDIN, THOMAS FROGNALL, 1824, *The Library Companion,* p. 64.

Lardner's works are still of very high worth, as stores both of learning and of thought.—SPALDING, WILLIAM, 1852–82, *A History of English Literature,* p. 330.

Lardner's apologetic works were especially planned for the benefit of the unlearned. He regarded the average reader as capable of judging for himself of the internal evidence for the historical character of the New Testament, and aimed at putting him in a position to form his own judgment respecting the external evidence, in place of relying on the authority of the learned. Without declaring any theory of inspiration, he undertook to show that all facts related in the New Testament are not only credible as a history, but narrated without any real discrepancies, and largely confirmed by contemporary evidence. His method is thorough, and his dealing with difficulties is always candid. When he meets with a difficulty he cannot remove, he exhibits much skill and cautious judgment, as well as ample learning, in his own various expedients for reducing it, leaving always the final decision with the reader. Of greatest value is his vast and careful collection of critically appraised materials for determining the date and authorship of New Testament books. Here he remains unrivalled. He may justly be regarded as the founder of the modern school of critical research in the field of early Christian literature, and he is still the leading authority on the conservative side.—GORDON, ALEXANDER, 1892, *Dictionary of National Biography, vol.* XXXII, *p.* 149.

William Falconer

1732-1769

Born, in Edinburgh, 11 Feb. 1732. At sea on merchant vessels in youth. Exchanged into Navy, 1749. On merchant vessel again, 1750. Contrib. poems to "Gentleman's Magazine." Re-entered Navy, 1760 [?]. Midshipman on "Royal George," 1762. Purser of frigate "Glory," 1763. Married Miss Hicks, 1763? Purser to "Swiftsure," 1767. Declined offer of partnership with John Murray, publisher, Oct. 1768. Purser of "Aurora" frigate, bound for India, with promise of secretaryship to Commissioners of H. E. I. C. Sailed, 2 Oct. 1869; ship was lost. *Works:* "A Poem, Sacred to the Memory of His Royal Highness, Frederick, Prince of Wales," 1751; "Ode on the Duke of York's Second Departure from England," 1762; "The Shipwreck," 1762; "An Universal Dictionary of the Marine," 1769. *Collected Poems:* first published in Johnson's "English Poets," 1790.—SHARP, R. FARQUHARSON, 1897, *A Dictionary of English Authors,* p. 96.

PERSONAL

In his person, he was about five feet seven inches in height; of a thin light make, with a dark weather-beaten complexion, and rather what is termed hard featured; being considerably marked with small-pox: his hair was of a brownish hue. In point of address, his manner was blunt, awkward, and forbidding: but he spoke with great fluency; and his simple, yet impressive, diction was couched in words which reminded his hearers of the terseness of Swift. Though Falconer possessed a warm and friendly disposition, he was fond of controversy, and inclined to satire. His observation was keen and rapid; his critcisms on any inaccuracy of language, or expression, were frequently severe; yet this severity was always intended eventually to create mirth, and not by any means to shew his own superiority, or to give the smallest offence. In his natural temper he was cheerful, and frequently used to amuse his messmates by composing acrostics on their favourites; in which he particularly excelled. As a professed man, he was a thorough seaman; and like most of that profession, was kind, generous, and benevolent.—CLARK, JAMES STANIER, 1804, *ed., The Shipwreck, Life.*

THE SHIPWRECK
1762

I have been reading Falconer's "Shipwreck"—a new humiliation for the ladies. I beg you may compare the close of that poem with Charlotte Smith's "Elegy," or with any female writer you ever saw, and glory you are a man. I fancy, while I weep over Arion, that I know him in real life. I figure also a Palemon to myself, but I would go twenty miles, if I had it in my power to do it with decency, to see William Falconer. Can you tell me is it he who is capt. on an East India ship? I shall rejoice to think it is. What a warmth of soul must he have originally possessed when the ocean was not able to quench it! Perhaps, Burns, such may be one day my poor Arion. I trace the resemblance in a thousand instances, and am resolved to have the book as a sacred remembrance I may brood over in secret, if it is not already out of print. Do write me what you think of this volume. Is my estimation fantastical, or does your judgment second mine? I hope it does, for I resolve, if I can find the "Shipwreck," it shall be placed close by your side on my shelf, at least for one month, my inseparable friend and companion. I will turn to it when the tempest howls, and pray for the poor wanderers of the wave with double hope and double fervor.—DUNLOP, FRANCES ANNE, 1789, *Correspondence with Robert Burns, Dec.* 24, *vol.* II, *p.* 24.

With two alone of all his clan
Forlorn the poet paced the Grecian shore,
No classic roamer, but a shipwrecked man!
Say then, what muse inspired these genial strains
And lit his spirit to so bright a flame?
The elevating thought of suffered pains,
Which gentle hearts shall mourn; but chief, the name
Of gratitude! remembrances of friend,
Or absent or no more! shades of the Past,
Which Love makes substance!

—COLERIDGE, SAMUEL TAYLOR, 1814? *To a Lady With Falconer's Shipwreck.*

His scholarship on the shores of Greece is only what we should accept of from a seaman; but his poem has the sensible charm of appearing a transcript of reality, and leaves an impression of truth and nature on the mind.—CAMPBELL, THOMAS, 1819, *Specimens of the British Poets.*

Falconer brought to the performance of his task a vigorous mind, a competent share of reading, strong powers of observation, and, what might least of all be expected from him, great felicity of numbers and expressions. He stands in need of no allowance for the scantiness of his education, or the nature of his employment. Whoever peruses the "Shipwreck" will be convinced, also, that the author is not a poet at second hand. His descriptions have a truth, a clearness, a freshness, which prove that he had seen and felt what he described. They are peculiarly his own. Of characters he has not many; but what he has are contrasted and supported with sufficient skill. The story is interesting, dramatically narrated, and has numerous touches of pathos. Attention is never suffered to flag. Even the scene of action contributes to shed a splendour over the poem.—DAVENPORT, R. A., 1822, *The British Poets, vol.* LVIII.

If the poem is estimated by a judgment lying between its positive merits, and the disadvantages under which it was composed,—undoubtedly the author will receive no slight portion of praise. And though, with the exception of some happier parts, it cannot satisfy the taste which has been formed on the finished writings of our leading poets, yet it is a singularly elegant production of a person who had received no education beyond the mere elements of language, and who was subsequently occupied in the severe duties and business of a seafaring life—equally without learning or leisure. The poetical powers of Falconer, in whatever rank they may be placed, were the gift of nature; for any assistance they may have derived from subsequent application, was only a proof that the original powers previously existed. The Milton of the village remained neither mute, nor inglorious.—MITFORD, JOHN, 1836, *The Poetical Works of William Falconer, Life.*

The merits of this celebrated composition are indeed undeniable. None but a great poet could have written "The Shipwreck," and that great poet must of necessity have been a thorough sailor. What home and its placid attractions are to the landsman, the sea and the storm were to Falconer. He delights in decking the ocean with all the terrific sublimity and wild beauty of which it is capable, and then calling upon us to admire the picture: our admiration may be enforced, but whilst we tremble, we cannot but applaud.—ALLIBONE, S. AUSTIN, 1854-58, *A Critical Dictionary of English Literature, vol.* I, *p.* 576.

It is too laboured and artificial to command permanent popularity.—ARNOLD, THOMAS, 1868-75, *Chaucer to Wordsworth, p.* 361.

There was largeness, and freedom and force in the subject he had chosen; and what is best in his treatment of it was learnt direct from the waves and winds. No one before Falconer had conceived or told in English poetry the long and passionate combat between the sea, roused to fury, and its slight but dexterous rival, with the varying fortunes of the strife. He had himself, like his Arion, been wrecked near Cape Colonna, on the coast of Greece; like Arion he was one of three who reached the shore and lived. For the material of his brief epic he needed but to revive in his imagination the sights, the sounds, the fears, the hopes, the efforts of five days the most eventful and the most vivid of his life. "The Shipwreck" is not a descriptive poem; it is a poem of action; each buffet of the sea, each swift turning of the wheel is a portion of the attack or defense; and as the catastrophe draws near, as the ship scuds past Falconera as the hills of Greece rise to view, as the pitiless cliffs of St. George grow clear, and the sound of the breakers is heard, the action of the poem increases in swiftness and intensity. Falconer was a skilful seaman; unhappily he was not a great poet. The reality, the unity, the largeness of his theme lend him support; and he is a faithful and energetic narrator. But the spirits of tempest and of night needed for their interpreter one of stronger and subtler speech than Falconer. —DOWDEN, EDWARD, 1880, *The English Poets, ed. Ward, vol.* III, *p.* 362.

Falconer's "Shipwreck" resembles most of the didactic poems of the time, and is marked by the conventionality common to them all. But it deserves a rather exceptional position from the obvious fidelity with which he has painted from nature; and though his use of technical terms is pushed even to ostentation, the effect of using the language of real life is often excellent, and is in marked contrast to the commonplaces of classical imitation which make other passages vapid and uninteresting. In this respect the poem made some mark, and Falconer had certainly considerable powers of fluent versification.—STEPHEN, LESLIE, 1889, *Dictionary of National Biography, vol.* XVIII, *p.* 165.

Falconer's work is most unequal. The verse at its best has an admirably easy flow, and at the same time a nervous energy beyond the reach of the mere copyist. But there are two very different accents in it. One is that of imitated classicism. The parts descriptive of the scenes through which the ship passes are poor. To make them good would have demanded a culture which Falconer had no opportunity to acquire. The classical similes, introduced by way of illustration, and the hackneyed loves are also poor. The other accent is that of nature; and to this the poem owes the whole of its value. The fact that Falconer relates what he himself saw and endured giving reality to his descriptions and speed and fire to his narrative. Sometimes, nay often, he so overloads his verse with technicalities that it sinks to mere prose; but in the happier passages he succeeds in throwing over the

hard facts of the sailor's life and lot the light of imagination. His fidelity to fact is the source of much that is bad, but likewise of all that is good in his poem. This too it is that connects him with the coming school. It is quite evident that he was troubled with no sense of discontent with the old. Versification and diction were imitated, as far as the author could imitate, from Pope; and where the matter suited he was ready to adopt the worst enormities of Pope's followers. But his choice of a subject introduced a vital difference. He had seen everything he described, had felt the agonies he painted, and was himself the hero of his poem.—
—WALKER, HUGH, 1893, *Three Centuries of Scottish Literature, vol.* II, *p.* 116.

The first and greatest of British marine poets.—EYRE-TODD, GEORGE, 1896, *Scottish Poetry of the Eighteenth Century, vol.* I, *p.* 209.

Thomas Chatterton

1752–1770

Born, at Bristol, 20 Nov. 1752. Educated at Colston's Hospital, Bristol, Aug. 1760 to July 1767. First poems printed in "Farley's Bristol Journal" 1763 and 1764. Apprenticed to a Bristol attorney, July 1767. First of "Rowley" poems written, 1768. Success with pseudo-antique poems. Apprentice indentures cancelled, April 1770. Left Bristol for London, 24 April 1770. Contributed to various periodicals, but resources gradually failed. Only one poem separately printed in lifetime. Committed suicide, 25 Aug. 1770. Buried in Shoe Lane Workhouse Churchyard. Afterwards transferred to graveyard in Gary's Inn Road. *Works:* "An Elegy on the much lamented death of William Beckford, Esq." (anon.), 1770. *Posthumous:* "The Execution of Sir Charles Baldwin" (ed. by T. Eagles), 1772; "Poems supposed to have been written at Bristol, by Thomas Rowley and others" (ed. by T. Tyrwhitt), 1777 (2nd edn., same year); "Miscellanies in Prose and verse" (ed. by J. Broughton), 1778; "Rowley" poems, ed. by Dean Milles, 1782; Supplement to "Miscellanies," 1784; "Rowley" poems, ed. by L. Sharpe, 1794; "The Revenge," 1795. *Poetical Works:* in 1 vol., 1795; in 3 vols., 1803; in 2 vols., 1875; in 1 vol., 1885. *Life:* by Gregory, 1789; by Davis (with letters) 1806; by Dix, 1837; by Wilson, 1869, and memoirs in edns. of works.—SHARP, R. FARQUHARSON, 1897, *A Dictionary of English Authors, p.* 53.

PERSONAL

Sir,—Upon recollection I don't know how Mr. Clayfield could come by his letter; as I intended to have given him a letter, but did not. In regard to my motives for the supposed rashness, I shall observe that I keep no worse company than myself. I never drink to excess; and have, without vanity, too much sense to be attracted to the mercenary retailers of iniquity. No! it is my pride, my damn'd native, unconquerable pride, that plunges me into distraction. You must know that 19-20ths of my composition is pride. I must either live a slave, a servant; have no will of my own, no sentiments of my own which I may freely declare as such; or die!—perplexing alternative. But it distracts me to think of it. I will endeavour to learn humility, but it cannot be here. What it will cost me on the trial Heaven knows!

I am your much obliged, unhappy, humble Servant, T. C.

—CHATTERTON, THOMAS, 1770, *Letter to Mr. Barrett.*

EDWIN CROSS, APOTHECARY, BROOK STREET, HOLBORN. Knew the deceased well, from the time he came to live with Mrs. Angell in the same street. Deceased used generally to call on him every time he went by his door, which was usually two or three times in a day: Deceased used to talk a great deal about physic, and was very inquisitive about the natures of different poisons. I often asked him to take a meal with us, but he was so proud that I could never but once prevail on him, though I knew he was half-starving. One evening he did stay, when I unusually pressed him. He talked a great deal, but all at once became silent, and looked quite vacant. He used to go very often to Falcon Court, Fleet Street, to a Mr. Hamilton, who printed a magazine; but who, he said, was using him very badly. I once recommended him to return to Bristol, but he only heaved a deep sigh; and begged me, with tears in his eyes, never to mention the hated name again. He called on me on the 24th August about half-past eleven in the morning, and bought some arsenic, which he said was for an experiment. About the same time next day, Mrs. Wolfe ran in for me, saying deceased had killed himself. I went to his room, and found him quite dead. On his window was a bottle containing arsenic and water; some of the little bits of arsenic were between his teeth. I believe if he had not killed himself, he would soon have died of starvation; for he was too proud to ask of anyone. Witness always considered deceased as an astonishing genius.—?CROSS, EDWIN, 1770, *Testimony at Inquest, Aug.* 27.

Unfortunate boy! poorly wast thou accommodated during thy short sojourning among us;—rudely wast thou treated,—sorely did thy feeling soul suffer from the scorn of the unworthy; and there are, at last, those who wish to rob thee of thy only meed, thy posthumous glory. Severe, too, are the censurers of thy morals. In the gloomy moments of despondency, I fear thou has uttered impious and blasphemous thoughts, which none can defend, and which neither thy youth, nor thy fiery spirit, nor thy situation, can extenuate. But let thy more rigid censors reflect, that thou wast literally and strictly but a boy. Let many of thy bitterest enemies reflect what were their own religious principles, and whether they had any, at the age of fourteen, fifteen, and sixteen. . . . In return for the pleasure I have received from thy poems, I pay thee, poor boy, the trifling tribute of my praise. Thyself thou has emblazoned; thine own monument thou has erected. But they whom thou has delighted, feel a pleasure in vindicating thine honours from the rude attacks of detraction.—KNOX, VESIMUS, 1777–1824, *Essays, Moral and Literary, No.* 144.

I am always intending to draw up an account of my intercourse with Chatterton, which I take very kindly you remind me of, but some avocation or other has prevented it. My perfect innocence on having indirectly been an ingredient in his dismal fate, which happened two years after our correspondence, and after he had exhausted both his resources and his constitution, have made it more easy to prove that I never saw him, knew nothing of his ever being in London, and was the first person, instead of the last, on whom he had practiced his impositions, and founded his chimeric hopes of promotion. My very first, or at least second letter, undeceived him in those views, and our correspondence was broken off before he quitted his master's business at Bristol; so that his disappointment with me was but his first ill success; and he resented my incredulity so much, that he never condescended to let me see him. Indeed, what I have said now to you, and which cannot be controverted by a shadow of a doubt, would be sufficient vindication. I could only add to the proofs, a vain regret of never having known his distresses, which his amazing genius would have tempted me to relieve, though I fear he had no other claim to compassion.—WALPOLE, HORACE, 1778, *Letter to Rev. William Cole, May* 21; *Letters, ed. Cunningham, vol.* VII, *p.* 70.

The activity of his mind is indeed almost unparalleled. But our surprise must decrease, when we consider that he slept but little; and that his whole attention was directed to literary pursuits; for he declares himself so ignorant of his profession, that he was unable to draw out a clearance from his apprenticeship, which Mr. Lambert demanded. He was also unfettered by the study of the dead languages, which usually absorb much of the time and attention of young persons; and though they may be useful to the attainment of correctness, perhaps they do not much contribute to fluency in writing. Mr. Catcott declared, that when he first knew Chatterton, he was ignorant even of Grammar. . . . The person of Chatterton, like his genius, was premature; he had a manliness and dignity beyond his years, and there was a something about him uncommonly prepossessing. His most remarkable feature was his eyes, which though grey, were uncommonly piercing; when he was warmed in argument, or otherwise, they sparkled with fire, and one eye, it is said, was still more remarkable than the other.—GREGORY, GEORGE, 1779–1803, *Life of Thomas Chatterton, ed. Southey, vol.* I, *pp.* lv, lxxi.

Oh, ill-starr'd Youth, whom Nature form'd in vain,
With powers on Pindus' splendid height to reign!

O dread example of what pangs await
Young Genius struggling with malignant fate!
—HAYLEY, WILLIAM, 1782, *An Essay on Epic Poetry.*

Yet as with streaming eye the sorrowing muse,
Pale Chatterton's untimely urn bedews;
Her accents shall arraign the partial care,
That shielded not her son from cold despair.
—PYE, HENRY JAMES, 1783, *The Progress of Refinement, pt.* ii.

Sweet Flower of Hope! free Nature's genial child!
That didst so fair disclose thy early bloom,
Filling the wide air with a rich perfume!
. . . .
Poor Chatterton! *he* sorrows for thy fate
Who would have praised and loved thee, ere too late,
Poor Chatterton! farewell! of darkest hues
This chaplet cast I on thy unshaped tomb;
But dare no longer on the sad theme muse,
Lest kindred woes persuade a kindred doom:
For oh! big gall-drops, shook from Folly's wing,
Have blackened the fair promise of my spring;
And the stern Fate transpierced with viewless dart
The last pale Hope that shivered at my heart!
. . . .
O Chatterton! that thou wert yet alive!
. . . .
We, at sober eve, would round thee throng,
Hanging, enraptured, on thy stately song,
And greet with smiles the young-eyed Poesy
All deftly masked as hoar Antiquity.
. . . .
Sweet Harper of time-shrouded Minstrelsy!
—COLERIDGE, SAMUEL TAYLOR, 1790–1829, *Monody on the Death of Chatterton.*

The Bard, to dark despair resign'd,
With his expiring art,
Sings, midst the tempest of his mind,
The shipwreck of his heart.
If Hope still seem to linger nigh,
And hover o'er his head,
Her pinions are too weak to fly,
Or Hope ere now had fled.
Rash Minstrel! who can hear thy songs,
Nor long to share thy fire?
Who read thine errors and thine wrongs,
Nor execrate the lyre?
The lyre, that sunk thee to the grave,
When bursting into bloom,
That lyre, the power to Genius gave
To blossom in the tomb.
Yes;—till his memory fail with years,
Shall Time thy strains recite;
And while thy story swells his tears,
Thy song shall charm his flight.
—MONTGOMERY, JAMES, 1802, *Chatterton.*

I thought of Chatterton, the marvellous Boy,
The sleepless Soul that perish'd in his pride.
—WORDSWORTH, WILLIAM, 1802, *Resolution and Independence.*

As to his person, his sister said that he was thin of body, but neatly made; that his features were by no means handsome, and yet, notwithstanding, the *tout-ensemble* was striking; which arose, she conceived, from the wonderful expression of his eyes, and more particularly of the left eye, which, to use her own words, seemed at times, from its brilliancy, "to flash fire." She then proceeded to acquaint me that some malevolent aspersions had been thrown out as to his moral character, and particularly his being partial to the society of abandoned women, which she positively denied, with tears in her eyes; stating that he was the best and most tender of brothers, never enjoying so much satisfaction as when he could present them some little token of his affection; that he always kept good hours at night, to her certain knowledge; and that by day he was by far too much taken up with books and his occupations to be a loose character.—As to his having a predilection for some female, she told me she believed that to have been the case; but, to the best of her knowledge, and from her soul (she assured me) she spoke it, no stain whatsoever could attach itself to his moral conduct.—IRELAND, WILLIAM-HENRY, 1805, *Confessions, p.* 15.

This boy [a nephew of Mr. Walmsley] who was the bedfellow of Chatterton, informed Mr. Croft that Chatterton used to sit up all night reading and writing; that he never came to bed till very late, often three or four o'clock, but that he was always awake when he waked, and got up at the same time. He lived chiefly upon a half-penny roll, or a tart and some water. . . . He did not, however, wholly abstain from meat, for he was once or twice known to take a sheep's tongue out of his pocket. . . . Early in July Chatterton left his lodgings in Shoreditch, and went to lodge with Mrs. Angel, a sock-maker, in Brook Street, Holborn. It were an injury not to mention historically the lodgings of Chatterton, for every spot he made his residence has become poetical ground. . . . Of his extreme indigence there is positive testimony. Mrs. Angel remembers that for two days, when he did not absent himself from his room, he went without food. . . . Pressed hard by indigence and its companions, gloom and despondency, the mind of Chatterton became disordered, and on the night of the 24th of August, 1770, he swallowed a large dose of opium, which caused his death. . . . The inquest of the jury was brought in insanity, and the body of Chatterton was put into a shell, and carried unwept, unheeded, and unowned to the burying-ground of the workhouse in Shoe Lane.—DAVIS, JOHN, 1806, *Life of Chatterton.*

He became an infidel, but whether this was in consequence of any course of reading into which he had fallen, or that he found it convenient to get rid of the obligations which stood in the way of his past or future schemes, it is not very material to inquire. . . . In his writings we find some passages that are more licentious than could have been expected from a young man unhackneyed in the way of vice, but not more so than might be expected in one who was premature in every thing, and had exhausted the stock of human folly at an age when it is usually found unbroken. All his deceptions, his prevarications, his political tergiversation, &c., were such as should have been looked for in men of an advanced age, hardened by evil associations, and soured by disappointed pride or avarice. — CHALMERS, ALEXANDER, 1814, *The Works of the English Poets.*

When we conceive the inspired boy transporting himself in imagination back to the days of his fictitious Rowley, embodying his ideal character, and giving to airy nothing a "local habitation and a name," we may forget the impostor in the enthusiast, and forgive the falsehood of his reverie for its beauty and ingenuity. —CAMPBELL, THOMAS, 1819, *Specimens of the British Poets.*

Marvellous boy, whose antique songs and unhappy story
Shall, by gentle hearts, be in mournful memory cherished
Long as thy ancient towers endure, and the rocks of St. Vincent,
Bristol! my birthplace dear.
—SOUTHEY, ROBERT, 1821, *A Vision of Judgment*, xi.

O Chatterton! how very sad thy fate!
Dear child of sorrow—son of misery!
How soon the film of death obscur'd that eye,
Whence Genius mildly flash'd, and high debate.
How soon that voice, majestic and elate,
Melting in dying numbers! Oh! how nigh
Was night to thy fair morning. Thou didst die
A half-blown flow'ret which cold blasts amate.
But this is past: thou art among the stars
Of highest Heaven: to the rolling spheres
Thou sweetly singest: nought thy hymning mars,
Above the ingrate world and human fears.
On earth the good man base detraction bars
From thy fair name, and waters it with tears.
—KEATS, JOHN, 1821? *To Chatterton.*

He would sometimes, for days together, go in and out of the house without speaking to any one, and seemingly absorbed in thought. After such occasions he frequently called some of his associates into his room, and read them some portions of Rowley. — DIX, JOHN, 1837–51, *Life of Chatterton.*

A native aptitude to self-sufficiency, pertinacity, and scorn of interference or censure, gave a ready admission into the formation of his character of the unmitigated effect of every thing that, in the circumstances of his situation, tended to create a predominance of the qualities we are describing. Growing up separate and alien, in a great degree, from the social interests and sentiments which bind men together, he was habitually ready and watchful for occasions to practise on their weakness and folly, and to indulge a propensity to annoyance by satire. He would play off the witty malice, no matter who was the object. He was a very Ishmael with this weapon. It is somewhere his own confession that, when the mood was on him, he spared neither foe nor friend. Very greatly amusing as it may well be believed that his company was when he chose to give it, nobody was safe against having his name, with his peculiarities, his hobby, his vanity, hitched into some sarcastic stanza. Men must not be expected to sympathize very kindly with the mortifications of a person, who, whatever be his talents, demands that such temper and habits shall be no obstruction to advancement in society.— FOSTER, JOHN, 1838–56, *Critical Essays, ed. Ryland, vol.* II, *p.* 520.

The house in which Chatterton was born

was behind a shop nearly opposite the northwest corner of the church; and the monument to the young poet, lately erected by subscription, has been very appropriately placed in a line between this house and the north porch of the church in which he professed to have found the Rowley MSS. This monument is a Gothic erection, much resembling an ancient cross, and on the top stands Chatterton, in the dress of Colston's school, and with an unfolded roll of parchment in his hand. This monument was erected under the care and from the design of John Britton, the antiquary, who, so much to his honor, long zealously exerted himself to rescue Chatterton's memory from apparent neglect in his native city. The man who can gaze on this monument; can contemplate the boyish figure and face of the juvenile poet; can glance from this quarter, where he was born in poverty, to that old porch, where he planned the scheme of his fame; and can call to mind what he was and what he did without the profoundest sensations of wonder and regret, may safely pass through life without fear of an astonishment. It is, in my opinion one of the most affecting objects in Great Britain. How much, then, is that feeling of sympathy and regret augmented when you approach, and, upon the monument, read the very words written by the inspired boy himself for his supposed monument, and inserted in his "will."

"To the Memory of
Thomas Chatterton.
Reader, judge not: if thou art a Christian—believe that he shall be judged by a Superior Power; to that Power alone is he now answerable."

—HOWITT, WILLIAM, 1846, *Homes and Haunts of the Most Eminent British Poets, vol.* I, *p.* 299.

A little beyond Snow Hill is Shoe Lane, running from Holborn into Fleet Street. In the burial ground of Shoe Lane workhouse was interred the ill-fated poet, Thomas Chatterton. The ground in which he lies buried now forms a part of Farringdon Market, immediately adjoining Shoe Lane, but the exact site of his resting place is unfortunately unknown.—JESSE, J. HENEAGE, 1850, *London and Its Celebrities, vol.* I, *p.* 438.

The first place that I visited was connected with a far deeper tragedy, the beautiful church of St. Mary Redcliffe. I climbed up to the muniment room over the porch, now and forever famous, and sitting down on the stone chest then empty, where poor Chatterton pretended to have found the various writings he attributed to Rowley, and from whence he probably did obtain most of the ancient parchment that served as his material, I could understand the effect that the mere habit of haunting such a chamber might produce upon a sensitive and imaginative boy. . . . A most painful irreligious paper, called his will, written, let us hope, under the influence of the same phrensy that prompted his suicide, is shown in a glass case in the museum at Bristol.—MITFORD, MARY RUSSELL, 1851, *Recollections of a Literary Life, pp.* 387, 389.

Although Walpole was very indignant at Chatterton's attempt to impose upon him, in the course of his own career he affords several instances of having indulged in similar deceptions. . . . Walpole quite forgot his own offences in the greatness of his anger at the offence of the Bristol apprentice—possibly imagining, that what was the most natural thing in the world, when done by a gentleman of family, was altogether unpardonable when attempted by a boy just emancipated from a charity school.—WARBURTON, ELIOT, 1852, *Memoirs of Horace Walpole, vol.* II, *p.* 346.

Besides being an antiquarian, and a creative genius in the element of the English antique, Chatterton was also, in the year 1769–70, a complete and very characteristic specimen of that long-extinct phenomenon, a thinking young Englishman of the early part of the reign of George III. In other words, reader, besides being, by the special charter of his genius, a poet in the Rowley vein, he was also, by the more general right of his life at that time, very much such a young fellow as your own unmarried great-great-grandfather was.—MASSON, DAVID, 1856–74, *Chatterton, A Story of the Year* 1770, *p.* 53.

That he was, in one sense of the word, profligate—that is, that he was a habitual and gross liar, and not restrained by any religious or moral principle from saying or writing that which he knew to be false, for the sake of gain,—is too clear; but that he was profligate as the word is used with reference to sensual immorality, at least in such way as should account for pecuniary distress, I do not believe.—MAITLAND, SAMUEL ROFFEY, 1857, *Chatterton: An Essay, p.* 47.

At every step it is needful to recall this fact of boyhood, apart from every other adverse element of orphanage, poverty, and misguidance. For the study is that of a child, a boy, a youth, running counter to all the tastes and habits of his age; acting in defiance of ordinary influences; at every stage doing a man's work: often unwisely, perversely, unaccountably; but still doing the work of a man, and baffling the astute selfishness of men, while yet a child. Viewed in its most unfavourable aspects, such an intellectual phenomenon may well attract our study, as a strange example of precocity, approximating, almost to genius acting by instinct: like those manifestations of irrational vital action, which puzzle us by their resemblance to the highest intelligence. But the brief existence here retraced has also its phases of sorrowful, and even tragic interest, on which we now look back as on a precious inheritance which that eighteenth century wasted and flung aside.—WILSON, DANIEL, 1869, *Chatterton: A Biographical Study, Introduction, p.* xvi.

Thomas Chatterton, whose forgery consisted in publishing his own compositions as the poems of Rowley, who lived in the fifteenth century, was an infidel in profession and a libertine in practice; and as he was the most precocious in genius, so was he the most circumstantial in falsehood, of the literary forgers of the age. That his suicide was premeditated is undoubted. . . . He chose to leave Bristol, where he had many friends, to seek his fortune in London, where he had none; and, when he failed, was too proud to return to his native city. To complain of the "cold neglect" of the world with regard to a boy of eighteen, however great his genius, is quite preposterous. But it was the fashion to consider he was neglected and starved, and epigrams, such as the following, were written on him ("Asylum for Fugitive Pieces," 1785, 118):

All think, now Chatterton is dead,
His works are worth preserving!
Yet no one, when he was alive,
Would keep the bard from starving!

Johnson, Goldsmith, and a hundred others, who were nearly starved at eighteen, persevered and won their way to fame, as Chatterton might have done, had his character been of a higher stamp.—DODD, HENRY PHILIP, 1870, *The Epigrammatists, pp.* 424, 425.

With Shakspeare's manhood at a boy's wild heart,—
Through Hamlet's doubt to Shakspeare near allied,
And kin to Milton through his Satan's pride,—
At Death's sole door he stooped, and craved a dart;
And to the dear new bower of England's art,—
Even to that shrine Time else had deified,
The unuttered heart that soared against his side,—
Drove the fell point, and smote life's seals apart.
Thy nested home-loves, noble Chatterton;
The angel-trodden stair thy soul could trace
Up Redcliffe's spire; and in the world's armed space
Thy gallant sword-play:—these to many an one
Are sweet for ever; as thy grave unknown
And love-dream of thine unrecorded face.
—ROSSETTI, DANTE GABRIEL, 1881, *Five English Poets, Ballads and Sonnets.*

Chatterton's remains, enclosed in a shell, were interred in the Shoe Lane workhouse burying-ground on 28 Aug. 1770, as appears from the register of burials at St. Andrew's, Holborn, where the name is entered as "William Chatterton," to which another hand has added "the poet." Years afterwards, when that site had to be cleared for the building up of the new Farringdon Market, the paupers' bones, all huddled together, were removed to the old graveyard in the Gray's Inn Road. A wildly improbable story about the exhumation and reinterment of his remains at Bristol was first told by George Cumberland in Dix's Appendix A (p. 299), and afterwards reiterated more in detail by Joseph Cottle in Pryce's "Memorials of the Canynges Family" (p. 293). A still wilder story was put forth in 1853 by Mr. Gutch in "Notes and Queries" (vii. 138, 139) and which purported to be an authentic record of the coroner's inquest on the occasion of Chatterton's suicide. Four years afterwards, however, Mr. Moy Thomas was able to demonstrate, from the parish books of St. Andrew's, Holborn, in the "Athenæum" of 5 Dec., 1857, the spurious character of the whole narrative. The books also showed that Chatterton died in the first house from Holborn on the left-hand side, the last number of all in Brooke Street, No. 39.—KENT, CHARLES, 1887, *Dictionary of National Biography, vol.* x, *p.* 150.

Below, an open window kept
  Old books in rare display,
Where critics drowsed and poets slept
  Till Grub Street's judgment-day.
One book brought care again to me,—
  The book of Rowley's rhyme,
That Chatterton, in seigneury
  Of song, bore out of time.
The merchant of such ware, unseen,
  Watched spider-like the street;
He came forth, gray, and spider-thin,
  And talked with grave conceit.
Old books, old times,—he drew them nigh
  At Chatterton's pale spell:
"'Twas Brook Street," said he, "saw him die,
  Old Holborn knew him well."
The words brought back in sudden sway
  That new-old tale of doom;
It seemed the boy but yesterday
  Died in his lonely room.
Without, the press of men was heard;
  I heard, as one who dreamed,
The hurrying throng, the singing bird,
  And yesterday it seemed.
And as I turned to go, the tale
  This pensive requiem made,
As though within the churchyard's pale
  The boy was newly laid:
Perhaps, who knows? the hurrying throng
  Gave hopeless thoughts to him;
I fancy how he wandered, long,
  Until the light grew dim.
The windows saw him come and pass
  And come and go again,
And still the throng swept by—alas!
  The barren face of men.
And when the day was done, the way
  Was lost in lethal deeps:
Sweet Life!—what requiem to say?—
  "'Tis well, 'tis well, he sleeps."

—RHYS, ERNEST, 1891, *Chatterton in Holborn, Century Magazine, vol.* 42, *p.* 350.

The public of 1830 permitted itself to be moved by the misfortune of Chatterton; it pitied that ulcerated soul, for whom the fatal result of genius is suicide. When the work is reproduced thirty years later, the audience advises the poor devil "to sell his boots."—PELLISSIER, GEORGES, 1897, *The Evolution of Realism, The Literary Movement in France During the Nineteenth Century, tr. Brinton, p.* 332.

Perhaps it may be more than an idle fancy to attribute to heredity the bent which Chatterton's genius took spontaneously and almost from infancy; to guess that some mysterious antenatal influence—"striking the electric chain wherewith we are darkly bound"—may have set vibrating links of unconscious association running back through the centuries. Be this as it may, Chatterton was the child of Redcliffe Church. St. Mary stood by his cradle and rocked it; and if he did not inherit with his blood, or draw in with his mother's milk a veneration for her ancient pile, at least the waters of her baptismal font seemed to have signed him with the token of her service. Just as truly as "The Castle of Otranto" was sprung from Strawberry Hill, the Rowley poems were born of St. Mary's Church.—BEERS, HENRY A., 1898, *A History of English Romanticism in the Eighteenth Century, p.* 339.

We all know the history of Chatterton: what would be the history of a Chatterton of the present day? I will tell it, taking a living example, from my own knowledge. As a boy he was bookish: he devoured all the books he could lay hands upon: he borrowed and read: at school he was easily first: at home he locked himself up and secretly wrote poetry: already he had joined the fraternity of those who write. When he left school, at which he had learned shorthand, he was placed in a newspaper office. Here he reported meetings and lectures and police cases: he picked up news; he shaped the paragraph: he made himself generally useful: presently he began to write descriptive papers: he reviewed books: all this time he was giving his leisure hours—which were not too many—to the cultivation of literature. And at last he brought out his first work—a volume of poems perhaps: or a volume of fiction or a volume of essays—with the help of which he introduced himself. His name now began to appear in magazines, and more and more frequently—yet he remained on his newspaper: he was not in the least danger of starving: he was, on the contrary, well fed and fairly prosperous. But he drifted more and more into authorship. He has now become well known as a writer. If he is wise he will continue to write for the papers as well as the magazines. Perhaps at last the day will come when he will be fully justified in trusting to himself, and can give up the newspaper work. But he will never quite give up his connection with journalism. Very likely he will be appointed editor of some magazine: he may be invited to advise on some great publishing firm: he may be appointed literary editor of a great morning paper. That would be the modern career of a new Chatterton.— BESANT, WALTER, 1898, *The Pen and the Book, p.* 23.

GENERAL

Johnson said of Chatterton, "This is the most extraordinary young man that has encountered my knowledge. It is wonderful how the whelp has written such things."—JOHNSON, SAMUEL, 1776, *Life by Boswell, ed. Hill, vol.* III, *p.* 59.

I think poor Chatterton was an astonishing genius. . . . The prematurity of Chatterton's genius is, however, full as wonderful, as that such a prodigy as Rowley should never have been heard of till the eighteenth century. The youth and industry of the former are miracles, too, yet still more credible. There is not a symptom in the poems, but the old words, that savours of Rowley's age —change the old words for modern, and the whole construction is of yesterday. —WALPOLE, HORACE, 1777, *Letter to Rev. William Cole, June* 19; *Letters, ed. Cunningham, vol.* VI, *p.* 447.

We find, among these Poems, Odes in irregular metres, Eclogues of the Pastoral kind, and Discoursing Tragedies; compositions, for not one of which any example could be found in England in the XVth century. Even in those compositions, of which the species was not entirely unknown, it is impossible not to observe a striking difference from the other compositions of that age, with respect to the *manner* in which they are constructed, and the *subjects* to which they are applied. Instead of tedious chronicles we have here interesting portions of history, selected and embellished with all the graces of epic poetry; instead of devotional hymns, legendary tales, and moralizations of scripture, we have elegant little poems upon *charitie* and *happinesse*, a *new church*, a *living worthy*, and other occurrences of the moment: no translations from the French, no allusions to the popular authors of the middle ages; nothing, in short, of what we see in so many other writers about that time. If Rowley really lived and wrote these poems in the XVth century, he must have stalked about, like Tiresias among the *Homeric ghosts*—

"He only wise, the rest mere fleeting shades."—

—TYRWHITT, THOMAS, 1777–84, *ed. Rowley Poems.*

On the whole, I am inclined to believe, that these poems were composed by the son of the school-master before mentioned; who inherited the inestimable treasures of Cannynge's chest in Radcliffe-church, as I have already related at large. This youth, who died at eighteen, was a prodigy of genius: and would have proved the first of English poets, had he reached a maturer age.—WARTON, THOMAS, 1778–81, *The History of English Poetry, sec.* XXVI.

Nor does my memory supply me with any human being, who, at such an age, with such disadvantages, has produced such compositions. Under the heathen mythology, superstition and admiration would have explained all, by bringing Apollo upon earth; nor would the god ever have descended with more credit to himself.—CROFT, SIR HERBERT, 1780, *Love and Madness.*

Gentlemen of the jury, the prisoner at the bar is indicted for the uttering certain poems composed by himself, purporting them to be the poems of Thomas Rowley, a priest of the fifteenth century, against the so frequently disturbed peace of Parnassus, to the great disturbance and confusion of the Antiquary Society, and likewise notoriously to the prejudice of the literary fame of the said Thomas Chatterton.—MATY, HENRY, 1782, *New Review.*

Chatterton's conduct and opinions were early tinctured with irreligion. How must his mind have laboured under the burden of describing pathetically the pleasures of virtue and the rewards of religion; which are so frequently mentioned in these poems, though they had not made their proper impression on his heart!—MILLES, JEREMIAH, 1782, *Preliminary Dissertation to Rowley's Poems.*

The greatest genius England has produced since the days of Shakespear.—MALONE, EDMOND, 1782, *Cursory Observations on the Poems Attributed to Rowley, p.* 41.

For Chatterton, he was a gigantic genius, and might have soared I know not whither.—WALPOLE, HORACE, 1785, *Letter to the Countess of Ossory, July* 4; *Letters, ed. Cunningham, vol.* VIII, *p.* 570.

On Monday, April 29, he [Johnson] and I made an excursion to Bristol, where I was entertained with seeing him enquire upon the spot, into the authenticity of "Rowley's Poetry," as I had seen him enquire upon the spot into the authenticity of "Ossian's Poetry." George Catcot, the pewterer, who was as zealous for Rowley, as Dr. Hugh Blair was for Ossian, (I trust my Reverend friend will excuse the comparison), attended us at our inn, and with a triumphant air of lively simplicity called out, "I'll make Dr. Johnson a Convert." Dr. Johnson, at his desire, read aloud some of Chatterton's fabricated verses, while Catcot stood at the back of his chair, moving himself like a pendulum, and beating time with his feet, and now and then looking into Dr. Johnson's face, wondering that he was not yet convinced. We called on Mr. Barret the surgeon, and saw some of the *originals* as they were called, which were executed very artificially; but from a careful inspection of them, and a consideration of the circumstances with which they were attended, we were quite satisfied of the imposture, which, indeed, has been clearly demonstrated from internal evidence, by several able critics.—BOSWELL, JAMES, 1791–93, *Life of Johnson, ed. Hill, vol.* III, *p.* 58.

That the Rowley-poems are thus printed as the Works of Chatterton, will not surprise the public, though it may perhaps renew a controversy in which much talent has been mis-employed. The merit of these poems has been long acknowledged. Whatever be the value of the others, the Editors hope they have performed an acceptable, as they know it to be a useful labour, in thus collecting, so far as they have been able, all the productions of the most extraordinary young man that ever appeared in this country. They have felt peculiar pleasure, as natives of the same city, in performing this act of justice to his fame and to the interests of his family.—SOUTHEY, ROBERT, 1803, *ed., The Works of Thomas Chatterton, Preface, vol.* I, *p.* vi.

As Rowley, Chatterton had put forth his whole strength, and exerted himself to the utmost, in describing those scenes of antique splendour which captivated his imagination so strongly. But when he wrote in his own character, he was under the necessity of avoiding every idea, subject, or expression, however favourite, which could tend to identify the style of Chatterton with that of Rowley; and surely it is no more to be expected that, thus cramped and trammelled, he should equal his unrestrained efforts, than that a man should exert the same speed with fetters on his limbs, as if they were at liberty.—SCOTT SIR WALTER, 1804, *Chatterton, Edinburgh Review, vol.* 4, *p.* 221.

Chatterton had written a political essay for "The North Briton," which opened with the preluding flourish of "A spirited people freeing themselves from insupportable slavery:" it was, however, though accepted, not printed, on account of the Lord Mayor's death. The patriot thus calculated the death of his great patron!

		£.	s.	d.
Lost by his death in this Essay, ...		1	11	6
Gained in Elegies, .	£2 2			
———in Essays, .	3 3			
		5	5	0
Am glad he is dead by .		£3	13	6

—DISRAELI, ISAAC, 1812–13, *A Mendicant Author, Calamities of Authors, note.*

I cannot find in Chatterton's works anything so extraordinary as the age at which they were written. They have a facility, vigour, and knowledge, which were prodigious in a boy of sixteen, but which would not have been so in a man of twenty. He did not shew extraordinary powers of genius, but extraordinary precocity. Nor do I believe he would have written better had he lived. He knew this himself, or he would have lived. Great geniuses, like great kings, have too much to think of to kill themselves; for their mind to them also "a kingdon is." With an unaccountable power coming over him at an unusual age, and with the youthful confidence it inspired, he performed wonders, and was willing to set a seal on his reputation by a tragic catastrophe. He had done his best; and, like another Empedocles, threw himself into Ætna, to ensure immortality.—HAZLITT, WILLIAM, 1818, *Lectures on the English Poets, Lecture* vi.

INSCRIBED,
WITH EVERY FEELING OF PRIDE AND REGRET
AND WITH "A BOWED MIND,"
TO THE MEMORY OF
THE MOST ENGLISH OF POETS EXCEPT SHAKESPEARE,
THOMAS CHATTERTON.

—KEATS, JOHN, 1818, *Original Inscription of Endymion.*

Had Chatterton possessed sufficient manliness of mind to know the magnanimity of patience, and been aware that great talents have a commission from Heaven, he would not have deserted his post, and his name might have been paged with Milton.—PORTER, JANE, 1819, *Letter to Keats.*

Chatterton's language is entirely northern. I prefer the native music of it to Milton's, cut by feet.—KEATS, JOHN, 1819, *Letter to George and Georgiana Keats, Sept.* 22; *Letters, ed. Colvin, p.* 313.

The inequality of Chatterton's various productions may be compared to the disproportions of the ungrown giant. His works had nothing of the definite neatness of that precocious talent which stops short in early maturity. His thirst for knowledge was that of a being taught by instinct to lay up materials for the exercise of great and undeveloped powers. Even in his favourite maxim, pushed it might be to hyperbole, that a man by abstinence and perseverance might accomplish whatever he pleased, may be traced the indications of a genius which nature had meant to achieve works of immortality. Tasso alone can be compared to him as a juvenile prodigy. No English poet ever equalled him at the same age.—CAMPBELL, THOMAS, 1819, *Specimens of the British Poets.*

We are told in the life of Chatterton, that, in his early boyhood, he was reckoned of very dull intellect, till he "fell in love," as his mother expressed it, with the illuminated capitals of an old musical manuscript, in French, from which she taught him his letters. . . . It is impossible to think of the subsequent history of this wonderful young man, without tracing a probable connexion of those accidental circumstances, which could not fail to give a peculiar importance to certain conceptions, with the character of that genius, which was afterwards to make grey-headed erudition bend before it, and to astonish at least all those on whom it did not impose.—BROWN, THOMAS, 1820, *The Philosophy of the Human Mind, Lecture* xliv.

Nothing indeed is more wonderful in the Rowley poems than the masterly style of versification which they frequently display. Few more exquisite specimens of this kind can be found in our language than the Ministrel's song in Ælla, beginning,

O sing unto my roundelay.

A young poet may be expected to describe warmly and energetically whatever interests his fancy or his heart; but a command of numbers would seem to be an art capable of being perfected only by long-continued and diligent endeavours. It must be recollected, however, that much might be done in the time which was at Chatterton's disposal, when that time was undivided by the study of any other language but his own.—CARY, HENRY FRANCIS, 1821-24-46, *Lives of English Poets, ed. Cary, p.* 408.

I have said that there was not a new book written within these ten years. In the days of our fathers, it would have been necessary, at least, to mention as a forgery the celebrated poems attributed to Thomas Rowley. But probably no one person living believes in their authenticity.—HALLAM, HENRY, 1837-39, *Introduction to the Literature of Europe, pt.* i, *ch.* iii, *par.* 43.

It may be observed, before we close the chapter, that Chatterton has used the Spenser-staves, in the poems which he ascribed to Rowley. This anachronism would, of itself, be sufficient to prove the forgery, even though it had baffled every other test, which modern criticism has applied to it.—GUEST, EDWIN, 1838, *A History of English Rhythms, vol.* II, *p.* 396.

We have never thought that the world lost more in the "marvellous boy," Chatterton, than a very ingenious imitator of obscure and antiquated dulness.—LOWELL, JAMES RUSSELL, 1845, *Edgar Allan Poe, Graham's Magazine, Feb.*

There can be no doubt of the admirable merit of the poems themselves; they are full of genius, and some of them are in the highest degree dignified and sublime; but this beauty and sublimity are certainly not of the fifteenth century; so that whatever glory Chatterton loses as an antiquarian, he more than recovers as a poet. As a poet alone he would, if he had lived, have been the greatest of his age. —SHAW, THOMAS B., 1847, *Outlines of English Literature, p.* 303.

Chatterton evinced how mighty his genius was, by the distance at which it anticipated experience. Why, when most of our boys are but blubbering their books, this superhuman youth was pouring out the thoughts, that swell and shake the breast of manhood. Still, there is no means by which genius can altogether anticipate experience. The faculties most powerful, therefore, in the youth of genius, are those which distinguish the writings of Chatterton. These are luxuriance of fancy and opulence of expression. The fancy of Chatterton is not only rich but strong; it has not only a plumage of dazzling splendor, but a pinion of daring flight; and his language reflects, perfectly, the brilliancy of his fancy and sustains him amidst the bravest of its soarings.—GILES, HENRY, 1850, *Lectures and Essays, vol.* II, *p.* 288.

Curious is it to note that in the long controversy, which followed on the publication by Chatterton of the poems which he ascribed to a monk Rowlie, living in the fifteenth century, no one appealed at the time to such lines as the following,

"Life, and all *its* goods I scorn,'

as at once decisive of the fact that the poems were not of the age which they pretended. Warton who rejected, although with a certain amount of hesitation, the poems, and gives reasons, and many of them good ones, for this rejection, yet takes no notice of this little word, which betrays the forgery at once; although there needed nothing more than to point to it, for the disposing of the whole question.—TRENCH, RICHARD CHENEVIX, 1855, *English Past and Present, p.* 101.

Up to a certain point, as it were, Chatterton could remain himself; but the moment he was hurried past that point, the moment he attained to a certain degree of sublimity, or fervour, or solemnity in his conceptions, and was constrained to continue at the same pitch, at that moment he reverted to the fifteenth century, and passed into the soul of Rowley. No one who has not read the antique poems of Chatterton can conceive what extraordinary things they are. . . . These antique poems of Chatterton (and there are about twenty shorter ones in the same series) are perhaps as worthy of being read consecutively as many portions of the poetry of Byron, Shelley, or Keats. There are passages in them, at least, quite equal to any to be found in these poets; and it is only the uncouth and spurious appearance of antiquity which they wear when the absurd spelling in which they were first printed is retained that prevents them from being known and quoted. . . . With no other evidence before us than is afforded by this and the other antique pieces which we have quoted, one may assert, unhesitatingly, not only that Chatterton was a true English poet of the eighteenth century, but also that, compared with the other English poets of the part of that century immediately prior to the new era begun by Burns and Wordsworth, he was, with all his immaturity, almost solitary in the possession of the highest poetic gift. Pope, Thomson, and Goldsmith, were poets of this century; and no sensible man will for a moment think of comparing the boy of Bristol, in respect of his whole activity, with those fine stars of our literature, or even with some of the lesser stars that shone along with them. But he had a specific fire and force of imagination in him which they had not.—MASSON, DAVID, 1856–74, *Chatterton: A Story of the Year* 1770, *pp.* 270, 274, 283.

Think you, no fond creatures
Draw comfort from the features
Of Chatterton, that Phaëthon pale, struck down to sunless soil?
Scorch'd with sunlight lying,
Eyes of sunlight hollow,
But, see! upon the lips a gleam of the chrism of Apollo!

—BUCHANAN, ROBERT, 1866, *To David in Heaven.*

Perhaps the clearest evidence of his high poetic gifts is to be found in the comparisons instituted between him and other poets. By reason of his very excellence he has been tried by the highest standards, without thought of his immaturity. Grave critics are found testing the Rowley Poems by Chaucer, or matching them with Cowley and Prior; and even finding in the acknowledged satires of a boy of sixteen "more of the luxuriance, fluency, and negligence of Dryden, than of the terseness and refinement of Pope." One of the strongest evidences of his self-originating power is, in reality, to be found in the contrast which his verse presents to that of his own day. In an age when the seductive charm of Pope's polished numbers captivated public taste, Chatterton struck a new chord and evolved principles of harmony which suggest comparison with Elizabethan poets, rather than with those of Anne's Augustan era. But he was no imitator. Amid all the assumption of antique thought, the reader perceives everywhere that he had looked on Nature for himself; and could discern in her, alike in her calm beauty, and in her stormiest moods, secrets hidden from the common eye. He had, moreover, patriotic sympathies as intense as Burns himself. His Goddwyn, Harold, Ælla, and Rycharde, his Hastings, Bristowe, or Ruddeborne, are all lit up with the same passionate fire, to which some of his finest outbursts of feeling were due; and which was still more replete with promise for the future.—WILSON, DANIEL, 1869, *Chatterton: A Biographical Study, p.* 316.

If he had really taken pains to *read* and *study* Chaucer or Lydgate or any old author earlier than the age of Spenser, the Rowley poems would have been very different. They would then have borne some resemblance to the language of the fifteenth century, whereas they are rather less like the language of that period than of any other. The spelling of the words is frequently too late, or too bizarre, whilst many of the words themselves are too archaic or too uncommon.—SKEAT, WALTER W., 1871, *ed. Chatterton's Poetical Works, Essay on the Rowley Poems, vol.* II, *p.* xxvii.

As to the Rowley series, I do not hesitate to say that they contain some of the finest poetry in our language, though they are unequal, just as the modern poems are. They are jewels set in the prose-romance of ancient Bristol as imagined by Chatterton; though Canynge, the old mayor, who is the central figure, was an actual person of importance.—NOEL, RODEN, 1872–86, *Chatterton, Essays on Poetry and Poets, p.* 39.

His genius was capable of great sweetness and tenderness, but it shows to greatest advantage where he gives a loose rein to his powers. His description of the battle of Hastings is widely magnificent, and his ballad "Dethe of Sir Charles Bawdin" ranks with the finest heroic lays of the old English and Scotch ballads.—SCHERR, J., 1874, *A History of English Literature, tr. M. V., p.* 164.

His name, indeed, is better known than that of many men who have filled large places in our literature; and there is a general conviction that he was a genius, although it is doubtful if anyone except his editor or biographer could be found who could quote a line of his works. Chatterton's fame has come primarily from the events of his own brief life, and the world has been content to take his genius on trust. . . . Apart from his marvellous fecundity, one finds buried in the mediæval débris passages of real beauty and strength both in thought and expression. The rarity of such qualities in juvenile verses entitles Chatterton to a high place among very young poets, and speculation may therefore fairly say that in the future—never reached—he might have been among the first.—LODGE, HENRY CABOT, 1875–97, *Certain Accepted Heroes and Other Essays, pp.* 119, 130.

Chatterton—the marvellous youth—seems to me to be marvellous chiefly from his youth. There is little, if anything, of permanent value in his writings. In one way, however, he showed an acuteness which may, perhaps, be fairly called marvellous. He showed an instinctive knowledge—remarkable in one so young—of the kind of intellectual food for which a demand was springing up in the country.—STEPHEN, LESLIE, 1876, *History of English Thought in the Eighteenth Century, vol.* II, *p.* 446.

So steeped indeed was Chatterton in romance, that, except in the case of the "African Eclogues," his imagination seems to be never really alive save when in the dramatic masquerade of the monk of Bristol. And here we touch the very core and centre of Chatterton's genius—his artistic identification.—WATTS, THEODORE, 1880, *English Poets, ed. Ward, vol.* III, *p.* 403.

As an unpublished poem by Chatterton the "Exhibition" is deserving of notice, but it would be unjust to regard it in any way as a fair sample of its author's genius. It was written in great haste, left uncorrected, and, like most of his satirical pieces on local personages, was not intended for publication.—INGRAM, JOHN H., 1883, *Chatterton and his Associates, Harper's Magazine, vol.* 67, *p.* 236.

His name has been coupled in good faith with that of Keats, a comparison inconceivably unjust to the latter. Hyperion to a Satyr, truth to falsehood, are not more unlike than was Keats to Chatterton. Keats was a sweet and noble spirit, a devotee of the beautiful, a Galahad circled about with snowy doves; Chatterton was a pestilent backbiter, a vain and moody egotist, a geniune product of an age of shams. . . . Chatterton's precocity is undeniable. If it be meritorious to write bad verses at eleven, that merit is certainly his. Few of his pieces, however, bear date prior to 1768, when Chatterton was nearly sixteen. Facility he possessed, and versatility. He imitated all styles in turn; now he smacks of Pope, now of Gray or Spenser, just as the schoolboy's clumsy copy bears a provoking resemblance to the master's elegant penmanship. The taint of insincerity runs through Chatterton's writings almost from the first. Upon this point he says himself, "He is a poor author who cannot write on both sides." He gives us alternately a hymn and an indecent lampoon, an elegy in the vein of Gray and a burlesque in the vein of Halévy. Lovesick ballads and mock heroics are addressed to the same lady. Satire was his forte, for in satire the unscrupulous egoism of his nature found a ready vent.—HARDING, EDWARD J., 1885, *The Apotheosis of Chatterton, The Critic, vol.* 7, *p.* 301.

The most extraordinary poet for his years who ever lived.—LANG, ANDREW, 1886, *Books and Bookmen, p.* 28.

In Chatterton's true poetry, as distinguished from his fugitive and occasional work, the two pre-eminent qualities are genius and imagination. If any mortal ever possessed genius—that divine mirage so inexplicably elusive—it was Chatterton; and, as in Byron's case, it must cover a multitude of sins. Artificial and affected as much of his work is, there can still be discerned in it the artistic power of the true poet; and had he written nothing else, "The Balade of Charitie" alone would have rescued his name from oblivion. . . . No poet—not even Coleridge—was ever so imbued with the romantic spirit; and, without giving him more than his due, we must acknowledge Chatterton to be the founder of the modern romantic school of poetry. That Coleridge was influenced to a considerable extent by Chatterton is patent to everyone, and that he was deeply impressed by the fate of the younger poet is also evident. . . . To try and ascertain the character of Chatterton from his works were as vain as to study Shakespeare with a like object. We cannot trace his personality: in vain do we rub the ring; the genius stubbornly refuses to appear. He belongs to the objective order of poets; his mind is creative rather than reflective. This power of concealing, or effacing, his own identity, while still preserving a thorough sympathy with the character he is delineating, is especially surprising in one so young.—RICHMOND, JOHN, 1888, *ed., The Poetical Works of Thomas Chatterton (Canterbury Poets), Prefatory Notice, pp.* 23, 24, 25.

It is not to be denied that, in relation of his years and equipments to the vigour and bulk of his work produced, Chatterton is—let us say it boldly—the most extraordinary phenomenon of infancy in the literature of the world. To an intellect so untrammelled, to a taste so mature, to an art so varied and so finished at the age of seventeen, twenty years more of life might have sufficed to put the possessor by the side of Milton and perhaps of Shakespeare. But when we come to think not of what was promised, but of what was actually achieved, and to compare it with the finished poems of Thomson and Goldsmith, of Collins and Gray, some moderation of our rapture seems demanded. . . . There are frequent flashes of brilliancy in Chatterton, and one or two very perfectly sustained pieces, but the main part of his work, if rigorously isolated from the melodramatic romance of his career, is surely found to be rather poor reading, the work of a child of exalted genius, no doubt, yet manifestly the work of a child all through. —GOSSE, EDMUND, 1888, *A History of Eighteenth Century Literature, p.* 334.

After a very brief period of controversy as to the genuineness of Rowley (which even at the time such mere pioneers and dilettanti in the study of Old English as Gray and Mason at once negatived), this had been entirely given up, and the patient exertions of Professor Skeat have shown the originals, the processes, and the entire machinery in the invention of the dialect. But it may be permitted to protest against the printing of the poems as a whole in modernised form, and still more against the extraordinary liberties which others have taken with Chatterton's text, even to the Bentleian extent of substituting words which to the individual critic "seem more appropriate." It is certain that if we wish to appreciate Chatterton's actual poetic powers, we must take the words he wrote in the spelling in which he wrote them; though linguistic inquiry may take its own course. Thus considering, we shall find him a distinct puzzle, showing in his ordinary English nothing of the charm which floats about his Rowleian dialect-pieces, and even in these not perhaps suggesting the certain possession of that charm had he lived. His metrical ability is great, though it is rather too much to claim for him that he fully anticipated Coleridge's reversion to the *Genesis* and *Exodus* scheme, and his phrase and word-music have now and then a singular romantic appeal. But there is something disquieting in this, since it exactly resembles the not infrequent, but always passing, gifts of very young children; and it makes him æsthetically a delight, but critically a problem. His antiques vary from *pastiches*, hardly more really antique than Thomson or Shenstone, though inspired by the study of somewhat older models, to things almost or wholly exquisite, like "Ælla's Dirge." The nature-touches are in the same way sometimes exquisite, sometimes conventional, and the whole is a strange medley of promise, performance, and failure.—SAINTSBURY, GEORGE, 1897, *A Short History of English Literature, p.* 586.

My only belief is that the Rowley poems are interesting principally as literary curiosities—the work of an infant phenomenon—and that they have little importance in themselves, or as models and inspirations to later poets. I cannot help thinking that, upon this subject, many critics have lost their heads.—BEERS, HENRY A., 1898, *A History of English Romanticism in the Eighteenth Century, p.* 362.

The Chatterton manuscripts are sadly scattered. Some are in the British Museum, some in the museum in Bristol, one or two at the Bodleian, at Oxford, and some in private hands. Many have perished. No collection of his writings, complete or even fairly complete, has been made; even his poems, although existent in many editions, have never been systematically collected. Oddly, the many attempts to modernize the Rowley poems have had only indifferent success. They must be read in the original to judge of their real beauties.—RUSSELL, CHARLES E., 1900, *The Marvelous Boy, Munsey's Magazine, vol.* 24, *p.* 676.

Mark Akenside

1721–1770

Mark Akenside was son of a butcher at Newcastle-on-Tyne. He was sent to the Edinburgh University, with aid of a fund for the purpose, to be educated as a Dissenting minister; but he made medicine his study, was proud of his oratory in the debates of the Medical Society, and aspired to a seat in Parliament. After three years at Edinburgh, Akenside went to Leyden, where he stayed another three years, took his degree as M. D., and found a friend in a student of law, Jeremiah Dyson, who came home with him. "The Pleasures of Imagination," in its first form, appeared in 1744, when Akenside's age was twenty-three. Its subject was suggested by Addison's essays on Imagination, in the "Spectator." Akenside wrote odes also, and worked at the elaboration of his chief poem throughout his life, publishing the enlargement of his First Book in 1757, and of the second in 1765; the enlargement of Book III., with an unfinished fragment of Book IV., appeared after his death.—MORLEY, HENRY, 1879, *A Manual of English Literature, ed. Tyler, p.* 603.

PERSONAL

Of all our poets, perhaps, Akenside was the best Greek scholar since Milton.—WARTON, JOSEPH, 1782, *Essay on Pope, vol.* II, *p.* 386.

Akenside used every endeavour to

become popular, but defeated them all by the high opinion he everywhere manifested of himself, and the little condescension he shewed to men of inferior endowments; by his love of political controversy, his authoritative censure of the public councils, and his bigoted notions respecting government, subjects foreign to his profession, and with which some of the wisest of it have thought it prudent not to concern themselves. In the winter evenings he frequented Tom's coffeehouse, in Devereux court, then the resort of some of the most eminent men for learning and ingenuity of the time, with some of whom he became entangled in disputes and altercations, chiefly on subjects of literature and politics, that fixed on his character the stamp of haughtiness and self-conceit, and drew him into disagreeable situations. . . . Akenside was a man of religion and strict virtue, a philosopher, a scholar, and a fine poet. His conversation was of the most delightful kind, learned, instructive, and without any affectation of wit, cheerful and entertaining. One of the pleasantest days of my life I passed with him, Mr. Dyson, and another friend, at Putney bowling-green house, where a neat and elegant dinner, the enlivening sunshine of a summer's day, and the view of an unclouded sky, were the least of our gratifications. In perfect good humour with himself and all around him, he seemed to feel a joy that he lived, and poured out his gratulations to the great dispenser of all felicity in expressions that Plato himself might have uttered on such an occasion.—HAWKINS, SIR JOHN, 1787, *Life of Samuel Johnson, pp.* 244, 247.

When Akenside's "Pleasures of the Imagination" first came out, he did not put his name to the poem. Rolt went over to Dublin, published an edition of it, and put his own name to it. Upon the fame of this he lived for several months, being entertained at the best tables as the ingenious Mr. Rolt. His conversation indeed, did not discover much of the fire of a poet; but it was recollected, that both Addison and Thomson were equally dull till excited by wine. Akenside having been informed of this imposition, vindicated his right by publishing the poem with its real authour's name.—BOSWELL, JAMES, 1791–93, *Life of Johnson, ed. Hill, vol.* I, *p.* 416.

Akenside, when a student at Edinburgh, was a member of the Medical Society, then recently formed, and was eminently distinguished by the eloquence which he displayed in the course of the debates. Dr. Robertson (who was at that time a student of divinity in the same university) told me that he was frequently lead to attend their meetings chiefly to hear the speeches of Akenside, the great object of whose ambition then was a seat in Parliament; a situation which he was sanguine enough to flatter himself he had some prospect of obtaining, and for which he conceived his talents to be much better adapted than for the profession he had chosen. In this opinion he was probably in the right, as he was generally considered by his fellow-students as far inferior in medical science to several of his companions.—STEWART, DUGALD, 1827, *Elements of the Philosophy of the Human Mind, vol.* III, *p.* 501

That "Akenside, when he walked in the streets, looked for all the world like one of his own Alexandrines set upright," was a saying of Henderson the actor, for which I am indebted to a true poet of our own day, Mr. Rogers, who heard it repeated many years ago.—DYCE, ALEXANDER, 1834, *Life of Akenside, Appendix.*

There were two Akensides—Akenside the poet, and Akenside the man; and of the *man* Akenside there were numerous subdivisions. Remarkable as a poet, he was even yet more noteworthy a private individual in his extreme inconsistency. No character is more commonplace than the one to which is ordinarily applied the word contradictory; but Akenside was a curiosity from the extravagance in which this form of "the commonplace" exhibits itself in his disposition and manners. By turns he was placid, irritable, simple, affected, gracious, haughty, magnanimous, mean, benevolent, harsh, and sometimes even brutal. At times he was marked by a childlike docility, and at other times his vanity and arrogance displayed him almost as a madman. Of plebeian extraction, he was ashamed of his origin, and was yet throughout life the champion of popular interests. Of his real humanity there can be no doubt, and yet in his demeanor to the unfortunate creatures whom, in his capacity of a hospital-physician, he had to attend, he was always supercilious, and often cruel.

. . . Akenside was never very successful as a physician, although he thoroughly understood his profession, and in some important particulars advanced its science.—JEAFFRESON, JOHN CORDY, 1861, *A Book About Doctors.*

A contemporary has left this portrait of the poet-physician: "One leg of Dr. Akenside was considerably shorter than the other, which was in some measure remedied by the aid of a false heel. He had a pale strumous countenance, but was always very neat and elegant in his dress. He wore a large white wig, and carried a long sword. He would order the servants (at Christ's Hospital), on his visiting days, to precede him with brooms to clear the way, and prevent the patients from too nearly approaching him."—GOSSE, EDMUND, 1885, *Dictionary of National Biography, vol.* I, *p.* 210.

His English acquaintances in Paris left a much less genial trace on "Peregrine Pickle." Mark Akenside and his unnamed friend the painter were the originals of the physician and Pallet. What the author of the "Pleasures of Imagination" had done to offend Smollett is not very clear. If it is true that he made "disparaging remarks on Scotland," that would be enough to account for the unmeasured attack made on him. Perhaps, however, Akenside's real offence was, that he was not a little of a prig, and very much of a bore. He quoted Greek, he was a great republican, he laid down the law, and annoyed Smollett by continual talk about the ancients; at least this is what he did, if the physician is even a gross caricature of the real Mark Akenside.—HANNAY, DAVID, 1887, *Smollett* (*Great Writers*), *p.* 83.

HYMN TO THE NAIADS

Throughout the range of English literature, there is nothing more deeply imbued with the spirit of the ancient world than our author's "Hymn to the Naiads." In its solemnity, its pomp of expression, and its mythologic lore, he has shown himself a more successful imitator of Callimachus; yet is far from being the mere echo of a Grecian hymn.—DYCE, ALEXANDER, 1834, *ed., The Poetical Works of Mark Akenside.*

Up to the days of Keats' "Endymion" and "Hyperion," Akenside's "Hymn to the Naiads" was thought one of the best attempts to reproduce the classical spirit and ideas. It now takes a secondary place; and at no time could be compared to an actual hymn of Callimachus or Pindar, any more than Smollett's "Supper after the Manner of the Ancients" was equal to a real Roman Cœna, the ideal of which Croly has so superbly described in "Salathiel."—GILFILLAN, GEORGE, 1857, *ed., The Poetical Works of Mark Akenside, Life, p.* xx.

Akenside's "Hymn to the Naiads" has the true classical spirit. He had caught the manner and feeling, the varied pause and harmony, of the Greek poets, with such felicity that Lloyd considered his "Hymn" as fitted to give a better idea of that form of composition, than could be conveyed by any translation of Homer or Callimachus.—CHAMBERS, ROBERT, 1876, *Cyclopædia of English Literature, ed. Carruthers.*

His "Hymn to the Naiads" is usually held, and with good cause, to be his best poem, the most graceful, the most sculpturesque specimen of his blank verse.—GOSSE, EDMUND, 1888, *A History of Eighteenth Century Literature, p.* 311.

PLEASURES OF THE IMAGINATION

Johnson. "I think we have had enough of Gray. I see they have published a splendid edition of Akenside's works. One bad ode may be suffered; but a number of them together makes one sick." *Boswell.* "Akenside's distinguished poem is his 'Pleasures of Imagination': but, for my part, I never could admire it so much as most people do." *Johnson.* "Sir, I could not read it through." *Boswell.* "I have read it through; but I did not find any great power in it."—JOHNSON, SAMUEL, 1772, *Life by Boswell, ed. Hill, vol.* II, *p.* 188.

In English, Dr. Akenside has attempted the most rich and poetical form of didactic writing in his "Pleasures of the Imagination," and though, in the execution of the whole, he is not equal, he has, in several parts, succeeded happily, and displayed much genius.—BLAIR, HUGH, 1783, *Lectures on Rhetoric and Belles-Lettres, ed. Mills, Lecture* xl.

It was welcomed as a work of such intrinsic worth ought to be welcomed. From its sale the author's finances were improved and his fame established. Dr. Johnson mentions, that he has heard Dodsley (by whom it was published) say, that when the copy was offered him, the price demanded for it, which was a hundred and twenty pounds, being such as he was not inclined to give precipitately, he carried the work to Pope, who having looked into it, advised him not to make a niggardly offer, for "this was no every day writer." —HUTCHINSON, BENJAMIN, 1789, *Biographia Medica.*

If his genius is to be estimated from this poem, it will be found to be lofty and elegant, chaste, correct, and classical.—BARBAULD, ANNA LETITIA, 1795, *ed., The Pleasures of Imagination.*

Akenside had in him the materials of poetry, but he was hardly a great poet. He improved his "Pleasures of the Imagination" in the subsequent editions by pruning away a great many redundances of style and ornament.—HAZLITT, WILLIAM, 1818, *Lectures on the English Poets, Lecture* vi.

Of Akenside (the most perfect builder of our blank verse) I know of no edition entitled to particular commendation. Why are his "Pleasures of the Imagination" so little perused? There are a hundred (I had well nigh said a thousand) electrical passages in this charming poem. —DIBDIN, THOMAS FROGNALL, 1824, *The Library Companion, p.* 735, *note.*

In his poem, as an elegant critic has observed with great propriety, he has united the grace of Virgil, the colouring of Milton, the incidental expression of Shakspeare, to paint the finest features of the human mind, and the most lovely forms of true morality and religion.—BUCKE, CHARLES, 1832, *Life, Writings and Genius of Akenside.*

Few English poets of the eighteenth century are to be ranked before the author of "The Pleasures of the Imagination."—CLEVELAND, CHARLES D., 1848, *A Compendium of English Literature, p.* 578.

The mischief is, that the poet, theorizing and poetizing by turns, loses his hold of his readers more than other writers whose topics are less abstract. The philosophical thinker finds better teaching elsewhere; and the poetical student, unless he is also metaphysically inclined, has his enthusiasm chilled by the obtrusive dissertations.—SPALDING, WILLIAM, 1852–82, *A History of English Literature, p.* 337.

The analysis of the pleasurable feelings which are awakened in the mind by whatever excites the imagination, though suitable enough as a subject for an essay, becomes insupportable when carried on through a poem of more than two thousand blank verses. Akenside had no sense of humour and no wit, but was an ardent lover of nature; he may be called a second-rate Wordsworth, whose style that of some of his "Odes" much resembles. —ARNOLD, THOMAS, 1868–75, *Chaucer to Wordsworth, p.* 355.

Whether his view of the imagination is always correct or not, his sentiments are always elevated; his language high sounding but frequently redundant, and his versification correct and pleasing. His descriptions of nature are cold but correct; his standard of humanity is high but mortal. Grand and sonorous, he constructs his periods with the manner of a declaimer; his ascriptions and apostrophes are like those of a high-priest.—COPPÉE, HENRY, 1872, *English Literature, p.* 351.

The poem is really Romantic only in its title.—PHELPS, WILLIAM LYON, 1893, *The Beginnings of the English Romantic Movement, p.* 39.

One cannot read "The Pleasures of Imagination" without becoming sensible that the writer was possessed of poetic feeling, and feeling of a kind that we generally agree to call romantic. His doctrine at least, if not his practice, was in harmony with the fresh impulse which was coming into English poetry. . . . But Akenside is too abstract. In place of images, he presents the reader with dissertations.—BEERS, HENRY A., 1898, *A History of English Romanticism in the Eighteenth Century, p.* 140.

GENERAL

Is this the land where Akenside displays
The bold yet temperate flame of ancient days?
—BEATTIE, WILLIAM, 1765, *On the Report of a Monument to be Erected in Westminster Abbey to the Memory of a Late Author.*

To his versification justice requires that praise should not be denied. In the general fabrication of his lines he is perhaps superior to any other writer of blank-verse; his flow is smooth, and his pauses are musical; but the concatenation of his verses is commonly too long continued, and the full close does not recur with sufficient frequency. The sense is carried on through a long intertexture of complicated clauses, and as nothing is distinguished, nothing is remembered.—JOHNSON, SAMUEL, 1779–81, *Akenside, Lives of the English Poets.*

——Be thou our guest,
Impetuous Akenside, some gloomy eve
When the red lightning scarce begins to glare,
And the mute thunder hardly designs to growl.
Raised by thy torrent song, we shall enjoy
The loud increasing horrors of the storm,
Awfully grand.
—HURDIS, JAMES, 1788, *The Village Curate.*

He possesses a warm imagination and great strength and beauty of diction. His poem, you know, does not, like Campbell's "Hope," consist of a number of little incidents told in an interesting manner, and selected to illustrate his positions,—it is little else than a moral declamation. Nevertheless I like it. Akenside was an enthusiastic admirer of the ancient republics and of the ancient philosophers. He thought highly of Lord Shaftesbury's principles, and had a bad opinion of Scotsmen. For this last peculiarity he has been severely caricatured by Smollett in his "Peregrine Pickle" under the character of the fantastic English doctor in France.—CARLYLE, THOMAS, 1815, *Early Letters, ed. Norton, p.* 23.

Akenside attempted a sort of classical and philosophical rapture, which no elegance of language could easily have rendered popular, but which had merits of no vulgar order for those who could study it. —JEFFREY, FRANCIS LORD, 1816, *Jonathan Swift, Edinburgh Review, vol.* 27, *p.* 7.

The sweetness which we miss in Akenside is that which should arise from the direct representations of life, and its warm realities and affections. We seem to pass in his poem through a gallery of pictured abstractions rather than of pictured things. He reminds us of odours which we enjoy artifically extracted from the flower instead of inhaling them from its natural blossom. It is true that his object was to teach and explain the nature of mind, and that his subject led him necessarily into abstract ideas, but it admitted also of copious scenes, full of solid human interest, to illustrate the philosophy which he taught.—CAMPBELL, THOMAS, 1819, *Specimens of the British Poets.*

Akenside was one of the fiercest and most uncompromising of the young patriots out of Parliament. When he found that the change of administration had produced no change of system, he gave vent to his indignation in the "Epistle to Curio," the best poem that he ever wrote; a poem, indeed, which seems to indicate, that, if he had left lyric composition to Gray and Collins, and had employed his powers in grave and elevated satire, he might have disputed the pre-eminence of Dryden.—MACAULAY, THOMAS BABINGTON, 1833, *Walpole's Letters to Sir Horace Mann, Edinburgh Review; Critical and Miscellaneous Essays.*

His genius was more allied to the sublime than the vivacious. He had a deep love for nature; but it was for her laws, her general effects and grand combinations rather than her special beauties. Hence his descriptions, although often winsome, are vague and partake more of thoughtful reverie than minute observation. He delighted to trace mental phenomena more than to paint elaborate landscapes. The metaphysician and naturalist are coevident with the scholar and aspirant in his verse. — TUCKERMAN, HENRY T., 1849, *Characteristics of Literature, p.* 253.

Akenside would have made a first-class metaphysical professor, particularly in the æsthetic department.—MILLER, HUGH, 1856, *Essays, p.* 451.

Akenside's rich, though diffuse, eloquence, and the store of fanciful illustration which he pours out, evidence a wonderfully full mind for so young a man.—CRAIK, GEORGE L., 1861, *A Compendious History of English Literature and of the English Language, vol.* II, *p.* 287.

A noble thinker.—TAINE, H. A., 1871, *History of English Literature, tr. Van Laun, vol.* II, *bk.* iii, *ch.* vii, *p.* 220.

He had the conceptions of a great poet with less faculty than many a little one, and is one of those versifiers of whom it is enough to say that we are always willing to break him off in the middle with an &c., well knowing that what follows is but the coming-round again of what went before, marching in a circle with the cheap numerosity of a stage-army.—LOWELL, JAMES RUSSELL, 1871, *A Good Word for Winter, My Study Windows, p.* 33.

Akenside, didactic in matter, stiffly classical in manner, with a coldly poetic elevation of diction, was not fitted to help his age onward either in freedom, depth or boldness.—BASCOM, JOHN, 1874, *Philosophy of English Literature, p.* 213.

A certain force and dignity of thought is perceptible beneath a rather cumbrous style; he is prompted to write by a full mind instead of an empty purse. He has a certain message to deliver to mankind, and the difficulty of his utterance is characteristic. . . . Akenside judged well in desiring a harmony between poetry and philosophy; but the attempt at a fusion was unfortunate. His formulas suffered a fate analogous to that of his master's writings. The rather stilted style and not very lucid thought have in both cases rendered the difficulty of penetrating to the real thought too great for cursory readers; and a poet suffers more than a philosopher for wrapping his meaning in sententious obscurity.—STEPHEN, LESLIE, 1876, *History of English Thought in the Eighteenth Century, vol.* II, *pp.* 364, 365.

Honour is due to Akenside for his homage to the mind and to things of the mind. And it would be unjust to say that his enthusiasm was not sincere. Since, however, he lived as poet so much among ideas, since apart from these ideas his poetry ceases to exist, one cannot but ask, Were his ideas true? Were they the best ideas? Do they still survive? And again, Did Akenside present his ideas in the best way, in a way at once philosophical and poetic? Did he indeed effect the use of reason and imagination? It must be answered that Akenside's theory as a whole will not bear investigation, that some of his ideas are commonplace, some fantastic. . . . Akenside's moral elevation was self-conscious, a dignity of attitude assumed deliberately, a constructive elevation. . . . He was deficient on the side of common human sympathy; he lacked geniality. He felt himself to be a "superior person," and he was so in fact; but he had the kind of superior fatuousness that such persons are readily betrayed into. His tone is too high-pitched; his ideas are too much in the air; they do not nourish themselves in the common heart, in the common life of man. Still Akenside really lifts up his head and tries to breathe empyreal gales. —DOWDEN, EDWARD, 1880, *The English Poets, ed. Ward, vol.* III, *p.* 342.

Akenside is stiffly classical in manner, and gives us too much foliage for the fruit.—WELSH, ALFRED H., 1883, *Development of English Literature and Language, vol.* II, *p.* 135.

At his very best Akenside is sometimes like a sort of frozen Keats.—GOSSE, EDMUND, 1888, *A History of Eighteenth Century Literature, p.* 312.

The poet, it may be added, wrote a great number of odes that lack all, or nearly all, the qualities which should distinguish lyrical poetry. Not a spark of the divine fire warms or illuminates these reputable verses, but the author states that his chief aim was to be correct, and in that he has succeeded.—DENNIS, JOHN, 1894, *The Age of Pope, p.* 118.

Akenside is a very fair touchstone of criticism. It is impossible to like or even to admire him very heartily; he belongs to a class of poets, represented in most days, who are plaster rather than marble, photograph rather than picture, pinchbeck rather than gold or even copper. And yet a reluctant confession must accompany all reasonable depreciation of him. It is a question whether Akenside wants much to have turned his statue into life, or at least his stucco into alabaster.—SAINTSBURY, GEORGE, 1898, *A Short History of English Literature p.* 579.

Alexander Cruden

1701–1770

Born at Aberdeen, 31st May, 1701, took his M. A. at Marischal College, but for a short time was under restraint. On his release he left Aberdeen, and, after ten years' tutoring, in 1732 started as a bookseller in London. In 1737 appeared his admirable "Concordance of the Holy Scriptures." It was dedicated to Queen Caroline, who promised to "remember him," but died a few days later. Cruden now relapsed into insanity, and for ten weeks was kept in a madhouse, as again for a fortnight in 1753. Earning meanwhile his livelihood as a press-reader he assumed the title of "Alexander the Corrector," and in 1755 began to go through the country reproving Sabbath-breaking and profanity. But many a good and kindly action was interwoven with his crack-brained courtships, his dreams of knighthood and a seat in parliament. He was just back from a visit to Aberdeen when he died at his prayers in his Islington lodgings, 1st November, 1770. See life by A. Chalmers, prefixed since 1824 to the "Concordance."—PATRICK AND GROOME, *eds.*, 1897, *Chambers's Biographical Dictionary, p.* 264

PERSONAL

Alexander Cruden, who compiled the great "Concordance," was one of the most unique eccentrics upon record. The man was of excellent and mild disposition, very piously inclined, of studious habit, and of an industry that cannot be surpassed, for it was incessant and lifelong. A thread of madness seems to have run through all that he did, and at times usurped the whole web of his life, so that confinement seemed to those who knew him to be indispensable. This idea was probably erroneous, and aggravated the disease it should have repressed, causing needless misery to a very gentle and harmless being. The facts of his life are few, but most instructive to those who delight in watching the occasional freaks and pranks of Nature in her *hors d'œuvres.* One of the most singular of these is to be found in Alexander Cruden. In his general conduct he is a model of method and routine, but, when driven by an impulse, no course of action is too much out of rule to deter him. He becomes at one and the same moment, as it were, a man of order that can surpass the most disorderly at a bound.—WARD, CHARLES A., 1888, *Memoir of Alexander Cruden, Temple Bar, vol.* 84, *p.* 242.

His biblical labours have justly made his name a household word among the English-speaking peoples; his earnest, gentle, and self-denying piety commanded in his later days, in spite of his eccentricities, the kindly and compassionate toleration, often the admiration, of his contemporaries. It is probable that his habits in later life improved his mental condition.—MACRAY, W. D., 1888, *Dictionary of National Biography, vol.* XIII, *p.* 251.

CONCORDANCE OF THE BIBLE

It is so complete as a Concordance that nothing remains materially deficient.—WILLIAMS, EDWARD, 1800, *The Christian Preacher.*

It is not unlikely that Cruden, corrected and improved, will still retain his place in English literature.—ORME, WILLIAM, 1824, *Bibliotheca Biblica.*

Of Cruden's "Concordance," there have been many abridgments, which profess to contain all that is valuable in the original, which makes us marvel at the stupidity of the author, who devoted so many days and nights to accumulate what we are now assured is entirely superfluous! Yet being old-fashioned in our ideas, we rather prefer having every line of this unnecessary matter.—ALLIBONE, S. AUSTIN, 1854–58, *A Critical Dictionary of English Literature, vol.* I, *p.* 456.

George Whitefield

1714–1770

Born at Gloucester, England, Dec. 27, 1714: died at Newburyport, Mass., Sept. 30, 1770. An English clergyman, one of the founders of Methodism: celebrated as a pulpit orator. He was educated at Gloucester and Oxford; became associated at Oxford with the Methodists; was ordained deacon in 1736; visited Georgia in 1738; returning to England in the same year to be ordained a priest; began open-air preaching at Bristol with great effect; again visited America 1739–41; preaching in New England, New York, Georgia, and elsewhere; separated from Wesley on doctrinal points in 1741 (Whitefield retaining his rigid Calvanism and Wesley leaning toward Arminianism); preached throughout Great Britian; was in America for the third time 1744–48 (and several times later); and became Chaplain to the Countess of Huntingdon. He returned to America for the last time in 1769, and died there.—SMITH, BENJAMIN E., 1894–97, *ed., The Century Cyclopedia of Names, p.* 1059.

PERSONAL

He would not allow much merit to Whitefield's oratory. "His popularity, Sir (said he), is chiefly owing to the peculiarity of his manner. He would be followed by crowds were he to wear a nightcap in the pulpit, or were he to preach from a tree."—JOHNSON, SAMUEL, 1769, *Life by Boswell, ed. Hill, vol.* II, *p.* 91.

I did not disapprove of the design; but, as Georgia was then destitute of materials and workmen, and it was proposed to send them from Philadelphia at a great expense, I thought it would have been better to have built the House here and brought the children to it. This I advised; but he was resolute in his first project, rejected my counsel, and I therefore refused to contribute. I happened soon after to attend one of his sermons, in the course of which I perceived he intended to finish with a collection, and I silently resolved he should get nothing from me. I had in my pocket a handful of copper money, three or four silver dollars, and five pistoles in gold. As he proceeded, I began to soften, and concluded to give the copper. Another stroke of his oratory made me ashamed of that, and determined me to give the silver; and he finished so admirably that I emptied my pocket wholly into the collector's dish, gold and all. At this sermon there was also one of our club, who, being of my sentiments respecting the building in Georgia, and suspecting a collection might be intended, had by precaution emptied his pockets before he came from home. Towards the conclusion of the discourse, however, he felt a strong desire to give, and applied to a neighbour, who stood near him, to borrow some money for the purpose. The application was fortunately made to perhaps the only man in the company who had the firmness not to be affected by the preacher. His answer was, "At any other time, Friend Hopkinson, I would lend to thee freely; but not now, for thee seems to be out of thy right senses."—FRANKLIN, BENJAMIN, 1790? *Autobiography, ch.* viii.

Mr. George Whitefield, of whom, though Dr. Johnson did not think very highly, it must be acknowledged that his eloquence was powerful, his views pious and charitable, his assiduity almost incredible; and, that since his death, the integrity of his character has been fully vindicated.—BOSWELL, JAMES, 1791–93, *Life of Johnson, ed. Hill, vol.* I, *p.* 88.

His voice excelled both in melody and compass, and its fine modulations were happily accompanied by that grace of action which he possessed in an eminent degree, and which has been said to be the chief requisite of an orator. An ignorant man described his eloquence oddly but strikingly, when he said that Mr. Whitefield preached like a lion. So strange a comparison conveyed no unapt a notion of the force and vehemence and passion of that oratory which awed the hearers and made them tremble like Felix before the apostle.—SOUTHEY, ROBERT, 1820, *Life of Wesley.*

Whitfield's zealous spirit exhausted all its energies in preaching, and his full dedication to God was honoured by unbounded success. The effect produced by his sermons was indescribable, arising in a great degree from the most perfect forgetfulness of self, during the solemn moment of declaring the salvation that is in Christ Jesus. His evident sincerity impressed every hearer.—SIDNEY, EDWIN, 1834, *Life of Rowland Hill.*

Must have been a man with great things in his heart. He had many dark contests with the spirit of denial that lay about him before he called his genius forth into action. All the *logic* in him was poor and trifling compared to the *fire* that was in him, unequalled since Peter the Hermit. First he went to Bristol, and preached to the neighboring coal miners, who were all heathens yet, but he preached to them till he saw, as he tells us, "their black cheeks seamed with white tears." He came to Scotland, and got money there to convert the heathen. This was a great thing to do, considering the hard, thrifty, cold character of the nation. He came to Glasgow and preached, and talked about the Indians and their perishing state; would they hesitate to contribute of their goods to rescue this poor people? And thus he warmed the icy people into a flame, insomuch that, not having money enough by them, they ran home for more, and brought even blankets, farm stuff, hams, etc., to the church, and piled them in a heap there! This was a remarkable fact, whether it were the work of a good spirit, or of the devil. — CARLYLE, THOMAS,

1838, *Lectures on the History of Literature, p.* 175.

From the days of Paul of Tarsus and Martin Luther to our own, history records the career of no man who, with a less alloy of motives terminating in self, or of passions breaking loose from the control of reason, concentrated all the faculties of his soul with such intensity and perseverance for the accomplishment of one great design. . . . Whitfield was a great and a holy man; among the foremost of the heroes of philanthropy; and as a preacher, without a superior or a rival.—STEPHEN, SIR JAMES, 1838, *The Lives of Whitfield and Froude, Edinburgh Review, vol.* 67, *pp.* 513, 514.

Often feeble, and assailed by violent disease threatening speedy dissolution, he was in perpetual journeyings, to which neither his wife nor his home seemed to have been regarded as the slightest obstacles. All his tastes and habits were itinerant, and, it must be confessed, they were necessary to one, whose field was the world, and who was conscious of gifts, for which not a single church but all christendom was the appropriate theatre. —PARKMAN, F., 1838, *Whitefield in America, Christian Examiner, vol.* 25, *p.* 102.

Whitefield had evidently made a deep impression on the imaginations of the men of his day; for, in every account they gave of his preaching, there was a distinct image of the man, of his look, his action, his fervor, and some particular point was remembered, that he had made in his discourse. It seemed as if there was, every time, some new effect or uncommon incident, to fix the sermon in every memory, to be transmitted to at least one generation. We remember hearing two of our public men describe Whitefield many years ago. They were then aged, and disposed to value the solid more than the showy. They were of ripe years and judgment when they heard him, and, though of strong passions, yet good masters of themselves and disposed to see the whole of things. And the imagination of the one was filled with his preaching a farewell sermon on Boston Common at sunrise, and investing the newborn day with a glory the eye had never seen; it became a religious memorial. The other dwelt upon the flight of the dove towards heaven, and gave Whitefield's action as his soul seemed to follow the waving of its wings. They had probably forgotten much of the doctrine, but the image was fixed forever. —FITCH, E. T., 1839, *Philip's Life and Times of Whitefield, North American Review, vol.* 48, *p.* 479.

The common impression is that Whitfield had revivalist rudeness and passion. On the contrary, he had extreme grace of manner. He had art as well as fervency, and the union made him irresistible to his hearers, to whatever parish they belonged. —HOLYOAKE, GEORGE JACOB, 1869–95, *Public Speaking and Debate, p.* 184.

Unlike Wesley, whose strongest enthusiasm was always curbed by a powerful will, and who manifested at all times and on all subjects an even exaggerated passion for reasoning, Whitefield was chiefly a creature of impulse and emotion. He had very little logical skill, no depth or range of knowledge, not much self-restraint, nothing of the commanding and organising talent, and, it must be added, nothing of the arrogant and imperious spirit so conspicuous in his colleague. At the same time a more zealous, a more single-minded, a more truly amiable, a more purely unselfish man it would be difficult to conceive.—LECKY, WILLIAM EDWARD HARTPOLE, 1878, *A History of England in the Eighteenth Century, vol.* II, *ch.* ix.

If one were asked who was the greatest pulpit orator that ever lived, it would be a nice question to determine, so various are the styles of sacred eloquence, and so different are the tastes of even the most competent judges. But if we were to judge by the effects produced, we should hardly need to hesitate in pronouncing George Whitefield the Demosthenes of the pulpit. . . . Not only the unlettered, but men of the highest culture, yielded to the fascination of his speech. The cold, skeptical Hume declared that he would go twenty miles on foot to hear Whitefield preach; and in his chapel might be seen the Duke of Grafton, not yet pierced by the arrows of Junius, the heartless George Selwyn, Lord North, Charles James Fox, William Pitt, and Soame Jenyns. John Newton, the friend of Cowper, used to get up at four in the morning to hear the great preacher at five; and he says that even at that early hour the Moorfields were as full of lanterns as the Haymarket of flambeaux on an opera night.—MATHEWS, WILLIAM, 1878, *Oratory and Orators, pp.* 379, 382.

Wesley's fame as a preacher was somewhat obscured by the extraordinary power of Whitefield, whose dramatic eloquence attracted all classes.—BUCKLEY, JAMES M., 1898, *A History of Methodism in the United States, p.* 329.

His printed sermons by no means explain his reputation; it should be remembered that he preached over eighteen thousand sermons; only sixty-three were published by himself, forty-six of them before he was twenty-five years of age. Eighteen other sermons in print were published from shorthand notes, unrevised. The warmth of his expressions, and an incautious frankness of statement in his autobiographical writings, laid him open to ridicule and undeserved reproach. It was primarily against Whitefield that the more persistent attacks upon methodism were levelled. Apart from his evangelistic work he was in many ways a pioneer. With none of the administrative genius by which Wesley turned suggestions to account, he anticipated Wesley's lines of action to a remarkable extent. He preceded him in making Bristol a centre of methodist effort; he was beforehand with him in publishing journals, in founding schools, in practicing open-air preaching, and in calling his preachers to a conference. His religious periodical, "The Christian History" (begun in 1740), may be looked upon as a predecessor of the "Arminian Magazine" (1778). Whitefield's complexion was fair, his eyes dark blue and small; originally slender, he became corpulent from his fortieth year, though his diet was spare, and a cow-heel his favourite luxury. Like Wesley, he rose at four; his punctuality was rigid, his love of order extreme; "he did not think he should die easy, if he thought his gloves were out of their place" (WINTER, p. 82). He was "irritable, but soon appeased" (ib. p. 81); his beneficence was the outcome of the generous glow of his affections.—GORDON, ALEXANDER, 1900, *Dictionary of National Biography, vol.* LXI, *p.* 91.

GENERAL

Whitefield never drew as much attention as a mountebank does; he did not draw attention by doing better than others, but by doing what was strange. Were Astley to preach a sermon standing upon his head on a horse's back, he would collect a multitude to hear him; but no wise man would say he had made a better sermon for that. I never treated Whitefield's Ministry with contempt; I believe he did good. He had devoted himself to the lower classes of mankind, and among them he was of use. But when familiarity and noise claim the praise due to knowledge, art, and elegance, we must bear down such pretensions.—JOHNSON, SAMUEL, 1779, *Life by Boswell, ed. Hill, vol.* III, *p.* 465.

It is clear fact, admitting of no manner of question, that Whitefield's writing, nay, that those specimens of his public addresses which were written down during this powerful delivery, bear but exceedingly slender marks of anything we are accustomed to denominate talent, in the intellectual sense. His reasoning is no more than just a common propriety in putting thoughts generally common together. His devotional sentiment is fervent, but not of elevated conception. His figures, as far as we recollect, are seldom new, or what critics mean when they speak of "felicity;" their analogy is the broad and obvious one, such as that between medicine and the gospel, considered as a remedical dispensation. The diction is quite plain, and does not appear to partake of eloquence, further than any easy freedom, and the genuine expression of sincerity and earnestness. The collection of letters, constituting about one-half of his printed works, must have exceedingly disappointed those who sought from them any other instruction, than that which may be imparted by one general emanation of pious zeal, undistinguished by any discriminative particularity of thought, or any but the most obvious kind of reflections, often repeated and in the same words, on the successive incidents and scenes of his life and labours. There are none of those pointed observations, either on human nature or individual character, which might have been suggested by the masses and the particles of the human kind so variously brought under his view, and which would have been made by such a sagacious man, for instance, as John Knox. And even the disclosures of the movements and principles of his own mind, on which subject there is no appearance of reserve, are, with a singular uniformity, for a man stimulated by the circumstances of so extraordinary a career, in the strain of pious commonplace. The reader's interest would soon subside in an irresistible sense of insipidity, but for the strong and constant indications of a genuine religious zeal, and the train of references proving an unremitted and most wonderful course of exertions. In short, there can be no hazard in asserting, that his collective writings would, in the minds of all cultivated and impartial readers, leave the *marvellous* of his successes to be accounted for on the ground of causes quite distinct from talent, in the intellectual sense of the term.—FOSTER, JOHN, 1812, *George Whitefield, Critical Essays, ed. Ryland, vol.* II, *p.* 64.

I never read a line of Whitfield's sermons which did not appear to me within the reach of the most ordinary capacity. But he addressed himsef to the sensitive rather than to the rational nature of the sensitivo-rational beings to whom he spoke. I take him to be one of the great examples of the truth, that the quantity of motion may compensate for the deficiency of matter in producing momentum in the moral as well as in the physical world.—STEPHEN, SIR JAMES, 1838, *Selection from the Correspondence of the Late Macvey Napier, Letter, May* 9.

The sermons of Whitfield have come down to us in a very imperfect form. They are, for the most part, mere notes of what he said. It has often been remarked that his sermons are strangely destitute of vigorous or original thought. Though it is certain they have greatly suffered from the mutilated form in which they have reached us, we must confess it does not appear to us that the sermons are very deficient in those qualities of thought or expression which we have represented as so essential to popular eloquence. It is true they often want method and arrangement, are disfigured by repetitions, extravagancies, and frequent and gross violations of taste. These are to be attributed partly to the cause above specified; that is, the imperfect manner in which his sermons have been preserved, partly to the character of his own mind, and partly to the age. If, indeed, any one look for profound speculation or continuous and subtle reasoning in these sermons, he will be disappointed; but so far from wondering on that account that they should have produced such an effect, he will feel, if he know any thing of the philosophy of popular eloquence, that they could not have produced such an effect, if they had been characterised by these qualities. But they could not have been destitute of the principal qualities, whether of thought or of style, which constitute popular eloquence; and we think that even now, amidst great deformities, those qualities may still be not obscurely traced in them.—ROGERS, HENRY, 1840, *The British Pulpit, Edinburgh Review, vol.* 72, *p.* 77, *note.*

I have taken some pains to examine the series of texts preached on by Whitefield and Wesley: few of them are odd, or even uncommon, they are the familiar, evangelical, everlasting verses, which God has owned in all ages.—ALEXANDER, JAMES W., 1844, *Familiar Letters, Jan.* 25, *ed. Hall, vol.* I, *p.* 387.

Of all the spiritual heroes of a hundred years ago none saw so soon as Whitefield what the times demanded, and none were so forward in the great work of spiritual aggression. I should think I committed an act of injustice if I placed any name before his.—RYLE, J. C., 1868, *The Christian Leaders of the Last Century, p.* 31.

His published sermons are far from equal to his reputation; the charm seems to have been in his voice, elocution, and gesture. — MINTO, WILLIAM, 1872–80, *Manual of English Prose Literature, p.* 429.

One of Whitefield's assistants, Cornelius Winter, tells us that Whitefield wept profusely during his sermons, that he stamped and was overcome by his feelings, and that the physical effort was frequently followed by a loss of blood. But the printed sermons, which appear indeed to have been imperfectly reported, will draw no tears from the most emotional nature. In fact, they are the most striking proof that can be given of the familiar fact that oratory depends for its instantaneous effect upon the dramatic, rather than upon the intellectual, power of the orator. Here and there, there are passages of which we can believe that their defects of thought and language would not necessarily destroy our pleasure in a voice and manner of extraordinary excellence. There are apostrophes to God or to the sinner or to the Devil, in which, if we attend only to the situation and abstract our minds resolutely from the actual words, we can believe that a great effect might be produced. But nothing except the unequivocal testimony of facts could convince us that the greatest oratorical capacity could inform those tattered shreds of sensational rhetoric which are strung together to form the bulk of Whitefield's published sermons. It is, we know, the strength of the arm, not of the weapon, which gives force to the arrows of eloquence; and when Whitefield smote men to the heart with such blunt and brittle weapons, the secret of his success must have lain as much in the hearers as in the orator.—STEPHEN, LESLIE, 1876, *History of English Thought in the Eighteenth Century, vol.* II, *p.* 425.

His failings were chiefly those of a somewhat weak nature, of overstrung nerves, and of a half-educated and very defective taste. He was a little irritable and occasionally a little vain. His theological opinions betrayed him into much narrowness of judgment, and his impulsive disposition into constant indiscretion and exaggeration of language. His letters, and indeed most of his writings, are intolerably tedious, and sometimes not a little repulsive. They are written for the most part with that exaggeration of sentiment, in that maudlin, ecstatic, effusive, and meretricious style which is so common among his co-religionists, and which appears to most cultivated minds to denote much vulgarity, not only of taste, but of feeling. It is a style crowded with ejaculations, interrogations, and quotations from Scripture, in which the simplest subject is expressed in strained Biblical language, in which the inmost and deepest feelings of the soul are ostentatiously paraded, and the most sacred subjects and the holiest names are treated with coarse familiarity.—LECKY, WILLIAM EDWARD HARTPOLE, 1878, *A History of England in the Eighteenth Century, vol.* II, *ch.* ix.

There is little in his printed sermons now extant to repay the trouble of perusing them; his literary remains do not entitle him to the consideration due even to a respectable mediocrity; and his Journals are a wearisome monotony of unmeaning rhapsodies, which could not be read by anyone less enthusiastic than himself without a feeling strongly akin to disgust. Yet to this man it was given, without the aid of worldly wisdom or the resources of extensive knowledge, to sway multitudes with a power to which Tully was a stranger, and for which we search in vain for a parallel, even in the greatest ages of Athenian eloquence.—MYALL, WILLIAM, 1880, *George Whitefield, International Review, vol.* 9, *p.* 270.

While destitute of Wesley's marvellous power of organisation, he was without rival as the pulpit orator of the century in which he lived. Men of the most varied orders of mind bore witness to the profound impression he produced. Those who listened to him were not only interested and convinced, but quickened with a new kind of life.—BROWN, J., 1896, *Social England, ed. Traill, vol.* V, *p.* 238.

John Jortin

1698–1770

John Jortin (1698–1770), a writer on theological subjects, was the son of a Protestant refugee from Brittany, and was born in London 23rd October 1698. In his tenth year he entered Charterhouse school, and in 1715 he became a pensioner of Jesus College, Cambridge, where his reputation as a Greek scholar led the classical tutor of his college to select him to translate certain passages from Eustathius for the use of Pope in his translation of Homer. He graduated B. A. in 1719 and M. A. in 1722. In the latter year he published a small volume of Latin verse entitled "Lusus Poetici." Having received priest's orders in 1724, he was in 1726 presented by his college to the vicarage of Swavesey in Cambridgeshire, an appointment which he resigned in 1730 to become preacher of a chapel in New Street, London. In 1731, along with some friends, he began a publication entitled "Miscellaneous Observations on Authors Ancient and Modern," which appeared at intervals during two years. In 1737 he was presented to the vicarage of Eastwell in Kent, and in 1751 he became rector of St. Dunstan's-in-the-East. Shortly after becoming chaplain to the bishop of London in 1762, he was appointed to a prebendal stall of St. Paul's, and to the vicarage of Kensington, and in 1764 he was made archdeacon of London. He died at Kensington, September 5, 1770. The principal works of Jortin are "Discussions Concerning the Truth of the Christian Religion," 1746; "Remarks on Ecclesiastical History," 1751; "Life of Erasmus," 2 vols., 1750, 1760, founded on the life by Le Clerc, but containing a large amount of new matter; and "Tracts Philological, Critical, and Miscellaneous," 1790. All his works display great learning and some acuteness both of research and criticism, but though written in a lively style they do not bear that stamp of originality which confers permanent interest.—BAYNES, THOMAS SPENCER, *ed.*, 1881, *Encyclopædia Britannica, vol.* XIII, *p.* 749.

PERSONAL

He was a man of great learning, fine taste, and much vivacity of imagination, an accomplished critic, and a warm friend to the diffusion of sound knowledge.—ALLIBONE, S. AUSTIN, 1854–58, *A Critical Dictionary of English Literature, vol.* I, *p.* 999.

The fact was that Jortin was a scholar in every sense of the word; Warburton is none: and in the matter of the disagreement between them, Jortin shows as much above Warburton in magnanimity as he is in learning.—PATTISON, MARK, 1863–89, *Life of Bishop Warburton, Essays, ed. Nettleship, vol.* II, *p.* 131.

GENERAL

Good sense and sound morality appear in them [Sermons], not, indeed, dressed out in the meretricious ornaments of a florid style, but in all the manly force and simple graces of natural eloquence. . . . Will always be read with pleasure and edification.—KNOX, VICESIMUS, 1777, *Essays, Moral and Literary, No.* CXV.

Jortin's sermons are very elegant.—JOHNSON, SAMUEL, 1778, *Life by Boswell, ed. Hill, vol.* III, *p.* 281.

The ease, simplicity, and vigour of this engaging writer (I speak of the biographer), who negligently scatters learning and vivacity on every subject which he treats, are here ["Life of Erasmus"] exercised on a most congenial topic.—GREEN, THOMAS, 1779–1810, *Diary of a Lover of Literature.*

As to Jortin, whether I look back to his verse, to his prose, to his critical or to his theological works, there are few authors to whom I am so much indebted for rational entertainment or for solid instruction.—PARR, SAMUEL, 1789, *Tracts by a Warburton and a Warburtonian.*

Once, and rarely more than once, he rose to eloquence; and that was in the preface of his "Remarks," &c., which the late Dr. Gosset told me he regularly read through, every year, with undiminished delight. . . . They are excellent,—pithy, learned, candid, and acute; presenting us with the *marrow* of his predecessors.—DIBDIN, THOMAS FROGNALL, 1824, *The Library Companion, pp.* 100, 116, *notes.*

Critical ["Remarks on Ecclesiastical History"] but wanting in more important things.—BICKERSTETH, EDWARD, 1844, *The Christian Student.*

Besides being a writer of elegant sermons in an age when pulpit literature had greatly decayed, may be remembered as the author of various contributions to ecclesiastical history, in which he showed liberality of thought. Jortin was persistent and fairly successful in controversy with Warburton.—GOSSE, EDMUND, 1888, *A History of Eighteenth Century Literature, p.* 362.

Jortin's "Erasmus," based on the life by Jean Le Clerc, is a respectable piece of work, but has long been superseded. His five volumes of contributions to ecclesiastical history are still valuable, not merely for the store of curious material which they contain, illustrating the history of Christian ideas up to the Reformation, but for keen judgments of men and manners, and an engaging lightness of style, spiced with epigram. "Wit without ill-nature and sense without effort," says Dr. Parr, "he could at will scatter upon every subject." By John Hey and later writers Jortin is unduly decried as flippant. He thought and wrote like a cultured layman. Though he regarded the niceties of theological speculation as "trifles," he treated them in detail,

DAVID GARRICK

From Original Painting by
Robert Edge Pine.

THOMAS GRAY

Engraving by W. Greatbatch.
From Drawing by Eckhardt.

with a mind utterly disengaged from ecclesiastical bias. From one of his posthumous tracts it is clear that he interpreted the obligations of subscription in the laxest sense. His personal character was remarkably gentle and kindly. He was fond of music, and played the harpsichord.—GORDON, ALEXANDER, 1892, *Dictionary of National Biography, vol.* XXX, *p.* 202.

Thomas Gray

1716–1771

Born, in London, 26 Dec. 1716. Early education at Burnham. To Eton, 1727 [?]. To Pembroke Hall, Camb., as Pensioner, summer of 1734; transferred to Peterhouse, 9 Oct. 1734. Took no degree; left University, Sept. 1738. Travelled abroad with Horace Walpole, March 1739 to Sept. 1740. Returned to Peterhouse, Camb., as Fellow-Commoner, Oct. 1742; LL. B., 1743. Lived chiefly at Cambridge for remainder of life. Removed to Pembroke Coll., 6 March 1756. In London, Jan. 1759 to June 1761. Prof. of History and Mod. Languages, Cambridge, 28 July 1768. Increasing ill-health. Died, at Cambridge, 30 July 1771. Buried at Stoke Pogis. *Works:* "Ode on a distant prospect of Eton College" (anon.), 1747; "An Elegy wrote in a Country Churchyard" (anon.), 1751 (2nd–4th edns., same year); "Six Poems," 1753; "The Progress of Poesy; and, The Bard," 1758; "Poems" (collected; two independent edns.), 1768; "Ode, performed . . . at the installation of . . . A. H. Fitzroy, Duke of Grafton" (anon.), 1769. *Posthumous:* "A Catalogue of the Antiquities . . . in England and Wales" (anon.; priv. ptd.), [1773]; "Life and Letters," ed. by W. Mason, 1774; "The Bard," ed. by J. Martin, 1837; "Correspondence with W. Mason," ed. by J. Mitford, 1853. *Collected Works:* "Poems," ed. by W. Mason, 1775; "Poems and Letters" (priv. ptd.), 1879; "Works," ed. by E. Gosse (4 vols.), 1884. *Life:* by E. Gosse, 1882.—SHARP, R. FARQUHARSON, 1897, *A Dictionary of English Authors, p.* 118.

PERSONAL

He is the worst company in the world. From a melancholy turn, from living reclusely, and from a little too much dignity, he never converses easily; all his words are measured and chosen, and formed into sentences; his writings are admirable; he himself is not agreeable.—WALPOLE, HORACE, 1748, *To George Montague, Sep.* 3; *Letters, ed. Cunningham, vol.* II, *p.* 128.

Mr. Gray, our elegant poet, and delicate Fellow-Commoner of Peter House, has just removed to Pembroke Hall, in resentment of some usage he met with at the former place. The case is much talked of, and is this:—He is much afraid of fire, and was a great sufferer in Cornhill; he has ever since kept a ladder of ropes by him, soft as the silky cords by which Romeo ascended to his Juliet, and has had an iron machine fixed to his bedroom window. The other morning Lord Percival and some Petreuchians, going a hunting, were determined to have a little sport before they set out, and thought it would be no bad diversion to make Gray bolt, as they called it, so ordered their man, Joe Draper, to roar out "fire." A delicate white night-cap is said to have appeared at the window; but finding the mistake, retired again to the couch. The young fellows, had he descended, were determined, they said, to have whipped the Butterfly up again.—SHARP, REV. JOHN, 1756, *Letter, March* 12, *Nichols' Illustrations of Literature of the Eighteenth Century, vol.* VI, *p.* 805.

I am sorry you did not see Mr. Gray on his return; you would have been much pleased with him. Setting aside his merit as a poet which, however, is greater in my opinion than any of his contemporaries can boast, in this or any other nation, I found him possessed of the most exact taste, the soundest judgment, and the most extensive learning. He is happy in a singular facility of expression. His composition abounds with original observations, delivered in no appearance of sententious formality, and seeming to arise spontaneously without study or premeditation. I passed two days with him at Glammis, and found him as easy in his manners, and as communicative and frank as I could have wished.—BEATTIE, JAMES, 1765, *Letter to Sir William Forbes.*

I regret that poor Mr. Gray is now no more than Pindar. One fatal moment sets two or three thousand years aside, and brings the account equal. I really believe our British Pindar not unequal in merit to the bard of Thebes. I hope Mr. Gray has left some works yet unpublished.—MONTAGU, ELIZABETH, 1772, *Letters, Aug.* 15; *A Lady of the Last Century, ed. Doran, p.* 177.

Perhaps he was the most learned man in Europe. He was equally acquainted with the elegant and profound parts of science, and that not superficially, but thoroughly. He knew every branch of history, both natural and civil; had read all the original histories of England, France, and Italy; and was a great antiquarian. Criticism, metaphysics, morals, politics, made a principal part of his study; voyages and travels of all sorts were his favourite amusements; and he had a fine taste in paintings, prints, architecture, and gardening. With such a fund of knowledge, his conversation must have been equally instructing and entertaining; but he was also a good man, a man of virtue and humanity. There is no character without some speck, some imperfection; and I think the greatest defect in his was an affectation in delicacy, or rather effeminacy, and a visible fastidiousness, or contempt and disdain of his inferiors in science.—TEMPLE, WILLIAM, 1772, *Letter to James Boswell, London Magazine, March.*

He was much admired for his singing in his youth; yet he was so sly in exercising this talent that Mr. Walpole tells me he never could but once prevail on him to give proof of it, and then it was with so much pain to himself that it gave him no manner of pleasure.—MASON, WILLIAM, 1774, *Memoirs of Thomas Gray.*

What has occurred to me, from the slight inspection of his letters in which my undertaking has engaged me, is, that his mind had a large grasp; that his curiosity was unlimited, and his judgment cultivated; that he was a man likely to love much where he loved at all; but that he was fastidious and hard to please.—JOHNSON, SAMUEL, 1779–81, *Gray, Lives of the English Poets.*

Gray could never compose voluntarily: his genius resembled the armed apparition in Shakspeare's master-tragedy. "He would not be commanded." When he wished to compose the "Installation Ode," for a considerable time he felt himself without the power to begin it: a friend calling on him, Gray flung open his door hastily, and in a hurried voice and tone, exclaiming in the first verse of that ode—

> Hence, avaunt! 'tis holy ground!—

his friend started at the disordered appearance of the bard, whose orgasm had disturbed his very air and countenance. —DISRAELI, ISAAC, 1796–1818, *Effect of Great Works, The Literary Character.*

Mr. Gray was in stature rather below the middle size. He had a pleasing countenance, in which, however, there was no extraordinary expression, consequently no indication of his internal powers. The print which is prefixed to his "Life" is rather a caricature, for his features were not so stiff and prominent, but more rounded and delicate.—BRYANT, JACOB, 1798, *Letter, Dec.* 24.

His faculties were endowed with uncommon strength; he thought with a manly nervousness; and he penetrated forcibly into every subject which engaged his attention. But his petty manners were disagreeably effeminate and fastidious: his habits wanted courage and hardiness; and his temper and spirits were a prey to feebleness, indolence, and trivial derangements. His heart was pure; and his conduct, I firmly believe, stained with no crime. He loved virtue for its own sake, and felt a just and never-slackened indignation at vice. But the little irritations of his daily temper were too much affected by trifles: he loved to assume the character of *the fine gentleman*, a mean and odious ambition in any one, but scarcely to be forgiven in a man of genius. He would shrug his shoulders and distort his voice into fastidious tones; and take upon himself the airs of what folly is pleased to call *high company.*—BRYDGES, SIR SAMUEL EGERTON, 1808, *Traits in the Character of Gray the Poet; Censura Literaria.*

As the life of Gray advanced, it was still marked by the same studious and secluded habits; but he appears gradually to have left his classical studies for a more extended circle of reading, including history, antiquities, voyages, and travels; and in many of the books in his library, as

Fabian's Chronicles, Clarendon, and others, the extreme attention with which he read is seen by his various and careful annotations, and by the margins being filled with illustrations and corrections drawn from State Papers, and other original documents. The latest period of his life seems to have been very much occupied in attention to natural history in all its varied branches, both in the study of books, and in the diligent observation of nature.—MITFORD, JOHN, 1814–43–53, *Life of Gray.*

I cannot, on looking through his memoirs, letters, and poems, discover the slightest trace of passion, or one proof or even indication that he was ever under the influence of woman.—JAMESON, ANNA BROWNELL, 1829, *The Loves of the Poets, vol.* II, *p.* 309.

In the even balance of all his emotions Gray preserved himself from every vice; —virtuous generally, inasmuch as he carried no one virtue into a passion. Ambition never allured, Pleasure never intoxicated, Love never engrossed him. His inspiration, as we before said, was a highly cultivated taste operating on a most harmonions ear.—LYTTON, EDWARD BULWER LORD, 1837–68, *Gray's Works, Miscellaneous Prose Works, vol.* I, *p.* 152.

Stoke Park, thus interesting both on account of these older associations, and of Penn and Gray, is about a couple of miles from Slough. The country is flat, but its monotony is broken up by the noble character and disposition of its woods. Near the house is a fine expanse of water, across which the eye falls on fine views, particularly to the south, of Windsor Castle, Cooper's Hill, and the Forest Woods. About three hundred yards from the north front of the house stands a column, sixty-eight feet high, bearing on the top a colossal statue of Sir Edward Coke, by Rosa. The woods of the park shut out the view of West End House, Gray's occasional residence, but the space is open from the mansion across the park, so as to take in the view both of the church and of a monument erected by the late Mr. Penn to Gray. Alighting from the carriage at a lodge, I entered the park just at the monument. This is composed of fine freestone, and consists of a large sarcophagus, supported on a square pedestal, with inscriptions on each side. Three of them are selected from the "Ode to Eton College" and the "Elegy." . . . The fourth bears this inscription:

"This Monument, in honor of
Thomas Gray,
Was erected A. D. 1799,
Among the scenery
Celebrated by that great Lyric and Elegiac Poet.
He died in 1771,
And lies unnoted in the adjoining Churchyard,
Under the Tomb-stone on which he piously
And pathetically recorded the interment
Of his Aunt and lamented Mother."

This monument is inclosed in a neatly-kept garden-like inclosure, with a winding walk approaching from the shade of the neighboring trees. To the right, across the park, at some little distance, backed by fine trees, stands the rural little church and churchyard where Gray wrote his "Elegy," and where he lies.—HOWITT, WILLIAM, 1846, *Homes and Haunts of the Most Eminent British Poets, vol.* I, *pp.* 318, 319.

Gray found very little gratification at Cambridge in the society and manners of the young university men who were his contemporaries. They ridiculed his sensitive temper and retired habits, and gave him the nickname of "Miss Gray," for his supposed effeminacy. Nor does Gray seem to have lived on much better terms with his academic superiors. He abhorred mathematics, with the same cordiality of hatred which Pope professed towards them, and at that time concurred with Pope in thinking that the best recipe for dulness was to

"Full in the midst of Euclid plunge at once,
And petrify a genius to a dunce."

—CREASY, SIR EDWARD, 1850–75, *Memoirs of Eminent Etonians, p.* 333.

Viewed through the medium of the interest which legitimately attaches to genius, we are confident that the few incidents in the life of such a man as Thomas Gray will appear important links of a chain of existence whose value was precious beyond all calculation.—WARBURTON, ELIOT, 1852, *Memoirs of Horace Walpole, vol.* II, *p.* 128.

The morose hermit of Cambridge.—TAINE, H. A., 1871, *History of English Literature, tr. Van Laun, vol.* II, *bk.* iii, *ch.* vii, *p.* 220.

What Gray owed to his mother may be

imagined. It was she who saved his life when he was a child; and it was she who sent him to Eton, where he remained six years, and to Cambridge, where he remained three or four years, and to the continent, where he traveled with Horace Walpole, living the life of a thoughtful and elegant scholar. She lived to see twelve—is it harsh to say—*happy* years after the death of her husband, to see her love repaid by the genius of her son. As devoted to her as she was to him, he never mentioned her without a sigh. And when she died, full of years, he placed over her loved remains this most pathetic inscription:

Beside her Friend and Sister,
Here sleep the Remains of
Dorothy Gray,
Widow; the careful, tender mother
Of many Children, one of whom alone
Had the Misfortune to survive her.
She died March XI., MDCCLIII.
Aged LXXII.

—STODDARD, RICHARD HENRY, 1874, *British Authors, Scribner's Monthly, vol.* 8, *p.* 456.

West End, the house in which Gray's mother lived, and he wrote much poetry and many letters, now called Stoke Court, is about one mile north of the church. Gray described it as "a compact neat box of red brick, with sash windows, a grotto made of flints, a walnut-tree with three mole-hills under it." The house was rebuilt by Mr. Penn about 1845, on a larger scale, and is now a gentleman's villa. The room in which Gray wrote was, however, preserved, and forms a part of the present house. The walnut-tree and grotto were retained, and the basin of gold-fishes greatly enlarged.—THORNE, JAMES, 1877, *Handbook of the Environs of London: Stoke Pogis.*

In one of Phillip Gray's fits of extravagances he seems to have had a full-length of his son painted, about this time, by the fashionable portrait-painter of the day, Jonathan Richardson the elder. The picture is in the Fitzwilliam Museum, at Cambridge. The head is good in colour and modelling; a broad, pale brow, sharp nose and chin, large eyes, and a pert expression give a lively idea of the precocious and not very healthy young gentleman of thirteen. He is dressed in a blue satin coat, lined with pale shot silk, and crosses his stockinged legs so as to display dapper slippers of russet leather. His father, however, absolutely refused to educate him, and he was sent to Eton, about 1727, under the auspices of his uncles, and at the expense of his mother. —GOSSE, EDMUND, 1882, *Gray (English Men of Letters), p.* 3.

"Knowledge, penetration, seriousness, sentiment, humour"—so Mr. Matthew Arnold counts over the five talents committed to Gray. Five talents; yet it is not easy to think of him as ever to be a ruler of five cities. With his gathered learning, his insight and his power of organising knowledge, his judgment at once delicate and solid, his feeling for beauty in nature and in art, his amiable irony and his brightness of style, why was Gray a failure, and why does the story of his life hang weights upon our courage and our hope? One can imagine his biographer protesting in lively tones against the word "failure." Gray created a style in English poetry; he was perhaps the most cultured Englishman of his generation; he interpreted Icelandic literature; he heralded the romantic revival; he felt the beauty of Gothic architecture; he revealed the wonders of lake and crag in Cumberland and Westmoreland; he sustained classical learning in his university; he made true friends and kept them. And, doubtless, compared with many lives, that of Gray may almost deserve to be called a success. Yet, on the other hand, there have been gallant defeats which, compared with such success as his, look like victories. After all contentions to the contrary, the settled conviction returns and maintains its hold upon our minds that Gray failed to work out the possibilities of his nature; that, for some enervating cause within, some retarding cause without, his powers must have carried him much farther than they actually did.—DOWDEN, EDWARD, 1882, *Gosse's Gray, The Academy, vol.* 22, *p.* 58.

His contemptuous hatred of theology and of creeds is marked; he had no patience with them; of worship he knew nothing. It has been said that he would have found a medicine for his unhappiness in wedded love; he would have found more than a medicine in religion. The stately pathos of such a life is indisputable. The pale little poet, with greatness written so largely on all his works, with keen, deep eyes, the long aquiline nose, the heavy chin, the thin compressed lips, the halting affected gait, is a figure to be contemplated with serious and loving interest, spoiled for life, as he said, by retirement. —BENSON, ARTHUR CHRISTOPHER, 1888, *Gray, Macmillan's Magazine, vol.* 59, *p.* 30.

I was FORTUNATE enough to obtain a few years ago the original manuscript of Gray's "Elegy in a Country Churchyard": I mention, merely for the sake of a historical record, that an American sent over to bid 200 pounds for it: I obtained it for 220. It would have been to the lasting shame of Britain to allow such a priceless treasure to cross the Atlantic. When a boy at Eton I made a pilgrimage each year to the Churchyard where Gray is entombed: no record of him exists there: he was buried in his mother's grave: the well-intentioned, but vulgar, monument in Stoke Pogis Park, close by, is unworthy of the beauty of his consummate Art, and exquisite Refinement.—FRASER, SIR WILLIAM, 1893, *Hic et Ubique, p.* 266.

The air of Stoke Pogis must promote longevity. The church itself is a marvel of loveliness, with its gray, ivy-clad walls, its many gables, its tall, graceful spire, and its general air of peaceful, honoured old age. Gray lies close to the western wall of the church, in the same tomb with the mother who was his idol. . . . We went down into the seven hundred year old church, to which we had come solely for Gray's sake, and found, as usual, that it was a palimpsest. Always one inscription on the parchment overlies another. . . . In one corner a square pew is pointed out, where Gray used to sit by his mother's side, thinking a boy's thoughts.—DORR, JULIA C. R., 1895, *The Flower of England's Face, pp.* 76, 78, 79.

He was sensitive to all fine influences that were in the literary air. One of the greatest scholars among English poets, his taste was equal to his acquisitions. He was a sound critic of poetry, music, architecture, and painting. His mind and character both had distinction; and if there was something a trifle finical and old-maidish about his personality—which led the young Cantabs on one occasion to take a rather brutal advantage of his nervous dread of fire—there was also that nice reserve which gave to Milton, when *he* was at Cambridge, the nickname of the "the lady of Christ's."—BEERS, HENRY A., 1898, *A History of English Romanticism in the Eighteenth Century, p.* 172.

Whichever way the eye turns in all the country between Windsor and Stoke Pogis there is in every place something that suggests chapters in Gray's life or famous and beloved lines from his poems; and the landscape in which so much of his life was set and with which so many of his works are associated, is one whose whole tone and character seem peculiarly in harmony with his own genius. But it is in the quiet churchyard that the memory of the poet lives in its greatest intensity. So long as the pathos of lowly life appeals to the heart, so long as there is a soul not wholly lost to the charm of peaceful days spent in the "cool sequestered vale of life," so long as the tender images of fading day and unavailing reminders of the dead have power to move the spirit, —so long will this God's Acre keep green the memory of that poet whose verse abounds with "sentiments to which every bosom returns an echo."—SHELLEY, HENRY C., 1898, *The Birthplace of Gray's Elegy, New England Magazine, vol.* 24, *p.* 672.

ELEGY IN A COUNTRY CHURCHYARD

1751

As you have brought me into a little sort of distress, you must assist me, I believe, to get out of it as well as I can. Yesterday I had the misfortune of receiving a letter from certain gentlemen (as their bookseller expresses it), who have taken the Magazine of Magazines into their hands. They tell me that an *ingenious* Poem, called reflections in a Country Church-Yard, has been communicated to them, which they are printing forth-with; that they are informed that the *excellent* author of it is I by name, and that they beg not only his *indulgence*, but the *honour* of his correspondence, etc. As I am not at all disposed to be either so indulgent, or so correspondent, as they desire, I have but one bad way left to escape the honour they would inflict upon me; and therefore am obliged to desire you would make Dodsley print it immediately (which may be done in less than a week's time) from your copy, but without my name, in what form is most convenient for him, but on his best paper and character; he must correct the press himself, and print it without any interval between the stanzas, because the sense is in some places continued beyond them; and the title must be,—Elegy, written in a Country Churchyard. If he would add a line or two to say it came into his hands by accident, I should like it better. If you behold the Magazine of Magazines in the light I do, you will not refuse to give yourself this trouble on my account, which you have taken of your own accord before now. If Dodsley do not do this immediately, he may as well let it alone.—GRAY, THOMAS, 1751, *Letter to Horace Walpole, Feb.* 11; *Works, ed. Gosse, vol.* II, *p.* 210.

The following Poem came into my hands by accident, if the general approbation with which this little Piece has been spread, may be called by so slight a term as accident. It is this approbation which makes it unnecessary for me to make an Apology but to the Author: as he cannot but feel some Satisfaction in having pleas'd so many Readers already, I flatter myself he will forgive my communicating that Pleasure to many more.—"THE EDITOR."—DODSLEY, ROBERT, 1751, *Elegy Written in a Country Church-yard, Advertizement.*

This is a very fine poem, but overloaded with epithet. The heroic measure, with alternate rhyme, is very properly adapted to the solemnity of the subject, as it is the slowest movement that our language admits of. The latter part of the poem is pathetic and interesting.—GOLDSMITH, OLIVER, 1767, *The Beauties of English Poetry.*

The "Church-yard" abounds with images which find a mirror in every mind, and with sentiments to which every bosom returns an echo. The four stanzas, beginning "Yet even these bones" are to me original: I have never seen the notions in any other place; yet he that reads them here persuades himself that he has always felt them. Had Gray written often thus, it had been vain to blame, and useless to praise him.—JOHNSON, SAMUEL, 1779–81, *Gray, Lives of the English Poets.*

Of smaller poems, the "Elegy" of Gray may be considered as the most exquisite and finished example in the world, of the effect resulting from the intermixture of evening scenery and pathetic reflection.—DRAKE, NATHAN, 1798–1820, *Literary Hours, No.* xxiv, *vol.* II, *p.* 17.

Gray's "Pindaric Odes" are, I believe, generally given up at present: they are stately and pedantic, a kind of methodical borrowed phrensy. But I cannot so easily give up, nor will the world be in any haste to part with, his "Elegy in a Country Churchyard;" it is one of the most classical productions that ever was penned by a refined and thoughtful mind, moralizing on human life. Mr. Coleridge (in his "Literary Life") says that his friend Mr. Wordsworth had undertaken to show that the language of the "Elegy" is unintelligible: it has, however, been understood.—HAZLITT, WILLIAM, 1818, *Lectures on the English Poets. Lecture* vi.

Had Gray written nothing but his "Elegy," high as he stands, I am not sure that he would not stand higher; it is the cornerstone of his glory; without it, his odes would be insufficient for his fame.—BYRON, LORD, 1821, *On Bowles's Strictures on Pope.*

I know not what there is of spell in the following simple line:

"The rude forefathers of the hamlet sleep;"

but no frequency of repetition can exhaust its touching charm. This fine poem overcame even the spiteful enmity of Johnson, and forced him to acknowledge its excellence.—BRYDGES, SIR SAMUEL EGERTON, 1834, *Imaginary Biography.*

There is a charm in metre, as there is in music; it is of the same kind, though the relation may be remote; and it differs less in degree, perhaps, than one who has not an ear for poetry can believe. . . . Gray's "Elegy" owes much of its popularity to its strain of verse; the strain of thought alone, natural and touching as it is, would never have impressed it upon the hearts of thousands and tens of thousands, unless the diction and meter in which it was embodied had been perfectly in unison with it. Beattie ascribed its general reception to both causes. . . . Neither cause would have sufficed for producing so general, and extensive, and permanent an effect, unless the poem had been, in the full import of the word, harmonious.—SOUTHEY, ROBERT, 1835, *Life of Cowper, ch.* xii.

At its very birth, it received the stamp of immortality.—LYTTON, EDWARD BULWER

LORD, 1837–68, *Gray's Works, Miscellaneous Prose Works, vol.* I, *p.* 146.

Gray's "Elegy" will be read as long as any work of Shakespeare, despite of its moping owl and the tin-kettle of an epitaph tied to its tail. It is the first poem that ever touched my heart, and it strikes it now just in the same place. Homer, Shakespeare, Milton, Dante, the four giants who lived before our last Deluge of poetry, have left the ivy growing on the church-yard wall.—LANDOR, WALTER SAVAGE, 1843, *Notes out of Letters, Life by Forster, p.* 570.

The work is a masterpiece of poetical handling. . . . But the poem, in spite of all his skill, has somewhat of an artificial and hot-bed air; the imagery, beautiful as it is, inspires the reader with an involuntary feeling of its having been painfully collected from a multitude of sources. It is a piece of rich mosaic; and though the parts of which it is composed are exquisite in themselves and dovetailed together with no ordinary art, the effect of the whole is rather of *construction* than *evolution.*—SHAW, THOMAS B., 1847, *Outlines of English Literature, pp.* 296, 297.

For wealth of condensed thought and imagery, fused into one equable stream of golden song by intense fire of genius, the Editor knows no poem superior to this "Elegy,"—none quite equal. Nor has the difficulty of speaking well on common topics, without exaggeration yet with unfailing freshness and originality, been ever met with greater success. Line after line has the perfection of a flawless jewel: it is hard to find a word that could have been spared, or changed for the better. This condensation, however, has injured the clearness of the poem: the specific gravity of the gem, if we may pursue the image, has diminished its translucent qualities. Many notes have hence been added;—the useful but prosaic task of paraphrase is best left to the reader, who may make one for his benefit, and then burn it for his pleasure.—PALGRAVE, FRANCIS TURNER, 1875, *ed., The Children's Treasury of English Song, Notes, p.* 292.

Of all short poems—or indeed of all poems whatsoever—in the English language, which has been, for a century and a quarter past, the one most universally, persistently, and incessantly reproduced and quoted from? I suppose, beyond rivalry and almost beyond comparison, the "Elegy in a Country Churchyard" of Thomas Gray. Such is the glory which has waited upon scant productiveness and relative mediocrity—though undoubtedly nobly balanced and admirably grown and finished mediocrity—in the poetic art. The flute has overpowered the organ, the riding-horse has outstripped Pegasus, and the crescent moon has eclipsed the sun.—ROSSETTI, WILLIAM MICHAEL, 1878, *Lives of Famous Poets, p.* 147.

A popularity due in great measure to the subject,—created for Gray a reputation to which he has really no right. He himself was not deceived by the favour shown to the "Elegy." "Gray told me with a good deal of acrimony," writes Dr. Gregory, "that the 'Elegy' owed its popularity entirely to the subject, and that the public would have received it as well if it had been written in prose." This is too much to say; the "Elegy" is a beautiful poem, and in admiring it the public showed a true feeling for poetry. But it is true that the "Elegy" owed much of its success to its subject, and that it has received a too unmeasured and unbounded praise. Gray himself, however, maintained that the "Elegy" was not his best work in poetry, and he was right. High as is the praise due to the "Elegy," it is yet true that in other productions of Gray he exhibits poetical qualities even higher than those exhibited in the "Elegy." He deserves, therefore, his extremely high reputation as a poet, although his critics and the public may not always have praised him with perfect judgment. We are brought back, then, to the question: How, in a poet so really considerable, are we to explain his scantiness of production?—ARNOLD, MATTHEW, 1880, *The English Poets, ed. Ward, vol.* III, *p.* 305.

Extreme elegance and careful composition are more conspicuous in the "Elegy" than in most other English poems of equal length. The art is not forced upon the reader's attention, but it has doubtless preserved a poem in which it is commonly said that there is no other quality of exceptional greatness. Yet there is a sort of ungraciousness in that remark, inasmuch as it resembles the well-known criticism of the man who, when he first saw Hamlet acted, commented on the large number of familiar quotations that it contained, for the "Elegy" is so well known that it seems thereby somewhat trite and valueless.—PERRY, THOMAS S., 1880, *Gray, Collins and Beattie, Atlantic Monthly, vol.* 46, *p.* 812.

It was whilst Gray was quietly vegetating in Bloomsbury that an event occurred of which he was quite unconscious, which yet has singularly endeared him to the memory of Englishmen. On the evening of the 12th of September, 1759—whilst Gray, sauntering back from the British Museum to his lodgings, noted that the weather was cloudy, with a south-southwest wind—on the other side of the Atlantic the English forces lay along the river Montmorency, and looked anxiously across at Quebec and at the fateful heights of Abraham. When night-fall came, and before the gallant four thousand obeyed the word of command to steal across the river, General Wolfe, the young officer of thirty-three, who was next day to win death and immortality in victory, crept along in a boat from post to post to see that all was ready for the expedition. It was a fine, silent evening, and as they pulled along with muffled oars, the General recited to one of his officers who sat with him in the stern of the boat nearly the whole of Gray's "Elegy in a Country Churchyard," adding as he concluded, "I would prefer being the author of that poem to the glory of beating the French tomorrow." Perhaps no finer compliment was ever paid by the man of action to the man of imagination, and, sanctified, as it were, by the dying lips of the great English hero, the poem seems to be raised far above its intrinsic rank in literature, and to demand our respect as one of the acknowledged glories of our race and language.—GOSSE, EDMUND, 1882, *Gray (English Men of Letters), p.* 143.

Gray's Elegy is better known and more widely loved than any single poem in our language. . . . It is because the original charm is still as fresh as ever, that we may call the "Elegy in a Country Churchyard" the central poem of the age. —HARRISON, FREDERIC, 1883–86, *The Choice of Books and Other Literary Pieces, pp.* 381, 382.

Its melancholy music gets somehow stamped on the brain of nearly all of us, and lends a poetic halo to every old graveyard that has the shadow of a church-tower slanted over it.—MITCHELL, DONALD G., 1895, *English Lands Letters and Kings, Queen Anne and the Georges, p.* 79.

Gray's famous "Elegy," 1751, which was originally sold for sixpence, jumped from £36 in 1888 to £59 in 1892, and when the next copy came into the market in December 1893 it sold for £74.—ROBERTS, W., 1896, *Rare Books and Their Prices, p.* 25.

It is the habit of anthologists to include the "Elegy" in collections of Lyric poetry, but no definition of a lyric poem that I have ever heard of can be so strained as to bring this long and almost perfect elegiac poem into such a collection as the present.—CRAWFURD, OSWALD, 1896, *ed. Lyrical Verse from Elizabeth to Victoria, note, p.* 431.

The fame of Thomas Gray is unique among English poets, in that, although world-wide and luminous, it springs from a single poem, a flawless masterpiece,—"The Elegy Written in a Country Churchyard." This is the one production by which he is known to the great mass of readers and will continue to be known to coming generations; yet in his own time his other poems were important factors, in establishing the high repute accorded to him then and still maintained in the esteem of critics. . . . Lowell says of the "Elegy" that it won its popularity "not through any originality of thought, but far more through originality of sound." There must, however, be some deeper reason than this for the grasp which it has upon the minds and hearts of all classes.—LATHROP, GEORGE PARSONS, 1897, *Library of the World's Best Literature, ed. Warner, vol.* XI, *pp.* 6623, 6625.

There is no poem in the English language more decidedly popular. It appeals to a feeling all but universal,—applicable to all ranks and classes of society. The poem exhibits the highest poetic sensibility and the most cultivated taste. No poem in the English language is more figurative, nor is there any of greater metrical beauty. The popularity which it first attained, today continues unabated. —JONES, WILLIAM C., 1897, *Elements and Science of English Versification, p.* 272.

The "Elegy" is the masterpiece of this whole "Il Penseroso" school, and has summed up for all English readers, for all time, the poetry of the tomb.—BEERS, HENRY A., 1898, *A History of English Romanticism in the Eighteenth Century, p.* 175.

ODES

Even my friends tell me they [the Odes] do not succeed, and write me moving topics of consolation on that head; in short, I have heard of nobody but a player [Garrick] and a doctor of divinity [Warburton] that profess their esteem for them.—GRAY, THOMAS, 1757, *Letter to Dr. Hurd, Aug.* 25; *Works, ed. Gosse, vol.* II, *p.* 325.

He speaks to a people not easily impressed with new ideas, extremely tenacious of the old; with difficulty warmed, and as slowly cooling again. How unsuited then to our national character is that species of poetry which rises upon us with unexpected flights! Where we must hastily catch the thought, or it flies from us; and, in short, where the Reader must largely partake of the Poet's enthusiasm in order to taste his beauties.—GOLDSMITH, OLIVER, 1757, *Odes by Mr. Gray, London Monthly Review, vol.* 17, *p.* 239.

Talking of Gray's "Odes," he said, "They are forced plants raised in a hotbed; and they are poor plants; they are but cucumbers after all." A gentleman present, who had been running down Ode-writing in general, as a bad species of poetry, unluckily said, "Had they been literally cucumbers, they had been better things than Odes."—"Yes, Sir (said Johnson), for a *hog*."—JOHNSON, SAMUEL, 1780, *Life by Boswell, ed. Hill, vol.* IV, *p.* 15.

I yet reflect with pain upon the cool reception which those noble odes, "The Progress of Poetry" and "The Bard," met with at their first publication; it appeared that there were not twenty people in England who liked them.—WHARTON, THOMAS, 1781, *Letter to Mason, May* 29.

No piece can now be selected from his works that can justly come into competition with the "Bard" of Gray; over his inimitable ode a tinge so wildly, awful, so gloomily terrific, is thrown, as without any exception to place it at the head of lyric poetry.—DRAKE, NATHAN, 1798–1820, *Literary Hours, No.* XXV, *vol.* II, *p.* 22.

Gray (to whom nothing is wanting to render him, perhaps, the finest poet in the English language but to have written a little more) is said to have been so much hurt by a foolish and impertinent parody of two of his finest odes, that he never afterwards attempted any considerable work.—SMITH, ADAM, 1801, *Theory of Moral Sentiments, vol.* I, *p.* 255.

"The Ode on a Distant Prospect of Eton College" is more mechanical and commonplace [than the "Elegy in a Country Churchyard]; but it touches on certain strings about the heart, that vibrate in unison with it to our latest breath. No one ever passes by Windsor's "stately heights," or sees the distant spires of Eton College below, without thinking of Gray. He deserves that we should think of him; for he thought of others, and turned a trembling, ever-watchful ear to the "still sad music of humanity."—HAZLITT, WILLIAM, 1818, *Lectures on the English Poets, Lecture* vi.

. . . I have this evening been reading a few passages in Gray's Odes. I am very much pleased with them. The "Progress of Poesy" and the "Ode on Eton College" are admirable. And many passages of "The Bard," though, I confess, quite obscure to me, seem to partake in a great degree of the sublime. *Obscurity* is the great objection which many urge against Gray. They do not consider that it contributes in the highest degree to sublimity; and he certainly aimed at sublimity in these Odes. Every one admires his Elegy, and if they do not his Odes, they must attribute it to their own want of taste.—LONGFELLOW, HENRY WADSWORTH, 1823, *Letter to His Mother, Life, ed. Longfellow, vol.* I, *p.* 29.

That beautiful stanza where he has made the founders of Cambridge to pass before our eyes like shadows over a magic glass.—HALLAM, HENRY, 1827–46, *Constitutional History of England.*

Who has not felt the sentiments and the regrets expressed here with all the sweetness of the Muse? Who has not been affected at the remembrances of the sports, the studies, the loves, of his early years! But can we recall them to life? The pleasures of youth reproduced by memory are ruins viewed by torch-light. —CHATEAUBRIAND, FRANÇOIS RENÉ VISCOUNT DE, 1837, *Sketches of English Literature, vol.* II, *p.* 259.

Overflies ["The Bard"] all other English lyrics like an eagle. . . . It was the prevailing blast of Gray's trumpet that more than anything else called men back to the legitimate standard.—LOWELL, JAMES RUSSELL, 1871, *Pope, My Study Windows, pp*, 337, 338.

Gray's Odes have a stately swing to their measures, which comes nearer to Pindar than any other poetry. He is the most successful copyist of the Greek metres, and he never fails to stir us by the mere power of style.—POOR, LAURA ELIZABETH, 1880, *Sanskrit and Its Kindred Literatures*, p. 436.

Compared, not with the work of the great masters of the golden ages of poetry, but with the poetry of his own contemporaries in general, Gray's may be said to have reached, in his style, the excellence at which he aimed; while the evolution, also, of such a piece as his "Progress of Poesy," must be accounted not less noble and sound than its style.—ARNOLD, MATTHEW, 1880, *The English Poets, ed. Ward, vol.* III, *p*. 316.

In the "Eton College," again, the change from emotion to emotion, the balance of the parts, the pathetic humor of the conclusion, which recalls and binds together and suffuses the whole, must strike everybody who reflects for a moment on the construction of the poem. The effect of the whole, and of each part as contributing to the whole, has been elaborately calculated, elaborately, and yet with such vividness of emotional insight that there is no trace of labor. Stanza follows stanza as if by spontaneous growth, and the concluding reflection arises as if by irresistible suggestion.—MINTO, WILLIAM, 1894, *The Literature of the Georgian Era, ed. Knight, p.* 96.

LETTERS

I find more people like the grave letters than those of humour, and some think the latter a little affected, which is as wrong a judgment as they could make; for Gray never wrote anything easily but things of humour. Humour was his natural and original turn—and though, from his childhood, he was grave and reserved his genius led him to see things ludicrously and satirically; and though his health and dissatisfaction gave him low spirits, his melancholy turn was much more affected than his pleasantry in writing. You knew him enough to know I am in the right.—WALPOLE, HORACE, 1775, *To Rev. William Cole, Letters; ed. Cunningham, vol.* VI, *p.* 206.

Read Gray's Letters on his Tour to the Lakes. He saw little, and that little hastily; but what he did see he sketched with the pen inimitably. The touches with which he occasionally gives life and spirit to the delineation are equisite. Yet in Gray's prose, as in his verse, there is some thing affected; and his wit, though very refined and pure, has the air of being forced. The description of the *sunrise* is incomparably fine.—GREEN, THOMAS, 1779–1810, *Diary of a Lover of Literature.*

Gray's letters very much resemble what his conversation was. He had none of the airs of either a scholar or a poet; and though on those and all other subjects he spoke to me with the utmost freedom, and without any reserve, he was in general company much more silent than one could have wished.—FORBES, SIR WILLIAM, 1806, *Life of Beattie.*

His letters are inimitably fine. If his poems are sometimes finical and pedantic, his prose is quite free from affectation. He pours his thoughts out upon paper as they arise in his mind; and they arise in his mind without pretence, or constraint, from the pure impulse of learned leisure and contemplative indolence. He is not here on stilts or in buckram; but smiles in his easychair as he moralizes through the loopholes of his retreat on the bustle and raree-show of the world, or "those reverend bedlams—colleges and schools!"—He had nothing to do but to read and think, and to tell his friends what he read and thought. His life was a luxurious, thoughtful dream.—HAZLITT, WILLIAM, 1818, *Lectures on the English Poets, Lecture* vi.

Delightful indeed are these "Letters:" evincing the taste of a virtuoso, the attainments of a scholar, and the gaiety of a classical wit.—DIBDIN, THOMAS FROGNALL, 1824, *Library Companion.*

Gray appears to us to be the best letter-writer in the language. Others equal him in particular qualities, and surpass him in amount of entertainment; but none are so nearly faultless. Chesterfield wants heart, and even his boasted "delicacy;" Bolingbroke and Pope want simplicity; Cowper is more lively than strong; Shenstone reminds you of too many rainy days, Swift of too many things he affected to despise, Gibbon too much of the formalist and the *litteratéur*. The most amusing of all our letter-writers are Walpole and Lady Mary Wortley Montagu; but though they have abundance of wit, sense, and animal spirits, you are not always sure of their veracity. Now, "the first quality in a companion," as Sir William Temple observes, "is truth;" and Gray's truth is as manifest as his other good qualities. He has sincerity, modesty, manliness (in spite of a somewhat effeminate body), learning, good-nature, playfulness, a perfect style; and if an air of pensiveness breathes all over, it is only of that resigned and contemplative sort which completes our sympathy with the writer. . . . Gray is the "melancholy Jaques" of English literature, without the sullenness or causticity.—HUNT, LEIGH, 1849, *A Book for a Corner, Second Series.*

Everyone knows the letters of Gray, and remembers the lucid simplicity and directness, mingled with the fastidious sentiment of a scholar, of his description of such scenes as the Chartreuse. That is a well-known description, but those in his journal of a "Tour in the North" have been neglected, and they are especially interesting since they go over much of the country in which Wordsworth dwelt, and of which he wrote. They are also the first conscious effort—and in this he is a worthy forerunner of Wordsworth—to describe natural scenery with the writer's eye upon the scene described, and to describe it in simple and direct phrase, in distinction to the fine writing that was then practised. And Gray did this intentionally in the light prose journal he kept, and threw by for a time the refined carefulness and the insistance on human emotion which he thought necessary in poetic description of Nature. In his prose then, though not in his poetry, we have Nature loved for her own sake.—BROOKE, STOPFORD, A., 1874, *Theology in the English Poets, p.* 36.

Kindly feeling, an indolent turn, intellectual fastidiousness, are traceable up and down the course of the correspondence, and present a genuine likeness of the man.—ROSSETTI, WILLIAM MICHAEL, 1878, *Lives of Famous Poets, p.* 158.

However people may differ in their estimate of Gray as a poet, as a man he is secure of our affection, so soon as we get to know him, and any one may know him who will read his letters. Here, surely, there is no want of speaking out. Indeed, there are few literary men of so attractive a nature as Gray. Perhaps he is the most lovable of all except Charles Lamb, and with Lamb, despite many obvious differences, he has many points in common. They were both solitary creatures, living a recluse life in the world, but not of it, their best friends among the dead; they were both exquisite critics and no mean writers of poetry; they were both a prey to melancholy or rather, as Gray says, to "leucocholy;" they had both a delicate and delightful humour; they were both the very soul of gentle goodness. And so it comes about that their letters, in which they live to us, are among the few external good things which are necessary to happiness. The charm of a letter of Gray's lies partly in this interest of his character, and partly in the perfect felicity with which everything is said.—BEECHING, H. C., 1885, *The Academy, vol.* 27, *p.* 53.

His letters are all but the best in the best age of letter-writing. They are fascinating not only for the tender and affectionate nature shown through a mask of reserve, but for gleams of the genuine humour which Walpole pronounced to be his most natural vein.—STEPHEN, LESLIE, 1890, *Dictionary of National Biography, vol.* XXIII, *p.* 27.

GENERAL

"What muse like Gray's shall pleasing, pensive, flow,
Attempered sweetly to the rustic woe;
Or who like him shall sweep the Theban lyre,
And, as his master, pour forth thoughts of fire?"

—LLOYD, ROBERT, 1762, *Epistle to Churchill.*

The author of the finest odes, and of the finest moral elegy in the world.—BEATTIE, JAMES, 1776–9, *On the Usefulness of Classical Learning, Essays on Poetry and Music, p.* 483, *note.*

I have been reading Gray's Works, and think him the only poet since Shakspeare entitled to the character of sublime.

Perhaps you will remember that I once had a different opinion of him. I was prejudiced. He did not belong to our Thursday society, and was an Eton man, which lowered him prodigiously in our esteem. I once thought Swift's letters the best that could be written; but I like Gray's better. His humour, or his wit, or whatever it is to be called, is never ill-natured or offensive, and yet, I think equally poignant with the Dean's.—COWPER, WILLIAM, 1777, *Letter to Joseph Hill, April* 20; *Works, ed. Southey, vol.* II, *p.* 223.

Not that her blooms are mark'd with beauty's hue,
My rustic Muse her votive chaplet brings;
Unseen, unheard, O Gray, to thee she sings!—
While slowly-pacing thro' the churchyard dew,
At curfeu-time, beneath the dark-green yew,
Thy pensive genius strikes the moral strings;
Or borne sublime on Inspiration's wings,
Hears Cambria's bards devote the dreadful clue
Of Edward's race, with murthers foul defil'd;
Can aught my pipe to reach thine ear essay?
No, bard divine! For many a care beguil'd
By the sweet magic of thy soothing lay,
For many a raptur'd thought, and vision wild,
To thee this strain of gratitude I pay.

—WARTON, THOMAS, 1777, *To Mr. Gray.*

As a writer he had his peculiarity, that he did not write his pieces first rudely and then correct them, but laboured every line as it arose in the train of composition; and he had a notion, not very peculiar, that he could not write but at certain times, or at happy moments; a fantastic foppery, to which my kindness for a man of learning and of virtues wishes him to have been superior. . . . To say that he has no beauties, would be unjust: a man like him, of great learning and great industry, could not but produce something valuable. When he pleases least, it can only be said that a good design was ill directed.—JOHNSON, SAMUEL, 1779–81, *Gray, Lives of the English Poets.*

It is no incurious subject to enquire, what is the spirit of lyric poetry? . . . The Greeks, the Greeks alone, my friend, are the masters, and their works the models of this kind of poetry. If we examine these models with care, we shall perceive that this species of poetry divides itself, in resemblance of the works of nature, into two kinds, the sublime, and the beautiful. In the first class Pindar stood without a rival till Gray appeared.—PINKERTON, JOHN (ROBERT HERON), 1785, *Letters of Literature, p.* 33.

Or pour, with Gray, the moving flow
Warm on the heart.

—BURNS, ROBERT, 1787, *The Vision, Duan,* ii.

When the taste has been almost exclusively cultivated, the character will be without energy, and its most prominent feature will be that delicacy of feeling against which Mr. Hume has entered so just a protest. Gray stripped of his genius is a tolerably fair model of a man of mere taste, and nothing can be well imagined less desirable than Gray's sickly constitution of mind. Nothing, I think, affords a more lively representation of intellect, thus puny and passive, than those masses of animated jelly which one sees at times scattered along the seashore without bone or tendon, that quiver to every blast and shrink at every touch.—BEDDOES, THOMAS, 1793, *Observations on the Nature of Demonstrative Evidence, with Reflections on Language, p.* 123.

The most costive of poets.—CUMBERLAND, RICHARD, 1806, *Memoirs, vol.* I, *p.* 23.

Of all English poets he was the most finished artist. He attained the highest degree of splendour of which poetical style seems to be capable. If Virgil and his scholar Racine may be allowed to have united somewhat more ease with their elegance, no other poet approaches Gray in this kind of excellence. The degree of poetical invention diffused over such a style, the balance of taste and of fancy necessary to produce it, and the art with which an offensive boldness of imagery is polished away, are not indeed always perceptible to the common reader, nor do they convey to any mind the same species of gratification which is felt from the perusal of those poems which seem to be the unpremeditated effusions of enthusiasm; but to the eye of the critic, and more especially to the artist, they afford a new kind of pleasure, not incompatible with a distinct perception of the art employed, and somewhat similar to the grand emotions excited by the reflection on the skill and toil exerted in the construction of a magnificent palace. They can only be classed among the secondary pleasures of poetry, but they never can exist without a great degree of its higher excellences.—MACKINTOSH, SIR JAMES, 1811, *Journal, Dec.* 22, *Life, ed. Mackintosh, vol.* II, *p.* 177.

He was indeed the inventor, it may be strictly said so, of a new lyrical metre in his own tongue. The peculiar formation of *his* strophe, antistrophe, and epode, was unknown before him; and it could only have been planned and perfected by a master genius, who was equally skilled by long and repeated study, and by transfusion into his own mind of the lyric composition of ancient Greek and of the higher "*canzoni*" of the Tuscan poets, "*di maggior carme e suono*," as it is termed in the commanding energy of their language. Antecedent to "The Progress of Poetry," and to "The Bard," no such lyrics had appeared. There is not an ode in the English language which is constructed like these two compositions; with such power, such majesty, and such sweetness, with such proportioned pauses and just cadences, with such regulated measures of the verse, with such master principles of lyric art displayed and exemplified, and, at the same time, with such a concealment of the difficulty, which is lost in the softness and uninterrupted flowing of the lines of each stanza, with such a musical magic, that every verse in it in succession dwells on the ear and harmonizes with that which is gone before.—MATHIAS, THOMAS JAMES, 1814, *ed., Works of Thomas Gray.*

That Mr. Gray, who never permitted any of his compositions to appear even to his friends before they were finished with the most elaborate exactness—who did not even trust himself with a sketch of his projected works, but wrought them line by line to the highest degree of perfection, till even his own industry was fatigued with the task—that a critic so fastidious should have committed to his executors a vast mass of indigested memoranda never intended for publication by himself, *vel cremanda vel in publicum emittenda*, more especially when his will was written in a state of perfect recollection, must be regarded as one of the anomalies of the human mind for which it is vain to seek any solution but in the general inconsistency of our nature.—SOUTHEY, ROBERT, 1814, *Thomas Gray, Quarterly Review, vol.* 11, *p.* 304.

Gray failed as a poet not because he took too much pains and so extinguished his animation, but because he had very little of that fiery quality to begin with, and his pains were of the wrong sort. He wrote English verses as his brother Eton school boys wrote Latin, filching a phrase now from one author and now from another. I do not profess to be a person of very various reading; nevertheless, if I were to pluck out of Gray's tail all of the feathers which I know belong to other birds, he would be left very bare indeed. Do not let anybody persuade you that any quantity of good verses can be produced by mere felicity; or that an immortal style can be the growth of mere genius. "*Multa tulit fecit que*" must be the motto of all those who are to last.—WORDSWORTH, WILLIAM, 1816, *Letter to Gillies.*

Gray, with the talents, rather of a critic than a poet—with learning, fastidiousness, and scrupulous delicacy of taste, instead of fire, tenderness, or invention—began and ended a small school, which we could scarcely have wished to become permanent, admirable in many respects as some of its productions are—being far too elaborate and artificial either for grace or for fluency, and fitter to excite the admiration of scholars, than the delight of ordinary men. However, they had the merit of not being in any degree French, and of restoring to our poetry the dignity of seriousness, and the tone at least of force and energy.—JEFFREY, FRANCIS LORD, 1816, *Jonathan Swift, Edinburgh Review, vol.* 27, *p.* 7.

The obscurity so often objected to in him is certainly a defect not to be justified by the authority of Pindar, more than anything else that is intrinsically objectionable. But it has been exaggerated. He is nowhere so obscure as not to be intelligible by recurring to the passages. And it may be further observed, that Gray's lyrical obscurity never arises, as in some writers, from undefined ideas or paradoxical sentiments. On the contrary, his moral spirit is as explicit as it is majestic; and deeply read as he was in Plato, he is never metaphysically perplexed. The fault of his meaning is to be latent, not indefinite or confused. When we give his beauties re-perusal and attention, they kindle and multiply to the view. The thread of association that conducts to his remote allusions, or that connects his abrupt transitions, ceases then to be invisible. His lyrical pieces are like paintings on glass, which must be placed in a strong light to give out the perfect radiance of their colouring.—CAMPBELL, THOMAS, 1819, *Specimens of the British Poets.*

No wonder he should describe so well what he saw, for he seems to be present at life rather as a spectator than an actor. When he wrote, it was more to exercise his mind, or entertain his fancy, than from any ambition to please or be admired by others. England had not sent abroad so elegant a scholar since the days of Milton; but he did not, like Milton, seek for distinction in the company of the learned. Whatever was going forward, he was anxious to observe, but cared not how little he was himself seen. The few incidents in his life are to be collected from his letters, which were written with no view to publication, and on that account show to more advantage the excellence of his character, his duty and affection as a son, his cordiality and sincerity as a friend, his diligence, accuracy and elegance as a scholar, and the high sense of probity and honour that actuated his whole conduct.—CARY, HENRY FRANCIS, 1823, *Notices of Miscellaneous English Poets, Memoir, ed. Cary, vol.* II, *p.* 293.

When we read Gray we are led into the ideal world: every thing is new to us, and novelty is always a source of admiration. . . . He writes nothing dictated by his feelings, or by his heart. He appeals to the understanding and the imagination alone. Even in his celebrated elegy he expresses only those sentiments which naturally occur to a philosophic mind in contemplating the final destiny of beings whose existence is limited to a contracted span. Whatever incidental remarks arise from this contemplation in his "Elegy," have no reference to the heart, or its affections. He looked only to the intellectual part of our nature, for he wrote not what his feelings, but what his understanding dictated.—M'DERMOT, M., 1824, *The Beauties of Modern Literature, p.* 99.

Talking of epitaphs, L. Smith said that Mackintosh thinks that of Gray on his mother the most perfect in the language. —MOORE, THOMAS, 1827, *Diary, Jan.* 4; *Memoirs, ed. Russell, vol.* V, *p.* 139.

The Lyrical crown of Gray was swept away at one fell swoop by the ruthless arm of Dr. Johnson. That the Doctor's celebrated critique was unduly severe must be admitted; but the stern censor had truth on his side, nevertheless. There is more of Art than Nature in Gray; more of recollection than invention; more of acquirement than genius. If I may use a colloquial illustration, I should say, that the marks of the tools are too evident on all that he does.—NEELE, HENRY, 1827, *Lectures on English Poetry, p.* 212.

A laborious mosaic, through the hard stiff lineaments of which little life or true grace could be expected to look; real feeling, and all freedom in expressing it, are sacrificed to pomp, cold splendour; for vigour we have a certain mouthing vehemence, too elegant indeed to be tumid, yet essentially foreign to the heart, and seen to extend no deeper than the mere voice and gestures. Were it not for his "Letters," which are full of warm exuberant power, we might almost doubt whether Gray was a man of genius; nay, was a living man at all, and not rather some thousand-times more cunningly devised poetical turning-loom, than that of Swift's Philosophers in Laputa.—CARLYLE, THOMAS, 1828–69, *Goethe, Miscellanies, vol.* I, *p.* 221.

Gray is one of the few, the very few, of our greatest poets, who deserves to be studied in every line for the apprehension of that wonderful sweetness, power, and splendour of versification which has made him (scholastic and difficult as he is) one of the most popular of writers, though his rhymes are occasionally flat, and his phrases heathen Greek to ordinary readers. The secret of his supremacy consists principally in the consummate art with which his diction is elaborated into the most melodious concatenation of syllables to form lines.—MONTGOMERY, JAMES, 1833, *Lectures on General Literature, Poetry, etc., p.* 173.

I think there is something very majestic in Gray's "Installation Ode;" but as to the "Bard" and the rest of his lyrics, I must say I think them frigid and artificial. —COLERIDGE, SAMUEL TAYLOR, 1833, *Table Talk, ed. Ashe, Oct.* 23, *p.* 264.

There is no doubt that Gray laboured some of his compositions too much, and that this often rendered him abrupt and obscure, and the train of his ideas interrupted, so that the reader cannot follow them without great pains, and without the aid of notes. This is an essential fault in poetry, and absolutely destroys eloquence, which, if it cannot carry the reader or hearer simultaneously along with it, fails in its purpose.—BRYDGES, SIR SAMUEL EGERTON, 1834, *Autobiography, vol.* II, *p.* 25.

Gray, as the inmate of a hall at Cambridge, as one seldom absent from the schools, might well have been forgiven for adhering implicitly to the common models. Yet his strain of the Welsh Bard, and his snatches from the Runic, show with how bold a flight he could soar into the open sky. It is needless to praise where there are none to disapprove. It is striking, however, to observe the beauty of that stanza which he expunged from his "Elegy on a Country Churchyard;" so that it might almost be said, that even the leavings of Gray are superior to the finished compositions of other men. Again, when we reflect how frequent the invasion of the Roman Empire by the Barbaric tribes has engaged the pen of other writers from Jornandes down to Gibbon, it is worthy of note that so much eloquence and imagery should remain to be compressed by this poet within the narrow compass of four lines.—STANHOPE, PHILIP HENRY (LORD MAHON), 1836–54, *History of England from the Peace of Utrecht to the Peace of Versailles, vol.* VI, *p.* 318.

Gray was ambitious to be thought gentleman-like; he could not bear to hear any one talk of his poetry, of which he was ashamed. He prided himself on being deeply versed in history, and so he really was; he turned his attention also to the natural sciences, and had pretensions to chemistry; as Sir Humphrey Davy lately aspired, but with reason, to poetical renown. Where are the gentle manlikeness, the history, and the chemistry of Gray? He lives only in a melancholy smile of those Muses whom he despised.—CHATEAUBRIAND, FRANÇOIS RENÉ VISCOUNT DE, 1837, *Sketches of English Literature, vol.* II, *p.* 259.

Painfully and minutely laborious, diffident of his own powers, weighing words in a balance, borrowing a thought here, and a phrase there, Gray wrote English as he wrote Latin. It was a dead language to him, in which he sought to acquire an elegant proficiency by using only the epithets and the phrases rendered orthodox by the best models. But he was no vulgar plagiarist—his very deficiency of invention became productive of a beauty peculiarly his own, and created a kind of poetry of association; so that in reading Gray we are ever haunted with a delightful and vague reminiscence of the objects of a former admiration or love, as early things and thoughts that are recalled to us by some exquisite air of music, and in some place most congenial to dreamlike recollections of grace and beauty. . . . In these contributions, levied from all lands, the excellence of Gray is felicitously displayed. That excellence was an admirable delicacy of taste; the ear of his mind was exquisitely attuned; all the notes he borrows he connects into perfect concord with each other;—and thought and rhyme are equally harmonious. His poems are like cabinets of curious and costly gems—the gems have been polished often by hands long mouldered into dust, and have glittered in the coronals of many a foreign muse, but it is for the first time that they have been so artfully disposed in one collection,—so well selected, so skillfully displayed.—LYTTON, EDWARD BULWER LORD, 1837–68, *Gray's Works, Miscellaneous Prose Works, vol.* I, *p.* 142.

In Gray, surely, we have lost a literary historian such as the world has not yet had; so rare is that genius who happily combines qualities apparently incompatible. In his superior learning, his subtle taste, his deeper thought, and his more vigorous sense, we should have found the elements of a more philosophical criticism, with a more searching and comprehensive intellect, than can be awarded to our old favorite, Thomas Warton.—DISRAELI, ISAAC, 1841, *Lydgate, Amenities of Literature.*

GRAY, while Windsor's antique towers shall
stand,
Or spring revisit Britain's favour'd land;
While those old bards whose praise he sung
so well
Shall keep their place in memory's haunted
cell;
When the green churchyard and the halow'd
tower
Attract your steps at eve's soft, solemn hour;
As long as men can read, and boys recite,
As long as critics sneer, and bards endite,

And lavish lords shall print their jingling
stuff,
Mid ample margin, leaving verge enough;
So long shall Gray, and all he said and sung,
Tang the shrill accents of the school-girl's
tongue;
So long his Ode, his Elegy, and Bard,
By lisping prodigies be drawl'd and Marr'd.
—COLERIDGE, HARTLEY, 1849, *Sketches of English Poets, Poems, vol.* II, *p.* 302.

His powers of humour are proved, not so much by "the Long Story" as by the two admirable political pasquinades, which are very puritanically excluded from the common collections of his poems. That on Lord Sandwich and the Cambridge University election which begins—

"*When sly Jemmy Twitcher;*"

is the very raciest and tartest piece of the kind in our language. Gray's translations from the Norse and Welsh are universally popular. The "Descent of Odin" is generally one of the first pieces of English poetry, which a clever child voluntarily learns by heart, nor is it less a favourite with grown up critics. It is worth while to compare a portion of it with the original Norse. We see thus what Gray's taste led him to adopt, and what to modify. It also shows his skill and genius in adding, when desirable, to the archaic simplicity of the original.—CREASY, SIR EDWARD, 1850–75, *Memoirs of Eminent Etonians, p.* 354.

Johnson's life of Gray is a disparaging performance, the work of a superior mind anxious to cavil and find fault; its depreciatory tone has, however, been far from catching, and Gray has had ample justice done him in the general admiration of the world.—CUNNINGHAM, PETER, 1854, *ed. Johnson's Lives of the English Poets, p.* xxiii.

How much do I not owe to Gray, and how I love *him.*—HUNT, LEIGH, 1855, *Correspondence, vol.* II, *p.* 206.

What sort of literatesque types are fit to be described in the sort of literature called poetry is a matter on which much might be written. Mr. Arnold, some years since, put forth a theory that the art of poetry could only delineate *great actions.* But though, rightly interpreted and understood,—using the word "action" so as to include high and sound activity in contemplation,—this definition may suit the highest poetry, it certainly cannot be stretched to include many inferior sorts and even many good sorts. Nobody in their senses would describe Gray's "Elegy" as the delineation of a "great action:" some kinds of mental contemplation may be energetic enough to deserve this name, but Gray would have been frightened at the very word. He loved scholar-like calm and quiet inaction; his very greatness depended on his *not* acting, on his "wise passiveness," on his indulging the grave idleness which so well appreciates so much of human life.—BAGEHOT, WALTER, 1864, *Wordsworth, Tennyson and Browning, Works, ed. Morgan, vol.* I, *p.* 211.

In spite of the dulness of contemporary ears, preoccupied with the continuous hum of the popular hurdy-gurdy, it was the prevailing blast of Gray's trumpet that more than anything else called men back to the legitimate standard.—LOWELL, JAMES RUSSELL, 1871, *Pope, My Study Windows, p.* 387.

Wordsworth has laid hold of a sonnet of Gray's as a text to preach against false poetic diction. And yet Gray, notwithstanding his often too elaborate diction, deserves better of lovers of English poetry than to have his single sonnet thus gibbeted, merely because, instead of saying the sun rises, it makes

"Reddening Phœbus lift his golden fire."

In the ode on Spring, it is "the rosy-bosomed hours, fair Venus' train," which bring spring in. Venus is thrust between you and the advent of spring, much as Adversity is made "the daughter of Jove." For the nightingale we have "the Attic warbler," as in another ode, for the yellow corn-fields we have "Ceres' golden reign." It is needless to say how abhorent this sort of stuff is to the modern feeling about Nature. And yet, notwithstanding these blemishes, Gray did help forward the movement to a more perfect and adequate style, in which Nature should come direct to the heart, through a perfectly transparent medium of art. When he is at his best, as in the Elegy, Nature and human feeling so perfectly combine that the mind finds in all the images satisfaction and relief. There is in the Elegy no image from Greece or Rome, no intrusive heathen deity, to jar upon the feeling. From the common English landscape alone is drawn all that is needed to minister to the quiet but deep pathos of the whole.—SHAIRP, JOHN CAMPBELL, 1877, *On Poetic Interpretation of Nature, p.* 210.

I always think that there is more Genius in most of the three volume Novels than in Gray: but by the most exquisite Taste, and indefatigable lubrication, he made of his own few thoughts, and many of other men's, a something which we all love to keep ever about us. I do not think his scarcity of work was from Design: he had but a little to say, I believe, and took his time to say it.—FITZGERALD, EDWARD, 1879, *Letters, vol.* I, *p.* 441.

Gray, a born poet, fell upon an age of prose. He fell upon an age whose task was such as to call forth in general men's powers of understanding, wit and cleverness, rather than their deepest powers of mind and soul. . . . Gray, with the qualities of mind and soul of a genuine poet, was isolated in his century. Maintaining and fortifying them by lofty studies, he yet could not fully educe and enjoy them; the want of a genial atmosphere, the failures of sympathy in his contemporaries, were too great. . . . A sort of spiritual east wind was at that time blowing; neither Butler nor Gray could flower. They *never spoke out.* Gray's poetry was not only stinted in quality by reason of the age wherein he lived, it suffered somewhat in quality also. —ARNOLD, MATTHEW, 1880, *The English Poets, ed. Ward, vol.* III, *pp.* 312, 313.

In 1768 he was appointed Professor of History there, an office for which he was well qualified, but he never discharged the duties of his situation, being too lazy to prepare a course of lectures. Gray was a literary voluptuary, refined, finical, indisposed to active exertions, and so terrified lest a faulty piece of work should go out of his hands that he wrote very little. He was an extensive and curious reader in all departments of literature, and prevented time from lying heavy on his hands by engaging in all those trifling occupations by which so many worthy indolent people try to persuade themselves that they are busy. He made annotations in the books which he read; he drew up (for his own edification) tables of chronology; during the chief part of his life he kept a *daily* record of the blowing of flowers, the leafing of trees, the state of the thermometer, the quarter from which the wind blew, the falling of rain, and other matters of the kind.—NICOLL, HENRY J., 1882, *Landmarks of English Literature, p.* 199.

Of Gray he said, "Gray in his limited sphere is great, and has a wonderful ear." —TENNYSON, ALFRED LORD, 1883, *Criticisms on Poets and Poetry, Memoir by his Son, vol.* II, *p.* 288.

In one point only did Gray excel Emerson,—in the art of versification; which is a lower gift than either poetic insight or poetic expression, in both which Emerson greatly excelled Gray.—SANBORN, F. B., 1885, *The Genius and Character of Emerson, p.* 205.

I would desire you not to forget the changes of what I may call the manners of Cambridge, since Gray's time; the approximations of social and domestic life, especially in relation to female society, which would, I believe, not only have softened the asperity of his judgments respecting you, but might have even so far cheered his stagnant spirits, and diverted the monotony of his lonely hours, as to have relieved me from the main difficulty I have to encounter in assigning to Thomas Gray his prime and proper place in English literature. This is, in simple phrase, the scantiness—in adverse criticism, the sterility—of his genius. This peculiarity need not affect our sense of the greatness or even of the wonder at the apparition which it even augments, but undoubtedly it changes the aspect of our judgment just as in our estimate of greatness in life we have a different standard for the hero of one magnanimous action whatever it may be, and of the man of a continuous heroic life. For this prominent problem of the genius of Gray every serious critic will attempt his own solution.—HOUGHTON, LORD (RICHARD MONCKTON MILNES), 1885, *Speech at the Unveiling of the Gray Memorial, Cambridge, May* 26.

You will rather ask me how the individuality of Gray may strike an artist in its relation to Art; well, I answer this: It is an individuality in which an artist finds something to forgive, but how much to love and to admire! and that wherein we dissent from him lay in his time, but in that which we love and admire he was a precursor and a prophet. If, after the manner of his day, he bowed in painting to Guido, in architecture his chastened taste rebelled against the tawdry antics of Horace Walpole's Gothic. But it is chiefly in relation to landscape that the modern feeling stirred in him. Nature knew in him a lover, and in her turn loved to unseal to him her inmost secrets. Her beauties for him revealed a new and richer meaning, for him a fuller charm breathed from the meadow and from the mere, and the mountains lost their antique terrors, and their gloom, fired by a new light, turned in his eyes to glory; a new dawn had arisen. Salvator Rosa and his kind were dead. His path was clear for Turner, for Constable, for Crome. It was well, sir, that artists should join in doing homage to a man who amongst the foremost heralded the day in which such men were given to our country.—LEIGHTON, SIR FREDERICK, 1885, *Speech at the Unveiling of the Gray Memorial, Cambridge, May* 26.

The bulk exhibited by his poetry may not seem imposing to the critic, but it does not frighten the reader. It is natural for us to wish that a writer of Gray's order of genius should have produced some one large work; not because size is essential to greatness, but because it is necessary to the display of invention on a grand scale, and to the development of passions and activities working through mighty agencies. Yet it is extremely doubtful if his fame would have been enhanced in the slightest measure if he had accomplished what is so natural for us to desire. He probably knew the limits of his own powers better than his friends or critics. The unpublished fragments which he left do not, on the whole, make us regret very deeply that he never completed long and ambitious works. They would certainly have contained many fine lines, and might have contained many fine passages; but the spread of his reputation would most probably have been hindered rather than helped by the weight it had to carry.—LOUNSBURY, THOMAS R., 1885, *Gray's Works, The Nation, vol.* 40, *p.* 205.

Elegance, sweetness, pathos, or even majesty he could achieve, but never that force which vibrates in every verse of larger-moulded men. Bonstetten tells us that "every sensation in Gray was passionate," but I very much doubt whether he was capable of that sustained passion of the mind which is fed by a prevailing imagination acting on the consciousness of great powers. That was something he could never feel, though he knew what it meant by observation of others, and longed to feel it. In him imagination was passive; it could divine and select, but not create. Bonstetten, after seeing the best society in Europe on equal terms, also tells us that Gray was the most finished gentleman he had ever seen. Is it over fine to see something ominous in that word *finished?* It seems to imply limitations; to imply a consciousness that sees everything between it and the goal rather than the goal itself, that undermines enthusiasm through the haunting doubt of being undermined. We cannot help feeling in the poetry of Gray that it too is finished, perhaps I should rather say limited, as the greatest things never are, as it is one of their merits that they never can be. They suggest more than they bestow, and enlarge our apprehension beyond their own boundaries. Gray shuts us in his own contentment like a cathedral close or college quadrangle. He is all the more interesting, perhaps, that he was a true child of his century, in which decorum was religion. He could not, as Dryden calls it in his generous way, give his soul a loose, although he would. He is of the eagle brood, but unfledged. His eye shares the æther which shall never be cloven by his wing. But it is one of the school-boy blunders in criticism to deny one kind of perfection because it is not another. Gray, more than any of our poets, has shown what a depth of sentiment, how much pleasurable emotion mere words are capable of stirring through the magic of association, and of artful arrangement in conjunction with agreeable and familiar images.—LOWELL, JAMES RUSSELL, 1886, *Gray; New Princeton Review, vol.* 1, *p.* 163.

Gray and Collins, distinct enough in character to the careful critical inspector, have to the outward eye a curious similarity. They were contemporaries; they wrote very little, and that mostly in the form of odes; they both affected personation and allegorical address to a very unusual extent; both studied effects which were Greek in their precision and delicacy; both were learned and exact students of periods of literature now reinstated in critical authority, but in their day neglected. Yet, while Gray was the greater intellectual figure of the two, the more significant as a man and a writer, Collins possessed something more thrilling, more spontaneous, as a purely lyrical poet. When they are closely examined, their supposed similarity fades away; and, without depreciating either, we discover that each was typical of a class—that Collins was the type of the poet who sings, as the birds do, because he must; and Gray of the artist in verse, who has learned everything which the most consummate attention to workmanship can teach him, when added to the native faculty of a singularly delicate ear. . . . The most important poetical figure in our literature between Pope and Wordsworth.—GOSSE, EDMUND, 1888, *A History of Eighteenth Century Literature, pp.* 235, 236.

I will admit that, although Gray is the author of what is perhaps the most imposing single short poem in the language, and although he has charm, skill, and distinction to a marvellous degree, his originality, his force of production, were so rigidly limited that he may scarcely be admitted to the first rank.—GOSSE, EDMUND, 1889, *What is a Great Poet? Questions at Issue, p.* 100.

It is scarcely a paradox to say that he has left much that is incomplete, but nothing that is unfinished. His handwriting represents his mind; I have seen and transcribed many and many a page of it, but I do not recollect to have noticed a single carelessly written word, or even letter. The mere sight of it suggests refinement, order, and infinite pains. A mind searching in so many directions, sensitive to so many influences, yet seeking in the first place its own satisfaction in a manner uniformly careful and artistic, is almost foredoomed to give very little to the world; it must be content, as the excellent Matthias says, to be "its own exeeding great reward". But what is given is a little gold instead of much silver; a legal tender at any time, though it has never been soiled in the market. He claims our honour as one of those few who in any age have lived in the pursuit of the absolute best, and who help us to mistrust the glib facility with which we are apt to characterize epochs. In all that he has left, there is independence, sincerity, thoroughness; the highest exemplar of the critical spirit; a type of how good work of any kind should be done.—TOVEY, DUNCAN C., 1890, *Gray and His Friends, Introductory Essay, p.* 31.

The smallness of his actual achievements is sufficiently explained by his ill-health, his extreme fastidiousness, his want of energy and personal ambition, and the depressing influences of the small circle of dons in which he lived. The unfortunate eighteenth century has been blamed for his barrenness; but probably he would have found any century uncongenial. The most learned of all our poets, he was naturally an eclectic. He almost worshipped Dryden, and loved Racine as heartily as Shakespeare. He valued polish and symmetry as highly as the school of Pope, and shared their taste for didactic reflection and for pompous personification. Yet he also shared the tastes which found expression in the romanticism of the following period. Mr. Gosse has pointed out with great force his appreciation of Gothic architecture, of mountain scenery, and of old Gaelic and Scandinavian poetry. His unproductiveness left the propagation of such tastes to men much inferior in intellect, but less timid in utterance, such as Walpole and the Wartons. He succeeded only in secreting a few poems which have more solid bullion in proportion to the alloy than almost any in the language, which are admired by critics, while the one in which he has condescended to utter himself with least reserve and the greatest simplicity, had been pronounced by the *vox populi* to be the most perfect in the language.—STEPHEN, LESLIE, 1890, *Dictionary of National Biography, vol.* XXIII, *p.* 27.

Why, then, with so many favorable conditions did Gray produce so little? The chief condition was unfavorable; the spirit of the age was alien to his genius. He was a poet of great gifts and defective impulse fallen upon a prosaic time. The atmosphere he breathed, instead of vitalizing, debilitated him. Nobly endowed, and richly furnished with knowledge, he lacked motivity, and the age was against him.—MABIE, HAMILTON WRIGHT, 1891–93, *Short Studies in Literature, p.* 66.

Although Gray's biographers and critics have very seldom spoken of it, the most interesting thing in a study of his poetry—and the thing, of course, that exclusively concerns us here—is his steady progress in the direction of Romanticism. Beginning as a classicist and disciple of Dryden, he ended in thoroughgoing Romanticism. His early poems contain nothing Romantic; his "Elegy" has something of the Romantic mood, but shows many conventional touches; in the Pindaric Odes the Romantic feeling asserts itself boldly; and he ends in enthusiastic study of Norse and Celtic poetry and mythology. Such a steady growth in the mind of the greatest poet of the time shows not only what he learned from the age, but what he taught it. Gray is a much more important factor in the Romantic movement than seems to be commonly supposed. This will appear from a brief examination of his poetry.—PHELPS, WILLIAM LYON, 1893, *The Beginnings of the English Romantic Movement, p.* 157.

Yet both in his poetry and, what now more closely concerns us, in his prose, he exhibits the art of concealing his art. We feel ourselves in the presence of a most finished artist, but we do not see him mixing his colours, or fingering his brushes. We enjoy the effect without having thrust upon our notice the process or processes by which it has been produced. In his Letters the habit of a refined and polished manner has become second nature. He writes like a scholar, but without stiffness or effort. He is classical, but never pedantic. In addition to all the culture that so eminently distinguished Gray, he possessed natural gifts without which all his culture would have done little to endear him to the general reader. He had a genuine vein of humour, which not only prevents his being dull, but makes him at times highly entertaining. He had a keen sense of the beauty of landscape, and one of his greatest pleasures was to gaze upon it and to describe it. He was Wordsworthian before Wordsworth was born. Lastly, though reserved and seemingly dry and cynical, he was a man of the tenderest affections. He does not wear his heart upon his sleeve; but it would be a gross mistake to conclude because he does not wear it, that he had none to wear.—HALES, JOHN W., 1895, *English Prose, ed. Craik, vol.* IV, *p.* 222.

Gray was not so well known as the others. The only one of his poems to be read in France was the "Elegy written in a country churchyard," which was translated by the "Gazette littéraire" in 1765, and was freely copied by French poets, from Lemierre to Marie-Joseph Chénier, and from Fantanes or Delille to Chateaubriand. The "Elegy" is quite the most popular of Gray's works, but it by no means represents the profound and unique originality of the author of "The Bard" and the "Descent of Odin," than whom few poets have been more sincere. Nevertheless, this work, so modern in the sentiments it expresses yet at the same time so subtly classical in taste, attained something like celebrity in France. Gray's studious and highly cultivated talent provided, as it were, a connecting link between new aspirations and the classical methods to which Frenchmen were accustomed; he was spoken of as a "sublime philosopher, and a child of harmony." . . . By virtue of the sincerity of his religious feelings, of the delicious vagueness of his impressions, and of his serene and lofty inspiration, Gray is beyond dispute the predecessor of Chateaubriand and Lamartine, and of Rousseau before them. "With him," says his translator, the author of "René," "begins that school of the melancholy poets, which in our day has been transformed into a school of poets of despair." A valuable testimony, considering the authority with which it comes.—TEXTE, JOSEPH, 1895–99, *Jean-Jacques Rousseau and the Cosmopolitan Spirit in Literature, tr. Matthews, pp.* 303, 304.

Every boy who leaves Eton creditably is presented with a copy of the works of Gray, for which everything has been done that the art of printers, bookbinders and photographers can devise. This is one of the most curious instances of the triumphs of genius, for there is hardly a single figure in the gallery of Etonians who is so little characteristic of Eton as Gray. His only poetical utterance about his school is one which is hopelessly alien to the spirit of the place, though the feelings expressed in it are an exquisite summary of those sensations of pathetic interest which any rational man feels at the sight of a great school. And yet, though the attitude of the teacher of youth is professedly and rightly rather that of encouragement than of warning, though he points to the brighter hopes of life rather than brandishes the horrors that infest it, yet the last word that Eton says to her sons is spoken in the language of one to whom elegy was a habitual and deliberate tone. —BENSON, ARTHUR CHRISTOPHER, 1896, *Essays*, p. 119.

Despite the beauty and skill of his natural painting in the Odes, Gray never describes Nature for her own sake. It is always with some moral, some human feeling in view. —PALGRAVE, FRANCIS TURNER, 1896, *Landscape in Poetry*, p. 173.

By far the most important example of the clogs and crosses of the time is to be found in Thomas Gray, a man of less original poetical inspiration than Collins, perhaps not much more gifted in this way even than Shenstone, but a far better and far wider scholar than either, and entirely free from all untoward circumstance. Neither Milton, nor Wordsworth, nor Tennyson had greater facility for developing whatsoever poetical gifts were in each than had Gray.—SAINTSBURY, GEORGE, 1898, *A Short History of English Literature*, p. 575.

Tobias George Smollett

1721–1771

Born, in the "Lennox," Dumbartonshire, 1721; baptized, 19 March 1721. Early education at school at Dumbarton. Apprenticed to a doctor. To London, 1739. Entered Navy as Surgeon's Mate, Oct. 1740. After Carthagena expedition, retired from Navy; settled in Jamaica. Married there Anne Lascelles, 1744 [?]. Returned to London, 1744; devoted himself to literature. Visit to Paris, 1749 [?]. M. D., Marischal Coll., Aberdeen, 1750. Edited "Critical Review," 1756–60. Imprisoned three months for libel, 1759. Edited "British Mag.," 1760–67; "The Briton," May 1762 to Feb. 1763. Travelled abroad, June 1763 to spring 1765. To Italy, 1768; settled at Monte Nuovo, near Leghorn. Died there, Sept. 1771. Buried at Leghorn. *Works:* "Advice" (anon.), 1746; "Reproof" (anon.), 1747; "Adventures of Roderick Random" (anon.), 1748; "The Regicide" (anon.), 1749; "The History and Adventures of an Atom" (anon.), 1749; "Adventures of Peregrine Pickle" (anon.), 1751; "Essay on the External Use of Water," 1752; "Adventures of Ferdinand, Count Fathom" (anon.), 1753; "The Reprisal" (anon.), 1757; "Compleat History of England . . . to the Treaty of Aix-la-Chapelle" (4 vols.), 1757–58; "Continuation" of preceding (5 vols.), 1763–65; "Adventures of Sir Launcelot Greaves" (anon.), 1762; "Travels Through France and Italy" (2 vols.), 1766; "The Present State of All Nations" (8 vols.), 1768–69; "The Expedition of Humphery Clinker" (anon.), 1771 (misprinted 1671 on title-page of 1st edn.). *Posthumous:* "Ode to Independence," 1773. He *translated:* "Gil Blas" (anon.), 1749; "Don Quixote," 1755; "Voltaire's Works" (with others), 1761–74; "The Adventures of Telemachus," 1776; and *edited:* "A Compendium of Authentic and Entertaining Voyages," 1756. *Collected Works:* in 6 vols., 1790. *Life:* by R. Anderson, 1796.—SHARP, R. FARQUHARSON, 1897, *A Dictionary of English Authors*, p. 263.

PERSONAL

Smollett was a man of very agreeable conversation and of much genuine humor; and, though not a professional scholar, possessed a philosophical mind, and was capable of making the soundest observations on human life, and of discerning the excellence or seeing the ridicule of every character he met with. Fielding only excelled him in giving a dramatic story to his novels, but, in my opinion, was inferior to him in the true comic vein. He was one of the many very pleasant men with whom it was my good fortune to be intimately acquainted. —CARLYLE, ALEXANDER, 1753–56–1860, *Autobiography*, p. 216.

Is there a man, in vice and folly bred,
To sense of honour as to virtue dead,
Whom ties nor human nor divine can bind,
Alien from God, and foe to all mankind;
Who spares no character; whose every word,
Bitter as gall, and sharper than the sword,
Cuts to the quick; whose thoughts with rancour swell;
Whose tongue on earth performs the work of hell?
If there be such a monster, the Reviews
Shall find him holding forth against abuse.
"Attack profession!—'tis a deadly breach!—
The Christian laws another lesson teach:—

Unto the end should charity endure.
And candour hide those faults it cannot cure."
Thus Candour's maxims flow from Rancour's throat,
As devils, to serve their purpose, Scripture quote.
—CHURCHILL, CHARLES, 1761, *The Apology*, v. 298–313.

A most worthless and dangerous fellow, and capable of any mischief.—WALPOLE, HORACE, 1770, *To Sir Horace Mann, March* 16; *Letters, ed. Cunningham, vol.* v, *p.* 231.

Dick Ivy carried me to dine with S— [Smollett], whom you and I have long known by his writings. He lives in the skirts of the town; and every Sunday his house is open to all unfortunate brothers of the quill, whom he treats with beef, pudding, and potatoes, port, punch, and Calvert's entire butt-beer. . . . I was civilly received in a plain yet decent habitation, which opened backwards into a very pleasant garden, kept in excellent order; and indeed I saw none of the outward signs of authorship, either in the house or the landlord, who is one of those few writers of the age that stand upon their own foundation, without patronage and above dependence. If there was nothing characteristic in the entertainer, the company made ample amends for his want of singularity. At two o'clock I found myself one of ten messmates at a table; and I question if the whole kingdom could produce such another assemblage of originals. . . . After dinner we adjourned into the garden, where I observed Mr. S—— gave a short, separate audience to every individual, in a small remote filbert walk, from whence most of them dropped off, one after another, without further ceremony; but they were replaced by other recruits of the class, who came to make an afternoon's visit.—SMOLLETT, TOBIAS GEORGE, 1771, *Humphrey Clinker, Letter of Jerry Mulford.*

Siste viator!
Si leporis ingeniique venam benignam,
Si morum callidissimum pictorem,
Unquam es miratus,
Immorare paululum memoriæ
TOBIÆ SMOLLETT, M. D.
Viri virtutibus hisce
Quas in homine et cive
Et laudes et imiteris,
Haud mediocriter ornati:
Qui in literis variis versatus,
Postquam, felicitate sibi propria
Sese posteris commendaverat,
Morte acerba raptus
Anno ætatis 51.
Eheu! quam procul a patria!
Prope Liburni portum in Italia,
Jacet sepultus.
Tali tantoque viro, patruelo suo,
Cui in decursu lampada
Se potius tradidisse decuit,
Hanc Columnam,
Amoris, eheu! inane monumentum
In ipsis Levinæ ripis,
Quas versiculis sub exitu vitæ illustratas
Primis infans vagitibus personuit,
Ponendam curavit
JACOBUS SMOLLETT de Bonhill.
Abi et reminiscere,
Hoc quidem honore,
Non modo defuncti memoriæ,
Verum etiam exemplo, prospectum esse;
Aliis enim, si modo digni sint,
Idem erit virtutis præmium!
—INSCRIPTION ON PILLAR, 1773, *On Leven.*

In the practice of physic, Smollett, though possessed of superior endowments, and eminent scientific qualifications, had the mortification, from whatever cause, to be unsuccessful, at a moment when perhaps the neglect he experienced was aggravated by the unaccountable success of many a superficial unqualified contemporary, reaping the harvest of wealth and reputation. It has been supposed, that this want of success in a profession where merit cannot always ensure fame and affluence, was owing to his failing to render himself agreeable to the fair sex, whose favour is certainly of great consequence to all candidates for eminence, whether in physic or divinity. But his figure and address, which were uncommonly elegant and prepossessing, and his unsullied manners, renders this supposition highly improbable. It is more likely that his irritable temper, increased by the teazing and uncomfortable circumstances of the profession, and his contempt for the low arts of servility, suppleness, and cunning, were the real causes of his failure. It may be supposed also, that his publications, as a general satirist and censor of manners, were far more calculated to retard his progress as a physician, than to augment his practice.—ANDERSON, ROBERT, 1794–1803, *The Life of Tobias Smollett, M. D.*, *p.* 47.

The person of Dr. Smollett was stout and

well proportioned, his countenance engaging, his manner reserved, with a certain air of dignity that seemed to indicate that he was not unconscious of his own powers. He was of a disposition so humane and generous that he was ever ready to serve the unfortunate, and on some occasions to assist them beyond what his circumstances could justify. . . . His learning, diligence, and natural acuteness, would have rendered him eminent in the science of medicine, had he persevered in that profession; other parts of his character were ill suited for augmenting his practice. He could neither stoop to impose on credulity nor humour caprice.—MOORE, JOHN, 1797, *ed., Works of Smollett, Memoir.*

Smollett, who is a great poet, though he has written little in verse, and whose rich genius composed the most original pictures of human life, was compelled by his wants to debase his name by selling it to voyages and translations, which he never could have read. When he had worn himself down in the service of the public, or the booksellers, there remained not, of all his slender remunerations, in the last stage of life, sufficient to convey him to a cheap country and a restorative air on the Continent. The father may have thought himself fortunate, that the daughter whom he loved with more than common affection was no more to share in his wants; but the husband had by his side the faithful companion of his life, left without a wreck of fortune. Smollett, gradually perishing in a foreign land, neglected by an admiring public, and without fresh resources from the booksellers, who were receiving the income of his works, threw out his injured feelings in the character of "Bramble;" the warm generosity of his temper, but not his genius, seemed fleeting with his breath. In a foreign land his widow marked by a plain monument the spot of his burial, and she perished in solitude! Yet Smollett dead—soon an ornamented column is raised at the place of his birth, while the grave of the author seems to multiply the editions of his works. There are indeed grateful feelings in the public at large for a favourite author; but the awful testimony of those feelings, by its gradual progress, must appear beyond the grave! They visit the column consecrated by his name, and his features are most loved, most venerated, in the bust.—DISRAELI, ISAAC, 1812–13, *Authors by Profession, Calamities of Authors.*

The person of Smollett was eminently handsome, his features prepossessing, and, by the joint testimony of all his surviving friends, his conversation in the highest degree instructive and amusing. Of his disposition, those who have read his works (and who has not done so?) may form a very accurate estimate; for in each of them he has presented, and sometimes under various points of view, the leading features of his own character, without disguising the most unfavourable of them. . . . We know not that Smollett had any other marked failing, save that which he himself has so often and so liberally acknowledged. When unseduced by his satirical propensities, he was kind, generous, and humane to others; bold, upright, and independent in his own character; stooped to no patron, sued for no favour, but honestly and honourably maintained himself on his literary labours.—SCOTT, SIR WALTER, 1821, *Tobias Smollett.*

We have before us, and painted by his own hand, Tobias Smollett, the manly, kindly, honest and irascible; worn and battered, but still brave and full of heart, after a long struggle against a hard fortune. His brain had been busied with a hundred different schemes; he had been reviewer and historian, critic, medical writer, poet, pamphleteer. He had fought endless literary battles; and braved and wielded for years the cudgels of controversy. It was a hard and savage fight in those days, and a niggard pay. He was oppressed by illness, age, narrow fortune; but his spirit was still resolute, and his courage steady; the battle over, he could do justice to the enemy with whom he had been so fiercely engaged, and give a not unfriendly grasp to the hand that had mauled him. He is like one of those Scotch cadets, of whom history gives us so many examples, and whom, with a national fidelity, the great Scotch novelist has painted so charmingly. Of gentle birth and narrow means, going out from his northern home to win his fortune in the world, and to fight his way, armed with courage, hunger, and keen wits. His crest is a shattered oak tree, with green leaves yet springing from it. On his ancient coat-of-arms there is a lion and a horn; this shield of his was battered and dinted in a hundred fights and brawls, through which the stout Scotchman bore it courageously. You see somehow that he is a gentleman, through all his battling and struggling, his poverty, his hard-fought successes, and his defeats.—THACKERAY, WILLIAM MAKEPEACE, 1853, *The English Humourists of the Eighteenth Century.*

He was by no means the idle half-reprobate he represents in his "Roderick Random." He was often wrong and always irascible, continually fancying himself aggrieved, and always with a quarrel on his hands; but he was as proud, warm-hearted, and mettlesome a Scot as had then crossed the Tweed—of a spirit so independent, we are told, that he never asked a favour for himself from any great man in his life; paying his way honestly, and helping liberally those about him who were in distress; and altogether, so far from being a mere pleasure-seeker, that there was probably no man then in or near London, who stayed more at home, or worked more incessantly and laboriously to prevent the world from being a shilling the worse for him. He ruined his health by over-work.—MASSON, DAVID, 1859, *British Novelists and Their Styles, p.* 133.

In the following year, Smollett died, leaving to his widow little beyond the empty consolations of his great fame. From her very narrow purse she supplied the means of erecting the stone that marks the spot where he lies; and the pen of his companion . . . [Dr. John Armstrong], furnished an appropriate inscription. The niggardly hands of government remained as firmly closed against the relief of Mrs. Smollett as they had been in answer to her husband's own application for himself; an application which must have cost a severe struggle to his proud spirit, and of which his most intimate literary friends were probably never aware. He sought favors for others, says Dr. Moore; but "for himself he never made an application to any great man in his life!" He was not intemperate, nor yet was he extravagant, but by nature hospitable and of a cheerful temperament; his house-keeping was never niggardly, so long as he could employ his pen. Thus his genius was too often degraded to the hackney-tasks of booksellers; while a small portion of those pensions which were so lavishly bestowed upon ministerial dependants and placemen would have enabled him to turn his mind to its congenial pursuits, and probably to still further elevate the literary civilization of his country.—SARGENT, W., 1859, *Some Inedited Memorials of Smollett, Atlantic Monthly, vol.* 3, *p.* 702.

Most obscure among the other items in that Armada of Sir Chaloner's, just taking leave of England; most obscure of the items then, but now most noticeable, or almost alone noticeable, is a young Surgeon's-Mate,—one Tobias Smollett; looking over the waters there and the fading coasts, not without thoughts. A proud, soft-hearted, though somewhat stern-visaged, caustic and indignant young gentleman. Apt to be caustic in speech, having sorrows of his own under lock and key, on this and subsequent occasions. Excellent Tobias; he has, little as he hopes it, something considerable by way of mission in this Expedition, and in this Universe generally. Mission to take Portraits of English Seamanhood, with the due grimness, due fidelity; and convey the same to remote generations, before it vanish. Courage my brave young Tobias; through endless sorrows, contradictions, toils and confusions, you will do your errand in some measure; and that will be something!—CARLYLE, THOMAS, 1858–65, *History of Friedrich II. of Prussia, bk.* xii, *ch.* xii, *p.* 394.

There is something noble and even engaging in the character of Smollett: he stooped to no patron; he sued for no favour; he compromised no opinions; he maintained himself by his talents, and lived and died an independent, dauntless Scot. Yet that stern heart was broken, it is said, by the death of that young, fondly-loved girl who preceded him to the tomb. What a conjunction of fierce and gentle qualities;—of a heart full of tenderness, yet proud; of a nature replete with satirical dispositions, yet candid and forgiving.—THOMSON, KATHERINE (GRACE WHARTON), 1862, *The Literature of Society, vol.* II, *p.* 253.

Mrs. Smollett did not exactly appreciate a husband who had no profession. Poor Nancy does not seem to have been a very suitable yokefellow for our busy *litterateur.*

She had no reverence for literature as such, or for its professors. She had all a woman's desire for social distinction. But in order to take any position in that society after which this poor little Eve of the eighteenth century panted as eagerly as those of the nineteenth, an indispensable desideratum was that her husband should belong to one of the recognised professions, even although it might be only "something in the City!" . . . In "Narcissa's" eyes—for there is little doubt that the character of Narcissa in "Roderick Random" was at least suggested by his wife—her husband's literary work was worse than degrading. In common with many others of her time, she deemed "a man of letters" to be synonymous with a gentleman who spent one-half his time in the Fleet or the Marshalsea for debt, and the other half in dodging bailiffs from post to pillar for the privilege of enjoying God's sunshine without the walls of a jail.—SMEATON, OLIPHANT, 1897, *Tobias Smollett (Famous Scots Series), pp.* 69, 72.

His grave is in the old English cemetry in the Via degli Elisi at Leghorn (the only town in north Italy where protestants at that time had rights of burial), and the sea lies to the west of him, as of Fielding at Oporto. A Latin inscription (inaccurate as to dates) was written for his tombstone by Armstrong, and has recently been recut. Three years later a monument was erected by the novelist's cousin, Commissary James Smollett, on the banks of the Leven—a tall Tuscan column, which still attracts the eye of tourists on their way between the Clyde and Loch Lomond. The inscription was revised and in part written by Dr. Johnson, who visited Bonhill with Boswell in 1774.—SECCOMBE, THOMAS, 1898, *Dictionary of National Biography, vol.* LIII, *p.* 180.

RODERICK RANDOM
1748

I guessed "R. Random" to be his, [Fielding's] though without his name. I cannot think "Ferdinand Fathom" wrote by the same hand, it is every way so much below it.—MONTAGU, LADY MARY WORTLEY, 1754, *Letter to the Countess of Bute, June* 23.

The most popular of all the novels on which his high reputation rests.—CAMPBELL, THOMAS, 1819, *Specimens of the British Poets.*

In none of his succeeding volumes has he equalled the liveliness, force, and nature of this his first essay. So just a picture of a seafaring life especially had never before met the public eye. Many of our naval heroes may probably trace the preference which has decided them in their choice of a profession to an early acquaintance with the pages of "Roderick Random." He has not, indeed, decorated his scenes with any seductive colours; yet such is the charm of a highly wrought description, that it often induces us to overlook what is disgusting in the objects themselves, and transfer the pleasure arising from the mere imitation to the reality.—CARY, HENRY FRANCIS, 1821–24–45, *Lives of English Poets, ed. Cary, p.* 123.

"Roderick Random," indeed, with its varied delineation of life, is almost a romance. Its hero is worthy of his name. He is the sport of fortune rolled about through the "many ways of wretchedness" almost without resistance, but ever catching those tastes of joy which are every where to be relished by those who are willing to receive them. We seem to roll on with him, and get delectably giddy in his company.—TALFOURD, THOMAS NOON, 1842, *On British Novels and Romances, Critical and Miscellaneous Writings, p.* 14.

Smollett's "Roderick Random" is better worth preserving than the same author's continuation of Hume.—PATTISON, MARK, 1872–89, *Pope and His Editors, Essays, ed. Nettleship, vol.* II, *p.* 356.

In spite of its indecency, the world at once acknowledged it to be a work of genius: the verisimilitude was perfect; every one recognized in the hero the type of many a young North countryman going out to seek his fortune. The variety is great, the scenes are more varied and real than those in Richardson and Fielding, the characters are numerous and vividly painted, and the keen sense of ridicule pervading the book makes it a broad jest from beginning to end. Historically, his delineations are valuable; for he describes a period in the annals of the British marine which has happily passed away,—a hard life in little stifling holds or forecastles, with hard fare, —a base life, for the sailor, oppressed on shipboard, was the prey of vile women and land-sharks when on shore. What pictures of prostitution and indecency! what obscenity of language! what drunken infernal orgies! We may shun the book as we would shun the company, and yet the one is the exact portraiture of the other.—COPPÉE, HENRY, 1872, *English Literature, p.* 293.

"Roderick Random" is an exceedingly interesting work of fiction, and it was long popular. Its interest and attraction does not depend on the development of a well-conceived and elaborated plot, but on the inventive power, the native humour, and knowledge of the author. The turns in the fortune of the hero of the novel are many and varied, and scene follows scene with amazing rapidity, so the attention of the reader never flags; but the morality of the novel is low, and some coarse passages occur in it.—MACKINTOSH, JOHN, 1878-83-96, *The History of Civilisation in Scotland, vol.* IV, *p.* 199.

In the year 1809 was interred, in the churchyard of St. Martin's-in-the-Fields, the body of one Hew Hewson, who died at the age of eighty-five. He was the original of Hugh Strap, in Smollett's "Roderick Random." Upwards of forty years he kept a hair-dresser's shop in St. Martin's parish; the walls were hung round with Latin quotations, and he would frequently point out to his customers and acquaintances the several scenes in "Roderick Random" pertaining to himself, which had their origin, not in Smollett's inventive fancy, but in truth and reality. The meeting in a barber's shop at Newcastle-upon-Tyne, the subsequent mistake at the inn, their arrival together in London, and the assistance they experienced from Strap's friend, are all facts. The barber left behind an annotated copy of "Roderick Random," showing how far we are indebted to the genius of the author, and to what extent the incidents are founded in reality.—SAUNDERS, FREDERICK, 1887, *The Story of Some Famous Books, p.* 123.

"Roderick Random" is intentionally modelled on the plan of Lesage, and here, as elsewhere, Smollett shows himself less original than either Richardson or Fielding. He can hardly be said to invent or to construct; he simply reports. He does this with infinite spirit and variety. Comedy and tragedy, piety and farce, follow one another in bewildering alternation. But although he dazzles and entertains us, he does not charm. The book is ferocious to a strange degree, and so foul as to be fit only for a very well-seasoned reader. The hero, in whom Smollett complacently could see nothing but a picture of "modest merit struggling with every difficulty," is a selfish bully, whose faults it is exasperating to find condoned. The book of course, is full of good things. The hero is three separate times hurried off to sea, and the scenes of rough sailor-life, though often disgusting, are wonderfully graphic. Tom Bowling, Jack Rattlin, and the proud Mr. Morgan are not merely immortal among salt-sea worthies, but practically the first of a long line of sailors of fiction.—GOSSE, EDMUND, 1888, *A History of Eighteenth Century Literature, p.* 259.

THE ADVENTURES OF AN ATOM
1749

From our knowledge of his character, we expect, what we find in his work, ideas that indicate a firm and lofty mind, irritated by disappointment and neglect, and a diction ardent and energetic, corresponding to the strength and acuteness of his feelings of indignation and resentment. Though it is inferior, upon the whole, to his other novels, for ingenuity and contrivance in the composition, and for observation of life, it is written, for the most part, with his usual humour, animation, and felicity of expression.—ANDERSON, ROBERT, 1794-1803, *The Life of Tobias Smollett, M. D., p.* 204.

His extremely clever and extremely coarse political satire, "The Adventures of an Atom," published in 1769, was probably inspired partly by resentment at the neglect of his own claims by successive ministries. — MINTO, WILLIAM, 1887, *Encyclopædia Britannica, Ninth Edition, vol.* XXII.

"The History of an Atom" was successful, but is to-day the portion of Smollett's writings with which we could most comfortably dispense. It is a satire, or intended for such, but accommodates itself to none of the known rules of any school of satiric writing. Neither to Swift, Arbuthnot, Steele, nor Butler does it exhibit affinity.—SMEATON, OLIPHANT, 1897, *Tobias Smollett (Famous Scots Series), p.* 117.

"The Adventures of an Atom" are mentioned with a shudder when it is necessary to mention them at all, yet they are scarcely worse than the occasional conversation of very reputable medical students in all times. It may be questioned, finally, whether it is any hurt to a language to have nothing but specifically vulgar names for vulgar things, and so escape the deification of lubricity to which the less robust nations commit themselves. Vigorous and outspoken, irreverent, and sometimes too high-tempered, Smollett is a pervading exemplar of the British humorist.—DUFFIELD, PITTS, 1897, *Library of the World's Best Literature, ed. Warner, vol.* XXIII, *p.* 13577.

PEREGRINE PICKLE
1751

At candlelight D. D., and I read by turns, and what do *you think* has been part of our study?—why truly "Peregrine Pickle!" We never undertook it before, but *it is wretched stuff;* only Lady V's. history is a curiosity.—DELANY, MRS. (MARY GRANVILLE), 1752, *Letter to Mrs. Dewes, Correspondence, ed. Llanover, vol.* III, *p.* 162.

It has been said, that Smollett was not successful in drawing female characters; yet the principal female in his romances is always of the strictest purity of mind and manners. The character of "Emilia" in "Peregrine Pickle," the gayest perhaps of them all, is at the same time watchful and spirited. She does not indeed lecture on virtue like a professor of moral philosophy, nor is she decked in all the flowery ornaments with which the heroines of romance are sometimes adorned. She always appears in the simple dress, so becoming, and so peculiarly natural to young English ladies of virtue and good sense.—MOORE, JOHN, 1797, *ed., Works of Smollett, Memoir.*

It was received with such extraordinary avidity that a large impression was quickly sold in England, another was bought up in Ireland, a translation was executed into the French language, and it soon made its appearance in a second edition with an apologetic "Advertisement" and "Two Letters" relating to the "Memoirs of a Lady of Quality," sent to the editor by "a Person of Honour." This first edition is in our day scarce enough, and sufficiently coarse to fetch an enhanced price.—HERBERT, DAVID, 1870, *ed., Works of Smollett, Life.*

Peregrine Pickle attacks by a most brutal and cowardly plot the honour of a young girl, whom he wants to marry, and who is the sister of his best friend. We got to hate his rancorous, concentrated, obstinate character, which is at once that of an absolute king accustomed to please himself at the expense of others' happiness, and that of a boor with only the varnish of education. We should be uneasy at living near him; he is good for nothing but to shock or tyrannise over others. We avoid him as we would a dangerous beast; the sudden rush of animal passion and the force of his firm will are so overpowering in him, that when he fails he becomes outrageous. He draws his sword against an innkeeper; he must bleed him, grows mad. Everything, even to his generosities, is spoiled by pride; all, even to his gaieties, is clouded by harshness. Peregrine's amusements are barbarous, and those of Smollett are after the same style.—TAINE, H. A., 1871, *History of English Literature, tr. Van Laun, vol.* II, *bk.* iii, *ch.* vi, *p.* 178.

Its brightness, and the hearty fun of many of its chapters, like that (ch. xliv.) which describes an entertainment in the manner of the ancients, made the book widely popular and Smollett famous. The pompous gentleman caricatured by Smollett, as the giver of this banquet, was Mark Akenside.—MORLEY, HENRY, 1873, *A First Sketch of English Literature, p.* 836.

The characters in "Peregrinus Pickle"
All teach us wisdom, while our sides they tickle;
They argue not from what their acts ensue,
But tell us what they are from what they do.
—JOYCE, ROBERT DWER, 1877, *Reflections, Scribner's Magazine, vol.* 14, *p.* 446.

He keeps the reader's attention even when he offends his taste. He impaired the literary merit of "Peregrine Pickle," but at the same time added to its dissolute character and its immediate popularity by the forced insertion of the licentious "Memoirs of a Lady of Quality." Now a serious blemish, these memoirs formed at the time an added attraction to the book. They were eagerly read as the authentic account of Lady Vane, a notorious woman of rank, and were furnished to Smollett by herself, in the hope, fully gratified, that her infamous career might be known to future generations.—TUCKERMAN, BAYARD, 1882, *A History of English Prose Fiction, p.* 214.

It is a laughter-provoking book, with abundance of incident and "go," but it is occasionally indefensibly coarse, and not unfrequently shows that want of gentlemanly feeling which Smollett's admirers have too often to regret —NICOLL, HENRY J., 1882, *Landmarks of English Literature, p.* 225.

The autobiographic method did not prove pleasing to Akenside and others, whose characters were burlesqued in this novel; and Smollett could hardly employ the excuse of Dr. John Shebbeare, who says that novelists are like army-tailors, they make suits for all mankind, to be taken and fitted on to their persons by Tom, Dick, and Harry. For Smollett fitted his descriptions to the individual, and took care that they should suit no one else. His method is minute and his satire savage and personal.—RALEIGH, WALTER, 1894, *The English Novel, p.* 187.

FERDINAND COUNT FATHOM
1753

I think "Count Fathom" (though a bad, affected style) written with a better intention, and Melvin's character a good one, but they none of them are to be named in a day with our good friend Richardson.—DELANY, MRS. (MARY GRANVILLE), 1753, *Letter to Mrs. Dewes; Correspondence, ed. Llanover, vol.* III, *p.* 223.

Smollett, notwithstanding his peculiar propensity for burlesque and broad humour, has, in his "Ferdinand Count Fathom," painted a scene of natural terror with astonishing effect; with such vigour of imagination indeed, and minuteness of detail, that the blood runs cold, and the hair stands erect from the impression. The whole turns upon the Count, who is admitted, during a tremendous storm, into a solitary cottage in a forest, discovering a body just murdered in the room where he is going to sleep, and the door of which, on endeavouring to escape, he finds fastened upon him.—DRAKE, NATHAN, 1798–1820, *Literary Hours, vol.* I, *No.* xvii, *p.* 274.

His "Adventures of Count Fathom" is a description of the career of a hideous and perhaps an anomalous scoundrel. The same tendency to exaggerate both incident and character pervades all Smollett's novels. He seems to write under the stimulus of brandy. It is the nature and fancy of madness. The atmosphere of atrocity that surrounds the principal character and his associates in the "Count Fathom" is so black and stifling, and their features are so horrible, that one's imagination takes refuge almost in contempt in order to relieve itself of the disgust they have excited. At the same time it must be owned that there are points in the work which answer to the stimulated energies of an undoubtedly powerful mind by nature. . . . No one of Smollett's works, or indeed of any other writer of fiction that I am acquainted with, contains stronger specimens of real power in invention and language, than this exhibits. —CLARKE, CHARLES COWDEN, 1872, *On the Comic Writers of England, The Gentleman's Magazine, n. s., vol.* 8, *pp.* 572, 573.

The Count is a scoundrel, or, at least, tries to be one; but he is so weak, so easily baffled, so utterly unable to succeed except where he is helped by the incredible folly of the virtuous characters; so much more in fact of a dupe than a villain, that whatever feeling he does arouse is one of a rather mild contempt. We hear much of his cleverness, but never see it. Smollett's literary fault in connection with him was not that he drew a greater sinner than any man should put into a book, but that, having introduced his hero as a villain of extraordinary ability, he entirely fails to convince the reader that Count Fathom was other than a very poor rogue indeed. The scene in the Robbers' Hut in the forest is sometimes spoken of as being original, and the model of many others of the same kind, but the praise can hardly have been given with the due recollection of much that is to be found in the "Spanish and French Authors" whom Smollett took as his masters.—HANNAY, DAVID, 1887, *Life of Tobias George Smollett, p.* 91.

His most sustained effort. The irony of the opening chapters, the ruthless characterisation of a scoundrel, and the description of the robbers' hut in the Black Forest exhibit a striking reserve of power. Few novels have been more imitated.—SECCOMBE, THOMAS, 1898, *Dictionary of National Biography, vol.* LIII, *p.* 176.

DON QUIXOTE
1753

I am sorry my friend Smollett loses his time in translations: he has certainly a talent for invention, though I think it flags a little in his last work. Don Quixote is a difficult undertaking: I shall never desire to read any attempt to new-dress him. Though I am a mere piddler in the Spanish language, I had rather take pains to understand him in the original than sleep over a stupid translation.—MONTAGU, LADY MARY WORTLEY, 1755, *Letter to the Countess of Bute, Jan.* 1.

Smollett inherited from nature a strong sense of ridicule, a great fund of original humour, and a happy versatility of talent, by which he could accommodate his style to almost every species of writing. He could adopt, alternately, the solemn, the lively, the sarcastic, the burlesque, and the vulgar. To these qualifications, he joined an inventive genius, and a vigorous imagination.—TYTLER, ALEXANDER FRASER (LORD WOODHOUSELEE), 1791, *Essay on the Principles of Translation.*

It wants that picturesque and romantic tone which is so great a charm in the original—that tenderness of feeling in the midst of, and modifying, the wildest extravagance of gaiety, which forms as it were the atmosphere of the southern humour, and distinguishes alike the frantic wit of the old comedy of Greece, the broad burlesque of the primitive Italian stage, and glows with such a steady and yet subdued radiance through the pages of the gentle Cervantes. Smollett's "Don Quixote" wants *sun*—the sun of La Mancha.—SHAW, THOMAS B., 1847, *Outlines of English Literature, p.* 268.

If in many ways not a faithful representation of Cervantes' immortal novel, is a lively and spirited production, showing Smollett's great command over language and power of fluent and vivacious narrative.—NICOLL, HENRY J., 1882, *Landmarks of English Literature, p.* 225.

HISTORY OF ENGLAND
1757–65

Robertson's History is, I think, extremely well written. — It was well observed, that nobody in the Augustan age could conceive that so soon after, a Horse should be made Consul: and yet matters were so well prepared by the time of Caligula, that nobody was surprised at the matter. And so when Clarendon and Temple wrote History, they little thought the time was so near when a vagabond Scot should write nonsense ten thousand strong.—WARBURTON, WILLIAM, 1759, *Letters from a Late Eminent Prelate, Jan.* 30, *No.* cxxv, *p.* 278.

I am reading again, the "History of England," that of Smollett. . . . I have to the reign of George the Second, and, in spight of the dislike I have of Smollett's language and style of writing, I am much entertained. — BURNEY, FRANCES, 1770, *Early Diary, ed. Ellis, vol.* I, *p.* 94.

Smollett had unquestionably talents, but his genius was entirely turned to the low and the ludicrous; of the dignity and beauty of historic composition, he had no conception, much less could he boast of possessing any portion of its all-pervading and philosophical spirit. His work is a dull and often malignant compilation, equally destitute of instruction and amusement.—BELSHAM, WILLIAM, 1793, *Memoirs of the Kings of Great Britain of the House of Brunswick; Memoirs of the Reign of George I., Preface.*

Respect for the great name of Smollett will not suffer me to pass over in silence his "History of England," the most important of his compilations. It is not to the purpose of the present enquiry to observe that the general concoction of the work reminds us rather of the promptings of the bookseller, than of the talents of its author. It is not however to be wondered at, that the style of a work, thus crudely composed, should not be such as to put contemporary authors to the blush. —GODWIN, WILLIAM, 1797, *Of English Style, The Enquirer, p.* 470.

In the beginning of the year 1758, Smollett published his "Complete History of England, deduced from the Descent of Julius Cæsar to the Treaty of Aix-la-Chapelle, in 1748;" in four volumes 4to. It is said that this voluminous work, containing the history of thirteen centuries, and written with uncommon spirit and correctness of language was composed and finished for the press within fourteen months, one of the greatest exertions of facility of composition which was ever recorded in the history of literature. . . . It cannot be denied that, as a clear and distinct narrative of facts, strongly and vigorously told with a laudable regard to truth and impartiality, the Continuation may vie with our best historical works. The author was incapable of being swayed by fear or favour; and where his judgment is influenced, we can see that he was only misled by an honest belief in the truth of his own arguments. —SCOTT, SIR WALTER, 1821, *Tobias Smollett.*

Warburton heard of its swift sale while his own "Divine Legation" lay heavy and quiet at his publisher's; and "the Vagabond Scot who writes nonsense," was the character vouchsafed to Smollett by the vehement proud priest. But Goldsmith keeps his temper, notwithstanding Smollett's great and somewhat easily-earned good fortune; and, in this as in former instances, there is no disposition to carp at a good success or quarrel with a celebrated name. His notice has evident marks of the interpolation of Griffiths, though that worthy's more deadly hostility to Smollett had not yet begun; but even as it stands, in the "Review" which had so many points of personal and political opposition to the subject of it, it is manly and kind. The weak places were pointed out with gentleness, while Goldsmith strongly seized on what he felt to be the strength of Smollett.—FORSTER, JOHN, 1848–71, *The Life and Times of Oliver Goldsmith, vol.* I, *p.* 109.

But such a work written in fourteen months could hardly compete in manner, and still less in matter, with the eight years' careful labour of Hume. The style is fluent and loose, possessing a careless vigour where the subject is naturally exciting, but composed too hastily to rise above dulness in the record of dry transactions. As regards matter, the historian can make no pretension to original research. He executed the book as a piece of hack-work for a London bookseller, availing himself freely of previous publications, and taking no pains to bring new facts to light.—MINTO, WILLIAM, 1872–80, *Manual of English Prose Literature, p.* 432.

The versatility of genius was never more fully proved than when Smollett turned historian. Put to the trade of book-making he became the ideal bookmaker. The language cannot show a more complete example of the dismal art than the history compiled by a prince of the domain of fiction, a master of fancy as fertile, and of a pen as vivid as English literature has ever produced. To Smollett's "Continuation of Hume," and the book trade which tyrannically forced it upon several much-enduring generations of readers, must be imputed not a little of the extraordinary superstition that the eighteenth century is the most tedious portion of English history.—STEBBING, WILLIAM, 1887, *Some Verdicts of History Reviewed, p.* 7.

It is superficial, inaccurate, and a dull and wearisome record.—AUBREY, W. H. S., 1896, *The Rise and Growth of the English Nation, vol.* III, *p.* 250.

Some critics have urged that Smollett might have taken a broader view of the sources and progress of national expansion and development. Minto rather off-handedly designates his style as "fluent and loose, possessing a careless vigour where the subject is naturally exciting," and concluded with the words, "the history *is said* to be full of errors and inconsistencies." Now, this last clause is taken word for word from Chambers "Cyclopaedia of English Literature," who took it from Angus's "English Literature," who borrowed it from Macaulay, who annexed it from the *Edinburgh Review*, which journal had originally adopted it with alterations from Smollett's own prefatory remarks in the first edition of the book. How many of these authors had read the history for themselves, to see if it really contained such errors and inconsistencies? Criticism conducted on that mutual-trust principle is very convenient for the critic; is it quite fair to the author? Now, anyone who faithfully reads Smollett's "History of England" and its "Continuation" will not discover a larger percentage of either errors or inconsistencies than appear in the works of his contemporary historians, Tytler, Hume, and Robertson. Smollett is as distinguishingly fair and impartial as it was possible for one to be, influenced so profoundly by his environment as were all the historians of the eighteenth century. The mind of literary Europe was already tinged by that spiritual unrest and moral callousness that was to induce the new birth of the French Revolution.—SMEATON, OLIPHANT, 1897, *Tobias Smollett* (*Famous Scots Series*), *p.* 143.

Another expedient for the rapid sale of

books was their issue in numbers. Smollett's "History of England" was published in sixpenny numbers, and had an immediate sale of 20,000 copies. This immense success is said to have been due to an artifice practised by the publisher. He sent down a packet of prospectuses carriage free (with half-a-crown enclosed) to every parish clerk in the kingdom, to be distributed by him through the pews of the church. This being generally carried out, a valuable advertisement was obtained, which resulted in an extensive demand for the work. — WHEATLEY, HENRY B., 1898, *Prices of Books, p.* 102.

SIR LAUNCELOT GREAVES
1762

In the first number of the *British Magazine* was the opening of the tale which contained his most feminine heroine (Aurelia Darnel), and the most amiable and gentlemanly of his heroes (Sir Launcelot Greaves); for, though Sir Launcelot is mad, wise thoughts made him so; and in the hope to "remedy evils which the law cannot reach, to detect fraud and treason, to a base insolence, to mortify pride, to discourage slander, to disgrace immodesty, and to stigmatise ingratitude," he stumbles through his odd adventures. There is a pleasure in connecting this alliance of Smollett and Goldsmith, with the first approach of our great humorist to that milder humanity and more genial wisdom which shed their mellow rays on Matthew Bramble.—FORSTER, JOHN, 1848–71, *The Life and Times of Oliver Goldsmith, vol.* I, *p.* 246.

It is only in externals that this work bears any resemblance to "Don Quixote." The author seems to have hesitated between making Sir Lancelot a mere madman and making him a pattern of perfectly sane generosity. The fun and the seriousness do not harmonize. The young knight's craze for riding about the country to redress wrongs armed *cap-a-pie* is too harshly out of tune with the rightness of his sympathies and the grave character of the real abuses against which his indignation is directed. In execution the work is very unequal and irregular, but the opening chapters are very powerful, and have been imitated by hundreds of novelists since Smollett's time.—MINTO, WILLIAM, 1887, *Encyclopædia Britannica, Ninth Edition, vol.* XXII.

An absurd and exaggerated satire which added nothing to his fame.—GOSSE, EDMUND, 1888, *A History of Eighteenth Century Literature, p.* 261.

Of "Sir Launcelot Greaves," originally contributed as a serial to "The British Review," the scheme, as one of the characters remarks, "is somewhat too stale and extravagant." The plot is the merest excuse for variety of scene, and the characters do not live. What he borrowed from Cervantes is as little put to its proper use by Smollett as what he borrowed from Fielding. His work loses its chief merit when he attempts to exchange his own method of reminiscence for a wider imaginative scheme.—RALEIGH, WALTER, 1894, *The English Novel, p.* 188.

TRAVELS THROUGH FRANCE AND ITALY
1766

I was best pleased with my old and excellent friend Smollett, testy and discontented as he is, he writes with perspicuity; his observations are generally sensible, and even his oddities are entertaining. —GARDEN, FRANCIS (LORD GARDENSTONE), 1792–95, *Travelling Memoranda, vol.* I.

Distinguished by acuteness of remark, and shrewdness of expression,—by strong sense and pointed humour.—SCOTT, SIR WALTER, 1821, *Life of Tobias Smollett.*

That Smollett, in recording the incidents of such a journey, should have put a good deal of gall into his ink, is not a matter of surprise; but it is rather remarkable that his journal should be so devoid of literary merit. The author of "Humphrey Clinker" seems to have packed his genius away at the bottom of his trunk, and not taken it out during his whole tour. His spirit is all put forth in vituperation; but otherwise he is tame and commonplace.—HILLARD, GEORGE STILLMAN, 1853, *Six Months in Italy p.* 512.

To see his selfwill, in its last soured and savage state, let us consult his "Travels," He was the "Smelfungus" of Sterne, who travelled from Dan to Beersheba, and found all barren. We are among the very few who have read the book. It is a succession of asthmatic gasps and groans.—GILFILLAN, GEORGE, 1855, *A Third Gallery of Portraits, p.* 230.

Wherever I have been able to test Smollett's accuracy, I have found him so invariably exact and truthful, that I should be inclined to take a good deal for granted on his mere assertion. It is beside my purpose—which is simply that of recalling attention to a book that has been extravagantly abused by some, and unreasonably neglected or forgotten by others—to follow the author through all his various wanderings by sea and land.—PROWSE, W. J., 1870, *Smollett at Nice, Macmillan's Magazine, vol.* 21, *p.* 533.

Concerning Smollett's "Letters from Abroad" much need not be said. They are far from being without glimpses of the man in his best style, and they light up objects and places to the untravelled man with many vivid touches and references; but they occupy small ground towards forming an estimate of the value of the novelist's intellectual labours.—SMITH, GEORGE BARNETT, 1875, *Tobias Smollett, Gentleman's Magazine, n. s., vol.* 14, *p.* 735.

HUMPHREY CLINKER
1771

A party novel written by that profligate hireling Smollett to vindicate the Scots and cry down juries.—WALPOLE, HORACE, 1797–1845, *Memoirs of the Reign of King George the Third.*

In this novel the author most successively executes, what had scarcely ever been before attempted—a representation of the different effects which the same scenes, and persons, and transactions, have on different dispositions and tempers. He exhibits through the whole work a most lively and humorous delineation, confirming strongly the great moral truth, that happiness and all our feelings are the result, less of external circumstances, than the constitution of the mind.—DUNLOP, JOHN, 1814–45, *The History of Fiction, p.* 413.

The very ingenious scheme of describing the various effects produced upon different members of the same family by the same objects, was not original, though it has been supposed to be so. Anstey, the facetious author of the "New Bath Guide," had employed it six or seven years before "Humphrey Clinker" appeared. But Anstey's diverting satire was but a light sketch compared to the finished and elaborate manner in which Smollett has, in the first place, identified his characters, and then fitted them with language, sentiments, and powers of observation, in exact correspondence with their talents, temper, condition, and disposition.—SCOTT, SIR WALTER, 1821, *Tobias Smollett.*

The novel of "Humphrey Clinker" is, I do think, the most laughable story that has ever been written since the goodly art of novel-writing began. Winifred Jenkins and Tabitha Bramble must keep Englishmen on the grin for ages yet to come; and in their letters and the story of their loves there is a perpetual fount of sparkling laughter, as inexhaustible as Bladud's well.—THACKERAY, WILLIAM MAKEPEACE, 1853, *The English Humourists of the Eighteenth Century.*

The poor peevish author was hastening to his end; but before he sank beneath this life's horizon, his genius shot forth its brightest beam. Disappointed in his last earthly hope—that of obtaining a consulship on some shore of the Mediterranean, where his last hours might be prolonged in a milder air—he travelled to the neighbourhood of Leghorn, and, settling in a cottage there, finished "Humphrey Clinker," which is undoubtedly his finest work. Lismahago is the best character in this picture of English life; Bath is the principal scene, upon which the actors play their various parts. Scarcely was this brilliant work completed, when Smollett died, an invalided exile, worn out long before the alloted seventy years. His pictures of the navy-men who trod English decks a century ago, are unsurpassed and imperishable. Trunnion, the one-eyed commodore; Hatchway and Bowling, the lieutenants; Ap-Morgan, the kind but fiery Welsh surgeon; Tom Pipes, the silent boatswain, remain as types of a race of men long extinct, who manned our ships when they were, in literal earnest, wooden walls, and when the language and the discipline, to which officers of the royal navy were accustomed, were somewhat of the roughest and the hardest.—COLLIER, WILLIAM FRANCIS, 1861, *A History of English Literature, p.* 319.

"Humphrey Clinker" is the best of his novels. It is pervaded by a manly tone of feeling, natural, caustic, and humorous observation, and fine discrimination of character. The descriptions of rural scenery, society, and manners are clear and fascinating. Smollett was gifted with a keen sense of the comic and ludicrous, which he deftly used, while touches of pathos also occur in his writings.—MACKINTOSH, JOHN, 1878–83–96, *The History of Civilisation in Scotland, vol.* IV, *p.* 199.

It is worth while noticing that in "Humphrey Clinker" the veritable British poorly-educated and poor-spelling woman begins to express herself in the actual dialect of the species, and in the letters of Mrs. Winifred Jenkins to her fellow maid-servant Mrs. Mary Jones at Brambleton Hall, during a journey made by the family to the North, we have some very worthy and strongly-marked originals not only of Mrs. Malaprop and Mrs. Partington, but of the immortal Sairey Gamp and of scores of other descendants in Thackeray and Dickens, here and there.—LANIER, SIDNEY, 1881, *The English Novel, p.* 185.

At Pisa he was visited by Sir Horace Mann, who did what he could for him; and among other work he wrote his charming novel of "Humphrey Clinker," in which he has evidently figured himself under the character of Matthew Bramble, whom Hannay calls "the most credible specimen of the *bourru bienfaisant* in literature." The charm of the book lies in its sweetness, which is the ripe product of Southern influence combined with ill health.—SCHUYLER, EUGENE, 1889–1901, *Smollett in Search of Health, Italian Influences, p.* 242.

Matthew Bramble and Obadiah Lismahago, the 'squire's sister and her Methodist maid, have passed permanently into literature, and their places are as secure as those of Partridge and Parson Adams, of Corporal Trim and "my Uncle Toby." Not even the Malapropoism of Sheridan or Dickens is quite as riotously diverting, as rich in its unexpected turns, as that of Tabitha Bramble and Winifred Jenkins, especially Winifred, who remains delightful even when deduction is made of the poor and very mechanical fun extracted from the parody of her pietistic phraseology. That it could ever have been considered witty to spell "grace" "grease," and "Bible" "byebill," can only be explained by the indiscriminate hostility of the earlier assailants of Enthusiasm. Upon this, as well as upon a particularly evil-smelling taint of coarseness which, to the honour of the author's contemporaries was fully recognized in his own day as offensive, it is needless now to dwell.—DOBSON, AUSTIN, 1894, *Eighteenth Century Vignettes, Second Series, p.* 140.

This charming work, with its multitudinous lights and shadows, its variety of incident and character, and its easy and picturesque style of narrative, besides being one of the most mirth-provoking stories in the language, is a vivid portraiture of the times. . . . Fielding's coarseness belongs to his own time, and is incidental; Smollett's is ingrained and inherent.—AUBREY, W. H. S., 1896, *The Rise and Growth of the English Nation, vol.* III, *p.* 250.

POETRY AND DRAMAS

This ode ["Tears of Scotland."] by Dr. Smollett does rather more honour to the author's feelings than his taste. The mechanical part, with regard to numbers and language, is not so perfect as so short a work as this requires; but the pathetic it contains, particularly in the last stanza but one, is exquisitely fine.—GOLDSMITH, OLIVER, 1767, *The Beauties of English Poetry.*

The few poems which he has left have a portion of delicacy which is not to be found in his novels: but they have not, like those prose fictions, the strength of a master's hand. Were he to live over again, we might wish him to write more poetry, in the belief that his poetical talent would improve by exercise; but we should be glad to have more of his novels just as they are.—CAMPBELL, THOMAS, 1819, *Specimens of the British Poets.*

Of Smollett's poems much does not remain to be said. The "Regicide" is such a tragedy as might be expected from a clever youth of eighteen. The language is declamatory, the thoughts inflated, and the limits of nature and verisimilitude transgressed in describing the characters and passions. Yet there are passages not wanting in poetical vigour. His two satires have so much of the rough flavour of Juvenal, as to retain some relish, now that the occasion which produced them has passed away. The "Ode to Independence," which was not published till after his decease, amid much of commonplace, has some very nervous lines. The personification itself is but an awkward one. The term is scarcely abstract and general enough to be invested with the attributes of an ideal being. In the "Tears of Scotland," patriotism has made him eloquent and pathetic; and the "Ode to Leven Water" is sweet and natural. None of the other pieces except the "Ode to Mirth," which has some sprightliness of fancy, deserves to be particularly noticed. —CARY, HENRY FRANCIS, 1821-24-45, *Lives of English Poets, ed. Cary, p.* 145.

As a poet, though he takes not a very high rank, yet the few poems which he has left have a delicacy which is not to be found in his novels.—CLEVELAND, CHARLES D., 1848, *A Compendium of English Literature, p.* 607.

The "Reprisal," which appeared in 1757, stands alone in two respects in Smollett's life. It was his only successful attempt to reach the stage, and it led to the soldering up of an old quarrel. The plot of this two-act comedy may have given Marryat the first idea of "The Three Cutters," and is worked up with no small liveliness. Its characters have a distinct comic *vis* of a rather broad kind. The sailors Lyon, Haulyard, and Block, are good as Smollett's sailors always were; Oclabber and Maclaymore, the exiled Jacobites in the French service, are first drafts of the immortal Lismahago. Like most of Smollett's work in those years, this comedy has its touch of journalism. —HANNAY, DAVID, 1887, *Life of Tobias George Smollett, p.* 144.

Except for some fiery passages, Smollett's "Regicide" is not of much account. Smollett was constitutionally able to express anger, and there are indignant explosions in almost every scene, often very forcible, but without real feeling. The persistent writing of irate lines made a fire in the author's ears, but his heart remained untouched.—DAVIDSON, JOHN, 1895, *Sentences and Paragraphs, p.* 46.

GENERAL

——Next Smollett came. What author dare resist
Historian, critic, bard, and novelist?
"To reach thy temple, honour'd Fame," he cried,
"Where, where's an avenue I have not tried?
But since the glorious present of to-day
Is meant to grace alone the poet's lay,
My claim I wave to every art beside,
And rest my plea upon the Regicide.
. . . .
But if, to crown the labours of my Muse,
Thou, inauspicious, should'st the wreath refuse,
Whoe'er attempts it in this scribbling age
Shall feel the Scotish pow'rs of Critic rage.
Thus spurn'd, thus disappointed of my aim,
I'll stand a bugbear in the road to Fame;
Each future minion's infant hopes undo,
And blast the budding honours of his brow."
—SHAW, CUTHBERT, 1766, *The Race.*

There was a third, somewhat posterior in time, not in talents, who was indeed a rough driver, and rather too severe to his cattle; but in faith he carried us at a merry pace, over land or sea; nothing came amiss to him, for he was up to both elements, and a match for nature in every shape, character, and degree; he was not very courteous, it must be owned, for he had a capacity for higher things, and was above his business; he wanted only a little more suavity and discretion to have figured with the best.—CUMBERLAND, RICHARD, 1795, *Henry, bk.* iii.

He has published more volumes, upon more subjects, than perhaps any other author of modern date; and, in all, he has left marks of his genius. The greater part of his novels are peculiarly excellent. He is nevertheless a hasty writer; when he affects us most, we are aware that he might have done more. In all his works of invention, we find the stamp of a mighty mind. In his lightest sketches, there is nothing frivolous, trifling and effeminate. In his most glowing portraits, we acknowledge a mind at ease, rather essaying its powers, than tasking them. We applauded his works; but it is with profounder sentiment that we meditate his capacity. The style of Smollett has never been greatly admired, and it is brought forward here merely to show in what manner men of the highest talents, and of great eminence in the *belles letres*, could write forty or fifty years ago.—GODWIN, WILLIAM, 1797, *Of English Style, The Enquirer, p.* 467.

Smollett had much penetration, though he is frequently too vulgar to please; but his knowledge of men and manners is unquestionable.—MATHIAS, THOMAS JAMES, 1798, *The Pursuits of Literature, Eighth ed., p.* 59.

There is a vein in Smollett—a Scotch vein—which is always disgusting to people with delicacy; but it is enough to say of him in his work, that he is an invalid with whom even invalids cannot sympathise—one has no patience with his want of patience.—HUNT, LEIGH, 1813, *Correspondence, vol.* I, *p.* 80.

It was his misfortune that the fair display of his talents, and perhaps the genuine sentiments of his heart, were perverted by the prejudices of friendship, or by the more inexcusable impulses of jealousy, revenge, and all that enter into the composition of an irritable character. He seems to have gladly embraced the opportunity, which secrecy afforded, of dealing his blows around without discrimination, and without mercy. It is painful to read the continual personal abuse he levelled at his rival Mr. Griffiths, and the many vulgar and coarse sarcasms he directed against every author, who presumed to doubt the infallibility of his opinion. It is no less painful to contemplate the self-sufficiency displayed on every occasion where he can introduce his own character and works.—CHALMERS, ALEXANDER, 1814, *The Works of the English Poets.*

You ask me what degrees there are between Scott's novels and those of Smollett. They appear to me to be quite distinct in every particular, more especially in their aims. Scott endeavours to throw so interesting and romantic a colouring into common and low characters as to give them a touch of the sublime. Smollett on the contrary pulls down and levels what with other men would continue romance. The grand parts of Scott are within the reach of more minds than the finest humours in Humphrey Clinker. I forget whether that fine thing of the Serjeant is Fielding or Smollett but it gives me more pleasure than the whole novel of the Antiquary. You must remember what I mean. Some one says to the Serjeant: "That's a non-sequitur!"—"If you come to that," replies the Serjeant, "you're another!"—KEATS, JOHN, 1818, *To George and Thomas Keats, Jan.* 5; *Letters, ed. Colvin, p.* 51.

In Smollett's Strap, his Lieutenant Bowling, his Morgan the honest Welshman, and his Matthew Bramble, we have exquisite humour,—while in his Peregrine Pickle we find an abundance of drollery, which too often degenerates into mere oddity; in short, we feel that a number of things are put together to counterfeit humour, but that there is no growth from within.—COLERIDGE, SAMUEL TAYLOR, 1818, *Wit and Humour; Miscellanies, ed. Ashe, p.* 123.

Smollett's humour often arises from the situation of the persons, or the peculiarity of their external appearance; as, from Roderick Random's carroty locks, which hung down over his shoulders like a pound of candles, or Strap's ignorance of London, and the blunders that follow from it. There is a tone of vulgarity about all his productions. The incidents frequently resemble detached anecdotes taken from a newspaper or magazine; and, like those in "Gil Blas," might happen to a hundred other characters. He exhibits the ridiculous accidents and reverses to which human life is liable, not "the stuff" of which it is composed. He seldom probes to the quick, or penetrates beyond the surface; and, therefore, he leaves no stings in the minds of his readers, and in this respect is far less interesting than Fielding. His novels always enliven, and never tire us; we take them up with pleasure, and lay them down without any strong feeling of regret.—HAZLITT, WILLIAM, 1818, *Lectures on the English Comic Writers, Lecture* vi.

Upon the whole, the genius of Smollett may be said to resemble that of Rubens. His pictures are often deficient in grace; sometimes coarse, and even vulgar in conception; deficient in keeping, and in the due subordination of parts to each other; and intimating too much carelessness on the part of the artist. But these faults are redeemed by such richness and brilliancy of colours; such a profusion of imagination,—now bodying forth the grand and terrible—now the natural, the easy, and the ludicrous; there is so much of life, action, and bustle, in every group he has painted; so much force and individuality of character,—that we readily grant to Smollett an equal rank with his great rival Fielding, while we place both far above any of their successors in the same line of fictitious composition.—SCOTT, SIR WALTER, 1821, *Tobias Smollett.*

The intellect of Smollett, acute and penetrating, enabled him to dive a certain way, but not as with the genius of a Fielding, into the very recesses of the human mind. His humour, lively and versatile as it was, lay rather in broad and strong painting, approaching caricature, than in situation and incident, which require no comment, which possess the soul and naked power of wit, without the ornament of language. Yet he could paint vividly and accurately the weaknesses and absurdities which presented themselves in ludicrous points of view. He had a clear conception, and he conveyed it in a perspicuous and forcible style. He combines simplicity with correctness, and elegance and ease with grace. His wit, bold and sudden, never fails to strike; and it is keen as it is strong and manly. His humour, though exquisite at times, and always lively, cannot compete with the innate power of Fielding, nor with that of Swift and Congreve. Nor as a general writer does he possess the delicate taste or chastened moral, with the poignant satire and pleasing variety of Addison, but his great forte lay in displaying the various incongruities of conduct and manners, as well as the sources of human actions, in all which he proved himself no unworthy rival of Theophrastus, of Bruyere, and Moliere. —ROSCOE, THOMAS, 1831–33, *The Complete Works of Tobias Smollett, Memoir*, p. xxxiii.

"Humphry Clinker" is certainly Smollett's best. I am rather divided between "Peregrine Pickle" and "Roderick Random," both extraordinary good in their way, which is a way without tenderness; but you will have to read them both, and I send the first volume of "Peregrine" as the richer of the two.—DICKENS, CHARLES, 1854, *Letter to Mr. Frank Stone; Letters, eds. Dickens and Hogarth, vol.* I, *p.* 416.

The "Briton," which probably suggested the title of Wilke's famous publication, was established also under the auspices of Bute, and conducted by Smollett. But no trace of the genius which produced "Roderick Random," and "Humphrey Clinker," is to be found in this production. Like his continuation of the "History of England," a vapid chronicle, put together by contract with the booksellers, these political essays, written for the wages of a minister, were among the dullest productions of their kind.—MASSEY, WILLIAM, 1855, *A History of England During the Reign of George the Third, vol.* I, *p.* 408.

Smollett, a practised writer for the press, had the command, indeed, of a style the fluency of which is far from being without force, or rhetorical parade either; but it is animated by no peculiar expressiveness, by no graces either of art or of nature. His power consists in the cordiality of his conception and the breadth and freedom of his delineation of the humourous, both in character and in situation. The feeling of the humourous in Smollett always overpowers, or at least has a tendency to overpower, the merely satirical spirit; which is not the case with Fielding, whose humour has generally a sly vein of satire running through it even when it is most gay and genial.—CRAIK, GEORGE L., 1861, *A Compendious History of English Literature and of the English Language, vol.* II, *p.* 298.

I have read over "Roderick Random," too—an odd contrast—but did not learn anything new from it. I found I knew Smollett well enough before. However, I shall get "Peregrine Pickle" for the sake of Trunnion and Pipes, who are grown very dim to me. Fielding's coarseness belongs to his time, Smollett's is of all time. But there are good sketches in him —LOWELL, JAMES RUSSELL, 1867, *Letter to C. E. Norton, July* 8; *Letters, ed. Norton, vol.* I, *p.* 391.

He reflects, in many respects, the character of the age more fully than any other writer—its material pleasures, its coarse amusements, its hard drinking, loud swearing, and practical jokes. His heroes are generally libertines, full of mirth and animal spirits, who make small account of woman's chastity, and whose adventures are intrigues, and their merriment broad farce. Such are the chief features of "Roderick Random" and "Peregrine Pickle," neither of which, however, is so offensive as the "Adventures of Ferdinand, Count Fathom," the hero of which is a blackguard and a scoundrel, without a redeeming virtue.—FORSYTH, WILLIAM, 1871, *The Novels and Novelists of the Eighteenth Century*, *p.* 274.

He exaggerates caricature; he thinks to amuse us by showing us mouths gaping to the ears, and noses half-a-foot long; he magnifies a national prejudice or a professional trick until it absorbs the whole character; he jumbles together the most repulsive oddities,—a Lieutenant Lismahago half roasted by Red Indians; old jack-tars who pass their life in shouting and travestying all sorts of ideas into their nautical jargon; old maids as ugly as monkeys, as withered as skeletons, and as sour as vinegar; maniacs steeped in pedantry, hypochondria, misanthropy, and silence.—TAINE, H. A., 1871, *History of English Literature, tr. Van Laun, vol.* II, *bk.* iii, *ch.* vi, *p.* 178.

Smollett's talent lay in vigorous descriptions of broad humour, whether in person, character, action, or scenery, and in these it may be said he has been surpassed by few. The scenes he had witnessed in life he described in the broadest sunlight of vividness. He had been a surgeon on board of a man-of-war, and every portion of his novels that have any reference to the seaman of a seafaring life may be given in upon evidence and sworn to. The whole scene on board the man-of-war is as minute and true as a Dutch painting. Smollett's language, moreover, is admirably adapted for humorous description, being natural, easy, concise, and home-striking to the point. He likewise possesses amazing power in narrations of terrific adventure, as, witness the forest scene with the robbers in "Count Fathom." And for his humour, all the night adventures in inns may be quoted. What can surpass in drollery of thought his making one of the landladies rush forth upon an occasion of alarm, installed in that never-described article of her husband's wardrobe, with the wrong side before? The humour of the circumstance may surely plead for this allusion to it.—CLARKE, CHARLES COWDEN, 1872, *On the Comic Writers of England, The Gentleman's Magazine, n. s., vol.* 8, *p.* 566.

He is full of wit and humour, but his humour is too broad and occasionally rather coarse. Smollett, however, is not only comic, he also possesses wonderful power for the representation of the pathetic and the horrible. The most original and the most carefully written of his novels is "Humphrey Clinker."—SCHERR, J., 1874, *A History of English Literature, tr. M. V., p.* 154.

Dickens in early childhood sat at the feet of Tobias Smollett. From the author of "Roderick Random" came to the author of "David Copperfield" the first inspiration of the story-teller. Each of these two men was the most popular fiction writer of his time, and there cannot be a doubt that the artist whose loss from among us we have not yet ceased to mourn gathered something both in style and substance from the novelist whose fictions so delighted his own childhood. It is not then quite wise in us, whose moral and intellectual lives have been largely influenced by Dickens, to pass by wholly unheeded the old master whom the child Dickens studied so intently and to such great purpose.—SMITH, GEORGE BARNETT, 1875, *Tobias Smollett, Gentleman's Magazine, n. s., vol.* 14, *p.* 729.

So long as his odes to "Leven Water" and to "Independence" exist, Smollett can never fail to be admired as a poet, nor can a feeling of regret be avoided that he did not devote more of his genius to poetic compositions. We cannot take leave of this distinguished Scotchman—distinguished as a historian, as a novelist, and as the author of lines which possess the masculine strength of Dryden—without alluding to a passage in his novel of "Peregrine Pickle," that passage so inexpressibly touching where the Jacobite exiles stand every morning on the coast of France to contemplate the blue hills of their native land, to which they are never to return!—WILSON, JAMES GRANT, 1876, *The Poets and Poetry of Scotland, vol.* I, *p.* 203.

There is a great similarity between Smollett and Lever. It rarely happens that the men who write prescriptions also write novels; but Smollett like Lever had combined the parts of physician and comic novelist. The tone of both is tinged by Tory tendencies. Smollett and Lever put their own adventures in books. Smollett introduced Dr. Akenside into "Peregrine Pickle" as Dr. Smellfungus. Lever puts Dr. Cusack into "O'Malley," and Dr. Finucane in "Lorrequer." Both started Tory journals in support of the Government; and both papers survived not many weeks; both wrote with ease and eschewed revision; both had a military bias; and martial scenes and rollicking adventure, with a relish of practical jokes, equally constitute their characteristics.—FITZPATRICK, W. J., 1879, *The Life of Charles Lever, vol.* II, *p.* 194.

It is in keeping with Smollett's deliberate dwelling on the more brutal phases of life, that the would-be sentimental parts of his stories are so terribly forced, cold, and prosaically positive. We are told that the physician listened with complacency to the ravings of Renaldo, Count de Melville, over the loss of the peerless Monimia, ravished from him by the machinations of the wicked Fathom. At this distance of time we do not listen to him with complacency, nor indeed to any of the amorous parts of Smollett's work. When posterity reads that "the lovers were seated; he looked and languished; she flushed and faltered; all was doubt and delirium, fondness and flutter," posterity laughs. There is no love scene in Smollett, though there are many which would be love-scenes if elaborate description and persistent filling up of adjectives could give them the spirit they lack. . . . To this prosaic accuracy of language ought to be attributed much of what is called Smollett's brutality. He certainly describes and almost insists on the merely physical sufferings and weakness of mankind. Disease and deformity, rags and vermin, are introduced by him with undesirable frequency—undesired, that is, by the taste of our time. Further, he is very apt to speak of mere brutal violence, done either in jest or in anger, with little or no appearance of indignation on his own part. For one thing, there are more blows given and received in Smollett; there is more flogging than could be paralleled in the work of any other writer who can fairly be called a man of letters.—HANNAY, DAVID, 1887, *Life of Tobias George Smollett, pp.* 77, 78.

While Smollett occasionally rises above Fielding, he does not maintain the same high level, and though free of digression, to which Fielding was prone, he is of coarser tastes. He is remarkable for a variety of incidents and characters almost bewildering in their abundance, and expressed in an easy, flowing style which is never obscure or tedious. If Fielding anticipated Thackeray, Smollett was the forerunner of Dickens. His love of fun leads him often to the verge of caricature. He painted a whole gallery of original characters, among which are the life-like portraits of Squire Bramble and Lieutenant Lesmahago, Commodore Trunnion and Jack Hatchway, Morgan and Tom Bowling, besides Strap, and Pipes, and Winifred Jenkins.—ROBERTSON, J. LOGIE, 1894, *A History of English Literature, p.* 234

A coarse anticipator of Captain Marryat.—RUSSELL, PERCY, 1894, *A Guide to British and American Novels, p.* 6.

Observation, and observation of the outside rather than of the inside, is Smollett's characteristic. He had seen much; he had felt much; he had desired, and enjoyed, and failed in, and been indignant at much. And he related these experiences, or something like them, with a fresh and vigorous touch, giving them for the most part true life and nature, but not infusing any great individuality into them either from the artistic or the ethical side. He was a good writer but not one of distinction. He never takes the very silghtest trouble about construction: his books are mere lengths cut off from a conceivably infinite bead-roll of adventurers. Vivid as are his sketches they all run (except perhaps in his last and best book) to types. His humour though exuberant is for the most part what has been called "the humour of the stick." He has no commanding or profound knowledge of human nature below the surface.—SAINTSBURY, GEORGE, 1895, *English Prose, ed. Craik, vol.* IV, *p.* 258.

The constructive power of Fielding is absent from Smollett, but in inventive tale-telling and in cynical characterisation, he is not easily equalled.—BROOKE, STOPFORD A., 1896, *English Literature, p.* 201.

As a novelist he stands among the British classics, probably unsurpassed in his own region—an amusing delineation of the stronger humours and absurdities of character.—EYRE-TODD, GEORGE, 1896, *Scottish Poetry of the Eighteenth Century, vol.* I, *p.* 151.

This rough and strong writer was troubled with no superfluous refinements of instinct. He delighted in creating types of eccentric profligates and ruffians, and to do this was to withdraw from the novel as Richardson, Fielding, and Sterne conceived it, back into a form of the picaresque romance. He did not realise what his greatest compeers were doing, and when he wrote "Roderick Random" (1748) he avowedly modelled it on "Gil Blas," coming, as critics have observed, even closer to the Spanish *picaros* spirit than did Le Sage himself. If Smollett had gone no further than this, and had merely woven out of his head one more romance of the picaresque class, we should never have heard of him. But his own life, unlike those of his three chief rivals, had been adventurous on land and under sail, and he described what he had seen and suffered. Three years later he published "Peregrine Pickle" (1751), and just before he died, in 1771, "Humphrey Clinker." The abundant remainder of his work is negligible, these three books alone being worthy of note in a sketch of literature so summary as this.—GOSSE, EDMUND, 1897, *Short History of Modern English Literature, p.* 245.

Smollett was placed in a very high rank by his contemporaries. Lady Wortley-Montagu praised her "dear Smollett" to all her friends (including Mrs. Delany and other pious people), Johnson commended his ability, Burke delighted in "Roderick Random," and Lydia Languish seems to have had an impartial affection for all his novels. Of later generations, Scott readily grants to him an equality with his great rival Fielding. Elia makes his imaginary aunt refer with a sigh of regret to the days when she thought it proper to read "Peregrine Pickle." Oblivious of Dickens, Leigh Hunt called Smollett the finest of all caricaturists. Talfourd puts his Strap far above Fielding's Patridge, and Thackeray gives to "Clinker" the palm among laughable stories since the art of novel-writing was invented. More critical is the estimate of Hazlitt. Smollett, he says, portrays the eccentricities rather than the characters of human life, but no one has praised so well the charm of "Humphrey Clinker" or the "force and mastery" of many episodes in "Court Fathom." Taine would appear to sympathise with Mr. Leslie Stephen in a much lower estimate of Smollett as the interpreter of the extravagant humours of "ponderous well-fed masses of animated beefsteak." Of the five great eighteenth century novelists, Defoe, Richardson, Fielding, Smollett, and Sterne, Smollett is now valued the least; yet in the influence he has exercised upon successors he is approached by Sterne alone of his contemporaries.—SECCOMBE, THOMAS, 1898, *Dictionary of National Biography, vol.* LIII, *p.* 181.

Smollett's realism is marked by the spot of decay. All his first novels have one characteristic of the fictions of Mrs. Manley and Mrs. Haywood, Tom Brown, and numerous other early eighteenth-century writers: he crowds his pages with well-known characters of his own time, usually for the purpose of fierce satire. He is a Swift without Swift's clear and wide vision. He ridicules Fielding for marrying his "cook-maid;" Akenside—a respectable poet and scholar—is a mere "index-hunter who holds the eel of science by the tail;" Garrick is "a parasite and buffoon, whose hypocrisy is only equalled by his avarice;" Lyttelton is "a dunce;" he insults Newcastle, Bute, and Pitt, and sneers at his king, and the "sweet princes of the royal blood." In making his characters at will the mouthpiece of his venom, he takes no pains to preserve their consistency; and frequently, under the excitement of his ferocious hate, he forgets they are there, and speaks out in his own name. This kind of work, though done brilliantly and under the inspiration of robust indignation, does not form a novel.—CROSS, WILBUR L., 1899, *The Development of the English Novel, p.* 65.

Christopher Smart

1722–1771

Born, at Shipbourne, Kent, 11 April 1722. Early education at Maidstone and at Durham, 1733–39. Matric. Pembroke Coll., Camb., 30 Oct. 1739; B. A., 1743; Fellow, 1745–53; M. A., 1747. Edited "The Student," 1750–51. Married Anna Maria Carnan, 1753. Contrib. to "The Universal Visitor," "The Midwife " "The Old Woman's Mag.," etc. Confined in a lunatic asylum for two years. Died in King's Bench Prison, 18 May 1770. *Works;* "On the Eternity of the Supreme Being," 1750; "A Solemn Dirge, sacred to the Memory of . . . Frederic, Prince of Wales," 1751; "An Occasional Prologue and Epilogue to Othello" [1751]; "On the Immensity of the Supreme Being," 1751; "On the Omniscience of the Supreme Being," 1752; "Poems on Several Occasions," 1752; second series [1763]; "The Hilliad," 1753; "On the Power of the Supreme Being," 1754; "Hymn to the Supreme Being," 1756; "On the Goodness of the Supreme Being," 1756; "A Song to David," 1763; "Poems" (priv. ptd.) [1763?]; "Hannah" [oratorio libretto] [1764?]; "Ode to . . . the Earl of Northumberland," 1764; "Abimelech" [oratorio libretto,] [1768?]. He *Translated:* "Carmen Alexandri Pope in S. Cæciliam latine redditum," 1743; Horaces' Works (2 vols.), 1756; "The Poems of Phædrus," 1765; "The Psalms of David," 1765; "The Parables of our Lord," 1768. *Collected Poems:* in 2 vols., with memoir, 1791.—SHARP, R. FARQUHARSON, 1897, *A Dictionary of English Authors, p.* 259.

PERSONAL

And as to Sm[art]: he must necessarily be abîmé, in a very short time. His debts daily increase (you remember the state they were in, when you left us). Addison, I know, wrote smartly to him last week; but it has had no effect, that signifies only I observe he takes hartshorn from morning to night lately: in the meantime he is amusing himself with a Comedy of his own writing, which he makes all the boys of his acquaintance act, and intends to borrow the Zodiack room, and have it performed publickly. Our friend Lawman, the mad attorney, is his copyist; and truly the author himself is to the full as mad as he. His piece (he says) is inimitable, true sterling wit, and humour by God; and he can't hear the Prologue without being ready to die with laughter. He acts five parts himself, and is only sorry, he can't do all the rest. He has also advertised a collection of Odes; and for his Vanity and Faculty of Lying, they are come to their full maturity. All this, you see, must come to a Jayl, or Bedlam, and that without any help, almost without pity.—GRAY, THOMAS, 1747, *Letter to Thomas Wharton; Works, ed. Gosse, vol.* II, *p.* 161.

We have a man here that writes a good hand; but he has little failings that hinder my recommending him to you. He is lousy, and he is mad: he sets out this week for Bedlam; but if you insist upon it, I don't doubt he will pay his respects to you.—GRAY, THOMAS, 1751, *Letter to Horace Walpole, Oct.* 8; *Works, ed. Gosse, vol.* II, *p.* 25.

Madness frequently discovers itself merely by unnecessary deviation from the usual modes of the world. My poor friend Smart shewed the disturbance of his mind, by falling upon his knees, and saying his prayers in the street, or in any other unusual place. Now although, rationally speaking, it is greater madness not to pray at all, than to pray as Smart did, I am afraid there are so many who do not pray, that their understanding is not called in question.—JOHNSON, SAMUEL, 1763, *Life by Boswell, ed. Hill, vol.* I, *p.* 459.

The author of the "Old Woman's Magazine" and of several poetical productions; some of which are sweetly elegant and pretty—for example: "Harriet's Birthday," "Care and Generosity,"—and many more. This ingenious writer is one of the most unfortunate of men—he has been twice confined in a mad-house—and but last year sent a most affecting epistle to papa, to entreat him to lend him half-a-guinea!—How great a pity so clever, so ingenious a man should be reduced to such shocking circumstances. He is extremely grave, and has still great wildness in his manner, looks, and voice; but 'tis impossible to *see* him and to *think* of his works, without feeling the utmost pity and concern for him.—BURNEY, FRANCES, 1768, *Early Diary, ed. Ellis, Sept,* 12, *vol.* I, *p.* 24.

The history of his life is but melancholy. Such was his habitual imprudence, that he would bring home guests to dine at his house, when his wife and family had neither a meal, nor money to provide one. He engaged, on one occasion, to write the Universal Visitor, and for no other other work, by a contract which was to last ninety-nine years. The publication stopped at the end of two years. During his bad health, he was advised to walk for exercise, and he used to walk for that purpose to the ale-house; but *he was always carried back.*—CAMPBELL, THOMAS, 1819, *Specimens of the British Poets.*

A type of one who has "no enemy but himself."—PALGRAVE, FRANCIS TURNER, 1889, *ed., The Treasury of Sacred Song, p.* 350, *note.*

In manner Smart seems to have been abnormally nervous and retiring, but when this shyness was overcome, he was particularly amiable, and had a frank and engaging air which, with children especially, often overflowed with drollery and high spirits. Latterly, however, owing to bad habits, penurious living, and his constitutional melancholia, he became a mere wreck of his earlier self.—SECCOMBE, THOMAS, 1897, *Dictionary of National Biography, vol.* LII, *p.* 388.

SONG TO DAVID

Neither Dr. Anderson, nor the present editor [Alexander Chalmers] has been able to discover a copy of the "Song of David," which Smart composed when confined in a mad-house, indenting the lines with a key upon the wainscot. The loss of a poem composed under such circumstances, by a man of such talents, is greatly to be regretted. The following are some of the few stanzas which have been preserved by the Reviewers; Smart has never written with more strength and animation,—and perhaps never with so much feeling.—SOUTHEY, ROBERT, 1814, *Chalmers's English Poets, The Quarterly Review, vol.* 11, *p.* 496.

It is only in our own day that attention has been recalled to the single poem by which he deserves to be not only remembered, but remembered as a poet who for one short moment reached a height to which the prosaic muse of his epoch was wholly unaccustomed. There is nothing like the "Song to David" in the eighteenth century; there is nothing out of which it might seem to have been developed. It is true that with great appearance of symmetry it is ill-arranged and out of proportion; its hundred stanzas weary the reader with their repetitions and with their epithets piled up on a too obvious system. But in spite of this touch of pedantry, it is the work of a poet; of a man so possessed with the beauty and fervour of the Psalms and with the high romance of the psalmist's life that in the days of his madness the character of David has become a "fixed idea" with him, to be embodied in words and dressed in the magic robe of verse when the dark hour has gone by. There are few episodes in our literary history more interesting than this of the wretched bookseller's hack, with his mind thrown off its balance by drink and poverty, rising at the instant of his deepest distress to a pitch of poetic performance unimagined by himself at all other times, unimagined by all but one or two of his contemporaries, and so little appreciated by the public that when an edition of his writings was called for it was sent into the world with this masterpiece omitted.—WARD, THOMAS HUMPHRY, 1880, *English Poets, vol.* III, *p.* 351.

When in the mad-house Christopher Smart wrote the "Song to David"—a poem which not only transcends anything he ever did or was supposed capable of doing in his saner moments, but actually stands alone in the literature of the age for beauty, intensity, and occasional sublimity. Smart is said to have inscribed the poem with a key upon the wainscot of the room in which he was confined—an obvious physical impossibility, unless the wainscot was unusually large or the key unusually small! Some of the eighty-five stanzas may thus have been written, and the whole afterwards committed to paper. In any case, the "Song" is one of the greatest curiosities and wonders of English literature; and Mr. Browning has been attracted to it, as by a congenial theme. That a writer of merely ordinary powers—a clever scribbler of miscellaneous commonplaces—should suddenly soar to so great a height, then as suddenly fall flat again, is just such a mental phenomenon as our philosophical modern poet delights in analysing.—GREEN, S. G., 1887, *Christopher Smart, Leisure Hour, vol.* 36, *p.* 234.

—Yourself who sang
A Song where flute-breath silvers trumpet-clang,
And stations you for once on either hand
With Milton and with Keats, empowered to claim
Affinity on just one point—(or blame
Or praise my judgment, thus it fronts you full)—
How came it you resume the void and null,
Subside to insignificance,—live, die
—Proved plainly two mere mortals who drew nigh
One momont—that, to Art's best hierarchy,
This, to the superhuman poet-pair?
. . . .
But let the dead successors worst and best
Bury their dead: with life be my concern—
Yours with the fire-flame: what I fain would learn
Is just—(suppose me haply ignorant
Down to the common knowledge, doctors vaunt)
Just this—why only once the fire-flame was:
No matter if the marvel came to pass
The way folks judged—if power too long suppressed
Broke loose and maddened, as the vulgar guessed,
Or simply brain-disorder (doctors said),
A turmoil of the particles disturbed,
Brain's workaday performance in your head,
Spurred spirit to wild action health had curbed,

And so verse issued in a cataract
Whence prose, before and after, unperturbed
Was wont to wend its way. Concede the fact
That here a poet was who always could—
Never before did—never after would—
Achieve the feat: how were such fact explained?
—BROWNING, ROBERT, 1887, *Parleyings with Certain People of Importance in Their Day, pp.* 61, 62.

Its power of metre and imaginative presentation of thoughts and things, and its mingling of sweet and grand religious poetry ought to make it better known. —BROOKE, STOPFORD A., 1896, *English Literature, p.* 221.

It is hardly disputable that the "Song to David" supplies a very remarkable link between the age of Dryden and the dawn of a new era with Blake; and it combines to a rare degree the vigour and impressive diction of the one with the spirituality of the other. There are few episodes in our literary history more striking than that of "Kit Smart," the wretched bookseller's hack, with his mind thrown off its balance by poverty and drink, rising at the moment of his direst distress to the utterance of a strain of purest poetry.—SECCOMBE, THOMAS, 1897, *Dictionary of National Biography, vol.* LII, *p.* 388.

GENERAL

As a poet his genius has never been questioned by those who censure his carelessness, and commiserated an unhappy vacillation of his mind. He is sometimes not only greatly irregular, but irregularly great. His errors are those of a bold and daring spirit, which bravely hazards what a vulgar mind could never suggest. Shakspeare and Milton are sometimes wild and irregular; but it seems as if originality alone could try experiments. Accuracy is timid and seeks for authority. Fowls of feeble wing seldom quit the ground, though at full liberty, while the eagle unrestrained soars into unknown regions. —ANDERSON, ROBERT, 1799, *ed., The British Poets.*

If Smart had any talent above mediocrity, it was a slight turn for humour. In his serious attempts at poetry, he reminds us of those

"Whom Phœbus in his ire
Hath blasted with poetic fire."

—CAMPBELL, THOMAS, 1819, *Specimens of the British Poets.*

Far from other fate was thine, unhappy Kit,
Luckless adventurer in the trade of wit.
A bitter cup was offer'd to thy lip,
Drugg'd with the wants and woes of authorship.
Untimely thrust upon this mortal stage,
No childish pastime could thy thoughts engage.
Books were thy playmates. In a happy dream
Thy hours unmark'd would glide along the stream
Of fancies numberless, and sweet, and fair;
Link'd like the notes of some voluptuous air,
For ever varying as the hues that deck
With changeful loveliness the ring-dove's neck.
Still rising, flitting, melting, blending,
For ever passing, and yet never ending.
Sweet life were this, if life might pass away
Like the soft numbers of a warbled lay;
Were man not doom'd to carefulness and toil,
A magic lamp with unconsuming oil.
Truth is a lesson of another school,
And duty sways us with a stricter rule.
The stream of life awhile that smoothest flows,
'Ere long is hurried down the steep of woes,
Or, lost in swamps of penury and shame
Leaves the foul vapour of a tainted name.
—COLERIDGE, HARTLEY, 1849, *Sketches of English Poets, Poems, vol.* II, *p.* 308.

The author of "David," under happier circumstances, might have conferred additional poetic lustre, even upon the college of Spenser.—BIRRELL, AUGUSTINE, 1887, *Obiter Dicta, Second Series, p.* 280.

No one can afford to be entirely indifferent to the author of verses which one of the greatest of modern writers has declared to be unequalled of their kind between Milton and Keats. . . . Save for one single lyric, that glows with all the flush and bloom of Eden, Smart would take but a poor place on the English Parnassus. His odes and ballads, his psalms and satires, his masques and his georgics, are not bad, but they are mediocre.—GOSSE, EDMUND, 1891, *Gossip in a Library, pp.* 185, 195.

Johnson defended him half-jocularly, but the piece of Smart's work which was least likely to appeal to Johnson is that which has secured him his vogue of late years. This is the now famous "Song to David," to which the praise given to it in Mr. Ward's "Poets," and Mr. Browning's allotment to the author of a place in the "Parleying with Certain People of Importance," have given a notoriety certainly not attained by the rest of Smart's work, familiar as, for a century or so, it ought to have been by its inclusion in Chalmers, where the "Song" is not. Smart, as there presented, is very much like other people of his time, giving some decent hackwork, a good deal of intentionally serious matter of no value, and a few light pieces of distinct merit.—SAINTSBURY, GEORGE, 1898, *A Short History of English Literature, p.* 582.

William Wilkie

1721-1772

William Wilkie, D. D., known among his friends by the title of "The Scottish Homer," was born at Echlin, County Linlithgow, Scotland, 1721; educated at the University of Edinburgh, and subsequently became a successful farmer; was ordained assistant and successor to Mr. Guthrie, minister of Ratho, 1753; Professor of Natural Philosophy in the University of St. Andrews, 1759; died 1772. 1. The "Epigoniad;" a Poem, in Nine Books, Edin., 1757, 8vo; 2d ed., with a "Dream, in the Manner of Spenser," Lon., 1759, 8vo. . . . 2. "Fables," 1768, 8 vo; Plates after S. Wale. —ALLIBONE, S. AUSTIN, 1870, *A Critical Dictionary of English Literature, vol.* III, *pp.* 2722, 2723.

PERSONAL

He is described as a very absent, eccentric person, who wore as many clothes as tradition assigns to the grave digger in "Hamlet" on the stage, and who used to lie in bed with two dozen pair of blankets above him! David Hume gives a humorous description of the circumstances under which Wilkie carried on his Homeric studies. The Scottish farmers near Edinburgh are very much infested, he says with wood-pigeons. "And Wilkie's father planted him often as a scarecrow (an office for which he is well qualified) in the midst of his fields of wheat. He carried out his Homer with him, together with a table, and pen and ink, and a great rusty gun. He composed and wrote two or three lines, till a flock of pigeons settled in a field, then rose up, ran towards them, and fired at them; returned again to his former station, and added a rhyme or two more, till he met with a fresh interruption." —CHAMBERS, ROBERT, 1876, *Cyclopædia of English Literature, ed. Carruthers.*

Regarded by his college friends as the ablest of the distinguished students of his day, Wilkie continued to impress later contemporaries by his originality, remarkable attainments, and conversational power, and to shock them by his eccentricity and slovenly habits.—BAYNE, THOMAS, 1900, *Dictionary of National Biography, vol.* LXI, *p.* 258.

EPIGONIAD

1757

"The Epigoniad," seems to be one of those *new old* performances; a work that would no more have pleased a peripatetic of the academic grove, than it will captivate the unlettered subscriber to one of our circulating libraries.—GOLDSMITH, OLIVER, 1757, *The Epigoniad, Monthly Review, vol.* 17, *p.* 228.

The execution of the "Epigoniad" is better than the design, the poetry superior to the fable, and the colouring of the particular parts more excellent than the general plan of the whole. Of all the great epic poems which have been the admiration of mankind, the "Jerusalem" of Tasso alone would make a tolerable novel, if reduced to prose, and related without that splendour of versification and imagery by which it is supported; yet, in the opinion of many able judges, the "Jerusalem" is the least perfect of all these productions; chiefly because it has least nature and simplicity in the sentiments, and is most liable to the objection of affectation and conceit. The story of a poem, whatever may be imagined, is the least essential part of it: the force of versification, the vivacity of the images, the justness of the descriptions, the natural play of the passions, are the chief circumstances which distinguish the great poet from the prosaic novelist, and give him so high a rank among the heroes in literature: and I will venture to affirm, that all these advantages are to be found in an eminent degree in the "Epigoniad." —HUME, DAVID, 1759, *Critical Review, April.*

There is nothing more wonderful in this admirable poem than the intimate acquaintance it displays, not only with human nature, but with the turn of manner of thinking of the ancients, their history, opinions, manners, and customs. There are few books that contain more learning than the "Epigoniad." To the reader acquainted with remote antiquity it yields high entertainment; and we are so far from thinking that an acquaintance with Homer hinders men from reading this poem, that we are of opinion it is chiefly by such as are conversant in the writings of that poet that the "Epigoniad" is or will be read. And as the manners therein described are not founded on any circumstances that are temporary and fugacious, but arise from the original frame and constitution of human nature, and are consequently the same in all nations and periods of the world, it is probable, if the English language shall not undergo very material and sudden changes, that the epic poem of Wilkie will be read and admired when others that are in greater vogue in the present day shall be overlooked and forgotten.—ANDERSON, ROBERT, 1799, *ed., The British Poets.*

The "Epigoniad" of Wilkie is the bold attempt of an energetic mind to try its powers in the most arduous path of poetry, the Epic; without that correctness of judgment, and previous discipline in the practice of harmonious numbers, which can alone ensure success in an age of polish and refinement. It has accordingly been measured by that standard of criticism, which the most unqualified judges can easily apply,—a comparison with the most perfect productions of its kind; and its palpable defects have involved in an indiscriminate condemnation its less obvious, but real merits.—TYTLER, ALEXANDER FRASER, 1806–14, *Memoirs of the Life and Writings of Henry Home of Kames, vol.* I, *p.* 246.

A poem . . . of great merit, not only as possessing much of the spirit and manner of Homer . . . but also a manly and vigorous style of poetry, rarely found in modern compositions of the kind.—MACKENZIE, HENRY, 1822, *Life of John Home.*

It is now no longer read, and is fast being consigned to oblivion.—BALDWIN, JAMES, 1882, *English Literature and Literary Criticism, Poetry, p.* 287.

"The Epigoniad" is moderately good; but it requires more than moderate merit to induce men to read an epic in nine books. . . . It was doubtless Pope's Homer which inspired Wilkie with the ambition to write a classical epic; but a translation of Homer, and a translation by Pope, was a very different thing from an orginal poem on a subject of ancient legend by William Wilkie. There are numerous faults in Wilkie's composition —glaring Scotticisms, bad rhymes, incapacity to attain that neatness and point without which the heroic couplet is indefensible. Worse than all is the absence of any great original ideas.—WALKER, HUGH, 1893, *Three Centuries of Scottish Literature, vol.* II, *pp.* 102, 104.

The "Epigoniad," Wilkie's chief work, an ambitious epic in nine books descriptive of the siege of Thebes, appeared in 1757. Its inspiration was obviously owed to Pope's translation of the Iliad and Odyssey, and it has many shortcomings not to be found in its model—Scotticisms, false rhymes and rhythm, and even flaws of language. Many passages, however, are conceived in singularly happy vein, and the story is vigorous and crisp.—EYRE-TODD, GEORGE, 1896, *Scottish Poetry of the Eighteenth Century, vol.* I, *p.* 160.

Wilkie has no genuine right to be called "the Scottish Homer," but as a mere achievement in verse his "epic" is creditable; it has a fair measure of fluency, its imagery is apt and strong, and it is brightened by occasional felicities of phrase, descriptive epithet, and antithetical delineation.—BAYNE, THOMAS, 1900, *Dictionary of National Biography, vol.* LXI, *p.* 259.

John Woolman

1720-1772

An eminent preacher of the Society of Friends, born in Northampton, Burlington Co., West Jersey, in 1720, after some experience in Mount Holly as a storekeeper, became a tailor, travelled on religious visits in several parts of America, not neglecting the Indians; died at York, England (where he was in attendance on the Quarterly Meeting), of the small-pox, Oct. 5, 1772. He partook of the excellent spirit which distinguished Thomas Chalkley, Stephen Grellet, William Allen, and Daniel Wheeler. 1. "Some Considerations on the Keeping of Negroes," 1754, "Part Second, Considerations," &c., 1762. 2. "Considerations on Pure Wisdom and Human Policy, on Labour, on Schools, and on the Right Use of the Lord's Outward Gifts," 1768. 3. "Considerations on the True Harmony of Mankind, and how it is to be Maintained," 1770. 4. "Epistle to the Quarterly and Monthly Meetings of Friends," 1772. 5. "Remarks on Sundry Subjects," 1773. 6. " A Word of Remembrance and Caution to the Rich," 1793. 7. "Serious Considerations; with some of his Dying Expressions," 1773. "The Works of John Woolman, in two parts," 1774, 1775; "Journal, and The Works of John Woolman, Part the Second, Containing his Last Epistle and his other Writings," 1775.—ALLIBONE, S. AUSTIN, 1870, *A Critical Dictionary of English Literature, vol.* III, *p.* 2834.

JOURNAL

A perfect gem! His is a *schöne Seele*, (beautiful soul). An illiterate tailor, he writes in a style of the most exquisite purity and grace. His moral qualities are transferred to his writings. Had he not been so very humble, he would have written a still better book; for, fearing to indulge in vanity, he conceals the events in which he was a great actor. His religion is love. His whole existence and all his passions were love! If one could venture to impute to his creed, and not to his personal character, the delightful frame of mind which he exhibited, one could not hesitate to be a convert. His Christianity is most inviting,—it is fascinating.—ROBINSON, HENRY CRABB, 1824, *Diary, Jan*, 22.

Its author was a tailor, living in a small village of New Jersey; and of tailoring he rejected all the more lucrative branches. He chiefly occupied himself with the smallest class of business by which, even in those economical days, a support could be won. Living before the commencement of any distinctively American literature, he expressed his thoughts in the English of the common schools. And yet these thoughts have won the attention and admiration of scholars and literary men, for they show, in humblest language, the desire of a conscience to be at peace with its Maker even in the smallest details of daily life. No mirror ever reflected more faithfully the lineaments of him who looked upon it, than does this "Journal" give back the moral likeness of its author. —HOOPER, WILLIAM R., 1871, *John Woolman, Appleton's Journal, vol.* 6, *p.* 606.

It is certain, therefore, that, considering the transformations among the Quakers themselves, the New Jersey preacher would be sadly out of place if he stepped down from his niche in their pantheon into their meeting-houses and homes at the present day. St. Simeon Stylites at the Fifth Avenue Hotel would hardly appear more anachronistic. Doubtless, the suggested contrasts between our age and his, joined to Woolman's childlike simplicity and naïveté, his often inconsequential discourse, and his half-pitiful, half-amusing bodily afflictions, were what made his Journal favorite reading with Charles Lamb. And if we do not misjudge, they strike a responsive chord in Mr. Whittier's humor (a greater possession than the world gives him credit for); and he takes up the book, not always that he may deepen his moral sense and renew his standard of duty—what every one may do who reads his "Journal" devoutly—but as one, not a Quaker, would open "Don Quixote" or "The Merry Wives of Windsor."—GARRISON, W. P., 1871, *Woolman's Journal, The Nation, vol.* 13, *p.* 45.

If we open the record at random we see a good man, living for God in the world, and ranging in his tender sympathies from little things to great.—RICHARDSON, CHARLES F., 1887, *American Literature*, 1607–1885, *vol.* I, *p.* 151.

His journal is remarkable for its simple and lucid style, as well as for its humanity.—HART, ALBERT BUSHNELL, 1896, *ed., American History told by Contemporaries, vol.* II, *p.* 302.

The purity of the gentle Quaker's soul has, as Whittier, his loving editor, says, entered into his language. The words are a transparent medium of spirit. Style and man are equally unconscious of themselves. Without art Woolman has attained, in his best passages, that beauty of simplicity, that absolute candor which is the goal of most studious art. As lucid as Franklin's "Autobiography," the "Journal" shines with a pearly lustre all its own.—BATES, KATHARINE LEE, 1897, *American Literature*, p. 90.

As we study John Woolman along the pages upon which he has made record of his inmost nature, we shall be inclined to infer that the traits which made him the man he was, were these: first, a singularly vivid perception of the reality and worth of things spiritual; secondly, such a passion of desire for all that is like God, that whatsoever he met with in himself or in others which was otherwise, grieved him with an ineffable sorrow; thirdly, love, taking every form of adoration for the Highest Love, and of sympathy and effort on behalf of all God's creatures, great and small; next, humility; next, directness, simplicity, sincerity; next, refinement.—TYLER, MOSES COIT, 1897, *The Literary History of the American Revolution*, 1763–1783, *vol.* II, *p.* 342.

GENERAL

Get the writings of John Woolman by heart; and love the early Quakers.—LAMB, CHARLES, 1821, *A Quakers' Meeting.*

Him, though we once possessed his works, it cannot be truly affirmed that we ever read. Try to read John we often did; but read John we did not. This, however, you say, might be our fault, and not John's. Very likely; and we have a notion that now, with our wiser thoughts, we *should* read John if he were here on this table. It is certain that he was a good man, and one of the earliest in America, if not in Christendom, who lifted up his hand to protest against the slave trade; but still we suspect that, had John been all that Coleridge represented, he would not have repelled us from reading his travels in the fearful way that he did. But again we beg pardon, and entreat the earth of Virginia to lie light upon the remains of John Woolman; for he was an Israelite indeed, in whom there was no guile.—DE QUINCEY, THOMAS, 1845–59, *Coleridge and Opium-Eating; Collected Writings, ed. Masson, vol.* V, *p.* 196.

The larger portions of Woolman's writings are devoted to the subjects of slavery, uncompensated labor, and the excessive toil and suffering of the many to support the luxury of the few. The argument running through them is searching, and in its conclusions uncompromising, but a tender love for the wrong-doer as well as the sufferer underlies all. They aim to convince the judgment and reach the heart without awakening prejudice and passion. To the slaveholders of his time they must have seemed like the voice of conscience speaking to them in the cool of the day. One feels, in reading them, the tenderness and humility of a nature redeemed from all pride of opinion and self-righteousness, sinking itself out of sight, and intent only upon rendering smaller the sum of human sorrow and sin by drawing men nearer to God and to each other. The style is that of a man unlettered, but with natural refinement and delicate sense of fitness, the purity of whose heart enters into his language. There is no attempt at fine writing, not a word or phrase for effect; it is the simple unadorned diction of one to whom the temptations of the pen seems to have been wholly unknown.—WHITTIER, JOHN GREENLEAF, 1871, *ed., The Journal of John Woolman, Introduction, p.* 33.

The gentle hearted Quaker, like Izaak Walton, a tailor, and like him, also, a lover of man, animal and plant. Although he was an irrepressible reformer, his writings have none of the pride of opinion and self-righteousness which are the besetting sins of reformers. Catholic, humble, receptive, his words are a benediction. Such Charles Lamb, the purest and manliest of modern English writers, found them, and as such he praised them.—MABIE, HAMILTON W., 1892, *The Memorial Story of America, p.* 585.

Philip Dormer Stanhope

1694-1773.

1694, Philip Dormer Stanhope, fourth Earl of Chesterfield, born 22nd September, 1712, Chesterfield entered Trinity Hall, Cambridge (as Stanhope). 1715, Appointed Gentleman of the Bed-chamber to the Prince of Wales. 1715, Entered the House of Commons as M. P. for St. Germains. 1723, Appointed Captain of the Guard. 1726, Succeeds to the Earldom, on the death of his father. 1727, Chesterfield appointed Ambassador at the Hague. 1730, Appointed Lord Steward and invested with the Garter.

1732, His son, Philip Stanhope, born. 1733, Dismissed from office by the King, in consequence of his opposition to Walpole's Excise Bill. 1733, Married Melosina de Schoulenberg, Countess of Walsingham (daughter, as supposed, of George I.). She died without issue in 1778. 1737, Speech against Bill for Licensing Theatres. 1739, Commencement of his "Letters to his Son;" continued to the death of the latter in 1768. 1744, Appointed Envoy to the Hague. 1745 and 1746, Lord Lieutenant of Ireland, from May, 1745, to Nov. 18, 1746—residing the last six months in England. 1746, Secretary of State, Offered a Dukedom. 1748, Resigns 6th February, owing to his opposition to the War. 1751, Proposed and carried the Reformation of the Calendar. 1752, His deafness commences. 1755, His Godson and successor, Philip Stanhope, son of Arthur Charles Stanhope, born 28th November. 1761, Commencement of his "Letters to his Godson." 1768, Death of his Son. 1773, Died 24th March.—MOULTON, CHARLES WELLS, 1902.

PERSONAL

Lord Chesterfield was allowed by everybody to have more conversable entertaining table-wit than any man of his time; his propensity to ridicule, in which he indulged himself with infinite humour and no distinction, and with inexhaustible spirits and no discretion, made him sought and feared, liked and not loved, by most of his acquaintance; no sex, no relation, no rank, no power, no profession, no friendship, no obligation, was a shield from those pointed, glittering weapons, that seemed to shine only to a stander-by, but cut deep in those they touched. . . . With a person as disagreeable as it was possible for a human figure to be without being deformed, he affected following many women of the first beauty and most in fashion; and, if you would have taken his word for it, not without success; whilst in fact and in truth, he never gained any one above the venal rank of those whom an Adonis or a Vulcan might be equally well with, for an equal sum of money. He was very short, disproportioned, thick and clumsily made; had a broad, rough-featured, ugly face, with black teeth, and a head big enough for a Polyphemus. One Ben Ashurst, . . . told Lord Chesterfield once that he was like a stunted giant which was a humorous idea and really apposite.—HERVEY, JOHN LORD, 1727–43? *Memoirs of the Reign of King George the Second, ed. Croker, ch.* iv.

Chesterfield is a little, tea-table scoundrel, that tells little womanish lies to make quarrels in families; and tries to make women lose their reputations, and make their husbands beat them, without any object but to give himself airs; as if anybody could believe a woman could like a dwarf baboon.—GEORGE II., 1743? *To Lord Hervey.*

He had early in his life announced his claim to wit, and the women believed in it. He had besides given himself out for a man of great intrigue, with as slender pretensions; yet the women believed in that too—one should have thought they had been more competent judges of merit in that particular! It was not his fault if he had not wit; nothing exceeded his efforts in that point; and though they were far from producing the wit, they at least amply yielded the applause he aimed at. He was so accustomed to see people laugh at the most trifling things he said, that he would be disappointed at finding nobody smile before they knew what he was going to say. His speeches were fine, but as much laboured as his extempore sayings. His writings were—everybody's: that is, whatever came out good was given to him, and he was too humble ever to refuse the gift. . . . In short, my Lord Chesterfield's being the instrument to introduce this new era into our computation of time will probably preserve his name in almanacs and chronologies, when the wit that he had but laboured too much, and the gallantry that he could scarce ever execute, will be no more remembered.—WALPOLE, HORACE, 1751? *Memoirs of the Last Ten Years of the Reign of George II.*

There was besides these two, another person of great rank, who came to have a considerable share in the design of ruining sir Robert Walpole, I mean the earl of Chesterfield: he was esteemed the wittiest man of the time, and of a sort that has scarcely been known since the reign of king Charles the second, and revived the memory of the great wits of that age, to the liveliest of whom he was thought not to be unequal. He was besides this, a very graceful speaker in publick, had some knowledge of affairs, having been ambassador in Holland, and when he was engaged in debates, always took pains to be well informed of the subject, so that no man's speaking, was ever more admired, or drew more audience to it, than his did, but chiefly from those, who either relished his wit, or were pleased with feeling the ministry exposed by his talent of ridicule, and the bitterness of jest, he was so much master of, and never spared. And this made him so very terrible to the ministers who were of the house of lords, that they dreading his wit upon them there, and his writings too, for he sometimes, as it was thought, furnished the weekly paper of the opposition, with the most poignant pieces it had.—ONSLOW, ARTHUR, 1752? *Remarks on Various Parts of Sir Robert Walpole's Conduct, and Anecdotes of the Principal Leaders of the Opposition; Coxe, Memoirs of Sir Robert Walpole, vol.* II, *p.* 570.

When, upon some slight encouragement, I first visited your Lordship, I was overpowered, like the rest of mankind, by the enchantment of your address; and could not forbear to wish that I might boast myself *Le vainqueur du vainqueur de la terre*;—that I might obtain that regard for which I saw the world contending; but I found my attendance so little encouraged, that neither pride nor modesty would suffer me to continue it. When I had once addressed your Lordship in publick, I had exhausted all the art of pleasing which a retired and uncourtly scholar can possess. I had done all that I could; and no man is well pleased to have his all neglected, be it ever so little. Seven years, my Lord, have now past, since I waited in your outward rooms, or was repulsed from your door; during which time I have been pushing on my work through difficulties, of which it is useless to complain, and have brought it, at last, to the verge of publication, without one act of assistance, one word of encouragement, or one smile of favour. Such treatment I did not expect, for I never had a Patron before. The shepherd in Virgil grew at last acquainted with Love, and found him a native of the rocks. Is not a Patron, my Lord, one who looks with unconcern on a man struggling for life in the water, and, when he has reached ground, encumbers him with help? The notice which you have been pleased to take of my labours, had it been early, had been kind; but it has been delayed till I am indifferent, and cannot enjoy it; till I am solitary, and cannot impart it; till I am known, and do not want it. I hope it is no very cynical asperity not to confess obligations where no benefit has been received, or to be unwilling that the publick should consider me as owing that to a Patron, which Providence has enabled me to do for myself. Having carried on my work thus far with so little obligation to any favourer of learning, I shall not be disappointed though I should conclude it, if less be possible, with less; for I have been long wakened from that dream of hope, in which I once boasted myself with so much exultation.

My Lord,
Your Lordship's most humble,
Most obedient servant.

—JOHNSON, SAMUEL, 1755, *Letter to the Right Honourable the Earl of Chesterfield, Feb.* 7.

Lord Chesterfield however by his perpetual attention to propriety, decorum, *bienséance*, &c., had so *veneered* his manners, that though he lived on good terms with all the world he had not a single *friend*. The fact was I believe that he had no warm affections. His excessive and unreasonable attention to decorum and studied manner attended him almost to his last hour.—MALONE, EDMOND, 1783, *Maloniana, ed. Prior, p.* 357.

Nature, it must be owned, had endowed him with fine parts, and these he cultivated with all the industry usually practised by such as prefer the semblance of what is really fit, just, lovely, honourable, to the qualities themselves; thus he had eloquence without learning, complaisance without friendship, and gallantry without love. . . . In addition to his character of an orator and a statesman, he was emulous of that of a poet, his pretensions to which were founded on sundry little compositions in verse that from time to time appeared in collections of that kind; elegant it must be confessed; but generally immoral and ofttimes profane.—HAWKINS, SIR JOHN, 1787, *Life of Samuel Johnson, pp.* 178, 180.

That Lord Chesterfield must have been mortified by the lofty contempt, and polite, yet keen satire with which Johnson exhibited him to himself in this letter, it is impossible to doubt. He, however, with that glossy duplicity which was his constant study, affected to be quite unconcerned. Dr. Adams mentioned to Mr. Robert Dodsley that he was sorry Johnson had written his letter to Lord Chesterfield. Dodsley, with the true feelings of trade, said "he was very sorry too; for that he had a property in the 'Dictionary,' to which his Lordship's patronage might have been of consequence." . . . Johnson having now explicitly avowed his opinion of Lord Chesterfield, did not refrain from expressing himself concerning that nobleman with pointed freedom: "This man (said he) I thought had been a Lord among wits; but, I find, he is only a wit among Lords!" And when his "Letters" to his natural son were published, he observed, that "they teach the morals of a whore, and the manners of a dancing master."—BOSWELL, JAMES, 1791-93, *Life of Johnson, ed. Hill, vol.* I, *pp.* 307, 308.

Lord Chatham:—Never since the conquest has Ireland passed so long a time in tranquility and contentment. In this, my lord, you stand high above the highest of our kings: and by those who are right minded, and who judge of men by the good they do and the difficulty of doing it, you will be placed by future historians in an elevated rank among the rulers of mankind. Pardon me: for to praise a great man in his presence is no slight presumption.—LANDOR, WALTER SAVAGE, 1824, *Lord Chesterfield and Lord Chatham; Imaginary Conversations, Second Series, p.* 142.

Chesterfield was, what no person in our time has been or can be, a great political leader, and at the same time the acknowledged chief of the fashionable world; at the head of the House of Lords and at the head of *ton*; Mr. Canning and the Duke of Devonshire in one. In our time the division of labor is carried so far that such a man could not exist. Politics require the whole of energy, bodily and mental, during half the year; and leave very little time for the bow window at White's in the day, or for the crush-room of the Opera at night. A century ago the case was different. Chesterfield was at once the most distinguished orator in the Upper House, and the undisputed sovereign of wit and fashion. He held this eminence for about forty years. At last it became the regular custom of the higher circles to laugh whenever he opened his mouth, without waiting for his *bon mot*. He used to sit at White's with a circle of young men of rank round him, applauding every syllable that he uttered. If you wish for a proof of the kind of position which Chesterfield held among his contemporaries. look at the prospectus of Johnson's Dictionary. Look even at Johnson's angry letter. It contains the strongest admission of the boundless influence which Chesterfield exercised over society.—MACAULAY, THOMAS BABINGTON, 1833, *To Hannah M. Macaulay, Aug.* 2; *Life and Letters, ed. Trevelyan.*

Lord Chesterfield's eloquence, the fruit of much study, was less characterized by force and compass than by elegance and perspicuity, and especially by good taste and urbanity, and a vein of delicate irony which, while it sometimes inflicted severe strokes, never passed the limits of decency and propriety. It was that of a man, who in the union of wit and good sense with politeness, had not a competitor. These qualities were matured by the advantage which he assiduously sought and obtained, of a familiar acquaintance with almost all the eminent wits and writers of his time, many of whom had been the ornaments of a preceding age of literature, while others were destined to become those of a later period.—STANHOPE, PHILIP HENRY EARL, (LORD MAHON), 1845, *ed., The Letters of Philip Dormer Stanhope, Earl of Chesterfield, Preface.*

Although one of the genuine aristocracy, owing his title to no modern creation, he made himself a reputation which few of his countrymen equalled in his own day; and, which is perhaps more remarkable, he left his mark upon the mind and manners of the English race so deep, that it will be long before it is entirely effaced. No man ever put into more attractive shape the maxims of a worldly Epicurean philosophy. No man ever furnished, in his own person, a more dazzling specimen of the theory which he recommended. If Cicero came more nearly than any person ever did to the image of the perfect orator which he described, Chesterfield is universally considered as having equally sustained his own idea of the perfect gentleman.—ADAMS, CHARLES FRANCIS, 1846, *The*

Earl of Chesterfield, North American Review, vol. 63, *p.* 166.

Having once satisfied himself that there was no insurrectionary movement in the country [Ireland] and none likely to be, he was not to be moved from his tolerant course by any complaints or remonstrances. Far from yielding to the feigned alarm of those who solicited him to raise new regiments, he sent four battalions of the soldiers then in Ireland to reinforce the Duke of Cumberland. He discouraged jobs, kept down expenses. . . . When some savage Ascendency Protestant would come to him with tales of alarm, he usually turned conversation into a tone of light *badinage*, which perplexed and baffled the man. One came to seriously put his lordship on his guard by acquainting him with the fact that his own coachman was in the habit of going to mass. "Is it possible?" cried Chesterfield—"Then I will take care the fellow shall not drive *me* there." A courtier burst into his apartment one morning, while he was sipping his chocolate in bed, with the startling intelligence that "the Papists were rising in Connaught." "Ah," he said, looking at his watch—"'tis nine o'clock—time for them to rise." There was evidently no dealing with such a viceroy as this who showed such insensibility to the perils of Protestantism and the evil designs of the dangerous Papist. Indeed, he was seen to distinguish by his peculiar admiration a Papist beauty, Miss Ambrose, whom he declared to be the only "dangerous Papist" he had met in Ireland.—MITCHEL, JOHN, 1868, *History of Ireland, ch.* xi.

But perhaps the most interesting apartment in the whole house (Chesterfield House) is the library; there, where Lord Chesterfield used to sit and write, still stand the books which it is only fair to suppose that he read,—books of wide-world and enduring interest, and which stand in goodly array, one row above another, by hundreds. High above them, in separate panels, are "Kit Kat" sized portraits of all the great English poets and dramatists, down to the time of Chesterfield. . . . In another room not far from the library, one seems to gain an idea of the noble letter-writer's daily life; for it is a room which has not only its antechamber, in which the aspirants for his lordship's favor were sometimes kept waiting, but on its garden side a stone or marble terrace overlooking the large garden, stretching out in lawn and flower-beds, behind the house. Upon this terrace Chesterfield doubtless often walked, snuff-box in hand, and in company with some choice friend.—WALFORD, EDWARD, 1869, *Chesterfield, Londoniana, vol.* II.

Lord Chesterfield was a man of extraordinary talents, for his own day the veritable king among men of the world, of whom life is built up with an infinity of care and skill upon well-organized, though worldly, self-love and consummate enjoyment of the world; with no negation of religion, but with no interest in it; with a toleration of it, conditional upon its abiding peaceably in its own place, as a hat abides in the hall until it is wanted for going out of doors.—GLADSTONE, WILLIAM EWART, 1896, *Studies Subsidiary to the Works of Bishop Butler, p.* 134.

Chesterfield incurred the dislike of three of the most influential writers of his day—Dr. Johnson, Horace Walpole, and Lord Hervey (Queen Caroline's friend). Their hostile estimates have injured his posthumous reputation, and inspired Dickens's ruthless caricature of him as Sir John Chester in "Barnaby Rudge." Chesterfield's achievements betray a brilliance of intellectual gifts and graces which discourages in the critic any desire to exaggerate his deficiency in moral principle. In matter and manner—in delicate raillery and in refinement of gesture—his speeches in parliament were admitted to be admirable by his foes. . . . Chesterfield's worldliness was in point of fact tempered by native common-sense, by genuine parental affections, and by keen appreciation of, and capacity for, literature. Even in his unedifying treatment of the relations of the sexes his solemn warnings against acts which forfeit self-respect or provoke scandal destroyed most of the deleterious effect of the cynical principles on which he took his stand. Nowhere did Chesterfield inculcate an inconsiderate gratification of selfish desires. Very sternly did he rebuke pride of birth or insolence in the treatment of servants and dependents. His habitual text was the necessity from prudential motives of self-control and of respect for the feelings of others. As a writer he reached the highest levels of grace and perspicuity, and as a connoisseur of literature he was nearly always admirable. His critical taste was seen to best advantage in his notices of classical writers.—LEE, SIDNEY, 1898, *Dictionary of National Biography, vol.* LIV, *p.* 34.

LETTERS TO HIS SON

I have declined the publication of Lord C's letters. The public will see them, and upon the whole, I think with pleasure; but the whole family were strongly bent against it; and especially on d'Eyverdun's account, I deemed it more prudent to avoid making them my personal enemies.—GIBBON, EDWARD, 1773, *Private Letters, vol.* I, *p.* 195.

I hope your Lordship's approbation of a work, written by the late Earl of Chesterfield, on so important a subject as Education, will not fail to secure that of the Public: and I shall then feel myself happy in the assured merit of ushering into the world so useful a performance.—STANHOPE, EUGENIA, 1774, *Letters Written by Lord Chesterfield to his Son, Dedication, March.*

I shall go to town to-morrow and send for my Lord Chesterfield's Letters, though I know all I wish to see is suppressed. The Stanhopes applied to the Chancellor for an injunction, and it was granted. At last his Lordship permitted the publication on two conditions that I own were reasonable, though I am sorry for them. The first, that the family might expunge what passage they pleased: the second, that Mrs. Stanhope should give up to them, without reserving a copy, Lord Chesterfield's Portraits [Characters] of his contemporaries, which he had sent to his son, and re-demanded of the widow, who gave them up, but had copied them. He burnt the originals himself, just before he died, on disgust with Sir John Dalrymple's book, a new crime in that sycophant's libel.—WALPOLE, HORACE, 1774, *To Rev. William Mason, Apr.* 7; *Letters, ed. Cunningham, vol.* VI, *p.* 73.

His diction is unaffected, and unlaboured. His wit is natural, and without effort, nay, even his most profound remarks upon human nature, of which he has many, seem rather to spring spontaneously from his subject, and to have risen from the conception of the moment, than to be the consequence of preconsideration or of study. Our author's education, his rank and consequent associates, his peculiar talent for conversation, the very best ingredient which can possibly enter into the espistolary style, and indeed the whole colour of his life, seem to have formed him expressly for this sort of composition, and, as this is perhaps the only species of writing in which it may be confessed that we are surpassed by our neighbors the French, it is not improbable that his predilection to the manners of that superficially ingenious people may have contributed not a little to his success.—CHARLEMONT, LORD, 1774, *Letter to Lord Bruce, July* 17.

No modern work, has perhaps been received with such avidity by the public as "Lord Chesterfield's Letters." The subject, the education of a man of the world, and the author, the most accomplished gentleman of his time, naturally engaged the public attention; and the elegance of composition has, we may say, justified the great expectations that were raised. We have not here simply the speculative opinions of a theorist in his closet, but the conduct and practice of a great master carrying his work into execution.—BURKE, EDMUND? 1774, *Annual Register.*

My good old new friend, Mr. Hutton, made me two visits while my mother was at Chesington. We had a good deal of conversation upon Lord Chesterfield's "Letters," which I have just read. I had the satisfaction to find, that our opinions exactly coincided; that they were extremely well written, contained some excellent *hints* for education; but were written with a tendency to make his son a man wholly unprincipled; inculcating immorality, countenancing all *gentleman-like* vices, *advising* deceit and *exhorting* to inconstancy. "It pleased me much," said Mr. Hutton, "in speaking to the King about these 'Letters,' to hear him say, '*For my part, I like more straight-forward work.*' "—BURNEY, FRANCES, 1774, *Early Diary, ed. Ellis, vol.* I, *p.* 305.

Thou polished and high-finished foe to truth,
Gray-beard corruptor of our listening youth;
To purge and skim away the filth of vice,
That so refined it might the more entice,
Then pour it on the morals of thy son;
To taint *his* heart was worthy of *thine own!*
Now, while the poison all high life pervades,
Write, if thou canst, one letter from the
shades;

One, and one only, charged with deep regret,
That thy worst part, thy principles, live yet;
One sad epistle thence may cure mankind
Of the plague spread by bundles left behind.
—COWPER, WILLIAM, 1782, *The Progress of Error.*

I have been reading for the first time Lord Chesterfield's "Letters," with more disgust than pleasure, and more pity than disgust. Such letters must have defeated their own main purpose, and made the poor youth awkward, by impressing him with a continual dread of appearing so. But it is painful to see what the father himself was—not, as it appears, from any want of good qualities, but because there was one *grace* a thought of which never entered his mind.—SOUTHEY, ROBERT, 1831, *Correspondence with Caroline Bowles, March* 8, *p.* 219.

Lord Chesterfield stands much lower in the estimation of posterity than he would have done if his letters had never been published.—MACAULAY, THOMAS BABINGTON, 1833, *Walpole's Letters to Sir Horace Mann, Edinburgh Review, Critical and Miscellaneous Essays.*

When I said that Chesterfield had lost by the publication of his letters, I of course considered that he had much to lose; that he has left an immense reputation, founded on the testimony of all his contemporaries of all parties, for wit, taste, and eloquence; that what remains of his Parliamentary oratory is superior to anything of that time that has come down to us, except a little of Pitt's. The utmost that can be said of the letters is that they are the letters of a cleverish man; and there are not many which are entitled even to that praise. I think he would have stood higher if we had been left to judge of his powers—as we judge of those of Chatham, Mansfield, Charles Townshend, and many others—only by tradition and by fragments of speeches preserved in Parliamentary reports.—MACAULAY, THOMAS BABINGTON, 1833, *Selection from the Correspondence of the Late Macvey Napier, Letter, Oct.* 14.

It is probable, that Chesterfield has been judged by the world, on all points, by the moral unsoundness exhibited in the "Letters to his Son." He has been held as responsible for the work as if he had published it. He came into our houses with his system, and sought the confidence of our boys and young men, and gave a pungency and authority to his instructions by offering them as the real communications of a parent to a cherished son. A vicious romance, or unsound theories and speculations upon life and character, conveyed in a didactic treatise, might not have so armed the world against him. We have here one of the cases, in which an able man excites more alarm, and does more mischief, by direct appeals to consciousness and experience, than by presenting glowing pictures to the imagination. It is not surprising, then, that he has been condemned in the mass. But the reader, who has forbearance enough to discriminate, will not deny, that these "Letters" contain a great amount of practical good sense; that the sketches of character and defects are in the first style of diverting and instructive satire; and that the composition has the animation and grace which we should expect from a highly cultivated mind, occupied with delightful visions of a young man rising into brilliant fame under its guidance.—CHANNING, E. T., 1840, *Lord Chesterfield, North American Review, vol.* 50, *p.* 427.

It is by these letters that Chesterfield's character as an author must stand or fall. Viewed as compositions, they appear almost unrivalled as models for a serious epistolary style; clear, elegant, and terse, never straining at effect, and yet never hurried into carelessness. While constantly urging the same topics, so great is their variety of argument and illustration, that, in one sense, they appear always different, in another sense, always the same. They have, however, incurred strong reprehension on two separate grounds: first, because some of their maxims are repugnant to good morals; and, secondly, as insisting too much on manners and graces, instead of more solid acquirements. On the first charge I have no defence to offer; but the second is certainly erroneous, and arises only from the idea and expectation of finding a general system of education in letters that were intended solely for the improvement of one man. Young Stanhope was sufficiently inclined to study, and imbued with knowledge; the difficulty lay in his awkward address and indifference to pleasing. It is against these faults, therefore, and these faults only, that Chesterfield points his battery of eloquence. Had he found his son, on the contrary, a graceful but superficial trifler, his letters would no doubt have urged with equal zeal how vain are all accomplishments when not supported by sterling information. In one word, he intended to write for Mr. Philip Stanhope, and not for any other person. And yet, even after this great deduction from general utility, it was still the opinion of a most eminent man, no friend of Chesterfield, and not proficient in the graces—the opinion of Dr. Johnson, "Take out the immorality, and the book should be put into the hands of every young gentleman."—STANHOPE, PHILIP HENRY EARL (LORD MAHON), 1845, *ed., The Letters of Philip Dormer Stanhope, Earl of Chesterfield, Preface, p.* xviii.

These letters were addressed to a natural son—and that circumstance should be constantly kept in mind; it is needful to explain many things that are said, and the only apology for many omissions; but at the same time we must say that if any circumstance could aggravate the culpability of a father's calmly and strenuously inculcating on his son the duties of seduction and intrigue, it is the fact of that son's unfortunate position in the world being the result of that father's own transgression. And when one reflects on the mature age and latterly enfeebled health of the careful unwearied preacher of such a code, the effect is truly most disgusting.—BROUGHAM, HENRY LORD, 1845, *Collective Edition of Lord Chesterfield's Letters, Quarterly Review, vol.* 76, *p.* 482.

Nescia mens hominum fati, sortisque futuræ: what would be the feelings of the all-accomplished, eloquent, and lettered Earl himself, were he to wake from the dead and find his reputation resting on his confidential letters to his son! He would be little less astonished than Petrarch, were *he* to wake up and find his *Africa* forgotten, and his Sonnets the key-stone of his fame.—HAYWARD, A., 1845, *Lord Chesterfield, Edinburgh Review, vol.* 82, *p.* 422; *Traveller's Library, vol.* XVII.

The letters of Lord Chesterfield are a remarkable instance of celebrity gained unintentionally, and superseding, in a great measure, other grounds of reputation. For one person acquainted with his character as a statesman, at home and in diplomacy, the rare ability displayed as Lord Lieutenant of Ireland in the administration of that most unmanageable section of the British empire, and the tradition of his oratory, twenty know of his letters to his son, written in perfect parental confidence, and published years afterwards surreptitiously. I cannot better or more briefly characterize the letters, than by saying that they make a book of the minor moralities and the major immoralities of life. They profess to deal with nothing higher than those secondary motives which, though poor and even dangerous substitutes for moral principle, are yet not to be despised in the formation of character—considerations of expediency, reputation, personal advantage; and being addressed to a youth of uncouth manners, they laid that stress upon grace of deportment which has given to the name of Chesterfield a proverbial use. The letters embody a great deal of sound advice, the result of the large worldly experience of an acute and cultivated nobleman, too acute not to know at least the impolicy of much of the world's wickedness.—REED, HENRY, 1855, *Lectures on English Literature from Chaucer to Tennyson, p.* 405.

Chesterfield, like all votaries of detail, repeats himself continually; he announces, with oracular emphasis, in almost every letter, proverbs of worldly wisdom and economical shrewdness, with an entire confidence in their sufficiency worthy of old Polonius, of which character he is but a refined prototype. The essence of these precepts is only a timid foresight utterly alien to a noble spirit.—TUCKERMAN, HENRY T., 1857, *Essays Biographical and Critical, p.* 36.

Chesterfield's "Letters" are excellent; and could we wring out of the choice web which he has woven, certain impurities, we should still think it, as it was in old times, the book for a Christmas present to a son or nephew. But this is impracticable. You cannot remodel Chesterfield: throughout almost every page, some trivial selfishness of character, some violation of sincerity, some entire ignoring of any high principle of religion, or even of honour, appears.—THOMSON, KATHERINE (GRACE WHARTON), 1862, *The Literature of Society, vol.* II, *p.* 231.

Of all depravity in the world there can

be none so great as that of the father who would corrupt his boy. And yet this devil's counsellor, with his wicked words on his lips, looked out over sea and land after his nursling with a yearning love that is almost divine. Such problems are beyond human power to solve. They can be cleared up only by One who knows and sees, not in part, but all.—OLIPHANT, MARGARET O. W., 1869, *Historical Sketches of the Reign of George Second*, *p.* 120.

The Letters were not designed for the press, but were published by the son's widow after Chesterfield's death. No doubt on their first appearance they were highly prized in the fashionable world, but their morality has from the first called forth the severest censures. Not only Johnson the Christian moralist, and Cowper the evangelical poet, but our own Dickens, have joined in its condemnation. Sir John Chester in "Barnaby Rudge" is a sort of later Chesterfield, who reads with delight the letters of his great exemplar, but finds in them a depth of worldliness he had never fathomed. Yet, perhaps, no work, to those who read them aright, enforces more effectually than these Letters the lesson, *Vanitas vanitatum.* — CAREY, CHARLES STOKES, 1872, *ed.*, *Letters Written by Lord Chesterfield to his Son, vol.* I, *p.* xii.

The moral of Chesterfield's instructions how to get on in the world is shortly this: almost everything is allowable, but it must be done in a becoming manner.—SCHERR, J., 1874, *A History of English Literature, tr. M. V.*, *p.* 150.

I am anxious, by recalling to the attention of some readers of this Review what really was the essential part of the teaching of Chesterfield, to do something towards making the study of his "Letters to his Son" what I think they ought to be, a regular portion of the education of every Englishman who is likely to enter public life tolerably early.—GRANT-DUFF, M. E., 1879, *Chesterfield's Letters to his Son, Fortnightly Review, vol.* 31, *p.* 824.

For us, he is interesting chiefly, if not solely, as the author of the "Letters to his Son," which were published after his death. Other letters have been published by the late Lord Carnarvon; but although they show different moods, they do not materially alter the impression made by the unique letters to his son, where we have Chesterfield's theory of life set forth with reiterated detail. . . . It is a work of supererogation to point out the defects of Chesterfield's philosophy. It is, of course, profoundly immoral, profoundly selfish, profoundly cynical. In literary taste he is almost as open to criticism. Shakespeare had scarcely any existence for him; Milton, he avows, is no favourite; and in Dante he finds nothing but laborious and misty obscurity. These are failures of taste that lie on the very surface. The real defect, and that of which Chesterfield would most have resented the imputation, is the absolute weight of conventionality under which he is borne down. His chief aim was the attainment of a sort of cynical independence of life: as a fact he tied himself hand and foot in a very neat network of conventionality and routine.—CRAIK, HENRY, 1895, *English Prose, vol.* IV, *pp.* 80, 81.

Though as a letter-writer he never equals Johnson at his best, yet in his general level he surpasses him. There is, indeed, more variety in Johnson's letters from the great variety of subjects on which he writes. Nevertheless, in the very uniformity of Chesterfield's there is a certain counter-balancing advantage. Not only are our attention and interest never distracted by sudden transitions, but, moreover, there is a real pleasure in seeing the wonderful dexterity with which, though playing on so few strings, he so rarely repeats the same tune.—HILL, GEORGE BIRKBECK, 1898, *Eighteenth Century Letters, Introduction, p.* xxix.

And one takes up the "Letters," written by such a man, which are on dreadfully twaddling subjects sometimes, as well as being tainted by that peculiarly unsavory morality, which contain very little information about the age in which they were written, which have scarcely any of the brilliant social wit of Horace Walpole, and none of the broad humor of Mary Montagu, and is fascinated by them. There is here and there indeed a maxim which is better than any of Rochefaucauld's; there is worldly wisdom; there is endless parental advice; but it is for none of these things one reads My Lord. That infinite dignity and grace of expression, that careful ease, charm, finish, polish, which are as far from the stiffness of Mr. Pope as from the colloquialism of the vulgar, that delicate suggestion of intimacy with all the great literatures of the world and that perfect air of good breeding, make his familiar correspondence into a classic.—TALLENTYRE, S. G., 1899, *Lord Chesterfield, Longman's Magazine.*

GENERAL

Nor would th' enamour'd Muse neglect to pay
To Stanhope's worth the tributary lay,
The soul unstain'd, the sense sublime, to paint
A people's patron, pride, and ornament,
Did not his virtues eterniz'd remain
The boasted theme of Pope's immortal strain.
—SMOLLETT, TOBIAS, 1747, *The Reproof.*

The few light, trifling things that I have accidentally scribbled in my youth, in the cheerfulness of company, or sometimes, it may be, inspired by wine, do by no means entitle me to the compliments which you make me as an author; and my own vanity is so far from deceiving me upon that subject, that I repent of what I have shown, and only value myself upon what I have had the prudence to burn.—CHESTERFIELD, LORD, 1748, *Letter to Dr. Madden.*

Yet Chesterfield, whose polish'd pen inveighs
Gainst laughter, fought for freedom to our plays;
Uncheck'd by megrims of patrician brains,
And damning dulness of lord chamberlains.
—BYRON, LORD, 1811, *Hints from Horace.*

The Chesterfield whom we chiefly love to study is therefore a man of wit and of experience, who had devoted himself to business and essayed all the parts of political life only in order to learn their smallest details, and to tell us the result; it is he who, from his youth, was the friend of Pope and of Bolingbroke, the introducer of Montesquieu and of Voltaire into England, the correspondent of Fontenelle and of Madam de Tencin; he whom the Academy of Inscriptions admitted among its members, who combined the spirit of the two nations, and who, in more than one sparkling Essay, but especially in the Letters to his son, exhibits himself to us as a moralist alike amiable and consummate, and one of the masters of life. It is the Rochefoucauld of England whom we are studying.—SANTE-BEUVE, C. A., 1850, *English Portraits.*

A nobleman who, whatever were his faults and shortcomings as a man, may be properly described as a jealous and enlightened friend of freedom, and one of the first and most intrepid of parliamentary orators. This speech of Lord Chesterfield's against the Licensing Bill is one of the few specimens of the parliamentary eloquence of the period that has come down to us in a perfect form.—LAWRENCE, FREDERICK, 1855, *The Life of Henry Fielding, p.* 97.

In spite of his faults and eccentricities, it is pleasant to discover something more of good to Chesterfield's credit than the world was hitherto aware of. He was neither altogether a cynic nor merely worldly-wise. That he could ever win our affection, like a Fox in politics or a Goldsmith in literature, is out of the question, but that there was a strain of human tenderness in him which has been too frequently ignored is abundantly demonstrated by these charming Letters to his Godson.—SMITH, GEORGE BARNETT, 1890, *A Philosopher in the Purple, Lippincott's Magazine, vol.* 46, *p.* 700.

Had a gift amounting almost to genius in the discovery of bad writers.—LOUNSBURY, THOMAS R., 1891, *Studies in Chaucer, vol.* 3, *p.* 201.

The name "Chesterfield" and his "Letters" are always associated together, but the "Chesterfield's Letters" known to our Grandfathers—to the men of last century and of the first half of this—are the "Letters to his Son," and it is as the author of these and with the character he bears as such, generally condensed into the epigrammatic but far from true and now unquotable saying of Dr. Johnson's that he is still thought of. Judging him from these famous Letters, the world long since saw in him merely "his delicate but fastidious taste, his low moral principle, and his hard, keen, and worldly wisdom;" and this is still the popular verdict, though recent criticism and the publication of the "Letters to his Godson" should go far to modify it.—BRADSHAW, JOHN, 1892, *ed., The Letters of Philip Dormer Stanhope, Earl of Chesterfield, with the Characters, Introduction, p.* xvii.

No shrewder men ever sat upon a throne, or on anything else, than the first two Georges, monarchs of this realm. The second George hated Chesterfield, and called him "a tea-table scoundrel." The phrase sticks. There *is* something petty about this great Lord Chesterfield.—BIRRELL, AUGUSTINE, 1894, *Essays about Men, Women and Books, p.* 23.

With the exception of Machiavelli, we know of no other writer whose opinions and precepts have been so ridiculously misrepresented, and that, unfortunately for Chesterfield's fame, not merely by the multitude, but by men who are among the classics of our literature. . . . In times like the present we shall do well to turn occasionally to the writings of Chesterfield, and for other purposes than the acquisition of style. In an age distinguished beyond all precedent by recklessness, charlatanry, and vulgarity, nothing can be more salutary than communion with a mind and genius of the temper of his. We need the corrective—the educational corrective—of his refined good sense, his measure, his sobriety, his sincerity, his truthfulness, his instinctive application of aristocratic standards in attainment, of aristocratic touchstones in criticism. We need more, and he has more to teach us. We need reminding that life is success or failure, not in proportion to the extent of what it achieves in part, and in accidents, but in proportion to what it becomes in essence, and in proportion to its symmetry.—COLLINS, J., C. 1895, *Essays and Studies, pp.* 196, 262.

Not only our present manners but our present speech would have seemed vulgar to Chesterfield.—TOVEY, DUNCAN C., 1897, *Reviews and Essays in English Literature, p.* 59.

As a letter-writer, in his few excursions into the essay, and in such other literary amusements as he permitted himself, he stands very high, and the somewhat artificial character of his etiquette, the wholly artificial character of his standards of literary, æsthetic, and other judgment, ought not to obscure his excellence. Devoted as he was to French, speaking and writing it as easily as he did English, he never Gallicised his style as Horace Walpole did, nor fell into incorrectnesses as did sometimes Lady Mary. The singular ease with which, not in the least ostentatiously condescending to them, he adjusts his writing to his boy correspondents is only one function of his literary adaptability. Nor is it by any means to be forgotten that Chesterfield's subjects are extremely various, and are handled with equal information and mother wit. He was not exactly a scholar, but he was a man widely and well read, and the shrewdness of his judgment on men and things was only conditioned by that obstinate refusal even to entertain any enthusiasm, anything high-strung in ethics, æsthetics, religion, and other things, which was characteristic of his age. Had it not been for Chesterfield we should have wanted many lively pictures of society, manner, and travel; but we should also have wanted our best English illustration of a saying of his time, though not of his —"If there were no God, it would be necessary to create one." — SAINTSBURY, GEORGE, 1898, *A Short History of English Literature, p.* 644.

John Hawkesworth

1715?-1773.

John Hawkesworth, LL. D., 1715 or '19-1773, a native of London, is best known as the editor of "The Adventurer," (published Nov. 7, 1752—March 9, 1754), and the author of 70 or 72 of its 140 numbers. He was also a contributor to the "Gentleman's Magazine;" published some Tales,—"Edgar and Emmeline," and "Almoran and Hamet,"—1761; edited Swift's "Works and Letters, with his Life," 1765-66; published a translation of Telemachus in 1768; wrote "Zimri," an excellent oratorio, and other plays; and in 1773 (3 vols. 4to) gave to the world, an "Account of the Voyages of Byron, Wallis, Cartaret, and Cook." By this last publication, for which he was engaged by the Government, he gained £6000,—not unalloyed by severe censure for moral improprieties in his description of savage life, for alleged nautical errors and scientific defects.—ALLIBONE, S. AUSTIN, 1854-58, *A Critical Dictionary of English Literature, vol.* I, *p.* 802.

PERSONAL

Hawkesworth was a man of fine parts, but no learning: his reading had been irregular and desultory: the knowledge he had acquired, he, by the help of a good memory retained, so that it was ready at every call, but on no subject had he ever formed any system. All of ethics that he knew, he had got from Pope's "Essay on Man," and Epistles; he had read the modern French writers, and more particularly the poets, and with the aid of Keill's Introduction, Chambers Dictionary, and other such common books, had attained such an insight into physics, as enabled him to talk on the subject. In the more valuable branches of learning, he was deficient. His office of curator of the Magazine gave him great opportunities of improvement, by an extensive correspondence with men of all professions; it increased his little stock of literature, and furnished him with more than a competent share of that intelligence which is necessary to qualify a man for conversation. He had a good share of wit, and a vein of humour. With all these talents, Hawkesworth could be no more than an instructive and entertaining companion.—HAWKINS, SIR JOHN, 1787, *Life of Samuel Johnson, p.* 252.

He was originally a watchmaker, or some other mechanick trade. By reading Dr. Johnson's writings he acquired his style, and a certain moral and sentimental air, though nothing mortified him so much as to suppose that he was an imitator of Johnson. He lived much with him, and Johnson was fond of him, but latterly owned that Hawkesworth—who had set out a modest, humble man—was one of the many whom success in the world had spoiled. He was latterly, as Sir Joshua Reynolds told me, an affected insincere man, and a great coxcomb in his dress. He had no literature whatever; and was so ignorant even of English history that, when he was employed in publishing three volumes of Swift's letters, the Bishop of Salisbury (as he told me) could not make him comprehend the difference between Lord Oxford and Lord Orford.—MALONE, EDMOND, 1793, *Maloniana, ed. Prior, p.* 441.

GENERAL

Let me add, that Hawkesworth's imitations of Johnson are sometimes so happy, that it is extremely difficult to distinguish them, with certainty, from the compositions of his great archetype. Hawkesworth was his closest imitator, a circumstance of which that writer would once have been proud to be told; though, when he had become elated by having risen into some degree of consequence, he, in a conversation with me, had the provoking effrontery to say he was not sensible of it.—BOSWELL, JAMES, 1791–93, *Life of Johnson, ed. Hill, vol.* I, *p.* 293.

Read Hawkesworth's "Life of Swift;" of whose character and conduct but an imperfect idea is given by the narrative of Johnson. Hawkesworth is much more communicative and interesting; and the minuteness and simplicity with which he details the few but deplorable incidents of the last four years of Swift's life are highly affecting. The circumstance of his struggling to express himself, after a silence broken but once for more than a year, and finding all his efforts ineffectual, heaving a deep sigh, quite cleaves the heart.—GREEN, THOMAS, 1796–1810, *Diary of a Lover of Literature, Oct.* 11.

Dr. Hawkesworth favoured the public with a whimsical, but beautiful little piece, called "Edgar and Emmeline." The machinery of fairies, who direct everything, is well managed, and by the addition of musical interludes, the piece afforded an elegant entertainment to a number of crowded audiences.—MURPHY, ARTHUR, 1801, *Life of David Garrick, vol.* I, *p.* 366.

His literature, though by no means deep or accurate, was elegant and various; his style was polished, his imagination ardent; his morals were pure, and he possessed an intimate knowledge of the world. . . . It is scarcely requisite to observe, that he formed his STYLE on that of Dr. Johnson; he was not, however, a servile imitator; his composition has more ease and sweetness than the model possesses, and is consequently better adapted for a work, one great object of which is popularity. He has laid aside the *sesquipedalia verba*, and, in a great measure, the monotonous arrangement and the cumbrous splendour of his prototype, preserving, at the same time, much of his harmony of cadence and vigour of construction.—DRAKE, NATHAN, 1810, *Essays, Illustrative of the Rambler, Adventurer, and Idler, vol.* II, *pp.* 4, 7.

His "Amurath" is, perhaps, the most instructive tale of the kind in any language, and has been reprinted in a variety of forms in books adapted for the use of children. The stories of Opsinous, of

Charlotte and Marie, of Eugenio, of Abulus, of Desdemona, and of Flavilla, are told with impressive elegance, and discover an accurate knowledge of the human heart, and an uncommon felicity in displaying the workings of the passions. That of Agamus cannot be read without exciting a powerful interest. It is to be feared it turns upon an incident more common than is generally suspected among those who extend their licentious indulgences to a late period of life. Everywhere, indeed, his practical morality is to be preferred to his philosophy of ethics; for the latter is frequently perplexed, and leads to erroneous conclusions. In treating the most common topics, Dr. Hawkesworth's illustrations are peculiarly striking.—CHALMERS, ALEXANDER, 1808–23, *The British Essayists, Preface to the Adventurer*, p. 30.

Hawkesworth had little learning, but considerable literary talent.—BARKER, G. F. RUSSELL, 1891, *Dictionary of National Biography, vol.* XXV, *p.* 205.

Dr. Hawkesworth's tale of "Almpran and Hamet" (1761) has a supernatural basis: the elder of the two kingly brothers is endowed by a genius with the power of exchanging forms with whomsoever he pleases, and thus is enabled to carry on a plot against his brother, and to attempt to supplant him in the affections of the beautiful Almeida. But the object of the tale is to show how powerless are fate and metaphysical aid to crush virtue, and how little magical power can add to the happiness of a vicious possessor. The author was the biographer of Swift and the admirer of Johnson; his tale is the offspring of "Gulliver" and "Rasselas."—RALEIGH, WALTER, 1894, *The English Novel*, p. 218.

The great ape of Johnson.—SAINTSBURY, GEORGE, 1898, *A Short History of English Literature*, p. 620.

George Lord Lyttelton

1709–1773.

Lord George Lyttelton (1709-73), son of Sir Thomas Lyttelton of Hagley in Worcestershire, entered parliament in 1730, soon acquired eminence as a speaker, held several high political offices, and was raised to the peerage in 1759. His poetry gained him a place in Johnson's "Lives of the Poets;" his best-known prose works are on "The Conversion and Apostleship of St. Paul" (1747), "Dialogues of the Dead" (1760), and "History of Henry II," (1764). See "Memoirs and Correspondence" (1845).—PATRICK AND GROOME, *eds.*, 1897, *Chambers's Biographical Dictionary*, p. 610.

PERSONAL

This unadorned stone was placed here
by the particular desire and express
directions of the Right Honorable
George Lord Lyttleton,
Who died August 22, 1773, aged 64.

—TOMBSTONE AT HAYDEN, 1773.

As disagreeable as his figure was, his voice was still more so, and his address more disagreeable than either.—HERVEY, LORD, 1743? *Memoirs.*

Sir George Lyttelton was an enthusiast both in religion and politics; absent in business, not ready in a debate, and totally ignorant of the world: on the other hand, his studied orations were excellent; he was a man of parts, a scholar, no indifferent writer, and by far the honestest man of the whole society. —WALDEGRAVE, LORD, 1763? *Memoirs*, p. 25.

Sir George Lyttelton and Legge were as opposite in their manners; the latter concise and pointed, the former diffuse and majestic. Legge's speeches seemed the heads of chapters to Sir George Lyttelton's dissertations.—WALPOLE, HORACE, 1797? *Memoirs of the Last Ten Years of the Reign of King George II.*

Pedantry was so deeply fixed in his nature, that the hustings, the treasury, the exchequer, the House of Commons, the House of Lords, left him the same dreaming schoolboy that they found him.—MACAULAY, THOMAS BABINGTON, 1834, *Mackintosh's History, Edinburgh Review; Critical and Miscellaneous Essays.*

His natural abilities were good; and though not of the highest order, were continually strengthened by careful and unremitting cultivation. His ambition of improvement, springing from a deep sense of the obligations which wealth and station imposes upon their possessor, was constant to the hour of his death—to press forward in the pursuit of knowledge, not diverted from the chase by early success and extravagant admiration of moderate efforts: "to scorn delights, and live laborious days," had been the occupation of his life. Its fruit was visible in the variety of his accomplishments, and the fullness of his information upon the subjects to which he had devoted himself. During the course of his life he had maintained an oral or epistolary intercourse with the most celebrated persons of his day, both in England and Europe. Making ample allowance for the language of cotemporaneous flattery, it is impossible to ascribe to that alone the very general estimation in which his opinions were held by all who had any pretensions to almost any kind of literature. Nor indeed is the verdict of posterity greatly at variance with the judgment of his own time. Of how few can it be said that they have left behind them works in History, Poetry, and Divinity, which, after the lapse of nearly a century, maintain an honourable place in the literature of their country? And of how very few, that they combined with success in these pursuits a laborious and distinguished share in the duties of public life?—PHILLIMORE, ROBERT, 1845, *ed., Memoirs and Correspondence of George Lord Lyttelton from* 1734 *to* 1773.

Lyttelton, who is known as "the good Lord Lyttelton," was an amiable, absent-minded man, of unimpeachable integrity and benevolent character, with strong religious convictions and respectable talents. In spite of his "great abilities for set debates and solemn questions," his ignorance of the world and his unreadiness in debate made him a poor practical politician. In appearance he was thin and lanky, with a meagre face and an awkward carriage. . . . Lyttelton was a liberal patron of literature. . . . His friendship with Pope . . . formed the subject of an attack upon him in the House of Commons.—BARKER, G. F. RUSSELL, 1893, *Dictionary of National Biography, vol.* XXXIV, *p.* 371.

OBSERVATIONS ON THE CONVERSION AND APOSTLESHIP OF SAINT PAUL
1747

I have read your religious treatise with infinite pleasure and satisfaction. The style is fine and clear, the arguments close, cogent, and irresistible. May the King of kings, whose glorious cause you have so well defended, reward your pious labours, and grant that I may be found worthy, through the merits of Jesus Christ, to be an eye-witness of that happiness which I don't doubt he will bountifully bestow upon you! In the meantime, I shall never cease glorifying God for having endowed you with such useful talents and giving me so good a son. Your affectionate father. — LYTTELTON, THOMAS, 1747, *Letter to George Lyttelton.*

The great advantage of this performance is, that the evidence for Christianity is here drawn to one point of view, for the use of those who will not attend to a long series of argument. The design is to show, that the conversion and apostleship of St. Paul, alone considered, is, of itself, a demonstration sufficient to prove Christianity to be a divine revelation. This design is very happily executed.—LELAND, JOHN, 1754–56, *A View of the Principal Deistical Writers.*

Lord Lyttleton has discussed the most illustrious instance of the conversion to this religion, in the person of St. Paul, a man of the highest natural talents and of the profoundest reasoning and erudition; and he has accompanied the whole with remarks of weight and dignity on the general subject of Revelation.—MATHIAS, THOMAS JAMES, 1798, *Pursuits of Literature, Eighth ed., p.* 204, *note.*

He successfully shows that St. Paul was not an *impostor* nor an *euthusiast* and that he *could not have been deceived* himself. From all which, his lordship infers the certainty of his conversion and call to the apostleship, and, consequently, the divine origin of the gospel. It is a well-reasoned and acute pamphlet, and discovers considerable acquaintance with the Scriptures.—ORME, WILLIAM, 1824, *Bibliotheca Biblica.*

DIALOGUES OF THE DEAD
1760–62

Were very eagerly read, though the production rather, as it seems, of leisure than of study;—rather effusions than compositions. The names of his persons too often enable the reader to anticipate their conversation; and, when they have met, they too often part without any conclusion. He has copied Fenelon more than Fontenelle.—JOHNSON, SAMUEL, 1779–81, *Lyttelton, Lives of the English Poets.*

KING HENRY II.
1764–67

I think your Lordship will have a great deal of pleasure in reading Lord Lyttleton's History. You will like to see a Gothic building by a Roman architect. The story is Gothic, but expressed with majesty, gravity and force, without anything dark or rude, or perplexed and confused. —MONTAGU, ELIZABETH, 1767, *Letter to Lord Kames, July* 30.

Lyttleton's "Henry II." is a learned and honest book.—SOUTHEY, ROBERT, 1805, *Letter to John May, Aug.* 5; *Life and Correspondence.*

Lord Lyttelton, in his "Life of Henry the Second," goes through a very candid and temperate inquiry into this question; and he thinks the Commons was originally a part of the national council or Parliament. The strongest evidence he produces is drawn from the two celebrated instances of the petitions sent, one by the borough of St. Alban's, the other by Barnstaple.—SMYTH, WILLIAM, 1840, *Lectures on Modern History, Lecture* vi.

The subject of it is well chosen, the arrangement is good, and the style clear. The great bulk of it is still useful; and an addition which should retrench some superfluities, correct some inaccuracies, and embody the pith of the best recent works on the same subjects, would be a standard book for every student of English or general medæival history.—CREASY, SIR EDWARD, 1850–76, *Memoirs of Eminent Etonians, p.* 307.

The work was, in fact, highly instructive, learned, careful, and accurate, but like many another of that description, wanted the crowning touch of genius to give it lasting importance. Its whole plan and form was tedious and uninviting. Lyttleton had pursued, through five dreary volumes, the life of a king who had been long forgotten by the public, and whose reign, with one or two striking episodes, had been dull and unimportant. His work is as long as the whole of Hume's History of England, and while that graceful writer had condensed in a few pages the Life of Henry II., Lyttleton gave to one reign labor and space sufficient for the history of the nation.—LAWRENCE, EUGENE, 1853, *The Lives of the British Historians, vol.* I, *p.* 378.

A prolix and ill arranged but elaborate and sensible performance, founded throughout on original authorities, and, from the detailed and painstaking investigations it contains of many fundamental points, still forming perhaps the best introduction we possess to the study of the English constitution.—CRAIK, GEORGE L., 1861, *A Compendious History of English Literature and of the English Language, vol.* II, *p.* 358.

GENERAL

Have you seen Lyttleton's Monody on his wife's death? There are parts of it too stiff and poetical; but others truly tender and elegiac, as one would wish. —GRAY, THOMAS, 1747, *Letter to Thomas Wharton, Nov.* 30.

Lord Lyttelton's Poems are the works of a man of literature and judgment, devoting part of his time to versification. They have nothing to be despised, and little to be admired.—JOHNSON, SAMUEL, 1779–81, *Lyttelton, Lives of the English Poets.*

In the "Persian Letters," as in all his other works, Lyttelton is but an imitator: —the idea, the name, and some of the details are borrowed from the "Lettres Persannes" of the President Montesquieu-then in high repute. Johnson, impressed perhaps with the idea that they were written by an Oxonian of eighteen, treats them slightingly as too "visibly the production of a very young man." They would not, it is true, thirty years later, have added much to the fame which Lyttelton had, rather by his rank than his writings, attained; but they are, we think, no contemptible production even for the age of twenty-five; and they may still be read with amusement and some information as to the manners of the time. Their most serious faults to modern readers, says Mr. Phillimore, "are occasional indelicacies, both of thought and expression—which, as well as their extreme political opinions, was a subject of regret to Lyttelton in after-life." The indelicacy, though probably now less visible than it was in the original edition, is still too obvious; but it was the style of that day, and hardly exceeds the freedoms of some papers in the "Spectator," and falls infinitely short of the licence of his original—the great French magistrate and *moralist,*

OLIVER GOLDSMITH

From a Painting by Alonzo Chappel, from Original Painting by Sir Joshua Reynolds.

as he is called.—CROKER, JOHN WILSON, 1845, *Phillimore's Lord Lyttelton, Quarterly Review, vol.* 78, *p.* 229.

His literary reputation in a great measure died with him; his poems are long since forgotten and his prose writings have little merit. The "Persian Letters," the most amusing of them all, were written while he was very young, and are a tolerable imitation of Montesquieu. They contain passages indelicate and coarse, and could hardly be placed in the hands of the young and pure of our own day. They probably gave rise, however, to Goldsmith's "Citizen of the World," and by their popularity led that delightful writer to imitate and surpass them. But Goldsmith's letters are the perfect and graceful productions of a man of genius, Lyttleton's those of a coarse and inferior artist.—LAWRENCE, EUGENE, 1853, *The Lives of the British Historians, vol.* I, *p.* 383.

Cruel sceptics, like Gibbon, have not failed to point out that his works are "not illuminated by a ray of genius." But his heart has spoken once or twice, in the loosely-strung Pindaric *Monody* to his wife, and in the elegiac prologue to "Coriolanus," Thomson's posthumous tragedy.—GOSSE, EDMUND, 1888, *A History of Eighteenth Century Literature, p.* 228.

Oliver Goldsmith

1728–1774

Born, at Pallas, Co. Longford, 10 Nov. 1728. Family removed to Lissoy, 1730. At village school, 1734–35; at school at Elphin, 1736–39; at Athlone, 1739–41; at Edgeworthstown, 1741–44. To Trin. Coll., Dublin, as Sizar, 11 June 1744; Symth Exhibition, 1747; B. A., 27 Feb. 1749. With his mother at Ballymahon, 1749–51. Rejected as a clergyman, 1751. Private tutorship, 1751–52. To Edinburgh to study medicine, autumn of 1752. To Leyden, 1754. Travelled on the Continent, 1755–56. Possibly took M. B. degree at Louvain or Padua. Returned to London, Feb. 1756. Set up in practice as physician. Master at school at Peckham, winter of 1756 to 1757. Contrib. to "Monthly Review," April to Sept., 1757, Dec. 1758; to "Literary Mag.," Jan. 1757, Jan. to May, 1758; to "Critical Review," Nov. 1757, Jan. to Aug., 1759, March 1760; to "The Busybody," Oct. 1759. Ed. "Lady's Mag.," 1759–60. Friendship with Johnson begun, 1761. Contrib. to "The Public Ledger," Jan. to Feb., 1760; to "The British Mag.," Feb. 1760 to Jan. 1763. Visit to Bath for health, 1762. Removed to Islington, winter of 1762. Tried again to set up as physician, 1765. Settled in Temple, 1767; lived there till death. "The Good-natured Man" produced at Covent Garden, 29 Jan. 1768; "She Stoops to Conquer," Covent Garden, 15 March 1773; "The Grumbler" (adapted from Sedley), Covent Garden, 8 May 1773. Contrib. to "Westminster Mag.," Jan. to Feb. 1773; to "Universal Mag.," April 1774. Died, in London, 4 Apr. 1774. Buried in the Temple. *Works:* "Memoirs of a Protestant" (anon.), 1758; "Enquiry into the Present State of Polite Learning" (anon.), 1759; "The Bee" (anon.; 8 nos.), 1759; "A History of the Seven Years' War," 1761; "A Poetical Dictionary" (anon.), 1761; "History of Mecklenburgh," 1762; "The Mystery Revealed," 1742 (1762); "A Citizen of the World" (anon.), 1762; "Life of Richard Nash" (anon.), 1762; "The Art of Poetry on a new Plan" (anon.; attrib. to Goldsmith), 1762; "The Martial Review" (anon.), 1763; "An History of England" (anon.), 1764; "The Traveller," 1765; "Essays," 1765; "The Vicar of Wakefield" (2 vols.), 1766; "History of Little Goody Two-Shoes" (anon. attrib. to Goldsmith), 1766; "The Good-natured Man," 1768; "The Roman History" (2 vols.), 1769 (abridged by Goldsmith, 1772); "The Deserted Village," 1770; "The Life of Thomas Parnell," 1770; "Life of . . . Viscount Bolingbroke" (anon.), 1770; "The History of England" (4 vols.) 1771 (abridged, 1774); "Threnodia Augustalis," 1772; "She Stoops to Conquer," 1773; "Retaliation," 1774 (2nd to 5th edns. same year); "The Grecian History" (2 vols.), 1774; "A History of the Earth" (8 vols.), 1774. *Posthumous:* "Miscellaneous Works," 1775; "The Haunch of Venison," 1776; "A Survey of Experimental Philosophy" (2 vols.), 1776, "Poems and Plays," 1777; "Poetical and Dramatic Works," 1780; "The Captivity," 1836; "Asem, the Man-Hater," 1877. He *translated:* (under pseud. of "James Willington") Bergeracs' "Memoirs of a Protestant,"

1758; Plutarch's "Lives" (with J. Collyer,) 1762; Formey's "Concise History of Philosophy," 1766; Scarron's "Comic Romance," 1776; and *edited:* Newbery's "Art of Poetry," 1762; "Poems for Young Ladies" (anon.), 1767; "Beauties of English Poesy," 1767; "T. Parnell's Poems," 1770.—SHARP, R. FARQUHARSON, 1897, *A Dictionary of English Authors, p.* 114.

PERSONAL

Of all solemn coxcombs Goldsmith is the first; yet sensible—but affects to use Johnson's hard words in conversation.—WARTON, THOMAS, 1766, *Letter to Joseph Warton, Jan.* 22.

Jarvis. A few of our usual cards of compliment—that's all. This bill from your tailor; this from your mercer; and this from the little broker in Crooked Lane. He says he has been at a great deal of trouble to get back the money you borrowed. *Honeywood.* That I don't know: but I am sure we were at a great deal of trouble in getting him to lend it. *Jarvis.* He has lost all patience. *Honeywood.* Then he has lost a good thing. *Jarvis.* There's that ten guineas you were sending to the poor man and his children in the Fleet. I believe that would stop his mouth for a while at least. *Honeywood.* Ay, Jarvis, but what will fill their mouths in the meantime?—GOLDSMITH, OLIVER, 1768, *The Good-Natured Man.*

Honors to one in my situation are something like ruffles to one that wants a shirt. —GOLDSMITH, OLIVER, 1770, *Letter to Maurice Goldsmith, January.*

From our Goldsmith's anomalous character, who
Can withhold his contempt, and his reverence too?
From a poet so polished, so paltry a fellow!
From critic, historian, or vile Punchinello!
From a heart in which meanness had made her abode,
From a foot that each path of vulgarity trod;
From a head to invent and a hand to adorn,
Unskilled in the schools, a philosopher born.
By disguise undefended, by jealousy smit,
This *lusus naturæ* nondescript in wit,
May best be compared to those Anamorphôses;
Which for lectures to ladies th' optician proposes;
All deformity seeming, in some points of view,
In others quite accurate, regular, true:
Till the student no more sees the figure that shocked her,
But all in his likeness,—our odd little doctor.
—PIOZZI, HESTER LYNCH, 1773? *The Streatham Portraits, Autobiography, ed. Hayward, p.* 254.

Here, Hermes, says Jove, who with nectar was mellow:
Go fetch me some clay—I will make an odd fellow:
Right and wrong shall be jumbled, much gold and some dross,
Without cause be he pleased, without cause be he cross
Be sure, as I work, to throw in contradictions,
A great love of truth, yet a mind turn'd to fictions;
Now mix these ingredients, which, warm'd in the baking,
Turn'd to *learning* and *gaming, religion* and *raking.*
With the love of a wench let his writings be chaste;
Tip his tongue with strong matter, his lips with fine taste:
That the rake and the poet o'er all may prevail,
Set fire to the head and set fire to the tail;
For the joy of each sex on the world I'll bestow it,
This scholar, rake, Christian, dupe, gamester and poet.
Though a mixture so odd he shall merit great fame,
And among brother mortals be Goldsmith his name;
When on earth this strange meteor no more shall appear,
You, *Hermes,* shall fetch him to make us sport here.
—GARRICK, DAVID, *Jupiter and Mercury.*

OLIVARII GOLDSMITH,
Poetæ, Physici, Historici,
Qui nullum ferè scribendi genus
Non tetigit,
Nullum quod tetigit non ornavit:
Sive risus essent movendi,
Sive lacrymæ,
Affectuum potens at lenis dominator:
Ingenio sublimis, vividus, versatilis,
Oratione grandis, nitidus, venustus:
Hoc monumento memoriam coluit
Sodalium amor,
Amicorum fides,
Lectorum veneratio,
Natus in Hiberniâ Forniæ
Longfordiensis,
In loco cui nomen Pallas,
Nov. xxix. MDCCXXXI;
Eblanæ literis institutus;
Obiit Londini,
April iv, MDCCLXXIV.
—JOHNSON, SAMUEL, 1776, *Epitaph on Tomb, Westminster Abbey.*

It may be improper to observe (as a kind of Apology for some particulars which are before related to have passed between me and Dr. Goldsmith), that he was bred a Physician, and therefore it was natural to converse with him on the subject of his disorder in a medical manner; but his attention had been so wholly absorbed by polite literature, that it prevented him from making any great progress in medical studies. As an elegant Writer, he will always be held in the highest esteem by persons of true taste. His "Traveller" and "Deserted Village" are deservedly numbered among the best poetical productions of the present age; and some of his essays, and other pieces, are very advantageously distinguished by general wit and native humour. It should also be remembered, that he was not only an excellent writer, but a most amiable man. His humanity and generosity greatly exceeded the narrow limits of his fortune; and those who were no judges of the literary merit of the Author, could not but love the Man for that benevolence by which he was so strongly characterised. . . . N. B. As my late respected and ingenious friend, Dr. Goldsmith, was pleased to honour Dr. Cogan and myself with his patronage and assistance in the Undertaking for the Recovery of persons apparently dead by Drowning, and other sudden accidents, now on the point of being established in this kingdom, I think I cannot shew a greater proof of my esteem for the deceased, than by applying the profits of this publication (if any should arise) to an institution, the design of which was favoured with his approbation. —HAWES, DR. WILLIAM, 1780, *An Account of the Late Dr. Goldsmith's Illness.*

He was such a compound of absurdity, envy, and malice, contrasted with the opposite virtues of kindness, generosity, and benevolence, that he might be said to consist of two distinct souls, and influenced by the agency of a good and bad spirit.—DAVIES, THOMAS, 1780, *Life of Garrick, vol.* II, *p.* 147.

Of Dr. Goldsmith he said, "No man was more foolish when he had not a pen in his hand, or more wise when he had." —JOHNSON, SAMUEL, 1780, *Life by Boswell, ed. Hill, vol.* IV, *p.* 35.

Goldsmith is well known by his writings to have been a man of genius and of very fine parts; but of his character and general deportment, it is the hardest task anyone can undertake to give a description. . . . He had some wit, but no humour, and never told a story but he spoiled it. . . . His poems are replete with fine moral sentiments, and bespeak a great dignity of mind; yet he had no sense of the shame, nor dread of the evils, of poverty. In the latter he was at one time so involved, that for the clamours of a woman, to whom he was indebted for lodging, and for bailiffs that waited to arrest him, he was equally unable, till he had made himself drunk, to stay within doors, or go abroad to hawk among the booksellers his "Vicar of Wakefield." In this distress he sent for Johnson who immediately went to one of them, and brought back money for his relief.—HAWKINS, SIR JOHN, 1787, *Life of Samuel Johnson, pp.* 416, 417, 420.

It has been generally circulated and believed that he was a mere fool in conversation; but, in truth, this has been greatly exaggerated. He had, no doubt, a more than common share of that hurry of ideas which we often find in his countrymen, and which sometimes produces a laughable confusion in expressing them. He was very much what the French call *un étourdi,* and from vanity and an eager desire of being conspicuous wherever he was, he frequently talked carelessly without knowledge of the subject, or even without thought. His person was short, his countenance coarse and vulgar, his deportment that of a scholar aukwardly affecting the easy gentleman. Those who were in any way distinguished, excited envy in him to so ridiculous an excess, that the instances of it are hardly credible. When accompanying two beautiful young ladies with their mother on a tour in France, he was seriously angry that more attention was paid to them than to him; and once at the exhibition of the "Fantoccini" in London, when those who sat next to him observed with what dexterity a puppet was made to toss a pike, he could not bear that it should have such praise, and exclaimed with some warmth, 'Pshaw! I can do it better myself." He, I am afraid, had no settled system of any sort, so that his conduct must not be strictly scrutinised; but his affections were social and generous, and when he had money he gave it away very liberally. His desire of imaginary consequence predominated over his attention to truth.—BOSWELL, JAMES, 1791-93, *Life of Johnson, ed. Hill, vol.* I, *p.* 477.

Goldsmith, though quick enough at prose, was rather slow in his poetry—not from the tardiness of fancy, but the time he took in pointing the sentiment and polishing the versification. . . . His manner of writing poetry was this: he first sketched a part of his design in prose, in which he threw out his ideas as they occurred to him; he then sat carefully down to versify them, and add such other ideas as he thought better fitted to the subject. He sometimes would exceed his prose design by writing several verses impromptu, but these he would take uncommon pains afterwards to revise, lest they should be found unconnected with his main design. The writer of these memoirs called upon the Doctor the second morning after he had begun "The Deserted Village," and to him he communicated the plan of his poem. . . . He then read what he had done of it that morning, beginning "Dear lovely bowers of innocence and ease," and so on for ten lines. "Come," says he, "let me tell you, this is no bad morning's work; and now, my dear boy, if you are not better engaged, I should be glad to enjoy a Shoemaker's holiday with you."—COOKE, WILLIAM, 1793, *European Magazine, vol.* 24.

In person he was short; about five feet five or six inches; strong, but not heavy in make; rather fair in complexion, with brown hair; such, at least, as could be distinguished from his wig. His features were plain but not repulsive,—certainly not so when lighted up by conversation. His manners were simple, natural, and perhaps on the whole, we may say, not polished; at least without the refinement and good-breeding which the exquisite polish of his compositions would lead us to expect. He was always cheerful and animated, often, indeed, boisterous in his mirth; entered with spirit into convivial society; contributed largely to its enjoyments by solidity of information, and the naïveté and originality of his character; talked often without premeditation, and laughed loudly without restraint.—DAY, JUDGE, 1801? *Letter to Prior.*

A friend of his paying him a visit at the beginning of March 1759, found him in lodgings there so poor and uncomfortable that he should not think it proper to mention the circumstance, if he did not consider it as the highest proof of the splendour of Doctor Goldsmith's genius and talents, that by the bare exertion of their powers, under every disadvantage of person and fortune, he could gradually emerge from such obscurity to the enjoyment of all the comforts and even luxuries of life, and admission into the best societies of London. The Doctor was writing his "Enquiry" &c., in a wretched dirty room in which there was but one chair, and when he, from civility, offered it to his visitant, himself was obliged to sit in the window. While they were conversing, some one gently rapped at the door and being desired to come in, a poor ragged little girl of very decent behaviour entered, who, dropping a curtsy, said "My mamma sends her compliments, and begs the favour of you to lend her a chamber-pot full of coals."—PERCY, THOMAS, 1801-7? *Memoir of Oliver Goldsmith, p.* 60.

That he was fantastically and whimsically vain all the world knows, but there was no settled and inherent malice in his heart. He was tenacious to a ridiculous extreme of certain pretensions, that did not and by human nature could not, belong to him, and at the same time inexcusably careless of the fame, which he had powers to command. His table-talk was, as Garrick aptly compared it, like that of a parrot, whilst he wrote like Apollo; he had gleams of eloquence, and at times a majesty of thought, but in general his tongue and his pen had two very different styles of talking. What foibles he had he took no pains to conceal, the good qualities of his heart were too frequently obscured by the carelessness of his conduct, and the frivolity of his manners.—CUMBERLAND, RICHARD, 1806, *Memoirs, vol.* I, *p.* 350.

Much of the attention which even Goldsmith personally met with was undoubtedly owing to the patronage of his admired friend; yet Sir Joshua used to say, that Goldsmith looked at, or considered, public notoriety, or fame as one great parcel, to the whole of which he laid claim, and whoever partook of any part of it, whether dancer, singer, slight-of-hand man, or tumbler, deprived him of his right, and drew off the attention of the world from himself, and which he was striving to gain. Notwithstanding this, he lamented that whenever he entered into a mixed company, he struck a kind of awe on them, which deprived him of the enjoyment and freedom of society, and which he then made it his endeavour to dispel by playing wanton and childish pranks in order to bring himself to the wished-for level. . . . Sir Joshua was much affected by the death of Goldsmith, to whom he had been a very sincere friend. He did not touch the pencil for that day, a circumstance most extraordinary for him, who passed *no day without a line.*—NORTHCOTE, JAMES, 1813, *Memoirs of Sir Joshua Reynolds, pp.* 126, 170.

The greatest real fault of Dr. Goldsmith was, that, if he had thirty pounds in his pocket, he would go into certain companies in the country, and, in hopes of doubling the sum, would generally return to town without any part of it.—CRADOCK, JOSEPH, 1826–28, *Miscellaneous Memoirs.*

Of his loves we know nothing; they were probably the reverse of poetical, and may have had some influence on his purse and respectability, but none on his literary character and productions.—JAMESON, ANNA BROWNELL, 1829, *The Loves of the Poets, vol.* II, *p.* 311.

His death, it has been thought, was hastened by "mental inquietude." If this supposition be true, never did the turmoils of life subdue a mind more warm with sympathy for the misfortunes of our fellow-creatures. But his character is familiar to every one who reads: in all the numerous accounts of his virtues and his foibles, his genius and absurdities, his knowledge of nature and his ignorance of the world, his "compassion for another's woe" was always predominant; and my trivial story of his humouring a froward child weighs but as a feather in the recorded scale of his benevolence.—COLMAN, GEORGE, 1830, *Random Records.*

"An inspired-idiot," Goldsmith, hangs strangely about him; though, as Hawkins says, "he loved not Johnson, but rather envied him for his parts; and once entreated a friend to desist from praising him, 'for in doing so,' said he, 'you harrow-up my very soul!'" Yet, on the whole, there is no evil in the "gooseberry-fool;" but rather much good; of a finer, if of a weaker, sort than Johnson's; and all the more genuine that he himself could never become *conscious* of it,—though unhappily never cease *attempting* to become so; the Author of the genuine "Vicar of Wakefield," nill he, will he, must needs fly towards such a mass of genuine Manhood; and Dr. Minor keep gyrating round Dr. Major, alternately attracted and repelled.—CARLYLE, THOMAS, 1832–69, *Boswell's Life of Johnson, Miscellanies, vol.* IV, *p.* 86.

His associates seem to have regarded him with kindness, which, in spite of their admiration of his writings, was not unmixed with contempt. In truth, there was in his character much to love, but very little to respect. His heart was soft, even to weakness: he was so generous, that he quite forgot to be just; he forgave injuries so readily, that he might be said to invite them, and was so liberal to beggars, that he had nothing left for his tailor and his butcher. He was vain, sensual, frivolous, profuse, improvident. —MACAULAY, THOMAS BABINGTON, 1843, *Critical and Historical Essays.*

He was privately interred in the Temple burying-ground, and a tabular monument to his honor placed on the walls of Westminster Abbey. That great and noble building does not hold the remains of a nobler or better heart. Oliver Goldsmith was a true Irishman, generous, impulsive, and improvident; but he was more, he was a true man and true poet. Whether we laugh with him or weep with him, we are still better for it.—HOWITT, WILLIAM, 1846, *Homes and Haunts of the Most Eminent British Poets, vol.* I, *p.* 378.

Oliver Goldsmith, whose life and adventures should be known to all who know his writings, must be held to have succeeded in nothing that his friends would have had him succeed in. He was intended for a clergyman, and was rejected when he applied for orders; he practised as a physician, and never made what would have paid for a degree. What he was not asked or expected to do, was to write: but he wrote, and paid the penalty. His existence was a continued privation. The days were few, in which he had resources for the night, or dared to look forward to the morrow. There was not any miserable want, in the long and sordid catalogue, which in its turn and in all its bitterness he did not feel. He had shared the experience of those to whom he makes affecting reference in his "Animated Nature," "people who die really of hunger, in common language of a broken heart;" and when he succeeded at the last, success was but a feeble sunshine on a rapidly approaching decay, which was to lead him, by its flickering light, to an early grave.—FORSTER, JOHN, 1848-71, *The Life and Times of Oliver Goldsmith, vol.* I, *p.* 1.

On examining narrowly the character of Goldsmith, we find, even in what are commonly regarded as its defects, and served to render him ridiculous in the circles of London, some clue to the enigma of the contrast between the habits of the man and the style of the writer. Goldsmith never, from the period at which he lounged at the college-gates as a sizar to the time when his peach-blossom coat attracted the mirth of Garrick, divested himself of the notion that he was a gentleman. This conviction was almost the strongest he possessed; the more it was invaded, the more he clung to it. He surrounded it with all the keenest susceptibilities of his sensitive nature. Nothing so galled and offended him as a hint to the contrary. To be liked as a jester, not companion—to be despised for his poverty—to be underrated as a sizar—to be taunted by a schoolboy with a question of his gentility—were cruelties beyond all others that fate could inflict. . . . Grasping at that respect of which he was so tenacious, he resorts to fine clothes to set off his homely person—to paradoxes in conversation to enforce attention; he gives breakfasts and suppers he can ill afford; he apologises for lodgings beneath his dignity. He is always keeping the hat off his head to hide some patch on his coat. This sensitiveness, proceeding from intense self-consciousness, is mixed up with the most amiable attributes of his nature, and has subjected even his lavish generosity, his cordial charity, to the imputation of a want of true feeling.—LYTTON, EDWARD BULWER LORD, 1848-68, *Goldsmith, Miscellaneous Prose Works, vol.* I, *pp.* 71, 74.

My trust is that Goldsmith lived upon the whole a life which, though troubled, was one of average enjoyment. Unquestionably, when reading at midnight, in the middle watch of a century which *he* never reached by one whole generation, this record of one so guileless, so upright, or seeming to be otherwise only in the eyes of those who did not know his difficulties, nor could have understood them, —when recurring also to his admirable genius, to the sweet natural gaiety of his oftentimes pathetic humour, and to the varied accomplishments, from talent or erudition, by which he gave effect to endowments so fascinating,—one cannot but sorrow over the strife which he sustained, and over the wrong by which he suffered. A few natural tears fall from every eye at the rehearsal of so much contumely from fools, which he faced unresistingly as one bareheaded under a hailstorm; and worse to bear than the scorn of fools was the imperfect sympathy and jealous self-distrusting esteem which he received to the last from friends. Doubtless he suffered much wrong; but so, in one way or other, do most men: he suffered also this special wrong, that in his lifetime he never was fully appreciated by any one friend: something of a counter movement ever mingled with praise for *him;* he never saw himself enthroned in the heart of any young and fervent admirer; and he was always overshadowed by men less deeply genial, though more showy than himself: but these things happen, and will happen forever, to myriads amongst the benefactors of earth. Their names ascend in songs of thankful commemoration, yet seldom until the ears are deaf that would have thrilled to the music. And these were the heaviest of Goldsmith's afflictions: what are likely to be thought such—viz. the battles which he fought for his daily bread—I do not number amongst them.—DE QUINCEY, THOMAS, 1848-57, *Oliver Goldsmith, Works, ed. Masson, vol.* IV, *p.* 289.

Goldsmith had no secrets: his follies, his weaknesses, his errors were all thrown to the surface; his heart was really too guileless and innocent to seek mystery and concealment. . . . He was no one's enemy but his own; his errors, in the main, inflicted evil on none but himself, and were so blended with humorous and even affecting circumstances, as to disarm anger and conciliate kindness. Where eminent talent is united to spotless virtue, we are awed and dazzled into admiration, but our admiration is apt to be cold and reverential; while there is something in the harmless infirmities of a good and great, but erring individual, that pleads touchingly to our nature; and we turn more kindly towards the object of our idolatry, when we find that, like ourselves, he is mortal and is frail. The epithet so often heard, and in such kindly tones, of "poor Goldsmith," speaks volumes. Few, who consider the real compound of admirable and whimsical qualities which form his character, would wish to prune away its eccentricities, trim its grotesque luxuriance, and clip it down to the decent formalities of rigid virtue. "Let not his frailties be remembered," said Johnson; "he was a very great man." But, for our part, we rather say, "Let them be remembered," since their tendency is to endear; and we question whether he himself would not feel gratified in hearing his reader, after dwelling with admiration on the proofs of his greatness, close the volume with the kind-hearted phrase, so fondly and familiarly ejaculated, of "Poor Goldsmith."—IRVING, WASHINGTON, 1849, *Oliver Goldsmith, pp.* 230, 426.

Who, of the millions whom he has amused, does not love him? To be the most beloved of English writers, what a title that is for a man! A wild youth, wayward but full of tenderness and affection, quits the country village where his boyhood has been passed in happy musing, in idle shelter, in fond longing to see the great world out of doors, and achieve name and fortune—and after years of dire struggle, and neglect and poverty, his heart turning back as fondly to his native place, as it had longed eagerly for change when sheltered there, he writes a book and a poem, full of the recollections and feelings of home—he paints the friends and scenes of his youth, and peoples Auburn and Wakefield with remembrances of Lissoy. Wander he must, but he carries away a home-relic with him, and dies with it on his breast. His nature is truant; in repose it longs for change: as on the journey it looks back for friends and quiet. He passes to-day in building an air castle for to-morrow, or in writing yesterday's elegy; and he would fly away this hour; but that a cage necessity keeps him. What is the charm of his verse, of his style, and humour? His sweet regrets, his delicate compassion, his soft smile, his tremulous sympathy, the weakness which he owns? Your love for him is half pity. You come hot and tired from the day's battle, and this sweet minstrel sings to you. Who could harm the kind vagrant harper? Whom did he ever hurt? He carries no weapon—save the harp on which he plays to you; and with which he delights great and humble, young and old, the Captains in the tents, or the soldiers round the fire, or the women and children in the villages, at whose porches he stops and sings his simple songs of love and beauty.—THACKERAY, WILLIAM MAKEPEACE, 1853, *The English Humourists of the Eighteenth Century.*

Forgettest thou thy bard who, hurried home
From distant lands and, bent by poverty,
Reposed among the quiet scenes he loved
In native Auburn, nor disdain'd to join
The village dancers on the sanded floor?
No poet since hath Nature drawn so close
To her pure bosom as her Oliver.
—LANDOR, WALTER SAVAGE, 1863, *Erin.*

It is his name only, not his dust, that is mingled with the Poets. He lies on the north side of the Temple Church, under a gravestone erected in this century. But "whatever he wrote, he did it better than any other man could do. He deserved a place in Westminster Abbey, and every year he lived would have deserved it better." It had been intended that he should have his burial in the Abbey, but the money which a public funeral would have cost was reserved for his monument. It is on the south wall of the South Transept—in a situation selected by the most artistic, and with an inscription composed by the most learned, of his admirers. Sir Joshua Reynolds fixed the place. Dr. Johnson exemplified, in his inscription, the rule which he had sternly laid down for others, by writing it not in English, but in Latin. In vain was the famous round-robin addressed to him by all his friends.—STANLEY, ARTHUR PENRHYN, 1867–96, *Historical Memorials of Westminster Abbey, p.* 278.

On this occasion [a trip to the Continent] he went as one of a family-party, with Mrs. Horneck, a widow lady, whose acquaintance he had recently made through Sir Joshua Reynolds, and her two daughters, beautiful girls of twenty and eighteen respectively. The elder, for whom Goldsmith had invented the playful name of "Little Comedy," was engaged to be married to a Mr. Bunbury; the younger, Mary Horneck, or "The Jessamy Bride," as Goldsmith called her, was unengaged, and—! Well, who knows? Of no feminine creature, at all events, save this "Jessamy Bride," do we hear, in all Goldsmith's life, so near to him, and in such circumstances, that the world can fancy he was in love with her and can wish that they had wedded. "The Jessamy Bride!" what a suggestion of the jasmine-flower, of gracefulness and white muslin, the very sound of her name! Poor, plain, mean-looking Goldy!—two-and-forty years of age, too!—did he only look and sigh, and know it to be hopeless? . . . When she was engaged, which was not till a year after Goldsmith's death, it was to a Colonel Gwyn, whose wife she became about three years after that. She was alive as late as 1840, having survived Goldsmith sixty-six years. She talked of him fondly to the last.—MASSON, DAVID, 1868, *The Miscellaneous Works of Oliver Goldsmith, Memoir, pp.* xlvii, xlviii.

Of no man who has left so great a reputation, who was possessed of so much wit, who had in so eminent a degree the power to delight, is there so little testimony to his genius to be found outside his books. Though conscious of his own incapacity for conversation, he persisted in talking and blundering. He had little literature, yet his vanity was too great to allow him to disguise his ignorance. He argued when he had no facts; he doubted when there was no room for disbelief; he affirmed where he had not the means to prove. His generosity was attributed to vanity; and even vanity, his friends thought, was too moderate a term to apply to a quality which rendered a man unjust to many that he might gain the applause of a few.—RUSSELL, WILLIAM CLARK, 1871, *The Book of Authors, p.* 279, *note.*

The 4th of April, 1874, was the centennial anniversary of Goldsmith's death; and the recurrence of the date has been made the occasion, in England, of rearing a public monument to him who, after the lapse of a hundred years, is still the best-known and best-beloved writer of his age. . . . Whatever affection we may have for the generous and great-hearted nature of the man, and whatever the admiration his literary masterpieces may command, the world is, after all, chiefly interested in Goldsmith's career as representing the condition of literature and literary men in the middle of the eighteenth century. —TOWLE, GEORGE M., 1874, *Oliver Goldsmith, Appleton's Journal, vol.* 11, *p.* 459.

It is amusing to find the harebrained character of the family repeated in the generation which succeeded Oliver Goldsmith. His nephew, Lieutenant Goldsmith, R. N., in 1824 resolved to try whether an ancient Cornish prophecy was true, that the famous Logan Stone would never be overturned by human strength: and, aided by a party of his seamen, he succeeded in rolling over this load of about seventy tons. The practical joke proved no joke to its perpetrator. He was ordered by the Admiralty to reinstate the Logan Stone in its proper site, and hence incurred debts which he only paid off shortly before his decease.—ROSSETTI, WILLIAM MICHAEL, 1878, *Lives of Famous Poets, p.* 162, *note.*

His name has been used to glorify a sham Bohemianism—a Bohemianism that finds it easy to live in taverns, but does not find it easy, so far as one sees, to write poems like the "Deserted Village." His experiences as an author have been brought forward to swell the cry about neglected genius—that is, by writers who assume their genius in order to prove the neglect. The misery that occasionally befell him during his wayward career has been made the basis of an accusation against society, the English constitution, Christianity—Heaven knows what. It is time to have done with all this nonsense. Goldsmith resorted to the hack-work of literature when everything else had failed him; and he was fairly paid for it. When he did better work, when he "struck for honest fame," the nation gave him all the honor that he could have desired. With an assured reputation, and with ample means of subsistence, he obtained entrance into the most distinguished society then in England—he was made the friend of England's greatest in the arts and literature—and could have confined himself to that society exclusively if he had chosen. His temperament, no doubt, exposed him to suffering; and the exquisite sensitiveness of a man of genius may demand our sympathy; but in far greater measure is our sympathy demanded for the thousands upon thousands of people who, from illness or nervous excitability, suffer from quite as keen a sensitiveness without the consolation of the fame that genius brings.—BLACK, WILLIAM, 1879, *Goldsmith (English Men of Letters)*, p. 150.

As fabled beasts before the lyre
  Fell prone, so want and hunger fled;
The way was free to his desire,
  And he like one with manna fed.
The world, the world, for him was meant;
  Cathedral towers, and Alpine torrents!
He trod a measure as he went,
  And piped and sang his way to Florence!
Great wit and scholar though he be,
  I love, of all his famous days,
This time of simple vagrancy
  Ere youth and bliss had parted ways.
With what a careless heart he strayed,
  Light as the down upon a thistle,
Made other hearts his own, and paid
  His way through Europe with a whistle!
—SPOFFORD, HARRIET PRESCOTT, 1887, *Goldsmith's Whistle, Ballads about Authors*, p. 25.

Near the Temple Church, in a green spot among the buildings, a plain stone laid flat on the turf bears these words: "Here lies Oliver Goldsmith." I believe doubt has been thrown upon the statement that Goldsmith was buried in that place, but, as some poet ought to have written,

Where doubt is disenchantment
'Tis wisdom to believe.

We do not "drop a tear" so often as our Della Cruscan predecessors, but the memory of the author of the "Vicar of Wakefield" stirred my feelings more than a whole army of crusaders would have done.—HOLMES, OLIVER WENDELL, 1887-91, *Our Hundred Days in Europe*, p. 154.

That Boswell had some prejudice against Goldsmith, partly due to jealousy of his intimacy with Johnson, talks of him with an absurd affectation of superiority, and dwells too much on his foibles, is no doubt true. The portrait may be slightly caricatured; but the substantial likeness is not doubtful. It would be as ill-judged to dispute Goldsmith's foibles as to assert that Uncle Toby was above a weakness for his hobby. Goldsmith, no doubt, often blundered in conversation; went on without knowing how he should come off, and displayed ignorance when trying to "get in and shine." Reynolds admitted the fact by explaining it as intended to diminish the awe which insolates an author. On such a question there can be no appeal from the unanimous judgment of contemporaries. But all this is perfectly compatible with his having frequently made the excellent hits reported by Boswell. The statements that he was jealous of the admiration excited by pretty women or puppet-shows, are probably exaggerations or misunderstandings of humorous remarks. But he was clearly vain, acutely sensitive to neglect, and hostile to criticism; fond of splendid garments, as appears from the testimony of his tailors' bills, printed by Prior; and occasionally jealous, so far as jealousy can coexist with absolute guilelessness and freedom from the slightest tinge of malice. His charity seems to have been pushed beyond the limits of prudence, and all who knew him testify to the singular kindliness of his nature. According to Cradock he indulged in gambling. He was certainly not retentive of money; but his extravagance went naturally with an expansive and sympathetic character open to all social impulses.—STEPHEN, LESLIE, 1890, *Dictionary of National Biography*, vol. XXII, p. 93.

A stolid physician, called in consultation in those last days, and seeing his disordered state, asked, "If his mind was at ease?" Mind at ease! Surely a rasping question to put to a man whose pulse is thumping toward the hundreds, whose purse is empty, plans broken up, credit gone, debts crowding him at every point, pains racking him, and the grimy Fleet Prison close by, throwing its shadow straight across his path. No, his mind is *not* at ease; and the pulse does gallop faster and faster, and harder and harder to the end; when, let us hope—ease did come, and—God willing—"Rest for the weary."—MITCHELL, DONALD G., 1895, *English Lands Letters and Kings, Queen Anne and the Georges*, p. 134.

Let him who wishes preach a sermon on this story. But there you have it. "A brother in Ireland who needs help." The brother in London, the brother in America, the brother in Ireland who needs help. All men were his brothers, and those who needed help were first in his mind.

—HUBBARD, ELBERT, 1895, *Little Journeys*, p. 336.

As those who knew Charles Lamb intimately, loved him and delighted in his friendship in spite of his weaknesses, his irregular life and his bad puns, so the personal friends of Oliver Goldsmith were always willing to pass by his many faults and admire and love the great and lovable qualities of the man. . . . Because among the virtues were also strewn some not inconsiderable vices, and because a bad name is less easy to be rid of than a good one, the character of "poor Goldy" has been more or less twisted and turned and warped out of shape during the years, and he is perhaps better known as the "inspired idiot" than as a man of many high and noble qualities.—CABLE, LUCY LEFFINGWELL, 1900, *Literary Biography, The Book Buyer*, vol. 20, p. 395.

POLITE LEARNING
1759

It is the first publication of Goldsmith's in which one need now look for anything of his real mind, and is still well worth reading.—MASSON, DAVID, 1868, *The Miscellaneous Works of Oliver Goldsmith, Memoir*, p. xxvii.

Clouds of adversity were about Goldsmith in April, 1759, when the "Enquiry into the Present State of Polite Learning in Europe" was published by Dodsley, in 12mo., without its author's name upon the title-page. The little book is interesting, as it represents the beginning of Goldsmith's true life as a writer. It was suggested by the fact that in his year of travel he had seen something of Europe. He blunders boldly, speaks of Celtic as the language of the Eddas, and finds in Dante, who "addressed a barbarous people in a method suited to their apprehensions," a strange mixture of good sense and absurdity. "The truth is, he owes most of his reputation to the obscurity of the times in which he lived. As in the land of Benin a man may pass for a prodigy of parts who can read, so in an age of barbarity a small degree of excellence ensures success." Of this first essay of Goldsmith's it may more certainly be said that there is a strange mixture in it of good sense and absurdity. He is right in the main: his sympathies are with the men of independent thought, and he sees clearly the fact that it is a poor time in Literature when criticism leads the way.—MORLEY, HENRY, 1885, *ed., The Vicar of Wakefield, Plays and Poems, Introduction.*

Even when wrong, Goldsmith is generally half-way right; and this is especially true of the critical judgments contained in his first published book. The impudence of "The Enquiry" (1759) is delicious. What this young Irishman, fluting it through Europe some five years before, had *not* learned about the "Condition of Polite Learning," in its principal countries, might fill a ponderous folio. What he did learn, eked out with harmless misstatement, flashes of inspiration, and a clever argument to prove that criticism has always been the foe of letters, managed to fill a respectable duodecimo, and brought him to the notice of publishers and scholars.—GAYLEY, CHARLES MILLS, 1897, *Library of the World's Best Literature, ed. Warner*, vol. XI, p. 6503.

An extraordinary compound of good writing, bad taste, ignorance, mother-wit, and literary originality.—SAINTSBURY, GEORGE, 1898, *A Short History of English Literature*, p. 617.

CITIZEN OF THE WORLD
1762

Goldsmith's "Citizen of the World," like all his works, bears the stamp of the author's mind. It does not "go about to cozen reputation without the stamp of merit." He is more observing, more original, more natural and picturesque than Johnson. His work is written on the model of the "Persian Letters," and contrives to give an abstracted and somewhat perplexing view of things, by proposing foreign prepossessions to our own, and thus stripping objects of their customary disguises. Whether truth is elicited in his collision of contrary absurdities, I do not know; but I confess the process is too ambiguous and full of intricacy to be very amusing to my plain understanding. For light summer reading it is like walking through a garden full of traps and pitfalls. . . . Beau Tibbs, a prominent character in this little work, is the best comic sketch since the time of Addison; unrivalled in his finery, his vanity, and his poverty.—HAZLITT, WILLIAM, 1818, *Lectures on the English Comic Writers, Lecture* v.

If in any of his writings Goldsmith could be truly said to have echoed the measured tone of Johnson, it was probably in his most varied and agreeable "Citizen of the World," a work written at a period when his genius was scarcely yet independent enough to allow of abjuring allegiance to the reigning powers in literature. Yet even here an imitation is but sometimes perceptible, and whenever it occurred was, perhaps, only the involuntary work of the ear taking up the rich and elaborate harmony which it was most accustomed to hear, and which, in those days, was seldom heard unaccompanied by unqualified manifestations of almost rapturous approval. . . . Of that gay and sparkling facetiousness which he himself was wont to admire so highly in other writers, the instances in this collection are innumerable.—BUTLER, PROF., 1836, *Gallery of Illustrious Irishmen, Dublin University Magazine, vol.* 7, *pp.* 44, 45.

One of the most exquisitely written books in any tongue.—MILLER, HUGH, 1850, *Essays, p.* 79.

If Goldsmith had to struggle socially against the disadvantages of poverty, intellectually it cannot be doubted that poverty very amply compensated him. His circumstances forced him to be an unwilling spectator of scenes, and the companion of men of whom affluence or his laziness would have kept him ignorant. His "Citizen of the World," indeed, is an epitome of London life as it was exhibited to the observer of that age.—RUSSELL, WILLIAM CLARK, 1868, *Goldsmith and La Bruyère, The Argosy, p.* 265.

As a satirist he was more like Juvenal than Horace, and we may well doubt whether he would have been able to set off the lucubrations of his Indian with the felicitous sportiveness that still makes the letters, now better known by the name under which they were subsequently published in a collected form, of "The Citizen of the World," the most popular work of their class.—YONGE, CHARLES DUKE, 1872, *Three Centuries of English Literature, p.* 65.

THE TRAVELLER

1765

Goldsmith being mentioned, Johnson observed, that it was long before his merit came to be acknowledged. That he once complained to him, in ludicrous terms of distress, "Whenever I write anything, the publick *make a point* to know nothing about it:" but that his "Traveller" brought him into high reputation. LANGTON. "There is not one bad line in that poem; not one of Dryden's careless verses." SIR JOSHUA. "I was glad to hear Charles Fox say, it was one of the finest poems in the English language." LANGTON. "Why was you glad? You surely had no doubt of this before." JOHNSON. "No, the merit of 'The Traveller' is so well established, that Mr. Fox's praise cannot augment it, nor his censure diminish it."—JOHNSON, SAMUEL, 1778, *Life by Boswell, ed. Hill, vol.* III, *p.* 286.

The partiality of his friends was always against him. It was with difficulty we could give him a hearing. Goldsmith had no settled notions upon any subject. so he talked always at random. It seemed to be his intention to blurt out whatever was in his mind, and see what would become of it. He was angry, too, when catched in an absurdity; but it did not prevent him from falling into another the next minute. I remember Chamier, after talking with him for some time, said, "Well, I do believe he wrote this poem himself: and, let me tell you, that is believing a great deal." Chamier once asked him, what he meant by *slow* the last word in the first line of "The Traveller,"

Remote, unfriended, melancholy, slow.

Did he mean tardiness of locomotion? Goldsmith, who would say something without consideration, answered, "Yes." I was sitting by, and said, "No, Sir; you do not mean tardiness of locomotion; you mean, that sluggishness of mind which comes upon a man in solitude." Chamier believed then that I had written the line as much as if he had seen me write it. Goldsmith, however, was a man, who, whatever he wrote, did it better than any other man could do. He deserved a place in Westminster Abbey, and every year he lived, would have deserved it better. He had, indeed, been at no pains to fill his mind with knowledge. He transplanted it from one place to another; and it did not settle in his mind; so he could not tell what was in his own books.—BOSWELL, JAMES, 1791–93, *Life of Johnson, ed. Hill, vol.* III, *p.* 286.

Neither the ideas nor the imagery are very new or striking, but it is exquisitely versified (in the rhymed couplet); and its ease, elegance, and tenderness have made many passages pass into the memory and language of society. It is peculiarly admirable for the natural succession and connection of the thoughts and images, one seeming to rise unforcedly, and to be evolved, from the other. It is also coloured with a tender haze, so to say, of soft sentiment and pathos, as grateful to the mind as is to the eye the blue dimness that softens the tints of a distant mountain-range. It is a relief to the reader after Pope, in whom the objects stand out with too much sharpness, and in whom we see too much intense activity of the mere intellect at work. Pope is daylight; Goldsmith is moonlight.—SHAW, THOMAS B., 1847, *Outlines of English Literature*, *p.* 275.

To point out the beauties of this poem, would be to comment upon every passage; and, indeed, it may be safely left to the admiration of its myriad readers. Though praised by Johnson and successful at the start, passing in a few months through four editions, it grew, by degrees, like all works of genius, in popular estimation. The best test of its merit is that now, after the extraordinary production of a new race of poets of the highest powers in the nineteenth century, it is as secure of admiration as ever.—DUYCKINCK, EVERT A., 1873, *Portrait Gallery of Eminent Men and Women, vol.* I, *p.* 39.

The very first line of the poem strikes a key-note—there is in it a pathetic thrill of distance, and regret, and longing; and it has the soft musical sound that pervades the whole composition.—BLACK, WILLIAM, 1879, *Goldsmith* (*English Men of Letters*), *p.* 71.

When Johnson prunes or interpolates lines in the "Traveller," we feel as though a woodman's axe was hacking at a most delicate piece of carving.—STEPHEN, LESLIE, 1879, *Samuel Johnson* (*English Men of Letters*), *p.* 78.

Leaves us cold, although there are good lines here and there. . . . We seem to be remote from the new spirit of poetry as we read this rhymed thesis with which the simple-hearted child-like, merry young Irishman made his appearance as a poet. In order to be esteemed he suppressed all naturalness and simplicity, and posed for a philosopher, with a full command of rhetorical devices.—PERRY, THOMAS SERGEANT, 1883, *English Literature in the Eighteenth Century*, *pp.* 396, 397.

VICAR OF WAKEFIELD
1766

The | Vicar of Wakefield. | A Tale. | Supposed to be written by himself. | Sperate miseri, cavete felices. | Salisbury: | Printed by B. Collins, | for F. Newbery, in Pater-Noster-Row, London. | mdcclxvi.—TITLE PAGE TO FIRST EDITION, 1766.

I received one morning a message from poor Goldsmith that he was in great distress, and as it was not in his power to come to me, begging that I would come to him as soon as possible. I sent him a guinea, and promised to come to him directly. I accordingly went as soon as I was drest, and found that his landlady had arrested him for his rent, at which he was in a violent passion. I perceived that he had already changed my guinea, and had got a bottle of Madeira and a glass before him. I put the cork into the bottle, desired he would be calm, and began to talk to him of the means by which he might be extricated. He then told me that he had a novel ready for the press, which he produced to me. I looked into it, and saw its merit; told the landlady I should soon return, and having gone to a bookseller, sold it for sixty pounds. I brought Goldsmith the money, and he discharged his rent, not without rating his landlady in a high tone for having used him so ill.—JOHNSON, SAMUEL, 1763, *Life by Boswell, ed. Hill, vol.* I, *p.* 481.

There are a hundred faults in this thing, and a hundred things might be said to prove them beauties. But it is needless. A book may be amusing with numerous errors, or it may be dull without a single absurdity. The hero of this piece unites in himself the three greatest characters upon earth: he is a priest, a husbandman, and the father of a family. He is drawn as ready to teach, and ready to obey; as simple in affluence, and majestic in adversity. In this age of opulence and refinement, whom can such a character please? Such as are fond of high life, will turn with disdain from the simplicity of his country fireside. Such as mistake ribaldry for humor, will find no wit in his harmless conversation; and such as have been taught to deride religion, will laugh at one whose chief stores of comfort are drawn from futurity.—GOLDSMITH, OLIVER, 1766, *The Vicar of Wakefield, Advertisement.*

I have this very moment finish'd reading a novel call'd the "Vicar of Wakefield." It was wrote by Dr. Goldsmith. His style is rational and sensible, and I knew it again immediately. This book is of a very singular kind—I own I began it with distaste and disrelish, having just read the elegant Letters of Henry,—the beginning of it, even disgusted me,—he mentions his wife with such indifference—such contempt—the contrast of Henry's treatment of Frances struck me—the more so, as it is real—while this tale is fictitious—and then the style of the latter is so elegantly natural, so tenderly manly, so unassumingly rational,—I own I was tempted to thro' the book aside—but there was something in the situation of his family, which if it did not interest me, at least drew me on—and as I proceeded, I was better pleased.—The description of his rural felicity, his simple, unaffected contentment—and family domestic happiness, gave me much pleasure—but still, I was not satisfied, a *something* was wanted to make the book satisfy me—to make me *feel* for the Vicar in ever line he writes, nevertheless, before I was half thro' the first volume, I was, as I may truly express myself, *surprised into tears,* and in the second volume I really sobb'd. It appears to me, to be impossible any person could read this book thro' with a dry eye, at the same time the best part of it is that which turns one's griefs out of doors, to open them to laughter.—BURNEY, FRANCES, 1768, *Early Diary, ed. Ellis, vol.* I, *p.* 12.

We had lately a poet of the same name with the person just mentioned, perhaps of the same family, but by no means of the same character. His writings, in general, are much esteemed; but his poetry is greatly admired. Few tragedies have been read with stronger emotions of pity than the distressful scenes in the "Vicar of Wakefield;" yet we cannot but regret that the author of the "Traveller" should have undervalued his genius so far as to write a romance.—GRANGER, JAMES, 1769–1824, *Biographical History of England, vol.* IV, *p,* 40, *note.*

In the meantime I will hope the best, and endeavour to pursue Oliver Cromwell, through all his crooked paths. I have gone but a short way, my attention having been completely engrossed by a book that has bewitched me for the time; it is the "Vicar of Wakefield," which you must certainly read. Goldsmith puts one in mind of Shakspeare; his narrative is improbable and absurd in many instances, yet all his characters do and say so exactly what might be supposed of them, if so circumstanced, that you willingly resign your mind to the sway of this pleasing enchanter; laugh heartily at improbable incidents, and weep bitterly for impossible distresses. But his personages have all so much nature about them! Keep your gravity if you can, when Moses is going to market with the colt, in his waistcoat of gosling-green; when the Vicar's family make the notable procession on Blackberry and his companion; or, when the fine ladies dazzle the Flamboroughs with taste, Shakspeare, and the musical glasses; not to mention the polemical triumphs of that redoubted monogamist the Vicar. 'Tis a thousand pities Goldsmith had not patience, or art, to conclude suitably a story so happily conducted; but the closing events which rush on so precipitately, are managed with so little skill, and wound up in such a hurried and really bungling manner, that you seem hastily awaked from an affecting dream.—GRANT, ANNE, 1773, *Letters from the Mountains, Letter* XX, *June* 20.

Now Herder came [in 1770?] and together with his great knowledge brought many other aids, and the later publications besides. Among these he announced to us the "Vicar of Wakefield" as an excellent work, with the German translation of which he would make us acquainted by reading it aloud to us himself. . . . The delineation of this character [that of the "excellent Wakefield"] on his course of life through joys and sorrows, the ever-increasing interest of the story, by the combination of the entirely natural with the strange and the singular, make this novel one of the best which has ever been written. . . . I may suppose that my readers know this work, and have it in memory; whoever hears it named for the first time here, as well as he who is induced to read it again, will thank me.

—GOETHE, JOHANN WOLFGANG, 1811–31, *From My Own Life, tr. Oxenford, vol.* I, *bk.* X, *pp.* 368, 369.

His "Vicar of Wakefield" has charmed all Europe. What reader is there in the civilized world who is not the better for the story of the washes which the worthy Dr. Primrose demolished so deliberately with the poker—for the knowledge of the guinea which the Miss Primroses kept unchanged in their pockets,—the adventure of the picture of the Vicar's family, which could not be got into the house,—and that of the Flamborough family, all painted with oranges in their hands—or for the story of the case of shagreen spectacles and the cosmogony?—HAZLITT, WILLIAM, 1818, *Lectures on the English Poets, Lecture* vi.

But whatever defects occur in the tenor of the story, the admirable ease and grace of the narrative, as well as the pleasing truth with which the principal characters are designed, make the "Vicar of Wakefield" one of the most delicious morsels of fictitious composition on which the human mind was ever employed. . . . We read the "Vicar of Wakefield" in youth and in age—we return to it again, and bless the memory of an author who contrives so well to reconcile us to human nature. . . . The wreath of Goldsmith is unsullied; he wrote to exalt virtue and expose vice; and he accomplished his task in a manner which raises him to the highest rank among British authors.—SCOTT, SIR WALTER, 1823, *Oliver Goldsmith.*

Our only English poet of the period was Goldsmith; a pure, clear, genuine spirit, had he been of depth or strength sufficient: his "Vicar of Wakefield" remains the best of all modern Idyls, but it is and was nothing more.—CARLYLE, THOMAS, 1828–69, *Goethe, Miscellanies, vol.* I, *p.* 250.

I lately chanced to fall in with "The Vicar of Wakefield," and felt compelled to read the little book over again, from beginning to end, being not a little affected by the vivid recollection of all that I have owed to the author, for the last seventy years. The influence Goldsmith and Sterne exercised upon me, just at the chief point of my development, cannot be estimated. This high, benevolent irony, this just and comprehensive way of viewing things, this gentleness to all opposition, this equanimity under every change, and whatever else all the kindred virtues may be termed,—such things were a most admirable training for me, and surely these are the sentiments, which in the end lead us back from all the mistaken paths of life. By the way, it is strange that Yorick should incline rather to that which has no Form, and that Goldsmith should be all Form, as I myself aspired to be when the worthy Germans had convinced themselves, that the peculiarity of true humour is to have no Form.—GOETHE, JOHANN WOLFGANG, 1829, *Letter to Zelter, Dec.* 25, *tr. Coleridge, p.* 381.

The sphere in which Goldsmith's powers moved, was never very extensive, but, within it, he discovered all that was good, and shed on it the tenderest lights of his sympathizing genius. No one ever excelled so much as he in depicting amiable follies and endearing weaknesses. His satire makes us at once smile at, and love all that he so tenderly ridicules. The good Vicar's trust in monogomy, his son's purchase of the spectacles, his own sale of his horse, to his solemn admirer at the fair; the blameless vanities of his daughters, and his resignation under his accumulated sorrows, are among the best treasures of memory. The pastoral scenes in this exquitsite tale are the sweetest in the world. The scents of the hay field, and of the blossoming hedge-rows, seem to come freshly to our senses. The whole romance is a tenderly-coloured picture, in little, of human nature's most genial qualities. — TALFOURD, THOMAS NOON, 1842, *On British Novels and Romances, Critical and Miscellaneous Writings, p.* 15.

The fable is indeed one of the worst that ever was constructed. It wants, not merely that probability which ought to be found in a tale of common English life, but that consistency which ought to be found even in the wildest fiction about witches, giants, and fairies.—MACAULAY, THOMAS BABINGTON, 1843, *Oliver Goldsmith, Critical and Historical Essays.*

Look ye now, for one moment, at the deep and delicate humor of Goldsmith. How simple at his touch the venial infirmities and vanity of this good Vicar of Wakefield live lovingly before the mind's eye! How we sympathize with poor Moses in that deep trade of his for the green spectacles!

How all our good wishes for aspiring rusticity thrill for the showman who would let his bear dance only to the genteelest tunes!—WHIPPLE, EDWIN P., 1845–71, *Wit and Humor, Literature and Life, p.* 118.

It had been published little more than four years, when two Germans whose names became afterwards world-famous, one a student at that time in his twentieth, the other a graduate in his twenty-fifth year, met in the city of Strasburg. The younger, Johann Wolfgang Goethe, a law-scholar of the university, with a passion for literature, sought knowledge from the older, Johann Gottfried Herder, for the course on which he was moved to enter. Herder, a severe and masterly, though somewhat cynical critic, laughed at the likings of the young aspirant, and roused him to other aspirations. Producing a German translation of "The Vicar of Wakefield," he read it out aloud to Goethe in a manner which was peculiar to him; and, as the incidents of the little story came forth in his serious, simple voice, . . . a new ideal of letters and of life arose in the mind of the listener. Years passed on; and while that younger student raised up and re-established the literature of his country, and came at last, in his prime and in his age, to be acknowledged for the wisest of modern men, he never ceased throughout to confess what he owed to those old evenings at Strasburg. The strength which can conquer circumstances; the happy wisdom of irony which elevates itself above every object, above fortune and misfortune, good and evil, life and death, and attains to the possession of a poetical world, first visited Goethe in the tone with which Goldsmith's tale is told. The fiction became to him life's first reality. . . . He remembered it, when, at the height of his worldly honour and success, he made his written Life (*Wahrheit und Dichtung*) record what a blessing it had been to him; he had not forgotten it, when, some twenty years ago, standing at the age of eighty-one on the very brink of the grave, he told a friend that in the decisive moment of mental development, "The Vicar of Wakefield" had formed his education, and that he had recently, with unabated delight, "read the charming book again from beginning to end, not a little affected by the lively recollection" of how much he had been indebted to the author seventy [sixty] years before.—FORSTER, JOHN, 1848, *The Life and Times of Oliver Goldsmith, vol.* I, *pp.* 422, 423.

How contradictory it seems that this, one of the most delightful pictures of home and homefelt happiness should be drawn by a homeless man; that the most amiable picture of domestic virtue and all the endearments of the married state should be drawn by a bachelor, who had been severed from domestic life almost from boyhood; that one of the most tender, touching, and affecting appeals on behalf of female loveliness should have been made by a man whose deficiency in all the graces of person and manner seemed to mark him out for a cynical disparager of the sex.—IRVING, WASHINGTON, 1849, *Oliver Goldsmith, p.* 191.

With that sweet story of the "Vicar of Wakefield," he has found entry into every castle and every hamlet in Europe. Not one of us, however busy or hard, but once or twice in our lives, has passed an evening with him, and undergone the charm of his delightful music.—THACKERAY, WILLIAM MAKEPEACE, 1853, *The English Humourists of the Eighteenth Century.*

His "Vicar of Wakefield" is "a prose idyl," somewhat spoilt by phrases too well written, but at bottom as homely as a Flemish picture.—TAINE, H. A., 1871, *History of English Literature, tr. Van Laun, vol.* II, *bk.* iii, *ch.* vi, *p.* 183.

Goldsmith alone amongst our later poets has left us a portrait that deserves to compare with one by Chaucer. It is that ever-charming portrait of the Village Preacher, a not unworthy *pendant* of the "Parson," by which, indeed, it was indirectly inspired. He has given us duplicates of it in prose in the persons of the Vicar of Wakefield and of the Man in Black. There is a tradition that he who sat to Chaucer for the Parson was no other than Wicliffe. It seems fairly certain that Goldsmith's original was his own father. That was the one figure he could draw with the utmost skill, the deepest feeling.—HALES, JOHN W., 1873, *Notes and Essays on Shakespeare, p.* 67.

Dante exhibits great fertility in situations and conjunctions; but, besides that many of them were ready to his hand, this kind of inventiveness denotes of itself no fine creative faculty. It is the necessary equipment of the voluminous novelist. In this facility and abundance Goldsmith could not have coped with James and Bulwer; and yet the "Vicar of Wakefield" (not to go so high as "Tristram Shandy" and "Don Quixote") is worth all their hundred volumes of tales put together.—CALVERT, GEORGE H., 1875, *Essays Æsthetical*, p. 120.

And the wonder is that Goldsmith of all men should have produced such a perfect picture of domestic life. What had his own life been but a moving about between garret and tavern, between bachelor's lodgings and clubs? Where had he seen—unless, indeed, he looked back through the mist of years to the scenes of his childhood—all this gentle government, and wise blindness; all this affection, and consideration, and respect? There is as much human nature in the character of the Vicar alone as would have furnished any fifty of the novels of that day, or of this.—BLACK, WILLIAM, 1879, *Goldsmith* (*English Men of Letters*), p. 82.

But to return to our sketch of English fiction, it is now delightful to find a snowdrop springing from this muck of the classics. In the year 1766 appeared Goldsmith's "Vicar of Wakefield."—LANIER, SIDNEY, 1881, *The English Novel*, p. 189.

No novelist has more deeply imbued his work with his own genius and spirit, and none have had a more beneficent genius, nor a more beautiful spirit to impart than the author of "The Deserted Village." The exquisite style, the delicate choice of words, the amiability of sentiment, so peculiarly his own, and so well suited to express the simple beauty of his thoughts, gave a charm to the work which familiarity can only endear.—TUCKERMAN, BAYARD, 1882, *A History of English Prose Fiction*, p. 238.

Dr. Primrose and his wife, Olivia and Sophia, Moses with his white stockings and black ribbon, Mr. Burchell and his immortal "Fudge," My Lady Blarney and Miss Carolina Wilhelmina Amelia Skeggs—have all become household words. The family picture that could not be got into the house when it was painted; the colt that was sold for a gross of green spectacles; the patter about Sanchoniathon, Manetho, Berosus, and Ocellus Lucanus, with the other humours of Mr. Ephraim Jenkinson—these are part of our stock speech and current illustration. Whether the book is still much read it would be hard to say, for when a work has, so to speak, entered into the blood of a literature, it is often more recollected and transmitted by oral tradition than actually studied. But in spite of the inconsistencies of the plot, and the incoherencies of the story, it remains, and will continue to be, one of the first of our English classics. Its sweet humanity, its simplicity, its wisdom and its common-sense, its happy mingling of character and Christianity, will keep it sweet long after more ambitious, and in many respects abler, works have found their level with the great democracy of the forgotten.—DOBSON, AUSTIN, 1888, *Life of Oliver Goldsmith*, p. 118.

"The Vicar of Wakefield" is remarkable for its single characters, remarkable for its incidents of pathos and humour, but has no substantial development of plot. The tangential property of Goldsmith's mind, the happy Irish inconsequence, that led him in his "Animated Nature" to include among the varieties of the human race dwarfs and giants, mummies and waxworks, because he had seen some of these in a show at Chelsea, made him averse to all rigid or reasoned structure in his novel. He is the gayest and wisest of companions on the road, all the more because he is unaccustomed to a destination.—RALEIGH, WALTER, 1894, *The English Novel*, p. 208.

When his landlady had Goldsmith arrested for debt, the only possible asset through which his friend Johnson could hope to extricate him was the manuscript of a tale which Goldsmith had written, but had never attempted to publish. This Johnson took to a publisher and advised him to buy it for sixty pounds. What would have been poor Goldsmith's emotion could he have looked into the future and witnessed a recent event which took place in Germany: the editor of a widely circulated journal there took the votes of his subscribers as to their favourite book, and this same tale of Goldsmith's—"The Vicar of Wakefield"—came in at the top of the poll.—KEPPEL, FREDERICK, 1894,

Sir Joshua Reynolds, Scribner's Magazine, vol. 15, *p.* 96.

When I first read the "Vicar of Wakefield" (for I have since read it several times, and hope yet to read it many times), I found its persons and incidents familiar, and so I suppose I must have heard it read. It is still for me, one of the most modern novels: that is to say, one of the best. It is unmistakably good up to a certain point, and then unmistakably bad, but with always good enough in it to be forever imperishable. Kindness and gentleness are never out of fashion; it is these in Goldsmith which make him our contemporary, and it is worth the while of any young person presently intending deathless renown to take a little thought of them. They are the source of all refinement, and I do not believe that the best art in any kind exists without them. The style is the man, and he cannot hide himself in any garb of words so that we shall not know somehow what manner of man he is within it; his speech betrayeth him, not only as to his country and his race, but more subtly yet as to his heart, and the loves and hates of his heart. As to Goldsmith, I do not think that a man of harsh and arrogant nature, of wordly and selfish soul, could ever have written his style, and I do think that, in far greater measure that criticism has recognized, his spiritual quality, his essential friendliness, expressed itself in the literary beauty that wins the heart as well as takes the fancy in his work.—HOWELLS, WILLIAM DEAN, 1895, *My Literary Passions, p.* 16.

It made its way, not because Goldsmith had written it, but by reason of its domesticity and the simple idyllic charm which attracts in any age. The story of good prevailing over evil as he told it was new-old, and the tale of sure reward for patient submission in adversity is as ancient as the Book of Job. Its motive is to enforce the truth that heroism of soul may rise triumphant over the vanities and trials of daily life.—RIGGS, JAMES GILBERT, 1896, *ed., The Vicar of Wakefield, Introduction, p.* 19.

The first edition of Goldsmith's "Vicar of Wakefield," 1766, a quarter of a century ago could have been purchased for £5; eight or nine years ago almost twice that sum would not have been considered excessive; in 1891 a copy sold at Sotheby's for £90, and in May 1892 another at the same place went to £94.—ROBERTS, W., 1896, *Rare Books and Their Prices, p.* 25.

Goldsmith's "Vicar of Wakefield," 1766, first edition. Mansfield-Mackenzie (1889), £67. T. B. T. Hildyard (1895), £56 (original calf). Alfred Crampton (1896), £65 (morocco extra by Bedford). Rare Books and MSS. (Sotheby, March 1897), £60 (original calf).—WHEATLEY, HENRY B., 1898, *Prices of Books, p.* 247.

Richardson, Fielding, Smollett, Walpole, had started English fiction upon many lines, dealing with life under the most varied aspects and from widely different points of view. But it was reserved for Goldsmith to initiate the idyllic novel—to portray with mingled humour and pathos the lives and doings of simple country folk, to touch the actualities of their existence with the transfiguring power of the poet, and to fill his descriptions with deep and genuine feeling, born of closest sympathy with the things of which he wrote. Thus, instead of following the course which others had marked out, he established a fresh point of departure. To recognize this is to appreciate something of his originality, and to understand why his work occupies a place by itself among the great novels of the time.—HUDSON, WILLIAM HENRY, 1898, *ed. Goldsmith's Vicar of Wakefield, Introduction, p.* xxii.

As a humorist, Goldsmith set himself squarely against his contemporaries, and, with what little gall there was in him, expressly against Sterne. He never twitches at our nerves with the sentimental scene, but relieves his deepest pathos with a kindly irony. To him there is no humor in the dash, the asterisk, the wink, and the riddle; his sentences always have their logic and their rhythm. He despises ribaldry, and implies, with a grain of truth, that Sterne is only a second Tom D'Urfey, one of the most profane of Restoration wits.—CROSS, WILBUR L., 1899, *The Development of the English Novel, p.* 80.

Little enough was Goldsmith like his own hero, the Vicar of Wakefield, save only that both were lovable; and in no sense is "The Vicar of Wakefield" an autobiography. It is an imperishable tale of the misfortunes of that compound of wisdom and simplicity, of vanity and unselfishness, of shrewdness and benevolence—the Vicar of Wakefield.—STODDARD, FRANCIS HOVEY, 1900, *The Evolution of the English Novel, p.* 48.

THE HERMIT
1766

The best things in it are some neat turns of moral and pathetic sentiment, given with a simple conciseness that fits them for being retained in the memory. As to the story, it has little fancy or contrivance to recommend it.—AIKIN, JOHN, 1805? *An Essay on the Poetry of Goldsmith.*

Any reader of the ballad who pleases may make a wry face, along with Kenrick of Grub street, at the insipidity of Dr. Goldsmith's negus, and may seek elsewhere some livelier liquor. We feel differently, for we have heard this ballad in the open air from Mr. Burchell's manly throat, while Sophia in her new ribbons languished in the hay. To us, the love-lorn stranger is an eighteenth-century cousin—and so perhaps a little modish—of Rosalind and Viola. Those earlier disguisers bore themselves no doubt more gallantly, with more of saucy archness; but none was more sweetly discovered than Goldsmith's pretty pilgrim by her mantling blush, and bashful glance, and rising breast.—DOWDEN, EDWARD, 1880, *The English Poets, ed. Ward, vol.* III, *p.* 372.

At most we can allow it accomplishment and ease. But its sweetness has grown a little insipid, and its simplicity, to eyes unannointed with eighteenth-century sympathy, borders perilously upon the ludicrous.—DOBSON, AUSTIN, 1888, *Life of Oliver Goldsmith, p.* 108.

THE DESERTED VILLAGE
1770

What true and pretty pastoral images has Goldsmith in his "Deserted Village!" They beat all: Pope, and Phillips, and Spenser too, in my opinion;—That is, in the pastoral, for I go no farther.—BURKE, EDMUND, 1780, *Letter to Shackleton, May* 6; *Correspondence, vol.* II, *p.* 347.

"The Deserted Village" is a poem far inferior to "The Traveller," though it contains many beautiful passages. I do not enter into its pretensions to skill in poetical economy, though, in that respect, it contains a strange mixture of important truths. My business is with the poetry. Its inferiority to its predecessor ["The Traveller"] arises from its comparative want of compression, as well as of force and novelty of imagery. Its tone of melancholy is more sickly, and some of the descriptions which have been most praised are marked by all the poverty and flatness, and indeed are peopled with the sort of comic and grotesque figures, of a Flemish landscape.—BRYDGES, SIR SAMUEL EDGERTON, 1808, *Life of Goldsmith, Censura Literaria.*

A little poem, which we passionately received into our circle, allowed us from henceforward to think of nothing else. Goldsmith's "Deserted Village" necessarily delighted every one at that grade of cultivation, in that sphere of thought. Not as living and active, but as a departed, vanished existence was described, all that one so readily looked upon, that one loved, prized, sought passionately in the present, to take part in it with the cheerfulness of youth. Highdays and holidays in the country, church consecrations and fairs, the solemn assemblage of the elders under the village linden-tree, supplanted in its turn by the lively delight of youth in dancing, while the more educated classes show their sympathy. How seemly did these pleasures appear, moderated as they were by an excellent country pastor, who understood how to smooth down and remove all that went too far,—that gave occasion to quarrel and dispute. Here again we found an honest Wakefield, in his well-known circle, yet no longer in his living bodily form, but as a shadow recalled by the soft mournful tones of the elegiac poet. The very thought of this picture is one of the happiest possible, when once the design is formed to evoke once more an innocent past with a graceful melancholy. And in this kindly endeavour, how well has the Englishman succeeded in every sense of the word! I shared the enthusiasm for this charming poem with Gotter, who was more felicitous than myself with the translation undertaken by us both; for I had too painfully tried to imitate in our language the delicate significance of the original, and thus had well agreed with single passages, but not with the whole.—GOETHE, JOHANN WOLFGANG, 1811–31, *From My Own Life, tr. Oxenford, bk.* xii, *vol.* I, *p.* 474.

In Goldsmith's "Deserted Village,"

much entertainment is afforded, and compassion excited, by the inimitable skill and pathos of the author in displaying the characters, pastimes, wrongs, and sufferings of the natives of "Auburn:" but still the reader *condescends* to be pleased, or to pity; and the poet is rather their advocate than their neighbour, or one of themselves: there is little of *fellow*-feeling in the case.—MONTGOMERY, JAMES, 1833, *Lectures on General Literature, Poetry, etc., p.* 165.

The "Deserted Village" is, of all Goldsmith's productions, unquestionably the favorite. It carries back the mind to the early seasons of life, and re-asserts the power of unsophisticated tastes. Hence, while other poems grow stale, this preserves its charm. . . . So thoroughly did the author revise the "Deserted Village," that not a single original line remained. The clearness and warmth of his style is, to my mind, as indicative of Goldsmith's truth, as the candor of his character or the sincerity of his sentiments. It has been said of Pitt's elocution, that it had the effect of impressing one with the idea that the man was greater than the orator. A similar influence it seems to me is produced by the harmonious versification and elegant diction of Goldsmith.—TUCKERMAN, HENRY THEODORE, 1846–51, *Thoughts on the Poets, pp.* xxii, xxiii.

The sweet and tender seriousness of the "Deserted Village" is relieved by touches of humor, as well as heightened by touches of pathos; if sorrow disturb the heart, it is more than half consoled by the thought, that gentle or happy natures will find or make for themselves such simple and unexacting pleasures, wherever their lot may be cast. And then the personality which we cannot help attaching to this poem, the reflex of Goldsmith's own character, private history, cherished opinions and tastes, and secret sorrow—what interest do they impart to every line of it! Spite of all the controversy about the identity of Auburn and Lissoy, we shall always feel that the former is the scene of the poet's early life, and the haven towards which, amid the storms of his struggling existence, his eyes were ever turned.—KIRKLAND, C. M., 1850, *Irving's Life of Goldsmith, North American Review, vol.* 70, *p.* 283.

It is in "The Deserted Village," his best known poem, that he has most fully shown the grace and truthfulness with which he could touch natural scenes. Lissoy, an Irish village where the poet's brother had a living, is said to have been the original from which he drew. In the poem, the church which crowns the neighboring hill, the mill, the brook, the hawthorn-tree, are all taken straight from the outer world. The features of Nature and the works of man, the parsonage, the school-house, the ale-house, all harmonize in one picture, and though the feeling of desolation must needs be a melancholy one, yet it is wonderfully varied and relieved by the uncolored faithfulness of the pictures from Nature and the kindly humor of those of man. It is needless to quote from a poem which every one knows so well. The verse of Pope is not the best vehicle for rural description, but it never was employed with greater grace and transparency than in "The Deserted Village." In that poem there is fine feeling for Nature, in her homely forms, and truthful descriptions of these, but beyond this Goldsmith does not venture. The pathos of the outward world in its connection with man is there, but no reference to the meaning of Nature in itself, much less any question of its relation to the Divine Being and a supersensible world.—SHAIRP, JOHN CAMPBELL, 1877, *On Poetic Interpretation of Nature, p.* 212.

In English literature there is nothing more thoroughly English than these writings produced by an Irishman.—BLACK, WILLIAM, 1879, *Goldsmith* (*English Men of Letters*), *p.* 123.

The matter is of more importance to him than the manner; and at the same time his ear for music, and familiar acquaintance with good models have enabled him to go on without jarring the reader's ear with crude or false lines. Figures of speech are introduced in sufficient variety, but always from well-understood sources, and never expressed in such a way as to cause any effort in following them or their application. We are not challenged to stop and admire new and glittering constructions, nor ingeniously improvised words. Common speech affords the most of his material; and thus his lines pass again into common speech, and enrich the thought of thousands who are unaffected by the more ambitious masters of verse. He is strikingly free from foreign airs, uses no metrical variations caught from the Continent, and yet, by skilfully varying his pauses, avoids monotony throughout. He has a poet's mastery of epithet. . . . "The Deserted Village" deserves our careful attention from the deep feeling in its thought, the music in its lines, and its entire freedom from affectation. It stands for itself, a graceful example of true English literature.—GREGORY, WARREN FENNO, 1894, *ed. Oliver Goldsmith's Traveller and Deserted Village, pp.* 43–44.

We do not read "The Deserted Village" for its Political Economy: we read it for its idyllic sweetness; for its portraits of the village preacher, of the village schoolmaster, of the country inn; for its pathetic description of the poor emigrants; for the tender and noble feeling with which Goldsmith closes the poem in his Farewell to Poetry.—SYLE, L. DUPONT, 1894, *From Milton to Tennyson, Notes, p.* 70.

HISTORY OF ENGLAND
1771

I have published, or Davies has published for me, an "Abridgment of the History of England," for which I have been a good deal abused in the newspapers, for betraying the liberties of the people. God knows I had no thought for or against liberty in my head; my whole aim being to make up a book of a decent size, that, as Squire Richard says, *would do no harm to nobody.* However, they set me down as an arrant Tory, and consequently an honest man. When you come to look at any part of it, you'll say that I am a sore Whig.—GOLDSMITH, OLIVER, 1772, *Letter to Bennet Langton, Sept.* 7.

The History on the whole, however, was well received; some of the critics declared that English history had never before been so usefully, so elegantly, and agreeably epitomized; "and, like his other historical writings, it has kept its ground" in English literature.—IRVING, WASHINGTON, 1849, *Oliver Goldsmith, p.* 301.

As a historian, Goldsmith accomplishes all at which he aims. He does not promise much, but he does more than he promises. He takes, it is true, facts which had been already collected, but he shapes them with an art that is all his own.—GILES, HENRY, 1850, *Lectures and Essays, vol.* I, *p.* 235.

In Goldsmith's "History of England" no mention is made of the great plague or the great fire of London.—KEDDIE, WILLIAM, 1854, *Cyclopædia of Literary and Scientific Anecdote, p.* 272.

RETALIATION
1774

In fact the poem, for its graphic truth, its nice discrimination, its terse good sense, and its shrewd knowledge of the world, must have electrified the club almost as much as the first appearance of "The Traveller," and let them still deeper into the character and talents of the man they had been accustomed to consider as their butt. "Retaliation," in a word, closed his accounts with the club, and balanced all his previous deficiencies.—IRVING, WASHINGTON, 1849, *Oliver Goldsmith, p.* 405.

Plutarch, as a character-painter, is a dauber to Oliver Goldsmith; nor has Reynolds himself, in those portraits of his in which, according to Burke, he has combined the invention of history and the amenity of landscape, "excelled these little sketches, where the artist not only draws the literal features, but gives at once the inner soul and the future history of his subjects." The character of Garrick and Burke have never been surpassed, and have been approached only by Lowell, in his "Fable for Critics"—a poem formed upon the model (and the motive, too), of "Retaliation."—GILFILLAN, GEORGE, 1854, *ed., The Poetical Works of Goldsmith, Collins and T. Warton, p.* xxv.

"Retaliation" is the most mischievous, and the most playful, the friendliest and the faithfulest of satires. How much better we know Garrick because Goldsmith has shown him to us in his acting off the stage! And do we as often think of Reynolds in any attitude as in that of smiling non-listener to the critical coxcombs.

"When they talked of their Raphaels, Correggios and stuff,
He shifted his trumpet and only took snuff."

Would that portraits of Johnson and Boswell had been added!—DOWDEN, EDWARD, 1880, *The English Poets, ed. Ward, vol.* III, *p.* 372.

ANIMATED NATURE
1774

Distress drove Goldsmith upon undertakings, neither congenial with his studies, nor worthy of his talents. I remember him, when in his chamber in the Temple, he shewed me the beginning of his "Animated Nature;" it was with a sigh, such as genius draws, when hard necessity diverts it from its bent to drudge for bread, and talk of birds and beasts and creeping things, which Pidcock's showman would have done as well. Poor fellow, he hardly knew an ass from a mule, nor a turkey from a goose, but when he saw it on the table.—CUMBERLAND, RICHARD, 1806, *Memoirs, Written by Himself, vol.* I, *p.* 352.

The descriptions and definitions are often loose and inaccurate, and the chief defect of the work arises from its being a mere compilation from books. It has therefore none of the freshness of personal observation; nothing which awakens the curiosity and inspires the confidence of the reader, as in the delightful pages of White, Montague, or Rennie.—MITFORD, JOHN, 1831, *Life of Goldsmith.*

Of all his hack labours for booksellers that which seems to have been written with the greatest good-will. The work contains many exquisite passages, and as it is not very probable that it will ever be reprinted *in extenso,* those passages in which the writer appears to the greatest advantage richly deserve to find a place in any edition of his writings.—CUNNINGHAM, PETER, 1853, *ed., The Works of Oliver Goldsmith, Preface, vol.* I, *p.* viii.

COMEDIES

Goldsmith in vain tried to stem the torrent by opposing a barrier of low humour, and dulness and absurdity, more dull and absurd than English sentimental Comedy itself.—PINKERTON, JOHN (ROBERT HERON), 1785, *Letters of Literature, p.* 47.

Goldsmith was, perhaps, in relation to Sheridan, what Vanburgh was to Congreve. His comedies turn on an extravagance of intrigue and disguise, and so far belong to the Spanish school. But the ease of his humorous dialogue, and the droll, yet true conception of the characters, made sufficient amends for an occasional stretch in point of probability. If all who draw on the spectators for indulgence, were equally prepared to compensate by a corresponding degree of pleasure, they would have little occasion to complain.—SCOTT, SIR WALTER, 1814–23, *The Drama.*

His two admirable Comedies of "The Good Natured Man," and "She Stoops to Conquer," are the greenest spots in the Dramatic waste of the period of which we are speaking. They are worthy of the Author of "The Vicar of Wakefield;" and to praise them more highly is impossible. Wit without licentiousness; Humour with out extravagance; brilliant and elegant dialogue; and forcible but natural delineation of character, are the excellencies with which his pages are prodigally strewn.—NEELE, HENRY, 1827, *Lectures on English Poetry, p.* 152.

Goldsmith's immediate predecessors were the playwrights of the sentimental school. His literary taste and keen sense of humour revolted against their general badness and their bathos, and he went back for models to the dramatists of the Restoration,—a term, be it observed, which has much more than a chronological significance,—and both Goldsmith and Sheridan may in a sense be taken to be the last representatives of the great Restoration School of Comedy.—CRAWFURD, OSWALD, 1883, *ed., English Comic Dramatists, p.* 214.

THE GOOD-NATURED MAN
1768

The town will not bear Goldsmith's low humour, and justly. It degrades his Good natur'd Man, whom they were taught to pity and have a sort of respect for, into a low buffoon; and, what is worse, into a falsifier, a character unbecoming a gentleman.—HOADLY, JOHN, 1768, *Letter to Garrick, Garrick Correspondence, vol.* I, *p.* 506.

Is labored and vaguely portrayed.—EMERY, FRED PARKER, 1891, *Notes on English Literature, p.* 78.

Honey-wood (the Good-Natured Man) is not a successful bit of painting; it is impossible to feel that there is reality or naturalness in the character. As the leading lover, also, Honey-wood should exact our sympathy in his misfortunes, instead of which he represses it. When he entertains the idea of giving up the woman he loves to such a creature as Lofty, we are offended with him, but later on, when he actually pleads for his rival to Miss Richland (she taking it for his own declaration), his conduct provokes disgust. Goldsmith seems to have felt that the character was not satisfactory, if we may judge by the attempts made to justify it, in the speeches at the end of the play given to Sir William Honey-wood. As it stands, Croaker (originally played by Shuter) is the best acting part in the piece. Collaboration would not have been easy with Goldsmith, but it might in many respects have improved "The Good-Natured Man."—ARCHER, FRANK, 1892, *How to Write a Good Play, p.* 83.

SHE STOOPS TO CONQUER
1773

Dr. Goldsmith has written a Comedy—no, it is the lowest of all farces. It is not the subject I condemn, though very vulgar, but the execution. The drift tends to no moral, no edification of any kind. The situations, however, are well imagined, and make one laugh, in spite of the grossness of the dialogue, the forced witticisms, and total improbability of the whole plan and conduct. But what disgusts me most is, that though the characters are very low, and aim at a lower humour, not one of them says a sentence that is natural or marks any character at all. It is set up in opposition to sentimental comedy, and is as bad as the worst of them.—WALPOLE, HORACE, 1773, *To Rev. William Mason, May* 27; *Letters, ed. Cunningham, vol.* V, *p.* 467.

The whole company pledged themselves to the support of the ingenious poet, and faithfully kept their promise to him. In fact he needed all that could be done for him, as Mr. Colman, then manager of Covent Garden theatre, protested against the comedy, when as yet he had not struck upon a name for it. Johnson at length stood forth in all his terrors as champion for the piece, and backed by us his clients and retainers demanded a fair trial. Colman again protested, but, with that salve for his own reputation, liberally lent his stage to one of the most eccentric productions that ever found its way to it, and "She Stoops to Conquer" was put into rehearsal. We were not over-sanguine of success, but perfectly determined to struggle hard for our author: we accordingly assembled our strength at the Shakespear Tavern in a considerable body for an early dinner, where Samuel Johnson took the chair at the head of a long table, and was the life and soul of the corps: the poet took post silently by his side with the Burkes, Sir Joshua Reynolds, Fitzherbert, Caleb Whitefoord and a phalanx of North-British pre-determined applauders, under the banner of Major Mills, all good men and true. Our illustrious president was in inimitable glee, and poor Goldsmith that day took all his raillery as patiently and complacently as my friend Boswell would have done any day, or every day of his life. In the meantime we did not forget our duty, and though we had a better comedy going, in which Johnson was chief actor, we betook ourselves in good time to our separate and allotted posts, and waited the awful drawing up of the curtain. As our stations were pre-concerted, so were our signals for plaudits arranged and determined upon in a manner, that gave every one his cue where to look for them, and how to follow them up. . . . All eyes were upon Johnson, who sate in a front row of a side box, and when he laughed everybody thought themselves warranted to roar. . . . We carried our play through, and triumphed not only over Colman's judgment, but our own.—CUMBERLAND, RICHARD, 1806, *Memoirs, vol.* I, *pp.* 366, 368, 369.

That delightful comedy, "She Stoops to Conquer," would indeed deserve a volume, and is the best specimen of what an English comedy should be. It illustrates excellently what has been said as to the necessity of the plot depending on the characters, rather than the characters depending on the plot, as the fashion is at present. . . . What a play! We never tire of it. How rich in situations, each the substance of a whole play! At the very first sentence the stream of humour begins to flow.—FITZGERALD, PERRY, 1870, *Principles of Comedy and Dramatic Effect, p.* 91, 98.

He at least lived long enough to witness the brilliant beginning of a dramatic triumph which has lasted till our day, and which only one other comedy written since, "The School for Scandal," can be said to have rivaled. Macaulay calls it "an incomparable farce in five acts;" its rollicking drollery and sparkling wit are fitting to amuse all generations, and its dramatic skill is a victory of true inventive genius.—TOWLE, GEORGE M., 1874, *Oliver Goldsmith, Appleton's Journal, vol.* 11, *p.* 461.

Night fell, and [Goldsmith] found himself at Ardagh, half-way on his journey. Casting about for information as to "the best house," that is to say, the best inn in the neighborhood, he unluckily lit upon one Cornelius Kelly, who had been fencing-master to the Marquis of Gramby, but, what is more to the purpose, was a confirmed wag and practical joker. Amused with Oliver's schoolboy swagger, he gravely directed him to the mansion of the local magnate, Squire Featherston. To Squire Featherston's the lad accordingly repaired, and called lustily for some one to take his horse. Being ushered into the presence of the supposed landlord and his family, he ordered a good supper, invited the rest to share it, treated them to a bottle or two of wine, and finally retired to rest, leaving careful injunctions that a hot cake should be prepared for his breakfast on the morrow. His host, who was a humorist, and moreover knew something of his visitor's father, never undeceived him; and it was not until he quitted the supposed inn next day that he learned, to his confusion, that he had been entertained at a private house. Thus early in Oliver Goldsmith's career was rehearsed the first sketch of the successful comedy of "She Stoops to Conquer."—DOBSON, AUSTIN, 1888, *Life of Oliver Goldsmith*, p. 18.

Is the best society comedy in our language.—JOHNSON, CHARLES F., 1900, *English and American Literature*, p. 282.

GENERAL

We do not mean to insinuate that his lucubrations ["The Bee"] are so void of merit as not to deserve the public attention. On the contrary, we must confess ourselves to have found no inconsiderable entertainment in their perusal. His stile is not the worst, and his manner is agreeable enough, in our opinion, however it may have failed of exciting universal admiration. The truth is, most of his subjects are already sufficiently worn out.—KENRICK, WILLIAM, 1760, *Monthly Review*, *vol.* 22, *p.* 39.

The trading wits endeavour to attain,
Like booksellers, the world's first idol—gain:
For this they puff the heavy Goldsmith's line,
And hail his sentiment, though trite, divine.
—CHATTERTON, THOMAS, 1770, *The Art of Puffing by a Bookseller's Journeyman.*

Goldsmith being mentioned: JOHNSON. "It is amazing how little Goldsmith knows. He seldom comes where he is not more ignorant than any one else." SIR JOSHUA REYNOLDS. "Yet there is no man whose company is more liked." JOHNSON. "To be sure, Sir. When people find a man of the most distinguished abilities as a writer, their inferiour while he is with them, it must be highly gratifying to them. What Goldsmith comically says of himself is very true,—he always gets the better when he argues alone; meaning, that he is master of a subject in his study, and can write well upon it; but when he comes into company, grows confused, and unable to talk. Take him as a poet, his 'Traveller' is a very fine performance; ay, and so is his 'Deserted Village,' were it not sometimes too much the echo of his Traveller.' Whether, indeed, we take him as a poet,—as a comick writer,—or as an historian, he stands in the first class."—JOHNSON, SAMUEL, 1773, *Life by Boswell, ed. Hill, vol.* II, *p.* 270.

No man had the art of displaying with more advantage as a writer, what ever literary acquisitions he made. *"Nihil quod tetigit non ornavit."* His mind resembled a fertile, but thin soil. There was a quick, but not a strong vegetation, of whatever chanced to be thrown upon it. No deep root could be struck. The oak of the forest did not grow there; but the elegant shrubbery and the fragrant parterre appeared in gay succession.—BOSWELL, JAMES, 1791–93, *Life of Johnson, ed. Hill, vol.* I, *p.* 477.

What can be more exquisite than the poetry of Goldsmith, whose versification is, without any exception, more sweet and harmonious than that of any other poet, and whose sentiments and imagery are equally beautiful and pathetic.—DRAKE, NATHAN, 1798–1820, *Literary Hours, No.* xxix, *vol.* II, *p.* 118.

Goldsmith was the most natural of cultivated poets. Though he retained the cadence, he softened and varied the style of his master, Pope. His ideas are often common-place and his language slovenly; but his simplicity and tenderness will always continue to render him one of the most delightful of our poets. Whatever excellence he possesses is genuine, neither the result of affectation nor even of effort; few writers have so much poetry with so little glare. His prose is of a pure school, but not of sufficient elegance to atone for the substantial defects of his writings, except indeed in one charming novel, in which if he had more abstained from common-place declamation, less indulged his national propensity to broad farce, and not at last hurried his personages out of their difficulties with improbable confusion, he would have reached nearly the highest rank in that species of composition.—MACKINTOSH, SIR JAMES, 1811, *Journal, Dec.* 22, *Life, ed. Mackintosh, vol.* II, *p.* 177.

Goldsmith wrote with perfect elegance and beauty, in a style of mellow tenderness and elaborate simplicity. He had the harmony of Pope without his quaintness, and his selectness of diction without his coldness and eternal vivacity.—JEFFREY, FRANCIS LORD, 1816, *Jonathan Swift, Edinburgh Review, vol.* 27, *p.* 7.

His whole manner has a still depth of feeling and reflection, which gives back the image of nature unruffled and minutely. He has no redundant thoughts or false transports; but seems, on every occasion, to have weighed the impulse to which he surrendered himself. Whatever ardour or casual felicities he may have thus sacrificed, he gained a high degree of purity and self-possession. His chaste pathos makes him an insinuating moralist, and throws a charm of Claude-like softness over his descriptions of homely objects that would seem only fit to be the subjects of Dutch painting. But his quiet enthusiasm leads the affections to humble things without a vulgar association; and he inspires us with a fondness to trace the simplest reflections of Auburn, till we count the furniture of its ale-house and listen to

"The varnish'd clock, that tick'd behind the door."

—CAMPBELL, THOMAS, 1819, *Specimens of the British Poets.*

He was a friend to virtue, and in his most playful pages never forgets what is due to it. A gentleness, delicacy, and purity of feeling, distinguishes whatever he wrote, and bears a correspondence to the generosity of a disposition which knew no bounds but his last guinea. It was an attribute almost essential to such a temper, that he wanted the proper guards of firmness and decision, and permitted, even when aware of their worthlessness, the intrusions of cunning and of effrontery.—SCOTT, SIR WALTER, 1823, *Oliver Goldsmith.*

Goldsmith did everything happily.—COLERIDGE, SAMUEL TAYLOR, 1823, *Table Talk, ed. Ashe, Jan.* 4, *p.* 22.

Goldsmith is, perhaps, the only English poet who can claim the exclusive merit of writing from the heart alone; not that he has not written pieces of wit and humour, but that his principal poems are the pure offspring of feeling and passion. It was, however, a subdued passion, for there is more pathos in Eloisa to Abelard, than in any of his productions, or in any other production of the English language. . . . Goldsmith possessed a considerable portion of patriot virtue, but it was not sufficiently ardent to be called patriotic fire. He was more a philanthropist than a patriot.—M'DERMOT, M., 1824, *The Beauties of Modern Literature, pp.* xv, xix.

Of Goldsmith, all praise were idle, and censure vain. For simplicity, sweetness, and tenderness, he has yet no rival: and he is always perspicuous and correct.—DIBDIN, THOMAS FROGNALL, 1824, *The Library Companion, p.* 735, *note.*

We do ourselves wrong to compare him injuriously with others. We are losers by it. We cannot and ought not to be satisfied with his poetry, and seek nothing higher and different; yet if we forget it, and even think less of it, the change will not be owing to our worship of greater genius, but to a feverish love to idols. Indeed, the relish of such poetry is some evidence of an uncorrupted taste. It owes nothing to affectation, and is in nothing more original than its serenity or tempered feeling. While the glory of greater artists is in subduing their inspiration to their conception of perfect workmanship, his distinction is that he is willing not to stimulate his powers to false efforts. He effects one purpose of all real poetry, by refining the perception and multiplying the sources of truth.—CHANNING, E. T., 1837, *Goldsmith, North American Review, vol.* 45, *p.* 116.

For accurate research or grave disquisition, he was not well qualified by nature or by education. He knew nothing accurately: his reading had been desultory; nor had he meditated deeply on what he had read. He had seen much of the world; but he had noticed and retained little more of what he had seen than some grotesque incidents and characters which happen to strike his fancy. But, though his mind was very scantily stored with materials, he used what materials he had in such a way as to produce a wonderful effect. There have been many greater writers; but perhaps no writer was ever more uniformly agreeable. His style was always pure and easy, and, on proper occasions, pointed and energetic. His narratives were always amusing, his descriptions always picturesque, his humour rich and joyous, yet not without an occasional tinge of amiable sadness. About everything that he wrote, serious or sportive, there was a certain natural grace and decorum, hardly to be expected from a man a great part of whose life had been passed among thieves and beggars, streetwalkers and merryandrews, in those squalid dens which are the reproach of great capitals. —MACAULAY, THOMAS BABINGTON, 1843, *Oliver Goldsmith, Critical and Historical Essays.*

We are obliged to confess that the Vicar, artless and delightful as he is, is an inferior brother of Parson Adams; and that there are great improbabilities in the story. But the family manners, and the Flamboroughs, and Moses, are all delicious; and the style of writing perfect. Again, we are forced to admit, that the "Traveller" and "Deserted Village" are not of the highest or subtlest order of poetry; yet they are charming of their kind, and as perfect in style as his prose. They are cabinets of exquisite workmanship, which will outlast hundreds of oracular shrines of oak ill put together. Goldsmith's most thoroughly original productions are his comedies and minor poems, particularly "She Stoops to Conquer."—HUNT, LEIGH, 1846, *Wit and Humor, p.* 247.

It is in the narrowness of his range, and in the close identity of his characters with his own heart and experience, that we are to find the main cause of Goldsmith's universal and unfading popularity. He had in himself an original to draw from, with precisely those qualities which win general affection. Lovable himself, in spite of all his grave faults, he makes lovable the various copies that he takes from the master portrait. His secret is this—the emotions he commands are pleasurable. He is precisely what Johnson calls him, "*affectuum lenis dominator*"—*potens* because *lenis*. He is never above the height of the humblest understanding; and, by touching the human heart, he raises himself to a level with the loftiest. He has to perfection what the Germans call *Anmuth.* His muse wears the zone of the Graces. . . . Whether you read "The Deserted Village," "The Vicar of Wakefield," "The Goodnatured Man," or "The Citizen of the World," you find at the close that much the same emotions have been awakened—the heart has been touched much in the same place. But with what pliant aptitude the form and mode are changed and disguised! Poem, novel, essay, drama, how exquisite of its kind! The humour that draws tears, and the pathos that provokes smiles, will be popular to the end of the world.—LYTTON, EDWARD BULWER LORD, 1848–68, *Goldsmith, Miscellaneous Prose Works, vol.* I, *pp.* 69, 70.

While, the productions of writers of loftier pretension and more sounding names are suffered to moulder on our shelves, those of Goldsmith are cherished and laid in our bosoms. We do not quote them with ostentation, but they mingle with our minds, sweeten our tempers, and harmonize our thoughts; they put us in good-humor with ourselves and with the world, and in so doing they make us happier and better men.—IRVING, WASHINGTON, 1849, *Oliver Goldsmith, p.* 14.

But gentler GOLDSMITH, whom no man could hate,
Beloved of Heaven, pursued by wayward fate,
Whose verse shall live in every British mind,
Though sweet, yet strong; though nervous, yet refined;—
A motley part he play'd in life's gay scene,
The dupe of vanity and wayward spleen;
Aping the world, a strange fantastic elf;
Great, generous, noble, when he was himself.
—COLERIDGE, HARTLEY, 1849, *Sketches of English Poets, Poems, vol.* II, *p.* 303.

His books, I think, must be always pleasant, as well as profitable, friends, provided we do not expect from them, as we ought not to expect from any friend, more than they profess to give.—MAURICE, FREDERICK DENISON, 1856, *The Friendship of Books and Other Lectures, p.* 27.

Goldsmith could not be termed a thinker; but everything he touched he brightened, as after a month of dry weather, the shower brightens the dusty shrubbery of a suburban villa.—SMITH, ALEXANDER, 1863, *Dreamthorp, p.* 44.

It is a sensible relief to turn from the maudlin sentimentality of Richardson and the coarseness of Fielding and Smollett, to the purity of the pages of Goldsmith. —FORSYTH, WILLIAM, 1871, *The Novels and Novelists of the Eighteenth Century, p.* 299.

Goldsmith, in his farm-house lodgings on the Edgeware road, used to sit writing in very loose apparel,—sometimes wandering into the kitchen, without noticing any one, where he would stand musing with his back to the fire, and then hurry off again to his room, to jot down whatever thought might have struck him. It was off at a tangent with him; but then whatever he touched (*tetigit*) he adorned. Rough jottings down are seldom so smooth as his.—JACOX, FRANCIS, 1872, *Authorship in the Act, Aspects of Authorship, p.* 6.

The elegant simplicity, the genial wisdom, the lambent humor, the melting tenderness, the perennial cheerfulness, and the fresh and uncloying sweetness, which charm us in every line of Goldsmith.—DESHLER, CHARLES D., 1879, *Afternoons with the Poets, p.* 171.

The most thoughtful, the most gentle, the most truly humourous of all the writers of his age or of any age, he is, on the whole, the most attractive figure in our literary history. He has touched every kind of composition, history, poetry, drama, fiction, and criticism, and he has touched them all with a master's hand.—FLETCHER, C. R. L., 1881, *The Development of English Prose Style, p.* 22.

The simplicity of his pathos and the gentleness of his humour have never been equalled.—SAINTSBURY, GEORGE, 1886, *Specimens of English Prose Style, p.* 223.

In Goldsmith we have a respectable degree of variability in sentence-length, and therefore of one chief element of proportion—though other sense of paragraphic proportion Goldsmith had none. The general sentence-length is low, and 15 per cent. of the sentences fall below 15 words; on the other hand there are a few periods of more than 100 words. Goldsmith's narrative sequence is perfect, little needing nor much using connectives. He has not such unity as some descriptive and narrative writers of the day, Fielding, for instance. He follows Fielding carelessly in the handling of dialogue.—LEWIS, EDWIN HERBERT, 1894, *The History of the English Paragraph, p.* 121.

Much of its attraction is of that native and personal kind which resists the resolvents of analysis. That he may have learnt something of phrase-building from the "Rambler" is possible, but he clearly, and fortunately, did not learn too much. It is demonstrable that, for certain of the qualities of his verse, he was largely indebted to French models and it is not unreasonable to conclude that French models generally, and Voltaire in particular, had also influenced him in prose. But when one has catalogued his peculiarities and noted his differences, when one has duly scheduled his gifts of simplicity, ease, gaiety, pathos, and humour, something still remains undefined and evasive—the something that is Genius.—DOBSON, AUSTIN, 1895, *English Prose, ed. Craik, vol.* IV, *p.* 348.

Goldsmith, doubtless, felt that his proper study was Man. Hence the Greek reserve in the treatment of the accessory landscape. Why, then, have these fragmentary glimpses so permanent a hold on our memories and hearts? We may find this in their perfect propriety of choice, their "keeping," as painters say, in their delightful simplicity of thought and expression,—perhaps above all, in the music, the equable balance of syllables, with which Goldsmith—and he only—by some mysterious gift of grace, has half-transformed the too monotonously accented decasyllable couplet of Pope.—PALGRAVE, FRANCIS TURNER, 1896, *Landscape in Poetry, p.* 174.

The one great writer whom Johnson could not eclipse was Oliver Goldsmith, who, amidst the general contamination, stood out as the exponent of a pure and almost faultless prose style. It is questionable whether Goldsmith's essays have generally received the attention they merit, for they are easily the best of their time.—LOBBAN, J. H., 1896, *English Essays, Introduction, p.* xlv.

By the side of Johnson, like an antelope

accompanying an elephant, we observe the beautiful figure of Oliver Goldsmith. In spite of Johnson's ascendency, and in spite of a friendship that was touching in its nearness, scarcely a trace of the elder companion is to be discovered in the work of the younger. . . . There is no ponderosity about Goldsmith, whose limpid and elegant simplicity of style defies analysis. In that mechanical and dusty age he did not set up to be an innovator. We search in vain, in Goldsmith's verse or prose, for any indication of a consciousness of the coming change. He was perfectly contented with the classical traditions, but his inborn grace and delicacy of temper made him select the sweeter and the more elegant among the elements of his time. As a writer, purely, he is far more enjoyable than Johnson; he was a poet of great flexibility and sensitiveness; his single novel is much fuller of humour and nature than the stiff "Rasselas;" as a dramatist he succeeded brilliantly in an age of failures; he is one of the most perfect of essayists. Nevertheless, with all his perennial charm, Goldsmith, in his innocent simplicity, does not attract the historic eye as the good giant Johnson does, seated for forty years in the undisputed throne of letters.—GOSSE, EDMUND, 1897, *Short History of Modern English Literature, pp.* 253, 254.

In the "Deserted Village" and the "Vicar of Wakefield" we have his love of nature and man, shot through with the characteristic elements of his varied and eventful life. They are graceful and touching in their revelation of the pleasures and pains of mortal life, and yet there is not an element of bitterness. In each nature and man are revealed with distinctness and color, with warmth and naturalness, entirely new to English literature. No changes of literary fashion can ever lessen the estimation in which these works are held by all who love simplicity and truth.—GEORGE, ANDREW J., 1898, *From Chaucer to Arnold, Types of Literary Art, p.* 642.

The slave of letters and the master of letters. — STODDARD, FRANCIS HOVEY, 1900, *The Evolution of the English Novel p.* 48.

Robert Fergusson

1750–1774

Robert Fergusson, Scottish poet, was born at Edinburgh, 5th September 1750, and educated at Dundee and St. Andrews University, where he wrote verses. He removed to Edinburgh, and was employed in the office of the commissary clerk, contributing to *Ruddiman's Weekly Magazine* poems which gained him such local reputation as proved his ruin—convivial excesses permanently injured his health. Religious melancholy became complete insanity after an accidental injury to his head. He died 16th October, 1774, and was buried in Canongate churchyard, where fifteen years later Burns erected a stone over his grave. His poems were collected in 1773. There are editions by Ruddiman (1779), Irving (1800), Robert Chambers (1840), and A. B. Grosart (1851). Fergusson possessed vigour, fancy, fluency, and comic humour, but lacked imagination and passion. —PATRICK AND GROOME, *eds.*, 1897, *Chambers's Biographical Dictionary, p.* 361.

PERSONAL

No sculptur'd Marble here, nor pompous lay,
No storied Urn nor animated Bust;
This simple stone directs pale Scotia's way
To pour her sorrow o'er the Poet's dust. . . .
She mourns, sweet tuneful youth, thy hapless fate:
Tho' all the powers of song thy fancy fir'd,
Yet Luxury and Wealth lay by in State,
And, thankless, starv'd what they so much admir'd.
This humble tribute with a tear he gives,
A brother Bard—he can no more bestow:
But dear to fame thy Song immortal lives,
A nobler monument than Art can show.
—BURNS, ROBERT, 1787, *On Robert Fergusson, On the Tombstone in the Canongate Churchyard, and Additional Stanzas not Inscribed.*

He was about five feet six inches high, and well shaped. His complexion fair, but rather pale. His eyes full, black, and piercing. His nose long, his lips thin, his teeth well set and white. His neck long and well proportioned. His shoulders narrow, and his limbs long, but more sinewy than fleshy. His voice strong, clear, and melodious. Remarkably fond of old Scots songs, and the best singer of the "Birks of Invernay" I ever heard.

When speaking, he was quick, forcible, and complaisant. In walking he appeared smart, erect, and unaffected.—SOMMERS, THOMAS, 1803, *Life of Robert Fergusson*, *p.* 45.

An incident strikingly illustrative of the unhappy destiny of the young poet, and at the same time of the honorable esteem in which he was held by those who knew him, must not remain untold. Shortly after his death a letter came from India directed to him, enclosing a draft for £100, and inviting him thither, where a lucrative situation was promised him. The letter and draft were from an old and attached school-fellow, a Mr. Burnet, whose name deserves to be forever linked with Fergusson's for this act of munificent, though fruitless, generosity.—WHITELAW, ALEXANDER, 1843, *ed.*, *Book of Scottish Song, Introduction.*

The poor, high-soaring, deep-falling, gifted, and misguided young man.—CARLYLE, THOMAS, 1850? *Letter to A. B. Grosart, Nov.* 25.

The simple stone which "directs Pale Scotia's way to pour her Sorrows o'er her Poet's Dust" is on the west side of the church, not many steps from the gateway, and on the left as one enters the church-yard. It is always well cared for, and a royal Scottish thistle, planted by some devout hand, rises, as if defiantly, to guard the spot.—HUTTON, LAURENCE, 1891, *Literary Landmarks of Edinburgh*, *p.* 36.

We are three Robins, who have touched the Scots lyre this last century. Well, the one is the world's. He did it, he came off; he is for ever; but I, and the other, ah! what bonds we have! Born in the same city; both sickly; both vicious; both pestered—one nearly to madness and one to the madhouse—with a damnatory creed; both seeing the stars and the moon, and wearing shoe-leather on the same ancient stones, under the same pends (—courts), down the same closes, where our common ancestors clashed in their armour, rusty or bright. . . . He died in his acute, painful youth, and left the models of the great things that were to come; and the man who came after outlived his green-sickness, and has faintly tried to parody his finished work. If you will collect strays of Robert Fergusson, fish for material, collect any last re-echoing of gossip, command me to do what you prefer—to write the preface, to write the whole if you prefer; anything so that another monument (after Burns's) be set up to my unhappy predecessor, on the causey of Auld Reekie. You will never know, nor will any man, how deep this feeling is. I believe Fergusson lives in me. I do. But "tell it not in Gath." Every man has these fanciful superstitions coming, going but yet enduring; only most men are so wise (or the poet in them so dead) that they keep their follies for themselves.—STEVENSON, ROBERT LOUIS, 1894? *Letter to Craibe Angus.*

As for the man distinct in so far as he can be made distinct from the poet, I have failed indeed if I have not thrown off from him for ever the Irving-originated moralising, and won for him not blame but pity; not sentencing but sympathy; not judging him by lapses through stress of circumstance but by what was best in him; and it is my hope that every reader will rejoice with me that well-nigh a century and a quarter after his poor wasted body was borne to its last resting-place in Canongate Churchyard, there are still multitudes of "brither Scots" all the world over to whom his memory is dear and tender.—GROSART, ALEXANDER B., 1898, *Robert Fergusson* (*Famous Scots Series*), *p.* 159.

GENERAL

Is the author of two tolerably pretty love songs.—RITSON, JOSEPH, 1794–1869, *A Historical Essay on Scotish Song, vol.* I, *p.* 71.

Robert Fergusson was the poet of Scottish city-life, or rather the laureate of Edinburgh. A happy talent in portraying the peculiarities of local manners, a keen perception of the ludicrous, a vein of original comic humour, and language at once copious and expressive, distinguished him as a poet. He had not the invention or picturesque fancy of Allan Ramsay, nor the energy and passion of Burns. His mind was a light warm soil, that threw up early its native products, sown by chance or little exertion; but it had not strength and tenacity to nurture any great or valuable production. A few short years, however, comprised his span of literature and of life; and criticism would be ill employed in scrutinising with severity any occasional poems of a youth of twenty-three, written from momentary feelings and impulses, amidst professional drudgery or midnight dissipation. . . . In one department—lyrical poetry, whence Burns draws so much of his glory—Fergusson does not seem, though a singer, to have made any efforts to excel. In English poetry he utterly failed; and if we consider him in reference to his countrymen, Falconer or Logan—he received the same education as the latter—his inferior rank as a general poet will be apparent. —CHAMBERS, ROBERT, 1876, *Cyclopœdia of English Literature, ed. Carruthers.*

Nothing can be more mawkish and vapid than Fergusson, when he makes Damon and Alexis discourse in his purely English pastorals. —SHAIRP, JOHN CAMPBELL, 1877, *On Poetic Interpretation of Nature, p.* 225.

His chief characteristics as a poet are—a keen sense of the ludicrous, a strong vein of original comic humour, a talent for describing the peculiarities of local manners, and a copious command of expressive language. He wrote poems both in English and Scotch; his Scotch pieces, however, are most esteemed.—MACKINTOSH, JOHN, 1878–96, *The History of Civilization in Scotland, vol.* IV, *p.* 178.

At the early age of twenty-four, sung of the Tweed in his poem "The Rivers of Scotland." Fine genius as he was, he has but caught some echoes of the theme, and his whole description is vague and characterless. But in "Hame Content," a satire, he has touched the true soul of Scottish scenery and music, and done much greater justice to Bangour than Hogg did.—VEITCH, JOHN, 1878, *The History and Poetry of the Scottish Border, p.* 457.

His range of subjects is narrowed by the narrow space of a career which began at twenty-four. He had a keen enjoyment of city life, with its clubs for a little dissipation, and its bailies and its "black banditti" for a constant occasion of laughter. Still more keen on his part was that enjoyment of the country, the pleasures of which he seldom tasted except in imagination, but which supplies the inspiration of some of his most touching verses, as well as some of his mock heroics. We alternate in his verse between these two sets of themes, and in his treatments of both we meet with the same vein of pure pathos, and its almost unfailing accompaniment of genuine humour.—SERVICE, JOHN, 1880, *The English Poets, ed. Ward, vol.* III, *p.* 503.

Some people are inclined to ask—Are we quite sure that we are worshipping the right poet? It is true that there are many poets, and I sometimes yield so far to the suggestion as to think that we might worship some of them a little more than we do. There is FERGUSSON, Burns's master, who died at twenty-four, a true poet, but so unfortunate after death as in life, that I doubt if we have a proper critical edition of Fergusson, and certainly we have not such an account of his life as might well be written.—LANG, ANDREW, 1891, *Burns Anniversary Dinner, Edinburgh.*

There have been considerable differences of judgment as to Fergusson's position among the poets; but on the whole the drift of political opinion has been against him. A much lower place is commonly assigned to him now than would once have been claimed. Perhaps this is due partly to a certain impatience of the more than generous praise of Burns, who habitually speaks of Fergusson as his own equal, and sometimes as more than his equal, and who proves the sincerity of his regard by imitating Fergusson more frequently than any other poet. . . . Fergusson, in his poetry as in his life, is less sane and sensible than Ramsay, in some respects perhaps less strong; but he is infinitely finer, he gives promise of things of which there is no hint from beginning to end in Ramsay; and in the course of a career which closed ere it had well begun, he displays a fervour and an elevation which the author of "The Gentle Shepherd" could never rival. Ramsay was acute and solid; but Fergusson was a genius. . . . All the verse he ever wrote can be contained within the covers of a small volume, and only a few of his pieces are of high merit. But some of those pieces bear the stamp of genius, immature indeed, but real, and justify the belief that had he lived even a few years longer his position as the inferior only of Burns would have been beyond dispute.—WALKER, HUGH, 1893,

Three Centuries of Scottish Literature, vol. II, *pp.* 39, 40.

This knack of making auld-warld wardies clack in hamespun rhyme Fergusson possessed in the highest degree. His vocabulary has a strength, a fulness, and a vigour about it which secure instant recognition. Fergusson wields the brave utterance of Scotia as the potter wields and moulds the finest clay. Like all noble and well-chosen speech, Fergusson's commended itself to every sort and condition of men, and readers of all classes instinctively recognised that a new magician had arisen; that in these thoroughly original and unique Scots poems it was indeed true of the words, in the fullest sense, that

ilk ane at his billy's back
Kept guid Scots time.

This gift of perfect manipulation of human speech, either in prose or verse, is one that has come very rarely in the history of genius to a writer so young as Fergusson. It has more usually been the growth of maturer years. This peculiar gift is something different from divine afflatus—the poet's inspiration; there may be less of genius in it, but there is infinitely more of talent. In a few lines, in a vivid word picture, Fergusson succeeds in giving us a living, breathing transcript from Nature. . . . The wonder of all this is increased when one recollects that Fergusson was but a lad of twenty or so when he obtained his supremacy. His English poems were almost, if not quite, worthless. They had the ring of the conventional, artificial period about them, without any redeeming felicity, or originality of genius; and though they obtained some vogue, they are now, except in the personal or antiquarian sense, absolutely without interest. I have read them and re-read them, and read them again, and I must honestly testify that from the first line to the last I have found but two or three stanzas which have struck me as having any genuine ring of true poetic metal.—GORDON, ALEXANDER, 1894, *Robert Fergusson, The Gentleman's Magazine, vol.* 277, *pp.* 392, 393.

Apart from the fact that he struck the keynote, which was afterwards accentuated by the Ayrshire poet, of all the modern vernacular verse of Scotland, he remains, by reason both of his genius and of his tragic story, one of the three most interesting figures of eighteenth century Scottish poetic annals. . . . In Fergusson's case it is unnecessary to make allowance for his youth: he was but twenty-three when he died. Had he lived longer, it is true, his genius might have developed higher imaginative power, and experience might have given him more artistic resource. But the fact remains that in the field of Scottish poetry which he essayed he has been surpassed only by two or three competitors. "Leith Races" and "Hallowfair" present pictures almost as racy and realistic, if indeed not so boisterous, as their great prototypes, King James's "Christ's Kirk on the Green" and "Peblis to the Play." The same pieces, with "The Election" and "The Setting of the Session," afford the most graphic impression extant of the Edinburgh life of his day. His "Elegies," "Braid Claith," "Hame Content," and "Torn Kirk Bell" were masterpieces in a rich vein of satiric humour. And his "Gowdspink" with his "Farmer's Ingle" depicted fields of homely charm in which Fergusson has been improved upon only by Burns himself. . . . The same commendation cannot be given to Fergusson's English poems, which comprise more than half his work. These are written for the most part in the affected and conventional taste of much of the Scoto-English verse of the time. But his pieces in the rich Lowland-Scottish dialect—pieces which were eagerly read by the common people everywhere in his own day—remain enough to furnish reputations for half a dozen poets.—EYRE-TODD, GEORGE, 1896, *Scottish Poetry of the Eighteenth Century, vol.* II, *pp.* 111, 113, 114.

Has been a good deal over-praised, though he has no small merit, especially in some Edinburgh pieces and in "The Gowdspink."—SAINTSBURY, GEORGE, 1898, *A Short History of English Literature, p.* 594.

My claim, therefore for Robert Fergusson, as I have all along stated, is a modest but a definite one. He is to be gratefully remembered for what his vernacular poems did for Robert Burns; for what he did in the nick of time in asserting the worth and dignity and potentiality of his and our mother-tongue; for his naturalness, directness, veracity, simplicity, raciness, humour, sweetness, melody; for his felicitous packing into lines and couplets sound common sense; for his penetrative perception that the man and not "braid claith" or wealth is "the man for a' that;" for his patriotic love of country and civil and religious freedom; and for the perfectness—with only superficial scratches rather than material flaws—of at least thirteen of his vernacular poems, and for sustaining the proud tradition and continuity of Scottish song.—GROSART, ALEXANDER B., 1898, *Robert Fergusson* (*Famous Scots Series*), *p.* 159.

Abraham Tucker

1705–1774

A metaphysical writer, was born in London in 1705, and was educated at Bishop's Stortford School and Merton College, Oxford. He studied for a while at the Inner Temple, but was not admitted to the bar. He died in 1774. He published, "Freewill, Fore-knowledge, and Fate; a Fragment" by Edward Search (London 1763): "Man in Quest of Himself, or a Defence of the Individuality of the Human Mind or Self," etc., by Cuthbert Comment, Gent. (1763). His great work, however, is "The Light of Nature Pursued," by Edward Search (1768–78).—M'CLINTOCK AND STRONG, *eds.*, 1881, *Cyclopædia of Biblical, Theological, and Ecclesiastical Literature, vol.* X, *p.* 574.

LIGHT OF NATURE PURSUED
1768–78

Read Tucker's "Introduction to his Light of Nature Pursued." There is a desultoriness in his style and manner for which I have no mercy on such topics as he has undertaken to treat.—GREEN, THOMAS, 1779–1810, *Diary of a Lover of Literature.*

I have found in this writer more original thinking and observation upon the several subjects that he has taken in hand, than in any other, not to say than in all others put together. His talent also for illustration is unrivalled. But his thoughts are diffused through a long, various, and irregular work. I shall account it no mean praise if I have been sometimes able to dispose into method, to collect into heads and articles, or to exhibit in more compact and tangible masses, what, in that otherwise excellent performance is spread over too much surface.—PALEY, WILLIAM, 1785, *Principles of Moral and Political Philosophy, Preface.*

I do not know of any work in the shape of a philosophical treatise that contains so much good sense so agreeably expressed. —HAZLITT, WILLIAM, 1807, *ed., The Light of Nature Pursued, Abridgment.*

But I must be permitted to add that as a metaphysician he seems to me much more fanciful and solid, and, at the same time, to be so rambling, verbose, and excursive as to be more likely to unsettle than to fix the principles of his readers. —STEWART, DUGALD, 1815–21, *First Preliminary Dissertation to Encyclopædia Britannica.*

A vast mine of thought.—WILSON, JOHN, 1823, *Blackwood's Magazine, vol.* 13, *p.* 331, *note.*

It is in mixed, not in pure philosophy, that his superiority consists. In the part of his work which relates to the intellect, he has adopted much from Hartley, hiding but aggravating the offence by a change of technical terms; and he was ungrateful enough to countenance the vulgar sneer which involves the mental analysis of that philosopher in the ridicule to which his physiological hypothesis is liable. . . . Take him all in all, however, the neglect of his writings is the strongest proof of the disinclination of the English nation, for the last half century, to metaphysical philosophy.—MACKINTOSH, SIR JAMES, 1830, *Second Preliminary Dissertation to Encyclopædia Britannica.*

Happy beyond all men in the power of illustrating the obscure by the familiar; but happier still in the most benevolent and cheerful temper, and in a style which beautifully reflects the constitutional gaiety and kindness of his heart. There is a charm even in his want of method, and in the very clumsiness of his paragraphs; for each sentence bears him testimony that he is too intent on his object to think of anything else, and that to teach controversialists to understand and to love each other was the single end for which he lived and wrote. Of his metaphysical speculations, the most original and curious is the "Enquiry into the Nature and the Operation of Motives." But his excellence consists in the brightness and in the variety of the lights he has thrown round the whole circle of those topics over which natural and revealed religion exercise a common and indivisible dominion. To rid them of mere logomachies, to show much the fiercest disputants may be unconsciously agreed, to prove how greatly Christianity is misrepresented by many of her opponents, and misunderstood by many of her friends—and, without ever assuming the preacher's office, to explain the depths of the great Christian canon of mutual love as the universal substratum of all moral truth,—this is the duty which he has undertaken, and which he executes, often successfully, and always with such courage, diligence, and vivacity, and with so unbroken a sunshine of a placid and playful temper, as to render the "Light of Nature" one of the most attractive books in our language, both to those who read to be themselves instructed on these questions, and to those who read with the view of imparting such instruction to others.—STEPHEN, SIR JAMES, 1840, *Works of the Author of Natural History of Enthusiasm, Edinburgh Review, vol.* 71, *p.* 242.

Tucker's style has several charms rarely met in philosophical works—charms, indeed, that are more or less incompatible with rigorous scientific precision. The diction is simple, thickly interspersed with colloquial idioms, and has an exquisitely musical flow. In every other sentence we are delighted with some original felicity of expression or of illustration. The loose and often ungrammatical structure of the sentences, and the diffusive rambling character both of the work as a whole and of the several divisions, forbid his being taken as a model for strict scientific exposition; but the popular expositor of practical wisdom might learn a great deal from his copious and felicitous language and imagery. Obviously, however, it will not do even for popular purposes to imitate him closely. The expense of his voluminous treatise may have something to do with the general neglect of so ingenious a writer; but at any rate it is significant against close imitation of his style that the views of Happiness and Virtue in Paley's "Moral Philosophy," which are simply Tucker's summarised and formulated, are never referred to their original author.—MINTO, WILLIAM, 1872–80, *A Manual of English Prose Literature, p.* 472.

The voluminous but fascinating "Light of Nature Pursued" a huge storehouse of thought that is not seldom original, put with constant vividness and much humour, though diffusely and without order.—SAINTSBURY, GEORGE, 1898 (*A Short History of English Literature, p.* 634.

GENERAL

The most agreeable of metaphysicians. —HUNT, LEIGH, 1847, *Garth, Physicians and Love-Letters; Men, Women and Books.*

Tucker is an example of a very rare species—the philosophical humorist, and is called by Mackintosh a "metaphysical Montaigne." The resemblance consists in the frankness and simplicity with which Tucker expounds his rather artless speculations, as he might have done in talking to a friend. He was an excellent country squire, not more widely read than the better specimens of his class, but of singularly vivacious and ingenious intellect. His illustrations, taken from the commonest events and objects, are singularly bright and happy. He has little to say upon purely metaphysical points, in which he accepts Locke as his great authority; but his psychological and ethical remarks, though unsystematic and desultory, are full of interest. He was obviously much influenced by Hartley, whom, however, he seems to have disliked. His chief interest was in ethical discussions.—STEPHEN, LESLIE, 1899, *Dictionary of National Biography, vol.* LVII, *p.* 278.

John Hill

1716?–1775

A voluminous writer, was born in 1716, at Peterborough. He was brought up as an apothecary, and practised as a physician; wrote numerous books with great rapidity, and was the inventor of several quack medicines. Under the auspices of the Earl of Bute he published a "System of Botany," in 17 vols. folio; and on presenting a

copy of it to the king of Sweden was invested with the order of Vasa. He also published a Supplement to Chambers' Cyclopaedia, "Essays on Natural History and Philosophy;" conducted a periodical called "The Inspector," and wrote several novels, farces, &c. He was a constant attendant at every place of public amusement; and, being a satirical "busybody," was often involved in quarrels with the wits of the day.
—CATES, WILLIAM L. R., *ed.*, 1867, *A Dictionary of General Biography*, p. 513.

PERSONAL

With sleek appearance and with ambling pace,
And, type of vacant head, with vacant face,
The Proteus Hill put in his modest plea,—
Let Favour speak for others, Worth for me.—
For who, like him, his various powers could call
Into so many shapes and shine in all?
Who could so nobly grace the motley list,
Actor, Inspector, Doctor, Botanist?
Knows any one so well—sure no one knows—
At once to play, prescribe, compound, compose?
—CHURCHILL, CHARLES, 1761, *The Rosciad.*

Dr. Hill was, notwithstanding, a very curious observer; and if he would have been contented to tell the world no more than he knew, he might have been a very considerable man, and needed not to have recourse to such mean expedients to raise his reputation.—JOHNSON, SAMUEL, 1767, *Conversation with George III., Life by Boswell, ed. Hill, vol.* II, *p.* 44.

He had received no academical education; but his ambition prompting him to be a graduate, he obtained, from one of those universities which would scarce refuse a degree to an apothecary's horse, a diploma for that of doctor of physic. After this, he engaged in a variety of works, the greater part whereof were mere compilations, which he sent forth with incredible expedition; and though his character was never in such estimation with the booksellers as to entitle him to an extraordinary price for his writings, he has been known by such works as those above mentioned, by novels, pamphlets, and a periodical paper called "The Inspector," the labour of his own head and hand, to have earned, in one year, the sum of £1500. He was vain, conceited, and in his writings disposed to satire and licentious scurrility, which he indulged without any regard to truth, and thereby became engaged in frequent disputes and quarrels that always terminated in his own disgrace.—HAWKINS, SIR JOHN, 1787, *The Life of Samuel Johnson, p.* 211.

The literary Proteus, Dr., afterwards Sir John Hill, who shared with Orator Henley the dubious honour of being the most notorious man of his age. Hill was originally an apothecary, but abandoning his business for the stage, he produced a few bad farces at the Haymarket, in which he appeared as an actor. . . . Having been hissed off the stage, he betook himself with industry to the study of medicine and natural history; and many works on these subjects, displaying considerable information and research, proceeded from his pen. As a consequence of his scientific labours, and armed with the cheap honours of a Scotch degree, he obtained a large practice as a physician, and was enabled to launch out into extravagances which increased his notoriety, and showed the shallowness of his character. . . . His activity and industry were indeed marvellous. Though he spent so much of his time in the amusements of the gay world, and in frequenting places of entertainment, his pen was never idle.
—LAWRENCE, FREDERICK, 1855, *The Life of Henry Fielding, pp.* 304, 305.

Hill was a versatile man of unscrupulous character, with considerable abilities, great perseverance, and unlimited impudence.—BARKER, G. F. RUSSELL, 1891, *Dictionary of National Biography, vol.* XXVI, *p.* 398.

GENERAL

See where my son, who gratefully repays
Whate'er I lavish'd on his younger days;
Whom still my arm protects to brave the town
Secure from Fielding, Machiavel, or Brown;
Whom rage nor sword e'er mortally shall hurt,
Chief of a hundred chiefs o'er all the pert!
Rescued an orphan babe from common sense,
I gave his mother's milk to Confidence;
She with her own ambrosia bronz'd his face,
And changed his skin to monumental brass.
—ANON, 1752, *The Pasquinade.*

The neutral nonsense, neither false nor true—
Should Jove himself, in calculation mad,
Still negatives to blank negations add;
How could the barren ciphers ever breed;
But nothing still from nothing would proceed.
Raise, or depress, or magnify, or blame
Inanity will ever be the same.
—SMART, CHRISTOPHER, 1753, *The Hilliad.*

For physics and farces,
His equal there scarce is;
His farces are physic,
His physic a farce is.

—GARRICK, DAVID, *On Dr. Hill Farce.*

Sir John Hill had just wrote a book of great elegance—I think it was called "Exotic Botany"—which he wished to have presented to the king, and therefore named it to Lord Bute. His lordship waived that, saying that "he had a greater object to propose;" and shortly after laid before him a plan of the most voluminous, magnificent, and costly work that ever man attempted. I tremble when I name its title—because I think the severe application which it required killed him; and I am sure the expense ruined his fortune —"The Vegetable System." This work was to consist of twenty-six volumes folio, containing sixteen hundred copperplates, the engraving of each cost four guineas; the paper was of the most expensive kind; the drawings by the first hands. The printing was also a very weighty concern; and many other articles, with which I am unacquainted. Lord Bute said that "the expense had been considered, and that Sir John Hill might rest assured his circumstances should not be injured." Thus he entered upon and finished his destruction. The sale bore no proportion to the expense. After "The Vegetable System" was completed, Lord Bute proposed another volume to be added, which Sir John strenuously opposed; but his lordship repeating his desire, Sir John complied, lest his lordship should find a pretext to cast aside repeated promises of ample provision for himself and family. But this was the crisis of his fate—he died.—HILL, HON. LADY, 1787, *An Address to the Public.*

One of the most extraordinary characters of the eighteenth century. . . . It cannot be denied, that, in many of these volumes, a considerable fund of information, especially on Botany, was communicated to the public; and though the mode in which it was conveyed was generally slovenly, and sometimes inaccurate and unscientific, our author must be allowed the merit of having greatly contributed to diffuse through the island a taste for natural history. . . . Under this form the "Inspector" includes one hundred and fifty-two numbers; many of which are written with vivacity, and a few exhibit traits of humour, character, and imagination. The most useful and interesting papers in the work are devoted to subjects of natural history, especially to microscopical observations on insects, fossils, &c. The style of this periodical paper, as might be expected from the hasty manner in which it was usually written, is often loose and slovenly, and frequently ungrammatical.—DRAKE, NATHAN, 1809, *Essays Illustrative of the Rambler, Adventurer and Idler, vol.* II, *pp.* 238, 241, 245.

This despised man, after all the fertile absurdities of his literary life, performed more for the improvement of the "Philosophical Transactions," and was the cause of diffusing a more general taste for the science of botany, than any other contemporary. His real ability extorts that regard which his misdirected ingenuity, instigated by vanity, and often by more worthless motives, had lost for him in the world.—DISRAELI, ISAAC, 1814, *Sir John Hill, Quarrels of Authors.*

A detailed account of these many publications would be of but small interest to the modern reader, who knows little of Sir John save his name, and this principally through his quarrels with the Royal Society, and with Garrick. He was a man of remarkable versatility of talent, but his moral character cannot be commended.—ALLIBONE, S. AUSTIN, 1854–58, *Critical Dictionary of English Literature, vol.* I, *p.* 846.

David Hume

1711–1776

Born, in Edinburgh, 26 April 1711. Probably educated at Edinburgh University. Lived in France, 1734–37. Settled at home, at Ninewells, Berwickshire, 1737. Tutor in household of Marquis of Annandale, April 1745 to April 1746. Sec. to Gen. St. Clair in expedition against Canada, 1746–47. With Gen. St. Clair on embassy to Austria and Italy, 1748. Returned to Ninewells, 1749. Removed with his sister to Edinburgh, 1751. Keeper of Advocates' Library, 28 Jan. 1752 to 1757. Prosecuted

DAVID HUME

Engraving by H. W. Smith.
Portrait by Ramsay.

historical studies. To Paris, as Sec. to Ambassador, Earl of Hartford, Oct. 1763. Pension of £400, 1765. To England, bringing Rousseau with him, Jan. 1766. Returned to Edinburgh, same year. In London, as Under Secretary of State, 1767–68. Settled in Edinburgh, 1769. Died there, 25 Aug. 1776. Buried in Calton Hill Cemetery. *Works:* "A Treatise of Human Nature" (anon.), vols. i, ii, 1739; vol. iii, 1740; "Essays, moral and political" (2 vols., anon.), 1741–42; "Philosophical Essays concerning Human Understanding" (anon.), 1748; " A True Account of the behaviour . . . of Archibald Stewart" (anon.), 1748; "An Enquiry concerning the Principles of Morals," 1751; "Political Discourses" 1752 (2nd edn. same year); "Essays and Treatises on Several Subjects" (4 vols.), 1753-54; "The History of England" [under the House of Stuart] (2 vols.), 1754–57; "Four Dissertations," 1757; "The History of England under the House of Tudor" (2 vols.), 1759; "The History of England from the Invasion of Julius Caesar to the accession of Henry VII." (2 vols.), 1762; "A Concise Account of the dispute between Mr. Hume and Mr. Rousseau" (anon.), 1766; "Scotticisms" (anon.), 1770. *Posthumous:* "Autobiography," 1777; "Two Essays," 1777; "Dialogues concerning Natural Religion," 1779.—SHARP, FARQUHARSON R., 1897, *A Dictionary of English Authors, p.* 141.

PERSONAL

Nature, I believe, never formed any man more unlike his real character than David Hume. The powers of physiognomy were baffled by his countenance; neither could the most skilful in that science pretend to discern the smallest trace of the faculities of his mind in the unmeaning features of his visage. His face was broad and flat, his mouth wide, and without any other expression than that of imbecility; his eyes vacant and spiritless; and the corpulence of his whole person was far better fitted to convey the idea of a turtle-eating alderman than that of a refined philosopher. His speech in English was rendered ridiculous by the broadest Scotch accent, and his French was, if possible, still more laughable; so that wisdom most certainly never disguised herself before in so uncouth a garb.—CHARLEMONT, JAMES CAULFIELD EARL, 1748, *Memoirs of Political and Private Life by Hardy, p.* 8.

At this time David Hume was living in Edinburgh and composing his "History of Great Britain." He was a man of great knowledge, and of a social and benevolent temper, and truly the best-natured man in the world. He was branded with the title of Atheist, on account of many attacks on revealed religion that are to be found in his philosophical works, and in many places of his History,—the last of which are still more objectionable than the first, which a friendly critic might call only sceptical. Apropos of this, when Mr. Robert Adam, the celebrated architect, and his brother, lived in Edinburgh with their mother, an aunt of Dr. Robertson's, and a very respectable woman, she said to her son, "I shall be glad to see any of your companions to dinner, but I hope you will never bring the Atheist here to disturb my peace." But Robert soon fell on a method to reconcile her to him, for he introduced him under another name, or concealed it carefully from her. When the company parted she said to her son, " I must confess that you bring very agreeable companions about you, but the large jolly man who sat next me is the most agreeable of them all." "This was the very Atheist," said he, "mother, that you was so much afraid of." "Well," says she, "you may bring him here as much as you please, for he's the most innocent, agreeable, facetious man I ever met with." This was truly the case with him; for though he had much learning and a fine taste, and was professed a sceptic, though by no means an atheist, he had the greatest simplicity of mind and manners with the utmost facility and benevolence of temper of any man I ever knew. His conversation was truly irresistible, for while it was enlightened, it was naïve almost to puerility.—CARLYLE, ALEXANDER, 1753, *Autobiography, p.* 221.

Ever since I was acquainted with your works, your talents as a writer have, notwithstanding some differences in abstract principles, extorted from me the highest veneration. But I could scarce have thought that, in spite of differences of a more interesting nature, even such as regard morals and religion, you could ever force me to love and honour you as a man. Yet no religious prejudices, as you would probably term them, can hinder me from doing justice to that goodness and candour which appeared in every line of your letter.—CAMPBELL, DR., 1762, *Letter to Hume, June.*

In attempting to throw some new light upon the abstruse subjects, I wish to preserve the due mean betwixt confidence and despair. But whether I have any success in this attempt or not, I shall always avow myself your disciple in metaphysics. I have learned more from your writings in this kind, than from all others put together. . . . Your friendly adversaries, Drs. Campbell and Gerard, as well as Dr. Gregory, return their compliments to you respectfully. A little philosophical society here, of which all the three are members, is much indebted to you for its entertainment. Your company would, although we are all good Christians, be more acceptable than that of St. Athanasius; and since we cannot have you upon the bench, you are brought oftener than any other man to the bar, accused and defended with great zeal, but without bitterness.—REID, THOMAS, 1763, *Letter to Hume, March.*

With respect to myself, I am sorry I cannot have the pleasure of taking leave of you in person, before I go into perpetual exile. I sincerely wish you all health and happiness. In whatever part of the earth it may be my fate to reside, I shall always remember with pleasure, and recapitulate with pride, the friendly intercourse I have maintained with one of the best men, and undoubtedly the best writer of the age.

Nos patriam fugimus: tu Tityre, lentus in umbrâ,
Formosam resonare doces Amaryllida silvas.

—SMOLLETT, TOBIAS GEORGE, 1768, *Letter to David Hume, Aug.* 31.

Sir, Hume is a Tory by chance as being a Scotchman; but not upon a principle of duty; for he has no principle. If he is anything he is a Hobbist.—JOHNSON, SAMUEL, 1773, *The Journal of a Tour to the Hebrides, by Boswell, ed. Hill, Sept.* 30, *p.* 309.

I was, I say, a man of mild dispositions, of command of temper, of an open, social, and cheerful humour, capable of attachment, but little susceptible of enmity, and of great moderation in all my passions. Even my love of literary fame, my ruling passion, never soured my temper, notwithstanding my frequent disappointments. My company was not unacceptable to the young and careless, as well as to the studious and literary; and as I took a particular pleasure in the company of modest women, I had no reason to be displeased with the reception I met with from them. In a word, though most men anywise eminent have found reason to complain of calumny, I never was touched or even attacked by her baleful tooth: and though I wantonly exposed myself to the rage of both civil and religious factions, they seemed to be disarmed in my behalf of their wonted fury. My friends never had occasion to vindicate any one circumstance of my character and conduct; not but that the zealots, we may well suppose, would have been glad to invent and propagate any story to my disadvantage but they could never find any which they thought would wear the face of probability. I cannot say there is no vanity in making this funeral oration of myself, but it is not a misplaced one; and this is a matter of fact which is easily cleared and ascertained.—HUME, DAVID, 1776, *My Own Life, p.* 32.

Dear Sir,—Yesterday, about four o'clock, afternoon, Mr. Hume expired. The near approach of his death became evident in the night between Thursday and Friday, when his disease became excessive, and soon weakened him so much that he could no longer rise out of his bed. . . . He never dropped the smallest expression of impatience; but, when he had occasion to speak to the people about him, always did it with affection and tenderness. . . . When he became very weak, it cost him an effort to speak; and he died in such a happy composure of mind that nothing could exceed it.—BLACK, DR., 1776, *Letter to Adam Smith, Aug.* 26.

The extreme gentleness of his nature never weakened either the firmness of his mind, or the steadiness of his resolutions. His constant pleasantry was the genuine effusion of good-nature and good-humour, tempered with delicacy and modesty, and without even the slightest tincture of malignity, so frequently the disagreeable source of what is called wit in other men. It never was the meaning of his raillery to mortify; and therefore, far from offending, it seldom failed to please and delight, even those who were the objects of it. To his friends, who were frequently the objects of it, there was not perhaps any one of all his great and amiable qualities, which contribute more to endear his conversation. And that gaiety of temper, so agreeable in society, but which is so often accompanied with frivolous and superficial qualities, was in him certainly attended with the most severe application, the most extensive learning, the greatest depth of thought, and a capacity in every respect the most comprehensive. Upon the whole, I have always considered him, both in his lifetime and since his death, as approaching as nearly to the idea of a perfectly wise and virtuous man, as perhaps the nature of human frailty will permit.—SMITH, ADAM, 1776, *Letter to William Strahan, Nov.* 9.

I always lived on good terms with Mr. Hume, though I have frankly told him, I was not clear that it was right in me to keep company with him. "But (said I), how much better are you than your books!" He was cheerful, obliging, and instructive; he was charitable to the poor; and many an agreeable hour have I passed with him: I have preserved some entertaining and interesting memoirs of him, particularly when he knew himself to be dying; which I may some time or other communicate to the world. I shall not, however, extol him so very highly as Dr. Adam Smith does, who says, in a letter to Mr. Strahan the Printer (not a confidential letter to his friend, but a letter which is published with all formality:) "Upon the whole, I have always considered him, both in his life time and since his death, as approaching as nearly to the idea of a perfectly wise and virtuous man as perhaps the nature of human frailty will permit." Let Dr. Smith consider. Was not Mr. Hume blest with good health, good spirits, good friends, a competent and increasing fortune? And had he not also a perpetual feast of fame? But, as a learned friend has observed to me, "What trials did he undergo to prove the perfection of his virtue? Did he ever experience any great instance of adversity?"—When I read this sentence delivered by my old "Professor of Moral Philosophy," I could not help exclaiming with the *Psalmist*, "Surely I have not more understanding than my teachers!"—BOSWELL, JAMES, 1785, *The Journal of a Tour to the Hebrides, ed. Hill, Aug.* 15, *p.* 32.

DAVID HUME

Born 1711. Died 1776.

Leaving it to Posterity to add the rest.
—INSCRIPTION ON TOMB, 1778, *Calton Hill, Edinburgh.*

Mr. Burke told me he was well acquainted with David Hume, and that he was a very easy, pleasant, unaffected man, till he went to Paris as secretary to Lord Hertford. There the attention paid him by the French *belles savants* had the effect of making him somewhat a literary coxcomb. Mr. Burke said that Hume in compiling his history did not give himself a great deal of trouble in examining records, &c.; and the part he most laboured at was the reign of King Charles II., for whom he had unaccountable partiality.—MALONE, EDMOND, 1787, *Maloniana, ed. Prior, p.* 368.

On the 15th August, 1776, Mr. Hume died in Edinburgh, after having been afflicted for more than a twelvemonth with a complaint which he himself believed would prove fatal. His death, therefore, he had foreseen for some considerable time; yet his cheerfulness and composure of mind remained unabated, and he even exerted, at times, a playful humour, not altogether decorous in so solemn a situation. The world was naturally not unsolicitous to see, whether Mr. Hume, in his dying moments, would express any sentiments different from those which he had published in his philosophical writings. But although he retained the full possession of his faculties to the last, he preserved a most cautious silence on that subject, and never uttered a word that could indicate whether any change had taken place in his opinions, or not. There is every reason to believe, however, that his sentiments remained still the same; for he left for publication, a treatise, entitled, "Dialogues on Natural Religion," of a similar strain with those which had been printed during his lifetime.—FORBES, SIR WILLIAM, 1806, *An Account of the Life and Writings of James Beattie, vol.* II, *p.* 141.

Mallet's wife, a foolish and conceited woman, one evening introduced herself to David Hume at an assembly, saying, "*We deists*, Mr. Hume, should know one another." Hume was exceedingly displeased and disconcerted, and replied, "Madam, I am no deist; I do not so style myself;

neither do I desire to be known by that appellation."—HARDY, FRANCIS, 1810, *Life of James Caulfield, Earl of Charlemont.*

His temper was calm, not to say cold; but though none of his feelings were ardent, all were engaged on the side of virtue. He was free from the slightest tincture of malignity or meanness; his conduct was uniformly excellent.—MACKINTOSH, SIR JAMES, 1811, *Memoirs, ed. Mackintosh, vol.* II, *p.* 167.

Hume is an author so celebrated, a philosopher so serene, and a man so extremely amiable, if not fortunate, that we may be surprised to meet his name inscribed in a catalogue of literary calamities. Look into his literary life, and you will discover that the greatest portion was mortified and angered; and that the stoic so lost his temper, that had not circumstances intervened which did not depend on himself, Hume had abandoned his country and changed his name!—DISRAELI, ISAAC, 1812–13, *The Miseries of Successful Authors, Calamities of Authors.*

Hume's character of himself was well drawn and full of candour; he spoke of himself as he ought, but added what surprised us all, that plain as his manners were, and apparently careless of attention, vanity was his predominant weakness. That vanity led him to publish his essays which he grieved over, not that he had changed his opinions, but that he thought he had injured society by disseminating them. "Do you remember the sequel of that affair?" said Hume. "Yes, I do," replied my mother, laughing. "You told me that although I thought your character a sincere one, it was not so; there was a particular feature omitted that we were still ignorant of, and that you would add it. Like a fool, I gave you the MS. and you thrust it into the fire, adding, 'Oh! what an idiot I had nearly proven myself to be to leave such a document in the hands of a parcel of women!'"—BARNARD, ANNE LADY, 1825–40, *Lives of the Lindsays, ed. Lindsay.*

Through the whole of the memorials of Hume's early feelings we find the traces of a bold and far-stretching literary ambition . . . "I was seized very early," he tells us in his "Own Life," "with a passion for literature, which has been the ruling passion of my life, and a great source of my enjoyments." Joined to this impulse, we find a practical philosophy, partaking far more of the stoical than of that sceptical school with which his metaphysical writings have identified him; a morality of self-sacrifice and endurance for the accomplishment of great ends. . . . He was an economist of all his talents from early youth. No memoir of a literary man presents a more cautious and vigilant husbandry of the mental powers and acquirements. There is no instance of a man of genius who has wasted less in idleness or in unavailing pursuits. Money was not his object, nor was temporary fame; . . . but his ruling object of ambition, pursued in poverty and riches, in health and sickness, in laborious obscurity and amid the blaze of fame, was to establish a permanent name, resting on the foundation of literary achievements, likely to live as long as human thought endured, and mental philosophy was studied.——BURTON, JOHN HILL, 1846, *Life and Correspondence of David Hume, vol.* I, *pp.* 17, 18.

We have no authenticated record of Hume ever opening to any human being the religious, or irreligious convictions of his soul. A good-natured and sociable man, kind and indulgent to those with whom he came in contact, he passed through life a solitary being, certainly with no God and apparently with no human being to whom to unbosom himself. —MCCOSH, JAMES, 1874, *The Scottish Philosophy, p.* 123.

In 1770, Hume built himself a house in the New Town of Edinburgh, which was then springing up. It was the first house in the street, and a frolicsome young lady chalked upon the wall "St. David's Street." Hume's servant complained to her master, who replied, "Never mind, lassie, many a better man has been made a saint of before," and the street retains its title to this day.—HUXLEY, THOMAS HENRY, 1879, *David Hume (English Men of Letters), p.* 37.

Those who differ most widely from the philosophy of Hume cannot fail to appreciate much in the character of the man. His life showed a consistent course of self-command. His passions were kept under the steady control of the reason. He was habitually generous, direct, and open as the day, with no twist in his nature, and with nothing servile. He may be truly described as a man "without dissimulation,"—which is more than can be said of some of his opponents,—as a man of his integrity and candour. His intellectual honesty showed itself in his love of all that could be verified, and in his hatred of what seemed to him to be unrealities. If he had no Celtic enthusiasm, he had in compensation the sunny Saxon temperament, and if never radiant, he was usually serene and cheerful. He had an almost equal appreciation of the Stoic and the Epicurean view of life; but it was towards the latter that his sympathies practically tended. Unaffected, easy-minded, bright, and sociable, but also eminently secular, we find no trace in him of introspection, or of the seriousness and moral thoughtfulness that attend it. He had a clear head, and a generous heart—add to this the absence of jealousy, that common failing of literary circles and coteries; but he lacked the elevation and the nobleness that are usually associated with the philosophy of idealism. He had a singularly keen intellect; but his intellectual vision was singularly limited.—KNIGHT, WILLIAM, 1886, *Hume (Philosophical Classics)*, *p.* 97.

Dr. Adam Smith relates how Hume diverted himself, a short time before his death, by inventing jocular excuses he might make to Charon, and Charon's surly answers in return. "I thought I might say to him, 'Good Charon, I have been correcting my works for a new edition; allow me a little time to see how the public receive the alterations.' But Charon would answer, 'Get into the boat this instant, you lazy, loitering rogue!' "—MORRILL, JUSTIN S., 1887, *Self-Consciousness of Noted Persons*, *p.* 109.

His thorough good nature, as well as his indifference, prevented him from obtruding his opinions upon any who did not sympathise; while no man was a heartier friend or more warmly appreciative of merit — especially in Scotsmen.—STEPHEN, LESLIE, 1891, *Dictionary of National Biography*, *vol.* XXVIII, *p.* 220.

He is with the full ardour of his being a man of society. He delights in the companionship of his fellows, works surely into the intimacy of close friendship, and is ever ready for rippling, glancing humour, giving and receiving electric impulse from casual acquaintance. These features are not commonly associated, but they were united in him. There are two natures in the man, two lives within this one life; the inner, that of the abstract thinker living within a charmed circle where he does not meet friends, save one or two, and where he cultivates an independence that owns no authority; and the outer life of the man who is free of spirit, ready for all occurrences, and given to a playfulness of disposition, and even joviality, which to most onlookers must seem inconsistent with the high philosophic gift. Yet these two natures are indissolubly united—they are constantly appearing in parallel relations as if they were distinct. Together they constitute a nature rarely met with. It were easy, looking now at the one feature, now at the other, to bring home a charge of inconsistency. In a sense, he is inconsistently a thinker who scorns the ordinary levels of thought; a humorist who revels in the pleasures of the passing hour as if life were a play. These apparently contradictory features are as prominent as they have ever appeared in any human life—together they constitute the actual David Hume—philosopher and man of the world.—CALDERWOOD, HENRY, 1898, *David Hume (Famous Scots Series)*, *p.* 18.

No man could have sought for a companion more delightful or entertaining than Hume. With wide experience, with the dignity of an independent thinker, with the concentration and abundant stores of the student, he united a simplicity which thought no evil, and an almost childlike pleasure in the happiness of social intercourse. He fenced himself in with no artificial barrier of haughtiness or reserve. He had an easy flow of humour, which was in his case accompanied, as it not always is, by that social tact which is rooted in good-nature and benevolence. "His conversation," says one of his friends, "was irresistible, for while it was enlightened, it was naïve almost to puerility." He excelled above all in that perfect form of raillery which Swift has described—the art of making apparent sarcasm suggest the best qualities of those against whom the sarcasm appears to be directed. No man could attract more successfully all characters and all ages. He could soothe the aged or the unfortunate as happily as he could please the young and frolicsome. With all his calmness of temper, and all his boldness of speculation, he was like a child in his discernment of character, and partook in no degree of that useful but not altogether pleasant faculty of reading character with a judicial eye. If he was an object of suspicion to those whose peace might be disturbed by rumors of his atheism, they were quickly disarmed by his irresistible personality.—CRAIK, SIR HENRY, 1901, *A Century of Scottish History, vol.* I, *p.* 411.

A TREATISE OF HUMAN NATURE
1739–40

Never literary attempt was more unfortunate than my "Treatise of Human Nature." It fell *dead-born from the press*, without reaching such distinction, as even to excite a murmur among the zealots.—HUME, DAVID, 1776, *My Own Life, p.* 7.

From what has been already said, it may be seen that we are not to look in Mr. Hume's "Treatise" for any regular or connected system. It is neither a scheme of Materialism nor a scheme of Spiritualism; for his reasonings strike equally at the root of both these theories. His aim is to establish a universal scepticism, and to produce in the reader a complete distrust in his own faculties. . . . With the single exception of Bayle, he has carried this sceptical mode of reasoning farther than any other modern philosopher. —STEWART, DUGALD, 1815-21, *First Preliminary Dissertation, Encyclopædia Britannica.*

The philosophy of Hume, as a whole, originated and fell with himself. A more partial and less daring scepticism might probably have gained many followers; but it is the inevitable result of every system, professing universal unbelief, to destroy itself. The man who by any process of reasoning involves every portion of human knowledge in doubt, instead of persuading any one to follow his conclusions, does little more than controvert his own principles by a "reductio ad absurdum."—MORELL, J. D., 1846–7, *An Historical and Critical View of the Speculative Philosophy of Europe in the Nineteenth Century.*

This treatise is by far the most important of all his philosophical works. If we except certain speculations in history and political economy, it contains nearly all his favourite ideas. He devoted to it all the resources of his mighty intellect. He had read extensively, pondered deeply, and taken immense pains in polishing his style. He could scarcely, indeed, be called a learned man, in the technical sense of the term, but he was well informed. We could have wished that he had possessed wider sympathies with earnest seekers after truth in all ages, but this was not in the nature of the man. His knowledge of Greek was very imperfect at this time (he afterwards renewed his acquaintance with that language); what he knew of greek philosophy was chiefly through Cicero (his very pictures of the Stoics and Epicureans are Roman rather than Grecian), and he never entered into the spirit of such deep and earnest thinkers as Socrates, Plato, and Aristotle, —he tells us somewhere that the fame of Aristotle is utterly decayed. In respect even of modern writers, he never comprehended the profundity of such men as Cudworth and Descartes in the previous century; and he had no appreciation of the speculations of Clarke and Leibnitz, who lived in the age immediately preceding his own. He belongs to the cold, elegant, doubting, and secular eighteenth century; and, setting little value on antiquity, he builds for the present and the future on the philosophy of his own time. —MCCOSH, JAMES, 1874, *The Scottish Philosophy, p.* 121.

Although it is characterised by a marked simplicity of arrangement, it presents some of the most subtle thought and searching reasoning to be found in any literature.—MACKINTOSH, JOHN, 1878–92, *The History of Civilization in Scotland, vol.* IV, *p.* 26.

The "Treatise of Human Nature" is clear, forcible, and untechnical. Its most striking characteristics are its spontaneity and individuality. Hume owed little to academic training, and wrote his earlier works at a distance from centres of learning, without access to large libraries. The literary beauties of the "Treatise," however, are marred by its structural defects. It is a series of brilliant fragments rather than a well-rounded whole, and is concerned more with criticism of metaphysical opinions from the point of view of Hume's theory of knowledge than with the construction of a complete system of philosophy.—MIKKELSEN, M. A., 1897, *Library of the World's Best Literature, ed. Warner, vol.* XIII, *p.* 7777.

Hume had taken his place in the literature of his country and of the world. He himself, however, was depressed with sense of failure, for he says, "Never was literary attempt more unfortunate than my 'Treatise of Human Nature.'" He felt disappointed that it did not even "excite a murmur among the zealots." His power had been concentrated to the utmost, but renown did not come to him, as he had anticipated. What he could do in philosophic thought was accomplished, and he was convinced that the writing was not of slight significance; but the reading public did not know what had been done—his contribution was not of the character to attract readers.—CALDERWOOD, HENRY, 1898, *David Hume (Famous Scots Series), p.* 24.

It was written when he was only twenty-five, and probably no book of the kind, destined to exercise such an extended influence, was ever written by a man of that age, certainly never with greater ease or more supreme command of his own ideas —CRAIK, SIR HENRY, 1901, *A Century of Scottish History, vol.* II, *p.* 188.

ESSAYS

I am strongly tempted too to have a stroke at Hume in parting. He is the author of a little book called "Philosophical Essays," in one part of which he argues against the being of a God, and in another (very needlessly you will say) against the possibility of miracles. He has crowned the liberty of the press. And yet he has a considerable post under the Government. I have a great mind to do justice on his arguments against miracles, which I think might be done in few words. But does he deserve notice? Is he known amongst you? Pray answer me these questions. For if his own weight keeps him down, I should be sorry to contribute to his advancement to any place but the pillory.—WARBURTON, WILLIAM, 1749, *Letters from a Late Eminent Prelate, Sept.* 28, *p.* 14.

I have not yet read the last *Review*, but dipping into it, I accidentally fell upon their account of Hume's "Essay on Suicide." I am glad that they have liberality enough to condemn the licentiousness of an author whom they so much admire: —I say liberality, for there is as much bigotry in the world to that man's errors as there is in the hearts of some secretaries to their peculiar modes and tenets. He is the Pope of thousands, as blind and presumptuous as himself. God certainly infatuates those who will not see. It were otherwise impossible, that a man, naturally shrewd and sensible, and whose understanding has had all the advantages of constant exercise and cultivation, could have satisfied himself, or have hoped to satisfy others with such palpable sophistry as has not even the grace of fallacy to recommend it.—COWPER, WILLIAM, 1784, *Letter to Rev. William Unwin, July* 12; *Works, ed. Southey, vol.* III, *p.* 122.

I like his "Essays" better than anything I have read these many days. He has prejudices, he does maintain errors,—but he defends his positions with so much ingenuity, that one would be almost sorry to see him dislodged. His essays on "Superstition and Enthusiasm," on "The Dignity and Meanness of Human Nature," and several others, are in my opinion admirable both in matter and manner, particularly the first, where his conclusions might be verified by instances with which we are all acquainted. The manner, indeed, of all is excellent; the highest and most difficult effect of art—the appearance of its absence—appears throughout.—CARLYLE, THOMAS, 1815, *Early Letters, ed., by Charles Eliot Norton, p.* 20.

Of the "Political Discourses" it would be difficult to speak in terms of too great commendation. They combine almost every excellence which can belong to such a performance. . . . The great merit, however, of these discourses, is their originality, and the new system of politics and political economy which they unfold. Mr. Hume is, beyond all doubt, the author of the modern doctrines which now rule the world of science, which are to a great extent the guide to practical statesmen, and are only prevented from being applied in their fullest extent to the affairs of nations, by clashing interests and the ignorant prejudices of certain powerful classes; for no one deserving the name of legislator pretends to doubt the soundness of the theory, although many held that the errors of our predecessors require a slow recourse to right principle in conducting the practical business of the world. . . . It is certain that Dr. Smith's celebrated work, with all its great merits, is less of a regular system than the detached essays of Mr. Hume. The originality of the latter's opinions is wholly undeniable: they were published full fourteen years before the "Wealth of Nations." —BROUGHAM, HENRY LORD, 1845–6, *Lives of Men of Letters of the Time of George III.*

"Essays on Commerce, Interest, Balance of Trade, Money, Jealousy of Trade, and Public Credit," display the same felicity of style and illustration that distinguish the other works of their celebrated author. His views of the commercial intercourse that should subsist among nations are alike enlightened and liberal: and he has admirably exposed the groundlessness of the prejudices then entertained against a free intercourse with France, and the fear of being deprived, were commercial restraints abolished, of a sufficient supply of bullion. . . . Hume and Smith saw and pointed out the injurious operation of the Methuen treaty, and exposed the absurdity of our sacrificing the trade with France to that of so beggarly a country as Portugal.—MCCULLOCH, JOHN RAMSAY, 1845, *Literature of Political Economy.*

Of all the English deistical works of the eighteenth century, the influence of two and only two survived the controversy. Hume's "Essay on Miracles," though certainly not unquestioned and unassailed, cannot be looked upon as obsolete or uninfluential.—LECKY, W. E. H., 1865, *History of the Rise and Influence of the Spirit of Rationalism in Europe.*

No writer on miracles omits to notice Hume. To refute him has been the ambition of every Christian apologist for the last hundred years; but what could really be said in reply was said in his lifetime. It is recorded of a professor in the University of Edinburgh that he annually refuted the great sceptic, and with as much complacency as regularity. A portion of his lectures was always introduced with the words—"Having considered these different systems, I will now, gentlemen, proceed to refute the ingenious theories of our late respected townsman, Mr. David Hume." As there really was but one answer, that answer has been repeated with variations and amplifications by all who have undertaken to meet his objections.—HUNT, JOHN, 1869, *David Hume, Contemporary Review, vol.* 11, *p.* 89.

"I flatter myself," says Hume, in the "Essay upon Miracles," "that I have discovered an argument of a like nature" (the reference is to Tillotson's argument on transubstantiation), "which, if just, will, with the wise and learned, be an everlasting check to all kinds of superstitious delusion, and, consequently, will be useful as long as the world endures." This preliminary trumpet-flourish, intended probably to startle the drowsy champions of the faith into some consciousness of the philosopher's claims, has been as nearly fulfilled as could have been expected. Hume's argument, neglected for the moment, soon attracted the assaults of theologians. Since his day eager apologists have denounced it, reasoned against it, passed it under the most rigid examination, and loudly and frequently proclaimed the discovery of some fatal flaw. The fact that the argument is being answered to this day proves that its efficacy is not exhausted. Every new assault is a tacit admission that previous assaults have not demolished the hostile works. It is needless to enquire how far this particular logical *crux* has contributed to the decay amongst rational thinkers of a belief in the miraculous. That belief forms part of a system of thought, and grows faint as the general system loses its hold upon the intellect. The prominence given to the essay, except as an admirable specimen of the dialectical art, may, therefore, be easily exaggerated. No single essay has sapped the bases of belief. On the other hand, the essay is but a small part of Hume's attack upon the fundamental dogmas of theology. His popular reputation, indeed, is almost exclusively based upon it; he is known as the author of this particular dilemma; all else that he wrote is ignored; and so exclusively has attention been fixed upon these particular pages, that few of his assailants take any notice even of the immediately succeeding essay, which forms with it a complete and connected argument.—STEPHEN, LESLIE, 1876, *History of English Thought in the Eighteenth Century, vol.* I, *p.* 309.

The germs of several of Adam Smith's economic doctrines, and some of Bentham's, are to be found in these "Essays." In literary form their merit is great; but it is greater as regards their substance. They are weighted with economic wisdom, with happy and suggestive thoughts on questions of Government; and on the relations of party to party their political sagacity is great. If the "Wealth of Nations" was the chief contribution to the economic literature of England of the eighteenth century, these "Essays" prepared the way for it; and Smith's debt to Hume was both direct and indirect.—KNIGHT, WILLIAM, 1886, *Hume (Philosophical Classics)*, p. 36.

HISTORY OF ENGLAND
1754–62

Hume has out-done himself in this new History, in shewing his contempt of Religion. This is one of those proof charges which Arbuthnot speaks of in his treatise of *political lying*, to try how much the publick will bear. If his history be well received, I shall conclude that there is even an end of all pretence to Religion.—WARBURTON, WILLIAM, 1759, *Letters from a Late Eminent Prelate, Mar.* 3, *p.* 282.

In 1752, The Faculty of Advocates chose me their librarian, an office for which I received little or no emolument, but which gave me the command of a large library. I then formed the plan of writing the "History of England;" but being frightened with the notion of continuing a narrative through a period of seventeen hundred years, I commenced with the accession of the House of Stuart, an epoch when, I thought, the misrepresentations of faction began chiefly to take place. I was, I own, sanguine in my expectations of the success of this work. I thought that I was the only historian, that had at once neglected present power, interest and authority, and the cry of popular prejudices; and, as the subject was suited to every capacity, I expected proportional applause. But miserable was my disappointment: I was assailed by one cry of reproach, disapprobation, and even detestation; English, Scotch, and Irish, Whig and Tory, churchman and secretary, freethinker and religionist, patriot and courtier, united in their rage against a man, who had presumed to shed a generous tear for the fate of Charles I. and the Earl of Strafford; and after the first ebullitions of their fury was over, what was still more mortifying, the book seemed to sink into oblivion. Mr. Millar told me, that in a twelvemonth he sold only forty-five copies of it. I scarcely, indeed, heard of one man in the three kingdoms, considerable for rank or letters, that could endure the book. I must only except the primate of England, Dr. Herring, and the primate of Ireland, Dr. Stone, which seem two odd exceptions. These dignified prelates separately sent me messages not to be discouraged.—HUME, DAVID, 1776, *My Own Life, p.* 17.

The "History" of Mr. Hume is indeed very far from being laudable. It is a mere apology for prerogative from beginning to end: and, tho' the best apology which hath been offered, is yet very weak; which shews the cause must be desperate when even so great an advocate utterly fails in its defence. At the same time that his political principles led him to exalt the prerogative, his philosophic opinions forced him to depress the church: while every body knows that *no church, no king*. Hence his work is one chaos of heterogeneous axioms, and misrepresented events. — PINKERTON, JOHN (ROBERT HERON), 1785, *Letters of Literature, p.* 366.

It is surprising, on examining any particular point, how superficial Hume is, and how many particulars are omitted that would have made his book much more entertaining; but perhaps we have no right to expect this in a general history.—MALONE, EDMOND, 1787, *Maloniana, ed. Prior, p.* 370.

For a judicious choice of materials, and a happy disposition of them, together with perspicuity of style in recording them, this writer was hardly ever exceeded; especially in the latter part of his work, which is by far the most elaborate. The earlier part of his history is too superficial. —PRIESTLY, JOSEPH, 1788, *Lectures on History, Lecture* xxvii, *p.* 176.

The perfect composition, the nervous language, the well-turned periods of Dr. Robertson, inflamed me to the ambitious hope that I might one day tread in his footsteps: the calm philosophy, the careless inimitable beauties of his friend and rival, often forced me to close the volume with a mixed sensation of delight and despair.—GIBBON, EDWARD, 1793, *Autobiography, ch.* xii.

The history of England was investigated

by Hume, not with the eyes of a patriot but of a philosopher; and from each author whom he consulted, selecting alternately the choicest diction, he constructed an artful narrative, in which strength, precision, elegance, and a copious simplicity are infinitely diversified; a narrative interspersed throughout with the most profound reflections; and, though partial, perhaps, to a particular system or party, enriched with the most philosophical views of the arguments and peculiar opinions of the times.—LAING, MALCOLM, 1800–4, *History of Scotland, vol.* IV, *p.* 391.

It is therefore in his "History of England," and principally in those parts of it which were the last composed, that we must look for that style of which the merit is universally confessed. Easy and natural as it appears to be, it was the cultivated fruit of long practice, and a sedulous attention to those models which he esteemed the best.—TYTLER, ALEXANDER FRASER, 1806–14, *Memoirs of the Life and Writings of Henry Home of Kames, vol.* I, *p.* 237.

His greatest work, and that which naturally claims most attention, was his "History of England," which, notwithstanding great defects, will probably be at last placed at the head of historical compositions. No other narrative seems to unite, in the same degree, the two qualities of being instructive and affecting. No historian approached him in the union of the talent of painting pathetic scenes with that of exhibiting comprehensive views of human affairs.—MACKINTOSH, SIR JAMES, 1811, *Memoirs, ed. Mackintosh, vol.* II, *p.* 168.

The great standards of historical composition which England produced during the eighteenth century are among the most important features of belles lettres. In this species of literature they have surpassed all other nations, if only in leading the way, and as historical models for foreign imitation. Unless I am mistaken, Hume ranks with the foremost in this department. . . . His description of earlier times is very unsatisfactory: having no affection for them, he could not sufficiently realize them. — SCHLEGEL, FREDERICK, 1815–59, *Lectures on the History of Literature.*

The name of Hume is far the more considerable which occurs in the period to which we have alluded. But, though his thinking was English, his style was entirely French; and being naturally of a cold fancy, there is nothing of that eloquence or richness about him which characterizes the writings of Taylor, and Hooker, and Bacon, and continues, with less weight of matter, to please in those of Cowley and Clarendon.— JEFFREY, FRANCIS LORD, 1816, *Swift, Edinburgh Review, vol.* 27, *p.* 8.

Hume was not, indeed, learned and well-grounded enough for those writers and investigators of history who judged his works from the usual point of view, because he was not only negligent in the use of the sources of history, but also superficial.—SCHLOSSER, FRIEDRICH CHRISTOPH, 1823, *History of the Eighteenth Century, tr. Davison.*

The author, indeed, wanted that resolute spirit of industry and research, which alone can lead an historian to become thoroughly acquainted with the valuable writers of the middle ages.— DIBDIN, THOMAS FROGNALL, 1824, *The Library Companion, p.* 235, *note.*

Hume often puts the names of the monkish writers in his margin; but I fear all he knew of them was through the media of other writers. He has some mistakes which could not have occurred had he really consulted the originals. . . . Hume is certainly an admirable writer: his style bold, and his reflections shrewd and uncommon; but his religious and political notions have too often warped his judgment.—FARMER, RICHARD, 1827, *Letter to a Friend on the Study of English History, Goodhugh's Library Manual, p.* 43.

Hume is an accomplished advocate. Without positively asserting much more than he can prove, he gives prominence to all the circumstances which support his case; he glides lightly over those which are unfavourable to it; his own witnesses are applauded and encouraged; the statements which seem to throw discredit on them are controverted; the contradictions into which they fall are explained away; a clear and connected abstract of their evidence is given. Every thing that is offered on the other side is scrutinized with the utmost severity; every suspicious circumstance is a ground for comment and invective; what cannot be denied is extenuated, or passed by without notice; concessions even are sometimes made; but this insidious candour only increases the effect of the vast mass of sophistry.—MACAULAY, THOMAS BABINGTON, 1828, *History, Edinburgh Review, Critical and Miscellaneous Essays.*

In Hume's narrative the earlier portions were the last composed. To go backwards is scarce less difficult in writing than in walking; and it is no small proof of his merit and ability as an historian, to have overcome that difficulty of his composition, and left it hardly perceptible to a common reader.—STANHOPE, PHILIP HENRY (LORD MAHON), 1836–54, *History of England from the Peace of Utrecht to the Peace of Versailles, vol.* XI, *p.* 304.

His readiness to rest satisfied with whatever first offered itself, provided it suited his present purpose, without either scrutinizing its internal evidence, or verifying it by reference to earlier and better authority, is forced upon our notice in his account of the battle of Shrewsbury.—TYLER, J. ENDELL, 1838, *Henry of Monmouth, or Memoirs of the Life and Character of Henry V., vol.* I, *p.* 158.

As to his methodicalness, no man ever had a larger view than Hume; he always knows where to begin and end. In his history he frequently rises, though a cold man naturally, into a kind of epic height as he proceeds. His description of the Commonwealth, for example, where all is delineated as with a crayon; one sees there his large mind, moreover, not without its harmonies.—CARLYLE, THOMAS, 1838, *Lectures on the History of Literature, p.* 183.

And now, when we enter upon the reign of William, we have no longer the assistance of the philosophic Hume. We have no longer within our reach those penetrating observations, those careless and inimitable beauties, which were so justly the delight of Gibbon, and, with whatever prejudices they may have been accompanied, and, however suspicious may be those representations which they sometimes enforce and adorn, still render the loss of his pages a subject of the greatest regret, and leave a void which it is impossible adequately to supply.—SMYTH, WILLIAM, 1840, *Lectures on Modern History, Lecture* xxii.

A man of his exceedingly inquiring and unrestrained mind, living in the midst of the eighteenth century, might have been expected to have espoused what is called the popular side in the great questions of English history, the side, in later language, of the movement. Yet we know that Hume's learning is the other way. Accidental causes may perhaps have contributed to this; the prejudice of an ingenious mind against the opinions which he found most prevalent around him; the resistance of a restless mind to the powers that be, as natural as implicit acquiescence in them is to an indolent mind. But the main cause apparently is to be sought in his abhorrence of puritanism, alike repugnant to him in its good and its evil. His subtle and active mind could not bear its narrowness and bigotry, his careless and epicurean temper had no sympathy with its earnestness and devotion. The popular cause in our great civil contests was in his eyes the cause of fanaticism: and where he saw fanaticism he saw that from which his whole nature recoiled, as the greatest of all conceivable evils.—ARNOLD, THOMAS, 1842, *Introductory Lectures on Modern History, Lecture* v.

Considered as calm and philosophic narratives, the histories of Hume and Robertson will remain as standard models for every future age. The just and profound reflections of the former, the inimitable clearness and impartiality with which he has summed up the arguments on both sides, on the most momentous questions which have agitated England, as well as the general simplicity, uniform clearness and occasional pathos, of this story, must forever command the admiration of mankind. In vain we are told that he is often inaccurate, sometimes partial; in vain are successive attacks published on detached parts of his narrative, by party zeal or antiquarian research, his reputation is undiminished; successive editions issuing from the press attest the continued sale of his work; and it continues its majestic course through the sea of time, like a mighty three-decker, which never even condescends to notice the javelins darted at its sides from the hostile canoes which from time to time seek to impede its progress.—ALISON, SIR ARCHIBALD, 1844, *Michelet's France, Foreign and Colonial Review; Essays, vol.* III, *p.* 419.

No one can be surprised if in so short a time alloted to the whole work, far more attention was given to the composition of the narrative than to the preparation of the materials. It was altogether impossible that, in so short a period, the duty of the historian should be diligently performed. The execution of the work answers to the mode of its performance. But if the "History" be not diligently prepared, is it faithfully written? There are numberless proofs of the contrary; but we have the most express evidence in the author's own statement to prove this position.—BROUGHAM, HENRY LORD, 1845-6, *Lives of Men of Letters of the Time of George III.*

Is it possible that this false pleader, this avowed traducer, this narrator of a garbled story, can be the first of British historians? That a writer so unreliable can have won the attention and applause of the best minds of his own and all succeeding ages? That Mackintosh and Brougham and Romilly can have united to place him where he now stands, first among his rivals; while the honest intellect of the Anglo-Saxons of every land cherishes as a priceless treasure this work, in which there is so much that is false and so much that is unworthy? There can only be applied to this singular problem in literature the simplest solution. What we admire in Hume's History is the display of intellectual power. We read it, not so much for information, as for an agreeable intellectual exercise. In this view it was written, in this it is read. We admire its subtile disputations, its artful array of facts, the genius which shines in its false narrative, and illuminates its unsound disputations. The consciousness that its narrative is unsound heightens the interest of the tale.—LAWRENCE, EUGENE, 1855, *The Lives of the British Historians, vol.* II, *p.* 209.

David Hume was not a philosophic historian, for many of his inaccuracies might have been avoided, had he been willing to sacrifice indolence to duty, and encounter the labor of research; he was not a philosophic historian, because his prejudices sometimes made him an eulogist, when he should have been an impartial judge. No man will ever form a correct opinion of any monarch of the house of Stuart from his pages. Hume has no sympathy with the deep-seated love of liberty and sense of justice that glowed in the bosoms of those who opposed the arbitrary claim of prerogative in his favorite kings. Poorer stuff than the Stuarts to make Kings of, never lived in England, and yet no one would learn it from Hume.—HAWKS, FRANCIS L., 1856, *History of North Carolina, vol.* I, *p.* 59.

His "History," notwithstanding some defects which the progress of time and of knowledge is every year making more considerable, or at least enabling us better to perceive, and some others which probably would have been much the same at whatever time the work had been written, has still merits of so high a kind as a literary performance that it must ever retain its place among our few classical works in this department, of which it is as yet perhaps the greatest. In narrative clearness, grace, and spirit, at least, it is not excelled, scarcely equalled, by any other completed historical work in the language.—CRAIK, GEORGE L., 1861, *A Compendious History of English Literature and of the English Language, vol.* II, *p.* 356.

For ease, beauty, and picturesque power of style, there was then nothing like it in the range of English historical literature: and for these qualities it yet holds an honoured place on our book-shelves. Yet the day of Hume as an authority on English history has long gone by. The light of modern research has detected countless flaws and distortions in the great book, which was carefully, even painfully, revised as to its style, but which was formed in great part of a mass of statements often gathered from very doubtful sources, and heaped together, almost unsifted and untried. . . . He wrote exquisitely; but he sometimes spent the beauty of his style upon mere chaff and saw-dust. Much the same thing it was, as if a jeweller should frame a costly casket and grace it with every ornament of art, that its rich beauty might at last enshrine a few worthless pebbles or beads of coloured glass.—COLLIER, WILLIAM FRANCIS, 1861, *A History of English Literature, pp.* 326, 327.

Happily, the influence of Hume's calumnies has long been an expiring influence. But one of their sources is likely to be perennial. It was not mere Jacobitism which made David Hume distort so perseveringly the career and character of Walter Ralegh. Fire and water are not more antipathetic than were the natures of Ralegh and of Hume. Amongst men of genius, it would be hard to find in more salient contrast breadth and narrowness. —EDWARDS, EDWARD, 1868, *The Life of Sir Walter Ralegh, vol.* I, *p.* 721.

David Hume was, like Machiavelli, a man of genius. His mind was one of great power and originality. He was a most acute and even subtle reasoner. It has been said that the object of his reasonings was not to attain truth, but to show that it was unattainable. I am inclined to think that his frequent failures in attaining truth are rather attributable to a bad habit he had acquired, through indolence, of carelessness or indifference about the accuracy of his facts.—BISSET, ANDREW, 1871, *Essays on Historical Truth, p.* 138.

The rapidity with which his history was executed, at a time when but little aid was to be derived from the labours of any predecessors in the same field, shows, not, if fairly considered, that he did not devote himself to such diligent research as is the boast of some modern historians; but that, in fact, the means for such investigation were not at that time accessible. Original documents, where they were known to exist, were jealously guarded. And Hume had to trust to his innate sagacity to extract the truth from sources which to a less penetrating intellect would scarcely have conveyed any indication of information. Yet so great was his native shrewdness that, while drawing only from materials open to all, he threw a perfectly new light on many of the most important transactions and greatest characters in our annals, which since his time has been generally admitted to be the true one.—YONGE, CHARLES DUKE, 1872, *Three Centuries of English Literature, p.* 121.

It still occupies a chief place among English histories, and rightly so, for it is based on the careful study of original sources, the materials are fully mastered and clearly developed, and due attention is paid to the lessons history teaches; persons and times are represented from an impartial point of view on the whole, and the style is fascinating throughout.—SCHERR, J., 1874, *A History of English Literature, tr. M. V., p.* 139.

The "History" as a whole is of no high authority. From first to last it is evidently the work of an essayist and "philosopher," who regarded truth as subordinate to effect, and looked to his own ends, personal and philosophical. To apologize for the misconduct of the Stuarts, to write down the British Constitution, as well as the Christian religion, or at least so much of both as were not then admired by the higher order of the state, were among the objects he sought to attain.—JENKINS, O. L., 1876, *The Student's Handbook of British and American Literature, p.* 238.

He was a man of large reading and profound thought, who could see more clearly than others into the relations of causes and effects, and into the relative significance of the events he had to describe in their reference to events elsewhere; and he had a peculiar gift in the discrimination of the true from the imaginary or the false. There was a universal testimony to the superiority of Hume's work in the countless editions of "Hume and Smollett's History,"—the inferior author being trusted of necessity when the superior was not available.—BURTON, JOHN HILL, 1880, *A History of the Reign of Queen Anne, vol.* II, *p.* 323.

It is the unstudied grace of Hume's periods which renders him, in spite of his unfairness and defective erudition, in spite of his toryism and infidelity, the popular historian of England.—MATHEWS, WILLIAM, 1881, *Literary Style, p.* 8.

This work, written more than a hundred years ago, has enjoyed the rank of a classic in historical literature from the day of its completion to the present time. In point of clearness, elegance, and simplicity of style it has never been surpassed. This peculiarity, however, united as it is with the calm and philosophical spirit with which the author contemplates the events he describes, has given the work a rank to which its strictly historical merits never would have entitled it. Indeed, Hume was not an historical investigator in any true sense of the term. He was under much greater obligations to some of his predecessors than he ever acknowledged. With some propriety it may be said that Carte was the miner, while Hume was only the finisher of the materials brought together by his more industrious and thorough predecessor. An historical work written as Hume wrote could hardly fail to abound in gross errors. For a long time many of the mistakes of this history escaped detection; but of late the errors have been shown to be so abundant and so flagrant that the opinion of scholars concerning the value of the work has been completely modified.—ADAMS, CHARLES KENDALL, 1882–88, *A Manual of Historical Literature, p.* 469.

The more closely it is looked into, it will be seen that Hume the Historian cannot be separated from Hume the Philosopher. The fundamental doctrine of empiricism may be seen underlying the whole of the "History." He wrote the latter work after he had explicitly abandoned a philosophy of *a priori* principles, and come thoroughly under contemporary influence. A Scotsman trained in France, and a follower of the experiential method, he read the history of his country under the prejudices of his system and position; and he wrote it far too quickly. While his brother historian, Robertson, spent more than six years over his "Scotland," Hume wrote the first volume of his "England" in little more than a year; and when revising it, he altered rapidly, without the necessary research. His bias against the Whigs grew with that on which it fed. If—as was the case—many of the Roundheads were fanatics, and the majority of the Cavaliers were of a more tolerant spirit, that was enough for Hume. He at once exaggerated both. His historical style is undoubtedly good. It is specially clear and vivid—not a dry digest of annals, but a picturesque narrative, lit up by gleams of happy characterisation, and many felicitous side-comments on men and things.—KNIGHT, WILLIAM, 1886 *Hume* (*Philosophical Classics*), *p.* 226.

Gave himself no time for such research as would now be thought necessary. He became more superficial as he receded further into periods with which he had little sympathy, and was studying merely for the nonce. His literary ability, however, made the book incomparably superior to the diluted party pamphlets or painful compilations which had hitherto passed for history; nor could the author of the "Political Discourses" fail to give proofs of sagacity in occasional reflections. His brief remarks upon the social and economical conditions of the time (see Appendix to James I) were then an original addition to mere political history. The dignity and clearness of the style are admirable. The book thus became, as it long continued to be, the standard history of England, and has hardly been equalled in literary merit.—STEPHEN, LESLIE, 1891, *Dictionary of National Biography, vol.* XXVIII, *p.* 219.

Is a classic; though it can hardly be said to be a good book.—HARRISON, FREDERIC, 1894, *Carlyle's Place in Literature, The Forum, vol.* 17, *p.* 537.

It is probable that his History will long hold place on our library shelves; its style might almost be counted a model historic style—if we were to have models (of which the wisdom is doubtful). It is clear, it is precise, it is perspicuous, it is neat to a fault. It might almost be called a reticent style, in its neglect of those wrappings of wordy illustration and amplification which so many historians employ. He makes us see his meaning as if we looked through crystal; and if the crystal is toned by his prejudices—as it is and very largely—it is altogether free from the impertinent decorative arabesques of the rhetorician.—MITCHELL, DONALD G., 1895, *English Lands Letters and Kings, Queen Anne and the Georges, p.* 156.

The old accusations against its partisanship are ridiculous. Hume's Toryism did not lead him nearly so far from absolute impartiality as Lingard's "Popery," as Macaulay's Whiggishness, as Mr. Green's neo-Liberalism; and he compensated it by a sort of transcendence of humour which, unfortunately, none of these three shared. Much more serious defects, the first more or less unavoidable, the second the taint of the time, were the incompleteness of his information, and the rather cavalier fashion in which he treated what information he had. But it may be doubted whether his mastery of a sort—and a very excellent sort—of style did not compensate even for these.—SAINTSBURY, GEORGE, 1896, *Social England, ed. Traill, vol.* V, *p.* 267.

Is, in the writer's endeavour to make it a philosophic whole, in its clearness of narrative and purity of style, our first literary history. But he is neither exact, nor does he care to be exact. He does not love his subject, and he wants sympathy with mankind and with his country. His manner is the manner of Voltaire, passionless, keen, and elegant.—BROOKE, STOPFORD A., 1896, *English Literature, p.* 202.

Modern critics have shown that Hume's pages swarm with inaccuracies, and that, what is a worse fault, his predilections for Tory ideas lead him to do wilful injustice to the opponents of arbitrary power. All this, however, is little to the point; Hume is no longer appealed to as an authority. He is read for his lucid and beautiful English, for the skill with which he marshals vast trains of events before the mental eye, for his almost theatrical force in describing the evolution of a crisis. If we compare his work from this point of view with all that had preceded it in English literature, we shall see how eminent is the innovation we owe to Hume. He first made history readable.—GOSSE, EDMUND, 1897, *Short History of Modern English Literature, p.* 257.

PHILOSOPHY

Hume, the most subtle, if not the most philosophical, of the deists; who, by perplexing the relations of cause and effect, boldly aimed to introduce a universal scepticism, and to pour a more than Egyptian darkness into the whole region of morals.—HALL, ROBERT, 1799, *Modern Infidelity Considered with Respect to Its Influence on Society, Works, ed. Gregory.*

Dr. Reid rendered good service to the cause of truth, in opposition to the sceptical philosophy of Hume, who dexterously availed himself of the authority of Locke in the support of his own mischievous dogmas.—WILLIAMS, EDWARD, 1800, *The Christian Preacher.*

In these investigations of Hume, philosophical scepticism stands forth with a power, depth, and logical consistency, such as had never before appeared; recommended, moreover, by great correctness, clearness, and elegance of diction.—TENNEMANN, WILLIAM GOTTLIEB, 1812, *A Manual of the History of Philosophy, tr. Johnson, ed. Morell, p.* 372.

His all-pervading and destructive scepticism determined the course of English philosophy. Since his day, nothing further has been effected in this department of inquiry than strenuous efforts to arrest pernicious influences, tending to sap the very foundations of moral order and to uphold the fabric of necessary convictions by means of various bulwarks. —SCHLEGEL, FREDERICK, 1815–59, *Lectures on the History of Literature.*

Those of my writings to which you refer will be read by no nation: a few speculative men will take them; but none will be rendered more gloomy, more dissatisfied, or more unsocial by them. Rarely will you find one who, five minutes together, can fix his mind even on the surface: some new tune, some idle project, some light thought, some impracticable wish, will generally run, like the dazzling haze of summer on the dry heath, betwixt them and the reader. A bagpipe will swallow them up, a strathspey will dissipate them, or Romance with the death-rattle in her throat will drive them away into dark staircases and charnel-houses.—LANDOR, WALTER SAVAGE, 1828, *David Hume and John Home, Imaginary Conversations, Third Series.*

The Scepticism of Hume, like an electric spark, sent life through the paralyzed opinions; philosophy awoke to renovated vigor, and its problems were again to be considered in other aspects, and subjected to a more searching analysis. . . . To Hume we owe the philosophy of Kant, and, therefore, also, in general, the latter philosophy of Germany. Kant explicitly acknowledges that it was by Hume's *reductio ad absurdum* of the previous doctrine of Casuality, he was first roused from his dogmatic slumber. . . . To Hume, in like manner, we owe the philosophy of Reid, and, consequently, what is now distinctively known in Europe as the Philosophy of the Scottish School.—HAMILTON, SIR WILLIAM, 1836, *Lectures on Metaphysics, Appendix.*

Hume, the prince of *dilettanti*, from whose writings one will hardly learn that there is such a thing as truth, far less that it is attainable; but only that the *pro* and *con* of everything may be argued with infinite ingenuity, and furnishes a fine intellectual exercise. — MILL, JOHN STUART, 1838–97, *Bentham, Early Essays, ed. Gibbs, p.* 331.

David Hume, however, was a very great man—great as a historian, as every one admits; but greater still as a philosopher; for it is impossible to calculate what a blank, but for him, the whole speculative science of Europe for the last seventy years would have been.—FERRIER, JAMES

FREDERICK, 1842–6, *Berkeley and Idealism, Lectures, vol.* II, *p.* 300, *note.*

The marvellousness, acuteness and subtlety of Hume have never been denied; and his influence upon speculation has been aided as much by the alarm his doctrines excited, as by the ingenuity with which they were upheld. If Berkeley met with no refuters, Hume could meet with none. Antagonists have generally been compelled to admit that the skeptical reasoning was unanswerable.—LEWES, GEORGE HENRY, 1845–46, *Biographical History of Philosophy, p.* 571.

The centre of Hume's philosophizing is his criticism of the conception of cause. Locke had already expressed the thought that we attain the conception of substance only by the *habit* of always seeing certain modes together. Hume takes up this thought with earnestness. Whence do we know, he asks, that two things stand together in the relation of cause and effect? . . . There needs no further proof, than simply to utter these chief thoughts of Hume, to show that his scepticism is only a logical carrying out of Locke's empiricism. Every determination of universality and necessity must fall away, if we derive our knowledge only from perceptions through the sense; these determinations cannot be comprised in sensation.—SCHWEGLER, ALBERT, 1848–55, *A History of Philosophy in Epitome, tr. Seelye, pp.* 199, 201.

It was acknowledged by Hume, that it was only in solitude and retirement that he could yield any assent to his own philosophy.—MILLER, HUGH, 1856, *Essays, p.* 447.

Hume's abstractions are not deep or wise. He owes his fame to one keen observation, that no copula had been detected between any cause and effect, either in physics or in thought; that the term cause and effect was loosely or gratuitously applied to what we know only as consecutive, not at all as casual.—EMERSON, RALPH WALDO, 1856, *English Traits, Works, Riverside ed., vol.* V, *p.* 232.

Hume, though a most accomplished reasoner, as well as a profound and fearless thinker, had not the comprehensiveness of Adam Smith, nor had he that invaluable quality of imagination without which no one can so transport himself into past ages as to realize the long and progressive movements of society, always fluctuating, yet, on the whole, steadily advancing. How unimaginative he was, appears, not only from the sentiments he expressed, but likewise from many traits in his private life. It appears, also, in the very colour and mechanism of his language; that beautiful and chiselled style in which he habitually wrote, polished as marble, but cold as marble too, and wanting that fiery enthusiasm and those bursts of tempestuous eloquence, which, ever and anon, great objects naturally inspire, and which rouse men to their inmost depths. This it was, which, in his "History of England,"—that exquisite production of art, which, in spite of its errors, will be admired as long as taste remains among us,—prevented him from sympathizing with those bold and generous natures, who, in the seventeenth century, risked their all to preserve the liberty of their country. . . . It was this which made him stop where he did, and which gave to his works the singular appearance of a profound and original thinker, in the middle of the eighteenth century, advocating practical doctrines, so illiberal, that, if enforced, they would lead to despotism, and yet, at the same time, advocating speculative doctrines, so fearless and enlightened, that they were not only far in advance of his own age, but have, in some degree, outstripped even the age in which we live.—BUCKLE, HENRY THOMAS, 1861–94, *History of Civilization in England, vol.* III, *pp.* 331, 332.

Such was Hume's psychology; an attempt to push analysis to its ultimate limits; valuable in its method, even if defective in its results; a striking example of the acuteness and subtle penetration of its author.—FARRAR, ADAM STOREY, 1862. *A Critical History of Free Thought, p.* 149.

The subtlest of all our metaphysicians.—LYTTON, EDWARD BULWER LORD, 1863–68, *Caxtoniana, Miscellaneous Prose Works, vol.* III, *p.* 83.

We shall now repeat the leading points of Hume's system, in the usual order. I.—The standard of Right and Wrong is Utility, or a reference to the Happiness of mankind. This is the ground, as well as the motive, of moral approbation. II.—As to the nature of the Moral Faculty, he contends that it is a compound of Reason, and Humane or Generous Sentiment. He does not introduce the subject of Free-will into Morals. He contends strongly for the existence of Disinterested Sentiment, or Benevolence; but scarcely recognizes it as leading to absolute and uncompensated self-sacrifice. He does not seem to see that as far as the approbation of benevolent actions is concerned, we are anything but disinterested parties. The good done by one man is done to some others; and the recipients are moved by their self-love to encourage beneficence. The regard to our own benefactor makes all benefactors interesting. III.—He says little directly bearing on the constituents of Human Happiness; but that little is all in favour of simplicity of life and cheap pleasures. He does not reflect that the pleasures singled out by him are far from cheap; "agreeable conversation, society, study, health, and the beauties of nature," although not demanding extraordinary wealth, cannot be secured without a larger share of worldly means than has ever fallen to the mass of men in any community. IV.—As to the substance of the Moral Code, he makes no innovations. He talks somewhat more lightly of the evils of Unchastity than is customary; but regards the prevailing restraints as borne out by Utility. The inducements to virtue are, in his view, our humane sentiments, on the one hand, and our self-love, or prudence, on the other; the two classes of motives conspiring to promote both our own good and the good of mankind. V.—The connexion of Ethics with Politics is not specially brought out. The political virtues are moral virtues. He does not dwell upon the sanctions of morality, so as to distinguish the legal sanction from the popular sanction. He draws no line between Duty and Merit. VI.—He recognizes no relationship between Ethics and Theology. The principle of Benevolence in the human mind is, he thinks, an adequate source of moral approbation and disapprobation; and he takes no note of what even sceptics (Gibbon, for example) often dwell upon, the aid of the Theological sanction in enforcing duties imperfectly felt by the natural and unprompted sentiments of the mind.—BAIN, ALEXANDER, 1868, *Moral Science*, p. 195.

It is rather curious that although David Hume's "still-born" "Treatise of Human Nature" had then been before the world for fourteen years, and his "Inquiry concerning Human Understanding" for nearly four years, no allusion to Hume is to be found either in the published or the hitherto unpublished writings of Berkeley. Yet he was Berkeley's intellectual successor in the leadership of European thought, as far as speculative power, subtlety, and the general line of inquiry pursued are concerned; and in both these works the Scotch philosopher gives his own negative solution of the chief questions which Berkeley had pursued from youth to old age. Berkeley's attack upon abstractions, as well as his metaphysical analysis of mathematical quantity and of the material world, largely influenced the philosophical education of Hume; as Hume in his turn awoke Kant, and through Kant modern Germany. Berkeley, Hume, and Kant were the three great speculative minds of the eighteenth century, connected in chronological and philosophical succession.—FRASER, ALEXANDER CAMPBELL, 1871, *ed., Life and Letters of George Berkeley*, p. 343.

Hume's philosophical significance is connected principally with his speculations concerning casualty. His skepticism is founded on the assertion, that the casual idea, owing to its origin in habit, admits of use only within the field of experience: to reason from data given empirically to that which is transcendent (or lies beyond the whole range of experience), like God and immortality, appears to Hume unlawful. To this is to be added that Hume, particularly in his earliest treatise, expresses an equally negative judgment concerning the idea of substance; that I, he argues, is a complex of ideas, for which we have no right to posit a single substratum or underlying substance. Hume's ethical principle is the feeling of the happiness and misery of man. The moral judgment is based on the satisfaction or disapprobation which an action excites in him who witnesses it. Owing to the natural sympathy of man for his fellows, an action performed in the interest of the common welfare calls forth approbation, and one of an opposite nature, disapprobation.—UEBERWEG, FRIEDRICH, 1871, *History of Philosophy, tr. Morris*, p. 134.

Everybody knows that Hume was a

sceptic. It is not so generally known that he has developed a full system of the human mind. Students of philosophy should make themselves acquainted with it. It has in fact been the stimulating cause of all later European philosophy: of that of Reid and his school; of that of Kant, and the powerful thinkers influenced by him; and of that of M. Cousin, and his numerous followers in France, in their attempt to combine Reid and Kant. Nor is it to be omitted that Mr. J. S. Mill, in his "Examination of Hamilton," has reproduced to a large extent the theory of Hume, but without so clearly seeing or candidly avowing the consequences.—McCosh, James, 1874, *The Scottish Philosophy, p.* 133.

Hume was the first writer who distinctly realized the limits within which a sensationalist individualism is confined, and also the first who carried out, with something like fidelity, that substitution of psychology for ontology, which his predecessors had been more ready to prescribe than to practice.—Caird, Edward, 1877, *A Critical Account of the Philosophy of Kant, p.* 64.

In Locke, Berkeley, and Hume, the three classic names in the history of British speculation, we have brought before us three very distinctly marked individualities. Characterized with reference to their philosophic tendencies, Locke is the serious, or, rather, the jejunely sober, inquirer; Berkeley, the philosophic seer and positivist, and Hume the academic sceptic. In their personal lives all three are, although in different ways, almost equally admirable. Locke combines gaiety and gravity in the good breeding of the gentleman. Berkeley unites transparent purity of nature with the eloquent defense of ideals and unflagging labor for their realization. Hume applies the brakes—always an ungrateful labor—to the precipitous train of human speculation; he is the sworn enemy of all enthusiasms; he is the Mephistopheles, or "spirit of denial," in British thought.—Morris, George S., 1880, *British Thought and Thinkers, p.* 234.

While so much of the career of this great thinker, in thought so clear, in heart so kindly, is on its spiritual side a darkness and a grief to Christian minds, let us remember the undoubted evidence of reaction and recoil from the gloom of doubt which no one has more eloquently expressed, and let us give as much acceptance as we can to the words uttered amidst the shock of his mother's death, and uttered as a reply to the charge of having broken with all Christian hope—"Though I throw out my speculations to entertain the learned and metaphysical world, yet in other things I do not think so differently from the rest of the world as you imagine."—Cairns, John, 1881, *Unbelief in the Eighteenth Century, p.* 111.

As a philosopher of religion Hume is the finisher and destroyer of deism. . . . Hume never denied the existence of God, never directly impugned revelation. His final word is doubt and uncertainty. . . . In his moral philosophy Hume shows himself the empiricist only, not the skeptic. . . . Only once since David Hume, in Herbert Spencer, has the English nation produced a mind of like comprehensive power. Hume and Locke form the culminating points of English thought. They are national types, in that in them the two fundamental tendencies of English thinking, clearness of understanding and practical sense, were manifested in equal force. In Locke these worked together in harmonious co-operation. In Hume the friendly alliance is broken, the common labor ceases; each of the two demands its full rights; a painful breach opens up between science and life.—Falckenberg, Richard, 1885–93, *History of Modern Philosophy, tr. Armstrong, pp.* 228, 230, 231, 236.

If you are to enjoy the inner life, you must bear also its burdens and its doubts. To become sure of yourself, you must first doubt yourself. And this doubt, this skepticism, which self-analysis always involves, who could express it better than the great Scotchman, David Hume? Hume is, I think, next to Hobbes, the greatest of British speculative thinkers, Berkeley occupying the third place in order of rank. I cannot undertake to describe to you in this place the real historical significance of Hume, his subtlety, his fearlessness, his fine analysis of certain of the deepest problems, his place as the inspirer of Kant's thought, his whole value as metaphysical teacher of his time. What you will see in him is merely the merciless skeptic, and, in this superficial sketch of the rediscovery of the inner consciousness, I don't ask you to see more. —ROYCE, JOSIAH, 1892, *The Spirit of Modern Philosophy, p.* 93.

The Philosophy of Hume was a destructive assault upon the main position of the Deists respecting the origin of all religions save what they called "the religion of nature." On the other hand, not only by its criticism of the basis of positive belief in general, but also by its dealing with the proofs of the Christian creed in particular, it presented to Christian Apologists problems of the gravest consequence. —FISHER, GEORGE PARK, 1896, *History of Christian Doctrine, p.* 388.

Although Hume's writings are so much better known at first hand than those of Cumberland and Gay,—the only two of his English predecessors who can really be said to have stated the Utilitarian principle,—it is more difficult than might be supposed to present his views on Ethics in a way to leave no room for misunderstanding. In the first place, one has to keep in mind Hume's relation to the "moral sense" school, and avoid attributing either too much or too little importance to this relation; and, in the second place,—what is much more important,—one has to decide, after the most careful examination and comparison, whether one shall accept his earlier or his later treatment of Ethics as the more adequately representing his system.—ALBEE, ERNEST, 1897, *Hume's Ethical System, Philosophical Review, vol.* 6, *p.* 338.

The theory of causation first set forth by David Hume has attracted more attention and led to more discussion than any other philosophical doctrine of modern times.—PETERSON, JAMES B., 1898, *The Empirical Theory of Causation, Philosophical Review, vol.* 7, *p.* 43.

GENERAL

The great David Hume.—GIBBON, EDWARD, 1758, *Private Letters, Dec.* 30.

If we may judge of him by his writings, will scarcely be charged with the fault of having carried humility to an excess. A pity it is that he hath not made a better use of his abilities and talents, which might have laid a just foundation for acquiring the praise he seems so fond of, as well as rendered him really useful to the world, if he had been so industrious as to employ them in serving and promoting the excellent cause of religion, as he hath unhappily been in endeavouring to weaken and expose it.—LELAND, JOHN, 1754–56, *A View of the Principal Deistical Writers, p.* 239.

"Why, Sir, his style is not English; the structure of his sentences is French. Now the French structure and the English structure may, in the nature of things, be equally good. But if you allow that the English language is established, he is wrong. My name might originally have been Nicholson, as well as Johnson; but were you to call me Nicholson now, you would call me very absurdly."—JOHNSON, SAMUEL, 1763, *Life by Boswell, ed. Hill, vol.* I, *p.* 508.

David, who there supinely deigns to lie,
The fattest hog in Epicurus' sty,
Though drunk with Gallic wine and Gallic praise,
David shall bless Old England's halcyon days.
—MASON, WILLIAM, 1773, *An Heroic Epistle to Sir William Chambers on his Book of Gardening.*

Next comes the Scotch Goliath, David Hume; but where is the accomplished stripling who can cut off his most metaphysical head? Who is he that can stand up before him, and prove the existence of the universe and its Founder? He hath an adroiter wit than all his forefathers in philosophy if he will confound this uncircumcised. The long and dull procession of reasoners that have followed since have challenged the awful shade to duel, and struck the air with their puissant arguments. But as each new comer blazons "Mr. Hume's objections" on his pages, it is plain they are not satisfied the victory is gained. Now, though every one is daily referred to his own feelings as a triumphant confutation of the glozed lies of this deceiver, yet it would assuredly make us feel safer to have our victorious answer set down in impregnable propositions.—EMERSON, RALPH WALDO, 1823, *Letters, ed. Cabot, vol.* I, *p.* 104.

Hume was a Tory; he was also a Scotchman:—this renders the almost uniform absence of Scotticisms, from his style, a subject of surprise—if not of astonishment.—DIBDIN, THOMAS FROGNALL, 1824, *The Library Companion, p.* 235, *note.*

Hume was too rich a man to borrow; and perhaps he reached on the French more than he was acted on by them: but neither had he aught to do with Scotland; Edinburgh, equally with La Flèche, was but the lodging and laboratory, in which he not so much morally *lived* as metaphysically *investigated.*—CARLYLE, THOMAS, 1828, *Burns.*

Hume's reputation as a philosopher and an historian has long been on the wane, his views in both are regarded as partial and one-sided; it is believed that in his science he gave exclusive prominence to one set of faculties and that in his estimate of facts he was almost as exclusively guided by one set of authorities. Praised by one school of critics beyond his merits, depreciated by another below his deserts, there is reason to suspect that he has been more frequently judged by the supposed consequences of his doctrines than by the doctrines themselves, and though in the examination of principles it is not possible to neglect their obvious tendency, yet there is a danger that these tendencies may be measured by our own preconceived notions rather than by the necessary and immediate inferences from the author's writings and statements.—TAYLOR, W. C., 1846, *The Philosophy of David Hume, Bentley's Miscellany, vol.* 19, *p.* 494.

Hume is considered also as one of the most dangerous and insidious enemies by whom the Christian religion has ever been attacked.—SHAW, THOMAS B., 1847, *Outlines of English Literature, p.* 282.

Morality survives, we know not well how, in Hume. . . . There is a cogency in this resting upon only the lowest grounds; the winter-vitality of the moral convictions of Hume is worth more than any summer exuberance of sentiment.—CLOUGH, ARTHUR HUGH, 1852, *Development of English Literature, Prose Remains, p.* 349.

The character of the true sceptic was never more clearly exhibited than by David Hume, the philosopher and historian, whose name is so well known and firmly established among the greatest of his century, and whose works and influence have produced as much effect upon men's minds and beliefs as it is possible for a perpetual negative to produce. He is not only a born representative of the class, but even to a great extent of his time, which was an unbelieving age, full of profanities, great and small, and an immense and astonishing indifference to everything spiritual and unseen. He was one of the most clear-sighted men of his day—keen in pursuit of truth, not moved by any throes of mental anguish because of his inability to believe one dogma or another, but still far from setting himself up as an authority above other authorities, or arrogating a superior judgment. He was no profligate, eager to cover his sins by the abrogation of moral laws—no revolutionary, bent upon satisfying his own ambition by the overturn of all things. Neither was his spirit affected by the gloomy nothingness of the system he believed. He was an honest, cheerful, comfortable, unexcited soul, full of a steady power of labour, much patience and good-humour, and a certain sober light-heartedness, whatever was his fortune. The devoutest believer, with all the succours of religion, could not have behaved with more composure and dignity in the presence of death; nor is the sober quiet of his life less remarkable.—OLIPHANT, MARGARET O. W., 1869, *The Sceptic, Historical Sketches of the Reign of George Second, p.* 417.

The autobiography of Hume is singularly interesting, as being the portrait of a modest, firm, independent, and just man. —UNDERWOOD, FRANCIS H., 1871, *A Hand-Book of English Literature, British Authors, p.* 162.

Hume is always idiomatic, but his idioms are constantly wrong; many of his best passages are, on that account, curiously grating and puzzling: you feel that they are very like what an Englishman would say, but yet that after all, somehow or other, they are what he never would say, —there is a minute seasoning of imperceptible difference, which distracts your attention and which you are forever stopping to analyze.—BAGEHOT, WALTER, 1876, *Adam Smith as a Person, Works, ed. Morgan, vol.* III, *p.* 296.

Hume, in style nearly perfect.—MORISON, JAMES COTTER, 1879, *Gibbon* (*English Men of Letters*), *p.* 102.

An accomplished reasoner, an original, profound, and fearless thinker, more remarkable for depth than for erudition. As a philosopher, the greatest in the school of materialism; as a historian, the first to treat the sequence of historical events in a philosophical manner; as a man, one of the leaders of the race.—WELSH, ALFRED H., 1883, *Development of English Literature and Language, vol.* II, *p.* 166.

Mr. Hume confessed himself the prince of sceptics, as Voltaire was the prince of scoffers. — PIERSON, ARTHUR TAPPAN, 1886, *Many Infallible Proofs, p.* 12.

Hume's place in literature is not, at the present moment, adequate to what we know of his powers of intellect or to his originality as a thinker. He is acknowledged to be a great man, but he is very little read. His "History," in fragments, and his "Essay on Miracles," which still enjoys a kind of success of scandal, are all that the general reader knows of Hume. If we deplore this fact, it must be admitted that his cool and unimpassioned criticism of belief, his perpetual return to the destructive standpoint, yet without vivacity, as one who undermines rather than attacks an opposing body, his colourless grace, the monotony of his balanced and faultless sentences, offer to us qualities which demand respect but scarcely awaken zeal, and, in short, that Hume although a real is a somewhat uninspiring classic. His great merit as a writer is his lucidity, his perfectly straightforward and competent expression of the particular thing he has it on his mind to say.—GOSSE, EDMUND, 1888, *A History of Eighteenth Century Literature, p.* 299.

A studied and artful—sometimes a strained—simplicity is the chief characteristic of his style. He never attempts the majestic periods of Johnson or Gibbon; while a certain air of stiffness and precision effectually prevents his being spirited on the one hand, or colloquial on the other. His prose flows on with a steady and even motion, which no obstacle ever retards, nor any passion ever agitates. In the whole of his writings there is scarce one of those outbursts of emotion which at times animate the pages even of the coolest metaphysicians. Scorn there is in abundance; but it is the amused and pitying contempt of a superior being who watches from afar the frailties and vices from which himself is consciously exempt. Enthusiasm, or righteous indignation, was a total stranger to Hume's cast of mind. But his sneer and his sarcasm, though by far less elaborate and less diligently sustained, are hardly less effective and pointed than Gibbon's. . . . Hume's vocabulary is copious and well chosen, but never picturesque. . . . Many men have written English prose with greater ease, fluency, and freedom, and many with greater dignity and effect; but few with more accuracy, purity, and elegance of diction than David Hume.—MILLAR, J. H., 1895, *English Prose, ed. Craik, vol.* IV, *pp.* 187, 188.

Hume is impeccable in paragraph unity from the point of view of subject analysis. His unity depends on the philosophic scheme, the previsedly careful articulation of framework. It is not the picturesque unity of Macaulay. In spite of occasional extreme sententiousness, and his very sparing use of sentence-connectives, Hume's coherence is always good. The sententiousness is never left unexplained. If the reader is ever delayed it is by the balance of the sentence, but he is never seriously checked by this. In Hume the formal balance breaks in upon the sequence as waves pass beneath a boat and lap it sharply, but only to drive it onward. Hume's favorite order is loose, with a tendency to eschew initiatory sentences. The topic sentence is likely to be somewhat indefinite, becoming clear with the first amplifying sentences. To sum up: Hume represents the long paragraph adapting itself to the Johnsonian balanced sentence. His integers of style are larger than Johnson's, but less unwieldy than Gibbon's. He is retrogressive in percentage of very short sentences.—LEWIS, EDWIN HERBERT, 1894, *The History of the English Paragraph, p.* 118.

His philosophical importance has lasted better than his historical, because his history, though full of ability, was written without access to many documents since laid open, and with a somewhat insufficient attention to careful use of those that were accessible; while his philosophy, needing nothing but the furniture of his own mind, and employing that in the best way on one side of perennially interesting and insoluble questions, remains a *point de repère* for ever. It is indeed admitted to have practically restarted all philosophical inquiry, being as much the origin of German and other theory as of the Scottish school and of later English negative materialism. Luckily, too, the value of literary work as such is far more enduring than that of either philosophy or history by themselves. For they may be superseded, but it never can. And Hume's expression was for his special purposes supreme—perfectly clear, ironical, but not to the point of suspicious frivolity, and as polished as the somewhat dead and flat colour of the style of the time would admit.—SAINTSBURY, GEORGE, 1898, *A Short History of English Literature, p.* 623.

David Hume was without question the man of greatest mental grasp whom Scotland produced in the eighteenth century. —CRAIK, SIR HENRY, 1901, *A Century of Scottish History, vol.* II, *p.* 186.

James Ferguson

1710–1776.

A native of Keith, Bamffshire, whilst yet very young, without the advantages of education, exhibited a remarkable genius for mechanical and astronomical investigations. Whilst employed in the humble capacity of a shepherd, he continued his studies with untiring zeal. In 1743 he came to London, where he attracted great attention by the publication of astronomical tables, and the delivery of lectures, repeated in many towns in England, on experimental philosophy. A list of his publications and contributions to Phil. Trans. will be found in Bibl. Brit. Works, edited by Sir David Brewster, Edinburgh, 5 vols. 8vo. "Lectures on select Subjects in Mechanics, Hydrostatics, &c.," edited by Sir D. B., 2 vols. 8vo. "Astronomy explained upon Sir Isaac Newton's principles," 1821, 2 vols. 8vo. New ed., 1841, 2 vols. 8vo.—ALLIBONE, S. AUSTIN, 1854–58, *A Critical Dictionary of English Literature, vol.* I, *p.* 587.

PERSONAL

Here
is interred the body of
JAMES FERGUSON,
F. R. S.
Who, blessed with a fine natural Genius,
by unwearied application (without a Master)
attained the Sciences.
Astronomy and Mechanics he taught
with singular success and reputation
He was modest, sober, humble, and religious,
and
His works will immortalize his Memory,
When this small Monument is no more.
He died 16th Nov. 1776, aged 66.
—INSCRIPTION ON TOMB, 1776.

The best machine I ever contrived is the Eclipsareon, of which there is a figure in the thirteenth plate of my "Astronomy." It shows the time, quantity, duration, and progress of solar eclipses, at all parts of the earth. My next best contrivance is the Universal Dialing Cylinder, of which there is a figure in the eighth plate of the supplement to my "Mechanical Lectures." It is now thirty years since I came to London; and during all that time, I have met with the instances of friendship from all ranks of people, both in town and country, which I do here acknowledge with the utmost respect and gratitude; and particularly the goodness of our present gracious Sovereign, who, out of his privy purse, allows me fifty pounds a year, which is regularly paid without any deduction. —FERGUSON, JAMES, c1776, *A Short Account of His Own Life, p.* 23.

Mr. Ferguson had a very sedate appearance, face and brow a little wrinkled; he wore a large full stuff wig, which gave him a venerable look, and made him to appear older than he really was. He usually wore a white neckerchief, especially when delivering his lectures. His coat had no neck, was of large dimensions, reaching down below the knee, and coming full round in front; was decorated with large buttons, and of course had the usual huge pockets and double folded-up sleeves fenced with shirt wrist ruffles. His waistcoat was also large; had likewise no neck; large pockets; and reached down to near his thighs. He wore knee breeches, generally of black velvet, or plush, and fastened at the knee with silver buckles; generally wore black stockings, full shoes with buckles. When walking about he wore the cocked hat of that day slightly trimmed with lace; and, in these, the latter days of his life, he walked about with the aid of a staff.—REID, ANDREW, 1833, *Personal Appearance and Dress of Mr. Ferguson about the Year* 1774, *Letter to E. Henderson, June* 7.

Among self-educated men there are few who claim more of our admiration than the celebrated James Ferguson. If ever any one was literally his own instructor in the very elements of knowledge, it was he. Acquisitions that have scarcely in any other case, and probably never by one so young, been made without the assistance either of books or a living teacher, were the discoveries of his solitary and almost illiterate boyhood. There are few more interesting narratives in any language than the account which Ferguson himself has given of his early history.—CRAIK, GEORGE L., 1845, *The Pursuit of Knowledge under Difficulties, vol.* I.

Ferguson was a man of very clear judgment, and of unwearied application to study; benevolent, meek, and innocent in his manners as a child; humble, courteous, and communicative. His religious character gave the tone to his general conduct. The anxieties and changes of his chequered life never effaced the religious impressions early produced by the piety of his parents, but rather strengthened his confidence towards God, and his belief in the great doctrines of our most holy faith. A lovely character was his, according to the testimony of all who knew him.—BRIGHTWELL, C. L., 1879, *Annals of Industry and Genius, p.* 300.

GENERAL

Mr. Ferguson may in some degree be regarded as the first elementary writer on Natural Philosophy, and to his labours we must attribute that general diffusion of scientific knowledge among the practical mechanics of this country, which has in a great measure banished those antiquated prejudices and erroneous manners of construction that perpetually misled the unlettered artist. But it is not merely to the praise of a popular writer that Mr. Ferguson is entitled; while he is illustrating the discoveries of others, and accommodating them to the capacities of his readers, we are frequently introduced to inventions and improvements of his own; many of these are well known to the public; and while some of them have been of great service to experimental philosophy, they all evince a considerable share of mechanical genius. To a still higher commendation, however, our author may justly lay claim; it has long been fashionable with a certain class of philosophers to keep the Creator totally out of view when describing the noblest of his works. But Mr. Ferguson has not imbibed those gloomy principles which steel the heart against its earliest and strongest impressions, and prompt to suppress those feelings of devotion and gratitude which the structure and harmony of the universe are so fitted to inspire. When benevolence and design are particularly exhibited in the works or in the phenomena of nature, he dwells with delight upon the goodness and wisdom of their Author; and never fails to impress upon the reader, what is apt to escape his notice, that the wonders of creation, and the various changes which the material world displays, are the result of that unerring wisdom and boundless goodness which are unceasingly exerted for the comfort and happiness of man.—BREWSTER, SIR DAVID, 1821, *ed. Ferguson's Lectures on Select Subjects.*

The faculties of distinct apprehension and luminous exposition belonged, indeed, to Ferguson in a pre-eminent degree. He doubtless owed his superiority here in a great measure to the peculiar manner in which he had been obliged to acquire his knowledge. Nothing that he had learned had been set him as a task. He had applied himself to whatever subject of study engaged his attention, simply from the desire and with the view of understanding it. All that he knew, therefore, he knew thoroughly, and not by rote merely, as many things are learned by those who have no higher object than to master the task of the day. On the other hand, as has often happened in the case of self-educated men, the want of a regular director of his studies had left him ignorant of many departments of knowledge in which, had he been introduced to them, he was probably admirably adapted to distinguish himself, and from which he might have drawn, at all events, the most valuable assistance in the prosecution of his favorite investigations.—HOWE, HENRY, 1846, *Eminent Mechanics, p.* 246.

Ferguson's "Astronomy explained on Sir Isaac Newton's Principles" was published in July, 1756, and met with immediate and complete success. The first issue was exhausted in a year; the thirteenth edition, revised by Brewster, appeared in 1811, and the demand for successive reprints did not cease until ten years later. It was translated into Swedish and German, and long excluded other treatises on the same subject. Although containing no theoretical novelty, the manner and method of its expositions were entirely original. Astronomical phenomena were for the first time described in familiar language. The book formed Herschel's introduction to celestial science. . . . Ferguson's great merit as a scientific teacher lay in clearness, both of thought and style, and in the extreme ingenuity with which by means of machines and diagrams he brought the eye to help the mind of the learner. Hutton recognized his "vary uncommon genius, especially in mechanical contrivances and executions." Brewster considered him as "in some degree the first elementary writer on natural philosophy."—CLERKE, MISS A. M., 1886, *Dictionary of National Biography, vol.* XVIII, *pp.* 345, 346.

James Granger

1723–1776.

Born at Shaston, Dorset, in 1723: died at Shiplake, Oxfordshire, April 4, 1776. An English writer and print-collector. He matriculated at Christ Church, Oxford, in 1743, but took no degree. He took holy orders, and was presented to the vicarage of Shiplake. About 1773 he made a tour through Holland. He wrote "A Biographical History of England . . . with a preface showing the utility of a collection of engraved portraits, etc." (1769). This was continued with additions at different times till in 1824 the work had increased to 6 volumes. In 1806 another continuation appeared from materials left by Granger and the collections of the Rev. Mark Noble, who edited it. The wholesale destruction of illustrated biographical works necessary to accomplish this gave rise to the term *grangerize.*—SMITH, BENJAMIN E., *ed.*, 1894–97, *The Century Cyclopedia of Names, p.* 454.

A BIOGRAPHICAL HISTORY OF ENGLAND

1769

I write neither for fame nor bread; but have taken up the pen for the same reason that some of my brethren have laid it down, that is, only to amuse myself. . . . This singular book, which has been the employment of my leisure hours for several years of my life, will, doubtless, be numbered among my idlenesses, perhaps my weaknesses; but, I hope, never amongst my sins.—GRANGER, JAMES, 1769, *A Biographical History of England, Dedication to Horace Walpole.*

I have, since I saw you, read every word of "Granger's Biographical History." It has entertained me exceedingly, and I do not think him the *Whig* that you supposed. Horace Walpole's being his patron is, indeed, no good sign of his political principles. But he denied to Lord Mountstuart that he was a Whig, and said he had been accused by both parties of partiality. It seems he was like Pope,

"While Tories call me Whig, and Whigs a Tory."

I wish you would look more into this book; and as Lord Mountstuart wishes much to find a proper person to continue the work upon Granger's plan, and has desired I would mention it to you, if such a man occurs, please to let me know.—BOSWELL, JAMES, 1776, *Letter to Samuel Johnson, Aug.* 30.

I have no hesitation in designating it as a delightful and instructive book; but whoever republishes it should *add* the portraits of the different characters which were unknown to the author. Considering that Granger may be said to have first walked the field alone, it is surprising what he has done. His catalogue of engraved heads is immense. His style is always clear, pointed, and lively: and if he talked and preached as he *wrote* in his biographical history, it would have been difficult to have withdrawn attention from so intelligent a quarter.—DIBDIN, THOMAS FROGNALL, 1824, *The Library Companion, p.* 509, *note.*

That a certain class of bibliomaniacs and bibliolaters should be denounced as biblioclasts and bibliophobians by all the great community of bibliocists, bibliophilists, bibliographers, bibliopolists, bibliologists, bibliopegists, bibliotaphists, bibliothecarys and bibliognostes would seem, to the lay mind, to imply a very serious condition of affairs. Yet this is, and has been, exactly the position of the Grangerites since the founder of this sect published his great work one hundred and eighteen years ago. . . . Granger's "History" was the first book extended by the introduction of extra prints illustrative of its text, and Mr. Granger was the original Extra-illustrator, the father of the noble band of Grangerites. Unlike his decendants he wrote his book to illustrate his portraits; he did not collect his portraits to illustrate his book.—HUTTON, LAURENCE, 1887, *Grangerism and the Grangerites, The Book Buyer, vol.* IV, *pp.* 93, 94.

Previously to the publication of the first edition of Granger's work in 1769 five shillings were considered a liberal price by collectors for any English portrait. After the appearance of the "Biographical History," books, ornamented with engraved portraits, rose in prices to five times their original value, and few could be found unmutilated. In 1856 Joseph Lilly and Joseph Willis, booksellers each offered for sale a magnificent illustrated copy of Granger's work. Lilly's copy, which included Noble's "Continuation," was illustrated by more than thirteen hundred portraits, bound in 27 vols. imperial 4to, price £42. The price of Willis's copy, which contained more than three thousand portraits, bound in 19 vols. fol., was £38. 10s. It had cost the former owner nearly £200.—COOPER, THOMPSON, 1890, *Dictionary of National Biography, vol.* XXII, *p.* 373.

Samuel Foote

1720–1777.

Born, in Truro, Jan. 1720 [?]; baptized 27 Jan. 1720. At school at Worcester. Matric. at Worcester Coll, Oxford, 1 July 1737; took no degree. Became an actor; first appeared at Haymarket Theatre, 6 Feb. 1744. Acted in Dublin same year. Acted in London, 1745-49. Lived in Paris, 1750-52. Acted in London, 1753-57; in Dublin, winter of 1757-58; in Edinburgh, spring of 1759; in Dublin, winter of 1759-60. Manager of Haymarket, 1760; of Drury Lane, 1761. Acted till 1766; in that year lost leg through accident. Granted patent to build a theatre. Opened new theatre in Haymarket, May 1767. Visited Dublin, 1768. Manager of Edinburgh theatre, 1770. Sold patent of London theatre, 16 Jan. 1777. Died, at Dover, 21 Oct. 1777. Buried in West Cloister of Westminster Abbey. *Works:* "The Genuine Memoirs. . . . of Sir J. D. Goodere" [1741?]; "A Treatise on the Passions" [1747]; "The Roman and English Comedy Consider'd," 1747; "Taste," 1752; "The Englishman in Paris," 1753; "The Knights," 1754; "The Englishman Returned from Paris," 1756; "The Author," 1757; "The Minor," 1760; "A Letter . . . to the Reverend Author of the 'Remarks . . . on the Minor,'" 1760; "The Orators," 1762; "The Comic Theatre; being a free Translation of all the best French Comedies, by S. Foote and others" (5 vols.), 1762; "The Lyar" (adapted from Corneille), 1764; "The Mayor of Garratt," 1764; "The Patron," 1764; "The Commissary," 1765; "The Lame Lover," 1770; "Apology for 'The Minor,'" 1771; "A trip to Calais" (under pseud.: "Timothy Timbertoe"), 1775; "The Bankrupt," 1776. *Posthumous:* "The Maid of Bath" (anon.), 1778; "The Devil upon Two Sticks," 1778; "The Nabob," 1778; "The Cozeners" (anon.), 1778; "The Capuchin," 1778. *Collected Works:* in 4 vols., 1763-78; in 3 vols., 1830. *Life:* "Memoirs" (anon.), [1778]; by W. Cooke, 1805; by J. Bee, in 1830 edn. of "Works." —SHARP, R. FARQUHARSON, 1897, *A Dictionary of English Authors, p.* 101.

PERSONAL

By turns transform'd into all kind of shapes,
Constant to none, Foote laughs, cries, struts, and scrapes:
Now in the centre, now in van or rear,
The Proteus shifts, bawd, parson, auctioneer,
His strokes of humour, and his bursts of sport,
Are all contain'd in this one word,—*Distort.*

—CHURCHILL, CHARLES, 1761, *The Rosciad, v.* 395–400.

Foote being mentioned, Johnson said, "He is not a good mimick." One of the company added, "A merry Andrew, a buffoon." JOHNSON. "But he has wit too, and is not deficient in ideas, or in fertility and variety of imagery, and not empty of reading; he has knowledge enough to fill up his part. One species of wit he has in an eminent degree, that of escape. You drive him into a corner with both hands; but he's gone, Sir, when you think you have got him—like an animal that jumps over your head. Then he has a great range for wit; he never lets truth stand between him and a jest, and he is sometimes mighty coarse. Garrick is under many restraints from which Foote is free." WILKES. "Garrick's wit is more like Lord Chesterfield's." JOHNSON. "The first time I was in company with Foote was at Fitzherbert's. Having no good opinion of the fellow, I was resolved not to be pleased; and it is very difficult to please a man against his will. I went on eating my dinner pretty sullenly, affecting not to mind him. But the dog was so very comical that I was obliged to draw down my knife and fork, throw myself back upon my chair, and fairly laugh it out. No, Sir, he was irresistible."—JOHNSON, SAMUEL, 1776, *Life by Boswell, ed. Hill, vol.* III, *p.* 79.

He was, perhaps, the only man among the set, totally independent of Johnson's monarchy; he had an intrepid wit and pleasantry of his own, and was fearless of any colloquial antagonist.—COLMAN, GEORGE, 1830, *Random Records.*

Foote's clothes were, then, tawdily splashed with gold lace; which, with his linen, were generally bedawbed with snuff; he was a Beau Nasty. They tell of him that, in his young days, and in the fluctuation of his finances, he walked about in boots, to conceal his want of stockings, and that, on receiving a supply of money, he expended it all upon a diamond ring, instead of purchasing the necessary articles of hosiery.—PEAKE, RICHARD BRINSLEY, 1841, *Memoirs of the Colman Family, vol.* I, *p.* 395, *note.*

The strength and predominance of Foote's humour lay in its readiness. Whatever the call that might be made upon it, there it was. Other men were humorous as the occasion arose to them, but to him the occasion was never wanting. Others might be foiled or disabled by the lucky stroke of an adversary, but he took only the quicker rebound from what would have laid them prostrate. To put him out was not possible.—FORSTER, JOHN, 1854, *Samuel Foote, Quarterly Review, vol.* 95, *p.* 487.

Was ever wit more audacious than Foote? Perspicacious and bold—seeing everything and stopping at nothing,—no wonder the great town shook with terror and laughter at his daring personalities and mimicries. As quick to say as to see, the strokes of his humour were as surprising as they were instantaneous, and his victims fell without staggering. There was no threatening, to forewarn or alarm; no waste by elaboration; and when the mischief was done, there was no smell of spent forces. On the stage, at the club, at the coffee-house, he took off everybody of prominence. Nobody seemed to escape him. At the Haymarket, for forty nights in succession, he imitated Whitefield. "There is hardly a public man in England," said Davies, "who has not entered Mr. Foote's theatre with an aching heart, under the apprehension of seeing himself laughed at." His rule was, that you ought not to run the chance of losing your friend for your joke unless your joke happens to be better than your friend.—RUSSELL, A. P., 1883, *Characteristics, p.* 234.

And wittiest among them all, creating roars of laughter by his sallies, or his mimicry of some well-known actor or politician, was a young gentleman of family and fortune, at this time a student of the Inner Temple. Dressed in a frock-suit of green, and silver lace, bag wig, sword, bouquet, and point ruffles, he frequented the place daily, until the carriage of some woman of quality would drive to the door, and Mr. Samuel Foote being inquired for, he would hasten out, hat in hand, and ride away with his lady fair.—MOLLOY, J. FITZGERALD, 1884, *The Life and Adventures of Peg Woffington, vol.* I, *p.* 28.

His humour was decidedly Aristophanic; that is to say, broad, easy, reckless, satirical, without the slightest alloy of *bonhomie*, and full of the directest personalities.—A meteor that delighted by the splendour of its blaze.—The meteor of the moment who possessed every species of wit.—He was of that sort that he would rather lose his friend than his jest.—He never stopped the career of his *bon-mot* out of respect to persons; it as readily struck a royal duke as a poor player.—His conversation was of such a description that "nought but itself could be its parallel!" Teeming with fancy, and various knowledge, fearless of consequences, and privileged in the character of a wit, he took his stand with confidence, and threw his shafts around him with the dexterity of a master, the first and last of his own school.—Whatever we talked about—whether fox-hunting, the turf, or any other subject—Foote instantly took the lead and delighted us all.—Very entertaining, with a kind of conversation between wit and buffoonery. —He has a great range for wit, he never lets truth stand between him and a jest, and he is sometimes mighty coarse.—He has wit to ridicule you, invention to frame a story of you, humour to help it about; and when he has set the town a-laughing, he puts on a familiar air and shakes you by the hand.—JERROLD, WALTER, 1894, ed., *Bon-Mots of Samuel Foote and Theodore Hook, Introduction, p.* 7.

GENERAL

BOSWELL. "Foote has a great deal of humour?" JOHNSON, "Yes, Sir." BOSWELL. "He has a singular talent of exhibiting character" JOHNSON. "Sir, it is not a talent; it is a vice; it is what others abstain from. It is not comedy, which exhibits the character of a species, as that of a miser gathered from many misers: it is farce, which exhibits individuals."—JOHNSON, SAMUEL, 1769, *Life by Boswell, ed. Hill, vol.* II, *p.* 109.

Foote was certainly a great and fertile genius, superior to that of any writer of the age; his dramatic pieces were most of them, it is true, unfinished, and several of them little more than sketches; but they are the sketches of a master, of one who, if he had labored more assiduously, he could have brought them nearer to perfection. Foote saw the follies and vices of mankind with a quick and discerning eye; his discrimination of character was quick and exact; his humour pleasant, his ridicule keen, his satire pungent, and his wit brilliant and exuberant. He described with fidelity the changeable follies and fashions of the times; and his pieces, like those of Ben Jonson, were calculated to please the audience of the day; and for this reason posterity will scarcely know anything of them. — DAVIES, THOMAS, 1780, *Life of David Garrick, vol.* II.

Other comic writers have merely shown "the body of the time its general form and pressure," but Foote has soared beyond this common flight, he has adventured to drag the objects of vice and folly individually before the public, and with a kind of dramatic boldness (unknown to any stage since the days of Aristophanes) to punish the delinquents in the first instance, as a warning to others: and here he has, generally, so regulated his satire, that although a single character may now and then be distinguished, it seems to embrace a whole genus. . . . Allowing for some instances of ill directed satire, taking Foote in general as a *dramatic writer*, an *actor*, a *wit*, an *humourist*, and *lively companion*, he stands on so high a scale of eminence, that all must exclaim, "This was a most extraordinary man!"—COOKE, WILLIAM, 1805, *Memoirs of Samuel Foote, vol.* I, *pp.* 2, 4.

The plays of Foote, the modern Aristophanes, who ventured, by his powers of mimicking the mind as well as the external habits, to bring living persons on the stage, belong to this period, and make a remarkable part of its dramatic history. But we need not dwell upon it. Foote was an unprincipled satirist; and while he affected to be the terror of vice and folly, was only anxious to extort forbearance-money from the timid, or to fill his theatre at the indiscriminate expense of friends and enemies, virtuous or vicious, who presented foibles capable of being turned into ridicule. It is a just punishment of this course of writing, that Foote's plays, though abounding in comic and humorous dialogue, have died with the parties whom he ridiculed. When they lost the zest of personality, their popularity, in spite of much intrinsic merit, fell into utter decay. —SCOTT, SIR WALTER, 1814–23, *The Drama.*

A careful examination of Foote's writings has satisfied us that they are not unworthy of a very high place in literature, though not perhaps in all respects the place he would have claimed.—FORSTER, JOHN, 1854, *Samuel Foote, Quarterly Review, vol.* 95, *p.* 486.

Some of Foote's apologists have almost worshipped him as the reformer of abuses, the scourge of hypocrites, and the terror of evil-doers. But Foote does not seem to have been moved by any higher principle than gain. If Mrs. Salmon, had a Chamber of Horrors, the more murders that were committed, the better she was pleased, for the more she made by the crime. Foote endeavored to crush Whitfield by personal ridicule; but Whitfield was a far more useful man in his very wicked generation than Foote, who did not denounce the wickedness, but mimicked the peculiarities of the reformer. . . . Except in ceasing to mimic Whitfield on the stage, after the death of that religious reformer, I can scarcely find a trait of delicacy in Foote's character. He seems to have been as unscrupulous in act, as he was cruel in his wit.—DORAN, JOHN, 1863, *Annals of the English Stage, vol.* II, *pp.* 131, 132.

If "The Liar" be his cleverest, "The Mayor of Garratt" retained the largest and the longest popularity: but, alas! it is now consigned to the tomb of the ungenteels. It has not been revived for many years; and when that admirable actor, Dowton, last appeared in Major Sturgeon (and in which performance I can believe that he never was surpassed in richness of humour—even by the author himself), and when Russell played Jerry Sneak (who avowedly exceeded all his predecessors in the part), the piece was pronounced "low," and even hissed. Our "bear-leaders" in society "hates everything as is low; their bears shall dance only to the genteelest of tunes—'Water parted from the sea,' and 'The minuet in *Harih*adne'" —and so they turned up their exclusive noses at the major's history of his campaign, and the death of Major Molasses. —CLARKE, CHARLES COWDEN, 1872, *On the Comic Writers of England, Gentleman's Magazine, N. S., vol.* 8, *p.* 315.

It is strange that while all the other English humorists of the eighteenth century have received such ample appreciation, the plays of Foote should be so little read. To those who would form a perfect conception of the manners of a hundred years ago, his works are invaluable; there is not a folly, a vice, a sham of the time, which they do not expose; they are frequently coarse, but so was the age, and a true mirror must reflect what is presented to it. But their coarseness is palliated by real wit and well-written dialogue; his characters, it is true, are too frequently caricatures founded on some physical deformity or eccentricity of manner, but they are usually typical, and their humour springs out of the absurdities common to all humanity; and if they display no very profound knowledge of the mainsprings of human nature, they are seldom unnatural, and are almost uniformly drawn with justness and vigor.—BAKER, HENRY BARTON, 1878, *English Actors from Shakespeare to Macready, vol.* I, *p.* 255.

Cibber had been succeeded by Foote (1721–1777), in whose numerous dramas the development of characteristic dialogue was entirely subordinated to the illustration of such oddities and whimsical singularities as could be emphasised by the talent for mimicry possessed by the author-actor himself; and not one of Foote's plays holds a niche in literature.—GOSSE, EDMUND, 1888, *A History of Eighteenth Century Literature, p.* 317.

Foote's prose tracts, like his letters, are forcibly, wittily, and logically written. It is, however, as a dramatist, a wit, and an actor that he has to be judged; in all these qualities he is noteworthy. No complete collection of his plays has been made, more than one of his pieces, chiefly his early entertainments, having never been printed. . . . As a rule the plays are invertebrate, and the manners they sketch are not to be recognised in the present day. Foote had, however, a keen eye to character, and on the strength of the brilliant sketches of contemporary manners which he afforded, and of the wit of the dialogue, they may be read with pleasure to this day. Foote's satire is direct and scathing. Much of it is directed against individuals, not seldom with no conceivable vindication, since Foote singled out those, such as Garrick, to whom he was under deepest obligations. During his lifetime and for some years subsequently Foote was known as the English Aristophanes. Without being deserved, the phrase is less of a misnomer than such terms ordinarily are. As an actor Foote seems to have attracted attention only in his own pieces. Tom Davies, who speaks with something not far from contempt of his general performances, praises his Bayes in the "Rehearsal." In this, however, Foote, like Garrick, used to introduce allusions to contemporary events.—KNIGHT, JOSEPH, 1889, *Dictionary of National Biography, vol.* XIX, *p.* 374.

Lays bare as with scalpel, in his farce of "The Author," the struggles, and expedients, and humiliations of the literary profession.—AUBREY, W. H. S., 1896, *The Rise and Growth of the English Nation, vol.* III, *p.* 113.

William Dodd

1729-1777

Dr. Dodd was a clergyman of the Church of England. He was educated at Cambridge, and rose rapidly in church preferments. He was tutor to the young Earl of Chesterfield and one of the King's chaplains. Being fond of display, and living beyond his means, he ran in debt and resorted to fraud to extricate himself. He wrote an anonymous letter to a lady of rank, offering her £3000 for her influence in obtaining for him an important rectory. The letter being traced to him caused him to be dismissed from the King's list of chaplains. He forged the name of Lord Chesterfield to a bond for £4200, and, being convicted of the crime, he was executed for it at Tyburn. *Works.*—Dr. Dodd's publications are numerous and valuable: "Discourses on the Miracles and Parables of Christ;" "Sermons to Young Men;" "The Visitor;" "Comfort for the Afflicted;" "Thoughts in Prison;" "Reflections on Death;" "Commentary on the Old and New Testament;" "Beauties of Shakespeare;" "Beauties of History," etc.—HART, JOHN S., 1872, *A Manual of English Literature, p.* 318.

PERSONAL

As soon as we entered the chapel the organ played, and the Magdalens sung a hymn in parts,—you cannot imagine how well. The chapel was dressed with orange and myrtle, and there wanted nothing but a little incense to drive away the devil, or—to invite him. Prayers then began, psalms and a sermon; the latter by a young clergyman, one Dodd, who contributed to the Popish idea one had imbibed, by haranguing entirely in the French style, and very eloquently and touchingly. He apostrophised the lost sheep, who sobbed and cried from their souls; so did my Lady Hertford and Fanny Pelham, till, I believe, the city dames took them for Jane Shores. The confessor then turned to the audience, and addressed himself to his Royal Highness (Prince Edward), whom he called *most illustrious prince,* beseeching his protection. In short, it was a very pleasing performance, and I got *the most illustrious* to desire it might be printed.—WALPOLE, HORACE, 1760, *To George Montague, Jan.* 28; *Letters, ed. Cunningham, vol.* III, *p.* 282.

Before I began my operations relative to the window-tax, I witnessed something memorable. It being much the fashion to go on a Sunday evening to a chapel of the Magdalen Asylum, we went there on the second Sunday we were in London, and had difficulty to get tolerable seats for my sister and wife, the crowd of genteel people was so great. The preacher was Dr. Dodd, a man afterwards too well known. The unfortunate young women were in a latticed gallery, where you could only see those who chose to be seen. The preacher's text was, "If a man look on a woman to lust after her," &c. The text itself was shocking, and the sermon was composed with the least possible delicacy, and was a shocking insult on a sincere penitent, and fuel for the warm passions of the hypocrites. The fellow was handsome, and delivered his discourse remarkably well for a reader. When he had finished, there were unceasing whispers of applause, which I could not help contradicting aloud, and condemning the whole institution, as well as the exhibition of the preacher, as *contra bonos mores,* and a disgrace to a Christian city.—CARLYLE, ALEXANDER, 1769-1850-60, *Autobiography, p.* 408.

The Doctor's powers are pretty well known about town; not a more popular preacher within the sound of Bow Bells; I do not mean for the nobility only—*those* every canting fellow can catch; the best people of fashion arn't ashamed to follow my Doctor. Not one, madam, of the hum-drum drawling, long-winded tribe; he never crams congregations, or gives them more than they can carry away—not more than ten or twelve minutes at most. . . . But then his wig, madam! I am sure you must admire his dear wig; not with the bushy, brown buckles, hanging and dropping like a Newfoundland spaniel, but short, rounded off at the ear, to shew his plump cherry cheeks, white as a curd, feather-topped, and the curls as close as a cauliflower.—FOOTE, SAMUEL, 1774, *The Cozeners.*

That which is appointed to all men is now coming upon you. Outward circumstances, the eyes and thoughts of men, are below the notice of an immortal being about to stand the trial for eternity, before the Supreme Judge of heaven and earth. Be comforted: your crime, morally or religiously considered, has no very deep dye of turpitude. It corrupted no man's principles; it attacked no man's life. It involved only a temporary and reparable injury. Of this, and all other sins, you are earnestly to repent; and may God, who knoweth our frailty, and desireth not our death, accept your repentance, for the sake of his Son JESUS CHRIST our Lord. In requital of those well-intended offices which you are pleased so emphatically to acknowledge, let me beg that you make in your devotions one petition for my eternal welfare. I am, dear Sir,

Your affectionate servant.
—JOHNSON, SAMUEL, 1777, *Letter to the Reverend Dr. Dodd, while in Prison, June* 26.

He had spent whole months with Mossop the actor, who drilled him into reading the Litany with such witching emphasis, that women went miles to hear him read the Litany. Mrs. Clive had made him pay rather dearly in dinners and suppers, and mulled claret and earrings, for instructing him in a pleasing delivery of the services for the solemnization of matrimony, the churching of women, and the private or public baptism of children. Palmer had taught him how to read a public notice from the pulpit with effect, and Woodward had enlightened him as to the achievement of distinctness with grace, in enunciating the "Dearly beloved," and in reading an Epistle. For all this Will was indebted to the players at Drury Lane,—but the necessary money was well laid out. It returned cent. per cent. Covent Garden was not backward in lending him a sort of fitness for his calling.—DORAN, JOHN, 1859, *New Pictures on Old Panels, p.* 5.

The wretched clergyman was the victim of the old British, stupid, mulish complacency, which has so often fancied it is doing something Spartan and splendid, when it is only cruel and ridiculous. It once shot an admiral "to encourage the rest," and it hanged Doctor Dodd to show the surrounding world a spectacle of stern, unflinching morality. For the offence which Doctor Dodd committed, such a punishment was wholly unsuited—even unmerited. Degradation would have been, at most, the suitable penalty. Even weighing the moral delinquency accurately there was no tremendous guilt involved in the offence—for it is clear that if he used the name of his patron, he meant to restore the money eventually. In justice to the man, his story should be considered.
—FITZGERALD, PERCY, 1864, *Unfortunate Doctor Dodd, Dublin University Magazine, vol.* 63, *p.* 257.

GENERAL

For my own part, better and more important things henceforth demand my attention; and I here, with no small pleasure, take leave of Shakespeare and the critics. As this work was begun and finished before I entered upon the sacred functions in which I am now happily employed, let me trust this juvenile performance will prove no objection, since graver, and some very eminent members of the Church have thought it no improper employ to comment, explain, and publish the works of their own country's poets.—DODD, WILLIAM, 1752, *Beauties of Shakespeare, Preface.*

The "Prison Thoughts," although written in blank verse, can scarcely be called poetry. They are the spasmodic, hysteric, and insincere utterances of a weak man under affliction. The power of self-deception in the writer is something to be wondered at. To read these thoughts without any other record of his life, you would gather that he had committed some crime, not perhaps a very black one; but that he was otherwise a good, pious, holy, persecuted man. He is constantly shrieking out his complaints against the world and its vices; and now that he can no longer participate in them and enjoy them, they have become the objects of his bitterest denunciations. You feel while reading "these wild and wayward cries," that the grapes are sour; and the pity you would otherwise have is changed into something akin to contempt. The true tone of Christian meekness, and sorrow, and repentance are wanting. Surely he who had tasted of these so much denounced pleasures, who had fallen so often and so thoroughly under their fascinations, might have had a little more charity for those who were still slaves in the garden of the Syrens! His objurgations are not so much those of one disgusted with the sins, as of one unable to be a participator in them. So striking is this air of superficial and ostentatious piety; so vehement is the assertion of this horror at the doings of the world; so apparent is it that noise, and shrieks, and groans are no true measure of the writer's true feelings; that all the time you read there is ringing in your ears the dreary, monotonous, and unpleasant old proverb:—

"When the devil was sick, the devil a monk
would be;
When the devil was well, the devil a monk
was he."

—LANGFORD, JOHN ALFRED, 1861, *Prison Books and Their Authors, p.* 273.

His "Beauties of Shakespeare," the work by which he is best known; which is reprinted down to this day, and which can boast of the honour of having been quoted by Schlegel.—MARKS, ALFRED, 1865, *Dr. Dodd, Once a Week, vol.* 12, *p.* 263.

Hugh Kelly

1739–1777

A native of the banks of the Lake of Killarney, wrote "Thespis, a Poem;" "False Delicacy, a Comedy," 1768, 8vo.; "A Word to the Wise, a Comedy," 1770, 8vo., and other comedies; "Clementina, a Tragedy," 1771, 8 vo.; and some other compositions. A Collective ed. of his "Works," with "Life," was published in London, 1778.—ALLIBONE, S. AUSTIN, 1854–58, *Critical Dictionary of English Literature, vol.* I, *p.* 1013.

PERSONAL

It is recorded in Johnson's "Works," that when some one asked Johnson whether they should introduce Hugh Kelly to him, "No, Sir," says he, "I never desire to converse with a man who has written more than he has read."—JOHNSON, SAMUEL, 1768, *Life by Boswell, ed. Hill, vol.* II, *p.* 55, *note.*

It may be justly said of Kelly that no man ever profited more by a sudden change of fortune in his favour; prosperity caused an immediate and remarkable alteration in his conduct; from a low, petulant, absurd, and ill-bred censurer, he was transformed to the humane, affable, well-bred, good-natured man. His conversation in general was lively and agreeable, he had an uncommon stock of ready language, and though not deeply read, yet what he said was generally worthy of attention. He sometimes, indeed, from an attempt to assume uncommon politeness, and a superabundance of benevolence, became rather tiresome and luscious in his compliments.—DAVIES, THOMAS, 1780, *Life of David Garrick.*

He was noted, however, for unconsciously imitating Goldsmith. He was so fond of displaying plate on his sideboard that he added to it his silver spurs; and he exhibited his fat little person in "a flaming broad silver-laced waist-coat, bag-wig, and sword." It was reported, however, that he had done Goldsmith, who admired Mrs. Kelly's amiability, the service of dissuading him from marrying Mrs. Kelly's bad-tempered sister.—GOODWIN, GORDON, 1892, *Dictionary of National Biography, vol.* XXX, *p.* 351.

GENERAL

This night presents a play, which publick
rage,
Or right or wrong, once hooted from the
stage:
From zeal or malice, now no more we dread,
For English vengeance *wars not with the dead.*
A generous foe regards with pitying eye
The man whom Fate has laid where all must
lie.
To wit reviving from its author's dust,
Be kind, ye judges, or at least be just:
Let no renewed hostilities invade
Th' obvious grave's inviolable shade.
Let one great payment every claim appease,
And him who cannot hurt, allow to please;
To please by scenes, unconscious to offence,
By harmless merriment, or useful sense.
Where aught of bright or fair the piece dis
plays,
Approve it only;—'tis too late to praise.
If want of skill or want of care appear,
Forbear to hiss;—the poet cannot hear.

—JOHNSON, SAMUEL, 1777, *A Word to the Wise, Prologue.*

A most masterly critic of our time, William Hazlitt, has disposed of Steele's pretensions as a comic dramatist; and poor Hugh Kelly, who has not survived to our time, must be disinterred to have his pretensions judged: yet the stage continues to suffer, even now, from the dregs of the sentimental school, and it would not greatly surprise me to see the comedy with which Kelly's brief career of glory began, again lift up a sickly head amongst us. It is not an easy matter to describe that comedy. ["False Delicacy."] One can hardly disentangle, from the maze of cant the make-believe in which all the people are involved, what it precisely is they drive at; but the main business seems to be, that there are three couples in search of themselves throughout the five acts, and enveloped in such a haze or mist of "False Delicacy" (the title of the piece), that they do not till the last succeed in finding themselves. . . . Examples need not be cited. Mr. Kelly's style will never want admirers. While it saves great trouble both to actor and author, it exacts from an audience neither judgment nor discrimination; and, with an easy indolent indulgence of such productions, there will always be mixed up a sort of secret satisfaction in their mouthing morals and lip-professions of humanity.—FORSTER, JOHN, 1848–71, *The Life and Times of Oliver Goldsmith, vol.* II, *pp.* 94, 95.

Hugh Kelly, the author of "The School for Wives," and some other second-rate dramas, produced during this interval a series of papers in a flashy, juvenile style under the title of "The Babbler."—CRAIK, GEORGE L., 1861, *A Compendious History of English Literature and of the English Language, vol.* II, *p.* 317.

William Pitt

Earl of Chatham

1708–1778

William Pitt, first Earl of Chatham. Born at Westminster, Nov. 15, 1708: died at Hayes, Kent, May 11, 1778. A famous English Whig statesman and orator. He was the son of Robert Pitt of Boconnock, in Cornwall; studied at Trinity College, Oxford; and obtained a cornet's commission in the dragoons. He entered Parliament in 1735, and in 1746 became vice-treasurer of Ireland in Pelham's administration. He was in the same year promoted to the office of paymaster-general, which he retained under the Duke of Newcastle. Disappointed in his hope of advancement, he attacked the Government in 1755, and was deprived of office. He was secretary of state under the Duke of Devonshire 1756–57. In 1757 he formed a coalition with the Duke of Newcastle, who became premier, although Pitt, as secretary of state, obtained the ascendancy in the government. He adopted vigorous measures in prosecution of the Seven Years' War, and the period which followed is one of the most brilliant in English history. He resigned in 1761, inasmuch as he failed to receive the support of the rest of the ministry for a war with Spain. He became premier on the fall of Rockingham in 1766, and was created Viscount Pitt and Earl of Chatham. He resigned in 1768, owing to ill health. He opposed the policy pursued toward the American colonies, although his last appearance in the House of Lords, on April 7, 1778, was in order to protest against the dismemberment of the British empire by the acknowledgment of their independence.—SMITH, BENJAMIN E., *ed.*, 1894–97, *The Century Cyclopedia of Names, p.* 810.

PERSONAL

Sir, the venerable age of this great man, his merited rank, his superior eloquence, his splendid qualities, his eminent services, the vast space he fills in the eyes of mankind, and, more than all the rest, his fall from power, which, like death, canonizes and sanctifies a great character, will not suffer me to censure any part of his conduct. I am afraid to flatter him; I am sure I am not disposed to blame him. Let those who have betrayed him by their adulation insult him with their malevolence.—BURKE, EDMUND, 1774, *Speech on American Taxation, April* 19.

I am sure you will be desirous to hear a true account of Lord Chatham's accident in ye House, and of his present condition of health. The newspapers are in but little credit in general, but their account of that affair has been very exact. His lordship had been long confined by a fit of the gout, so was debilitated by illness and want of exercise. The House was invaded by numbers who went to hear him on so critical a state of affairs. The thunder of his eloquence was abated, and the lightning of his eyes was dimmed in a certain degree, when he rose to speak; but the glory of his former administration threw a mellow lustre around him, and his experience of publick affairs gave the force of an oracle to what he said, and a reverential silence reigned through the senate. He spoke in answer to the Duke of Richmond. The Duke of Richmond replied. Then his lordship rose up to speak again. The genius and spirit of Britain seemed to heave in his bosom, and he sank down speechless. He continued half an hour in a fit. His eldest and second sons and Lord Mahon were in great agony, waiting the doubtful event. At last, he happily recovered; and though he is very weak still, I am assured by his family, that he looks better than he did before this accident.—MONTAGU, ELIZABETH, 1778, *Letter, April* 10, *A Lady of the Last Century, p.* 238.

On the stage, he would have been the finest Brutus or Coriolanus ever seen. . . . His figure, when he first appeared in Parliament, was strikingly graceful and commanding, his features high and noble, his eyes full of fire. His voice, even when it sank to a whisper, was heard to the remotest benches; when he strained it to its fullest extent, the sound rose like the swell of the organ of a great cathedral, shook the house with its peal, and was heard through lobbies and down staircases, to the Court of Requests and the precincts of Westminster Hall. He cultivated all these eminent advantages with the most assiduous care. His action is described by a very malignant observer as equal to that of Garrick. His play of countenance was wonderful; he frequently disconcerted a hostile orator by a single glance of indignation or scorn. Every tone, from the impassioned cry to the thrilling aside, was perfectly at his command. It is by no means improbable that the pains which he took to improve his great personal advantages had, in some respects, a prejudicial operation, and tended to nourish in him that passion for theatrical effect which, as we have already remarked, was one of the most conspicuous blemishes in his character.—MACAULAY, THOMAS BABINGTON, 1834, *Thackeray's Chatham, Edinburg Review, Critical and Miscellaneous Essays.*

It is this personal and solitary grandeur which strikes us most as we look back to William Pitt. The tone of his speech and action stands out in utter contrast with the tone of his time. In the midst of a society critical, polite, indifferent, simple even to the affectation of simplicity, witty and amusing but absolutely prosaic, cool of heart and of head, skeptical of virtue and enthusiasm, skeptical above all of itself, Pitt stood absolutely alone. The depth of his conviction, his passionate love for all that he deemed lofty and true, his fiery energy, his poetic imaginativeness, his theatrical airs and rhetoric, his haughty self-assumption, his pompousness and extravagance, were not more puzzling to his contemporaries than the confidence with which he appealed to the higher sentiments of mankind, the scorn with which he turned from a corruption which had till then been the great engine of politics, the undoubting faith which he felt in himself, in the grandeur of his aims, and in his power to carry them out.—GREEN, JOHN RICHARD, 1874, *A Short History of the English People, p.* 717.

"Power arising from popularity" was, of course, represented by Chatham, the head of the last great party in the State. By the energy of his haughty will he stands out above all contemporary politicians. Scorning the wretched intrigues which passed for statesmanship amongst his rivals, he placed himself for a brief period at the head of the nation. For a moment England was ruled by its natural king, and had its reward in a blaze of military glory. During his later years, disease, the distrust of his rivals, or his own arrogance, kept Chatham for the most part in melancholy retirement. For another brief period he tried, but failed grievously, to weld together the jarring elements of party into a powerful administration. The popular will could only impose a Chatham upon the king and the aristocracy at a time of fierce excitement. In calmer periods, and when his powers were failing, the politicians were too strong for him. Chatham, as the representative of the popular favour, and by the natural turn of a vehement mind, intuitive rather than discursive, and more eloquent than logical, was inclined towards the absolute dogmas of the revolutionary school. He was not, indeed, a believer in the rights of man in a revolutionary sense; for his ardent patriotism often took the form of almost melodramatic loyalty. But he judged the issues of the time by principles which easily assimilated with those of the revolutionists. Wilkes and the patriots of the City revered him as their natural head, though a head generally wrapped in clouds and darkness. Camden, his favourite lawyer, was the great judicial defender of popular rights. Shelburne, his lieutenant, was the patron of Priestley and Price; and it is not difficult to suppose that, under other circumstances, Chatham might have developed into a Mirabeau.—STEPHEN, LESLIE, 1876, *History of English Thought in the Eighteenth Century, vol.* II, *p.* 205.

Though Chatham's character is absolutely free from suspicion of corruption, no statesman ever exhibited greater inconsistencies during his political career. Pride rather than principle seems to have actuated his conduct on more than one occasion. He consulted no judgment but his own. His haughtiness to his colleagues was only equalled by his abject servility to the king. His vanity was excessive, and he delighted in pomp and ostentation. He was always playing a part.—BARKER, G. F. RUSSELL, 1896, *Dictionary of National Biography, vol.* XLV, *p.* 365.

GENERAL

What parent, anxious for the character and success of a son would not in all that related to his education, gladly have resorted to the advice of such a man? What youthful spirit, animated by any desire of future excellence, and looking for the gratification of that desire, in the pursuits of honorable ambition, or in the consciousness of an upright, active, and useful life, would not embrace with transport any opportunity of listening on such a subject to the lessons of Lord Chatham? —GRENVILLE, LORD, 1804, *Chatham's Letters to Thomas Pitt, Preface.*

The most interesting relic that we have of this greatest of statesmen, is his "Letters to his Nephew, Thomas Pitt (afterwards Lord Camelford), then at Cambridge." No volume of equal size contains more valuable instructions for a young student than these letters.—CLEVELAND, CHARLES D., 1848, *A Compendium of English Literature, p.* 639.

Five speeches were written out from notes taken on the spot by Sir Philip Francis and Mr. Hugh Boyd. One of them is said to have been revised by Lord Chatham himself. These are the best specimens we possess of his style and diction, and it would be difficult, in the whole range of our literature, to find more perfect models for the study and imitation of the young orator.—GOODRICH, CHAUNCEY A., 1852, *Select British Eloquence.*

In elementary studies like ours, we cannot undertake to deal with the Parliamentary Eloquence of our country. But we ought to learn, that the earliest specimens of its greatness may be said to have been given before the middle of the eighteenth century, in the commanding addresses of the elder Pitt, more commonly known as Earl of Chatham.—SPALDING, WILLIAM, 1852–82, *A History of English Literature, p.* 350.

His speeches, as they have come down to us, are confessedly fragments; but even these "shreds of unconnected eloquence" are without a parallel. They blaze with the authentic fire of the imagination, —of the imagination in the full sweep of excited and overmastering feeling. They are the masterful words of a great man; haughty and arrogant words sometimes, no doubt, but haughty and arrogant because the speaker, in the pride of his integrity, scorned from the depths of his soul all meanness, and baseness, and *finesse.*—MATHEWS, WILLIAM, 1878, *Oratory and Orators, p.* 233.

If examined word by word and sentence by sentence his speeches are full of instruction. The style is natural, easy, and varied, with short clauses expressing vivid ideas—the style of a man pressing right onward to the end he has in view, diverted by no by-play and checked by no inferior purpose. He had faults belonging to a self-confident and somewhat arrogant disposition, but they were faults of taste and not of motive. Counterbalancing and overwhelming all these minor defects was an impetuous earnestness, based upon deep conviction, which could not be expressed without the stamp of absolute sincerity. It was this quality that could not be hid by the wealth of poetic utterance nor obscured by the emotion which sometimes accompanied it.—SEARS, LORENZO, 1893, *The History of Oratory, p.* 271.

The idol of the nation, whose genius raised him head and shoulders above all competitors.—CRAIK, SIR HENRY, 1901, *A Century of Scottish History, vol.* I, *p.* 461.

Augustus Montague Toplady

1740–1778

Augustus Montague Toplady, (1740–78), hymn-writer, born at Farnham, and educated at Westminster and Trinity College, Dublin, in 1768 became vicar of Broad Hembury, Devon, and in 1775 preacher in a chapel near Leicester Fields, London. A strenuous defender of Calvinism, he was a bitter controversialist. His "Church of England vindicated from Arminianism" (1774) is forgotten; but no hymn is better known than "Rock of Ages." In 1759 he published "Poems on Sacred Subjects;" his "Psalms and Hymns" (1776) was a collection with but few of his own.—PATRICK AND GROOME, *eds.*, 1897, *Chambers's Biographical Dictionary, p.* 922.

PERSONAL

Mr. Augustus Toplady I know well; but I do not fight with chimney-sweepers. He is too dirty a writer for me to meddle with; I should only foul my fingers. . . . I leave him to Mr. Sellon. He cannot be in better hands. . . . Your affectionate brother,—WESLEY, JOHN, 1770, *Letter to Mr. Merryweather, June* 24.

He died young; and the piety and diligence of his life is somewhat overshadowed by a personal virulence in controversy which more advanced years would probably have tempered. He spoke of what he supposed to be Wesley's theological errors as if they were so many unpardonable sins, the very thought of which almost drove him into frenzy.—ABBEY, CHARLES J., 1887, *The English Church and Its Bishops,* 1700–1800, *vol.* II, *p.* 142.

GENERAL

Toplady dwelt much on the importance of Calvinistic principles, which he defended with great energy of language and argument. But he too often indulged in controversy to an asperity of manner, and sometimes a ludicrous representation of his antagonist, altogether inconsistent with the dignity of the subject.—WILLIAMS, EDWARD, 1800, *The Christian Preacher.*

A strenuous defender of Calvinistic views, but not in the spirit of the gospel. His "Historic Defence" is full of information, and worth reading. It has been examined by the Anglo-American Bishop White in his "Comparative Views of the Controversy between the Calvinists and the Arminians," and the fidelity of his quotations questioned. Some of the "Hymns" are beautiful.—BICKERSTETH, EDWARD, 1844, *The Christian Student.*

Toplady was the author of that most precious lyric,

"Rock of Ages! cleft for me!" etc.,—

one of the most popular hymns in the English language, and one that has found its way into nearly all the Collections. It has been adopted by the Roman Catholic Church, in its English original; and, in the admirable Latin version of it by the Right Hon. William Ewart Gladstone, is likely to find a place in the Breviary.—HATFIELD, EDWIN F., 1884, *The Poets of the Church, p.* 615.

His fervour of nature, when directed to worthier purpose, inspired Toplady with this splendid Lyric; ["Rock of Ages"] which, in beauty and intensity of feeling, has a rival in ["Compared With Christ, in all beside,"]—a hymn truly sublime through the simplicity of its absolute self-surrender.—PALGRAVE, FRANCIS TURNER, 1889, *ed., The Treasury of Sacred Song, p.* 351, *note.*

His splendid and expressive hymns, a rich embodiment of religious experience, are his imperishable memorial.—SAUNDERS, FREDERICK, 1885, *Evenings with the Sacred Poets, p,* 351.

When the *Sunday at Home* took the plebiscite of 3,500 of its readers as to which were the best hymns in the language, the "Rock of Ages" stood at the top of the tree, having no fewer than 3,215 votes. Only three other hymns had more than 3,000 votes. They were, "Abide with me," "Jesus, Lover of my soul," and "Just as I am." . . . Toplady was a sad polemist, whose orthodox soul was outraged by the Arminianism of the Wesleys. He and they indulged in much disputation of the brickbat and Billingsgate order, as was the fashion in those days. Toplady put much of his time and energy in the composition of controversial pamphlets, on which the good man prided himself not a little. The dust lies thick upon these his works, nor is it likely to be disturbed now or in the future. But in a pause in the fray, just by way of filling up an interval in the firing of polemical broadsides, Augustus Montague Toplady thought he saw a way of launching an airy dart at a joint in Wesley's armour, on the subject of Sanctification. So without much ado, and without any knowledge that it was by this alone he was to render permanent service to mankind, he sent off to the *Gospel Magazine* of 1776 the hymn "Rock of Ages."—STEAD, W. T., 1897, *Hymns that Have Helped, pp.* 139, 140.

Toplady was the author of the fine hymn, "Rock of ages cleft for me," which was published in the "Gospel Magazine" in Oct. 1775, probably soon after it was written, although a local tradition associates its symbolism with a rocky gorge in the parish of Blagdon, his first curacy. It does not appear in his early volume, "Poems on Sacred Subjects," 1759. It was translated into Latin by Mr. Gladstone in 1839. Montgomery puts Toplady's hymns on a level with those of Charles Wesley, but that is too high an estimate. The best, after "Rock of Ages," is "Deathless Principle, arise," a soliloquy to the soul of the type of Pope's "Vital Spark." Of the contemporary Calvinist writers Toplady was the keenest, raciest, and best equipped philosophically.—BENNETT, LEIGH, 1899, *Dictionary of National Biography, vol.* LVII, *p.* 58.

William Warburton

1698–1779

Born at Newark, 24 Dec. 1698. At school at Newark, and at Oakham Grammar School, till 1714. Articled to an attorney, 23 April 1714, for five years. Before long gave up legal profession, and was ordained Deacon, 1723; Priest, 1727. Vicar of Greaseley, 1727–28. Created M. A., Camb., April 1728. Rector of Brant-Broughton, 1728–46. Rector of Frisby, 1730–56. Chaplain to Prince of Wales, 1738. Married Gertrude Tucker, 5 Sep. 1745. Preacher to Lincoln's Inn, 1746. Prebendary of Gloucester, 1753–55. Chaplain-in-Ordinary to the King, 1754. D. D., 1754. Prebendary of Durham, 1755–57. Dean of Bristol, 1757. Bishop of Gloucester, Dec. 1759. Founded a Lectureship at Lincoln's Inn, 1768. Died, at Gloucester, 7 June 1779. Buried in the Cathedral. Works [exclusive of separate sermons]: "Miscellaneous Translations" (anon.), 1724; "Critical and Philosophical Enquiry into the Causes of Prodigies and Miracles" (anon)., 1727; "The Legal Judicature in Chancery" (anon.; with S. Burroughs), 1727; "The Alliance between Church and State" (anon.,) 1736; "The Divine Legation of Moses" (2 vols.), 1738–41; "A Vindication of Mr. Pope's Essay on Man," 1740; "Remarks on Several Occasional Reflections" (2 pts.), 1745–46; "Two Sermons," 1746; "Apologetical Dedication to . . . Dr. H. Stebbing," 1746; "Letter from an Author to an M. P., " 1747; "Remarks upon the Principles . . . of Dr. Rutherford's Essay," 1747; "Letter to the Editor of the Letters on the Spirit of Patriotism" (anon.), 1749; "Letter to Viscount Bolingbroke" (anon.), 1749; "Julian," 1750; "The Principles of Natural and Revealed Religion" (3 vols.), 1753–67; "A View of Lord Bolingbroke's Philosophy" (anon.), 1756; "Remarks on Mr. D. Hume's Essay on the Natural History of Religion" (anon.; with R. Hurd), 1757; "A Rational Account . . . of the Lord's Supper," 1761; "An Enquiry into the Nature . . . of Literary Property" (anon.), 1762; "The Doctrine of Grace," 1763. *Posthumous:* "Tracts by Warburton and a Warburtonian," 1789; "Letters . . . to one of his friends," 1808; "Letters to the Rt. Hon. Charles Yorke" (priv. ptd.), 1812; "Selection from his Unpublished Papers," ed. by F. Kilvert, 1841. He *edited*, Pope's "Essay on Man," 1729; "Dunciad," 1749; "Shakespeare's Plays," 1747; "Essay on Criticism," 1751; "Works," 1751, and "Additions to Works," 1776. *Collected Works:* ed. by R. Hurd, new edn. (14 vols.), 1811–41. Life: by J. S. Watson, 1863.—SHARP, R. FARQUHARSON, 1897, *A Dictionary of English Authors, p.* 292.

PERSONAL

Who is Mr. Warburton? What is *his* birth, or whence *his* privilege, that the reputations of men both living and dead, of men in birth, character, station, in every instance of true worthiness, much his superiors, must lie at the mercy of his petulant satire, to be hacked and mangled as his ill-mannered spleen shall prompt him, while it shall be unlawful for

WILLIAM WILBERFORCE

Engraving by H. Adlard, from a Painting by Hoare in Gloucester Palace.

JAMES FERGUSON

Engraving by Holl, from Original by Townsends.

anybody, under penalty of degradation, to laugh at the unscholar-like blunders, the crude and far-fetched conceits, the illiberal and indecent reflections, which he has endeavoured, with so much self-sufficiency and arrogance, to put off upon the world as a standard of true criticism?—EDWARDS, THOMAS, 1747, *Canons of Criticism, Preface.*

Rev. Sir,—I had the favour of yours, which gave me a mixture of pain and pleasure,—of pain for ever having been at variance with you; of pleasure from some prospect of seeing an end of it, unless I deceive myself. You complain; I could complain too; but to what purpose would that serve? To irritate, perhaps; but that is not my present design. You say that you never was concerned in the attacks made upon me. I ought to believe you; and I do believe you. But before you informed me of it, I thought otherwise; and so did many a person besides me. That you recommended me to persons who had it in their power to do me service, I doubt not. Vouchers are needless. Your own word suffices with me, and I thank you for it.—JORTIN, JOHN, 1758, *Letter to Warburton.*

Was so proud, that, should he meet
The twelve Apostles in the street,
He'd turn his nose up at them all,
And shove his Saviour from the wall:
Who was so mean (Meanness and Pride
Still go together side to side)
That he would cringe, and creep, be civil,
And hold a stirrup for the devil. . . .
Brought up to London, from the plough
And pulpit, how to make a bow
He tried to learn; he grew polite,
And was the Poet's Parasite. . . .
A heart, which virtue ne'er disgrac'd;
A head, where learning runs to waste;
A gentleman well-bred, if breeding
Rests in the article of reading;
A man of this world, for the next
Was ne'er included in his text;
A judge of genius, though confess'd
With not one spark of genius bless'd;
Amongst the first of critics plac'd,
Though free from every taint of taste;
A Christian without faith or works,
As he would be a Turk 'mongst Turks;
A great divine, as lords agree,
Without the least divinity.
To crown all, in declining age,
Inflamed with church and party rage,
Behold him, full and perfect quite,
A false saint, and true hypocrite.
—CHURCHILL, CHARLES, 1764, *The Duellest.*

To have made a proper use of the advantages of a good education, is a just praise; but to have overcome the disadvantages of a bad one, is a much greater. Had I not your lordship's example to justify me, I should think it a piece of extreme impertinence to inquire where *you* were bred. It is commonly said your lordship's education was of that particular kind concerning which it is a remark of that great judge of men and manners, Lord Clarendon, that it particularly disposes them to be proud, insolent, and pragmatical. "Colonel Harrison was the son of a butcher, and had been bred up in the place of a clerk, under a lawyer of good account in those parts; which kind of education introduces men into the language and practice of business; and if it be not resisted by the great ingenuity of the person, inclines young men to more pride than any other kind of breeding, and disposes them to be pragmatical and insolent." Now, my lord, as you have in your whole behaviour, and in all your writings, remarkably distinguished yourself by your humility, lenity, meekness, forbearance, candour, humanity, civility, decency, good manners, good temper, moderation with regard to the opinions of others, and a modest diffidence of your own, this unpromising circumstance of your education is so far from being a disgrace to you, that it highly redounds to your praise.—LOWTH, ROBERT, 1765, *Letter to the Author of the Divine Legation.*

Upon which the King said, that he heard Dr. Warburton was a man of such general knowledge, that you could scarce talk with him on any subject on which he was not qualified to speak; and that his learning resembled Garrick's acting, in its universality. His Majesty then talked of the controversy between Warburton and Lowth, which he seemed to have read, and asked Johnson what he thought of it. Johnson answered, "Warburton has most general, most scholastick learning; Lowth is the more correct scholar. I do not know which of them calls names best." The king was pleased to say he was of the same opinion; adding, "You do not think, then, Dr. Johnson, that there was much argument in the case." Johnson said, he did not think there was. "Why truly, (said the King), when once it comes to calling names, argument is pretty well at an end."—JOHNSON, SAMUEL, 1767, *Life by Boswell, ed. Hill, vol.* II, *p.* 41.

To the Memory of
WILLIAM WARBURTON, D. D.,
For more than nineteen years Bishop of this Sce;
A Prelate
Of the most sublime Genius and exquisite Learning,
Both which Talents
He employed, through a long life,
in the support
of what he firmly believed,
the Christian Religion,
and of what he esteemed the best Establishment of it,
the Church of England.
He was born at Newark-upon-Trent,
Dec. 24, 1698:
was consecrated Bishop of Gloucester,
Jan. 20, 1760;
Died at his Palace, in this City, June 7, 1779,
and was buried near this place.

—HURD, RICHARD, 1779, *Inscription on Monument, Gloucester Cathedral.*

He was rather a tall, robust, large-boned man, of a frame that seemed to require a good supply of provisions to support it; but he was sensible, if he had lived as other people do, he must have used a good deal of exercise, and, if he had used a good deal of exercise, it must have interrupted the course of his studies, to which he was so devoted as to deny himself any other indulgence, and so became a singular example, not only of temperance, but even of abstinence, in eating and drinking; and yet his spirits were not lowered or exhausted, but were rather raised and increased, by his low living.—NEWTON, THOMAS, 1782? *Life by Himself, p.* 155.

Mr. Burke, who avowed he knew little of art, though he admired it and knew many of its professors, was acquainted with Blakey the artist, who made the drawing for the frontispiece to Warburton's edition of Pope's works. He told him it was by Warburton's particular desire that he made him the principal figure, and Pope only secondary; and that the light, contrary to the rules of art, goes upward from Warburton to Pope. A gentleman who was present when Mr. B. mentioned this circumstance, remarked that it was observable the poet and his commentator were looking different ways.—MALONE, EDMOND, 1789, *Maloniana, ed. Prior, p.* 370.

Churchill hated Warburton, for no apparent cause, except that he thought himself bound in friendship to take up all Wilkes's quarrels, and the Bishop had complained in the House of Lords of a gross and flagitious insult which that profligate had offered him. Yet there were more points of resemblance between Warburton and Churchill than any other two men of their age; they resembled each other in strength of character, in vigour and activity of mind, in their contemptuous sense of superiority over all who oppose them, and in a certain coarseness of nature, which was marked in the countenance of both, . . . which Churchill did not fail to note in the object of his enmity, . . . and of which he was not unconscious in himself.—SOUTHEY, ROBERT, 1835, *Life of Cowper, vol.* I, *p.* 327.

How, indeed, could Pope have expected Bolingbroke to like Warburton? The author of the "Divine Legation" was the embodiment of all that Bolingbroke detested in divines; and his bold, paradoxical, learned, and elaborate work must have appeared to Bolingbroke one of those compilations of artificial theology which he considered it his especial mission to destroy. The two men stood in natural antagonism. Bolingbroke's hatred was not softened by the suspicion, that whatever might be his other qualifications, his learning on those theological questions on which he pronounced so decidedly, was not to be compared with that of this proud and scornful attorney's son, who was working his way up to the bench of bishops.—MACKNIGHT, THOMAS, 1863, *The Life of Henry St. John, Viscount Bolingbroke, p.* 658.

His life was a succession of battles,—battles of the pen. All Warburton's books, like those of St. Augustine, are written against some adversary. But instead of handling the great public themes of Divinity, natural and revealed, Warburton is always defending some peculiar notion of his own, to which no one attached any importance, himself as little as any. The zest lay in the fighting, of which, while he was young, he never could get enough. The most famous of Warburton's battles,—and the most serious; indeed the Waterloo of his critical empire,—was that with Lowth. In this celebrated encounter, in which the whole reading public, from the king downwards, participated with the liveliest interest, the points of sacred antiquity debated are mostly of no moment. Or where they are of moment, as *e. g.*, the date of the Book of Job, the disputants lack the requisite knowledge for throwing even the feeblest ray of light upon them.—PATTISON, MARK, 1863–89, *Life of Bishop Warburton, Essays, ed. Nettleship. vol.* II, *p.* 120.

A Blazing Star,—A Colossus of Literature,—The Great Preserver of Pope and Shakespeare,—The Literary Bull-dog,—A Literary Revolutionist,—The Modern Stagirite,—The Most Impudent Man Living,—A Mountebank in Criticism,—The Poet's Parasite,—A Quack in Commentatorship,—The Scaliger of the Age,—A Universal Piece-Broker.—FREY, ALBERT R., 1888, *Sobriquets and Nicknames, p.* 476.

ALLIANCE BETWEEN CHURCH AND STATE

1736

The first edition of the "Alliance" was presented to all the bishops; when nothing came of that, the second was addressed to both the Universities; and when nothing came of that, the third was dedicated to a noble earl; and nothing has yet come of that.—EDWARDS, THOMAS, 1747–48, *Canons of Criticism.*

His work is one of the finest specimens that are to be found, perhaps, in any language, of scientific reasoning applied to a political subject.—HORSLEY, SAMUEL, 1786, *Review of the Case of the Protestant Dissenters.*

His once famous book on "The Alliance between Church and State," in which all the presumption and ambition of his nature was first made manifest.—JEFFREY, FRANCIS LORD, 1809, *Warburton's Letters, Edinburgh Review, vol.* 13, *p.* 345.

Of the minor works of Warburton, perhaps the most useful, at *this time* unquestionably the most important and interesting, is "The Alliance between Church and State." . . . This acute and comprehensive work.—WHITAKER, THOMAS D., 1812, *Hurd's Edition of Warburton, Quarterly Review, vol.* 7, *p.* 402.

The greatest intellectual defect of [the "Alliance," &c.] appears to be the absolute and rigid form of its propositions in indeterminate subject-matter. The writer argues for his particular scheme of the support of an establishment with full toleration of dissent, and the maintenance of an exclusive test, as though it were the single and mathematically necessary result of all general arguments from the nature of the State and the Church; whereas his is, in fact, only *one* mode of constructing the social equation; adapted perhaps to one particular stage of the progression of religious freedom, but not distinguished by any inherent properties of truth from other modes, which may be equally suitable to the preceding or the following stages.—GLADSTONE, WILLIAM EWART, 1838–41, *The State in its Relations with the Church.*

Is perhaps the most really valuable of his works.—LECKY, WILLIAM EDWARD HARTPOLE, 1887, *A History of England in the Eighteenth Century, vol.* V, *ch.* xix.

This book has often been considered his best. He accepts in the main the principles of Locke; and from the elastic theory of a social contract deduces a justification of the existing state of things in England. The state enters into alliance with the church for political reasons, and protects it by a test law and an endowment. In return for these benefits the church abandons its rights as an independent power. The book, representing contemporary ideas and vigorously written, went through several editions. It was highly praised afterwards by Horsley ("Case of Protestant Dissenters," 1787); by Whitaker in the "Quarterly" for 1812; and has some affinity with the doctrine of Coleridge in his "Church and State."—STEPHEN, LESLIE, 1899, *Dictionary of National Biography, vol.* LIX, *p.* 303.

DIVINE LEGATION OF MOSES

1738–41

"The table is always full, Sir. He brings things from the north, and the south, and from every quarter. In his 'Divine Legation,' you are always entertained. He carries you round and round, without carrying you forward to the point; but then you have no wish to be carried forward." He said to the Reverend Mr. Straham, "Warburton is perhaps the last man who has written with a mind full of reading and reflection."—JOHNSON, SAMUEL, 1781, *Life by Boswell, ed. Hill, vol.* IV, *p.* 57.

A work in all views, of the most transcendent merit, whether we consider the invention or the execution. A plain, simple argument, yet perfectly new, proving the divinity of the Mosaic law, and laying a sure foundation for the support of Christianity is there drawn out to great length by a chain of reasoning, so elegantly connected, that the reader is carried along it with ease and pleasure; while the matter presented to him is so striking for its own importance, so embellished by a lively fancy, and illustrated from all quarters by exquisite learning and the most ingenious disquisition, that, in the whole compass of modern and ancient theology there is nothing equal or similiar to this extraordinary performance.—HURD, RICHARD, 1794, *Life of Warburton.*

His "Divine Legation of Moses,"—the most learned, most arrogant, and most absurd work, which has been produced in England for a century.—JEFFREY, FRANCIS LORD, 1809, *Warburton's Letters, Edinburgh Review, vol.* 13, *p.* 346.

To the composition of this prodigious performance Hooker and Stillingfleet could have contributed the erudition, Chillingworth and Locke the acuteness, Taylor an imagination even more wild and copious, Swift, and perhaps Eachard, the sarcastic vein of wit; but what power of understanding, excepting that of Warburton, could first have amassed all these materials, and then compacted them into a bulky and elaborate work so consistent and harmonious? The principle of the work was no less bold and original than the execution. That the doctrine of a future state of reward or punishment was omitted in the books of Moses, had been insolently urged by infidels against the truth of his mission, while divines were feebly occupied in seeking what was certainly not to be found there, otherwise than by inference and implication. But Warburton, with an intrepidity unheard of before, threw open the gates of his camp, admitted the host of the enemy within his works, and beat them on a ground which was now become both his and theirs. In short, he admitted the proposition in its fullest extent, and proceeded to demonstrate from that very omission, which in all instruments of legislation merely human, had been industriously avoided, that a system which could dispense with a doctrine the very bond and cement of human society, must have come from God, and that the people to whom it was given must have been placed under his immediate superintendence. . . . Warburton's "Divine Legation" is one of the few theological, and still fewer controversial works, which scholars perfectly indifferent to such subjects will ever read with delight.—WHITAKER, THOMAS D., 1812, *Hurd's Edition of Warburton, Quarterly Review, vol.* VII, *pp.* 397, 399.

Parts of his system are true, and important, and well supported; but his main principle is a fallacy: unfounded in itself, and incapable of demonstrating the Divine Legation of Moses, were it even true.—ORME, WILLIAM, 1824, *Bibliotheca Bibleca.*

Warburton, with all his boldness and ingenuity, was not profoundly read in the Greek philosophers: he caught at single sentences which favoured his own views, rather than fully represented the spirit and opinions of his authors. The great proof of the discernment of Warburton was his dim second-sight of the modern discoveries in hieroglyphics.—MILMAN, HENRY HART, 1839, *Life of Gibbon.*

The intrinsic merit and ingenuity of the "Divine Legation" must ultimately have won it attention; but an immediate and exaggerated *éclat* was conferred upon it by the cloud of insect assailants who immediately fastened upon it. The liberal section of the clergy, represented by Hare, commended, but with an evident coldness. The moderate orthodox, represented by the feeble Sherlock, timidly gave in their adhesion, rather as if they feared to alienate so much power than as heartily appropriating it. But the high-church party, standing aloof in sullen opposition, felt at once, by an instinct far surer than intelligence, that the new candidate in the field of theology, however carefully he might have avoided committing himself against them, yet was not of them. They fell upon him immediately, to bury and to stifle, with the usual arms of the party—denunciation, not argument. —PATTISON, MARK, 1863–89, *Life of Bishop Warburton, Essays, ed. Nettleship, vol.* II, *p.* 125.

The book is remarkable for its arrogance and lack of "sweet reasonableness." It claims no attention from the student of

English literature, neither would Warburton himself were it not for his association with Pope.—DENNIS, JOHN, 1894, *The Age of Pope*, p. 239.

A strange feeling accompanies the modern reader on his way through the book; the mere count of years that have passed since it was written is no measure of the mental interval that separates us from the author; the whole problem has altered beyond recognition, the whole horizon of thought is changed. His curious multifarious learning, his subtile lawyer-like method in speculative matters, his almost incredible confidence in the torch of logic to light the way to truth, these are now subjects of antiquarian rather than of living interest.—DIXON, W. MACNEILE, 1895, *English Prose, ed. Craik, vol.* IV, *p.* 95.

His famous "Divine Legation of Moses," which would have been one of the most brilliant paradoxes in literature if the author had kept it down in size, and one of the most learned of works if he had attended a little more to accuracy.—SAINTSBURY, GEORGE, 1898, *A Short History of English Literature, p.* 632.

EDITION OF SHAKESPEARE
1747

Such is the felicity of his genius in restoring numberless passages to their integrity, and in explaining others which the author's sublime conceptions, or his licentious expression, kept out of sight, that this fine edition of Shakespeare must ever be highly valued by men of sense and taste; a spirit, congenial to the author, breathing throughout, and easily atoning, with such, for the little mistakes and inadvertencies discoverable in it.—HURD, RICHARD, 1794, *Life of Warburton.*

At length, when the public had decided on the facts of Warburton's edition, it was confessed that the editor's design had never been to explain Shakspeare! and that he was even conscious he had frequently imputed to the poet meanings which he never thought! Our critic's great object was to display his own learning! Warburton wrote for Warburton, and not for Shakspeare! and the literary imposture almost rivals the confessions of Lauder or Psalmanazar!—DISRAELI, ISAAC, 1814, *Warburton, Quarrels of Authors.*

Always striving to display his own acuteness, and scorn of others, deviates more than any one else from the meaning. —HALLAM, HENRY, 1837-39, *Introduction to the Literature of Europe, pt.* iii, *ch.* vi, *par.* 54.

If it were not painful to associate Shakspere, the great master of practical wisdom, with a critic who delights in the most extravagant paradoxes, we might prefer the amusement of Warburton's edition to toiling through the heaps of verbal criticism which later years saw heaped up. Warburton, of course, belonged to the school of slashing emendators.—KNIGHT, CHARLES, 1845, *Studies of Shakspere.*

This prelate, not then mitred, was undeniably learned and able; but he was as undeniably assuming and arrogant in his personal demeanor, and he treated Shakespeare's works as he probably would have treated the player himself, had he been his contemporary. He set himself not so much to correcting the text, as to amending the writings of Shakespeare. His tone is that of haughty flippancy. Does he find a passage in which the thought, or the expression of William Shakespeare is at variance with the judgment of William Warburton?—he immediately alters it to suit the taste of that distinguished scholar and divine, saying: "Without a doubt, Shakespeare wrote, or meant, thus."—WHITE, RICHARD GRANT, 1854, *Shakespeare's Scholar, p.* 10.

In 1744 Theobald died, and three years afterwards appeared Warburton's edition of Shakspeare. It is to be hoped for the honour of human nature that there are few parallels to the meanness and baseness of which Warburton stands convicted in this work. His object was two-fold. The first and most important was to build the reputation of his own edition on the ruin of his predecessor's, and the next to insinuate that any merit which is to be found in Theobald's edition is to be attributed not to Theobald but to himself. After observing in the Preface that Theobald "succeeded so ill that he left his author in ten times a worse condition than he found him," he goes on to say that "it was my ill-fortune to have some accidental connection with him;" that "I contributed a great number of observations to him," and these, "as he wanted money, I allowed him to print." . . . Having thus disposed of his dead friend in the Preface, he proceeds to appropriate his labours. He adopts Theobald's text as the basis of his own; he steals his illustrations; he incorporates, generally without a word of acknowledgment, most of Theobald's best emendations, carefully assigning to him such as are of little importance, while in his notes he keeps up a running fire of sneers and sarcasms.—COLLINS, JOHN CHURTON, 1895, *The Porson of Shakspearian Criticism, Essays and Studies, pp.* 269, 270.

Though a few of Warburton's emendations have been accepted, they are generally marked by both audacious and gratuitous quibbling, and show his real incapacity for the task. Though this was less obvious at the time, a telling exposure was made by Thomas Edwards in "a Supplement" to Warburton's edition, called in later editions "Canons of Criticism." Johnson compared Edwards to a fly stinging a stately horse; but the sting was sharp, and the "Canons of Criticism" is perhaps the best result of Warburton's enterprise.—STEPHEN, LESLIE, 1899, *Dictionary of National Biography, vol.* LIX, *p.* 306.

EDITIONS OF POPE

You have signalised yourself by affecting to be the bully of Mr. Pope's memory, into whose acquaintance, at the latter end of the poor man's life, you were introduced by your nauseous flattery; and whose admirable writings you are about to publish, with commentaries worthy of Scriblerus himself; for we may judge of them beforehand by the specimens we have already seen of your skill in criticism.—MALLET, DAVID? 1749, *Epistle to the Most Impudent Man Living.*

Soon after Pope's acquaintance with Warburton commenced, and the latter had published some of his heavy commentaries on that poet, his friend Lord Marchmont told him that he was convinced he was one of the vainest men living. "How so?" says Pope. "Because, you little rogue," replied Lord Marchmont, "it is manifest from your close connection with your new commentator you want to show posterity what an exquisite poet you are, and what a quantity of dulness you can carry down on your back without sinking under the load."—MALONE, EDMOND, 1789, *Maloniana, ed. Prior, p.* 385.

Dr. Warburton, endeavouring to demonstrate, what Addison could not discover, nor what Pope himself, according to the testimony of his intimate friend, Richardson, ever thought of or intended, that this Essay was written with a methodical and systematical regularity, has accompanied the whole with a long and laboured commentary, in which he has tortured many passages to support this groundless opinion. Warburton had certainly wit, genius, and much miscellaneous learning; but was perpetually dazzled and misled, by the eager desire of seeing everything in a new light unobserved before, into perverse interpretations and forced comments. It is painful to see such abilities wasted on such unsubstantial objects. Accordingly his notes on Shakspeare have been totally demolished by Edwards and Malone; and Gibbon has torn up by the roots his fanciful and visionary interpretation of the sixth book of Virgil. And but few readers, I believe, will be found that will cordially subscribe to an opinion lately delivered, that his notes on Pope's Works are the very best ever given on any classic whatever. For, to instance no other, surely the attempt to reconcile the doctrines of the "Essay on Man" to the doctrines of revelation, is the rashest adventure in which ever critic yet engaged. This is, in truth, to divine, rather than to explain an author's meaning.—WARTON, JOSEPH, 1797, *ed. Pope.*

Warburton had more to do with Pope's satires as an original suggester, and not merely as a commentator, than with any other section of his works. Pope and he hunted in couples over this field: and those who know the absolute craziness of Warburton's mind, the perfect frenzy and *lymphaticus error* which possessed him for leaving all high-roads of truth and simplicity, in order to trespass over hedge and ditch after coveys of shy paradoxes, cannot be surprised that Pope's good sense should often have quitted him under such guidance. . . . The Doctor was latterly always the instigator to any outrage on good sense, and Pope, from mere habit of deference to the Doctor's theology and theological wig, as well as from gratitude for the Doctor's pugnacity in his defence (since Warburton really was as good as a bull-dog in protecting Pope's advance or retreat), followed with docility the leading of his reverned friend into any excess of folly.—DE

QUINCEY, THOMAS, 1848–58, *The Poetry of Pope, Works, ed. Masson, vol.* XI, *pp.* 69, 71.

Warburton, Pope's first editor, had a vigorous understanding, and possessed the enormous advantage that he carried on the work in concert with the poet, and could ask the explanation of every difficulty. A diseased ambition rendered his talents and opportunities useless. Without originality he aspired to be original, and imagined that to fabricate hollow paradoxes, and torture language into undesigned meanings was the surest evidence of a fertile, penetrating genius. He employed his sagacity less to discover than to distort the ideas of his author, and seems to have thought that the more he deviated from the obvious sense the greater would be his fame for inventive power. He has left no worse specimen of his perverse propensity than the spurious fancies, and idle refinements he fathered upon Pope. They are among his baldest paradoxes, are conveyed in his heaviest style, and are supported by his feeblest sophistry. His lifeless and verbose conceits soon provoke by their falsity, and fatigue by their ponderousness.—ELWIN, WHITWELL, 1871, *ed., The Works of Alexander Pope, Introduction, vol.* I, *p.* xx.

It will thus be seen that Warburton not only slurred over the explanation of difficult passages in Pope's text, but that to promote his interest, or to gratify his spite, he did not scruple to misrepresent the plain intention of his author, and to introduce into his notes irrelevant sarcasms of his own. Such a perversion of his trust of course raises the further presumption that he may have tampered with the text itself, which we know differs in several important respects from all the editions published in Pope's lifetime. . . . Quite enough evidence, however, remains of the untrustworthiness of Warburton's work to make us deplore the fact that his editions should have been taken as the starting-point for all succeeding investigations.—COURTHOPE, WILLIAM JOHN, 1881, *ed., The Works of Alexander Pope, Introductory Notice to Moral Essays and Satires, vol.* III, *pp.* 12, 13.

GENERAL

Mr. Warburton is the greatest general critic I ever knew, the most capable of seeing through all the possibilities of things.—POPE, ALEXANDER, 1730? *Spence's Anecdotes, Supplement, p.* 256.

He joined, to a more than athletic strength of body, a prodigious memory; and to both a prodigious industry. He had read almost constantly twelve or fourteen hours a day, for five-and-twenty or thirty years; and had heaped together as much learning as could be crowded into a head. In the course of my acquaintance with him, I consulted with him once or twice,—not oftener, for I found this mass of learning of as little use to me as to the owner. The man was communicative enough, but nothing was distinct in his mind. How could it be otherwise? he had never spared time to think,—all was employed in reading. His reason had not the merit of common mechanism. When you press a watch or pull a clock, they answer your question with precision. . . . But when you ask this man a question, he overwhelmed you by pouring forth all that the several terms or words of your question recalled to his memory; and if he omitted anything, it was that very thing to which the sense of the whole question should have led him and confined him. To ask him a question was to wind up a spring in his memory, that rattled on with vast rapidity and confused noise, till the force of it was spent; and you went away with all the noise in your ears, stunned and uninformed. I never left him that I was not ready to say to him, "Dieu vous fassel a grace de devenir moins savant!"—BOLINGBROKE, HENRY SAINT-JOHN LORD, 1735? *Letters on the Study and Use of History, Letter* iv.

It is my misfortune, in this controversy, to be engaged with a person who is better known by his *name* than his *works;* or, to speak more properly, whose *works are more known than read.*—EDWARDS, THOMAS, 1747, *Canons of Criticism, Preface.*

He was a man of vigorous faculties, a mind fervid and vehement, supplied by incessant and unlimited inquiry with wonderful extent and variety of knowledge, which yet had not oppressed his imagination nor clouded his perspicacity. To every work he brought a memory full-fraught, together with a fancy fertile of original combinations, and at once exerted the powers of the scholar, the reasoner, and the wit. But his knowledge was too multifarious to be always exact, and his pursuits too eager to be always cautious. His abilities gave him a haughty confidence, which he disclaimed to conceal or modify; and his impatience of opposition disposed him to treat his adversaries with such contemptuous superiority as made his readers commonly his enemies, and excited against the advocate the wishes of some who favoured the cause. He seems to have adopted the Roman emperor's determination, *orderint dum metuant;* he used no allurements of gentle language, but wished to compel rather than persuade. His style is copious without selection, and forcible without neatness; he took the words that presented themselves; his diction is coarse and impure, and his sentences are unmeasured.—JOHNSON, SAMUEL, 1779–81, *Pope, Lives of the English Poets.*

And whom we may compare, not altogether improperly, to a blazing star that has appeared in our hemisphere, obscure his origin, resplendent his light, irregular his motion, and his period quite uncertain. With such a train of quotations as he carries in his tail, and the eccentricity of the vast circuit he takes, the vulgar are alarmed, the learned puzzled. Something wonderful it certainly protends, and I wish he may go off without leaving some malignant influence at least among us, if he does not set us on fire.—CUMING, WILLIAM, c1785, *Letter, Illustrations of the Literatures of the Eighteenth Century, ed. Nichols, vol.* II, *p.* 840.

While they (Leland and Jortin) were living, no balm was poured into their wounded spirits by the hand that pierced them; and if their characters after death remain unimpaired by the rude shocks of controversy and the secret crimes of slander, their triumph is to be ascribed to their own strength, and to the conscious weakness of their antagonists, rather than to his love of justice, or his love of peace.—PARR, SAMUEL, 1789, *ed., Tracts by Warburton and a Warburtonian.*

The learning and abilities of the author (of the Divine Legation) had raised him to a just eminence; but he reigned the Dictator and tyrant of the World of Literature. The real merit of Warburton was degraded by the pride and presumption with which he pronounced his infallible decrees; in his polemic writings he lashed his antagonists without mercy or moderation; and his servile flatterers (see the base and malignant Essay on the Delicacy of Friendship), exalting the master critic far above Aristotle and Longinus, assaulted every modest dissenter who refused to consult the oracle and to adore the Idol. In a land of liberty, such despotism must provoke a general opposition, and the zeal of opposition is seldom candid or impartial.—GIBBON, EDWARD, 1793, *Autobiography.*

Warburton had that eagle-eyed sagacity, which pierces through all difficulties and obscurities; and that glow of imagination which gilds and irradiates every object it touches.—HURD, RICHARD, 1808? *Commonplace Book, ed. Kilvert, p.* 249.

Warburton, we think, was the last of our *great* divines—the last, perhaps, of any profession who united profound learning with great powers of understanding, and, along with vast and varied stores of acquired knowledge, possessed energy of mind enough to wield them with ease and activity. The days of the Cudworths and Barrows—the Hookers and Taylors, are gone by. . . . He was not only the last of our reasoning scholars, but the last also, we think, of our powerful polemics. This breed, too, we take it, is extinct;—and we are not sorry for it. . . . The truth is, that this extraordinary person was a Giant in literature—with many of the vices of the Gigantic character.—JEFFREY, FRANCIS LORD, 1809, *Warburton's Letters, Edinburgh Review, vol.* 13, *pp.* 343, 344, 345.

Nor is there, in the whole compass of our literary history, a character more instructive for its greatness and its failures; none more adapted to excite our curiosity, and which can more completely gratify it. . . . Warburton was a literary Revolutionist, who, to maintain a new order of things, exercised all the despotism of a perpetual dictator. The bold unblushing energy which could lay down the most extravagant positions, was maintained by a fierce dogmatic spirit, and by a peculiar style of mordacious contempt and intolerant insolence, beating down his opponents from all quarters with an animating shout of triumph, to encourage those more serious minds, who, overcome by his genius, were yet often alarmed by the ambiguous tendency of his speculations.—DISRAELI, ISAAC, 1814, *Warburton, Quarrels of Authors.*

It is not a little painful to observe on the disingenuousness of petty critics, who would deny to such a man as Warburton the claim of literary abilities. I will maintain, however, that those abilities were really *first-rate*, whether he be considered as a religionist and a philosopher (characters which, unhappily, are not always found together) a polemic, or a writer of notes.—BECKET, ANDREW, 1815, *Shakspeare's Himself Again, Preface, p.* xix.

Warburton's love of paradox is well known. His levity, dogmatism, and surliness have often been exposed. His love of notoriety and of the marvellous was certainly stronger than his attachment to truth. While his talents will always be admired, his character will never be respected.—ORME, WILLIAM, 1824, *Bibliotheca Biblica.*

The currents of life had drifted Warburton on divinity as his profession, but nature designed him for a satirist; and the propensity was too strong to yield even to the study of the Gospels.—STEPHEN, SIR J., 1838, *Oxford Catholicism, Edinburgh Review, vol.* 67, *p.* 507.

That it is possible to have all the powers of Warburton, and be greatly in the dark on the truths of the gospel, is made sufficiently evident by his "Treatise on the Doctrine of Grace."—BICKERSTETH, EDWARD, 1844, *The Christian Student.*

A divine of almost unrivalled erudition (Jortin excepted) in his day.—MILMAN, HENRY HART, 1854? *History of Latin Christianity, vol.* VIII, *bk.* xiv, *ch.* viii, *note.*

In his literary character, he was of a bold and determined English spirit, ready to resist all opponents, and willing to consider the state of authorship as a state of war. If any deduction be made from this part of his character, it must be on account of his conduct towards Pope, in his advances to whom there appears no great magnanimity, and whom he has always been suspected of defending rather from hope of possible advantage than from sincerity of settled opinion. . . . . Whatever faults he had, he was no bigot. With bigots he professed to be at perpetual war. His mind, certainly, was not of the class in which bigotry fixes itself. —WATSON, JOHN SELBY, 1863, *Life of William Warburton, pp.* 618, 631.

We have already related some of Warburton's more signal enmities. They are samples only of a whole career. Nay, the man himself is in this but the representative man of his age. Theological literature was a babel of loud vociferation, coarse contradiction, and mean imputation. The prize in this *mêlée* was to the noisiest lungs and the foulest tongue. The Warburtonians must not bear the blame alone; nor was the disease of distraction confined to divines. The progress of refinement cannot tame the passions, but has curbed the directness with which they then vented themselves in words. Even now malignant imputation, banished from higher literature, still lingers in clerical controversy. But, after every deduction made, we still find there rests upon the Warburtonian school an extraordinary opprobrium on the score of dirt-throwing. Warburton's superiorty and his generous temper ought to have exempted him from this weakness of inferior writers. Instead of that he is the worst offender. . . . The vigour of his thought does not concentrate itself in telling paragraphs. It is a rude—we had almost said brute—force penetrating the whole. And his English style is so slipslop, that it would be difficult to find in all the thirteen volumes of his works half a dozen passages which might be taken as fair specimens of his peculiar powers.—PATTISON, MARK, 1863–89, *Life of Bishop Warburton, Essays, ed. Nettleship, vol.* II, *pp.* 160, 175.

Bishop Warburton wrote "Remarks on Hume's 'Natural History of Religion.'" They are not of much value; in fact, this is one of Warburton's poorest performances. His words were many and strong, his arguments few and feeble. Warburton defended Christianity by throwing mud at its opponents.—HUNT, JOHN, 1869, *David Hume, Contemporary Review, vol.* 11, *p.* 95.

Warburton was a fortunate author. Though he published a host of paradoxical notions, his opponents, if we are to trust his repeated assertions, were always fools and knaves.—ELWIN, WHITWELL, 1871, *ed., The Works of Alexander Pope, vol.* I, *p.* xiv, *note.*

In Warburton force predominated very much over judgment. He delighted in upholding paradoxes and hopeless causes —arguing with great ingenuity, eking out his argument with plentiful abuse, and, when violently excited, even going the length of threatening his opponent with the cudgel. His command of language, if used with greater discretion, would have given him one of the highest places in literature. His style is simple, emphatic, and racy; diversified with clever quotations and pungent sarcasm (often taking the form of irony).—MINTO, WILLIAM, 1872–80, *Manual of English Prose Literature, p.* 427.

He cultivated the majestic air of a tyrant in literature; he argued, he denounced, he patronised the orthodox, and he bellowed like a bull at the recalcitrant. He was so completely certain of his own intellectual supremacy, that the modern reader feels almost guilty in being able to feel but scant interest in him and in his writings. . . . Warburton was very learned, but so headstrong, arrogant, and boisterous, that he stuns the reader, and those who now examine the vast pile of his writings are not likely to be gratified. What he might gain by his vigour he more than loses by his coarseness, and the student sickens of his ostentation and his paradox.—GOSSE, EDMUND, 1888, *A History of Eighteenth Century Literature, p.* 281.

Is as tricky as Pope himself when it suits his purpose to be so. . . . . . . Warburton's stupendous self-assertion concealed to some extent his heavy style and poverty of thought. His aim was to startle by paradoxes, since he could not convince by argument. No one could call an opponent names in the Billingsgate style more effectively, and every man who ventured to differ from him was either a knave or a fool. "Warburton's stock argument," it has been said, "is a threat to cudgel anyone who disputes his opinion." He was a laborious student, and the mass of work he accomplished exhibits his robust energy, but he has left nothing which lives in literature or in theology. He was, however, a man of various acquisitions, and won, for that reason, the praise of Dr. Johnson.—DENNIS, JOHN, 1894, *The Age of Pope, pp.* 56, 240.

Is the typical controversialist of his age; strong, uncompromising, vigorous with something of the sinewy force of the athlete, direct and even brutal in manner, swollen with the self-satisfied pride of the combatant, and without anything of sentiment or feeling.—CRAIK, HENRY, 1895, *ed., English Prose, Introduction, vol.* IV, *p.*3.

To take by storm the Temple of Fame seems to have been the valiant resolve of the once-renowned author of "The Divine Legation of Moses." He flung its warders a loud defiant summons to surrender, and thundered at its doors. Had violence sufficed for the achievement, so fierce and arrogant a knight of the pen would assuredly have added enduring reputation to his wordly success; but though he proved himself an effective soldier in the controversial campaigns of his own day, it was inevitable that the judgment of time should go in his disfavour. The sword and lance of Warburton's mental equipment, however fitted to put an adversary to silence, were powerless to overawe "the incorruptible Areopagus of posterity." Churchman as he was, and in the end prelate, the weapons of his warfare were not spiritual, nor the virtues of his character and temper the distinctive Christian graces.—DIXON, W. MACNEILE, 1895, *English Prose, ed. Craik, vol.* IV, *p.*93.

Who would care a picayune in these degenerate days what Dr. Warburton said pro or con a book? It was Warburton (then Bishop of Gloucester) who remarked of Granger's "Biographical History of England" that it was "an odd one." This was as high a compliment as he ever paid a book; those which he did not like he called sad books, and those which he fancied he called odd ones.—FIELD, EUGENE, 1896, *The Love Affairs of a Bibliomaniac, p.* 184.

William Warburton was a rather typical divine of the age, who, after perhaps occupying too high a position in it, has been unduly depreciated in this. . . . Warburton just came short of being a great theologian and a great man of letters. His controversial manners cannot be defended, but we should probably have heard a good deal less of them if he had been on the unorthodox side.—SAINTSBURY, GEORGE, 1898, *A Short History of English Literature, p.* 632.

To his admirers he represented the last worthy successor of the learned divines of the preceeding century. His wide reading and rough intellectual vigour are undeniable. Unfortunately he was neither a scholar nor a philosopher. Though he wrote upon the Old Testament, his knowledge of Hebrew was, as Lowth told him, quite superficial; and his blunders in Latin proved that he was no Bentley. His philosophical weakness appears not only in his metaphysical disquisitions, but in the whole conception of his book. The theological system presupposed in the "Divine Legation" is grotesque, and is the most curious example of the results of applying purely legal conceptions to such problems. Warburton, as Lowth pointed out, retained the habits of thought of a sharp attorney, and constantly mistakes wrangling for reasoning. He was ingenious enough to persuade himself that he had proved his point when he had upset an antagonist by accepting the most paradoxical conclusions. Freethinkers such as Walpole and Voltaire thought him a hypocritical ally; and no one, except such personal friends as Hurd and Towne, has ever seriously accepted his position. He flourished in a period in which divines, with the exception of Butler, were becoming indifferent to philosophical speculation. For that reason he found no competent opponent, though his pugnacity and personal force made many enemies and conquered a few humble followers.—SPEPHEN, LESLIE, 1899, *Dictionary of National Biography, vol.* LIX, *p.* 309.

David Garrick

1717–1779

Born. in Hereford, 19 Feb. 1717. Educated at Lichfield Grammar School, 1727. At Lisbon for a short time to learn wine trade, 1727. Pupil of Samuel Johnson, at Edial, 1736. To London with Johnson, March 1737. Entered at Lincoln's Inn, 9 March 1737. Set up wine business with his brother, 1738. Play "Lethe" produced at Drury Lane, April 1740. Became an actor, 1741. Wrote plays, 1741–75. Played at Goodman's Fields Theatre, 1741–42; in Dublin, 1742; at Drury Lane, 1742–45; in Dublin in 1745 and 1746; at Covent Garden, 1745–47. Joint manager of Drury Lane with Lacy, 1747. Played at Drury Lane, 1747–63, 1765–76. Married Eva Marie Violetti, 22 June 1749. Visited Paris, 1752. Tour in France and Italy, 1763–65. Retired from stage, 1776. Buried in Westminster Abbey. *Works:* "The Lying Valet," 1741; "Lethe," 1741; "Lilliput" (anon.), 1747; "Miss in her Teens," (anon.), 1747; "To Mr. Gray on his Odes" (anon.), [1757?]; "The Guardian" (anon.), 1759; "The Enchanter" (anon.), 1760; "The Fribbleraid" (anon.), 1761; "The Farmer's Return from London" (anon.), 1762; "The Sick Monkey" (anon.) 1765; "The Clandestine Marriage" (with G. Colman), 1766; "Neck or Nothing" (anon.), 1766; "Cymon" (anon.), 1767; "A Peep behind the Curtain" (anon.), 1767; "Ode upon dedicating a Building . . . to Shakespeare" (anon.), 1769; "The Theatres" (anon.), 1772; "Love in the Suds" (anon.), 1772; "The Irish Widow" (anon.), 1772; "Albumazar" (anon.), 1773; "A Christmas Tale" (anon.), 1774; "The Theatrical Candidates" (anon.), 1775; "May Day" (anon.), 1775; "Bon Ton" (anon.), 1775; "The Fairies," 1775. He *adapted* plays by Shakespeare, Beaumont and Fletcher, Wycherley, Jonson, Fagan, Southern, etc. *Collected Works:* "Poetical Works" (2 vols.), 1785; "Dramatic Works" (3 vols.), 1798; "Private Correspondence" (2 vols.), 1831–32. *Life:* by T. Davies, 1780; by Murphy, 1801; by P. Fitzgerald, 1868; by Jos. Knight, 1894.—SHARP, R. FARQUHARSON, 1897, *A Dictionary of English Authors, p.* 108.

PERSONAL

There is a little simple farce at Drury Lane, called "Miss Lucy in Town," in which Mrs. Clive mimics the Muscovita admirably, and Beard Amorevoli tolerably. But all the run is now after Garrick, a wine-merchant, who is turned player at Goodman's-Fields. He plays all parts, and is a very good mimic. His acting I have seen, and may say to you, who will not tell it again here, I see nothing wonderful in it—but it is heresy to say so; the Duke of Argyll says he is superior to Betterton.—WALPOLE, HORACE, 1742, *Letter to Sir Horace Mann, May* 26; *Letters, ed. Cunningham, vol.* I, *p.* 168.

I am as much an admirer of Mr. Garrick, and his excellences, as I ought to be: and I envy him no part of his good fortune. But then, though I am free to acknowledge he was made for the stage, I cannot be brought to think the stage was made only for him; or that the fate of every dramatic writer ought either to be at his mercy, or that of any other manager whatever; and the single consideration that there is no alternative but to fly from him, in case of any neglect or contempt, to Mr. Rich, is enough to deter any man in his senses from embarking a second time on such a hopeless voyage.—RALPH, J., 1758, *Case of Authors by Profession.*

The favor I meet with from ye Greatest men, has made me far from repenting of my choice. I am very intimate with Mr. Glover, who will bring out a Tragedy next winter upon my acc^t^. Twice I have sup'd wth ye Great Mr. Murray, Consell^r^, and shall wth Mr. Pope, by his Introduction. I sup'd with ye Mr. Littleton y Prince's Favourite, last Thursday night, and that with ye highest Civility and complaisance. He told me he never knew what Acting was till I appeared, and said I was only born to act w^t^ Shakespear writ. These things daily occurring give me Great Pleasure. I din'd with Ld Hallifax and Ld Sandwich, two very ingenious Noblemen, yesterday, and am to dine at Ld Hallifax's next Sunday with Ld Chesterfield. I have the Pleasure of being very intimate, too, with Mr. Hawkins Browne of Burton. In short, I believe nobody (as an Actor) was ever more caress'd, and my Character as a private Man makes 'em more desirous of my Company. (All this *entre nous*, as one Broth^r^ to another). I am not fix'd for next year, but shall certainly be at ye Other End of ye Town. I am offered 500 guineas and a Clear Benefit, or part of ye Management.—GARRICK, DAVID, 1759, *Letter to Peter Garrick, Apr.* 19.

I have known *one little man* support the theatrical world like a David Atlas upon his shoulders, but Préville can't do half as much here, though Mad. Clairon stands by him and sets her back to his. . . . You are much talked of here, and much expected, as soon as the peace will let you. These two last days you have happened to engross the whole conversation at the great houses where I was at dinner. 'Tis the greatest problem in nature in this meridian that one and the same man should possess such tragic and comic powers, and in such an *equilibrio* as to divide the world from which of the two Nature intended him.—STERNE, LAURENCE, 1762, *Letter to David Garrick from Paris.*

If manly sense; if Nature link'd with Art;
If thorough knowledge of the human heart;
If powers of acting vast and unconfin'd;
If fewest faults with greatest beauties join'd;
If strong expression, and strange powers which lie
Within the magic circle of the eye;
If feelings which few hearts like his can know,
And which no face so well as his can show,
Deserve the preference: Garrick! take the chair;
Nor quit it till thou place an equal there.
—CHURCHILL, CHARLES, 1763, *The Rosciad, v,* 1081–1090.

WILKES.—"Garrick would have made the small-beer still smaller. He is now leaving the stage; but he will play *Scrub* all his life." I knew that Johnson would let nobody attack Garrick but himself, as Garrick once said to me, and I had heard him praise his liberality; so to bring out his commendation of his celebrated pupil, I said, loudly, "I have heard Garrick is liberal." JOHNSON.—"Yes, Sir, I know that Garrick has given away more money than any man in England that I am acquainted with, and that not from ostentatious views. Garrick was very poor when he began life; so when he came to have money, he probably was very unskilful in giving away, and saved when he should not. But Garrick began to be liberal as soon as he could; and I am of opinion, the reputation of avarice which he has had, has been very lucky for him, and prevented his having many enemies. You despise a man for avarice but do not hate him. Garrick might have been much better attacked for living with more splendour than is suitable to a player: if they had had the wit to have assaulted him in that quarter, they might have galled him more. But they have kept clamouring about his avarice, which has rescued him from much obloquy and envy."—JOHNSON, SAMUEL, 1776, *Life by Boswell, ed. Hill, vol.* III, *p.* 80.

Here lies David Garrick, describe me who can,
An abridgment of all that was pleasant in man;

As an actor, confess'd without rival to shine:
As a wit, if not first, in the very first line:
Yet, with talents like these, and an excellent heart,
The man had his failings, a dupe to his art.
Like an ill-judging beauty, his colours he spread,
And beplaster'd with rouge his own natural red.
On the stage he was natural, simple, affecting;
'Twas only that when he was off he was acting.
With no reason on earth to go out of his way,
He turn'd and he varied full ten times a day:
Though secure of our hearts, yet confoundedly sick,
If they were not his own by finessing and trick:
He cast off his friends, as a huntsman his pack,
For he knew when he pleas'd he could whistle them back
Of praise a mere glutton, he swallow'd what came,
And the puff of a dunce, he mistook it for fame;
Till his relish grown callous, almost to disease,
Who pepper'd the highest was surest to please.
But let us be candid, and speak out our mind,
If dunces applauded, he paid them in kind.
Ye Kenricks, ye Kellys, and Woodfalls so grave,
What a commerce was yours, while you got and you gave!
How did Grub-street re-echo the shouts that you rais'd,
While he was be-Roscius'd, and you were be-prais'd!
But peace to his spirit, wherever it flies,
To act as an angel, and mix with the skies:
Those poets, who owe their best fame to his skill,
Shall still be his flatterers, go where he will,
Old Shakespeare, receive him, with praise and with love,
And Beaumonts and Bens be his Kellys above!

—GOLDSMITH, OLIVER, 1774, *The Retaliation.*

Splitt me if I'd not a hundred times rather be spoken to by Garrick in public than His majesty, G—d bless him!—BURNEY, CHARLOTTE ANN, 1777, *Journal, ed. Ellis, p.* 277.

Nature had done so much for him, that he could not help being an actor; she gave him a frame of so manageable a proportion, and from its flexibility so perfectly under command, that, by its aptitude and elasticity, he could draw it out to fit any sizes of character that tragedy could offer to him, and contract it to any scale of ridiculous diminution, that his Able Drugger, Scrubb, or Fribble, could require of him to sink it to. His eye, in the meantime, was so penetrating, so speaking; his brow so moveable, and all his features so plastic, and so accommodating, that wherever his mind impelled them, they would go; and before his tongue could give the text, his countenance would express the spirit and the passion of the part he was encharged with.—CUMBERLAND, RICHARD, 1806, *Memoirs, Written by Himself, p.* 245.

Garrick's appearance forms an epoch in the history of the English theatre, as he chiefly dedicated his talents to the great characters of Shakspeare, and built his own fame on the growing admiration of the poet. Before his time, Shakspeare had only been brought on the stage in mutilated and disfigured alterations. Garrick returned on the whole to the true originals, though he still allowed himself to make some very unfortunate changes. It appears to me that the only excusable alteration of Shakspeare is, to leave out a few things not in conformity to the taste of the time. Garrick was undoubtedly a great actor. Whether he always conceived the parts of Shakspeare in the sense of the poet, I from the very circumstances stated in the eulogies on his acting should be inclined to doubt. He excited, however, a noble emulation to represent worthily the great national poet; this has ever since been the highest aim of actors, and even at present the stage can boast of men whose histrionic talents are deservedly famous.—SCHLEGEL, AUGUSTUS WILLIAM, 1809, *Dramatic Art and Literature, ch.* xiii.

Goldsmith, who played to please the boy, whereas Garrick always seemed playing to please himself, as he did in a theatre. . . . He diverted and dazzled me, but never made me love him; and I had always this feeling for him, though I was too young to define it.—COLMAN, GEORGE, 1830, *Random Records, vol.* I, *pp.* 117, 118.

Garrick, too, was a frequent visitor in Poland Street and St. Martin's Lane. That wonderful actor loved the society of children, partly from good nature, and partly from vanity. The ecstasies of mirth and terror which his gestures and play of countenance never failed to produce in a nursery, flattered him quite as much as the applause of mature critics. He often exhibited all his powers of mimicry for the amusement of the little Burneys, awed them by shuddering and crouching, as if he saw a ghost, scared them by raving like a maniac in St. Luke's, and then at once became an auctioneer, a chimney sweeper, or an old woman, and made them laugh till the tears ran down their cheeks. —MACAULAY, THOMAS BABINGTON, 1842, *Madame D'Arblay, Edinburgh Review; Critical and Miscellaneous Essays.*

He was a sprightly dramatist, a man of wit, and no doubt a generous man, though the endless matters of business in which he was concerned, and the refusals of all kinds which he must have been often forced into, got him, with many, a character for the reverse. Johnson, who did not spare him, pronounced him generous. Fine as his tragedy must have been, we suspect his comedy must have been finer; because his own nature was one of greater sprightliness than sentiment. We hear nothing serious of him throughout his life; and his face, with a great deal of acuteness, has nothing in it profound or romantic.—HUNT, LEIGH, 1848, *The Town, p.* 294.

But David—I fear me—was a sad little sneak. He was grossly penurious, and consequently left behind him a hundred thousand pounds. He was an autocrat in the theatre; jealous of the applause that even the women obtained, when he was on the stage with them; submissive in the presence of a peer, a poet, or a news-writer; equally fearing to elbow the position of the one or to cross the power or caprice of the other. I have seen MS. letters of Garrick's manœuvring for puffs and laudatory notices that have given me the lowest opinion of his mental dignity. —CLARKE, CHARLES COWDEN, 1872, *On the Comic Writers of England, Gentleman's Magazine, N. S. vol.* 8, *p.* 317.

As a man, the detraction of his age has branded him with defects, of which it is sufficient to say that they are now known to have been greatly exaggerated. It is possible that he was not exempt from vanity; and it would have been strange if, in the almost unique eminence he enjoyed, he had wholly escaped it. If, as alleged, early poverty had left him over mindful of small things, let it also be remembered that he was capable of the most splendid generosity, and that, too, in cases where his kindness must have been coals of fire. As to his reported jealousy and envy, as many tales are told on one side as on the other. But if the worst be admitted, it can hardly be denied that he brought to the uneasy throne of theatrical management administrative talents of the rarest kind. He gathered round him a magnificent constellation of dramatic talent, to which he himself was sun and centre. When Pope said of him at Goodman's Fields that "he never had an equal, and would never have a rival," the epigram was a prophecy; and Quin uttered a truer thing than he knew when he named him the "Whitfield of the stage."—DOBSON, AUSTIN, 1886, *Actors and Actresses of Great Britain and the United States, ed. Matthews and Hutton, vol.* I, *p.* 66.

He had no enduring hostility, however, his temper generally being devoid of gall. He carried caution to an excess. Davies says that he acquired through this a hesitation in speech which did not originally characterise him. As a rule he was fairly accessible to authors, and if he produced few masterpieces, the fault was in the writers. In dramatists generally he displayed genuine interest, and after his retirement he took great pains to advance the fortunes of Hannah More. In his disputes the impression conveyed is generally that he was in the right. He generally treated the ebullitions of mortified vanity on the part of authors with tenderness. He kept the masculine portion of his company in fair order, though the feminine portion was generally mutinous. He made many important reforms, some of them learned during his journeys abroad, in discipline, in stage arrangement, and in matters of costume, in which he effected some improvement, pleading as a not very convincing reason for going no further that the public would not stand it. In many cases of difficulty he showed magnanimity, which his enemies sought vainly to stamp as prudence. Fortune fluctuated during his managerial career, but the result was that the property he conducted increased steadily in value during his management, that he retired with a larger fortune than any English actor except

Alleyn had made in a similar enterprise, and with the respect and friendship of all the best men of his epoch.—KNIGHT, JOSEPH, 1890, *Dictionary of National Biography, vol.* XXI, *p.* 25.

GENERAL

Garrick's portentous "Ode," as you truly call it, has but one line of truth in it, which is where he calls Shakespeare the God *of our Idolatry:* for *sense* I will not allow it; for that which is so highly satirical, he makes the topic of his hero's encomium. The "Ode" itself is below any of Cibber's. Cibber's nonsense was something like sense; but this man's sense, whenever he deviates into it, is much more like nonsense.—WARBURTON, WILLIAM, 1769, *Letter to Hurd, Sept.* 23

As a writer, we can hardly tell what to say of his powers: we do not know, touching either character, thought, or expression, how much was really in *his* the plays of others. The two-act comedy, at least, was his own. Prologue was his chief province, and his fertility in such compositions, was inexhaustible. *Epigram* he made vigorous court to; and *epitaph*, in some instances, owned no superior. In the light measures of Prior he frolics like that poet himself, or Voltaire, or Gresset in the enchanting *Ver-Vert.*—BOADEN, JAMES, 1831, *Private Correspondence of David Garrick, Memoir, p.* lxiv.

It is as an actor that Garrick appeals to us, and not as a dramatist. A list of the plays, which were assigned him, or the authorship of which he claimed, may be seen in the "Biographia Dramatica" of Baker, Reed and Jones, to which list of 39 pieces must be added an alteration of "Mahomet" and some similar experiments. A few of Garrick's plays have, as has been said, ingenuity of construction and vivacity. On the whole, like that of Christian in the "Pilgrim's Progress," his march towards immortality will be the speedier and the more comfortable when the burden of his general dramas falls from him. His occasional verses are sometimes happy. What Johnson said of his talk is almost true of his verses—"Garrick's conversation is gay and grotesque. It is a dish of all sorts, but all good things. There is no solid meat in it: there is a want of sentiment in it." A curiously complex, interesting, and diversified character is that of Garrick. Fully to bring it before the world might have taxed his own powers of exposition.—KNIGHT, JOSEPH, 1894, *David Garrick, p.* 335.

John Armstrong

1709–1779

John Armstrong, physician and poet, was born about 1709 in Castleton manse, Liddesdale, Roxburghshire. He took the Edinburgh M. D., in 1732, and soon after commenced practice in London. In 1736 he published a nauseous poem, "The Œconomy of Love;" in 1744 his principal work, "The Art of Preserving Health," a didactic poem in four books. In 1746 he was appointed physician to the London Soldiers' Hospital, in 1760 physician to the forces in Germany, whence he returned on half-pay in 1763, to resume practice. With Fuseli, the painter, he made a continental tour (1771); and he died in London from a fall, 7th September 1779. The friend of Thomson, Mallet, Wilkes, &c. Armstrong seems to have been a reserved, indolent, and splenetic man, "who quite detested talk;" kind-hearted withal, and frugal.—PATRICK AND GROOME, *eds.*, 1897, *Chambers's Biographical Dictionary, p.* 42.

PERSONAL

With him was sometimes joined in silent walk
(Profoundly silent, for they never spoke),
One shyer still, who quite detested talk:
Oft stung by spleen, at once away he broke,
To groves of pine and broad o'ershadowing oak;
There, inly thrilled, he wandered all alone,
And on himself his pensive fury wroke;
He ever uttered word, save, when first shone
The glittering star of eve—"Thank Heaven! the day is done."

—THOMSON, JAMES, 1744, *The Castle of Indolence.*

Armstrong, another poet and physician and not unworthy of either class, for genius and goodness of heart, though he had the weakness of affecting a bluntness of manners, and of swearing, drew his last breath in this street. He is well known as the author of the most elegant didactic poem in the language,—the "Art of Preserving Health." The affectations of men of genius are sometimes in direct contradiction to their best qualities, and assumed to avoid a show of pretending what they feel. Armstrong, who had bad health, and was afraid perhaps of being thought effeminate, affected the bully in his prose writings; and he was such a swearer, that the late Mr. Fuseli's indulgence in that infirmity has been attributed to his keeping company with the Doctor when a youth.—HUNT, LEIGH, 1848, *The Town, p.* 320.

ART OF PRESERVING HEALTH
1744

To describe so difficult a thing, gracefully and poetically, as the effects of distemper on a human body, was reserved for Dr. Armstrong, who accordingly hath executed it at the end of his third book of his "Art of Preserving Health," where he hath given us that pathetick account of the sweating sickness. There is a classical correctness and closeness of style in this poem, that are truly admirable, and the subject is raised and adorned by numberless poetical images.—WARTON, JOSEPH, 1753–78, *Reflections on Didactic Poetry.*

Dr. Armstrong, in his "Art of Preserving Health," has not aimed at so high a strain as the other [Akenside]. But he is more equal; and maintains throughout a chaste and correct elegance.—BLAIR, HUGH, 1783, *Lectures on Rhetoric and Belles-Lettres, ed. Mills, Lecture* xl.

His "Art of Preserving Health" is the most successful attempt, in our language, to incorporate material science with poetry. Its subject had the advantage of being generally interesting; for there are few things that we shall be more willing to learn, either in prose or verse, than the means of preserving the outward bulwark of all other blessings. At the same time, the difficulty of poetically treating a subject, which presented disease in all its associations, is one of the most just and ordinary topics of his praise. Of the triumphs of poetry over such difficulty, he had no doubt high precedents, to show that strong and true delineations of physical evil are not without an attraction of fearful interest and curiosity to the human mind; and that the enjoyment, which the fancy derives from conceptions of the bloom and beauty of healthful nature, may be heightened, by contrasting them with the opposite pictures of her mortality and decay. Milton had turned disease itself into a subject of sublimity, in the vision of Adam, with that intensity of the fire of genius, which converts whatever materials it meets with into its ailment: and Armstrong, though his powers were not Miltonic, had the courage to attempt what would have repelled a more timid taste. His Muse might be said to show a professional intrepidity in choosing the subject; and, like the physician who braves contagion (if allowed to prolong the simile), we may add, that she escaped, on the whole, with little injury from the trial. By the title of the poem, the author judiciously gave his theme a moral as well as a medical interest. He makes the influence of the passions an entire part of it. By professing to describe only how health is to be preserved, and not how it is to be restored, he avoids the unmanageable horrors of clinical detail; and though he paints the disease wisely spares us its pharmaceutical treatment. His course through the poem is sustained with lucid management and propriety.—CAMPBELL, THOMAS, 1819, *Specimens of the British Poets.*

His sentences are generally short and easy, his sense clear and obvious. The full extent of his conceptions is taken at the first glance; and there are no lofty mysteries to be unravelled by repeated perusal. What keeps his language from being prosaic, is the vigour of his sentiments. He thinks boldly, feels strongly, and therefore expresses himself poetically. Where the subject sinks, his style sinks with it; but he has for the most part excluded topics incapable either of vivid description, or of the oratory of sentiment. He had from nature a musical ear, whence his lines are scarcely ever harsh, and are usually melodious, though apparently without much study to render them so. Perhaps he has not been careful enough to avoid the monotony of making several successive lines close with a rest or pause in the sense. On the whole, it may not be too much to assert, that no writer in blank verse can be found more free from stiffness and affectation, more energetic without harshness, and more dignified without formality.—AIKIN, JOHN, 1820, *An Essay on Dr. Armstrong's Poem on the Art of Preserving Health.*

Has the rare merit of an original and characteristic style, distinguished by raciness and manly grace.—CRAIK, GEORGE L., 1861, *A Compendious History of English Literature and of the English Language, vol.* II, *p.* 287.

Warton has praised the "Art of Preserving Health" for its classical correctness and closeness of style, and its numberless poetical images. In general, however, it is stiff and laboured, with occasional passages of tumid extravagance; and the images are not unfrequently echoes of those of Thomson and other poets. The subject required the aid of ornament, for scientific rules are in general bad themes for poetry, and few men are ignorant of the true philosophy of life, however they may deviate from it in practice. — CHAMBERS, ROBERT, 1876, *Cyclopædia of English Literature, ed. Carruthers.*

On the whole however the merits of "The Art of Preserving Health" far outweigh its defects. It may indeed be urged by a devil's advocate that it is but a left-handed compliment to say that a man has done better than could be expected a task which, as sense and taste should have shown him, ought not to have been attempted at all. But Armstrong must always have, with competent judges, the praise which belongs to an author who has a distinct and peculiar grasp of a great poetical form.—SAINTSBURY, GEORGE, 1880, *The English Poets, ed. Ward, vol.* III, *p.* 184.

In the class of poetry to which it belongs, the "Art of Preserving Health" holds a distinguished place. No writer of the eighteenth century had so masterful a grasp of blank verse as is shown in parts of this poem. The powerful passage descriptive of the plague (book iii.) has been highly praised. As in all didactic poetry, the practical directions are of little interest; but those who value austere imagination and weighty diction cannot afford to neglect Armstrong's masterpiece. —BULLEN, A. H., 1885, *Dictionary of National Biography, vol.* II, *p.* 95.

A poem containing some powerful passages, and many which are better fitted for a medical treatise than for poetry.—DENNIS, JOHN, 1894, *The Age of Pope, p.* 242.

GENERAL

Let them with Armstrong, taking leave of sense,
Read musty lectures on Benevolence,
Or con the pages of his gaping Day,
Where all his former fame was thrown away,
Where all but barren labour was forgot,
And the vain stiffness of a letter'd Scot;
Let them with Armstrong pass the term of light,
But not one hour of darkness.
—CHURCHILL, CHARLES, 1764? *The Journey, Poems, ed. Tooke, vol.* II, *p.* 296.

On the whole, he is likely to be remembered as a poet of judicious thoughts and correct expression; and, as far as the rarely successful application of verse to subjects of science can be admired, an additional merit must be ascribed to the hand which has reared poetical flowers on the dry and difficult ground of philosophy. —CAMPBELL, THOMAS, 1819, *Specimens of the British Poets.*

The "Œconomy of Love," 1736, 8vo, was published anonymously; and it is indeed a production which not many men would care to claim. A more nauseous piece of work could not easily be found. When the author reissued the poem in 1768, he had the good sense to cancel some of the worst passages.—BULLEN, A. H., 1885, *Dictionary of National Biography, vol.* II, *p.* 94.

Armstrong's diction was absurdly tumid; he calls a wild briar-rose "a cynorrhodon," and a cold bath "a gelid cistern." But his merits of dignity and melody are at present underrated. The structure of Armstrong's blank verse is excellent, and though founded upon Thomson's, has a certain independent stateliness.—GOSSE, EDMUND, 1888, *A History of Eighteenth Century Literature, p.* 227.

Armstrong's early imitation of Shakespeare and his critical panegyrics on the great dramatists reveal his true leanings. He was indeed indebted to Thomson, but only in a slight degree; and the influence of his country is rather seen in the independence of the fashionable mode which it helped him to maintain, than in positive features of his style. He was one of the earliest students of the Elizabethans who went so far as to make them his models, and acknowledge them as supreme masters of poetic art. He owes to the school in which he studied the daring of his sombre imagination, the manliness of his style, and the strength of his verse.—WALKER, HUGH, 1893, *Three Centuries of Scottish Literature, vol.* II, *p.* 90.

No one now would write on Armstrong's subjects in Armstrong's manner, but his grasp of the peculiar Thomsonian diction and versification was extraordinary.—SAINTSBURY, GEORGE, 1898, *A Short History of English Literature, p.* 579.

John Langhorne

1735-1779

An English divine, poet, and historian, was born at Kirkby Stephen, in Westmoreland, in 1735. He published several popular pieces, particularly a poem, entitled "Genius and Valor," and having therein defended Scotland from the scurrility thrown out by Churchill in his "Prophecy of Famine," he was complimented with the degree of D. D. by the university of Edinburgh. In 1770 in conjunction with his brother, he published a translation of Plutarch, which is still a very popular work: in 1777 he was presented to a prebendal stall in the cathedral of Wells, and died in 1779.—GODWIN, PARKE, 1852, *Hand-Book of Universal Biography, p.* 567.

PERSONAL

He died in the flower of his prime, when the promises of his youth were on the verge of their full accomplishment. That such a man should take pains to put out the lamp that lights up the chamber of speculation and thought within him, is as lamentable as it is censurable; and little more can be said for him but that his guilt and folly appear harmless in comparison with the malignity of those of our day who abuse the arts of composition and the power of song, to spread a moral blight around them.—ROBERTS, WILLIAM, 1834, *Memoirs of the Life and Correspondence of Hannah More, pt.* i.

GENERAL

It is but a cheerless task of criticism, to pass with a cold look and irreverent step, over the literary memories of men, who, though they may rank low in the roll of absolute genius, have yet possessed refinement, information, and powers of amusement, above the level of their species, and such as would interest and attach us in private life. Of this description was Langhorne; an elegant scholar, and an amiable man. He gave delight to thousands, from the press and the pulpit; and had sufficient attraction, in his day, to sustain his spirit and credit as a writer, in the face of even Churchill's envenomed satire. Yet, as a prose writer, it is impossible to deny that his rapidity was the effect of lightness more than vigour; and, as a poet, there is no ascribing to him either fervour or simplicity. His Muse is elegantly languid. She is a fine lady, whose complexion is rather indebted to art than to the healthful bloom of nature. It would be unfair not to except from this observation several plain and manly sentiments, which are expressed in his poem "On the Enlargement of the Mind," and some passages in his "Country Justice," which are written with genuine feeling.—CAMPBELL, THOMAS, 1819, *Specimens of the British Poets.*

There is a period in youth when the mere power of numbers has a more strong effect on ear and imagination than in afterlife. At this season of immature taste, the author was greatly delighted with the poems of Mickle and Langhorne.—SCOTT, SIR WALTER, 1821, *Kenilworth, Preface.*

His [Scott's] youthful admiration of Langhorne has been rendered memorable by his own record of his first and only interview with his great predecessor, Robert Burns.—LOCKHART, JOHN GIBSON, 1836, *Life of Sir Walter Scott, ch.* v.

For LANGHORNE, Reverend let him still continue,
Although his mind had very little sinew.
'Twas his to ape our reverend ancient lays
With mincing prettiness of modern phrase,
As some fine ladies mimic in their dress
The simple finery of a shepherdess;
And shape their silks and muslins to the cut
That decks the dwellers of the mud-built hut.
—COLERIDGE, HARTLEY, 1849, *Sketches of English Poets, Poems, vol.* II, *p.* 309.

Langhorne, an amiable man, and highly popular as well as warmly beloved in his day, survives now in memory chiefly through his Plutarch's Lives, and through a few lines in his "Country Justice," which are immortalised by the well-known story of Scott's interview with Burns. Campbell puts in a plea besides for his "Owen of Carron," but the plea, being founded on early reading, is partial, and has not been responded to by the public. —GILFILLAN, GEORGE, 1860, *Specimens with Memoirs of Less-Known British Poets.*

The only poem of Langhorne's which has a cast of originality is his "Country Justice." Here he seems to have anticipated Crabbe in painting the rural life of England in true colours. His picture of the gipsies, and his sketches of venal clerks and rapacious overseers, are genuine likenesses. He has not the raciness or the distinctness of Crabbe, but is equally faithful, and as sincerely a friend to humanity. He pleads warmly for the poor vagrant tribe.—CHAMBERS, ROBERT, 1876, *Cyclopædia of English Literature, ed. Carruthers.*

Langhorne was a popular writer in his day, but his sentimental tales and his pretty verses have long ceased to please, and he is now best remembered as the joint translator of "Plutarch's Lives."—BARKER, G. F. RUSSELL, 1892, *Dictionary of National Biography, vol.* XXXII, *p.* 101.

That he had a tender feeling towards animals is shown by his poems on birds and by his protest against the cruelty of confining birds in cages. The most striking characteristic of Langhorne's poems is his direct expression of the excellence of the gift that nature's hand bestows. . . . Langhorne's perception of the power of nature over man, and his passionate sense of personal indebtedness to nature are the keynotes of his work. In a narrow way and with feeble speech he shows a mental and spiritual experience of the same type as that which Wordsworth records of his own youth. His motive in writing "an unaffected wish to promote the love of nature and the interests of humanity," is likewise Wordsworthian.—REYNOLDS, MYRA, 1896, *The Treatment of Nature in English Poetry, Between Pope and Wordsworth, pp.* 132, 133.

Langhorne at least sometimes has a melancholy clangour of verse too rare in his century.—SAINTSBURY, GEORGE, 1898, *A Short History of English Literature, p.* 587.

William Kenrick

1725?-1779

A critic of equal ability, impudence, and literary ferocity, was for a long time—first in the *Monthly* and subsequently in the *London Review*—the terror of the new scribes, and the object of disgust to the old authors, of his own day. Goldsmith, Akenside, Johnson, Colman, Boswell, Garrick, and a host of others, were in turn made to suffer for having gained that popularity or notoriety which the public denied to him. We have already had something to say of this "Literary Ishmaelite" in our lives of Goldsmith and Dr. Johnson, and have little to add in this place. His productions—consisting of poems, poetical epistles, philosophical and philological speculations, comedies, letters, &c., pub. from 1751 to 1773—are now forgotten, save in connexion with the better men whom he attacked; nor would the world be much benefited by a revival of this lost knowledge. But those who desire to explore further may consult the *Monthly Review* (Kenrick's own child) the *London Review; Gent. Mag.;* Chalmers's Biog. Dict.; Boswell's "Life of Johnson," and other literary records of the day, and the "Encyc. Brit." His most ambitious publication was "A New Dictionary of the English Language: to which is prefixed a Rhetorical Grammar," Lon., 1773, 4to. "The Rhetorical Grammar" was also pub. separately in 1784, 8vo.— —ALLIBONE, S. AUSTIN, 1854-58, *A Critical Dictionary of English Literature, vol.* I, *p.* 1022.

PERSONAL

Dreaming of genius which he never had,
Half wit, half fool, half critic, and half mad;
Seizing like Shirley on the poet's lyre,
With all the rage, but not one spark of fire;
Eager for slaughter and resolved to tear
From others' brows that wreath he must not wear,
Next Kenrick came; all furious and replete
With brandy, malice, pertness, and conceit.
Unskill'd in classic lore, through envy blind
To all that's beauteous, learned, or refined;
For faults alone behold the savage prowl,

With Reason's offal glut his ravening soul;
Pleas'd with his prey, its inmost blood he drinks,
And mumbles, paws, and turns it—till it stinks.
—SHAW, CUTHBERT, 1766, *The Race.*

He was brought up as a scale-maker, or in some such employment, but early became a hack writer. He had a strong love of notoriety, a jealous and perverse temper, and was often drunk and violent. He became the enemy of every decent and successful person, and so notorious as a libeller that few condescended to answer him. His vanity led him to fancy himself equal to any task with serious study. . . . In his later years Kenrick seldom wrote without a bottle of brandy at his elbow. Though a superlative scoundel, he was clever, and especially proud of the rapidity of his writing, even his more serious works.—GOODWIN, GORDON, 1892, *Dictionary of National Biography, vol.* XXXI, *pp.* 16, 19.

GENERAL

Though he certainly was not without considerable merit, he wrote with so little regard to decency and principles, and decorum, and in so hasty a manner, that his reputation was neither extensive nor lasting. I remember one evening, when some of his works were mentioned, Dr. Goldsmith said, he had never heard of them; upon which Dr. Johnson observed, "Sir, he is one of the many who have made themselves *publick*, without making themselves *known*."—BOSWELL, JAMES, 1791–93, *Life of Johnson, ed. Hill, vol.* I, *p.* 576.

The turn of his criticism, the airiness or the asperity of his sarcasm, the arrogance with which he treated some of our great authors, would prove very amusing, and serve to display a certain talent of criticism. . . . He was a man of talents, who ran a race with the press; could criticise all the genius of the age faster than it could be produced; could make his own malignity look like wit, and turn the wit of others into absurdity by placing it topsy-turvy,—DISRAELI, ISAAC, 1812–13, *Calamities of Authors.*

It may be well, however, in passing, to bestow our mite of notoriety upon the miscreant who launched the slander. [On Goldsmith] He deserves it for a long course of dastardly and venomous attacks, not merely upon Goldsmith, but upon most of the successful authors of the day.—IRVING, WASHINGTON, 1849, *Life of Goldsmith, p.* 135.

Sir William Blackstone

1723-1780

Born at London, July 10, 1723: died at London, Feb. 14, 1780. A celebrated English jurist, appointed Vinerian professor of common law at Oxford in 1758, and Justice in the Court of Common Pleas in 1770. His chief work is "Commentaries on the Laws of England" (1765–68). Eight editions appeared in the author's lifetime, and for sixty years after his death they followed in quick succession. These editions were edited and annotated by Coleridge, Chitty, Christian, and others. An American edition was printed in 1884, but the text has not been reprinted in England since 1844. There are various adaptations of it for modern use.—SMITH, BENJAMIN E., *ed.*, 1894–97, *The Century Cyclopedia of Names, p.* 160.

PERSONAL

If I were personally your enemy, I should dwell with a malignant pleasure upon those great and useful qualities you certainly possess, and by which you once acquired, though they could not preserve to you, the respect and esteem of your country. I should enumerate the honours you have lost, and the virtues you have disgraced; but, having no private resentments to gratify, I think it sufficient to have given my opinion of your public conduct, leaving the punishment it deserves to your closet and to yourself.—JUNIUS, 1769–72, *Letter* xviii.

He was a believer in the great truths of Christianity, from a thorough investigation of its evidence: attached to the church of England from conviction of its excellence, his principles were those of its genuine members, enlarged and tolerant. His religion was pure and unaffected, and his attendance on its public duties regular, and those duties always performed with seriousness and devotion.—CLITHEROW, J., 1781, *ed., Reports, Memoir.*

Sir William Blackstone, as Sir. Wm. Scott of the Commons observed to me a few days ago, was extremely irritable. He was the only man, my informant said, he had ever known who acknowledged and lamented his bad temper. He was an accomplished man in very various departments of science, with a store of general knowledge. He was particularly fond of architecture, and had written upon that subject. The notes which he gave me on Shakspeare show him to have been a man of excellent taste and accuracy, and a good critick. The total sum which he made by his "Commentaries," including the profits of his lectures, the sale of the books while he kept the copyright in his own hands, and the final sale of the proprietorship to Mr. Cadell, amounted to fourteen thousand pounds. Probably the bookseller in twenty years from the time of that sale will clear ten thousand pounds by his bargain, and the book proved to be an estate to his heirs.—MALONE, EDMOND, 1791, *Maloniana, ed. Prior, p.* 431.

Judge Blackstone composed his "Commentaries" (he was a poet too in his youth) with a bottle of port before him. —BYRON, LORD, 1821, *On Bowles's Strictures on Pope.*

The private character of Sir William Blackstone is represented in very favourable colours by his biographer, but seems to have been misunderstood by those who did not enjoy an intimate acquaintance with him. His appearance was not prepossessing. The heaviness of his features and figure, and the contraction of his brow, gave a character of moroseness to his countenance which did not exist in fact. He was not, however, free from occasional irritation of temper, which was increased by the nervous complaints to which he was subject. In his own family he was cheerful, agreeable, and even facetious, and a diligent observer of those economical arrangements upon which so much of the respectability and comfort of life depends. The disposal of his time was so skilfully managed, that, though he was a laborious student, he freely mingled in the amusements and relaxations of society. This he effected by his rigid punctuality.—ROSCOE, HENRY, 1830, *Lives of Eminent British Lawyers, p.* 256.

A formal, precise, and affected lecturer —just what you would expect from the character of his writings; cold, reserved, and wary—exhibiting a frigid pride.— BOWRING, SIR JOHN, 1838, *Works of Jeremy Bentham, vol.* x, *p.* 45.

The politician and the judge are forgotten now, and only the commentator remains. But his life was consistent throughout. He had a reverence for authority and a respect for formalities; his mind turned more readily to apology than to criticism; and destitute of ideals he lived in a narrow groove, contented with himself and the world. When he and Serjeant Nares were calling for the expulsion of Wilkes because he was a blasphemer, Burke described their arguments as "solid, substantial, roast-beef reasoning." The phrase paints to the life the worshipper of the constitution, who staked the fate of England upon trial by jury.— MACDONELL, G. P., 1885, *Blackstone, Macmillan's Magazine, vol.* 51, *p.* 360.

COMMENTARIES ON THE LAWS OF ENGLAND
1765–68

Correct, elegant, unembarrassed, ornamented, the style is such as could scarce fail to recommend a work still more vitious in point of matter to the multitude of readers. He it is, in short, who, first of all institutional writers, has taught jurisprudence to speak the language of the scholar and the gentleman; put a polish upon that rugged science; cleansed her from the dust and cobwebs of the office: and if he has not enriched her with that precision which is drawn only from the sterling treasury of the sciences, has decked her out, however, to advantage, from the toilet of classical erudition; enlivened her with metaphors and allusions; and sent her abroad in some measure to instruct, and in still greater measure to entertain, the most miscellaneous, and even the most fastidious, societies. The merit to which, as much perhaps as to any, the work stands indebted for its reputation, is the enchanting harmony of its numbers; a kind of merit that of itself is sufficient to give a certain degree of celebrity to a work devoid of every other. So much is man governed by the ear.—BENTHAM, JEREMY, 1776, *A Fragment on Government; being an Examination of what is Delivered on the Subject in Blackstone's Commentaries, Preface.*

I recommend the "Commentaries" of Blackstone as a general book. The intention of that ingenious writer was to give a comprehensive outline; and when we consider the multiplicity of doctrine which he embraced, the civil, the criminal, the theoretical and practical branches of the law, we must confess the hand of a master. But in the minutiæ he is frequently, very frequently, inaccurate. He should, therefore, be read with caution. The student, in reading him, will often require explanation from him whose duty it is to instruct. — WATKINS, CHARLES, 1800, *Principles of Conveyancing.*

I suppose you will now go in earnest to law. I do not know much of the matter, but I suspect that a regular attendance (and with attention) to the courts, is still more important than any reading whatever; you, of course, read Blackstone over and over again; and if so, pray tell me whether you agree with me in thinking his style of English the very best among our modern writers; always easy and intelligible; far more correct than Hume, and less studied and made up than Robertson.—FOX, CHARLES JAMES, 1802, *Letter to John Bernard Trotter, Oct.* 28, *Memoirs, ed. Trotter, p.* 318.

Of Blackstone's Commentaries it would be presumptuous in us to attempt an eulogium, after Sir William Jones has pronounced it to be the *most beautiful outline* that was ever given of any science. Nothing can exceed the luminous arrangement, the vast comprehension, and, we may venture to add from the best authorities, the legal accuracy of this wonderful performance, which, in style and composition, is distinguished by an unaffected grace, a majestic simplicity, which can only be ecclipsed by the splendour of its higher qualities.—HALL, ROBERT, 1808, *Miscellaneous Works, ed. Gregory, p.* 449.

Perhaps no professional writer has suffered more from the zeal of injudicious admirers than Blackstone in his celebrated "Commentaries." They were not designed for students at law, but for students at the University; they were not addressed to professional, but to unprofessional, readers. He was not a lecturer of an Inn of Court, but a University professor—not to inform lawyers, but to render the law intelligible to the uninformed minds of beginners. Addressing himself to persons of this description, like an experienced actor, he accommodated himself to the temper and character of his audience, rather for effect than with a view to demonstrate. Like the gnomon upon the sun-dial, he takes no account of any hours but the serene. A man may read Blackstone's "Commentaries" from one end to the other, and yet have no notion that a proposition in law is as capable of being resolved and demonstrated as a proposition in mathematics. In the rank of elementary composition they might forever have reposed beneath undisturbed laurels; but he who would make them the institute of his professional education imprudently forces them into an element which is not their own, and lays the foundation for those perilous misunderstandings—that unlawyer-like, jejune smattering, which informs without enlightening, and leaves its deluded votary at once profoundly ignorant and contented.—RITSO, FREDERICK, 1815, *Introduction to the Science of the Law.*

Blackstone—a great master of classical and harmonious composition, but a feeble reasoner, and a confused thinker.—MACKINTOSH, SIR JAMES, 1830, *Dissertation on the Progress of Ethical Philosophy.*

Good authority. The "Commentaries" are still quoted, and as frequently as ever in the Courts of Law and Equity; if possible, with increased respect for the value of Blackstone's opinions, and of the evidence which his pages afford, of the former state of the law.—WARREN, SAMUEL, 1835, *Popular and Practical Introduction to Law Studies.*

When we reflect upon the vastness and complication of our legislative and executive system, and the thousand elements, Roman, mediæval, municipal, feudal, and parliamentary, which combine to form that wonderful compound, the British constitution, it is impossible to express too warmly the gratitude which not only every Englishman, but every civilized man, should feel towards Blackstone for having placed, in an intelligible and accessible form, the history of what can never be devoid either of philosophical interest, or influence upon the destinies of human liberty.—SHAW, THOMAS B., 1847, *Outlines of English Literature, p.* 410.

I have followed your advice, and I have

read, or rather re-read, Blackstone. I studied him twenty years ago. Each time he has made upon me the same impression. Now, as then, I have ventured to consider him (if one may say so without blasphemy) an inferior writer, without liberality of mind or depth of judgment; in short, a commentator and a lawyer, not what *we* understand by the words *jurisconsulte* and *publiciste.* He has, too, in a degree which is sometimes amusing, a mania for admiring all that was done in ancient times, and for attributing to them all that is good in his own. I am inclined to think that, if he had had to write, not on the institutions, but on the products of England, he would have discovered that beer was first made from grapes, and that the hop is the fruit of the vine—rather a degenerate product, it is true, of the wisdom of our ancestors, but as such worthy of respect. It is impossible to imagine an excess more opposite to that of his contemporaries in France, for whom it was enough that a thing was old for it to be bad.—TOCQUEVILLE, ALEXIS DE, 1853, *Correspondence with Nassau William Senior, ed. Simpson, vol.* II, *p.* 44.

There are men in the prime of life who fancy that Sir William Blackstone must have been the intensest of the Old-World "fogies," in a state of preternatural dryness, and that he was always to be found in the same place, writing heavy treatises on Law, and making interminable extracts from musty authors, dryer, if possible, than himself; that he was in short a machine, which when he died had only run down, and could have been made to go for ever with an occasional winding. This is the absurdest idea of all. There are men—I do not fear to say it—who have read every page of Blackstone's "Commentaries," and are now living. They never speak of the feat as a thing extraordinary, and seem even to have formed something of an attachment for their author, and profess to admire his style. These men have never been charged with insanity, and with moderate care will be certain to escape the horrors of the strait-jacket.—MAURICE, JACQUES, 1856, *Blackstone, Knickerbocker Magazine, vol.* 47, *p.* 288.

What Lyttleton and his crabbed expositor were to our legal ancestors, Blackstone is to modern students: and though some of the more earnest or more ambitious of them may seek honours by endeavouring to fathom the mysteries of the "Tenures," the οἱ πολλοί of the profession are content to earn an easy degree by mastering the more attractive lessons conveyed in the "Commentaries." So popular have they become, that, where the study was confined in former times to those who pursued it as an avocation, few men of rank or fortune now consider their education complete without gaining an insight into the constitution of the country through Blackstone's easy and perspicuous pages; and abridgments are even introduced into schools for the instruction of the young.—FOSS, EDWARD, 1864, *The Judges of England, vol.* VIII, *p.* 243.

He never knew the civil law otherwise than superficially, and frequently states it inaccurately; and even in English law his work is not more remarkable for original research than for the singular skill which it shows in making a happy use of the labours of previous text-writers.—MACDONELL, G. P., 1886, *Dictionary of National Biography, vol.* V, *p.* 137.

I have not hesitated to speak plainly of the defects and limitations of Blackstone's works. . . . I have dwelt, at what may be thought needless length, upon the mistake in his definition of law, and on the relation between law and rights, because the most important change in our science within the last century seems to me to be that by which we have got rid of the notion of law as essentially a command, obedience or disobedience to which makes rights and wrongs, and substituted for it the conception of human rights, and duties. . . . Much of the work done by the so-called school of analytical jurists in England, I believe to have been in the wrong direction, leading farther away from the true sense of law, as we now understand it, than Blackstone's own view.—HAMMOND, WILLIAM G., 1890, *ed. Blackstone's Commentaries, Preface, p.* xix.

Nowhere, it is said, has the chief work of Sir William Blackstone been more widely read than in America. . . . Blackstone was not without his critics, who remarked upon some disproportion in the parts of his great work, which closes with a chapter on the rise, progress and gradual improvements of the laws of England, suggesting to Reeves the utility of a history of English law, filled up with some minuteness upon the outline thus drawn. Thomas Jefferson questioned the wisdom of Blackstone's plan of smoothing the path of the student of law. He was also opposed to citing English authorities after the declaration of independence, and is reported to have said that to exclude them would be "to uncanonize Blackstone, whose book, although the most eloquent and best digested of our law catalogues, has been perverted more than all others to the degeneracy of legal science; a student finds there is a smattering of everything, and his indolence easily persuades him that if he understands that book he is master of the whole body of the law."—SINGLETON, ROY, 1890, *Sir William Blackstone and His Works, Magazine of American History, vol.* 24, *p.* 31.

GENERAL

An early taste for literature has too often misled the student from the ruder and more rugged paths of his profession; but the taste and genius of Blackstone rendered his literary acquirements subservient to his professional success. . . . The acquirements of Sir William Blackstone as a scholar were, doubtless, very considerable. He had always been in the habit of employing much of his time in reading, and, possessing a powerful memory, with a mind very capable of arranging its stores, he was remarkable for the variety and extent of his information. It is to be regretted that he never applied himself to any undertaking of a purely literary nature, in which there can be little doubt that he would have been eminently successful.—ROSCOE, HENRY, 1830, *Lives of Eminent British Lawyers, pp.* 243, 256.

Of his "History of the Charters" it is in vain to attempt any abridgment; for such is the precision of his taste, and such the importance of the subject, that there is not a sentence in the composition that is not necessary to the whole, and that should not be perused. Whatever other works may be read slightly, or omitted, this is one the entire meditation of which can in no respect be dispensed with. The claims which it has on our attention are of no common nature. The labour which this eminent lawyer has bestowed on the subject is sufficiently evident.—SMYTH, WILLIAM, 1840, *Lectures on Modern History.*

His copy of octosyllabics, entitled "The Lawyer's Farewell to his Muse," is one of the best minor poems of the time, and suggests that so skilful a versifier might have taken his place with the professional lyrists.—GOSSE, EDMUND, 1888, *A History of Eighteenth Century Literature, p.* 307.

Thomas Hutchinson

1711–1780

The last royal governor of Massachusetts. An historian of great ability but whose merits as such were not recognized by his contemporaries. His "History of the Colony of Massachusetts Bay," the third and last volume which was not published till nearly fifty years after his death, begins with the year 1628, and closes with the year 1774. He published also a "Collection of Original Papers" relating to the same subject.—ADAMS, OSCAR FAY, 1897, *A Dictionary of American Authors, p.* 202.

PERSONAL

Fled, in his old age, from the detestation of a country, where he had been beloved, esteemed, and admired, and applauded with exaggeration—in short, where he had been everything from his infancy—to a country where he was nothing; pinched by a pension, which, though ample in Boston, would barely keep a house in London; throwing round his baleful eyes on the exiled companions of his folly; hearing daily of the slaughter of his countrymen and conflagration of their cities; abhorred by the greatest men and soundest part of the nation, and neglected, if not despised by the rest, hardened as had been my heart against him, I assure you I was melted at the accounts I heard of his condition. Lord Townsend told me that he put an end to his own life. Though I did not believe this, I know he was ridiculed by the courtiers. They laughed at his manners at the levee, at his perpetual quotation of his brother Foster, searching his pockets for letters to read to the king, and the king turning away from him with his head up, etc.— ADAMS, JOHN, 1817, *Letter to William Tudor, Works, vol.* X, *p.* 261.

Few who sat upon the bench in the last century were more deserving of commendation than Judge Hutchinson. His character in this capacity was irreproachable. His learning, even in the science of the law, was highly respectable, and, when we consider his early education, was indeed remarkable. He possessed great clearness of thought, and excelled in that most difficult property of a good judge, a clear and intelligible statement of the case upon which he was to pass. It is a traditionary anecdote that, after listening to the charges given his associates, juries were in the habit of remarking when Hutchinson rose to address them, "Now we shall have something which we can understand." . . . . In his official character he had great readiness and capacity for business, and was faithful and laborious in the performance of his duties. He was a fluent and graceful speaker, a vigorous writer, and a respectable scholar. . . . Had he lived at almost any other period of our history, with the same industry and application of his powers, his fame would have survived as that of an useful, honorable, and honored man. — WASHBURN, EMORY, 1840, *Sketches of Judicial History of Massachusetts, pp.* 304, 305.

No servant of the Crown ever received more slander, personal abuse, and misrepresentation, than Thomas Hutchinson in Massachusetts, and yet his descendants have allowed a whole century to elapse without making an effort to defend his character. Time will show that it did not need defending, and the delay is an advantage to all parties, for we can now examine the situation calmly and dispassionately, which it was impossible to do during the prevalence of political excitement. We would wish, therefore, to speak without offence, and endeavour to re-unite in the bonds of friendship those ties which were unfortunately loosened at the time of the dispute. — HUTCHINSON, PETER ORLANDO, 1883, *ed., The Diary and Letters of Thomas Hutchinson, Preface, p.* iii.

Few Americans of the Revolutionary period have had a more lasting renown than Thomas Hutchinson, and few have been more leniently judged on a second hearing. Abused for his virtues, condemned in his absence, feared, hated, and maligned to a degree which now seems absurd, the lapse of a century has left his fellow Bostonians ready to see and acknowledge the really attractive side of his character. . . . One can almost affirm that he was a loyalist by stress of reason rather than by conviction or sympathy. His soul yearned for his native land, his best wishes were for his countrymen, he felt himself an alien in the England which swallowed him. But the conviction of the absolute correctness of his position in regard to the logical supremacy of Parliament paralyzed every movement of his heart or of his intellect.—WHITMORE, W. H., 1884, *Thomas Hutchinson, The Nation, vol.* 38, *pp.* 298–299.

Hutchinson's good breeding and high character made him popular in society, where he made the acquaintance of Gibbon and General Paoli, and he paid frequent visits to court; but as a consistent Calvinist, he regarded Garrick and playgoing with only qualified approval. He was also engaged in writing the third volume of his "History," covering the period "from 1749 to 1774, and comprising a detailed narrative of the origin and early stages of the American revolution"; but it was not published until 1828, when his grandson, the Rev. John Hutchinson, edited it. He was created D. C. L. at Oxford, in 1776. During the last years of his life he bore with fortitude the loss of his property and the ingratitude of his countrymen; but the death of his daughter Peggy, followed by that of his son Billy, broke him down, and he died on 3 June, 1780. He was buried at Croydon.— SANDERS, LLOYD C., 1891, *Dictionary of National Biography, vol.* XXVIII, *p.* 345.

He was buried at Croydon on the 9th of June. It would scarcely be possible for a human life to close among circumstances of deeper gloom. He and his children, to be sure, were not in want; his balance at his banker's was £6387 15s 3d. In every other way utter wreck had overtaken his family and himself. His daughters and his youngest son, dispirited, dropped prematurely at the same time with him into the grave. The prospects of the elder sons seemed quite blasted. In daily contact with him, a company of Loyalist exiles, once men of position and substance, now discredited and disheartened, were in danger of starvation. The country he had loved had nothing for him but contumely. To a man like Hutchinson public calamity would cause a deeper pang than private sorrows. No more threatening hour for England has probably ever struck than the hour when the soul of this man passed. It was becoming apparent that America was lost, a rending which easily might be fatal to the empire, and which her hereditary enemies were hastening to make the most of. To America herself the rending seemed to many certain to be fatal. While the members were thus being torn away, destruction seemed to impend at the heart. At the moment of the death, London was at the mercy of the mob in the Gordon riots. The city was on fire in many places; a drunken multitude murdered right and left, laying hands even upon the noblest of the land. Mansfield, because he had recommended to the mercy of a jury a priest arrested for celebrating mass, saved his life with difficulty, his house with all his possessions going up in conflagration. The exile's funeral passed on its way through smoke and uproar that might easily have been regarded as the final crash of the social structure. No one foresaw then what was immediately to come; that England was to make good her loss twice over; that America was to become the most powerful of nations; that the London disorders were on the surface merely and only transient. In Hutchinson's latest consciousness, every person, every spot, every institution dear to his heart, must have seemed to be overwhelmed in catastrophe. Such was the end of a life thoroughly dutiful and honorable!—HOSMER, JAMES K., 1896, *The Life of Thomas Hutchinson*, p. 348.

GENERAL

Hutchinson, whose writing is more worthy of the dignified title of history than any other American composition during our colonial state.—SAVAGE, RICHARD, 1816, *Hubbard's History of New England, North American Review, vol.* 2, *p.* 223.

The only monument of his mind is his "History of Massachusetts," written with lively inquisitiveness and a lawyer-like criticism; though without a glimpse of the great truths which were the mighty causes of the revolutions he describes. He was philosophic, if to know somewhat of the selfish principles in man be philosophy; otherwise he was blind, except to facts.—BANCROFT, GEORGE, 1838, *Documentary History of the Revolution, North American Review, vol.* 46, *p.* 477.

His "History of the Province of Massachusetts Bay," which, in its completed form, brings the story down to the very year of the author's exit from the colony, may fairly be called a praiseworthy production, even from the literary standpoint. One old book may be valuable as an original authority, another may be prized for its quaintness of autobiographical detail or social chronicle. Hutchinson's work offers something more than this, and deserves some credit for its literary style. Notwithstanding the marked political opinions of the author, one feels a confidence in his statements greater than that reposed in the writings of the professional moralist Cotton Mather. Naturally, Hutchinson never attained a tithe of the popularity enjoyed by Increase and Cotton Mather in their capacity of historians; politics had crowded literature to the wall, and Hutchinson was not the man to get an impartial hearing in his lifetime. But it is now apparent that he possessed an ability shared but never fully displayed by Thomas Prince: that of accumulating, studying, and assimilating historical materials, and placing them before the reader in an orderly and intelligible form. It is this ability that makes the historian; and in the maturity and thoroughness of Hutchinson's work we find the beginning of the second and principal period of historical literature in America. More than this one cannot claim; to say less than this would be injustice. In Hutchinson's diary and miscellaneous papers are sometimes to be found a loftiness of thought and a transparency of diction which are similar to the good literary qualities of the "History."—RICHARDSON, CHARLES F., 1887, *American Literature*, 1607–1885, *vol.* I, *p.* 448.

Governor Hutchinson was fortunate in respect to materials for his work, having access to many documents and sources of information long since lost. From these he compiled, with excellent judgment and rare scholarship, a work which will always be regarded as the highest authority.—PATTEE, FRED LEWIS, 1896, *A History of American Literature*, p. 52.

That in these volumes Hutchinson has illustrated the fundamental virtues of an historian, and that he deserves to be ranked as, upon the whole, the ablest historical writer produced in America prior to the nineteenth century, are conclusions as to which there is now substantial agreement among scholars. . . . A great historian, Hutchinson certainly was not, and, under the most favorable outward conditions, could not have been. He had the fundamental virtues of a great historian—love of truth, love of justice, diligence, the ability to master details and to narrate them with accuracy. Even in the exercise of those fundamental virtues, however, no historian in Hutchinson's circumstances could fail to be hampered by the enormous preoccupations of official business, or to have his judgment warped and colored by the pre-possessions of his own political career. While Hutchinson was, indeed, a miracle of industry, it was only a small part of his industry that he was free to devote to historical research. However sincere may have been his purpose to tell the truth and to be fair to all, the literary product of such research was inevitably weakened, as can now be abundantly shewn, by many serious oversights and by many glaring misrepresentations, apparently through his failure to make a thorough use of the important sources of information then accessible to him, such as colonial pamphlets, colonial newspapers, the manuscripts of his own ancestors and of the Mathers, and especially the general court records of the province in which he played so great a part. As to the rarer intellectual and spiritual endowments of a great historian,—breadth of vision, breadth of sympathy, the historic imagination, and the power of style,—these Hutchinson almost entirely lacked. That he had not the gift of historical divination, the vision and the faculty divine to see the inward meaning of men and of events, and to express the meaning in gracious, noble, and fascinating speech—Hutchinson was himself partly conscious.—TYLER, MOSES COIT, 1897, *The Literary History of the American Revolution*, 1763–1783, *vol.* ii.

James Harris

1709–1780

Born at Salisbury, studied at Wadham, Oxford, and Lincoln's Inn. On his father's death (1733) left master of an ample fortune, he devoted himself to the classics, but in 1761 entered parliament, and in 1763 became a Lord of the Admiralty and of the Treasury, in 1764 secretary and comptroller to Queen Charlotte. In 1774 he published "Art and Happiness;" in 1751 "Hermes," an inquiry into universal grammar. See his works edited in 1801–3 with a Memoir by his son, the diplomatist, James, first Earl of Malmesbury (1746–1820).—PATRICK AND GROOME, *eds.*, 1897, *Chambers's Biographical Dictionary, p.* 465.

GENERAL

His profound knowledge of Greek, which he applied more successfully, perhaps, than any modern writer has done, to the study and explanation of ancient philosophy, arose from an early and intimate acquaintance with the excellent poets and historians in that language. . . . The deep sense of moral and religious obligation which was habitual to him, and those benevolent feelings which were so great a happiness to his family and friends, had the same powerful influence over his public as his private life.—MALMESBURY, EARL, 1801, *ed. Works, Memoirs of the Life and Character of the Author, vol.* I, *pp.* XXIX, XXXV.

We ought not either to admit the mention of Mr. James Harris, the learned and accomplished author of one of the most beautiful specimens of metaphysical analysis of the theory of Language, which exist in our language—I mean the work entitled "Hermes."—MORELL, J. D., 1846–47, *An Historical and Critical View of Speculative Philosophy of Europe in the Nineteenth Century, p.* 144.

Mr. Harris had *long* left the University of Oxford before he began even to read Aristotle, or to inquire into the Greek philosophy; and he was led to the consideration of universal grammar by no book of the academical cycle, either then or since, but by the "Minerva" of Sanctius. That Mr. Harris was a tardy student of philosophy, is shown, perhaps, in his want of self-reliance, in his prejudice in favor of authority—at least of ancient authority.

But truth is not the property of the old or of the new; "nondum occupata," it frequently belongs to neither.—HAMILTON, SIR WILLIAM, 1853, *Oxford as it Might Be, Discussions on Philosophy and Literature.*

The definitions of Harris are considered arbitrary, and often unnecessary, and his rules are complicated; but his profound acquaintance with Greek literature, and his general learning, supplying numerous illustrations, enabled him to produce a curious and valuable publication. Every writer on the history and philosophy of grammar must consult "Hermes." Unfortunately the study of the ancient dialects of the northern nations was little prevalent at the time of Mr. Harris, and to this cause—as was the case also with many of the etymological distinctions in Johnson's Dictionary—must be attributed some of his errors and the imperfection of his plan. — CHAMBERS, ROBERT, 1876, *Cyclopædia of English Literature, ed. Carruthers.*

Richard Challoner

1691-1781

Born at Lewes, Sussex, Sept. 29, 1691: died at London, Jan. 12, 1781. An English Roman Catholic Divine, made bishop of Debra in 1740, and vicar apostolic of London in 1758. He was educated at the English College at Douai, and was professor of philosophy there 1713-20, and vice-president and professor of divinity 1720-30, returning to London in the latter year. He published a large number of polemical and theological works, including "The Rheims New Testament and the Douay Bible, with Annotations" (1749-50). His version of the Douay Bible is substantially that since used by English-speaking Catholics.—SMITH, BENJAMIN E., *ed.*, 1894-97, *The Century Cyclopedia of Names, p.* 232.

GENERAL

Challoner published an English bible, being in some sense a new version, and differing considerably in its diction from that of the Rheims-Douay. Dr. Challoner's version has been followed more than others by English-speaking Catholics since his day, and his influence upon the language of religion and devotion among Catholics has been accordingly very great. His influence in this respect has been still further increased by the great and continued popularity of his books on practical religion, such as "The Catholic Christian Instructed," "Meditations," and other devotional works, some of which have been circulated by millions. So familiar, indeed, is the language of Challoner to Catholic Christians generally, that whenever, in any diocese, the question arises as to which English version of the Vulgate shall be authorized for use in that diocese, the preference is given to Challoner's, rather than to the Rheims-Douay, notwithstanding the traditional veneration to which the latter is held. This was the decision of the late Cardinal Wiseman, and has been that of most English-speaking Bishops of the Catholic Church for the last hundred years. . . . Dr. Challoner writes with great vigor and freshness of thought, and in a style remarkable for its sparkling clearness and the purity of his English.—HART, JOHN S., 1872, *A Manual of English Literature, pp.* 322, 323.

In history, we are indebted to Dr. Challoner for the valuable "Memoirs of Missionary Priests and other Catholics that have Suffered Death in England on Religious Accounts, from the Year 1577 to 1684." He gives us an account of 180 martyrs who suffered during the reign of Elizabeth alone. The "Memoirs" are a monument of the accuracy, research, and moderation of their author. The style, suited to this kind of narrative, is simple and concise. Another important work of Dr. Challoner is his revision of the Rheims-Douay Bible, in which he substituted modern for antiquated terms. His revision is generally used by Catholics, but the admirers of the old Anglo-Saxon would willingly return to the earlier version.—JENKINS, O. L., 1876, *The Student's Handbook of British and American Literature, p.* 273.

One of the most learned and best known English Catholic writers of the eighteenth century.—MURRAY, JOHN O'KANE, 1877-84, *Lessons in English Literature, p.* 217.

Challoner inaugurated a new era in

English catholic literature, and many of his publications are to this day regarded by his co-religionists as standard works of doctrine or devotion.—COOPER, THOMPSON, 1887, *Dictionary of National Biography, vol.* IX, *p.* 442.

Henry Home
Lord Kames
1696-1782

Scottish philosopher, born at Kames in Berwickshire, was called to the bar in 1723, and raised to the bench as Lord Kames in 1752. Besides books on Scots law, he published "Essays on Morality" (1751), "An Introduction to the Art of Thinking" (1761), "Elements of Criticism" (his best-known work, 1762), and "Sketches of the History of Man" (1774).—PATRICK AND GROOME, *eds.*, 1897, *Chambers's Biographical Dictionary, p.* 546.

PERSONAL

Lord Kames and Mrs. Drummond, his wife, came from Edinburgh, which is an hundred miles from Denton, on purpose to spend a few days with me. His lordship is a prodigy. At eighty-three he is as gay and as nimble as he was at twenty-five. His sight, hearing, and memory perfect. He has a great deal of knowledge and a lively imagination, and is a most entertaining companion. I have promised to return his visit two years hence. I think as he has not grown old in the space of eighty-three years, two years more cannot have much effect. If it should abate a little of his vivacity, he would still have enough left.—MONTAGU, ELIZABETH, 1778, *A Lady of the Last Century, ed. Doran, p.* 246.

He received from nature an extraordinary activity of mind, to which his multiplied occupations allowed no remission, even in his advanced age; we find him as indefatigable in his eightieth year, as in the most vigorous and ambitious season of his life. The versatility of his talents were accompanied by a strength and acuteness, which penetrated to the essence of the subjects to which they were applied. The intentions with which he prosecuted such a wide diversity of studies, appear often excellent; very few men so ingenious, so speculative, so systematic, and occasionally so fanciful, have kept practical utility so generally in view. The great influence which he exerted over some of the younger philosophers of the time, several of the most distinguished of whom were proud to acknowledge themselves his pupils, was employed to determine their speculations to useful purposes. His conduct in the office of judge appears to have impressed every impartial man that witnessed it, with an invariable opinion of his talents and integrity. As a domestic and social man, his character was that of frankness, good humour, and extreme vivacity. His prompt intelligence continually played around him, and threw its rays on every subject that even casualty could introduce into conversation.—FOSTER, JOHN, 1807, *On Memoir-Writing, Critical Essays, ed. Ryland, vol,* I, *p.* 64.

Lord Kames was in his person extremely tall, and of a thin and slender make. In his latter years, he had a considerable stoop in his gait; but when in the vigour of life, and particularly when in his dress of a barrister, his appearance is said to have been uncommonly becoming. His countenance, though not handsome, was animated and intelligent, and was strongly marked by that benignity of disposition which was a prominent feature of his mind. In ordinary discourse, his accent and pronunciation were like those of the better educated of his countrymen of the last age. The tone was not displeasing from its vulgarity; and though the idiom, and frequently the phrases, were peculiar to the Scottish dialect, his language was universally intelligible. . . . A strong feature of Lord Kames's disposition, was an artless simplicity and ingenuity, which led him at all times to express without reserve both his feelings and his opinions. This propensity gave frequently an appearance of bluntness of manner, which was apt to impress a stranger unfavourably, as erring against those lesser proprieties of behaviour, so necessary in the commerce of the world. But this impression was momentary; the same frankness of nature displayed at once both the defect and its cause: it laid open the integrity of his character, and that perfect candour, which judging always most favourably of others, was unconscious of harbouring a thought which required concealment or disguise. —TYTLER, ALEXANDER FRASER, 1814, *Memoirs of the Life and Writings of Henry Home of Kames, vol.* II, *pp.* 329, 331.

Sceptical as we may well be of any high estimate of his mental calibre, he was a characteristic figure in his day, and accentuates many of its traits by exaggeration and by travesty. He represented all the indomitable energy of the race, and its persevering struggle against odds. When he attained to the dignity of the Bench, the long tension brought a reaction, and he turned with zest to the pursuits of what he deemed elegant literature and lofty speculation, undeterred by any consciousness of the limitations of his early training. . . . As was often the case with his countrymen, he relieved the long restraint of toil by indulgence in antics that frequently fell to the ridiculous, and cultivated with assiduity the reputation of a wit, which degenerated not rarely into the indecency of the buffoon, and suffered the restraints neither of dignity nor of good taste. . . . He was not a great lawyer; he was in no sense a philosopher; his literary taste was frequently perverse; his political speculations were whimsical and often absurd; his wit had often much of boyish mischief, asserting itself against the restraints of authority, and never rose to the serenity of humour. But in his indomitable energy, in his industry, in his freedom from timidity or any bashfulness bred of his own defects, he was characteristic of his age.—CRAIK, SIR HENRY, 1901, *A Century of Scottish History, vol.* II, *pp.* 195, 196.

GENERAL

In my passage to America, I read your excellent work, the "Elements of Criticism," in which I found great entertainment: much to admire, and nothing to reprove. I only wish you had examined more fully the subject of Music, and demonstrated, that the pleasure which artists feel in hearing much of that composed in the modern taste, is not the natural pleasure arising from melody or harmony of sounds, but of the same kind with the pleasure we feel on seeing the surprising feats of tumblers and rope-dancers, who execute difficult things.—FRANKLIN, BENJAMIN, 1765, *Letter to Lord Kames.*

Among Mr. Hume's numerous disciples, I do not know one who ever read his "Treatise on Human Nature." In order, therefore, to be read, you must not be satisfied with reasoning with justness and perspicuity; you must write with pathos, with elegance, with spirit, and endeavour to warm the imagination, and touch the heart of those who are deaf to the voice of reason. . . . What has made Lord Kames's "Elements of Criticism" so popular in England, is his numerous illustrations and quotations from Shakespeare. If his book had wanted these illustrations, or if they had been taken from ancient or foreign authors, it would not have been so generally read in England.—GREGORY, JOHN, 1768, *Letter to Dr. Beattie, Beattie's Life by Forbes, vol.* I, *p.* 141.

He had too much liberality of mind not to allow to others the same liberty in judging which he claimed to himself. It is difficult to say, whether that worthy man was more eminent in active life or in speculation. Very rare surely have been the instances where the talents for both were united in so eminent a degree. His genius and industry, in many different branches of literature, will, by his works, be known to posterity. His private virtues and public spirit, his assiduity through a long and laborious life in many honourable public offices with which he was entrusted, and his zeal to encourage and promote every thing that tended to the improvement of his country, in laws, literature, commerce, manufactures, and agriculture, are best known to his friends and contemporaries. — REID, THOMAS, 1785, *Essays on the Intellectual Powers of Man, Dedication.*

The "Historical Law Tracts" of Lord Kames are conducted upon a very judicious system of investigating the natural principles of some of the most important objects of judicial science, and tracing the application of them in the Laws of Rome, of Scotland, and of England; but a comparison between the Laws of Scotland and England, conducted, I think, with great fairness, is apparently the leading object of the undertaking.—EVANS, WILLIAM DAVID, 1806, *Pothier on Law of Obligations, Introduction.*

The "Elements of Criticism," considered as the first systematical attempt to investigate the metaphysical principles of the fine arts, possesses, in spite of its numerous defects both in point of taste and philosophy, infinite merits, and will ever be regarded as a literary wonder by those who know how small a portion of his time it was possible for the author to allot to the composition of it, amidst the imperious and multifarious duties of a most active and useful life.—STEWART, DUGALD, 1815–21, *First Preliminary Dissertation to Encyclopædia Britannica.*

His works are generally all an awkward compound of ingenuity and absurdity, and in this volume ["Essays on the Principles of Morality"] the latter quality, it appears to me, considerably preponderates. It is metaphysical—upon Belief, Identity, Necessity, etc. I devoutly wish that no friend of mine may ever come to study it, unless he wish to learn,

"To weave fine cobwebs, fit for skull
That's empty, when the moon is full."

—CARLYLE, THOMAS, 1815, *Letter, Aug.* 22; *Life by Conway, p.* 162.

His diction is tolerably copious, and his turns of expression often have something of the crisp ingenuity of Hume's, but his sentences are not very skilfully put together; his style wants flow. Curiously enough, his analysis of the mechanical artifices of sentence-making is one of the most substantial parts of his "Elements;" it supplied both Campbell and Blair with all that they have to say on sentence-mechanism, and contains some ingenuities that they did not see fit to adopt.—MINTO, WILLIAM, 1872–80, *Manual of English Prose Literature, p.* 475.

In the present day, if Lord Kames is read at all, it is for his ingenious and acute speculation into the sources of æsthetic pleasure.—GOSSE, EDMUND, 1888, *A History of Eighteenth Century Literature, p.* 281.

Kames was an ingenious and voluminous writer, with a considerable knowledge of law and a great taste for metaphysics. His style, however, is crabbed and wanting in variety, while his learning is frequently superficial and inaccurate.—BARKER, G. F. RUSSELL, 1891, *Dictionary of National Biography, vol.* XXVII, *p.* 232.

Lord Kames was a man whose words have been voiceless to any generation beyond his own. Even by his own friends his speculations can hardly have carried real weight, however indulgently they were treated as the efforts—earnest enough in their way—of an acute and ingenious, but ill-trained and ill-balanced intellect.—CRAIK, SIR HENRY, 1901, *A Century of Scottish History, vol.* II, *p.* 194.

Henry Brooke

1703?–1783

Henry Brooke, dramatist and novelist, was born in 1708, at Rantavan, County Cavan, the son of a wealthy clergyman. In 1720 he entered Trinity College, Dublin; in 1724 went to study law in London, where he became the chosen friend of Pope and Lyttelton; in 1728 married his cousin and ward, a girl of fifteen; in 1740 returned in ill health to Rantavan, and in 1745 was made barrackmaster of Mullingar, a post worth £400 a year. He died in Dublin, 10 October, 1783. His poem, "Universal Beauty" (1735), is supposed to have suggested Erasmus Darwin's "Botanic Garden." "Gustavus Vasa" (1739), the acting of which was prohibited at Drury Lane, was afterwards produced in Dublin as the "*Patriot.*" The sonorous eloquence of his plays has not saved them from oblivion; and his novel, "The Fool of Quality" (5 vols. 1766), is the sole survivor of his numerous works.—PATRICK AND GROOME, *eds.*, 1897, *Chambers's Biographical Dictionary, p.* 136.

PERSONAL

The accounts of his private circumstances, in that kingdom, are given rather confusedly by his biographers; but it appears, upon the whole, that they were unfortunate. He supported an only brother in his house, with a family as numerous as his own; and ruined himself by his generosity. At last the loss of his wife, after a union of fifty years, the death of many of his children, and his other misfortunes, overwhelmed his intellect. Of this imbecility there were indeed some manifestations in the latest productions of his pen.—CAMPBELL, THOMAS, 1819, *Specimens of the British Poets.*

The pupil of Swift and Pope; the friend of Lyttelton and Chatham; the darling of the Prince of Wales; beau, swordsman, wit, poet, courtier, the minion once of fortune, yet unspoilt by all her caresses, he had long been known to Irishmen only as the saintly recluse of Longfield.—KINGSLEY, CHARLES, 1859, *The Fool of Quality, Preface.*

A pure and noble-minded Christian gentleman, he lived in the world but not of it. Surrounded by its attractions, versed in its accomplishments, his heart was ever most faithful to his divine Master. It is almost hard to realise, knowing what court and city manners were in the reigns of the first two Georges, that he could have preserved his life so untainted and true.—ABBEY, CHARLES J., 1887, *The English Church and Its Bishops*, 1700–1800, *vol.* I, *p.* 299.

A visitor to Brooke in 1775 described him as "dressed in a long blue cloak, with a wig that fell down his shoulders. He was a little man, neat as wax-work, with an oval face, ruddy complexion, and large eyes full of fire." Brooke sank into a state of mental depression on the deaths of his wife and of his children, of whom the sole survivor (out of a family of twenty-two) was his daughter Charlotte, who devoted herself entirely to him. Disease and grief rendered him at times incapable of mental or physical exertion.—GILBERT, J. T., 1886, *Dictionary of National Biography, vol.* VI, *p.* 426.

UNIVERSAL BEAUTY
1735

Having paid another visit to London, he renewed his acquaintance with Pope; and, with his encouragement, published his poem, entitled, "Universal Beauty." This poem forms a curious, but unacknowledged prototype of Darwin's "Botanic Garden." It has a resemblance to that work, in manner, in scientific spirit, and in volant geographical allusion, too striking to be supposed accidental; although Darwin has gone beyond his original, in prominent and ostentatious imagery.—CAMPBELL, THOMAS, 1819, *Specimens of the British Poets.*

A brilliant but obscure metaphysical and scientific poem, entitled "Universal Beauty," was published in no less than six anonymous folio instalments in the course of 1735, and is now very rarely met with complete. It was from the pen of an Irish squire, Henry Brooke (1703–1783), long afterwards author of an unimportant sentimental novel, "The Fool of Quality." His poem deserves attention. It is written in very musical couplets, with, however, too frequent indulgence in the alexandrine. It is manifestly inspired by the optimistic philosophy of Shaftsbury. . . . Brooke never fulfilled the promise of this remarkable first poem.—GOSSE, EDMUND, 1888, *A History of Eighteenth Century Literature, pp.* 218, 219.

Worth notice, though it has been too highly praised.—SAINTSBURY, GEORGE, 1898, *A Short History of English Literature, p.* 610.

THE FOOL OF QUALITY
1766

But the greatest excellence of all is that it continually strikes at the heart. It perpetually aims at inspiring and increasing every right affection; at the instilling gratitude to God and benevolence to man. And it does this not by dull, dry, tedious precepts, but by the liveliest examples that can be imagined; by setting before your eyes one of the most beautiful pictures that ever was drawn in the world. The strokes of this are so delicately fine, the touches so easy, natural and affecting, that I know not who could survey it with tearless eyes, unless he had a heart of stone. I recommend it, therefore, to all those who are already, or desire to be, lovers of God and man.—WESLEY, JOHN, 1780, *ed., History of Earl of Moreland, Preface.*

That best of religious romances, the "Fool of Quality." The piety there is at once most deep and most benign. There is much, indeed of elegant mysticism, but all evidently most heartfelt and sincere. The yearnings of the soul after universal good and intimate communion with the divine nature were never more nobly shown. The author is most prodigal of his intellectual wealth, "his bounty is as boundless as the sea, his love as deep." He gives to his chief characters riches endless as the spiritual stores of his own heart. It is, indeed, only the last which gives value to the first in his writings. It is easy to endow men with millions on paper, and to make them willing to scatter them among the wretched; but it is the corresponding bounty and exuberance of the author's soul, which here makes the money sterling, and the charity divine. The hero of this romance always appears to our imagination like a radiant vision encircled with celestial glories. The stories introduced in it are delightful exceptions to the usual rule by which such incidental tales are properly regarded as impertinent intrusions.—TALFOURD, THOMAS NOON, 1842, *On British Novels and Romances, Critical and Miscellaneous Writings, p.* 16.

There is full and conscious consistency in Mr. Brooke's method, whether or not there be dramatic unity in his plot. By that time also one may hope the earnest reader will have begun to guess at the causes which have made this book forgotten for a while; and perhaps to find them not in its defects but in its excellencies; in its deep and grand ethics, in its broad and genial humanity, in the divine value which it attaches to the relations of husband and wife, father and child; and to the utter absence both of that sentimentalism and that superstition which have been alternately debauching of late years the minds of the young. And if he shall have arrived at this discovery, he will be able possibly to regard at least with patience those who are rash enough to affirm that they have learnt from this book more which is pure, sacred, and eternal, than from any which has been published since Spenser's "Fairy Queen."—KINGSLEY, CHARLES, 1859, *ed. The Fool of Quality, Preface.*

A book I remember as among my father's loves—one of the few novels in our old library at Stockbridge. How well do I remember the five duodecimo volumes, in their dark leather bindings. The favourite books of that time stand around the chambers of memory, each a shrine. In this there is much wit and pathos, nature and wisdom (nature *is* wisdom when it is evolved from the human heart and from life). The style seems to me admirable—something in the fashion of the quaint old coats of our grandfathers, fashioned for ease and use, and of the best broadcloth garnished with velvet. It seems to me an admirable book might be made out of it for children, and I have a great mind to try my hand at it. It might, perhaps, flatter a little too much the dynasties of the present day, the young usurpers of their father's thrones.—SEDGWICK, CATHARINE M., 1860, *Life and Letters, p.* 379.

A more horribly dull and tedious book it was never my misfortune to read; and as a fiction, or a story, or a work of art, it is beneath criticism. . . . I willingly rank myself among the average readers as regards my estimate of the book, and can only wonder at Mr. Kingsley having taken the trouble to republish it, and still more at the praise which he lavishes upon it. It is made up of dull sermons and dull disquisitions on morality and the British Constitution, with an absurd attempt at a story, in which it is impossible to take interest, running through it.—FORSYTH, WILLIAM, 1871, *The Novels and Novelists of the Eighteenth Century, pp.* 168, 169.

Brooke's intellectual genealogy seems to be traceable to Behmen on the one hand and to Rousseau on the other; whilst a curious strain of Irish eccentricity runs through the whole, tempered by touches of the grace and tenderness of his greater countryman Goldsmith. The book resembles in some respects the friend of our infancy, "Sanford and Merton," though in that excellent performance the Rousseau element is not tempered by any theological admixture. Such performances indicate a current of vague feeling in search of some mode of utterance less constrained than that sanctioned by the practice of the Pope school, but equally ready to flow along the channels marked by Wesley or by Rousseau.—STEPHEN, LESLIE, 1876, *History of English Thought in the Eighteenth Century, vol.* II, *p.* 439.

His "Earl of Moreland," or "Fool of Quality," in five volumes, is over-long and over-exuberant, not in length only, but in fancy and expression. But it is full of noble thoughts—for which the education of an ideal nobleman gives ample scope—in morals, politics, and theology.—ABBEY, CHARLES J., 1887, *The English Church and Its Bishops,* 1700–1800, *vol.* I, *p.* 300.

The author has so many interests, such width of mind, so keen a desire to further a vast variety of political and social reforms, that his story is completely overlaid by moral digressions; he is so occupied in works of public benevolence that he starves his child.—RALEIGH, WALTER, 1894, *The English Novel, p.* 213.

James Otis

1725-1783

The Patrick Henry of New England, was one of the earliest, boldest, and most eloquent advocates of the rights of the Colonies, in the dispute with the mother country. Otis was a native of West Barnstable, Massachusetts, and a graduate of Harvard, of the class of 1743. He was a fine classical scholar, and among other things, published a work on Latin Prosody, and a dissertation on "The Power of Harmony in Prosaic Composition." His chief publications, however, were of a political character, namely, "A Vindication of the Conduct of the House of Representatives of Massachusetts Bay;" "The Rights of the British Colonies Asserted and Proved;" "Considerations on Behalf of the Colonists;" "A Vindication of the British Colonies."—HART, JOHN S., 1872, *A Manual of American Literature, p.* 62.

PERSONAL

The Honorable James Otis having by advise of his physician, retired into the country for the recovery of his health; *Voted,* That the thanks of the town be given to the Honorable James Otis for the great and important services, which, as a representative in the General Assembly through a course of years, he has rendered to this town and province; particularly for his undaunted exertions in the common cause of the colonies, from the beginning of the present glorious struggle for the rights of the British constitution. At the same time, the town cannot but express their ardent wishes for the recovery of his health, and the continuance of those public services, that must long be remembered with gratitude, and distinguish his name among the patriots of America.—*Resolutions at Town Meeting, Boston,* 1770, *May* 8.

Otis was a flame of fire!—with a promptitude of classical allusion, a depth of research, a rapid summary of historical events and dates, a profusion of legal authorities, a prophetic glance of his eye into futurity, and a torrent of impetuous eloquence, he hurried away every thing before him. American independence was then and there [1761] born. . . . Every man of a crowded audience appeared to me to go away, an I did, ready to take of arms against writs of assistance. . . . Mr. Otis . . . breathed into this nation the breath of life.—ADAMS, JOHN, 1817, *Letters.*

Six weeks exactly after his return, on Friday afternoon the 23d day of May 1783, a heavy cloud suddenly arose, and a greater part of the family were collected in one of the rooms to wait till the shower should have past. Otis, with his cane in one hand, stood against the post of the door which opened from this apartment into the front entry. He was in the act of telling the assembled group a story, when an explosion took place which seemed to shake the solid earth, and he fell without a struggle, or a word, instantaneously dead, into the arms of Mr. Osgood, who, seeing him falling, sprang forward to receive him. This flash of lightning was the first that came from the cloud, and was not followed by any others that were remarkable. There were seven or eight persons in the room, but no other was injured. No mark of any kind could be found on Otis, nor was there the slightest change or convulsion in his features. It is a singular coincidence, that he often expressed a wish for such a fate. He told his sister, Mrs. Warren, after his reason was impaired, "my dear sister, I hope when God Almighty in his righteous providence shall take me out of time into eternity, that it will be by a flash of lightning," and this idea he often repeated.—TUDOR, WILLIAM, 1823, *The Life of James Otis, p.* 485.

All through the great struggle for independence, to which his eloquence had excited his countrymen, James Otis was like a blasted pine on the mountains—like a stranded wreck in the midst of the billows. It was just as the sunlight of peace burst upon his disenthralled country, that his spirit departed for the realm of unclouded intelligence. —LOSSING, BENSON J., 1855-86, *Eminent Americans, p.* 163.

He was like the huge cannon on the man-of-war, in Victor Hugo's story, that had broken from its moorings in the storm, and became a terror to those whom it formerly defended. — HOSMER, JAMES KENDALL, 1885, *Life of Samuel Adams, p.* 355.

In his prime he was esteemed the chief orator of the Revolutionary movement. His fat figure was not ungraceful; his voice was strong and well modulated; his plump face was courtly and handsome; his eye was piercing; and he was likened by the elder President Adams to a "flame of fire." . . . He was neither consistent nor discreet, but the public, often inconsistent and indiscreet, is apt to favor a spokesman of similar temper. Like Charles Sumner, the great Boston orator of the later century, he was dictatorial and vain, and like Sumner, he was made more popular by an unjust personal assault which he suffered. His eccentricities and misfortunes actually increased his temporary influence, and the public reluctantly gave up his leadership, even when his insanity was manifest. — RICHARDSON, CHARLES F., 1887, *American Literature, 1607–1885, vol.* I, *pp.* 182, 183.

His five-hour speech against taxation without representation, delivered in the council chamber of the old town hall in Boston, was a masterly performance, making him famous as the bold and brilliant advocate of colonial rights. No summary or abstract of this speech can do justice to the whole, which can be estimated only by reading in its integrity. Even then how much is lost, as in the case of so many other great orators, in the lack of their presence and of the occasion which inspired them, and which they in turn made memorable.—SEARS, LORENZO, 1895, *The History of Oratory, p.* 310.

His eloquence was bold, witty, pungent, and practical. He communed with other minds, but more with his own. He was learned, and yet original, courteous in debate, and always treating the opinions of his adversaries with the respect they deserved; but he was bold and daring in his own investigations. He always listened to appeals which were conciliating, and motives that were just. In the presence, however, of arrogance and oppression, he was as firm as a rock. . . . Mr. Otis always forgot himself in the subject he discussed. He explored all the resources at his command, and was tireless in preparation. He appeared to be completely absorbed by his theme while speaking, and thought as little of the skill he should display as an orator, as one fighting for his life thinks of the grace he shall exhibit in the flourish of his weapons. He was enthusiastic, sincere, forceful, natural, and spoke the language of a powerful mind under high but well-regulated excitement.—HARDWICKE, HENRY, 1896, *History of Oratory and Orators, pp.* 336, 337.

GENERAL

Otis was not content with employing his eloquence alone, but he took up his pen also in defence of our rights; and if his pen was not equal to his tongue, it was sufficiently pointed and powerful to arouse his countrymen, and to excite the vengeance of those he called our oppressors. Otis affixed his name boldly to whatever he wrote; before this time, most political writings had come to the world anonymously. Others followed the example which Otis had set them, and wrote over their own names, when it was thought they could do more good by this course, than by taking an assumed name. He was not only a patriot, but, what is more to my immediate purpose, he was a splendid scholar, and wrote several elementary works, and works of taste. — KNAPP, SAMUEL L., 1829, *Lectures on American Literature, p.* 90.

His abilities, perhaps, were overrated in the admiring judgment of his contemporaries. His style as a writer was copious and energetic; but it was careless, incorrect, and defective in taste and method. As a speaker, he was fluent, animated, coarse, and effective; his eloquence was better adapted to popular assemblies than to the graver occasions of legislative debate; and, in the halls of justice, we may suppose that it produced a greater effect on the jury than the judge. His voice and manner were very impressive, and seemed to force conviction upon his hearers, even when his arguments did not reach their judgment. The few fragments of his speeches, that were reported, and are now extant, give no idea of the enthusiasm that was created by their delivery. The elevation of his mind, and the known integrity of his purposes, enabled him to speak with decision and dignity, and commanded the respect as well as the admiration of his audience. His arguments were not comprehensive or varied; they related only to a few points in the subject, which they placed in a very clear and convincing light; but he had not the wide grasp of mind necessary for considering the affair as a whole, and examining it in all its aspects and relations. His eloquence showed but little imagination, yet, it was instinct with the fire of passion. His learning was neither extensive nor profound; but his writings show something of the taste of a scholar, and he was tolerably familiar with the classics and with English history.—BOWEN, FRANCIS, 1844, *James Otis, Library of American Biography, ed. Sparks, vol.* XII, *p.* 197.

Unfortunately, few of his rhetorical productions are now extant. A sad fatality attended all his manuscripts. None of his speeches were fully recorded, and he himself being cut off from active life before the Revolution actually commenced, his name is connected with none of the public documents of the nation. His memorials as an orator are rather traditionary than actual; we are compelled to estimate his merits chiefly through the imperfect description, but boundless admiration, of his time. But the mutilated fragments that yet survive are colossal, and with these for our guide we can, in faint idea reconstruct the noble proportions of the original work, as Cuvier built up the Mastedon from a few relics, and Michael Angelo, with the Torso of the Vatican before him, projected anew the masterpiece of Grecian genius on a scale of artistic grandeur which threw into insignificance all the conceptions of contemporary minds.—MAGOON, E. L., 1848, *Orators of the American Revolution, p.* 80.

His pamphlet on "The Rights of the Colonies" is worthy of constant study; his speeches were eloquent with the lasting impulses of freedom. —LAWRENCE, EUGENE, 1880, *A Primer of American Literature, p.* 41.

He can hardly be termed a writer, and we know his speeches by the effects they produce rather than in themselves. His pamphlet on the "Rights of the British Colonists" is probably his best literary production.—HAWTHORNE, JULIAN AND LEMMON, LEONARD, 1891, *Americon Literature, p.* 35.

He was, above all things, an orator; and his oratory was of the tempestuous kind—bold, vehement, irregular, overpowering. When he took pen in hand, he was an orator still; and the habit of extemporaneous, impetuous, and reckless expression which he had long indulged in at the bar, controlled him at his desk. In writing upon any subject of controversy, he seemed to storm across his own pages in mighty rage, even as he had been accustomed to pace stormily up and down before a jury; to throw to the winds all the classic virtues in expression,—temperance, order, lucidity; to catch at bold allusions, flaming images, grotesque comparisons; and to leave unrevised upon the paper, and in all its original extravagance and inaccuracy, whatsoever in the fury of composition he had once flung down upon it. He seemed even to despise the correction of his own work, perhaps to be incapable of it . . . But great as are the literary blemishes upon Otis's work, that work is still full of power. . . . His learning on many subjects was considerable, even if disorderly; and he had instant command over the resources of his own memory. He had, moreover, the ability to grasp quickly all the principles and facts of a given case, to pierce to the core of them, and to perceive the logic which controlled them; and even while pressing forward in his track along a zigzag path of his own choosing, and with many a wide and dangerous sweep of digression, he yet never lost sight of the logical goal which he had set out to reach. In his pamphlets, too, as in his speeches, he gave free rein to his enjoyment of humor, and to his uncommon faculty of sarcasm. A serious discomfiture of his opponent was never quite enough to appease his ambition in debate: he must also cover his antagonist with ridicule, and drive him from the field amid shouts of derision.—TYLER, MOSES COIT, 1897, *The Literary History of the American Revolution,* 1763–1783, *vol.* I, *pp.* 38, 39.

Alexander Ross

1699–1784

Born in Aberdeenshire, 1699; died at Lochlee, Forfarshire, May 20, 1784. A Scottish schoolmaster and poet. He wrote "Helenore, or the Fortunate Shepherdess" (1768: a narrative poem), and a number of songs ("Wooed an' Married an' a'," etc.) and other poetical pieces, in the rural dialect of Aberdeenshire.—SMITH, BENJAMIN E., *ed.* 1894–97, *The Century Cyclopedia of Names, p.* 868.

PERSONAL

His money income, from all sources, did not much exceed twenty pounds a-year, besides a free house; yet, considering the fewness of his wants, and several perquisites in kind, with six acres of grazing and arable land, and an unlimited supply of peat fuel, his circumstances present nothing to excite our commiseration. Indeed, few poets have enjoyed a more equable share of happiness, and endures less of the cankering cares incident to the battle of life. Nothing that he has written bears the slightest trace of discontent.—ROSS, J., 1884, *ed., The Book of Scottish Poems, p.* 433.

GENERAL

The poem which gives its name to this volume, "Helenore, or the Fortunate Shepherdess," seems to have been written before 1740, in direct rivalry with Allan Ramsay. It is in some respects unique particularly as being the most ambitious narrative work in Scots written, perhaps, down to the present time; it is composed in the heroic measure, and extends to more than four thousand verses. An elaborate story of homely Scottish life is told with some skill, an almost Chaucerian simplicity, and much occasional picturesqueness, disguised by the rough dialect. . . . Alexander Ross eked "Helenore" out with some good songs.—GOSSE, EDMUND, 1888, *A History of Eighteenth Century Literature, pp.* 338, 339.

The meanness which is visible in the *dénouement* of the story is indicative of the limitation of Ross's poetical faculty. There is little in him of "the consecration and the poet's dream." His is a matter-of-fact mind: he tells the reader plainly of the nausea which afflicts both his principal female characters from eating berries in their wanderings among the hills. But this, which is his weakness, is at the same time his strength. He is always true. Even in his unfortunate conclusion he is only depicting, perhaps a little too faithfully, the ambitions of the class from which his characters are drawn—ambitions which after all do not differ in kind from those cherished in higher ranks of life. It has even been suggested that the story of "Helenore" was probably based on fact, and that the infidelity may not have been of Ross's invention. At any rate, if he is destitute of some of the virtues which are always expected and generally found in pastoral poetry, he possesses others which are extremely rare. His narrative is vigorous, the interest well sustained, and the characters of the shepherd people not ill-drawn. In these respects Ross followed, and followed well, his master Ramsay. He added however little to what Ramsay had done. His powers were in the main similar, and they were less considerable.—WALKER, HUGH, 1893, *Three Centuries of Scottish Literature, vol.* II, *p.* 32.

To the present day "Helenore" remains popular in the north, but in spite of its frequent touches of nature and the stamp of truth about its characters, its many incongruities destroy its effect as a work of art. The poem is written in the Buchan dialect, and possesses some interest on that account; but the reader is startled to find a Helenore and a Rosalind (in this case the hero's name) among the peasantry of Scotland, and still more so to come upon these high-sounding titles contracted with easy familiarity into "Nory" and "Lindy." The pastoral, however, has not been without an influence upon the work of later poets, and Burns has acknowledged that Scota, the muse to whom Ross addresses his invocation, afforded the suggestion for his own Coila. —EYRE-TODD, GEORGE, 1896, *Scottish Poetry of the Eighteenth Century, vol.* I.

Burns wrote, "Our true brother Ross of Lochlee was a wild warlock," one of the "suns of the morning;" and he said that he would not for anything that "The Fortunate Shepherdess" should be lost. Dr. Blacklock and John Pinkerton were loud in their praise, and the poem was for many years, and indeed is still, very popular in the north of Scotland. The Buchan dialect in which it is written will repel readers of the south; and the text of most editions, including that edited in 1812 by Ross's grandson—the Rev. Alexander Thomson of Lenthrathan—is very corrupt. The poem abounds in weak lines, and the plot is not very happy. But though the whole is very inferior to its model—Allan Ramsay's "Gentle Shepherd"—it contains pleasant descriptions of country life and scenery.—AITKEN, GEORGE A., 1897, *Dictionary of National Biography, vol.* XLIX, *p.* 255.

Samuel Johnson

1709-1784

1709, Sep. 18, Johnson born at Lichfield. 1728, goes to Oxford. 1735, translates Lobo's "Abyssinia;" Marries. 1737, goes to London with Garrick. 1738, publishes "London." 1739, publishes two political pamphlets: "The Complete Vindication and Marmor Norfolciense." 1740-3, writes Debates in Magna Lilliputia for "Gentleman's Magazine." 1744, "Life of Mr. Richard Savage." 1745, "Miscellaneous Observations on Macbeth." 1747, "Plan for a Dictionary of the English Language." 1748, writes "Vanity of Human Wishes." 1749, "Vanity of Human Wishes" published, "Irene" (written 1736) acted. 1750-2, "The Rambler." 1752, his wife dies. 1752-3, contributes to Hawkesworth's "Adventurer." 1755, publishes "The Dictionary." 1756, issues "Proposals for an Edition of Shakespeare." 1758-60, writes "The Idler" for the "Universal Chronicle." 1759, his mother dies; publishes "The Prince of Abyssinia." 1762, granted a pension. 1763, meets Boswell. 1764, the Literary club is founded; Johnson meets the Thrales. 1765, "Edition of Shakespeare." 1770, "The False Alarm." 1771, "Thoughts on the Late Transactions respecting the Falkland Islands." 1773, tour to Scotland and the Hebrides. 1774 "The Patriot;" tour to North Wales. 1775, "Taxation no Tyranny;" "Journey to the Western Islands." 1776, "Political Tracts." 1777, begins "Lives of Poets." 1779, publishes four volumes of "Lives;" 1781, last six volumes of "Lives;" Thrale dies. 1784, Mrs. Thrale becomes Mrs. Piozzi; Dec. 13, Johnson dies. 1785, Johnson's "Prayers and Meditations" published; Boswell publishes "Journal of a Tour to the Hebrides;" 1788-9, Johnson's "Sermons." 1791, Boswell's "Life of Johnson." 1816, Johnson's "Diary in North Wales."—SCOTT, FRED N., 1891, *ed. Rasselas, p.* 25.

PERSONAL

He and another neighbour of mine, one Mr. Johnson, set out this morning for London together: Davy Garrick to be with you early the next week; and Mr. Johnson to try his fate with a tragedy, and to see to get himself employed in some translation, either from the Latin or the French. Johnson is a very good scholar and poet, and I have great hopes will turn out a fine tragedy writer.—WALMSLEY, GILBERT, 1736-7, *Letter to Rev. Mr. Colson, March* 2.

That great CHAM of literature.—SMOLLETT, TOBIAS GEORGE, 1759, *Letter to Wilkes, March* 16.

I hope Johnson is a writer of reputation, because, as a writer, he has just got a pension of 300*l.* per annum. I hope, too, that he has become a friend to this constitution and the family on the throne, now he is thus nobly provided for; but I know he has much to *unwrite*, more to *unsay*, before he will be forgiven by the true friends of the present illustrious family for what he has been writing and saying for many years.—WILKES, JOHN, 1762, *The North Briton, No.* 11, *Aug.* 14.

The day after I wrote my last letter to you I was introduced to Mr. Johnson by a friend: we passed through three very dirty rooms to a little one that looked like an old counting-house, where this great man was sat at his breakfast. The furniture of this room was a very large deal writing-desk, an old walnut-tree table, and five ragged chairs of four different sets. I was very much struck with Mr. Johnson's appearance, and could hardly help thinking him a madman for some time, as he sat waving over his breakfast like a lunatic. He is a very large man, and was dressed in a dirty brown coat and waistcoat, with breeches that were brown also (though they had been crimson), and an old black wig: his shirt collar and sleeves were unbuttoned; his stockings were down about his feet, which had on them, by way of slippers, an old pair of shoes. He had not been up long when we called on him, which was near one o'clock: he seldom goes to bed till near two in the morning; and Mr. Reynolds tells me he generally drinks tea about an hour after he has supped. We had been some time with him before he began to talk, but at length he began, and, faith, to some purpose! everything he says is as *correct* as a *second edition:* 'tis almost impossible to argue with him, he is so sententious and so knowing.—HUMPHRY, OZIAS, 1764, *Letter to Rev. William Humphry, Sept.* 19.

SAMUEL JOHNSON

Painting by Alonzo Chappel.
From Original by Sir Joshua Reynolds.

Here Johnson comes—unblest with outward grace,
His rigid morals stamped upon his face;
While strong conceptions struggle in his brain,
(For even wit is brought to bed with pain).
To view him porters with their loads would rest,
And babes cling, frightened, to the nurses' breast;
With looks convuls'd he roars in pompous strain,
And like an angry lion shakes his mane.
Thy Nine, with terror struck, who ne'er had seen
Aught human with so terrible a mien,
Debating, whether they should stay or run—
Virtue steps forth and claims him for her son.
—SHAW, CUTHBERT, 1766, *The Race.*

Johnson, you are the very man Lord Chesterfield describes:—a Hottentot indeed, and tho' your abilities are respectable, you never can be respected yourself. He has the aspect of an Idiot, without the faintest ray of sense gleaming from any one feature—with the most awkward garb, and unpowdered grey wig, on one side only of his head—he is for ever dancing the devil's jig, and sometimes he makes the most driveling effort to whistle some thought in his absent paroxysms. He came up to me and took me by the hand, then sat down on a sofa, and mumbled out that he had heard two papers had appeared against him in the course of this week—one of which was—that he was to go to Ireland next summer in order to abuse the hospitality of that place also. His awkwardness at table is just what Chesterfield described, and his roughness of manners kept pace with that. When Mrs. Thrale quoted something from Foster's Sermons, he flew in a passion and said that Foster was a man of mean ability, and of no original thinking. All which tho' I took to be most true, yet I held it not meet to have it so set down.—CAMPBELL, THOMAS, 1775, *A Diary of a Visit to England in* 1775, *by an Irishman, March* 11.

The time is again at which, since the death of my poor dear Tetty, on whom God have mercy, I have annually commemorated the mystery of Redemption, and annually purposed to amend my life. My reigning sin, to which perhaps many others are appendant, is waste of time, and general sluggishness, to which I was always inclined, and in part of my life have been almost compelled by morbid melancholy and disturbance of mind. Melancholy has had in me its paroxysms and remissions, but I have not improved the intervals, nor sufficiently resisted my natural inclination, or sickly habits. I will resolve henceforth to rise at eight in the morning, so far as resolution is proper, and will pray that God will strengthen me. I have begun this morning.—JOHNSON, SAMUEL, 1776, *Prayers and Meditations, Apr.* 7.

He is, indeed, very ill-favoured; is tall and stout; but stoops terribly; he is almost bent double. His mouth is almost [constantly opening and shutting], as if he was chewing. He has a strange method of frequently twirling his fingers, and twisting his hands. His body is in continual agitation, *sea-sawing* up and down; his feet are never a moment quiet; and, in short, his whole person is in *perpetual motion.* His dress, too, considering the times, and that he had meant to put on his *best becomes*, being engaged to dine in a large company, was as much out of the common road as his figure; he had a large wig, snuff-coloured coat, and gold buttons; but no ruffles to his [shirt] doughty fists, and black worsted stockings. He is shockingly near-sighted, and did not, till she held out her hand to him, even know Mrs. Thrale.—BURNEY, FRANCES, 1777, *Letter to Mr. Crisp, March* 28, *Early Diary, ed. Ellis, vol.* II, *p* 154.

Dr. Johnson is as correct and elegant in his common conversation as in his writings. He never seems to study either for thoughts or words; and is on all occasions so fluent, so well-informed, so accurate, and even eloquent, that I never left his company without regret. Sir Josh. Reynolds told me that from his first outset in life, he had always had this character; and by what means he had attained it. He told him he had early laid it down, as a fixed rule, always to do his best, *on every occasion* and in *every company*, to impart whatever he new in the best language he could put it in; and that by constant practice, and never suffering any careless expression to escape him, or attempting to deliver his thoughts without arranging them in the clearest manner he could, it was now become habitual to him. I have observed, in my various visits to him, that he never relaxes in this respect.

When first introduced I was very young; yet he was as accurate in his conversation as if he had been talking with the first scholar in England. I have always found him very communicative; ready to give his opinion on any subject that was mentioned. He seldom however starts a subject himself; but it is very easy to lead him into one.—MALONE, EDMOND, 1783, *Maloniana, ed. Prior, March, p.* 92.

I have lately been in the almost daily habit of contemplating a very melancholy spectacle. The great Johnson is here, labouring under the paroxysms of a disease which must speedily be fatal. He shrinks from the consciousness with the extremest horror. It is by his repeatedly expressed desire that I visit him often: yet I am sure he neither does, nor ever did, feel much regard for me; but he would fain escape, for a time, in any society, from the terrible idea of his approaching dissolution. I never would be awed, by his sarcasm or his frowns, into acquiescence with his general injustice to the merits of other writers, with his national or party aversions; but I feel the truest compassion for his present sufferings, and fervently wish I had power to relieve them. . . . His memory is considerably impaired, but his eloquence rolls on in its customary majestic torrent, when he speaks at all. My heart aches to see him labour for his breath, which he draws with great effort. It is not improbable that this literary comet may set where it rose, and Lichfield receives his pale and stern remains.—SEWARD, ANNA, 1784, *Letters, Oct.* 29.

Poor dear Johnson! he is past all hope. The dropsy has brought him to the point of death; his legs are scarificed: but nothing will do. I have, however, the comfort to hear that his dread of dying is in a great measure subdued; and now he says "the bitterness of death is past." He sent the other day for Sir Joshua; and after much serious conversation told him he had three favours to beg of him, and he hoped he would not refuse a dying friend, be they what they would. Sir Joshua promised. The first was that he would never paint on a Sunday; the second that he would forgive him thirty pounds that he had lent him, as he wanted to leave them to a distressed family; the third was that he would read the bible whenever he had an opportunity; and that he would never omit it on a Sunday. There was no difficulty but upon the *first* point; but at length Sir Joshua promised to gratify him in all. How delighted should I be to hear the dying discourse of this great and good man, especially now that faith has subdued his fears. I wish I could see him.—MORE, HANNAH, 1784, *Letter, Memoirs, vol.* I, *p.* 213.

45 minutes past 10 P. M.—While I was writing the adjoining articles I received the fatal account, so long dreaded, that Dr. Johnson was no more! May those prayers which he incessantly poured from a heart fraught with the deepest devotion, find that acceptance with Him to whom they were addressed, which piety, so humble and so fervent, may seem to promise!—WINDHAM, WILLIAM, 1784, *Diary, Dec.* 13.

Went to Bolt Court at eleven o'clock in the morning; met a young lady coming down stairs from the Doctor, whom, upon inquiry, I found to be Miss Morris (a sister to Miss Morris, formerly on the stage). Mrs. DeMoulins told me that she had seen the Doctor; that by her desire he had been told she came to ask his blessing, and that he said, "God bless you!" I then went up into his chamber, and found him lying very composed in a kind of doze: he spoke to nobody. Sir John Hawkins, Mr. Langton, Mrs. Gardiner, Rev. Mr. Strahan and Mrs. Strahan, Doctors Brocklesby and Butter, Mr. Steevens, and Mr. Nichols the printer, came; but no one chose to disturb him by speaking to him, and he seemed to take no notice of any person. While Mrs. Gardiner and I were there, before the rest came, he took a little warm milk in a cup, when he said something upon its not being properly given into his hand: he breathed very regular, though short, and appeared to be mostly in a calm sleep or dozing. I left him in this state, and never more saw him alive. In the evening I supped with Mrs. Hoole and my son at Mr. Braithwaite's, and at night my servant brought me word that my dearest friend died that evening about seven o'clock: and next morning I went to the house, where I met Mr. Seward; we went together into the chamber, and there saw the most awful sight of Dr. Johnson laid out in his bed, without life!—HOOLE, JOHN, 1784, *Diary, Dec.* 13.

Yesterday, my dear Sir, I followed our ever-lamented friend Dr. Johnson to his last mansion. . . . He was followed to the Abbey by a large troop of friends. Ten mourning-coaches were ordered by the executors for those invited. Besides these, eight of his friends or admirers clubbed for two more carriages, in one of which I had a seat. But the executor, Sir John Hawkins, did not manage things well; for there was no anthem or choir service performed, no lesson, but merely what is read over every old woman that is buried by the parish. Surely, surely, my dear Sir, this was wrong, very wrong. Dr. Taylor read the service, but so-so. He lies nearly under Shakspere's monument, with Garrick at his right hand, just opposite to the monument erected not long ago for Goldsmith by him and some of his friends. —BURNEY, CHARLES, 1784, *Letter to Dr. Parr, Dec.* 21; *Life and Works of Dr. Samuel Parr.*

In the name of God. Amen. I SAMUEL JOHNSON, being in full possession of my faculties, but fearing this night may put an end to my life, do ordain this my last will and testament. I bequeath to God a soul polluted with many sins, but I hope purified by repentance, and I trust redeemed by Jesus Christ. I leave seven hundred and fifty pounds in the hands of Bennet Langton, Esq.; three hundred pounds in the hands of Mr. Barclay and Mr. Perkins, brewers; one hundred and fifty pounds in the hands of Dr. Percy, bishop of Dromore; one thousand pounds, three per cent. annuities in the public funds, and one hundred pounds now lying by me in ready money; all these before-mentioned sums and property I leave, I say to Sir Joshua Reynolds, Sir John Hawkins, and Dr. Wm. Scott, of Doctors Commons, in trust for the following uses; That is to say, to pay to the representatives of the late William Innys, bookseller, in St. Paul's Church Yard, the sum of two hundred pounds; to Mrs. White, my female servant, one hundred pounds stock in the three per cent. annuities aforesaid. The rest of the aforesaid sums of money and property, together with my books, plate, and house-hold furniture, I leave to the before-mentioned Sir Joshua Reynolds, Sir John Hawkins, and Dr. William Scott, also in trust, to be applied, after paying my debts, to the use of Francis Barber, my man-servant, a negro, in such manner as they shall judge most fit and available to his benefit. And I appoint the aforesaid Sir Joshua Reynolds, Sir John Hawkins, and Dr. William Scott, sole executors of this my last will and testament, hereby revoking all former wills and testaments whatsoever. In witness whereof I hereunto subscribe my name, and affix my seal, this eighth day of December, 1784.

SAM. JOHNSON (L. S.)

Signed, sealed, published, declared, and delivered by the said testator, as his last will and testament, in the presence of us, the word *two* being first inserted in the opposite page.

GEORGE STRAHAN.
JOHN DES MOULINS.

—JOHNSON, SAMUEL, 1784, *Will.*

Samuel Johnson, LL.D.
obiit xiii die Decembris,
Anno Domini
MDCCLXXXVI.
Ætatis suæ LXXV.

—INSCRIPTION ON GRAVE, WESTMINSTER ABBEY, 1784.

At this time, having survived the tempest by which the capital and the court had been so long agitated, expired Dr. Samuel Johnson, a name which cannot be pronounced without veneration. I consider him as the most illustrious and universal man of letters whom I have personally known in my time; because I contemplate Burke more as an orator than an author, whatever fame he may have acquired by his writings. Gibbon's reputation, however deservedly high, is limited to a single branch of composition, and to a single work. With Hume and Robertson, I was not acquainted. Adam Smith, Jacob Bryant, and Horace Walpole—all of whom I knew—eminent as were their talents, could not, on the whole sustain a competition with Johnson.—WRAXALL, SIR NATHANIEL WILLIAM, 1784, *Posthumus Memoirs of my Own Time.*

He was born with a scrophulous habit, for which he was touched, as he acknowledged, by good Queen Anne, whose piece of gold he carefully preserved. . . . Though he seemed to be athletic as Milo himself, and in his younger days performed several feats of activity, he was to the last a *convulsionary.* He has often stept aside, to let nature do what she would with him. His gestures, which were a degree of St. Vitus's dance, in the street, attracted the notice of many: the stare of the vulgar, but the compassion of the better sort. This writer has often looked another way, as the companions of Peter the Great were used to do, while he was under the short paroxysm. He was perpetually taking opening medicines. He could only keep his ailments from gaining ground. He thought he was worse for the agitation of active exercise. He was afraid of his disorders seizing his head, and took all possible care that his understanding should not be deranged. *Orandum est, ut sit mens sana in corpore sano.* When his knowledge from books, and he knew all that books could tell him, is considered; when his compositions in verse and prose are enumerated to the reader (and a complete list of them wherever dispersed is desirable) it must appear extraordinary he could abstract himself so much from his feelings, and that he could pursue with ardour the plan he laid down of establishing a great reputation. —TYERS, THOMAS, 1784, *A Biographical Sketch of Dr. Samuel Johnson, Gentleman's Magazine, Dec.*

Dr. Johnson was a pious man; attached, I confess, to established system, but it was from principle. In company I neither found him austere nor dogmatical; he certainly was not polite, but he was not rude; he was familiar with suitable company; but his language in conversation was sententious; he was sometimes jocular, but you felt as if you were playing with a lion's paw. His body was large, his features strong, his face scarred and furrowed with the scrophula; he had a heavy look; but when he spoke it was like lightning out of a dark cloud.—LETTSOM, JOHN COAKLEY, 1785, *Memorials, Jan.* 13, *vol.* I, *p.* 78.

At one period of the Doctor's life, he was reconciled to the bottle. Sweet wines, however, were his chief favourites. When none of these were before him, he would sometimes drink Port, with a lump of sugar in every glass. The strongest liquors, and in very large quantities, produced no other effect on him than moderate exhilaration. Once, and but once, he is known to have had his dose; a circumstance which he himself discovered, on finding one of his sesquipedalion words hang fire. He then started up, and gravely observed—"I think it time we should go to bed." After a ten years' forbearance of every fluid, except tea and sherbet, "I drank," said he, "one glass of wine the health of Sir Joshua Reynolds, on the evening of the day on which he was knighted. I never swallowed another drop till old Madeira was prescribed to me as a cordial during my present indisposition, but this liquor did not relish as formerly, and I therefore discontinued it." . . . His knowledge in manufactures was extensive.—STEEVENS, GEORGE, 1785, *Johnsoniana, European Magazine, Jan.*

As Johnson was the firmest of believers without being credulous, so he was the most charitable of mortals without being what we call an active friend. Admirable at giving counsel, no man saw his way so clearly; but he would not stir a finger for the assistance of those to whom he was willing enough to give advice: besides that, he had principles of laziness, and could be indolent by rule. To hinder your death, or procure you a dinner, I mean if really in want of one; his earnestness, his exertions could not be prevented, though health and purse and ease were all destroyed by their violence. If you wanted a slight favour, you must apply to people of other dispositions; for not a step would Johnson move to obtain a man a vote in a society, to repay a compliment which might be useful or pleasing, to write a letter of request, or to obtain a hundred pounds a year more for a friend, who perhaps had already two or three. No force could urge him to diligence, no importunity could conquer his resolution of standing still. . . . Promptitude of thought indeed, and quickness of expression, were among the peculiar felicities of Johnson: his notions rose up like the dragon's teeth sowed by Cadmus all ready clothed, and in bright armour too, fit for immediate battle. He was therefore (as somebody is said to have expressed it) a tremendous converser, and few people ventured to try their skill against an antagonist with whom contention was so hopeless.—PIOZZI, HESTER LYNCH, 1786, *Anecdotes of the Late Samuel Johnson During the Last Twenty Years of his Life.*

Here lies poor Johnson! Reader, have a care,
Tread lightly, lest you rouse a sleeping bear!
Religious, moral, generous, and humane
He was; but, self-sufficient, rude, and vain.
Ill-bred, and over-bearing in dispute,
A scholar, and a Christian, and a brute.
—JENYNS, SOAME, 1787? *Epitaph on Dr. Johnson.*

Methinks I view his full, plain suit of brown,
The large gray bushy wig, that grac'd his crown;
Black worsted stockings, little silverbuckles;
And shirt, that had no ruffles for his knuckles.
I mark the brown great-coat of cloth he wore,
That two huge Patagonian pockets bore,
Which Patagonians (wondrous to unfold!)
Would fairly both his Dictionaries hold.
—WALCOT, JOHN (PETER PINDAR), 1787, *A Poetical and Congratulatory Epistle to James Boswell, Esq.*

As Johnson lived the life of the righteous, his end was that of a Christian: he strictly fulfilled the injunction of the apostles, to work out his salvation with fear and trembling; and, though his doubts and scruples were certainly very distressing to himself, they give his friends a pious hope, that he, who added to almost all the virtues of Christianity, that religious humility which its great teacher inculcated, will, in the fulness of time, receive the reward promised to a patient continuance in well-doing.—HAWKINS, SIR JOHN, 1787, *The Life of Samuel Johnson, p.* 590.

Johnson, it is said, was superstitious; but who shall exactly ascertain to us, what superstition is? . . . There was no occasion that Johnson should teach us to dance, to make bows, or turn compliments. He could teach us better things. To reject wisdom, because the person of him who communicates it is uncouth, and his manners are inelegant;—what is it, but to throw away a pineapple, and assign for a reason the roughness of its coat? That Johnson was generous and charitable, none can deny. But he was not always judicious in the selection of his objects: distress was a sufficient recommendation, and he did not scrutinize into the failings of the distressed. May it be always my lot to have such a benefactor! . . . For the mixture of power and weakness in the composition of this wonderful man, the scholar should learn humility. It was designed to correct that pride which great parts and great learning are apt to produce in their possessor. In him it had the desired effect. For though consciousness of superiority might sometimes induce him to carry it high with man (and even this was much abated in the latter part of life), his devotions have shewn to the whole world, how humbly he walked at all times with his God. . . . His eminence and his fame must of course have excited envy and malice: but let envy and malice look at his infirmities and his charities, and they will melt into pity and love.—HORNE, BISHOP GEORGE, 1787, *The Olla Podrida, No.* 13.

His necessary attendance while his play was in rehearsal, and during its performance, brought him acquainted with many of the performers of both sexes, which produced a more favourable opinion of their profession than he had harshly expressed in his "Life of Savage." With some of them he kept up an acquaintance as long as he and they lived, and was ever ready to show them acts of kindness. He for a considerable time used to frequent the *Green Room*, and seemed to take delight in dissipating his gloom, by mixing in the sprightly chit-chat of the motley circle then to be found there. Mr. David Hume related to me from Mr. Garrick, that Johnson at last denied himself this amusement, from considerations of rigid virtue; saying "I'll come no more behind your scenes, David; for the silk stockings and white bosoms of your actresses excite my amorous propensities."—BOSWELL, JAMES, 1791–93, *Life of Johnson, ed. Hill, vol.* I, *p.* 233.

I shall remark such qualities only as his works cannot convey. And among those the most distinguished was his possessing a mind which was, as I may say, always ready for use. Most general subjects had undoubtedly been already discussed in the course of a studious thinking life. In this respect few men ever came better prepared into whatever company chance might throw him, and the love which he had to society gave him a facility in the practice of applying his knowledge of the matter in hand in which I believe he was never exceeded by any man. It has been frequently observed that he was a singular instance of a man who had so much distinguished himself by his writings that his conversation not only supported his character as an author, but, in the opinion of many, was superior. Those who had lived with the wits of the age know how rarely this happens. I have had the habit of thinking that this quality, as well as others of the same kind, are possessed in consequence of accidental circumstances attending his life. What Dr. Johnson said a few days before his death of his disposition to insanity was no new discovery to those who were intimate with him. The character of Imlac in "Rasselas," I always considered as a comment on his own conduct, which he himself practised, and as it now appears very successfully, since we know he continued to possess his understanding in its full vigour to the last. Solitude to him was horror; nor would he ever trust himself alone but when employed in writing or reading. He has often begged me to go home with him to prevent his being alone in the coach. Any company was better than none; by which he connected himself with many mean persons whose presence he could command. . . . We are both of Dr. Johnson's school. For my part, I acknowledge the highest obligations to him. He may be said to have formed my mind, and to have brushed from it a great deal of rubbish. Those very people whom he has brought to think rightly will occasionally criticise the opinions of their master when he nods. But we should always recollect that it is he himself who taught us and enabled us to do it.—REYNOLDS, SIR JOSHUA, 1792? *Life and Times of Sir Joshua Reynolds by Leslie and Taylor, vol.* II.

It may be said, the death of Dr. Johnson kept the public mind in agitation beyond all former example. . . . As a man, Dr. Johnson stands displayed in open day-light. Nothing remains undiscovered. What ever he said is known; and without allowing him the usual privilege of hazarding sentiments, and advancing positions, for mere amusement, or the pleasure of discussion, criticism has endeavoured to make him answerable for what, perhaps, he never seriously thought. His diary, which has been printed, discovers still more. We have before us the very heart of the man, with all his inward consciousness. And yet neither in the open paths of life, nor in his secret recesses, has any one vice been discovered. We see him reviewing every year of his life, and severely censuring himself, for not keeping resolutions, which morbid melancholy, and other bodily infirmities, rendered impracticable. We see him for every little defect imposing on himself voluntary penance, going through the day with only one cup of tea without milk, and to the last, amidst paroxysms and remissions of illness, forming plans of study and resolutions to amend his life. Many of his scruples may be called weaknesses; but they are the weaknesses of a good, a pious, and most excellent man.—MURPHY, ARTHUR, 1792, *An Essay on the Life and Genius of Samuel Johnson.*

With a lumber of learning and some strong parts, Johnson was an odious and mean character—by principle a Jacobite, arrogant, self-sufficient, and overbearing by nature, ungrateful through pride, and of *feminine bigotry.* His manners were sordid, supercilious, and brutal, his style ridiculously bombastic and vicious; and in one word, with all the pedantry he had all the gigantic littleness of a country schoolmaster.—WALPOLE, HORACE, 1797? *Memoirs of the First Ten Years of George III.*

Mrs. Williams was a person extremely interesting. She had uncommon firmness of mind, a boundless curiosity, retentive memory, and strong judgment. She had various powers of pleasing. Her personal afflictions and slender fortune she seemed to forget, when she had the power of doing an act of kindness: she was social, cheerful, and active, in a state of body that was truly deplorable. Her regard to Dr. Johnson was formed with such strength of judgment and firm esteem, that her voice never hesitated when she repeated his maxims, or recited his good deeds; though upon many other occasions her want of sight led her to make so much use of her ear, as to affect her speech. Mrs. Williams was blind before she was acquainted with Dr. Johnson.—KNIGHT, LADY, 1799, *European Magazine, Oct.*

Johnson's manner of composing has not been rightly understood. He was so extremely short-sighted, from the defect of his eyes, that writing was inconvenient to him; for whenever he wrote, he was obliged to hold a paper close to his face. He, therefore, never composed what we call a foul draft on paper of any thing he published, but used to revolve the subject in his mind, and turn and form every period, till he had brought the whole to the highest correctness and the most perfect arrangement. Then his uncommonly retentive memory enabled him to deliver a whole essay, properly finished, whenever it was called for. The writer of this note has often heard him humming and forming periods, in low whispers to himself, when shallow observers thought he was muttering prayers, &c.—PERCY, THOMAS, 1805? *Anecdotes and Remarks of Samuel Johnson.*

Herculean strength and a stentorian voice,
 Of wit a fund, of words a countless choice;
In learning rather various than profound,
 In truth intrepid, in religion sound;
A trembling form and a distorted sight,
 But firm in judgment and in genius bright;
In controversy seldom known to spare,
 But humble as the publican in prayer;
To more than merited his kindness, kind,
 And though in manners harsh, of friendly mind;
Deep tinged with melancholy's blackest shade,
 And though prepared to die, of death afraid—
Such Johnson was; of him with justice vain,
 When will this nation see his like again?

—CUMBERLAND, RICHARD, 1806, *Memoirs Written by Himself.*

There never, indeed, was a human being of whom more may be known by those who have had no opportunity of personal acquaintance, and perhaps never a man whose failings, after having been exposed by imprudence or exaggerated by malice, were sooner forgotten in the esteem excited by his superior talents, and steady virtues.—CHALMERS, ALEXANDER, 1806, *ed., The Works of Samuel Johnson, Advertisement.*

His good deeds were as many as his good sayings. His domestic habits, his tenderness to servants, and readiness to oblige his friends; the quantity of strong tea that he drank to keep down sad thoughts; his many labours reluctantly begun, and irresolutely laid aside; his honest acknowledgment of his own, and indulgence to the weaknesses of others; his throwing himself back in the post-chaise with Boswell, and saying, "Now I think I am a good-humoured fellow," though nobody thought him so, and yet he was; his quitting the society of Garrick and his actresses, and his reason for it; his dining with Wilkes, and his kindness to Goldsmith; his sitting with the young ladies on his knee at the Mitre, to give them good advice, in which situation, if not explained, he might be taken for Falstaff; and last and noblest, his carrying the unfortunate victim of disease and dissipation on his back up through Fleet street (an act which realises the parable of the good Samaritan)—all these, and innumerable others, endear him to the reader, and must be remembered to his lasting honour. He had faults, but they lie buried with him. He had his prejudices and his intolerant feelings, but he suffered enough in the conflict of his own mind with them; for if no man can be happy in the free exercise of his reason, no wise man can be happy without it. His were not time-serving, heartless, hypocritical prejudices; but deep, inwoven, not to be rooted out but with life and hope, which he found from old habit necessary to his own peace of mind, and thought so to the peace of mankind. I do not hate, but love him for them. They were between himself and his conscience, and should be left to that higher tribunal

"Where they in trembling hope repose,
The bosom of his father and his God."

In a word, he has left behind him few wiser or better men.—HAZLITT, WILLIAM, 1818, *Lectures on the English Comic Writers, Lecture* v.

Having mentioned some literary characters, who became personally known to me in the university, I will not omit, although extraneous to it, that giant of genius and literature, Dr. Samuel Johnson. My introduction to him was a letter from the Rev. Jonathan Odel, formerly missionary at Burlington. The Doctor was very civil to me. I visited him occasionally; and I know some who would be tempted to envy me the felicity of having found him, one morning, in the act of preparing his dictionary for a new edition. His harshness of manners never displayed itself to me, except in one instance; when he told me that had he been prime-minister, during the then recent controversy concerning the stamp-act, he would have sent a ship-of-war, and levelled one of our principal cities with the ground. On the other hand, I have heard from him sentiments expressive of a feeling heart; and convincing me, that he would not have done as he said. —WHITE, WILLIAM, 1819, *Letter to Bishop Hobart, Sept.; Memoirs of the Life of Bishop White.*

There was a pith about old Samuel which nothing could stand up against. His influence was not so much that of an author as of a thinker. He was the most powerful intellect in the world of books. He was the Jackson of the literary ring—the judge—the emperor—a giant—acknowledged to be a Saul amongst the people. Even David Hume would have been like a woman in his grasp; but, odd enough, the two never met.—WILSON, JOHN, 1822, *Noctes Ambrosianæ, April* 2.

In the vicissitudes of twenty-seven years, no estrangement occurred to interrupt their mutual admiration and regard. Burke followed Johnson to the grave as a mourner; and in contemplating his character, applied to it a fine passage from Cicero, which might equally suit his own: —*Intentum enim animum quasi arcum habebat, nec languescens succumbebat senecuti.* When some one censured Johnson's general rudeness in society, he replied with equal consideration and truth, "It is well, when a man comes to die, if he has nothing worse to accuse himself of than than some harshness in conversation."—PRIOR, SIR JAMES, 1824, *Memoirs of the Life and Character of the Right Hon. Edmund Burke.*

When first I remember Johnson I used to see him sometimes at a little distance from the house, coming to call on my father; his look directed downwards, or rather in such apparent abstraction as to have no direction. His walk was heavy, but he got on at a great rate, his left arm always fixed across his breast, so as to bring the hand under the chin; and he walked wide, as if to support his weight. Getting out of a hackney-coach, which had set him down in Fleet Street, my brother Henry says he made his way up Bolt Court in the zig-zag direction of a flash of lightning; submitting his course only to the deflections imposed by the impossibility of going further to right or left. His clothes hung loose, and the pocket on the right hand swung violently, the lining of his coat being always visible. I can now call to mind his brown hand, his metal sleeve-buttons, and my surprise at seeing him with plain wristbands, when all gentlemen wore ruffles; his coat-sleeve being very wide, showed his linen almost to the elbow. His wig in common was cut and bushy; if by chance he had one that had been dressed in separate curls, it gave him a disagreeable look, not suited to his years or character. I certainly had no idea that this same Dr. Johnson, whom I thought rather a disgraceful visitor at our house, and who was never mentioned by ladies but with a smile, was to be one day an honour not only to us but to this country. I remember a tailor's bringing his pattern-book to my brothers, and pointing out a purple, such as no one else wore, as the doctor's usual choice. We all shouted with astonishment, at hearing that Polyheme, as, shame to say, we had nicknamed him, ever had a new coat; but the tailor assured us he was a good customer.—HAWKINS, LETITIA, 1827, *Memoirs, vol.* I, *p.* 86.

Johnson, it is well known, professed to recruit his acquaintance with younger persons, and, in his latter days, I, with a few others were more frequently honoured by his notice. At times he was very gloomy, and would exclaim, "Stay with me, for it is a comfort to me"—a comfort that any feeling mind would wish to administer to a man so kind, though at times so boisterous, when he seized your hand, and repeated, "Ay, Sir, but to die and go we know not where," &c.—here his morbid melancholy prevailed, and Garrick never spoke so impressively to the heart. Yet, to see him in the evening (though he took nothing stronger than lemonade), a stranger would have concluded that our morning account was a fabrication. No hour was too late to keep him from the tyranny of his own gloomy thoughts. A gentleman venturing to say to Johnson, "Sir, I wonder sometimes that you condescend so far as to attend a city club." "Sir, the great chair of a full and pleasant club is, perhaps, the throne of human felicity."—CRADOCK, JOSEPH, 1828, *Literary Memoirs.*

In early youth I knew Bennet Langton, *of that ilk*, as the Scotch say. With great personal claims to the respect of the public, he is known to that public chiefly as a friend of Johnson. He was a very tall, meagre, long-visaged man, much resembling, according to Richard Paget, a stork standing on one leg, near the shore, in Raphael's cartoon of the miraculous draught of fishes. His manners were in the highest degree polished; his conversation mild, equable, and always pleasing. He had the uncommon faculty of being a good reader. I formed an intimacy with his son, and went to pay him a visit at Langton. After breakfast we walked to the top of a very steep hill behind the house. When we arrived at the summit, Mr. Langton said, "Poor, dear Dr. Johnson, when he came to this spot, turned to look down the hill, and said he was determined 'to take a roll down.' When we understood what he meant to do, we endeavoured to dissuade him; but he was resolute, saying, he had not had a roll for a long time; and taking out of his lesser pockets whatever might be in them—keys, pencil, purse, or penknife, and laying himself parallel with the edge of the hill, he actually descended, turning himself over and over until he came to the bottom." The story was told with such gravity, and with an air of such affectionate remembrance of a departed friend, that it was impossible to suppose this extraordinary freak of the great lexicographer to have been a fiction or invention of Mr. Langton.—BEST, H. D., 1829, *Personal and Literary Memorials, vol.* I, *p.* 62.

Johnson grown old, Johnson in the fulness of his fame and in the enjoyment of a competent fortune, is better known to us than any other man in history. Everything about him, his coat, his wig, his figure, his face, his scrofula, his St. Vitus's dance, his rolling walk, his blinking eye, the outward signs which too clearly marked his approbation of his dinner, his insatiable appetite for fish-sauce and veal pie with plums, his inextinguishable thirst for tea, his trick of touching the posts as he walked, his mysterious practice of treasuring up scraps of orange-peel, his morning slumbers, his midnight disputations, his contortions, his mutterings, his gruntings, his puffings, his vigorous, acute, and ready eloquence, his sarcastic wit, his vehemence, his insolence, his fits of tempestuous rage, his queer inmates, old Mr. Levett and blind Mrs. Williams, the cat Hodge and the negro Frank—all are as familiar to us as the objects by which we have been surrounded from childhood. . . . The club-room is before us, and the table on which stands the omelet for Nugent and the lemons for Johnson. There are assembled those heads which live for ever on the canvas of Reynolds. There are the spectacles of Burke and the tall thin form of Langton; the courtly sneer of Beauclerk and the beaming smile of Garrick; Gibbon tapping his snuff-box, and Sir Joshua with his trumpet in his ear. In the foreground is that strange figure which is as familiar to us as the figures of those among whom we have been brought up—the gigantic body, the huge massy face, seamed with the scars of disease; the brown coat, the black worsted stockings, the gray wig with a scorched foretop; the dirty hands, the nails bitten and paired to the quick. We see the eyes and mouth moving with convulsive twitches; we see the heavy form rolling; we hear it puffing; and then comes the "Why, sir!" and the "What then, sir?" and the "No, sir!" and the "You don't see your way through the question, sir!"—MACAULAY, THOMAS BABINGTON, 1831, *Boswell's Life of Johnson, Edinburgh Review; Critical and Miscellaneous Essays.*

Leaving now this our English *Odyssey*, with its Singer and Scholiast, let us come to the *Ulysses;* that great Samuel Johnson himself, the far-experienced, "much-enduring man," whose labours and pilgrimage are here sung. A full-length image of his Existence has been preserved for us: and he perhaps of all living Englishmen, was the one who best deserved that honour. . . . Seldom, for any man, has the contrast between the ethereal heavenward side of things, and the dark sordid earthward, been more glaring: whether we look at Nature's work with him or Fortune's, from first to last, heterogeneity, as of sunbeams and miry clay, is on all hands manifest. Whereby indeed, only this was declared, That *much life* had been given him; many things to triumph over, a great work to *do.* Happily also he did it; better than the most. Nature had given him a high, keen-visioned, almost poetic soul; yet withal imprisoned it in an inert, unsightly body: he that could never rest had not limbs that would move with him, but only roll and waddle: the inward eye, all-penetrating, all-embracing, must look through bodily windows that were dim, half-blinded; he so loved men, and "never once *saw* the human face divine!" Not less did he prize the love of men; he was eminently social; the approbation of his fellows was dear to him, "valuable," as he owned, "if from the meanest of human beings:" yet the first impression he produced on every man was to be one of aversion, almost of disgust. By Nature it was farther ordered that the imperious Johnson should be born poor: the ruler-soul, strong in its native royalty, generous, uncontrollable, like the lion of the woods, was to be housed, then, in such a dwelling-place: of Disfigurement, Disease, and lastly of a Poverty which itself made him the servant of servants. Thus was the born king likewise a born slave: the divine spirit of Music must awake imprisoned amid dull-croaking universal Discords; the Ariel finds himself encased in the coarse hulls of a Caliban. So is it more or less, we know (and thou O Reader, knowest and feelest even now), with all men: yet with the fewest men in any such degree as with Johnson.—CARLYLE, THOMAS, 1832, *Boswell's Life of Johnson, Critical and Miscellaneous Essays, vol.* IV, *pp.* 51, 57.

I love the Doctor as much as Bos. did, certainly. He was a noble fellow, saturated with knowledge; a magazine of satire, a powder-house of wit.—APPLETON, THOMAS GOLD, 1832, *Life and Letters, p.* 79.

Johnson's malady and Cowper's were precisely similar in the early period of each, as we have before remarked; the only difference was in the strength of mind of either sufferer. Cowper at once surrendered himself up to the tyranny of his disorder, and took a pleasure in parading the chains of his melancholy before the eyes of his correspondents, even when "immuring himself at home in the infected atmosphere of his own enthusiasm;" while Johnson struggled with his disease, sometimes indeed in a spirit of ferocious independence, and very seldom complained to his most intimate friends of his "humiliating malady." In no point was the vigour of his intellect shown in so strong a light as in this particular; for in no malady is there so great a disposition to complain of the sufferings that are endured, and to over-state their intensity, lest, by any possibility, they should be underrated by others.—MADDEN, R. R., 1833, *Infirmities of Genius, vol.* I, *p.* 228.

Dr. Johnson's fame now rests principally upon Boswell. It is impossible not to be amazed with such a book. But his "bow-wow" manner must have had a good deal to do with the effect produced;—for no one, I suppose, will set Johnson before Burke,—and Burke was a great and universal talker;—yet now we hear nothing of this except by some chance remarks in Boswell. The fact is, that Burke, like all men of genius who love to talk at all, was very discursive and continuous; hence he is not reported; he seldom said the short things that Johnson almost always did, which produce a more decided effect at the moment and which are so much more easy to carry off. Besides, as to Burke's testimony to Johnson's powers, you must remember that Burke was a great courtier; and after all, Burke said and wrote more than once that he thought Johnson greater in talking than writing, and greater in Boswell than in real life.—COLERIDGE, SAMUEL TAYLOR, 1833, *Table Talk, ed. Ashe, July* 4, *p.* 239.

If then it be asked, who first, in England, at this period, breasted the waves and stemmed the tide of infidelity,—who, enlisting wit and eloquence, together with argument and learning, on the side of revealed religion, first turned the literary current in its favour and mainly prepared the reaction which succeeded,—that praise seems most justly to belong to Dr. Samuel Johnson. Religion was to him no mere lip-service nor cold formality: he was mindful of it in his social hours as much as in his graver lucubrations; and he brought to it, not merely erudition such as few indeed possessed, but the weight of the highest character, and the respect which even his enemies would not deny him. It may be said of him that, though not in Orders, he did the Church of England better service than most of those who at that listless era ate her bread.—STANHOPE, PHILIP HENRY (LORD MAHON), 1836–54, *History of England, vol.* IV, *p.* 313.

His youth was one of extreme poverty; yet when a person who knew of his condition had a pair of old shoes placed in his belongings, as soon as Johnson discovered them he flung them out the window. This incident is an expressive type of the man's conduct through life; he never would stand in another's shoes; he preferred misery when it was his own, to anything derivable from others. He was in all respects a ponderous man,—strong in appetite, powerful in intellect, of Herculean frame, a great passionate giant. There is something fine and touching too, if we will consider it, in that little, flimsy, flippant, vain fellow, Boswell, attaching himself as he did to Johnson: before others had discovered anything sublime, Boswell had done it, and embraced his knees when the bosom was denied him. —FOX, CAROLINE, 1840, *Memories of Old Friends, ed. Pym, Journal, May* 19, *p.* 106.

Our English neighbors, as a people at least, are much less literary than ourselves. The fame of their best writers has scarce at all reached the masses of their population. They know nothing of Addison with his exquisitely classic prose, or of Pope with his finished and pointed verse. We have been struck, however, by finding it remarked by an English writer, who lived long in London, and moved much among the common people, that he found in the popular mind well-marked though indistinct and exaggerated traces of at least one great English author. He could learn nothing, he observed, from the men who drove cabs and drays, of the wits and scholars of Queen Anne, or of the much greater literati of the previous century; nay, they seemed to know scarce anything of living genius; but they all possessed somehow an indistinct, shadowy notion of one Dr. Samuel Johnson,—a large, ill-dressed man, who was a great writer of they knew not what; and almost all of them could point out the various places in which he had lived, and the house in which he died. Altogether independently of his writings—for these are far from being of a popular cast—the doctor had made an impression by the sheer bulk and energy of his character; he loomed large and imposing simply as a man.—MILLER, HUGH, 1844, *Essays, p.* 146.

Another paradox of Mr. Gilfillan's under this head is that he classes Dr. Johnson as indolent; and it is the more startling because he does not utter it as a careless opinion upon which he might have been thrown by inconsideration, but as a concession extorted from him reluctantly: he had sought to evade it, but could not. Now, that Dr. Johnson had a morbid predisposition to decline labour from his scrofulous habit of body is probable. The question for us, however, is not what nature prompted him to do, but what he did. If he had an extra difficulty to fight with in attempting to labour, the more was his merit in the known result,—that he *did* fight with that difficulty, and that he conquered it. This is undeniable. And the attempt to deny it presents itself in a comic shape when one imagines some ancient shelf in a library, that has groaned for nearly a century under the weight of the doctor's works, demanding "How say you? Is this Sam Johnson, whose Dictionary alone is a load for a camel, one of those authors whom you call idle? Then Heaven preserve us poor oppressed bookshelves from such as you will consider active." George III, in a compliment as happily turned as any one of those ascribed to Louis XIV, expressed his opinion upon this question of the Doctor's industry by saying that he also should join in thinking Johnson too voluminous a contributor to literature were it not for the extraordinary merit of the contributions. Now, it would be an odd way of turning the royal praise into reproach if we should say: "Sam, had you been a pretty good writer, we, your countrymen, should have held you to be also an industrious writer; but, because you are a *very* good writer, therefore, we pronounce you a lazy vagabond." —DE QUINCEY, THOMAS, 1845–57, *Gilfillan's Literary Portraits, Works, ed. Masson, vol.* XI, *p.* 381.

Dr. Johnson's essays on politeness are admirable; yet his "You lie, sir!" and "You don't understand the question, sir!" were too common characteristics of his colloquies. He and Dr. Shebbeare were both pensioned at the same time. The report immediately flew, that the king had pensioned two bears,—a he-bear and a she-bear.—WHIPPLE, EDWIN P., 1846, *Authors in their Relations to Life, Literature and Life, p.* 34.

He brought, into common talk, too plain an anticipation of victory and triumph. He wore his determination not to be thrown or beaten, whatever side he might please to take, somewhat defiantly upon his sleeve; and startled peaceful society a little too much with his uncle Andrew's habits in the ring at Smithfield. It was a sense, on his own part, of this eagerness to make every subject a battleground, which made him say, at a moment of illness and exhaustion, that if he were to see Burke then, it would kill him. From the first day of their meeting, now some years ago, at Garrick's dinner-table, his desire had been to measure himself with Burke on all occasions.—FORSTER, JOHN, 1848–71, *The Life and Times of Oliver Goldsmith, vol.* I, *p.* 319.

Johnson once lived in Fetter Lane, but the circumstances of his abode there have not transpired. We now, however, come to a cluster of his residences in Fleet Street, of which place he is certainly the great presiding spirit, the *Genius loci.* He was conversant for the greater part of his life with this street, was fond of it, frequented its Mitre Tavern above any other in London, and has identified its name and places with the best things he ever said and did. It was in Fleet Street, we believe, that he took the poor girl up in his arms, put her to bed in his own house, and restored her to health and her friends; an action sufficient to redeem a million of the asperities of temper occasioned by disease, and to stamp him, in spite of his bigotry, a good Christian. Here, at all events, he walked and talked, and shouldered wondering porters out of the way, and mourned, and philosophised, and was "a good-natured fellow" (as he called himself), and roared with peals of laughter till midnight echoed to his roar. —HUNT, LEIGH, 1848, *The Town, p.* 121.

Next I told the driver to take me to Fleet street, to Gough Square, and to Bolt court, where Johnson lived and died. Bolt court lies on Fleet street, and it is but a few steps along a narrow passage to the house, which is now a hotel, where Johnson died; but you must walk on farther through the narrow passage, a little fearful to a woman, to see the place where he wrote the dictionary. The house is so completely within a court, in which nothing but brick walls could be seen, that one wonders what the charm of London could be, to induce one to live in that place. But a great city always draws to itself the great minds, and there Johnson probably found his enjoyment.—MITCHELL, MARIA, 1857, *Life, Letters and Journals, p.* 104.

I was but little interested in the legends of the remote antiquity of Lichfield, being drawn thither partly to see its beautiful cathedral, and still more, I believe, because it was the birthplace of Dr. Johnson, with whose sturdy English character I became acquainted, at a very early period of my life, through the good offices of Mr. Boswell. In truth, he seems as familiar to my recollection, and almost as vivid in his personal aspect to my mind's eye, as the kindly figure of my own grandfather. . . . Beyond all question I might have had a wiser friend than he. The atmosphere in which alone he breathed was dense; his awful dread of death showed how much muddy imperfection was to be cleansed out of him, before he could be capable of spiritual existence; he meddled only with the surface of life, and never cared to penetrate farther than to plough-share depth; his very sense and sagacity were but a one-eyed clear-sightedness. I laugh at him sometimes, standing beside his knee. And yet, considering that my native propensities were toward Fairy Land, and also how much yeast is generally mixed up with the mental sustenance of a New Englander, it may not have been altogether amiss, in those childish and boyish days, to keep pace with this heavy-footed traveller, and feed on the gross diet that he carried in his knapsack. It is wholesome food even now. And, then, how English! Many of the latent sympathies that enable me to enjoy the Old Country so well, and that so readily amalgamated themselves with the American ideas that seemed the most adverse to them, may have been derived from, or fostered and kept alive by, the great English moralist. Never was a descriptive epithet more nicely appropriate than that! Dr. Johnson's morality was as English an article as a beefsteak. —HAWTHORNE, NATHANIEL, 1863, *Lichfield and Uttoxeter, Our Old Home.*

Communion, though but for a short while, with the spirit of this man's life, fellowship with his sufferings, sympathy with his sorrows, the sense of his virtues, and the felt presence of his genius, will surely bring a touch of healing to some wounded heart, or a word of strength to some weary brain. It has been well said, "*The first condition of human goodness is, something to love; the second, something to reverence,*" both these conditions meet, and meet grandly, in the life of Doctor Samuel Johnson.—MAIN, ALEXANDER, 1874, *Life and Conversations of Dr. Samuel Johnson, p.* 441.

Dr. Johnson was a man of no profound mind,—full of English limitations, English politics, English Church, Oxford philosophy; yet, having a large heart, mother-wit, and good sense which impatiently overleaped his customary bounds, his conversation as reported by Boswell has a lasting charm. Conversation is the vent of character as well as of thought; and Dr. Johnson impresses his company, not only by the point of the remark, but also, when the point fails, because *he* makes it. —EMERSON, RALPH WALDO, 1880–83, *Clubs; Works, Riverside ed., vol.* VII, *p.* 223.

Johnson had the warmest of hearts. He was tender and even gallant, love was almost a weakness with him. When an uncouth youth, he was in love with a local belle. There was a certain Molly Aston, with whom he was desperately smitten; and his gallantry to ladies when advanced in life makes up some pretty scenes in Boswell. The real attachments of his life were two: the first for his wife; the second, the well-known devotion to Mrs. Thrale. Mrs. Johnson was a singularly coarse, painted creature, much older than he was, without a charm to recommend her. Yet he was really infatuated by her. Garrick, attending his school, used to make much mirth out of the clownish attempts at adoration on the part of the Edial pedagogue, and would later mimic the uncouth love-making of the future dictionary-writer. To her he was all through the devoted husband, just as he had been the devoted son; and his grief at her loss showed that this almost grotesque affection was based on the most substantial and enduring grounds.—FITZGERALD, PERCY, 1883, *Kings and Queens of an Hour, vol.* II, *p.* 300.

Is it possible to feel as deep an interest in and admiration for Carlyle, apart from his works, as we do in Johnson? Different temperaments will answer differently. Some people have a natural antipathy to Carlyle, based largely, no doubt, on misconception. But misconception is much easier in his case than in Johnson's. He was more of an exceptional being. He was pitched in too high a key for the ordinary uses of life. He had fewer infirmities than Johnson, moral and physical. Johnson was a typical Englishman, and appeals to us by all the virtues and faults of his race. Carlyle stands more isolated, and held himself much more aloof from the world. On this account, among others, he touches us less nearly. Women are almost invariably repelled by Carlyle; they instinctively flee from a certain hard, barren masculinity in him. If not a woman-hater, he certainly had little in his composition that responded to the charms and allurements peculiar to the opposite sex; while Johnson's idea of happiness was to spend his life driving briskly in a postchaise with a pretty and intelligent woman. Both men had the same proud independence, the same fearless gift of speech, the same deference to authority or love of obedience. In personal presence, the Englishman had the advantage of mere physical size, breadth, and a stern forbidding countenance. Johnson's power was undoubtedly more of the chest, the stomach, and less of the soul, than Carlyle's, and was more of a blind, groping, unconscious force; but of the two men he seems the more innocent and child-like. His journal is far less interesting and valuable as literature than Carlyle's, but in some way his fervent prayers, his repeated resolutions to do better, to conquer his laziness, "to consult the resolve on Tetty's coffin," "to go to church," "to drink less strong liquors," "to get up at 8 o'clock," "to reject or expel sensual images and idle thoughts," "to read the Scriptures," etc., touch one more nearly than Carlyle's exaggerated self-reproaches and loud bemoanings of the miseries of life. Yet the fact remains that Johnson lived and moved and thought on a lower plane than Carlyle, and that he cherished less lofty ideals of life and of duty. It is probably true also that his presence and his conversation made less impression on his contemporaries than did Carlyle's; but, through the wonderful Boswell, a livelier more lovable and more real image of him is likely to go down to succeeding ages than of the great Scotchman through his biographer. — BURROUGHS, JOHN, 1886, *Dr. Johnson and Carlyle, The Critic, N. S., vol.* 5, *p.* 2.

Concerning the portraits of Dr. Johnson alone, many pages might be written.

His face is as familiar to-day as that of Bonaparte, Shakespeare or Mary Queen of Scots. In one private collection of Johnson there are one hundred and fifty-three prints, no two of which are alike; and this collection is known to be incomplete. When the Neophyte comes to this name on his list he will be at a loss where to begin and how soon to stop. He will certainly be tempted to gather as many as his purse will buy.—HUTTON, LAURENCE, 1887, *Grangerism and the Grangerites, The Book Buyer, vol.* 4, *p.* 290.

The Blaspheming Doctor,—Blinking Sam,—The Bolt Court Philosopher,—The Cerberus of Literature,—The Classic Rambler,—The Colossus of English Philology,—The Giant of Literature,—The Great Bear,—Great Caliban,—The Great Cham of Literature,—The Great Moralist,—The Great Seer,—The Incomprehensible Holofernes,—A Learned Attila,—Our Letter'd Polypheme,—The Leviathan of Literature,—The Literary Anvil,—The Literary Castor,—The Literary Colossus,—Our Literary Whale,—Pomposo,—The Respectable Hottentot,—Sir Charles Easy,—Sober,—Surly Sam,—Ursa Major.—FREY, ALBERT R., 1888, *Sobriquets and Nicknames, p.* 426.

That dear Old Doctor! fierce of mien,
Untidy, arbitrary, fat,
What gentle thoughts his name enfold!
So generous of his scanty gold,
So quick to love, so hot to scorn,
Kind to all sufferers under heaven—
A tenderer despot ne'er was born;
His big heart held a corner even
For Hodge the cat.

—COOLIDGE, SUSAN, 1889, *Hodge the Cat.*

Given thus, on the one hand, a man of vigorous intellect, strong, though controlled passions, and fascinating conversation, and, on the other, a woman of talent, able and quick to appreciate his merits, and let the two be thrown together intimately for the period of sixteen years, nothing would be more natural than for a feeling to spring up, at least on the part of the man, warmer than mere friendship. Difference of age counts for little in such cases for it is a common saying that the heart never grows old. A man in Johnson's position readily forgets how he actually appears to the woman who flatters and pleases him, and, conscious only of his own youthful feelings, is prone to imagine that he seems to her as young as he does to himself. There is no proof that Mrs. Thrale ever entertained any sentiment for Johnson other than the esteem which in Madame d'Arblay became reverent adoration. Indeed, when spoken to about her supposed passion for him some years afterwards by Sir James Fellows, she ridiculed the idea, saying that she always felt for Johnson the same respect and veneration as for a Pascal. But if the long-continued manifestation of these sentiments, coupled with the most assiduous devotion and tender, wifelike care, had not awakened in him some response beyond mere gratitude, he would have been the most insensible of beings. Love, moreover, is frequently the result of propinquity and habit, and to both these influences Johnson was subjected for more than sixteen years. If he misinterpreted the attentions he received, and was emboldened by them to hope for a return of the passion they aroused, he did only what many a wise man has done under the same circumstances, and will do again.—HITCHCOCK, THOMAS, 1891, *Dr. Johnson and Mrs. Thrale, Unhappy Loves of Men of Genius, p.* 66.

Johnson had a tall, well-formed, and massive figure, indicative of great physical strength, but made grotesque by a strange infirmity. Madame d'Arblay speaks of his "vast body in constant agitation, swaying backwards and forwards;" Miss Reynolds describes his apparently unconsciousness "antics," especially when he crossed a threshold. Sometimes when he was reading a book in the fields a mob would gather to stare at his strange gestures. Reynolds mentioned that he could constrain them when he pleased, though Boswell called them St. Vitus's dance. He had queer tricks of touching posts and carefully counting steps, even when on horseback. He was constantly talking or muttering prayers to himself. His face, according to Campbell, had "the aspect of an idiot." He remained in silent abstraction till roused, or, as Tyers said, was like a ghost, who never speaks till he is spoken to. In spite of his infirmities he occasionally indulged in athletic performances. Mrs. Piozzi says that he sometimes hunted with Thrale. He understood boxing, and regretted the decline of prize-fighting, jumped, rowed, and shot, in a "strange and unwieldy" way, to show that he was not tired after a "fifty miles' chase," and, according to Miss Reynolds, swarmed up a tree and beat a young lady in a foot-race when over fifty. Langton described to Best how at the age of fifty-five he had solemnly rolled down a hill. His courage was remarkable; he separated savage dogs, swam into dangerous pools, fired off an overloaded gun, and defended himself against four robbers single-handed. His physical infirmities were partly accountable for roughness of manner. He suffered from deafness and was shortsighted to an extreme degree, although by minute attention he could often perceive objects with an accuracy which surprised his friends. He was thus often unable to observe the failings of his companions. Manners learnt in Grub Street were not delicate; his mode of gratifying a voracious appetite was even disgusting; while his dress was slovenly, and he had "no passion for clean linen." He piqued himself, indeed, upon his courtesy; and, when not provoked by opposition, or unable to perceive the failings of others, was both dignified and polite. Nobody could pay more graceful compliments, especially to ladies, and he was always the first to make advances after a quarrel. His friends never ceased to love him; and their testimony to the singular tenderness which underlay his roughness is unanimous. He loved children, and was even too indulgent to them; he rejoiced greatly when he persuaded Dr. Sumner to abolish holiday tasks, and was most attentive to the wants of his servants. He was kind to animals, and bought oysters himself for his cat Hodge, that his servants might not be prejudiced against it. He loved the poor, as Mrs. Piozzi says, as she never saw any one else do; and tended to be indiscriminate in his charity.—STEPHEN, LESLIE, 1892, *Dictionary of National Biography, vol.* XXX, *p.* 44.

Johnson's experiences of Booksellers were very varied. He had not quite the same opinion of Osborne that he had of Davies. But probably poor Osborne could not afford the extravagance of a pretty wife like Tom Davies. The story is well known how, when Johnson was earning the most miserable pittance as a Cataloguer for Osborne, he fell out with his employer, and, knocking him down with a folio, called him a blockhead. "Sir, he was impertinent to me, and I beat him," was the Doctor's version of the story afterwards.—HUMPHREYS, ARTHUR L., 1893, *Piccadilly Bookmen: Memorials of the House of Hatchard, p.* 20.

In the whole company of English writers from Chaucer to Carlyle there is no more sharply defined and vigorous personality; none more pronounced, more clearly shown, more easily understood. Evidently the failure of Johnson's work to impress us adequately is in no sense due to lack of individuality behind it; the fact that we are transferring our interest more and more from the work to the man shows clearly enough that the man possessed qualities which his work fails to convey. Johnson's defect as a writer lay in his inability to make his voice distinct; it does not ring clear in perfectly natural tones. When he talked, his words were charged with the electric current of his tremendous personality; when he wrote, the circuit was broken; at some point the current escaped into the air, and the reader never receives any emotion or impulse approaching a shock in intensity. It is probable that the only saving quality in Johnson's work is due to the fact that it helps us to understand him. In most cases we remember the man because of the work he did; in Johnson's case we shall remember the work because of the man who did it.—MABIE, HAMILTON WRIGHT, 1893, *Essays in Literary Interpretation, p.* 21.

He had other intimates, other disciples. But these were Gay Heart [Topham Beauclerk] and Gentle Heart [Bennet Langton] who drove his own blue-devils away with their idolatrous devotion, and whose bearing towards him stands ever as the best possible corroboration of his great and warm nature. With him and for him, they so fill the air of the time that to whomsoever has but thought of them that hour, London must seem lonely without their idyllic figures.

—"Our day is gone;
Clouds, dews, and dangers come; our deeds are done."

There are gods as good for the after years; but Odin is down, and his pair of unreturning birds have flown west and east.—GUINEY, LOUISE IMOGEN, 1894, *A Little English Gallery, p.* 226.

His brain was as big, or bigger, than his heart; it had made itself felt all over England by long, honest work—by brave, loud speech. He had snubbed the elegant Lord Chesterfield, who would have liked to see his name upon the first page of the great Dictionary. Not an outcast of the neighborhood but had heard of his audacious kindness; not a linkboy but knew him by the chink of his half-pence; not a beggar but had been bettered by his generous dole; not a watchman but knew him by his unwieldly hulk, and his awkward, intrepid walk; and we know him,—if we know him at all—not by his "Rambler" and his "Rasselas," so much as by the story of his life.—MITCHELL, DONALD G., 1895, *English Lands Letters and Kings, Queen Anne and the Georges, p.* 105.

We were engaged at extra-illustrating Boswell's life of Johnson, and had already got together somewhat more than eleven thousand prints when we ran against a snag, an obstacle we never could surmount. We agreed that our work would be incomplete, and therefore vain, unless we secured a picture of the book with which the great lexicographer knocked down Osborne, the bookseller at Gray's Inn Gate.—FIELD, EUGENE, 1895, *The Love Affairs of a Bibliomaniac, p,* 149.

"If I had no duties, and no reference to futurity, I would spend my life driving briskly in a post-chaise with a pretty woman." Such was the deliberate pronouncement of a philosopher verging on seventy; and, despite the ominous hint about futurity, it is surely one of the finest compliments ever paid to the sex. What is more, it accurately represents, which few compliments do, the honest conviction of the speaker. We know from his own lips, and the testimony of his friends, that there were two things in which the Doctor's soul delighted—rapid motion, and the society of agreeable young women. Whirling along in a post-chaise was his notion of true enjoyment from a physical point of view; conversing with some sprightly beauty who could understand him and add something to the conversation, his acme of intellectual happiness. For this ordinarily uncouth and quarrelsome old man; this rampaging, browbeating controversialist—who, at other times, betrayed a savage pleasure in flouting the amenities of social intercourse—could change himself into a vastly different monster when in the company of women,—could sheathe his claws, smooth his bristles, and moderate his roar, when they patted and fondled him. What is stranger, he was always ready to forsake his predatory pursuits to the patting and fondling in question.—CRAIG, W. H., 1895, *Doctor Johnson and the Fair Sex, p.* 1.

All competent critics—and he has occupied the most competent—have found it not merely necessary to admit that the man was greater than his works, but not specially easy to indicate the special character of his human greatness. . . . In mere knowledge he might sometimes go wrong; in mere taste, frequently; in crotchet, perpetually. But he was perfectly honest; there was not an atom or a shred of cant in him; his moral nature in his best moments was of the noblest, the kindest, the sanest ever known or even conceivable. We are sometimes told that his greatness is the creation of Boswell. His own age, the age of Burke and Gibbon, was neither foolish nor credulous; it had not read Boswell, and it made no mistake about Johnson. He is not the greatest or the most universal of our men of letters, but he is by far the most English; and very little shame need we take to ourselves so long as we can point to him as our literary embodiment, if not exactly our literary exemplar or masterpiece-—SAINTSBURY, GEORGE, 1896, *Social England, ed. Traill, vol.* V, *p.* 256.

Dr. Samuel Johnson's library, which was sold in 1785, was not a very valuable one. It consisted of 650 lots, which sold for £100. Among them was the second Shakespeare folio, now in the possession of Sir Henry Irving.—WHEATLEY, HENRY B., 1898, *Prices of Books, p.* 141.

POEMS

Perused Johnson's "London" and "Vanity of Human Wishes." His numbers are strong in sense, and smooth in flow, but want that varied grace and inextinguishable spirit which constitute the essential charm of Pope's.—GREEN, THOMAS, 1779–1810, *Diary of a Lover of Literature.*

Dr. Johnson, born no doubt with violent passions, yet with the organs of his senses, thro' which the fancy is stored, if not imperfect, surely far from acute, had from a very early age most cultivated his powers of ratiocination, till by degrees he grew to esteem lightly every other species of excellence: and carrying these ideas into poetry, he was too much inclined to think that to reason in verse, when the harmony of numbers, and especially if something of the ornament of poetical language, was added to the force of truth, was to attain the highest praise of the art.—BRYDGES, SIR SAMUEL EGERTON, 1800, *ed. Phillips's Theatrum Poetarum Anglicanorum, Preface, p.* xlii.

The fame of Dr. Johnson would not have been less widely diffused if the few poetical productions contained in the following pages had never been written; and yet the "Two Satires," and the "Prologue for the Opening of Drury Lane Theatre," are noble productions; and would have been sufficient to throw no mean lustre on the reputation of an ordinary writer. He, like Pope, chose to be the poet of reason; not because he was deficient in imagination, for his Oriental fictions contain much of the elements of the most fanciful poetry, but his mind was so constituted that "he condemned all that had not a direct practical tendency." That he knew how to appreciate the creative faculty of the poet is evident from the character he has drawn of Shakspeare; and he would have done justice to Milton, if his prejudices against the man had not blinded his judgment to the merits of the poet. He had diligently studied the works of Dryden and Pope, and has caught the spirit, vigour and terseness of his great models. . . . Of his lyric effusions much cannot be said: they want the enthusiasm and feeling which is the soul of such compositions. When we recollect the imperfection of two of the senses, sight and hearing, in Johnson, we shall not be surprised that he has not a keen perception of the beauties of nature, or of the powers of harmony; his want of relish for descriptive poetry, and pastoral cannot therefore be wondered at; nor his want of success in his "Odes on the Seasons." He does not paint from nature, but from books.—SINGER, S. W., 1822, *British Poets, Chiswick, ed. vol.* 67, *pp.* 148, 149.

That his Tragedy ("Irene") was a great failure on the stage has been already related; that it is of extreme dulness, of a monotony altogether insufferable, and therefore tires out the reader's patience quite as much as it did the auditor's, is true; that most of his lesser pieces are only things of easy and of fairly successful execution is likewise certain, with perhaps the exception of his verses on Robert Levett's death, which have a sweetness and a tenderness seldom found in any of his compositions. But had he never written anything after the "Imitations of Juvenal," his name would have gone down to posterity as a poet of great excellence,—one who only did not reach equal celebrity with Pope, because he came after him, and did not assiduously court the muse. In truth, these two pieces are admirable, both for their matter, their diction, and their versification. . . . Of Johnson's Latin verses it remains to speak, and they assuredly do not rise to the level of his English, nor indeed above mediocrity. The translation of Pope's "Messiah," however, a work of his boyhood, gave a promise not fulfilled in his riper years.—BROUGHAM, HENRY LORD, 1845, *Lives of Men of Letters of the Time of George III.*

He was a poet of no mean order. His resonant lines, informed as they often are with the force of their author's character—his strong sense, his fortitude, his gloom—take possession of the memory, and suffuse themselves through one's entire system of thought.—BIRRELL, AUGUSTINE, 1887, *Obiter Dicta, Second Series, p.* 130.

Dr. Johnson's epitaph on his friend Levett is as prosaic a poem as ever was written, and as strong a one. It is perhaps the only friendly epitaph in the language that contains no compliment to the object of it, in excess of the bare truth, and what Dr. Johnson could do with no other fuel to feed a genius that was never poetic in its essence, than the bare truth, is shown by the splendid culmination of the last four lines.—CRAWFURD, OSWALD, 1896, *ed., Lyrical Verse from Elizabeth to Victoria, p.* 431, *note.*

His work in verse is very small, and though all of it is scholarly and some elegant, it is universally composed in obedience to a very narrow and jejune theory of English versification and English poetics generally. Nothing perhaps but the beautiful epitaph on his friend Levett, and the magnificent statement of his religious pessimism in the "Vanity of Human Wishes," distinctly transcends mediocrity. — SAINTSBURY, GEORGE, 1898, *A Short History of English Literature*, p. 615.

LONDON
1739

"London" is to me one of those few imitations that have all the ease and all the spirit of an original. The same man's verses on the opening of Garrick's theatre are far from bad.—GRAY, THOMAS, 1751? *Letter to Horace Walpole; Works, ed. Gosse, vol.* II, *p.* 220.

This poem of Mr. Johnson's is the best imitation of the original that has appeared in our language, being possessed of all the force and satirical resentment of Juvenal. Imitation gives us a much truer idea of the ancients than ever translation could do. — GOLDSMITH, OLIVER, 1767, *The Beauties of English Poetry*.

Dr. Johnson's "London, a Satire," is a noble poem. But his great moral genius was constrained in composition by the perpetual parody on his powerful prototype, Juvenal. To have shown so much genius and so much ingenuity at one and the same tlme, to have been so original even in imitation, places him in the highest order of minds. But his range was here circumscribed; for he had to move parallel with the Roman,—finding out in every passage corresponding and kindred sins,—and in order to preserve—which he did wondrously—the similitude—

"To bridle in his struggling muse with pain,
Which long'd to launch into a nobler strain."

—WILSON, JOHN, 1828, *The Man of Ton, Blackwood's Magazine, vol.* 23, *p.* 835.

"London" is marked by genuine public spirit; at the same time we see quite as much of the man as of the moralist in the poet's characteristic allusions to the penalties of poverty, his antipathy to the Whigs, and his dislike of foreigners. The story that "Thales" was meant for Savage, and that the occasion of the poem was the departure of the latter from London after his trial, is confuted by dates, but we may be sure that the poem gives us a real representation of Johnson's feelings as a struggling author and a political partisan. — COURTHOPE, WILLIAM JOHN, 1880, *English Poets, ed. Ward, vol.* III, *p.* 246.

LIFE OF SAVAGE
1744

No finer specimen of literary biography existed in any language, living or dead; and a discerning critic might have confidently predicted that the author was destined to be the founder of a new school of English eloquence.—MACAULAY, THOMAS BABINGTON, 1843, *Samuel Johnson, Critical and Historical Essays*.

In its early days Johnson was the chief contributor to its pages. [*The Gentleman's Magazine*]. He had a room set apart for him at St. John's Gate, where he wrote as fast as he could drive his pen, throwing the sheets off, when completed, to the "copy" boy. The "Life of Savage" was written anonymously, in 1744, and Mr. Harte spoke in high terms of the book, while dining with Cave. The publisher told him afterwards: "Harte, you made a man very happy the other day at my house by your praise of 'Savage's Life.'" "How so? none were present but you and I." Cave replied, "You might observe I sent a plate of victuals behind the screen; there lurked one whose dress was too shabby for him to appear; your praise pleased him much."—CURWEN, HENRY, 1873, *A History of Booksellers*, p. 59.

The best extant illustration of the life of the struggling authors of the time.—STEPHEN, LESLIE, 1879, *Samuel Johnson* (*English Men of Letters*), *p.* 29.

It is the longest and most elaborate of Johnson's essays in biography, and may still be read with great pleasure, in spite of various patent faults. It recounted, with all detail, a scandal, into the truth of which Johnson had not taken the pains to inquire; it was but careless in the statement of fact which lay easily within the writer's circle of experience; and it treated with extreme indulgence a character which, in a stranger, would have called down the moralist's sternest reproof. The critical passages now escape censure only because so few in the present day read the works examined. But the little book was undeniably lively; it contained several anecdotes admirably narrated, and its graver parts displayed the development of Johnson's studied magnificence of language. Good biography was still rare in England, and "The Account of Savage" attracted a great deal of notice.—GOSSE, EDMUND, 1888, *A History of Eighteenth Century Literature, p.* 285.

VANITY OF HUMAN WISHES
1749

"The Vanity of Human Wishes" is, in the opinion of the best judges, as high an effort of ethick poetry as any language can shew. The instances of variety of disappointment are chosen so judiciously and painted so strongly, that, the moment they are read, they bring conviction to every thinking mind. That of the scholar must have depressed the too sanguine expectations of many an ambitious student. That of the warrior, Charles of Sweden, is, I think, as highly finished a picture as can possibly be conceived.—BOSWELL, JAMES, 1791–93, *Life of Samuel Johnson, ed. Hill, vol.* I, *p.* 225.

The "Vanity of Human Wishes," the subject of which is in a great degree founded on the Alcibiades of Plato, possesses not the point and fire which animates the "London." It breathes, however, a strain of calm and dignified philosophy, much more pleasing to the mind, and certainly much more consonant to truth, than the party exaggeration of the prior satire. The poet's choice of modern examples, in place of those brought forward by the ancient bard, is happy and judicious; and he has everywhere availed himself, and in a style the most impressive, of the solemnity, the pathos, and sublime morality of the christian code. In consequence of this substitution of a purer system of ethics, and of a striking selection of characters, among which that of Charles of Sweden is conspicuously eminent, the whole has the air of an original, and, to be understood, requires not to be collated with its prototype.—DRAKE, NATHAN, 1809, *Essays Illustrative of the Rambler, Adventurer, and Idler, vol.* I, *p.* 135.

Read Johnson's "Vanity of Human Wishes,"—all the examples and mode of giving them sublime, as well as the latter part, with the exception of an occasional couplet. I do not so much admire the opening. I remember an observation of Sharpe's (the *Conversationist*, as he was called in London, and a very clever man), that the first line of his poem was superfluous, and that Pope (the very best of poets, I think), would have begun at once, only changing the punctuation,—

"Survey mankind from China to Peru."

The former line, "Let observation," &c., is certainly heavy and useless. But 'tis a grand poem—and so *true!* true as the tenth of Juvenal himself. The lapse of ages *changes* all things,—time—language—the earth—the bounds of the sea—the stars of the sky, and every thing "about, around, and underneath" man, *except man himself*, who has always been, and always will be, an unlucky rascal. The infinite variety of lives conduct but to death, and the infinity of wishes lead but to disappointment.—BYRON, LORD, 1821, *Diary, Ravenna, Jan.* 9.

The deep and pathetic morality of which has often extracted tears from those whose eyes wander dry over pages professedly sentimental.—SCOTT, SIR WALTER, 1823, *Samuel Johnson.*

Tennyson admired Samuel Johnson's grave earnestness, and said that certain of his couplets, for these qualities and for their "high moral tone," were not surpassed in English satire. However, he ventured to make merry over:

"Let observation, with extensive view,
Survey mankind, from China to Peru."

"Why did he not say 'Let observation, with extended observation, observe extensively?' "—TENNYSON, ALFRED LORD, 1869, *A Memoir by His Son, vol.* II, *p.* 73.

Its strong Stoical morality, its profound and melancholy illustrations of the old and ever new sentiment, *Vanitas Vanitatum*, make it perhaps the most impressive poem of the kind in the language.—STEPHEN, LESLIE, 1879, *Samuel Johnson (English Men of Letters), p.* 35.

IRENE
1749

Though uninteresting on the stage, was universally admired in the closet, for the propriety of the sentiments, the richness of the language, and the general harmony of the whole composition.—MURPHY, ARTHUR, 1792, *An Essay on the Life and Genius of Samuel Johnson.*

In his tragedy, the dramatis personæ are like so many statues "stept from their pedestal to take the air." They come on the stage only to utter pompous sentiments of morality, turgid declamation, and frigid similes. Yet there is throughout, that strength of language, that heavy mace of words, with which, as with the flail of Talus, Johnson lays everything prostrate before him. — CARY, HENRY FRANCIS, 1821-24-45, *Lives of English Poets*, *p.* 90.

Even the mighty intellect, the eloquent morality, and lofty style of Johnson, which gave too tragic and magnificent a tone to his ordinary writing, failed altogether to support him in his attempt to write actual tragedy; and "Irene" is not only unworthy of the imitator of "Juvenal" and the author of "Rasselas" and the "Lives of the Poets," but is absolutely, and in itself, nothing better than a tissue of wearisome and unimpassioned declamations.—JEFFREY, FRANCIS LORD, 1822-44, *Contributions to the Edinburgh Review, vol.* II, *p.* 334.

One of the heaviest and most unreadable of dramatic performances, interesting now, if interesting at all, solely as a curious example of the result of bestowing great powers upon a totally uncongenial task.—STEPHEN, LESLIE, 1879, *Samuel Johnson* (*English Men of Letters*), *p.* 36.

There are several accounts extant by those who were present on the first night, but that which Dr. Adams gave Boswell is perhaps the most trustworthy. "Before the curtain drew up there were catcalls whistling which alarmed Johnson's friends. The prologue, which was written by himself in a manly strain, soothed the audience, and the play went off tolerably till it came to the conclusion, when Mrs. Pritchard, the heroine of the piece, was to be strangled on the stage, and was to speak two lines with the bow-string round her neck. The audience cried out 'Murder! Murder!' She several times attempted to speak, but in vain. At last she was obliged to go off the stage alive." The author's annoyance at this interruption must have been a good deal alleviated by the triumph it gave him over Garrick, at whose suggestion the strangling scene had been arranged. Dr. Burney's version is more favourable, but he speaks of a curious story circulated at the time of the author's being "observed at the representation to be dissatisfied with some of the speeches and conduct of the play himself, and, like La Fontaine, expressing his disapprobation aloud." Old Aaron Hill, one of the heroes of "The Dunciad," who had composed much bad poetry and worse prose, and whose critical judgment may be estimated by his prediction of his own posthumous fame and of Pope's speedy oblivion, wrote to Mallet: "I was at the anomalous Mr. Johnson's benefit, and found the play his proper representative; strong sense, ungraced by sweetness or decorum." Though Irene was not a great success, it escaped positive failure, and Johnson received from copyright and "author's nights," very nearly three hundred pounds.—GRANT, FREDERICK RICHARD CHARLES, 1887, *Samuel Johnson* (*Great Writers*), *p.* 56.

THE RAMBLER
1750-52

I am inexpressibly pleased with them. . . . I hope the world tastes them; for its own sake I hope the world tastes them. . . . I would not, for any consideration, that they should be laid down through discouragement.—RICHARDSON, SAMUEL, 1750, *Letter to Cave, Aug.* 9.

"The Rambler," is certainly a strong misnomer: he always plods in the beaten road of his predecessors, following the "Spectator" (with the same pace as a packhorse would do a hunter) in the style that is proper to lengthen a paper. These writers may, perhaps, be of service to the public, which is saying a great deal in their favour. There are numbers of both sexes who never read anything but such productions, and cannot spare time, from doing nothing, to go through a sixpenny pamphlet. Such gentle readers may be improved by a moral hint, which, though repeated over and over, from generation to generation, they never heard in their lives. I should be glad to know the name of this laborious author.—MONTAGU, LADY MARY WORTLEY, 1754, *Letter to the Countess of Bute, June* 23; *Works, ed. Dallaway, vol.* IV, *p.* 220.

I have lately been reading one or two volumes of "The Rambler;" who, excepting against some few hardnesses in his manner, and the want of more examples to enliven, is one of the most nervous, most perspicuous, most concise (and) most harmonious prose writers I know. A learned diction improves by time.—SHENSTONE, WILLIAM, 1760, *Letter to Mr. Graves, Feb.* 9.

The "Rambler" may be considered as

Johnson's great work. It was the basis of that high reputation which went on increasing to the end of his days. The circulation of those periodical essays was not, at first, equal to their merit. They had not, like the "Spectators," the art of charming by variety; and indeed how could it be expected? The wits of Queen Anne's reign sent their contributions to the "Spectator;" and Johnson stood alone. A stage coach, says Sir Richard Steele, must go forward on stated days, whether there are passengers or not. So it was with the "Rambler," every Tuesday and Saturday, for two years. In this collection Johnson is the great moral teacher of his countrymen; his essays form a body of ethics; the observations on life and manners are acute and instructive; and the papers, professedly critical, serve to promote the cause of literature It must, however, be acknowledged, that a settled gloom hangs over the author's mind; and all the essays, except eight or ten, coming from the same fountain-head, no wonder that they have the raciness of the soil from which they spring. Of this uniformity Johnson was sensible. . . . It is remarkable, that the pomp of diction, which has been objected in to Johnson, was first assumed in the "Rambler." His "Dictionary" was going on at the same time, and, in the course of that work, as he grew familiar with technical and scholastic words, he thought that the bulk of his readers were equally learned; or at least would admire the splendour and dignity of the style.—MURPHY, ARTHUR, 1792, *An Essay on the Life and Genius of Samuel Johnson.*

His "Ramblers" are in everybody's hands; about them opinions vary, and I rather believe the style of these essays is not now considered as a good model, this he corrected in his more advanced age, as may be seen in his "Lives of the Poets," where his diction, though occasionally elaborate and highly metaphorical, is not nearly so inflated and ponderous as in the "Ramblers."—CUMBRELAND, RICHARD, 1806, *Memoirs Written by Himself, vol.* I, *p.* 362.

The mass of intellectual wealth here heaped together is immense, but it is rather the result of gradual accumulation, the produce of the general intellect, labouring in the mine of knowledge and reflection, than dug out of the quarry, and dragged into the light by the industry and sagacity of a single mind. I am not here saying that Dr. Johnson was a man without originality, compared with the ordinary run of men's minds, but he was not a man of original thought or genius, in the sense in which Montaigne or Lord Bacon was. He opened no new vein of precious ore, nor did he light upon any single pebbles of uncommon size and unrivalled lustre.—HAZLITT, WILLIAM, 1818, *Lectures on the English Comic Writers, Lecture* v.

Dr. Johnson seems to have been really more powerful in discoursing *vivâ voce* in conversation than with his pen in hand. It seems as if the excitement of company called something like reality and consecutiveness into his reasonings, which in his writings I cannot see. His antitheses are almost always verbal only; and sentence after sentence in the "Rambler" may be pointed out to which you cannot attach any definite meaning whatever. In his political pamphlets there is more truth of expression than in his other works, for the same reason that his conversation is better than his writings in general. He was more excited and in earnest.—COLERIDGE, SAMUEL TAYLOR, 1833, *Table Talk, ed. Ashe, Nov.* 1, *p.* 266.

It would not be easy to name a book more tiresome, indeed, more difficult to read, or one which gives moral lessons, in a more frigid tone, with less that is lively or novel in the matter, in a language more heavy and monotonous. The measured pace, the constant balance of the style, becomes quite intolerable; for there is no interesting truth to be inculcated remote from common observation, nor is there any attack carried on against difficult positions, nor any satirical warfare maintained either with opinions or with persons.—BROUGHAM, HENRY LORD, 1845, *Lives of Men of Letters of the Time of George III.*

It has been asked, with emphasis, "Who now reads the 'Rambler?' " And it is indubitable that this book, which once exerted so mighty an influence on the English language and people, has given place, at least in general reading, to works of far inferior merit and interest. The reason seems to be, that its object is well nigh accomplished. It commenced with a standard of morals and language elevated far above the prevailing style of morals and of writing. It has elevated both, and has brought the English language and notions of morality to its *own level.* Nor is it wonderful that men should regard with less interest a work which *now* is seen to have no very extraordinary elevation. It is a component part of English literature, having *fixed* itself in the language, the style, and the morals of the English people, and taken its place as an integral, almost undistinguished, part of the national principles of writing and morality. The result is that, while the *benefits* of the "Rambler" may be diffusing themselves, unperceived, to almost all the endearments of the fireside and virtues of the community, the book itself may be very imperfectly known and unfrequently perused. Johnson may be almost forgotten, except in praise; but his mighty power is yet sending forth a mild influence over lands and seas, like the gentle movements of the dew and the sunbeam.—BARNES, ALBERT, 1855, *Miscellaneous Essays and Reviews, vol.* I, *p.* 126.

The "Rambler" is not a book to be opened in a careless moment, for the style is out of fashion; but it requires a reader of little sagacity to penetrate to its profound stores of thought and feeling; and as he pursues his way through apologues and allegories, he will be rewarded by many delightful sketches of character, enlivened by jest and humor.—DUYCKINCK, EVERT A., 1873, *Portrait Gallery of Eminent Men and Women, vol.* I, *p.* 19.

The pompous and involved language seems indeed to be a fit clothing for the melancholy reflections which are its chief staple, and in spite of its unmistakable power it is as heavy reading as the heavy class of lay-sermonizing to which it belongs.—STEPHEN, LESLIE, 1879, *Samuel Johnson (English Men of Letters), p.* 40.

The wonder is that Johnson should have managed to continue it for two years, and that with its many obvious defects he should have been able to win for it at last a very substantial popularity. Too much stress is sometimes laid on the pomposity of his diction. For serious topics, which were avowedly his chief aim, his style is well suited, and his use of a balanced, periodic structure, if ludicrous when misapplied, is certainly impressive when it is made the vehicle of his moralizings. . . . Johnson was far from being a pedant, but he wanted the agility to make a graceful descent from the pinnacles of art, and he had not the supreme requisite of being able to conceal the condescensions of learning.—LOBBAN, J. H., 1896, *English Essays, Introduction, pp.* xli, xlii.

Although his essays have been oftener under—than over-valued of late, they are far from original in conception, and those at least of the "Rambler" are too often injured by the excessively stiff and cumbrous style which has been rather unjustly identified with Johnson's manner of writing generally.—SAINTSBURY, GEORGE, 1898, *A Short History of English Literature, p.* 615.

DICTIONARY
1755

I think the publick in general, and the republick of letters in particular, are greatly obliged to Mr. Johnson, for having undertaken, and executed, so great and desirable a work. Perfection is not to be expected from man; but if we are to judge by the various works of Johnson already published, we have good reason to believe, that he will bring this as near to perfection as any man could do. The *plan* of it, which he published some years ago, seems to be a proof of it. Nothing can be more rationally imagined, or more accurately and elegantly expressed. I therefore recommend the previous perusal of it to all those who intend to buy the Dictionary, and who, I suppose, are all those who can afford it. . . . It must be owned, that our language is, at present, in a state of anarchy, and hitherto, perhaps, it may not have been the worse for it. During our free and open trade, many words and expressions have been imported, adopted, and naturalized from other languages, which have greatly enriched our own. Let it still preserve what real strength and beauty it may have borrowed from others; but let it not, like the Tarpeian maid, be overwhelmed and crushed by unnecessary ornaments. The time for discrimination seems to be now come. Toleration, adoption, and naturalization have run their lengths. Good order and authority are now necessary. But where shall we find them, and, at the same time, the obedience due to them? We must have recourse to the old Roman expedient in times of confusion, and chuse a dictator. Upon this principle, I give my vote for Mr. Johnson to fill that great and arduous post. And I hereby declare, that I make a total surrender of all my rights and privileges in the English language, as a free-born British subject, to the said Mr. Johnson, during the term of his dictatorship. Nay more, I will not only obey him, like an old Roman, as my dictator, but, like a modern Roman, I will implicitly believe in him as my Pope, and hold him to be infallible while in the chair, but no longer. More than this he cannot well require; for, I presume, that obedience can never be expected, when there is neither terrour to enforce, nor interest to invite it. . . . But a Grammar, a Dictionary, and a History of our Language through its several stages, were still wanting at home, and importunately called for from abroad. Mr. Johnson's labours will now, I dare say, very fully supply that want, and greatly contribute to the farther spreading of our language in other countries. Learners were discouraged, by finding no standard to resort to; and, consequently, thought it incapable of any. They will now be undeceived and encouraged.—CHESTERFIELD, PHILIP DORMER STANHOPE LORD (ADAM FITZ-ADAM), *The World*, 1754, *Nov.* 28, *Dec.* 5.

Talk of war with a Briton, he'll boldly advance,
That one English soldier will beat ten of France;
Would we alter the boast from the sword to the pen,
Our odds are still greater, still greater our men:
In the deep mines of science though Frenchmen may toil,
Can their strength be compared to Locke, Newton, and Boyle?
Let them rally their heroes, send forth all their pow'rs,
Their verse-men, and prose-men; then match them with ours.
First Shakespeare and Milton, like gods in the fight,
Have put their whole drama and epic to flight;
In satires, epistles, and odes would they cope,
Their numbers retreat before Dryden and Pope;
And Johnson, well-arm'd, like a hero of yore,
Has beat forty French, and will beat forty more.

—GARRICK, DAVID, 1755, *On Johnson's Dictionary.*

Johnson's Dictionary is a most important, and, considered as the work of one man, a most wonderful performance. It does honour to England, and to human genius; and proves, that there is still left among us a force of mind equal to that which formerly distinguished a Stephanus or a Varro. Its influence in diffusing the knowledge of the language, and retarding its decline, is already observable:

Si Pergama dextra
Desendi possent, etiam hac defensa fuissent.

And yet, within the last twenty years, and since this great work was published, a multitude of new words have found their way into the English tongue, and, though both unauthorised and unnecessary, seem likely to remain in it.—BEATTIE, JAMES, 1769, *Remarks on the Usefulness of Classical Learning.*

Such is the merit, . . . that our language does not possess a more copious, learned, and valuable work.—HARRIS, JAMES, 1781, *Philological Inquiries.*

The definitions have always appeared to me such astonishing proofs of acuteness of intellect and precision of language, as indicate a genius of the highest rank. This it is which marks the superiour excellence of Johnson's "Dictionary" over others equally or even more voluminous, and must have made it a work of much greater mental labour than mere Lexicons, or *Word-books*, as the Dutch call them. They, who will make the experiment of trying how they can define a few words of whatever nature, will soon be satisfied of the unquestionable justice of this observation, which I can assure my readers is founded upon much study, and upon communication with more minds than my own. A few of his definitions must be admitted to be erroneous. Thus, *Windward* and *Leeward*, though directly of opposite meaning, are defined identically the same way; as to which inconsiderable specks it is enough to observe, that his Preface announces that he was aware there might be many such in so immense a work; nor was he at all disconcerted when an instance was pointed out to him. A lady once asked him how he came to define *Pastern* the *knee* of a horse: instead of making an elaborate defense, as she expected, he at once answered, "Ignorance, Madam, pure ignorance."—BOSWELL, JAMES, 1791–1793, *Life of Samuel Johnson.*

From a careful examination of this work, and its effect upon the language, I am inclined to believe that Johnson's authority has multiplied instead of reducing the number of corruptions in the English language. . . . I can assure the American public that the errors in Johnson's "Dictionary" are ten times as numerous as they suppose; and that the confidence now reposed in its accuracy is the greatest injury to philology that now exists. I can assure them further that if any man, whatever may be his abilities in other respects, should attempt to compile a new dictionary, or amend Johnson's, without a profound knowledge of etymology, he will unquestionably do as much harm as good.—WEBSTER, NOAH, 1807, *A letter to Dr. David Ramsay, of Charleston, Respecting the Errors in Johnson's Dictionary.*

Had Johnson left nothing but his "Dictionary," one might have traced there a great intellect, a genuine man. Looking to its clearness of definition, its general solidity, honesty, insight, and successful method, it may be called the best of all dictionaries. There is in it a kind of architectural nobleness; it stands there like a great solid square-built edifice, finished, symmetrically complete: you judge that a true builder did it.—CARLYLE, THOMAS, 1841, *On Heroes and Hero-Worship.*

The public, on this occasion, did Johnson full justice, and something more than justice. The best lexicographer may well be content if his productions are received by the world with cold esteem. But Johnson's Dictionary was hailed with an enthusiasm such as no similar work has ever excited. It was indeed the first dictionary which could be read with pleasure. The definitions shows so much acuteness of thought and command of language, and the passages from poets, divines, and philosophers are so skilfully selected, that a leisure hour may always be very agreeably spent in turning over the pages. The faults of the book resolve themselves, for the most part, into one great fault. Johnson was a wretched etymologist. He knew little or nothing of any Teutonic language except English, which indeed, as he wrote it, was scarcely a Teutonic language; and thus he was absolutely at the mercy of Junius and Skinner.—MACAULAY, THOMAS BABINGTON, 1843, *Samuel Johnson, Critical and Historical Essays.*

What the middle of the last century has to be proud of is, Dr. Johnson's colossal work, the first great Dictionary of our language.—REED, HENRY, 1855, *Lectures on English Literature from Chaucer to Tennyson*, p. 240.

Dr. Johnson was the Magnus Apollo of lexicographers then, and his bulky fame still casts a large shadow over the world of words. To rebel against his autocratic rule at the beginning of this century was to write one's self down an audacious and presuming sciolist. It is not surprising, therefore, that Webster's criticism of Johnson in this Dictionary and in other places should have exposed him to censure.—SCUDDER, HORACE E., 1881, *Noah Webster (American Men of Letters)*, p. 218.

An ignorant philologist, following in the track of still more ignorant predecessors.—MACKAY, CHARLES, 1887, *Through the Long Day, vol.* II, *p.* 395.

The publication of Johnson's Dictionary was as the cloud no bigger than a man's hand, heralding the downfall of the patronage system; and the indignant though dignified letter of wounded pride and surly independence which he wrote on February 7, 1755, to the courtly Earl of Chesterfield, who had professed much but had performed little for him at a time when he was friendless and unknown, was as the shrill blast of a trumpeter proclaiming in plain and unmistakable terms that the winter of individual patronage was past and that the summer of public patronage had begun.—SIDNEY, WILLIAM CONNOR, 1891, *England and the English in the Eighteenth Century, vol.* II, *p.* 128.

It was a great advance upon its predecessors. The general excellence of its definitions and the judicious selection of illustrative passages make it (as often observed) entertaining as well as useful for reference. Its most obvious defect arises from Johnson's ignorance of the early forms of the language and from the conception then natural of the purpose of a dictionary. Johnson (see his preface) had sensibly abandoned his first impression that he might be able to "fix the language," as he came to see that every living language must grow. He did not aim, however, at tracing the growth historically, but simply at defining the actual senses of words as employed by the "best authors." He held that the language had reached almost its fullest development in the days of Shakespeare, Hooker, Bacon, and Spenser, and thought it needless to go further back than Sidney. He also, as a rule, omitted living authors. The dictionary, therefore, was of no philological value, although it has been the groundwork upon which many later philologists have worked. Taking for granted the contemporary view of the true end of a dictionary, it was a surprising achievement, and made an epoch in the study of the language.—STEPHEN, LESLIE, 1892, *Dictionary of National Biography, vol.* XXX, *p.* 37.

That Dictionary did ultimately give him a great lift—as it has to a good many, since. The ponderous volume furnished very many New England households seventy years ago; and I can remember sitting upon it, in my child-days, to bring my head properly above the level of the table.—MITCHELL, DONALD G., 1895, *English Lands Letters and Kings, Queen Anne and the Georges, p.* 97.

RASSELAS
1759

I have lately read the "Prince of Abyssinia"—I am almost equally charm'd and shocked at it—the style, the sentiments are inimitable—but the subject is dreadful —and handled as it is by Dr. Johnson, might make *any* young, perhaps old, person tremble.—BURNEY, FRANCES, 1768, *Early Diary, ed. Ellis, July* 17, *vol.* I, *p.* 14.

I wish I were not warranted in saying, that this elegant work is rendered, by its most obvious moral, of little benefit to the reader. We would not indeed wish to see the rising generation so unprofitably employed as the Prince of Abyssinia; but it is equally impolitic to repress all hope, and he who should quit his father's house in search of a profession, and return unprovided, because he could not find any man pleased with his own, would need a better justification than that Johnson, after speculatively surveying various modes of life, had judged happiness unattainable, and choice useless.—HAWKINS, SIR JOHN, 1787, *The Life of Samuel Johnson, p.* 371.

To those who look no further than the present life, or who maintain that human nature has not fallen from the state in which it was created, the instruction of this sublime story will be of no avail. But they who think justly, and feel with strong sensibility, will listen with eagerness and admiration to its truth and wisdom. Voltaire's "Candide," written to refute the system of Optimism, which it has accomplished with brilliant success, is wonderfully similar in its plan and conduct to Johnson's Rasselas; Insomuch, that I have heard Johnson say, that if they had not been published so closely one after another that there was not time for imitation, it would have been in vain to deny that the scheme of that which came latest was taken from the other. Though the proposition illustrated by both these works was the same, namely, that in our present state there is more evil than good, the intention of the writers was very different. Voltaire, I am afraid, meant only by wanton profaneness to obtain a sportive victory over religion, and to discredit the belief of a superintending Providence: Johnson meant, by shewing the unsatisfactory nature of things temporal, to direct the hopes of man to things eternal. "Rasselas," as was observed to me by a very accomplished lady, may be considered as a more enlarged and more deeply philosophical discourse in prose, upon the interesting truth, which in his "Vanity of Human Wishes" he had so successfully enforced in verse.—BOSWELL, JAMES, 1791–93, *Life of Samuel Johnson, ed. Hill, vol.* I. *p.* 396.

No prig shall ever persuade me that "Rasselas" is not a noble performance, in design and in execution. Never were the expenses of a mother's funeral more gloriously defrayed by a son than the funeral of Samuel Johnson's mother by the price of "Rasselas," written for the pious purpose of laying her head decently and honourably in the dust.—WILSON, JOHN, 1829, *Noctes Ambrosianæ, April.*

The reader who first attempts the "Abyssinian Candide" feels that he has imposed on himself a task rather than found a pleasure, or even a relaxation. The manner is heavy, and little suited to the occasion; the matter is of a very ordinary fabric, if it is safe and wholesome; there is nothing that shines except the author's facility of writing in a very artificial style, as soon as we are informed, by external evidence, of the whole having been written in a few nights. He, perhaps, had some kind of misgiving that it was not a successful effort, for he had never looked at it till two-and-twenty years after it was written, when a friend happening to have it who was travelling with him, Johnson read it with some eagerness.—BROUGHAM, HENRY LORD, 1845, *Lives of Men of Letters of the time of George III.*

So on the story rolls, poetic and gloomy, like a bit of the Black Sea!—MASSON, DAVID, 1859, *British Novelists and Their Styles, p.* 151.

All the sterner traits of Johnson's character, his uncompromising rectitude, his steadiness of outlook on unrelieved gloom, his hatred of sentimental and unthinking optimism, have left their mark on "Rasselas."—RALEIGH, WALTER, 1894, *The English Novel, p.* 205.

This elephantine novelette has a host of excellent and eloquent moral reflections in it, shouldering and elbowing themselves out from its flimsy dress of fiction.—MITCHELL, DONALD G., 1895, *English Lands Letters and Kings, Queen Anne and the Georges, p.* 106.

"Rasselas," struck off at a heat when his mother lay dying, tells in prose what the "Vanity of Human Wishes" tells in verse. It is little known to the modern reader, who is not easily reconciled to its style. At no time could it have been a favorite with the young and thoughtless. Nevertheless, as years steal over us, we own, as we lay it down with a sigh, that it gives a view of life as profound and true as it is sad.—HILL, GEORGE BIRKBECK, 1897, *Library of the World's Best Literature, ed. Warner, vol.* XIV, *p.* 8288.

EDITION OF SHAKESPEARE
1765

The praise is due of having first adopted and carried into execution Dr. Johnson's admirable plan of illustrating Shakspeare by the study of writers of his own time. By following this track, most of the difficulties of the author have been overcome, his meaning (in many instances apparently lost) has been recovered, and much wild unfounded conjecture has been happily got rid of. By perseverance in this plan, he effected more to the elucidation of his author than any if not all his predecessors, and justly entitled himself to the distinction of being confessed the best editor of Shakspeare.—REED, ISAAC, 1785–1803, *ed. Shakspeare, vol.* I, *p.* 3.

Johnson compares him who should endeavour to recommend this poet by passages unconnectedly torn from his works, to the pedant in Hierocles who exhibited a brick as a sample of his house. And yet how little, and how very unsatisfactorily, does he himself speak of the pieces considered as a whole! Let any man, for instance, bring together the short characters which he gives at the close of each play, and see if the aggregate will amount to that sum of admiration which he himself, at his outset, has stated as the correct standard for the appreciation of the poet.—SCHLEGEL, AUGUSTUS WILLIAM, 1809, *Dramatic Art and Literature, Lecture* xii.

Johnson explained much well, but there is something magisterial in the manner wherein he dismisses each play like a boy's exercise, that irritates the reader. His criticism is frequently judicious, but betrays no ardent admiration for Shakspeare.—HALLAM, HENRY, 1837–39, *Introduction to the Literature of Europe, pt.* iii, *ch.* vi, *par.* 54.

Garrick got a better hold of Shakespeare's thought than Dr. Johnson, the John Bull of erudition on whose nose Queen Mab must have skipped about queerly enough, whilst he was writing about the "Midsummer Night's Dream." He certainly did not know why Shakespeare occasioned him more involuntary irritation and desire to sneeze than any other of the poets he criticised.—HEINE, HEINRICH, 1838–95, *Notes on Shakespeare Heroines, tr. Benecke, p.* 34.

When Johnson had issued his proposals twenty years before for an edition of Shakespeare, he pointed to a great novelty for the elucidation of the poet. His intuitive sagacity had discerned that a poet so racy and native required a familiarity both with the idiom and the manners of his age. He was sensible that a complete explanation of an author, not systematic and consequential, but desultory and vagrant, abounding in casual allusions and slight hints, is not to be expected from any single scholiast. He enumerates, however, the desiderata for this purpose; among which we find that of reading the books which Shakespeare read, and to compare his works with those of writers who lived at the same time, or immediately preceded, or immediately followed him. This project, happily conceived, inferred comprehensive knowledge in the proposer; but it was only a reverie,—a dim Pisgah view which the sagacity of the great critic had taken of that future Canaan, which he himself never entered. With this sort of knowledge, and these forgotten writers, which the future commentators of Shakespeare revelled in, Johnson remained wholly unacquainted. But what proved more fatal to the editorial ability of Johnson than this imperfect knowledge of the literature and the manners of the age of Shakespeare, was that the commentator rarely sympathized with the poet; for his hard-witted and unpliant faculties, busied with the more palpable forms of human nature, when thrown amid the supernatural and the ideal, seemed suddenly deserted of their powers: the magic knot was tied which cast our Hercules into helpless impotence; and, in the circle of imaginative creation, we discover the baffled sage resisting the spell by apologizing for Shakespeare's introduction of his mighty preternatural beings!—DISRAELI, ISAAC, 1841, *Shakespeare, Amenities of Literature.*

He would doubtless have admitted that it would be the height of absurdity, in a man who was not familiar with the works of Æschylus and Euripides to publish an edition of Sophocles. Yet he ventured to publish an edition of Shakspeare, without having ever in his life, as far as can be discovered, read a single scene of Massinger, Ford, Decker, Webster, Marlow, Beaumont, or Fletcher.—MACAULAY, THOMAS BABINGTON, 1843, *Samuel Johnson, Critical and Historical Essays.*

The larger portion of Johnson's Preface not only to a certain extent represented the tone of opinion in Johnson's age, but was written with so much pomp of diction, with such apparent candour, and with such abundant manifestations of good sense, that, perhaps more than any other production, it has influenced the public opinion of Shakspere up to this day. That the influence has been, for the most part, evil, we have no hesitation in believing.—KNIGHT, CHARLES, 1849, *Studies of Shakspere.*

It is giving the Doctor but little praise to say that he was a better editor than his Reverend predecessor. The majority of his emendations of the text were, nevertheless, singularly unhappy; and his notes, though often learned and sometimes sensible, were generally wanting in just that sort of learning and sense most needful for his task. Strange as it may seem, no one who himself appreciates Shakespeare, can read Johnson's comments and verbal criticisms upon his plays without the conviction that to the "great moralist," the grandest inspirations and most exquisitely wrought fancies of the great dramatist were as a sealed book. Many an humble individual whom the learned bear growled at—we do not hesitate to include even "Bozzy" himself—appreciated Shakespeare better than the literary dictator did.— WHITE, RICHARD GRANT, 1854, *Shakespeare's Scholar, p.* 12.

JOURNEY TO THE WESTERN ISLANDS OF SCOTLAND
1775

Dr. Johnson has just published his Journey thro' the western isles; I have read it, and you should read it. It is quite a sentimental Journey, divested of all natural history and antiquities; but full of good sense, and new and peculiar reflections.—WHITE, GILBERT, 1775, *Letter to Rev. John White, Feb.* 1; *Life and Letters of Gilbert White, ed. Holt-White, vol.* I, *p.* 277.

His "Journey to the Western Islands of Scotland" is a most valuable performance. It abounds in extensive philosophical views of society, and in ingenious sentiment and lively description. A considerable part of it, indeed, consists of speculations, which many years before he saw the wild regions which we visited together, probably had employed his attention, though the actual sight of those scenes undoubtedly quickened and augmented them. Mr. Orme, the very able historian, agreed with me in this opinion, which he thus strongly expressed:—"There are in that book thoughts, which, by long revolution in the great mind of Johnson, have been formed and polished like pebbles rolled in the ocean!"—BOSWELL, JAMES, 1791–93, *Life of Johnson, ed. Hill, vol.* II, *p.* 343.

It is to Johnson that we go to see the life, the houses, the food, the garments—nay, the very speech and manners of the Scotsmen amongst whom he passed, and who were attracted to his personality by the magnetic force of a master-mind. . . . Johnson's Journal has the indescribable but irresistible charm of a monument of literary genius.—CRAIK, SIR HENRY, 1901, *A Century of Scottish History, vol.* II, *pp.* 40, 41.

TAXATION NO TYRANNY
1775

Of this performance I avoided to talk with him; for I had now formed a clear and settled opinion, that the people of America were well warranted to resist a claim that their fellow-subjects in the mother-country should have the entire command of their fortunes, by taxing them without their own consent; and the extreme violence which it breathed, appeared to me so unsuitable to the mildness of a christian philosopher, and so directly opposite to the principles of peace which he had so beautifully recommended in his pamphlet respecting Falkland's Islands, that I was sorry to see him appear in so unfavourable a light. Besides, I could not perceive in it that ability of argument, or that felicity of expression, for which he was, upon other occasions, so eminent. Positive assertion, sarcastical severity, and extravagant ridicule which he himself reprobated as a test of truth, were united in this rhapsody. That this pamphlet was written at the desire of those who were then in power, I have no doubt; and, indeed, he owned to me, that it had been revised and curtailed by some of them.—BOSWELL, JAMES, 1791–93, *Life of Johnson, ed. Hill, vol.* II, *p.* 357.

His political tracts must have exercised the very minimum of influence for the productions of so great a writer. He was the last man in the world to conciliate opposition, and his strong powers of argument were warped by prejudice. His "Taxation no Tyranny," written to defend the taxation of the American colonists against their will, is at once overbearing and sophistical. It might inflame and imbitter partisans, but it was too abusive and too unreasonable to make converts.—MINTO, WILLIAM, 1872–80, *Manual of English Prose Literature, p.* 424.

There was, indeed, one matter in which Johnson showed such a monstrous perversity that even the faithful Boswell fell away from him. He could not away with the claims of America. "Taxation no Tyranny" is indeed a lamentable pamphlet, but it is not Toryism. . . . In fact, much of the argument of his pamphlet is not so much wrong in itself as hopelessly beside the mark; and it is beside the mark not because Johnson was a Tory, but just because he was indifferent to the forms of government. Thus he was distracted from the main issue to subsidiary points, and at such a crisis subsidiary points could have no weight.—SARGEAUNT, JOHN, 1898, *Dr. Johnson's Politics, The Bookman, vol.* 6, *pp.* 421, 422.

LIVES OF THE POETS
1779–81

Johnson, to occasional felicity of diction, great purity of moral, and energy of thought, united a very considerable portion of critical acumen, and his Lives of Dryden and Pope are noble specimens of his powers of discrimination; yet, notwithstanding this rare combination of striking qualities, he was deficient in that sensibility to, and enthusiasm for, the charms of nature, in that relish for the simple and pathetic, so absolutely necessary to just criticism in poetry. To these defalcations were superadded an unreasonable antipathy to blank verse, a constitutional ruggedness of temper, and a bigoted, though well-meant, adhesion to some very extravagant political and religious tenets. His biographical details have suffered much from these peculiarities of temper and of taste; and a Milton, an Akenside, a Collins, a Dyer, and a Gray, might upbraid the Literary Dictator for his bitter and illiberal invective, his churlish and parsimonious praise, his great and various misrepresentations. — DRAKE, NATHAN, 1798–1820, *Literary Hours, vol.* I, *No.* xii, *p.* 160.

There are parts of the "Lives of the Poets" which every lover of literary or moral justice would be glad to see stamped with an indelible brand of reprobation, with a disgrace so signal and conspicuous as to be a perpetual warning against the perversion of criticism and private history by political and religious bigotry and personal spleen.—FOSTER, JOHN, 1808, *Criticism on the English Poets, Essays.*

Throughout his "Lives of the Poets," he constantly betrays a want of relish for the more abstracted graces of the art. When strong sense and reasoning were to be judged of, these he was able to appreciate justly. When the passions or characters were described, he could to certain extent decide whether they were described truly or no. But as far as poetry has relation to the kindred arts of music and painting, to both of which he was confessedly insensible, it could not be expected that he should have much perception of its excellences. . . . When he is most strong, he gives us some good reason for his being so. He is often mistaken, but never trivial and insipid. It is more safe to trust to him when he commends than when he dispraises; when he enlarges the boundaries of criticism which his predecessors had contracted, than when he sets up new fences of his own.—CARY, HENRY FRANCIS, 1821–24–45, *Lives of English Poets, pp.* 84, 88.

Dr. Johnson's "Lives of the Poets" are necessarily a prominent ornament of every library; as they have been the common theme of admiration of all countries. The style and the reflections are the chief charm of this popular work. Many of the facts must be cautiously admitted. Not that Johnson designedly falsified; but he always wanted time, diligence, and patience, in the collection of his materials; and, he rejoiced to find the fact as he *wished* to find it: without sufficiently weighing it in the balance of impartiality. He *hugged* every thing which he thought might throw a shade on a republican, a whig, or a dissenter; and spared no pains in executing such a picture in his most powerful and overwhelming colours. But toryism and orthodoxy neither require nor recommend such intemperate conduct. Even the very loose reports which had reached him of Dryden's funeral, were inserted without a suspicion of their veracity; and it remained for Mr. Malone (in his admirable edition of Dryden's prose works, to which a biography of the poet is prefixed) to dispel and dissipate this idle story as a barefaced fiction. But Johnson, had he been living, would not have surrendered it without a *growl*. Much that he has inserted in the life of Pope, and more in that of Milton, has been, and will continue to be, corrected and disproved: but who that reads Johnson's criticisms on certain portions of the "Paradise Lost," is not convinced that he is reading one of the most masterly performances of the human intellect? exhibiting an extent of power of conception—a vigour and felicity of diction—such as one knows not where to find equalled in any modern production. His life of Savage, the first in the order of execution, is considered to be the chef-d'œuvre; but this may be because it *was* the first; and because we have long known that Sir Joshua Reynolds read it with such intense interest, as to be unconscious that he was nearly dislocating his arm against a chimney piece, all the time! In consequence, he sought Johnson's acquaintance, and respected and loved the great philologist to his dying day. Still, the lives of Dryden and Pope abound with some of the happiest specimens of Johnson's powers of narrative and criticism. The whole set of Lives is indeed charming: fraught with wisdom and excellent taste.—DIBDIN, THOMAS FROGNALL, 1824, *The Library Companion, p.* 510, *note.*

We could find no pleasure in sacrificing one great man to the *manes* of another. . . . He did not and he could not appreciate Milton. We doubt whether two other minds, having so little in common as those of which we are now speaking, can be found in the higher walks of literature. Johnson was great in his own sphere, but that sphere was comparatively "of the earth," whilst Milton's was only inferior to that of angels. It was customary, in the day of Johnson's glory, to call him a Giant, to class him with a mighty but still an earth-born race. Milton we should rank among Seraphs.—CHANNING, WILLIAM ELLERY, 1826, *Remarks on the Character and Writings of John Milton.*

A life of Milton is yet a desideratum in our literature. Johnson hated his democratic principles, and despised his impracticable philosophy: the severity with which he handled him was only restrained by a veneration for his piety, and perhaps ignorance of his ariaism.—SOUTHEY, ROBERT, 1827, *Todd's ed. of Milton, Quarterly Review, vol.* 36, *p.* 42.

He had his prejudices, and his partialities, and his bigotries, and his blindnesses, but on the same fruit-tree you see shrivelled pears or apples on the same branch with jargonelles or golden pippins worthy of Paradise. . . . Show me the critique that beats his on Pope and on Dryden,—nay, even on Milton; and hang me if you may not read his "Essay on Shakspeare" even after having read Charles Lamb, or heard Coleridge, with increased admiration of the powers of all three, and of their insight through different avenues, and as it might seem, almost with different bodily and mental organs, into Shakspeare's "old exhausted" and his "new imagined worlds." He was a critic and a moralist who would have been wholly wise had he not been partly constitutionally insane.—WILSON, JOHN, 1829, *Noctes Ambrosianæ, April.*

"The Lives of the Poets" has been by far the most popular of his works, and is doubtless the one for which he will be reverenced in future times. It afforded room for the display of every kind of talent; of his critical sagacity, his burning imagination, his learned research, and that memory by which he retained many curious anecdotes and traits of character, which would otherwise have been lost. No doubt a prejudiced air is given to the work by his political prepossessions, and he has done injustice to some distinguished names; but he wrote what he thought, and treated his subjects as he believed they deserved. It is now clear that he was wrong in some respects; but he did not err in malice, and how was it reasonable to expect, that he should follow the prejudices of others in preference to his own.—PEABODY, W. B. O., 1832, *Croker's Boswell, North American Review, vol.* 34, *p.* 103.

A production more discreditable to the author is not to be found in the whole of his voluminous works; equally discreditable, whether regarded in an historical light or as a sample of literary criticism. . . . His "Life of Milton" is a humiliating testimony of the power of political and religious prejudices to warp a great and good mind from the standard of truth, in his estimation not merely of contemporary excellence, but of the great of other years, over whose frailties Time might be supposed to have drawn his friendly mantle.—PRESCOTT, WILLIAM HICKLING, 1839, *Chateaubriand's Sketches of English Literature, North American Review, vol.* 49, *pp.* 337, 338.

The critic was certainly deficient in sensibility to the more delicate, the minor beauties of poetic sentiment. He analyzes verse in the cold-blooded spirit of a chemist, until all the aroma, which constituted its principal charm, escapes in the decomposition. By this kind of process, some of the finest fancies of the Muse, the lofty dithyrambics of Gray, the ethereal effusions of Collins, and of Milton too, are rendered sufficiently vapid. In this sort of criticism, all the effect that relies on *impressions* goes for nothing. Ideas are alone taken into the account, and all is weighed in the same hard, matter-of-fact scales of common sense, like so much solid prose.—PRESCOTT, WILLIAM HICKLING, 1839, *Chateaubriand's Sketches of English Literature, Biographical and Critical Miscellanies.*

Wrote the lives of the poets and left out the poets.—BROWNING, ELIZABETH BARRETT, 1842–63, *The Book of the Poets.*

The lives of the Poets are, on the whole, the best of Johnson's works. The narratives are as entertaining as any novel. The remarks on life and on human nature are eminently shrewd and profound. The criticisms are often excellent, and, even when grossly and provokingly unjust, well deserve to be studied. For, however erroneous they may be, they are never silly. They are the judgments of a mind trammelled by prejudice and deficient in sensibility, but vigorous and acute. They therefore generally contain a portion of valuable truth which deserves to be separated from the alloy; and, at the very worst, they mean something, a praise to which much of what is called criticism in our time has no pretensions.—MACAULAY, THOMAS BABINGTON, 1843, *Samuel Johnson, Critical and Historical Essays.*

You know, of course, that Swift has had many biographers; his life has been told by the kindest and most good-natured of men, Scott, who admires but cannot bring himself to love him, and by stout old Johnson, who, forced to admit him into the company of poets, receives the famous Irishman, and takes off his hat to him with a bow of surly recognition, scans him from head to foot, and passes over to the other side of the street. . . . Johnson truly admires Swift: Johnson does not quarrel with Swift's change of politics, or doubt his sincerity of religion: about the famous Stella and

Vanessa controversy the Doctor does not bear very hardly on Swift. But he could not give the Dean that honest hand of his; the stout old man puts it into his breast, and moves off from him.—THACKERAY, WILLIAM MAKEPEACE, 1853, *The English Humourists of the Eighteenth Century.*

Johnson did not care for facts:—too indolent for research, it was enough if what he said of Pope were true of human nature,—true as to the motives and feelings that influence men,—and the comment was of universal application. Johnson's speculation on the incidents or assumed incidents in the "Life of Pope" is philosophy teaching by example; and would be instructive had no such man as Pope ever lived,—had the work been a romance, like the "Life of Robinson Crusoe," "Tom Jones," or "The Vicar of Wakefield." But the abstract and imperishable value of Johnson's Memoir is no apology for another and for every other writer.—DILKE, CHARLES WENTWORTH, 1854–75, *Pope's Writings, The Papers of a Critic, vol.* I, *p.* 95.

A cry was raised on more grounds than one against his Life of Milton. "I could thrash his old jacket," writes Cowper, "till I made his pension jingle in his pocket." All Cambridge was in arms against what Mackintosh has called "that monstrous example of critical injustice which he entitles the life of Gray." The same feeling was expressed against his criticism on Collins, and only less generally because the reputation of that poet was but then upon the rise. The friends of Lord Lyttelton were annoyed at the contempt, artful and studied as they called it, thrown upon the character of a nobleman who, with all the little foibles he might have, was, in their eyes, one of the most exalted patterns of virtue, liberality, and benevolence. Great displeasure was expressed with equal justice at his account of Thomson, while his censure of Akenside was thought by many what it really is, illiberal, and his criticism on Prior was condemned as "severe and unjust."—CUNNINGHAM, PETER, 1854, *ed. Johnson's Lives of the Poets, vol.* I, *p.* ix.

A work which, with all its faults, is the most masculine and massive body of criticism in the English tongue.—GILFILLAN, GEORGE, 1855, *A Third Gallery of Portraits, p.* 245.

The worst enemy that Milton and his great cause have ever been called on to confront; the worst as regards undying malice: in which qualification for mischief Dr. Johnson was not at all behind the diabolical Lauder or the maniacal Curran; and the foremost by many degrees in talents and opportunities for giving effect to his malice. I will here expand the several steps in the process of the case, so that the least attentive of readers, or least logical, may understand in what mode and in what degree Dr. Johnson, hunting for a triumph, allowed himself to trespass across the frontiers of calumny and falsehood, and at the same time may understand how far my own exposure smashes the Doctor's attempt in the shell.—DE QUINCEY, THOMAS, 1859, *Johnson's Life of Milton, Collected Writings, ed. Masson, vol.* IV, *p.* 105.

The Doctor was a capital judge of the substantial value of the goods he handled, but his judgment always seems that of the thumb and forefinger. For the shades, the disposition of colors, the beauty of the figures, he has as good as no sense whatever. The critical parts of his "Life of Dryden" seem to me the best of his writing in this kind. There is little to be gleaned after him. He had studied his author, which he seldom did, and his criticism is sympathetic, a thing still rarer with him. As illustrative of his own habits, his remarks on Dryden's reading are curious.—LOWELL, JAMES RUSSELL, 1868–90, *Dryden; Prose Works, Riverside ed., vol.* III, *p.* 140, *note.*

His "Lives of the Poets" do indeed truly stand for what Boswell calls them, "the work which of all Dr. Johnson's writings will perhaps be read most generally and with most pleasure." And in the lives of the six chief personages of the work, the lives of Milton, Dryden, Swift, Addison, Pope, and Gray, we have its very kernel and quintessence; we have the work relieved of whatever is less significant, retaining nothing which is not highly significant, brought within easy and convenient compass, and admirably fitted to serve as a *point de rèpere*, a fixed and thoroughly known centre of departure and return, to the student of English literature. I know of no such first-rate piece of literature, for supplying in this way the wants of the literary student, existing at all in any other language; or existing in our own language, for any period except the period which Johnson's six lives cover. A student cannot read them without gaining from them, consciously or unconsciously, an insight into the history of English literature and life.—ARNOLD, MATTHEW, 1878, *Johnson's Lives, Macmillan's Magazine, vol.* 38, *p.* 155.

The child of his old age—the "Lives of the Poets"—a book in which criticism and biography are combined, is an admirable performance in spite of serious defects. It is the work that best reflects his mind, and intelligent readers who have once made its acquaintance, will be apt to turn it into a familiar companion.—STEPHEN, LESLIE, 1879, *Samuel Johnson* (*English Men of Letters*), *p.* 167.

It has generally been acknowledged that Johnson's life of Gray is the worst section in his delightful series. It formed the last chapter but one in the fourth volume of the "Lives of the Poets," and was written when its author was tired of his task, and longed to be at rest again. It is barren and meagre of fact to the last degree.—GOSSE, EDMUND, 1882, *Gray* (*English Men of Letters*), *p.* 215.

This was a literary task for which he was exactly qualified. Originally he designed to give only a paragraph to minor poets, and four or five pages to the greater; but the flood of anecdote and criticism, as Macaulay happily says, overflowed the narrow channel; and sheets were expanded into volumes. It is instructive to note that, whereas the author's remuneration was three hundred guineas, the publishers reaped nearly six thousand pounds. *Sic vos non vobis!* With this supreme effort of his genius, which continues to be a text-book to literary students to the present day, Johnson's intellectual activity came to an end.—MONTAGU, R. W., 1884, *ed. Johnsoniana.*

It is no matter that Johnson's standards and view-points are extravagantly and exclusively of his time, so that occasionally—the cases of Milton and Gray are the chief—he falls into critical errors almost incomprehensible except from the historical side. Even these extravagances fix the critical creed of the day for us in an inestimable fashion, while in the great bulk of the Lives this criticism does no harm, being duly adjusted to the subjects. Johnson's estimate of Chaucer doubtless would have been, as his "Rambler" remarks on Spenser actually are, worthless, except as a curiosity. But of Dryden, of Pope, and of the numerous minor poets of their time and his, he could speak with a competently adjusted theory, with admirable literary knowledge and shrewdness, and with a huge store of literary tradition which his long and conversation-loving life had accumulated, and which would have been lost for us had he not written.—SAINTSBURY, GEORGE, 1898, *A Short History of English Literature, p.* 616.

LETTERS

There is little (in "Johnson's Letters") to gratify curiosity, or to justify impatience. They are such letters as ought to have been *written*, but ought never to have been *printed*. Still they are the true letters of friendship, which are meant to show kindness rather than wit. Every place to which he was invited, every dose of physic he took, everybody who sent to ask how he did, is recorded. I can read them with a degree of interest, because I knew and loved the man, and besides was often a party concerned in the dinners he mentions. A few of these letters are very good; sometimes he is moral, and sometimes he is kind—two points of view in which it is always agreeable to consider Johnson. I am often named, never with unkindness, sometimes with favour. The impudence of editors and executors is an additional reason why men of parts should be afraid to die. Burke said to me the other day in allusion to the innumerable lives, anecdotes, remains, etc., which have been published of Johnson—"How many maggots have crawled out of that great body!"—MORE, HANNAH, 1788, *Letter to Sister.*

He who found it so easy to talk, rarely took of his own accord to the task of composition. Nor will Johnson, in spite of the plea set up for him by the present editor, be ever known as a great letter-writer, hardly even as a good one. This is not saying that in these two volumes there is not much weighty observation, much acute comment, much that would be found interesting in itself, even did it not have the additional interest of having been written by the most famous literary man that England then possessed. But the indefinable charm of unconscious self-revelation which sets off the hastiest productions of the born letter-writer, is not to be found either among the valuable reflections or the dry details that make up no small share of this correspondence. —LOUNSBURY, THOMAS R., 1892, *Dr. Johnson's Letters, The Nation, vol.* 54, *p.* 415.

As a letter-writer, Johnson has great merits. Let no man despise the epistolary art. It is said to be extinct. I doubt it. Good letters are always scarce. It does not follow that because our grandmothers wrote long letters, they all wrote good ones, or that nobody nowadays writes good letters because most people write bad ones. Johnson wrote letters in two styles. One was monumental—more suggestive of the chisel than the pen. In the other there are traces of the same style, but, like the old Gothic architecture, it has grown domesticated, and become the fit vehicle of plain tidings of joy and sorrow—of affection, wit, and fancy.—BIRRELL, AUGUSTINE, 1885, *Dr. Johnson, Contemporary Review, vol.* 47, *p.* 38.

GENERAL

Of this Johnson, you and I, I believe, think much alike. (?)—WARBURTON, WILLIAM, 1765, *Letters from a Late Eminent Prelate, Oct.* 31, *p.* 368.

Auctioneer.—This is the Leviathan of Literature, the Colossus Doctor—and his friend the Head of the Press; a technical pair fit to fill up any lady's library. The first was secretary to Rasselas, Prince of Abyssinia, but, turning out both an Idler and a Rambler, and giving False Alarms to the city by which he frightened into fits the Queen of Irene, he was immediately ordered to be sold by public auction. His compassion was thought to be Good-natured Man, till he injured a Vicar of Wakefield, deluding the poor priest with a False Prospect of Society: since which he has crawled among the ruins of a Deserted Village, and employed his time in castrating the Roman History. These are the Literary Castor and Pollux; the benevolent, celebrious, convivial associates, the incomprehensible Holofernes and the impenetrable Goodman Dull.—ANON, 1770, *St. James Chronicle, June* 14.

So pleads the tale that gives to future times
The son's misfortunes and the parent's crimes;
There shall his fame (if own'd to-night) survive,
Fix'd by the hand that bids our language live.
—SHERIDAN, RICHARD BRINSLEY, 1777, *Prologue to Sir Thomas Overbury.*

The distinguishing excellence of Johnson's *manner*, both in speaking and writing, consists in the apt and lively illustrations by example with which, in his vigorous sallies, he enforces his just and acute remarks on human life and manners, in all their modes and representations; the character and charm of his *style*, in a happy choice of dignified and appropriate expressions, and that masterly *involution* of phrase by which he contrives to bolt the prominent idea strongly on the mind. —GREEN, THOMAS, 1779–1810, *Diary of a Lover of Literature.*

Here Johnson lies—a sage by all allow'd,
Whom to have bred, may well make England proud;
Whose prose was eloquence, by wisdom taught,
The graceful vehicle of virtuous thought;
Whose verse may claim—grave, masculine and strong,
Superior praise to the mere poet's song;
Who many a noble gift from Heaven possess'd,
And faith at last, alone worth all the rest.
O man, immortal by a double prize,
By fame on earth—by glory in the skies!
—COWPER, WILLIAM, 1785, *Epitaph on Dr. Johnson.*

By nature's gifts ordain'd mankind to rule,
He, like a Titian, form'd his brilliant school;
And taught congenial spirits to excel,
While from his lips impressive wisdom fell.
Our boasted Goldsmith felt the sovereign sway;
From him deriv'd the sweet, yet nervous lay.
To Fame's proud cliff he bade our Raphael rise;
Hence Reynolds' pen with Reynolds' pencil vies.
With Johnson's flame melodious Burney glows,
While the grand strain in smoother cadence flows.
And you, Malone, to critick learning dear,
Correct and elegant, refin'd though clear,
By studying him, acquir'd that classick taste,
Which high in Shakspeare's fane thy statue plac'd.
Near Johnson Steevens stands, on scenick ground,
Acute, laborious, fertile, and profound.
Ingenius Hawkesworth to this school we owe,
And scarce the pupils from the tutor know.
Here early parts accomplish'd Jones sublimes,
And science blends with Asia's lofty rhymes:
Harmonious Jones! who in his splendid strains

Sings Camdeo's sports, on Agra's flowery plains:
In Hindu fictions while we fondly trace
Love and the Muses, deck'd with Attick grace.
Amid these names can Boswell be forgot,
Scarce by North Britons now esteem'd a Scot'?
Who to the sage devoted from his youth,
Imbib'd from him the sacred love of truth;
The keen research, the exercise of the mind,
And that best art, the art to know mankind—
Nor was his energy confin'd alone
To friends around his philosophick throne;
Its influence wide improv'd our letter'd isle,
And lucid vigour marked the general style:
As Nile's proud waves, swoln from their oozy bed,
First o'er the neighbouring meads majestick spread;
Till gathering force, they more and more expand,
An with new virtue fertilise the land.

—COURTENAY, JOHN, 1786, *A Poetical Review of the Literary and Moral Character of the Late S. Johnson.*

Of literary merit, Johnson, as we all know, was a sagacious but a most severe judge. Such was his discernment, that he pierced into the most secret springs of human actions; and such was his integrity, that he always weighed the moral characters of his fellow-creatures in the "balance of the sanctuary."—PARR, SAMUEL, 1789, *ed., Tracts by Warburton and a Warburtonian.*

No need of Latin or of Greek to grace
Our Johnson's memory, or inscribe his grave;
His native language claims this mournful space,
To pay the Immortality he gave.

—FLOOD, HENRY, 1789, *Epitaph on Johnson.*

Overbearing pedant and bully, whose reputation was proof of the decline of British taste and learning.—BUCHAN, LORD, 1791? *Address at the Coronation of the Bust of Thomson, Sep.* 22.

We are reading in idle moments, or rather dipping into, a very different work, Boswell's long-expected "Life of Johnson." It is like going to Ranelagh; you meet all your acquaintance: but it is a base and a mean thing to bring thus every idle word into judgement—the judgement of the public. Johnson, I think, was far from a great character; he was continually sinning against his conscience, and then afraid of going to hell for it. A Christian and a man of the town, a philosopher and a bigot, acknowledging life to be miserable, and making it more miserable through fear of death; professing great distaste to the country, and neglecting the urbanity of towns; a Jacobite, and pensioned; acknowledged to be a giant in literature, and yet we do not trace him, as we do Locke, or Rousseau, or Voltaire, in his influence on the opinions of the times. We cannot say Johnson first opened this vein of thought, led the way to this discovery or this turn of thinking. In his style he is original, and there we can track his imitators. In short, he seems to me to be one of those who have shone in the *belles lettres*, rather than, what he is held out by many to be, an original and deep genius in investigation. — BARBAULD, ANNA LÆTITIA, 1791, *Works, vol.* II, *p.* 157.

After the Doctor's death, Burke, Sir Joshua Reynolds, and Boswell sent an ambling circular-letter to me, begging subscriptions for a Monument for him—the two last, I think, impertinently; as they could not but know my opinion, and could not suppose I would contribute to a Monument for one who had endeavoured, poor soul! to degrade my friend's superlative poetry. I would not deign to write an answer; but sent down word by my footman, as I would have done to parish officers with a brief, that I would not subscribe. In the two new volumes Johnson says, and very probably did, or is made to say, that Gray's poetry is *dull*, and that he was a *dull* man! The same oracle dislikes Prior, Swift, and Fielding. If an elephant could write a book, perhaps one that had read a great deal would say, that an Arabian horse is a very clumsy ungraceful animal. Pass to a better chapter!—WALPOLE, HORACE, 1791, *To Miss Berry, May* 26; *Letters, ed. Cunningham, vol.* IX, *p.* 319.

I remember Mr. Burke, speaking of the Essays of Sir Francis Bacon, said, he thought them the best of his works. Dr. Johnson was of opinion, that "their excellence and their value consisted in being the observations of a strong mind operating upon life; and in consequence you find there what you seldom find in other books." It is this kind of excellence which gives a value to the performances of artists also. It is the thoughts expressed in the works of

Michael Angelo, Correggio, Raffaelle, Parmegiano, and perhaps some of the old Gothic masters, and not the inventions of Pietro da Cortona, Carlo Marati, Luca Giordano, and others, that I might mention, which we seek after with avidity: from the former we learn to think originally. May I presume to introduce myself on this occasion, and even to mention, as an instance of the truth of what I have remarked, the very Discourses which I have had the honour of delivering from this place? Whatever merit they have, must be imputed, in a great measure, to the education which I may be said to have had under Dr. Johnson. I do not mean to say, though it certainly would be to the credit of these Discourses, if I could say it with truth, that he contributed even a single sentiment to them; but he qualified my mind to think justly. No man had, like him, the faculty of teaching inferior minds the art of thinking Perhaps other men might have equal knowledge; but few were so communicative.—REYNOLDS, SIR JOSHUA, 1792? *On Johnson's Influence.*

Johnson's partiality for old English manners and practices was unbounded; nor can there be produced from the annals of our literature a more fervent anti-whig and anti-gallican.—GODWIN, WILLIAM, 1797, *Of English Style, The Enquirer, p.* 379.

Every one of tolerable education feels the *imitability* of Dr. Johnson's and other-such's style, the imitability of Shakspere's, etc. Hence, I believe, arises the partiality of thousands for Johnson. They can imagine *themselves* doing the same. Vanity is at the bottom of it. The number of imitators proves this in some measure.—COLERIDGE, SAMUEL TAYLOR, 1805, *Anima Poetæ, p.* 97.

Johnson's style has pleased many from the very fault of being perpetually translatable; he creates an impression of cleverness by never saying any thing in a common way.—COLERIDGE, SAMUEL TAYLOR, 1818, *Style, Miscellanies Æsthetic and Literary, ed. Ashe, p.* 182.

The structure of his sentences, which was his own invention, and which has been generally imitated since his time, is a species of rhyming in prose, where one clause answers to another in measure and quantity, like the tagging of syllables at the end of a verse; the close of the period follows as mechanically as the oscillation of a pendulum, the sense is balanced with the sound; each sentence, revolving round its centre of gravity, is contained within itself like a couplet, and each paragraph forms itself into a stanza. Dr. Johnson is also a complete balance-master in the topics of morality. He never encourages hope, but he counteracts it by fear; he never elicits a truth, but he suggests some objection in answer to it. He seizes and alternateley quits the clue of reason, lest it should involve him in the labyrinths of endless error: he wants confidence in himself and his fellows. He dares not trust himself with the immediate impressions of things, for fear of compromising his dignity; or follow them into their consequences, for fear of committing his prejudices. His timidity is the result, not of ignorance, but of morbid apprehension.—HAZLITT, WILLIAM, 1818, *Lectures on the English Comic Writers, Lecture* v.

It is a great defect in the education of our youth in both the Universities that they do not sufficiently apply themselves to the study of their mother tongue. By this means it happens, that some very learned men and polite scholars are not able to express themselves with propriety in common conversation, and that when they are discoursing on a subject which they understand perfectly well. I have been acquainted with three persons only who spoke English with that eloquence and propriety, that if all they said had been immediately committed to writing, any judge of the English language would have pronounced it an excellent and very beautiful style—Atterbury, the exiled bishop of Rochester; Dr. Gower, provost of Worcester College; and Samuel Johnson.—KING, WILLIAM, 1819, *Anecdotes of My Own Times.*

Rough Johnson, the great moralist.
—BYRON, LORD, 1823, *Don Juan, canto,* xiii.

Of all the men distinguished in this or any other age, Dr. Johnson has left upon posterity the strongest and most vivid impression so far as person, manners, disposition, and conversation are concerned. We do but name him, or open a book which he has written, and the sound and action recall to the imagination at once his form, his merits, his peculiarities, nay, the very uncouthness of his gestures, and the deep impressive tone of his voice. We learn not only what he said, but form an idea how he said it; and have, at the same time, a shrewd guess of the secret motive why he did so, and whether he spoke in sport or in anger, in the desire of conviction, or for the love of debate. It was said of a noted wag, that his bon-mots did not give full satisfaction when published, because he could not print his face. But with respect to Dr. Johnson, this has been in some degree accomplished; and, although the present generation never saw him, yet he is, in our mind's eye, a personification as lively as that of Siddons in Lady Macbeth, or Kemble in Cardinal Wolsey.—SCOTT, SIR WALTER, 1823, *Samuel Johnson.*

Perhaps you do not know of my profound veneration for this surly sage; but I am such an admirer of his peculiar style of excellence, that I can easily endure defects that bring him within my reach, and save me the effort of standing on tiptoe to contemplate his gigantic mind.—GRANT, MRS. ANNE, 1823, *Letters, May* 15; *Memoir and Correspondence, ed. Grant, vol.* III, *p.* 2.

At length rose the Colossus of English Philology, Samuel Johnson; having secretly and unremittingly formed his style upon the basis of that of Sir Thomas Browne; a name, in every respect to be held in grateful remembrance. But Johnson, as a philologist, is almost an original; and doubtless among the very foremost in the ranks of the literature of his country. And yet, I know not how it is, but, as years creep on, we do not read his pages with that devoted enthusiasm which we did in our College days: for where is the man, who, having turned his thirtieth year, peruses "Rasselas" or the "Rambler?" It is as a *Colloquialist* and *Biographer* that Johnson has scarcely a rival —especially when prejudices did not spread a film over those intellectual orbs, which were constructed to gaze uninjured upon the sun!—DIBDIN, THOMAS FROGNALL, 1824, *The Library Companion, p.* 608.

The judgments which Johnson passed on books were in his own time regarded with superstitious veneration; and in our own time are generally treated with indiscriminate contempt. They are the judgments of a strong but enslaved understanding. The mind of the critic was hedged round by an uninterrupted fence of prejudices and superstitions. Within his narrow limits he displayed a vigour and an activity which ought to have enabled him to clear the barrier that confined him. . . . He was no master of the great science of human nature. He had studied, not the *genus* man, but the *species* Londoner. Nobody was ever so thoroughly conversant with all the forms of life, and all the shades of moral and intellectual character, which were to be seen from Islington to the Thames, and from Hyde-Park corner to Mile-end green. But his philosophy stopped at the first turnpike gate. Of the rural life of England he knew nothing; and he took it for granted that everybody who lived in the country was either stupid or miserable.—MACAULAY, THOMAS BABINGTON, 1831, *Boswell's Life of Johnson, Edinburgh Review, Critical and Miscellaneous Essays.*

His imagination was not more lively than was necessary to illustrate his maxims; his attainments in science were inconsiderable, and in learning far from the first class; they chiefly consisted in that sort of knowledge which a powerful mind collects from miscellaneous reading, a various intercourse with mankind. From the refinement of abstruse speculation he was withheld, partly, perhaps, by that repugnance to such subtleties which much experience often inspires, and partly also by a secret dread that they might disturb those prejudices in which his mind had found repose from the agitation of doubt. He was a most sagacious and severly pure judge of the actions and motives of men, and he was tempted by frequent detection of imposture to indulge somewhat of that contemptuous scepticism, respecting the sincerity of delicate and refined sentiments, which affected his whole character as a man and writer.—MACKINTOSH, SIR JAMES, 1835, *Memoirs, ed. Mackintosh, vol.* II, *p.* 166.

No man contemplates with greater tenderness than we do the frailties of Dr. Johnson; none respects more the sound parts of his moral system; or admires more the vigor of the elephantine step with which he sometimes tramples down insolent error and presumptuous sophistry. But let no young man, who wishes to write well study his style.—EVERETT, EDWARD, 1835, *Washington Irving, North American Review, vol.* 41, *p.* 3.

Samuel Johnson, in some respects, stood entirely alone in Europe. In those years there was no one in Europe like him. . . . Was a large minded man, an entirely sincere and honest man. Whatever may be our differences of opinion is here entirely insignificant; he must inevitably be regarded as the brother of all honest men. One who held this truth among the insincerities that lay around him, that, after all, "life was true yet," and he was a man to hold by that truth, and cling to it in the general shipwreck on the sea of Eternity.—CARLYLE, THOMAS, 1838, *Lectures on the History of Literature, p.* 180.

His brilliant style has been the ambition of every schoolboy, and of some children of larger growth, since the days of the "Rambler." But the nearer they come to it, the worse. The beautiful is turned into the fantastic, and the sublime into the ridiculous.—PRESCOTT, WILLIAM HICKLING, 1839, *Chateaubriand's Sketches of English Literature, North American Review, vol.* 49, *p.* 334.

A love of hard and learned words prevailed throughout; and a fondness for balanced periods was its special characteristic. But there was often great felicity in the expression, occasionally a pleasing cadence in the rhythm, generally an epigrammatic turn in the language, as well as in the idea. Even where the workmanship seemed most to surpass the material, and the *word-craft* to be exercised needlessly and the diction to run to waste, there was never any feebleness to complain of, and always something of skill and effect to admire. The charm of nature was ever wanting, but the presence of great art was undeniable. Nothing was seen of the careless aspect which the highest of artists ever give their masterpieces,—the produce of elaborate but concealed pains; yet the strong hand of an able workman was always marked; and it was observed, too, that he disdained to hide from us the far less labour which he had much more easily bestowed. There is no denying that some of Johnson's works, from the meagerness of the material and the regularity of the monotonous style, are exceedingly little adapted to reading. They are flimsy, and they are dull; they are pompous, and, though full of undeniable—indeed, self-evident—truths, they are somewhat empty; they are, moreover, wrapped up in a style so disproportioned in its importance, that the perusal becomes very tiresome, and is soon given up. This character belongs more especially to the "Rambler," the object of such unmeasured praises among his followers, and from which he derived the title of the Great Moralist.—BROUGHAM, HENRY LORD, 1845, *Lives of Men of Letters of the Time of George III.*

As a writer, he is the very incarnation of good sense; and as a man, he was an example of so high a degree of virtue, magnanimity, and self-sacrifice, that he has been justly placed by a profound modern speculator among the *heroes* of his country's annals. . . . Johnson's style during the whole of his career was exceedingly peculiar and characteristic both in its beauties and defects, and when he arrived at eminence may be said to have produced a revolution in the manner of writing in English; and as this revolution has to a certain degree lasted till the present day, it will be well to say a few words on the subject. It is in the highest degree pompous, sonorous, and, to use a happy expression of Coleridge, hyper-latinistic; running into perpetual antithesis, and balancing period against period with an almost rhythmical regularity, which at once fills and fatigues the ear. . . . The prevailing defect of Johnson's style is uniformity: the combinations of his kaleidoscope are soon exhausted; his peal of bells is very limited in its changes; and there is necessarily, in so artificial a style, an air of pretention and ambitiousness, the sameness is more fatiguing than would be the snipped periods and tuneless meanness of a more unostentatious mode of expression. . . . His mind, admirably adapted as it was for the scientific part of criticism, was impotent to feel or appreciate what is picturesque or passionate. He is like a deaf man seated at a symphony of Beethoven—a sense is wanting to him. . , . The character of Shakspeare's genius, given in the preface, is a noble specimen of panegyric; and it is singular to see how far the divine genius of the dramatist almost succeeds in overcoming all the prejudices of Johnson's age and education. As a moralist, as a painter of men and minds, Johnson has done Shakspeare (at least as far as any man could) ample justice; but in his judgment of the great creative poet's more romantic manifestations he exhibits a callousness and insensibility which was partly the result of his education and of the age when he lived, and partly, without doubt, the consequence of the peculiar constitution of his mind—a mind which felt much more sympathy with men than with things, and was much more at home in the "full tide of London existence" than in the airy world of imagination—among the everyday crowds of Fleet Street, than in Prospero's enchanted isle, or the moonlit terraces of Verona.—SHAW, THOMAS B., 1847, *Outlines of English Literature, pp.* 242, 243, 244, 247, 248.

Dr. Johnson, gravely supporting an aristocratic public policy, while he powerfully and pathetically rebuked aristocratic private conduct. Let the name of Dr. Johnson never be mentioned among scholars without a sad respect; but is he, distinctively, *the scholar* in English history?—CURTIS, GEORGE WILLIAM, 1856, *The Duty of the American Scholar, Orations and Addresses, ed. Norton. vol.* I, *p.* 11.

Doctor Johnson's written abstractions have little value; the tone of feeling in them makes their chief worth.—EMERSON, RALPH WALDO, 1856–84, *English Traits, Works, Riverside ed., vol.* V, *p.* 232.

Dr. Johnson's English style demands a few words. So peculiar is it, and such a swarm of imitators grew up during the half century of his greatest fame, that a special name—Johnsonese—has been often used to donate the march of its ponderous classic words. Yet it was not original, and not a many-toned style. There were in our literature, earlier than Dr. Johnson's day, writers who far outdid their Fleet Street disciple in recruiting our native ranks with heavy-armed warriors from the Greek phalanx and the Latin legion. Of these writers Sir Thomas Browne was perhaps the chief. Goldy, as the great Samuel loved to call the author of the "Deserted Village," got many a sore blow from the Doctor's conversational sledge-hammer; but he certainly contrived to get within the Doctor's guard and hit him home, when he said, "*If you were to write a fable about little fishes, Doctor, you would make the little fishes talk like whales.*" Macaulay tells us that when Johnson wrote for publication, he did his sentences out of English into Johnsonese. — COLLIER, WILLIAM FRANCIS, 1861, *A History of English Literature, p.* 349.

There is perhaps no subsequent prose-writer upon whose style that of Johnson has been altogether without its effect.—CRAIK, GEORGE L., 1861, *A Compendious History of English Literature and of the English Language, vol.* II, *p.* 328.

His true genius lay in the masculine strength of his common sense; and in spite of his prejudices, of his dogmatism, of his frequent intolerance and occasional paradox—in spite, still more, of a style in prose strangely contrasting the cold severity of his style in verse—unfamiliar, inflated, artificially grandiose—still that common sense has such pith and substance that it makes its way to every plain, solid understanding. And while all that Johnson owed to his more imaginative qualities has faded away from his reputation; while his poems are regarded but as scholastic exercises; while his tragedy is left unread; while the fables and tales scattered throughout his essays allure no popular imitation, and even "Rasselas" is less admired for its loftiness of purpose and conception than censured for its inappropriate dialogue or stilted diction, and neglected for the dryness of its narrative and the frigidity of its characters; while his ablest criticisms, composed in his happiest style, rarely throw light upon what may be called the metaphysics of imaginative art,—his knowledge of the world has a largeness and at times a depth which preserve authority to his opinions upon the general bearings of life and the prevalent characteristics of mankind—a knowledge so expanded, by its apprehension of generical truths, from mere acquaintanceship with conventional manners, and the sphere of the town life which enthralled his taste, that at this day it is not in capitals that his works are most esteemed as authoritative, but rather in the sequestered homes of rural book-readers. To men of wit about town, a grave sentence from Johnson upon the philosophy of the great world would seem old-fashioned pedantry, where, to men of thought in the country, it would convey some truth in social wisdom too plain to be uttered by pedants, and too solid to be laughed out of fashion by wits.—LYTTON, EDWARD BULWER LORD, 1863–68, *Caxtoniana, Miscellaneous Prose Works, vol.* III, *p.* 451.

Johnson neither in amplitude of literature nor exactness of scholarship could be deemed a match for Lessing; but they were alike in the power of readily applying whatever they had learned, whether for purposes of illustration or argument. They resemble each other, also, in a kind of absolute common-sense, and in the force with which they could plant a direct blow with the whole weight both of their training and their temperament behind it. As a critic Johnson ends where Lessing begins. The one is happy in the lower region of the understanding: the other can breathe freely in the ampler air of reason alone. Johnson acquired learning, and stopped short through indolence at a certain point. Lessing assimilated it, and accordingly his education ceased only with his life. Both had something of the intellectual sluggishness that is apt to go with great strength; and both had to be baited by the antagonism of circumstances or opinions, not only into the exhibition, but into the possession of their entire force. Both may be more properly called original men than, in the highest sense, original writers.—LOWELL, JAMES RUSSELL, 1866–90, *Lessing; Prose Works, Riverside ed., vol.* II, *p.* 191.

In fact, his phraseology rolls always in solemn and majestic periods, in which every substantive marches ceremoniously, accompanied by its epithets; great, pompous words peal like an organ; every proposition is set forth balanced by a proposition of equal length; thought is developed with the compassed regularity and official splendour of a procession. Classical prose attains its perfection in him, as classical poetry in Pope. Art cannot be more consummate, or nature more forced. No one has confined ideas in more strait compartments; none has given stronger relief to dissertation and proof; none has imposed more despotically on story and dialogue the forms of argumentation and violent declamation; none has more generally mutilated the flowing liberty of conversation and life by antitheses and technical words. It is the completion and the excess, the triumph and the tyranny, of oratorical style. We understand now that an oratorical age would recognise him as a master, and attribute to him in eloquence the primacy which it attributed to Pope in verse.—TAINE, H. A., 1871, *History of English Literature tr. Van Laun, vol.* II, *bk.* iii, *ch.* vi, *p.* 188.

Johnson first taught literary men the lesson of self-reliance and independence. Of all men of genius he is the only typical Englishman in whose strength, as also in his weakness, we see the national character. He was absolutely free from meanness and jealousy; a mighty soul which disdained tricks and subterfuges. "Like the Monument," in his own language, he stood upright and never stooped; no human power could have torn him from his base. Yet in this strongest of natures there was the gentlest affection, and the deepest reverence and humility. The giant has a heart like a woman or a child.—JOWETT, BENJAMIN, 1871–72, *Life by Abbott and Campbell, vol.* II, *p.* 33.

Johnson wrote almost all his "Ramblers" just as they were wanted for the press; he sent a certain portion of the copy of an essay, and wrote the remainder while the earlier part was printing. When it was wanted, and he had fairly sat down to it, he was sure, he said, it would be done.—JACOX, FRANCIS, 1872, *Authorship in the Act, Aspects of Authorship, p.* 6.

Doctor Samuel Johnson was poet, dramatist, essayist, lexicographer, dogmatist, and critic, and, in this array of professional characters, played so distinguished a part in his day that he was long regarded as a prodigy in English literature. His influence has waned since his personality has grown dim, and his learning been superseded or over-shadowed; but he still remains, and must always remain, the most prominent literary figure of his age. . . . His style is full-sounding and antithetic, his periods are carefully balanced, his manner eminently respectable and good; but his words, very many of them of Latin derivation, constitute what the later critics have named *Johnsonese*, which is certainly capable of translation into plainer Saxon English, with good results. . . . As a critic, his word was law: his opinion was clearly and often severely expressed on literary men and literary subjects, and no great writer of his own or a past age escaped either his praise or his censure. Authors wrote with the fear of his criticism before their eyes; and his pompous diction was long imitated by men who, without this influence, would have written far better English. But, on the other hand, his honesty, his scholarship, his piety, and his championship of what was good and true, as depicted in his writings, made him a blessing to his time, and an honored and notable character in the noble line of English authors.—COPPÉE, HENRY, 1872, *English Literature, pp.* 324, 330, 331.

The style of Johnson, deemed so admirable at the time, seems to us now intolerably artificial, pedantic, constrained, and ponderous. His periods are carefully considered and balanced, its proportionate length, emphasis, and weight of heavy words being given to each member: homely and familiar words and phrases, however apposite or expressive, are rejected as undignified; antithesis does duty for brilliancy, and an occasional reversal of the syntax for variety. Each point is handled in the style of a solemn argument: step by step the demonstration proceeds, often leading to a conclusion which would have been admitted upon statement. His utterances are too frequently elaborately dressed-up commonplaces; and a laborious paragraph is employed to evolve a thought which might have been more forcibly expressed in a single terse idiomatic phrase. Thus, his style has no freshness, no individual coloring; we feel that it is the result of a multitude of heterogeneous minds, all ground together in the mill of omnivorous learning. Johnson's criticisms are learned, carefully weighed, but deficient in insight. He had no faculty of entering into other men's natures, and justly appreciating views which he did not himself hold. He was an infatuated, though perfectly honest and disinterested, Tory; and his intense political bias often led him into absurd injustice. In his eyes Voltaire was merely an infidel and cynical buffoon, and Rousseau a miscreant deserving the gallows. Being absolutely destitute of the poetic faculty, he lacked the essential qualification for a critic of poetry; and, while sure to detect a fallacy in reasoning, or a blemish in morals, the finer spirit of poetry he could not appreciate. On the other hand, his writings are everywhere pervaded by a perfect love of truth and justice, and an utter abhorrence of falsehood and fraud; by a pure morality, enforced with the strongest emphasis; by a warm admiration for all things good and noble; and by the sincerest spirit of Christian piety; all which qualities he exemplified in his own brave and blameless life. His style, ponderous and constrained as it now appears, was not without many good qualities.—JOHNSTON, RICHARD MALCOLM, AND BROWNE, WILLIAM HAND, 1872, *English Literature, p.* 229.

Robert Hall, in his early days, made Johnson a model, but soon gave him up, complaining of a want of fervour in his morality. Though profoundly convinced of the doctrines of Religion, he seldom dilates on her "august solemnities," or on the grandeur of her hopes and fears. What he keeps principally in view is the beneficial effect of religious belief on human conduct, laying down the law in sonorous dogmas. In the presence of objects that raise emotions of sublimity in other men, he was on the watch to lay hold of general rules. Instead of giving way to the æsthetic influence of the situation, he pondered on the causes of the moral value of them, and meditated dictatorial, high-sounding, general propositions.—MINTO, WILLIAM, 1872–80, *Manual of English Prose Literature, p.* 419.

A solid Doric column, chipped into outline and assigned position by circumstances, he nevertheless chiefly interests us by the rugged strength of his own native texture.—BASCOM, JOHN, 1874, *Philosophy of English Literature, p.* 206.

His prose writings are noted for their formality of style and vigor of thought. Like Addison, he has furnished an adjective descriptive of literary style; and to be "Johnsonian" is to be ponderous and grandiose. "Rasselas, Prince of Abyssinia," an allegorical story from which we take our extracts, is perhaps the most familiar of his compositions to the general reader. Dr. Johnson was a man of vigorous intellect, acute and argumentative, but narrow in his views, dogmatic and positive in his assertions.—CATHCART, GEORGE R., 1874, *The Literary Reader, p.* 26.

He presented "common-sense" in the most prosaic sense of the word.—SCHERR, J., 1874, *A History of English Literature tr. M. V., p.* 150.

Now that we are out of reach of his terrible voice and his overbearing demeanour, and regarding him thus from a safe distance, we do not find it so difficult to designate his capacity for judging in literary matters as often shallow and pretentious. . . . The formidable lexicographer was of that class of men who are almost prepared to find fault with the sun because of the spots upon his surface. —SMITH, GEORGE BARNETT, 1875, *Henry Fielding, Poets and Novelists, pp.* 255, 257.

He was as good a moralist as a man can be who regards the ultimate foundations of morality as placed beyond the reach of speculation. "We know we are free, and there's an end on't" is the answer to the great metaphysical difficulty. He "refutes" Berkeley by kicking a stone. He thinks that Hume is a mere trifler, who has taken to "milking the bull" by way of variety. He laughs effectually at Soame Jenyns's explanation of the origin of evil; but leaves the question as practically insoluble, without troubling himself as to why it is insoluble, or what consequences may follow from its insolubility. Speculation, in short, though he passed for a philosopher, was simply abhorrent to him. He passes by on the other side, and leaves such puzzles for triflers. He has made up his mind once for all that religion is wanted, and that the best plan is to accept the established creed. And thus we have the apparent paradox that, whilst no man sets a higher value upon truthfulness in all the ordinary affairs of life than Johnson, no man could care less for the foundations of speculative truth. His gaze was not directed to that side. Judging in all cases rather by intuition than by logical processes, he takes for granted the religious theories which fall in sufficiently with his moral convictions. To all speculation which may tend to loosen the fixity of the social order he is deaf or contemptuously averse. The old insidious Deism seems to him to be mere trash; and he would cure the openly aggressive Deism of Rousseau by sending its author to the plantations. Indifference to speculation generates a hearty contempt for all theories. He has too firm a grasp of facts to care for the dreams of fanciful Utopians; his emotions are too massive and rigid to be easily excited by enthusiasts. He ridicules the prevailing cry against corruption. The world is bad enough in all conscience, but it will do no good to exaggerate or to whine.—STEPHEN, LESLIE, 1876, *History of English Thought in the Eighteenth Century, vol.* II, *p.* 374.

That great Luminary of Learning, the English Lexiphanes.—STODDARD, RICHARD HENRY, 1876, *Lord Macaulay and His Friends, Harper's Magazine, vol.* 53, *p.* 85.

No writer delivers moral maxims and dictatorial sentences with greater force, or lays down definitions with more grave precision. His critical acumen, setting aside personal and political prejudices, was likewise very great; but he is utterly averse to the easy and familiar, both in style and sentiment. His style formed an era in English composition. Its balanced pomp and antithetical clauses had with many an irresistible charm. However, the admiration for its exuberance of words of Latin etymology, and its sonorous rotundity of phrase, after having betrayed some writers into an injudicious imitation, has at length subsided; and the share of influence which remains, has certainly improved the general language.—JENKINS, O. L., 1876, *The Student's Handbook of British and American Literature, p.* 244.

One clever writer has lately attempted a defence of Dr. Johnson's pompous style, saying that the sage drew distinctions as he drew his breath, and that he could not express these distinctions without couching his diction in Latin-born phrases. The answer is most simple: he drew distinctions with equal subtility when he was talking, and he expressed them in the homeliest Teutonic. He has had his reward: his "Rambler" lies unread on our book-shelves; his talk, as recorded by Boswell, is perused every year by thousands of delighted students. Any writer of our day, who has a mind to be read a hundred years hence, should lay the lesson to heart.—OLIPHANT, T. L. KINGTON, 1878, *The Old and Middle English, p.* 589, *note.*

Johnson gained his reputation by his unrivalled power of concentrating his own forces, of defending himself against the aggression of outer influences,—and striking a light in the process. Of course Johnson was a man of very strong general understanding. Had he not been so, he could not have commanded the respect he did, for those who do not in a considerable degree understand others, will never be themselves understood. Still, admitting freely that it both takes a man of some character as well as insight, to understand distinctly what is beyond his own sphere, and a man of some insight as well as character, to teach others to understand distinctly what is within himself, it is clear that Johnson's genius lay in the latter, not in the former direction,—in maintaining himself against the encroachments of the world, and in interpreting himself to that world, not in enlarging materially the world's sympathies and horizons, except so far as he taught them to include himself. The best things he did of any kind were all expressions of himself.—HUTTON, RICHARD HOLT, 1878, *Criticisms on Contemporary Thought and Thinkers, vol.* I, *p.* 164.

Merely a man of keen perception and shrewd reasoning. — BLACK, WILLIAM, 1879, *Goldsmith (English Men of Letters), p.* 95.

Johnson unites in his own style many of the opposite excellences exhibited by his predecessor and his friend. It was impossible that the bias of his strong character should be altogether concealed in his verse, and "London" in particular appears to have been largely inspired by personal motives like those which suggested to Pope his "Imitations of Horace." But the different genius of the two poets is seen in the selection of their respective originals. Pope was struck by the many superficial points of resemblance between himself and the lively egotistical Horace, and seized eagerly on the opportunity of presenting his own virtues, friendships, and enmities to the public under a transparent veil of imitation. Johnson, on the contrary, who, as an unknown writer, could not hope to interest the public in his personal concerns, chose a general theme, and imitated the satirist whose denunciations of Roman vice offered, in many respects, an apt parallel to the manners of his own age. . . . "The Vanity of Human Wishes" marks a calmer and more prosperous epoch in the poet's life, and its philosophical generalising spirit is an anticipation of Goldsmith's "Traveller." Johnson was now relieved from the immediate pressure of want; and in his second "Imitation" he takes a wider survey of mankind; he suppresses all personal satire, and fetches the illustrations of his argument from distant times. The style of this poem is also completely different from that of "London:" in the latter he is ardent, animated, and colloquial, while in the "Vanity of Human Wishes" he speaks with the gravity of a moralist, making his periods swelling and sonorous, balancing his verses against each other, and equaling Pope himself in the condensation of his language. Nevertheless, the whole spirit of the composition, though professedly an imitation, is highly characteristic of the man: we see in it the melancholy gloom that darkened all his views of human existence, while at the same time the noble lines of the conclusion recall the language of those touching fragments of prayer which Boswell discovered among his papers and has preserved in his "Life." His Prologues are of the highest excellence; indeed it may be confidently affirmed that he is the best writer of prologues in the language. No man was ever so well qualified to strike that just mean between respectfulness and authority which such addresses to the public require. His sound critical power and elevated feeling are well exemplified in the "Prologue spoken at the opening of Drury Lane Theatre;" and there is true greatness of spirit in his Prologue to "Comus," in which he claims the liberality of the audience for Milton's granddaughter as a tardy redress for the injustice shown by the nation to the genius of the poet himself. His admirable independence of the character is perhaps even better seen in the Prologue to "A Word to the Wise," a play which at its first exhibition was damned in consequence of political prejudices against the author, but was revived after his death. Nothing can be better than the dignity with which Johnson, in this address, while reccognising the judicial authority of the audience, indirectly reproves them for their previous disregard of the laws of humanity by which all their verdicts ought to be determined.—COURTHOPE, W. J., 1880, *English Poets, ed. Ward, vol.* III, *p.* 246.

Johnson did more than any other one man in English letters to make literature a working profession—to take it out of the hands of patrons, and make the dealings of author and publisher a substantial business relation. He was one of the first English authors who lived by his work, and the honest independence with which he inspired the profession, has been a help to authors ever since his time. His dictionary, too, was one of the great works of the century. While we can not help wishing that the *Johnsonian* tendency in language had been towards greater simplicity and not towards the introduction of so many Latin words, still we must see that he did a great work for language. In his time there was no standard dictionary—the best one very imperfect—and Johnson in arranging and defining the words of the language, brought it into order and gave it form. He singly and alone attempted to do for England what the French Academy did for France, and although it is a question whether it is not better to have so important a work done by a body of scholars rather than by one man alone, yet nobody in raising that question, will doubt the value and honesty of Samuel Johnson's labors.—RICHARDSON, ABBY SAGE, 1881, *Familiar Talks on English Literature, p.* 321.

He taught others to look, like himself, through all the fleeting accidents of life to that in which a man can really live, and there were none who came to know him without learning how pure a spring of love and tenderness kept the whole nature fresh within. Firmly attached to the established Church, Johnson was a stout Tory on the religious side of his life and held the First Georges in such contempt as, it may be said, their lives had duly earned for them. But no delusions of party feeling dimmed his sense of human brotherhood, and of the large interests of humanity. Negro slavery was to his mind so gross a wrong that he startled a polite company one day with a toast "to the next Insurrection of the Blacks." The political corruption of his time caused Johnson in his Dictionary, which appeared in 1755, to define "Pension" as "a grant made to any one without an equivalent," and "Pensioner" as "a slave of state, hired by a stipend to obey his master." . . . Johnson's power had grown with the time, and he so far shared the reaction against formalism in his style, that the English of his "Lives of the Poets" differs distinctly from the English of his "Rambler."—MORLEY, HENRY, 1881, *Of English Literature in the Reign of Victoria with a Glance at the Past, pp.* 83, 85.

The most able criticism of the 18th century was Johnson's; he may be called in fact the first really systematic critic of English literature; for, although his remarks on other authors are scattered all about his own miscellaneous writings, it may be confidently stated that he made criticism his profession, and earned his living by it. He is an important link in the chain of English prose writers, for he is the first author whose whole thoughts were turned to the works of his predecessors.—FLETCHER, C. R. L., 1881, *The Development of English Prose Style, p.* 19.

In morals and criticism, it will ever be to his praise that he has assailed all sentimentalism and licentiousness. His wit, eloquence, and logic were always enlisted on the side of revealed religion, to deepen and extend, in heart and practice, the human faith in God. In the fields of Literature, which were now beginning to be cultivated on all sides, he did more than any of his contemporaries to create a pure and invigorating atmosphere. His balanced pomp of antithetic clauses soon had for others, as it had for him, an irresistible charm, and caused a complete revolution, for a time, in English style. Unhappily, it was too often imitated by inferior writers, who had not the glow to kindle the massive structure —little fishes talking like whales. There has been no English prose writer, onward to the present day, whose style has not been influenced by that of Johnson.—WELSH, ALFRED H., 1883, *Development of English Literature and Language, vol.* II, *p.* 178.

I never for an instant compared Johnson to Scott, Pope, Byron, or any of the really great writers whom I loved. But I at once and forever recognized in him a man entirely sincere, and infallibly wise in the view and estimate he gave of the common questions, business, and ways of the world. I valued his sentences not primarily because they were symmetrical, but because they were just, and clear; it is a method of judgment rarely used by the average public, who ask from an author always, in the first place, arguments in favour of their own opinions, in elegant terms; and are just as ready with their applause for a sentence of Macaulay's, which may have no more sense in it than a blot pinched between doubled paper, as to reject one of Johnson's, telling against their own prejudice,—though its symmetry be as of thunder answering from two horizons. I hold it more than happy that, during those continental journeys, in which the vivid excitement of the greater part of the day left me glad to give spare half-hours to the study of a thoughtful book, Johnson was the one author accessible to me. No other writer could have secured me, as he did, against all chance of being misled by my own sanguine and metaphysical temperament. He taught me carefully to measure life, and distrust fortune; and he secured me, by his adamantine commonsense, for ever, from being caught in the cobwebs of German metaphysics, or sloughed in the English drainage of them. —RUSKIN, JOHN, 1885, *Præterita, vol.* I, *p.* 416.

There is hardly any among the great men of history who can be called so emphatically and distinctively "a man of letters," undoubtedly none who has won so high a personal position and so large a contemporary influence by sheer strength of pen. The literary life is not generally considered to be especially favorable to the cultivation of piety; and Johnson's peculiar circumstances were not of a kind to make it more favorable in his case than usual. He was poor, neglected, struggling during a great part of his career against the heaviest odds. His natural disposition was by no means such as to predispose him to religion. He was afflicted from childhood with a hypochondriac and irritable humor; a proud domineering spirit, housed in an unwieldy and disordered body; plagued by inordinate physical appetites; inclined not unnaturally to rely with overconfidence upon the strength and accuracy of his reasoning powers; driven by his impetuous temper into violent assertion and bitter controversy; deeply wounded by his long years of obscurity, and highly elated by his final success,—he was certainly not one whom we would select as likely to be a remarkably religious man. Carlyle had less to embitter him. Goethe had no more to self-deify him. And yet, beyond a doubt, Samuel Johnson was a sincere, an humble, and, in the main, a consistent Christian.—VAN DYKE, JR., HENRY J., 1886, *A Sturdy Christian, Andover Review, vol.* 5, *p.* 491.

Among Johnson's numerous writings the ones best entitled to remembrance are, perhaps, his "Dictionary of the English Language," 1755; his moral tale, "Rasselas," 1759; the introduction to his "Edition of Shakspere," 1765; and his "Lives of the Poets," 1781. Johnson wrote a sonorous, cadenced prose, full of big Latin words and balanced clauses. . . . There is more of this in Johnson's "Rambler" and "Idler" papers than in his latest work, the "Lives of the Poets." In this he showed himself a sound and judicious critic, though with decided limitations. His understanding was solid, but he was a thorough classicist, and his taste in poetry was formed on Pope. He was unjust to Milton and to his own contemporaries, Gray, Collins, Shenstone, and Dyer. He had no sense of the higher and subtler graces of romantic poetry, and he had a comical indifference to the "beauties of nature." When Boswell once ventured to remark that poor Scotland had, at least, some "noble, wild prospects," the doctor replied that the noblest prospect a Scotchman ever saw was the road that led to London.—BEERS, HENRY A., 1886, *An Outline Sketch of English Literature, pp.* 200, 201.

The unfading interest in Dr. Johnson is one of the good signs of English character. Men do not read his books, but they never cease to care about him. It shows what hold the best and broadest human qualities always keep on the heart of man. This man, who had to be coaxed into favor before a request could be asked, and whose friends and equals were afraid to remonstrate with him except by a round-robin, was yet capable of the truest delicacy, the purest modesty, the most religious love for all that was greater and better than himself. But the great value of him was his reality. He was a perpetual protest against the artificialness and unreality of that strange eighteenth century in which he lived.—BROOKS, PHILLIPS, 1886–94, *Biography, Essays and Addresses, p.* 433.

Johnson has never been highly estimated as a critic, and on this point he has hardly received fair consideration. His hasty remarks, uttered in the heat of controversy, have been handed down as the result of deliberate judgment, but his literary instincts were more correct than has generally been imagined. Personal feelings undoubtedly often influenced his opinions, and he was unwilling to allow praise to writers of whose principles he disapproved. He could see little merit in the vigorous irony of Swift, and would never acknowledge him to be the author of "The Tale of a Tub!" but there is scarcely any writer from whom Johnson quoted so often in his dictionary. . . . On the other hand, he spoke too favourably of writers whose personal characters he respected. Beattie he loved, and he mentioned his writings in terms which now appear ludicrous. He was under obligations to Richardson, and thought highly of the moral tendency of his works, which in consequence he immensely over-rated, but he admitted that anybody who read Richardson's novels for the sake of the story would be compelled to hang himself, and forgot the fact that it is exactly *for the sake of the story* that novels are generally read, and that, however excellent may be the sentiment, the reader of a work of fiction will soon close the volume if there is no amusement in the plot.—GRANT, FREDERICK RICHARD CHARLES, 1887, *Life of Samuel Johnson, pp.* 154, 155.

His sagacious words and suggestions are likely to last with the literature of the language, for they embody great living truths and principles which are and must continue superior to the changes which affect and rule in the minor affairs of life.—SAUNDERS, FREDERICK, 1887, *The Story of Some Famous Books, p.* 94.

Johnson was never designed to be a successful periodical essayist. He had a better field in biography, lexicography and general criticism. He was far more than a miscellaneous essayist, and in this respect was the superior of Addison. Such critics as DeQuincey are led to speak in high terms of Johnson's style not so much on the basis of his periodical work as on that of his entire work as an author and commentator.—HUNT, THEODORE W., 1887, *Representative English Prose and Prose Writers, p.* 320.

The hold that Johnson has on the esteem of mankind, after the lapse of a century, proves that he was no unreal giant, but a hater of shams, and ever striving after the eternal verities, although unquestionably indebted to Boswell for his highest fame. He could not endure undeserved praise, and knew well enough that his tragedy of "Irene" added neither to his literary fame nor to the sum of his real merits. When a gentleman by the name of Pot was reported as having said that it "was the finest tragedy of modern times," Johnson at once replied, "If Pot says so, Pot lies;" and that verdict the public has never reversed. Goldsmith really touched Johnson in his most vulnerable point when he said, "He makes his little fishes talk like whales."—MORRILL, JUSTIN S., 1887, *Self-Consciousness of Noted Persons, p.* 106.

Johnson has contributed many imperishable sayings to the English language. Unfortunately, in literary matters he had a divided life. Macaulay has exaggerated the contrast between Johnson talking at his ease in the club or at Mrs. Thrale's tea-table, and Johnson penning "Ramblers" in the study. Still, there was a difference. Talk was to the Doctor the wine of life; it stirred his pulses, quickened his powerful but rather sluggish intellect, brought out his humour, drove off his besetting melancholy. Alone in Bolt Court, with blue devils, his pen lagged, and he produced, with some profoundly interesting work, a good deal of lumber. Though he raised the tone of the essay, he disimproved its form, as the masterly hand of Addison left it. The "Ramblers" and "Idlers," for instance, are, on the whole, failures, for want of the salt of personality which make the club talks successes. "Rasselas" is almost charming, but it resembles a theatrical performance by Mr. and Mrs. Vincent Crummles and Company. One was all Crummles; the other is all Johnson. Pakuah, Imlac, Rasselas, and the rest, all wear knee-breeches and buckles; their speech bewrayeth them. Here and there, especially in the "Idlers," there is a lively personal touch worthy of the "Spectator"; and weighty satire and vigorous criticisms of life are never wanting. . . . As a critic Johnson is excellent—intelligent, shrewd, knowing—and his worth may be well gauged by comparing him with his contemporaries, and even with the critical school of the earlier years of the nineteenth century. He has been abused for his mistakes. What critic is without them? What about the Edinburg Reviewers? How many of Francis Jeffrey's literary verdicts remain? . . . What will Carlyle's historical criticism be worth fifty years hence? What are Mr. Froude's worth now? Of Johnson, it may be said that as he produced the best dictionary in an age when philology was in its infancy, so he was the best literary critic of an age when there was very little criticism to speak of. Look at the stuff which passes for literary judgments with Horace Walpole, who was always sneering at Johnson's "tasteless pedantry!" Johnson was, in fact, a good deal better than his age and his prejudices.—MASSINGHAM, H. W., 1890, *Some Johnson Characteristics, The Gentleman's Magazine, vol.* 268, *pp.* 160, 161.

When the coffin was lowered into the grave, one able to read the outward signs of coming change might have seen buried with it the whole of the eighteenth century literature, as Johnson understood literature, and not to speak of frivolous productions such as those of Fielding and Smollett, who had also gone before. After Johnson's name in the list of English poets, scholars, and essayists may be drawn a thick black line such as in railway guides they use to indicate that here the train stops. Johnson's train of literature, which started merrily with Pope, Addison, Steele, and a glorious company of wits, had been running slowly of late, and has now come to a final stop. Not only was the old order changing, as happens continually, by the laws of being, but it was completely dead, and its successor as yet was not born. There was to be no more literature of the old school: nothing worth reading on the old lines was to be published; and the world must wait until the new men should begin their work with new thoughts, new ways of looking at things, and new forms of expression.—BESANT, SIR WALTER, 1891, *Over Johnson's Grave, Harper's Magazine, vol.* 82, *p.* 927

Johnson, in addition to his other great achievements, was capable of making colossal errors without the slightest help from others.—LOUNSBURY, THOMAS R., 1892, *Studies in Chaucer, vol.* I, *p.* 149.

There was an intellectual dress, as it were, put on by the man of genius of those times. It hung loosely upon Goldsmith's irregular frame. It sat close, well-fitting and fashionable upon Addison, but Samuel Johnson's mighty limbs almost burst its seams and betrayed at every movement the giant who wore it.—CRAWFORD, F. MARION, 1893, *The Novel, What Is It? p.* 101.

While he wrote some strong and quotable verse, full of vigorous and telling rhetoric, he is pre-eminently a prose writer in an age of prose. The uninspired and practical temper of his time found prose rather than poetry its natural medium. . . . While Johnson thus stands as the bulwark of the old order, both by his own work and by his critical verdicts on that of others, all about him new agitations were already rife. Absolute as was his literary dictatorship, his throne was reared on the verge of that revolution which begins the modern period of our literary history.—PANCOAST, HENRY S., 1893, *Representative English Literature, pp.* 318, 319.

Johnson's paragraph is remarkably short. In the "Rambler" there are but 2.32 sentences to the paragraph; the two rises to three in "Rasselas." The fewness of the sentences per paragraph and the high percentage (27 per cent.) of paragraphed sentences are phenomena not due in either case to dialogue. Johnson was exceedingly particular that each paragraph should form an integer; beyond this he cared not how few the sentences. His favourite order is loose, with a large share of deductive paragraphs. He loves a short introductory sentence, and when the chance permits he likes to make this sentence a generalization far wider than can be substantiated from the subsequent details. In the matter of proportion by varying short sentences with long, Johnson in his later work is by no means weak. Even in the earlier works the percentage of sentences of less than 15 words is considerable—9 per cent. in "Rambler" and "Rasselas," while the "Lives" shows 16 per cent. of simple sentences.—LEWIS, EDWIN HERBERT, 1894, *The History of the English Paragraph, p.* 116.

To attempt the Johnsonian period without a familiar knowledge of the Latin tongue is to practice diving before learning to swim; thereafter there is life to be saved at sea.—RALEIGH, WALTER, 1894, *The English Novel, p.* 260.

Johnson's weighty and impressive style suits well with a subject of moral grandeur such as not seldom employed his pen; but it grows monotonous, and becomes even ludicrous, when applied on occasions of ordinary or trifling importance. It was to this uniform pomposity of style that Goldsmith alluded when he said that Dr. Johnson would make little fishes talk like whales. But while Johnson's style of writing is overloaded with long words from the Latin, and ponderous with rolling sentences, his speech presented a contrast in pithy and pointed idiomatic Saxon English. He was to his century what Dryden had been to the seventeenth—a literary dictator whose verdict was final. The moral integrity of Johnson gave weight to his decisions.—ROBERTSON, J. LOGIE, 1894, *A History of English Literature, p.* 217.

Perhaps a little over-fond of trumpeting; loving so much his long sonorous roll of Ciceronian vocables.—MITCHELL, DONALD G., 1895, *English Lands Letters and Kings, Queen Anne and the Georges, p.* 98.

In style alone, we may justly claim that he is the vertebrate column of our prose. He could not accomplish the impossible. Once more I venture to express the conviction that the highest conceivable perfection of English prose was possible only to the Elizabethans, and that when the task passed unaccomplished from their hands, the hopes of it vanished beyond recall. But what Johnson could do, he did with consummate power. To him it was left to establish a code, to evolve order out of disorderly materials, to found a new ideal of style in absolutely logical precision, adding to that precision dignity and eloquence of force. To ascribe to him a slavish propensity to cumbrous and pedantic sesquipedalianism is to mistake the travesty for the original. His dictatorship in literature, based on native strength, was most unquestioned in the sphere of style; and it is not too much to say that all that is best in English prose since his day is his debtor in respect of not a few of its highest qualities, above all in respect of absolute lucidity, unfailing vigour, and saving common sense.—CRAIK, HENRY, 1895, *ed., English Prose, Introduction, vol.* IV, *p.* 10.

What, then, was Johnson's method? and what its practical application? The method is nothing if not magisterial. It takes for granted certain fixed laws—whether the laws formulated by Aristotle, or by Horace, or the French critics, is for the moment beside the question—and passes sentence on every work of art according as it conforms to the critical decalogue or transgresses it. The fault of this method is not, as is sometimes supposed, that it assumes principles in a subject where none are to be sought; but that its principles are built on a miserably narrow and perverted basis. That there are principles of criticism that the artist's search for beauty must be guided by some idea, is obvious enough. It can be questioned only by those who are prepared to deny the very possibility of criticism; who would reduce the task both of critic and of artist to a mere record of individual impressions. It need hardly be said that the very men who are most ready to profess such a doctrine with their lips, persistently and rightly, give the lie to it in their deeds. No creative work, no critical judgment, either is or can be put forward as a mere impression; it is the impression of a trained mind—that is, of a mind which, instinctively or as a conscious process, is guided by principles or ideas. So far, then, as he may be held to have borne witness to the need of ideas, Johnson was clearly in the right. It was when he came to ask, What is the nature of those ideas, and how does the artist or the critic arrive at them? that he began to go astray. Throughout he assumes that the principles of art—and that, not only in their general bearing (proportion, harmony, and the like), but in their minuter details—are fixed and invariable. To him they form a kind of case-law, which is to be extracted by the learned from the works of a certain number of "correct writers," ancient and modern; and which, once established, is binding for all time both on the critic and on those he summons to his bar. In effect, this was to declare that beauty can be conceived in no other way than as it presented itself, say, to Virgil or to Pope. It was to lay the dead hand of the past upon the present and the future. . . . Yet again. In the hands of Johnson—and it was a necessary consequence of his critical method—poetry becomes more and more a mere matter of mechanism. . . . As has already been said, Johnson is nothing if not a hanging judge; and it is just where originality is most striking that his sentences are the most severe.—VAUGHAN, C. E., 1896, *ed., English Literary Criticism, Introduction, pp.* lvi, lviii, lix.

The gradual tendency of the century had more and more come to be concentrated upon attention to common-sense, and in Johnson a character was developed, of noble intelligence, of true and tender heart, of lambent humour, in whose entire philosophy every impulse was subordinated to that negative virtue. Johnson became, therefore, the leading intellect of the country, because displaying in its quintessence the quality most characteristic of the majority of educated men and women. Common-sense gave point to his wit. balance to his morality, a Tory limitation to his intellectual sympathy. He keeps the central path; he is as little indulgent to enthusiasm as to infidelity; he finds as little place in his life for mysticism as for coarse frivolity. *Vita fumus,* and it is not for man to waste his years in trying to weigh the smoke or puff it away; bravely and simply he must labour and acquiesce, without revolt, without speculation, in "all that human hearts endure." This virile hold upon facts, this attitude to conduct as a plain garment from which the last shred of the Shaftesbury gold-lace optimism had been torn, explains the astounding influence Johnson wielded during his lifetime. His contemporaries knew him to be thoroughly honest, profoundly intelligent, and yet permeated by every prejudice of the age. They loved to deal with facts, and no man had so large a stock of them at his disposal as Johnson.—GOSSE, EDMUND, 1897, *Short History of Modery English Literature, p.* 249.

Thus, inured in life-long struggles, fortified in spirit by a robust faith, exalted in mind by the loftiest expression of Greek philosophy, Johnson was one of those few who are numbered among the immortals while still in this life: even as that other great Englishman and greatest of modern men, whom the world has just mourned with you, but whom immortality now claims as one of her noblest ornaments.—GENNADIUS, J., 1898, *Dr. Johnson as a Grecian, Johnson Club Papers, p.* 48.

Johnson's style is formal, balanced, and Latinized, and his manner is rather oracular. He influenced English prose greatly for fifty years. His writing now

"Neglected and deserted lie,
As they were not of nature's company.'

But he is full of good sense, often expressed in apt and forcible language. His range of thought is limited and insular, he is a typical eighteenth-century writer, —a good deal of a Philistine, but a great deal of a man.—JOHNSON, CHARLES F., 1900, *Outline History of English and American Literature, p.* 279.

Some wits of the day said that he used long words to make his "Dictionary" a necessity. If we read much of Johnson, we are in danger of imitating him unconsciously. A critic in the latter part of the nineteenth century, describing Johnson's style, says: "He delivers himself with severe majestical dignity and vigorous authoritative brevity." This critic was unconsciously writing Johnsonese. In the second place, Johnson loved formal balance so much that he used too many antitheses. Many of his balancing clauses are out of place or add nothing to the sense. . . . As a rule, Johnson's prose is too abstract and general, and it awakens too few images.—HALLECK, REUBEN POST, 1900, *History of English Literature, pp.* 299, 300.

All true Johnsonians treat with an amused contempt the statement so freely circulated in newspapers that nobody nowadays reads Johnson's writings. People are, of course, free to read what they like, and (if they like) not to read at all. Some of us keep books, other poultry. One man drives a motor car, whilst his brother is perhaps an amateur photographer. All the tastes are respectable. But if it so happens that you are fond of English literature, you will be a reader of Johnson, and from his works, whether in prose or verse, you will be infected and become possessed with a perception of a strong character, and a constant habit of mind presented in the pages of Boswell and Burney and Thrale, and indeed all the other sources of our knowledge.—BIRRELL, AUGUSTINE, 1901, *Do We Really Know Dr. Johnson, Outlook, vol.* 69, *p.* 914.